Other Disorders of Infancy, Childhood, or Adolescence

313.23 Elective mutism
313.82 Identity disorder
313.89 Reactive attachment disorder of infancy or early childhood
307.30 Stereotype/habit disorder
314.00 Undifferentiated attention-deficit disorder

ORGANIC MENTAL DISORDERS

Dementias Arising in the Senium and Presenium
Primary degenerative dementia of the Alzheimer type, senile onset
290.30 with delirium
290.20 with delusions
290.21 with depression
290.00 uncomplicated

(Note: code 331.00 Alzheimer's disease on Axis III)

Code in fifth digit:
1 = with delirium, 2 = with delusions, 3 = with depression, 0 = uncomplicated

290.1x Primary degenerative dementia of the Alzheimer type, presenile onset, _____

(Note: code 331.00 Alzheimer's disease on Axis III)

290.4x Multi-infarct dementia, _____
290.00 Senile dementia NOS
        Specify etiology on Axis III if known
290.10 Presenile dementia NOS
        Specify etiology on Axis III if known (e.g., Pick's disease, Jakob-Creutzfeldt disease)

Psychoactive Substance-Induced Organic Mental Disorders
Alcohol
303.00 intoxication
291.40 idiosyncratic intoxication
291.80 Uncomplicated alcohol withdrawal
291.00 withdrawal delirium
291.30 hallucinosis
291.10 amnestic disorder
291.20 Dementia associated with alcoholism
Amphetamine or similarly acting sympathomimetic
305.70 intoxication
292.00 withdrawal
292.81 delirium
292.11 delusional disorder
Caffeine
305.90 intoxication
Cannabis
305.20 intoxication
292.11 delusional disorder

Cocaine
305.60 intoxication
292.00 withdrawal
292.81 delirium
292.11 delusional disorder
Hallucinogen
305.30 hallucinosis
292.11 delusional disorder
292.84 mood disorder
292.89 Posthallucinogen perception disorder
Inhalant
305.90 intoxication
Nicotine
292.00 withdrawal
Opioid
305.50 intoxication
292.00 withdrawal

Phencyclidine (PCP) or similarly acting arylcyclohexylamine
305.90 intoxication
292.81 delirium
292.11 delusional disorder
292.84 mood disorder
292.90 organic mental disorder NOS
Sedative, hypnotic, or anxiolytic
305.40 intoxication
292.00 Uncomplicated sedative, hypnotic, or anxiolytic withdrawal
292.00 withdrawal delirium
292.83 amnestic disorder
Other or unspecified psychoactive substance
305.90 intoxication
292.00 withdrawal
292.81 delirium
292.82 dementia
292.83 amnestic disorder
292.11 delusional disorder
292.12 hallucinosis
292.84 mood disorder
292.89 anxiety disorder
292.89 personality disorder
292.90 organic mental disorder NOS

Organic Mental Disorders associated with Axis III physical disorders or conditions, or whose etiology is unknown.
293.00 Delirium
294.10 Dementia
294.00 Amnestic disorder
293.81 Organic delusional disorder
293.82 Organic hallucinosis
293.83 Organic mood disorder
        Specify: manic, depressed, mixed
294.80 Organic anxiety disorder
310.10 Organic personality disorder
        Specify if explosive type
294.80 Organic mental disorder

PSYCHOACTIVE SUBSTANCE USE DISORDERS
Alcohol
303.90 dependence
305.00 abuse
Amphetamine or similarly acting sympathomimetic
304.40 dependence
305.70 abuse
Cannabis
304.30 dependence
305.20 abuse
Cocaine
304.20 dependence
305.60 abuse
Hallucinogen
304.50 dependence
305.30 abuse
Inhalant
304.60 dependence
305.90 abuse
Nicotine
305.10 dependence
Opioid
304.00 dependence
305.50 abuse
Phencyclidine (PCP) or similarly acting arylcyclohexylamine (183)
304.50 dependence
305.90 abuse
Sedative, hypnotic, or anxiolytic
304.10 dependence
305.40 abuse
304.90 Polysubstance dependence
304.90 Psychoactive substance dependence NOS
305.90 Psychoactive substance abuse NOS

Abnormal Psychology

Abnormal Psychology

The Problem of Maladaptive Behavior

SIXTH EDITION

Irwin G. Sarason
University of Washington

Barbara R. Sarason
University of Washington

PRENTICE HALL, Englewood Cliffs, New Jersey 07632

Editorial/production supervision: Joe O'Donnell
Interior design: Christine Gehring-Wolf
Manufacturing buyer: Ray Keating
Cover design: Bruce Kenselaar
Cover art: Ross Neher, "Persistence." Oil on linen, 1988; 24″ x 24″.
        Collection of Mr. and Mrs. Ronald W. Moore.
        Courtesy of David Beitzel Gallery, New York.

 © 1989 by Prentice-Hall, Inc.
A Division of Simon & Schuster
Englewood Cliffs, New Jersey 07632

Printed in the United States of America

10 9 8 7 6 5 4 3 2 1

ISBN 0-13-004284-6

Prentice-Hall International (UK) Limited, *London*
Prentice-Hall of Australia Pty. Limited, *Sydney*
Prentice-Hall Canada Inc., *Toronto*
Prentice-Hall Hispanoamericana, S.A., *Mexico*
Prentice-Hall of India Private Limited, *New Delhi*
Prentice-Hall of Japan, Inc., *Tokyo*
Simon & Schuster Southeast Asia Pte. Ltd., *Singapore*
Editora Prentice-Hall do Brasil, Ltda., *Rio de Janeiro*

Contents

Instructor's Edition

Contents

Preface

This manual is designed for those using the sixth edition of Irwin and Barbara Sarason's text, *Abnormal Psychology: The Problem of Maladaptive Behavior*. The manual is designed to meet the needs of instructors with varying levels of experience in teaching a course in abnormal psychology. Experienced instructors may choose to use the chapter overviews to obtain a quick sense of the main topics in the text. An inspection of the chapter outlines will enable the experienced instructor to integrate his or her lecture material and the essential information presented in the text. Novice instructors should find the outlines helpful in organizing their own reading of the text chapter and in choosing discussion or supplementary lecture topics.

A set of learning objectives is presented for each chapter. These objectives highlight the major points presented in the chapter and have been developed from many semesters' use of earlier editions of this text, as well as a careful reading of new material in this edition. The objectives can be used by the instructor as a checklist of his or her own lecture coverage. They also are appropriate as class goals, for use as study guide questions, or for exam review sessions.

Discussion questions and class participation projects should help students to think more pointedly about salient, current, or intriguing issues and to take a more active role in their own learning process. In addition, supplementary lecture material is presented for each chapter. This material has been chosen to complement and at times to expand on material in the text. Source references have been included with the material, although every effort has been made to enable the instructor to prepare a lecture or discussion from the available information included in this manual. Experienced and novice instructors alike should find something in the supplementary material to enhance their lectures. Finally, an appendix contains a list of audiovisual materials to support an undergraduate course in abnormal psychology.

Robert J. Jueger
Marquette University

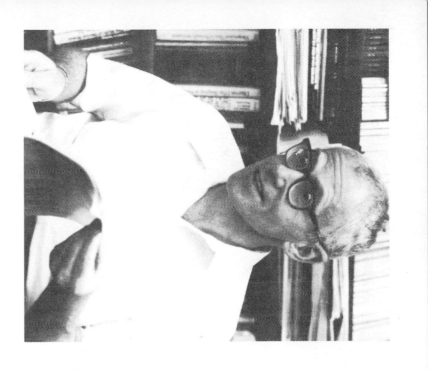

As is evident from their being coauthors of an Abnormal Psychology book that has gone through six editions, the Sarasons have a deep interest in the things that go wrong in human lives and result in psychological pain and behavioral problems. In addition to their textbook writing, the Sarasons have done extensive research on training and therapeutic programs that have proven useful for people who have several types of personal and social problems. They have worked with juvenile delinquents, high school students with poor academic motivation, and college students who experience uncomfortably high levels of test anxiety. The Sarasons are deeply concerned about finding ways in which communities can be made better, more compassionate places to live. Recently, they devised a technique to increase citizens' donations to the community's blood supply. Another of their active research interests is health psychology. Just underway is a large-scale project to use psychological principles in a community setting to help people adopt more healthy lifestyles.

Irwin G. Sarason, who received his B.A. degree from Rutgers University and Barbara R. Sarason, who received her B.A. degree from Depauw University, met while graduate students at the University of Iowa. Each of them was awarded a Ph.D. degree with a specialization in Clinical Psychology from Indiana University. They moved to Seattle in 1956, after completing internships at the West Haven, Connecticut, Veteran's Administration Hospital.

At present, Irwin is a professor and chairperson and Barbara is a research associate professor in the Psychology Department at the University of Washington.

In their current research, the Sarasons are investigating how our relationships with family and friends help us to cope with the stresses and strains of daily life. This topic of social support has implications for understanding individual development, abnormal behavior and health status, as well as aspects of the psychotherapeutic relationship that contributes to positive clinical outcomes. The Sarasons' work suggests that people who feel accepted and valued by others are more likely to be good stress copers. They believe that an important ingredient of psychotherapy is the therapist's communication of acceptance and positive evaluation of the patient.

The Sarasons have contributed extensively to the psychology literature. They have written and edited several books and have published numerous scholarly articles. Irwin, a past president of the Western Psychological Association, has written articles on anxiety, coping skills useful in dealing with stress, and the assessment of life stress. Barbara has written articles dealing with the acquisition and strengthening of social skills and the use of videotapes for the analysis of interpersonal relations. The Sarasons have lectured extensively about their work in the United States, England, Germany, the Netherlands, Belgium, France, Norway, and Sweden.

Abnormal Psychology

Overview

In Chapter One, an overview of abnormal behavior is presented. Abnormal behavior, which is viewed as maladaptation, is a function of situationally induced stress, personal vulnerability, and coping skills. The prevalence and incidence of abnormal behavior in the population is discussed. The types and functions of professional clinical workers are presented, followed by the main research strategies used in the study of abnormal behavior.

Outline

I. Introduction
    1. Case of Bob Cates
  A. What is Abnormal Behavior?
    1. Box 1-1: Father Kills Two Sons: Bart Dobben
    2. People differ in degrees of differentness
  B. The Stigma of Abnormal Behavior
    1. Many people continue to be frightened of "mental illness," even though the public knows more about abnormal behavior
    2. The media contributes to the public's fear by presenting mentally ill as violent and by building misconceptions about what is normal or typical behavior
  C. Adaptive and Maladaptive Behaviors
    1. Adaptation refers to survival, whereas adjustment refers to individual mastery of the environment and a sense of peace
    2. Maladaptive vs. deviant behavior: all maladaptive behavior is deviant behavior but the opposite is not true
II. Stress, Coping, and Vulnerability
  A. Stress: Reactions to Situations That Pose Demands, Constraints, or Opportunities

  B. Coping: How People Deal With Difficulties and Attempt to Overcome Them
  C. Vulnerability: Likelihood of Responding Maladaptively
    1. Influenced by:
      a. heredity
      b. personality characteristics
      c. lack of certain skills
      d. past experiences
    2. Table 1-1: Negative life events and personal maladjustment
    3. Stress, coping, and vulnerability interact
      a. As stress increases (decreases), the less (more) vulnerability is needed to display maladaptive behavior
      b. Coping skills keep one strong when vulnerable
      c. Clinical interventions help cope with stress and/or vulnerability
III. Reasons for Clinical Contacts
  A. Personal Unhappiness: Case of Jack Farmer
    1. A case in which deviance is not obvious but personal concerns lead to professional help
  B. Concerns of Others: Case of Mary Waverly
    1. Some cases may be deviant but not clearly maladaptive
  C. Legal and Community Problems: Case of Charles Clay
    1. A personal maladaptation becomes a social maladaptation
IV. The Epidemiology of Maladaptive Behavior
  A. Epidemiological Research
    1. To obtain information about the physical and psychological maladaptations of groups
  B. Prevalence, Incidence and Risk Factors
    1. Prevalence is the frequency of occurrence at a particular point in time
    2. Incidence is the number of new cases that arise in a period

3. Risk factor indicates a statistical association between a disorder and a factor
C. Cause and Prevention
1. Moving from obtaining estimates of maladaptive behavior to determining the causes and preventions
2. Social change and diagnostic fashions can affect statistics
V. Sources of Help
A. Types of Treatment Facilities
1. Community-based treatment facilities have become more available to disturbed individuals
2. Deinstitutionalization of chronic patients has been implemented as government policy
3. As much as 20 percent of the population are struggling with psychological impairment; however, few seek mental health services
B. Types of Mental Health Specialists
1. Characteristics of professionals trained to work with abnormal behavior
   a. Clinical psychologists: Hold a Ph.D., a research degree, and are trained to diagnose and treat abnormal behavior, affect, and cognitions
   b. Psychiatrists: Physicians with specialized training in prescriptions of drugs
   c. Psychiatric social workers: hold advanced degrees, usually a master's degree, and are often concerned with the relationship between the person and the community
2. Clinicians emphasize the case-study method, which involves an in-depth study of the individual whether subject receives drugs
E. Ethical Aspects of Research
1. Ethical standards do not allow experimenters to place people in jeopardy without their informed consent
VII. Study Outline

Learning Objectives

Students should know:
1. How attitudes and knowledge about abnormal behavior have changed over the past three decades.
2. The meaning of "adaptation" and how it differs from "adjustment."

3. That not all deviant behavior is maladaptive, but that all maladaptive behavior is deviant; that coping effectiveness, personal distress, and social consequences are important variables in determining whether a deviant behavior is maladaptive.
4. How stress, coping, and vulnerability are defined and related.
5. What the reasons are that people seek professional help.
6. What the goals of epidemiological research are. They should also be aware of the similarities and differences between prevalence and incidence data.
7. Recent prevalence and incidence statistics of abnormal behavior for adults and children.
8. How psychologists, psychiatrists, and social workers, although all concerned with the assessment and treatment of abnormal behavior, are different in terms of training and function.
9. What the important steps are in conducting research.
10. The strengths and weaknesses of the case study, correlational, longitudinal, and cross-sectional research strategies.
11. The kinds of experimental studies and why experimental studies enable researchers to examine cause-effect relationships.
12. Ethical standards for conducting research and the procedures which must be followed to insure informed consent.

Discussion Questions

1. The text directs attention to the ways in which the media has portrayed people with maladaptive behavior. Specifically, those with emotional disorders have been portrayed as dangerous more frequently than is the actual case. Also, the media portray alcohol problems, promiscuity, divorce, and anxiety as being more common than surveys of the public would indicate. Are media viewers able to discount this incorrect information? What effects do such portrayals have on public attitudes toward and knowledge about those with maladaptive behavior? Should the media be encouraged to make a more veridical presentation of the relationship between maladaptive behavior and violence? If so, how could this be accomplished—corrective promotional efforts by the media? Government censorship or regulation? Political action such as boycotting sponsors' products?

2. Albert Einstein was a well-known figure whose behavior was deviant but not maladaptive. Another well-known person, the artist Renoir, was generally acknowledged to be both highly creative and to manifest maladaptive behavior. What criteria can be used to distinguish deviant creativity from deviant maladaptive behavior?

Class Participation Project

The policy of deinstitutionalizing chronic mental patients by referring them to community-based residential facilities has resulted in an increased number of contacts between former mental patients with chronic conditions and the public. Compared to 25 years ago, it is now more likely that a person with a chronic mental disorder will be encountered in the supermarket, the shopping mall, on the bus, or on the street corner. Ask the students in the class to recall one incident in which they personally have encountered a chronic "mentally ill" person, to think about what happened, and then to write down the details of that encounter. Then ask whether the students felt comfortable or uncomfortable, whether the mentally disordered person seemed to be dangerous or nondangerous, and whether the behavior of the person seemed predictable or unpredictable. It might also be interesting to note where the encounter occurred, whether other people were present, and whether the chronically mentally disordered person actually approached or spoke to the student. Collect the accounts and tabulate the percent of students who found the encounter to be uncomfortable, unpredictable, and dangerous.

Judith Rabkin, in a review of public attitudes toward maladaptive behavior ("Who is called mentally ill: Public and professional views," *Journal of Community Psychology*, 1979, 7, 253-258.) has indicated that members of the public feel uncomfortable with the mentally ill and that the public finds those with maladaptive behavior to be unpredictable and dangerous. Were these the reactions observed by the students in their recollections of encounters with chronic mentally disordered persons? If not, how might the setting, the presence or absence of other people, and the actions of the chronic mentally disordered person change one or more of their reactions?

Supplemental Lecture Material

Theoretical models of normal and abnormal behavior both conceptualize adaptive and maladaptive behavior along a continuum that varies in the degree or severity. However, those same models sometimes disagree on how the continuum should be labeled. The psychoanalytic and humanistic-existential models provide, perhaps, the greatest contrast. In Table 1.1, a continuum of maladaptive behavior is presented from the psychoanalytic perspective as provided by Karl Menninger. The continuum clearly includes degrees of maladaptive behavior. One might conclude that adaptive behavior is an ideal state and that certainly is the message that many receive from reading Freud's popular book *The Psychopathology of Everyday Life*.

The humanistic-existential position is perhaps best embodied in the hierarchy of needs proposed by Abraham Maslow. The existentialists' position is that maladaptive behavior stems from an alienation from our true selves and a failure to have our love and belongingness needs satisfied. Adaptive behavior is viewed as a fulfillment of our increasingly higher order needs in the realization of our potentials. Thus, we all have varying degrees of adaptive behavior, and maladaptive behavior is merely an indica-

TABLE-1.1

Karl Menninger's Unitary Concept of Mental Health Disorders (*The Vital Balance*. New York: Viking Press, 1963)

Mental Health ⟷ Mental Illness

Normal coping devices: crying, working, sleeping, boasting, use of beverages, daydreaming

First level of dysfunction: worry, instability, inhibition, minor somatic symptoms, mild sexual dysfunction

Second level of dysfunction: fainting, phobias, intoxication, compulsion, self-mutilation, perverse sexual behavior, inadequate personality, use of addictive drugs

Third level of dysfunction: breakdown in control of aggressive impulses leading to chronic or episodic acts of violence

Fourth level of dysfunction: pervasive feelings of despondency and hopelessness; erratic disorganized excitement; bizarre behavior, mutism, posturing, incoherent speech, paranoid delusional themes; confused delirious states

Fifth level of dysfunction: gross deterioration, suicide, continuous wild excitement leading to death from exhaustion

tion that an individual has failed to develop higher-level adaptive behavior.

The labels of these two continua are quite different. The psychoanalytic model is a scale of *maladaptiveness* varying from less to more, whereas the humanistic-existential model is a scale of *adaptiveness* varying from less to more. One might ask whether important information could be obtained by combining the continua so that individuals might be seen as more maladaptive and more adaptive (the eccentric artist such as Van Gough), as well as less maladaptive and more adaptive (the average cit-

izen?), and other combinations of maladaptiveness and adaptiveness. Of course, a theoretical model establishes a conclusion about the nature of maladaptive behavior by following philosophical postulates on the characteristics of human nature. The psychoanalytic tradition sees human nature as essentially irrational, affective, and negative. The humanistic-existential model views human nature as rational, cognitively determined, and as essentially positive. A unification of continua of maladaptive behavior and adaptive behavior must reconcile these opposing fundamental postulates about human nature.

CHAPTER 2

The Historical Background of Abnormal Psychology

Overview

This chapter presents views on the causes and treatment of abnormal behavior from a thousand years B.C.E., to the early part of the 20th century. Many conceptions of abnormal behavior and treatment have been recurring throughout history. Notable individuals and movements who were part of these recurring themes are highlighted. The roots of the controversies about organic psychological causation are traced through the 19th century.

Outline

I. Historical Views of Abnormal Behavior
  A. Historically Recurring Theories
    1. Supernatural and mystical forces cause abnormal behavior
      a. The witch doctor or *shaman* has contact with and exorcises these forces
    2. Organic defects that affect specific organs have been thought to cause deviance
      a. Skull trephination was a treatment consistent with this approach
    3. The psychological perspective views abnormal behavior as a result of inadequate perceptual, cognitive, or emotional abilities
  B. The Ancient Greeks
    1. Homer (ca. 800 B.C.E.) viewed disturbed behavior as punishment for offending the gods
    2. Hippocrates (460-377 B.C.E.) held that behavior is determined by the brain
      a. Treatment consisted of rest, bathing, and dieting

3. Socrates (470-399 B.C.E.) held that proper reasoning brings personal happiness
4. Plato (427-347 B.C.E.) introduced the organismic view
  a. behavior is a product of the totality of psychological processes
  b. conflicts between emotion and reason result in abnormal behavior
5. Aristotle (384-322 B.C.E.) placed value on reason

C. The Middle Ages
  1. Early Middle Ages were a time of unrest and constant warfare
    a. St. Augustine (354-430 C.E.) held that psychological knowledge can be gained through introspectionism; laid the groundwork for modern psychoanalytic theories
    b. Christianity served to comfort people
  2. The Church in the 13th and 14th centuries supported demonology as the cause of abnormal behavior; deviance was no longer tolerated
    a. *Malleus Maleficarum* published in 1484, became the basic reference for investigation of diabolical phenomena
  3. Recent research suggests that "witches" were not mentally disturbed
  4. Only a few islands of enlightenment existed; notably, Paracelsus, Heárte, and the English government

D. The Renaissance
  1. A less-than-compassionate view of insanity persisted despite increased humanism, scholarship
    a. Those obviously disordered were still often punished in the 17th century

2. An exception was Johann Weyer (1515-1576) who asserted that deviance should be treated medically

E. The Age of Reason and Enlightenment
1. Baruch Spinoza (1632-1677) wrote that mind and body are inseparable
2. Shakespeare included examples of mental problems especially in *Hamlet*
3. Robert Burton (*Anatomy of Melancholy*) focused on depression
4. Franz Joseph Gall (1758-1828) formulated the Theory of Phrenology, that faculties are located in particular areas of the brain
5. William Cullen (1712-1790) espoused *physiognomy*, that is, judging personality from the face
6. Anton Mesmer (1734-1815) developed hypnosis to treat iron ion imbalances in the body

F. The Reform Movement
1. In 1792, Phillipe Pinel, a physician, took charge of the institutionalized insane in Paris
   a. He advocated care rather than punishment and removed the chains from the patients
   b. He developed a classification system
2. British reforms began in the early 1800s in the way of protests against conditions at Bethlehem Hospital ("Bedlam")
3. The Reform Movement in America, which began in the early 1800s, was spawned by Benjamin Rush, a physician who introduced new treatment methods in the first American hospital for the mentally ill; Dorothea Dix, whose efforts led to the construction of many mental hospitals; and Clifford Beers (*A Mind That Found Itself*), who organized reform movements in the early 20th century

II. Psychological vs. Organic Views
A. The Psychological Approach
1. In early 1800s, irrational romanticism replaced the scientific, rational thinking of the 18th century
2. Johann Christian Heintoth (1773-1843) held that mental illness stems from largely unconscious, personal conflicts between unacceptable impulses and the guilt they cause
   a. This idea set the stage for Freud's views

B. The Organic Approach
1. The later 1800s were noted for organic theories of cause
   a. Wilhelm Griesinger (1817-1868) held that mental illness was caused by brain disturbances
   b. Emil Kraepelin (1856-1926) developed a classification system based on the belief that mental illness is caused by organic disease

C. The Approaches Converge
1. Jean Charcot (1823-1893), the "Napolean of neurosis," studied hysteria, organic symptoms with no organic disorder, and suggested psychological causes
2. Treatment of hysteria with hypnosis
3. Pierre Janet (1859-1947) extended Charcot's work and broadened scope of what is considered abnormal behavior
4. Sigmund Freud (1856-1939) studied with Charcot and further developed psychological explanations for abnormal behavior

III. The Stage is Set
A. A Few Conceptions About Abnormality Are New
1. Conceptions have been influenced by scientific evidence and by community values
2. Also influenced by trying to solve problems before scientific evidence is compiled
3. Often the public has sought a quick or dramatic solution to a problem

IV. Study Outline

Learning Objectives

Students should know:

1. That three commonly recurring themes in the history of causes of abnormal behavior include evil spirits, organic defects, and psychological factors.
2. That the ancient practice of trephining and medieval witchburning were aimed at releasing evil spirits from the body.
3. How the ancient Greeks conceptualized organic and psychological factors as causing abnormal behavior.

4. About the changes in the treatment of people exhibiting deviant behavior during the Middle Ages.

5. That a few rational perspectives such as St. Augustine and Paracelsus existed during the Dark Ages.

6. That scientific and humanistic ideals of the Renaissance had little impact on the treatment of the insane until the latter part of the 16th century. How Johann Weyer contributed to this reform.

7. How during the 1700s science and rationalism replaced spiritual conceptions as theories of abnormal etiology.

8. Who Anton Mesmer was and how his therapeutic approach as a physician was a throwback to earlier times.

9. How the views of reformers like Pinel, Rush, Dix, and Beers influenced the institutional treatment of abnormal behavior.

10. How the views of physicians like Heinroth, Kraepelin, Charcot, and Freud ushered in the controversy between organic and psychological explanations of abnormal behavior.

Discussion Questions

1. Literature and the media have capitalized on the concept of possession by spirits as an explanation of irrational behavior. A notable recent example of this was the popularity of the movie *The Exorcist*. Does the popularity of such stories reflect a lingering fascination or belief in spiritual possession as a cause of abnormal behavior? Just how strong and widespread among the lay public is the belief in spiritual explanations?

2. In Chapter One, it was noted that since 1955 deinstitutionalization of the mentally disordered has been practiced. In Chapter Two, we see that institutionalization and deinstitutionalization each have been periodically emphasized throughout history. What feelings and attitudes among the public lead to a policy of placing those with serious abnormal behavior in residential custodial institutions?

3. Survey the class to see who believes that there is a genetic basis to alcoholism; to schizophrenia; to depression; to hypertension; to "neurosis." How many believe that as technology advances a biolog-

ical cause will be found for each and every type of abnormal behavior?

Supplementary Lecture Material

Trephining

In 1883, an American anthropologist, E.G. Squire, found part of a human skull that had a rectangular shaped hole cut into it. Since that time, at least 1500 skulls with evidence of surgery (trephining or trepanning) have been found. Discovering the reasons for these operations has been the work of archaeologists and anthropologists, but it has relevance to the history of abnormal psychology. This demonstration is aimed at leading students to ask questions about skull surgery that will help them learn more about its practice and the reasons for it.

Social scientists often work retrospectively to determine the causes of a behavioral outcome, as noted by Freud when he said that the process of psychoanalysis:

…resembles to a great extent an archaeologist's excavation of some dwelling-place that has been destroyed and buried…. The two processes are in fact identical, except that the analyst works under better conditions and has more material at his command to assist him, since what he is dealing with is not something destroyed, but something that is still alive…. But just as the archaeologist builds the walls of the building from the foundations that have remained standing, determines the number and position of the columns from the depressions in the floor and reconstructs the mural decorations and paintings from the remains found in debris, so does the analyst proceed when he draws his inferences from the fragments of memories, from the associations and from the behavior of the subject of analysis.

The most extensive review of skull surgery was conducted by T.D. Stewart as the curator of physical anthropology at the Smithsonian Institute's National Museum. (A number of pictures of skull surgery appear in an article by Stewart, "Stone-Age survey: A general review with emphasis on the new world," in W.P. True (Ed.), *Smithsonian Treasury of Science*, New York: Simon and Schuster, 1960.)

The types of information that Stewart and others have searched for include the geographic location and age of the skull findings; the sex and age of the person operated on, the position, shape, and size of the operation; signs of the kinds of instruments used in surgery; signs of bone regrowth; and other artifacts that provide information about these operations. Here are some of Stewart's findings:

- The largest numbers (approximately 1000) of trephined skulls have been found in Peru. These operations took place from 500 B.C.E. to 1500 C.E.
- Approximately 400 skulls have been discovered in Europe, ranging in age from 3000 B.C.E. to 200 B.C.E. The major center was in southern France (connecting this custom with the beginning of modern surgery?). Some skulls have cross-shaped scars resulting from cauterization.
- Trephining of the skull was practiced by Stone-Age people in the South Pacific during the 19th century.
- Trephining was unknown in Africa, but was practiced in parts of Asia (west of the Caspian Sea). The reasons for the Asian practice were verbally described by people practicing surgery in the late 19th century: A cross was cauterized on the skull to prevent illness and trephining was performed for many circumstances.
- Medieval European medical records reveal that cauterization was used in cases of dementia and epilepsy.
- Many operations were performed after a skull fracture (to alleviate pressure on the brain?).
- Some operations in Europe resulted in round pieces of skull being polished and worn as amulets.
- The ages of people operated on range from 6 years to old age.
- Almost all areas of the skull were operated on and perhaps as many as 55 percent show complete healing.

Thus, there may have been many reasons for performing these surgeries. One reason can be stated with some certainty; trephining and cauterization was a treatment for illnesses like dementia and epilepsy.

The Role of the French in the Classification of Mental Illness

Philippe Pinel (1745-1826) is well-known for his reform of Bicetre and Salpetirere, the French Asylums for Insane. He promoted the view that the insane were not possessed by demons but, rather, had illnesses of the mind. In that Pinel believed the insane to be ill, it is not surprising that he was also one of the first to classify these mental illnesses. The four basic clinical types of illness named by Pinel included the following:

- *mania*, which was characterized by marked excitement or fury
- *melancholia*, with the symptoms of depression and limited delusions
- *dementia*, marked by the lack of cohesive ideas
- *idiotism*, which included dementias of organic etiology.

Pinel's start of a nosological system was furthered by the work of one of his students and his successor as physician in charge of Salpetriere, Jean Esquirol (1772-1840). Esquirol presented the most accurate description of idiocy of the time, refining Pinel's category. He also laid the groundwork for the current conceptualization of schizophrenia when he referred to *hallucination* in the way the term is used today, described cases that today would be classified schizophrenia, and coined the term *monomania*, which has been seen as a type of schizophrenia.

Jean Pierre Falret (1794-1870) was a student of Esquirol who carried on the work begun by Pinel. Falret noted that two people can engage in the same delusions and can exhibit similar mental symptoms. This illness he named *folie à deux*.

The last of the famous lineage of students of Pinel to be concerned with classification was Benedict Augustin Morel (1809-1873), Falret's student. Morel originated the term *dementia praecox* to refer to a degenerative illness of the mind.

CHAPTER 3

Theoretical Perspectives on Maladaptive Behavior

Outline

I. The Role of Theory in Abnormal Psychology
  A. The Usefulness of Theories
    1. They help organize facts
    2. Even incomplete theories are useful
    3. Each theory explains some behavior but no theory explains all behavior
    4. Dangers exist in adopting a theory too rigidly
    5. New theories develop out of weaknesses of old theories

II. The Biological Perspective
  A. Overview
    1. An outgrowth of 17th and 18th century scientific advances
    2. Studies the relationship between bodily impairment and disordered behavior
    3. Biological factors are important in some but not all conditions
    4. Extreme position holds that all abnormal behavior is caused by disordered body structure or function
  B. Biological Determinants of Body Function
    1. Genetic factors
      a. Chromosomes contain genes in which the basis for gene action is DNA; chromosomal abnormalities produce abnormalities in the brain
      b. Faulty genes can cause metabolic or biochemical abnormalities
      c. Penetrance is the percentage of cases in which a characteristic appears when a specific gene is present
      d. In the past, the importance of nature vs. nurture has been debated; now the emphasis is on the interaction between genes and environment

      e. Population and behavior genetics are rapidly developing fields
      f. Research on effects of inheritance depends on degree of concordance: relationship between two twins or family members on a behavioral trait
        (1) monozygotic and dizygotic twins are studied for the degree of concordance

    2. The brain and nervous system
      a. Peripheral nervous system
        (1) somatic: transmits from sense organs to muscles
        (2) autonomic: directs the activity of glands and internal body organs
      b. Central nervous system: brain, including the cerebrum, cortex, and spinal cord
      c. The neuron, which consists of the axon, dendrites, synapses, and neurotransmitters, is the fundamental unit of the nervous system
      d. limbic system, which is associated with emotional and motivational functions, includes hypothalamus
      e. chemical receptors are activated by endorphins
    3. The endocrines
      a. Include pituitary, thyroid, adrenal, and gonadal glands
      b. Hormones secreted by glands act as messengers to correlate external events with internal events
      c. Especially concerned with stress and stressors
  C. Research on Biological Factors and Abnormal Behavior
    1. Goals are to determine the causal role of biological factors in maladaption, and to identify effective forms of chemotherapy

2. Psychoimmunology: a search for links between psychological and immunological events
   a. theory: stress disrupts the body's immune system
   b. the immune system influences a person's susceptibility to the course of a disease
3. Psychopharmacology involves the study of the effects of drugs on behavior
   a. Five major drug types
      (1) antipsychotic
      (2) antianxiety
      (3) antidepressant
      (4) pain-relieving
      (5) perceptual-process altering drugs
D. Integration of Biological and Psychological Systems
   1. Many operations are influenced by both systems
   2. Biological systems have plasticity

III. The Psychodynamic Perspective
A. Basic Assumptions
   1. Emotions and thoughts are important sources of behavior
   2. Observable behavior is a function of intrapsychic events
   3. Feelings and thoughts must be inferred from behavior
B. Freud and Psychoanalysis
   1. Assumes psychic determinism and the conscious, preconscious, and unconscious dimensions of mental events
   2. Stages of psychosexual development
      a. libido is focused on a particular erogenous zone in each stage
      b. stages include oral, anal, phallic, latency period, genital
      c. problems at a stage result in fixation
   3. The psychic apparatus
      a. structures include, id, ego, superego
      b. primary-process and secondary-process thinking reflect id-ego influences
   4. Anxiety
      a. two types: from excessive external stimulation; from excessive accumulation of internal psychic energy
      b. can be in anticipation of danger, thereby serving as an alarm signal, or an indication of inability to cope
   5. Defense mechanisms
      a. used by ego to ward off anxiety
      b. include repression, displacement, intellectualization, reaction formation, denial, projection, regression, sublimation
C. Clinical Psychoanalysis
   1. Psychoanalysis is a clinical technique and a theoretical perspective
   2. Maladaptive behavior is caused by developmental experiences that persist into later life
   3. Free association and dream analysis are important therapeutic elements
D. The Neo-Freudians
   1. Rejected emphasis on sexuality and the role of biology
   2. Focused on ego and interpersonal relations
   3. Theorists included Jung, Adler, Erikson among others
E. Evaluating Psychoanalytic Theory
   1. Difficult to evaluate objectively
   2. Still influential and controversial

IV. The Behavioral Perspective
A. The Experimental Approach
   1. Behavior is a product of stimulus-response relationships
   2. Deterministic: every act, event is caused by an antecedent event
   3. Behavior change occurs through environmental change
   4. Behavior is changed through positive and negative reinforcement, punishment, and extinction
B. Classical Conditioning
   1. A neutral (conditioned) stimulus is paired with a natural (unconditioned) stimulus in order to evoke a response (conditioned) to the neutral stimulus that is similar to the response (unconditioned) to the natural stimulus
   2. Systematic desensitization is a therapeutic procedure based on classical conditioning principles
C. Operant Conditioning
   1. Reinforcement occurs after the response, unlike classical conditioning, where reinforcement occurs regardless of response
   2. Shaping is a basic process in operant conditioning
D. Modeling
   1. Learning can occur through observation of others; performance is influenced by reinforcement
   2. Modeling: behavior change through observation of other

3. Modeling also contributes to formation of concepts, attitudes, needs

E. Learning and Mediational Processes
1. Radical behaviorists hold that all references to inner processes must be avoided
2. Social learning theorists agree that thoughts mediate external stimuli and overt behavior

V. The Cognitive Perspective
A. Origins of the Cognitive Perspective
1. Grew out of learning and psychodynamic theories
2. Concerned with thoughts and problem-solving strategies
3. Behavior is a function of the way a person attends to, interprets, and uses available information
4. Schemata fill the mental life of the individual
5. Self-efficacy is based on convictions of personal effectiveness

B. Cognitive Approaches to Personality
1. John Dollard and Neal Miller
a. Translated Freudian theory into learning terms
b. Emphasized cognitive resolution of conflicts
2. George Kelly
a. Personal constructs represent the ways in which a person interprets the world
b. People are problem solvers, predicting the world around them
c. Rejected Freudian notions of unconscious and the influence of past socialization experiences
d. Personal constructs determine emotions
3. Albert Bandura
a. Emphasizes modeling and symbolic, cognitive processes of learning
b. Problems can be solved symbolically without trial and error behavior
c. Self-regulation (internal reinforcement) emphasized over external reinforcement

C. Cognitive Therapies
1. Albert Ellis
a. Developed Rational Emotive Therapy
b. Stresses role of belief in causing behaviors
c. Maladaptive behaviors and emotions are a result of faulty beliefs
2. George Kelly
a. Fixed-role therapy is used to modify constructs

3. Aaron T. Beck
a. People make false assumptions and feel badly

VI. The Humanistic-Existential Perspective
A. Humanistic Point-of-View
1. Emphasizes inherent goodness of human nature and free will in contrast to psychoanalytic and learning perspectives
2. Emphasizes inherent need for self-actualization
3. Abraham Maslow's hierarchy of needs
a. Needs include: physiological, safety, love and belongingness, esteem, self-actualization
b. Deficiency vs. Growth needs
c. Neurotics have not attained basic needs
4. Carl Roger's conception of self
a. Self-understanding and self-actualization are related to self-regard and acceptance
b. Anxiety results from inconsistencies between self-perceptions and self-ideals
c. Therapists must understand the feelings of clients and must accept clients as persons of worth and dignity

B. The Existential Point-of-View
1. Basic concepts
a. Each person is free to choose to act authentically
b. Inauthenticity results in unhappiness and dissatisfaction
2. Rollow May
a. Anxiety is indicative of a choice; unconstructive use of anxiety results in guilt
b. Therapist helps people make constructive choices

VII. The Community Perspective
A. Basic Ideas
1. Maladaptive behavior is a result of inability to cope effectively with stress
2. This reflects a failure of person's social support system
3. Efforts are directed toward preventing maladaptive behavior
4. Holds that social disorganization is a major cause of personal problems
5. Social causation: unfavorable environment increases the stress of an already vulnerable person
6. Social selection: people who do not function well experience downward mobility
B. Social Roles and Labeling

    1. Social roles are functions that people play as members of social groups

    2. Labels can have a negative effect

  C. Contributions of Community Perspective

    1. Ties to others are an important influence on development of maladaptive behavior

    2. Has led to creative service approaches

VIII. The Value of the Interactional Approach

  A. The Author's Perspective

    1. Abnormal behavior can result from any or all of a large number of factors

    2. Influence of situations and vulnerabilities and strengths of an individual exert interactive and joint effects on behavior

    3. Thoughts serve as mediators linking information from environment and behavior

    4. Personal characteristics and experience determine how people respond to a situation

IX. Study Outline

Learning Objectives

Students should know:

1. How theories of maladaptive behavior can be useful.

2. The kinds of physiological causes of abnormal behavior from the biological perspective.

3. The meaning of genetic penetrance and genetic concordance.

4. The main research strategy used to study human inheritance.

5. The underlying assumptions regarding the causes of behavior from the psychodynamic perspective.

6. The functions of id, ego, and superego psychic structures.

7. Some of the ego defense mechanisms and how they are used to reduce anxiety.

8. The major ideas of the neo-Freudians.

9. How learning theorists view behavior to be a function of environmental factors like positive and negative reinforcement, punishment, and extinction.

10. The principles and key terms of classical and operant conditioning.

11. The role of modeling and covert mediators in social learning explanations of abnormal behavior.

12. How cognitive psychologists differ in their study of the psychodynamic perspective in their study of psychological processes of abnormal behavior.

13. How learning theorists like Dollard and Miller, Kelly, Bandura have incorporated cognitions into their approaches.

14. That Ellis stresses the role of irrational beliefs as a cause of maladaptive behavior and that rational emotive therapy attempts to alter those beliefs.

15. The types of maladaptive thoughts Beck attempts to alter with his cognitive therapy;

16. The role and meaning of personal constructs; how Kelly's view of abnormal behavior differed from that of the psychodynamic perspective.

17. How the humanistic-existential theories' view of human nature differs from those of the psychodynamic and learning perspectives.

18. That Maslow's hierarchy of needs culminates in self-actualization and Rogers' approach to therapy focuses on helping people to become more fully functioning.

19. That the community perspective emphasizes social support for those vulnerable to stress and the prevention of abnormal behavior.

20. The difference between social causation and social selection explanations of the relationship between socioeconomic status and the presence of abnormal behavior.

21. The usefulness of an interactive approach to studying abnormal behavior.

Discussion Questions and Classroom Participation

Having reviewed the major perspectives of abnormal behavior, it might be useful to elicit the a priori or naive views toward the causes of abnormal behavior that the students of the class currently hold. In doing so, students will be tapping what Fritz Heider has referred to as "intuitive theories" of behavior. Undoubtedly, students have read and heard, prior to this course, some information about the explanations and treatment orientations toward abnormal behavior. Likewise, they may have varying degrees of experience with abnormal behavior. Naive or intuitive theories of behavior become most evident when there is partial knowledge of an event, when the facts of the event are ambiguous or unknown, and when there is a sense of urgency to obtain closure on an event. Students can tap their a priori beliefs about the causes of abnormal behavior by discussing the following questions and engaging in the exercises described below.

1. Ask the students to think of a person who has had severe problems with alcohol abuse. In that person's case, to what extent were biological or psychological

factors at the root of the problem? Social environment or individual "weakness" factors?

2. The psychodynamic and learning advocates have argued about the effectiveness and efficiency of each other's therapeutic techniques. The issue boils down to whether the behavioral "symptom" or the "underlying cause" should be treated. Consider the case of a person who has a fear of meeting new people. One could treat the behavioral symptom by helping the person relax in the company of a stranger and by teaching the student how to be appropriately assertive with strangers. But would that be sufficient to help the student deal with strangers in the future, or would the fear reappear?

3. The psychodynamic and cognitive perspectives differ in that the former emphasizes the developmental antecedents of a current problem whereas the latter emphasizes the current cognitions or thinking of the person. Have the students consider the situation of an overly suspicious person. Is suspiciousness a result of developmental experiences prior to a problematic episode or the result of a maladaptive thought style?

Supplemental Lecture Material

Irrational Beliefs and RET

Albert Ellis edited, with Russell Grieger, *The Handbook of Rational-Emotive Therapy* (New York: Springer, 1977), in an attempt to present in some source the major tenets and practices consistent with RET. In the first chapter of this book, Ellis outlines the "ABCs" of RET. According to Ellis:

Because of our innate and biological tendencies, we largely (though not exclusively) control our own destinies, and particularly our emotional destinies. And we do so by our basic values or beliefs.

How do our beliefs determine our emotions? According to the ABC framework, A is the activating experience or event, and C is the emotional and/or behavioral consequent. Consider the freshman who gets all Cs at the end of the first semester (point A) and then (point C) feels depressed about school and perhaps even drops out. This student might falsely assume that A caused C and say, "I did poorly in school. That poor performance makes me depressed and makes me not want to go back."

A rational-emotive therapist would claim that such thinking is irrational and illogical. It is not getting all Cs that caused the depression, it is what this student *thought* about those grades that led to depression. If the student

did not think that school was important or thought that Cs were good grades, she would not be upset. However, if she believed that she *had* to get As and Bs in order to be a worthwhile or self-respecting person, *must* be in the top 10% of her class, or that Cs are awful, then these beliefs would cause the depression. Thus, events do not cause feelings, but beliefs about events do, or A (activating event) – B (belief) – C (consequential emotion). Further, when these beliefs are irrational, they cause emotional upset.

The first step in detecting irrational beliefs, according to Ellis, is to look for signs of "musterbation"—statements which include musts, oughts, shoulds, or have tos. But not all irrational beliefs are "musturbatory," some of them reflect beliefs that just don't correspond with reality. Ellis states that there are four forms of irrational beliefs that involve musterbation, awfulizing, intolerance, and damnation:

1. you think that someone or something should, ought, or must be different from the way it actually does exist

2. you find it awful, terrible, or horrible when it is this way

3. you think that you can't bear, stand, or tolerate this person or thing that you concluded should not have been as it is

4. you think that you or some other person (or persons) have made or keep making horrible errors and that because you or they must not act the way they clearly do act, you or they deserve nothing good in life, merit damnation, and can legitimately receive the label of louse, rotten person, or turd.

After detecting irrational beliefs, the RET therapist disputes or challenges those beliefs (D) and ends with the client acquiring a new effect or philosophy (E) that will result in less emotional upset and more effective actions. The process of RET, in sum, consists of A (activating event) – B (belief) – C (emotional consequent) – D (disputation) – E (effect).

Mature and Immature Ego-Defense Mechanisms

George Vaillant (*Adaptation to Life*, New York: Brown, 1977), has conducted in-depth studies of Harvard graduates in middle age as a part of a continuing longitudinal study of men's lives. From interviews, questionnaires, tests, and autobiographical accounts, nearly 300 pages of data were assembled on each man studied. From this data were obtained about 20 crises and the essential response of each man to each crisis. Clinical raters then determined whether ego-defense mechanisms were evident in responses to crises. Vaillant categorized the ego-defense mechanisms the men used as "mature," "neurotic," "immature," or "psychotic" as follows:

Mature Ego-Defenses
  sublimation, altruism, suppression, anticipation, and humor
Neurotic Ego-Defenses
  intellectualization, repression, reaction-formation

Immature Ego-Defenses
  fantasy, projection, hypochondriasis, passive-aggressive behavior
Psychotic Ego-Defenses
  denial of external reality, distortion, delusional projection

Overview

The classification for diagnosis and assessment of abnormal behavior is the topic of this chapter. The latest diagnostic system, DSM-III-R, is presented in detail along with research findings on classification. This is followed by a review of the major assessment techniques.

Outline

I. Classification
  A. Pluses and Minuses of Classification
    1. Enables communication
    2. Allows statistical analysis
    3. Contributes to treatment planning
    4. Labels can create difficulties
    5. Diagnostic categories are imperfect, nor useful
    6. On balance, case for diagnosis is strong
    7. Sources of unreliability
       a. Differences among diagnosticians in training and theoretical orientation
       b. Differences among patients; no two individuals' problems are exactly alike
       c. Burden of heavy case loads
       d. Restricted range of disorders is seen in a particular clinic
  B. The Roles of Stress, Vulnerability, and Coping Resources
    1. Classification is most useful when it provides a *characterization* of personal problems
    2. *Context* of the problem is important
II. DSM-III-R
  A. Overview
    1. Gives different types of information
       a. Notes etiology when identifiable
       b. Notes assets and liabilities
       c. Describes subjective experience
       d. Describes context in which behavior occurs
    2. Differences from earlier versions of DSM
       a. Describes rather than interprets problems
       b. Uses more precise language
       c. Increased coverage
       d. Provides more examples
  B. The Multiaxial Approach
    1. Axis 1: primary diagnosis
    2. Axis 2: developmental and personality disorders
    3. Axis 3: physical disorders
    4. Axis 4: severity of psychosocial stress
    5. Axis 5: psychological functioning, social relationships, and occupational activities
  C. The Major Diagnostic Categories
    1. Axis 1 categories
       a. Disorders of infancy, childhood, or adolescence
       b. Organic Mental Disorders
       c. Psychoactive substance-use Disorders
       d. Sleep Disorders
       e. Schizophrenia
       f. Psychotic Disorders Not Elsewhere Classified
       g. Mood (Affective) Disorders
       h. Anxiety Disorders
       i. Somatoform Disorders
       j. Dissociative Disorders
       k. Sexual Disorders
       l. Factitious Disorders
       m. Impulse Control Disorders Not Classified Elsewhere
       n. Adjustment Disorders
       o. Psychological Factors Affecting Physical Condition

2. Axis 2 categories
   a. Developmental Disorders
   b. Personality Disorders
D. Evaluation of DSM-III-R
   1. Is more specific about the criteria for various diagnostic categories
   2. Increased the number of dimensions for making diagnosis
   3. Increased reliability
   4. High level of diagnostic agreement on broad categories but low reliability for finer distinctions
   5. Emphasizes single point in time over history
   6. Descriptions ignore etiology
   7. Integrates vulnerabilities, assets, and stressful life events

III. Research on Classification
   A. Clinical Judgment
      1. Some disorders are more easily classified than others
      2. Certain factors contribute to disagreement and error
         a. patient factors
         b. method factors
         c. criteria
         d. clinicians

IV. Assessment: The Basis of Classification
   A. Interviews
      1. Types of interviews
         a. Assessment interviews are used to gather information
         b. Therapeutic interviews are used to modify behavior
      2. Content of the interview
         a. Are fairly unstructured
         b. Many aspects of behavior must be observed and noted
            (1) who is the client
            (2) how does the client think and feel about life at this time
            (3) what is the history of the problem
            (4) what is the client's present psychological state
      3. The role of the interviewer
         a. interviewer characteristics influence the interview
         b. interviewers often distort or misinterpret what goes on in an interview
         c. a relationship between interviewer and interviewee develops

      4. The standardized interview
         a. Same questions are asked of all persons
         b. Limit flexibility
      5. The Diagnostic Interview Schedule
         a. Used to diagnose DSM-III-R categories
         b. Good reliability and potential to make comparability across studies
   B. Psychological Tests
      1. Intelligence tests
         a. Binet tests
         b. Wechsler tests: WAIS-R, WISC-R, WPPSI
            (1) Verbal IQ
            (2) Performance IQ
         c. Controversies in intelligence testing
         d. See Box 4-1: Recent Developments in the Assessment of Intelligence
      2. Personality assessment
         a. Personality inventories ask people questions about themselves: The MMPI is the most widely used test
         b. Rating scales allow respondent to choose one of a number of descriptors but are complicated by halo effects
         c. Projective techniques
            (1) Are thought to be sensitive to unconscious personality dimensions
            (2) Ask the respondent to give meaning to ambiguous stimuli
            (3) Include Rorschach, TAT, word-association, and sentence-completion techniques
   C. Behavioral Assessment
      1. Grew out of behavior therapy
      2. The assessment focus
         a. avoids references to unconscious processes
         b. behaviors under observation must be relevant
         c. baseline observations often made prior to intervention
   D. Cognitive Assessment
      1. Provides information about thoughts that precede, accompany, and follow maladaptive behavior
      2. Provides information about adaptive thinking too
   E. Bodily Assessment
      1. Bodily functions reflect motivations, concerns, feelings
      2. Include measurement of pupil dilation, blood pressure, perspiration, heart rate,

blood volume, blood analysis, blood pressure

3. Polygraph is much used and abused instrument

4. Biofeedback can be used successfully with certain bodily complaints

V. Study Outline

Learning Objectives

Students should know:

1. That classification is useful as a means of communication, in record-keeping, and in the planning of treatment programs.

2. The major sources of diagnostic systems.

3. The purpose of having a multiaxial classification system in DSM-III-R. What the five Axes of this system are.

4. How the diagnosis of personality disorders and developmental disorders on Axis 2 meshes with the primary diagnosis on Axis 1.

5. How DSM-III-R improves over previous diagnostic systems. The weaknesses of DSM-III-R that have been identified to date.

6. Some of the factors that influence the quality of clinical judgments.

7. The major assessment methods used in gathering information about clients.

8. What general types of information are sought during an assessment interview. The differences between a diagnostic and a therapeutic interview.

9. The types of information yielded by the Wechsler intelligence tests that make them more popular than the Binet test.

10. How the MMPI scales were developed and how the MMPI is used in clinical practice.

11. The rationale underlying the use of projective techniques. The materials, administrative procedures, and general interpretational goals of the Rorschach, TAT, sentence completion, and word-association techniques.

12. How behavioral assessment differs from more traditional forms of assessment. The goals of conducting a behavioral assessment and the kinds of questions asked when conducting this procedure.

13. Some of the bodily functions that are measured through bodily assessment. Some of the

advantages and limitations of this form of assessment.

Discussion Questions

An effective way to get students involved in a debate on clinical diagnosis is to ask them to list, on a sheet of paper, their objections to using a diagnosis and a label. After this, have the students list the advantages of having a classification system to define the animal and plant kingdoms. Then ask them to ponder how well the advantages of classifying animals and plants would generalize to clinical and behavioral phenomena. Usually advantages and disadvantages can be divided into a) categorizing behavior, b) using labels, and c) the current diagnostic system.

Classroom Demonstration

One of the criticisms of projective techniques is that they lead to invalid clinical judgments of psychopathology. The open-ended nature of projective techniques can become a disadvantage unless specific scoring procedures are followed prior to their interpretation. This necessity is nicely illustrated by Loren and Jean Chapman's work on "illusory correlation" in clinical judgment. An illusory correlation occurs when a professional assumes that certain responses on a projective technique are associated with certain behaviors, but there is, in fact, no real relationship between the test sign and the behavior. For example, the elaboration of eyes in figure drawings is thought to be indicative of paranoid thoughts; however, the research evidence is that paranoid people do not draw eyes differently than nonparanoid people. The basis of an illusory correlation lies in the verbal associative connection between the test sign and the behavioral symptom, and in the culturally popular ideas about what people with a particular behavior say and do. The Chapmans have demonstrated the presence of illusory correlations in clinical judgments based on the Draw-A-Person technique and on the Rorschach. Others have demonstrated this error on word-association techniques, the TAT, and even the MMPI.

The illusory correlation phenomenon can be nicely demonstrated with the Draw-A-Person test. To prepare the demonstration, obtain nine overhead transparency sheets. On each, draw a human figure, making sure that the figures below the neck are as nearly alike as possible. For three of the figures draw an enlarged head, for another three, a medium-sized head, and for the last third, a small-sized head. Draw small eyes, medium eyes, and enlarged eyes for each of the three figures at each size of head. Announce to the students that you have figure drawings that are indicative of two problems. Ask the students to assume that each figure is made by a person who 1) is worried about how intelligent he is or 2) is overly suspicious of others. Then present each transparency on an overhead projection screen for approximately ten seconds each. Instruct the students to look for aspects of the drawings that might be signs of the two problems. After viewing all three figures, ask the students to indicate how likely each of six drawing signs are indicative of each of the two problems. Use the following scale: 4, very likely; 3, somewhat likely; 2, somewhat unlikely; 1, very unlikely. The six drawing signs are 1) broad shoulders, 2) detail in clothing, 3) ears enhanced, 4) eyes enlarged, 5) head enlarged, 6) hands well-defined. The most popular illusory correlation for "suspicious of others" is enlarged eyes. The most popular illusory correlation for "worried about intelligence" is enlarged head size. Note that the factorial pairings of the two variables on the nine cards did not produce any positive correlation of test sign with worry or concern.

Supplementary Material

Classical vs. Prototypic Diagnosis

Many beginning students of abnormal behavior tend to think of types of abnormal behavior as distinct, discrete categories. Much as chicken pox is different from measles and mumps, attention-deficit hyperactivity disorder is thought to be different from conduct disorder, and antisocial personality disorder is considered separate from borderline personality disorder. These assumed distinctions reflect a *classical* approach to diagnosis. Disorders are considered to have necessary and sufficient symptoms that indicate its occurrence. Research, however, indicates that most DSM-III-R diagnostic categories probably are *prototypic*. This means that considerable overlap of symptoms occurs across diagnostic categories and that symptoms are sufficient, but not necessary, to the occurence of a particular disorder. This allows many permutations of symptoms combinations and allows considerable variation within a diagnostic category. Also, the unique presentation of symptom patterns is still diagnosable with the prototypic approach, and a new category need not be designed with each exceptional case.

Computerized Test Reports

In the last two decades, the computer has been more widely used in psychological testing. Computers are used in all three phases of individual assessment: 1) test administration, 2) scoring, and 3) test interpretation. All kinds of tests, including major tests such as the MMPI, have been programmed for presentation on the computer. Even test takers unfamiliar with computers can easily be taught to press a few keys to respond "True" or "False" and to advance the next item of the test. Unobtrusive measures such as time-to-completion can be recorded as part of the program. The interactive nature of the computer-presented testing might actually enhance the motivation of the client, especially for those who have negative motivational associations with paper-and-pencil tests.

Programs for scoring tests have two major advantages, 1) speed of scoring and 2) accuracy. Machine-scored tests are less likely to contain human scoring errors. Moreover, computer-assisted scoring permits an examination of many ratios and subscale comparisons that would otherwise be tedious to compute by hand.

To produce test interpretations, programmers take an *actuarial* approach to interpretation. The actuarial approach uses descriptions of typical behavior drawn from a large number of respondents with particular test scores or test score configurations. Whenever a score or configuration is identified, the corresponding description is printed. This is sometimes called a "cookbook" method of interpretation. There are several advantages and disadvantages to the method. First, the advantages: 1) Comparisons of the individual with large classes of similarly scoring test takers can be made. 2) The method is more time efficient. 3) The approach avoids clinician biases and errors of interpretation likely to happen because of limitations in human information-processing capabilities; especially, availability heuristics are avoided, and there is less tendency to see all clients alike. Disadvantages include the following: 1) The special circumstances of the test taker cannot be fully computed. 2) Some of the interpretations are likely to be more relevant to the test taker than are other interpretations; alternative scenarios with corresponding "if not this behavior, then this behavior" are seldom available.

Most clinicians develop a *characterization* of the client by drawing on their clinical experience with a particular type of client, and most clinicians attempt to describe the behavior of the individual in the *context* of his/her current social/physical environment. To do so requires *clinical judgment*. Thus, most test interpreters prefer to add an interview or some other sample of behavior to the actuarial results of computer scored and interpreted tests. Although the research evidence strongly supports an actuarial approach for the *prediction* of behavior, clinical judgment can greatly enhance the *description* of behavior.

Computer-based psychological testing has been criticized by clinical psychologists for its misuse by professionals and by persons untrained in test interpretation. Among the major concerns are the following issues: 1) The test-taking circumstances and the response set of the test taker are too infrequently taken into consideration. 2)

CHAPTER 4   Classification and Assessment   *I*-19

Interpretations do not account for the idiosyncrasies of the test taker. 3) Interpretations are made available to test takers without any opportunity to sit down with a clinician and get a fuller explanation that would alleviate their fears and would put the test data in perspective. Many of the classic and standard psychological tests are restricted to trained professionals to reduce their misuse as much as possible.

CHAPTER 5

Vulnerability,
Stress, and Coping:
Maladaptive Reactions

Overview

In this chapter, the role of stress in maladaptive behavior is discussed. Sources of stress include stress-arousing situations, stressful developmental transitions, and the interactive influences of those two sources. The role of coping techniques and social support in adjustive responses is reviewed. Failures of coping with stress that lead to adjustment disorders, posttraumatic disorders, and the dissociative disorders are discussed.

Outline

I. Vulnerability and Coping
   A. Stress Appraisal
      1. Primary appraisal: interpret the situation as either threatening or harmless
      2. Secondary appraisal: consider the kind of action called for and the nature and potency of resources to cope with
      3. behavioral coping: what we do when confronted with a stressor
         (1) confronting stressor
         (2) feeling anxious
         (3) becoming angry
         (4) being defensive
   B. Vulnerability and Adjustment to Stress
      1. Vulnerability is related to coping skills and social support
      2. Coping skills
         a. characteristic ways of dealing with situations
         b. personal characteristics, confidence, experience, influence coping
         c. behavioral coping: what we do when confronted with a stressor
            (1) confronting stressor
            (2) feeling anxious
            (3) becoming angry
            (4) being defensive
         d. coping resources: capabilities not actual behavior
      e. personal vulnerabilities influence stress experience
      f. denial of significance is common response
   C. Coping Techniques
      1. Successful copers have a variety of techniques
         a. seek information
         b. share concerns
         c. redefine a situation
         d. consider alternatives and consequences
         e. use humor
      2. Foreknowledge helps coping with stress effectiveness
      3. Learning specific skills
      4. Self-statements
      5. Social support
         a. having close relationships buffers stress and provides security and self-confidence
         b. strong family ties encourage self-reliance
         c. Social Support Questionnaire

II. Stress Arousal
   A. Stress-Arousing Situations
      1. Dimensions of variability
         a. duration
         b. severity
         c. predictability
         d. degree of loss of control
         e. individual's level of self-confidence
         f. suddenness of onset
      2. Stress is a highly personal response
      3. Disasters: common reactions
         a. disaster syndrome: dazed, aimless wandering, severe physical symptoms; experienced by one-third of survivors
         b. death anxiety
         c. terrifying dreams
         d. death guilt
         e. psychological numbing

f. impaired social relationships

g. search for meaning

h. similarities of stressful situations: prestress period's lack of concern about occurrence of event; impact period's excessive excitation; intense anxiety, confusion, heightened physiological personality

B. Life Transitions

1. Molly's mastery of fear of thunderstorms involved

   a. expressing fearfulness

   b. seeking comfort

   c. developing comforting self-statements

   d. taking pride in mastery

2. Adolescence

   a. late-maturing boys and early physically maturing girls show more personal social maladjustment

   b. middle adolescence includes increasing social responsibilities and priviledges; also, here-and-now perspective shifts to more future oriented perspective

   c. in late adolescence, development of personal identity and separation from the family are paramount

   d. loneliness is experienced as parents are relinquished as primary attachment figures

3. Old age

   a. depression is the most prevalent disorder

   b. paranoid thinking increases

   c. sleep disturbances and physical complaints are more common

   d. positive adjustment is associated with ability to enjoy oneself, gratification from social relationships, ability to express feelings, positive self image, sense of purpose in life

   e. effects of bereavement are harder on men than women

C. Multiple Stressors

1. Depression, anxiety, physiological overreactivity are most common effects

2. Life Experiences Survey measures recent events

3. Stress-related disorders increase with declining economy

III. Clinical Reactions to Stress

A. Adjustment Disorders

1. One or more stressors within range of common experience have occurred in past 3 months and resulted in poor adjustment

2. Maladaptive reactions dissipate when stressful events pass or coping skills are learned

3. Case of Mark Catton: interaction between past and present experiences led to stressful transition in marriage

4. Extremely bizarre behavior usually is not evident

5. Is not part of a lifelong pattern of adjustment

6. Bereavement comes with the loss of someone through death

   a. grief is an emotional response to loss

   b. expressions of grief vary widely

   c. common pattern

      (1) shock and denial

      (2) intense suffering and crying

      (3) despair and acceptance

      (4) sadness, anger, self-reproach, withdrawal, tenseness, anxiety are common

      (5) harder on men than women

B. Postraumatic Disorders

1. Uncommon experiences produce long-term effects

2. Acute: within 6 months of event; delayed: more than 6 months later

3. Characteristics

   a. reexperiencing of traumatic event

   b. recurrent dreams or nightmares

   c. emotional numbing

   d. flood of thoughts

   e. excessive autonomic arousal, hyperalertness, concentration difficulties

   f. cues related to traumatic event trigger reactions

   g. decreased interest in social relationships, sexuality

   h. guilt feelings: survivor guilt

   i. impulsivity, alcohol and drug use increases

4. Case of Harry: how denial blunts feelings

5. PTSD is established disorder but is controversial

   a. prevalence is 1 percent in general population

   b. prevalence is 3.5 percent in civilians exposed to physical attack

   c. prevalence is 20 percent in wounded Vietnam veterans

C. Dissociative Disorders

1. Common characteristics

   a. sudden, temporary alterations of consciousness

b. sudden beginning and ending
c. past history of serious family turmoil
d. feelings of unreality, estrangement, depersonalization, some loss of self identity

2. Psychogenic amnesia
   a. extensive, selective memory losses
   b. usually precipitated by accident or emotionally traumatic event
   c. more common in females, adolescents, and young adults
   d. rare disorder with rapid recovery

3. Psychogenic fugue
   a. sudden loss of sense of identity
   b. wander far from home
   c. ends with sudden waking up without recollection
   d. precipitated by intolerable stress
   e. of brief duration

4. Multiple personality
   a. very dramatic but very rare (approximately 150 cases described since early 1800s)
   b. more common with females (4:1); separate memories and typical behaviors; personalities often lack awareness of each other
   c. family history of active, abusive parent and passive, onlooking parent is common
   d. case of Margaret B.
   e. original personality often shy, introverted, unable to deal with strong feelings of anger, sexual passion; secondary personalities are opposite

5. Depersonalization
   a. no memory disturbance
   b. "as if" feelings involving temporary loss of sense of reality; sense of estrangement from oneself
   c. rapid onset involving partial loss of control over actions

6. Interpreting dissociative disorders
   a. often difficult to separate dissociation and psychotic state
   b. source of stress not immediately evident
   c. often explained in psychodynamic and cognitive terms
   d. therapists seek to uncover dissociated memories
   e. hypnosis and sedatives also used as therapy adjuncts

IV. Treating Stress-Related Problems
   A. Supportive Therapy
      1. All major schools of psychotherapy emphasize strengthening client's ego
      2. Clinician must provide support and strengthen coping skills
   B. Drugs and Sedatives
      1. Do not cure but help overcome panic states
      2. Tranquilizers often prescribed along with supportive therapy
   C. Relaxation Training
      1. Regulating autonomic nervous system can affect emotional state
      2. Tension cannot be present when relaxed
   D. Systematic Desensitization
      1. Combination of relaxation training and hierarchy of anxiety-producing stimuli
   E. Cognitive Modification
      1. Learning new internal dialogues and ways of thinking about situations and oneself
   F. Social Intervention
      1. Family therapy is a form of intervention involving the social context

V. Study Outline

Learning Objectives

Students should know:

1. That a two-stage cognitive process involving primary and secondary appraisal occurs in response to stress.
2. Coping techniques that are effective with stressors.
3. How social supports facilitate coping with stress.
4. The characteristics of situations that arouse stress.
5. The phases that people go through in response to unforeseen, stressful events. That some situations are so threatening that most individuals who encounter them experience high levels of stress. These situations include accidents, disasters, wars, and physical illness.
6. What some of the transitions in the life cycle are and how they can be stressful.
7. The characteristics of adjustment disorders.

8. The characteristics of posttraumatic stress disorders.

9. What dissociative disorders are and how they differ from adjustment disorders and posttraumatic disorders.

10. The characteristics of conditions—psychogenic amnesia, psychogenic fugue, multiple personality, depersonalization—that comprise the category of dissociative disorders.

11. Therapeutic techniques for treating stress related disorders.

Supplementary Lecture Material

Scales for Measuring Life Stress

The textbook presents an example of a recently developed life-stress scale entitled the "Life Experiences Survey." In their introductory course of their reading, students probably have come across one or more other scales to measure stress. The most frequently referenced scale is the "Social Readjustment Rating Scale" (SRRS) introduced by Holmes and Rahe. (Holmes, T.H., & Rahe, R.H., 1967. The Social Readjustment Rating Scale. *Journal of Psychosomatic Research, 11,* 213-218.) Students will recall that the SRRS consists of 43 items, each of which is assigned a "life change unit" value (LCU) from 11 to 100. The items include events that are usually positive for most people (e.g., Christmas) and events that are usually negative for most people (e.g., death of a spouse). Students might also be aware that Holmes and Rahe developed the SRRS by following the ideas of Hans Selye in his general adaptation syndrome, which is a theory of stress reactivity. In his original theory, Selye postulated that any change, be it positive or negative, was stressful to an organism. Collective changes, whether positive or negative, result in the physical decomposition that prolonged resistance to stress entails. It was this point that Holmes and Rahe wished to investigate with their SRRS. Specifically, they wanted to see whether a large number of life changes preceded a decline in physical health. In developing the SRRS, Holmes and Rahe used a psychophysical scaling method. They selected a modal event, marriage, and assigned it an arbitrary value of 500 LCUs. Many adults were then asked to judge each event in relation to the modal event and to indicate how much change in one's life that event caused. Conversions were then made so that "marriage" received an LCU of 50, "death of a spouse" an LCU of 100, and "minor violations of the law" an LCU of 11. Subsequent research with the SRRS identified a positive correlation between total LCUs experienced in the past 12 months and the number

of health problems experienced. Other research extended this concept to study the relationship between life change and maladaptive behavior, principally anxiety and depression.

Selye's model of stress reactivity was challenged almost at its inception by those who argued that the effects of life change depend on whether the change is positive or negative. Their argument has been that life changes that are positive are not detrimental to one's physical and psychological well-being and that it is only the negative events that are likely to result in physical and psychological deterioration. The experience of positive life change was thought to have a buffer effect that could offset the experience of negative life change. A review of these arguments can be found in an article by Vinokur and Selzer. (Vinokur, A., & Selzer, M.L., 1975. Desirable versus undesirable life events: their relationship to stress and mental distress. *Journal of Personality and Social Psychology, 32,* 329-337.)

Another important change in measurement of life stress has been the emphasis on subjective versus objective definitions of what is positive or negative. Thus, normative determinations of whether an event is positive or negative were thought to be less predictive of health problems and anxiety and depression than an individual's determination of an event's stress as positive or negative. Subsequent research generally has supported the argument that subjectively determined negative events are most predictive of health problems, anxiety, and depression. The role of positive life experiences as a growth experience and a buffer of negative events has not been as clearly established. However, Selye, in a revision of his original theory, has recognized the possibility of growth experiences, that is positive life changes such as enrolling in college, and has coined the term "eustress" to account for these experiences.

The Life Experiences Survey, developed by the author of the textbook (Sarason, I.G., Johnson, J.H., & Siegal, J.M., 1978. Assessing the impact of life changes: development of the Life Experience Survey. *Journal of Consulting and Clinical Psychology, 46,* 932-946.) represents the latest technology in the measurement of life events-caused stress. Specifically, it allows the respondent to indicate whether the event was positive or negative ("good" or "bad"), and the amount of impact that the event had on the respondents' behavior. Norms are available that enable a comparative statement to be made about the level of stress. The Life Experiences Survey has become popular with researchers and some clinicians.

Other parallel developments in the evolution of stress scales have focused on whether a particular event is controllable or uncontrollable and desirable or undesirable. There is evidence that the experience of undesirable but controllable events is most highly correlated with health problems, anxiety, and depression. Other researchers have argued for the use of local norms in the interpretation of stress levels. The argument goes that what is stressful in rural North Carolina might not be stressful in New York City or in San Diego. Unfortunately, few researches have used local norms to interpret levels of stress caused by life change.

Finally, an astute student might wonder aloud how the life stress scales are related to the assessment of psychosocial stressors on Axis IV of DSM-III-R. To date, there is little evidence available to indicate that clinicians use formal life-stress scales to make a diagnostic assessment on Axis IV. The complexity of issues surrounding the development of scales to measure life stress might leave the clinician trusting in his or her own judgment about the impact of experienced changes rather than using stress scales.

Stress *in Combat*

The experience of combat is cited in the textbook as an event that is found stressful by most people who engage in it. Recent attention to the post-Vietnam syndrome has highlighted the residual effects of combat experience. Actually, psychiatrists and clinical psychologists had made major studies in their understanding of combat stress prior to the Vietnam experience. In World War I, disability due to combat-induced stress was called "shell shock." In World War II, it was called "war neurosis." In the Korean War, the label was "combat fatigue." And in Vietnam (and currently), the term used is "combat exhaustion."

The symptoms of combat stress initially develop with signs of irritability, including overreactions to minor annoyances, abrupt expressions of anger, profane language, and tearful release of feelings. These symptoms develop into hypersensitivity as evidenced in startle-like reactions to noises, sudden movements, or light flashes. Sleep disturbances—including insomnia, nightmares, and recurrent dreams—often follow. This pattern of responses probably is more prevalent than realized by the public. In a study of World War II combat soldiers, Karl Menninger reported that the normal battle reaction included a pounding heart (50%), a sinking stomach (45%), cold sweat (30%), nausea (25%), vomiting (20%), general weakness (20%), involuntary bowel movements (10%), and involuntary urination (6%). This initial phase of combat exhaustion can last for a relatively long period of time or until an additional severe stress experience leads to unresponsive or uncontrollable behavior. Studies of military personnel under prolonged combat exposure have indicated that no one is completely immune from the psychological effects of war. Some are able to withstand

the effects of combat for a longer period than others, but eventually even they will show this initial phase of combat exhaustion. War neurosis, as the phenomenon was called then, was the single greatest loss of manpower in World War II. In a particularly detailed study of stress experience by combat aircrews, Grinker and Spiegel (Grinker, R.R., & Spiegel, J.P., 1945. *Men under stress.* New York: McGraw-Hill.) pointed out that 50 percent of combat airmen in the Eighth Air Force were disabled by combat exhaustion. In the Korean War, the frequency of combat fatigue was less, ranging from four to six percent. In the Vietnam War, the rate declined to 1.2 percent. This improved rate has been attributed to several factors, including improved methods of screening and more timely recognition and treatment. Others have pointed to the specified time commitment (13 months for Marines, 12 months for other service branches) and the more ready access to "creature comforts" such as showers, cold milk and beer, television, and recreational opportunities.

One of the major questions in the study of psychological breakdowns in combat is why some individuals are better able to cope with this source of stress than others. Many have pointed to premorbid personality characteristics (pre-combat developmental histories) as a possible explanation. However, studies of Israeli solders during the 1973 Yom Kippur War and American soliders in the Vietnam War indicate that over 60 percent of those who became psychiatric casualties were clear of premorbid problems and thus low in vulnerability to the effects of stress. One study investigated the *meaning* of an intense combat experience to the individual and the coping mechanisms normally used by that individual to handle similar situations. (Hendin, H., Pollinger, A., Singer, P., & Ulman, R.B., 1981. Meanings of combat and the development of posttraumatic stress disorder. *American Journal of Psychiatry, 138,* 1490-1493.) Although inconclusive, this study is representative of research that sees psychiatric casualties to be a result of the interactive influence of personality characteristics such as usual coping strategies and parameters of the stressful situation that overwhelm those strategies.

Preventative methods to treat combat exhaustion include the principles of *immediacy, expectancy, simplicity,* and *centrality.* Immediacy refers to the early recognition of signs of combat exhaustion. Expectancy refers to the clearly stated attitude that combat exhaustion patients will return to duty and that the importance of the symptoms is minimal. Simplicity means that treatment consists of proper diet, rest and relaxation, a clean environment, verbal reassurance, and encouragement of open expression of feelings. Centrality means that the treatment occurs close to the battle stations of the casualties. In general, then, treatment efforts are directed at preserving the soldier's identification with the group, the reduction of self-preservation tendencies that result in psychiatric symptoms, maintaining the image of what is expected of the soldier, and conveying a sense of normalcy and expectation of recovery.

Despite the low rate of psychiatric casualties during the Vietnam War, great attention has been focused on the posttraumatic disorders of those veterans. Is the rate of such disorders higher for Vietnam veterans than veterans in previous wars? Estimates of residual stress effects among Vietnam veterans have ranged from 20 to 60 percent. However, estimates of posttraumatic symptoms in World War II and the Korean War veterans indicated that depression, irritability, easy fatigue, nightmares, bad memories, and interpersonal difficulties were also heavily represented among those ex-soldiers. One study, conducted at a veterans hospital in Minnesota, compared Korean War veterans with Vietnam War veterans for the presence of posttraumatic stress disorder symptoms. The target symptoms included recurrent, intensive recollections, recurrent dreams, sudden feelings of reexperiencing stress, diminished interest in hobbies, feelings of estrangement, constriction, and hyperalertness. Control symptoms included persecutory delusions, grandiosity, suicidal urges, and anxiety. About 42 percent of each group of veterans had posttraumatic stress disorder symptoms, and 58 percent of each group manifested the control symptoms. The obvious conclusion to be drawn from this study is that Vietnam veterans do not differ from veterans of other wars in the number and kind of posttraumatic stress symptoms.

Others have challenged this study, saying that drawing a representative sample of Vietnam veterans, many of whom have not visited veterans hospitals, would yield very different results. At least one such large-sclae study has been conducted and may yet yield valuable information on this question. Vietnam veterans cite the special conditions of entering and leaving the war zones. Soldiers were frequently inserted as individual replacements and also left the combat zone individually. In a matter of hours, soldiers could exit a combat area and arrive in the United States without fanfare. This sudden transition without the company of comrades-in-arms to talk out experiences may have contributed greatly to suppressed feelings leading to delayed stress reactions. It is becoming clear that posttraumatic disorders cannot be predicted by precombat levels of adjustment of Vietnam War veterans. It is also evident that those in combat roles have experienced more symptoms than those who were not in combat zones. Moreover, those with heavy combat experience and wounds have more symptoms than those with light combat experience. Of course, the question of whether Vietnam produced more cases of posttraumatic stress disorders than other wars may never be completely answered. Historical differences in attitudes toward admission to and expression of psychiatric symptoms might make true comparisons impossible.

CHAPTER 6

Anxiety Disorders

Overview

This chapter discusses anxiety disorders, which are characterized by intense feelings of apprehension in the absence of appropriate external stimuli. Four types of anxiety disorders are examined: general anxiety disorder, panic disorder, phobic disorder, and obsessive-compulsive disorder. These disorders are then viewed from the psychodynamic, learning, cognitive, and biological perspectives.

Outline

I. Anxiety
  A. Overview
    1. As many as one-third of all adults suffer nervous complaints
    2. Common features
      a. experience of strong anxiety
      b. worry
      c. tension
      d. discomfort
    3. Can be adaptive if it motivates learning adaptive behaviors
    4. Is abnormal to feel anxiety in the absence of a visible cause
  B. Characteristics of Anxiety
    1. Feelings of uncertainty, helplessness
    2. Nervous, tense, jumpy, irritable
    3. Difficulty falling asleep
    4. Easily fatigued
    5. "Butterflies in stomach", headaches, muscle tension
    6. Difficulty concentrating
  C. Anxiety Disorders
    1. Anxiety is disproportionate to external event
    2. Includes generalized anxiety disorders, panic disorders, phobias, obsessive-compulsive disorders
    3. Called "neuroses" by DSM-II, but changed to "anxiety disorders" in DSM-III

II. Generalized Anxiety Disorder
  A. Characteristics
    1. Anxiety persists for at least a month
    2. Is not attributable to recent life experiences
    3. Described as prolonged, vague, unexplained but intense fears not attached to any particular object
  B. Symptoms
    1. Motor tension
    2. Autonomic reactivity
    3. Apprehensive feelings about the future
    4. Hypervigilance

III. Panic Disorder
  A. Characteristics
    1. Range in length from seconds to days
    2. Differ in severity and degree of incapacitation
    3. Unanticipated attacks followed by normal functioning
    4. Severe palpitations, shortness of breath, chest pains, trembling, sweating, dizziness
    5. Fear of dying or going crazy
    6. Runs in families; twice as frequent in women as men
    7. May occur with specific environmental stimuli or without obvious cues
    8. Psychotic disorganization with impaired reality testing may follow a panic attack
  B. Differential Diagnosis
    1. Similar to generalized anxiety disorder except not anxious all the time and sudden onset with more severe attack
    2. Multiple types of maladaptive behavior—

obsessions, phobias, compulsions—occur simultaneously

C. Comparisons of Panic and Anticipatory Anxiety
1. Case of Mr. E.
   a. either generalized anxiety disorder or panic disorder
   b. recurrent attacks make panic disorder likely
2. Imipramine prevents recurrence of panic but has no effect on anticipatory anxiety
3. Generalized anxiety disorder has fewer bodily symptoms and earlier, more gradual onset
4. Generalized anxiety disorder is more chronic but has more favorable outcome
5. Sodium lactate may be involved in provoking panic attacks

IV. Phobias
A. Phobias
   Characteristics
1. Highly specific fears of objects, people, situations
2. No gross distortion of reality
3. Fears out of proportion with reality and beyond voluntary control
4. No physical explanations
5. Fears are related to disturbing qualities of events
6. Begin as generalized anxieties and crystallize around specific objects
7. Interfere with normal living patterns
   a. Separations
   b. animals
   c. bodily mutilation
   d. social situations
   e. nature
8. Tend to generalize and grow broader
9. Occur gradually but not in isolation from other symptoms
10. Account for 2 to 3 percent of presenting complaints in clinics
11. Do not require hospitalization
B. Simple Phobia
1. Relatively rare
2. Irrational fears not elsewhere classified
   a. Snakes, dogs, rats, claustrophobia
3. Treated by learning nonanxiety responses
C. Social Phobia
1. Fear and embarrassment in dealing with other people
   a. asserting oneself
   b. making a mistake
   c. public speaking
   d. criticism

2. Begin in late childhood or early adolescence
3. Incidence for men, 1.25 percent; for women, 2.00 percent
4. General feeling of inadequacy in life
   a. social and interpersonal difficulties
   b. feel like an imposter
5. Fear of public speaking and public eating are primary complaints
6. Depression is common
D. Agoraphobia
1. Most common type
2. Fear of unfamiliar situations; open spaces, traveling; crowds
3. Also accompanied by panic attacks, generalized anxiety
4. More common in women
5. Onset in late teens
6. Waxes and wanes with changing object of fear
7. Organize lives to minimize exposure to fearful stimuli
8. Two groups: with or without panic attack
9. Treated with antidepressant medication (tricyclics and monoamine oxydase inibitors)
   a. but drugs do not reduce anticipatory anxiety
   b. behavioral techniques such as gradual exposure are effective in treating agoraphobia
10. Often clinging, dependent; 50 percent have had separation anxiety in childhood

V. Obsessive-Compulsive Disorder
A. Characteristics
1. Obsessives: unable to get an idea out of mind
2. Compulsives: feel compelled to perform an act or series of acts
3. Obsessions involve doubt, hesitation, fear of contamination, fear of own aggression
4. Compulsions include counting, ordering, checking, touching, washing
B. Types of Obsessive-Compulsive Preoccupations
1. Checking
2. Cleaning
3. Slowness
4. Doubting-conscientiousness
C. Other Characteristics
1. Become problem when they interfere with important routines of daily life
2. Fear of loss of control and need for structure are believed to be the core

3. Not psychotic because he/she is aware of irrationality
4. Sometimes become phobias but there are differences
   a. Fear is directed at consequences of involvement with a situation
   b. more elaborate set of beliefs

VI. Interpreting and Treating Anxiety Disorders
A. The Psychodynamic Perspective
   1. Major causes
      a. intrapsychic events and unconscious motivations
      b. anxiety experienced by ego due to excessive environmental demands or id-ego-superego conflict
      c. defenses are inadequate to control anxiety
   2. Causes of anxiety that reaches clinical proportions
      a. perceptions of self as helpless to cope with demands
      b. separation or anticipation of abandonment
      c. privation, loss of emotional support
      d. unacceptable impulses close to becoming conscious
      e. threats or anticipations of approval and withdrawal of love
   3. Phobias
      a. object of fear is symbolic of unresolved psychological conflict
   4. Obsessive-compulsive disorders
      a. aggression and rage bottled up by defense mechanisms of isolation, undoing, reaction formation
   5. Psychotherapy
      a. gaining insight into the roots of anxiety
      b. difficult to measure therapeutic success
B. The Learning Perspective
   1. Acquired responses and response tendencies
   2. Behavior therapy
      a. exposure therapy used with phobic and obsessive-compulsive disorders
      b. implosive therapy: recreate original situation to experience it without pain
      c. in vivo exposure: exposure in real life settings
      d. flooding: more sudden than in vivo
      e. modeling: acquiring skills or competency
   3. Behavior therapy: modeling emphasizes acquiring skills and competence

a. participant modeling, therapist modeling, and corrective feedback as client performs same behavior
b. guided mastery over frightening situations and maladaptive behavior directed at mastery, self-efficacy
C. The Cognitive Perspective
   1. Cognitive behavior therapy: changes in thinking occur as a consequence of acquiring new responses
   2. Cognitive factors in maladaptive behavior
      a. thinking disturbances occuring only in certain places or in relation to certain problems are sources of anxiety
         (1) unrealistic appraisals of situations
         (2) consistent overestimation of dangerousness
         (3) person scans the environment for danger
      b. unreasonable beliefs and assumptions of obsessives
         (1) I should be perfectly competent
         (2) I must avoid criticism or disapproval
         (3) I will be severely punished for mistakes and imperfections
   3. Cognitive therapy
      a. cognitive restructuring: review irrational beliefs and develop more rational ways of looking at lives
      b. thought stopping: sudden distracting stimulus is used to terminate obsessive thoughts
      c. cognitive rehearsal: mentally rehearsing adaptive approaches to problematic situations
      d. Aaron Beck
         (1) 5-20 sessions
         (2) task-oriented
         (3) Socratic method
         (4) based on premise that each of us has an inner voice
D. The Biological Perspective
   1. Genetic and environmental factors: no direct organic cause has been found for most types of anxiety disorders, but there are physical correlates of anxiety disorders including
      a. hypersensitive nervous system
      b. 15 percent of parents and siblings of people with anxiety disorders are similarly affected
      c. heritability of timidity, fearfulness, aggressiveness

d. 40 percent concordance for monozygotic twins, 4 percent for dizygotic twins

2. Drug therapies

a. benzodiazepines: Librium, Valium; used to treat anxiety, tension, behavioral excitement, insomnia

b. side effects include drowsiness, lethargy, motor impairment, reduced concentration

c. bind to receptor sites in receiving neuron; receptors are specific to certain chemicals

d. antidepressants are used to treat panic and obsessive-compulsive disorders

(1) tricyclics (imipramine, clomipramine) might improve the positive effects of exposure therapy

VII. Study Outline

Learning Objectives

Students should know:

√ 1. That everyone feels anxious at times and that anxiety can facilitate adaptation.

√ 2. How an anxiety disorder differs from the simple experience of anxiety.

√ 3. The major symptoms most likely to be manifested in generalized anxiety disorders.

√ 4. The differences between generalized anxiety disorders and panic disorders.

√ 5. That phobias are unrealistic fears of specific people, situations, or objects. They should also know the three general types of phobias.

√ 6. That obsessions are preoccupying thoughts, and compulsions are overwhelming desires to behave in certain ways. They should know the most common features of obsessive-compulsive disorders.

√ 7. How the psychodynamic perspective views anxiety disorders primarily as manifestations of intrapsychic conflicts.

√ 8. That learning theory views anxiety disorders as learned responses to environmental stimuli. Also, the theoretical rationale for using systematic desensitization, implosion, in vivo desensitization, flooding, and modeling.

√ 9. What causes anxiety from the cognitive perspective and some of the cognitive treatment strategies for anxiety, including cognitive restructuring, thought stopping, and cognitive rehearsal.

10. That although no direct organic cause has been isolated for anxiety disorders, the prescription of tranquilizers and antidepressants is effective in reducing panic, but not anticipatory anxiety, and in making the individual more amenable to exposure therapy.

Classroom Demonstration

Systematic desensitization and relaxation training have been used with great success to treat simple phobias. These procedures are easy to demonstrate in a classroom setting. A run through part of Jacobson's muscle relaxation technique will give students a feeling for the effects of this intervention strategy.

Instruct the students with the following relaxation script:

Make yourself as comfortable as you can. Close your eyes. Now stretch your legs as far as they can go and turn the toes under and tighten the muscles very tight and hold it. (5-second pause) Now also tighten the muscles in your calves and those in your thighs. Make your entire leg as tight as a drum and hold it. (5-second pause) Hold it. (5-second pause) And now relax all the muscles in your toes, all the muscles in your calves, all the muscles in your thighs. Let your legs go completely limp. And now feel that wonderful relaxation coming up from your toes, up your calves, up your thighs, and you are feeling wonderfully relaxed, beautifully relaxed, very calm, very relaxed. (5-second pause) Now I want you to stretch out your hands and make a fist. Feel the tightness. And now make it tighter, tighter, tighter, and hold it. (5-second pause) And now also tighten the muscles in your wrists, in your forearms, in your upper arms. (5-second pause) Hold it. (5-second pause) Now let go and get the wonderful feeling of relaxation right through your fingers, your hands, and now through your forearms and your upper arms. Let your arms go completely limp, and you are feeling wonderfully relaxed, beautifully relaxed, very calm, very relaxed, and feeling just beautiful.... (Instructions are discontinued at this point but would include additional tension relaxation of the torso, face, back, stomach muscles.) You are feeling calm, feeling relaxed, feeling like you are floating on a sea of tranquility; completely calm and at ease. (5-second pause) And now, just enjoy that wonderful feeling of relaxation and well-being for a few moments. (15-second pause) Soon I will count to five, and you will open your eyes. You will continue feeling as calm and wonderfully in control of your feelings as you feel now. Your mind will be clear and alert and your body will feel very well in every way. One—feeling fine. Two—coming up now, feeling very good. Three—feeling very relaxed, but alert. Four and five—open your eyes, feel relaxed, feel calm, feel wonderfully well.

A hierarchy of fears can easily be constructed around the anxiety of school examinations. A volunteer from the class might be solicited in order to construct a personal hierarchy of fearful stimuli leading up to school examinations. If no volunteer is forthcoming, the fear hierarchy in Table 6.1 can be presented to the students.

The three steps involved in conducting systematic desensitization are 1) training the individual in the use of progressive relaxation until a state of relaxation can be induced and maintained relatively easily; 2) constructing a hierarchy of anxiety-inducing events that lead up to the feared major event (most hierarchies will begin at 0 and

end at 100 and probably will not have equal intervals); and 3) alternating exposure (in vivo or imaginary) to items on the hierarchy and to the relaxation response, starting each time from the beginning and continuing up the hierarchy until the individual feels uncomfortably anxious. The fearful individual should be asked to rerate the items of the hierarchy at the close of the session. Successive sessions involving progressively greater exposure to the most anxiety producing events usually result in lowered ratings of anxiety. Frequently, however, the ratings do not reach zero but stabilize at a more manageable level.

Supplemental Lecture Material

Distinguishing between Anxiety Disorders and Personality Disorders

As was noted in the text, DSM-III dropped the label "neurosis" and substituted the term "anxiety disorders" to make the classification system more atheoretical. Previous DSM classifications had been heavily influenced by the psychodynamic perspective, especially for disorders with anxiety as a principle characteristic. It is rather instructive to review the history of the concept of "neurosis" and to trace its differentiation from the similar category of personality disorders. This has been done nicely in an article by Townsend and Martin (Townsend, J.S., & Martin, J.A. 1983. Whatever happened to neurosis? An overview. *Professional Psychology: Research and Practice, 14,* 323-329.) and is presented in Table 6.2.

The term neurosis is derived from the Greek word *neupov*, which means nerve. The word *neurosis* was first used in a clinical sense by William Cullen (1772) to refer to functional impairment that had no evidence of physiological pathology. A little over a century later, Freud developed the concept of neurosis by distinguishing between actual neurosis and psychoneurosis. The former referred to a physical disorder brought about by repressed sexual tension, whereas the latter term was used to refer to the formation of psychological symptoms (behavioral, cognitive, and affective) caused by the repression of inner conflicts. Much of Freud's later work was with psychoneurosis. He identified subtypes of anxiety neurosis, anxiety, and hysteria. In all of these disorders, the symptoms manifested the conflict between id and superego functions.

Neo-Freudians made a distinction between character neurosis (personality disorder) and symptom neurosis (psychoneurosis). Again, it has been the latter term, symptom neurosis, that includes the neurotic disorders

TABLE-6.1

Hierarchy of Fearful Events Leading Up to a School Examination

Fear Rating	Event
0	Beginning the course
15	Hearing the instructor announce the first exam three weeks hence
20	Trying to decide how to study for the exam
25	Reading and reviewing the material that will be on the exam
50	Hearing the instructor announce that the exam is one week away
55	Hearing a fellow student ask what kinds of questions will be on the exam
70	Studying the night before the exam
80	Cramming alone in the library right before the exam
85	Walking to the room just before the exam
90	Hearing other students talk just before class begins
95	Waiting for copies of the exam to be passed down the row
100	Looking at the exam and seeing that the first page is all multiple choice questions
100	Seeing that there are seven pages including two pages of essay questions
100	Reading the first question and not being sure about it

TABLE-6.2

Evolution of the Term "Neurosis"

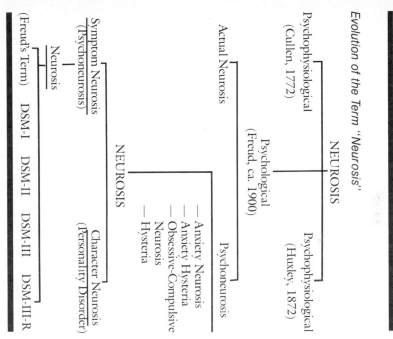

The research is fairly clear that there is no correlation between having an obsessive-compulsive personality character style and experiencing the symptoms of an obsessive-compulsive anxiety disorder. (Carr, A.T., 1974. Compulsive neurosis: A review of the literature. *Psychological Bulletin, 81*, 311-318.) Moreover, the research is more supportive of a social-learning theory of obsessive-compulsive personality development than of a psychoanalytic theory. The evidence seems to indicate that obsessive-compulsive personality traits are modeled by parents to their children as desirable. Psychoanalytic notions of fixations around toilet training experiences largely have not been supported. In contrast, there is more support for psychoanalytic interpretations of the development of obsessive-compulsive anxiety disorders. Despite sharing a similar name, then, the evidence raises the question of whether the two disorders are different entities.

Obsessive-Compulsive Anxiety Disorder versus Obsessive-Compulsive Personality Disorder

Students often confuse obsessive-compulsive anxiety disorder with obsessive-compulsive personality disorder. To be fair, professionals are not always sure what these syndromes are, as witnessed by the change of names from DSM-II to DSM-III, and DSM-III-R (neurosis to anxiety disorders; obsessive-compulsive personality disorder to compulsive personality disorder, back to obsessive-compulsive personality disorder). In an anxiety disorder, the individual experiences the persistent intrusion of undesired thoughts (obsessions) or urges and actions (compulsions) that he or she finds difficult, if not impossible, to control and manage. Although the individual is aware of the inappropriateness and irrationality of the thoughts or actions and wants to stop, he or she cannot. In the personality disorder, the individual is asymptomatic, that is without psychiatric symptomatology, but has a style of adaptation that includes straits, defenses, and a characteristic life style. Those individuals with obsessive-compulsive personality disorder usually manifest both compulsive thinking ("obsessive") and compulsive motor behavior ("compulsions"). Research indicates that they are exceedingly systematic and methodical people who prefer a well-ordered life, who are themselves consistent and punctual, meticulous in their use of words, who dislike unfinished tasks and interruptions in their plans and goal-directed behavior. (Pollak, J.M., 1979. Obsessive-compulsive personality: A review. *Psychological Bulletin, 86*, 225-241.) These characteristics are well-integrated, considered consonant with ideal-self, and thus a source of pride and positive self-esteem. In contrast, the symptoms of the anxiety disorder—the unwanted thoughts and compulsive acts—severely disrupt the individual's life, are accompanied by worry, doubt, and procrastination, and are experienced as alien and disturbing. To use the language of the psychodynamic perspective, the symptoms of the personality disorder are ego-syntonic, and those of the anxiety disorder are ego-dystonic.

described in DSM-I and DSM-II and anxiety disorders described in DSM-III and DSM-III-R.

CHAPTER 7

Psychological Factors and Physical Symptoms

Overview

The relationship between psychological and biological factors in determining symptoms of physical illness is explored. Theories concerning this relationship initially are discussed. Three general disorders that are influenced by psychological and biological interactions are then examined. Psychophysiological disorders involve physical impairment exacerbated by psychological factors. In somatoform disorders, there are physical complaints that are not accompanied by physical impairment. People who voluntarily produce physical symptoms in order to manipulate others are classified as having a factitious disorder.

Outline

I. Concepts of Psychological, Social, and Bodily Interaction
  A. Awareness That Mind Can Influence the Body
    1. Concept dates to ancient Greeks and Romans
    2. In 18th and 19th centuries, Mesmer and Charcot treated bodily complaints with hypnosis
    3. Freud applied psychoanalytic concepts
  B. Psychosomatic Hypothesis
    1. Psychosomatic hypothesis held that physical symptoms can be caused by blocking of emotional expression
    2. Specific emotional conflicts and stressors were thought to be associated with particular physical conditions
    3. Organ-susceptibility hypothesis stated that a weak organ would break down under stress

  4. General adaptation syndrome refers to 3-phase pattern of reaction to prolonged stress
    a. shock or alarm response
    b. resistance phase
    c. exhaustion phase
  C. Biopsychosocial Model
    1. Current emphasis
    2. Person is a system with psychological states, social and biological subsystems
    3. Homeostasis refers to mechanism by which organism struggles to restore equilibrium
II. Psychological Factors Affecting Physical Health
  A. Interactive Effects of Psychological and Physical Factors
    1. Psychological states play a role in susceptibility to physical illness
    2. Physical illness affects state of mind
  B. Stress and Illness
    1. Two factors influence stress reaction
      a. meager, distorted psychological resources
      b. perceived severity of situations
    2. Psychological factors that play a role in physical illness
      a. inability to adapt to changes in environmental demands
      b. inability to handle and express realistically strong feelings and emotions
      c. inability to interpret demands, constraints, opportunities correctly
      d. inability to form rewarding, long-lasting interpersonal ties, particularly love relationships
    3. Temperament and personality early in life may be predictive of illness susceptibility decades later, e.g., self-confidence in adolescence

4. Not all people biologically predisposed become ill
5. Community and social variables—poverty, migration, occupation—affect health

C. Longevity
1. Social isolation, sudden loss of a loved one, death of a parent, chronic loneliness shorten the life span
2. See Table 7-1 for predictors of longevity
3. Nonbiological factors play a role in longevity
   a. mortality rates are higher for socially isolated
   b. women live longer than men
   c. psychological hardiness describes people more resistant to stress and less susceptible to illness: stronger sense of personal control, greater involvement, more open to change

III. Behavioral Medicine and Health Psychology
A. Introduction
1. Behavioral medicine
   a. using psychological techniques to treat illness
   b. goal: to improve service delivery
2. Health psychology
   a. using techniques to prevent illness
   b. strengthens behaviors that lead to good health
3. Common to both is the emphasis to maximize health

B. Interpreting Bodily Signals
C. Using Health-Related Information
D. Psychological Processes and the Immune System
1. Stress and emotional arousal can lower the immune system's resistance to disease

IV. Psychophysiological Disorders
A. Cardiovascular Disorders
1. Coronary heart disease (CHD)
   a. 20 percent develop CHD before age 60
   b. produced by lesions of coronary arteries
   c. angina pectoris: periodic chest pains caused by insufficient supply of blood to heart due to plaque buildup (atherosclerosis)
   d. myocardial infarction: more complete curtailment of blood supply ("heart attack")
   e. catecholamines (epinephrine and norepinephrine) secreted under arousing conditions accelerate rate of arterial damage

f. although rate of mortality has dropped recently—30 percent in last 30 years—heart disease is leading cause of death after age 45
2. Life style patterns
   a. twin studies indicate that life experiences cause CHD
   b. cross-cultural studies also support role of life experience
   c. social losses and isolation are related to CHD
   d. Occupational stress correlated with CHD
3. Type-A coronary-prone behavior pattern
   a. heart attack-prone personality pattern includes competitiveness, striving for achievement, aggressiveness
      (1) talking rapidly, explosively
      (2) moving, walking, eating rapidly
      (3) unduly irritated at delay
      (4) scheduling more in less time
      (5) guilty while relaxing
      (6) doing two things at once
   b. one of strongest single predictors of heart disease
   c. more common with middle-level managers than top business executives
   d. prospective studies support role of behavior in CHD
      (1) Framingham Study of 5,127 adults
   e. contradictory findings exist and methodological problems abound
   f. efforts to modify CPB have been successful
4. Hypertension
   a. high blood pressure: greater than $150/90$
   b. related to environmental stress, anxiety, sustained anger
   c. relaxation training and biofeedback treatments are often effective in reducing blood pressure
   d. most common chronic indicator—10 percent of adults
   e. anger and anger suppression accompany inadequate social expression

B. Cancer
1. Psychological factors associated with cancer
   a. emotional constrictedness: people who deny strong feelings are prone to developing cancer
   b. uncontrollable stress
   c. how anger is dealt with: expressed too directly or bottled up too tight

    d. depression has predicted later cancer

2. Research encouraging but longitudinal studies needed

C. Headaches
1. Most commonly reported bodily complaint (10 to 20 percent of those who see a physician)
2. Pain components
   a. physiological changes
   b. subjective experience of pain
   c. behavior motivated by pain
3. Tension headaches distinguished by skeletal-muscle change, often in response to stress
4. Migraine headaches are on one side or on front of head, are severe, are caused by dilation of cranial artery
   a. usually preceded by aura
   b. perfectionistic personality, driven traits
   c. drugs constrict arteries; behavior therapy helps others

D. Allergies
1. Cause of asthma is unknown but involves allergic reaction
2. 3 percent of population have asthma
3. Psychological and situational factors maintain or worsen asthmatic attacks
   a. panic and fear
   b. overcontrolling parents
      (1) Purcell's study of children separated from parents supports this

E. Gastrointestinal Disorders
1. Abnormalities of the digestive system including diarrhea and ulcers
2. Lack of control over environment leads to ulceration in animals
3. Heredity is a predisposing factor in ulcers but stress brings them on

F. Rheumatoid Arthritis
1. May be affected by stress, disturbed interpersonal relationships, or lowered self-esteem

V. Somatoform Disorders
A. DSM-III-R Categories
1. Bodily complaints exist, but psychological factors rather than physiological factors are responsible
2. Include somatization disorder, conversion disorder
3. Psychogenic pain disorder: severe prolonged pain in excess of normal organic symptoms

4. Hypochondriasis: unrealistic fear of disease; obsessive preoccupation with health

B. Somatization Disorder
1. Marked by multiple somatic complaints
2. Called "Briquet's Syndrome"
3. Complaints are vague, exaggerated, dramatic
4. Most frequent complaints: headache, fatigue, heart palpitations, fainting
5. History of doctor shopping
6. Patients believe they are sickly and provide detailed histories to support their claims
7. Show many features of histrionic personality disorder
8. More frequent among women; pattern begins in early adulthood

C. Conversion Disorder
1. Loss of part or all of basic bodily function
   a. e.g., glove anesthesia
2. Not under voluntary control
3. Psychoanalytic perspective: symptom has symbolic value and represents an underlying psychological conflict
4. Self-reports of symptoms do not correspond with neuroanatomy
5. Frequently traced to specific precipitating stressors
6. La belle indifférence describes lack of concern about disability
7. Secondary gains include attention, affection, disability pension
8. Most outbreaks are referred to as group hysteria

VI. Factitious Disorders and Malingering
A. Voluntary Production of Symptoms
1. Desire to assume a patient's role is goal of factitious disorder
   a. Lying, demanding, and dramatic traits
   b. More common among men
   c. frequent hospitalizations
2. Munchausen Syndrome: marked by repeated knowing simulation of disease for sole purpose of obtaining medical attention
3. Malingerers seek medical care in order to obtain a specific goal
4. Occur in people with severe, lifelong personality disturbances

VII. Study Outline

Learning Objectives

Students should know:

1. The implications of the psychosomatic hypothesis and the organ susceptibility hypothesis. The weaknesses of these theories.

2. The three phases of the general adaptation syndrome.

3. The interactive nature of the effects of biological and psychosocial factors on health.

4. The similarities and differences between behavioral medicine and health psychology.

5. The principle characteristics of psychophysiological disorders.

6. Biological and psychological variables contributing to coronary heart disease. Sociocultural factors associated with coronary heart disease and hypertension.

7. The characteristics of the Type A coronary-prone behavior pattern.

8. Some psychological factors that have been associated with cancer.

9. The characteristics of tension headaches and migraine headaches.

10. That asthma is an allergic condition that is maintained or worsened by psychological factors in a majority of cases.

11. That heredity predisposes and stress brings on the development of ulcers.

12. That somatoform disorders are the result of psychological rather than physiological factors.

13. The characteristics of somatization disorder.

14. The characteristics of conversion disorder.

15. That factitious disorders and malingering involve the voluntary production of symptoms to obtain gains.

Supplementary Lecture Material

Personality Characteristics of Hypertensives

Researchers have been interested for a long time in the personality characteristics of those who develop hypertension. One of the earliest theories, developed by Franz Alexander from the psychoanalytic perspective (Alexander, F., 1950. *Psychosomatic medicine*. New York: Norton.), proposed that specific psychophysiological dis-

orders were associated with specific unconscious conflicts. For example, a person with hypertension has unconscious hostile impulses. Control of those impulses waxes and wanes so that the person fluctuates between excessive control to outbursts of aggression. These hostile impulses are controlled through repression, which leads to chronic blood pressure elevation. According to Alexander, other disorders are associated with other specific conflicts. For example, a person with asthma has an unresolved dependency on his or her mother. Research on Alexander's *specific conflict theory* of psychophysiological disorders has not been very supportive so that the theory is no longer popular with most clinicians.

Graham (Grace, W.J., & Graham, D.T., 1952. Relationship of specific attitudes and emotions to certain bodily diseases. *Psychosomatic Medicine, 14,* 243-251.) tried to match specific attitudes to specific disorders. Based on interviews with 128 people with 12 different kinds of psychophysiological disorders, she discovered that people with hypertension feel threatened with harm and must be ready and on guard, whereas people with asthma feel left out and want to shut other people or situations out. Once again, Graham's *specific attitude* hypothesis has not been supported by subsequent research.

A third approach, also from the psychodynamic perspective, has produced more fruitful results. David McClelland has developed a theory of hypertension which focuses on intrapsychic needs and the expression of those needs. In particular, he has identified suppressed anger as an explanation of hypertension. Three factors are thought to be related to the development of high blood pressure. There is 1) a high need for power, that is, a need to influence others or have an impact on them; 2) a strong tendency to inhibit the overt expression of this need through aggression (power inhibition); and 3) strong situational pulls to use power. He has found that college students who have stronger power needs than affiliation needs (desire to be friends with others, to avoid disapproval) and who are high in power inhibition have higher diastolic blood pressure than students with other combinations of needs, including inhibition. In a longitudinal study, McClelland found that elevated blood pressure at the ages of 51 to 53 could be predicted by the need patterns of these same men at the age of 30. (McClelland, D.C., 1979. Inhibited power motivation and high blood pressure in men. *Journal of Abnormal Psychology, 88,* 182-190.) In this study, 78 men had responded to TAT pictures in their early 20s and had their blood pressure checked every five years from approximately the age of 20. At the age of 30, men who had power scores greater than affiliation scores and who also had high power inhibition scores had significantly higher diastolic blood pressure at their later ages of 51 and 53 compared to men with other combinations of motive patterns. Of the 23 men with the suppressed anger motive pattern, six were under treatment for hypertension in their early 50s, five had died of cardiovascular disease, and 14 had elevated diastolic blood pressures. In all, 61 percent had shown signs of hypertension by their early 50s, whereas only 23 percent of the other 47 men showed signs of hypertension. The longitudinal design of this study lends strength to these findings and suggests that suppressed anger is one variable that can contribute to hypertension. Unfortunately, situational challenges to use power were not examined in the study, nor were alternative contributions to hypertension such as physiological predisposition and occupational stress ruled out.

McClelland's findings, then, appear to support Alexander's specific conflict theory of hypertension. Research has yet to determine whether this motive pattern is associated only with hypertension or whether it produces other psychophysiological disorders as well. There is evidence that the suppressed power motive is involved in other maladaptive behavior such as excessive alcohol use.

Conversion Disorder

Case History. The case of "The Girl Who Couldn't Breathe" was one of Freud's earlier cases on hysteria, originally published in his book with Joseph Breuer, *Studies in Hysteria* (1895). This was Freud's first case in which he did not use hypnosis. It very clearly shows Freud's views on the sexual etiology of hysteria.

One summer, while vacationing in the Alps, Freud hiked to the top of a mountain to stay at an inn. He was approached by a young woman, Miss Katharina, who complained of having difficulty breathing. She elaborated by saying that her attacks began with pressure on her eyes, her head would feel heavy, she would hear humming noises, she would become dizzy, her throat would feel tight, and then she would have trouble breathing. Freud felt that these were anxiety attacks and asked her about their origin. Miss Katharina began telling Freud about how, two years earlier, she had seen her uncle in bed with her cousin. At that time, Katharina said that she had trouble breathing, she tightened her eyes, and felt her head throb and hum. She didn't tell anyone about the incident at that time.

Three days after that incident, she woke up feeling dizzy and vomited. She stayed in bed, vomiting for three days. After she finally told her aunt, her aunt and uncle fought. The aunt and her children left the uncle with the cousin, who had become pregnant. In relating this story to Freud, Katharina told two other stories regarding her uncle that preceded the traumatic event. One story told of how, when she was 14, she went on an overnight trip with her uncle, who made sexual advances toward her during the night (although she did not know that the advances were sexual at that time). She then told of two instances in which she stayed overnight with her uncle and cousin and noted strange goings-on between them, again, not knowing what it all meant. Nevertheless, she had experienced symptoms like the present ones, but less intense during these earlier episodes.

After hearing these stories, Freud said to Katharina:

Now I know what you thought at the time you looked into the room. You thought, "Now he does with her what he wished to do with me on that night and the other time." It disgusted you, because you recalled the feeling how you awakened in the night and felt his body.

Freud never saw miss Katharina again and so could not complete his analysis. He hypothesized that the vomiting, which had been the first hysterical symptom after seeing her uncle and cousin in bed, had disappeared because Katharina had told her aunt what had happened, resulting in an emotional release or abreaction. Her aunt, however, did not want to hear any more and Katharina couldn't continue to discuss her feelings. This caused a damming up of tension, and unreleased, the other symptoms continued. Freud could only hope that by providing Katharina an opportunity to release these tensions he had helped her overcome her symptoms.

Freud believed this to be a typical case of hysteria where memories of sexual experiences in childhood become traumatic when triggered by an event which occurs when the person is old enough to understand sexuality. Katharina's symptoms were believed to be hysterical in that they were linked to reproductions of the anxiety she experienced during each of the events associated with her uncle that were sexual in nature.

Common symptoms. Textbooks on abnormal behavior frequently give examples of conversion disorder that include paralysis, blindness, and deafness. Such examples often nicely demonstrate the principles of conversion disorder reaction. It is dramatic to ponder how an individual could suddenly lose a major sensory function, that it not be under voluntary control, and that he or she not be overly distressed by this great sensory loss. But are these the physical symptoms most frequently seen in diagnosed cases of conversion disorder? Watson and Buranen (Watson, C.G., & Buranen, C., 1979. The frequencies of conversion reaction symptoms. *Journal of Abnormal Psychology, 88,* 209–211.) examined the relationships between the frequency of mention in 18 popular textbooks in abnormal psychology and the frequency of appearance in 40 cases of conversion disorder diagnosed at VA hospitals. Paralysis was mentioned in all of the textbooks but was found in only eight percent of the diagnosed cases. Blindness and deafness were mentioned in 94 percent and 72 percent of the textbooks, respectively, but were found in one of the cases identified by Watson and Buranen. The physical symptoms found most frequently in the diagnosed cases were hyperesthesia (58 percent), paresis (42 percent), anesthesia (38 percent), headache (32 percent), and paresthesia (25 percent). The respective frequency mentions by textbooks for these symptoms were 39 percent, 11 percent, 49 percent, 17 percent, and 50 percent. The rank order correlation between symptoms listed in textbooks and those identified in research was a nonsignificant .27. In addition, Watson and Buranen have pointed out that diagnosed cases of conversion disorder rarely contain a single physical symptom. Rather, the

presenting picture is one of multiple physiological complaints and with a gradual onset rather than a sudden appearance of symptoms. One might easily conclude from this study that textbooks have presented an overly simplified view of conversion disorders. Some, however, have criticized the sample of the Watson and Buranen study. First of all, the VA patients were all males, whereas the conversion disorder is more frequently diagnosed in the population at large among women. Secondly, the strictness of the diagnostic criteria might have varied over the years of the study that were represented by the cases of this study. Nevertheless, one is left wondering whether and how frequently textbook versions of conversion disorder actually do occur.

CHAPTER 8

Sexual Variations and Disorders

Overview

This chapter considers two types of sexual behaviors, those that are often personally troublesome and those that deviate from societal norms. Historical, current legal, and psychological attitudes toward sex are traced, and the pioneering work of Havelock Ellis, Freud, Kinsey, and Masters and Johnson are briefly discussed. Sexual dysfunctions are viewed as a result of experienced stress and various treatments are discussed. Homosexuality as a preference is distinguished from homosexuality as a disorder; transexual behavior, issues of gender identity, and sexual deviations involving paraphilias and pedophilia are considered.

Outline

I. Changing Views of Sexual Behavior
  A. Historical Concepts
    1. Ancient Greeks regarded sex as a part of nature
    2. In the 15th century, sex was viewed as sinful
    3. Sexual liberation occurred in 18th century
    4. In Victorian era, sex was viewed as beautiful, but only after marriage and only for men
    5. Havelock Ellis and Freud brought topic of sex into public consciousness
II. Gathering Objective Information About Sexual Behavior
  A. Surveys
    1. Kinsey's surveys
      a. first objective study of sexual behavior through interviews

      b. stimulated scientific study of sexual behavior
      c. led to change in society's acceptance of sexual behaviors
      d. premarital sex, extramarital sex, and oral-genital stimulation all have increased
    2. Other surveys have appeared in magazines or through newspaper recruitment
  B. Observational Research
    1. Masters and Johnson are pioneers in laboratory study of sexual behavior
    2. Described 4-stage pattern of sexual response
      a. excitement
      b. plateau
      c. orgasm
      d. resolution
    3. Challenged popular beliefs such as presumed differences between clitoral and vaginal orgasms
    4. Developed treatment techniques
  C. Case Studies
    1. Interesting but limited in scientific value
  D. Experimental Findings
    1. Research suggests that alcohol consumption affects sexual response
III. Sexual Variations
  A. Overview
    1. Lesbianism: female homosexuality
    2. Females less likely to have homosexual experience
    3. Kinsey estimates 4 to 10 percent homosexual behavior among males
      a. Kinsey has 7-point scale reflecting degree of homosexuality
    4. Rates have not changed through 20th century
  B. Research on Homosexuality

1. Some evidence that foundation of sexual preference is seen in childhood
2. Self-identification as homosexual comes about over a long period of time
3. Cross-cultural studies find homosexuality normative in some cultures
4. Majority of homosexuals are well-adjusted
5. There is no single personality or life style

C. Bisexuality
1. About 5 percent of adults have sexual activity with both males and females
2. Both bisexuals and gays may have conventional marriages

D. How Sexual Preference Develops
1. Animal research shows that prenatal hormone treatments play role in preference
2. Freud believed all are innately bisexual and attraction for the same sex is caused by a variation in sexual development
3. May be related to being rewarded by certain sexual experiences
4. Bell found no evidential support for psychodynamic or behavioral perspectives

IV. Sexual Dysfunction
A. Types of Sexual Dysfunction
1. DSM-III-R four-phase sexual response cycle
   a. appetitive: inhibition of sexual desire
   b. excitement: impotence, frigidity
   c. orgasm: premature ejaculation, retarded ejaculation, inhibited orgasm
   d. resolution
2. Erectile dysfunction
   a. performance anxiety
   b. also physical causes such as diabetes, hormonal imbalances
   c. usually occurs early in adult life
3. Functional vaginismus
   a. involuntary contraction of vaginal muscles preventing insertion of penis
4. Functional dyspareunia
   a. genital pain lasting for minutes or days
   b. occurs for both sexes
5. Half of marriages experience sexual dysfunction of some kind

B. The Treatment of Sexual Dysfunction
1. Masters and Johnson pioneered short-term treatment directed primarily at sexual problems
2. Therapeutic team approach including a physician and a behavioral scientist
3. Sensate focus technique
   a. reacquainting couples to the pleasures of tactile touch
   b. enhance erotic factors and diminish inhibiting distractions
4. Semans approach
   a. used to treat premature ejaculation
5. Low failure rates reported for sexual dysfunction programs
6. Behavior therapists use relaxation and modeling
7. For those whose sexual dysfunctions are rooted in more profound conflicts: Helen Singer Kaplan's psychodynamic therapy

C. The Effectiveness of Sex Therapy
1. Reported success rates range from 39 to 98 percent
   a. success is poorly defined
2. Must determine which therapeutic elements are most helpful

V. Gender Identify Disorder
A. Overview
1. Encompasses individual's conviction of being male or female
2. Part of self-concept, expressed through behavior, attitudes, fantasies

B. Childhood Problems of Gender Identity
1. Intense desire to be opposite sex continues into adulthood, then becomes transsexualism
2. Characterized by cross-gender clothing preferences and engaging in activities typical of opposite sex
3. Many candidates for sexual reassignment show considerable psychological disturbance

C. Transsexualism
1. Adults who intensely desire to change their sexual status and anatomical structure
2. Many applicants for sexual-reassignment therapy have considerable psychological disturbance

VI. The Paraphilias
A. Fetishism
1. Nonliving object serves as primary source of sexual arousal and consummation
2. Rubber fetishes are popular
3. Chronic disorder that is not well understood
   a. do not seek therapy

B. Transvestism
1. Cross-dressing to achieve sexual stimulation

2. Usually limited to men
3. More inhibited, less involved, more independent
4. Covert sensitization a useful treatment technique

C. Sexual Sadism and Masochism
   1. Inflicting or experiencing pain and indignity is linked to sexual gratification
   2. Little understood; more common in males

D. Autoerotic Asphyxia
   1. 500–1,000 deaths per year in United States; majority in teenagers or young adult males
   2. Warning signs listed in Table 8-3

E. Voyeurism
   1. Irresistible, repetitive urge to spy on others
   2. Male; usually harmless; begins in early childhood

F. Exhibitionism
   1. Always males who expose their genitals
   2. Heightened arousal by seeing others amazed or shocked
   3. Peaks during 20s

G. Obscene Telephone Callers
   1. Obtain sexual gratification through talking or masturbation

H. Pedophilia
   1. Heterosexuals attempting to gain sexual gratification from a child
   2. Children more often upset by parents' horrified reaction than by act itself
   3. Fixated pedophiles are attracted to children starting with adolescence
   4. Regressed pedophiles are attracted only after negative life event

I. Perspectives on the Paraphilias
   1. No single theory adequately explains

J. Treatment of the Paraphilias
   1. No one type of treatment is superior
   2. Behavioral treatment reduces paraphilias sexual behavior and increases appropriate sexual behavior
   3. Drug medroxy progesterone acetate may be effective in reducing sexual urges

VII. Study Outline

2. The findings and impact of the Kinsey surveys.
3. The four-stage pattern of sexual response observed by Masters and Johnson.
4. The technique of sensate focus.
5. The incidence of homosexual behavior and the distinctions between homosexuality and maladjusted gender identity.
6. The major types of sexual dysfunction experienced by men and women. The various treatment approaches available for treating each of the dysfunctions.
7. The characteristics of gender identity problems from mild forms to transsexualism.
8. The varieties of paraphilia, the extent to which paraphilias are problematic, and some of the treatments for paraphilias.
9. The causes of pedophilia and the impact on child victims.

Discussion Questions

1. Men and women hold somewhat different attitudes toward homosexuality. The latter are more lenient and accepting of homosexual behavior among men. What might account for the different attitudes toward homosexual behavior?

2. Considerable attention has been devoted recently to the relationship between pornography and aggression. Recent publications in social psychological journals, particularly articles and chapters by Edward Donnerstein, provide useful information for discussing the pornography-aggression relationship.

3. Reports of therapist-client sexual encounters have been increasing in the past decade. A consensus exists among practicing clinicians who have uncovered such episodes, usually through client self-report, that the encounter invariably causes psychological trauma for the client. What sanctions exist against such professional misconduct? How does a professional organization determine whether a therapist is guilty of misconduct or a victim of an unresolved transference involving wish-fulfillment? What precautions can and do therapists take to reduce the ambiguity that might lead to such a transference?

4. Assume that you are a caseworker/counselor who has just learned that your client is sexually abusing his child. What are your ethical obligations? Your legal obligations? How far does confidentiality with your adult client extend?

Learning Objectives

Students should know:

1. The cultural and historical bases of attitudes toward sex.

Supplementary Lecture Material

In an article that was part of a special series of the evaluation and treatment of sexual disturbance in the *Journal of Counseling and Clinical Psychology* (1986, pp. 139–189), Richard Lanyon reviewed evidence regarding the parsimony of various theories to explain child molestation and various treatments deriving from those theories. A number of conclusions were drawn based on this evidence.

1. Child molestation is not necessarily based in a character disorder.
2. A distinction must be made between preference molesters, or pedophiles, whose basic preference is for children, and situational molesters, whose basic preference is mainly for adults.
3. Molesters can be distinguished by how they control their victims; one type uses psychological means, whereas another group uses coercion or force.

4. The family-systems approach to therapy is widely used and generally considered the most useful clinically.
5. Behavioral techniques, including aversive conditioning procedures, have shown a high success rate for eliminating deviant behaviors, thoughts, and feelings.
   Several factors are related to good prognosis. These include the following:
1. manageability of life crises and financial needs
2. good heterosocial and heterosexual skills and experiences, plus a cooperative and committed adult sexual partner
3. motivation and willingness to persist in treatment and follow therapeutic instructions
4. relative freedom from other disorders (alcohol abuse, psychosis)
5. Relative freedom from constricting religious or moral beliefs about acceptable adult sexuality.

CHAPTER 9

Personality Disorders

Overview

In this chapter the personality disorders are introduced. They are grouped into three kinds of behavior—1) odd or eccentric; 2) dramatic, emotional, or erratic; and 3) fearful or anxious. Two additional newly proposed categories also are reviewed. The reasons for the maladaptive nature of a personality are explained. Similarities and differences are made between personality disorders and other disorders such as anxiety disorders and schizophrenia.

Outline

I. Classifying Personality Disorders
   A. Definition
      1. Personality disorders are longstanding, maladaptive, and inflexible ways of relating to the environment
      2. Because personality does not affect behavior similarly in all situations, personality disorders are not always evident
   B. Axis II
      1. This diagnosis is made only when inflexible, maladaptive behaviors due to personality style are evident
      2. Problem behaviors must be evident in social situations, on the job, or in a high level of individual distress
   C. Categorization
      1. Twelve personality disorders can be grouped into three kinds of behavior
         a. odd or eccentric
         b. dramatic, emotional, or erratic
         c. fearful or anxious

   2. DSM-III-R has added five new types of personality disorders
   3. Evidence for categorization is largely clinical rather than controlled research
   4. Personality disorders provide least reliable diagnoses
      a. ⅔ of patients meet two or more diagnoses of personality disorder
      b. prototypic descriptions of DSM-III-R contribute to difficulty

II. Odd or Eccentric Behaviors
   A. Paranoid Personality Disorder
      1. Characteristics
         a. unwarranted feelings of suspiciousness and mistrust of others
         b. hypersensitivity
         c. restricted emotional response
      2. Problems are most evident in interpersonal conflicts in work situations
      3. Effective problem-solving is impaired by thought rigidity
      4. These individuals rarely develop intimate relationships
   B. Schizoid Personality Disorder
      1. Characteristics
         a. socially withdrawn but not disturbed by a lack of social relationships
         b. do not have behavioral eccentricities of schizotypal category
      2. Tend to be loners who rarely express feelings directly
      3. Often have problems in jobs because of necessary contacts with others
   C. Schizotypal Personality Disorder
      1. Characteristics
         a. oddities of thinking, perceiving, communicating, behaving
         b. socially unskilled, seclusive
         c. difficulty communicating clearly or thinking under stress

2. Have greater than average risk of a schizophrenic episode

III. Dramatic, Emotional, or Erratic Behaviors
   A. Histrionic Personality Disorder
      1. Attitude-seeking behaviors involving exaggerated emotional expression
      2. Drug overdose and suicide attempts are the most frequent referral problems
      3. Impressionistic; distractible thinking style is evident
   B. Narcissistic Personality Disorder
      1. Characteristics
         a. an exaggerated sense of self-importance
         b. need for consistent attention
         c. fragile self-esteem
         d. lack of empathy
      2. Psychoanalytic contributions
         a. Freud's theory holds that as infants narcissists turn inward to avoid rejection
         b. Kernberg believes narcissism is the produce of cold, indifferent, subtly aggressive, spiteful parents
         c. Kohut holds that parental indifference toward the child's needs results in low self-esteem and periodic self-absorbtion
      3. Social learning perspective emphasizes parental overrating of children's worth and subsequent unrealistic self images
   C. Borderline Personality Disorder
      1. Defining characteristics
         a. intensive but unstable relationships
         b. impulsive, self-destructive behaviors
         c. emotional instability with sudden shifts in mood
         d. identity disturbances
         e. chronic feelings of boredome and emptiness and a fear of being alone
      2. Much overlap with mood disorders
      3. Similar to histrionic, schizotypal, antisocial personality disorders
      4. Possible causes include early attachment experience, parental abuse, neurobiological factors
      5. Treatment includes intensive face-to-face, three times per week
      6. Kernberg emphasizes splitting, which is a failure to integrate positive and negative experiences usually with other people
   D. Antisocial Personality Disorder
      1. Adult antisocial personality disorder
         a. at least 18 years old
         b. evidence of conduct disorder before age 15

         c. pattern of irresponsible anti-social behavior since age of 15 years
      2. DSM-III-R criteria are too liberal in that they describe 3/4 of all imprisoned criminals
      3. More conservative definitions identify 1/3 of imprisoned criminals as antisocial
      4. Conduct disorder, the equivalent for those under age 18, is made on Axis I
      5. Psychopath
         a. Cleckly's criteria of psychopathy are the most universally respected by researchers
      6. Perspectives on antisocial behavior
         a. adopted children separated at birth show more antisocial behavior like their parents
         b. may be related to neurotransmitters, abnormal EEG recordings
      7. Disturbed adolescents sometimes commit a single violent act
      8. Treatment
         a. not helped by traditional psychotherapy
         b. residential treatment seeks to increase feeling of emotion

IV. Anxious or Fearful Behaviors
   A. Avoidant Personality Disorder
      1. Characteristics
         a. extreme sensitivity to rejection or humiliation
         b. low self-esteem
      2. Although seclusive, avoidant people want to enter relationships
      3. Hypervigilant for rejection by others
   B. Dependent Personality Disorder
      1. Typical characteristics
         a. allow others to govern their lives
         b. subordinate their own needs to those of others
      2. Feel empty, anxious if left on own
      3. Meekness may result in physical and verbal abuse from spouse
      4. Causes are unclear
   C. Obsessive-Compulsive Personality Disorder
      1. Characteristics
         a. inability to express tender emotions
         b. perfectionism with details resulting in subsequent inability to gain perspective
         c. excessive concentration on work and productivity
         d. indecisiveness in decision making
         e. insistence that their way of doing things be followed
      2. Although appearing rigid and constricted,

obsessional thinking and compulsive behaviors are not evident as in obsessive-compulsive anxiety disorder

D. Passive Aggressive Personality Disorder
  1. Resist demands for adequate performance in vocational and social endeavors
  2. Resistance is indirect and passive
  3. Treatment efforts largely have been unsuccessful

V. Additional Proposed Categories
  A. Sadistic Personality Disorder
    1. Pervasive pattern of cruel, demanding, aggressive behavior toward others
       a. directed toward those who cannot fight back
       b. enjoyment gained from watching others suffer
  B. Self-Defeating Personality Disorder
    1. Avoids pleasureable experiences and seeks out relationships in which person will ultimately suffer
    2. Positive personal events result in feelings of guilt or depression
    3. Fail to accomplish for themselves

VI. Treatment of Personality Disorders
  A. Common Characteristics that Make Treatment Unlikely
    1. These individuals tend to be satisfied with their behavior
    2. Perceive the environment as the cause of any difficulties encountered
    3. Each disorder is characterized by the frequency and intensity with which behaviors occur
  B. Therapies
    1. Not responsive to drugs
    2. Behavioral techniques train skills
    3. Family therapy often used

VII. Study Outline

3. The history of diagnostic categories for personality disorders.
4. How the diagnosis of personality disorders on Axis II of DSM-III-R meshes with the primary diagnosis on Axis I.
5. The major categories of personality disorders and the characteristics of each.
6. The degree of success in treating various personality disorders.
7. Psychodynamic cognitive, learning, and biological approaches to personality disorders.
8. Some of the reasons for the relatively limited knowledge of personality disorders.
9. The differences between obsessive-compulsive anxiety disorders and compulsive personality disorder.
10. Why information on antisocial personality disorder that is obtained from incarcerated populations is questionable.
11. The difficulties of the antisocial personality disorder criteria including the question of how to distinguish sociopathic individuals from the broader category of antisocial personality disorder.

Discussion Questions

1. DSM-III-R does not allow a diagnosis of personality disorders before the age of 18 on the grounds that personalities are not well-established until late adolescence or early adulthood. Is there evidence that personalities can be reliably identified before the age of 18? How does one account for differences of temperament which are evident in infant behavior?

2. Therapeutic efforts with personality disorders largely have not been very successful; that is, personality disorders are resistant to treatment efforts. Can one ethically justify an intensive and expensive effort to alter someone's style of life? What conditions make this therapeutic effort more justifiable?

3. Use of the antisocial personality disorder category means that some people who have committed criminal behaviors may have a psychiatrically recognized disorder. Does this mean that these people should be treated for their psychiatric disorder or for their criminal behaviors?

4. In the past, the histrionic personality disorder has been attributed more frequently to women than to men. Does this reflect a sex-role bias in diagnosis, or do more women actually have this set of characteristics?

Learning Objectives

Students should know:
1. That the characteristic behaviors of personality disorders are episodic and dependent on the influence of different situations.
2. That personality disorders can be identified by the frequency and intensity with which certain behaviors appear when coping behaviors are called for.

Supplemental Lecture Material

Classification of Antisocial Subtypes

The sociopathic disorder is one subtype of the antisocial personality disorder that has been identified by researchers. More recent efforts have focused on sensation-seeking behavior, antisocial attitudes, a lack of empathy for others, and a low level of physical anxiety as the identifying characteristics of the sociopath. David Lykken (Lykken, D.T., 1957. A study of anxiety in the sociopathic personality. *Journal of Abnormal and Social Psychology, 55,* 6-10.) referred to this individual as a "primary sociopath," who could be contrasted with a second subtype of antisocial personality disorder that he called a "secondary sociopath." The latter, although sharing the antisocial behaviors of the former, demonstrates greater vulnerability and higher anxiety levels. Lykken's research, as well as that of Schmauk (Schmauk, F.J., 1970. Punishment, arousal, and avoidance learning in sociopaths. *Journal of Abnormal Psychology, 76,* 325-335.), showed that primary and secondary sociopaths differed in avoidance learning and in learning as a function of physical, monetary, and social punishment. In both studies, subjects were given the task of learning the correct path through a maze that involved 15 choice points. At each choice point there were four alternatives, each of which was represented by four levers on a control panel. One of the four levers was correct and the other three were wrong. One of the three wrong levers was programmed as the punishment lever. Lykken paired a mild electric shock to the calf of the leg with this punishment lever. Schmauk used mild electric shock for one condition but had subjects in another condition lose one quarter from a starting pile of 40 quarters for each punished, wrong response. In a third condition, still other subjects heard "wrong" in a disapproving tone every time the punished lever was pulled. Although the task was presented as a maze-learning task, the experimenters were really interested in how well the subjects learned to avoid punished errors. Schmauk's findings indicated that the loss of money has a greater effect on the behavior and physiological responsivity of primary sociopaths than either physical or social punishment. A similar pattern was observed with secondary sociopaths except that they were more responsive to physical punishment than were primary sociopaths.

Research on these delinquent subtypes has identified differences in their stimulation-seeking, moral reasoning, avoidance-learning, and transgression behavior following physiological arousal. Conduct-problem delinquents prefer greater stimulation, reason at lower levels of moral development, are more responsive to tangible punishment, and are more likely to transgress in states of boredom. Such differences in behavior by subtypes of delinquents have indicated that different treatments are more likely to be effective with each type. Conduct-problem delinquents are most responsive to response-cost contingency problems in which positive tangible reinforcers are lost for undesirable behavior. Personality problem delinquents benefit from treatment environments that include a supportive, anxiety reducing orientation. Subcultural delinquents are most responsive to a change of group identities and are likely with the demands of early adulthood to reduce the frequency of their aggressive antisocial behaviors.

Robert S. Hare at the University of British Columbia has developed a behavioral checklist for assessing psychopathy. This checklist has provided reliable and valid assessments of psychopathy in a male prison population. (See Hare, R.D., 1980. A research scale for the assessment of psychopathy in criminal populations. *Personality and Individual Differences, 1,* 111–119.) The items of the scale are listed below.

1. Glibness/superficial charm
2. Previous diagnosis as a psychopath
3. Egocentricity/grandiose sense of self worth
4. Proneness to boredom/low frustration tolerance
5. Pathological lying and deception
6. Conning/lack of sincerity
7. Lack of remorse or guilt
8. Lack of affect and emotional depth
9. Callous/lack of empathy
10. Parasitic lifestyle
11. Short-tempered/poor behavioral controls
12. Promiscuous sexual relations
13. Early behavior problems
14. Lack of realistic long-term plans
15. Impulsivity
16. Irresponsible behavior as parent
17. Frequent marital relationships
18. Juvenile delinquency
19. Poor probation or parole risk
20. Failure to accept responsibility for own actions
21. Many types of offenses
22. Drug/alcohol abuse not direct cause of antisocial behavior

Antisocial Personality Disorder and Predictions of Dangerousness

According to some researchers (Wulach, J.S., 1983. Diagnosing the DSM-III antisocial personality disorder. *Professional Psychology: Research and Practice, 14,* 330-340.), the DSM-III criteria for diagnosing antisocial personality disorder are broad enough to include the majority of criminals. They say that the diagnosis ignores individual differences in chronicity of behavior, the degree of violence, the role of situational factors in producing criminal behavior, and the probability of recidivism or the commission of further violence. Others, particularly John Monahan (Monahan, J., 1981. *The clinical prediction of violent behavior.* Rockville, Md.: National Institute of Mental Health.), would argue that clinicians and law enforcement personnel have not been able to predict dangerousness with any satisfactory degree of success anyhow. The use of a psychiatric diagnosis to describe criminal behavior, especially with its implications of cross-situational consistency and psychiatric etiology, is part of the confusion about the dangerousness potential of psychiatric populations. This problem has become more acute with the recent increase in the number of court-ordered psychiatric admissions in public-supported psychiatric institutions.

Judith Rabkin (Rabkin, J.G., 1979. Criminal behavior and discharged mental patients. *Psychological Bulletin, 86,* 1-27.) has reviewed the evidence on the relationship between psychopathology and violent behavior. She has provided at least partial answers for several pressing questions. First, are released psychiatric patients more likely than the normal population to engage in acts of violence against others? Rabkin's answer is that it depends on the year of admission. For admissions prior to the 1970s, the answer is no, but in the 1970s, and presumably in the 1980s, the answer is yes. Having a prior arrest record before psychiatric hospitalization is the best predictor of violence by released psychiatric patients. The high number of court-ordered admissions relative to the number of voluntary admissions in recent years has resulted in an increase in the level of violence by released psychiatric patients. Second, is violent behavior more often associated with any particular kind of disorder? The typical expsychiatric offender is male, in his 20s, and is of non-white ethnic and lower socioeconomic status. The most frequent diagnoses are schizophrenia and alcohol disorders. However, one should be cautious about inferring a causal relationship between these two diagnoses and subsequent dangerous behavior by expsychiatric patients. Once again, only those with a prior arrest record and the diagnosis of schizophrenia or substance abuse disorders are more likely than the normal population to engage in dangerous acts. Some evidence is available that schizophrenics without prior arrest records might even be less likely than the normal population to engage in behavior that is dangerous to others.

Diagnostic identification of those with a prior arrest record and with psychiatric problems such as schizophrenia and substance use disorders is now possible with the multiaxial format of DSM-III-R. For example, an individual might receive a diagnosis of undifferentiated schizo-

phrenia on Axis I and a diagnosis of antisocial personality disorder on Axis II because of evidence of psychiatric maladjustive behavior and because of a record of criminal behavior. Such an individual can be earmarked as having a higher probability of engaging in dangerous behavior than a person diagnosed only as psychiatrically maladjusted. In the end, then, DSM-III-R may provide a means of identifying those psychiatric and criminal individuals who are more likely to commit acts of violence against others.

Defining the Borderline Personality

The borderline personality disorder is a new diagnostic category in the DSM-III-R. However, clinicians with a psychoanalytic orientation found this category to be useful and had been using it diagnostically for treatment. Unfortunately, the diagnostic level began to be used more widely so that it has become something of a catch-all category that includes individuals who would have been diagnosed as "pseudoneurotic," "simple schizophrenia," "schizoid personality disorder," and "adjustment reaction" under previous diagnostic systems. In order to clarify the identifying characteristics of the borderline personality disorder, John Gunderson (Gunderson, J.G., & Kolb, J.E., 1978. Discriminating features of borderline patients. *American Journal of Psychiatry, 137,* 792-796.) studied psychiatric inpatients with mixed, schizophrenic, depressive, and borderline diagnoses. Using discriminant function analysis, he identified seven characteristics that are useful for differential diagnosis. These characteristics include impulsivity, low achievement in work and school, manipulative suicide attempts, heightened affectivity, a need to be with others, marginal to mild psychotic experiences, and disturbed close relationships involving dependency, psychological masochism, and efforts to manipulate others. With these characteristics, borderline could be reliably distinguished from other psychiatric groups.

Subsequent research by Gunderson has brought his prescription of treatment near to that of Masterson. Treatment should involve the family because that is a primary source of socialization problems. Parents of borderline patients are frequently indifferent to the emotional needs of their children. Although the parents of borderlines are more likely to have intact marriages compared to the parents of other hospitalized psychiatric groups, the parents are likely to have more psychopathology. Thus they cling to each other, lean on each other for emotional support, and give little support to their children. Treatment of the borderline individual must be intensive and may require several years of residential living away from the parents and family. The borderline patient is likely to respond initially with much anger followed by depression before a consistent, positive sense of self-esteem and identity begins to emerge. During this period it is often necessary to keep the borderline patient in a relatively confined treatment environment and to have a professional treatment staff who work well together and are able to identify the splitting and manipulation efforts of the borderline patient and to confront him or her about these actions. The addition of individual therapy facilitates the emergence of a more positive self-identification. Coordinated family therapy with the parents becomes important at this point in order to rejoin the borderline patient and the maladjusted parents. Obviously, a protracted treatment program of this sort is an expensive effort. Moreover, some would argue that the confinement and restrictions necessary early in treatment are a violation of patient rights. Many who work with borderline patients in intensive treatment programs would counter by pointing to the likely negative consequences of not making an intensive intervention and to the low success rate of maintenance programs of outpatient treatment in attempting to treat borderline personality disorder.

The work by Masterson and Gunderson described in the foregoing paragraphs constitutes a classical definition of the borderline personality disorder. These definitions attempt to specify necessary and sufficient conditions for the diagnosis of borderline disorder. DSM-III-R actually takes a prototypic approach to classification. In prototypic classification, the defining features are correlated as common members of a category but are not individually necessary or collectively or jointly sufficient to define a disorder. John F. Clarkin (Clarkin, J.F., Widiger, T.A., Frances, A., Hurt, S.W., & Gilmore, M., 1983. Prototypic typology and the borderline personality disorder. *Journal of Abnormal Psychology, 92,* 263-275.) conducted a study of 20 psychiatric outpatients with borderline personality disorder and found that most patients had less than seven of the eight diagnostic criteria specified by DSM-III-R. Moreover, even with a low base rate of occurrence in a patient population (25%), the diagnosis could still be made reliably with three, two, or even one diagnostic feature. Unstable/intense relationships, a single diagnostic feature of DSM-III-R, can reliably diagnose borderline personality disorder if one knows that the disorder is a personality disorder. That feature plus an identity disturbance diagnoses borderline disorder with certainty.

CHAPTER 10

Mood Disorders

Overview

Depression, characterized by dysphoria and loss of interest in previously pleasureable activities, and mania, characterized by extreme excitement, are the mood disorders discussed in this chapter. The etiology and treatment of unipolar depression is considered from the biological, psychodynamic, learning, cognitive, and humanistic—existential theories. Evidence suggests that bipolar disorders are genetically based and can be successfully treated with lithium. The chapter ends with a discussion of suicide and parasuicide.

Outline

I. Defining Mood Disorders
   1. A disturbance in mood that is not due to other physical or mental reaction
   2. Table 10-1 defines major categories of mood disorders

II. Depression
  A. Depressed Mood
    1. Feeling the "blues"
    2. "Black cloud" of depression
  B. Grief and Loss
    1. Sadness from death in one's family includes
     a. physical distress
     b. preoccupation with image of deceased
     c. feelings of guilt, hostility, loss
     d. gradual disappearance with grieving
  C. The Frequency of Depression
    1. 6 percent of U.S. residents fit diagnosis of depression in any 6-month period
    2. 80 percent of these people are never treated

    3. Worldwide disorder with economic consequences
  D. Risk Factors for Depression
    1. Twice as many women as men
     a. not explained as an artifact of seeking treatment
    2. Separation, divorce is highest risk factor
    3. Stress, family history of depression, depressed parent of young child
    4. Birth cohorts of younger people more depressed than older people

III. Depressive Disorder
    1. Must separate sadness from depression
    2. Key elements of thoughts of depressed people
     a. think of themselves as unworthy or blameful
     b. think they are helpless to change situation
     c. do not think things will be better in future
  A. Dysthymia
    1. "Defective or diseases mood" (Greek)
    2. Tends to be chronic, lasts throughout the day
    3. Most do not come to attention of physician
    4. Multiple problems include
     a. difficulties eating
     b. difficulties sleeping
     c. constant feeling of tiredness
     d. difficulty thinking or making decisions
     e. low opinion of self
     f. hopelessness
  B. Major Depression
    1. Marked by depressed mood and/or physical problems
     a. see Table 10-2 for list of characteristics
    2. Episodes are without mania

3. May last 6 months

4. Reoccurrence most likely within 2 years

  a. average reoccurrence of 7 episodes in lifetime

5. 15 percent have some psychotic symptoms

IV. Theories of Depression

  A. Biological Theories

    1. Role of heredity

      a. results of twin studies indicate that bipolar disorders are more strongly linked to heredity

      b. Figure 10-4 illustrates genetic role

        (1) relatives of depressed have 8 times more likelihood than normals under age 20

        (2) relatives over age 40 are equal to normals

      c. exact mechanisms of inheritance are unclear

    2. Biochemical aspects of depression

      a. probably lack of neurotransmitters in brain

      b. neurons, synapses, synaptic vescicles

      c. neurotransmitters include

        (1) monoamines

          (a) norepinephrine (NE)

          (b) dopamine (DA)

          (c) serotonin (5-HT)

      d. catecholamine theory holds that decreased levels of NE cause depression

      e. indolamine theory holds that decreased levels of 5-HT

      f. possibly due to failure to regulate neurotransmitter system

    3. The search for markers of depression

      a. Dexamethasone Suppression Test

        (1) not enough support to use on a routine basis

        (2) reported for other conditions as well, alcoholism, schizophrenia

      b. scanning technologies

      c. biological rhythms involving temperature, sleep

    4. Treatments based on biological theories

      a. See Table 10-3

      b. Tricyclics and MAO inhibitors increase amount of norepinephrine

      c. MAOs have greater side effects such as high blood pressure

      d. Lithium used to treat bipolar disorder

      e. 2 to 3 weeks lag time before drugs become effective

      f. electroconvulsive therapy (ECT) may be used until drugs become active but results in memory loss and temporarily retarded learning

  B. The Psychodynamic View

    1. Depression is a complex reaction to loss

      a. Freud and Karl Abraham

      b. Causal factor is emotional, not sexual

      c. Punishing superego to control anger and aggressive feelings

    2. Disturbance in early childhood relationships often leaves person with dependent orientation

      a. Harlow's monkeys' separation resulted in depressive behaviors

      b. Bowlby: early separation creates feelings of sadness, anger

      c. Brown: women who lose mothers before age 11 are more likely to be depressed

    3. Loss affecting self-esteem may be more symbolic than real

    4. Therapy is aimed at modifying existing associations between thoughts and feelings

      a. long-term therapy: uncovering unconscious basis in childhood experiences

      b. short-term therapy: opportunity to verbalize thoughts and feelings

  C. The Behavioral Perspective

    1. Lack of reinforcement

      a. may be either lack of reinforcement or negative reinforcement

    2. Lewinsohn emphasizes low rate of behavior output, feelings of sadness due to low rate of positive experiences or high rate of unpleasant experiences

      a. environment could be the problem

      b. person might lack social skills

    3. Depressed people have more unpleasant events and find these events more unpleasant than do nondepressed people

    4. Depressed people have negative effects on others

    5. Depressed people delay and attempt to get emotional support from others when stressed

    6. Try to maintain relationships by clinging, dependent behavior

    7. Depressives are capable of acting differently in different roles

      a. long-term relationships receive depressed mood

b. couples depress each other
8. Depressives show bigger differences between ideas of self-efficacy and their behavioral standards
9. Treatment based on behavioral theories
  a. pinpoint specific person-environment interactions related to depression
  b. observe person at home
  c. use lists of pleasant/unpleasant events
  d. daily mood ratings
  e. social skills training
  f. case of Alice in text
D. The Cognitive Perspective
  1. Currently, the most influential theory
  2. Same experience affects people differently depending on how they think about it
  3. Beck's cognitive distortion model
    a. depressed people have erroneous and exaggerated ways of thinking (See Table 10–5)
    b. also have negative view of self, world, the future (cognitive triad)
    c. negative cognitions cause the depressed state
    d. overgeneralization, unrealistically high goals, magnify personal faults, minimize personal qualities
    e. depressed people compare themselves with others
    f. modified theory includes sociotropic and autonomous depressive types
  4. Cognitive therapy for depression
    a. interviews and activity scales used in assessment
    b. daily activities are rated for mastery and pleasure
  5. Attributional models of depression
    a. learned helplessness (Seligman): dogs exposed to inescapable shock subsequently did not act to avoid shock in later experiments
    b. revised theory (Abramson): depression occurs when negative qualities are attributed to self as a result of helpless experiences; internal, global, stable attributions are associated with depression
    c. life-stress models suggest that having negative experiences may cause depression
    d. the information-processing analysis suggests that depression is represented by a primitive emotion node which is

activated by a variety of events such as a meaningful loss
    e. theory best explains depression associated with achievement
    f. learned helplessness might be a product rather than a cause of depression
  6. Life stressors activate cognitive set
  7. Information-processing activated theory holds that memories are linked to primitive emotion nodes
    a. depression is activated by appraisal of events involving subjective losses
  8. Cognitive accuracy in depression
    a. depressed people are more accurate than nondepressed people
    b. nondepressed people attribute good outcomes to themselves and bad outcomes to others
    c. realism of depressed people decreases as therapy progresses
E. The Humanistic-Existential Perspective
  1. Loss of self-esteem, real or symbolic
  2. External verifications of identity include who they are and what they have
  3. Emphasize difference between ideal self and perception of actual state of things
    a. depression results when this difference becomes too great
F. Contrasting Psychological Theories of Depression
  1. Despite different theoretical perspectives, many treatments for depression are similar
  2. Existential therapy is less structured, oriented on here and now, is essentially a talking therapy; other therapies have become more alike
G. An Interactive View
  1. No one type of therapy is best for unipolar depression
  2. Collaborative Research Program found no differences between cognitive and interpersonal therapies
V. The Bipolar Disorders
  A. Characteristics of Bipolar Disorders (See Table 10–8)
    1. Characterized by phases of both depression and mania
    2. Mania
      a. flight of ideas
      b. elevated mood
      c. increased psychomotor activity
      d. incidence is 1.2 percent

c. only a very few experience only mania
f. impairment of judgment and grandiose ideas
3. Bipolar II includes no manic episodes but has at least one hypomanic episode

B. Manic Episodes
1. Environmental factors can set off
2. High stress, lack of sleep, lack of emotional support can set off

C. Causes of Bipolar Disorders
1. The role of heredity
  a. hereditary risk is 5 times that of unipolar depression
  b. dominant gene of tip of short arm of chromosome 11 is associated with inherited bipolar disorder
  c. X chromosome also has been implicated
2. Brain metabolism
  a. 6 percent of those originally diagnosed as unipolar will have subsequent manic episode
  b. helped by lithium but not by tricyclics
3. Sleep disturbance studied as potential cause of disorder
  a. partial sleep deprivation or shifting time of sleep earlier helps major depression
  b. sleep deprivation produces mania
4. 2 to 4 hours phototherapy per day is effective for treating winter depression, but positive effects wear off rapidly

D. Treatment of Bipolar Disorders
1. Lithium helps two thirds of all manic patients by preventing manic episodes
  a. also helps depressed relatives of bipolars
  b. many patients discontinue use against orders

VI. Suicide and Parasuicide
A. Characteristics
1. Hopelessness is a good predictor of eventual suicide
2. Suicide occurs as people recover from depression
3. 15 percent of clinically depressed will kill self
4. Suicide rate of depressed is 22 to 36 times greater than normal population
5. Rate of suicide among young age groups has increased since 1949
6. Cultural values about suicide differ
B. Causes of Suicide
1. Focus is split between society and the individual
2. Sociological theories emphasize social isolation
3. Psychological theories emphasize decision to commit suicide
  a. psychodynamic theory: extreme expression of inward-turned aggression
  b. learning theory: past suicidal attempts, threats, models
  c. cognitive theory: problem solving of negative event experiences
4. Parasuicides have rigid, narrow perceptions of world as good and bad

C. Suicide and the Media
1. 10 percent of population may have thoughts of suicide
2. Excessive publicity of suicide encourages impulsive suicide acts

D. Impact of Suicide on Others
1. Traumatic for survivors
2. Demonstrating care, expression of feelings helps recovery

VII. Study Outline

Learning Objectives

Students should know:

1. How to differentiate diagnostic categories of affective disorders.
2. How to differentiate clinical depression and sadness.
3. The catecholamine and indolamine theories of depression. How norepinephrine, receptor sites, and dopamine are thought to cause depression. How serotonin might be involved.
4. The appropriate use of electroconvulsive therapy (ECT) in depression.
5. The psychodynamic perspective's several etiological views of depression.
6. Lewinsohn's reinforcement-based learning theory of depression. The role of interpersonal behaviors in maintaining depression. Behavioral treatment procedures for depression.
7. Beck's cognitive explanation of depression. Cognitive therapy procedures for treating depression.
8. The revised learned helplessness explanation of depression and the kind of attributions that depressives more commonly make.
9. How the existential-humanistic theory of depression differs from other theories of

depression. How other theories of depression are similar to each other.

10. The characteristics of manic states. That mania can be produced by drugs and physiological causes in addition to the psychiatric disorder.
11. That the genetic bases of bipolar disorders are different from those of unipolar depression.
12. The therapeutic effects of lithium.
13. Variables that are predictive of suicide. The differences between sociological and psychological approaches to suicide.

mental health professionals to prevent suicides among those with clinical depressive disorders makes them important professional questions for the students to consider.

Supplementary Lecture Material

Etiological studies examining the causes of depression largely have been developed from correlational studies or from analogue studies simulating aspects of depressive disorders. Many times these studies describe concurrent thoughts, feelings, or behaviors of depressives. In order to demonstrate a causal relationship between a variable and depression, it must be demonstrated that the variable preceded the onset of depression in time. That is, there must be a positive correlation between the hypothesized antecedent variable and the subsequent state of depression. If we call the antecedent time Time 1 and the subsequent state of depression Time 2, then the correlation between the level of depression at Time 2 and the variable of interest at Time 1 should not be stronger than the correlation between the variable of interest at Time 1 and the level of depression at Time 2. A statistical technique useful in analyzing these relationships is cross-lagged panel correlation analysis. A typical model is presented in Figure 10.1. In this design, r_Y should be significantly greater than r_X if evidence for a cause-effect relationship is to be found. The measures of depression and the hypothesized causal variable should be stable over time, that is, have acceptable levels of test-retest reliability if the desired relationship is to be identified. These correlations are represented by r_D for depression and r_B for the hypothesized variable. Actually, the cross-lagged panel correlation technique will not allow one to conclude that a cause-effect relationship definitely exists. Rather, it allows the researcher to rule out the possibility that the relationship is spurious, or attributable to some third unmeasured and unidentified variable.

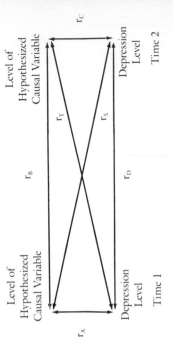

Figure 10-1
Cross-Lagged Panel Correlation Model

Discussion Questions

1. The fundamental attribution error identified by researchers of attribution processes is that normal individuals take more responsibility than warranted for good outcomes and less responsibility than warranted for bad outcomes. In contrast, as the text indicated, depressives often are more accurate in their attributions of self responsibility. This observation has been made in several studies. In addition, it has been demonstrated that depressives view themselves more similarly to how others rate them than do nondepressives. That is, depressives are more realistic in their self-perceptions than nondepressives. How can this puzzling phenomenon be explained? Is it maladjustive to be too rational and objective? If so, does this indicate a limit to cognitive and ego-psychodynamic theories of adjustive behavior? Or, given that the above studies have been based on college students, is the effect an artifact of the subject population? Are there skills, such as being an effective conversationist at a party, or being successful in an occupation such as sales, that require an element of self-deception?

2. Existentialists have argued that suicide is sometimes a normal response to a distressing world. Consider the experiences of the elderly who often have declining health, loss of loved ones and close friends, and reduced opportunities for positive self expression. Can the students of the class identify any circumstances in which suicide is not a maladjustive behavior? Can the students identify similar circumstances for the elderly? Is there a point at which suicide in the elderly due to clinical depression cannot be conscienced but suicide due to rational problem-solving responses to negative life experiences can be? Although these are inherently ethical questions that each individual must address with reference to his or her own values, the interaction of theories of behavior and the mandate of

Sanford Golin, David Schaeffer, and Paul Sweeney have used the cross-lagged panel correlation technique to determine whether there is support for antecedent-consequent relationships between attributions for stress-ful negative events and depression (Golin, S., Sweeney, P.D., & Schaeffer, D.E., panel correlational analysis. *Journal of Abnormal Psychology, 84, 718-721.*) (Sweeney, P.D., Schaeffer, D.E., & Golin, S., 1982. Pleasant events, unpleasant events, and depression. *Journal of Personality and Social Psychology, 43,* 136-144.) In essence, they have compared the antecedent-consequent evidence supporting the Lewinsohn learning theory of depression with the cognitive attribution theory of depression deriving from the reformulated learned helplessness approach. In their studies, they failed to find support for a simple antecedent-consequent relationship between the lack of pleasant events or the number of unpleasant events and subsequent levels of depression. They did find support for the cognitive attributional model of depression. Specifi-

cally, antecedent attributions of stability and globality for bad-outcome events were related to later depression and could not be attributed to a third variable. Thus, the Lewinsohn theory of depression was not supported, whereas the cognitive theory was.

Golin and his colleagues have suggested that the relationship between the lack of reinforcing pleasant events or the increase in negatively reinforcing unpleasant events and level of depression might be mediated by a third variable, perhaps a cognitive one. That is, a decrease in positive reinforcement or an increase in negative reinforcement will not result in depression unless the individual somehow interprets the changes in a certain way. Such a mediating variable is yet to be established, but if it should accumulate, then the learning theory of depression might have to be revised much as the original theory of learned helplessness theory was by the addi-tional attention to cognitive attributional processes.

CHAPTER 11

Schizophrenic Disorders

Overview

This chapter focuses on a definition of the concept of schizophrenia. Characteristic symptoms of schizophrenia are presented along with incidence rates and historical trends. The subtypes of disorganized, catatonic, and paranoid schizophrenia are discussed. Positive and negative indicators of outcome and the therapeutic approaches to the treatment of schizophrenia are reviewed.

Outline

I. Some Facts About Schizophrenia
  1. Found in all races and cultures
  2. 1 percent of population has schizophrenia at some time in their lives
    a. 46 percent have active symptoms
    b. 18 percent are in remission
    c. only half receive treatment
  3. 40 percent of beds in mental hospitals are occupied by schizophrenics
    a. stay in hospital longer than any other disorder except depression
    b. picture is one of short hospitalizations with frequent readmissions
  4. Most serious of psychiatric disorders
II. Characteristics of Schizophrenic Disorders
  A. Thought Content
    1. Delusion is a faulty interpretation of reality despite clear evidence to the contrary
      a. See Table 11–2 for differences in delusions
  B. Form of Thought

    1. "Formal-thought disorder" refers to organization of thoughts
    2. Loosening of associations refers to shifts of ideas from topic to topic
    3. Autistic thinking is so self-centered as to be intelligible only to person doing thinking
      a. schizophrenics ask inappropriate questions
      b. repetitions and predictability of meaning found in normal speech are missing
    4. Majority of schizophrenics speak coherently most of the time
    5. Poverty of content refers to much speech with little transmission of information
  C. Perception
    1. Hallucinations involve projection of internal impulses into perceptual images of external world
      a. auditory hallucinations are most common type
      b. touch, smell and vision might also be present
    2. Hallucinations have been linked to abnormal brain excitability
    3. Wish fulfillment, aggression, critical superego are psychoanalytic interpretations
    4. Auditory hallucinations occur more frequently in people with low intelligence
  D. Lack of Appropriate Emotion
    1. Either loss of all signs of emotion or unpredictable outbursts of inappropriate emotions
    2. Flattened affect is a symptom but also may be a side effect of medications
  E. Unclear Boundaries of the Self

1. Loss of ego boundaries includes feelings of uniqueness, being a separate individual

F. Unpredictable Motor Behavior
1. May be wildly aggressive, move about constantly, or remain motionless

G. Motivational Level
1. Withdrawal from activities
2. Patients notice a slowing down of thoughts

H. Impaired Interpersonal Functioning
1. Social withdrawal and emotional detachment are present in all phases of schizophrenia
2. Sometimes unable to comprehend most basic social conventions

I. Attention: An Organizing Concept
1. Hallucinations, thought content, disturbance in sense of self might result in inability to screen out distracting stimuli
2. Appearance of first symptoms produces great anxiety
3. Uncertain whether focus is too broad or too narrow

J. Diagnostic Criteria
1. Deterioration from previous level of functioning is work, social relations, self care
2. Continuous signs for at least 6 months
3. Psychotic behavior present at some point

III. Historical View of Schizophrenic Disorders
A. Dementia Praecox
1. Emil Kraepelin among the first to classify schizophrenia as a distinct disorder
a. called it dementia praecox
b. recovery unlikely because of irreversible organic deterioration

B. The Schizophrenias
1. Eugen Bleuler used term "schizophrenia"
a. symptoms represent a group of disorders with different causes
b. some people with schizophrenia improve, some stay the same, others get worse
c. differentiated acute and chronic schizophrenia
d. emphasized role of environment
e. focused on loss of integration of thinking, emotion, motivation
f. four As: alterations in affect, associations, ambivalence, autism
2. Adolf Meyer and Harry Stack Sullivan

continued to emphasize broad concept of schizophrenia and psychosis in general
3. Bleuler's broad definition predominated through much of the twentieth century and led to overdiagnosis of schizophrenia

C. First-Rank Symptoms
1. Kurt Schneider described first-rank and second-rank symptoms
a. easily recognized by clinicians with greater agreement
b. however, symptoms found not only in schizophrenia; one-fourth of bipolars show these symptoms
2. DSM-III criteria are an amalgam of Kraepelin, Bleuler, Schneider

IV. Types of Schizophrenia
A. Traditional and DSM-III-R Subtypes
1. Kraepelin described three subtypes: catatonic, hebephrenic, paranoid
2. Bleuler added simple type, which now is called schizotypal personality disorder
a. lifelong inability to function independently
b. lack of assertiveness; have communication difficulties
3. Residual types no longer have prominent psychotic features
4. Disorganized schizophrenia (hebephrenic)
a. profuse delusions, visual hallucinations, grimacing, gesturing
b. childish disregard for social conventions
(1) inappropriate emotions such as silly giggling
5. Catatonic schizophrenia
a. motor activity disturbance ranging from immobility to extreme agitation
6. Paranoid Schizophrenia
a. primary cognitive symptoms: delusions, sustained extreme suspiciousness
b. loose thinking and blunted emotional responses

B. Schizophrenic Spectrum Disorders
1. Families of schizophrenics include more than expected number of unusual, eccentric relatives
2. Schizotypal and paranoid personality disorders are more common among relatives
3. Schizoaffective disorders include depression, mania
4. Atypical psychoses and paranoid disorder are other spectrum disorders

V. Positive and Negative Symptoms
   1. Behavioral excesses that include hallucinations, delusions, bizarre behavior, disordered thinking
   2. Respond well to drug therapy that blocks dopamine
   3. Usually functioned well before symptoms appeared
   4. Disturbed behaviors come and go
   B. Negative Symptoms
   1. Poor functioning before and after initial episode
   2. Antipsychotic drugs do not produce much improvement

VI. Outcome Indicators and Long-Term Studies
   A. Predictors of Outcome
   1. Include type of disorder, acute vs. chronic onset, and premorbid adjustment
      a. hebephrenics have poorest chance of recovery
      b. sudden onset has best prognosis
      c. good premorbid adjustment is positive sign
   B. Long-term Follow-up Studies
   1. Manfred Bleuler followed progress of 208 schizophrenics over 20-year period
      a. deterioration occurred in first 5 years
      b. after 5 years, proportions of recovered, improved, unimproved cases remained the same
      c. overall recovery rate remained constant
   2. Watts found that one third of Type I schizophrenics made social recovery
   3. In a Vermont study, Harding found one half to two thirds of schizophrenics were recovered

VII. Therapeutic Approaches
   A. Biological Therapies
   1. Most universal treatment by use of drugs
   2. One third relapse in first year; one half relapse in 2 years
   3. Can cause tardive dyskinesia
      a. 10 to 20 percent in mental hospitals; 40 percent in chronic hospitalization
   B. Psychodynamic Therapies
   1. When each used alone, drug therapy is more effective
   C. Behavioral Therapy
   1. Token economy to reward patients for desired behavior
   2. Social-skills training
   3. Behavioral self-instruction
   D. Milieu Therapy and Family Therapy
   1. Family attitudes and support influence recovery
   2. Social-learning generally superior to milieu
   3. Include half-way houses or group homes, day-care facilities, and mental-health clinics
   4. Train family members to modify controlling attitudes

VIII. Study Outline

Learning Objectives

Students should know:
1. Incidence rates of schizophrenia. That schizophrenics are now treated in community settings but with frequent rehospitalizations.
2. The defining characteristics of schizophrenia including inappropriate emotions, thoughts, perceptions and attention, contact with reality, and motivation.
3. The essence of Kraepelin's definition of schizophrenia, and of Bleuler's definition of schizophrenia. The differences between the two diagnoses.
4. The contributions of Schneider's criteria to the DSM-III criteria.
5. The characteristic symptoms of disorganized, catatonic, and paranoid subtypes of schizophrenia.
6. The predictors of outcome of schizophrenic disorder.
7. Some of the findings of long-term follow-up studies of schizophrenia. That definitive conclusions are hard to make because of changes in diagnostic criteria and the initiation of antipsychotic drugs.
8. Some of the therapeutic approaches to schizophrenia, their differences and effectiveness.
9. How the therapeutic communities and family training programs help to treat schizophrenics.

Discussion Questions

1. As was indicated in the text, schizophrenia is largely treated on an outpatient basis with recurrent brief hospitalizations for many individuals. Those individuals with relatively chronic symptoms often lose what occupational, social, and self-care skills they might have had prior to the initial onset of the schizophrenic symptoms. As a result, those without adequate family resources often end up in half-way houses, boarding houses, hotels for transients, or intermediate-care nursing homes. Although a vari-

able quality of life ensues, this system of treatment is financially preferable over the one practiced before the 1950s, namely, the large state hospital systems. Do students feel that the current system is defensible given the deprivations experienced by many chronic schizophrenics? What attitude changes are necessary to improve the quality of life of these individuals? Is the current outpatient system better than the maintenance programs of state hospitals? Where do individual rights and community responsibilities begin and end?

2. The term "nervous breakdown" sometimes has been used to describe an individual who has experienced a psychotic state. It might be interesting to collect students' interpretaations of the term "nervous breakdown" or of what a psychotic state consists. Does the consensus difinition of the class include schizophrenic symptoms? Is the term "nervous breakdown" limited to schizophrenic disorders, or can it be used with anxiety disorders such as panic disorder or obsessional neurosis and with affective disorders such as major depressive disorder or bipolar disorder?

3. Evidence suggests that schizophrenia is episodic, that some people have one episode of schizophrenia never to have another. Do the students know of people—relatives, neighbors, work associates, friends' relatives—who had diagnosed schizophrenia? Was it a single episode or did recurrent or continuous episodes occur?

Class Participation Project

There are a number of accounts in the popular literature of individuals who supposedly have experienced schizophrenia or who have written about the subjective experience of what is described as schizophrenia. Mark Vonnegut's autobiography, *The Eden Express,* Sylvia Plath's *The Bell Jar,* Deborah Blau's *I Never Promised You a Rose Garden,* Marguerite Sechehaye's *Autobiography of a Schizophrenic Girl,* and Clifford Beers' *A Mind That Found Itself* are a few of the more popular examples. There is, however, some question about whether these accounts describe purely schizophrenic disorders. All were labeled schizophrenic under the more broadly defined category emanating from the approach taken by Bleuler and prevalent in psychiatric practice until DSM-III. Many of these accounts include symptoms of affective disorders (Vonnegut, Sechehaye, Beers) or of somatization disorder (Blau) as well. The instructor might want to assign at lease several students to read each of the books mentioned above. With DSM-III criteria for schizophrenia and for affective disorders in hand, students could be asked to

detail the symptoms of each disorder and to make an overall diagnosis based on the symptoms described. How well do the students agree in their observation of symptoms? In their overall diagnosis? It might be interesting to schedule a day of short presentations on each of the literary sources reviewed by the class.

Supplementary Lecture Material

In Appendix A of DSM-III, a decision tree has been provided to illustrate the process of diagnostic decision-making when using DSM-III categories. As was indicated in the text, DSM-III takes a more conservative approach

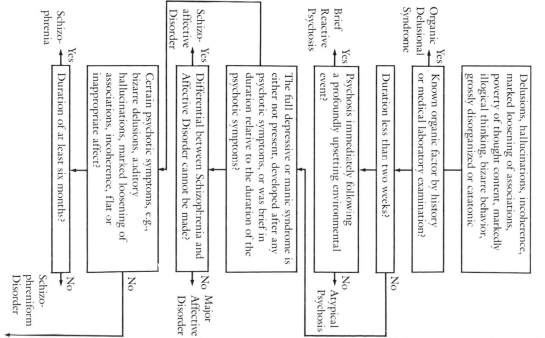

Figure 11-1
Differential Diagnosis of Psychotic Features

to the diagnosis of schizophrenia that requires that organic and affective disorders be ruled out before the disorder be labeled schizophrenia. A portion of that decision tree has been reproduced in Figure 11.1. It might be instructive to the students to follow this decision-making guideline to learn what the critical questions are and to gain some understanding of the use of the term "rule out" in clinical diagnosis.

CHAPTER 12

Causes and Markers
of Schizophrenia

Overview

I. Genetic Factors
A. Risk and Relatives
   1. Greater for relatives of schizophrenic than for nonrelatives
   2. Research has established an heredity risk factor in schizophrenia
B. Family Studies
   1. Probands, who are close in heredity, should be at greatest risk
   2. Risk for relatives is 2 to 46 times greater than for nonrelatives
      a. however, many schizophrenics do not become parents
   3. Assortive mating is tendency for people to mate with others more similar to themselves
      a. might result in "double doses" of genetic predisposition
   4. Genetic specificity and the spectrum concept are useful with schizophrenia
      a. monogenic theories state that a single gene pair determines schizophrenia
      b. polygenic theories suggest that the inheritance of schizophrenia is the cumulative effect of many genes
      c. theory of genetic homogeneity holds that more than one gene is necessary, but there is no cumulative effect
C. Twin Studies
   1. Compare concordance rates for dizygotic and monozygotic twins
   2. Concordance rates are much higher for monozygotic twins than for dizygotic twins
D. Adoption Studies

   1. Support genetic factor more than environmental factor
   2. Cross-fostering studies indicate that being raised by a schizophrenic foster parent is less of a factor than heredity in the development of schizophrenia
   3. Twin and family studies do not take environment into account whereas adoption studies do
E. A Genetic Model
   1. Schizophrenia not explained in terms of monogenetic model, maybe because of penetrance, which posits that environmental stress will bring on schizophrenia when individuals have potential for it
   2. Polygenic models state that many genes have an additive effect in that, if they exceed threshold, then schizophrenia is evident
F. Genetic Counseling
   1. Counselor presents what is known about risk factors

II. Vulnerability/Stress Factors
   1. Zubin states that each person has a vulnerability to stress but must have an interaction with stressful events
   2. Emphasis on the episodic nature of the disorder
   3. Finnish adoption study supports vulnerability/stress hypothesis

III. High-Risk Studies and the Search for Markers
A. Selecting a Group
   1. Target group is thought to have a higher potential for developing schizophrenia
      a. Mednick and Schulsinger studying 311 Danish children
      b. general psychopathology but not as

much schizophrenia identified in the high-risk group

2. One big problem: 90 percent of all schizophrenics do not have a schizophrenic parent

3. Garmezy and Devine found children vulnerable when they engaged in aggressive behavior

IV. Understanding the Schizophrenic Process

A. Structural Abnormalities in the Brain

1. CT scans have found schizophrenics have larger cerebral ventricles and present negative signs

2. Also found group with smaller ventricles that present positive signs

B. Biochemical Abnormalities in the Brain

1. Problem with research is control of extraneous variables

2. New research is dealing with biochemical functioning

3. PET scans: (positron emission tomography) observe brain chemical activity after radiation from glucose injections

a. can distingush controls and affective and schizophrenic disorders

4. The Dopamine Hypothesis

a. excess of dopamine at brain synapses causes schizophrenia

b. due to excess production or to faulty regulation or to oversensitive dopamine receptors or to too many receptors

c. low doses of amphetamines make schizophrenic symptoms worse

d. antipsychotic drugs are thought to block dopamine receptors

e. other biochemicals—MAO, endorphins—have also been implicated

f. evidence for brain biochemicals is indirect; also, these substances are produced elsewhere in the body

C. Psychophysiological Abnormalities

1. BEAM used to measure brain wave activity; schizophrenics may have slower activity

2. Half of schizophrenics are more responsive to stimuli and half are nonresponders

D. Attention

1. Eye-movements, related to information processing, are abnormal for schizophrenics

2. The Continuous Performance Test: schizophrenics have low sustained visual attention

E. Cognitive Functioning

1. Memory: problem in coding material

2. Disordered thinking

a. disordered thinking not unique to schizophrenia

b. drug treatment reduces thought disorder

F. Language

1. Language of schizophrenics is adult-like and rules of grammar are understood

2. Schizophrenics fail to provide necessary information, use ambiguous phrases, omit logical links between sentences

a. manics have links; schizophrenics do not

V. Family Relationships

A. Family Communication Deviance

1. Family relationships suggest that vulnerability to schizophrenia may be caused by frustrating interpersonal relationships in early life

B. Expressed Emotion

1. The attitudes expressed by family members whose behavior is disturbed

2. Parental affective style

a. schizophrenic children have parents who are more critical, intrusive, and guilt-inducing

VI. The Role of the Community

A. Schizophrenia More Often Found in Lower Classes

1. Social-selection theory

a. people become part of lower social class because of poor coping skills

2. Increased-stress theory

a. environment causes schizophrenia

b. community perspective takes this approach

VII. Study Outline

Learning Objectives

Students should know:

1. That the two main approaches to studying the genetic basis of schizophrenia involve examining concordance rates for twins and for adopted children. The rationale behind each of these

approaches and the strengths and weakness of each type of study are important to know.

2. That rather than using retrospective inference of genetic contributions, high-risk studies predict future behavior.

3. The conclusions that can be made about the genetic contribution to schizophrenia.

4. What role the vulnerability/stress factor plays in the etiology of schizophrenia.

5. The current biochemical research involves investigating dysfunctions of neural transmitters. The variations of the dopamine hypothesis of schizophrenia. Some of the limitations of biochemical research that prevent firm conclusions from being drawn.

6. Some of the psychophysiological measures that are used to measure the attention, information processing, and conditioning processes of schizophrenics.

7. How attention, language, and cognitive functioning are measured in schizophrenics and how they differ in these areas.

8. The role of family factors, including negative affect, poor communication, marital schism and marital skew, in schizophrenia.

9. The process by which an individual develops schizophrenic symptoms according to the humanistic-existential theory of R.D. Laing.

10. The meanings of the social-selection theory and increased-stress theory of schizophrenia. The community perspective of schizophrenia.

Discussion Questions

1. The text raises some questions about the real impact of antipsychotic drugs, by wondering whether the use of drugs creates a positive expectation of outcome rather than any substantive physiological changes. How might the double-blind experimental design be used to test this question?

2. Cross-cultural comparisons of developing and industrialized nations have indicated that schizophrenics have a better prognosis in developing countries than in industrialized nations. What factors might account for such differences?

3. Studies of family processes have identified several possible variables that might contribute to schizophrenia. However, some of these same faulty processes are found with other disorders. Nevertheless, the belief is strong among many lay people that

family factors are the principal cause of psychotic conditions, including schizophrenia. What would have to be done experimentally to establish that family factors were a *necessary and sufficient* cause of schizophrenia?

Supplementary Lecture Material

Cognitive Deficits of Schizophrenics

Much research has been conducted on the cognitive processes of schizophrenics. This research has focused on attentional processes; association processes, including concept formation; and verbal responses, including language, of the schizophrenic. After several decades of intensive study, researchers are unable to say definitely whether the cognitive deficits are primary or are due to some underlying neural and biochemical abnormalities. Nevertheless, much information of a descriptive nature has been collected about information-processing styles and thinking of schizophrenics. Three cognitive functions—concept formation, association, and reasoning—are highlighted here.

It has been observed that schizophrenics have a tendency to think that more objects belong to a class of events than is actually the case. Cameron and Epstein have labelled this tendency "overinclusion." For example, if the following item were given to a schizophrenic: Underline all the words necessary to complete the key word:

MAN: arms, shoes, hat, toes, head, none

the nonschizophrenic would probably underline arms, toes, and head. The schizophrenic would underline those words but would include shoes and hat as well. Thus, schizophrenics' concept-formation processes differ from those of nonschizophrenics.

Another example of differences in concept formation can be observed on the BRL Sorting Task originally developed by Kurt Goldstein. In this task, the examinee is given a large number of objects including a knife, fork, spoon, screwdriver, pliers, nail, hammer, cardboard circle, toy knife, toy spoon, toy fork, toy screwdriver, toy pliers, toy hammer, rubber ball, cigarette, cigar, rubber cigar, rubber eraser, among other items. These items are laid out in front of the individual, and he or she is asked to select and set to one side all those items that comprise a particular concept. For the concept "silverware," a normal adult would select the knife, fork, spoon. A schizophrenic might select these items but add the toy knife, fork, and spoon as well. This represents an expansion of the technical category "silverware" and represents another kind of overinclusion.

Another task of the BRL Sort is to apply a category label to objects selected by the examiner. For example, if a knife, fork, and spoon were selected, the examiner might label these objects according to their abstract category label ("silverware"), their function, or use ("use them to eat"), or their concrete physical properties ("shiny," or "made of metal"). Normal adults typically alternate between abstract category labels and functional labels for events. Brain-damaged individuals may use concrete properties to form concepts. Not infrequently, schizophrenics will use overly abstract conceptual categories that mimic concrete concept formation ("all things found in the universe," "matter," "man-made objects"). Thus, the concept-formation processes of schizophrenics often are overly abstract and too inclusive.

Association deficits also have been observed in schizophrenic thinking. Bleuler provides an illustration of associative interference or the inability to suppress responses that have a high associative connection to a previous word or thought. In this example, the individual is attempting to extend a New Year's greeting.

"I wish you then a good, happy, joyful, healthy, blessed, and fruitful year, and many good wine-years to come, as well as a healthy and good apple-year, and sauerkraut and cabbage and squash and seed year."

Loren and Jean Chapman, in researching related thinking processes of schizophrenics, have described an apparent breakdown in associative hierarchies. The speaker appears to perseverate along the chain of associations normally associated with each other. Unfortunately, the further associations are inappropriate for the current situation. In fact, schizophrenics often appear to be responding in a word-association fashion or to free-association instructions.

One clinical measure of associative thinking is the Whitaker Index of Schizophrenic Thinking (WIST). The WIST is divided into three parts: Similarities, Word Pairs, and New Inventions. One item from each subtest is provided here.

Similarities:

CAR
a. tires
b. automobile
c. jar
d. smickle
e. my transportation

Word Pairs:

RED AND BLUE
a. I have seen these
b. bright clothes
c. bed and glue
d. colors
e. lorp

New Inventions:

STRONG, ATTRACTIVE HOUSES WILL BE MADE FROM A NEW PLASTIC FOR ONLY HALF THE COST OF REGULAR HOUSES.
a. No house will be made of wood.
b. The plastic will be sarcastic.
c. More people will own houses.
d. The pink of will.
e. They will put plastic in my house.

Responses to these items are scored "0" if the correct answer is chosen, "1" if a lose association is selected, "2" for a self-reference association, "3" for a clang association, and "4" for a nonsense association. According to Whitaker, three characteristics of schizophrenic thinking can be measured by the WIST. *Illogical* thinking is manifested in the relationships between ideas and the logical requirements of a given task; *impaired* thinking reflects a marked discrepancy between an individual's capacity to think and the level of adequacy of thinking in a given instance; and *unwitting* thinking is indicated by a lack of awareness or control in relation to a given instance of thinking.

Does the WIST describe the thinking of schizophrenic individuals? The research findings are in dispute about this point. There is some evidence that schizophrenics are more likely to show thinking impairments on items that are affectively loaded on sex or aggression themes. Other research has indicated that WIST scores can be used to identify those who are brain-injured but that it cannot adequately identify those who have a schizophrenic disorder.

Another way of measuring schizophrenic thinking is to focus on responses to proverbs. Of course, a proverb is a saying that illustrates a particular moral, truth, or rule of living. Consider the following common proverb:

"People who live in glass houses should not throw stones."

Different interpretations of this proverb are classified below.

Literal: "People shouldn't throw rocks—they might get hurt, hurt people with rocks, or break the glass."

Concrete: "You're not always going to be the one looking out; other people will be looking at you occasionally."

Abstract: "People who are easily hurt should not try to hurt others."

Bizarre: "You shouldn't do something like work for the FBI which will disrupt your life."

The thinking of schizophrenics may be characterized by extreme concreteness or literalness as well as by bizarreness. The literal and concrete focus helps the

schizophrenic avoid runaway associations mentioned earlier. Research has demonstrated the presence of literal and concrete interpretations in the thinking of schizophrenics. Once again, however, the thinking of brain-injured individuals shows similar characteristics. Often, then, the key diagnostic question in examining the thinking of obviously impaired individuals is not whether they are impaired but whether the impairment is due to schizophrenia or organicity.

CHAPTER 13

Brain Disorders
and Changes Related to Aging

Overview

Disorders of the brain resulting in cognitive, affective, and behavior problems are presented in this chapter. Methods for assessing brain injury or disease are reviewed. Delirium is described. Dementia that occurs in the elderly is called senile dementia; in middle-age people it is called presenile dementia. Genetically-based disorders, neurotransmitter defective disorders, infection, nutritional deficiencies, brain injuries, and tumors also are reviewed. Different types of epilepsy are examined, and the interaction of personality and brain function in the elderly is discussed.

Outline

I. The Brain: An Interactive Perspective
  1. Each area of the brain develops in unique ways throughout a lifetime
  2. People in midlife may be more able to benefit from psychotherapy
  3. Interactive approach currently is favored

II. Vulnerability to Brain Disorders
  1. Complex integration rather than independent functions
  2. Factors that influence vulnerability to brain changes
    a. age: infant more susceptible than adult
    b. social support: isolation increases deficits
    c. stress: increases impact of deficits
    d. personality factors: many conditions impair cognitive performance
    e. physical condition: general health contributes to adjustment

III. Assessing Brain Damage
  A. Procedures
    1. Attempt to assess the extent of damage and deterioration
    2. Mental Status Examination: an interview supplemented by psychological testing
    3. Neuropsychological tests to assess impaired function of various brain regions
  B. Brain Imaging
    1. Computerized Axial Tomography (CAT): more sensitive than X-ray; identifies specific regions of brain damage
    2. Positron Emission Tomography (PET scan): x-ray of glucose utilization in the brain; shows the strength of biochemical processes in different areas of the brain

IV Organic Mental Disorders
  A. Delirium
    1. Global cognitive impairment: disorientation, confusion
    2. Result of acute and chronic brain conditions
    3. Stress, sleep, sensory deprivation also contribute to onset of delirium
    4. Delirium tremens results from excessive alcohol consumption
      a. interference with metabolism
      b. occurs in 5 percent of alcoholics
  B. Dementia
    1. Gradual loss of general intellectual abilities severe enough to interfere with social or occupational functioning
      a. senile dementia refers to this condition in people over 65
      b. in younger people, is called presenile dementia
      c. a common symptom is confabulation
    2. Primary degenerative dementia
      a. insidious onset, gradual course of deterioration

b. after age 65, is called senile dementia (Alzheimer's Disease)

c. called presenile dementia under age 65

d. previous personality characteristics are accentuated

3. The aging process

a. transient depressions occur in 30 percent or more of elderly

b. paranoid and hypochondriacal problems also more frequent

c. important points

(1) there are many examples of successful old people

(2) people can adapt successfully to developmental transitions

(3) there has been unfortunate clinical neglect of older people

4. Alzheimer's Disease occurs in one third of adults

a. affects 5 to 10 percent of people over 65

b. lasts average of 7 years

c. results in total physical and behavioral deterioration

d. caused by plaques and tangles in nerve cells

e. exact cause as yet unknown but probably involves reduced production of acetylcholine

f. researchers are finding ways to treat family members because of the stress they endure

5. Pick's Disease

a. peaks in 60s, less common than Alzheimer's, more common in women

b. brain atrophy; no cure

6. Multi-infarct dementia: minor strokes

a. "patchy" pattern of deficits

C. Other Organic Brain Syndromes

1. Amnestic syndrome involves memory disturbance related to inability to learn new information

2. Organic delusional syndrome involves delusions

3. Organic hallucinosis involves persistent hallucinations due to use of hallucinogens

4. Organic affective syndrome involves mood disorder

5. Organic personality syndrome involves changes in motivation, emotion, impulse control

V. Brain Disorders With a Variety of Causes

A. Huntington's Disease: A Genetically Based Disorder

1. Rare hereditary disease transmitted by a single dominant gene

2. Choreiform movements are prominent; memory loss is great

3. Chromosome pair 4 implicated by Venezuela study

4. Genetic counseling is used to discuss problems related to the occurrence of a genetically influenced mental disorder

B. Parkinson's Disease: Neurotransmitter Deficit

1. Progressive disorder beginning as early as age 50

2. Tremor, rigidity, mask-like face

3. Social withdrawal, emotional overcontrol, rigid coping styles

4. Successfully treated with L-dopa

C. General Paresis: Infection

1. Untreated syphilis results in dementia paralytic

a. progressive deterioration in psychological and motor functioning

2. Prompt diagnosis of syphilis is best preventive approach

D. Pellagra and Korsakoff's Syndrome: Nutritional Deficiencies

1. Pellagra caused by deficiency of vitamin niacin

2. Skin disorders, memory loss, concentration difficulties

3. Korsakoff's syndrome occurs in chronic alcoholics because of thiamine vitamin deficiency

E. Brain Injuries and Tumors

1. Traumatic neurosis describes reactions that follow a startling or traumatic event

2. Concussions do not involve structural damage and produce momentary transient states

3. Contusions involve fine structural damage

4. Lacerations involve tears or ruptures of brain tissue

5. Tumors interfere with blood supply to brain; symptoms depend on location in brain

6. Post-traumatic psychosis can follow brain injury

F. Epilepsy: Multiple Causal Factors

1. Incidence is 0.3 percent

2. Half of epilepsies result from birth injuries or brain traumas

3. Results from a transient electrical instability of some brain cells

4. Acquired, or symptomatic, epilepsy refers to seizures where cause is unknown
5. Grand mal and petit mal seizures
   a. lasts 2 to 5 minutes
   b. uncontrollable spasms
   c. preceded by vivid aura; tonic and clonic phases follow
   d. petit mal, common in children, has no convulsion but involves lapse of consciousness, lack of attention
6. Psychomotor epilepsy involves loss of good judgment
   a. visual hallucinations and confused state often accompany
G. Psychological Factors
   1. Seizures increase with increasing challenges, pressures
   2. Combination results in much stress
   3. Treatment of epilepsy involves drugs, surgery, psychological management
      a. Dilantin, phenobarbital reduce frequency and severity of seizures
      b. surgical interventions, although extreme, may be used as last resort
      c. conditioning has reduced frequency of seizures
H. Cerebrovascular Accidents: Blockage of Blood Supply
   1. Strokes involve blockages or ruptures of cerebral blood vessels
   2. Aphasia, inability to use words, often results
   3. Abrupt onset
VI. An Integrative Approach to Brain Disorders
   A. Psychological Factors
      1. More outgoing people have better likelihood of improvement
      2. Memory-aiding techniques
      3. Cognitive therapies for depression
VII. Study Outline

Learning Objectives

Students should know:

1. That brain function involves complex integration rather than discrete independent functions.
2. The factors that influence vulnerability to brain changes.
3. The major procedures used to assess brain damage.
4. The deficits associated with delirium. The causes of delirium tremens.
5. The deficits associated with dementia. Characteristics of senile dementia and presenile dementia.
6. The similarities and differences between Alzheimer's disease, Pick's disease, and multi-infarct dementias.
7. The causes and characteristics of Huntington's disease and Parkinson's disease.
8. The causes of general paresis and Korsakoff's syndrome. The effects of tumors.
9. The difference between brain concussions, contusions, and lacerations. That maladaptive behavior as a result of brain injury is usually explained by the location and extent of damage.
10. That aphasia involves loss of language functions due to brain dysfunction.
11. The differences between grand mal seizures, petit mal seizures, and psychomotor epilepsy. The several treatments that have been successful with epilepsy disorders. The origins and incidence of epilepsy.
12. That cerebrovascular accidents are abrupt in onset and that they usually occur after age 65. The symptoms and prognosis of small and large CVAs.
13. How pretraumatic personality and adjustment to an injury or tumor influence the individual's subsequent rehabilitation from the brain disorder. The importance of an interactive approach between brain dysfunction and psychological factors.
14. The demographic facts of the increasing number of elderly people. The functional disorders that often go hand-in-hand with brain deterioration.

Discussion Questions

1. Psychosurgery has been a very controversial medical procedure since it was first initiated on a wide scale worldwide in the 1930s. Nevertheless, an estimated 100,000 such operations were performed prior to the 1960s. Some clinicians and researchers have made a distinction between neurosurgery and psychosurgery on the basis of the goal of the surgery. Efforts to control neurological dysfunction, such as excision of regions of the thalamus to control Parkinson's disease and removal of parts of cerebral lobes ("lobectomy") to control the spread of epileptic seizures, which have been somewhat successful, would be categorized as neurosurgery. Efforts to control behavior such as violent aggressive outbursts would be labeled psychosurgery. Often, however, it is more difficult to determine whether the goal is neurological correction or psychological change as

in the amelioration of intractable pain. At any rate, the number of psychosurgeries performed has dropped dramatically so that an estimated 300 are now performed in the United States each year. Psychosurgery is usually an intervention of last resort so that prior drugs and behavioral therapies have failed to relieve the individual of the negative symptoms. Psychosurgery appears to be most successful in treating cases of chronic depression, excessive panic disorders, and persistent obsessive-compulsive anxiety disorders. The rather radical procedures of frontal lobotomy that are associated in many people's minds with psychosurgery are seldom practiced today. Rather stereotactic surgery involving implantation of fast decaying radiological substances and electrocoagulation of blood supply to particular neurons are the interventions of choice. However, given the many questions that are still unanswered about localization of brain function and the interdependent nature of brain function, many clinical neuropsychologists feel that psychosurgery is still a relatively crude procedure. It might be interesting to elicit students' opinions of neurosurgery and psychosurgery before giving them information about the more modern procedures. Does that information change their opinions? Under what circumstances, if any, would students be willing to accept brain surgery as an intervention technique?

2. Over the next 20 years, the number of people over the age of 65 will increase from approximately 20 million to 30 million. And one might assume that, since the frequency of senile dementia is correlated with age, the number of cases of senile dementia will increase by 50 percent. Barring any revolutionary medical discoveries, this increase might well occur. It need not necessarily occur, however, because personal and social factors affect deterioration, and they can be altered. This discussion focuses on factors that potentially slow down deterioration. Ask students to generate a list of personal and social factors that might contribute to the rate of deterioration of intellectual abilities in old people. (Some possible contributing factors include stress, social isolation, and lack of control over one's life.) Then have them consider ways of altering those factors that lead to deterioration.

Supplementary Lecture Material

Psychological Intervention in the Control of Epilepsy

Approximately 7 out of every 100,000 children have seizures and 90 percent of adult epileptics began having seizures before the age of 20. While anticonvulsant drugs have been shown to be effective in reducing seizure activity, these drugs produce undesirable side effects, and half of the children who take these drugs continue to have some seizures. Given that physical injury can result from seizures (e.g., from falling) and that pharmacological treatment is not fully effective for some, there is considerable value in finding alternative and supplemental treatments for this disorder.

Recently, the interactive nature of psychosocial and biological causes and treatments of epilepsy has been emphasized. For example, stress is now considered to be a major precipitator of seizures. In the way of treatment, a number of different and effective behavioral programs that have been developed to help control (most often in conjunction with drugs) seizures was reviewed in an article by Mostofsky, (Mostofsky, D.I., & Balaschak, B.A., 1977. Psychological control of seizures. *Psychological Bulletin*, 84, 723–750.) He has classified these procedures into three categories: reward-and-punishment programs, self-control programs, and physiological techniques. These procedures are outlined below.

A. Reward and punishment programs
  1. Denial of reward following the occurrence of a seizure
  2. Institution of penalties for seizures
  3. Relief from the application of noxious stimuli upon seizure reduction
  4. Punishment administration following seizures
  5. Rewards (either tangible or imagined) for periods of no seizure activity
B. Self-control
  1. Relaxation to reduce stress
  2. Traditional psychotherapy
  3. Self-control training
C. Psychophysiological methods
  1. Extinction by repeatedly presenting seizure eliciting stimuli
  2. Biofeedback

An illustrative case study of the psychological modification of seizures is provided by Barbara Balaschak. (Balaschak, B., 1976. Teacher-implemented behavior modification in a case of organically based epilepsy. *Journal of Consulting and Clinical Psychology, 44*, 218–223.) Joan, at the time of the study, was 11 years old and had been having seizures since she was 18 months old. Neither drugs (Dilantin and Phenobarbital) nor drugs in combination with psychotherapy had been effective in eliminating these seizures. Balaschak devised a program to reward Joan with candy for periods of no seizures during school. This program was implemented by Joan's fourth-grade teacher.

A baseline of seizures was obtained by compiling teacher and nurse reports for the first 50 days of school.

During this period, Joan had 30 seizures, which, when compared to the percentage of days on which there were seizures, indicated a rate of 60 percent. When treatment was instituted, the teacher recorded seizures on a "good times" chart, and the rate dropped to four seizures in 24 days, or a rate of 16.7 percent (drug treatment was maintained during this period). The treatment continued for the next 28 school days, after a vacation and change in medication, with 7 seizures occurring—a rate of 25 percent. Joan was absent from school for two months with mononucleosis. When she returned, the teacher discontinued the program. During this no-treatment period, she had 25 seizures in 40 days, or a rate of 62.5 percent.

This study lacked the adequate experimental controls necessary for definitive conclusions to be drawn. Nevertheless, it is highly suggestive, for there was a dramatic decline in seizure activity during treatment (16.7 to 25 percent) when compared to pretreatment (60 percent) and posttreatment (62.5 percent). It is notable that this program was successfully carried out by a teacher in a school setting. Unfortunately, after Joan's illness, the teacher decided that it was more important for Joan to concentrate on her school work than the seizure program and so the program was terminated.

Stages of Deterioration in Primary Degenerative Dementia

Severe symptoms of primary degenerative dementia occur in 5 percent of people over the age of 65, with mild to moderate symptoms occurring in another 11 percent of that population. Three phases of the progressive deterioration have been identified—an early "forgetfulness" phase, a "confusional" phase, and a "dementia" phase. These phases have been broken down to seven stages of clinically identifiable behaviors. (Reisberg, B., Ferris, S.H., DeLeon, M.J., & Cook, T., 1982. The Global Deterioration Scale for assessment of primary degenerative dementia. *American Journal of Psychiatry, 139*, 1136-1139.)

At the first stage, individuals do not complain of memory deficits, and interviews do not elicit evidence of memory deficit; however, tests of memory dysfunction show some mild problems. In the second stage, the "forgetfulness" stage, the individual complains of memory deficit, especially in forgetting names and where things have been placed. The interview does not yield evidence of memory deficits, and social and occupational functioning are intact; however, tests of memory show mild dysfunction.

Clear-cut deficits are evident in the third stage. Individuals may have difficulty concentrating, forget names of people, and remember little of what they have just read. Objects are misplaced, and the individual may

become lost when traveling to an unfamiliar place. The individual shows mild to moderate anxiety, and social and occupational functioning may become difficult to meet. Moderate memory dysfunction is evident on psychological tests, but mental status interviews are intact.

At stage four, the "confusional stage," deficits are manifested in many areas. The individual may have difficulty concentrating; for example, he or she might experience difficulty counting backwards by 7s (serial subtractions). They may fail to remember personal history information, be unable to travel alone, have difficulty managing personal finances, and fail on complex tasks requiring accuracy and efficiency. They are oriented in time and person and can recognize familiar faces. Individuals may deny the loss of psychological functions at this point. Also, flattening of affect and social withdrawal become evident. Impairments are evident in the mental status interview.

The phase of early dementia, stage five, involves a moderately severe cognitive deficit. Individuals have difficulty remembering important information such as their address or telephone number and the names of family members. Thus, they require support and cannot live independently. Their concentration is diminished (serial subtractions), and they may be disoriented in time or place. They do remember many things about themselves, including their own names and those of their spouses and children. They may need help in getting dressed, but they can go to the toilet by themselves.

The middle phase of dementia, stage six, involves severe cognitive deficits. Individuals may forget spouses' names, retain only sketchy knowledge of their own lives, and be unaware of recent life experiences. They require substantial assistance in living. They need help in traveling and may become incontinent. They do know their own names and are frequently capable of distinguishing familiar people but not recalling their names. Delusional behavior, compulsive symptoms, anxiety symptoms, and lack of purposeful behavior may become evident in this stage.

In the seventh stage, late dementia, verbal abilities are lost, and the individual is frequently incontinent, requires assistance in toileting and eating, and often loses control of psychomotor skills such as the ability to walk.

The mental status interview that is mentioned in the text is useful for identifying dementia in stages four and five but not in stages one, two, and three. Of course, the extent of the cognitive, behavioral, and affective deterioration is too obvious to make the mental status interview useful at stages six and seven. Thus, one might question how much the mental status interview adds to the detection of brain dysfunction, especially in relation to stages of primary degenerative dementia.

CHAPTER 14

Addictive Disorders

Overview

The effects, use, and treatment of alcohol and other drugs are covered in this chapter. The terms "abuse" and "dependence," "tolerance" and "withdrawal" are clarified. Substances are classified according to whether they produce abuse, physiological, or psychological withdrawal. The effects of alcohol use are described, and theoretical perspectives on the development of drinking problems are reviewed. Treatment from each of these theoretical perspectives is followed, and the issues of relapse prevention, barbiturates and tranquilizers, opiates, cocaine, amphetamines, hallucinogens, cannabis, caffeine, and nicotine follow.

Outline

I. Substance Dependence
  A. Psychoactive Substance Disorder
    1. Significant, ongoing maladaptive behavior that interferes with social functioning or job effectiveness
    2. Intoxication leads to belligerence, poor judgment
    3. Prolonged use results in reduction of goal-directed behaviors, cognitive deficits, flashbacks
  B. Substance Dependence
    1. Criteria
      a. some symptoms must continue for one month or occur frequently for six months
      b. anticipation of use
    2. Physiological dependence on a substance
      a. tolerance: doses must be higher or more frequent to produce previous effect

      b. withdrawal: physical symptoms that occur when use of substance is cut down or stopped

II. Alcohol
  A. Alcohol Abuse
    1. Incidence
      a. 70 percent of Americans drink on occasion
      b. more men than women
      c. highest in 21 to 34 age range
    2. Abuse referred to as problem drinking
    3. Dependence or addiction is called alcoholism
  B. Alcohol and Health
    1. Abusers have increased risk of death
      a. accidents, especially drunken driving
      b. over 50 percent of total nontraffic accidents: falls, fires, drowning
      c. illnesses, including cancer, high blood pressure, cirrhosis of liver
    2. Moderate alcohol use lessens chances of heart attack
    3. Extensive abuse may result in left hemisphere brain damage
    4. Heavy use by pregnant women may result in fetal alcohol syndrome
  C. Perspectives on Alcohol Abuse
    1. The biological view
      a. E.M. Jellinek was "founder" of this view
      b. alcoholism is a disease
      c. alcoholics experience irresistable physical cravings for alcohol
      d. satisfaction of cravings leads to physical dependence, which leads to loss of control
      e. complete abstention is only way for alcoholics to return to a normal life
    2. Genetic factors of alcohol susceptibility
      a. strong evidence that alcoholism runs in families

b. one type of inherited alcohol problem is called male-limited
   (1) son of affected father likely to show alcohol problems
   (2) occurs regardless of environment
c. second type of inherited alcohol problem is called mileu-limited
   (1) susceptibility appears to be hereditary, both sexes
   (2) environmental factors significantly affect frequency and severity of the drinking problem

3. Sensitivity to alcohol
   a. great variability due to differences in metabolism
   b. Orientals are more sensitive than Caucasians
   c. sensitivity of neural system differs

4. The psychodynamic view
   a. typical alcohol dependent person has an oral-dependent personality
   b. personality characterized by self-doubt, passivity, dependence
   c. lack of satisfaction of oral needs leads to oral gratification by devices such as drinking
   d. Jones: personality characteristics are consistent from adolescence to adulthood and include hostile, submissive, socially unsuccessful, anxious for males; impulsive, difficulty forming friendships

5. Learning factors
   a. people drink as a way of coping with problems of living
   b. through reinforcement and modeling people learn to use alcohol to cope with problems

6. Cognitive factors
   a. problem drinkers learn to expect positive effects from drinking
   b. problem drinkers interpret the experience positively even though it is predominantly negative

7. Social and community factors
   a. values and customs of the community influence attitudes toward drinking
   b. certain sociocultural conditions minimize alcohol problems
      (1) exposure to children at early age in strong family or religious setting
      (2) beverage is considered a food and served mainly at meals
      (3) drinking is not considered a virtue or a sin
      (4) abstinence is socially acceptable but drunkenness is not

D. Treatment
   1. First step is detoxification
      a. physiological withdrawal symptoms begin 6 to 24 hours after heavy drinking has stopped
      b. withdrawal signs include tremors, delirium, sweating, confusion, increased blood pressure, agitation
      c. insomnia, depression, anxiety may persist for weeks, months after completion of detoxification
   2. Most recoveries are not the result of treatment
      a. 40 percent recover on own; only 10 percent of abusers are treated
      b. acknowledgement of disorder is essential
      c. denial, obliviousness mask seriousness
   3. The biological approach
      a. outgrowth of view that alcoholism is a disease
      b. emphasis on need to avoid alcoholic beverages completely
      c. Alcoholics Anonymous widely recommended to adherents of disease model
         (1) Twelve Steps
         (2) AA effective for 50 percent who stay in for 2 years
      d. use of anti-abuse drug, Disulfiram, causes extreme discomfort upon having a drink
   4. The psychodynamic approach
      a. definitive conclusions supporting psychodynamic therapy are difficult to obtain
      b. probably provided very little benefit
   5. The learning approach
      a. aversive conditioning is based on classical conditioning principles and often includes use of nausea-producing drug
      b. covert sensitization often used when aversive conditioning is objectionable
   6. The cognitive approach
      a. clients monitor their behavior by noting the situational and environmental antecedents and consequences of heavy drinking
         (1) which places
         (2) with whom
         (3) when
         (4) emotional feeling just prior

b. client and therapist work together to develop cognitive coping techniques to deal with the tempting situations

7. Relapse prevention: Marlatt has developed cognitive program to prevent relapse

a. abstinence-violation effect is important factor in promoting a continuing relapse

b. requires a voluntary decision to change

c. assumes a sense of perceived control over own behavior as long as abstinence or rules of program are followed

d. encountering high risk situations involves frustration, anger, depression, interpersonal arguments with employers and family, social pressure to drink; requires assertiveness skills to disengage

c. conflict and guilt follow relapse; self-blame attribution follows

f. train individuals to recognize early warning signals that precede relapse and carry out trained coping strategies

8. Abstinence versus controlled drinking

a. some alcoholics, those above age 40, must abstain entirely in order to successfully cope with their alcohol problems

b. others, under age 40, can successfully resume drinking on a controlled basis

c. level of abuse before treatment plays role in which treatment strategy will be most effective

E. Preventing Alcohol Abuse

1. As many as 50 percent of people in treatment drop out

2. Studies have failed to find treatment effectiveness

III. Other Drugs

A. Barbiturates and Tranquilizers

1. Both have depressing effect on central nervous system

a. reduce anxiety and insomnia and affect a wide range of bodily functions

2. Body quickly develops a tolerance

a. after addiction, sudden abstinence results in withdrawal symptoms

3. Three types of barbiturate abuse

a. chronic intoxication

b. episodic intoxication

c. intravenous injections

B. The Opioids

1. Natural opioids are called endorphins

2. Opiates are derived from opium:

morphine, heroin, codeine, methadone, haloperidol

3. Effects of opioids have both sedative and analgesic effects

4. Opioids produce both tolerance and dependence; withdrawal reaction can be severe

5. Causes of opioid addiction

a. exposure orientation: view says cause is simply exposure to opioids

b. adaptive orientation: view focuses on interaction of person and situation

6. Treatment of opioid dependence

a. although hospitalization is common, it is ineffective as treatment

b. methadone maintenance is most widely used form of treatment

c. detoxification is first step for all nonmethadone maintenance treatments

C. Cocaine

1. An "upper" that increases heartbeat, raises blood pressure and body temperature, decreases appetite; should be classified as a narcotic

2. Can be snorted, smoked, or injected

3. Produces feelings of wittiness and hyperalertness

4. High doses can cause state resembling mania, impaired judgment, acute anxiety attacks

5. Small doses not physiologically addictive, does not lead to withdrawal symptoms, but feelings of gloom experienced after a high seem to be remedied only by more cocaine

6. Tolerance develops quickly

7. One form of treatment is through aversive conditioning

a. patient must be convinced that treatment is necessary

b. supportive psychotherapy

c. Cocaine Anonymous

D. Amphetamines

1. Stimulants that share many properties of cocaine

2. High doses can have considerable effect on central nervous system and cardiovascular system

3. Regular use of large amounts leads to tolerance

4. Thinking is characterized by paranoia with full-blown hallucinations possible

5. Withdrawal symptoms, if they occur, are quantitatively and qualitatively different from those found when opiate use ceases

E. Psychedelics
  1. Act on central nervous system to produce alterations of time, consciousness of self, and space
  2. Auditory, visual, tactile hallucinations also occur
  3. Natural hallucinogenic substances include DMT, STP, LSD
  4. Can produce extreme anxiety or panic attacks

F. Phencyclidine (PCP)
  1. Often called "angel dust," can cause hallucinations and dissociation
  2. Effects include flushing, sweating, dizziness, numbness
  3. Large doses produce drowsiness, convulsions, coma
  4. Is a dissociative anesthetic

G. Marijuana
  1. Most common illegal drug in United States; 20 percent have used once or more
  2. Not pharmacologically a narcotic; THC is active ingredient
  3. Produces psychological dependence
    a. produces stress-like coardiovascular effects
    b. may produce respiratory problems
    c. suppresses production of male hormones
    d. potentially harmful to infant in pregnant, nursing women
  4. Useful in treatment of glaucoma
  5. Peer pressure is strongest factor in introducing marijuana to adolescents

H. Nicotine
  1. Stimulant that is physically hazardous
  2. Withdrawal effects of nicotine: irritability, anxiety, headache, concentration problems begin two hours after last ingestion, peaks 24 hours after last cigarette
  3. Addiction to cigarettes is hard to overcome on a long-term basis
    a. negative reinforcement occurs when taking another cigarette reduced withdrawal effects
    b. heavy smokers may require pharmacological substitute such as tobacco gum
    c. lighter smokers can learn control of stimulus factors or cognitive controls
    d. aversive techniques include mild electric shock, rapid smoking
    e. cognitive program helps identify smoking situations and learning of

coping techniques as alternatives; use of self-reinforcement when resistance to smoking has been successful.
    f. combination of behavioral and cognitive coping responses is most effective, especially when alcohol is involved

IV. Study Outline

Learning Objectives

Students should know:
  1. How to define abuse and dependence, tolerance and withdrawal. How the various drugs are classified in their potential for abuse, physiological dependence, and psychological dependence.
  2. The impact of alcohol on health and behavior. That the amount of alcohol consumed, the social setting, and the person's expectations have a large effect on behavioral changes related to drinking.
  3. That there is strong evidence for a genetic basis to alcoholism; the two views of genetic contribution.
  4. The implication and assumptions of the biological and disease perspective of alcoholism.
  5. The psychodynamic focus on personality characteristics and processes associated with alcoholism.
  6. The learning and cognitive factors found in problem drinking. The roles of expectations in producing desirable effects from drinking and of negative reinforcement in maintaining problem drinking.
  7. The effects of alcohol detoxification. Treatment from the biological approach. The role of Alcoholics Anonymous in the treatment of alcoholism.
  8. How aversive conditioning and covert sensitization are used to treat alcohol use problems.
  9. The cognitive approach to treatment. Marlatt's cognitively oriented relapse prevention approach.
  10. The issues for and against abstinence and controlled drinking approaches to treatment.
  11. The characteristic effects of barbiturates and tranquilizers, their potential for addiction, and the effects of withdrawal from them.
  12. Some of the effects of amphetamines and cocaine in terms of the social and psychological consequences of prolonged use.
  13. Some of the treatments available for narcotic users, such as hospitalization and methadone maintenance.

14. The psychological and physiological negative effects of cannabis use.

15. Withdrawal effects associated with nicotine. The different approaches to stopping smoking and the relative success of each treatment.

Discussion Questions

1. How does each of us contribute to excessive drinking? (e.g., encouraging someone to stop for a drink after an event, offering multiple drinks to visitors, attending parties that we know will be wild)

2. What could or would you do if you thought someone was drunk? (e.g., take away car keys; insist they sleep before leaving for home) If you thought that they had a drinking problem? (tell them of your concern)

3. Should the use of alcohol be regulated by the government in the same way that other drugs are? Should there be a lower age limit on alcohol use? An upper age limit?

4. What can each of us do to contribute to a resistance to alcohol problems? (educate children in proper use; ignore associations of power and virility with alcohol use and emphasize negative behaviors of problem drinkers; encourage party-going drivers not to drink)

Class Participation Project

The cognitive approach to treating problem drinking is to identify the expectations of alcohol effects; to monitor one's daily activities in order to identify the situations and environmental antecedents and the consequences of drinking; and to identify and rehearse coping strategies that can be implemented in the place of drinking behavior. It can be instructive to students if a cognitive analysis like the forgoing is conducted.

The first step is to identify expectations associated with alcohol use. Questions of the following type could be rated on a seven-point scale ranging from strongly disagree to strongly agree: 1) Having a drink helps me relax after a tense experience. 2) I am a more sociable person after I've had a drink or two. 3) I am more inhibited when I have a drink or two. 4) I become overly aggressive when I've had too much to drink. 5) Sexual feelings are enhanced with a drink or two. 6) I am less aware of pleasurable sensations from the environment after a drink or two. 7) I can drive just as well as usual after I've had much to drink. 8) I feel more sure of myself after a drink. 9) People see the real me when I've had a lot to drink. 10) After having a few drinks, I have no trouble saying "no" to another drink. The results of this little survey might be compared against the findings of researchers. College students typically expect that moderate drinking results in relatively greater stimulation, feelings of greater control and dominance, and less inhibition for pleasurable experiences. However, heavy drinking is associated with a greater degree of perceived impairment. Studies also suggest that expectancy effects are strongest for behaviors believed to be positive or desirable such as lower social anxiety, greater assertiveness, sexual pleasure, and goal-directed aggression. In contrast, negative or undesirable acts such as making errors on a complex task or making mistakes while driving are not subject to the same expectancy effects.

The next step is to have the students monitor their behavior every day for a one-week period. For each event, have them record when, where, with whom, what, and how many drinks were consumed. In addition, have them record physical and social cues that promote drinking behavior. For example, any beer ads in magazines or on television, attention to a neighborhood bar to and from school, being with others who talked about drinking, who modeled drinking, who urged the student to drink, who made a critical remark or sarcastic remark that encouraged drinking.

Finally, have students describe their thinking, feeling, and actions during and after each drinking experience. Then have the students divide those reactions into pleasant reactions and unpleasant reactions. Some students, of course, will not have drinking experiences during the monitoring period. It might be useful for them to focus on the events that enable them to not have a drink in the same situations that others do have drinks. The class might attempt to identify precipitating events that elicit drinking behavior and positive feelings that maintain drinking behavior. How could they use alternative coping strategies and what strategies would they use in place of drinking alcohol?

CHAPTER 15

Maladaptive Behaviors of Childhood and Adolescence

Overview

I. The Scope of the Problem
   A. Incidence
      1. At least 13 percent of children in the United States have severe psychological problems requiring intervention
      2. See Box 15–1 for effects of child abuse and neglect
      3. Outcome of disorders in childhood is unclear
         a. have poor understanding of nature of childhood disorders and their relationship to adult disorders
         b. children's physical and intellectual development proceeds at different speeds than adults
         c. irregular patterns of development characterize some developmental periods

II. Disruptive Behaviors
   A. Attention-Deficit Hyperactivity Disorder
      1. Restlessness is a major complaint of school personnel
         a. 10 percent of boys and 1 percent of girls
         b. most frequent reason for children's referral to mental health facilities
      2. Easily distracted, difficulty concentrating, interrupt others
      3. Treatment
         a. use of psychostimulant drugs, methylphenidate (Ritalin) and destroamphetamine (Dexedrine)
            (1) stimulants have positive short-term effects with improved classroom behavior

   (2) stimulants do not improve long-term social, academic, personal problems
   (3) side effects include insomnia, headaches, nausea, tearfulness, decreased height
   (4) 30 to 40 percent of stimulant users do not improve or have unpleasant side effects
         b. behavior therapy may be an alternative treatment to drug treatment
            (1) gives children message that they can control their behavior
            (2) improves academic work more than social behavior
         c. research on too much sugar and food additives do not have sufficient evidence to support theories
         d. cognitive modeling of impulse control and aggression
   B. Conduct Disorders
      1. Behavior violates basic rights of others or major social rules
      2. Defining characteristics
         a. experts disagree about subtypes
         b. not to be confused with socialized delinquency
      3. More common in males and families with antisocial personality disorder or alcoholic problems
      4. Long-term outcome is worse than emotional disorders
      5. Treatment: prevention is most effective
         a. children who are aggressive are more likely to interpret causes of social interactions as hostile acts

III. Emotional Disturbances
   A. Anxiety Disorders of Childhood

1. Anxiety disorders are most frequent emotional disorders, are equal among boys and girls
   a. number of fears declines with age, peaks at age two
   b. cognitive development results in anticipatory fears
2. Fears and phobias
   a. focus changes from animals, dark to school, social
   b. Freud's case of "Little Hans" epitomizes psychodynamic displacement and repression
   c. learning theorists' reanalysis of Hans's case focused on classical conditioning
3. Generalized anxiety
   a. excessive worries of six months or longer
   b. routine events
   c. poor self concept
4. Obsessive-compulsive disorders
   a. rituals, obsessions, compulsions are relatively common
   b. outlook for severe form of the disorder is not good
   c. severe disorder is a rare event in childhood, accounting for less than one percent of clinic-attending children

B. Depression in Children and Adolescents
   1. Frequency
      a. about 15 percent of children show signs of depression
      b. less than 2 percent meet diagnostic criteria
      c. 30 to 60 percent of clinic-attending children are depressed
      d. 75 percent relapse within five years
   2. Changes in adolescence
      a. more girls show mood disorders in adolescence
      b. hypomania also begins to appear
   3. Long-term patterns
      a. can be either brief or reoccurring
   4. Suicidal behavior in childhood and adolescence
      a. one third of six to 12 year olds attending clinic have thought of suicide
      b. not all who kill self are depressed
      c. suicide before ten is rare but is second cause of death among adolescents
   5. Treating childhood depression
      a. psychoanalytic and family therapy used

   b. families high in conflict and low in emotional support
   c. cognitive therapy treats sense of hopelessness
   d. tricyclic medication used for adolescents, severely depressed younger children

IV. Problems With Physical Symptoms
   A. Anorexia Nervosa
      1. Feelings of hunger and preoccupation with food
      2. Characteristics include
         a. extreme weight loss
         b. disturbed body image involving intense fear of getting fat
      3. Predominantly white, middle and upper class adolescent females
      4. Causes
         a. most attention is now on psychological and family causes
      5. Depression is a continuing problem; anorexia–bulimics have substance abuse problems
      6. Family therapy and operant conditioning have been used as successful therapies
   B. Bulimia Nervosa
      1. Binge eating accompanied by laxative use or self-induced vomiting
         a. twice a week for at least three months
      2. Often accompanied by depression
      3. Binge-purge cycle represents "falling off the wagon"
         a. common among college women but not clinically significant
      4. Treatment
         a. relaxation training helps prevent binging
         b. positive thoughts are trained
         c. antidepressants given

V. Therapy With Children and Adolescents
   A. Differences Between Adult and Childhood Disorders
      1. Children rarely initiate treatment for themselves
      2. Children's problems a more direct result of family problems
      3. Goals and methods of treatment are more complex
      4. Use of developmental norms with children
   B. Play Therapy
      1. Play is substituted for verbal free-association

2. Expression of feelings is cathartic
C. Cognitive and Behavioral Therapies
  1. Parents are trained as therapists
D. Family Therapy
  1. Family systems approach deemphasizes individual
E. Results of Therapy
  1. About same with children as with adults
     a. treated children's outcomes are two thirds standard deviation better than nontreated children
     b. parents' reports of success are more positive than teachers' reports

Learning Objectives

Students should know:
1. Some of the reasons why the outcomes of interventions with troubled children are often unsatisfactory.
2. The characteristics of attention-deficit disorder. The use of age-appropriate behavioral norms to make the diagnosis. Treatment involves stimulant medication and behavioral therapy. The likely outcome for those with attention-deficit disorder.
3. The characteristics and outcomes of children with conduct disorder.
4. That the number and focus of fears in childhood change with age.
5. That phobias are interpreted differently and treated accordingly by psychodynamic and behavioral therapists.
6. That separation anxiety often involves school refusal, which can technically be distinguished from school phobia.
7. That rituals, obsessions, and compulsions are relatively common in childhood but that obsessive-compulsive anxiety disorders are very rare.
8. That historically, depression has not been diagnosed in childhood. That, nevertheless, many clinic-attending children show depressive symptoms.
9. That symptoms of childhood depression can vary with age.
10. The characteristics of anorexia nervosa. Some of the hypotheses about cause and treatments that have been successful.
11. The features of bulimia.
12. How therapy for children and adolescents differs from that of adults.

Discussion Questions

1. The use of stimulant medications has developed as one of the more effective treatments for attention-deficit disorder. Stimulant drugs reduce the activity level problems of attention deficit disorder, thus making the child more manageable in the classroom. These drugs appear to work in about 65 percent of those children with overactive behavior symptoms. As the text has indicated, long-lasting effects such as academic improvement and improved social relationships are not acquired through use of medication alone. The overuse of stimulant medication in the schools in the 1970s certainly points to the potential misuse of stimulant drugs. Ask students to put themselves in the roles of parents, of teacher, of child to think about the implications, both positive and negative, of using or not using stimulant medication to control the symptoms of attention deficit disorder.

2. Have any of the students worked with a child with early infantile autism? It might be helpful to other class members to hear about their experiences. Does the child exhibit all the classic features of early infantile autism?

3. Several paradoxes occur with anorexia nervosa. The disorder occurs in less than one-half of one percent of adolescent girls, but many students report having known or knowing of an anorexic from their high school experiences. Ask students to describe the cases they encountered. Were these classic cases of anorexia nervosa? Were bulimia symptoms also present?

Supplemental Lecture Material

One of the difficult questions to answer about the relationship between childhood disorders and adult disorders is whether children with disorders grow up to be adults with disorders or whether the two classes represent different people. The question is made more difficult by diagnostic categories and by the shift of attention to adolescent and child disorders following a period of relative neglect. To ask the question in another way, how stable are childhood and adolescent disorders?

The text has indicated that many problem behaviors of childhood are normative for that age and are "outgrown" or disappear with increasing age. Said in another way, the presence of problem behaviors in childhood does not necessarily indicate the presence of developmental disturbance. Studies have indicated only two problem behaviors, truancy and running away, that are more common in adolescence than in the childhood period. In contrast, many problem behaviors—aggressiveness, restlessness, temper tantrums, sleep difficulty, excessive fearfulness—are more common before the age of 12 than during adolescence.

In making a judgment of whether a developmental psychopathology is present, four criteria are helpful to clinicians: 1) The problems being displayed are not appropriate or common to the individual's age group; 2) the individual displays many problems rather than few; 3) the problem behaviors involve cognitive difficulties and antisocial behavior rather than only emotional distress age. Studies indicate that approximately 13 percent of children have severe disorders, 65 percent have mild-to-moderate disorders, and 22 percent have no discernible disorders. By comparison, 20 percent of adolescents have severe disorders, 60 percent have mild-to-moderate disorders, and 20 percent have no discernible disorders. Interestingly, these figures are also similar for adults—25 percent have severe disorders, 54 percent have mild-to-moderate disorders, and 19 percent have no disorder during their adult lifetimes.

Once again, do the same individuals occupy the same categories at their respective ages? The answer is yes. Children who have severe disorders are likely to be the adolescents with severe disorders, who in turn become the adults with serious disorders. This is not to say that

category exchanges do not take place. Rather, there is strong evidence of rather remarkable stability in psychological disorders from childhood through adulthood.

An examination of recovery rates provided by Weiner (Weiner, I., 1982. *Disorders of Childhood and Adolescence.* New York: Wiley.) and given in Table 15.1 indicates the stability of serious disorders in childhood and adolescence.

—

TABLE-15.1

—

Recovery Rates of Selected Childhood Disorders

Childhood Schizophrenia (Pervasive Developmental Disorder)

30-50%	achieve mode tely good social adjustment
20%	recover completely
75%	do poorly
50%	are prematurely institutionalized by adulthood

Adolescent Schizophrenia

25%	recover
25%	improve but have lingering symptoms or relapses
50%	make little or no progress

Affective Disorders (Unipolar Depression)

35%	recover
65%	have recurrences without hospitalization there is a 100% spontaneous remission rate

Phobias

90%	get over their excessive fears

CHAPTER 16

Developmental Disorders

Overview

The characteristics, prospects for change, therapy, research, and the cognitive and biological perspectives on autism are highlighted. Mental retardation is caused by genetic changes, prenatal environment, birth complications, physical hazards, and psychosocial disadvantage. Two models of cognitive development of the retarded are reviewed. The impact of federal laws and court rulings on the education of the mentally retarded are discussed. Finally, the impact of deinstitutionalization and prospects for independent living with self-help skills are examined.

Outline

I. Autistic Disorder
   A. Incidence
      1. Occurs in two to four children out of 10,000
      2. Boys more likely to be autistic
   B. Characteristics of Autistic Behavior
      1. Impairment of social relationships
      2. Impairment of communication skills
         a. echolalia
         b. absence of speech
      3. Narrow range of interests and activities
         a. sameness and routine are very important
         b. repetitive touching and smiling appear later
   C. Prospects for Change
      1. Key to predicting future adjustment is whether language skills are developed by age five
      2. About 90 percent are retarded; two thirds cannot care for themselves

      3. A few autistic children make a good adjustment later in life
   D. Therapy
      1. Behavior modification programs have been used to train language and self-help skills
      2. It takes several hours a day for months at a time
      3. Intensive training might allow a subgroup of children to reach average functioning
   E. Research on Autism
      1. First described thoroughly by Leo Kanner in 1943
      2. Important to separate autistic children who are retarded from those with average intelligence
      3. Cognitive perspective
         a. either under or over responsive to many kinds of stimuli
         b. language deficits include echolalia, reversal of pronouns
         c. trouble with higher order cognitive processing involving stimuli organized in meaning
         d. lack of symbolic play
         e. short-term memory recall is not deficient
      4. Biological perspective
         a. theories for etiology of autism are
            (1) damage to both hemispheres
            (2) damage of limbic system
            (3) dysfunction in brain stem
         b. so far there are no specific findings of brain damage
         c. possibility that autism may be inherited
         d. also suggested that parents of autistic children share human leucoyte antigens
   F. Autism vs. Childhood Schizophrenia
      1. Once thought of as a psychosis, autism is now considered a developmental disorder

2. Unclear whether schizophrenia in childhood is same as in adulthood

II. Mental Retardation

A. Features of Retardation

1. Intellectual functioning at least two standard deviations below average

2. Impaired adaptive behavior

3. Onset before age 18

B. Degrees of Retardation

1. Mild: IQ range, 50 to 69; 85 percent

2. Moderate: IQ range, 35 to 49; 10 percent

3. Severe: IQ range, 20 to 34; four percent

4. Profound: IQ range, below 20; less than one percent

C. Biological Causes

1. Overlapping terms

a. hereditary

b. innate

c. congenital

d. constitutional

D. Hereditary Disorders

1. Disorders caused by specific dominant genes

a. Tuberous Sclerosis produces internal and external skin tumors

b. are very few known disorders due to dominant genes

2. Disorders due to specific recessive genes

a. Phenylketonuria (PKU), results in severe retardation but can be prevented with restrictive diet

b. Tay Sachs disease is usually fatal by age four and occurs in Ashkenazi Jews of Eastern European descent

3. Disorders caused by sex cells

a. disorders of sex cells, abnormality not as severe as for autosome or nonsex cells

b. Fragile X Syndrome accounts for 10 percent of all retardation and is more severe in men than women

E. Disorders Due to Mutation

1. Down Syndrome

a. trisomy 21

b. considerable variability in degree of retardation, physical characteristics

c. Mosaicism also produces Down Syndrome

d. translocation produces a few cases of Down Syndrome

F. Amniocentesis

1. Other trisomies (trisomy 13, trisomy 18) also produce retardation

2. Amniocentesis can detect Down

Syndrome after fourth month of pregnancy

3. Pregnant women over 35 are at greater risk for delivering Down Syndrome child

4. Chorionic villus sampling, a new procedure, can be performed after fetus is nine weeks old

5. Alpha-fetoprotein and anecphaly also can be performed

G. Disorders Caused by Prenatal Environment

1. Maternal infections

a. Rubella virus: half of fetuses of mothers with rubella in first three months of pregnancy are infected; one third are retarded

b. herpes virus passed on during birth and can cause mental retardation

2. Blood incompatibilities and other chronic maternal conditions

a. antibody response such as Rh incompatibility can result in brain damage

b. hypertension and diabetes can also interfere with nutritional supply

3. Drugs

a. pass through the placenta to the fetus

b. fetal alcohol syndrome occurs in 40 percent of children born to alcoholic mothers

c. results in moderate mental retardation

H. Problems at Birth and After Birth

1. Asphyxia or lack of oxygen at birth

a. do poorly in thinking and perception and have more neurological problems

2. Prematurity occurs with lower-class mothers who smoke heavily and have poor diets

a. infants under three pounds at birth usually cannot attend regular school classes later

3. Infections include meningitis, encephalitis; cause inflammation of brain tissue

4. Head injuries frequently stem from automobile accidents and child abuse; swelling cuts off blood supply

I. Psychosocial Disadvantage

1. Three quarters of all retarded are in mild category and are without clear causal factors

2. Come from lower socio-economic class parents

3. Parents of mildly mentally retarded are often retarded

a. adopted children are not usually retarded

4. Effects of environmental change can be quite positive for mildly retarded
   a. North Carolina study showed that early intervention raised IQs

J. Cognitive Functioning in Retarded
1. Identification of retardation
   a. mildly retarded are identified later than moderate, severe, profound
2. Developmental and difference models
   a. developmental model assumes that process of cognitive development is no different for mildly retarded than for normals
      (1) mentally retarded make slower progress through stages of cognitive development
   b. difference model suggests qualitative differences between retarded and normals
      (1) uneven patterns of development characterized retarded

K. Public Educational Programs
1. Education for all Handicapped Children Act
   a. Public Law 94-124 (1975) required public schools to provide free, appropriate education to all handicapped children
      (1) basic communication and social skills programs offered to retarded
      (2) more retarded are cared for at home in early years
2. Court case of *Brown vs. Board of Education* (1954)
   a. resulted in subsequent efforts to provide "least restrictive" education
3. Mainstreaming has not brought improvement in academic performance and does not improve the social status of the child

L. New Approaches to Intelligence Testing
1. Kaufman Assessment Battery measures abilities unaffected by cultural factors
2. New intelligence tests have been devised to assess social competence as well (e.g., SOMPA)

M. Deinstitutionalization
1. Discipline and occupational employment are the chief problems of deinstitutionalized retarded
2. Community living programs and group homes offer mixture of management of behavior and job opportunities
3. Best predictor of success in a community setting is a measure of adaptive behavior
4. Lives are often lonely; they have low incomes

N. Vocational and Social Skills Training
1. Behavioral methods
   a. basic skills taught include use of money, housekeeping, use of telephone, appropriate use of leisure time
2. Training for leisure time enjoyment; take bus, shop, eat at restaurants through behavioral methods

O. Psychological Problems
1. Retarded children experience more failure and depend more on cues from adults rather than on own independent efforts
   a. ability to make transition from dependent to independent is critical
2. About 40 percent of retarded have emotional disturbance as well
   a. anxiety disorders are common among mildly retarded
3. Overacquiescense is negative correlated with IQ and can cause the retarded person interpersonal communication difficulties

III. Study Outline

Learning Objectives

Students should know:
1. The characteristics of autism.
2. Research, therapy, and future outlook of autism.
3. The three criteria for classifying someone as mentally retarded.
4. The distinguishing characteristics of mild, moderate, severe, and profound retardation.
5. The different types of genetic causes of mental retardation. The features of Down Syndrome.
6. Some of the prenatal environmental factors that can result in retardation.
7. The characteristics and causes of fetal alcohol syndrome.
8. The effects of birth complications and hazards after birth on cognitive functioning.
9. What adoption studies and early intensive intervention studies contribute to the heredity-environment controversy about the cause of mild mental retardation.

10. The problems of early detection of mild retardation and some of the difficulties in choosing tests to assess intellectual functioning and to find appropriate normative standards.
11. The implications of the developmental and difference models of cognitive development.
12. The impacts that Public Law 94-142 and court cases such as *Larry P. vs. Riles* have had on education of the retarded.
13. Some problems in adjustment that the retarded must overcome to achieve independent living. The effectiveness of community living programs on the quality of the retarded individuals' lives.

and moderately retarded. Are there any features of anxiety disorders that would be different? What about depressive disorders?
3. Mainstreaming mentally retarded into regular classrooms has been a controversial issue since its inception, largely because of court decisions. This is especially so because subsequent research has failed to find any related gains in academic performance or social relationships. Try to get students to examine this issue from a variety of perspectives: that of the mentally retarded child, the parents and siblings of that child, the teacher of that classroom, the other pupils of the classroom, the parents of other pupils of the classroom, a school board member who must find funds for special programs. Are there other acceptable alternatives?

Discussion Questions

1. Students sometimes have a difficult time comprehending the relationship between organicity or brain damage and mental retardation. Use of the following example and questions might help illustrate the important similarities and differences:

A ten-year-old boy was riding his bicycle home from the park when he was struck by a car coming off a side street. The boy suffered a severe contusion and was unconscious for nearly a week after the accident. After rehabilitation lasting about six months, the boy returned to school. Prior to the accident he had been doing average classroom work and a school examiner had found an IQ score of 102 with an individual intelligence test. A year after the accident, a rehabilitation psychologist tested the boy and found a measured IQ of 50 in addition to some difficulty in self-help skills such as dressing completely, being overly aggressive in social relationships, and occasional urine and feces incontinence. Subsequent years found the boy unable to keep up with his classmates in his academic work so that by the age of fourteen he was at least two years behind them in academic work.

Is this boy brain-injured? Mentally retarded? Both? Why? What is necessary to make the diagnosis of mental retardation? If the age were changed to that of a 20-year-old college student, would he be mentally retarded?

2. Some students will be surprised to hear that about half of the mentally retarded have emotional disturbances in addition to their cognitive and self-care deficits. Perhaps the class would like to consider the experience of anxiety disorders among the mildly

Supplementary Lecture Material

Assessing Adaptive Behavior

The diagnosis of mental retardation technically cannot be made unless there is evidence of serious deficits in adaptive behavior. Although the measurement of intellectual functioning and the choice of a normative comparison group has not been without controversy, agreement on an index of adaptive behavior has posed a more serious challenge for psychologists assessing the possibility of mental retardation. The IQ score without question has been the most frequently used outcome measure for treatment, early intervention, and preschool preparation programs. Nevertheless, the level of adaptive behavior is the best predictor of quality of community adjustment and degree of independent living. Edward Zigler (Zigler, E., & Trickett, P.K., 1978. IQ, social competence, and evaluation of early childhood intervention programs. *American Psychologist, 37*, 789-798.) has argued that social competence rather than IQ should be the primary measure of outcome in these intervention efforts. Zigler has suggested an index of social competence that includes measures of physical health, IQ, school achievement, motivational and emotional variables, school attendance, and incidence of conduct problems.

Several measures have been popular in the assessment of adaptive behavior of mentally retarded individuals. These include the Vineland Social Maturity Scale, and the System of Multi-cultural Pluralistic Assessment (SOMPA). None of these measures is as comprehensive as the measure of social competence proposed by Zigler. However, they have met psychometric criteria, are scored fairly easily, and are familiar to most psychologists working with the mentally retarded. Examples of items from the Vineland and Adaptive Behavior Scale are given in Table 16.1.

TABLE-16.1

Examples of Items Measuring Adaptive Behavior

Vineland Social Maturity Scale

Age Period 0-1

_____ Stands alone

_____ Does not drool

_____ Follows simple instructions

Age Period 1-2

_____ Marks with pencil or crayon

_____ Pulls off socks

_____ Eats with spoon

Age Period 2-3

_____ Asks to go to toilet

_____ Removes coat or dress

_____ Gets drink unassisted

Adaptive Behavior Scale

Self-care at Toilet (Check all that apply)

_____ Lowers pants at toilet without help

_____ Sits on toilet seat without help

_____ Uses toilet tissue appropriately

_____ Flushes toilet after use

_____ Puts on clothes without help

_____ Washes hands without help

_____ None of the above

CHAPTER 17

Therapies and Their Evaluation

Overview

The major therapeutic approaches to treatment are reviewed in this chapter. These approaches include psychodynamic, cognitive, humanistic–existential, behavioral, and cognitive-behavioral, and group therapies. Methodological issues on the study of psychotherapy effectiveness are reviewed and therapy effectiveness is discussed. Biological therapies and hospitalization also are reviewed.

Outline

I. Psychotherapy
   A. Psychoanalysis and Psychodynamic Therapy
      1. Takes a long time and is expensive
      2. Psychoanalysts must undergo analysis themselves before analyzing others
      3. Most analyses require two to five years
      4. Free association is used extensively
      5. Goal is to provide insight into one's inner life
      6. Transference and countertransference are used to resolve interpersonal conflicts and to reveal the meaning of anxiety
      7. Therapists prefer to let client evolve on interpretations but do offer their interpretations
      8. Hypnosis is used in therapy to suggest changes in behavior or to enhance relaxation
   B. Humanistic and Existential Therapies
      1. Humanists emphasize people's need for self-respect and the fundamental desire to achieve it

2. Existentialists emphasize need to confront basic questions of existence
3. Client-centered therapy introduced by Carl Rogers
   a. individual is seeking personal growth but needs support of an appreciative, accepting therapist
   b. therapist is nondirective facilitator who encourages self-exploration, enhanced self-confidence
   c. psychotherapy is a growth process in which client is restructuring his/her view of world
   d. therapist must demonstrate unconditional positive regard, nonjudgmental emphatic listening
4. Existential therapy emphasizes here-and-now of existence
   a. therapists are partners with their clients
   b. help clients come to terms with basic issues concerning meaning and directions of their lives
   c. therapists work with anxious and depressed clients
   d. help lonely people make constructive choices
5. Gestalt therapy is concerned with client's perceptions of self and world
   a. use role playing to stimulate expression of strong emotions
   b. therapist frustrates client, making him/her fight our conflicts and develop self-worth
   c. anxiety and personality disorders are due to dissociations of selves
   C. The Cognitive Psychotherapies
      1. Assume that maladaptive behavior is product of unrealistic perceptions and cognitions

2. Reject role of unconscious drives but use conversations between client and therapist to effect change

3. George Kelly's fixed role therapy involves having client examine roles he/she plays in interacting with others
   a. by examining constructs and social roles, therapist helps client reevaluate aspects of life that arouse anxiety

4. Albert Ellis uses rational emotive therapy to change self-defeating thoughts
   a. preoccupation with "musts" based on arbitrary, inaccurate assumptions
   b. therapist demonstrates how unrealistic self-verbalizations can worsen problem

5. Aaron Beck's cognitive therapy focuses on automatic thoughts that arise without reasoning
   a. these thoughts are accepted as valid without questioning by client
   b. therapy goal is to terminate automatic thinking and replace it with rationally derived thoughts
   c. especially useful with depressed people

II. Cognitive-Behavioral Therapies
   A. Relaxation Training
      1. Helps people who are tense and generally anxious
      2. Muscular relaxation training
      3. Meditative procedures involve mental concentration
      4. Autogenic training
   B. Systematic Desensitization
      1. Combines muscle relaxation with distressing thoughts and images
      2. Begins with induction of relaxed state
      3. Images ranging from mild to severe anxiety arousing are gradually introduced
      4. Works best with physiologically hyperreactive individuals
      5. In vivo desensitization is superior to imaging
   C. Exposure Therapies
      1. Flooding operates on principle that continued exposure to anxiety-provoking stimuli will decrease anxiety
      2. Implosive therapy involves experiencing of successively higher levels of imagined anxiety
   D. Modeling
      1. Social skills are shown to be successful to client

2. Guided rehearsal involves imitation supplemented by coaching from the model
   a. live modeling
   b. symbolic modeling: observation of another
   c. covert modeling: imagining observing a model

E. Assertiveness Training
   1. Designed to enchance certain interpersonal skills
   2. Modeling and behavioral rehearsal plays a role

F. Paradoxical Intention
   1. Performing behaviors that are in opposition of client's goal

G. Behavior Modification
   1. Fading involves gradual elimination of cues no longer needed
   2. Positive reinforcers strengthen desirable behavior
   3. Extinction procedures and punishment are used to eliminate undesirable behaviors
   4. Biofeedback can supplement reinforcement therapy

III. Group Therapy
   A. Cognitive Behavioral Group Therapy
      1. Focus is on increasing skills and comfort of people in social situations
      2. Modeling, social reinforcement, feedback, homework assignments are used to remedy specific difficulties
   B. Family Therapy
      1. Often begins with one member of family
      2. Attitudes and feelings toward each other, cooperation and sharing can be examined
      3. The family is often treated as a system
      4. Marital therapy
   C. Psychodrama
      1. Group therapies offer ideal opportunity to compare own attitude with others and to use social transference
      2. Jacob Moreno introduced psychodrama in 1920s
      3. Group enacts events of emotional significance
         a. role playing is spontaneous
         b. is a vehicle for expressing strong emotions

IV. Integration of Therapeutic Approaches
   A. Behavioral Change of Insight?

B. Performance-Based Therapies and Insight Are Both Effective

V. Research on the Psychological Therapies
  A. Methodological Considerations
    1. Deciding on an acceptable outcome variable is difficult
    2. Similarity of subjects and therapists must be assured
    3. Enthusiasm effect may produce confounds
  B. Outcome Studies
    1. Comparisons between two groups have often been used
    2. Eysenck questioned whether positive outcomes are due to spontaneous remissions
    3. Spontaneous remissions can reflect informal help from nonprofessional sources
    4. Therapists and clients can view their level of therapeutic change differently
  C. Meta Analysis
    1. Method involves finding the overall effectiveness of a therapy by grouping many studies that evaluate the therapy
    2. Average client receiving therapy is better off than 75 percent of those not receiving treatment
    3. Less fear and anxiety than 83 percent of untreated controls
  D. Comparing Therapies
    1. Despite theoretical differences, superiority of one therapy over another has not been demonstrated conclusively
      a. therapies often emphasize the same factors: insight into problems, client-therapist relationship, opportunity to vent emotions, sense of trust, development of confidence
    2. Psychological therapies most useful with milder, nonpsychotic disorders involving feelings of unhappiness, anxiety states, nonpsychotic forms of depression
    3. Therapies not successful with schizophrenia, severe affective disorders, alcoholism, drug abuse
      a. do play a role in treatment of these disorders
    4. Problems, expectations, amount of possible change varies from person to person
    5. Many are helped by therapy but some do get worse

E. The Ingredients of Effective Therapy
  1. Success may be related more to personalities than to theories
  2. Technique factors are procedures used by therapist
  3. Interpersonal factors refer to social chemistry between therapist and client
    a. favorable outcomes most prevalent for anxiety disorders among clients whose therapists actively provided information, encouragement, opinions; made special efforts to facilitate discussion of problems, focused on here-and-now, encouraged new social activities
  4. Which activities bring about change?
    a. therapist characteristics: warmth, friendliness, genuineness, interpersonal style, beliefs, values, prejudices
F. Improving The Design of Psychotherapy Research
  1. Large sample size
  2. Homogeneous patients
  3. Treatment specificity
  4. Relevant outcome
  5. Control group measures

VI. Biological Therapies
  A. Electro-Convulsive Therapy
    1. Use has declined over past 20 years
      a. three to five percent of psychiatric inpatients receive ECT
    2. Effective with severe depression, acute mania
    3. Safe when used with muscle relaxants
    4. Unclear how or why ECT works
    5. Provides quick clinical improvement but may produce some memory impairment
  B. Drug Therapies
    1. Depression is treated with tricyclics, MAO inhibitor, stimulants, lithium
    2. Schizophrenia treated with neuroleptics or major tranquilizers such as phenothiazines
    3. Anxiety is treated with anxiolytic drugs or minor tranquilizers
    4. Effects are not always predictable
    5. Drug research requires carefully designed procedures
      a. animal studies are used to assess effects of various doses
      b. large-scale clinical trials must rule out enthusiasm, placebo effects

   c. double-blind method used to conceal from client and therapist which drug is being administered

6. Comparative studies of psychotherapy and drug therapy
   a. Camarillo State Hospital study of schizophrenics
      (1) careful controls implemented, including first admissions
      (2) did not use double-blind
      (3) 228 subjects randomly assigned to five treatments
      (4) Discharge rate was measure of success
      (5) drug alone and psychotherapy-plus-drug approaches provided best treatments, but drugs alone was cheaper

VII. Hospitalization
1. May include psychotherapy, drug therapy, social, educational, recreational programs
2. Public hospitals do not always have enough activities to keep patients engaged
3. Much variability in needs, quality and scope of programs, resources available to clients
4. Hospitalizations have declined and stays are shorter
5. Deinstitutionalization has emphasized quick returns to the community
   a. living conditions are often undesirable for hospital-released patients

VIII. Study Outline

humanistic therapies. The meaning of unconditional positive regard.
4. The focus and the therapist techniques of Gestalt and existential therapies.
5. Some of the relaxation behavioral techniques. The uses of modeling and behavior modification therapies.
6. Why therapy in groups and families is used to treat some disorders.
7. Some of the methodological issues that must be considered in studies of psychotherapy effectiveness.
8. The difficulty of accounting for spontaneous remission effects in psychotherapy. The findings of meta analyses of psychotherapy outcome studies.
9. That the effectiveness of one therapeutic approach over all others has not been demonstrated. That therapies share many characteristics even though they label and conceptualize them differently.
10. Characteristics of therapists that contribute to successful therapeutic outcomes.
11. That electroconvulsive therapy is most useful with severe depression and the conditions under which ECT might be used in the initial stages of treatment for depression.
12. The effectiveness of various drugs with various problems. The difficulties of determining the success of drugs in treatment and the necessity of using double-blind procedure.
13. The method and outcome of the Camorillo study, as well as the methodological problems of this study.
14. The changing role of hospitalization in the treatment process.

Learning Objectives

Students should know:
1. That psychoanalysis and psychodynamic therapies are usually long-term therapies with the goal of providing insight into inner functioning. The meaning of major terms such as free association, dream analysis, transference, and countertransference.
2. The assumptions of each of the cognitive therapies—fixed-role, rational-emotive, Becks cognitive therapy—and the kinds of psychological problems that are addressed by each of the therapies.
3. The role and assumptions of the therapist in Rogers' client-centered therapy. The goal of

Discussion Questions

1. Getting help for a family member, coworker, or friend who is experiencing problems of a serious maladaptive nature can be a very difficult, delicate, and frustrating process. This is particularly so when the individual in question is unaware or unwilling to admit the seriousness of his or her behaviors. It might be well at this point to review the disorders represented in Chapters 5 through 16 in order to categorize the likely response of the individual with that problem as "resistant" or "amenable." Try to outline a sequence of steps of increasing forcefulness that would enable a "resistant" individual to seek therapy.

2. The experiences of colleagues often are instructive for those who have never formally encountered a mental health professional. Using an anonymous "ballot" procedure, have students write down any source of professional help obtained for maladaptive behavior or problems of adjustment. Also have them characterize that help as belonging to one or another family of therapies. Discuss the frequency and nature of each type of intervention.

3. How does one pay for a psychotherapy service? Students have a broad range of knowledge about this question; some are very naive and some are quite experienced. How do health maintenance organizations and health insurance companies reimburse for psychotherapy? Which professionals are capable of receiving benefits for which kinds of services? How much do various services cost?

CHAPTER 18

Society's Response to Maladaptive Behavior

Overview

This chapter, with its focus on prevention, begins with distinctions between primary, secondary, and tertiary prevention and situation-focused and competency-focused prevention. The roles of three social institutions in prevention—the school, the family, and the community—then are discussed. The legal aspects of treatment and prevention include a discussion of criminal and civil commitment and recent court rulings enhancing patients' rights. The challenge of prevention is examined in terms of community resources and motivations.

Outline

I. Situation-Focused and Competency-Focused Prevention
   1. Situation-focused prevention reduces environmental causes of disordered behavior
   2. Competency-focused prevention enhances ability to cope with conditions that might lead to deviant behavior

II. Types of Prevention
   A. Primary Prevention
      1. Concerned with reduction of new cases of disorder
   B. Secondary Prevention
   C. Tertiary Prevention
      1. Attempts to reduce the impairment that may result from a given disorder

III. Sites of Prevention
   A. The Family
      1. Parents have crucial effect on child's behavior
      2. Child abuse is most blatant parental failure

   a. See Table 18–1
   b. incidence is difficult to estimate
   c. effects may be long term
   d. parental education, parents-as-therapists, Parents Anonymous are examples of preventative efforts
   3. Spouse abuse has received much attention only recently
      a. abusive husbands are less assertive in social relationships, more likely to have been abused as children
   4. Effects of divorce, which has increased dramatically recently, are seen in increased suicides, alcohol problems, depression
   5. Parents-as-therapists creates favorable environment for child
      a. applied to autism, mental retardation, aggressive behavior

   B. The School
      1. Larger schools have enabled new programs to be implemented
      2. Try to identify and help children with emotional problems that handicap academic learning
      3. Early education interventions help prevent or reduce problems later on
         a. Project Head Start has contributed to later school performance
         b. cognitive problem-solving skills can be taught to enhance behavioral adjustment
      4. Dropping out is a social problem as well as an educational one

   C. The Community
      1. Work world is major post-school activity for most adults
      2. Community agencies
         a. crisis-intervention agencies are skilled in handling crises
      3. Suicide prevention programs encourage troubled people to seek help

a. effective among white females

b. see Table 18–2 for warning signs of suicide

D. Treatment in the Community

1. Half-way house and community lodges provide social support and supervision

2. The case of Sylvia Frumkin shows how community "help" is unhelpful

3. A mix of available mental health services can improve treatment

4. Deinstitutionalization failures have resulted in an increase in state hospital readmissions

a. has not been helpful to many individuals

5. Increasing tendency to put people with criminal records in mental hospitals

IV. Legal Aspects of Treatment and Prevention

A. Institutionalization

1. Criminal commitment may occur when it is demonstrated beyond a reasonable doubt that person committed the prohibited act but that the act was committed without criminal intent due to mental disorder

a. incompetent person is one who cannot assist in own trial

b. insanity refers to someone's state of mind at time act was carried out

c. M'Naughten Rule holds that person must know right from wrong at the time of the act

d. Durham decision held that accused is not responsible if his/her actions were the result of a mental disease or mental defect

e. American Law Institute clarifies and combines M'Naughten and Durham rulings

f. 1983, Jones vs. United States ruled that people who are found not guilty by reason of insanity can be held indefinitely in a mental hospital under less rigorous proof of dangerousness

2. Civil commitments are based on doctrine of *parens patriae*

a. state takes into account best interest of a minor or an adult who is incapacitated

b. Addington vs. Texas (1979) ruled that state must present a clear and convincing case

c. decision is based on (1) whether individual is suffering from a disabling mental illness, and (2) whether he/she is dangerous

d. clinicians cannot predict dangerousness with accuracy

3. Rights of patients have been upheld in several recent court cases

a. Wyatt vs. Stickney (1971) held that state must provide adequate treatment for involuntarily confined mental hospital patients

b. O'Connor vs. Donaldson (1975) hospitalized patients who are not dangerous have a right to treatment

c. Rennie vs. Klein (1978) involuntarily admitted patient may decline drug treatment

d. "least restrictive treatment" is only as restrictive and confining as is necessary to achieve purposes of commitment

e. safety and effectiveness of present treatment methods are being questioned by patients and judges

f. informed consent requires patients receive adequate information about nature of planned treatment before undergoing it

V. The Challenge of Prevention

1. Identification of opportunities for growth and stability involves examining resources in community

2. Paraprofessionals can carry out many services

3. Self-help groups contribute to prevention

4. Community psychologists wear a number of different hats in promoting prevention

VI. A Final Word

A. Formula for Achieving Prevention

1. $P = K \times W$

a. P = prevention

b. K = needed knowledge

c. W = will to use what is known

2. Challenge is to motivate society to improve happiness, personal effectiveness, common good

Learning Objectives

Students should know:

1. The difference between situation-and competency-focused prevention.

2. The goals of primary, secondary, and tertiary prevention.

3. The impact of family variables such as child abuse, parent abuse, and divorce on the development of abnormal behavior. Prevention efforts that might limit the impact of these variables.

4. The goals of early education and screening programs in the educational process.

5. The types of community programs that can facilitate living in the community as opposed to in institutions. The relative success of deinstitutionalization.

6. The requirements of a criminal commitment.

7. The rulings derived from the M'Naughten Rule, the Durham Decision, and the American Law Institute guidelines.

8. The two judgments that must be made before a civil commitment can be ordered.

Supplementary Lecture Material

Detention and Rearrest Rates of Persons Found Insane

Richard Pasewark recently conducted a review of 50 cases of people in New York State who had been found not guilty by reason of insanity under the American Law Institute guidelines, (Pasewark, R.A., Pantle, M.L., & Steadman, H.J., 1982. Detention and rearrest rates of persons found not guilty by reason of insanity and convicted felons. *American Journal of Psychiatry, 139,* 892–897. These 50 cases were matched in criminal offenses, age, education, marital status, previous arrests, and sex with a group of convicted felons. The insanity subjects spent significantly less time in the hospital than the convicted felons spent in prison. Also, the rearrest rates of insanity subjects and convicted felons after their releases from, respectively, hospital and prison were not different. However, many more released insanity subjects were rehospitalized than were the released convicted felons.

Film, Videocassette, and Audiocassette List

A Boy Named Terry (CBS and Indiana University) Profile of a young boy with early infantile autism and the treatment program provided by the Loyola University Clinic. (58 min.)

Addiction and the Family (Films for the Humanities and Sciences) Examines the effects of a father's alcoholism on the family. (19 min.)

A Family in Grief (Research Press) Provides insights into parental, sibling, and family bereavement. (26 min.)

Aging (CRM Educational Films) Discusses the stereotypes regarding the abilities of the aged and describes the activity theory and the disengagement theory of aging. (21 min.)

Alcohol Addiction (Films for the Humanities) Explores the nature of addiction by focusing on laboratory studies, Alcoholics Anonymous, and Phoenix House. (28 min.)

Alcoholism: A Model Drug Dependency (CRM Educational Films) Alcohol is used as a model for understanding a variety of drug problems. Describes both psychological and physiological effects. (20 min.)

Alzheimer's Disease: The Long Nightmare (Films for the Humanities) Shows the emotional and financial drain of caring for those with Alzheimers. (19 min.)

Anorexia and Bulimia (Films for the Humanities) Explains the addictive nature of anorexia and bulimia. (19 min.)

A Psychopath (McGraw-Hill Text Films) The case history of a psychopath is reconstructed through interviews with mental health and law enforcement personnel. (30 min.)

Autism: Breaking Through (Films for the Humanities and Sciences) Examines various treatments available. (26 min.)

Autism: Childhood and Beyond (Films for the Humanities and Sciences) Examines therapies currently in use and profiles a 26-year-old. (19 min.)

Behavior: Disturbing and Disturbed (Beacon Films) A series of 13 video programs including two on schizo-phrenia and one on depression. (13 video programs, 60 min. each)

Behaviorism and Beyond (CRM Educational Films) Describes the origins and basic principles of behaviorism. (20 min.)

Behavior Modification: Teaching Language to Psychotic Children (Prentice Hall Film Library) Examines the uses of contingency management and imitation with psychotic children. (43 min.)

Behavior Theory in Practice (Prentice Hall Film Library) Describes and illustrates the principles of operant conditioning. (70 min.)

Behavior Therapy in Practice (University of Kansas) Part I is a general introduction to operant and respondent paradigms and extinction. Part II covers schedules, shaping, and programmed instruction. Part III presents generalization, discrimination, avoidance, and punishment. (3 films, 20 min. each)

Bulimia (Research Press) Shows causes and effects of bulimia. (20 min.)

Childhood Depression (Films for the Humanities and Sciences) Profiles a three-year-old boy and his mother, both of whom have depression. (19 min.)

Child Abuse (Films for the Humanities and Sciences) A therapist who deals with sex offenders describes the common characteristics of offenders who sexually or physically abuse children. (19 min.)

Coping with Loss (Films for the Humanities and Sciences) Uses the Challenger spacecraft tragedy to show how children deal with grief and loss. (19 min.)

Depression (Films for the Humanities and Sciences) Explains the difference between occasional mood swings and depression. (19 min.)

Eating Disorders (Research Press) Shows how young people become victims of eating disorders. (21 min.)

Everything to Live for (Films for the Humanities and Sciences) This documentary features the stories of four adolescents, two who attempt suicide but live and two who succeed at suicide. (52 min.)

Stress: A Disease of Our Times (Time-Life Films) Describes the effects of stress and includes illustrative experiments. (35 min.)

Stress and Immune Function (Films for the Humanities and Sciences) Examines the relationship between stress and breakdown of the immune system. (26 min.)

The Man Who Mistook Himself For a Hat (Films for the Humanities and Sciences) A collection of case studies of Alzheimer's disease. (75 min.)

The Mental Status Exam (U.S. Public Health Service) Demonstrates a mental status exam and shows how intake information is used to design a treatment plan. (40 min.)

The Obsessive-Compulsive Neurosis (McGraw-Hill Text Films) A case history. (28 min.)

The Psychotic Child (Psychological Cinema Register) Shows the efforts of a therapist to develop a relationship with a seven-year-old psychotic boy. (25 min.)

The Roots of Criminality (Indiana University) Examines the developmental history of the antisocial personality. (30 min.)

Three Approaches to Psychotherapy (Psychological Films) These are the classic "Gloria tapes," in which Carl Rogers, Fritz Perls, and Albert Ellis each interview the same woman. (3 films, 50 min. each)

Treating Phobias (Films for the Humanities and Sciences) Shows the incapacitating fear of agoraphobia through the eyes of a victim. (19 min.)

Fear Itself (Films for the Humanities) Focuses on agoraphobia and shows treatments including an agoraphobic group. (26 min.)

Harry (Research Press) A mildly retarded man who has spent nearly all of his 24 years in institutions is the recipient of behavior therapy techniques. (38 min.)

Managing Stress (Films for the Humanities and Sciences) Shows how different types of stress can affect productivity. (19 min.)

Maslow: Self-Actualization (Psychological Films) Abraham Maslow discusses his theory of self-actualization. Includes case material. (60 min.)

Nervous Breakdown (Films for the Humanities and Sciences) Profiles a father who chronicles his overwhelming feelings of depression. (19 min.)

Paranoid Schizophrenic (McGraw-Hill Text Films) Shows the assessment and treatment of a man suffering delusions of persecution. (30 min.)

Phobias (Time-Life Films) Depicts several typical phobic reactions. (17 min.)

Psychoanalysis (Psychological Cinema Register) Two practicing psychoanalysts enact episodes from several analytic settings. (30 min.)

Sigmund Freud: The View from Within (University of Southern California) Describes Freud's life and gives attention to what motivated Freud's theories. (29 min.)

Stress (Contemporary Films) Describes Selye's general adaptation syndrome. (11 min.)

Media Resource Addresses

Beacon Films
P.O. Box 575
Norwood, MA 02062

CRM/McGraw-Hill Films
110 Fifteenth Street
Del Mar, CA 92014

Contemporary Films
McGraw-Hill Book Company
1221 Avenue of the Americas
New York, NY 10020

Filmmaker's Library
133 East 58th Street
New York, NY 10022

Films for the Humanities and Sciences
P.O. Box 2053
Princeton, NJ 08543

Geigy Pharmaceuticals
Division of Geigy Chemical
Ardsley, NY 10502

Human Relations Media (HRM)
Room GFI
175 Tompkins Avenue
Pleasantville, NY 10570

Indiana University
Audio-Visual Center
Division of University Extension
Bloomington, IN 47401

Iowa State University
Media Resource Center
121 Pearson Hall
Ames, IA 50011

Michigan Media Resources Center
University of Michigan
400 Fourth Street
Ann Arbor, MI 48103

Michigan State University
Instructional Media Center
East Lansing, MI 48824

National Association of Mental Health Film Library
267 West 25th Street
New York, NY 10019

Penn State University
Audio-Visual Services
6 Willard Building
University Park, PA 16802

Prentice Hall Film Library
Englewood Cliffs, NJ 07632

Psychological Films
189 North Wheeler Street
Orange, CA 92669

Research Press
Box 31775
Champaign, IL 61820

Time-Life Films
43 West 16th Street
New York, NY 10011

University of California
Extension Media Center
2223 Fulton Street
Berkeley, CA 94720

University of Kansas
Film Rental Library
Continuing Education Building
Lawrence, KS 66045

University of Wisconsin
University Extension
432 North Lake Street
Madison, WI 53706

U.S. National Audiovisual Center
National Archives and Record Service
Washington, D.C. 20014

Instructor's Notes

Instructor's Notes

Instructor's Notes

Instructor's Notes

Instructors' Notes

Abnormal Psychology

SIXTH EDITION

Abnormal Psychology

The Problem of Maladaptive Behavior

Irwin G. Sarason
University of Washington

Barbara R. Sarason
University of Washington

PRENTICE HALL, Englewood Cliffs, New Jersey   07632

Library of Congress Cataloging-in-Publication Data

Sarason, Irwin G.
  Abnormal psychology : the problem of maladaptive behavior / Irwin
G. Sarason, Barbara R. Sarason.—6th ed.
      p.   cm.
  Bibliography: p.
  Includes indexes.
  ISBN 0-13-003765-6
  1. Psychology, Pathological.   I. Sarason, Barbara R.   II. Title.
  [DNLM: 1. Psychopathology.   2. Social Behavior Disorders.   WM 100
S242a]
RC454.S28   1989
616.89—dc19
DNLM/DLC
for Library of Congress   88-25467
                                                                          CIP

*To three individuals whose ability to adapt we admire
(in order of their appearance) Sue, Jane, and Don*

Editorial/production supervision: Joe O'Donnell
Manufacturing buyer: Ray Keating
Photo research: Christine Pullo
Photo editor: Lorinda Morris
Cover art: Ross Neher, "Persistence." Oil on linen, 1988; 24″ x 24″.
  Collection of Mr. and Mrs. Ronald W. Moore.
  Courtesy of David Betzel Gallery, New York.

ISBN 0-13-003765-6 01

Prentice-Hall International (UK) Limited, *London*
Prentice-Hall of Australia Pty. Limited, *Sydney*
Prentice-Hall Canada Inc., *Toronto*
Prentice-Hall Hispanoamericana, S.A., *Mexico*
Prentice-Hall of India Private Limited, *New Delhi*
Prentice-Hall of Japan, Inc., *Tokyo*
Simon & Schuster Southeast Asia Pte. Ltd., *Singapore*
Editora Prentice-Hall do Brasil, Ltda., *Rio de Janeiro*

(Acknowledgments appear on pp. 602, which constitutes a continuation of the copyright page.)

Brief Contents

Contents

8 Sexual Variations and Disorders   204

xiv

Preface

What excites us the most about abnormal psychology and the opportunity to publish a new edition of this book is that things are really happening in the field. Although the overall structure of the book is the same as in the fifth edition, every chapter has been revised with regard to theory, research, case material, and the way in which topics are introduced and presented. The sixth edition contains the most current material on research evidence and state-of-the-art techniques pertinent to maladaptive behavior, its treatment, and prevention.

We continue to believe that students must be helped to go beyond the mere acquisition and cataloging of facts. For that reason, we continue to emphasize the integrative and generative contributions of the major theoretical perspectives of abnormal psychology. The six theoretical perspectives described in previous editions as integrative threads throughout the book—the biological, behavioral, cognitive, psychodynamic, humanistic/existential, and community perspectives—continue to stimulate and guide the study of abnormal behavior. Our experience has been that students really value and like the use of the perspectives as a pedagogical feature. In the sixth edition, we carry the perspectives a step farther by showing how each of them contributes to understanding abnormal behavior as an interactional multi-determined product. Rarely is abnormality explicable in terms of the effects of only one cause. More often, abnormality manifests itself because several factors—reflected in the theoretical perspectives—have operated interactively. We view as decidedly salutary the increasing attention being given within the field of abnormal psychology to maladaptation as an interactional product. Although the concepts of stress and vulnerability can be used in a generalized way that may seem to explain everything (and nothing), we believe that, correctly applied, the use of these concepts can help students understand the complex interactions of biological, psychological, and environmental factors.

We have made a special effort in this edition to provide numerous examples of how theoretical perspectives influence the topics that are researched and the investigative approaches employed in their study. Obviously, all research areas are not developing at the same rate. We have given special emphasis to those areas that are experiencing the most explosive growth. Among these is biological research. For example, the array of brain-imaging techniques, with their associate provocative findings, seems to be expanding almost on a monthly basis. We define and describe these techniques, illustrate them, and present relevant research examples. The most recent findings on the role of biochemical factors in schizophrenia and the affective disorders are presented, and the value of incorporating them within an interactional framework is illustrated. Again as a reflection of recent research, we have discussed the role played by genetic factors in several types of abnormal behavior including alcoholism, autism, and anxiety disorders. Other biologically related topics that we discuss include psycho-immunology, noninvasive blood-pressure measurement, neuro-transmission processes together with their pharmacological implications, and the role of sodium lactate infusions in inducing panic attacks.

While biological progress may seem to be most dramatic, perhaps because of its high-tech features, progress in other areas is also encouraging and is important—particularly when viewed within an interactional framework. Especially pertinent to our emphasis on interactional processes is recent work on the role personality plays in immune-system functioning, how lifestyle factors relate to health and illness, and the effects on clinical outcomes of psychological preparation for surgery. Also, we describe existing recent work on the roles of intrusive thinking and denial in stress reactions, symptom overlaps in anxiety and depression, the effectiveness of self-directed exposure therapy in agoraphobia, self-help approaches to the treatment of social phobias, and convergences among seemingly different psychotherapeutic approaches. One burgeoning area of abnormal psychology concerns the effects of maladaptation in one individual on family functioning. Maladaptation rarely affects only one person. Family, friends, and co-workers also feel impacts.

While family causes of abnormal behavior have been discussed for many years, recent research on the impact of a disturbed spouse, sibling, or child on family members and their reciprocal influences on the affected individual adds a valuable dimension to the interpersonal and social aspects of disturbed psychological functioning.

In addition to providing state-of-the-art reviews of numerous research topics, we have also provided accounts of the important relationship between research design and the resulting empirical evidence. The evidence can't be better than the design out of which it emerged. Evidence that arises from research with a faulty design can be the source of misinformation and confusion. These unfortunate effects can be avoided if the data are examined critically in the light of the research that produced it.

In this edition, we review research methods specific to several particular disorders, as well as general methodological issues. We discuss such topics as what is involved in carrying out a clinical trial, pitfalls in interpreting long-term outcome studies, how to plan high-risk studies, and how to use the balanced placebo design. Several recently developed methodologies are influencing research design in abnormal psychology and we introduce students to them. They include the use of the research interview in the diagnostic process, meta-analysis, and the concept and identification of markers of behavior disorders. For example in schizophrenia, attention deficits assessed using the Continuous Performance Test may serve as markers of a vulnerability to schizophrenic disorder.

Not too many years ago, textbooks on abnormal psychology often were mainly descriptive encyclopedias of mental disorders. No such book would be written today—or, if it were written, it wouldn't be very well received. There are simply too many theoretical, research, and clinical frontiers that are being sensitively and intensively explored and that students must know about. Tough mindedness and innovation mark virtually all areas of study. New findings require revising our understanding of many clinical phenomena. For example, each of the last several editions of this book has devoted increasing attention to the contributions epidemiological studies are making to our understanding of specific disorders, as well as the scope of mental and behavioral disorders, their antecedents, and sequelae. Similarly, the powerful contributions of structured interview schedules to diagnostic reliability and clinical judgment are shedding light on previously neglected aspects of disorders. Abnormal psychology is alive with findings, leads, and controversies. We have tried to deal in a balanced way with both answers that are emerging from empirical study and questions about which there is disagreement.

A balanced approach is particularly important because of the increasing sophistication of students who are taking courses in abnormal psychology. They ask questions, and express doubts about the conventional

wisdom, and want to get to the core of issues. They are not impressed by jargon and are suspicious of discussions that seem to oversimplify complex issues. Through clear exposition, simple language, relevant case studies, and stimulating illustrations and examples, we hope to involve students in the subject matter of abnormal psychology and to help them achieve a realistic, integrated view of current thinking about maladaptive behavior. We have tried to achieve a proper and stimulating balance of clinical and research emphases and to avoid oversimplifying the complex realities of disordered behavior. The text facilitates the student's learning through the use of chapter outlines, understandable tables, graphs, chapter objectives, and a comprehensive glossary of essential terms.

Just as we have added, revised, and deleted sections of the book having to do with particular research topics, so also have we rethought every clinical vignette and case example. We continue to believe that clinical material is of critical importance in making the topic of abnormal behavior come alive for students. We have been fortunate in finding several new cases—some published, some unpublished—that enable us to more effectively illustrate important phenomena and processes. Almost 300 new references have been added to the bibliography since we last rewrote these chapters two years ago. Although we have added a considerable amount of material, we have also pruned and honed. No matter how interesting the presentation, students need a straight-forward, rather than a sprawling, organization and a text of manageable length. Throughout the work of revising we have kept quality, not quantity, as a goal.

If we could select only one word to characterize the sixth edition from the student's point of view, that word would be *accessibility.* Some contributors to this accessibility are features of previous editions that have stood the test of time; others are new. Because students have found them to be useful, this edition continues to use the **end of chapter study outlines** begun in the fifth edition. What students have perhaps liked the most about these outlines is that they serve to emphasize the most important points in each major section of each chapter and, thus, provide a standard with which students can compare their impressions. New to the sixth edition are beginning of chapter **learning objectives** that facilitate focus of the student's attention on the key information to be learned and the most important ideas to be understood in that chapter. These chapter objectives quickly and succinctly make the student aware of the organizing principles that help integrate the phenomena covered in each chapter. **Brief chapter outlines** begin each chapter to help students orient themselves to the material to be presented. Throughout the book, **important terms are highlighted** in bold face. These and other terms are defined in the **glossary,** which has been expanded in this edition. Probably, most students are not in the habit of routinely looking up terms in the glossary. In teaching the course, we have found that some gentle encouragement to use the glossary as a study tool serves as a valuable eye-opener for many students.

There are frequent tables that contain concise summaries of the key features of particular disorders (for example, one table lists the key triggers of migraines); other tables permit easy contrast between disorders that are in some ways similar. Many new tables have been added to either present new evidence, summarize clinical features, or explain processes. For example, Chapter 6 now has a table showing the similarities and differences between phobias and obsessive-compulsive disorders. Chapter 14 has new tables listing the criteria of dependence on psychoactive substances, the effects of alcohol on bodily functions, and the roles denial and motivation play in changing the behavior of alcoholics. Chapter 17 has new tables summarizing the basic features of behavior therapy and the various types of measures used in therapy outcome studies.

The book contains many graphic interpretations of research findings so that students can grasp their basic meaning without the distraction of digits and decimal points. The same thoughtful consideration given to the tables has also been applied with regard to the illustration program including photographs, diagrams, and cartoons. For example, Chapter 3 now has a new diagram of Freud's model of the mind, Chapter 13, a new box on Alzheimer's disease and ways of helping Alzheimer's patients, and Chapter 14, a new box on the scope of the alcohol problem. The illustration program of the fifth edition and its extensive use of color were highly successful and received many enthusiastic comments from both instructors and students. We believe that the production of this edition improves on the fine presentation of standard and special features of the fifth edition.

Accompanying the sixth edition is a useful package of ancillary materials. The Instructor's Edition begins with an overview of each chapter, followed by each chapter's objectives, discussion questions, class projects, and lecture suggestions. All this is bound to the book to provide ultimate accessibility, which should prove useful to new instructors as well as those veterans interested in freshening their presentation of material. A complete test bank is available, both on floppy disks and in booklet form, along with a Student Study Guide. New to this edition, we are providing transparency acetates and videos to qualifying adoptors.

Many people have helped us in preparing this edition. We have benefited from the insights and suggestions of our colleagues both at the University of Washington and elsewhere. Many clinicians and researchers have shared their unpublished cases and findings with us. We are also indebted to the authors of published work that has enabled us to be as up-to-date as possible. We thank all these direct and indirect contributors to our understanding of abnormal behavior, its underlying processes, and relevant therapies. We also wish to thank the following reviewers whose suggestions and comments were very helpful: Professor Anne Harris, Arizona State University; Professor Scott Henggeler, Memphis State University; Professor Robert Lueger, Marquette University; Professor Tom Marsh, Pitt Community College; Professor W.G. Murphy, Winthrop College; Professor Linda Musum-Miller, University of Arkansas at Little Rock; Professor Clive Robins, New York University; Professor J. Sidney Shrauger, State University of New York at Buffalo; Professor Michael D. Spiegler, Providence College; and Professor Robert Tipton, Virginia Commonwealth University.

The team at Prentice Hall has been both effective and supportive. We especially want to thank Susan Finnemore, Joseph O'Donnell, and Lorinda Morris for their contributions and thoughtfulness to us. An example of the special efforts made by Prentice Hall to make this book a truly valuable educational tool was an all-day meeting of the two of us, Susan, Joe, and Lori. The sole agenda of the meeting was a detailed review of the illustration program that enabled us to get feedback concerning our ideas for specific illustrations and to benefit from the ideas of Prentice Hall's experts. An outcome of this meeting was something that we feel is very important: a book that contains an illustration program, every element of which has been given thoughtful consideration. We—and many undergraduate students—have seen too many books that are full of smiling, angry, or worried adults, children, and babies whose pictures relate only tangentially to the text.

We also want to thank Betty Johnson, who somehow was able to convert our scribbles and sketches into readable copy. Honora Hanley developed her investigative talents to a high degree of effectiveness as she helped us track down many new references. Both she and David Pierce worked diligently in helping us compile the author and subject indices. We also appreciate Sue Sarason's valuable suggestions about content and organization.

Irvin G. Sarason
Barbara R. Sarason

Abnormal Psychology

O. Schlemmer, *Bauhaus Stairway*, 1932. Oil on canvas, 63 7/8 × 45". Collection, Museum of Modern Art, New York. Gift of Philip C. Johnson.

1

OBJECTIVES FOR CHAPTER ONE:

To learn:

1. How abnormal behavior is defined
2. How researchers study abnormal behavior

To understand:

The variety of reasons people seek help for abnormal behavior

P*ain of mind is worse than pain of body*

Latin Proverb

Bob Cates had felt tense, anxious, and worried a lot of the time during his entire stay at the large university he attended. There seemed to be so much to do. However, in his senior year, despite the fact that he was usually an energetic person, even small things seemed to require a major effort. He felt particularly overwhelmed at pressure points like exams, writing papers, and having to say things in class.

For reasons that were not clear, Bob became increasingly depressed and be began to feel that be couldn't go on much longer. His classes, and life in general, seemed less and less worth the effort they required. He couldn't concentrate on his school work and spent several hours each day sitting in his dormitory room—sometimes, just staring into space.

Bob Cates' friends noticed the changes in his behavior and mood and were concerned. As a result of their encouragement, Bob went to the University Counseling Service and had a series of sessions with a counselor. The questions that passed through the counselor's mind included the following:

What is Bob experiencing at the present time— what is he feeling and thinking about?

How serious is the problem that he is experiencing and to what degree is he aware of its seriousness?

What are the causes of Bob's problem—is the problem due to something that has arisen in his current situation or is it a continuation of a long-term, perhaps lifelong, pattern?

What can be done to help Bob overcome his unhappy state?

What is going on in a particular person's life that results in unhappiness and disordered behavior? What can be done to alleviate the problem? These questions are the focus of abnormal psychology. In the case of Bob Cates, the problem was part of a long-term pattern, but was also related to things going on in his current life situation. His parents had always emphasized the importance of hard work and achievement. His excellent high school record showed to what degree he had learned to strive for success. What seemed to have happened at the university (many of the facts were far from clear) was that for the first time he began to question the values on which his need to achieve was based. As the counseling proceeded, he came to see that in many subtle ways his parents had shaped him to be a "producer." During his junior year, when he was beginning to think about what to do after completing his education, Bob began to feel that he could never achieve as much as his parents wanted him to. This thought had a nagging, depressing effect on him. The future seemed hopeless, and he felt helpless to do anything about it. After several counseling sessions Bob admitted that he had had suicidal thoughts, although he had never seriously considered taking his own life.

us uncomfortable and even a little frightened. A mentally ill person should not be seen as evil, however, merely as different. Abnormal psychology deals with how it feels to be different, the meanings that get attached to being different, and how society deals with people whom it considers to be different. The spectrum of differentness is wide, ranging from reality-defying delusions and severe debilitation to worries and behavioral quirks that we would be better off not having but that do not interfere significantly with our daily lives.

An example of this milder end of the spectrum is a man who was an outstandingly successful district attorney, was elected governor of New York on three occasions, and was almost elected president of the United States in 1948. This man, Thomas E. Dewey, reached the pinnacle of success, displaying such qualities as rectitude, efficiency, precision, and a nearly limitless capacity for hard work. Yet it was just this combination of traits that made Dewey seem too good to be true. For example, he was never late or absent in his first twelve years of schooling. He lacked a sense of humor and seemed to enjoy life only when he was achieving some goal. He also had personal rigidities that restricted the spontaneity so important in public figures. For example, he had a phobia about germs. When he toured prisons, he would not touch a doorknob without first wiping it off with a folded handkerchief concealed in his palm. He also drank three quarts of water a day because of its presumed healthful effects. Dewey achieved much, but had he been less rigid he might have achieved even more; perhaps more important, he might have been a happier person (R. N. Smith, 1982).

Just as Bart Dobben's problems (Box 1–1) exceeded those of Bob Cates', so also were Joan Houghton's greater than Thomas E. Dewey's. Joan Houghton's break with reality required intensive treatment during a 5-week period of hospitalization. After her recovery she wrote an account of her experiences.

My mother and I sat next to each other in the waiting room while my father investigated admission procedures. A young man was seated near us. Perspiration dripped across his brow and down his cheeks. In silence I took a tissue from my purse, moved close to him and gently wiped the moisture from his face. I reassured him that everything would be fine.

Soon my father rejoined us. We went together to a small room where I met Kay, the psychiatric social worker assigned to my case, and a psychiatrist (whose name I don't recall). We talked a few minutes. I was presented with a piece of paper and instructed to sign my name. Obediently, I wrote "Saint Joan" on the paper, not realizing that I was voluntarily admitting myself to a state mental hospital. . . .At the time of my hospitalization I had both a sense of death and a

What Is Abnormal Behavior?

How abnormal is Bob Cates? While there is no basis for concluding that Bob is "crazy," he definitely has had serious difficulties in adjusting to college. Just how much pressure his parents actually placed on him is not answered by the available information. The fact that he spent hours just sitting in his room, together with his suicidal thoughts, suggests that he was experiencing adjustment difficulties that were much greater than those that are typical for college students.

In this book we will see cases of abnormal behavior both more and less serious than that of Bob Cates. Box 1–1 describes a man whose psychological problems dwarf those of Bob Cates and require that the community respond to them. Because our goal is not simply the description of abnormal behavior, we will review theoretical frameworks within which instances of human failure, inadequacy, and unhappiness have been conceptualized. At the same time we will also review basic research, pertinent to theories of abnormal behavior. This review of existing theory and research will give us a general framework within which to interpret the wide variety of human problems that find expression in abnormal behaviors. This framework emphasizes the roles played by stress, coping skills, and personal vulnerabilities.

Mental disorders, like anything unusual, may make

BOX 1-1
Father Kills Two Young Sons

Sometimes people who have led a reasonably ordinary life begin to develop unusual behaviors. These changes may come about very quickly or they may be gradual. The case reported here shows a gradual buildup of pressures that finally brought about a tragedy.

In some ways, the life of Bart Dobben was like that of everyone else on Amity Street. He mowed the lawn, tinkered with the car and doted on his two young sons.

Mr. Dobben was popular and active in school, said his mother, Mari Dobben. Like many young men in town, he went to work in the foundry, starting as a janitor after high school.

He soon moved into production, operating a huge vessel that purified and treated 10,000 pounds of molten iron at a time to produce various alloys, said Paul White, his partner in the vessel's control room for five years.

"He took a lot of abuse from people he worked with," Mr. White said. "I felt a lot of people would take advantage of his nature and inability to come back with a lot of vulgar talk."

"He wasn't disliked," Mr. White said. "He was a friendly, outgoing person." He was energetic, his friend said, adding that Mr. Dobben would ask the foreman for work when operations were slow.

Mr. Dobben had a new house and a year-old baby when things began to unravel in late 1985. Mr. White, 31, said he noticed the change.

Mr. Dobben's wife, Susan, told officials that one day in September 1985, her husband took the family on a harrowing drive down twisting roads at speeds of up to 80 miles an hour "because he felt God told him that our baby was in danger."

The police were called and Mr. Dobben was taken to the psychiatric unit of a local hospital. But he refused psychiatric treatment.

Mrs. Dobben later filed a petition seeking to have her husband committed to the Kalamazoo Regional Psychiatric Hospital. In the petition, she said her husband once covered the house windows and the television set with towels, hung diapers over baby pictures and "anointed the baby and things in his room with olive oil."

Dr. Jadimpalli V. Raju, a psychiatrist, diagnosed

Mr. Dobben as a schizophrenic who exhibited an "overreligious preoccupation" and who believed "God is going to come soon and take care of things."

On Thanksgiving Day, the police say, Mr. Dobben took his two sons, Bartley Joel, 2 years old, and Peter David, 15 months old, to the Cannon-Muskegon Corporation foundry where he worked and put them inside a giant ladle used to carry molten metal.

He then heated it to 1,300 degrees while his wife, unknowing, waited outside in the car. . . . (New York Times, 27 December 1987, p. 21—national edition)

So despite the outward similarity of his earlier life to that of his neighbors, Mr. Dobben was not like the rest of the people on Amity Street. His story culminated in a family tragedy.

rebirth about me. My first psychotic episode appeared as a private mental exorcism, ending with the honor of sainthood and the gifts of hope and faith. (Houghton, 1982, pp. 548–549)

Although Houghton's recovery enabled her to obtain and hold a job at the National Institute of Mental Health and to write sensitively about her experience, she faced many barriers that made the recovery process

who are known to have a history of mental disorder, regardless of whether they have recovered or not, or only by those who continue to engage in abnormal behaviors. In general, the more visible the abnormal behavior, the greater the probability that the person will experience prejudice and rejection.

For many years researchers have studied the public's attitudes toward abnormal behavior. The evidence shows that people know more about behavioral abnormalities today than they did twenty years ago and that overt rejection has declined. Nevertheless, ex-mental patients who continue to be identified as such by their behavior or history are not treated in the same way as ex-medical patients when it comes to housing, school admission, jobs, or general goodwill. Many people continue to be frightened of former mental patients, although it is becoming less socially acceptable to say so.

Some segments of the mass media may contribute to the public's fear of mental disorder. One study showed that 17 percent of prime-time programs involve the theme of mental illness and 3 percent of the major characters have some sort of mental disorder (Gerbner and others, 1981). Of these characters, 73 percent are portrayed as violent, compared with 40 percent of normal characters. Eighty-one percent of them fall victim to violence compared with 44 percent of normal characters. Of women who are depicted as mentally ill, 73 percent are violent compared with 24 percent of normal characters. Among all prime-time characters portrayed this way, one-fourth will be killed and one-fourth will kill someone else. Highly publicized acts, such as that of would-be presidential assassin John Hinckley, further reinforce the stereotype that mental disorder equals violence.

TV also builds misconceptions concerning what behaviors are normal or typical (Gerbner and others, 1981). More than three-quarters of all dramatic characters are shown eating, drinking, or talking about food—often more than once. Alcohol is mentioned in 80 percent of prime-time programs, aside from the commercials (see Figure 1-1). A child may see 10 scenes of alcohol consumption on TV during one day's viewing. The world of soap operas literally floats in alcohol. An average of nearly three 1-minute periods per each 21-minute program showed an alcohol-related event—a rate of about 6 per hour. Another recent study has shown that televised violence and crime have significant effects on crime rates (Henningan and others, 1982).

Adaptive and Maladaptive Behavior

The bulk of the behaviors studied by abnormal psychology is related to human failures and inadequacies. These failures in living are due mainly to failures in adaptation

more difficult than it had to be. Her ordeal continued after discharge from the hospital.

The crisis of mental illness appeared as a nuclear explosion in my life. All that I had known and enjoyed previously was suddenly transformed, like some strange reverse process of nature, from a butterfly's beauty into a pupa's cocoon. There was a binding, confining quality to my life, in part chosen, in part imposed. Repeated rejections, the awkwardness of others around me, and my own discomfort and self-consciousness propelled me into solitary confinement.

My recovery from mental illness and its aftermath involved a struggle—against my own body, which seemed to be without energy and stamina, and against a society that seemed reluctant to embrace me. It seemed that my greatest needs—to be wanted, needed, valued—were the very needs which others could not fulfill. At times, it felt as though I were trying to swim against a tidal wave. (Houghton, 1980, p. 8)

The following incident illustrates what swimming against that tidal wave was like.

One Sunday I went to church alone after being absent for several weeks. The minister (who knew of my history, faith, and strong belief in God) began his sermon with reference to the devil. He said, "If you ever want to be convinced of the existence of the devil, you should visit a mental institution." To illustrate his point, he described people who had lost control of their bodily functions, who screamed out obscenities. I left church after the sermon, drove home vowing never to return to that church as long as that minister preached from the pulpit. At home, however, I began to replace my anger with doubt. Maybe I misunderstood.

At my invitation the minister visited our home to discuss his philosophy about mental illness and the mentally ill. His visit was our last encounter. Not only did he see evil in mental illness but he conveyed an unforgiving attitude to those who have the misfortune of residing in mental hospitals. (Houghton, 1980, p. 10)

The Stigma of Abnormal Behavior

As Houghton's account makes clear, people who are noticeably deviant may experience prejudice and discrimination. However, it is not clear whether the stigma associated with mental illness—the sense of disgrace, or the reality of rejection—is experienced by most people

(a)

(b)

(c)

FIGURE 1-1
Television and the movies influence people's view of what behaviors are acceptable and desirable. An example of this is the media's portrayal of alcohol consumption.

(see Figure 1–2). Adaptation involves the balance between what people do and want to do, on the one hand, and what the environment (the community) wants, on the other.

Adaptation is a dynamic process. Each of us responds to our environment and to the changes that occur within it. How well we adapt depends on two factors: our personal characteristics (skills, attitudes, physical condition) and the nature of the situations that confront us (for example, family conflict or natural disaster). These two factors jointly determine whether we survive, are content, and prosper, or whether we fall by the wayside. Because nothing—neither ourselves nor

the environment—stays the same for very long, adaptation must take place all the time. The extremely rapid rate of change in the modern world puts a particular strain on our ability to adapt. Moreover, successful adaptation to one set of conditions is not a guarantee of successful adaptation to others.

Adaptation and Adjustment

A distinction is sometimes drawn between **adaptation** and **adjustment.** Adaptation refers to survival of the species, whereas adjustment refers to individual mastery of the environment and the sense of being at peace with

(a)

(c)

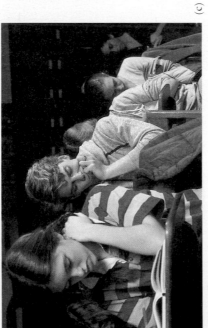

(b)

FIGURE 1–2

Maladaptation can arise in a variety of situations and can vary in severity. (a) The homeless man lying on the street in the first photo is unable to function well in society, his level of adaptation is very low. (b) This man, who suffers from an obsessive compulsive disorder is a "checker," someone with a need continually to check on the status of a situation. Here he is checking his front door—for the tenth time to make sure he has really locked it. (c) Some of the students in this photo may also be functioning maladaptively. They may be so worried about getting a good score that they cannot concentrate on their performance on the test. Although this is a much milder level of maladaptation, it may still be very important to some of the students.

oneself. In many instances this is a valid and useful distinction. In certain cases, however, it oversimplifies the human situation. Unlike those of animals, the adaptive successes and failures of human beings cannot be measured simply in terms of the survival and reproduction of the species. For most people in the modern world, concerns about quality of life and level of contentment far overshadow the need to satisfy biological requirements. Human beings have developed subtle language forms, a refined level of thinking, superior problem-solving skills, intricate social relationships, and complex communication processes, all of which affect behavior and its interpretation. Individuals' feelings of failure

may damage their social relationships, and the human gene pool might be significantly affected by the failure of such people to marry and have children. On the other hand, many individuals with certain types of inadequacies, who would probably be unable to hold their own in a subsistence economy, can survive and reproduce in the modern world because of social institutions such as welfare programs, Social Security, and health insurance.

Biological factors aside, how we live and how we feel about the way we live are important factors in human adaptation. For us, adaptation refers to people's ability or inability to modify their behavior in response to changing environmental requirements. In this book, therefore, we devote most of our attention to people's personal and social adaptations.

Maladaptive vs. Deviant Behavior

All maladaptive behavior is deviant behavior. However, deviant or unusual behavior is not necessarily maladaptive. This can be seen in the case of Albert Einstein. At the age of 12 Einstein decided to devote his life to solving the "riddle of the huge world." Early in his career, while working as a patent office examiner, he wrote five papers that eventually changed our view of the universe. Although public recognition of the importance of Einstein's theory was many years away, his ability to think about the properties of matter in a completely new way began almost at once to influence the thought of physicists. Other kinds of deviant behaviors, such as wearing very bright ties, refusing to travel by airplane, drinking ten cups of coffee a day, and needing to read in bed for two hours before falling asleep, are not as productive as Einstein's behavior and may seem odd or annoying, but people who act in these ways do not need major rehabilitative efforts to live happy, productive lives.

Describing behavior as **maladaptive** implies that a problem exists; it also suggests that either vulnerability in the individual, inability to cope, or exceptional stress in the environment has led to problems in living. Students of maladaptive behavior are especially interested in behavior that is not merely different or deviant but that also represents a source of concern to the individual, to his or her family and friends, or to society. This means, for example, that students of maladaptive behavior direct more of their attention toward those with very low IQs than toward those with high IQs, or toward those who are not happy rather than toward those who are.

There are many causes of maladaptations. In some instances—for example, in certain forms of brain damage—an organic cause is uncovered. In other cases, undesirable present or past social relationships—for example, an incestuous relationship—may be implicated. In still other cases, a combination of these factors along with a stressful event, such as the death of a loved one or the birth of a child, plays a decisive role.

Maladaptations range from chronic fears that are troubling but not disabling to nearly complete loss of orientation, severe distortion of reality, and inability to communicate. The individual may be unhappy about his or her maladaptive behavior, or the community may be worried about what might happen if the person is not removed from society. Throughout this book many different kinds of maladaptive behavior will be described, along with the social reactions they evoke.

Stress, Coping, and Vulnerability

When we talk about how well people adapt, it is important to consider the conditions under which the adaptations are made. The same person may handle a frightening or difficult situation well at one time and maladaptively at others. Some people may behave adaptively in the same situation that others handle poorly. Why is this the case? Three concepts—stress, coping, and vulnerability—help us to understand these differences in behavior. Seven-year-old Denton may adapt well when he has a sympathetic teacher, when his parents are getting along well, and when he is healthy. However, if he has a teacher whom he hates, if his parents bicker half the night and are on the edge of divorce, and if he is constipated, he may become much more upset about not being a starting player in his soccer team than we might have predicted. Or if Mrs. Block has just lost an important client for her firm and comes home to find someone has smashed into her car as it sat parked in the carport, and then her 12-year-old child tells her he has just left his violin on the school bus, she may not respond as constructively as she might have under other circumstances.

Stress refers to people's reactions to situations that pose demands, constraints, or opportunities. For example, a person could feel stressed by seeing a child fall into a rapidly flowing river, by being awakened by a fire alarm and smelling smoke, or by being promoted to a new job with more responsibility. People are likely to experience psychological stress when they have to deal with an unexpected or unusual change, such as a natural disaster. They are likely to experience even greater stress than usual when the change occurs at the same time as a severe life crisis (such as the death of a loved one) or at the beginning of a critical development period (such as adolescence). As Table 1–1 shows, the average number of stressful life events (such as family disturbances, serious illness of a parent, brother, or sister) is greater for clinical cases than for comparable control persons. (Based on Goodyer, Kolvin, and Garzanis, 1985)

Coping refers to how people deal with difficulties and attempt to overcome them. Coping skills are the techniques that are available to an individual in making such attempts. A number of general skills are useful in handling stressful situations. These include thinking constructively, dealing with problems as they arise, behaving flexibly, and providing feedback to oneself about which tactics work in a given situation and which ones do not. How useful any particular skill will be depends upon the nature of the situation and the individual's

TABLE 1–1

Negative Life Events and Personal Maladjustment

Clinical Group		Average Number of Negative Life Events
Conduct disorders	Cases	1.18
	Controls	.36
Mild mood disorders	Cases	1.13
	Controls	.36
Severe mood disorders	Cases	.84
	Controls	.22
Somatic symptoms disorders	Cases	1.04
	Controls	.19

Based on Goodyer, Kolvin, and Gatzanis, 1985. Reprinted with permission from the *British Journal of Psychiatry*.

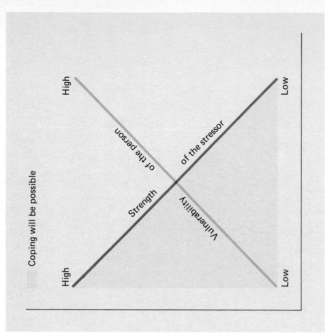

FIGURE 1–3

The interaction between stress and vulnerability determines whether coping will be possible. Whether a person has adequate coping skills determines whether coping will occur.

vulnerabilities and assets. Having an effective repertory of coping skills strengthens a person's sense of self-control and self-direction. By gaining greater control over our behavior, we may be able to alter environmental conditions that influence us.

Vulnerability refers to how likely we are to respond maladaptively to certain situations. An individual can be an effective coper in one situation but not in another. Vulnerability may be increased by having a particular kind of heredity such as a schizophrenic parent, by certain personality characteristics such as a tendency to worry or feel anxious, by the lack of certain skills such as the ability to make decisions calmly, or by a buildup of unexpected negative experiences. Some people are more vulnerable in all situations because they deal less effectively with what happens to them in daily life. Others are more vulnerable simply because of a combination of recent stressful events. Certainly people are more vulnerable in particular kinds of situations that remind them of former problems or difficulties. For example, upon seeing a child swept away in a river, a person who has seen one of her younger brothers killed in an accident when she was 5 might freeze, while someone who has not had such an experience would be able to act in time to save the child.

Certain life conditions in and of themselves increase people's vulnerability and increase their risk of maladaptive behavior. They become a part of a high-risk group of people who, because they share these life conditions, are more likely than the rest of the population to experience the negative effects of stress. Population groups that may be at high risk for certain conditions include children and adolescents, the aged and the disabled, and disadvantaged minority groups.

Stress, coping, and vulnerability are interrelated (see Figure 1–3). The greater the stress, the less vulnerability is required for a person to display maladaptive

behavior. The less severe the stress, the greater the vulnerability needed to produce maladaptive behavior. The better people's coping repertories, the less likely they are to fall apart in situations in which they are vulnerable. Generally, it is easier and more effective to help people learn better ways of dealing with stress than to prevent the stresses to which they are vulnerable. Chapter 5 presents a more in-depth view of the effects of stress and the variety of ways people deal with them.

Clinical interventions are ways of helping people cope with stress more effectively. The intervention selected for someone who is experiencing a short-term crisis, such as the serious illness of a loved one, might be a tranquilizing drug. In this case, the tranquilizer reduces vulnerability to intense anxiety experienced over a period of time. In other cases, insight into the person's desires, motivations, and conflicts is needed in order to help the individual cope more effectively with stress and become less vulnerable to the crises that are the inevitable ingredients of every human life. Sometimes the person needs to learn new skills or behaviors that are effective in dealing with difficult situations. For some people, the way they think about a situation needs to be changed. If a low grade makes you think, "I'm dumb; it's no use trying to finish this course," the results may be very different than they would if you thought, "I didn't study very effectively; I'd better organize my work better and check with the professor before the test to ask about the points that aren't clear." The particular approach taken by the clinician depends on his or her assessment of the factors in a given case and the psychological perspective or viewpoints he or she favors.

In this book we will present a number of different perspectives on why maladaptive behavior occurs and how adaptive behavior can be substituted for it. Running through our discussion of abnormal psychology will be a consideration of the effects of stress and individual vulnerability on the outcome of any particular situation. The more we understand what causes an individual to feel stressed, and the more we can identify the factors that produce vulnerability, the clearer the sources of the maladaptive behavior will be and the more likely we will be to come up with effective treatment procedures. That is what the study of abnormal psychology is all about.

Reasons for Clinical Contacts

Some people seek professional help because they are dissatisfied with themselves and certain aspects of their lives; others do so because of concerns expressed by family members, friends, or co-workers; still others are forced to see clinicians because they have gotten into trouble with the community.

Personal Unhappiness

In the following case, personal unhappiness seems to have been the factor that led the person to seek help.

Jack Farmer is a 35-year-old executive in a large multinational corporation. From all outward appearances, any differences he might have from other people are positive. Whatever weaknesses he has are minor. For example, his coordination in physical activities, such as playing tennis, is probably below average. The opinion of his company and community is that Jack Farmer is a very well-functioning individual. While he and his wife and two children get along reasonably well, Jack has had some concerns that have shaped his family role, particularly as his children approach high school age. These concerns have to do with the burdens of family responsibility, especially the need he feels to ensure his family's happiness should anything happen to him. He has occasionally commented to his wife that television commercials about the need to have plenty of life insurance seem to have been written specifically with him in mind. However, Jack is concerned about more than money. He feels that he should be a closer friend

to his children and less distant from his wife than he often is. He is also very concerned about the issue of nuclear waste and the pollution of the natural environment. His concerns often lead to his feeling blue and hopeless about the future.

One Sunday Jack read a newspaper article about a local mental health center that had opened recently. The article pointed out that the center's services were not restricted to severely disturbed individuals, that perfectly normal people who have hit a rough spot in their lives might find it valuable to talk with an expert about their personal problems. After several weeks of internal debate ("Could I be a little crazy?" "I'd be ashamed if my friends ever found out that I went to a shrink"), Jack decided to go to the mental health center.

By conventional standards, Jack Farmer's case is not serious. He sought help because of personal dissatisfactions and concerns. Wrestling further with his personal tensions seemed worse to him than his fear of being stigmatized if he sought professional help.

The Concerns of Others

Sometimes it is difficult even for professionals to decide what the dividing line should be between maladaptive and merely unusual behavior. In the following case, there was no agreement about whether the woman concerned was psychotic (out of touch with reality) and needed institutionalization, or whether her behavior was simply unusual and presented no hazard to her or her family.

Mary Waverly was in her late twenties. A university graduate, she had run a successful boutique in a large western city until shortly before the birth of her daughter, who is now 2 years old. During the year before Mary's daughter was born, Mary's mother had been treated for cancer. She died when Alice, her granddaughter, was fourteen months old. During the baby's first year and a half, she had surgery several times to correct a birth defect.

Recently, Mary's husband attempted to have her committed to a psychiatric hospital. He said he was concerned about their daughter's welfare. Mary had become a religious fanatic. Although she came from a very religious family, until recently, when she joined a cult group, her behavior had not seemed unusual. Since joining the group she refused to have sexual relations with her husband because he was not a "believer." Although she seemed to take good care of

her child, she made all decisions only after listening to the "voice of the Lord."

When Mrs. Waverly was examined, her judgment did not seem impaired, her intelligence was above average, and her religious thoughts, although they took up a great deal of her time, did not seem to differ from those of other enthusiastic converts to a cult group. A pediatrician examined her daughter and reported that she was well cared for. A question was raised about what Mrs. Waverly might do if she thought God told her to harm her child or someone else. Neither of the clinicians who examined her was willing to give a definite answer.

Mrs. Waverly didn't think she had a mental disorder and didn't think she needed treatment. One of the clinicians agreed. He believed that her behavior was unusual but that she was not mentally ill. Another clinician thought she was a paranoid schizophrenic who should be hospitalized for drug therapy. What should be done when professionals disagree? In this case, after hearing the conflicting views Mr. Waverly decided not to press for hospitalization.

ran from the store and summoned the police. The police investigation led Mr. Clay to seek advice from his lawyer, who had been a friend since high school. Although Clay insisted that "there is nothing the matter with me," his anger and suspiciousness bothered the lawyer. Using tact and persuasion, the lawyer got Mr. Clay to agree to visit a psychiatrist. Unfortunately, the visit did not work out well. Clay was reluctant to talk about his concerns and was angered by what he viewed as the psychiatrist's inquisitiveness. He refused to return for a second visit. Nevertheless, the lawyer was able to get Clay out of trouble with the police. Unfortunately, several months later Clay was arrested and convicted of physically attacking another customer.

Legal and Community Problems

Mild personal maladaptations like Jack Farmer's affect the lives of the individual and possibly a small number of other people. Mary Waverly's behavior was a matter of concern to her husband because he was worried about the possibility that she might harm their daughter. In the case of Charles Clay, a legal problem arose over something he had done.

Charles Clay, aged 45, owned what had been a successful 24-hour-a-day grocery store. Now, however, he was having increasing difficulty containing his anger toward his customers. Until five years ago he had been a cheerful, friendly merchant. Then his wife died, and his personality seemed to change.

Increasingly he worried that people were trying to shoplift his merchandise. (There was a problem with a few high school students who frequented his store right after school.) As time went on, he began to confront customers with his suspicions and even to demand that some of them submit to being searched.

Not surprisingly, Mr. Clay's business began to decline. When this happened, he got very angry and even more suspicious. The culminating event occurred when a woman entered the store, walked around for a few minutes, and then bought a newspaper. When Clay tried to search her (at the same time yelling, "Don't tell me you were just looking around!"), she

Many people saw Charles Clay as having problems that he refused to recognize. In spite of the social consensus about the maladaptive quality of his behavior, he gave himself a clean bill of health. In part because of his failure to perceive his own behavior accurately, Clay eventually got into trouble with the law. His first contact with the police did not result in formal charges; the community's agents recognized his psychological difficulties, and the focus of their attention was on helping a citizen with his personal problems. The second contact, however, resulted in punishment for a crime. Society had decided that Clay was not going to help himself and moved to protect itself.

Gross failure to see oneself accurately, as illustrated by the case with Charles Clay, is characteristic of several of the most serious forms of maladaptive behavior. In such cases, it is a highly positive development if the person begins to suspect that his or her behavior is contributing to difficulties in getting along with other people.

The Epidemiology of Maladaptive Behavior

The aim of epidemiological research is to obtain information about the physical and psychological maladaptations of populations and groups. Epidemiologists are interested in identifying the environmental causes of particular conditions, especially those causes associated with a community's way of life. The Broad Street pump incident is one of the most famous examples of epidemiological inquiry and its use in furthering public health. In 1848, during a severe cholera epidemic in London, a study of the disease's distribution within the city was carried out. The study showed that the outbreak had a geographical center, a water pump in Broad Street (see Figure 1–4). It was further found that two groups—inmates of an institution and employees of a brewery—did not develop the illness in anything like epidemic proportions. Each of these groups had its own well, and brewery workers drank beer rather than water at work. On the basis of this information, the Broad Street pump was dismantled and the epidemic brought under control. This example is especially interesting because it shows how epidemiological work can contribute to human well-being even when the cause of a condition is unknown—the microorganisms that cause cholera had not been identified in 1848.

Prevalence, Incidence, and Risk Factors

Epidemiologists conduct surveys to estimate the extent of a health problem. Two types of information are obtained in these surveys. **Prevalence** data describe the frequency of occurrence of a given condition at a particular point in time. For example, if, on a given date, 100

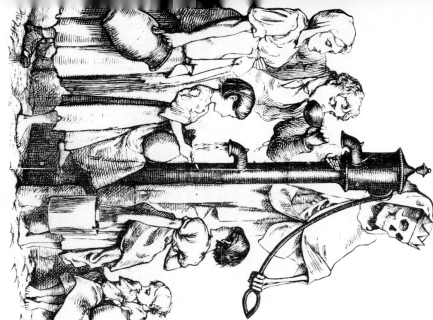

FIGURE 1–4
Epidemiological detective work can reveal the source of disease.

cases of depression were counted in a community of 1,000 people, the prevalence rate would be 10 percent. **Incidence** data relate to the number of new cases of a specific condition that arise during a particular period of time. For example, if 10 people who had not been depressed at the time of the prevalence study became depressed during the next year, the incidence rate would be 1 percent. Epidemiological research has identified a number of factors that must be attended to in order to ensure the accuracy of survey results. These include representative sampling of the population, clearly worded questions asked, and careful training of interviewers (Eaton and others, 1984). Table 1–2 gives the definitions of a number of concepts used in epidemiological research.

The concept of risk factor (Table 1–2) is based on the finding of a statistically significant association between a disorder and a factor (for example, lung cancer and smoking; cardiovascular disease and high cholesterol level). The following are risk factors that have been identified for violent behavior (Reid and Balis, 1987):

- History of aggressive, destructive behavior
- History of repeated traffic violations (reckless driving, etc.)
- History of child abuse and neglect
- Childhood history of severe hyperactivity and restlessness
- Habitual alcohol use and dependence
- Suicidal attempts and gestures
- Hypersexuality
- Low frustration tolerance
- Low self-esteem and failure to achieve
- Inability to examine one's own behavior
- Impulsivity
- Self-centeredness

TABLE 1–2

Epidemiological Concepts

Incidence. The rate of new cases during a defined period of time (for example, one year).

Prevalence. The rate of both new and old (existing) cases for a defined period of time (for example, 6-month prevalence).

Lifetime prevalence. The proportion of people in the general population who ever had a particular disorder.

Risk factor. A specific characteristic or condition whose presence is associated with an increased likelihood that a specific disorder is present, or will develop at a later time.

TABLE 1–3

Factors Associated with Rates of Diagnosed Mental Disorder

1. *Age.* Younger people have higher rates than older people.
2. *Marital Status.* Separated, divorced, and single people have higher rates than the married and widowed.
3. *Education.* Less educated people have higher rates than people who have more education.
4. *Personal Income.* The lower the income, the higher the rates.
5. *Employment Status.* Unemployed people have higher rates than employed people.
6. *Contact with Friends.* Lack of social contacts is associated with relatively high rates.
7. *Satisfaction with Relationships with Friends and Relatives.* The greater the satisfaction, the lower the rates.
8. *Marital Happiness.* The greater the degree of marital happiness, the lower the rates.

Based on Leaf and others, 1984.

When risk factors are identified, they may be useful in suggesting prevention efforts. For example, children who have been abused or neglected might be given the opportunity to express their psychological pain as a step toward preventing long-term frustration and anger. Risk factors can serve as early warning signs of the need for intervention regarding particular conditions.

The scope of mental health problems is reflected in findings from a survey of nearly 10,000 people living in Baltimore, Maryland; New Haven, Connecticut; and St. Louis, Missouri (Myers and others, 1984). The findings suggest that at any given time about 29 million Americans—nearly one in five adults—suffer from mental disorders ranging from mildly disabling anxiety to severe schizophrenia. Anxiety disorders (not depression as was previously thought) are the most common psychiatric problem, occurring in about 8 percent of those surveyed. Abuse or dependence on drugs afflicts about 6 to 7 percent of the population (most of these cases involve alcohol). Mood disorders, which include depression and alternating periods of depression and mania (intense excitement), affected 6 percent of the adults studied. Schizophrenia, the most severely disabling of mental illnesses, was found in about 1 percent of the population.

The same survey showed that, while the overall rates of mental illness for men and women are similar, the most common diagnoses for women are phobias and depressions, whereas for men the most common diagnoses are alcohol abuse and dependence on drugs. The study also found that the rate of mental disorders drops sharply after 45 years of age. Other evidence suggests that the prevalence of persistent handicapping mental health problems among children aged 3 to 15 ranges from 5 to 15 percent (Commission on Mental Health, 1978). A recent epidemiological study showed that, in addition to those with diagnosed mental disorders, another 15 percent of the population show high levels of demoralization and unhappiness that are not accompanied by a diagnosable disorder (Dohrenwend and Dohrenwend, 1982). It must also be noted that the lives of 30 to 40 million people are affected because of their close ties with mentally ill individuals (*Research on Mental Illness and Addictive Disorders*, 1985). In this book, we will focus not only on the effect of maladaptive behavior on the person whose problems are described but also on the effects of the problem on family members—parents, husbands, wives, and children. Table 1–3 lists several factors that are significantly related to the presence of mental illness. It seems clear that interpersonal, economic, and educational factors play important roles in the frequency of abnormal behaviors. There is also evidence that people who have good coping skills and supportive friends and relatives are less likely to suffer psychological distress than those who do not (Horwitz, 1984).

Cause and Prevention

A major epidemiological challenge in abnormal psychology is the need to move from obtaining accurate and meaningful estimates of different types of maladaptation to determining their causes and preventing them. Epidemiologists were acting to prevent illness when they traced cholera to the Broad Street pump. The challenge to abnormal psychology is whether the same kind of detective work can prevent and eventually aid in unraveling the complex cause-and-effect relationships involved in maladaptive behavior. For example, we know that there are significant correlations between depression and being female, between suicide and being an older white male, between drug addiction and being a member of an urban black group, and between schizophrenia and failure. Why do these relationships exist? Answers to questions like these should lay the groundwork for better treatment and prevention.

One can compare the types and recorded frequencies of disorders in a population by using statistics from different time periods. However, these comparisons are confusing, because in addition to any real changes that may occur, statistics reflect many other things, such as changes in diagnostic fashions or criteria as well as social and political changes. **Diagnosis,** or the way disorders are defined and patients labeled, changes from time to time, and as a result different frequencies are reported for certain disorders.

The effects of social changes, together with changes in diagnostic fashions, can be seen in the following examples.

1. The number of cases diagnosed as alcoholism has increased sharply, to the point where alcoholism is now one of the most frequently used diagnostic categories.

2. The number of children who receive treatment for childhood disorders has increased sharply.

In the first case, in many states alcoholism is now treated as a maladaptive behavior rather than as a crime. This means that many people who would have been dealt with in the criminal justice system are now showing up as mental health cases. In the second example, facilities for treating children are more available, and a variety of effective psychological methods now exist to deal with many childhood problems; as a result of both of these factors, figures showing increases in treatment for childhood disorders do not necessarily indicate any change in the prevalence of such disorders.

Many other examples of the effect of social change on statistics could be cited. In the past, many old people who could not care for themselves ended up in state mental hospitals. The recent use of nursing homes for this group has reduced the rate of hospitalization of the elderly for mental disorders. However, there have been increases in the admission rates for younger age groups, probably also as a result of social change. The age groups under 24 years have shown the greatest percent-

age increase in mental hospital admission in recent years. At present the rate of admissions for the 25- to 44-year-old group is 2,727 per 100,000, followed by the rate for the 18- to 24-year-old group of 2,299 per 100,000. Figure 1–5 shows the percent distribution of admissions to mental health facilities by age.

Another variable that affects the number of cases reported is the availability of mental health services. While the number of beds reserved for patients with mental health problems (often called psychiatric beds) varies from one state to another, the total number of such beds available has declined (Greene and others, 1986; Redick and others, 1984). From 1974 to 1984 there was a decrease of 58.4 percent in the number of available beds. To some extent the decrease in hospital beds is linked with an increase in community outpatient facilities in many areas. These offer crisis intervention or short-term treatment focused on specific problems for which appropriate help might not have been available in the past.

The number of community treatment and care facilities has increased over threefold since 1955, and the trend toward treating people in the community is now firmly established. Of the estimated 3.6 million people served in mental health facilities in 1975, over 65 percent were treated on an outpatient basis (outpatient psychiatric clinics and community mental health centers combined). Figure 1–6 shows the variety of mental health facilities that are available today.

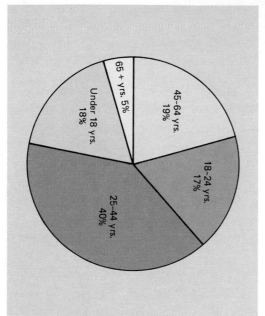

FIGURE 1–5

Percentages of people in different age groups who are admitted to mental health facilities. The percentages do not add to 100 because of rounding. (Adapted from Rosenstein and Millazo-Sayre, 1981)

45–64 yrs. 19%

65 + yrs. 5%

Under 18 yrs. 18%

18–24 yrs. 17%

25–44 yrs. 40%

(a)

FIGURE 1–6

Many communities have several mental health services available to residents. Community mental health centers (a) provide many services, ranging from traditional, individual, group, and behavioral therapy

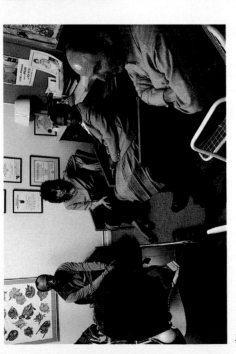

(e)

FIGURE 1–6 (b–g) (continued)
(b), to supportive activities that help integrate isolated people into the community, as well as day hospital centers that permit structured activities and socialization for clients (c). With this kind of help, families often are able to care for the mentally ill at home over a long period. General medical hospitals (d) often have mental health units that provide emergency care and long-term treatment, while private practitioners (e), such as clinical psychologists and psychiatrists, treat many people who seek help in coping with the problems of daily life.

(c)

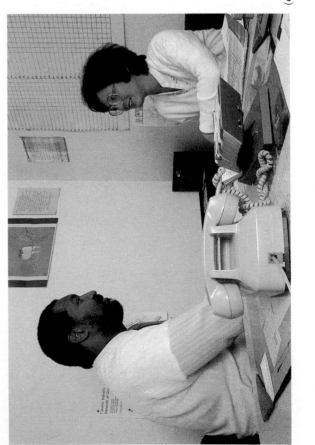

(d)

(b)

Sources of Help

Types of Treatment Facilities

Despite the decrease in number of beds in state mental hospitals, these institutions continue to play an important role in caring for the most disturbed and troublesome patients in the U.S. mental health system. State hospitals serve as 24-hour emergency backups, the institutions of last resort and ultimate responsibility (Rosenstein and others, 1986). Nevertheless, most experts agree about the desirability of treating people in the community as early as possible so as to avoid institutionalization. Community-based treatment has become a more realistic possibility for some disturbed individuals because of an increase in the availability of community facilities, changes in state laws regarding involuntary hospitalization and the detaining of disturbed individuals in mental hospitals, and the discovery that a variety of drugs effectively control much of the violent and bizarre behavior associated with mental patients.

In recent years there has been a movement to **deinstitutionalize**, or return to the community, mental patients whose problems can be expected to continue for long periods. Under the banner of community-based care, many of them now live in nursing homes, boarding houses, residential hotels (often in undesirable neighborhoods), and subsidized apartments. This change, based partly on concern for the civil rights of the individual, is also a result of scientific advances like the use of antipsychotic drugs. These make it possible for many people to function adaptively enough so that they don't need to be institutionalized, although many of these individuals still behave in marginal, ineffective fashion.

Most authorities agree that one in five people engage in some form of maladaptive behavior, although only a small percentage of these people come into contact with mental health services. This is true despite the fact that a recent survey of the utilization of both general medical and mental health services showed that, during the 6-month period studied, 16 to 25 percent of the visits to these services were for psychological problems and a large proportion of those cases were handled by mental health specialists (Shapiro and others, 1984). The number of workers involved in providing services for these troubled people is well over 400,000. When the income losses of the clients are added to the salaries of health care personnel, the cost of mental health care comes to tens of billions of dollars per year.

Types of Mental Health Specialists

Most of the behavior patterns with which this book deals are of special interest to three groups of mental health specialists: clinical psychologists, psychiatrists, and psychiatric social workers. A **clinical psychologist** is a psychologist with a graduate degree, usually a Ph.D., who specializes in abnormal behavior. Clinical psychologists are trained to diagnose and treat personality problems that are not medical or organic in nature. They also plan and conduct research investigations. A **psychiatrist** is a physician (an M.D.) with postgraduate training and experience in treating emotional disorders. Psychiatrists have legal responsibilities in commitment proceedings and in the supervision of mental hospitals. Somatic therapies, such as drugs and electroconvulsive therapy, are administered by psychiatrists. Psychiatric social workers are most often concerned with the link between a person who displays problematic behavior and his or her home environment. The activities of psychiatrists, clinical psychologists, and social workers often overlap. For example, all three are trained to conduct psychotherapy and counseling.

This account by a clinical psychologist accurately reflects the diversity of activities in which most clinicians engage.

> *I wish the time passed more slowly because there is just so much to do. From talking to my clinician friends I know I'm not alone in feeling that way.*
>
> *Part of the problem is that most of us don't just do one thing. Sure, some do mainly therapy and others are primarily diagnosticians. But most of us do many things.*
>
> *Take me, for example. I work in a big-city general hospital that has two wards for psychiatric cases and a large outpatient clinic. Many of these patients are not in very good contact with reality. In some cases police officers picked them up because they were wandering aimlessly around town in the middle of winter, in the dead of night. In other cases, they are people who have had some recent situational stress and are just not able to come to terms with it.*
>
> *In still other cases, physicians who have patients on other wards in the hospital ask us for help. Yesterday, for example, a surgeon referred a case to me because the patient, who is supposed to undergo abdominal*

have replaced beliefs and hope in the effort to help people suffering from behavior disorders.

Some scientists have contributed to clinical progress either by accident or as an offshoot of some other interest. For example, some advances in developing tranquilizing drugs came from the observation that drugs that were being used for other purposes also decreased anxiety. However, most of the scientific information on which contemporary abnormal psychology is based comes from in-depth studies of deviant people. Although researchers may differ on their interpretation of data, they agree that careful observation is essential for scientific progress.

Observing Behavior

Certain sciences, such as astronomy and anatomy, are basically descriptive in nature. Scientists in those two disciplines concentrate on using careful observations to describe heavenly or earthly bodies. Psychologists also do research that is descriptive in nature. By describing various behaviors and the specific circumstances under which they seem to occur, researchers can obtain important information about potential cause-and-effect relationships. Observation and description are often the first steps in the scientific process; eventually they lead to the formulation of hypotheses that can be tested experimentally and applied in clinical situations. As can be seen in the following description, observation plays an important role in psychological treatment:

I noticed that Mr. R never looked directly at me. He answered my questions but always looked the other way. He seemed terribly shy and afraid. I was tempted to ask him what he was afraid of, but decided not to because he might take my comment as a criticism.

Some clinicians might have decided to ask Mr. R. about his apparent fearfulness. However, all would agree on the importance of carefully observing and noting his anxious behavior.

Some observations are easier to make than others. It doesn't take years of scientific training to objectively evaluate how well or poorly a dog or tulip has adapted to its environment. In a sense, the researcher is a disinterested observer in the world of the robin and the redwood. For example, the behavior of lemmings, which periodically throw themselves into the sea in what appears to be mass suicide, arouses no public outcries.

People cannot be completely disinterested observers of themselves, however. Personal values, goals, and interests, together with cultural norms, influence our judgments about the success or failure of human adaptation. For example, in a society that does not make

surgery tomorrow, has been in such a psychological panic that the doctor felt something had to be done—and he didn't know what to do. So far, I've talked with the patient twice. Really, all I did was listen and let her ventilate her feelings. You'd be amazed how much just listening in a sympathetic and supportive manner does to help a person who is going through a stressful situation. When I told the surgeon that this patient was very worried about getting too strong a dose of anesthetic and dying he was amazed. He said the patient had never mentioned that worry to him.

About 20 percent of my time is spent dealing with problems nonpsychiatric physicians need help with. Perhaps 30 percent is spent doing therapy either on the wards or in the outpatient clinic. Another 20 percent involves administering psychological tests to patients with particular problems. The rest of the time I do research. That's what usually gets squeezed out when a number of pressing clinical problems arise. That's when I most need a time-stretcher. But all the pressure is nothing compared to how much I like what I'm doing. I wouldn't trade with anybody.

The work of professionals in the mental health field is especially challenging because it requires the ability to think on one's feet correctly and quickly size up a problem ("Is this person depressed enough to be thinking about suicide?"), and devise appropriate and sometimes unusual treatment plans for clients. This means that while clinicians strive for complete objectivity in their work and try to use proven techniques, they often must devise on-the-spot tactics to deal with the particular problem confronting them.

Clinicians emphasize the clinical or case-study method, which involves an in-depth study of the individual. Each case seems to be different because of the particular circumstances surrounding the case, and cases are made more complicated because troubled people more often than not leave out important information in telling their stories to clinicians. They frequently fail to remember significant experiences and the feelings and thoughts related to them. Each case study thus is unique, although with experience clinicians become sensitive to commonalities that aid them in understanding and helping people.

Research in Abnormal Psychology

The scientific method has greatly increased our understanding of abnormal behavior, how to treat it, and how to present it. As a consequence, observation and fact

judgments about the private sexual activities of its members, homosexuals would be seen as unusual but not as objects of concern. On the other hand, a society that believes homosexuality to be undesirable and illegal creates for itself, in a manner of speaking, a problem of maladaptation. Maladaptation is therefore neither a universal nor a timeless concept. Behavior that may be quite adaptive in one society may be a failure in another.

With this in mind, how do scientists study human behavior objectively? They record responses, describe events and the conditions surrounding them, and then draw inferences about causes. In order to overcome the effects of personal bias, several observers make reports on each of the individuals or events under study. Reliability increases when these observers have a common frame of reference, agree on which particular aspects of behavior to emphasize (and which not to emphasize), and when they do not have to draw too many inferences from their observations. Observational methods are used in specially created laboratory conditions as well as in naturally occurring situations.

Observation is more than simply using one's eyes in a seemingly straightforward way. Certain questions must be asked first: What types of responses should be selected for observation? How capable is the observer of making reliable and unbiased observations? Will the observer's presence influence the behavior that he or she wants to study? Is it preferable to observe behavior within naturally occurring settings or under controlled laboratory conditions? Should observations be limited to motor responses (walking, running), verbal responses (phone conversations, requests for help), or expressive behavior (smiling, crying)? How long a period of time is needed for reliable observation? Is time sampling needed—that is, should observations be gathered during several different time intervals? Even mental patients who hallucinate frequently do not engage in this kind of behavior all the time; time sampling can provide data on the conditions under which certain types of responses are most likely to occur.

Reliable observations can provide useful records of both the incidence of behavior in a given environment and the events that elicit and maintain it. An example of how observational research can correct commonsense but incorrect assumptions is found in a study of the frequency of interactions between patients and staff on a mental hospital ward (Eldred and others, 1964). One might assume that the staff members' goal of helping their patients would lead them to spend most of their time interacting with the patients. However, as Figure 1–7 shows, the rate at which staff members interacted with other staff members was approximately double the rate of interaction between patients and staff. The low rate of interaction between patients also seems surprising, but it is typical of the social isolation found on the wards of many mental hospitals.

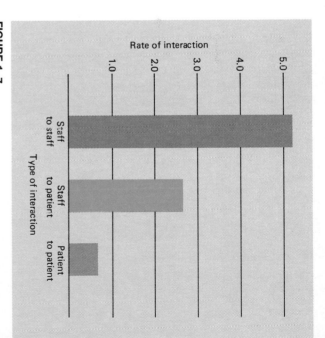

FIGURE 1–7
Rates of interaction for different patient and staff relationships. (Adapted from Eldred and others, 1964, p. 4)

Although they are subjective and therefore are susceptible to personal bias, **self-observations** can be useful in clinical research. For example, a patient who had been admitted to a mental hospital because of depression was asked to keep track of her mood (level of sadness) and activity (number of social exchanges with hospital staff or other patients). Figure 1–8 shows a progressively less depressed mood and increased social activity during her first 15 days of hospitalization. In this case, there was good agreement between the patient's self-observations and the observations made by the hospital staff. This will not always be the case. As we all know, the people with whom we come into con-

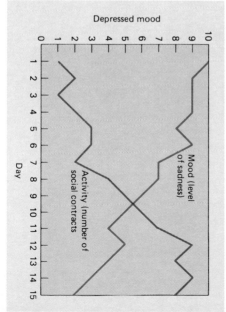

FIGURE 1–8
The mood and activity changes in a patient treated for depression. The patient's mood ratings are based on her self-observations.

tact in our daily lives may not see us as we see ourselves (see Figure 1–9).

Self-observations are useful in keeping records of the responses to clinical treatment. In the case of the patient whose self-observations are recorded in Figure 1–8, the treatment was complex, consisting of a benign hospital environment, daily individual and group psychotherapy, and medication. It would be interesting to compare the self-observation records of groups of comparable patients whose treatment consisted of only one of these elements—the hospital environment, psychotherapy, or medication alone—as well as all the possible combinations of these treatments.

Studies conducted in ongoing clinical settings often do not permit complete control over all relevant factors. Although the inability to exercise full control over the situation may pose some methodological problems, the fact that research is conducted in the "real world" probably increases the applicability of the findings. A study entitled *On Being Sane in Insane Places* provides an example. The researcher wanted to know what happens when people who have been diagnosed as mentally ill begin to act completely sane after they have been hospitalized (Rosenhan, 1973). Are they immediately recognized as sane and released from the hospital, or does the label "mentally ill" affect the way their behavior is perceived by the staff?

Eight normal individuals were admitted to mental hospitals when they telephoned the hospitals and complained that they were hearing voices. They falsified their names and occupations (several were psychiatrists or psychologists) but otherwise gave their true life histories, except for their descriptions of their "symptoms." All except one received a diagnosis of schizophrenia, a serious behavior disorder that is characterized by disorganized thought processes and inappropriate emotional response. Once they had been admitted to the hospitals, however, the "patients" acted as normal as possible.

Were these "patients" immediately detected as imposters? Not at all. No staff member in any of the hospitals ever expressed any suspicion of them. (It is interesting to note, however, that other patients on the wards frequently suspected that the false patients were imposters.) Although the false patients were soon highly motivated to obtain a release from the hospital, their hospitalization periods ranged from 7 to 52 days, with an average stay of 19 days.

The hospital staffs were understandably conditioned to see their patients as mentally ill, since most of their patients are truly disturbed, and this conditioning strongly influenced their perceptions of the false patients. They sometimes saw evidence of mental illness in the most innocent behaviors. For example, at one hospital mealtimes were the most exciting events of the day,

MANKOFF

"You are fair, compassionate, and intelligent, but you are perceived as biased, callous, and dumb."

FIGURE 1–9

"You are fair, compassionate, and intelligent, but you are *perceived* as biased, callous, and dumb." Drawing by Mankoff; © 1985 The New Yorker Magazine, Inc.

and patients would often start gathering before it was time to eat. One psychiatrist pointed to a group of patients waiting outside the lunchroom and remarked to a group of staff members that this behavior reflected the unconscious "oral-incorporative needs" that are symptomatic of schizophrenia. If patients became justifiably angry with staff members, their anger was almost always attributed to their illness rather than to the behavior of the staff. A later examination of hospital records also disclosed that because the clinicians who wrote the diagnostic reports were aware that the false patients had complained of hearing voices, they often distorted the facts in the patients' life histories to fit their belief that the patients were schizophrenic.

Thus the label of schizophrenic persisted long after the behaviors that led to the original diagnosis had ceased. Every false patient except one (who was still diagnosed as schizophrenic) was discharged with the diagnosis of *schizophrenia in remission* which meant that the disorder was still assumed to be present but not in an active form. Perhaps one of the most damaging effects of labels like "crazy" and "mentally ill" is that the patients themselves may come to accept them and behave accordingly. The effects of labeling (having a diagnosis attached to the individual) influence the observations of both patients and clinicians and also influence how those observations are interpreted.

The value of observations is greatest when what is to be observed is defined explicitly. Four types of data are of special interest in observational research:

1. The stimuli that elicit particular types of responses—for example, the influence of family members' behavior (such as criticism or hostility) on a person who is prone to become depressed.
2. The subjective response to the stimuli—for example, the person's feelings when he or she is criticized.
3. The behavioral response to the stimuli—for example, the person's level of social activity after receiving criticism.
4. The consequences of the behavior—for example, how does the environment respond when the person behaves in a depressed manner?

The types of observations made and the observational methods employed depend on a number of factors, including the hypothesis being investigated and the situations in which the observations must be made. Observations might be made by means of hidden videotaping equipment, by visible observers who do not interact with the people they are studying, or by participant observers who become actively involved in the behavior they are observing. Each of these methods has advantages and disadvantages. For example, secret videotap-

ing allows us to observe behavior without the knowledge of the individual who is being observed, but many scientists object to this technique on ethical grounds. Participant and nonparticipant observations have been used by anthropologists and sociologists as well as by psychologists. However, any observer may affect people's behavior simply by being present. Participant observers may damage their objectivity by becoming overinvolved with the people they are studying. Nonparticipant observers may come to superficial conclusions because they are not involved enough. Each of these techniques can be valuable, and each has both supporters and critics.

The Role of Theory

Scientists like to proceed from observation to theory because they want to figure out why or how a particular phenomenon occurs. Behaving just as lay people would, they use reason, logic, and sometimes simple guesswork to arrive at an initial and tentative explanation. However, whereas casual observers may be satisfied with such a tentative answer, scientists recognize it as only tentative and go on to test their understanding by "if . . . then . . ." hypotheses that can be evaluated (for example, "if children are frustrated, then they are likely to behave aggressively"). They then proceed to collect the observations needed to either support or refute the hypothesis. If the hypothesis is supported by their observations, they return to their original "Why?" question and attempt to formulate increasingly broad concepts and principles that go beyond their observations. This is the way theories are developed.

Good theories have a number of functions. First, they are able to incorporate many existing facts, observations, and relationships within a single, broad explanatory framework. Second, additional hypotheses may be derived from the theory and tested, and may lead to new observations. In this way theories provide a foundation on which to build knowledge. If new observations do not support the theory, it may be modified or discarded. However, it will still have served a valuable function by leading to the discovery of new knowledge and to the development of an even better and more inclusive theory.

In order for a theory to be useful, it must be capable of being tested and refuted. It should be able to specify the types of relationships that are not possible as well as those that are. If it seems able to account for everything and anything, even seemingly contradictory facts, it is not a good scientific theory. The essence of the scientific method is systematic observation and the use of objective procedures to identify cause-and-effect relationships.

The Research Journey

Saying that research goes from observation to theory is a little like going on an automobile trip. There is a lot more to the journey than knowing where one is and where one wants to go. What route should be followed? Will there be detours? Would bad weather make a difference? How should one prepare for the trip? Following are some of the important steps in the scientist's research journey:

1. *Specifying the topic as clearly as possible.* Suppose you are intrigued by psychotherapy. Why are you drawn to that topic? Is it because you think verbal interchanges are crucial to achieving therapeutic change? Or are you more interested in the interpersonal relationship between client and therapist?

2. *Reviewing the relevant literature.* Some library work can save a researcher a lot of time and frustration. Studying the pertinent books and journals can answer many questions: How have other people dealt with this idea? What were the outcomes of their research?

3. *Defining the variables.* A variable is any aspect of a person, group, or setting that is measured for the purposes of the study in question. **Independent variables** are manipulated by the researcher in order to investigate their effects on particular outcomes that are called **dependent variables.**

4. *Developing a specific hypothesis.* A hypothesis is a statement to be proved, an idea that has been formulated so that it may be evaluated using scientific methods. A hypothesis is a kind of educated guess that states a predicted relationship between events or variables. It is typically stated in the form "If A occurs, then B will occur."

5. *Selecting a research strategy.* What plan of action will permit the hypothesis to be tested? Does the researcher plan to see each subject on one occasion (for example, at the beginning or end of psychotherapy), or will several observations be necessary in order to test your hypothesis? Should an experiment be conducted? Conducting an experiment means systematically varying one or more conditions for some groups but not for others. Is experimental research possible in a particular clinical setting?

6. *Conducting the study.* The research should be carried out objectively enough to permit others to repeat (replicate) it. Therefore, all the steps in the research process must be specified. For example, how was the sample of subjects selected? Were the subjects chosen on the basis of age, sex, or intelligence? If so, the selection variables must be specified.

7. *Analyzing the results.* How did the group or groups perform? What is the likelihood that the results are simply due to chance? An analysis of research results usually includes making a distribution of the scores obtained by subjects; calculating relevant **descriptive statistics**, the numerical measures (scores) that enable a researcher to describe certain aspects of subjects' performance (for example, the mean or average); and calculating **inferential statistics**, the statistics that are used for judgments about the probability that the results are due to chance.

8. *Reporting research findings.* Writing up a piece of research not only permits communication of ideas and findings to others but also forces the researcher to think through all that he or she has done and the meaning that might be attached to it. Going public serves an important communication function. The scientific journey would be much less valuable if research results were not written up and published.

Types of Research

In evaluating an hypothesis it is important to decide on the observations that are relevant to it and the conditions under which those observations should be made. The conditions might be the same for all subjects or different for designated groups. In **assessment** studies, the conditions are the same, the aim being to gather information under standard conditions for purposes of description and prediction. In **experimental** studies, the conditions are varied so as to test hypotheses about the effects of the conditions.

Assessment Studies

The purpose of **assessment** is to provide an objective account of behavior at any given time. Assessment methods range from recording how often certain responses occur in natural situations to noting the types of behavior displayed in specially created settings such as interviews. Assessment is not simply a measuring device; it is a general approach to observing and interpreting behavior. As such, it extends beyond traditional procedures such as interviews and tests in much the same way that the concept of intelligence and the judgments based on it extend beyond the tests used to measure it.

Assessment data can be used in a number of ways. They might be used to predict future behavior, to identify correlates of present behavior, or to measure the likelihood of a positive reaction to therapeutic procedures. For example, a study of junior high school students might indicate the type of person who is most likely to engage in antisocial behavior in the future; a comparison of the assessed characteristics of depressed individuals might point out those who are most likely to commit suicide; and a comparison of the personality traits of people who respond positively to psychotherapy and those who respond negatively might help in screening candidates for therapy. Assessment research ranges from in-depth studies of one or a few people to surveys of large populations.

When people are assessed, several kinds of data are usually gathered, including age, sex, personal history, and number of previous hospitalizations. This information can be intercorrelated and the degree of relationship among the various items determined. This type of study—called a **correlational study**—can be useful in a limited way. Correlational studies tell us only that two factors are related: they do not tell us how or why. Just knowing that variable A and B have a high degree of association does not tell us whether A causes B or B causes A, as Figure 1–10 humorously illustrates. Perhaps another variable, C, has caused the correlation between A and B. There is also a fourth possibility, that the correlation is simply a coincidence with no causality involved. As example, a study done in eleven countries

found that anxiety was positively correlated with the rate of alcoholism (Lynn and Hampson, 1970). In other words, the more anxiety the population attributed to itself, the higher the alcoholism rate. This is a provocative finding, but its meaning requires extensive inquiry. Does it mean that anxiety causes alcoholism, that alcoholism causes anxiety, that some other factor (such as income level or marital status) might cause both alcoholism and anxiety, or that the relationship between anxiety and alcoholism is accidental?

Despite their limitations, correlation studies have much to contribute to the study of abnormal behavior. This is particularly true when, for practical or ethical reasons, it is not possible to manipulate conditions experimentally. Suppose, for example, that we wanted to study the possibility that having been abused as a child increases the likelihood that one will abuse one's own children. It would be highly unethical as well as impractical to subject an experimental group of children to severe abuse and then wait twenty years to see whether or not they beat their own children. However, information about such a correlation could be of great value in un-

"WHICH IS IT—DO PEOPLE HATE US BECAUSE WE DRESS THIS WAY, OR DO WE DRESS THIS WAY BECAUSE PEOPLE HATE US?"

FIGURE 1–10
"Which is it—do people hate us because we cress this way, or do we dress this way because people hate us?" (By permission of Sidney Harris and *Saturday Review World.* © 1987 by Sidney Harris)

ticular conditions. For example, a follow-up study might be carried out to determine how well people who have been discharged from a mental hospital have adjusted to life in the community. Figure 1–11 summarizes the results of a study that explored the relationship between the amount of TV viewing at 8 years of age and the seriousness of criminal acts at age 30. The figure shows that the seriousness of crimes was proportional to TV-viewing frequency at age 8 for both males and females. While this relationship may not be causal, the fact that child TV viewing was predictive of crime seriousness in adulthood suggests the need to investigate the TV-viewing experiences of children. What are the characteristics of children who do a lot of TV viewing? What sorts of programs do they watch?

The **cross-sectional study** is a useful way to assess the views or status of one or more groups of people at any given point in time. Cross-sectional studies are the most common assessment method used by social scientists. Because no follow-up is required, these studies are less time-consuming and expensive than longitudinal studies. A public opinion poll is an example of a cross-sectional study that is carried out in the field. Developmental psychologists often use the cross-sectional approach in the laboratory or in natural settings to compare children's behavior, attributes, abilities, and concerns at different ages.

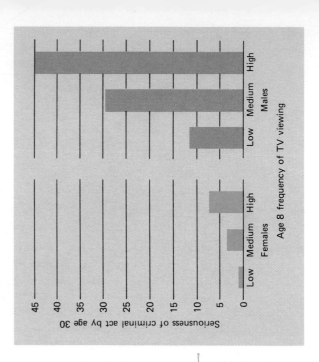

FIGURE 1–11
Seriousness of criminal acts by age 30 as a function of frequency of TV viewing at age 8. (Eron, 1987, p. 440. Copyright © 1987 by the American Psychological Association. Reprinted by permission of the author.

derstanding the causes of abuse, and could perhaps be used in selecting high-risk parents for programs designed to prevent abuse.

As an alternative, we might find ways to measure the amount of abuse parents received when they were children as well as the extent to which they now abuse their own children. For each of a large group of parents, we could obtain a score for each of the two abuse variables—each parent's reports of being abused as a child and some measure of his or her abusiveness as a parent—and then determine what kind of relationship, if any, exists between the two sets of measures. The knowledge that being abusive and having been abused are correlated provides a potentially useful clue to how child abuse could be prevented. Perhaps parental counseling and training for people who were abused as children would be of preventive value.

If we find a positive correlation, we might be tempted to conclude from the data that child abuse is caused by parents having been abused as children. This is certainly a possibility, but there are other possible explanations for the positive correlation. It may be, for example, that guilt about abusing their own child causes parents to exaggerate the extent to which they were abused as children. Another possibility is that some other variable that was not measured in the study (such as some form of psychological disturbance) actually caused the person to be the target of abuse as a child and causes him or her to become a child abuser as an adult. We simply cannot be certain which of these and other possible causal relationships may account for the positive correlation between recalled childhood experiences and present adult behavior.

One way to deal with a problem of this kind is the **longitudinal study**, whose goal is to observe and record the behavior of people over long periods—perhaps twenty or thirty years. This type of study is costly, time-consuming, and often frustrating to the investigator, who may not live to see the study completed. There are other problems as well. The nature of the group under study may change greatly as people move or die. The methods chosen at the beginning of the study may become outdated. The importance of new variables that were ignored in the study may become recognized by the scientific community. For these reasons, few longitudinal studies are done. Nevertheless because they deal so directly with the developmental process, the value of such studies is widely recognized.

One type of research that avoids some of these problems but still has longitudinal features is the **follow-up study.** In such studies, people are given an initial assessment and then are contacted again months or years later to see whether there have been any changes in their behavior during that time. Follow-up studies are used to assess the effects of different therapeutic approaches as well as to observe the development of par-

BOX 1-2
Understanding Abnormal Behavior through Animal Research

For obvious reasons, certain types of experimentation cannot be carried out using human subjects. For example, it would be impossible—and unethical, even if it were possible—to try to observe and control the course of a person's life. However, the telescoped life-span of nonhuman primates like monkeys makes it possible to study the long-term consequences of early experiences. Under controlled conditions these experiences can be observed either as they unfold or after experimental manipulations. Animal studies permit levels of control and ways of carrying out experimental manipulations that are not possible with humans. As a consequence, animal experimentation plays an important role in the study of abnormal behavior.

Animal studies can be used to investigate both biological and social factors in behavior. One example of a research with a biological focus is the investigation of the effects of drugs. Researchers have fed monkeys large doses of drugs that are believed to cause depression and have noted their effects on the animals' behavior. Such experiments have shown that depression-inducing drugs lead to decreases in the general activity and exploratory behavior of monkeys.

A group of drugs called amphetamines, which function as stimulants, produce psychotic symptoms in people. If the effects of amphetamines on animals were known, animals that had been injected with amphetamines could then be given antipsychotic drugs to determine whether they are able to counteract the amphetamine's psychosis-inducing action. Research has shown that rats and humans exhibit some similar symptoms when treated with amphetamines, and we now know that certain antipsychotic drugs are effective in reversing the effects of amphetamines on rats.

People who abuse amphetamines frequently engage in ritualized stereotyped behavior such as repetitively disassembling complex objects like radios. Not surprisingly, reassembly of such objects requires more concentration than they can muster. Rats that are given high doses of amphetamines develop a similar syndrome called **stereotypy**. They pace back and forth, sniffing the corners of their cages and chew repetitively on the bars. Studies are being conducted on the brains of rats treated with either or both amphetamines and antipsychotic drugs. These studies will help identify the areas of the brain and the mechanisms related to the drug effects.

Animal subjects have been used in another aspect of research on amphetamines and other stimulants. In a number of studies, stimulant drugs have been shown to increase an animal's sensitivity to reinforcement. That is, the drug increases the effects of reward and possibly even punishment so that the animal learns habits more quickly and with greater success. This finding is provocative because stimulant drugs often make

hyperactive children more responsive to reward and punishment.

In the course of their research on dogs, Samuel Corson and his co-workers (1976) noticed that some of the dogs were quite restless and not very responsive to rewards and punishments. They administered a variety of drugs to the dogs with no beneficial effect until they tried amphetamine. The researchers found that the stimulant medication quieted the dogs and that, like hyperactive children, they were then better able to learn. An examination of the hyperactive dogs' brains showed that they were deficient in certain neurotransmitters, chemicals that make possible the movement of nerve impulses. The identification of this deficiency opens up the possibility of a better understanding of the nervous-system abnormalities that cause hyperactivity and the way therapeutic drugs like amphetamine act to alleviate this condition.

Another example of animal studies with a biological focus can be seen in the work of Harry Harlow and his co-workers. They were interested in the effects of early experience on the later development of monkeys. Infant monkeys show a number of innate behaviors, such as clinging and sucking. When the infants are separated from their mothers and reared with other young monkeys, their clinging behavior lasts much longer than it does for mother-reared monkeys (see Figure 1–12a). Young monkeys also begin to show innate fear behavior when they are about 2 months old. When they are

FIGURE 1–12
(a) All monkeys go through a clinging stage, but monkeys who are reared without their mothers show a greatly prolonged period of clinging.

BOX 1-2 (CONTINUED)

reared with other monkeys, the fear behaviors do not disappear but last into adulthood (Suomi and Harlow, 1978).

When infant monkeys are not only separated from their mothers but reared in isolation for 6 months, they show several disturbed behaviors. They suck themselves, constantly rock back and forth, and are very timid. When their isolation ends, they behave very aggressively toward other monkeys. The research showed, however, that monkeys that are reared in isolation for 6 months can later develop normally if they are "treated" by therapist monkeys. The most successful therapist monkeys were 3-month-olds who still showed a great deal of clinging behavior. They clung to the isolates affectionately (see Figure 1–12b). The isolates soon responded, and within 6 months their behavior was hard to distinguish from that of their therapists (Suomi and Harlow, 1972).

Young monkeys separated from their mothers often show symptoms similar to depression in humans. Depression in young monkeys may be preceded by a protest phase characterized by immediate frantic activity that appears to reflect attempts to communicate with and locate the missing mother. The depression is often followed by a detachment phase in which the young monkey shows an emotional detachment or aloofness from its mother upon reunion. This phase has been ob-

FIGURE 1–12 (b) (continued)
(b) A young monkey, still in the clinging stage, can be an effective therapist for an older monkey who was reared in isolation.

served in human children when in the presence of mothers from whom they have been separated (Rosenblum and Paully, 1987).

Experimental Studies

Experimental research involves the observation and assessment of behavior, but with an important additional ingredient. In **experiments,** variables can be manipulated. This degree of control is impossible in many real-life situations. Because experimenters can control the variables in the laboratory, they can more easily isolate and record the causes of the behavior they observe. For certain purposes research with animals is valuable because it permits the manipulation of experimental variables and the control of unwanted factors to an extent usually not possible with people (see Box 1–2).

The variables that are manipulated by researchers in experiments are **independent variables; dependent variables** are any observed changes in behavior due to the manipulation. Psychological experiments are designed to discover relationships between environmental conditions and behavior. For example, an experiment might be done to discover the relationship between the temperature in a room and people's performance on a test. In this experiment the independent variable would be the temperature. The experimenter would use a different temperature for each experimental group. The dependent variable would be the test scores. If the average

test scores for the groups were different, the experimenter would conclude that this result was related to the different temperatures in the rooms in which the groups worked. Asking people how they felt under both conditions would be simpler, but the results would not be nearly as accurate or objective.

A study by Abrams and Wilson (1979) illustrates the power of the experiment in identifying a factor that is relevant to a particular type of behavior. The researchers were interested in the relationship between alcohol and social anxiety in women. The subjects were paid female undergraduates selected from volunteers who reported only moderate drinking. Two independent variables, alcohol dose and expectancy, were manipulated by randomly assigning subjects to one of four groups: expect alcohol and receive alcohol, expect alcohol and receive placebo, expect placebo and receive alcohol, or expect placebo and receive placebo. (A **placebo** is an inactive substance whose effect on a person's behavior depends on his or her expectations.) The experimental manipulation was **double-blind;** that is, neither the subject nor the experimenter knew what the subject was drinking. All of the subjects were told that both alcohol and nonalcohol groups would be tested in the study and that they had been randomly assigned to either the alcohol-only group or the nonalcohol-only group. Under the guise of preparing for a breathalyzer test, the subjects gargled with a mouthwash that reduced their sensitivity to taste. The drinks were mixed from labeled bottles in full view of the subject, and the glasses in the "receive placebo" group were surreptitiously smeared with vodka. Finally, the breathalyzer was altered to give false feedback.

After the drink manipulation and breathalyzer test, the subjects were placed in a controlled social interaction with a male confederate. The dependent variables included physiological measures of anxiety (heart rate and skin conductance) taken before, during, and after the interaction; self-report measures of anxiety taken before and after the interaction; and observer ratings of the anxiety shown by each subject during the interaction.

The experiment showed that women who believed that they had consumed alcohol, whether or not their drinks actually contained alcohol, showed significantly increased levels of physiological arousal compared with those who believed that they had drunk only tonic water. According to ratings made by observers, subjects who believed that they had consumed alcohol showed greater discomfort in the social interaction (see Figure 1–13). This experiment highlights the decisive role that

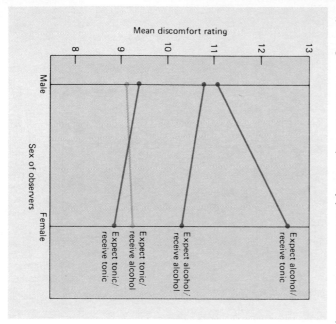

FIGURE 1–13
Mean discomfort ratings by drink content, expectancy, and sex made by observers who rated videotapes of subjects' social interactions. (From Abrams, D. B., and Wilson, O. T. [1979]. Effects of alcohol on social anxiety in women. *Journal of Abnormal Psychology* 88: 161–173. Copyright © 1979 by the American Psychological Association. Reprinted by permission of the author.)

subjects' expectations can play in their behavior and in their ability to cope.

There are two general types of experiments. The first type is the **hypothesis-testing experiment**, in which the researcher makes a prediction based on a theory and then conducts an experiment to see whether the prediction is correct.

I'm interested in determining whether, if children have an early close, secure relationship with an adult, what psychologists call attachment, they will have fewer problems getting along with other children when they enter school. My hypothesis is that if children are securely attached when they are very young, their social skills will be better and they will be less likely to be described as having behavior problems.

I have some records of nursery school children's behavior in a situation designed to measure attachment. In that research setup, a young child and his or her mother sit together in an attractive room with some playthings. Then a "stranger" (a research worker) comes into the room and sits down. After awhile the mother leaves; she comes back a short time later. The way the child behaves, both while the mother is gone and when she returns, is a measure of attachment. If the child does not cling to the mother when the stranger enters, and if the child continues to play with the toys, is not distressed when she leaves, and greets her warmly but does not cling to her when she returns, the child is said to be securely attached.

Now those children are in the first grade, and I want to determine whether those who were securely attached in nursery school behave differently from the other children in either stressful or nonstressful situations. For one-half of each of the attachment groups, I am observing the children in a frustrating situation where they are given an impossible task to solve. For the other half of each group, I will give the children another task that is not difficult but takes a fairly long time to do. My hypothesis is that children who are securely attached will work longer at the impossible task than the other attachment group. For the other task, I expect no difference between the two groups. I base these predictions on the idea that children who are securely attached in their early years develop feelings of competence and tolerance of frustration superior to those of children who did not have a positive attachment experience.

The second type of experiment, the **behavior-change experiment** is concerned primarily with the development of therapeutic techniques. It is also designed to test hypotheses, but in this case the goal is to make an immediate contribution to the development of practical rehabilitative techniques. For example, a behavior-change experiment might test the hypothesis that supervised work experiences are significantly more effective than group psychotherapy in changing the attitudes and behavior of convicted criminals. The researcher who wrote the following account is studying schizophrenics. However, his goal is a very practical one: improving the social skills of schizophrenics.

I'm trying to devise procedures that will help hospitalized schizophrenics return to the community more quickly and be more effective when they make their return. My approach is to start with one obvious deficiency of schizophrenics: inadequate social skills. They just don't do a very good job of relating to other people. What I've been doing is finding out, by asking them questions and observing them, what social skills schizophrenics lack; for example, they have a lot of trouble introducing themselves to strangers and making small talk. I'm modeling—that is, demonstrating—for them various ways of being effective in social situations. I also have a control group that doesn't get the social skills training, as well as a group that participates in discussions about how to handle social situations but gets no modeling. If I'm on the right track, follow-ups should show that the modeling group is better able to adjust back into the community than the control group and maybe also better than the discussion group.

Ethical Aspects of Research

Regardless of the scholarly reasons for doing research, researchers should not place people in either physical or psychological jeopardy without their informed consent. Subjects should be informed regarding what the experiment is about and any hazards associated with participation in it. They also must be clearly told that they are free to withdraw from the experiment at any time. If deception must be used, the subjects must be completely debriefed after the experiment, and the entire procedure explained to them. Special measures must be taken to protect confidentiality.

As a result of the increasing emphasis on the protection and welfare of both human and animal subjects used in psychological research, psychologists now must restrict their experimentation with certain groups of people who are not in a position to give their consent, such as children, the mentally retarded, and seriously disturbed mental patients. When such people, or others who are not able to give consent, are involved, consent must be obtained from their parents or guardians. Strict guidelines are also being developed for research in prisons. No prisoner can be forced to participate in research or penalized for refusal to do so, and in the case of rehabilitative programs, prisoners must be permitted to share in decisions concerning program goals. Researchers must adhere to the ethics of research or risk serious legal and professional consequences.

Study Outline

WHAT IS ABNORMAL BEHAVIOR?

1. Abnormal psychology deals with how it feels to be different, the meanings that get attached to being different, and how society deals with people whom it considers to be different.

2. Overt rejection of abnormal behavior has declined, yet there is still prejudice toward people who are noticeably deviant or have a history of mental disorder. Television and other mass media build misconceptions about what behavior is normal and what is abnormal.

3. **Adaptation** is an ongoing process that involves a balance between what people want and what their environment wants. How well a person adapts depends on his or her personal characteristics and the nature of the situations confronting him or her.

4. Maladaptive behavior not only is deviant but also causes concern in the individual, his or her family and friends, or society. Maladaptation has many causes and can range from mildly troubling fears to severe distortion of reality and inability to communicate.

STRESS, COPING, AND VULNERABILITY

1. **Stress** refers to people's reactions to situations that pose demands, constraints, or opportunities. It is increased by unexpected change, severe crises, or critical developmental periods. **Coping skills** are techniques, such as constructive thinking and flexibility, that enable people to deal with stress, giving them some control over their behavior and over the environment. **Vulnerability**, or the likelihood of maladaptive responses, is

affected by heredity, personality, lack of certain skills, negative experiences, and certain life conditions.

2. Stress, coping, and vulnerability interact and affect a person's adaptive behavior. Clinical intervention can help people cope with stress.

REASONS FOR CLINICAL CONTACTS

People may seek professional help because they are unhappy, because others are concerned about them, or because they are in trouble with the community or the law.

THE EPIDEMIOLOGY OF MALADAPTIVE BEHAVIOR

1. Epidemiologists seek information about the physical and psychological adaptation of groups, especially environmental causes of conditions associated with a community's way of life. They obtain two types of information: **prevalence data**, or the frequency of occurrence of a condition at a given point in time, and **incidence data**, or the number of new cases occurring during a given period. Comparisons of statistics from different periods are confusing because of changes in the definition and labeling of disorders, as well as social and political changes such as care of the aged and availability of mental health services.

SOURCES OF HELP

1. Federal and local laws now encourage psychiatric treatment within the community rather than in large institutions. Community care for chronic patients is supplied by nursing homes and other special residences and is facilitated by antipsychotic drugs. Only a small percentage of people who engage in maladaptive behaviors are in contact with mental health services.

2. **Clinical psychologists** have postgraduate degrees and specialized knowledge of abnormal behavior. They diagnose and treat nonmedical personal problems and do research. **Psychiatrists** (physicians who specialize in emotional disorders) have legal responsibilities in commitment proceedings, supervision of mental hospitals, and administration of drugs. **Psychiatric social workers** have graduate degrees in social work. They work with families and help them utilize community resources. Clinicians from all these fields are trained to do therapy and counseling.

RESEARCH IN ABNORMAL PSYCHOLOGY

1. Observation and description of behavior, either under controlled laboratory conditions or in natural set-

tings, can lead to inferences about its causes. Personal biases can be counteracted by the use of more than one observer. Self-observation can also be useful in clinical research. The data obtained in these ways include the stimuli that elicit particular responses, subjective and behavioral responses to particular stimuli, and the environmental consequences of certain behaviors.

2. To develop theories about why particular phenomena occur, scientists apply reason, logic, and even guesswork to their observations in order to arrive at a tentative explanation that can be tested with further observations. Good theories lay a foundation on which to build further knowledge; they must be testable and capable of being refuted.

3. The steps in scientific research are (a) specifying the topic; (b) reviewing the literature; (c) defining the variables to be measured—both **independent variables**, those that are manipulated by the researcher, and **dependent variables** or outcomes; (d) developing a hypothesis; (e) selecting a research strategy; (f) conducting the study; (g) analyzing the results (which involves calculating **descriptive statistics**, or numerical measures, and **inferential statistics**, which are used in judging the probability that the results are due to chance); and (h) reporting the findings of the research.

4. **Assessment studies** describe and predict behavior under specific conditions. They include correlational, longitudinal, follow-up, and cross-sectional studies. **Correlational studies** tell the degree of relationship among various factors; they can be useful when it is not possible to manipulate experimental conditions. **Longitudinal studies** record behavior over long periods. In **follow-up studies**, people are contacted some time after an initial assessment to determine whether there have been any changes in their behavior. **Cross-sectional studies** assess one or more groups at a particular time.

5. In **experimental studies**, independent variables are manipulated and changes in behavior (the dependent variables) are observed in order to discover their relationships to the independent variables. In a **hypothesis-testing experiment** the researcher makes a prediction based on a theory and then conducts an experiment to see whether the prediction is correct. **Behavior-change experiments** test hypotheses that are related to possible therapeutic techniques.

6. Various ethical considerations in psychological research involve disclosing the nature of the experiment, protecting subjects' anonymity, obtaining the consent of the subjects, and not forcing participation.

CHAPTER 2

The Historical Background of Abnormal Psychology

Louis Leopold Boilly, *Reunion de Têtes Diverses*, Color lithograph, 19 3/4 × 14 1/2". Clements Fry Collection, Yale University.

OBJECTIVES FOR CHAPTER TWO:

To learn:

1. The history of explanations of abnormal behavior
2. How treatment has changed over time as a result of these explanations

To understand:

How the pendulum swings back and forth from biological to psychological explanations of abnormal behavior

---

Historical Views of Abnormal Behavior

*A*t this point, what you know about abnormal psychology could be compared to what you would know about your friends if all you had was current information such as their majors in college and how they furnish their rooms. To really know them, you would need to know a lot about what their life was like before you met them. The same is true for the study of abnormal psychology. Until you learn about its origins and history, you will be unable to understand it fully.

You may feel that an excursion into history is irrelevant. Because modern techniques are no doubt much more effective, enlightened, and sophisticated than those used in earlier times, why not concentrate on them instead of getting bogged down in accounts of the past? The trouble with this approach is that it misses important links between the past and the present. Much of what seems modern is an outgrowth of the past, not a rejection of it. In abnormal psychology, as in other fields of study, there are fewer completely new ideas than one might think. A review of the history of abnormal psychology provides a context within which the best of the modern discipline can be understood.

People have always been concerned about their physical well-being, their social relationships, and their place in the universe. They have posed many questions about these issues and have evolved theories about them. Some of those theories seem almost universal. They can be observed in many parts of the world and in many periods of human history. Perhaps the greatest benefit of studying the history of abnormal psychology is the awareness that certain theories of deviance have occurred over and over again.

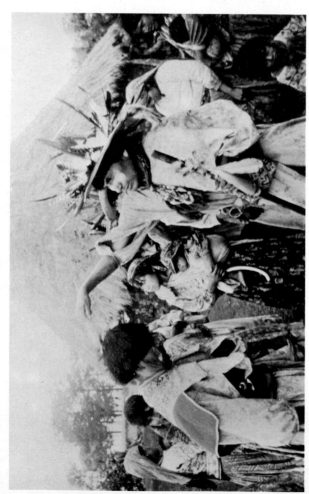

FIGURE 2–1
A shaman anoints a man with holy water as the latter embarks on a pilgrimage.

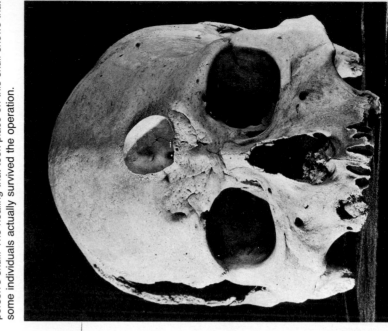

FIGURE 2–2
The technique of trephining involved chipping a hole in the person's skull. The healing that took place on this skull shows that some individuals actually survived the operation.

One ancient theory that is still encountered today holds that abnormal behavior can be explained by the operation of supernatural and magical forces such as evil spirits or the devil. In societies that believe in this theory, therapy generally involves **exorcism**, that is, removing the evil that resides in the individual through countermagic and prayer. Although this view is most prevalent in nonliterate cultures, it is still found in industrialized societies and often exists side by side with more modern approaches. For example, many people who use folk healers also seek assistance from health care professionals (Ness and Wintrob, 1981). Professionals can improve the effectiveness of the help they provide by understanding what folk healers do and why their patients seek them out.

In many societies the **shaman** or medicine man, a magician who is believed to have contact with supernatural forces, is the medium through which spirits communicate with human beings (see Figure 2–1). Through the shaman, an afflicted person can learn which spirits are responsible for his or her problem and what needs to be done to appease them. To accomplish this, the shaman conducts a seance in which he displays intense excitement and often mimics the abnormal behavior he seeks to cure. Through mystical utterances, violent movements, and by acting out his dreams, the shaman reveals messages from spirits. Often the liberation of an evil spirit from the patient's body is expressed through what appears to be the actual expulsion of an object, such as a stone, from the patient's ear or mouth. These rituals are based on specific theories about magic as the cause of abnormal behavior and as the basis of therapeutic change.

It is tempting to view seemingly primitive beliefs about mental illness as part of the dead past. Yet the fact is that even in a relatively advanced and enlightened society like the United States there is a wide range of views about the causes of personal problems. The following case, reported in 1977, concerned a 33-year-old man from a rural area near Little Rock, Arkansas:

The patient had been having seizures recently and had become increasingly irritable and withdrawn from his family. When he could no longer be detained safely on the neurology service, he was transferred to the psychiatric ward, where he became increasingly more agitated, confused, and almost delirious. He became very fearful whenever people approached him, and he began to hallucinate. He finally slowed down after being given 1000 mg of chlorpromazine (a tranquilizer), but the necessity for bed restraint remained. All neurological findings, including a brain scan, proved normal. After two weeks of hospitalization the patient suffered a cardiac arrest. All efforts to revive him failed. An autopsy provided no reason for the death. After he died, the patient's wife told staff members that her husband had been seeing a "two-headed," an older woman considered by the community to be a witch who cast spells and healed people. The widow stated that her husband had angered the two-headed and that she had caused his death. (Golden, 1977, p. 1425)

Reports of "two-headeds" in Africa and other places describe them as people with voodoo powers that are able to cause sickness, insanity, and death. The power of such beings apparently is related to the victim's belief in them.

Another recurring theme in the history of abnormal behavior is the belief that individuals behave strangely because their bodies are not working right. Such people have something wrong with them, an organic defect that affects a specific organ rather than the whole body. The source of the presumed defect varies according to the nature of the abnormality, the society's cultural beliefs, and—particularly in the modern era—scientific knowledge.

The finding of ancient skulls with holes in them that were not caused by battle wounds has led some writers to conjecture that abnormal behavior was sometimes treated by means of a procedure called **trephination.** In this technique a sharp tool such as a stone was used to make a hole in the skull about 2 centimeters in diameter (see Figure 2–2). Evidence that trephination was performed as early as 3000 to 2000 Æ.œ. has been uncovered in eastern Mediterranean and North African countries. Studies of trephined skulls suggest that the operation often was not fatal, a remarkable achievement given the difficulty of the procedure. Trephination may have been done to permit demonic spirits to escape. However, because of the absence of written records and the fact that our only data are the trephined skulls themselves, we need to be cautious in speculating about their significance (see Figure 2–3).

FIGURE 2–3
A modern mural depicting the Incas of Peru performing trephination.

A third general approach reflects what might be called the psychological perspective. According to this point of view, behavioral disturbances are caused by inadequacies in the way an individual thinks, feels, or perceives the world. According to the psychological perspective, people are at least potentially capable of examining their own thinking and modifying their behavior in light of that examination. Many modern psychotherapists see their task as helping people learn to think more rationally about themselves and their social relationships.

All three of these perspectives—mystical, organic, and psychological—have recurred throughout the history of Western civilization, beginning with the Greeks.

The Ancient Greeks

The earliest writers about the psychological and organic approaches to deviance were the philosophers of ancient Greece. At the height of their civilization, the Greeks emphasized the rational analysis of the natural world. The concepts of motivation and intelligence were among those that they invented in their efforts to explain the behavior they observed in everyday life. We tend to see the modern era as the period in which human beings have sought to push back the boundaries of human understanding through the application of reason. The main difference between us and the ancient Greeks is that we have access to all the knowledge that has accumulated in the past 2000 years, as well as the tools of the scientific method.

Even in ancient Greece, however, knowledge evolved over a period of several centuries. At the time that Homer created the *Iliad* and the *Odyssey* (about 800 B.C.E.), disturbed or psychotic behavior was interpreted as a form of punishment for offenses against the gods. ("Those whom the gods would destroy, they first make mad.") In the battle scenes in the *Iliad*, Homer typically described his heroes as suddenly possessed by feelings of power that are engendered in them by the gods. States of insanity were believed to be created in the same way. Therapy took place in a group of temples dedicated to Asclepius, the god of healing. Each temple was a maze-like structure in which mental patients walked and slept and ultimately reached the center. In the process it was believed that Asclepius attended to their dreams and healed them.

In the centuries after Homer the idea that a person's life is in the hands of the gods gradually declined, at least among educated citizens. The Greek philosophers became increasingly curious about aspects of the individual that might explain normal as well as abnormal behavior. Extreme mental deviations and disorders came to be viewed as natural phenomena for which rational treatments might be developed.

The ancient Egyptians, as well as the Mesopotamians and Hebrews, believed the seat of the mind to be in the heart. When the Pharaohs were embalmed, the heart was venerated, but the brain was scooped out and thrown away. For the Greeks, the brain was the seat of the mind. (Shakespeare referred to the lingering heart-mind controversy in Act III of *The Merchant of Venice* when he wrote: "Tell me where is fancie bred or in the heart or in the head.") Despite his lack of anatomical knowledge, Hippocrates (460–377 B.C.E.) looked to the brain in his efforts to explain why people behave as they do. He described the brain as the interpreter of consciousness and the body's most important organ.

From the brain and the brain only, arise our pleasures, joys, laughter and jests, as well as our sorrows, pains, griefs and tears. Through it, in particular, we think, see, hear, and distinguish the ugly from the beautiful, the bad from the good, the pleasant from the unpleasant. . . .

In these ways I hold that the brain is the most powerful organ of the human body, for when it is healthy it is the interpreter to us of the phenomena caused by the air, as it is the air that gives it intelligence. Eyes, ears, tongue, hands and feet act in accordance with the discernment of the brain.

Hippocrates described epileptic seizures and concluded that they were caused by a diseased brain. He also wrote about depression, states of delirium, psychosis, irrational fears (what we now call phobias), and hysteria (organic symptoms in the absence of an organic disturbance). He and his followers became known for their ability to recognize and treat mental illness. Their therapeutic techniques consisted of rest, bathing, and dieting. There is even a record of Hippocrates appearing as an expert witness at the trial of an insane person. Today physicians continue to pay their debt to Hippocrates by taking the Hippocratic oath when they graduate from medical school (see Figure 2–4).

Three other Greek philosophers—Socrates (470–399 B.C.E.), Plato (427–347 B.C.E.), and Aristotle (384–322 B.C.E.)—also deserve mention for their contributions to abnormal psychology. Socrates was interested in self-exploration and considered reasoning to be the cornerstone of the good life and personal happiness. He believed in using inquiry to further knowledge; his goal was to teach by asking questions instead of giving answers. Today this procedure—called the Socratic method—is a valuable teaching tool as well as a component of the scientific method.

Socrates' most famous student, Plato, developed the **organismic point of view.** In his view, behavior is a product of the totality of psychological processes. Like many modern writers, Plato believed that disturbed be-

FIGURE 2–4
Hippocrates, an older contemporary of Plato, was born in 460 B.C. He attended the medical school on the island of Cos and traveled to many cities both to practice and to teach. Over the centuries his fame grew. His writings include material that today would be called textbooks, articles, case histories, and speeches. The following comments reflect his belief in the value of trying to understand mental life in terms of the physical functioning of the brain:

And men should know that from nothing else but from the brain come joys, laughter and jests, and sorrows, griefs, despondency and lamentations. And by this, in an especial manner, we acquire wisdom and knowledge, and see and hear and know what are foul and what are fair, what sweet and what unsavory . . . and by the same organ we become mad and delirious and fears and terrors assail us, some by day, and dreams and untimely wanderings, and cares that are not suitable and ignorance of present circumstances, disquietude and unskillfulness.

havior grew out of conflicts between emotion and reason. In contrast to those who saw abnormal behavior as having a physical cause, he stressed the power of ideas, going so far as to say that the mind is the only true reality of human existence. According to Plato, the ideal

individual is, above all, guided by reason. In his *Laws*, he expressed the belief that people who have lost their reason should be separated from society: "No lunatic shall be allowed to be at large in the community; the relatives of such persons shall keep them in safe custody at home by such methods as they contrive, on penalty of fine."

Aristotle, a pupil of Plato and the teacher of Alexander the Great, wrote extensively on the nature of reasoning and consciousness and also sought to analyze human emotions. He described and speculated about a number of emotional and motivational states, including anger, fear, envy, courage, hatred, and pity. He believed that anger occurred when a person was subjected to what he or she experienced as injustice and wrongdoing; he saw fear as the awareness of danger with an expectation of loss, defeat, or rejection. Like most of the Greek philosophers, Aristotle placed the highest value on reason and application. He also believed that the various forces in the body need to be in balance for reason to prevail.

The rational approach of the Greek philosophers laid the groundwork for modern science. It led to attempts to classify abnormal behavior according to some consistent scheme. It temporarily replaced magic and religious explanations of abnormal behavior with a quest, through observation and reason, for natural causes. Except for a break during the Middle Ages, that quest has continued until the present time.

The Middle Ages

A host of changes accompanied the decline of ancient Greek culture and the rise and fall of the Roman Empire. Perhaps the two most obvious causes of these changes were the invasions of Western Europe by barbarian tribes and the growth of the Christian religion. The invaders, whose ideas were primitive compared to those of the Greeks and Romans, caused great social unrest; the Christian religion served to comfort people in troubled times. The church also acted as a unifying force when the civil government of Rome finally fell.

The unrest of the Middle Ages was intensified by nearly constant warfare as well as by the Black Death and other epidemics that came without warning and wiped out hundreds of thousands of people. During this period fear and terror spread like brush fires, causing many outbreaks of group hysteria. The nature of these outbreaks varied. Some groups of people behaved like packs of wolves (lycanthropy), and others danced in the streets, making spiderlike movements (tarantism).

During the early Middle Ages the importance of the Christian spirit of charity, particularly toward stigmatized groups such as the severely mentally disturbed, cannot be overestimated. For example, in Gheel, Belgium, the church established a special institution for the care of retarded and psychotic children. As they improved, these children were often placed with sympathetic families in the neighborhood of the institution (see Figure 2–5). Also during this period, music and dance were thought to cure insanity by restoring the chemical balance within the body (see Figure 2–6).

One figure in the early Christian era, the theologian and philosopher Saint Augustine (A.Ø. 354–430), stands out because he helped lay the groundwork for modern psychodynamic theories of abnormal behavior. Writing extensively about feelings, mental anguish, and human conflict, he was perhaps the earliest forerunner of today's psychoanalysts. It was not so much the topics he dealt with as the way he approached them that most resembles the psychoanalytic method of today. Saint Augustine used introspection, or examination of his own thoughts, feelings, and motives, to discuss mental processes like the conflict between pleasure and discipline. He worked almost ruthlessly toward a complete, if painful, self-analysis, and in his *Confessions* he revealed his innermost thoughts, temptations, and fears.

By demonstrating that introspection and exploration of the individual's emotional life could be valuable sources of psychological knowledge, Saint Augustine made an important contribution to modern abnormal psychology. Unfortunately, these efforts were not followed up during the late Middle Ages. As the church's control and influence increased, so did its role in governmental affairs, and it was religious dogma, not civil law, that became the supreme voice of authority. The church came to control the practice of medicine, defining its goals and prescribing treatments for various conditions. To the degree that this control reflected a feeling of charity toward people suffering hardships of various kinds, the church played a positive role. To the degree that it was intolerant, authoritarian, and repressive, its role was decidedly negative.

The legacy of rationality that the Middle Ages had inherited from the Greek philosophers was soon abandoned. Demonology and superstition gained renewed

FIGURE 2–5
One place where moral therapy has survived is Gheel, Belgium. Founded after the miracle cure of five "lunatics" at the shrine of St. Dymphna in the thirteenth century, the colony has continued its work to the present. Over 2,000 patients like this man live in private homes under few restrictions; there they work with the inhabitants at everyday tasks until they have recovered.

FIGURE 2–6
In this engraving, the insane are shown being led through a dance in an effort to improve their mental condition.

FIGURE 2–7
This late fifteenth-century painting by Girolamo Di Benvenuto, *St. Catherine Exorcising a Possessed Woman,* shows St. Catherine of Siena casting the devil out of a possessed woman. The devil is seen fleeing from the woman's head.

importance in the explanation of abnormal behavior. Church authorities felt the need for a definitive document on the apprehension and conviction of witches and sorcerers, whom they saw as the primary agents of evil. That need was met in 1484 with the publication *Malleus Maleficarum* (*The Witches' Hammer*), by Fathers Henry Kramer and James Sprenger, a highly influential work that became a basic reference for investigators of diabolical phenomena.

In the late Middle Ages, although many people continued to take a benign, naturalistic view of mental illness, antintellectualism and belief in magic and witchcraft increased. Many people believed strongly in **exorcism**, the casting out of evil spirits from the body of an afflicted person (see Figure 2–7). Nevertheless, it is difficult to draw firm conclusions about the mental status of the witches who were put on trial during the Middle Ages, since the available evidence is sparse and scattered. However, recent research has shown that many of the "witches" who were put on trial in New England during the sixteenth and seventeenth centuries were persecuted social outcasts rather than people suffering from mental disorders (Demos, 1982; Schoenman, 1984; Spanos, 1978).

History does not move in a simple, uncomplicated way. The *Malleus Maleficarum* described a case of a young man who could not restrain himself from protruding his tongue or shouting obscenities whenever he tried to pray. It attributed this problem, which today would in all likelihood be described as an obsessive–compulsive disorder, to demonic possession. However, Paracelsus (1493–1541) vigorously attacked such notions as possession by the devil. Like the Greeks before him, he pictured maladaptations as natural phenomena, although, as a believer in astrology, he felt that such phenomena lay within the stars and planets, not within the individual. In the sixteenth century another rational thinker, Juan Huarte (1530–1589), wrote one of the first treatises on psychology, *Probe of the Mind.* In it he distinguished between theology and psychology and argued forcefully for a rational explanation of the psychological development of children.

In addition to thoughtful individuals like Paracelsus and Huarte, there were some relatively enlightened governments and some serious efforts to care for mentally troubled individuals. In England, for example, the Crown had the right and duty to protect the mentally impaired, who were divided into two categories: natural fools and persons *non compos mentis*. A **natural fool** was a mentally retarded person whose intellectual capacities had never progressed beyond those of a child. **Persons non compos mentis** did not show mental disability at birth. Their deviant behavior was not continuous, and they might show long periods of recovery. (For reasons that are not clear, by the fifteenth century the term *lunatic* replaced the phrase *non compos mentis* and *idiot* replaced *natural fool*.)

There is also evidence that hearings to judge a person's mental status and legal competency were held as early as the thirteenth century (Neugebauer, 1979). Such examinations were designed to assess a person's orientation, memory, and intellect. The following description of Emma de Beston, which dates from 1383, is typical of the reports that were based on such examinations.

The said Emma, being caused to appear before them, was asked whence she came and said that she did not know. Being asked in what town she was, she said that she was at Ely. Being asked how many days there were in the week, she said seven but could not name them. Being asked how many husbands she had had in her time she said three, giving the name of one only and not knowing the names of the others. Being asked whether she had ever had issue by them, she said that she had had a husband with a son, but did not know his name. Being asked how many shillings were in forty pence, she said she did not know. Being asked whether she would rather have twenty silver groats than forty pence, she said they were of the same value. They examined her in all other ways which they thought best and found that she was not of sound mind, having neither sense nor memory nor sufficient intelligence to manage herself, her lands or her goods. As appeared by inspection she had the face and countenance of an idiot.

—(O'Donoghue, 1914, pp. 127–128)

The Renaissance

The Renaissance was a period of increased humanism, curiosity about nature, and interest in scholarship. Yet persecution of people society did not like continued. Figure 2–8 is an example of the less than compassionate view of insanity that was commonplace. Many medical authorities devoted much time to investigating skin blemishes, which were believed to indicate points of contact with Satan. The idea of magical cures embodied in shamanism survived in the popular therapy of removing stones from the head (see Figure 2–9).

Although the influence of *Malleus Maleficarum* continued to be felt for centuries, gradually the idea that irrational behavior could be explained rationally gained renewed attention. It followed that detailed descriptions of the behavior in question were needed. Johann Weyer (1515–1576), a sixteenth-century physician, was one of the major contributors to this development. In an age of unbridled superstition, Weyer emphasized psychological conflict and disturbed interpersonal relationships as causes of mental disorder. His enlightened humanism undoubtedly saved countless mentally ill people from death at the stake. Weyer had the courage to insist that witches were mentally disturbed individuals rather than creatures of Satan. He vigorously asserted the need to treat such people medically rather than theologically.

On the basis of careful psychological examination of mental patients, Weyer described a wide range of abnormal behavior, including paranoia, epilepsy, psychosis, depression, and persistent nightmares. In *The Deception of Demons* he specifically attacked the preposterous claims of the *Malleus Maleficarum*. He argued that clinical treatment must be oriented toward meeting the needs of disturbed people rather than merely following rules of institutions like the church. He spent much time talking with and observing his patients because he

FIGURE 2–8
This sixteenth-century woodcut shows a method for curing insanity. An insane man's head is held in an oven while demons and troublesome thoughts exit through the top of the oven.

FIGURE 2–9

This early sixteenth-century painting by Hieronymus Bosch shows an operation for stones in the head. An old phrase that is used even today describing a mentally unbalanced person is "He has stones (or rocks) in his head." In the sixteenth and seventeenth centuries quacks took advantage of this superstition and pretended to cure insanity by making a superficial incision in the patient's scalp and "extracting" small stones that were supplied by a confederate standing behind the patient.

The Age of Reason and the Enlightenment

The seventeenth century, known as the Age of Reason, and the eighteenth century, known as the Enlightenment, have been so labeled because during these two centuries reason and the scientific method came to re-

felt that he could not treat psychopathology without firsthand knowledge of it. The knowledge led him to the conclusion that inner experiences (such as psychological conflict) and disturbed relationships with others were significant causes of mental illness. Weyer's writings represent a major step toward the separation of abnormal psychology from theology.

place faith and dogma as ways of understanding the natural world. During these two centuries major advances were made in such diverse fields as astronomy, biology, and chemistry. The aspect of the scientific method that received the greatest emphasis was the need to support assertions with observations of natural phenomena.

Although human emotions and motivations are less accessible to direct observation than the moon, the stars, and the human circulatory system, a number of philosophers and scientists focused on the subjective experiences of human beings. Baruch Spinoza (1632–1677) anticipated modern approaches to psychology and physiology with his argument that mind and body are inseparable. In terms that were reminiscent of much current writing in psychology, Spinoza wrote about psychological causation and the roles of emotions, ideas, and desires in human life. He even referred to unconscious mechanisms that influence behavior. Spinoza's main contribution to abnormal psychology was his argument that psychological processes, though they are not directly observable, are equal in importance to the material processes of the natural world. William Harvey (1578–1657), best known for his work on the circulatory system, also wrote about the relationships between the psychological and physiological sides of life.

Among the perceptive observers of the human experience have been playwrights, novelists, and poets. During the Age of Reason, a number of authors probed especially deeply into the problems of human motivation and emotions. The clearest examples can be found in the plays of William Shakespeare (1564–1616), particularly *Hamlet*. Hamlet wants to take revenge on his uncle but consistently hesitates to act. Psychoanalysts have interpreted this hesitation as a reflection of Hamlet's neurotic conflicts concerning his mother, who had married the uncle after the death of Hamlet's father. Another literary work that dealt with human emotions was the *Anatomy of Melancholy*, by Robert Burton (1577–1640) (see Figure 2–10). In this book Burton focused on the emotional core of depression and called attention to an observation that clinical workers have often made: depressed people tend to be very angry not only with themselves but with all others as well. Burton, a professor of divinity at Oxford, based his description and analysis of depression on personal experience.

These developments mirror the longstanding conflict between the psychological and physical explanations of abnormal behavior. However, during the seventeenth and eighteenth centuries both groups—those who analyzed subjective experience and those who sought to identify physical defects—finally rejected the idea that demons and supernatural forces were the causes of abnormal behavior. As a consequence, by the end of the eighteenth century superstition had been almost totally replaced by a commitment to rationality,

FIGURE 2–11

These statues, originally on the gates of the Bethlehem Hospital in England, are generally taken as representations of Raving Madness (top) and Melancholy Madness (bottom).

FIGURE 2–10

The title page from Burton's book, which was written under the name of Democritus Junior. At the top center is a picture of Democritus the Elder in his garden, a portrait of the author at the bottom. The three larger pictures on each side illustrate some of the causes of melancholy. Jealousy, love, and superstition are on the left; solitude, hypochondriasis, and mania are on the right. At the bottom are two herbs, borage and hellebore, that are thought to help cure melancholia.

scientific observation, and humane treatment of the mentally ill.

In England the movement toward humane treatment gained impetus as a result of the psychotic breakdown suffered by King George III in 1765. This event precipitated a constitutional crisis and made many people aware that even prominent individuals were not immune to mental derangement. Madhouses had existed in England for many years, but only in 1774 did Britain pass its first parliamentary act licensing such institutions and regulating the admission of patients to them.

From the late seventeenth to the nineteenth century interest rose in **physiognomy**, the art of judging

character, personality, and feelings from the form of the body, particularly the face (see Figure 2–11). In the early nineteenth century a new approach to abnormal psychology emerged. Franz Joseph Gall (1758–1828), a physician, studied the brains of different kinds of people (young, old, deranged) and gathered evidence suggesting that brain size and mental development are related. On the basis of this evidence he formulated the theory of **phrenology**, according to which discrete psychological "faculties" were located in specific areas of the brain. Gall believed that bumps and indentations on the surface of the skull were accurate reflections of the underlying brain parts. Figure 2–12 shows a device that was used to measure these irregularities. Interest in this now-discredited theory lasted a long time: the journal of the Ohio State Phrenological Society was published until 1938, and the British Phrenological Society was in existence until 1967.

Two additional examples that illustrate the growing interest in physical approaches to mental illness are the ideas of Cullen and Mesmer. The Scottish physician William Cullen (1712–1790) believed that neurotic behavior was caused by physical defects of the nervous sys-

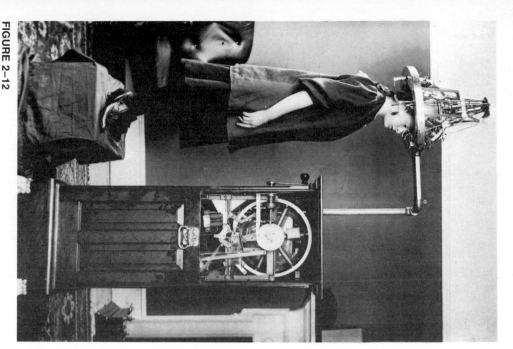

FIGURE 2–12
The Lavery electric phrenometer, invented in 1907, was designed to measure bumps on the head.

FIGURE 2–13
Mesmer treated his patients using a *baquet*, a round tub in which he placed bottles of magnetized water. This eighteenth-century engraving shows patients using rods and ropes connected to the tub to touch the afflicted areas on their bodies.

tem. Cullen's therapeutic efforts seem naive, but they were a logical outgrowth of his organic orientation. He treated his patients with cold dousings, bloodletting, vomiting, special diets, exercise programs, and physiotherapy. Like most of his contemporaries, Cullen used severe restraints and straitjackets to control violently disturbed individuals.

An even more famous example of the quest for organic explanations of abnormal behavior is the career of a Viennese physician, Franz Anton Mesmer (1734–1815). In 1774 Mesmer heard of the work of some English physicians who were treating certain diseases with magnets. He then treated a patient by making her swallow a preparation containing iron and attaching three magnets to her body, one on her stomach and two on her legs. Following her dramatic recovery, Mesmer speculated about the mechanisms that had brought about the cure. We would all agree with his first conclusion: the favorable result could not reasonably be explained by the action of the magnets alone. But Mesmer, a flamboyant and ambitious man, went on to assert that the magnets had simply reinforced or strengthened the primary cause of the cure: his personal or animal magnetism.

While Mesmer's idea of animal magnetism seems ridiculous today, it fit reasonably well with some of the scientific beliefs of his time. In the eighteenth century it was widely believed that the planets influenced both physiological and psychological aspects of behavior. Mesmer contended that all human beings were endowed with a special magnetic fluid, a kind of sixth sense that, when liberated, could cure and prevent all illnesses (see Figure 2–13). Furthermore, he was convinced that he possessed an unusual abundance of the fluid. Mesmer believed that a gesture with his hands was enough to make his patients feel the transmission of his magnetic force.

Mesmer's patients entered a thickly carpeted, dimly lit room amid soft music and perfumed air. They held hands, forming a circle around the *baquet*, a tub filled with magnetized water. Mesmer entered, dressed in an elegant cloak and carrying a sword. These dramatics were deliberately created to accomplish the emotional crisis needed for the cure.

Many testimonials claimed that Mesmer's treatment had been helpful. However, the mechanism of his therapy had more to do with the power of suggestion than with the planets. His animal magnetism was a forerunner not of an organic cure, but rather of a complex psychological means of influencing attitudes and behavior. Mesmer thus was an important figure in the history of hypnosis, a clinical technique that, while far removed from Mesmer's *baquet*, still relies on suggestion as a means of influencing the patient's state of awareness.

The Reform Movement

Along with the growth of a scientific attitude toward mental disorders, there was an increase in compassion for people who suffered from them. Philippe Pinel (1745–1826), a leader in the reform of French mental hospitals, had expressed great sympathy for the plight of the deranged. He firmly believed that they required humane care and treatment. Although this orientation is widely accepted by both professional workers and the public today, Pinel's ideas were far from commonplace in his time. Pinel had to fight against the view that institutions for the insane are needed more to protect society than to help the deranged.

An interesting aspect of the growth of Pinel's humanism was the influence of Jean-Baptiste Pussin, a former patient at a hospital where Pinel worked. After being discharged Pussin was given a job at the Hospice de Bicêtre, where he eventually became superintendent of the ward for incurable mental patients. Recent research has shown that it was Pussin, not Pinel, who removed the chains from patients at the Bicêtre. Pussin forbade cruelty toward patients and routinely dismissed attendants who mistreated them. Pinel learned much from Pussin, and when he was appointed head of the Salpêtrière, he insisted that Pussin come with him.

Other reformers in Europe and America also had to fight many battles to achieve their goals. An example of the less-than-human methods that they opposed were the ships of fools, or ships whose captains were paid to take the mentally ill away from the offended community. The community usually managed to ignore the fact

FIGURE 2–14

It may be difficult to believe that a mental hospital would sell admission tickets, but this is exactly what was done until the late eighteenth century at Bethlehem Hospital in London. Visitors were charged a penny a visit, for which they could view the antics of the inmates and tease them to their hearts' content. Part of the figure shows one artist's conception of Bethlehem Hospital as it was in 1710. Note the visitors looking at the patients through the barred windows.

that the lives of the passengers often ended at the bottom of the sea thousands of miles from home.

An important step toward humane treatment of the mentally ill occurred on May 25, 1815, when the British House of Commons ordered a "Parliamentary Inquiry into the Madhouses of England." One of these, the Hospital of St. Mary of Bethlehem in London, had become known for the noise and chaos prevailing within it (see Figure 2–14). The activities in this "madhouse" were of such great interest to the public that visitors often came to observe the antics of the patients. Tickets were even sold to this popular tourist attraction

FIGURE 2-15

George Cruikshank's dramatic pictures of the mistreatment of mental patients helped bring about reform legislation. His portrait of William Norris, who was bound by foot-long chains to an iron rod at the head of his bed for 12 years, is an example of those illustrations.

(see Figure 2–15), from which the word *bedlam* is derived. A full-scale investigation was initiated after incidents of physical abuse at Bethlehem Hospital were revealed by a citizen's committee, which rallied public support for enlightened legislation on behalf of the mentally ill.

One of the leaders of the reform committee was William Hone, a political satirist. Hone described the formation of the committee as follows.

I was at a Coffee Shop in Fleet Street sitting next to Alderman Waithman, when the illustrator, George Cruikshank, came in. We talked, as we often did, on the subject of madhouses, of the abuses and cruelty to the patients—

I then proposed forming a committee to investigate the Lunatic Asylums.

Thus self-authorized, we knocked at the door of one Asylum after another. George Cruikshank drew the pictures and I took notes.

Cruikshank's graphic portrayals of the inhuman conditions endured by the mentally ill were a major factor in bringing about reform (see Figure 2–15).

By the middle of the nineteenth century, the growing acceptance of humanitarian ideas had led to a broad recognition of the need to reform social institutions. Vigorous movements were begun to establish protective and benign asylums for the mentally ill. These movements were given impetus by Pinel's *Treatise on Insanity,* in which he called for the application of scientific principles in place of guesswork in arriving at treatments for disturbed behavior. Classifying his patients according to observable characteristics, such as melancholy and delirium, Pinel sought to devise specific treatments for them. For example, here is how he described the optimal treatment of melancholia and depression:

Patience, firmness, humane feeling in the manner of directing them, continuous watchfulness in the wards to prevent outbursts of anger and exasperations, pleasant occupations varied according to differences in taste, various types of physical exercise, spacious quarters among trees, all the enjoyments and tranquillity of country living, and from time to time soft and melodious music, all the easier to obtain since there is almost always in these establishments some distinguished musician whose talents languish for want of exercise and cultivation.

—(Pinel, 1809, pp. 258–260)

The sometimes huge asylums for the insane that were built in the nineteenth century came into existence because it was felt that the only way to treat mentally disturbed people was to isolate them from the damaging influences of family, friends, and community. Accompanying this view was the belief in **moral treatment.** This approach sought to control and rehabilitate the patient through a fixed schedule that encouraged regular habits; kind treatment with a minimum of restraint; a daily visit from the hospital superintendent, who assumed the role of persuader and inspirational leader; calm, pleasant surroundings; accommodations that separated patients with different degrees of disturbance; proper diet; some medication; and organized physical and mental activities (see Figure 2–16).

The programs of hospitals that employed moral-treatment approaches seemed to be most effective when the patients and staff shared common religious, ethnic, and cultural values; when caseloads were held to a relatively small size; when the hospital superintendent was charismatic and inspirational; and when adequate funds to run the hospitals were available (Morrissey and Goldman, 1986).

The Reform Movement in America

The eighteenth century was not a good time to be insane in the fledgling British Colonies; often the mentally ill simply languished in jail. Gradually, however, a reform movement took hold in the Colonies. Virginia's royal governor, Francis Fauquier, persuaded the House of Burgesses to build a hospital for "ideots and lunaticks"; the hospital opened on October 12, 1773 (see Figure 2–17).

(c)

FIGURE 2–17

A reconstruction of the Public Hospital for Persons of Insane and Disordered Minds in Williamsburg, Virginia, America's first public institution exclusively for the mentally ill, recently opened for public viewing (a). In the eighteenth century the inmates inhabited bare, depressing cells (b). By the midnineteenth century, comfortable housing had become an important part of treatment (c).

FIGURE 2–16

This lithograph, called Lunatic's Ball, shows a dance that was held for patients at a county asylum in 1848. The contrast between this illustration and those of Bethlehem Hospital illustrates the advances made in the 1800s. Note also the continued belief in the beneficial effects of music and the arts, also illustrated in Figure 2–6.

(a)

(b)

Benjamin Rush (1745–1813), a signer of the Declaration of Independence, is often credited with the founding of American psychiatry. He believed that "madness" was caused by engorgement of the blood vessels of the brain. Although the treatment methods that he advocated (bleeding, purging, and water cures) seem more like punishment than therapy, his work took place in a hospital rather than in a custodial institution and his methods were intended to reduce pressure on the brain's blood vessels and thus reduce mental illness. The Pennsylvania Hospital, where Rush introduced his new treatment methods, was the first hospital in America to admit mentally ill patients. His *Medical Inquiries and Observations upon the Diseases of the Mind* published in 1812 was the first American textbook on psychiatry and was used as a basic reference for over fifty years.

The lack of humane treatment and decent facilities for the insane in America (see Figure 2–18) appalled Dorothea Dix (1802–1887), a Boston schoolteacher who devoted much of her life to visiting institutions for the indigent. By 1847 she had visited 18 penitentiaries, 300 county jails and houses of correction, and 500 almshouses where the mentally ill were kept. Through her personal efforts 32 mental hospitals were constructed.

At the turn of the century, an American businessman named Clifford Beers recorded his experiences as a mental patient in *A Mind that Found Itself*, published in 1908 (see Box 2–1). After his recovery Beers became determined to make changes in the conditions of mental hospitals, and his book helped him gather support for a citizens' reform group, the National Committee for Mental Hygiene (now called the National Association

for Mental Health), which was founded in 1909. The group promoted social programs aimed at preventing mental illness as well as ensuring humane treatment of the mentally ill.

Despite the progress toward more humane treatment of mental patients in the nineteenth century, the mentally ill continued to be persecuted well into the twentieth century. An example is provided by Albert Deutsch, who published a shocking exposé of the mistreatment of patients at the Philadelphia State Hospital for Mental Diseases during the 1940s:

The male "incontinent ward" was like a scene out of Dante's Inferno. Three hundred nude men, stood, squatted and sprawled in this bare room. . . . Winter or Summer, these creatures never were given any clothing at all. . . . Many patients . . . had to eat their meals with their hands. There weren't nearly enough spoons or other tableware to go around. . . . Four hundred patients were herded into one barn-like dayroom intended for only 80. There were only a few benches; most of the men had to stand all day or sit on the splintery floor. There was no supervised recreation, no occupational therapy. . . . Only two attendants were on this ward; at least 10 were needed. The hogs in a near-by pigpen were far better fed, in far greater comfort than these human beings.

—(Deutsch, 1948, pp. 49–50)

Today such conditions are unlikely to exist and many institutions provide a high standard of care. Figure 2–20 shows scenes from contemporary mental hospitals.

FIGURE 2-18
The crib was one of the prescientific "therapies" for violent patients that Dorothea Dix sought to abolish.

BOX 2-1

A Protest That Had an Effect

Clifford Beer's book, *A Mind That Found Itself*, is the story of his treatment in mental hospitals during a period of psychosis. Its description of what Beers endured gripped the imagination of readers and helped gain popular support for the American mental health movement. After his recovery Beers carried on a lifelong crusade that helped revolutionize the care of the mentally ill (see Figure 2–19). In the following excerpt Beers describes how he was restrained in a camisole or straitjacket, a canvas device that was used to restrain unruly patients. In this case Beers believed that the attending physician had laced the jacket unnecessarily tight because of his anger at Beers's behavior.

No incidents of my life have ever impressed themselves more indelibly on my memory than those of my first night in a straitjacket. Within one hour of the time I was placed in it I was suffering pain as intense as any I ever endured, and before the night had passed it had become almost unbearable. My right hand was so held that the tip of one of my fingers was all but cut by the nail of another, and soon knifelike pains began to shoot through my right arm as far as the shoulder. After four or five hours the excess of pain rendered me partially insensible to it. But for fifteen consecutive hours I remained in that instrument of torture; and not until the twelfth hour, about breakfast time the next morning did the attendant so much as loosen a cord.

During the first seven or eight hours, excruciating pains racked not only my arms, but half of my body. Through I cried and moaned, in fact, screamed so loudly that the attendants must have heard me, little attention was paid to me. . . . I even begged the attendants to loosen the jacket enough to ease me a little. This they refused to do, and they even seemed to enjoy being in a position to add their considerable mite to my torture.

After fifteen interminable hours the straitjacket was removed. Whereas just prior to its putting on I had been in a vigorous enough condition to offer stout resistance when wantonly assaulted, now, on coming out of it, I was helpless. When my arms were released from their constricted position, the pain was intense. Every joint had been racked. I had no control over the fingers of either hand, and could not have dressed myself had I been promised my freedom for doing so.

For more than the following week I suffered as already described, though of course with gradually decreasing intensity as my racked body became accustomed to the unnatural positions it was forced to take. The first experience occurred on the night of October 18th, 1902. I was subjected to the same unfair, unnecessary, and unscientific ordeal for twenty-one consecutive nights and parts

FIGURE 2–19

Clifford Beers became an effective advocate for human treatment of mental disorders after his own experiences in a mental institution.

of the corresponding twenty-one days. On more than one occasion, indeed, the attendant placed me in the straitjacket during the day for refusing to obey some trivial command. This, too, without an explicit order from the doctor in charge, though perhaps he acted under a general order.

During most of the time I was held also in seclusion in a padded cell. A padded cell is a vile hole. The side walls are padded as high as a man can reach, as is also the inside of the door. One of the worst features of such cells is the lack of ventilation, which deficiency of course aggravates their general unsanitary condition. The cell which I was forced to occupy was practically without heat, and as winter was coming on, I suffered intensely from the cold. (Beers, 1981 [1907], pp. 107, 110–111)

FIGURE 2-20
Present-day mental institutions range from barren facilities for "warehousing" patients, to pleasant and stimulating institutions. These patients are in a well-run hospital whose staff recognizes the importance of positive social interactions in the recovery process.

Psychological vs. Organic Views

The causes of abnormal behavior have yet to be determined fully, and debates on this issue recur continually. Is abnormal behavior caused by disturbances in bodily functioning or by subjective experiences, thoughts, and motivations? This question remains high on the agenda of contemporary clinicians and researchers, and the way it is approached today owes much to the way it has been phrased over the years, particularly during the nineteenth century.

The Psychological Approach

Eighteenth-century theories emphasized **rational thinking** as the way to achieve personal and social adjustment. During the first half of the nineteenth century, however, the important role of **irrational thought** in both normal and abnormal behavior attracted much more attention. This took place as part of the so-called Romantic reaction against the view of philosophers and scientists who gave little weight to the role of emotions, motivations, and internal conflicts in human behavior. Many clinical workers and researchers began to view internal conflicts as a major cause of personal unhappiness and failure to adapt socially. This focus on emotion and irrational feelings laid the groundwork for Sigmund Freud's theories about mental processes and their relationship to disturbed behavior.

The reaction against pure rationalism directed more attention to the inner life of the person than to

any other aspect of human existence. The German psychiatrist Johann Christian Heinroth (1773–1843) theorized that mental illness resulted from internal conflicts between unacceptable impulses and the guilt generated by those impulses, and that the individual is often unaware of these conflicts. What distinguished theories like Heinroth's from those of his predecessors was their attempts to provide an account of the whole person, the inner life, and the mental stresses and strains that underlie observable behavior. This was in contrast to the rationalist view that the scientific study of abnormal behavior primarily required meticulous observation and description of disordered behaviors and classification of those behaviors.

Heinroth's ideas are strikingly similar to Freud's notion that impulses clash with conscience and result in anxiety, unhappiness, and socially inappropriate behavior. Freud, like Heinroth, recognized that this clash might take place at an unconscious level and that awareness of these conflicts was a means of understanding and resolving them, and hence a way of correcting maladaptive behavior. Despite these similarities, Freud seems to have been only slightly acquainted with Heinroth and the other participants in the Romantic reaction. One reason for this was that by midcentury, long before Freud's work began, the pendulum had begun to swing in a quite different direction—toward the search for biological causes of abnormal behavior.

The Organic Approach

Just as Heinroth was the champion of the psychological approach to abnormal behavior, another German psychiatrist, Wilhelm Griesinger (1817–1868), led the search for bodily causes. He argued that most mental disorders were caused by the direct or indirect influence of disturbances in brain function. While he was a staunch advocate of humane treatment and was himself a sensitive observer of human conflict, Griesinger firmly believed that the organic, rather than the psychological, origins of human maladaptation and unhappiness were predominant. His slogan was "mental diseases are brain diseases."

Behind this perspective was the assumption that the material (brain cells) almost invariably causes the mental manifestation (personal unhappiness). The major implication of this viewpoint was that it was necessary to find out more about how the body (particularly the nervous system) works. One way of doing so was to dissect the brains of mentally disturbed individuals after their death. Researchers reasoned that the unusual behaviors exhibited by those individuals had been caused by structural abnormalities in the brain. Through direct examination of the brains of such people, they hoped to discover relationships between the brain and behavior. From this point of view, introspection as a path to understanding psychological disturbance held little appeal. Nor was there much interest in how thought directs observable behavior.

Emil Kraepelin (1856–1926), who was influenced by Griesinger, also believed that abnormal behavior was caused by organic disturbances. Kraepelin's major contribution was his attempt to construct a classification system that would encompass most of the disorders that required treatment and hospitalization. He distinguished between two especially serious and debilitating conditions, dementia praecox and manic-depressive psychosis, and believed that they were specific diseases with specific organic causes.

The Approaches Converge

Toward the end of the nineteenth century, important developments took place on both the physical and psychological fronts. The French neurologist Jean Martin Charcot (1825–1893) continued to believe that organic disturbances were of crucial importance, but he used a psychological approach in studying and treating his patients. The patients in whom Charcot was most interested were **hysterics,** people who suffered from organic complaints for which no organic causes could be found. Hysterics complained of loss of sensation in the skin, pains in various parts of the body, blindness and other visual impairments, tics, muscular contractions that resembled epileptic seizures, difficulty in walking, or paralysis. In addition to this wide variety of inexplicable symptoms, Charcot observed some psychological consistencies in hysterical patients, notably what he called *la belle indifférence:* although a person who had become paralyzed could be expected to be depressed about it, Charcot's patients seemed unconcerned about their condition. Charcot also noticed that hysterical patients had their own incorrect theories of bodily functioning and that their physical symptoms were compatible with those theories. He diagnosed many of these cases as "traumatic paralysis."

Despite his orientation toward organic causes, Charcot became impressed with his psychological observations and came to the conclusion that mental states were indeed related to hysterical symptoms. He therefore developed a technique for hypnotizing hysterical patients. While they were in a hypnotic trance, he suggested to them that their symptoms (for example, paralysis of a part of the body) would disappear. In many

FIGURE 2–21
This portrait of Charcot shows him lecturing to a group of colleagues at the Salpêtrière, the same institution where Pinel had unchained the patients. In this scene Charcot is demonstrating the typical behavior of a hysteric, using a female patient as an example. Notice her fainting posture. Such dramatic behavior is typical of a hysterical episode.

cases the symptoms disappeared completely. Charcot also was able to induce hysterical symptoms in normal individuals by giving them appropriate suggestions while they were under hypnosis.

Throughout France and Europe Charcot gained great prestige; he was referred to as the "Napoleon of neuroses." He became known as a charismatic clinician and teacher (see Figure 2–21). The following account describes some of his miraculous cures:

Many patients were brought to Charcot from all over the world, paralytics on stretchers or wearing complicated apparatuses. Charcot ordered the removal

FIGURE 2-22

Charcot presented this inscribed photograph of himself to Freud after Freud's visit to Paris. The visit had been possible because the University of Vienna had approved Freud's application for a travel grant (Macmillan, 1986):

If the Honourable College of Professors will award me the travelling grant, it is my intention to spend 3–4 months with Professor Charcot in Paris studying the wealth of material provided by the Salpêtrière Clinic, such a favourable opportunity not being available to me in the Departments of the General Hospital.

of those appliances and told the patients to walk. There was, for instance, a young lady who had been paralyzed for years. Charcot bade her stand up and walk, which she did under the astonished eyes of her parents and of the Mother Superior of the convent in which she had been staying. Another young lady was brought to Charcot with a paralysis of both legs. Charcot found no organic lesion; the consultation was not yet over when the patient stood up and walked back to the door where the cabman, who was waiting for her, took off his hat in amazement and crossed himself.

—(Ellenberger, 1970, p. 95)

One of Charcot's students, Pierre Janet (1859–1947), extended his work and concluded that hysteria was due to a splitting off from conscious experience of certain ideas that continued to influence behavior. He observed that under hypnosis many patients recalled upsetting events that seemed to be related to the onset of their symptoms. He found that in some cases, when patients expressed the strong feelings they had experienced at the time the original events took place, their symptoms weakened temporarily or disappeared.

Besides strengthening the view that psychological causes played a role in a significant number of behavioral disorders, Charcot and Janet helped broaden the scope of behavior that was studied by abnormal psychology. Their patients, though they were troubled people who needed help, were not thought of as insane or crazy.

One of the many clinical workers who came to France especially to study with Charcot was Sigmund Freud (1856–1939) (Figure 2–22). Freud had received his medical training as a neurologist and initially believed that the ultimate causes of abnormal behavior were biological. Like Charcot, however, he chose to explore aspects of mental life that seemed to be related to psychological discomfort and maladaptive behavior. Also like Charcot, Freud became increasingly interested in noncatastrophic conditions such as hysteria and phobias.

The Stage is Set

The history of abnormal psychology is the story of how communities have responded to people who were different and did not fit in. The ups and downs, the advances and retreats, leave us with a feeling of cautious optimism about the power of the intellect to comprehend and devise ways of helping individuals who are unable to adapt to community norms.

Ideas about abnormality are almost never brand new. As we have seen, they have a past that in some cases is very long. Moreover, they are often complex. Attitudes toward deviant individuals have always reflected the social dynamics that prevailed at the time. An example of the link between what is going on in a society (its values, prejudices, and the like) and how it conceives of mental illness has been provided by studies of the role of women in the nineteenth century. Theories that asserted that there were sex-based differences in the tendency to engage in abnormal behavior were clearly an outgrowth of cultural stereotypes and the social status quo. Not only were women regarded as subordinate to men, they were also believed to be more prone to nervous and emotional disorders. Biological factors were assumed to play a role in these differences. Some of Sigmund Freud's writings reflect this sexist assessment; for example, early in his career he assumed that the strong sexual repression he observed in women was the cause of what he viewed as their intellectual inferiority (Ellenberger, 1970).

Because we are so close to our own times, we tend to lose sight of many of the basic assumptions and beliefs that direct the thinking of our contemporaries, about a wide variety of topics. If we look back at earlier periods, these assumptions and beliefs are easier to see, and they often seem strange. For example, during the 1880s and 1890s, Freud's developing theories had to compete with ideas that seem naive today. One such idea was the notion that masturbation is a sign of serious personality disorder. People who masturbated were described as moral degenerates, as deceitful, selfish, and full of cunning. Excessive masturbation was believed to result in "masturbational insanity." Another popular idea was that there was a connection between blushing and psychological functioning: excessive blushing indicated inner moral failings, whereas inability to blush reflected psychological weakness (Skultans, 1979).

Policies regarding the treatment of abnormal behavior have been influenced by the public's concerns and priorities. For example, the American public puts a premium on speed and often seems to feel that a quick solution is best. Thus in the 1960s and 1970s public opinion favored a drastic reduction in the number of residents in mental hospitals. Because an effective system of halfway houses and other support services had not been established, masses of hurriedly discharged mental patients had to make their own way into unprepared and largely hostile communities. Few were able to make the transition successfully.

This book is devoted to modern theory, research, and practice concerning abnormal behavior. Everyone has read dozens of newspaper and magazine articles describing breakthroughs that will soon eliminate certain types of mental disorders. Too often the solutions do not materialize, because the breakthrough has been interpreted too simplistically. As the scientific method has uncovered information on a variety of fronts, the need to recognize the complexity of most forms of maladaptation has become clearer.

Study Outline

HISTORICAL VIEWS OF ABNORMAL BEHAVIOR

1. One of the oldest theories of maladaptive behavior attributes it to supernatural and magical forces. In societies that accept such beliefs, therapy generally involves exorcism of the evil spirits by a **shaman** or medicine man.
2. Maladaptive behavior has also been explained by the presence of organic defects that affect only a specific organ, not the whole body. **Trephination,** an extremely ancient therapy that apparently involved the release of evil spirits through a hole made in the skull, is based on the organic approach to abnormal behavior.
3. A third general approach to abnormal behavior is the psychological perspective. According to this point of view, behavioral disturbances are caused by inadequacies in the way an individual thinks, feels, or perceives the world.
4. In ancient Greece during the ninth century Æ.Œ., therapy took place in the temple of the god Asclepius. Hippocrates recognized the importance of the brain in explaining abnormal behavior and developed a therapy based on resting, bathing, and dieting. The trend toward rational explanations of behavior was strengthened by Socrates, Plato, and Aristotle. Socrates saw reason as the cornerstone of the good life. Plato developed the **organismic point of view**, which explains behavior as an expression of the totality of a person's psychological processes; he held that disturbed behavior grew out of internal conflicts between emotion and reason. Aristotle analyzed the emotions and wrote extensively on the nature of consciousness.
5. During the Middle Ages there were many instances of shocking treatment of the mentally ill as well as humane attitudes toward disturbed individuals. Superstitious beliefs in devils and demons were strengthened under the auspices of the Catholic church, but at the same time the idea of Christian charity encouraged more humane treatment of the mentally ill. Saint Au-

gustine's *Confessions* serve as a prototype of modern psychological tools such as introspection and self-analysis. Paracelsus and Juan Huarte attacked superstitious beliefs, and some governments were relatively enlightened in their treatment of the mentally ill. Nevertheless, the best-selling book of the time was *Malleus Maleficarism* (*The Witches' Hammer*), a treatise on diabolical phenomena.

6. Although it was characterized by increasing humanism and scholarship in many areas, the Renaissance was not a period of major change in people's attitudes toward maladaptive behavior. However, in *The Deception of Demons* Johann Weyer called for the separation of abnormal psychology from theology.

7. In the seventeenth century (the Age of Reason) and the eighteenth century (the Enlightenment), reason and the scientific method finally supplanted superstition as the primary ways of understanding human behavior. Baruch Spinoza argued that internal psychological processes were just as worthy of scientific examination as directly observable natural processes. At the same time, the belief that neurotic behavior was caused by physical defects remained current, leading to Franz Anton Mesmer's idea of animal magnetism and eventually to the use of hypnosis in treating psychological problems.

8. The movement toward more humane treatment of the mentally ill began in France with Philippe Pinel, who developed his **moral treatment** at the end of the eighteenth century. William Hone and George Cruikshank spearheaded a governmental review of conditions in London's Bethlehem Hospital in 1815. Benjamin Rush, Dorothea Dix, and Clifford Beers led the reform movement in America.

PSYCHOLOGICAL VS. ORGANIC VIEWS

1. The causes of abnormal behavior have not been established, and the debate over the relative importance of bodily functioning and psychological experiences continues. The eighteenth-century emphasis on **rational thought** was answered by the romantics' emphasis on the role of **irrational thought.** According to Johann Christian Heinroth, mental illness was caused by internal conflicts between unacceptable impulses and the guilt aroused by those impulses.

2. Wilhelm Greisinger led the search for the bodily causes of mental problems; he said that "mental diseases are brain diseases." Emil Kraepelin also stressed organic causes, but his major contribution was a classification system for disorders that required hospitalization. Jean Martin Charcot continued to believe in organic causes, but he treated his patients from a psychological perspective. Pierre Janet first made the observation that hysteria seemed to develop in response to past traumatic events that the patient could recall under hypnosis.

THE STAGE IS SET

1. Attitudes toward deviant individuals reflect the social dynamics of the time, that is, the society's prevailing values and prejudices. Policies regarding the treatment of abnormal behavior are influenced by the public's concerns and priorities.

Paul Giovanopoulos, *Mona Lisa X36*, 1988. Mixed mediums on canvas, 72 × 54″. Courtesy Louis K. Meisel Gallery, New York.

THE ROLE OF THEORY IN ABNORMAL PSYCHOLOGY

THE BIOLOGICAL PERSPECTIVE
Biological Determinants of Abnormal Behavior
Research on Biological Factors and Abnormal Behavior
Integration of Biological and Psychological Systems

THE PSYCHODYNAMIC PERSPECTIVE
Freud and Psychoanalysis
Freud's Theories of Personality
Clinical Psychoanalysis
The Neo-Freudians
Evaluating Psychoanalytic Theory

THE BEHAVIORAL PERSPECTIVE
Classical Conditioning
Operant Conditioning
Modeling
Learning and Mediational Processes

THE COGNITIVE PERSPECTIVE
Cognitive Approaches to Personality

THE HUMANISTIC–EXISTENTIAL PERSPECTIVE
Maslow's Hierarchy of Needs
Rogers' Conception of the Self
The Existential Point of View

THE COMMUNITY PERSPECTIVE
Social Roles and Labeling
Contributions of the Community Perspective

THE VALUE OF AN INTERACTIONAL APPROACH

STUDY OUTLINE

_f_ red Price, age 38, has been experiencing occasional pain in his chest for two months. He is a high school vice-principal in a large city, a high-pressure job requiring many daily contacts with teachers and students. The teachers often have complaints and the students almost always are having problems or causing them. Fred's assignment is to handle the problems effectively and quickly. He has put off seeing a doctor, attributing the pain to indigestion associated with stress at work. In fact, Alka Seltzer seemed to help somewhat. Recently he and his wife have been arguing a lot, often about money: braces for one child's teeth, tuition and living expenses for his oldest child who wants to go to college away from home, and nursing home expenses for his wife's mother. Last night, during an especially fierce argument with his wife, he had another bout of chest pains that took several hours to subside even after he took Alka Seltzer. Afterwards Fred began thinking about the fact that his father had his first heart attack when he was 47. Like Fred, his father had had a high-pressure job that took a lot out of him, leaving him exhausted at night. In the morning Fred called his doctor for an appointment.

It would be difficult to summarize Fred Price's problems in a neat straightforward manner. Is he simply a man who is about to have a heart attack? If so, is it because he has "bad" genes that make him prone to have one? Or, might his somatic problems simply be expressions of a high anxiety level engendered by a stressful job situation. Are his physical resources or stress-coping skills inadequate to handle the demands of being a vice-principal of an inner-city high school?

The Role of Theory in Abnormal Psychology

What role do family pressures and marital discord play in his symptoms? Like most of us, Fred Price is a complex person. His thoughts, behavior, and physical status probably have multiple determinants. From the information provided, it is not possible to decide on the likely cause or causes of his symptoms and apparent unhappiness.

Clinicians and researchers have developed theories they hope will be helpful in identifying the causes of behavioral maladaptation and physical illness. These theories guide clinicians as they inquire into the determinants of maladaptation. In Chapter 1 we said that stress, ways of coping, and vulnerability play important roles in maladaptive behavior. Stress arises when we must respond to challenges that are unexpected or for which we do not feel prepared. The beginning of a new school year, a death in the family, and living in an area with a high crime rate are examples of such challenges. People respond to stress by trying to do something about it. How they respond reflects the effectiveness of their coping skills. For example, a person might install an alarm system after a neighbor's house has been robbed. Some people, however, choose less constructive responses. They may deal with the stress of living in a crime-ridden area by buying guns and vicious dogs or by never leaving their houses after dark. Abnormal psychology deals with behavior that results from failures to cope constructively with the demands, constraints, and opportunities that we all experience as we go through life.

The failures to adapt that are the concern of abnormal psychology usually cannot be explained by the presence of stress alone. It is necessary to investigate the coping styles and vulnerabilities of people who exhibit such failures if we are to understand their maladaptive behavior and help them correct it. There are large differences in how well particular individuals cope with stress. We are all vulnerable to experiences that are related to sensitive areas in our personalities. When these personally relevant buttons are pushed, our capacity for handling stress declines and we feel less competent and content than usual. The war hero who falls apart when his wife threatens to divorce him, the child who is the delight of her teachers but cannot get along with her playmates—both show that an individual may be more vulnerable to certain situational and developmental challenges than to others.

A variety of theories have been offered to explain the vulnerabilities and coping failures that increase the likelihood of personal breakdown. In this chapter we will review the major theoretical approaches as they apply to the relationships among stress, coping, and vulnerability and to other important aspects of maladaptive behavior.

Everyone wants to know why things happen. Fred Price's symptoms certainly raised a number of questions in our minds. Scientific theories are created to organize what we know and explain what it means. Theories are never complete, because there are different ways of looking at what we do know and also because there are some pieces missing from our knowledge. Even an incomplete theory is useful, however, if it provides a perspective for examining the information we have. A good theory will also help us decide what new information we need.

Clinical workers and researchers operate on the basis of formal theories, but they also use informal theories or hunches based on past experience. A psychiatrist, clinical psychologist, or social worker who is assigned a case will use a particular theoretical perspective to analyze the available information. Theoretical perspectives serve as lenses that reflect and shape our conceptions of human nature. Thus according to one theoretical perspective a bad cold may be thought of as a viral infection; according to another it may be simply "God's will"; and according to your mother it may be "you own fault for getting your feet wet."

The diversity of theories in abnormal psychology is wide. We will review six theoretical perspectives that are particularly influential today: (1) the **biological perspective**, which emphasizes the role of bodily processes; (2) the **psychodynamic perspective**, which emphasizes the role of anxiety and inner conflict; (3) the **behavioral perspective**, which examines how the environment influences behavior; (4) the **cognitive perspective**, which looks to defective thinking and problem solving as causes of abnormal behavior; (5) the **humanist-existentialist perspective**, which emphasizes our uniqueness as individuals and our freedom to make our own decisions; and (6) the **community perspective**, which is concerned with the roles of social relationships and the impact of socioeconomic conditions on maladaptive behavior.

Which of these theoretical perspectives is right? In Jewish lore there is a story about a couple who came to their rabbi for marriage counseling. The rabbi interviewed each partner separately and then met with them together. They asked him who was right and who was wrong. The rabbi told the puzzled couple, "You are both right." The rabbi's observation also applies to these theoretical perspectives. Each one deals with pieces of reality, but the pieces are often quite different. Some theories are more pertinent to an understanding of the causes of stress, others to the ways in which we cope, and still others to the nature of human vulnerabilities. Consequently, there is no reason why we should commit ourselves to a particular theoretical position and feel called upon to explain all abnormal behavior in terms of its concepts. With a topic as complex as abnormal behavior, it is a good idea to remember that even a respected theory may be too simple an explanation.

There are many examples of the dangers of adopting too rigid a theoretical position. Consider the case of the elderly. The relatively high incidence of severe behavioral disorders in older people represents a major social problem. A high percentage of these disorders are related to bodily changes that are part of the aging process. However, it would be a mistake to say that psychotic behavior among old people is due simply to deterioration of the brain and disorders of the circulatory system. Two people with the same type of brain disorder might behave quite differently, depending on their life histories, self-concepts, present circumstances, coping styles, and worries about death and dying.

It is also important to note that theories are not static. In the previous chapter we saw that through the centuries explanations of deviance have undergone wide swings. New facts exerted an influence on existing theories, but so did people's beliefs, which may or may not have scientific validity. Besides accommodating new facts or changes in public attitudes, a new theory may be developed as a reaction to weaknesses in a currently popular theory. Although all of the basic theoretical viewpoints discussed in this chapter are important and are actively used and researched today, it is worthwhile to keep in mind that each was a reaction to the situation prevailing at the time it was initially proposed.

The Biological Perspective

In our review of the history of abnormal psychology in Chapter 2, we saw that the idea that bodily disturbances cause disordered behavior has been around for a long time. It is not surprising that the biological perspective gained renewed popularity in the eighteenth and nineteenth centuries, when great leaps forward in anatomy, physiology, and genetics made it seem reasonable that a biological cause might eventually be found for every disorder, be it physical or behavioral.

Major impetus for the biological point of view came from findings about the relationship between bodily infections and defects, on the one hand, and disordered behavior, on the other. Perhaps the most dramatic of these was the discovery of the link between syphilitic infection in early adulthood and general paresis, a serious deterioration of the brain that often appeared when the infected person reached middle age.

Recent information about the role of biological factors supports the argument that such factors are important to some, but certainly not all, mental conditions. Modern advances in several areas of biology and medicine have continued to motivate researchers. For example, equipment and techniques like the PT scan and the CT scan, which make it possible to see how the brain works without the use of surgical or other invasive procedures, are beginning to permit previously unthought-of studies of the relationships between behavior and the brain. And research on heredity and genetics has shown that certain chromosome defects are responsible for metabolic disorders, such as phenylketonuria, that in turn lead to specific forms of mental retardation. The list of behavioral problems in which biological processes play at least some role is lengthening, as is the list of biologically based therapies.

Most people distinguish between the body and the mind, although the meanings attached to these words vary widely. **Body** usually refers to organs, muscles, bones, and brain; **mind** usually refers to attitudes, feelings, and thoughts. We generally speak as if the worlds of body and mind were totally separate, as if the body were something in which the mind rides around, like a car. However, the separation between body and mind is an intellectual invention rather than a reality. Cognitive and bodily processes are closely intertwined, though how much weight one assigns to each process in accounting for maladaptive behavior depends on one's view of human beings. New evidence may alter the prevailing views from time to time.

At its most extreme, the biological viewpoint assumes that all maladaptive behavior is due to a disordered body structure or function. Such a disorder can be explained by an inherited defect, by a defect acquired through injury or infection before or after birth, or by a more or less temporary physiological malfunction caused by some condition that is present at a particular time. A less extreme view, which still emphasizes the importance of biological functioning, recognizes that maladaptive behavior is a joint product of three types of disordered processes: in the body (for example, a hormonal deficiency), in psychological functioning (for example, a tendency toward shyness), and in the social environment (for example, a high unemployment rate in the community).

Biological Determinants of Abnormal Behavior

A number of biological factors influence the behavior of organisms. How we behave and think depends not only on the action of each by itself but also on the interrelationships between them. Genetic factors, the brain and nervous system, and the endocrine glands all play important roles in psychological processes and have been shown to be involved in abnormal behavior.

Genetic Factors

Few fields have expanded as rapidly as genetics. Evidence that genetic abnormalities account for a significant number of medical problems has led researchers to seek hereditary roots for maladaptive behavior as well. Available evidence suggests that genetic factors may play a role in such diverse disorders as schizophrenia, depression, criminality, and mental retardation. The idea that people can inherit certain behavioral tendencies arouses skepticism among some people who feel it conflicts with egalitarian ideals and conjures up a specter of "biological determinism." Yet research, particularly within the past two decades, has shown that few dimensions of behavior seem to be immune to the effects of genetic factors.

A major factor in some genetic abnormalities is irregularities in the structure or number of an individual's chromosomes. **Chromosomes** are threadlike bodies that are present in pairs in all body cells. Humans have 46 chromosomes in each cell. Chromosomal abnormalities, or **chromosomal anomalies,** are likely to produce abnormalities in the brain. For instance, in Down syndrome, a type of mental retardation, there are three #21 chromosomes instead of two.

Arranged linearly along the chromosomes are the **genes,** each of which occupies its own characteristic position or **locus.** Faulty genes, or genes that are defective in some way, can exist in the absence of obvious chromosomal deviations and may cause metabolic or biochemical abnormalities. Particular genes influence behavior through a long series of steps. Their influence may be modified by events that happen before and after birth, as well as by the actions of other genes. The basis for gene action is a complex substance, **deoxyribonucleic acid** (DNA), that is found in the chromosomes. The discovery that DNA is the means by which genetic information is transferred led to the discovery of how genes work.

Behavior is not inherited. What we receive from our parents are molecules of DNA. Your DNA may carry the blueprint for a strong, sturdy body, but this will not automatically make you an athlete. For example, your nutrition, the amount of exercise and training you get, and your motivation, as well as any illnesses or injuries you experience before or after your birth, will all influence how your genetic predisposition toward physical strength is expressed. Sometimes a specific gene is present that has been identified as causing a certain characteristic or disease, yet the person may show no sign of the problem or perhaps only mild symptoms. The term **penetrance** has been used to refer to the percentage of cases in which, if a specific gene is present, a particular trait, characteristic, or disease will actually manifest itself in the fully developed organism.

The extent to which genes affect behavior has been a subject of debate for at least the last two centuries. In the nineteenth century fierce battles were fought in what has come to be known as the nature–nurture controversy. Heredity (nature) and environment (nurture) were seen as separate and distinct forces that worked in an either/or fashion. Either nature determined a certain behavior, or nurture did; you couldn't have it both ways. More in line with reality, however, is the view that the interaction of many forces—in particular the interaction between the information carried by genes and that provided by the environment—determines behavioral patterns.

A young but rapidly developing field is **population genetics,** the study of the distribution of genes throughout groups of people who mate with each other. Such information is used in predicting the incidence of certain genetically carried disorders. (For example, Tay Sachs disease is a form of retardation that is caused by genes carried by some Jews whose ancestors came from a particular area of Europe.) Related to population genetics is **behavior genetics.** Research in this field involves breeding animals selectively and uncovering the effects of inbreeding on behavior patterns such as those related to emotionality and maze learning. Horse breeders who attempt to raise Derby winners by mating the fastest mare to the fastest stallion are essentially behavior geneticists.

Research on the effects of inheritance on human behavior usually takes one of two forms: analysis of family histories and twin studies. Pedigree and family tree studies begin with an individual who manifests a particular trait. His or her relatives are then assessed to see whether they have the same trait. When such an analysis is carried out over at least two generations, some inferences about family genetics can be drawn. Twin studies are a more direct way of studying the effects of heredity on behavior. **Monozygotic** (identical) twins have been compared with **dizygotic** (fraternal) twins with respect to a variety of behaviors. Because monozygotic twins develop from the same fertilized egg, they have identical genes and hence identical heredities. Dizygotic twins, on the other hand, are the products of two entirely different eggs. If monozygotic twins exhibit a particular behavior disorder more often than dizygotic twins do, the identical heredity of the monozygotic pair may be the important factor.

The degree of **concordance** in twin studies refers to the relationship between twins or other family members with respect to a given characteristic or trait. If both twins show the trait, the pair is described as concordant (see Figure 3–1). If they do not, the pair is described as discordant. For example, studies have shown that the concordance rate of schizophrenics is high for monozygotic twins and drops precipitously for dizygotic twins of the same sex. The drop is even greater for dizygotic twins of opposite sexes. The fact that the concordance rate is not 100 percent for monozygotic twins suggests that environmental influences play a role. Although there is a very strong suggestion of a genetic component in schizophrenia, we must not forget that experience can lessen or emphasize the effects of any hereditary tendency.

The latter point is illustrated by a study of a set of identical triplets, all of whom suffered from serious chronic disorders (McGuffin, and others, 1982). Two of the brothers had periods of auditory hallucinations and other clear schizophrenic symptoms. Between these periods they functioned at a low level and were unable to work. The third brother also had psychotic periods (although not as clearly schizophrenic), but he was able to function at a relatively high level and could hold a job

between his psychotic episodes. His IQ was higher than that of his brothers, and his relationship with his father was much less stormy than theirs. This case demonstrates that even when people have identical heredities, their levels of functioning may vary in important ways.

The Brain and Nervous System

The nervous system has two major divisions: the **central nervous system,** which includes all the nerve cells (neurons) of the brain and spinal cord, and the **peripheral nervous system,** which includes all the neurons connecting the central nervous system with the glands, muscles, and sensory receptors (see Figure 3–2). The peripheral nervous system also has two divisions; the **somatic system,** which transmits information from sense organs to the muscles responsible for voluntary movement, and the **autonomic system,** which directs the activity of the glands and internal organs.

The fundamental unit of the entire nervous system is the **neuron,** or nerve cell, which has a long extension called the **axon** and several shorter extensions called **dendrites.** The function of nerve cells is to transmit electrical impulses to other nerve cells and to structures outside the nervous system (such as muscles and glands). A typical nerve cell receives a messenger chemical, or **neurotransmitter,** from other nerve cells through specific receptor sites on its dendrites. It changes the chemical signal to an electrical signal and

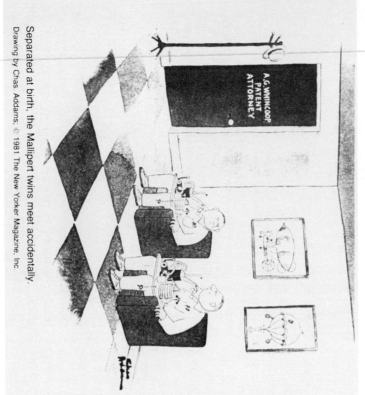

FIGURE 3–1

Some twins show a remarkable degree of concordance.

Separated at birth, the Mallipert twins meet accidentally.

Drawing by Chas. Addams; © 1981 The New Yorker Magazine, Inc.

A.G.WINNICOOP
PATENT
ATTORNEY

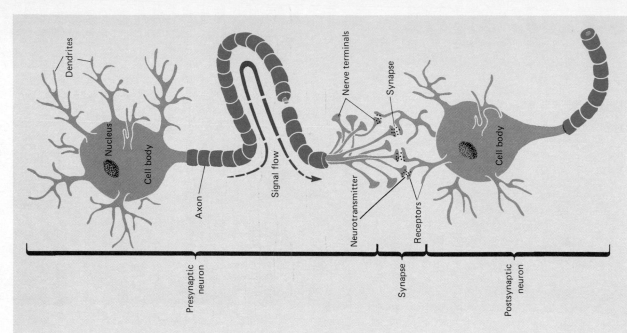

FIGURE 3–3

The relationship between a pair of typical neurons. A neuron consists of a cell body and two types of extensions—dendrites and an axon. Specific receptors or dendrites receive neurotransmitter molecules from the axons of adjacent neurons. This sets up an electrical impulse in the receiving neuron that is transmitted through the neuron at the nerve terminal at the tip of its axon. The arrival of the impulse at the nerve terminal causes the release of neurotransmitter molecules (shown by dots), which diffuse across a small gap (the synapse) to receptors on the dendrites of the next neuron. The process can be repeated many times to send signals throughout the brain and the rest of the nervous system.

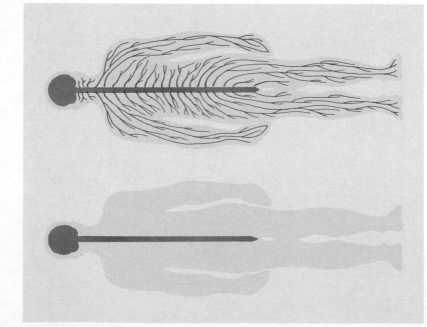

FIGURE 3–2

The central nervous system and the peripheral nervous system. The central nervous system (CNS) (left) consists of the brain, brain stem, and spinal cord; the peripheral nervous system (PNS) (right) includes all nerve fibers extending to and from the rest of the body. The CNS acts on the world through the PNS (a brain without a mouth cannot speak); it also learns about the world through the PNS (a brain without eyes cannot see).

sends it through the axon. When the electrical signal reaches the tip of the axon, the nerve cell releases molecules of neurotransmitters that pass through a tiny region called the **synapse** and are taken up by specific receptors on the dendrites of adjacent nerve cells. This process can be repeated many times to transmit signals throughout the nervous system (see Figure 3–3).

The brain is easily the most complex structure in the body (see Figure 3–4). Its two cerebral hemispheres are highly developed centers for processing sensory information. The **cerebral cortex,** the convoluted layer of gray matter that covers each hemisphere, controls our distinctively human behavior. The cortex has areas that monitor hearing, vision, body sensations, and other processes. Disturbances in specific parts of the brain (caused, for example, by tumors) will result in specific behavioral deficits (for example, loss of speech). Electrical stimulation of certain areas of the cerebral cortex also produces specific motor responses or sensory effects.

The brain and its neurons are active continuously. This activity occurs spontaneously as well as in response to external stimulation. The activity of nerve cells gen-

erates electrical energy, and the voltage differences between cells or regions can be amplified and measured as brain potentials. A record of these brain potentials, called an **electroencephalogram** (EEG), shows a pattern of brain waves. Researchers have found that most behavioral states have distinct brain wave patterns. For example, beta waves dominate during wakefulness, whereas theta and delta waves characterize deep sleep. Researchers have also been able to correlate brain wave patterns with psychological functions such as dreaming and attention, and with abnormalities caused by tumors or by the unusual electrical activity found in epilepsy (see Figure 3–5).

There is abundant evidence that various behavioral deficits result from defects in the central nervous system, but many questions remain unanswered. Frequently, neither the particular type of deficit nor the available information about possible organic damage is sufficiently clear-cut to permit a high degree of certainty about the causes of behavior. A person who experiences memory losses and thought disturbances may have fallen on his or her head, but the actual effects of the fall on brain tissue may not be obvious. In such a case, clinicians exercise caution in weighing the relative importance of organic damage and psychological factors. Full understanding of the brain's role in abnormal behavior will require extensive research on the interrelationships among psychological and biological processes.

The time and effort required for such research is illustrated by recent studies of the frontal lobes, the largest and most impressive parts of the brain. It is only natural to assume that such a large area would perform some important function. For many years it was assumed that the frontal lobes must be a "seat of intelligence." In recent years this view of the frontal lobes has been modified considerably. The frontal system now appears to be an important coordinator of emotion, volition, judgment, and creativity. A more refined charting of the functions of the frontal system is currently under way, and the results indicate that the frontal system may be quite important in major mental illnesses such as schizophrenia and affective disorders. For example, signs of damage to the frontal lobes have been noticed in schizophrenics. Much more research will be needed to determine whether some schizophrenics do indeed have defective frontal-lobe functioning or whether there is a breakdown in the communication between their frontal lobes and other important systems.

An important part of current brain research concerns recently identified systems within the brain. For example, work on the basic psychology and biology of motivation has resulted in the discovery of the brain reward system in higher animals. The brain reward system involves the hypothalamus and structures of the limbic system. The **limbic system** is part of the primitive, lower part of the cortex and is associated with emotional and motivational functions; the **hypothalamus,** located above the roof of the mouth, plays a role in motivation and emotions but also has connections with many other areas of the brain. Activation of the brain reward system by electrical stimulation produces an intense feeling of

pleasure that is much more powerful than ordinary reinforcers, such as food and sex. In experimental work with rats it has been found that if an electrode is implanted so that an animal can deliver a weak shock to its own brain reward system by pressing a lever (electrical self-stimulation), it will do so at a very fast rate. If the animal is starved and then given a choice between food and electrical self-stimulation, it will self-stimulate until it starves to death.

Early researchers who studied the brain reward system had no idea that their work might be related to addiction to substances like opium, but unexpected recent evidence is rapidly changing the situation. Researchers have discovered that there are chemical receptors on neurons in certain regions of the brain that respond to opiates. In fact, the greatest concentration of these opiate receptors is in the brain reward system. Moreover, the brain produces substances called **endor-**

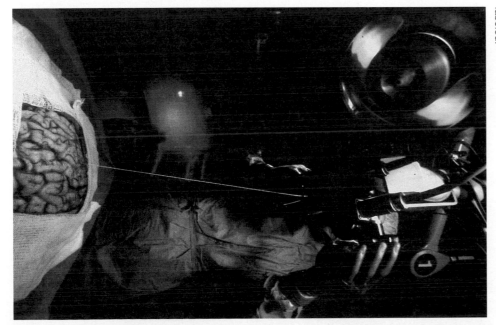

FIGURE 3–4a
The human brain. (a) View of exposed human brain during surgery. (b) The surface of the left hemisphere with major areas and their functions labeled. (c) A midline view of the right hemisphere with major areas/structures and their functions labeled.

FIGURE 3–4*b* and c

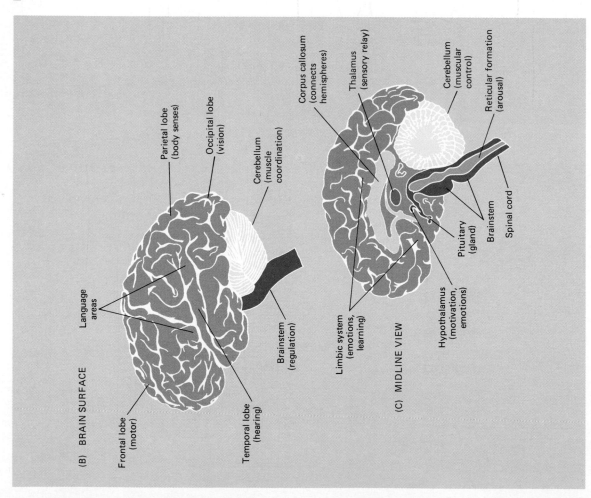

(B) BRAIN SURFACE

Language areas

Parietal lobe (body senses)

Occipital lobe (vision)

Cerebellum (muscle coordination)

Frontal lobe (motor)

Temporal lobe (hearing)

Brainstem (regulation)

Corpus callosum (connects hemispheres)

Thalamus (sensory relay)

Cerebellum (muscular control)

Reticular formation (arousal)

Limbic system (emotions, learning)

Hypothalamus (motivation, emotions)

Pituitary (gland)

Brainstem

Spinal cord

(C) MIDLINE VIEW

phins that activate these receptors; they are even more powerful analgesics (pain relievers) than opium and, when administered directly, are addictive.

The endorphins work like keys in a lock. They fit only into sites, or receptors, that are specifically designed to accept them. Because the endorphins are similar to opium and related chemicals, knowledge of how they work may lead to a better understanding of drug addiction and its treatment. There are, of course, equally important environmental, psychosocial, and personality factors that influence the actual addictive behaviors. If scientists can create nonaddictive chemicals that function like the opiates, they may be able to ease pain of all kinds, including the pain connected with stopping a heroin habit. Before this can happen, however, much more information about the brain reward system and endorphins is needed.

The Endocrines

Your body contains a marvelous system of glands and nerves which quickly organizes your heart, lungs, liver, kidneys, blood vessels, and bowels, causing them to work at top efficiency in an emergency (see Figure 3–6). And when the threat ends, that same glandular system calms everything down.

Several glands, including the pituitary, thyroid, adrenal, and gonadal (sex) glands, as well as the part of the pancreas that produces insulin, make up the endocrine system (Figure 3–7). These glands are ductless: the endocrines, unlike the salivary glands or tear glands, have no ducts for delivery of the substances they produce. Instead, they discharge those substances directly into the bloodstream, which carries them to all parts of the body. Hormones secreted by the endocrine glands

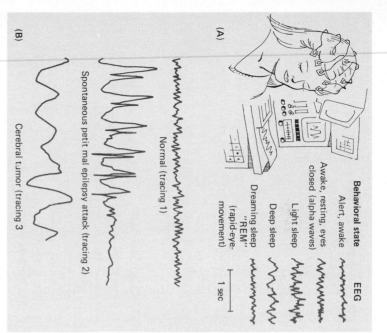

FIGURE 3–5
An EEG and three EEG tracings. (a) An electroencephalogram (EEG) uses scalp electrodes to measure the activity of specific types of neurons. Particular EEG patterns are associated with certain behavioral states as depicted here. (b) EEG tracings from patients who have different disorders are often visually distinguishable from one another and from those of normal subjects. Tracing 1 shows a normal EEG. Tracing 2 shows the onset of wave and spike discharges that are characteristic of petit mal epilepsy, a disorder in which sudden transitory disturbances of brain function may cause brief periods of loss of consciousness. Tracing 3 demonstrates the slow wave activity that is often associated with a cerebral tumor.

act as chemical messengers (the word "hormone" is derived from a Greek word meaning "messenger"). They correlate our reactions to external events and coordinate bodily growth and development.

Hormones are very potent, so it takes very little of them to exert an influence over their specific target cells. Cells that respond to hormones are genetically endowed with special surface molecules, or "receptors," that detect even very low hormone concentrations. Once these cells receive a hormone, they initiate a series of adjustments within the cell that are dictated by the hormone. Hormones will usually increase the cell's activity temporarily.

In the study of abnormal psychology there is particular interest in the role played by the endocrine glands in dealing with stress. The word **stressor** is often used to refer to a condition that makes it harder to achieve or maintain biological and psychological adaptation. Examples of stressors to which the endocrine

FIGURE 3–6
As you walk down the street, a large, ferocious dog suddenly jumps from behind a bush and directly in your path. Your heart begins thumping wildly. Your blood pressure peaks. Your body mobilizes its energy resources. You are ready to stand firm and do battle or to flee—ready for fight or flight. Of course, your brain acts first. The brain acts as a switchboard between your mental and physical life. By releasing hormones to travel to distant organs, your brain translates your emotional upsets into physical responses—a rapid heartbeat, a stomachache, inflamed intestines. Through your senses, generally your eyes, the brain recognizes the dog as a threat, sizes up the danger, and then releases chemicals to trigger the complex web of glands posted throughout your body. The glands pour out more chemicals—messengers that start the other organs working at top speed.

glands respond are biological factors such as disease germs and psychological experiences such as receiving an insult or engaging in combat. The hormones secreted by the glands help us mobilize our physical resources to deal with stressors by fighting or escaping.

The stress response involves the pituitary gland and the part of the adrenal gland called the **adrenal cortex**. In times of stress the brain is activated and sends messages to one of its structures, the hypothalamus, which is close to the pituitary gland. The hypothalamus releases a substance called **corticotrophin-releasing factor** (CRF), which goes to the pituitary to form and release another chemical, **adrenocortico-trophic hor-**

biological defects, and research on the connection between biochemical factors and depression. In the triplet study, the fact that the three brothers showed important differences in behavior, intelligence, and social adaptation serves as a stimulus for further research aimed at identifying variables that might account for the differences among people who have identical genes.

The other line of biological research has a therapeutic orientation. Drug studies illustrate this approach. Although the pill that will cure mental illness, like the process that will turn lead into gold, has not yet been invented, great strides are being made in biological therapies.

Psychoimmunology: A Search for Causes

Fred Jackson, a 50-year-old divorced high school teacher, had had a series of infections and fevers, swollen lymph nodes, and a nagging cough ever since his high-school-age daughter had died four years previously. Recently he had experienced severe respiratory difficulties, as a result of which he had been hospitalized. The three months prior to the hospitalization had been particularly stressful because of disagreements with the school principal, who seemed always to be annoyed with him. While he was in the hospital, treatment with antibiotics resulted in some symptomatic improvement, but he continued to feel weak and the lymph node swelling persisted. A lymph node biopsy showed the existence of a cancerous condition. His physician was not sure whether it was related to Jackson's physical condition, but the doctor concluded, after several conversations with his patient, that Jackson had not yet gotten over his daughter's death. Jackson seemed to work very hard at denying his grief over the daughter's death. He never expressed the feelings that the doctor felt would be normal under the circumstances.

Many physicians have noted associations between significant losses, like a daughter's death, and subsequent illness. The association often seems greatest when the person experiencing the loss is unable to express strong emotions, for example, the grief that normally accompanies personal tragedies. Cases like Jackson's have led researchers to the hypothesis that the stress evoked by major losses and separations disrupts the body's immune system and thereby contributes to a host of physical illnesses.

The immune system has two major tasks: recognition of foreign materials (called **antigens**), and inactivation and/or removal of these materials. The immune system influences a person's susceptibility to the course of a disease. It consists of several distinct groups of cells called **lymphocytes**. Recent research has provided a preliminary understanding of how stress and emotional fac-

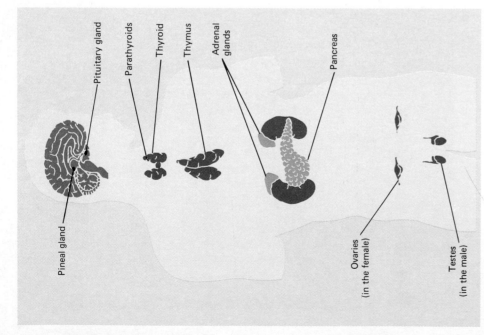

Pineal gland

Pituitary gland

Parathyroids

Thyroid

Thymus

Adrenal glands

Pancreas

Ovaries (in the female)

Testes (in the male)

FIGURE 3–7
The endocrine glands and their location in the body.

mone (ACTH). ACTH is released into the bloodstream and can go directly to the adrenal cortex, where it causes the adrenal cortex to form and release **adrenal corticosteroids**, which affect the brain's and the body's response to mental and physical stress. Some researchers have used the level of these steroids as an indicator of the degree of stress experienced by the individual.

Research on Biological Factors and Abnormal Behavior

The enormous growth in knowledge about biological processes has strengthened beliefs concerning their relationship to abnormal behavior and has stimulated two promising lines of research. In one, an effort is made to determine the causal role of biological factors in maladaptation. The study of identical triplets mentioned earlier illustrates this approach, as does research on certain forms of mental retardation that are clearly related to

tors lead to hormonal changes that can sometimes decrease the efficiency of the immune system and thus increase susceptibility to disease.

The first demonstration of a relationship between bereavement and alterations in the functioning of the immune system was a study of 26 surviving spouses of patients who either had been fatally injured or had died after a prolonged illness (Bartrop and others, 1977). Although the effects were not large, the evidence suggested diminished immune system functioning among the survivors. Subsequent research has shown that bereavement associated with the death of a spouse is associated with a suppression of immunity and that the absence of a supportive social network contributes to suppression of the immune system (Stein, Schleifer, and Keller, 1987). Furthermore, certain psychological states, such as loneliness, depression, and feelings of helplessness, have a negative impact on the immune system. In this connection it is noteworthy that Jackson's divorce had occurred a year before his daughter's death. The divorce had greatly restricted his social network. He had fewer contacts with other people and lacked social relationships that made it easy for him to express his grief, loneliness, and anger at the terrible things that had happened to him.

Psychoimmunology is a new field of study that links psychological and immunological events. While much research in this field involves the relationship between experimentally created stress and the immune systems of animals, increasing emphasis is being placed on studies of humans. There is reason to believe that behavioral factors can alter immunity and susceptibility to disease through direct central nervous system mechanisms and disruptions in the way the endocrine system functions. The challenge facing psychoimmunologists is to specify the mechanisms involved in the process that begins with a major stressful life event and ends with disease and perhaps even death.

The search for psychological factors in the onset of cancer has focused increased attention on the immune system. One difficulty in studying the development of cancer is that it occurs over a relatively long period; consequently, patients are not studied until clinical symptoms are evident. However, studies have suggested that the loss of a close and important person is associated with reduced immune competence, which contributes to the onset of cancer (Laudenslager and Reite, 1984). These results are reinforced by the finding that lack of social support or close interpersonal ties is also associated with the occurrence of cancer. In one study, almost 1,000 medical students were interviewed and then their medical records were monitored for 10 to 15 years (Thomas and Duszynski, 1974). Those who originally reported that they had few family ties were the most likely to have developed cancer during the 15-year period. Stress in general appears to be involved in the development of cancer, and lack of social support is associated with greater stress impact.

Psychopharmacology

For many years chemicals have been known to influence behavior—for example, to reduce pain and induce sleep. Only in recent years have chemicals been used extensively in treating maladaptive behavior. Several kinds of psychoactive drugs (antipsychotic, antianxiety, and antidepressant drugs) are often highly effective in reducing particular types of maladaptive behavior. Figure 3-8 illustrates how the use of antipsychotic drugs allows many individuals to be treated as outpatients instead of during long stays in mental hospitals.

Psychopharmacology is the study of the effects of drugs on behavior. This fast-growing area of investigation requires the skills of the chemist, physiologist, and psychologist. Psychopharmacologists study five major types of drugs. Some of these are therapeutic agents and others are important because of the social and health problems arising from their illegal use. In addition to the three types of psychoactive drugs already mentioned, psychopharmacologists study substances that have pain-relieving properties (such as opium) or that influence perceptual processes (such as LSD). These drugs do not create new responses in the organism; they simply modify processes that are already going on. They exert their effects by blocking or modifying certain bio-

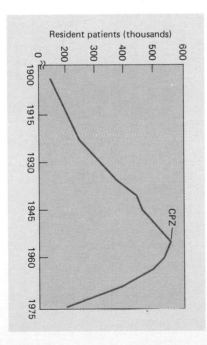

FIGURE 3–8

The introduction of antipsychotic drugs resulted in a sharp decline in the number of patients in mental hospitals. This figure shows the number of resident patients in state and county mental hospitals before and after the introduction of chlorpromazine (CPZ), a drug that is particularly effective in treating schizophrenia. Prior to the introduction of the antipsychotic drugs, there had been a steady increase in the number of hospitalized mental patients. The use of those drugs has greatly reduced and even eliminated hospital stays for many individuals. (Based on data from National Institute of Mental Health)

chemical and physiological processes, particularly those involved in neural transmission within the brain.

Integration of Biological and Psychological Systems

The biological perspective has proven fruitful because of the therapies, such as drugs, that it has produced, and also because of the questions it has raised. If the bizarre behavior of schizophrenics can be muted or eliminated by certain chemical compounds, can schizophrenia be regarded merely as a sign of a specific chemical disorder in the nervous system? Unfortunately, this sort of question can almost never be answered in a true-or-false fashion. For example, there are also instances in which purely psychological treatment of schizophrenics has led to marked reductions in bizarre behavior.

To what degree can maladaptive behavior be viewed as a disease? The boundaries between health and disease are far from clear, partly because of the roles played by psychological, social, and cultural factors. Given the multiple factors that affect people, an extreme organic perspective is likely to be simplistic. More likely to stand the test of time is a model that views maladaptive behavior as a product of these interacting factors. Although it does not provide a final answer, the biological perspective has enhanced our understanding of one of these sets of factors.

Virtually all fields of science and technology are marked by progressively increasing levels of specialization. This means that some people have much deeper knowledge about particular problems than others. As researchers involve themselves in the complexities of specific areas, they may tend to lose sight of the relationship of "their" topic to other topics.

The need for an integrated view of biological systems is illustrated by the endocrine glands. Traditionally, the endocrine system was viewed as separate from the nervous system but parallel to it in its activities. The traditional view also held the pituitary to be the "master gland" of the endocrine system. However, research has shown that certain pituitary cells are themselves subject to control by the hypothalamus in the brain. Specific neurons exert potent control over the pituitary. Thus, the brain in general, and the hypothalamus in particular, is the real "master gland" of the endocrine system. Awareness of the entire process by which the brain integrates the needs of the body with the demands of the environment has led to greater emphasis on neuroendocrine functions.

The organism behaves as an integrated unit. Exactly how the integration is achieved is an important but difficult question to answer. In an organism as complex as a human being, everything is related to everything else. These interrelationships extend beyond purely biological systems; each system enters into relationships with the behavioral and mental spheres of life, and those are not always one-way relationships. The amounts of certain chemicals in our bodies influence how much we are in contact with reality and how happy or sad we feel. However, our experiences and psychological reactions seem to influence how our immune system functions. An important goal in the study of the relationships between bodily systems and behaviors is to develop a theoretical framework that encompasses all of these types of relationships.

From the standpoint of abnormal psychology, it is important to relate biological processes to maladaptive behavior. Theories about these relationships range from those that reject the importance of the relationship for most disorders, to those that see value in exploring them but do not draw many firm conclusions, to those that argue that mental illnesses are diseases in the same sense as cancer or high blood pressure. However, there is growing evidence that cancer and high blood pressure are not pure illustrations of physically caused conditions. Most diseases are probably caused by multiple determinants, including physical, environmental, psychological, and hereditary factors. Disentangling these various kinds of causes from one another can be a difficult scientific problem.

It is clear that mental illness has multiple causes, and that these, like cancer and high blood pressure, are only partially understood. The biological perspective implies that many types of abnormal behavior are due largely to factors beyond people's control—that they are due primarily to the type of brain and body people are born with and the environment in which they are nourished. While this point of view may seem extremely deterministic, it is not totally so. Most theorists recognize that, to varying degrees, biological systems have plasticity. For example, the brain has built into it the ability to adapt and change in response to injury or changes in the environment. The limits that biological processes place on behavior and the degree to which those processes can be influenced represent topics of current research and theory.

The Psychodynamic Perspective

The psychodynamic perspective is based on the idea that thoughts and emotions are important causes of behavior. Sigmund Freud, the originator of this perspective, believed that eventually all behavior could be explained by bodily changes; however, because so little was known about the relationships between the body and the personality, he actually gave biological factors little emphasis. Most of his followers also have paid little attention to biology and have not thought of it as an important factor in the development of behavioral problems.

Psychodynamic approaches to behavior assume that, to varying degrees, observable behavior (overt responses) is a function of intrapsychic processes (covert events). Not all psychodynamic theorists emphasize the same inner events and the same sources of environmental stimulation, but they do agree that personality is shaped by a combination of inner and outer events, with emphasis on the inner ones.

Because thoughts and feelings are not directly observable, psychodynamic theorists must infer them. They relate their inferences about inner processes to important features of overt behavior. The following account by a psychotherapist illustrates how this is done:

By the fourth session I realized that he had never mentioned his father. It seemed as if there wasn't and never had been a father. I asked myself: How could it be that this man who is so unhappy and so many problems fails to even mention his father? I guessed that he was either so ashamed of his father that he couldn't talk about him or he harbored so much anger toward him that consciously or unconsciously he couldn't deal with it. I decided to wait and see what would happen rather than push the client in the direction of talking about something that was very sensitive for him.

During the ninth session he told me about a dream he had had the night before. A large dark man sat at a table and a small child watched from a corner as the man ate great quantities of food and ordered a small, frightened woman to bring him more and more. After he ate each helping he would raise a gun and shoot down a few people who were standing in a row against the wall.

The client reported how frightened he had felt during the dream. As we discussed his associations to the dream, it became clear to me that the man in the dream represented his father. After several more sessions he told me he felt very angry with me because I constantly told him what to do and verbally cut him down. After pointing out that in reality I had said almost nothing, I asked him if I seemed like the man in the dream. Finally the dike burst. For the rest of the session and the next one all of his seething hatred toward his father came out. He blurted out that when he was a child he had seen his father strike his mother several times. When he saw this happen, he had wanted to kill his father.

Apart from the contribution that psychodynamic theories have made to our understanding of human behavior, they seem especially influential because they are the systems out of which all types of psychotherapy developed. While clinical psychoanalysis as originated by Freud is infrequently used today, its basic elements and the theory of mental events underlying it have greatly influenced the development of the entire field of psychotherapy.

Freud and Psychoanalysis

Sigmund Freud, a Viennese neurologist, is clearly one of the most influential writers of this century, admired for his wit, intellect, and willingness to revise and improve his theories as his clinical experience grew. Freud began his practice at a time when there were few effective forms of treatment in most fields of medicine (see Figure 3–9). Effective treatment generally depends on an understanding of the causes of a disorder, and at that time, although accurate diagnoses could sometimes be made, little was known about the causes of disease, whether physical or mental. A disorder that was particularly common during the late 1800s was hysteria, the presence of physical problems in the absence of any physical causes. Like other well-trained neurologists of his time, Freud originally used hypnosis to help his hysterical patients loose their symptoms. Then a friend, Joseph Breuer, told Freud that while under hypnosis one of his patients had recalled and understood the emotional experience that had led to the development of her symptoms, and that her symptoms had then disappeared. For a time Freud and Breuer used this method of recapturing memories with some success. However, because some patients were not easy to hypnotize and sometimes the positive effects did not last long, Freud began to develop his method of psychoanalysis, in which the patient recaptures forgotten memories without the use of hypnosis.

Freud's Theories of Personality

Freud's theories of personality seem complicated because they incorporate many interlocking factors, but two basic assumptions underlie them all; psychic determinism and the conscious–unconscious dimension.

The principle of **psychic determinism** states that all behavior, whether overt (a muscle movement) or covert (a thought), is caused or determined by prior mental events. The outside world and the private psychic life of the individual combine to determine all aspects of behavior. As a clinical practitioner, Freud

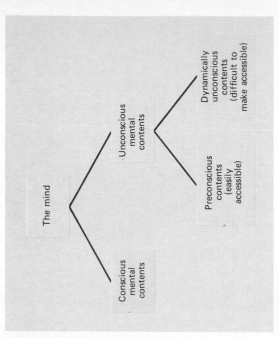

FIGURE 3–10
Freud's model of the mind. He viewed the mind as having conscious and unconscious portions. Material in the unconscious portion varies in the ease with which it can be brought to consciousness.

Freud was especially intrigued by thoughts and fantasies that seem to go underground but then reappear at the conscious level. He asserted that the level of intrapsychic conflict was a major factor in determining our awareness of particular mental events. According to Freud, the classic example of intrapsychic conflict results when a young boy desires to take his father's place in relation to his mother but at the same time feels love and affection for his father. Freud believed that the greater the degree of intrapsychic conflict, the greater the likelihood that the mental events connected with it would remain unconscious. The more massive the unconscious conflict, the greater the person's vulnerability to stress. Freud believed that behavior disorders that occur after childhood are caused by a combination of early traumatic experiences and later experiences which trigger the emotions and unresolved conflicts associated with the early events.

Freud contended that hidden impulses or drives are involved in human conflict. He referred to these drives as **libido** and believed that they were a form of psychic energy analogous to the individual's supply of physical energy. Just as some people are more athletic, some have stronger libido. Freud also believed that the psychic energy or drive level of the individual sets up an inner state of tension that must somehow be reduced. In general, libido can be seen as desire for pleasure, particularly sexual gratification.

One novel feature of Freud's theory was his emphasis on sexuality. This emphasis was no doubt related to the often prudish, repressive atmosphere of Vienna at that time. The concept of sexuality within psychoanalytic theory is very broad and, rather than referring

FIGURE 3–9
Sigmund Freud and his future wife, Martha Bernays, in September of 1885. Freud, a promising physician, had not yet begun his psychoanalytic inquiries. At the time that the photograph was taken, he was experimenting with cocaine. After taking repeated small doses of cocaine, Freud found that it was able to relieve depression as well as stimulate his capacity for concentrated work. He wrote an article in which he recommended the use of the drug as a stimulant, as a local anesthetic, and as a means of withdrawal from morphine addiction. Although these ideas seemed useful at the time, today we know more about the problems and serious consequences associated with cocaine use.

sought to modify unwanted behavior by identifying and eliminating its psychic determinants.

Freud assumed that mental events such as thoughts and fantasies vary in the ease with which they come to the individual's awareness. For example, aspects of mental life that are currently in awareness are **conscious.** Mental contents that are not currently at the level of awareness but can reach awareness fairly easily are **preconscious.** Mental contents that can be brought to awareness only with great difficulty are **unconscious.** Freud was interested mainly in how these unconscious mental contents could influence overt behavior (see Figure 3–10).

orily to sexual intimacy, can be equated with the individual's total quest for pleasure and gratification. Freud also saw the process of development as being expressed in sexual terms.

Stages of Psychosexual Development

Freud's theory of personality development placed tremendous emphasis on the effects of experiences that occur during the first five years of life. During this period children pass through a number of stages during which their libido is focused on a series of pleasure-giving or erogenous zones in the body. Those zones are the mouth, the anus, and the genitals, resulting in the **oral, anal, and phallic psychosexual stages.** In the phallic period, which occurs at about age 3, the child's pleasure in touching his or her genitals is accompanied by fantasies related to the sexual and aggressive impulses the child feels toward his or her parents. The child then enters a more or less sexually inactive latency period, which lasts until adolescence, when the sexual impulses are once again activated. If all has gone well to this point, the individual reaches the **genital stage,** in which pleasure comes from a mature heterosexual relationship.

What happens to children during these psychosexual stages helps mold their adult personalities. If they are unsuccessful in resolving the psychosexual conflicts that accompany a given stage or are severely deprived or overindulged, they may become fixated at one stage or another. **Fixation** is an arrest in personal development caused by the unresolved difficulties experienced at a given stage. Moreover, even if people resolve their conflicts successfully, severe difficulties later in life may cause them to **regress,** or adopt some of the feelings or behavior of earlier, more satisfying stages.

In well-socialized adults the self-centered sexuality of earlier psychosexual stages blossoms into mature love and the individual becomes capable of genuine caring and adult sexual satisfaction. Freud's ideas about psychosexual development are undoubtedly the most controversial aspect of his theory. Although many theorists agree that childhood experiences are very important in personality development, many of them reject Freud's assertions about childhood sexuality.

The Psychic Apparatus

For Freud, the mental world of the individual is divided into three structures: the **id,** the **ego,** and the **superego.** A basic distinction is made between the ego and the id. The id is a completely unorganized reservoir of psychic energy. The ego, on the other hand, is a problem-solving agent. Whereas the id is concerned simply with maximizing pleasure, the ego's efforts are directed toward maximizing pleasure within the constraints of reality. The id says, "I want it now." The ego says, "Okay, but first we have to do our homework" or "No, that's illegal." The ego performs the valuable functions of avoiding danger or coping with it when avoidance is not possible. There are three major sources of danger for the individual: the environment, his or her id impulses, and guilt. Guilt comes from the third structure of the psychic apparatus, the superego, which represents the person's moral code and reflects social values as expressed by parents, schools, and so on. The superego uses guilt to keep the id in line. The superego might say, "You know that's wrong" or "Work is more important than pleasure" (see Figure 3–11).

In early infancy the id is in control of all phases of behavior. Freud described the thought processes of the infant as **primary process thinking,** or thinking that is characterized by inability to discriminate between the real and the unreal, between the "me" and the "nonme," as well as by inability to inhibit impulses. Primary process thinking reflects uninhibited adherence to the **pleasure principle**—the immediate satisfaction of needs and desires without regard for the requirements of reality. The desire for immediate gratification that characterizes primary process thinking is dominant in childhood. Thus, most children, when given a piece of candy, eat it immediately, whereas an adult might wait until after lunch. A child who can't get immediate gratification often shifts its goal in order to achieve gratification in some other way. Thus, a baby that is crying for its bottle may gratify itself at least temporarily by sucking vigorously on its thumb.

Secondary process thinking is characteristic of older children and adults and is dependent on the development of the ego. The adult has learned to wait for gratification. Saving money for a goal—a new stereo system, a nest egg for old age—rather than going out for an expensive dinner on payday would be an example. The adult is also less likely than the child to substitute another object for gratification. An adult will generally keep working for the originally desired object even if setbacks occur.

Primary process thinking is still found in adults. It can be seen in cartoons, in dreams, in the parent who feels better after coming home and hitting the children because her boss criticized her on the job, and in the person who eats a pint of ice cream out of the container right in front of the refrigerator. However, maladaptation is considered to exist only when the primary process plays an overriding role in the adult's behavior.

Anxiety

Freud defined **anxiety** as a response to perceived danger or stress. He distinguished between two kinds of anxiety-provoking situations. In one, of which birth might be the best example, anxiety is caused by stimulation that exceeds the organism's capacity to handle it. In the other, Freud assumed that psychic energy (libido) ac-

IN A QUANDARY

FIGURE 3–11

The id, ego, and superego can give very different messages. See if you can identify which is the source of each message in this cartoon. The answers are at the bottom. (*New Yorker* magazine)

Answers: a, c b q id p superego b ego

cumulates if inhibitions and taboos keep it from being expressed. This accumulated energy may build up to the point where it may overwhelm the controls of the ego. When this happens, a panic or traumatic state results. Psychoanalysts believe that these traumatic states are likely to occur in infants and children who do not know how to cope with much of their environment.

Anxiety often arises in anticipation of danger rather than after a dangerous situation has actually occurred. Anxiety, like physical pain, thus serves a protective function by signaling the approach of danger and warning us to prepare our defenses. Anxiety can also indicate inability to cope with danger. The meaning of anxiety is a central problem of psychoanalysis.

Defense Mechanisms

Freud believed that the ego was not helpless in the face of the demands of the id, the outside world, and the superego. Anxiety alerts the individual to danger, such as the presence of an intense unconscious conflict or unacceptable wish. If this anxiety cannot be managed by direct action, so that the wish can be gratified, the ego

initiates unconscious defenses in order to ward off awareness of the conflict. A variety of defensive responses to perceived danger are possible. Since everyone experiences danger, the use of these responses, called **defense mechanisms,** clearly is not a special characteristic of maladaptive behavior. Defense mechanisms are used by all people, either singly or in combination, at one time or another. The level of adaptive behavior depends on the repertory of defenses available to the individual under study.

Freud never cataloged all the defense mechanisms, but he recognized that his use of repression as an all-encompassing concept needed clarification. In 1936 he focused on this need: "There are an extraordinarily large number of methods (or mechanisms, as we say) used by our ego in the discharge of its defensive functions. My daughter, the child analyst, is writing a book about them" (S. Freud (1936), 1964, p. 245). Shortly afterward, his daughter, Anna Freud, published her book, *The Ego and the Mechanisms of Defense.* There she defined and illustrated most of the defense mechanisms that are still referred to today (see Figure 3–12). Later in her

FIGURE 3–12
Anna Freud (1895–1982) made several contributions to psychoanalysis. In addition to her writings on defense mechanisms, she pioneered in adapting psychoanalysis for the treatment of children and the use of psychoanalytic concepts in child-rearing and education. She is shown here addressing a meeting at the Sorbonne, in Paris.

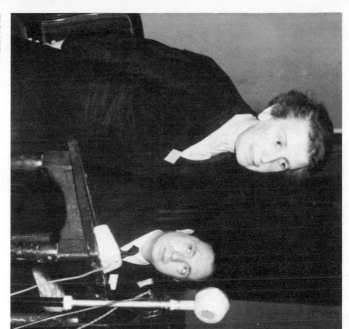

life, Anna Freud described her ideas about the role of defense mechanisms in this way:

> When I speak of successful defense I look at it from the point of view of the ego. If the ego defends itself successfully, it means that it achieves the aim of not allowing the forbidden impulse to enter into consciousness and that it does away with the anxiety connected with it and escapes unpleasure of any kind. That is a successful defense, although it may also have disastrous consequences for health and for later development. But from the point of view of defending oneself it is successful. You know, if somebody attacks you and you kill that person, the defense has been immensely successful, but it may not be approved of and have very disagreeable consequences. It all depends on your viewpoint. That is what I had in mind. (Sandler and Freud, 1985, p. 194)

The most important and basic of the defense mechanisms is **repression**. Freud called it the cornerstone on which psychoanalysis rests. Repression, like other defenses, is directed at both external dangers, such as fear-arousing events, and internal dangers, such as wishes, impulses, and emotions that cry out for gratification but arouse guilt. Repression reduces anxiety by keeping anxiety-laden thoughts and impulses out of the person's consciousness. Thus, a boy who experiences sexual desire for his mother and fear of retaliatory castration by his father could repress (render unconscious) both his unacceptable desire and his fear. The effort required to achieve such repression sometimes makes other behavior less effective. The person is, in a sense, preoccupied with the effort to maintain the repression. Sometimes repressed thoughts and wishes leak out and are expressed indirectly.

Repression is often described as motivated forgetting. It is necessary to distinguish between two kinds of forgetting: forgetting neutral mental content such as an unimportant telephone number is not the same as forgetting a traumatic childhood experience. Psychoanalysts are not nearly as interested in neutral material as they are in personally significant events. For instance, a recent college graduate may forget to go for a job interview if she is afraid that she will fail and not be hired, or a man may forget to attend the wedding of his brother to a woman that he himself was attracted to. In each case, the forgetting is real. The person is not making an excuse but actually is unaware of the engagement at the time. Table 3–1 lists some other defense mechanisms.

Clinical Psychoanalysis

Psychoanalysis is both a theoretical perspective and a clinical technique. As a clinical technique, it takes time. One of its conditions usually is that both patient and analyst make a commitment to the process for an indefinite period. Freud believes that much unhappiness and ineffectiveness are caused by forgotten conflicts that occurred long ago. Many a psychoanalyst has commented that a lifetime of difficulty cannot be straightened out in a few months.

Today most psychoanalysts are physicians who receive special training in the field of psychiatry and even more specialized analytic training. Some people without medical training, including psychologists, are also qualified to do psychoanalysis. All psychoanalysts believe that the roots of maladaptive behavior may be found in early childhood experiences and in infantile thoughts and feelings that persist into later life. They believe that insight into what went on in childhood enables the individual to adopt more mature and effective ways of living a happier, more productive adult life.

Many of Freud's ideas emerged from his studies of the dreams, fantasies, and memories of his patients. He developed the technique of **free association**, which calls for patients to express their thoughts and feelings as freely as possible during psychotherapy. With censorship (defense) reduced in this way, Freud hoped to gain a clearer picture of the conflicts underlying maladaptive

TABLE 3–1

Some Defense Mechanisms Used in Addition to Repression

Freud mentioned a number of defense mechanisms but he devoted most of his attention to repression as an all-inclusive defense. His daughter, Anna Freud, defined most of the concepts we refer to today as defense mechanisms.

DISPLACEMENT

A shift of feelings and attitudes from one object to another, more acceptable substitute.

Examples:

A man is criticized by his boss and then feels angry. He comes home and yells at his wife (yelling at the boss might be too dangerous).

A young girl feels sexually attracted to her older brother. She finds a person in her office who has the same dry sense of humor and curly hair as her brother and quickly becomes very attracted to him.

INTELLECTUALIZATION

Dealing with problems as interesting events which can be explained rationally and which have no anxiety or emotional content attached to them.

Examples:

A woman whose husband has just died discusses the inadequacy of America's mourning rituals, rather than her anger at her husband for leaving her.

A man who has just seen a bank robbery in which five people near him were gunned down talks about how interesting it was to observe the variety of ways that the people present reacted to the murders.

REACTION FORMATION

Expressing an unacceptable impulse by transforming it into its opposite.

Examples:

A person who is attracted by the excitement and brutality of war becomes an overly zealous pacifist.

A mother who feels angry and rejecting toward her child checks many times to see if the child is all right during the night and worries excessively about her safety on the way to and from school.

DENIAL

Refusal to acknowledge the anxiety-arousing aspects of the environment. The denial may be related only to the emotions connected to an idea or event or it may involve failure to acknowledge the event itself. Denial is most often seen in psychosis. It is seen in adults only under very severe stress.

Examples:

A husband, when told that his wife has incurable cancer, remains convinced that she will recover.

A student who has to take a final exam on material she doesn't understand, tells herself the exam is really not important and goes to a movie instead of studying the material with which she is having trouble.

IDENTIFICATION WITH THE AGGRESSOR

Adopting the traits or mannerisms of a feared person.

Examples:

A child who is afraid of his father takes on certain of his characteristics.

A member of the American Nazi Party who was the son of a concentration camp survivor.

PROJECTION

Characteristics or impulses that arouse anxiety are externalized by attributing them to others. Psychotics are particularly likely to use projection.

Examples:

Nazis in Germany who started World War II insisted that they did so because of aggressive threats from other countries.

A man who has a strong desire to have extramarital affairs but feels guilty about it constantly accuses his wife of being unfaithful to him even though he has no evidence.

REGRESSION

Going back to earlier ways of behaving that were characteristic of a previous development level. Typical of people who go to pieces under stress.

Examples:

A wife goes home to her mother every time she and her husband have a quarrel.

A student consoles himself, whenever things get rough, with several hot fudge sundaes, repeating behavior learned when his mother gave him ice cream to make him feel better after a scraped elbow or a disappointment.

SUBLIMATION

A socially useful course of action developed when more direct forms of gratification are blocked.

Examples:

A teenager with strong aggressive feelings expresses them without danger by becoming a football player.

Someone with strong erotic feelings expresses them in a socially approved way by becoming a painter of exotic nudes.

behavior. As his work proceeded, it occurred to him that dreams might provide evidence about the workings of unconscious impulses. Clinical psychoanalysis places great weight on the interpretation of dreams and other types of fantasy and their relationship to thought and behavior (see Figure 3–13).

Psychotherapists agree that not all cases of maladaptive behavior are suitable for psychoanalysis. There are several reasons why psychoanalysis might not be recommended. For example, a person might not have adequate financial resources to pay for the many sessions needed, or might lack the necessary intellectual resources, particularly the verbal skill to engage in the required level of communication. Freud believed that the most severe mental disorders, psychoses, could not be treated successfully with psychoanalysis. In addition, some analysts believe that people over the age of 40 lack sufficient flexibility for major personality change, and some personal problems are of such pressing urgency that there is not enough time to complete a lengthy psychoanalysis.

The Neo-Freudians

Theorists who follow Freud in general terms but disagree with certain of his ideas are often called **neo-Freudians** or neo-analysts because they have sought to revise most of Freud's basic ideas. Among the early neo-Freudians were Carl Jung (1875–1961) and Alfred Adler (1870–1937), both of whom were originally members of Freud's inner circle of supporters. Both men had much more optimistic conceptions of human nature

than Freud did. Jung did not think that all behavior is determined by earlier events. His emphasis on the need to emphasize spiritual qualities as well as rational ideas and his interest in Eastern religious thought have made him popular with many people today. Adler believed that people could be changed for the better through the creation of social conditions designed to develop realistic and adaptive lifestyles. For example, children have to be helped to overcome the inferiority that they naturally feel in comparison to adults. Consequently, Adler attached great importance to training parents in effective child-rearing techniques, and to the early education of children. He was a strong believer in the need to prevent psychological disorders rather than simply treat them after they occur.

Erik Erikson (b. 1902) is a central figure in contemporary psychoanalytic theory. His theory is a psychosocial one that emphasizes the "mutual fit between the individual and environment—that is, of the individual's capacity to relate to an ever-changing life space of people and institutions, on the one hand, and, on the other, the readiness of these people and institutions to make him part of an ongoing cultural concern" (Erikson, 1975, p. 102). Erikson stresses the role Freud assigned to the ego, but he gives it additional qualities such as the needs for trust and hope, industry, intimacy and love, and integrity. He thinks of the ego as a strong creative force that can deal effectively with problems.

Of special interest to psychologists is Erikson's idea of stages of development. Unlike Freud, who believed that development was essentially completed early in life, Erikson sees development as a lifelong process

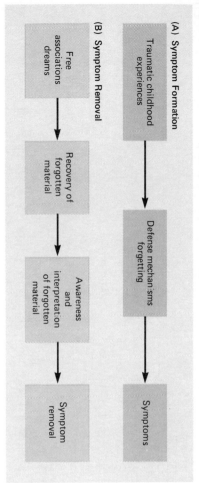

FIGURE 3-13

Processes hypothesized by Freud to be involved in symptom formation and removal. Symptoms (abnormal behavior, worries, unhappiness) result from traumatic childhood experiences that are defended against and forgotten but continue to exert unconscious influences that distort behavior, thought, and emotions. In the accepting, benign atmosphere of the psychoanalytic session, clues to the forgotten material come to the fore and are interpreted. Realization of the infantile quality of the forgotten material permits the individual to give up the symptoms.

(A) Symptom Formation

Traumatic childhood experiences → Defense mechanisms forgetting → Symptoms

(B) Symptom Removal

Free associations dreams → Recovery of forgotten material → Awareness and interpretation of forgotten material → Symptom removal

consisting of eight stages. The first four stages occur during infancy and childhood, the fifth during adolescence, and the last three during adulthood and old age.

The neo-Freudians helped broaden the perspectives of psychodynamic theory, particularly through their emphasis on the role of distorted interpersonal relationships in maladaptive behavior. They insisted that disordered behavior and thought must be viewed as outgrowths of the individual's efforts to cope with personal crises in a world peopled by others. The neo-Freudians deemphasized the role of biology in personality and instead looked to the social environment for explanations of maladaptive behavior.

Evaluating Psychoanalytic Theory

Psychoanalytic theory contains many ideas about the nature of perception and thought, human development, psychopathology, and treatment. However, its formulations are difficult to study scientifically because the events they hypothesize are not directly observable. Because psychoanalytic theory contains many general and somewhat unclearly defined concepts, it is hard to evaluate objectively. It seems to be better at explaining what has already happened than at predicting future events.

Because psychoanalytic concepts are difficult to prove experimentally, some researchers have tended to reject them out-of-hand. Others recognize that certain psychoanalytic concepts are vaguely stated and in fact untestable, but nevertheless they feel that scientific investigations should be conducted whenever possible.

Is psychoanalysis a theoretical framework within which human behavior can be studied scientifically, or is it a therapeutic method? These two possibilities are not inconsistent, as Freud pointed out on several occasions. A full evaluation of psychoanalysis will be possible only when its effectiveness as a therapy for maladaptive behavior has been objectively assessed and its links with the scientific method have been strengthened.

In recent years two research areas pertinent to the psychoanalytic perspective have seemed particularly promising. One concerns efforts to relate hypothesized psychodynamic processes to specific areas of brain function (Winson, 1985); and the other seeks to test experimentally such specific psychoanalytic concepts as primary process thinking, repression, and the superego's role as censor (Erdelyi, 1985; Bowers and Meichenbaum, 1985).

The Behavioral Perspective

Give me a dozen healthy infants, well-formed, and my own specified world to bring them up in and I'll guarantee to take any one at random and train him to become any type of specialist I might select, doctor, lawyer, artist, merchant-chief, and yes, even beggarman and thief, regardless of his talents, penchants, tendencies, abilities, vocations, and race of his ancestors.

—(Watson, 1925, p. 82)

For John B. Watson (1878–1958), the founder of behaviorism, development was a thoroughly mechanical affair. The complete personality—by which Watson meant the whole system of overt behavior—was built up out of the conditioning process. Although many contemporary learning theorists are not as confident as Watson about the simplicity of the processes of behavior acquisition and behavior change, the behavioristic approach continues to exert a powerful influence.

Just as dissatisfaction with a narrow biological orientation was one factor in the development of the psychodynamic perspective, the **behavioral perspective** developed in part because psychologists found many of Freud's ideas about the mind vague, complicated, and untestable. These theorists thought that the same behavior studied by Freud could be explained in a simpler fashion and in a way that would make it possible to study them experimentally.

Both the psychoanalytic and behavioral approaches are deterministic, but each finds the source of behavior in a different place. (**Determinism** means that every event or act is caused by what has happened before, not by the decisions of the individual.) Psychologists using the behavioral perspective focus on learning. They view behavior as a product of stimulus–response (S–R) relationships, not of intrapsychic events. They do not delve into the past or try to get people to figure out why they are the way they are. To change behavior, they concentrate on changing the relevant aspects of the environment, particularly sources of reinforcement.

A **reinforcer** is an event whose occurrence increases the probability that a certain stimulus will evoke a certain response. Reinforcers reward the individual for doing the right thing or not doing the wrong thing. If the reward is desirable enough, the individual is likely to keep on performing properly as long as the response is reinforced. The response can be either an approach response (asking for another glass of milk) or an escape or avoidance response (running from a pursuer or refusing to go out at night). A **positive reinforcer** increases the probability that the proper response will be made by giving the individual something pleasant. A **negative reinforcer**, on the other hand, increases the probability that the proper response will be made by taking away something unpleasant as soon as the proper response occurs.

Punishment, another way of changing behavior, is an unpleasant consequence for a wrong response. For example, a wife may positively reinforce her husband for not drinking by having sex with him only when he is sober; she may negatively reinforce his drinking by nagging when he stops drinking; and she may punish him for drunkenness by locking him out of the house. Table 3–2 illustrates the differences between reinforcement and punishment and contrasts them with **extinction**, still another way of changing behavior.

Positive and negative reinforcers and punishment have been applied to a variety of situations. Smiles, gold stars, and hugs are often highly effective in stimulating productive behavior in schoolchildren, and frowns or scolding may be used to discourage undesirable behavior. However, punishment, a negative consequence of behavior that is intended to discourage its repetition, is not very effective when used alone. It may cut down on undesired behavior, but it does not necessarily stimulate productive activity, since the person does not learn an acceptable substitute behavior.

The use of reinforcement in research on maladaptive behavior has followed two general paradigms: classical conditioning and operant conditioning.

Classical Conditioning

In **classical conditioning**, the response that an organism automatically makes to a certain stimulus is transferred to a new stimulus through an association between the two stimuli. The most famous classical conditioning experiment was Ivan Pavlov's (1849–1936) investigation of salivation in dogs. Pavlov placed a hungry dog in a harness and turned on a light at certain intervals. The dog did not salivate in response to the light, which was the **conditioned stimulus** (CS). After a few such trials, meat powder was delivered immediately after the light had been turned on. Since the dog was hungry, it salivated—an **unconditioned response** (UR)—upon presentation of the **unconditioned stimulus** (US), the meat powder. After a number of trials in which turning on of the light was followed by delivery of meat powder, Pavlov found that the dog salivated when the light

TABLE 3–2

Some Mechanisms of Behavior Change

	Definition	**Examples**
POSITIVE REINFORCEMENT	"Stamping in" any behavior by using a desired reinforcer as a reward.	Giving a child candy when he brings in a homework assignment. Saying "good girl" when the baby swallows a spoonful of cereal.
NEGATIVE REINFORCEMENT	"Stamping in" any behavior by removing an aversive stimulus when the behavior occurs.	Ceasing to scold a child when he hangs up his coat after throwing it on the floor. Allowing a child to go out if the child is having a tantrum because she must stay home.
PUNISHMENT	Aversive stimulus given as a result of an undesired behavior in an attempt to suppress that behavior in the future.	Slapping a child for swearing at you. Sending a child to her room because she broke her brother's toy.
EXTINCTION	Suppressing behavior by removing the reinforcers for it.	Ignoring a child when he has a temper tantrum. Removing all rock records from the record collection if your roommate, who likes only rock music, plays the stereo too often for your comfort.

was turned on even if food did not follow. A **conditioned response** (CR) to the light had been established. Other experiments showed that sounds, such as bells, also were capable of eliciting a conditioned response (see Figure 3–14).

In some classical conditioning experiments, the goal is to strengthen **escape** or **avoidance responses.** Conditioned responses that are not reinforced periodically through the presence of the US become weaker and ultimately disappear from the organism's repertory of responses. This disappearance of a previously learned response is called **extinction.**

Students of maladaptive behavior have been intrigued by the process of classical conditioning because it seems to explain fear, anxiety, and other types of emotional reactions. Some of these reactions may come about because of accidental classical conditioning. A child who has been bitten by a dog may fear all dogs and, through generalization, other types of animals as well. Classical conditioning is also the basis for some therapies. An example is **systematic desensitization,** a therapeutic procedure whose goal is to extinguish a conditioned response. This procedure might be used to help a woman who has been afraid of cars ever since she was injured in a serious auto crash. At first she was merely uncomfortable in a car, but finally she became so fearful that she could not even look at a picture of a car.

A diagram of the classical conditioning situation would look like this:

Unconditioned stimulus → Unconditioned response
Car crash and injury   *Fear*

Conditioned stimulus   → Conditioned response
Car   *Fear*

Through a series of steps that break down the bond between the conditioned stimulus and the conditioned response and substitute another conditioned response, the woman's unrealistic fear could be removed. First she would be taught to relax, then to imagine she was looking at an automobile ad in a magazine. Her relaxed state would counteract the anxiety response. Once she could do this successfully, she might be asked to look at a real car, to touch a car, to imagine herself in a car, and so on. At each step she would relax first and then experience the conditioned stimulus. In this way a new conditioning bond would be built up between a car and a relaxed state.

Operant Conditioning

In **operant conditioning,** the organism must make a particular response before the reinforcement occurs. The organism "operates" on its environment and produces an effect. A rat in a Skinner box, a device developed by B. F. Skinner (b. 1904) (Figure 3–15), will press a bar repeatedly if this activity is reinforced by pellets of food falling into a dish. Whereas classical conditioning makes use of natural as well as contrived responses, operant conditioning deals with responses that occur relatively infrequently prior to being reinforced.

A diagram of operant conditioning looks like this:

Response→Reinforcement→Increased probability that the response will be repeated

For example, in teaching a child to talk, parents reward the child with smiles and hugs whenever it says a desired word. These parental behaviors are positive reinforcements; they increase the chance that the child will repeat the word.

We hear over and over again how complex human behavior is. With pride we point to our lofty thoughts, fine feelings, and obscure motives. But those who use the behavioral perspective see human behavior as complex for other reasons. Even the simplest act can be seen as a chain of responses, each of which needs to be learned. Few of us get things right the first time. Children are particularly likely to become discouraged and give up if reinforcement is withheld until they do something perfectly. Thus, **shaping**—obtaining the desired response by reinforcing successfully better approxima-

FIGURE 3–14
Some mechanisms of behavior change.
(*Science* 238 (October 1987): 454)

FIGURE 3-15
B. F. Skinner, one of the most influential psychologists of the twentieth century, is shown here demonstrating the famous Skinner box used in many of his operant-conditioning experiments.

tions of it—is one of the basic processes in operant conditioning.

Considerable thought and planning are needed to decide what sorts of reinforcers are best for achieving particular behavior-shaping goals. In some situations an effective reinforcer may be rejected for purely practical reasons. A teacher who wanted to control disruptive behavior in the classroom probably could not use candy as a reinforcer, because it might have an undesirable effect on the pupils' appetites. In addition to deciding which reinforcers would be most effective and practical, it is necessary to decide on a **schedule** for reinforcing particular types of responses. The following case, which involves shaping verbal behavior in a 13-year-old boy with a suspected hearing problem, illustrates these elements.

Benjie, who wore a hearing aid, had never been observed to make verbal responses (except for occasional grunts). He did not smile, cry, or interact meaningfully with others in any way. A reinforcement program was instituted in which candy was used as both a positive reinforcer and a negative reinforcer. In addition to negative reinforcement (removal of a previously earned piece of candy), mild punishment (a slap on the hand) was used. This was how the operant treatment of Benjie began:

a. The experimenter sat across from Benjie and said, "Do you hear me, Benjie? If you do, nod your head." The experimenter nodded his head in the hope that Benjie would imitate him. Initially, Benjie made no head-nodding response.

b. Next, the basic procedure remained the same; however, candy was made contingent on the head-nodding response. Soon, Benjie was making 100 percent imitative head-nodding responses.

c. In the next procedure, the experimenter stood behind Benjie when giving the verbal cue. Benjie responded by nodding his head. This was the first indication to the experimenters that Benjie did, in fact, have the ability to hear verbalizations given at a normal conversational volume. From that point on Benjie did not wear his hearing aid in the laboratory or at home.

Discouragingly, Benjie made no discernible progress in vocalization. Because he seemed unresponsive to rewards, the experimenters decided to try a food deprivation schedule as a means of modifying Benjie's behavior. At breakfast, as soon as he made a sound he received a bite of food. This procedure proved to be effective. When he was hungry, he would make sounds at the command, "Benjie, tell me something." Eventually he came to respond to the command even when he was not hungry. After several months Benjie responded with a vocal sound every time a verbal command was directed toward him.

—(Knowles and Prutsman, 1968, p. 2)

Modeling

Reinforcement is not always necessary for learning to occur. Modeling can be used to change behavior because people are able to learn by watching how other people do things. Opportunities for observational learning arise when another person—a model—performs some response or group of responses. The observer does not need to have had practice in making the observed response and does not necessarily have to be reinforced in order to learn it. Exposure to models whose behavior and skills we admire plays an important role in our personal development and contributes to our self-esteem (see Figure 3-16). Models may have desirable or undesirable effects on those who observe their behavior.

Clinical studies support the conclusion that observational learning plays a part in the acquisition of maladaptive behavior. Anxiety in patients can often be

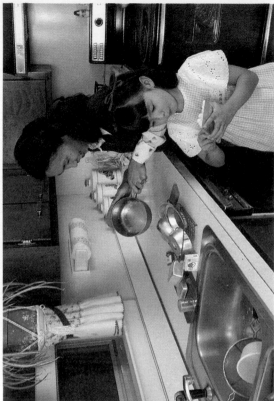

FIGURE 3–16
While modeling behavior can occur at all ages, it is seen most clearly in children.

traced to modeling experiences. A severe phobia, for example, may represent an exaggeration of a major or minor fear observed in a parent. Watching television is basically a symbolic modeling experience, especially for children. Noticeable and sometimes dramatic changes in behavior can result from modeling experiences. Terms like **vicarious learning, social facilitation, copying,** and **identification** have been used to characterize this process.

Modeling exposes the observer to the specific responses displayed by the model. Even more important, it provides the observer with food for thought. A child who observes continual arguing between parents forms a concept of what marriage is like. Poor people who observe the parade of commercials on television think that most other people are free from financial worries. Modeling, then, not only illustrates possible overt behavior but also contributes to the formation of concepts, attitudes, and needs. **Role playing,** or practicing

behavior shown by a model, is another important learning technique.

The way in which modeling and role playing can strengthen adaptive behavior is illustrated by the case of John R., an unemployed 18-year-old who had been institutionalized for stealing a car. Therapists noted that his problem was not simply a failure to adhere to social norms but a weak behavioral repertory.

A particularly serious deficiency was his fear about and inadequacy in job interview situations. He had never had an opportunity to observe the effective behavior of others in situations that required putting one's best foot forward. In the institution be was given the opportunity to observe job interview behavior as modeled by persons (noninmates) who were effective in this area. On several occasions John observed simulated job interviews and then practiced being interviewed himself. After leaving the institution, he found that the modeling experience had helped him. He reported that while waiting for an actual job interview he had remembered and thought about the behavior he had observed. He then mentally rehearsed how he might handle himself when confronted by the personnel manager. He was hired, he felt, because of the new skill and security he brought to the previously traumatic job interview situation. His increased skill and security seemed to result from his having a better idea of what to expect in a job interview.

Learning and Mediational Processes

Over the years there have been many theories about the learning process. In general, these theories can be divided into two camps. The first says that covert events, such as thoughts and feelings do not count because they cannot be directly observed and measured. This group, led by B. F. Skinner, believes that unless all references to inner processes are avoided, it will be impossible to develop a truly scientific approach to behavior. This strict environmental approach bases explanations of behavior only on observed events. From this perspective, therapy involves manipulating the person's environment so as to reinforce adaptive responses and extinguish maladaptive ones. Theorists who support this viewpoint, often called **radical behaviorists**, describe people as being more or less at the mercy of their environment.

Theorists of the second camp feel that environmentalism may be adequate to explain the behavior of pigeons and laboratory rats but is not sufficient to explain the complexity of human behavior, especially the qualities that distinguish humans from less complex animals. Members of this group, called **social learning theorists**, emphasize the idea that a number of factors combine to shape social behavior and mediate the influence of learning experiences. Although social learning theorists generally agree that covert events serve as mediators between external stimuli and overt behavior, the nature of the process is not clear.

An area of research that has received considerable attention from social learning theorists is modeling. The modeling approach does not consider either practicing of the desired behavior or immediate reinforcement of that behavior to be necessary for learning to take place. What a person observes can be essentially stored away and brought out in the form of a behavior when a situation occurs that is similar to the one faced by the model. Thus, although they recognize the importance of past events in the formation of present behavior, social learning therapists focus on the current maladaptive behavior that troubles the client.

The Cognitive Perspective

People are disturbed not by things, but by the views which they take of them.

—(Epictetus, first century B.C.)

If Epictetus were alive today, he would be a cognitive psychologist. The word "cognitive" comes from the Latin word **cognitare**, meaning "to have known." Cognitive psychology deals with human beings as information processors and problem solvers. The cognitive view seeks to account for behavior by studying the ways in which the person attends to, interprets, and uses available information.

The **cognitive perspective** in abnormal psychology has grown out of new directions in learning and psychodynamic theory. Some learning theorists have become increasingly interested in what goes on in the individual between the application of a stimulus and the response, and certain psychodynamic theorists have emphasized the need to focus on thinking and problem solving as well as on feelings and emotions (Bieber, 1980). This perspective has been given added impetus by a group of clinicians (such as Albert Ellis and George Kelly) who have derived cognitive theories from their own therapeutic experiences with clients.

Like the psychodynamic perspective, the cognitive perspective is concerned with internal processes. Rather than stressing urges, needs, and motivations, however, it emphasizes how people acquire and interpret information and use it in solving problems. Unlike psychoanalysis, it places great emphasis on mental processes that we are aware of or can rather easily be made aware of, as opposed to hidden motivations, feelings, and conflicts. Its approach has been contrasted with the learning perspective's emphasis on the external environment as a prime cause of behavior. Typically, the cognitive perspective pays more attention to our present thoughts and problem-solving strategies than to our personal histories. However, histories of cognitions are now receiving some attention (Sarason, 1979). The relationships among emotions, motivations, and cognitive processes are also being studied more intensively. The overlap between the cognitive perspective and other approaches is becoming more evident.

A special emphasis of the cognitive perspective is the concept of the person as information processor. According to this view, people are continually collecting, storing, modifying, interpreting, and understanding both internally generated information and environmental stimuli. Humans are viewed as active, selective seekers, creators, and users of information, and behavior is viewed as both a product and an initiator of mental acts and environmental changes. The mental life of the individual is conceived of as consisting of **schemata** (plural of schema) that contain information in particular domains such as parents, work, and pets. Through their influence on cognitive processes, schemata enable people to identify stimuli quickly, cluster them into manageable units, fill in missing information, and select a strategy for obtaining further information, solving a problem, or reaching a goal.

From a clinical standpoint, self-schemata are especially important. They organize and guide not only our social experiences but any experiences that are personally relevant. Personally relevant experiences are often laden with emotions and are likely to reflect an individual's prior learning history. Self-schemata are capable of distorting a person's perceptions of reality. Schemata that concern our self-evaluations influence not only how we feel about ourselves but also how we relate to others. For example, **self-efficacy** refers to the strength of our convictions about our personal effectiveness. People may imagine potential difficulties as more formidable than they are in reality if they perceive themselves as ineffective in important types of situations. Inappropriate or maladaptive behavior in those situations may confirm the individual's self-perception as inadequate, helpless, or cowardly. This confirmation may cause the person to avoid problematic situations or reduce his or her task-relevant efforts. A vicious cycle is thereby created and perpetuated (Turk and Salovey, 1985).

Cognitive Approaches to Personality

The cognitive perspective on personality has led to a variety of theories. Among the best known of these are those of Dollard and Miller, Kelly, and Bandura.

John Dollard and Neal Miller

John Dollard (1900–1980) and Neal Miller (b. 1909) tried to relate human learning to psychodynamic processes as well as to external events. Although thinking, feeling, perceiving, and other covert processes cannot be observed, they can be inferred. They are usually called **hypothetical constructs** (because there is no way to prove that they really exist) or **intervening variables** (because they are presumed to intervene between environmental stimuli and behavior).

Dollard and Miller (1950) thought they saw parallels between learning theory and Freudian theory in the area of personality development. For example, the reinforcement principle and Freud's pleasure principle have the same general function: people are more likely to do what makes them feel good. Dollard and Miller also made use of cognitive concepts by describing mal-adaptive behavior as a joint product of unfortunate life experiences and maladaptive thinking. They viewed gaining insight into the roots of one's behavior as acquiring self-awareness responses. Despite their preference for describing behavior in terms of habits and learning, they emphasized the individual's cognitive resolution of conflicts.

Dollard and Miller suggested that the use of labeling, a cognitive device that enables one to classify emotional responses, is a way of controlling one's own reactions in a particular situation. This sort of labeling can help a person cope with what otherwise might be a stress-producing situation. For example:

[A young man] had invited a girl whom he particularly liked but did not know very well to a formal dance. The girl had declined the invitation but said she would be glad to go to dinner before the dance. Trapped by her suggestion and his attraction to her, he had agreed to take her to dinner. The boy found the dinner rough going. He was immediately attacked by a stomach-ache so severe that he thought he would be forced to leave the table.

—(Dollard and Miller, 1950, p. 443)

He was able to use an understanding of his reactions and a cognitive technique learned in psychotherapy to improve the situation.

He recalled that aggression against a woman frequently took gastric form in his case. Could it be that he was angry at the girl, and if so, why? He realized immediately that he was angry and had repressed his anger. He had felt exploited by her suggesting dinner when she could not go with him to the dance. He was just being used to fill in a chunk of time before the dance. When these thoughts occurred, ones contradictory to them came up also. The girl did not seem like an exploitative type. Maybe she wanted to show that she really liked him. There would, after all, be another dance, so why not ask her then and there for another date. This he did, and she accepted with evident pleasure. The combination of this lack of cause for aggression and hope of the future brought relief; the stomach-ache disappeared. . . .

Once the stomach-ache was labeled as aggression-produced, the rest of the solution appeared rapidly.

—Ibid.

George Kelly

The product of George Kelly's (1905–1966) extensive study of the nature of personal experience was his psychology of **personal constructs**. Kelly (1955) concluded that people's personal constructs reflect how they interpret or develop ideas about themselves, the world, and future events. Personal constructs are the way in which each person builds his or her own reality by sorting people and events into categories. Kelly believed that each person is constantly engaged in problem solving and that personal constructs are an important means of organizing information about interpersonal relationships.

There are wide differences between the personal constructs of different individuals. People may perceive the same event in entirely different ways. For example, suppose two lovers break up. One observer may describe the event as simple incompatibility, while another may believe that one person "jilted" the other. Another might say that the breakup was due to "parental meddling"; still another might see it as a "blessing in disguise."

Kelly was not a supporter of the concepts of hidden psychodynamics and the unconscious. He often referred to what he whimsically termed "Kelly's first principle": "If you don't know what is wrong with clients, ask them, they may tell you." Although he recognized that we might not be aware of all of our personal constructs at any given time, he tended to reject Freud's belief that the greater part of mental life is hidden from view. He also tended to reject the emphasis placed by psychoanalysis on what happened to a person in the past. For Kelly, the important thing was the distinctive set of personal constructs that guide a person's life at the present time.

Kelly stressed the role of personal constructs as causes of emotional reactions. We feel anxious when we don't know how to handle a situation, when we become aware that our system of constructs does not encompass a problem that has arisen. Thus, Kelly believed that cognitions precede emotions. He saw psychotherapy as a way of demonstrating to clients that their constructs are hypotheses rather than facts. Once clients realized this, he encouraged them to test their constructs so that the maladaptive ones could be replaced with more useful ones.

Albert Bandura

In addition to his emphasis on social learning theory, Albert Bandura (b. 1925) has more recently emphasized the symbolic and cognitive aspects of learning as opposed to the stimulus–response aspects (see Figure 3–17). According to Bandura (1982), we can solve problems symbolically without having to resort to trial-and-error behavior because we can foresee the consequences of our behavior and act accordingly. For example, we buy fire insurance because we think about what might happen if our house burned down. Similarly, in preparing for our first winter camping trip, we assemble protective gear because we can anticipate the effects of a blizzard. The ability to anticipate consequences operates in more routine behaviors as well as in special instances like these.

Bandura (1978) has become interested in studying

FIGURE 3–17

Albert Bandura's work on modeling, as well as his more recent work on self-regulation, has been important not only theoretically but also in the development of new therapeutic approaches.

self-regulation or learning by internal reinforcement as opposed to the idea of modifying behavior by external reinforcement alone. Many cognitive psychologists are developing techniques by which people who lack behavioral self-control can be helped to acquire it. The following examples illustrate techniques for strengthening self-control that make use of cognitive mechanisms.

1. A student studies every night even though no test has been announced.
2. A heavy smoker teaches herself nonsmoking behavior.

In the first case, the student may motivate himself by means of cognitive representation of future consequences. That is, he may think about how bad he would feel if he scored poorly on the next test or how stressful it would be to try to learn all the information the night before the test. Another motivation may be his own goal-setting behavior. He wants to receive a high grade for the course. Whenever he feels like turning on the television set or stopping for a snack, he visualizes how he will feel if he attains his goal. When people evaluate their own behavior in this way, they tend to persist until they achieve their goals.

In the second example, each time the former smoker has the impulse to smoke, she may imagine an

X-ray of lungs afflicted by cancer, or she may see herself coughing and unable to breathe. Such self-generated cognitive mechanisms would provide negative reinforcement for her thoughts about smoking.

In addition to their application to the self-control of behavior, cognitive mechanisms are important in problem solving. If you were an engineer designing a bridge, you wouldn't try out different construction methods until you arrived at one that didn't collapse. Instead, after considering information about materials, climatic conditions, and the technical data on different designs and then performing complex cognitive operations, you would come up with a plan. Or suppose you have a chance to get a job as a summer trainee with a firm you'd like to work for after graduation. It would be a good experience, but the pay is low and it would mean moving to another state for the summer. Your finances would be stretched and you would have to work part time for the next winter to make up for the extra cost. You couldn't simply try out the job. Instead you would probably do some financial figuring, see what jobs are available in town, and after thinking about all the options and consequences, make a decision.

Cognitive Therapies

The idea that maladaptive thoughts are the cause of maladaptive behavior and that people must be taught new ways of thinking has been used as a basic approach by many therapists. Several forms of therapy are based on the cognitive perspective.

Rational–emotive therapy, developed by Albert Ellis, is based on the belief that behavior depends more on individual belief systems and ways of interpreting situations than on objective conditions. Ellis contends that all effective psychotherapists, whether or not they realize it, function as teachers for their clients. They help their clients to review, reperceive, and rethink their lives; to question their irrational beliefs; and to modify their unrealistic and illogical thoughts, emotions, and behaviors. Ellis regards both intense emotions and maladaptive behavior as the modifiable consequences of thoughts. He admits that faulty beliefs are probably formed in childhood. However, he feels that finding out how people got to be the way they are is less important than helping them respond more constructively to their present situation.

In rational–emotive therapy the clinician explains and demonstrates productive thinking, persuades the client to think and behave in more effective ways, and discusses homework assignments. Through such assignments the client might practice ways of behaving more assertively with co-workers or family members without alienating them (Ellis, 1962, 1970; Smith, 1982).

George Kelly used a variety of tactics to help his clients explore and modify their personal constructs.

Most often he used a traditional interview format in which he and his client talked about specific personal constructs and the roles they led the client to play in social relationships. In addition, he used **fixed-role therapy,** in which clients experimented with (by acting out) new roles that might result from particular revisions in their personal-construct systems. Kelly believed that people have difficulty simply trying out new ways of behaving; hence he was very supportive of these experimental efforts (Niemeyer, 1986).

Aaron Beck (1976) also thinks that the job of the therapist is to help clients restructure their thinking and replace maladaptive thoughts with thoughts that are more helpful in coping with stressful situations. Beck's work was originally focused on the cognitions of depressed individuals; but recently his approach has been extended to the problem of anxiety (Beck and Emery, 1985). Beck thinks that people's emotions and behavior are based largely on the way they view the world. In his view, depressed and anxious people exaggerate their difficulties and minimize the possibility that anything can be done about them.

The Humanistic–Existential Perspective

The humanistic–existential perspective presents a sharp contrast to the theoretical approaches described so far. Its roots are found in a number of philosophical and religious systems that have stressed the dignity, inherent goodness, and freedom of human nature. The growth of this perspective within psychology was partly a product of this tradition and partly a reaction to the less flattering conceptions of human nature that are characteristic of psychoanalysis and radical behaviorism.

One of the central assumptions of the humanistic view is that in every person there is an active force toward **self-actualization,** toward being "all that you can be." When the human personality unfolds in a benign environment that gives these creative forces free rein, the positive inner nature of the human being emerges. Human misery and pathology, on the other hand, are fostered by environments that frustrate the individual's tendencies toward self-actualization.

Closely related to the humanistic movement is the existential perspective, which became popular in Europe as psychologists and philosophers sought to understand how the horrors of World War II could have occurred and how certain people were able to rise above them and find meaning in life. While the humanistic theories focus on the process of self-actualization, existential theorists emphasize self-determination, choice, and the responsibility of the individual to rise above environmental forces. "We are our choices," maintains the existentialist. "Our existence and its meaning are squarely in our own hands, for we alone can decide what our attitudes and behaviors will be."

Humanistic–existential theorists believe that scientific psychology is missing the mark when it dwells only on observable behavior and neglects the person's inner life. They believe that inner experiences and the search for the meaning of existence are the core of the individual's being-in-the-world and hence should be the focus of psychology. They therefore regard introspection as a valid and, indeed, indispensable source of psychological information.

Maslow's Hierarchy of Needs

Abraham Maslow (1908–1970) was a leader in the effort to integrate a humanistic philosophy into the traditional scientific approach. His vehicle for accomplishing this was the **hierarchy of needs** (1968). Figure 3-18 shows Maslow's hierarchy as a five-layer pyramid. The needs in each layer must be satisfied before those in the next higher layer become important.

Maslow assumed that needs direct behavior. When we are hungry (need food), we direct our behavior toward getting food. When the most basic requirements, or **deficiency needs** (the two lower levels of Figure 3-18), are not met, they exert a dominant influence over our thinking and behavior. Physiological needs include those for food, water, and air. Safety needs take in freedom from pain, fear, and insecurity. When these basic needs are satisfied, we can turn to the needs at higher levels of the pyramid. Needs for identification with others and the feeling of being loved come next. When

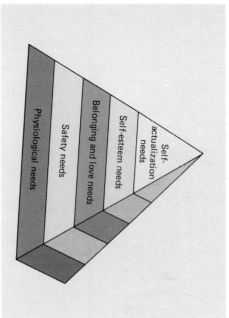

FIGURE 3-18
Maslow's hierarchy of needs.

Self-actualization needs
Self-esteem needs
Belonging and love needs
Safety needs
Physiological needs

these are satisfied, the person's [...] and in control of the environm[ent.] Finally, when all these needs a[re] turn to **self-actualization need**[s...] lems that we create for ourselv[es] and the scientist must inquire actualization. Maslow says self ization and fulfillment of peo[ple] tentialities.

Maslow viewed neurotics as people who have been prevented or are preventing themselves from attaining their basic needs, which means that they are also barred from self-actualization. As a result, they feel threatened and insecure. To correct this situation, therapists must give their clients enough respect and love to satisfy those basic needs. In addition, the client must be encouraged to display affection toward the therapist and others. Once this reciprocal relationship has been established, the client can begin the process of growth.

Rogers' Conception of the Self

Along with Maslow, Carl Rogers (1902–1987) is one of the leaders of humanistic psychology (see Figure 3-19). The centerpiece of his perspective on personality is the self-image (1951, 1959, 1980). Rogers relates the ability to achieve self-understanding and self-actualization to the individual's self-regard and perception of acceptance by others. An adult who felt wanted and highly valued as a child is likely to have a positive self-image, to be thought well of by others, and to have the capacity for self-actualization. Optimal adjustment results in what Rogers calls the fully functioning person and is characterized by a low level of anxiety. Anxiety is due to uneasiness or tension resulting from inconsistencies between people's self-perceptions and their ideas of what they would like to be.

Although the ways in which they conceptualize behavior contrast sharply, both Rogers and Freud developed their theoretical positions on the basis of similar observational data: the behavior of clients and therapists in psychotherapy. However, Rogers rejects the psychoanalytic notion that people are irrational and unsocial by nature. He asserts, on the contrary, that each person is basically rational, socialized and constructive.

For Rogers, psychotherapy is a situation in which anxious, troubled people with low self-regard and distorted perceptions of themselves and the world seek help. Rogers thinks that healthy people are those who move away from roles created by the expectations of others, that is, from pretending to be something they are not. Instead, they learn to trust themselves and reject the false selves that they have created. Neurotic and psychotic people, on the other hand, have self-concepts that

FIGURE 3–19
Carl Rogers, shown seated second from the right, spent much of the later part of his life working with groups of clients who wanted to get more out of their lives. Rogers believed that "there is no such thing as scientific knowledge; there are only individual perceptions of what appears to each person to be such knowledge." (1959, p. 192) This statement expressed the humanistic/existentialist view that inner experience and a search for individual meaning should be the focus of psychology.

do not match their experiences. They are afraid to accept their own experiences as valid, so they distort them, either to protect themselves or to win approval from others. A therapist can help them give up these false selves.

The task for Rogerian therapists is neither to provide interpretations nor to give advice. Rather, the therapist must accept clients as having worth and dignity in their own right despite their problems. This acceptance means that the therapist must understand the client's feelings, no matter how positive or negative they are or how much they contradict the therapist's own attitudes.

The Existential Point of View

Existentialists believe that people are free to choose among alternative courses of action. If this is true, why are so many people unhappy and dissatisfied? Why does maladaptive behavior exist? For one thing, not everyone chooses wisely. A person can choose to act either authentically or inauthentically. To act **authentically**

means to freely establish one's own goals. To act **inauthentically** means to let other people dictate those goals. For each person there are also certain givens that place definite limits on what he or she may become. These may be characteristics that are present at birth, such as learning ability, physical appearance, or the presence of a disabling disease, or they may be environmental, including the influence of parents and later of school. These expand or contract the individual's chances for fulfillment based on the qualities present at birth. The primary task of the therapist, according to this view, is to help empty, lonely people expand their experiences and fulfill their own uniqueness, that is, to help them make constructive choices.

The Community Perspective

Most people see mental illness as a personal health problem or as a character defect. In contrast, from the **com-**

munity perspective, maladaptive behavior results from inability to cope effectively with stress. It is not viewed as a disease or problem that exists only within the individual; instead, it is seen as at least partly a failure of the individual's social support system. This system includes the person's spouse, parents, siblings, relatives, friends, teachers, employer, religious adviser, and others, as well as community organizations and government agencies.

Community psychologists do not deny the role of life history or genetic makeup in causing maladaptive behavior, but these are not seen as necessarily sufficient to produce such behavior. For example, a schizophrenic may develop hallucinations for many reasons: biochemical factors, traumatic early experiences, or unusual social relationships are all possibilities. However, the presence of an especially strong stressor or the breakdown of the person's social support system may be equally important in producing the schizophrenic behavior.

The community approach attempts to reduce maladaptive behavior through preventive measures, by intervening in people's lives before catastrophes occur. Such measures include a variety of special programs: discussion or mutual support programs for recently separated, divorced, or widowed people; preschool enrichment programs for children from low-income, single-parent homes; day-care centers for the care of elderly people who need help in solving problems of living. Implicit in community psychology is the belief that the effects of social disorganization (such as slums, bad schools, and high unemployment rates) are a major cause of many personal problems. For this reason, mental health professionals with a community orientation tend to become involved in efforts to change society by lobbying for legislation and becoming actively involved in community affairs.

Community psychologists study the social environment and factors related to it, such as socioeconomic status. When the living places of people who are identified as psychologically and socially impaired are plotted on a map, it can be shown that the frequency of such problems is much higher in certain areas than in others. **Social-causation theories** argue that the poor schools, crime, poor housing, and prejudice often found in low-income, deteriorating neighborhoods may increase the stress experienced by already vulnerable people. The **social-selection theory**, on the other hand, argues that lower socioeconomic groups show a greater incidence of maladaptive behavior because people who do not function well tend to experience downward social mobility.

Those who believe in the community perspective are more likely to support the social-causation theory. They point out that, while social selection may be a factor, the theory does not rule out the stress-producing situations of lower-class living that may aggravate existing disorders. Lower-class people may have less power to control their environment as well as fewer resources for dealing with stress. For a variety of reasons, not the least of which is the difficulty of carrying out controlled research in community settings, one cannot completely rule out either the social-selection or the social-causation theory. One or the other might apply to certain types of disorders. In either case, psychologists with a community perspective see a need to develop special programs aimed at counteracting undesirable aspects of urban life such as poverty and overcrowding. Such programs would improve the lives of the general population as well as those of people with specific psychological problems.

Social Roles and Labeling

All individuals belong to social groups. These groups shape people's behavior by providing the distinctive reinforcement, punishments, and models that are part of life in a particular cultural setting. The members of a social group share a set of meanings or symbols, experience a feeling of unity, and participate in a network of mutual obligations. The group or groups to which a person belongs influence nearly every aspect of his or her life.

Social roles are particular functions that a person plays as a member of a social group. Some writers have maintained that we always attempt to project an image and that, in fact, we have no true self. This position is presented by Erving Goffman (1959), who argues that in all of our encounters with other people we adopt particular roles. Each role is accompanied by a script that includes different actions and signals. In effect, we vary our behaviors continuously as the situation requires. This viewpoint implies that there is no such thing as a fixed personality.

Less extreme than this position, and more widely accepted, is the composite position: there is a basic personality that is overlaid with situational role playing. Research has shown that a number of factors influence the roles people play in social relationships. These factors are often important because they serve to label an individual in a particular way. **Labeling** occurs whenever people are categorized on some basis, whether that basis is relevant and fair or not. Labels can be destructive because they draw attention to one aspect of the person while ignoring other aspects that make him or her unique.(Would you like to be labeled as a slob simply because you don't like to put your shoes away at night?) Some labels, such as "good student" and "loyal friend," are desirable, but many others carry negative social connotations. For example, the role of mental patient is widely viewed as socially unacceptable, and the label of mentally ill often causes permanent damage. The damage takes many forms, including discrimination by others and feelings of self-doubt and inadequacy.

In an experiment that demonstrated the effects of labeling on people's behavior (Farina and others, 1971), the subjects were psychiatric patients who had been hospitalized in the past but at the time of the study were outpatients living in the community. They were told that the study was designed to find out whether prospective employers would be less likely to hire former psychiatric patients than to hire individuals without a known history of mental illness. Half of the subjects were told that the interviewer knew their true status; the other half were told that the interviewer thought they were "medical" patients. The interviewer (who was actually a confederate of the experimenter) worked with each subject on a cooperative task. The subjects who thought they had been described as medical patients made higher scores on the task, rated the task as easier, and thought the interviewer appreciated them more than did those who had been labeled as psychiatric patients. The interviewer, who did not know what the subjects had been told, rated the mental-patient group as more anxious, tense, and poorly adjusted than the so-called medical patients. This experiment demonstrates that knowing how one is labeled can change one's behavior even if the label is known to be false.

Contributions of the Community Perspective

What we know at present supports the emphasis that community psychology has given to the role of the social environment in emotions and maladaptive behavior. For example, children's levels of distress and oppression increase sharply when they live in an environment in which adults express high levels of anger and behave aggressively. There is some evidence that this responsiveness to family discord is greater for boys than it is for girls (Cummings and others, 1985; Farber and others, 1985).

Rutter and Quinton (1984) studied 137 psychiatric patients who had children under the age of 15. They found that there was a high rate of psychological distress among the patients' spouses, which could be attributed to the tense family environment. One-third of the children of psychiatric patients were found to have a persistent psychiatric—usually conduct—disorder that was derived not from the parental illness itself but from the associated disturbance within the family. (A conduct disorder is one in which a child or adolescent habitually violates the rights of others through violent or antisocial behavior.) Evidence of this type suggests that once serious disorders are established within a family, these are incorporated into the child's personality and functioning, and the child's disordered behavior may continue even when the parental disorder improves.

The community perspective has been influential in producing creative new approaches to maladaptive behavior and in reaching segments of the population whose psychological needs have been ignored. It has been effective both in changing the perspective of academic thinking and in altering social policy.

The Value of an Interactional Approach

We have reviewed six widely varying perspectives on the causes and treatment of maladaptive behavior. You may be wondering how these perspectives relate to the rest of the book. Which one is emphasized most? We think you should know our biases and how our views will effect what you learn in this book.

We have attempted to use the most valuable contributions of each viewpoint in our discussions of abnormal behavior. Abnormal behavior can result from any or all of a large number of factors. One perspective may contribute more than another under one set of conditions; under a different set, another viewpoint may be more useful. Our approach, which is shared by many other psychologists, is interactional. The way a situation influences behavior depends on the particular vulnerabilities, capabilities, and preoccupations of the person experiencing the particular set of conditions. These conditions and the person's characteristics can be thought of as interacting or combining to produce a special product, the individual's behavior. Why maladaptive behavior occurs in some people and not others can be understood in this way (see Figure 3–20). For example, there is evidence that many people do not become depressed for either purely mental or purely environmental reasons (Oatley and Bolton, 1985). A full understanding of depression requires information about both the person's internal state and the state of his or her social and community ties. Depression can be viewed as despair over a severe loss or disappointment from which, for a longer or shorter time, there seems to be no escape. Recovery from this crisis depends on whether the situation changes and how the person's cognitions about the situation change.

Clinical interventions that help people cope more effectively with stress can also take many forms, depending on the client's problems and vulnerabilities and on the theoretical viewpoint of the clinician. For example, a tranquilizing drug might be prescribed for someone who is experiencing a temporary crisis such as the serious illness of a loved one. In that case, the tranquilizer

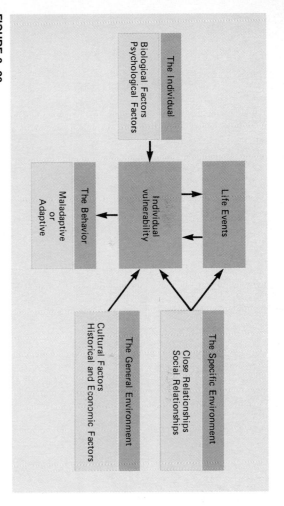

reduces the person's vulnerability to intense anxiety experienced over a limited period. In other cases, insight into the client's desires, motivations, and conflicts is needed in order to help him or her cope more effectively with stress and be less vulnerable to the crises that are the inevitable ingredients of every human life. In still another case, a person might never have learned the behavior needed to cope with a given situation. The best procedure in such a case might be to teach that behavior. Or perhaps the client is in an intolerable situation—for example, he or she is the child of an abusive parent. In such a case, the child's environment must be modified by removing the parent or helping the parent avoid abusive behavior. Or it may be that a person habitually misinterprets situations; here, retraining in how to think about problems might be appropriate.

Each of us has expectations and goals that color our thoughts. A stamp collector probably has different thoughts when going to the post office than a noncollector does. Our thoughts serve as **mediators:** they provide links between informational inputs and behavioral outputs, just as an intermediary in the business world

links a manufacturer and a retailer. Several theories of abnormal behavior deal with the mediating process, though there are differences of opinion about which ones are most important. The various theoretical perspectives reflect these differences by focusing on such different mediators as chemical processes in the body, drives and emotions, thinking styles, values and needs, or the social milieu.

Each of us confronts diverse situations each day. They provide us with information (pleasant, unpleasant, frightening, worrisome) and often call forth certain reactions. The information available to us influences our way of looking at things. At the same time, our personal characteristics—our skills and vulnerabilities—help determine how we handle the situations to which we must respond. The authors of this textbook are interested in what makes an individual vulnerable to particular situations, what kind of stressors cause maladaptive behavior to appear, and how people can build coping skills that enable them to deal better with stressors and compensate for their vulnerabilities.

Study Outline

THE ROLE OF THEORY IN ABNORMAL PSYCHOLOGY

Clinicians use a number of theories to explain vulnerabilities that lead to maladaptation and to plan therapies. Existing theories are continually changing, and new ones emerge frequently.

THE BIOLOGICAL PERSPECTIVE

1. The biological perspective emphasizes the idea that bodily disturbances cause disordered behavior. Irregularities in the genes may be responsible for some maladaptive behaviors. Through a substance called DNA, people may inherit a *tendency* toward a particular char-

acteristic or disease. Research on heredity in humans makes use of family histories and twin studies.

2. Another biological determinant of behavior is the brain and nervous system. Disturbances in specific parts of the brain can result in specific behavioral deficits. Researchers use electroencephalograms to analyze the brain wave patterns that are characteristic of different behavioral states. Research on the brain reward system, particularly substances called **endorphins,** may lead to a better understanding of drug addiction.

3. The **endocrine system,** which consists of various glands, affects the body's responses through the secretion of hormones. The pituitary gland and the adrenal cortex play roles in biological and psychological adaptation to stress.

4. **Psychoimmunology** links psychological and immunological events. It has been noted that bereavement and other stressors are frequently followed by illness, possibly caused by an alteration in the immune system. **Psychopharmacology** is the study of the effects of drugs on behavior.

THE PSYCHODYNAMIC PERSPECTIVE

1. The psychodynamic perspective is based on the idea that thoughts and emotions are important causes of behavior. Clinicians must infer these covert, unobservable thoughts and emotions from overt behavior.

2. According to Freud's method of **psychoanalysis,** it is important for patients to be helped to recapture emotionally laden memories that have been forgotten.

3. Freud's theory of **psychic determinism** states that all behavior is caused by prior mental events, which may be conscious (the individual is aware of them), preconscious (the individual can be made aware of them easily), or unconscious (they are difficult to bring to awareness). The level of awareness of mental events is determined by the amount of intrapsychic conflict surrounding those events.

4. During the first five years of life, the **libido** focuses on specific erogenous zones, resulting in the **oral, anal,** and **phallic** psychosexual stages, which eventually lead to the mature **genital** stage. Unresolved conflicts may cause a person to become **fixated** or arrested at one stage or to **regress** to a previous stage.

5. Freud believed that the mental world is divided into three structures: the pleasure-seeking **id;** the **ego,** which avoids or copes with danger; and the **superego,** which represents the society's moral code. During infancy, **primary process thinking,** characterized by the **pleasure principle** and desire for immediate gratification, is dominant. Later, **secondary process thinking** develops and gratification can be postponed. Some primary process thinking is found in adults.

6. **Anxiety** is a response to perceived danger that exceeds the organism's capacity to handle it. Because anxiety arises in anticipation of danger, it can serve a protective function.

7. The ego initiates **defense mechanisms** to ward off awareness of conflict. The most important of these mechanisms is **repression,** which reduces anxiety by keeping thoughts and impulses out of awareness.

8. In clinical psychoanalysis, the causes of maladaptive behavior are sought in early childhood experiences through such techniques as free association and the analysis of dreams, fantasies, and memories.

9. Neo-Freudians, including Jung, Adler, and more recently Erikson, have revised some of Freud's ideas and broadened the psychodynamic perspective. However, psychoanalytic theory remains difficult to evaluate scientifically.

THE BEHAVIORAL PERSPECTIVE

1. According to the behavioral perspective, behavior is a response to stimuli in the environment. **Positive reinforcers** increase the probability of particular responses by giving a reward for those responses; **negative reinforcers** take away something unpleasant; **punishment** gives an unpleasant consequence for the wrong response; **extinction** suppresses behavior by removing the reinforcers.

2. In **classical conditioning,** the response that is automatically made to a particular stimulus is transferred to a new stimulus through contiguity. In Pavlov's experiment based on the salivation of dogs, the light was the **conditioned stimulus,** the salivation was an **unconditioned response** to the food, which was the **unconditioned stimulus,** and the eventual salivation in response to the light alone was the **conditioned response.** Some maladaptive behaviors can be explained in terms of classical conditioning.

3. In **operant conditioning,** the response must precede the reinforcement; the organism operates on the environment and produces an effect. Using operant conditioning, B. F. Skinner taught rats to press a bar in order to receive food. **Shaping** of behavior involves reinforcing successively better approximations of a desired response.

4. Learning also occurs through **modeling,** or watching how other people do things, and **role playing,** or practicing the observed behavior. Models may have both desirable and undesirable effects on anxiety and fear, personal development, and self-esteem.

5. **Radical behaviorists** like B. F. Skinner believe that all behavior can be affected by manipulation of the environment. **Social learning theorists** believe that cognitive factors also influence behavior.

THE COGNITIVE PERSPECTIVE

1. The cognitive perspective focuses on how people acquire and interpret information and use it to solve problems. In this view, mental life consists of **schemata**, which contains information that people process in order to select strategies for solving a problem or reaching a goal. Self-schemata contain personally relevant information as well, including emotions, which can distort perceptions of reality.

2. John Dollard and Neal Miller combined elements of the psychodynamic, learning, and cognitive perspectives. They saw maladaptive behavior as the joint product of unfortunate life experiences and maladaptive thinking.

3. George Kelly believed that emotional reactions are based on **personal constructs**; that is, each person builds a view of the world by sorting people and events into categories. He saw the role of psychotherapy as replacing maladaptive constructs with more useful ones.

4. Albert Bandura believes that people can solve problems symbolically by foreseeing the consequences of their behavior. He has focused on **self-regulation** through the use of internal rather than external reinforcement.

5. There are several cognitive therapies. In **rational-emotive therapy**, developed by Albert Ellis, people are helped to question and modify their belief systems. George Kelly developed **fixed-role therapy**, in which people explore new ways of behaving. Aaron Beck, who has focused on depression and anxiety, believes that therapists can help people restructure their thoughts so as to cope better with stress.

THE HUMANISTIC–EXISTENTIAL PERSPECTIVE

1. The humanistic–existential perspective focuses on self-examination and the desire for freedom. In the humanistic view, there is a force toward self-actualization, or being "all that you can be." Existential theorists emphasize **self-determination**.

2. Abraham Maslow established a five-layer **hierarchy of needs**—physiological, safety, belonging and love, self-esteem, and self-actualization. Lower level needs must be satisfied before higher needs become important.

Maslow viewed neurotics as people who h[as]fied the lower levels of needs, especially longing and self-esteem. They thus are [...] seeking self-actualization.

3. According to Carl Rogers, personal adjustment de[...] pends on people's self-image. Therapists can help them accept themselves for what they are.

4. Existentialists believe that people are free to act either **authentically**, establishing their own goals, or in-**authentically**, letting others dictate their goals. Innate or environmental factors may limit or expand their potential for fulfillment. Rollo May believes that anxiety, which is caused when a person faces an important choice, either results in personal growth or may cause guilt. Therapists can help people make constructive choices.

THE COMMUNITY PERSPECTIVE

1. Community psychologists see maladaptation as resulting from the failure of social support systems. These systems can reduce such problems through preventive intervention, including special programs in the community. Community psychologists are likely to support **social-causation theories**, which argue that low socioeconomic status and poor living conditions cause stress that leads to psychological and social impairment; the **social-selection theory**, on the other hand, says that maladaptive behavior can lead to downward social mobility.

2. Behavior is shaped by a person's social group and the roles he or she plays within that group. Behavior is also affected by **labeling**, or categorizing people on some general basis.

THE VALUE OF AN INTERACTIONAL APPROACH

The interactional approach uses contributions from all of the six perspectives discussed in the chapter. Every person confronts diverse situations each day. The resulting behavior depends on the meshing of personal characteristics and both specific and general environmental factors. These produce individual vulnerabilities. Life events impact these vulnerabilities and are impacted by them.

*Classification
and Assessment*

Jennifer Bartlett, *Rhapsody,* 1975–76. Baked enamel and silkscreen grid on 16 gauge steel, enamel, each plate: 12 × 12". Overall: 7'6" × 153'9". Private collection, courtesy Paula Cooper Gallery, New York.

To learn:

1. The axes and major categories of DMS-III-R
2. The major methods of assessment

To understand:

1. Why classification is important
2. The negative aspects of classification

R obert Frank, a 37-year-old married man, came to a community mental health center because some of his thoughts had been bothering him.

For as long as he can recall, he has been introverted and somewhat fearful of people. He has desired social contact but, because of his fearfulness, has usually been unsuccessful in forming relationships. At the time that he came to the center, he was keeping certain disturbing thoughts to himself. In the past he had discussed these thoughts with his wife and with clinicians at a mental hospital. He thinks he is being spied upon by some unknown group, which he believes to be a government intelligence agency. He also feels that his television set is providing him with special messages and that an attempt is being made to control his will and thoughts. He has a job in a large corporation. In the judgment of his supervisor, he has performed well in the past but recently his work has deteriorated somewhat.

Frank has been hospitalized on two occasions, after which he seemed to make a good adjustment to the community. Six months ago his mother's death upset him greatly. During the past few months he has increasingly restricted his social activities to members of his family and has been somewhat withdrawn even with them. He came to the community mental health center because the thoughts were becoming more persistent. His discomfort level was increasing, he realized that he was becoming more incoherent, and he wanted to avoid another hospitalization if at all possible.

The clinical worker who talked with Frank wanted to get all this background information so that she could recommend the most practical and effective therapeutic program. She went through a series of steps in which information about Frank was gathered and interpreted. To increase the accuracy of their interpretations, clinicians often make use of the experiences of others in evaluating behavior. Classification systems are particularly valuable because they represent attempts to organize what a great many clinical workers know about the various types of problems they deal with.

The classification of personal problems is based on assessments of what clients say and how they behave. Both present life conditions and past experiences are taken into account. Classification is not simply an intellectual exercise, however. It has far-reaching effects on the lives of people who exhibit maladaptive behavior and on the activities of clinical workers.

Classification

The need to classify various types of personalities and personal problems has been recognized for a long time. Since the time of Hippocrates, classification systems have continually been revised to incorporate new knowledge and changing viewpoints. Nevertheless, the classification of abnormal behavior is still in an early stage of evolution, partly because of the arbitrary nature of the process of attaching labels to people. For example, there is no precise point at which an excessive drinker becomes a full-blown alcoholic, or when the tension you feel when you are alone in a strange room becomes the intense dread known as claustrophobia.

A classification statement or **diagnosis** places a disorder within a system of conventional groupings based on significant similarities in symptoms. Most classification systems are organized in hierarchical fashion. Thus, in the system that is used to classify animal life, human beings are members of the species *sapiens*, genus *Homo*, which is a subdivision of the family Hominidae, of the order *Primate*, of the class Mammalia, of the phylum Chordata, of the kingdom Animalia. Similarly, manic episode is a subdivision of bipolar disorder, which in turn is one of the major disorders in the family of mood disorders.

Pluses and Minuses of Classification

General use of a widely recognized classification system is very important. If every clinical worker made up his or her own system, communication problems would be enormous. It would be difficult to make use of research data on effective treatment, for example. Classification systems are also useful for statistical purposes. Government and other planning agencies need records of how often various types of maladaptation occur. Without such records, it would be impossible to say whether the incidence of certain forms of maladaptation was increasing or decreasing. Moreover, to the extent that the categories used in established classification systems are distinctive and can be rated reliably, they contribute to the planning of treatment programs and facilities.

The idea of classifying maladaptive behaviors has been criticized on several counts. Most important to many people is the fact that a diagnosis puts a label on a person. Labeling might make it difficult for a former patient to get a job, gain admission to a professional program, obtain custody of a child, and the like. Another argument is that many diagnoses are not useful because the diagnostic categories are imperfect and the same label may be assigned to behaviors that appear similar but have different causes and different treatments.

On balance, the case for classification is a strong one. It is easy to defend the idea that each patient is unique, yet nothing can be done to help an individual without referring to general principles. What is known about an individual case, however detailed, can be utilized only if the case is viewed within the context of existing knowledge. At the same time, general principles will have validity only if they are based on observation of individuals.

There are two major sources of unreliability in diagnoses. One concerns clinical judgment: differences in therapists' clinical training and theoretical orientation may lead to different diagnoses. The other major source of unreliability is the fact that diagnostic labels are attached to people, and no two people (or their problems) are alike. The same person might even describe his or her problem differently on two separate occasions. Diagnosticians may change their original assessment of a case, or two people with similar problems might describe their conditions differently and therefore be classified differently.

Ambiguities and inconsistencies also arise because most clinics and hospitals are burdened with more cases than they can handle. Leisurely and protracted study aimed at accurate classification is often impossible. Another factor is the range of problems treated by a particular clinical facility. The staff of a facility that treats a narrow range of disorders may tend to describe and interpret its cases differently than the staff of a more broadly based institution would. Diagnostic methods will achieve a firmer scientific basis as assessment becomes more standardized and less susceptible to distortion by such factors.

The Roles of Stress, Vulnerability, and Coping Resources

The authors' approach to abnormal psychology has some definite implications for the process of classification. This approach argues that abnormal behavior must be understood in the context of several factors: the recent stressful events in a person's life, such as a bereavement or loss of a job; the person's general vulnerabilities, such as a tendency toward low self-esteem that may have been engendered by early childhood experiences or a highly reactive nervous system; and what the individual has going for him or her, such as coping skills, intellectual ability, and family and friends who are willing and able to help.

Classifying abnormal behavior should be a matter of drawing a picture of a person rather than simply marking a point on a graph. In classifying a person who is experiencing a problem, we want to know not only what the problem is (for example, Frank's belief that he is being spied on) but also the context of the problem. The context includes (1) recent experiences that may have aroused stress and led to the worsening of his condition, (2) his vulnerabilities or weaknesses, and (3) his assets or strengths. The fact that Frank has experienced long periods of good adjustment (for example, being able to hold a job) is encouraging and should not be ignored. Optimally, the way we classify people should tell us something about their future prospects and likely responses to therapeutic efforts.

DSM-III-R

The most commonly used classification system for abnormal behaviors is the revised third edition of the American Psychiatric Association's *Diagnostic and Statistical Manual of Mental Disorders* (DSM-III-R). This manual, published as DSM-III in 1980 and revised in 1987 is used as a basis for communication among clinicians, for the maintenance of statistical records on the incidence of various types of problems, and for the planning of therapeutic programs. DSM-III-R might best be viewed as a set of guidelines for characterizing clinical problems, and it is concerned primarily with the description of these problems. Its categories take note of the etiology, or cause, of the disorder when it can be identified, as well as the subjective experiences of clients (for example, how worried or angry they seem to be) and their assets and liabilities. Thus, DSM-III-R provides information about the context in which abnormal behavior occurs as well as a description of the behavior in question.

DSM-III and DSM-III-R differ from earlier classification manuals in their emphasis on describing clinical problems rather than interpreting them. This change came about as a result of widespread concern that psychiatric diagnoses are often unreliable because they are based on guesses about the underlying causes of problems. The clinicians and researchers who developed DSM-III introduced more precise language into the classification system, increased its coverage to include additional types of maladaptive behavior, and provided more examples of the various categories. As a consequence, its revision, DSM-III-R, is about ten times longer than DSM-II, which was published in 1968.

Although it represents an advance in clinical classification, no one believes that DSM-III-R is the final word on the subject. Among its limitations is its continued reliance on impressionistic clinical judgments (for example, in estimating the severity of a disorder). An improved manual, DSM-IV, is scheduled to appear in the 1990s.

The Multiaxial Approach

DSM-III-R uses what is called a **multiaxial classification system**. This means that each case is not merely assigned to a category (for example, schizophrenia); instead, it is characterized in terms of a number of clinically important factors, which are grouped into the following five axes.

- AXIS I contains the **primary classification** or diagnosis of the problem that requires attention (for example, fear of heights).

- AXIS II classifies any **developmental and personality disorders** that begin in childhood or adolescence and usually persist in stable form into adult life. Examples are mental retardation and personality disorders such as an unwarranted tendency to interpret the actions of other people as threatening.

- AXIS III refers to any **physical disorders** that seem relevant to a case (for example, the client's history of heart attacks).

- AXIS IV rates the severity of **psychosocial stressors** in the client's recent past that may have contributed to the clinical problem and might influence the course of treatment (for example, divorce, death of a parent, loss of a job). Whether the stress is acute or chronic is also noted.

• AXIS V contains a global assessment of **psychological functioning, social relationships, and occupational activities** attained by the client. Ratings are made for both current functioning and the highest level of functioning during the past year. The behavior of two severely disturbed people would probably be interpreted differently and even treated differently if one had a history of good relationships with others and an excellent work record while the other had a history of social inadequacy and inability to hold a job.

The case presented at the beginning of the chapter might be classified as follows.

• Axis I: Paranoid schizophrenia
• Axis II: Avoidant personality disorder
• Axis III: No apparent medical problems
• Axis IV: Extreme
• Axis V: Serious impairment in several areas

Axes IV and V are innovations in that they can be quantitatively coded using criteria provided in DSM-III-R. Tables 4–1 and 4–2 describe the scales used in quantifying Axes IV and V.

The more complete the available information about a given case, the more reliable the DSM-III-R categorizations and ratings will be. Often, particularly in acute or emergency cases, a classification is made even though there are big informational gaps. In these cases, the classification is considered to be tentative and may be revised as more information is acquired.

The Major Diagnostic Categories

The first three axes constitute the official diagnostic categories of the American Psychiatric Association. Axes IV and V are regarded as supplementary categories for use in clinical and research settings.

DSM-III-R lists factors that are known to be relevant to particular diagnostic categories. These include the typical features of the disorder, the age at which it usually develops, its likely progression or outcome, the amount of social and occupational impairment involved, possible complications (for example, suicide attempts by

TABLE 4–1

Axis IV Scale for Rating Severity of Psychosocial Stressors

The codes can be applied for either acute life events or enduring circumstances and for adults or children.

| | | Type of Stressor | |
Code	Term	Specific Recent Events	Long Lasting Circumstances
		Adults	
1	None	None apparent	None apparent
2	Mild	Broke up with romantic partner	Job dissatisfaction
3	Moderate	Retirement	Marital discord
4	Severe	Divorce	Unemployment
5	Extreme	Victim of rape	Serious chronic illness in self or child
6	Catastrophic	Death of a child	Captivity as a hostage
0	Inadequate information or no change in condition		
		Children and Adolescents	
1	None	None apparent	None apparent
2	Mild	Change of school	Family arguments
3	Moderate	Birth of sibling	Chronic illness in parent
4	Severe	Divorce of parents	Multiple foster home placements
5	Extreme	Death of a parent	Recurrent sexual or physical abuse
6	Catastrophic	Death of both parents	Chronic life-threatening illness
0	Inadequate information or no change in condition		

Adapted from DSM-III-R (American Psychiatric Association, 1987, p. 11).

TABLE 4-2
Axis V Global Assessment of Functioning Scale (GAF)

The GAF is based on information concerning psychological, social, and occupational functioning on a hypothetical continuum of mental illness.

Code	Description	Example
90	Absent or minimal symptoms	None
80	Slight impairment	Occasional difficulty in concentration
70	Some mild symptoms	Depressed mood (feels blue)
60	Moderate symptoms	Conflict with co-workers
50	Serious symptoms	Frequent shoplifting
40	Impaired reality testing or communication	Illogical or obscure speech
30	Serious impairment	Suicidal; no home or friends
20	Some danger	Violent to self or others
10	Persistent danger	Frequently violent

Adapted from DSM III-R (American Psychiatric Association, 1987, p. 12).

depressed individuals), aspects of a person's life that increase the risk of a severe disorder, sex differences, and relevant family patterns. Table 4–3 lists indicators the clinician attends to in making a DSM-III-R classification.

Axis I Categories

Axis I includes all the major clinical disorders except personality and specific developmental disorders. These disorders are broken down as follows.

- DISORDERS OF INFANCY, CHILDHOOD, OR ADOLESCENCE. Conditions first evident in these periods include disruptive behavior, gender identity disorders, and certain eating disorders.

- ORGANIC MENTAL DISORDERS. Transient or permanent brain dysfunction attributable to such factors as the aging process or ingestion of a substance that affects the brain—for example, psychoses due to effects of excessive intake of alcohol, difficulty in directing attention, memory loss.

- PSYCHOACTIVE SUBSTANCE USE DISORDERS. Personal and social problems with use of certain substances—for example, dependence on and abuse of heroin, marijuana, and tobacco.

- SLEEP DISORDERS. Insomnia or difficulty in going to sleep or staying asleep, excessive daytime sleepiness, complaints of sleep disturbance without objective evidence, impairment of respiration during sleep, disturbance of the sleep-wake schedule, sleepwalking, sleep terrors.

- SCHIZOPHRENIA. Chronic disorganized behavior and thought of psychotic proportions (delusions, hallucinations), incoherence, and social isolation.

- DELUSIONAL (PARANOID) DISORDER. Well-organized system of delusions (often of being persecuted) without the incoherence, bizarreness, and social isolation seen in schizophrenia.

- PSYCHOTIC DISORDERS NOT CLASSIFIED ELSEWHERE. Includes schizophreniform disorders (similar to schizophrenia but currently of less than six months' duration), brief psychosis in reaction to a particular stress and schizoaffective disorders (a combination of disorganization and delusional behavior with feelings of depression and elation).

- MOOD (AFFECTIVE) DISORDERS. Depression or manic excitement, or both.

- ANXIETY DISORDERS. Anxiety, tension, and worry are major aspects of the clinical picture, with psychotic features (delusions, hallucinations) absent. Included also are posttraumatic (reactive, stress-caused) disorders. These may be brief or chronic.

- SOMATOFORM DISORDERS. Physical symptoms

TABLE 4-3
Clinical Observations and Symptoms Used in DMS-III-R Diagnosis

While a given symptom may be part of several different clinical pictures (for example, headaches may be present in cases marked by high anxiety, hypochondriasis, or somatic complaints), this list suggests the kinds of data clinicians attend to and that go into a psychiatric diagnosis. The presence of *groups* of symptoms characteristic of a particular disorder increases the likelihood of accurate classification.

Motor activity
Anxiety
Personal appearance
Behavior
Cognitive functioning ('attention, memory)
Eating disturbance
Energy level
Mood
Speaking manner
Occupational and social impairment
Perceptual disturbance
Personality traits
Physical symptoms
Sleep disturbance
Thought content

for which no medical causes can be found. These symptoms are apparently not under voluntary control and are linked to psychological factors or conflicts.

- DISSOCIATIVE DISORDERS. Sudden, temporary change in the normal functions of consciousness (for example, loss of memory, sleepwalking).
- SEXUAL DISORDERS. Deviant sexual thoughts and behavior that are either personally anxiety-provoking or socially maladaptive.
- FACTITIOUS DISORDERS. Physical or behavior symptoms that are voluntarily produced by the individual, apparently in order to play the role of patient, and often involving chronic, blatant lying.
- IMPULSE CONTROL DISORDERS NOT CLASSIFIED ELSEWHERE. Maladaptations characterized by failure to resist impulses (for example, pathological gambling, chronic stealing of desired objects, habitual fire-setting).
- ADJUSTMENT DISORDER. Maladaptive reactions to identifiable life events or circumstances that are expected to lessen and cease when the stressor ceases. The reactions may be dominated by depressed mood, anxiety, withdrawal, conduct disorder such as truancy, or lessening in work or job performance.
- PSYCHOLOGICAL FACTORS AFFECTING PHYSICAL CONDITION. Used to describe what have been referred to as either psychophysiological or psychosomatic disorders. Common examples include migraine headaches, painful menstruation, asthma, and duodenal ulcer.

Axis II Categories

The disorders listed on Axis II begin in childhood or adolescence and continue into adult life without much change. Axis I and II are separated so that when adults are evaluated, these continuing characteristics, which may affect personality or cognitive, social, or motor skills, will be taken into consideration. Axis II contains two major categories, *Developmental Disorders* and *Personality Disorders*. In some instances, the classification statements of Axis II are used to provide additional information about the primary diagnosis of Axis I. In others, the disorder referred to on Axis II is the individual's major problem.

Developmental Disorders. These include *Mental Retardation*, a significantly subaverage level of general intellectual functioning; *Pervasive Developmental Disorders*, in which there is an impairment in social interaction and communication that is accompanied by odd stereotyped behavior; and *Specific Developmental Disorders*, in which there are problems in particular aspects of speech, academic skills such as reading or arithmetic, or physical coordination.

Personality Disorders. These are characterized by enduring, inflexible, and maladaptive patterns of relating to, perceiving, and thinking about the environment and oneself. They cause impairment in social and occupational functioning. Personality disorders may resemble personality characteristics that occur in people who are functioning adaptively. They may also resemble many different behaviors associated with anxiety disorders, psychoses, or mood disorders.

Axis II may not distinguish clearly enough between personality styles or traits that are commonly seen in the general population and the rigid and clearly maladaptive personality styles that lead to personal unhappiness or ineffectiveness. Imperfect as it may be, however, the attempt to include personality factors in psychiatric classification is a step forward.

Evaluation of DSM-III and DSM-III-R

Although much more research evidence is needed if one is to make a definitive evaluation of DSM-III, some of its strengths and weaknesses have already been identified. DSM-III-R attempts to correct many of these by redefining some categories. Work to assess the impact of these changes has already begun.

One of the major objectives of DSM-III was to be quite specific about the criteria for using each diagnostic category. Table 4-4 illustrates DSM-III-R's emphasis on specifying criteria. It seems to have succeeded in achieving this objective. By emphasizing descriptions of behavior rather than theoretical ideas about its cause, DSM-III also seems to have succeeded in reducing the amount of inference needed to make a particular diagnosis.

In addition to increasing the dimensions used in describing particular disorders, DSM-III had greatly increased its coverage of the range of disorders. This increase is especially evident in the way it deals with childhood disorders.

DSM-III sought to increase its reliability by focusing on observable behavior rather than requiring inferences about what is going on inside the individual. Research studies have suggested that there may be adequate agreement in making Axis I and Axis V classifications but that there is less agreement for Axis II and Axis IV classifications (Spitzer, Forman, and Nee, 1979; Spitzer and Forman, 1979). Some of the changes in DSM-III-R are intended to increase the reliability of classification.

Related to the matter of reliability is the degree to which most clinicians would agree that the diagnostic categories are the "right" ones, that is, that they are meaningful and important. The developmental disorders

TABLE 4–4

Diagnostic Criteria for Separation Anxiety in Children from DSM-III-R

A. Excessive anxiety concerning separation from those to whom the child is attached, as evidenced by at least three of the following:

(1) unrealistic and persistent worry about possible harm befalling major attachment figures or fear that they will leave and not return

(2) unrealistic and persistent worry that an untoward calamitous event will separate the child from a major attachment figure, e.g., the child will be lost, kidnapped, killed, or be the victim of an accident

(3) persistent reluctance or refusal to go to school in order to stay with major attachment figures or at home

(4) persistent reluctance or refusal to go to sleep without being near a major attachment figure or to go to sleep away from home

(5) persistent avoidance of being alone, including "clinging" to and "shadowing" major attachment figures

(6) repeated nightmares involving the theme of separation

(7) complaints of physical symptoms, e.g., headaches, stomachaches, nausea, or vomiting, on many school days or on other occasions when anticipating separation from major attachment figures

(8) recurrent signs or complaints of excessive distress in anticipation of separation from home or major attachment figures, e.g., temper tantrums or crying; pleading with parents not to leave

(9) recurrent signs or complaints of excessive distress when separated from home or major attachment figures, e.g., wants to return home, needs to call parents when they are absent or when child is away from home

B. Duration of disturbance of at least two weeks.

C. Onset before the age of 18.

D. Occurrence not exclusively during the course of a Pervasive Developmental Disorder, Schizophrenia, or any other psychotic disorder.

American Psychiatric Association, 1987, pp. 60–61.

---

included in Axis II exemplify these problems. To what extent should children's reading and arithmetic difficulties be regarded as clinical problems? The inclusion of these developmental problems in a psychiatric classification system seems questionable.

It is possible that DSM-III's comprehensiveness is a mixed blessing. Research on agreement among clinicians in classifying patients has shown that there is a high level of agreement on broad general diagnostic categories, such as depression and juvenile delinquency, and low reliability for finer subdivisions within these general categories (Rutter and Shaffer, 1980). Much research will be required in order to determine the breadth and specificity needed to maximize the value of DSM-III and its revision (Williams, 1985).

DSM-III aroused considerable controversy (Klerman, 1984). Its supporters point to its recognition of the multiple problems that produce abnormal behavior, its effort to specify the bases for a particular classification, its superior reliability compared with DSM-II, and its use of the concept of multiaxial classification. Critics argue that it pays too much attention to how a person appears at a particular point in time (for example, upon admission to a clinic or hospital) and not enough to his or her prior history and developmental crises. DSM-III has also been criticized for providing little information

about the causes of abnormal behavior. Several writers argue that the manual ignores etiology and that both description and inferences about the processes involved in maladaptive behavior are needed (Bayer and Spitzer, 1985; Vaillant, 1984).

By introducing axes that pertain to severity of stress and previous level of adjustment, as well as to long-lasting personality patterns, DSM-III recognized the need for integrating what is known about people's vulnerabilities, assets, and stressful life events with what is observed in their behavior. No doubt modifications of the existing axes will be made in the light of research findings and the needs of practicing clinicians. For example, Axis V provides a global rating of the individual's highest level of adaptive functioning, but greater specificity would probably make this axis more useful. Separate ratings of level of adaptive functioning for social and occupational contexts would provide for more detailed characterization of an individual's problems. Separate ratings on Axis V for the past week and the past year might also be helpful.

Despite criticisms like those just noted, there seems little doubt that DSM-III was an improvement over previous diagnostic systems. Many of its limitations grew out of limitations in our understanding of what mental health and mental disorder are. Any classification system can be no better than available knowledge and attitudes about what is being classified. As we will see later in the chapter, experts who have devoted their entire careers to studying a specific topic such as schizophrenia have strong differences about what types of behavior should be studied.

The following comments by an experienced clinician show that even the concept of classification is controversial.

You would think that after working with troubled people for twenty years I'd know what their major problems are and what I should be diagnosing. Yet I'm not really sure what diagnosis is, what it should be, or how it can do more than just name and pigeonhole. I classify cases because it helps me keep records and communicate with other clinicians. At the same time, my major job is to treat people, to decide what I can do that will help them figure out what they should do to make their lives happier and more worthwhile. People are more different than they are similar. Two people may come in with a similar symptom, like delusions of grandeur, but the mechanisms that produce the symptom may be different. I wish diagnosis helped me better understand the basis for the conditions I diagnose.

DSM-III's greatest contribution may turn out to be the new knowledge that results from the arguments it has stimulated (Millon and Klerman, 1986).

Research on Classification

Research on the classification of abnormal behavior has focused on the role of clinical judgment in classification and on the effects of the labeling process. Information is also needed on how complex a classification system should be. How many categories should it have? Which variables must be assessed in making a diagnosis? Which ones should be optional? In what way should an individual's life story be taken into account in assessing his or her present behavior? The psychoanalytic perspective might lead to the conclusion that information about early childhood is essential to assessment, whereas a behavioristic viewpoint might emphasize a detailed description of present-day behavior. A diagnosis is not simply a label that is attached to a client by a clinician; it is a complex product of present knowledge and opinion about maladaptive behavior. As such, diagnosis is not an immutable process. Rather, it changes with advances in knowledge and alternations in what society defines as a problem.

Clinical Judgment

A variety of data go into classification statements. In arriving at a diagnosis, the clinician goes through a series of problem-solving and decision-making steps. The more complete and standardized the data and the more explicit the intervening cognitive steps, the greater the reliability of the diagnosis. This holds true whether we are talking about a clinician making a diagnosis on two different occasions using the same data or about two clinicians making independent diagnoses on the basis of the same information.

Studies of clinical judgment have been carried out in order to determine just how the clinician's role affects the reliability of classification. When diagnostic criteria are described clearly and intensive training is given in their use, and when the clinicians using them employ comparable methods, the reliability of diagnoses increases significantly. Additional factors also affect clinical judgments. One of these is the fact that certain disorders are more easily classified than others (for example, the reliability of diagnoses for organic brain disorders is higher than those for schizophrenia). Irrelevant or tangential information, such as labels, may throw a clinician off course. In addition, the attitudes and characteristics of diagnosticians often influence the judgments they make.

Research on clinical judgment suggests that even though they may not carry out formal research projects, clinicians use a research process in making their judgments. Like more research-oriented scientists, clinicians make observations, integrate them, and draw conclusions on the basis of the evidence they have gathered.

Evidence gathered in formal research on clinical judgment has helped identify factors that contribute to disagreement and error in day-to-day clinical research. Among them are the following.

1. *Patient factors.* The patient is not a constant. In fact, the patient may contribute to differences in clinical opinion by behaving in different ways at different times. If one clinician assesses an individual who is in the midst of an alcoholic delirium whereas another clinician's assessment is carried out several days after the delirium has lifted, differences in classification would not be surprising.

2. *Method factors.* Clinicians who use different assessment techniques might describe people who are actually similar as being different.

3. *Criteria factors.* Clinicians who have different standards for classifying cases might differ in their diagnoses.

4. *Clinician factors.* Clinicians differ in how they assess data. Personality differences, as well as differences in

training and theoretical orientation, influence the clinician's information processing.

Clinicians differ in how they process information and in how much they can keep track of. The computer may prove to be a valuable aid to clinical assessment because it is capable of scanning and retaining larger amounts of information than a human diagnostician can. Whether or not clinicians are aided by computers, the process by which they form judgments and make decisions is an important part of research on classification.

Assessment: The Basis of Classification

While efforts are made to improve classification systems, clinical workers must employ currently available methods in their work. The major methods used to assess behavior in clinical settings include interviews, psychological tests, behavioral assessment, cognitive assessment, and bodily assessment.

The Interview

The interview continues to be the most widely used assessment tool. Clinical interviews are of two types: assessment and therapeutic. The purpose of the **assessment** or **diagnostic interview** is to gather information and assess behavior. On the basis of the client's verbal and nonverbal behavior during the interview, the interviewer tries to figure out why the client is seeking help and what might be done from a therapeutic standpoint. The **therapeutic interview** occurs after a preliminary assessment has been made. Its aim is the actual modification of maladaptive behavior and attitudes.

Interviews usually involve two individuals, the interviewer and the client, although other people, such as family members, are sometimes included. Family members may also be interviewed separately. Treatment decisions are often based largely on the data gathered in an assessment interview, which may begin as a telephone call and then be followed up in a face-to-face setting.

Content of the Interview

Assessment interviewers seek to identify problems and determine the nature and extent of maladaptive behavior. Typically, interviewers begin by trying to find out how the client describes, understands, and interprets his or her problem. In some cases, the complaint is nonspecific, such as "I feel tense and worried all the time." In other cases, it may seem deceptively clear, as in "My child is hyperactive—I can't control him." Then the interviewer may inquire into the history of the problem. In the course of obtaining this information, the interviewer may get a better understanding of the stressing agents that were present in the client's life as the problem was developing.

Assessment interviews generally are relatively unstructured. Depending on the problem and how it is described, the interviewer may have to move back and forth among a number of topics. However, an attempt is made to answer the following questions:

1. *Who is the client?* That is, what is his or her name, age, ethnic and cultural background, marital status, and occupation? What led to his or her decision to obtain help from the clinic, hospital, or private consulting office?

2. *How does the clinic think and feel about his or her problem?* What are the client's preoccupations and feelings?

3. *What is the history of the problem and the client's developmental background?* Depending on the particular problem, an inquiry might be made into the physical and emotional climate of the home during the client's infancy and childhood, as well as the client's sleep patterns, physical and motor development, and sexual and social development.

4. *What is the client's present psychological state?* What is noteworthy about the client's speech, thought, judgment, cooperativeness, and social skills?

During an assessment interview, many aspects of behavior must be observed and noted. These include the client's general appearance and grooming, voice and speech patterns, and the kinds of thoughts described, as well as facial expression, posture, and style of movement.

People with serious problems state facts, opinions, attitudes, and, in some cases, distortions and lies. They behave in a variety of ways: they may sigh, gesture, avert their eyes, tap their feet, smile, or grimace at the interviewer. As a consequence of this flood of responses, the interviewer usually can extract and use only a small percentage of the data presented during the interview. On the other hand, some clients hesitate to discuss their problems openly and provide very little information. Answers to questions such as, "How does your wife get on your nerves?" can differ widely in honesty, clarity, and feeling. Unanticipated reactions by the interviewee must also be noted.

Much of the behavior that is sampled in an interview is self-description. To facilitate the planning of treatment, the interviewer must establish valid relationships between the responses made during the interview and the interviewee's behavior in current or future life situations. If the interview behavior is not representative of the client's characteristic response tendencies, inappropriate treatment decisions may be made. The interviewer attempts to construct a situation that, within a short period, provides reflections of complex lifelong patterns.

In most applied settings assessment interviewers make mental and written notes, subjectively interpreting the behavior sample as it unfolds. Are they accurate observers of the interviewee's behavior? Do they unduly influence the behavior of the person being interviewed? These questions arise frequently in discussions of interviewing. Interviewers don't always note or interpret correctly much of what goes on in an interview.

A truly objective evaluation of an interview cannot focus on the interviewee alone. Each interview involves a developing and distinctive relationship between the interviewer and the interviewee, and their characteristics jointly influence what takes place during the interview. Research supports clinical impressions that the interviewer is a major factor in the interview. The interviewer's behavior may influence the data obtained in an interview as well as how those data are analyzed. This is true for both assessment and therapeutic interviews. The following are some interviewer characteristics that might influence the course of an interview and its content (Beutler and others, 1986):

- age
- gender
- ethnicity
- professional background
- interviewing style
- personality pattern
- attitudes and values
- expectations

As the following case suggests, the unique characteristics and styles that both the client and interviewer bring to the clinical situation make it difficult to perfectly standardize clinical interviews.

The interviewer knew nothing about Robert Hatton except that he was 19 years old, had just begun his studies at a large university, and had a skin condition of apparently recent origin. The skin condition included redness, breaking out in large welts, and itchiness. Hatton had come to the Student Health Service for the skin condition, but the

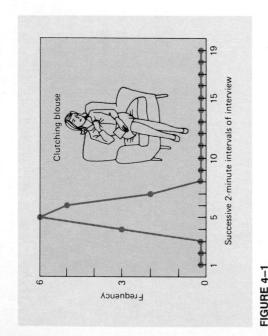

FIGURE 4–1
Frequency of one nonverbal response (blouse clutching) during an interview.

Interviewers need to observe the relationship between their clients' verbal and nonverbal behaviors. Often what interviewers hear contradicts what they see. The client's verbal manner may be calm and dispassionate even though tension is evident from nonverbal signs such as sweating and hand-wringing. In some cases, gestures, movements, and facial expressions yield clues to the sources of a client's anxiety. Experienced clinicians are adept at observing nuances of behavior that clients are unaware of or believe they are suppressing successfully, as can be seen in the following interview.

During the interview she held her small son on her lap. The child began to play with his genitals. The mother without looking directly at the child, moved his hand away and held it securely for a while. Later in the interview the mother was asked what she ordinarily did when the child played with himself. She replied that he never did this—he was a very "good" boy. She was evidently entirely unconscious of what had transpired in the very presence of the interviewer.

—(Maccoby and Maccoby, 1954, p. 484)

Another interviewer recorded the frequency of a client's "blouse-clutching" behavior during an assessment interview (see Figure 4–1) and noted a particularly high frequency of this behavior during one portion of the interview. The client had at that time been describing how, at the age of 8, she and her twin sister had been told that they had "killed their mother" during their birth.

The Role of the Interviewer

Every type of assessment involves taking a behavior sample for the purpose of predicting future behavior.

ointment prescribed gave only minor, temporary relief. The physician who had treated him recommended that he talk with a clinical psychologist who was on staff of the Student Health Service.

The first thing Hatton mentioned to the psychologist was the skin condition, how annoying and disruptive it was because of the incessant itching, and his puzzlement at being referred to a psychologist. During the initial interview he sweated a lot, occasionally had to catch his breath, and tapped his foot continually. Noting the stigma Hatton seemed to feel about talking with what he called "a mental specialist," the psychologist made the following analysis of the situation: "If Robert's skin condition does have a psychological component, he has to learn that it is okay to talk to me. My main job right now is to listen and not to ask a lot of questions that make Robert think he's crazy."

The psychologist did ask some questions ("Have you had skin problems in the past? Under what circumstances?" "How do you like it at the University"), but mainly she listened patiently, avoiding making quick judgments about what the client had to say, and carefully observed what the client said and did, as well as what topics seemed to be upsetting to him. While avoiding aloofness, the psychologist maintained a detached but friendly attitude. When the client expressed concern about his ability to succeed at the university, the clinician did not say, "You're obviously intelligent enough to be very successful at this university," even though Hatton's vocabulary and manner of expressing himself were obviously outstanding. ("What good would it do if I told Robert what all his friends and relatives tell him? What he is saying is that he's scared and really is worried about flunking out. I've got to let him know I realize what he is going through. The flip reassurance of other people hasn't done him one bit of good.")

The interview was uncomfortable for both Hatton and the psychologist. Hatton was tense, and there were long pauses during which he seemed unable to think of anything to say. Each of these pauses posed a conflict for the interviewer. ("If the pause is too long and too uncomfortable, he might decide not to come to see me again. On the other hand, what clients say after pauses is often very significant. I've got to steer along just the right path with Robert.") The interviewer increased her level of activity whenever she detected that the client was experiencing too much anxiety or felt that he needed a show of interest and support.

The clinical psychologist had seen many cases in which physical problems (such as skin conditions) were related to the stress of university life. But she did not want to pigeonhole Hatton. Her main goal in the intake interview was to establish a relationship of mutual trust with him. She liked him, wanted to help him, and thought she could. But the first task was to accept him as a likable, unique person and hope that he would want to come back. Apparently her approach worked, because Hatton came back four times, as a result of which much information was brought out and the clinical picture became clearer.

What emerged was a person of exceptional potential for whom the university was an intense stress because of the need he felt to be worthy of all the sacrifices his family was making for him. While he wanted to reward his parents for their help, he was also deeply angered at the way in which they blithely assumed he would make Phi Beta Kappa if he avoided being lazy.

On the basis of the series of assessment interviews, the psychologist pieced together a picture of an intense stress reaction because of all the pressures to which Hatton felt he was being subjected. The psychologist did not know for sure what had caused the skin condition, but she felt that it might have been an accompaniment of the anxious thoughts connected with going to the university. Her recommendation was that Hatton be seen by a psychotherapist who might help him decide on his own goals in life, rather than uncritically accepting his parents' goals for him. After a series of twenty therapy sessions, Hatton was much less anxious, his skin condition was no longer in existence, and he felt more accepting of both himself and his parents.

The Standardized Interview

We noted earlier that standardized procedures increase the reliability of classifications of abnormal behavior. This makes a lot of sense, since standardization guarantees that clinicians will at least ask the same questions of each person they interview. An argument against standardized interviews is that they do not give the clinician the flexibility needed to form a productive relationship with a client. However, there is no reason why a clinical worker could not use a standardized format in one interview and a more flexible one in another.

Standardized interviews are used to determine whether specific symptoms are present. Standardization is achieved by providing the interviewer with a glossary of symptom definitions, a series of questions that are pertinent to symptoms, a set of topics about which information should be obtained, and cut-off points that indicate when to stop probing on a particular topic. The clinician also is given instructions for rating the presence and severity of symptoms in numerical terms. Most structured interviews permit the interviewer to depart from the standardized form under specified circumstances. The interviewer also has the option of pursuing lines of inquiry (including a return to a former line of questioning or a jump to a completely different section) that are suggested by the client's responses.

The Diagnostic Interview Schedule

The Diagnostic Interview Schedule (DIS) illustrates the potential of the standardized interview (Robins and others, 1981). The DIS is designed to permit diagnosis of selected DSM-III-R categories such as panic disorder. A person who has a panic disorder has recurrent anxiety attacks that often occur unpredictably, though certain situations, such as riding on a bus, may become associated with a panic attack. Panic attacks are noted for their frequency, severity, and symptoms, which include sweating, trembling, faintness, and heart palpitations. The section of the DIS that pertains to panic disorder provides answers to the following questions and offers procedures for deriving the appropriate classification.

- Did a panic attack occur?
- How many attacks have occurred?
- What are the symptoms?
- Are the attacks repetitive rather than isolated?
- Are the attacks characteristic of the person's life rather than confined to a brief, atypical period?
- At what age did the attacks begin?
- Are the attacks explainable as symptoms of another disorder?
- Is the person tense, nervous, or high-strung between attacks?

The DIS has continued to evolve and now includes procedures, probes, and criteria appropriate for use with specific clusters of symptoms. New clusters are added periodically. For example, certain anxiety, stress, and eating disorders are included in the latest DIS format, Version IV, which not only describes symptoms but provides information about recent and past life experiences that are associated with their onset. For bulimia, whose main symptoms is binge eating, questions are asked about the types of food eaten, the respondent's mood during and after the binge, the environment in which the eating is done, how the binges are terminated, associated weight gain, and efforts to prevent weight gain. The onset and most recent occurrence of the disorder are determined from the dates of the first and most recent binges.

The DIS can be employed by professional and nonprofessional interviewers who have been trained in its use. The types of questions used are illustrated in Table 4–5. Training (a week-long course), supervision, quality control in the use of the interview, and periodic retraining sessions are emphasized. Programs for com-

TABLE 4–5

Examples of Questions Used in Standardized Interviews

How old were you the first time you were bothered by these particular fears?

Has there ever been a period of two weeks or more when you felt worthless, sinful, or guilty?

Have you ever gotten into physical fights while drinking?

For how many weeks, months, or years did you continue to have no interest in an activity that had meant a lot to you before?

Has there ever been a period of two weeks or more when you had a lot more trouble concentrating than is normal for you?

Has there ever been a period of two weeks or more when you wanted to die?

puter scoring of interview data are available. Studies are being carried out to determine the feasibility of using computers either to directly administer the DIS or to aid the interviewer in administering it.

Research has shown that both professional and nonprofessional DIS users tend to agree with each other and with the impressions gained by clinicians in more usual psychiatric interviews (Helzer and others, 1985). However, while the goal of an instrument like the DIS is to assess the occurrence of specific symptoms, deciding whether that goal has been achieved is not a simple matter since there is no objective and absolute standard against which to measure results. Nevertheless, clear specification of diagnostic definitions is a major achievement because it makes possible uniform diagnostic methods for diverse populations and places.

Instruments like the DIS, based on specific clinical criteria, have the potential to make comparability across studies a reality. However, much more research will be needed to determine whether this potential can be fully realized. Research on the DIS and similar instruments is proceeding at an accelerating pace. One of the findings of that research is that lay interviewers (that is, nonprofessionals) are able to use the DIS in a reliable fashion and that their judgments tend to agree with those of professionals (Anthony and others, 1985; Wittchen and others, 1985).

Psychological Tests

Although there is agreement about the need to develop valid ways of characterizing individuals, clinicians disagree on how this can best be accomplished. Because no single assessment tool is considered foolproof, assessment is commonly approached in more than one way in order to yield a more complete and accurate description of the individual. Over the past several decades an array of techniques for classifying behavior had been developed, mostly in the form of psychological tests.

Psychological tests differ from interviews in that they restrict the client's freedom of expression. Just as it is easier to quantify and compare scores on a multiple-choice test than on an essay test, the responses obtained on psychological tests can be more readily quantified and compared than the more open-ended and unstructured responses obtained in interviews. To achieve a well-rounded picture of the individual, most clinicians interpret quantified psychometric results in light of behavioral observations made in less restricted situations. We will discuss three types of psychological tests: intelligence tests, personality inventories, and projective techniques.

Intelligence Tests

Intelligence tests were the first widely recognized psychological assessment tool. During the latter part of the nineteenth century, intelligence was equated with fast reflexes and sensitivity to the environment. Efforts to assess intelligence relied heavily on sensory and other discrimination tasks. The English scientist Francis Galton sought to evaluate intelligence by measuring such things as reaction time, ability to discriminate between weights, sensitivity to pain, and ability to differentiate tones.

The Binet Tests. In the late nineteenth and early twentieth centuries, the French psychologist Alfred Binet developed a series of tests that differed noticeably from those that had previously been used to measure intelligence. Binet viewed intelligence as something that grows with age; older children are, on the average, more intelligent than younger ones. He sought to measure reasoning, ability to understand and follow directions, and the exercise of judgment or good sense. The child's score on the original Binet test was expressed as a mental level corresponding to the age of normal children whose performance reached the same level.

Later the term "mental age" was substituted for "mental level" and an intelligence quotient (IQ) was computed by dividing the person's test score, or mental age (MA), by his or her chronological age (CA) and multiplying the result by 100. In equation form,

$$IQ = \frac{MA}{CA} \times 100$$

The current test, called the Stanford-Binet scales, has undergone periodic revisions. Stanford-Binet scores are now derived from norms based on how much the individual's score deviates from the mean score for a particular age.

In its first three editions the Binet test yielded one overall score. Use of the Binet-type tests declined, partly

because the tasks on the Binet scales did not lend themselves to separate, reliable, quantitative analyses. Perhaps the most important reason for the relative decline in the use of the Binet scales was that they were designed primarily for work with children. As a result of these criticisms, the fourth edition (Stanford-Binet, 1985) yields several different scores, and many of the items have been rewritten to appeal to adults as well as children. This edition resembles the widely used Wechsler tests more than did the earlier editions (Vernon, 1987).

The Wechsler Tests. David Wechsler (1955, 1958) regarded the Binet tests as deficient because they produced only a single score. He believed that intelligence is an aggregate of abilities and should be measured as such. The **Wechsler Adult Intelligence Scale** (WAIS-R), published in 1981, consists of eleven subtests, of which six are verbal and five nonverbal. An important advantage of a test like the WAIS is that in addition to being able to compute a score for the entire test, one can score each of the subtests separately.

Three IQs are obtained on the Wechsler scales. **Verbal IQ** reflects level of attainment on subtests dealing with general information, comprehension, ability to think in abstract terms, and arithmetic. **Performance IQ** reflects level of attainment or tasks requiring solution of puzzles, substitution of symbols for digits, and reproduction of designs. The third type of IQ is the **Full Scale IQ**, which represents the total score on the test.

The success of Wechsler's Adult Intelligence Scales led to the development of the **Wechsler Intelligence Scale for Children** (WISC) (see Figure 4–2). In 1974 a revision of the children's test, WISC-R, was published; in this version not only were the test items improved, but the group whose score formed the norms or comparison group for evaluating performance was more representative of the total population (Kaufman, 1979). For use with ever younger children, the **Wechsler Preschool and Primary Scale of Intelligence (WPPSI)** was developed.

For many years intelligence testers have employed the Wechsler, Binet, and similar batteries in making clinical assessments. Recently, however, new theories have been suggested that may lead to different approaches to the assessment of intelligence. Box 4–1 describes recent developments in the assessment of intelligence.

Personality Assessment

Research on personality has stimulated the development of a variety of tests, rating scales, and questionnaires aimed at measuring personality differences. These devices can be useful shortcuts to understanding behavior. Think how long it takes you to get to know a person; in many situations psychologists do not have that kind of time.

exam—might be used to divide people into groups according to how upset they get while taking exams. Researchers have investigated whether more test-anxious students behave differently than less anxious ones in an experimental situation. A less common use of personality tests is as a dependent variable. One group of subjects might see a war movie showing violent battle scenes while another views a nature film. A personality test might then be used to determine which group had the higher aggression score.

Personality Inventories. The success of intelligence tests in predicting future achievement led researchers to try to develop similar ways to measure personality. But personality isn't something that can be measured by a total score that is high, medium, or low. The testlike measures used in personality assessment are meant to indicate the types of characteristics that combine to make up an individual's personality.

Rather than testing general knowledge or specific skills, **personality inventories** ask people questions about themselves. These questions may take a variety of forms. When taking such a test, you might have to decide whether each of a series of statements is accurate as a self-description, or you might be asked to respond to a series of true–false questions about yourself and the world. Several inventories require the respondent to rate a set of statements on a scale based on how well they reflect his or her characteristics. Modern personality inventories yield several scores, each of which is intended to represent a distinct aspect of the personality.

The diversity of items found in personality inventories is illustrated by the following statements, which are drawn from the *Minnesota Multiphasic Personality Inventory* (MMPI) (Hathaway and McKinley, 1967). The test taker responds to each statement with "True," "False," or "Cannot say."

a. I believe there is a God.
b. I would rather win than lose a game.
c. I am worried about sex matters.
d. I believe I am being plotted against.
e. I believe in obeying the law.
f. Everything smells the same.

The MMPI, the most widely used personality inventory today, was developed at the University of Minnesota during the 1930s in response to the need for a practical, economical means of characterizing the personalities of psychiatric patients who had been given different diagnoses.(Graham, 1987). It originally consisted of nine scales related to different groups of clinical disorders: hypochondriasis (Hs), depression (D), hysteria (Hy), psychopathic deviate (Pd), masculinity–femininity (Mf), paranoia (Pa), psychasthenia (Pt), schizo-

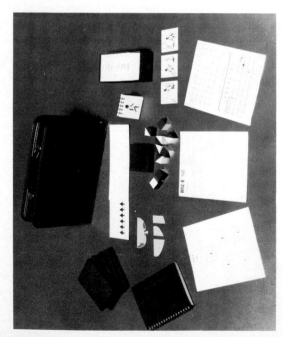

FIGURE 4–2a
The Weschsler Intelligence Scales contain a variety of subtests. This photo shows subtests from the performance section of the revised Weschsler Intelligence Scale for Children (WISC-R).

FIGURE 4–2b
This child is working on the Object Assembly subtest.

Personality tests and other assessment methods are used in clinical settings in making diagnoses, in deciding whether treatment is required, and in planning the treatment to be used. Personality tests are also used in selecting employees. A third major use of personality measures is in psychological research, where the tests may be used as either independent or dependent variables. For example, as an independent variable, scores on a measure of test anxiety—that is, the feeling of tenseness and worry that people experience before an

TABLE 4–6

phrenia (Sc), and hypomania (Ma). The more recently developed social introversion (Si) scale is now considered to be part of a standard 10-scale battery. There are also numerous special scales.

In developing each clinical scale, Hathaway and McKinley, the authors of the MMPI, looked at how groups of individuals with the appropriate diagnosis responded to the items on the MMPI. They also gave the test to people who were not psychiatric patients. The latter group included college students, nonpsychiatric patients, medical personnel, and visitors to the University of Minnesota Hospital. The responses of this normal group were compared with those of people who had been diagnosed as having a particular psychiatric disorder, such as a schizophrenic disorder. Items on which the scores were significantly different for the two groups came to constitute the scale for the disorder in question—in our example, this would be the schizophrenia scale. A high score on this scale indicates that the person's responses were similar to those of the schizophrenics in the original group tested by Hathaway and McKinley.

In addition to the clinical scales, there are three control scales. The L (or Lie) scale was devised to measure people's tendency to make themselves look good by attributing socially desirable characteristics to themselves. One L scale item is "I never tell a lie." An answer of "True" to this and similar items would cast doubt on how honest the rest of the person's answers are. People with high L scores appear impossibly good and virtuous.

For F scale was included to reflect people's carelessness and confusion in taking the MMPI. High scores on the F scale indicate that people described themselves as having a number of rare and improbable characteristics. For example, one F scale item is "There is an international plot against me."

The K scale is more subtle than the L and F scales. Its construction was based on the observation that some open and frank people may obtain high scores on the clinical scales while others who are very defensive may obtain low scores. The K scale was devised to reduce these biasing factors. People who get high K scores are defensive; they tend to answer "False" to items like "I feel bad when others criticize me." K corrections are made on a number of clinical scales in order to compare the scores obtained by people who differ in these tendencies.

Table 4–6 describes the MMPI's clinical and control scales. The principal application of the MMPI is in deciding how to classify a given case. In general, the greater the number and magnitude of deviant scores on the MMPI, the more likely it is that the individual is severely disturbed. In making diagnostic decisions, the MMPI user must be adept at interpreting not only the scores on the individual scales but also the pattern of

The name, abbreviation, and number of each scale is given. (Clinical workers typically refer to the scales by number rather than by name or abbreviation.) Interpretations of high scores for the scales are also given.

The MMPI: Clinical and Control Scales

Name and Abbreviation	Scale Number	Interpretation of High Scores
Clinical Scales		
Hypochondriasis (Hs)	1	Bodily preoccupation; pessimistic
Depression (D)	2	Depressed; lacks self-confidence
Hysteria (Hy)	3	Psychologically motivated physical symptoms; lacks insight
Psychopathic deviate (Pd)	4	Antisocial tendencies: impulsive
Masculinity-femininity (Mf)	5	Sex-role conflict
Paranoia (Pa)	6	Suspiciousness; resentful
Psychasthenia (Pt)	7	Anxious; insecure
Schizophrenia (Sc)	8	Bizarre thinking; withdrawn
Hypomania (Ma)	9	Excessive psychomotor activity; unrealistic goals
Social introversion (Si)	0	Social anxiety; shy
Control Scales		
L scale	—	Need to present unrealistically favorable impression
F scale	—	Severe psychological disturbance
K scale	—	Defensive; inhibited

those scores in a particular person's profile. For example, the assessor cannot assume that a high score on the schizophrenia scale indicates the presence of schizophrenia. Other psychotic groups may show high elevation on this scale, and schizophrenics often score higher on other scales than on the Sc scale.

Rating Scales. There are many other personality assessment techniques. The **rating scale** is one of the most venerable and versatile of these. Rating scales present respondents with an item (a concept, person, or situation) and ask them to select from a number of choices. The rating scale is similar in some respects to a multiple choice test, but its options represent degrees of a particular characteristic.

BOX 4-1

Recent Developments in the Assessment of Intelligence

CONTRIBUTIONS FROM COGNITIVE AND DEVELOPMENTAL PSYCHOLOGY

Cognitive and developmental psychologists have sought to create models of the structure of intelligence. Jean Piaget directed attention to how cognitive behavior changes in the course of a child's development. He suggested that the child passes through a series of cognitive stages, each of which is distinguished by the appearance of concepts that the child was unable to grasp earlier. Piaget was interested not so much in the correctness of children's responses as in the way they reason in arriving at the response. For example, if a child was asked whether a hammer is more like a nail or more like a screwdriver, Piaget would focus on whether the child selected a nail because a hammer and a nail are often used together or a screwdriver because both it and the hammer are tools. Most 4-year-olds would give the first answer, whereas older children would give the second. According to Piaget, as children become older they progress to symbolic thought and

FIGURE 4-3a

Perceptual performance in a case of organic brain damage. The Bender Visual–Motor Gestalt Test (1938) is a deceptively simple task in which the subject is asked to copy geometric forms like these. (From Bender Visual–Motor Gestalt Test, published by American Orthopsychiatric Association, 1938)

later to a final stage, that of logical, rational thought.

Cognitive psychologists have also studied how individuals with widely differing scores on intelligence tests solve problems. One of the most dramatic differences in problem-solving skills seems to deal with strategies of learning or **metacognition.** Low scores on intelligence tests are related to deficiencies in these strategies. For example, most people learn a variety of memorization strategies without any particular instruction. Those who are retarded need to have these strategies explicitly taught and explained to them. Teaching the strategies to retarded individuals improves their performance on a particular task, but the training cannot readily be applied to other tasks.

NEUROPSYCHOLOGICAL APPROACH TO INTELLIGENCE

Biological factors play a role in intelligence, also. One theorist, Howard Gardner (1983), believes that there are a small number of separate human intelligences,

FIGURE 4-3b

This is the Bender–Gestalt protocol of a patient suffering from organic brain damage. (From Lacks [1984], p. 34. Copyright 1984 by John Wiley & Sons. Reprinted by permission.)

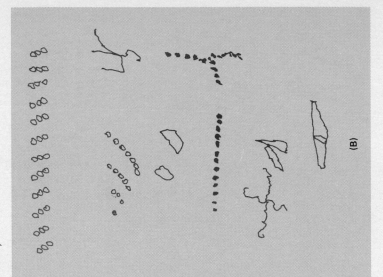

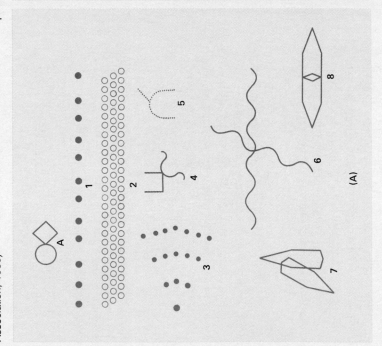

each of which is controlled by a specific region of the brain. His list includes the ability to use language, the ability to reason logically or mathematically, spatial skills, bodily talents like dance or mime, awareness of one's own feelings, and the ability to understand the feelings of others. Gardner describes his theory by saying that "the normal human being is so constituted as to be sensitive to certain informational content; when a particular form of information is presented, various mechanisms in the nervous system are triggered to carry out specific operations upon it. And from the re-

peated use of, elaboration of, and interaction among, these various computational devices, eventually flow forms of knowledge that we would readily term 'intelligent' " (Gardner, 1983, p. 279).

Neuropsychologists are interested in differentiating among intellectual functions and identifying their biological bases. For example, one group of researchers studied the effects of lowered oxygen intake on the performance of members of an expedition to Mt. Everest (West, 1984). Using a neuropsychological test battery and tests of memory and coordination, they measured

FIGURE 4–4
Some of the tasks from the Kaufman-ABC. In the Face Recognition subtest, the child is shown a picture of one or two faces such as (a) for 5 seconds. The child is then asked to select that face or faces from a group picture such as (b). The Gestalt Closure subtest, illustrated by (c) consists of a series of partially completed drawings. The child's task is to name the object pictured, in this case a bicycle. In the Word Order subtest (d) the child is shown a group of pictures and asked to touch them in the order they are named. Later the task is made more difficult by having the examiner name the items and then ask the child to do another task before pointing to the pictures in the correct sequence.

BOX 4–1 CONTINUED

the expedition members' performance at various altitudes on the mountain and one year after the expedition. There was a significant decline in verbal learning, verbal expression, short-term memory, and finger-tapping speed at high altitudes. Memory, verbal expression, and learning had returned to pre-expedition levels a year later, but most of the subjects still showed impairment in finger-tapping speed. Although the reason for this finding is unclear, it is likely that prolonged severe oxygen deprivation was related to a continuing dysfunction in the cerebrum.

One approach to the neuropsychological aspects of intelligence is to examine the ways in which individuals with known organic brain damage respond on performance tests. Figure 4–3 provides an example of this approach.

A NEW APPROACH TO INTELLIGENCE TESTING

The general approach to intelligence testing that has been dominant for at least fifty years has been challenged by these new ideas. One new test that has come into frequent use, the Kaufman Assessment Battery for Children (K-ABC), is designed to incorporate these new ideas from cognitive psychology and neuropsychology into the assessment of intelligence (Kaufman and Kaufman, 1983). The K-ABC consists of 16 subtests, some for older and some for younger chil-

dren. The tests fall into several categories: sequential processing, such as remembering a series of digits or hand movements; simultaneous processing, such as arranging a series of related pictures in the correct order; and tests that measure school experience more directly, such as naming pictures of well-known places and objects (see Figure 4–4). Many of the tests do not require a verbal response, and those that do require a few words at most. In most cases, the child can respond by pointing or in other nonverbal ways. The test has been described as a way to learn more about the child's approach to problem-solving and learning tasks. The test's emphasis on short-term memory has been questioned by some critics, but the Kaufmans argue that what is being measured is not memory as such but the sequential and simultaneous processing abilities that are defined as intelligence by cognitive psychologists.

Although the K-ABC tests have been described as being particularly fair to minority children, scores on these tests show the same black–white differences that are seen on other intelligence tests. However, the K-ABC tests do demonstrate that if parental education is taken into account there is little racial or ethnic difference on many nonverbal reasoning tasks. When the education of the parents is taken into account, blacks of preschool age and Hispanics of preschool and school age perform as well as whites. These similarities are due primarily to the tests' emphasis on short-term memory.

An example of a rating scale item is "To what degree are you shy?" People might be asked to place this item on a scale ranging from "Not at all" to "Extremely." They can do this graphically by placing a check mark at an appropriate point on a continuum:

Not at all	Slightly	Moderately	Very	Extremely

Unlike the MMPI, which can be used only for self-reporting, rating scales can be used to rate other people's behavior as well as one's own. For instance, a teacher might use rating scales to rate his or her students. In this case the item above might read "To what degree is this student shy?"

Rating scales, like self-report questionnaires, are not immune to inaccuracy. One possible biasing factor, the **halo effect**, results when an individual rates a person more favorably than is realistic on a specific

characteristic because the rater has a generally favorable reaction to the person (Cooper, 1981). Other methodological problems include the tendency to want to say only nice things about oneself or someone else, and the tendency to use the midrange of the scales. Research has shown that many of these problems can be reduced through careful wording of items, instructions to the rater, use of minimally ambiguous concepts and scales, and in some cases, actual training in making ratings.

An example of the use of rating scales in clinical work is the assessment of children's ability to pay attention to what is going on around them and to exercise self-control. The degree to which children possess these abilities is an indicator of their personal development. Many clinical problems in children are related to the inability to delay responding until the desired time, to plan activities, and to engage in socially appropriate behavior. Kendall and Wilcox (1978) devised a convenient series of rating scales to assess children's self-control. Their measure, the Behavior Rating Scale for Children, has proven reliable and can be used in a variety of settings and by untrained observers such as parents.

The Behavior Rating Scale for Children presents the rater with 33 questions, each of which is responded to on a 7-point rating scale (1 = always, 7 = never). The following are some representative items from the scale.

- Does the child sit still?
- Does the child disrupt games?
- Does the child think before he or she acts?
- Does the child grab for the belongings of others?
- Is the child easily distracted from his or her work or chores?

Projective Techniques. One group of assessment specialists believes that the more freedom people have in picking their responses, the more meaningful the description and classification that can be obtained. Because personality inventories do not permit much freedom of

choice, some clinical psychologists prefer to use **projective techniques,** in which a person is shown ambiguous stimuli and asked what he or she thinks they are about. Some clinicians believe that projective techniques are very sensitive to unconscious dimensions of personality. Defense mechanisms, latent impulses, and anxieties have all been inferred from data gathered in projective situations.

The *Rorschach inkblots,* developed by the Swiss psychiatrist Hermann Rorschach (1884–1922), consist of ten cards, half colored and half black and white (see Figure 4–5). The test is administered by showing the cards, one at a time, and asking the person to describe what he or she sees in them. There are no right or wrong answers. After the person has responded to the inkblots in a free-association manner, the examiner asks questions about particular responses ("What gave you that impression?" "What made it seem like a _____?"). Besides recording what is said in response to the inkblots,

FIGURE 4–5a
As the client responds to the Rorschach card, the clinician records both verbal responses and behavior.

FIGURE 4–5b
This inkblot, similar to those used in the Rorschach test, produced a variety of responses, including: 1. "Looks like a long tunnel or channel in the center." 2. "On its side, I see a crabby old man frowning, with a long nose. I don't like him." 3. "There is a head of a camel in the middle there—no body, just the head."

the examiner also notes the person's mannerisms, gestures, and attitudes.

Rorschach developed the inkblot test as part of an experimental effort to relate perception to personality. He believed that people's responses to inkblots could serve as clues to their basic personality traits. However, negative research findings have caused many users of projective techniques to become dubious about the validity of the Rorschach inkblots as perceptual indicators of personality. Even if the inkblots are useless for this purpose, however, the test can be used in analyzing people's social behavior and the content of their verbal productions. Attempts to elicit assistance from the examiner and the use of stereotyped verbal responses are examples of the types of behavior that can be observed in the Rorschach situation.

Like the Rorschach test, the *Thematic Apperception Test* (TAT) employs ambiguous stimuli to which people can respond in a free manner. The TAT uses pictures that show people engaging in a variety of activities; hence, it is less ambiguous than the Rorschach inkblots (see Figure 4–6). The total test consists of 30 picture cards and one blank card, although in most test situations not all of the cards are used. The cards are presented one at a time, and the person is asked to make up a story describing the scene in each picture, the events that led up to that scene, and the events that will grow of it. The person is also asked to describe the thoughts and feelings of the people in the story.

Henry A. Murray (1893–1988), the author of the TAT, described the picture in Figure 4–6a (Card 12-F) as a portrait of a young woman, with a weird old woman grimacing in the background. Following is a story about that picture that was told by a 37-year-old woman who was diagnosed as a paranoid schizophrenic and was also depressed. How might it be interpreted? Note the perceptual distortion that changed the usual mother–daughter relationship into a father–son relationship. (The examiner's questions are indicated in parentheses.)

It's an old man standing behind a young man thinking, or knows what this young man should do, what he has ahead of him. He is very tired [old man] and the young man has a lot more—I can't

FIGURE 4–6a
Cards from the Thematic Apperception Test are more structured than the Rorschach stimuli yet they also produce many different responses. This card, produced the two very different stories in the text.

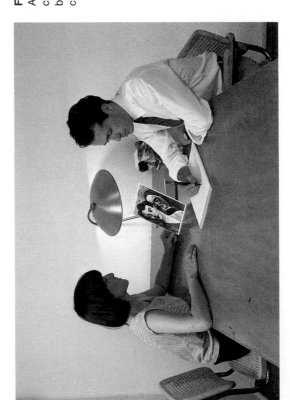

FIGURE 4–6b
As the client looks at the card and tells the story, the clinician not only records the story itself but notes behavior such as pauses, facial expressions, and changes in tone of voice.

explain it. The young man hasn't had the experience and gone through as much as the old man. That's all I think of now. (Relationship?) There is no relationship. I said father and son though didn't I? (Related?) No. (Happening?) They're both concentrating on life. (Explain?) Well, the old man, as I said, is concentrating on what the young man has ahead of him. (?) Whatever he chooses. (What did old man go through?) He looked like he had gone through suffering. (Explain?) Suffering from living. (?) Working hard. (Else?) No. (?) Well, I thought of other things. The trouble he'd had. (?) Family troubles. (Story?) They lived way out in a lonely place, worked and existed. Nothing much to do, and they became very tired, and that's all.

—(Schafer, 1948, pp. 188–189)

This is the response to the same card that was given by a 27-year-old married woman who would probably be diagnosed as having an anxiety disorder. How does it compare with the first response?

[Shakes head, swallows.] The old woman must be either the mother or the grandmother of the young woman. The young woman has a strong face. She has lots of character. The old woman has a sly expression on her face or around her mouth. If it wasn't for that expression on her face, I might try to interpret it. I can't imagine why she looks that way. The old woman looks like she worked hard all her life. (?) I don't know, just can't imagine. If this old lady had a different expression on her face, say, one of worry . . . (?) Then I'd say she must be cherishing a lot of ambitions for the girl. Maybe she would be hoping that the girl would do things she always wanted to do. Maybe her ambitions would be realized in this woman.

—(Schafer, 1948, p. 258)

Clinical interpretation of a TAT story usually begins with an effort to determine the character with whom the person seems to have identified. Attention is paid to such variables as the person's behavior in the testing situation, characteristics of his or her utterances, the way the stories are told, the stories' emotional tone, and the conscious and unconscious needs that are revealed by the story content.

Whereas Rorschach viewed his test as an experimental perceptual task, Murray conceived of the TAT as a probe of the unconscious. Most contemporary users of projective techniques consider them to be methods of tapping unconscious processes, an emphasis that is derived largely from the influence of psychoanalytic theory. Some psychotherapists use TAT responses as clues to hidden problem areas that require in-depth exploration.

In addition to the Rorschach and the TAT, many types of tasks are used as projective stimuli. In a **word-association test**, for example, a list of words is presented one at a time, and the person is asked to respond with the first word or idea that comes to mind. Clinicians are most interested in how long it takes a person to respond and how unusual the associations are. The **sentence-completion technique** is a logical extension of word associations. Here the subject is presented with a series of incomplete sentences and asked to complete them. Sentences are typically analyzed in terms of the attitude, conflicts, and motives reflected in them. The following are typical sentence stems.

- I worry about _____.
- My mother _____.
- What makes me mad is _____.
- My greatest regret is _____.

Other widely used projective methods include asking people to draw pictures of themselves and others, to finger paint, and to tell stories. These approaches have been used as means of increasing knowledge about fantasy, its determinants, and its behavioral correlates. At times their clinical use has been based more on theoretical usefulness than on objectively demonstrated validity. Researchers who are concerned with the evaluation of clinical tools continue to study these techniques.

Behavioral Assessment

Consider the case of a 7-year-old boy who, according to his teacher, is doing poorly in his schoolwork and, according to his parents, is difficult to manage at home and doesn't get along with other children. Among the types of assessment that might be considered in this case are the following: (1) a measure of the boy's general intelligence, which might help explain his poor schoolwork; (2) an interview with him to provide insights into his view of his problem; (3) personality tests, which might reveal trends that are related to his inadequate social relationships; (4) observations of his activities and response patterns in school; (5) observations of his behavior in a specially created situation, such as a playroom with many interesting toys and games; (6) an interview with his parents, since the boy's poor behavior in school may be symptomatic of problems at home; and (7) direct observation of his behavior at home.

Making all of these assessments would be a major undertaking. Because of the variety of data that are potentially available, the assessor must decide which types of information are most feasible and desirable under a given set of circumstances. In most cases, the clinician is interested in both subjective and objective information. Subjective information includes what clients think about, the emotions they experience, and their worries and preoccupations. Interviews, personality inventories, and projective techniques provide indications of subjective experience, although considerable clinical judgment is needed to infer what is going on within the client from the way he or she responds to a test. Objective information includes the person's observable behavior and usually does not require the assessor to draw complex inferences about such topics as attitudes toward parents, unconscious wishes, and deep-seated conflicts. **Behavioral assessment** is directed toward this type of observation (see Figure 4–7).

Behavioral assessment has grown out of the behavioral-therapy movement. It is often used to identify response deficits, which are then treated through the use of behavioral methods such as reinforcement schedules and modeling. Clinicians often use behavioral observations to get information that cannot be obtained by other means. Examples of such observations include the frequency of a particular type of response, such as physical attacks on others or observations by ward attendants

of certain behaviors of psychiatric patients. In either case, observational data must meet the same standards of reliability as data obtained by more formal measures.

The Assessment Focus

The following are some of the questions that are likely to be covered in behavioral assessments. Notice the absence of references to unconscious motivations or intrapsychic tensions.

1. What is the problem as described by the clinician?
2. Who are the people involved in the problem (parents, spouse)?
3. Under what circumstances is the problem most in evidence?
4. What reinforcers contribute to maintenance of the problematic behavior?
5. What is the developmental history of the problem?
6. What are the assets and liabilities of the client's behavioral repetoire.
7. How modifiable are aspects of the client's situation that bear on the problem, and how can modification be made?

The value of behavioral assessment depends on the behaviors selected for observation. For example, if the goal of assessment is to detect a tendency toward

FIGURE 4–7b
Children's behavior can also be observed in a natural setting. Aggressive behavior on a playground can be rated by observers. Because the situation is less standardized and other children are involved, these naturalistic ratings may be less easily compared. At the same time, the observed behavior may give important information about the child's everyday behaviors.

Cary Wolinsky, Stock, Boston

FIGURE 4–7a
This child's aggressive behavior in a playroom situation is being rated by observers through a one-way mirror. Behavioral observations made in a standardized situation are helpful to clinicians because the controlled environment makes comparisons among children more meaningful.

depression, the responses recorded should be those that are relevant to that tendency, such as smiling, motor activity, and talking. In one study of severely depressed individuals, daily observations of these types of responses were useful in judging how well clients were responding to treatment (Williams and others, 1972).

Baseline or **operant observations** are a type of behavioral observation that is becoming increasingly popular. These are recordings of response frequencies in particular situations before any treatment intervention has been made. They can be used in several ways. Observations might be made simply to describe a person's response repertory at a given time. For example, the number of aggressive responses made by children of different ages might be recorded. Such observations also provide a baseline for judging the effectiveness of behavior modification techniques. A similar set of observations made after behavior modification procedures have been used, could be compared with the baseline measurement as a way of determining how well the therapy worked.

Cognitive Assessment

Just as it is important to know what a person does and how his or her behavior affects other people, it is also necessary to assess the thoughts that may lie behind the behavior. **Cognitive assessment** provides information about thoughts that precede, accompany, and follow maladaptive behavior. It also provides information about the effects of procedures whose goal is to modify both how someone thinks about a problem and how he or she behaves.

An example of cognitive assessment is provided by Krantz and Hammen's (1979) study of the distortions in thinking that play a role in depression. Their work grew out of research and theory suggesting that depression-prone individuals tend to commit certain errors in thinking that stimulate feelings of depression (see Chapter 10). Krantz and Hammen developed a questionnaire consisting of several stories that dealt with interpersonal relationships and achievement of goals. For each story the subjects answered questions pertaining to the central character's feelings, thoughts, and expectations. The answers were scored for various types of distorted thinking (for example, a tendency to draw a general conclusion either from a single incident or from no evidence whatever; failure to attend to relevant aspects of a situation; and distortion of an incident or its significance).

On the basis of the subjects' interpretations of the central characters, Krantz and Hammen were able to show that subjects who were depressed were more likely than nondepressed subjects to make certain types of thinking errors. Their findings, together with those of

other researchers, suggest that people with a tendency toward depression are particularly prone to accept more responsibility than they should in difficult situations, as well as to feel more self-blame and to expect the worst.

Cognitive assessment can be carried out in a variety of ways (Kendall, 1985). For example, questionnaires have been developed to sample people's thoughts after an upsetting event. Beepers have been used to signal subjects to record their thoughts at certain times of the day. There are also questionnaires to assess the directions people give themselves while working on a task and their theories about why things happen as they do.

Cognitions play an important role when a person is trying to concentrate on an intellectual task (see Figure 4-8). Anyone who has taken exams knows that worrying about one's ability, the possibility of failure, and what other students might be doing interferes with effective performance. Whereas thoughts that reflect worry have undesirable effects, thoughts that are directed toward the task at hand are helpful. The Cognitive Interference Questionnaire (Sarason and Stoops, 1978) was developed to assess the degree to which people working on important tasks have thoughts that interfere with their concentration. Subjects respond to the questionnaire by indicating how often thoughts like the following ones enter their minds while they are working on an assigned task.

• I thought about how others have done on this task.
• I thought about things completely unrelated to this task.
• I thought about how poorly I was doing.
• I thought about something that made me angry.
• I thought about something that happened earlier in the day.

The assessment of thoughts and ideas is a relatively new development. It has received impetus from the growing evidence that thought processes and the content of thoughts are related to emotions and behavior. Cognitive assessment provides information about adaptive and maladaptive aspects of people's thoughts and the role their thoughts play in the processes of planning, making decisions, and interpreting reality.

Tests that measure maladaptive behavior are beginning to focus on the situations in which the behavior occurs and on how a particular individual deals with difficult situations. The approach helps relate certain difficulties to particular types of treatment. Such tests are designed to measure stress, coping skills, and social or interpersonal skills. It is likely that in the near future, many of these tests will move from experimental to clinical use as research data accumulate.

FIGURE 4–8
People have different kinds of thoughts while taking an exam. Worries or thoughts that are unrelated to the exam interfere with good performance.

FIGURE 4–9a
The portable blood pressure monitor allows a person's blood pressure to be recorded automatically at predetermined times without interfering with his or her normal daily activities.

Bodily Assessment

An individual's expressive behavior may reveal his or her feelings and motivations, and clinicians pay particular attention to these nonverbal messages. Bodily functions may also reflect motivations and concerns, and some clinicians pay attention to these as well. Sophisticated devices have been developed to measure such physiological changes such as pupil dilation, blood pressure, and electrical skin responses under specific conditions.

Technological advances are making it possible to monitor an individual's physiological state on a continuous basis. Sweat, heartbeat, blood volume, the amounts of different substances in the bloodstream, and blood pressure can all be recorded and correlated with the presence or absence of certain psychological conditions such as stress. Although the automated assessment of bodily processes that are pertinent to behavior disorders is just getting under way, this approach seems promising.

An example of the use of automated assessment can be seen in the measurement of blood pressure. It is now possible to measure blood pressure while a person is engaged in everyday activities. This represents a considerable advance, since resting blood pressure readings may not give a full picture of changes in pressure or provide an accurate 24-hour average. Ambulatory monitors can show changes in a patient's blood pressure throughout the day and during sleep (see Figure 4–9). Such data are useful in diagnosing cases of high blood pressure in which cognitive and behavioral factors play important roles. They may also be important in the selection and evaluation of treatment programs.

Figure 4–9b shows the pattern of blood pressure changes for a 45-year-old woman during a typical day. The patient had been diagnosed as having chronically elevated blood pressure, but as the figure shows, the readings actually covered a wide range. Other studies of patients who had been diagnosed as having high blood

FIGURE 4–9b

An ambulatory blood pressure monitor was used to record the changes in a 45-year-old woman's blood pressure during a one-day period. The top line charts systolic blood pressure and the bottom line diastolic blood pressure. The systolic pressure represents the higher point in the blood pressure cycle as the heart contracts and sends the blood through the circulatory system. The diastolic pressure represents the low point in the pressure cycle, which occurs as the heart fills with blood. (Werdegar and others, 1967, p. 103)

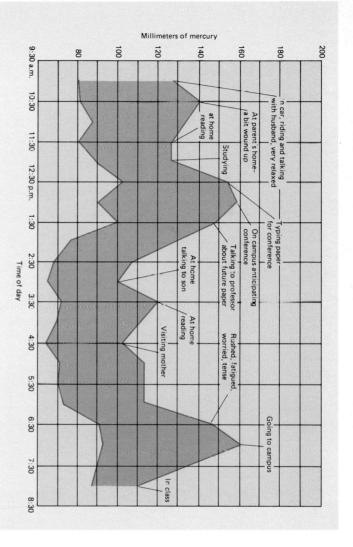

pressure have shown that blood pressure readings taken in the doctor's office may be significantly higher than readings taken during normal activity, even though the office readings are usually taken after a period of rest.

Another measure of emotional response is the **polygraph**, or lie detector. It records physiological reactions (heartbeat, blood pressure, breathing, and galvanic skin response). Its use has been criticized because it violates the right of privacy and the right to avoid self-incrimination. Even more important, questions have been raised about its reliability and validity. Criminal cases suggest that the accuracy of the polygraph in judging guilt can be made with 75- to 97-percent accuracy, but the rate of false-positives (people who are innocent but whose polygraph records suggest guilt) is too high to use the polygraph as the sole basis of determining guilt or innocence (Council on Scientific Affairs, 1986).

Research might suggest novel applications of the polygraph in the field of mental health. For example, it may be possible to use the polygraph to determine what situations or topics caused a particular emotional reaction on the part of a client. This knowledge might provide some clues about areas that should be explored during therapy. In one study (Abrams, 1973), the polygraph was used in much the same way that a word-association test would be used. Stimulus words—some neutral, some thought to be especially relevant—were read to each of 20 psychiatric patients while they were attached to a polygraph. Figure 4–10 shows a typical set of polygraph tracings. Respiration is at the top, galvanic skin response (GSR) in the center, and a combination of heartbeat and blood pressure at the bottom. Stimulus word 23, *window*, was included as a neutral word. However, instead of the expected lack of response, the patient showed a definite reaction to it. On the other hand, while there is a response to *sex*, it does not compare with the GSR to *window*. The patient later disclosed that he had considered committing suicide by jumping out a window. Word 26, the therapist's name, resulted in a large GSR, a slight rise in blood pressure, and suppression of breathing. In contrast, the patient reacted relatively little to neutral word 27, *pen*.

Biofeedback, which is described in Chapter 7, is being used increasingly often in the treatment of certain bodily complaints. The patient receives continuous reports of a particular index of bodily functions, such as blood pressure, and is helped to find ways of bringing the index within normal limits. Thus, the opportunity to monitor one's own behavior and bodily functioning can have a therapeutic effect.

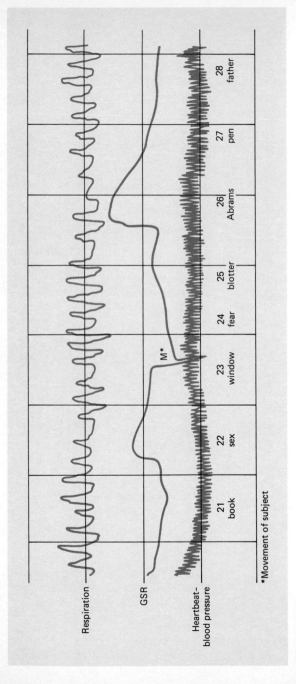

FIGURE 4–10
Polygraph tracing for one psychiatric patient. Stimulus words are numbered. (Abrams, 1973, p. 95)

Assessment techniques help in defining the nature and scope of clinical problems, selecting appropriate treatments, and evaluating the results from treatment. The use of multiple techniques (e.g., interview, projective techniques, and bodily assessment) may provide a particularly firm basis for valid clinical judgments.

As theories of maladaptive behavior become more comprehensive and more firmly based on scientific find-

ings, approaches to classification can be expected to change. Assessment and classification methods help clinicians describe disordered behavior and plan therapeutic interventions to change it. What is assessed and how people are classified and treated depend on what we know about the factors involved in abnormal behavior.

Study Outline

CLASSIFICATION

1. The **classification** of personal problems is based on assessments of what clients say and how they behave. It takes into account life conditions and past experiences. A classification statement or **diagnosis** places a disorder within a system of conventional groupings. Classification is useful for statistical purposes and enhances communication among clinicians and researchers.
2. Good classification characterizes a personal problem within the context of the person's stresses, vulnerabilities, and assets such as coping skills and support system.

DSM-II-R

1. The most commonly used classification system for abnormal behavior is DSM-III-R, the revised third edition of the American Psychiatric Association's *Diagnostic*

and Statistical Manual of Mental Disorders. It describes clinical problems rather than interpreting them, and is considered more reliable than earlier editions.
2. DSM-III-R uses a **multiaxial classification system** that characterizes each case in terms of a number of factors. Axis I is the primary diagnosis; Axis II classifies developmental and personality disorders that begin in childhood or adolescence and persist into adult life; Axis III refers to relevant physical disorders; Axis IV rates the severity of psychosocial stressors; and Axis V provides a global assessment of functioning.
3. Axis I includes disorders of infancy, childhood, or adolescence, organic mental disorders, psychoactive substance use disorders, sleep disorders, schizophrenia, delusional disorder, psychotic disorders not classified elsewhere, mood disorders, anxiety disorders, somatoform disorders, dissociative disorders, sexual disorders, facti-

tious disorders, impulse control disorders not classified elsewhere, adjustment disorder, and physical conditions affected by psychological factors.

4. Axis II includes disorders that begin in childhood or adolescence and continue into adulthood. There are two general categories of disorders classified on this axis: developmental disorders and personality disorders. Developmental disorders include mental retardation, pervasive development disorders, and specific developmental disorders. Personality disorders include a number of disorders. Personality disorders differ from personality traits or styles because in personality disorders the behavior is more rigid and maladaptive.

5. DMS-III-R has provided more specific criteria for using the various diagnostic categories and has reduced the amount of inference needed to make a particular diagnosis. It also has increased its coverage of the range of disorders. Further research is needed to evaluate its reliability.

RESEARCH ON CLASSIFICATION

Research has shown that unreliability in classification is due to inconsistencies in patient's behavior, unreliability of classification systems, differences in assessment techniques, and differences among clinicians in training, theoretical orientation, and personality.

ASSESSMENT: THE BASIS OF CLASSIFICATION

1. The basis of classification is assessment. The major assessment methods include interviews, psychological tests, behavioral assessment, cognitive assessment, and bodily assessment.

2. **Interviews** can be used for both diagnosis and therapy. Interviewers typically observe nonverbal as well as verbal behavior. In assessment, the clinician tries to use the interview as a sample of the client's behavior. Standardized, structured interviews like the Diagnostic Interview Schedule increase the reliability of results.

3. The three general types of **psychological tests** are intelligence tests, personality inventories, and projective techniques.

4. The first standardized **intelligence tests** were developed by Alfred Binet to measure the reasoning ability and judgment of children. Some of these tests expressed the score as an intelligence quotient (IQ), derived by dividing **mental age** by chronological age and multiplying by 100. The current Stanford-Binet scales use an IQ score based on deviations from a norm. The revised Wechsler Adult Intelligence Scale (WAIS-R), originally developed to overcome some of the shortcomings of the Binet test, can be broken down into **Verbal IQ, Performance IQ,** and **Full-Scale IQ.** Forms of the Wechsler test for children in several age groups are also available. The best known is the Wechsler Intelligence Scale for children (WISC).

5. Low test scores have been shown to be related to deficient learning strategies, or **metacognition.** The Kaufman Assessment Battery for Children (K-ABC) is designed to reduce cultural bias in intelligence tests by tapping a variety of basic cognitive processing abilities.

6. **Personality inventories** ask people questions about themselves. They usually yield several scores, each representing an aspect of personality. The Minnesota Multiphasic Personality Inventory (MMPI) is a widely used personality inventory. Another technique is the **rating scale,** in which the test taker chooses options representing degrees of a particular characteristic; these can be used to rate someone else's behavior as well as one's own.

7. In **projective techniques** people are asked to respond to ambiguous stimuli; these responses often express unconscious feelings. In the Rorschach inkblots, the individual is asked to tell what the ten inkblots look like in a free-association manner. In the Thematic Apperception Test (TAT), which consists of pictures of people in various situations, the individual makes up stories to explain what is going on in each picture. Other projective techniques were **word-association tests** and **sentence-completion tasks.**

8. In **behavioral assessment,** which has grown out of the behavioral therapy movement, direct observations are made of a person's behavior. **Baseline** or **operant observation,** establishes the frequency of a particular behavior before treatment is begun. Nonprofessionals and clients themselves can be trained to do behavioral assessment.

9. **Cognitive assessment** provides information about thoughts that precede, accompany, and follow maladaptive behavior, as well as about the effectiveness of various treatment procedures. The individuals being assessed may be asked to complete questionnaires, write down their thoughts at various times, or respond to stories.

10. **Bodily assessment** involves determining a person's inner state by measuring bodily functions such as pupil dilation and blood pressure. Sophisticated devices are now being used to monitor these functions. The **polygraph,** or lie detector, is a highly controversial device that measures heartbeat, blood pressure, respiration rate, and galvanic skin response.

CHAPTER 5

Vulnerability, Stress,
and Coping:
Maladaptive Reactions

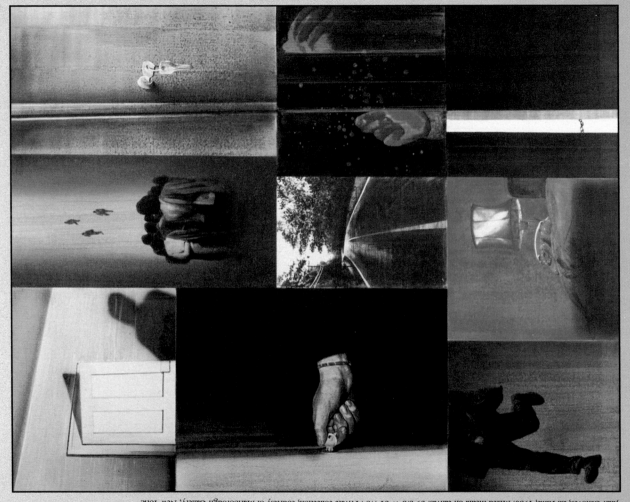

Juan Genovés, *La Ruta*, 1980. Mixed media on canvas, 39 3/8 × 31 7/8". Private collection, courtesy of Marlborough Gallery, New York.

To learn:

1. To identify the different types of stress-related disorders and be able to describe each

To understand:

1. That stress can be a result of a particular event, of a continuing difficulty, or of a life transition

2. How vulnerability, coping skills, and social support interact to determine how much stress a person experiences in any situation

O ne morning, while brushing her teeth, Sheila Mason noticed a small lump on her gum. It didn't hurt, but she was sure that it had not been there before. She wondered whether it might be related to an upset stomach or a cold, but there had been no recent changes in her diet and she felt fine. She was worried about the lump, but at the same time she didn't want to bring a trivial symptom to the attention of her physician or dentist. After three days the lump was still there. It was no bigger than it had been when she had first noticed it, and it still didn't hurt. Sheila concluded that it was not her responsibility to decide whether or not the lump was a trivial symptom. That was the professional's job. Having decided to get an expert to look at the lump, Sheila was left with only one question: Should she call her physician or her dentist?

Grace Dolby, married and the mother of two children, felt a small but noticeable lump in her right breast. Her first reaction was one of alarm bordering on panic, but she said nothing to anyone for two months. Grace was usually outgoing and cheerful, but during those months her husband, Jack, noticed that she had become moody, tense, and depressed. At times she also seemed distant and preoccupied. Toward the end of the two-month period, Grace's moodiness and distance from others (including her children) increased. Her sleep became fitful, and she had frequent headaches (even though previously she had almost never had them). If her husband insisted that she tell him what the matter was, her reply was always, "Nothing's the matter. I'm perfectly normal." Finally, one evening during lovemaking Jack felt the lump in her breast, and despite Grace's protests that it was "nothing" he insisted that she see the family physician.

Just about the only thing that Sheila Mason and Grace Dolby have in common is that they discovered lumps that worried them. The two women dealt with their worries in quite different ways. After some doubt about whether she should undergo a clinical examination, Sheila made a rational decision to seek help. She realized that there was a possibility that the lump could be serious but that she could not evaluate the possibility herself and that the longer she waited, the worse it would be.

In contrast, Grace Dolby seemed unable to act realistically and decisively. She first attempted to cope with the discovery of the lump in her breast by trying to deny that it was really there. But this was not completely successful. She then tried to tell herself that it "wasn't anything." The stress aroused by her discovery could be reduced only temporarily by denial and secrecy. She was still unable to deal with the reality of the lump.

Such a situation would be stressful for anyone. Most people who find themselves in such a situation go to a doctor immediately. Grace Dolby's response to her stressful situation is considered maladaptive mainly because it did not work; the lump (or reality) did not go away. In fact, Grace's behavior simply increased the amount of stress she experienced. A clinician working with Grace would want to understand the personal needs, motivations, and dispositions that combined with the situation (discovery of the lump) to produce her decision not to act. What made Grace Dolby so much more vulnerable to stress than Sheila Mason?

In this chapter we describe ways in which people react to stress. We emphasize examples of maladaptive behavior in response to two types of situations: those, like Sheila Mason's and Grace Dolby's, that arise suddenly, and those that develop more gradually and represent turning points in life, such as making a career decision. We examine the concept of stress, explore the different ways in which people handle it, and review three clinical conditions (adjustment disorders, posttraumatic disorders, and dissociative disorders) in which stress plays an identifiable role. Even though the behavioral reactions observed in the three conditions seem quite different, stress plays a crucial role in each, and its removal is often followed by improvement.

Because this is the first chapter in which we study particular disorders in some depth, it is worthwhile to anticipate an observation that has been made many times by both experienced clinicians and students: the various disorders are not conveniently arranged so that they have mutually exclusive features. Stress is the main topic of this chapter, but we will also refer to stress as we discuss other forms of maladaptation. What is distinctive about the disorders discussed here is that the exact sources of stress are more evident than they usually are in most forms of abnormal behavior. In the next chapter, where we review the anxiety disorders, we will find it more difficult to specify the exact sources of stress that result in intense anxiety.

Vulnerability and Coping

In Chapter 1 we said that the term "stress" refers to situations that pose demands, constraints, or opportunities. However, a situation that is stress-arousing for one person might be a neutral event for another. Whether a certain situation is stressful for us or not depends on how we appraise it and how we rate our ability to deal with it. There are two stages in the appraisal of any situation. During **primary appraisal,** individuals interpret a situation as either threatening or harmless. During **secondary appraisal,** they consider the kind of action that is called for, as well as the nature and potency of their resources for managing or coping with it. The extent to which people feel threatened depends on their estimate of the resources, which in turn is based largely on the information provided by the environment and by their own experiences and characteristics.

Vulnerability and Adjustment to Stress

People differ not only in the life events they experience but also in their vulnerability to them. A person's **vulnerability** to stress is influenced by his or her coping skills and the social support available. Vulnerability increases the likelihood of a maladaptive response to stress. For example, unloved children are more vulnerable and generally at greater risk of developing behavior disorders than those who are loved (Werner and Smith, 1982).

Coping skills are characteristic ways of dealing with situations. Successful copers are not just people who know how to do things. They also know how to approach situations for which they do not have a readily available response.

The characteristics that people bring with them to life experiences (their expectations, fears, skills, hopes) influence how much stress they feel and how well they cope with it. Experience and success in coping with similar situations, well-founded self-confidence, and the ability to remain composed and "think on one's feet" instead of falling to pieces when faced with a problem, all contribute to realistic appraisals of and responses to situations. These characteristics are products of personality development, which, in turn, is influenced by social relationships.

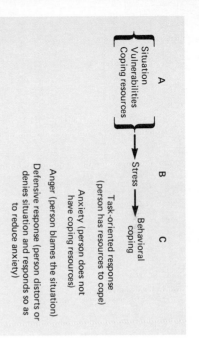

A
Situation
Vulnerabilities
Coping resources

B
Stress

C
Behavioral coping

Task-oriented response
(person has resources to cope)

Anxiety (person does not
have coping resources)

Anger (person blames the situation)

Defensive response (person distorts or
denies situation and responds so as
to reduce anxiety)

FIGURE 5-1
The stress process: ways of dealing with demands, constraints, and opportunities.

Figure 5-1 traces the steps involved in reactions to stress. On the right side of the figure are the four major types of overt reactions or **behavioral coping:** matter-of-factly confronting the situation, feeling anxious, becoming angry, and being defensive. Behavioral coping is what we actually do when confronted with a demand, constraint, or opportunity. Notice that the word "coping" appears twice in Figure 5-1, on the right side (C) and on the left (A), in the term **coping resources.** This term refers to capabilities, not to what a person will actually do in a given situation. People frequently fail to use their knowledge and skills in handling stressful situations. When this happens, we wonder why the person's coping resources were not enough to permit effective behavioral coping.

A task-oriented, matter-of-fact response to a tough situation is usually more effective than becoming anxious, angry, or defensive. Failure to be task-oriented can happen for a variety of reasons. It could be that we simply lack the coping resources we need if we are to take a matter-of-fact approach. In that case, the situation is beyond our capabilities. It could also be that certain elements of the situation prevent us from taking a constructive approach to it. For example, a man might have the coping resources needed to be assertive with other men but not with women. His vulnerability with regard to women might keep him from complaining about being shortchanged by a waitress, whereas he would be quick to complain if he were shortchanged by a waiter. In trying to identify the basis for a particular behavioral coping response, it is necessary to analyze carefully what is going on in the situation, together with the person's assets and liabilities (coping resources and vulnerabilities). In addition, attention must be paid to how the person sizes up the situation (primarily appraisal) and his or her coping resources (secondary appraisal).

Personal vulnerabilities and past experiences influence how much stress we experience in a given situation and how we deal with it. For example, Grace Dolby had had many experiences that involved doing something about a physical symptom (high temperature, skin rash). The lump in her breast, however, was different because of its life-threatening implications. Her mother had died when Grace was 4 years old, and Grace was concerned about depriving her children of the maternal love and attention that she had missed as a result of her mother's early death. Perhaps her intense concern about abandoning her children made Grace particularly vulnerable to her symptom and resulted in her denial of its significance.

Like Grace, many people with bodily symptoms either fail to attend to them or misinterpret them. The common response to the chest pain of a heart attack is denial of its significance. It has been estimated that 80 to 90 percent of people who experience such pain attribute it to other causes, usually indigestion (Hackett and Cassem, 1975). Once the possibility that it might be a heart attack strikes them, they think, "It couldn't be happening to me." This thought alone seems to be enough to keep them from seeking medical help. Even some physicians, who should know better, have gone jogging when they experienced chest pains in order to "prove it's nothing." Thus, there is a common tendency to deny the true significance of pain despite its severity, intensity, or duration.

This is true for psychological pain as well. Many people deny the reality of an unhappy or unsatisfying marriage rather than seek counseling or even a divorce. People who have lost their jobs may blame their employers instead of recognizing their own inadequacies as employees. They may put off looking for work because they "deserve a rest," denying even to themselves that they are afraid of being fired again. As Table 5-1 shows, denial can play a reality-distorting role at various stages of the stress experience.

Particular conditions might arouse stressful reactions in some people but not in others. At a memorial concert honoring the famous jazz musician Louis "Satchmo" Armstrong, his widow was stricken with a fatal heart attack as she played the final chord of a song that was identified with her husband, "The St. Louis Blues." According to a newspaper report, a 38-year-old father collapsed and died when his efforts to revive his 2-year-old daughter, who had fallen into a wading pool, failed. The report suggested that the girl had fallen into the pool while the fathers' attention wandered. An obituary noting the sudden death, at 51, of the newly appointed president of a television network stated that he was on his way to attend the funeral of his father, who had died the day before. Each of these examples suggests the importance of the appraisal process for each individual who experiences a particular type of event.

Another example of the importance of the appraisal process is found in hospitals, places to which we

thoughts (fears, plans) are aroused and coping strategies are considered. The end product is some response that reflects the level of stress as well as the person's resources and vulnerabilities.

TABLE 5-1

Types of Denial

Type of Denial	Example
1. Denial of provided information	"No one ever told me about it."
2. Denial of information about a threat	"No one ever told me there was anything to worry about."
3. Denial of personal relevance	"It doesn't apply to me."
4. Denial of urgency	"No need to hurry."
5. Denial of vulnerability	"No matter what happens, it can't happen to me."
6. Denial of emotion	"I'm not scared."
7. Denial of the emotion's relevance	"I'm scared, but there is no reason to feel that way."

Adapted from Breznitz, 1988. Courtesy of Hemisphere Publishing Corporation.

Coping Techniques

In coping, people use their personal resources to master a problem, overcome or sidestep an obstacle, answer a question, or resolve a dilemma. Successful copers are not just people who know how to do things. They also know how to probe situations for which they do not have a readily available response. Different coping strategies are effective in different types of situations. People who are generally successful copers have a varied array of personal resources, which include the ability to:

1. seek pertinent information.
2. share concerns and find consolation when needed.
3. redefine a situation so as to make it more solvable.
4. consider alternatives and examine consequences.
5. use humor to defuse a situation.

A growing body of research is devoted to the question of how people can be helped to cope with stress more effectively. One finding of this research is that what you don't know *can* hurt you. People who know what to expect beforehand are better able to cope with stress than people who do not know what lies ahead. Many surgical patients, for example, suffer unnecessarily because they have not been warned that they will have considerable pain after the operation. It has been shown that patients are less anxious and recover faster when they understand beforehand how the surgery will be done and have a clear idea of what the recovery process will be like.

The trauma of surgery, part biological and part psychological, can be greatly eased by psychologically preparing patients before the operation takes place. These preparatory steps aid physical recovery and lessen the pain and anxiety that surgery brings. A variety of preparations, ranging from hypnosis and relaxation training to educational videotapes, seem to help. The benefits, though, seem due to a psychological factor that underlies them all: heightening patient's feelings that they have some control over their recovery and that they are not passive victims.

In one recent study, 60 men undergoing coronary bypass grafts were divided into three groups. One group received the hospital's standard preparation: a brochure on the procedures and a short visit from a nurse to answer questions (Anderson, 1987). The other groups watched a videotape that followed a patient through the operation and recovery. In addition, one of

turn in times of great stress. Hospitals are supposed to be places where people can recover from illness, but in fact hospitalization can be a highly stressful experience. For instance, the continuous monitoring of a patient's physical status in the intensive care unit can be a highly stressful experience. The knowledge that one has a condition that is serious enough to require placement in an intensive care unit may be even more stressful. Probably the most stressful aspect of hospitalization for both the patient and for family members is the frequently occurring uncertainty about what the outcome of the treatment may be (see Box 5-1). Under such conditions frustrations from dealing with bureaucratic hospital procedures can be stressful even to a patient who is familiar with hospital routines and who has excellent coping skills.

Heightened stress levels have detectable, although usually not immediately noticeable, psychological consequences. For example, a significantly higher percentage of depressed and suicidal people than of people with other disorders have had undesirable recent experiences. The undesirable events that contribute most to depression include the departure or loss of significant people in one's life during the previous year (see Chapter 10).

The psychological disorders discussed in this chapter begin with a specific event that has definable characteristics and has special meaning for the person involved. This event is then appraised or processed, and as a result of the appraisal, the person's emotions or

BOX 5-1
Two Weeks in the Hospital

John A. Talbott, the author of this account, was not just "any" patient. At the time of the accident he was President of the American Psychiatric Association. Although as a physician he was familiar with medical procedures, being a patient gave him a quite different view of his condition and treatment than he would have had as a hospital staff member. The effect of injuries and the hospitalization itself may be stressful (see Figure 5-2), but this account shows how hospital procedures and medical personnel can add significantly to the problems of hospitalization.

"On November 30, 1981, while standing on the sidewalk near the Museum of Natural History in New York, I was hit by one of two cabs that had collided at the nearby intersection. . . . It was early in the morning. My physical injuries were substantial . . . but in retrospect, it was the way I was subsequently cared for, rather than treated, that sticks most in mind. . . ."

Some of Talbott's experiences show how interpersonal interactions can add to stress. For instance:

"Each morning a new nurse would bounce cheerily into the room, introduce herself, and take a history. I assumed on the second day that my first day's nurse had the day off. But by the third or fourth day I realized that some bizarre rotational system ensured that no nurse would ever get to know me, my needs, and my care, since I'd never see the same one twice.

One evening I received no dinner. After calls to the kitchen from the nursing staff produced no result, they

urged me to call—"they'll listen to you, you're a doctor." The nutrition person announced that it was too late for dinner, they were already immersed in setting up the breakfast trays. I asked if it wasn't possible to alter the routine so that I might be fed before 10 p.m. She then blew up at me for not understanding all the pressures she was under, and only after I reminded her that I was the patient and her job was to help patients, did she apologize and relent.

Finally, the day arrived, my few meager belongings marking a two-week stay were packed, and I was ready for the trip home. I eagerly awaited my physician's arrival to deliver some parting words—I awaited his optimistic view on my recovery, his good cheer, his clinical enthusiasm. Instead, he said he hoped he'd be able to "save" my leg, since the damage done was extensive, the healing complicated, and the prognosis uncertain. But, if he wasn't, all sorts of things could be done, including bone grafts. And if worse came to worse there was always the possibility of an amputation. But I shouldn't worry, that wouldn't happen for a while. When my wife arrived I was in tears.

Going home was no picnic—with an enormous, heavy cast and limited energy, I could barely make it to the bathroom—but it was home, without the surly aides, constantly rotating nurses, inadequate medication, dashing house staff, uncoordinated treatment team, incredibly unappealing food, and dehumanized physicians."

(Talbott, 1985, pp. 2, 31)

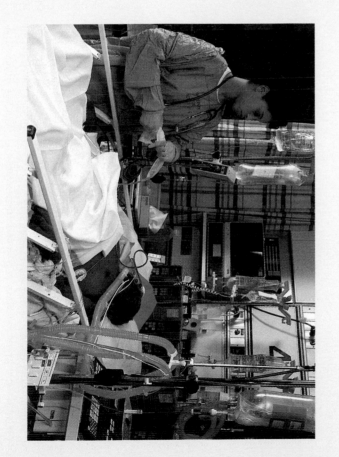

FIGURE 5-2
A hospital intensive-care unit, although it contains a variety of life-saving equipment, can be a frightening place that increases the stress already experienced by a patient.

these groups received advanced instructions in the physical therapy exercises—such as deep breathing to expand their lung capacity—that they would be doing to help recovery.

While 75 percent of those with the standard preparation suffered after the surgery from acute hypertension—a condition that can endanger coronary bypass patients in the first 12 hours after surgery—less than 45 percent of those who saw the tape had the problem. The patients who viewed the tape also had less anxiety as they waited in the hospital before the surgery and reported less stress and seemed more relaxed to nurses in the week after the surgery. The group that received extra instruction in the physical therapy went into surgery feeling less anxious than the other groups.

Learning the specific skills needed in stressful situations also helps individuals cope more effectively. Many people enter dangerous situations without proper training. For example, many hiking and mountain climbing accidents are a result of poor training and preparation. Besides learning specific skills, individuals can be trained for stressful situations by being put through a series of experiences that are graded from relatively low to relatively high in stress. In addition, observing a model who copes with stress in an effective way can help people who are about to enter a strange or dangerous situation.

People sometimes fail to cope with stress because a high level of arousal interferes with their ability to concentrate on adaptive thoughts. These people do not observe their own thoughts, feelings, and behaviors in challenging situations, and they fail to engage in constructive problem solving. Learning general skills for coping with stress involves learning how to think constructively, solve problems, behave flexibly, and provide feedback to oneself about which tactics work and which do not (see Table 5–2).

The following are examples of useful statements that people can make to themselves in preparing for and dealing with stressful situations. Such statements have been used in training programs directed toward strengthening cognitive skills. In this training, the statements are modeled for each participant, who is then given an opportunity to rehearse them while imagining being in stressful situations.

PREPARING FOR A STRESSFUL SITUATION

- "I should work out a plan for dealing with this problem."
- "I'm not going to worry about what happens; I'll just prepare myself in the best way I can."

CONFRONTING A STRESSFUL SITUATION

- "I'm just going to take one step at a time. I can do it."
- "I want to be sure to stick to what's really important."

COPING WITH FEELINGS OF BEING OVERWHELMED

- "Sure I'm scared—but that's normal."
- "I know I'm afraid, but I've got to do things that will help me cope."

REINFORCING SELF-STATEMENTS

- "I controlled my tension—and I did it."
- "I must be pretty good to be able to handle a crisis like that one."

People who cope effectively with stressful situations have learned to direct their thoughts along productive lines and to avoid being distracted by fear and

---

TABLE 5–2

Aids to Behavioral Coping

1. *Be task-oriented.* Focus only on the task confronting you. It is not productive to spend time with thoughts or feelings that are unrelated to accomplishing the task. Being task-oriented means that you are concentrating completely on the job at hand. Negative or disruptive thoughts and emotions are the enemies of task orientation.

2. *Be yourself.* Don't role play. You will be more effective acting naturally than trying to fit a role. Place your confidence in *yourself*, not in the role.

3. *Self-monitor.* Pay attention to the way you are thinking and feeling in a given situation. It is important to learn about what causes stress for you and about your personal reactions to stress. Effective self-monitoring is your early warning system. It can alert you to the necessity of using the other coping skills to prevent a blowup.

4. *Be realistic about what you can achieve.* Know your own limits as well as your strengths. At times, laughter is the best medicine—don't lose your sense of humor.

5. *Have a constructive outlook.* Try to look for the positives in the people around you. Don't be too quick to conclude that people are behaving the way they are just to upset you. Put yourself in the other person's shoes—from that point of view his or her behavior may make perfect sense.

6. *Use supportive relationships.* Compare notes, blow off steam, and get support from your friends. Don't draw into yourself when you are feeling stressed. Remember that we all get by with a little help from our friends.

7. *Be patient with yourself.* Don't punish yourself for not achieving perfection. Your mistakes should be learning experiences, not times for heavy self-criticism. Keep your expectations of yourself at a reasonable level.

worry. Actors, quarterbacks, and other people who are often in the limelight soon learn that attention to the task at hand is more constructive than self-preoccupied thoughts ("There are 100,000 people out there waiting for me to fumble that ball"). They also learn to antici- pate problems that might complicate a stressful situation and to think about the way to deal with them. Actors come to accept that they will occasionally get their lines mixed up and that deemphasizing their mistakes and moving on to the next line reduces the impact of their errors. On the other hand, the thoughts of some people who are prone to stress disorders are saturated with self- blame and catastrophizing ("The worst will surely hap- pen").

Social Support

"It isn't what you know, it's who you know" is a some- what cynical saying, but there is some unintended wis- dom in it. The traditional Danish proverb, "No one is rich enough to do without a neighbor" makes the point more positively. Recent research on social support has focused attention on the positive side of social relation- ships, or those interpersonal ties that are desired, re- warding, and protective.

Our social network includes people on whom we

can rely, people who let us know that they care about, value, and love us. Someone who believes that he or she belongs to a social network experiences **social support.** Evidence is increasing that maladaptive ways of thinking and behaving occur disproportionately among people with few social supports. The amount and adequacy of social support available to a person plays a part in both vulnerability and coping (Sarason and Sarason, 1985). Vulnerability to physical and psychological breakdown increases as social support decreases. That is, social sup- port serves as a buffer against the upsets of living in a complex world. Not only is social support very helpful during a period of stress (it is nice to know that there are people pulling for us in a tough situation), but it is also helpful in times of relative calm. It gives us the se- curity and self-confidence to try out new approaches and gain additional coping skills. With an expanded reper- tory of coping skills, we are in a better position to han- dle demands, frustrations, and challenges when they do arise.

Research aimed at measuring social support is un- der way. The Social Support Questionnaire (SSQ) pro- vides information about how much social support peo- ple think they have and how satisfied they are with it (Sarason and others, 1983). Table 5–3 lists some of the items on the SSQ. One interesting finding of research using the SSQ is that there is only a moderate correla-

---

TABLE 5–3

The Social Support Questionnaire

The *Social Support Questionnaire* (SSQ) consists of 27 items, four of which are presented here. After answering each item, the test taker is asked to indicate his or her level of satisfaction with the support available by marking a 6-point rating scale that ranges from "very satisfied" to "very unsatisfied." The SSQ yields scores relating to *Availability of* and *Satisfaction with* social support.

Whom do you know whom you can trust with information that could get you in trouble? (This item is completed as an example.)

— No one	A) R.N. (brother)	D) T.N. (father)	G)
	B) L.M. (friend)	E) L.M. (employer)	H)
	C) R.S. (friend)	F)	I)

Whose lives do you feel that you are an important part of?

— No one	A)	D)	G)
	B)	E)	H)
	C)	F)	I)

Whom can you really count on to distract you from your worries when you feel under stress?

— No one	A)	D)	G)
	B)	E)	H)
	C)	F)	I)

Who helps you feel that you truly have something positive to contribute to others?

— No one	A)	D)	G)
	B)	E)	H)
	C)	F)	I)

Stress Arousal

The reason it is important to build up a person's resources for behavioral coping is that stress has undesirable effects on behavior, thought, and bodily functioning. Uncomfortable psychological feelings are present when people experience stress, and there is a strong tendency to avoid situations that bring about distress. Blood pressure, hormone levels, and brain waves are also affected by stress. Very high levels of stress can result in trembling, stuttering, and a decline in the effectiveness with which tasks are carried out.

There is often little consistency in people's reactions to stress. That is, one person might react to stress primarily in a bodily way, another might develop psychological symptoms (such as excessive worry), and yet another might show a profound deterioration in performance. Responses to stress involve bodily, psychological, and behavioral systems, but the correlations among these systems is often low. Table 5–4 lists ways in which the three systems may react to stress.

TABLE 5–4

Some Psychological, Bodily, and Behavioral Reactions to Stress

Psychological Responses

feeling upset
inability to concentrate
irritability
loss of self-confidence
worry
difficulty making decisions
racing thoughts
absent-mindedness

Bodily Responses

rapid pulse
pounding heart
increased perspiration
tightened stomach
tensing of arm and leg muscles
shortness of breath
gritting of teeth

Behavioral Responses

deterioration in performance effectiveness
smoking and use of alcohol or other "recreational" drugs
accident proneness
nervous mannerisms (foot tapping, nail biting)
increased or decreased eating
increased or decreased sleeping

---

tion between the Availability and Satisfaction scores. There appears to be no minimum number of social supports that ensures satisfaction for everyone. For some people, a small number of close friends and relatives is satisfying, whereas others seem to need ties to many different people.

Research with the SSQ has also revealed relationships between social support and physical health. In general, people who have had many recent undesirable experiences are more likely to get sick than those who have been more fortunate. However, people who have high levels of social support are less vulnerable to illness even when they have experienced a recent misfortune (Sarason and others, 1985).

Maladaptive ways of thinking and behaving are more common among people who have few social supports, particularly within their families. After an extensive review of the relevant literature, John Bowlby (1973) concluded that, rather than sapping self-reliance, strong family ties seem to encourage it. Self-reliance and reliance on others are not only compatible but complementary. The "apron strings" become a hindrance only when the family exerts too much control over a person's life. However, even though lack of social support in one's early years can be damaging, the possibility exists that new social relationships can have stress-buffering and therapeutic value. Psychotherapy, from this perspective, is a special social relationship directed at helping people face and overcome obstacles.

Social support facilitates coping with crisis and adapting to change. Why do some people have many rewarding ties that help them smooth out the rough spots in their lives, while others are lonely and socially isolated? Are the number and quality of social ties simply a matter of luck? There is evidence that people with high and low levels of social support as assessed by the SSQ differ in the social skills needed to attract the interest of others (B. R. Sarason and others, 1985). When engaging in a conversation with a stranger, people who are high in social support feel more competent, comfortable, and assured than people who report having few social supports. In addition, people who are low in social support tend to be perceived by others as being less interesting, dependable, friendly, and considerate than people who are high in social support. They are also less wanted as friends and co-workers and report feeling more lonely. There appears to be a strong link between social skills and social support. People with low levels of support may not believe that other people could be interested in them. This belief would tend to increase their vulnerability to stress especially in situations that called for interactions with other people. Training in social skills might not only increase their interpersonal effectiveness but also help reduce their perception of social isolation.

TABLE 5-5

A variety of circumstances can evoke stress and require the individuals to adjust to it. Two broad types of stress-arousing conditions that require adjustment are (1) situations that arise in life, often unexpectedly, and (2) developmental transitions. The death of a close friend illustrates the need for a situational adjustment; going to college is an example of a transitional adjustment.

Stress-Arousing Situations

Events and circumstances that arouse stressful responses have varying characteristics. Following are some of the ways in which challenging situations and circumstances vary.

1. *Duration.* Stressful situations differ in duration. A job interview lasts for a short time, whereas a marital quarrel might last for hours or days.

2. *Severity.* Situations vary in the severity of the circumstances confronting the individual. In general, a minor injury is easier to cope with than a major injury.

3. *Predictability.* In some cases we know what is going to happen (predictability is high), whereas in others predictability is low. The amount of stress caused by a request to give an oral presentation in class would depend on whether the request was made on the spot or was a previously given assignment.

4. *Degree of loss of control.* One of the most upsetting aspects of a situation is the feeling that one is unable to exert any influence on the circumstances. For example, earthquake victims can do nothing to prevent or control the quake's initial impact and aftershocks.

5. *The individual's level of self-confidence.* Lack of self-confidence often results in reduced personal effectiveness, even though the person may really know how to handle the situation. For example, a recently divorced woman may feel ill at ease in social situations that she was able to handle very well during her marriage.

6. *Suddenness of onset.* Suddenness of onset influences how prepared we are to cope with a particular situation. An accident is usually completely unexpected, whereas the crises of adolescence build up gradually.

Stress is a highly personal response, whether the event that causes it happens to one person, a group of persons, or an entire community. One example of a stress reaction occurs when a police officer uses a weapon in the line of duty. The use of deadly force is emphasized as a last resort in confrontation situations in police work, and its use can have serious negative psychological impacts on the officer involved. One study examined the postshooting stress reactions of members of the Royal Canadian Mounted Police (RCMP) (Loo, 1986). Table 5-5 lists the most frequent postshooting stress impacts.

Accidents, natural disasters, and military combat are examples of situations that typically evoke high levels of stress and may result in posttraumatic stress disorders. Their psychological impact comes from actual physical injury or threat of injury and from the possibility of loss of life. An accident can happen to anyone, and whether we are directly involved, know someone who is involved, or merely see a report on TV of a disaster such as an airplane crash, it exerts an impact on us.

An airplane crash has some special features that must be recognized if its victims are to be psychologically helped. The passengers on a flight are usually strangers to one another, often come from a variety of areas, and are far from home. Whereas natural disasters are frequently perceived as "acts of God," air crashes engender reactions of anger and, even more striking, of guilt on the part of some survivors.

Along with passengers and crew members, other groups may feel the emotional effects of an airplane crash. These include ground crew members, air controllers, and relatives and friends of the victims. There may also be serious long-range problems related to airplane crashes. Survivors and crew members are likely to experience such chronic problems as psychological withdrawal from their work, family life, or society in general, as well as physical symptoms and habitual anxiety. Special problems may be felt by certain groups, such as children, the elderly, and ethnic minorities.

Survivors often torture themselves with such questions as "Why didn't I do more to save those who perished?" and "Why did I survive when others did not?" Victims may experience an "anniversary syndrome"—episodes of depression and anxiety on the anniversary of the disaster. This may happen without the victim's un-

TABLE 5-5

Most Frequent Impacts of Shooting Incidents on Police Officers and the Percentages of Officers Affected

Adverse Effect	Percentage
Preoccupation with the incident	39
Anger over the incident	25
Sleep disturbances	20
Flashbacks to the incident	20
Reexamination of personal values	18
Guilt feelings	14
Wishes that what happened could be undone	14
Depression	13

Adapted from Loo, 1986.

ground and, if so, how could he have hit from that angle? Why did they put a sheet over him when there were so many other bodies and parts lying around and when "gawkers" just kept lifting the sheet off anyway?) He had attempted to remain busy and mentally occupied in order to keep his mind off these images. The woman experienced multiple somatic disturbances including, most prominently, anorexia, nausea, and frequent sighing respirations. They both talked intensively and openly for an hour and a half, at the end, both agreed that they felt better having had the opportunity to get some of these thoughts out in the open.

—(Shuchter and Zisook, 1984, p. 296)

FIGURE 5–3

Sometimes death strikes suddenly. This passenger jet has just collided with a small plane near the San Diego airport. The photographer snapped it as it plunged toward the ground in a crash that killed all 136 passengers aboard. The two passengers in the small plane were also killed.

derstanding the source of the strong feelings that well up at about the time of the anniversary.

After the collision of a commercial airliner and a small private plane, wreckage and bodies fell into a suburban area (see Figure 5–3). Efforts were made to obtain information about witnesses' psychological reactions and to help them return to normal as quickly as possible. The following account of the experience of a young couple illustrates some of the psychological, behavioral, and bodily reactions found in disaster victims.

At first they responded with great reservation, saying that they had been eye witnesses to the crash from their home in North Park. They added that although their house was still intact, there had been approximately seventeen bodies scattered around their yard, trees, and roof. They had decided that they never wanted to live in the house again and had called the Salvation Army for help in finding a new home. After some initial reluctance to talk at all about their reactions, they began to freely disclose every detail. They were obviously quite anxious and angry, focusing their hostility at the media, police, and the councilman who was present. Recurrent images of bodies lying around their home were reported by the man, as were obsessions with the details of the tragedy. (Where did the body come from that hit their car and did $700 worth of damage? Did he die on impact or before? Was he on the

As more becomes known about what disasters like airplane accidents do to people, steps can be taken to improve the effectiveness of personnel who have the job of dealing with them. Training in the ability to recognize emotional problems and provide emotional support would be of great value in the efforts of such personnel to reduce both the short-term and long-term effects of these events.

Natural disasters (floods, earthquakes, and the like) threaten people's homes and property as well as their physical well-being. When there is warning of a disaster, the impending threat exerts a strong psychological influence. The disaster itself is extremely stressful because one has no control over it. The immediate postdisaster period can also be very emotionally arousing. Some survivors have difficulty picking up the pieces of their lives. Others may be troubled by strong feelings of guilt because they survived while others did not (see Table 5–6).

Military personnel in **combat** must deal with the constant fear of capture, death, or mutilation. Loss of sleep, physical exhaustion, separation from family, and concern about the killing of others heighten the stress of war (see Figure 5–4). Stress reactions are also seen

TABLE 5–6

Disasters that Result in Homelessness and Death Leave an Imprint on Survivors

Some Common Survivor Experiences

1. Death anxiety
2. Exaggerated reactions to ordinary life events
3. Terrifying dreams
4. Death guilt (self-condemnation for having lived while others died)
5. Psychological numbing (a reduced capacity for feelings of all kinds)
6. Impaired social relationships
7. Search for meaning (seeking meaning in the disaster)

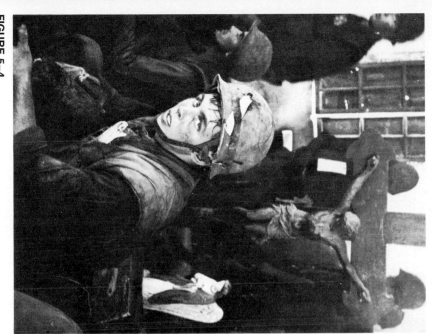

FIGURE 5-4
The stress-producing experiences of combat are clearly reflected on this soldier's face.

in wartime when soldiers who are not yet in combat think about what may be in store for them.

In his book *A Rumor of War*, the Pulitzer Prize-winning journalist Philip Caputo has written a sensitive account of his experience as a Marine Corps lieutenant in the Vietnam War. In the following excerpt Caputo describes in an especially clear way the intrusive thoughts aroused by being in combat and seeing death all around him.

I did not go crazy, not in the clinical sense, but others did. Malaria and gunshot and shrapnel wounds continued to account for most of our losses, but in the late summer the phrases acute anxiety reaction and acute depressive reaction started to appear on the sick-and-injured reports sent out each morning by the division hospital. I noticed, in myself and in other men, a tendency to fall into black, gloomy moods and then to explode out of them in fits of bitterness and rage. It was partly caused by grief, grief over the deaths of friends. I thought about my friends a lot; too much. That was the trouble with the war then: the long lulls between action gave us too much time to think.

—(Caputo, 1977, pp. 190–191)

Caputo also describes the anger aroused by the combat experience.

One of its symptoms is a hatred for everything and everyone around you; now I hated myself as well, plunging into morbid depressions and thinking about committing suicide in some socially acceptable way—say, by throwing myself on an enemy hand grenade. At other times, I felt urges to kill someone else. When in those moods, the slightest irritation was likely to set me off.

—(Caputo, 1977, pp. 190–191)

Research on the psychological effects of extreme stressors, such as wars, has shown that they set in motion a cycle of reactions aimed at restoring an equilibrium between the person's self-concept and the new realities of his or her life. Preexisting personality characteristics may interfere with an adaptive response after a disaster. People who see themselves as incompetent, who tend to respond defensively to challenges (for example, by using denial or projection), who have conflicts involving themes similar to some aspect of the disaster, or who believe that their past thoughts might somehow have influenced what happened—such people are likely to have long-lasting maladaptive reactions to traumatic situations. These prolonged reactions usually include feeling dazed and having intrusive thoughts and images about the traumatic event. These thoughts and images may interfere with the ability to sleep.

The type of stress and its characteristics, together with the circumstances of the situation and each person's resources and vulnerabilities, determine the long-range influences, if any, of stressful life events. Philip Caputo, whose account of the effects of combat was presented earlier, has also described the intense post-stress anxiety he experienced after leaving the combat area.

It was a quiet day, one of those days when it was difficult to believe a war was on. Yet, my sensations were those of a man actually under fire. Perhaps I was suffering a delayed reaction to some previous experience. Perhaps it was simply battle fatigue. Whatever the cause, I was outwardly normal, if a little edgier than usual; but inside, I was full of turbulent emotions and disordered thoughts, and I could not shake the weird sensation of being split in two.

—(Caputo, 1977, p. 297)

Life Transitions

Whereas disasters are imposed on people from outside, other crises grow out of the individual's own path of personal development. Beginning with birth into a complex, often confusing world and continuing through childhood, adolescence, adulthood, and advanced age, crises build up and are resolved in either adaptive or maladaptive ways. In early childhood the transitions seem to be both momentous and frequent. Lois Murphy's (1974) study of 2-year-old Molly's adjustment to the stress of thunderstorms illustrates how easy it is for adults to underestimate the challenges involved in the growing-up process.

1. As a 2-year-old, Molly cried many times and was completely terrified during thunderstorms or when a jet plane passed overhead.

2. A year later she was able to get into bed with her older sister during a thunderstorm and accept comfort from her.

3. At about the same time Molly began to reassure herself (and her baby brother), saying, "It's just noise and it won't really hurt you a bit."

4. A month after this storm Molly was again terrified as a jet plane flew unusually low overhead; she cried and clung to her sister for comfort. A few hours later she repeated several times to herself, "Thunder really doesn't hurt you; it just sounds noisy. I'm not scared of planes, only thunder."

5. The next month she opened the door to her parents' room during a thunderstorm, saying that her younger brother was afraid (although he was really fast asleep).

6. Nine months later, at four years and two months, she was awakened from a nap during a thunderstorm, but remained quietly in bed. Afterward she said to her sister, "There was lots of thunder, but I just snuggled in my bed and didn't cry a bit."

7. Four months later, at four and a half years, Molly showed no open fear herself during a storm, and comforted her frightened little brother, saying, "I remember when I was a little baby and I was scared of thunder and I used to cry and cry every time it thundered." (Murphy, 1974, p. 76)

As she progressed developmentally, the following factors probably contributed to Molly's successful transition:

1. Expressing her fearfulness and sense of helplessness

2. Seeking comfort from a supporting person

3. Developing comforting things to say to herself, which permitted her to provide her own support

4. Formulating a self-image that emphasized pride in her mastery of her fear

The two-steps-forward-one-step-backward process shown by Molly is also characteristic of later developmental transitions.

Stressful transitions come about because of changes in the operation of biological, personal, cultural, environmental, and historical variables. Adaptation to one life crisis often influences success in adaptation later on. Many people are able to weather these crises, but some develop a clinically significant degree of inappropriate behavior that usually disappears after the transition has been made.

Following are some of the transitions in the life cycle that can cause stress.

1. Birth and attainment of coordination between mother and infant

2. Initial steps toward independence and transition to an out-of-home facility (school, day-care center)

3. Puberty, with all the biological and social changes that mark the adolescent years

4. Major educational transitions, such as going to college

5. Entry into the world of work

6. Marriage

7. Bearing and rearing children

8. Moving to a new place of residence

9. Children's milestones

10. Retirement

We will illustrate transitional stress with two examples: adolescence and old age.

Adolescence

The role of cultural factors in adolescence cannot be overestimated. As a reasonably distinct period of life, adolescence might be described as a by-product of the Industrial Revolution. Prior to that event there had been no need to provide a special niche for people who were biologically no longer children but to whom society did not find it convenient to assign adult roles. Since the Industrial Revolution, the age at which individuals are admitted to adult occupational roles has repeatedly been raised, with the result that the period of adolescence has been lengthened. The stress experienced by adolescents has been increased by the lack of agreement about when adolescence ends as well as by the greater number of life choices young people have to make.

Adolescence can be divided into early, middle, and late periods. The dominant theme of early adolescence is the individual's response to changes in sex hormone levels and a general growth spurt. The onset of puberty comes at an increasingly early age—the average age at first menstruation has declined from 16.5 years in 1860 to 12.5 years today. The comparable events of puberty for boys lag approximately 2 years behind those for girls.

By the end of this early period, the person has acquired a body that is quite different from the one he or she had as a child. Changes in body image have a significant effect on an adolescent's self-concept. How well an adolescent likes his or her body often depends on how other people respond to it. For example, late-maturing boys generally show more personal and social maladjustment at all stages of adolescence than those who mature early. They tend to be characterized by negative self-concepts, prolonged dependency, and feelings of rejection by social groups that are important to them. The picture is different for girls. Early-maturing girls often lack poise and are submissive in their social relationships. Late-maturing girls, on the other hand, seem more outgoing and self-assured.

The extent to which the unpredictable moodiness, depression, anger, and emotionality often seen in early adolescence are related to changes in sex hormone levels is unclear. It has been shown, however, that adolescence does not necessarily have to be a stormy and stressful time. Parental interest, reasonable guidelines, and support, particularly from the same-sex parent, play important roles in helping the younger teenager make the necessary developmental transitions.

During midadolescence (roughly 15 to 18 years of age), the individual receives increasing responsibility and more privileges (for example, holding down a part-time job; driving a car). There are also increases in stress created by the fact that the adolescent is in many ways a marginal character: too old to be treated as a child, too young to have the rights of an adult. For example, the percentage of individuals who report that they have engaged in premarital intercourse has increased markedly in the last decade, especially among females. Although there is increasing moral acceptance of premarital intercourse, this does not remove the social issues related to this behavior. Thus, the incidence of venereal disease is at an all-time high, and the increasing number of high school students who are mothers is a source of both personal and social problems.

Perhaps the most noteworthy developmental occurrence in midadolescence is the gradual shift from a here-and-now perspective to a point of view that is oriented toward the future. In addition, the individual becomes less self-absorbed and grows increasingly concerned with values and ideals.

Graduation from high school is usually taken as the high point of late adolescence. Living with the family, which is seen as protection by some adolescents and as restraint by others, can now come to an end. Some individuals move directly into the adult roles of marriage and full-time work, whereas others enter a more or less extended adolescence through college or job-training experience. Major tasks of this period include development of a personal identity, renegotiation of the relationship to the family, and the development of stable and enduring ties to others. Late adolescence can be difficult for a variety of reasons, including high unemployment rates among teenagers and young adults as well as high crime rates and the problems posed by alcoholism and drug abuse.

One of the major events of adolescence occurs when parents are relinquished as primary attachment figures. During this period adolescents often feel isolated and in limbo. In a study of over 9,000 adolescents in ten U.S. cities (Brennan and Auslander, 1979), 54 percent of the subjects agreed with the statement, "I often feel lonely." There was a significant sex difference in this sense of isolation: 61.3 percent of the boys but only 46.5 percent of the girls agreed with the statement. The adolescents' sense of isolation involved relationships with parents, teachers, and peers. Ten percent of the adolescents sampled felt that their parents were not interested in them; 36 percent felt that their parents did not understand their problems; 33 percent felt that their teachers did not understand them well enough; 12 percent felt that they had no one to turn to for help; and 25 percent indicated that they spent less than half an hour a day with their friends.

Various factors contribute to adolescent loneliness (Brennan, 1982). The adolescent experiences new desires and expectations that may not be readily satisfied but that disrupt existing personal relationships. A predisposition to loneliness may originate in such personality characteristics as shyness and low self-esteem and may be intensified by cultural factors such as the social network within the high school.

Because of the inevitable changes that occur during adolescence, some degree of loneliness may be unavoidable. Moreover, the pain of loneliness can have a positive function. Lonely individuals may be more motivated to develop or upgrade social and emotional relationships and to do something about meeting the challenges of becoming an adult. One study of first-year college students found that those who overcome their initial loneliness and their future relationships with others despite the stress of moving to a new social environment (Cutrona and others, 1979).

Loneliness is not the same thing as social isolation. It is a subjective experience. A person can be alone without being lonely, and a person can be lonely in the middle of a crowd. Essentially, we are lonely when our current social relationships do not satisfy our needs or do not live up to our expectations. The psychological study of loneliness is growing in importance. People go through periods of loneliness at many points in their lives, not just during adolescence. Researchers are intensively studying loneliness and interpersonal skills, as a product of unsatisfying social relationships and interpersonal skills, as an attribute that can be measured and influenced by interventions (such as counseling), and as a state that is precipitated by specific conditions.

Old Age

As people grow older, they often seem to slow down because of physiological changes. For example, chemical changes in the bone structure make the bones more brittle. Age also seems to cause decreases in adrenal gland secretion, which results in hair loss. Changes in the central nervous system may result from the loss of cells that do not replace themselves, as well as from changes in hormone levels, oxygen deficiencies caused by impaired blood circulation, or changes in cell components. Finally, aging seems to be associated with increased susceptibility to disease.

Increased susceptibility to psychological disorders accompanies the physical debilities of old age. Depression is the most prevalent psychological disorder among older people, and paranoid thinking (for example, the belief that people are eavesdropping on one) seems to increase in the later years. Sleep patterns also change with age. Older people need less sleep and are more likely to awaken spontaneously during the night. A wide variety of physical complaints in the absence of a diagnosed physical problem is also frequent. A significant portion of old people in hospitals and nursing homes have brain disorders that interfere with their psychological and social effectiveness. Elderly people, who often have diminished physical and mental reserves, may face especially strong stressors, including illness and the adverse changes that typically accompany growing old, such as loss of loved ones, forced relocation, and increased dependence on others (*Research on Mental Illness and Addictive Disorders*, 1984).

What makes for good adaptation to old age? People who adjust well to old age appear to have been able to enjoy themselves and to obtain gratification from social relationships throughout their lives. They are also able to express their feelings, have a positive self-image, and feel a sense of purpose in life. Maladjusted elderly people express distress and discontent and are problems for their family and often for their community. The following factors seem to encourage adaptation to old age.

1. Economic security
2. High educational level
3. Social independence (including the capacity for solitary enjoyment)
4. Good health

Multiple Stressors

There seems to be some truth to the commonly held belief that everyone has a breaking point. The more stress people experience, the more likely they are to break down either physically or psychologically. Dealing with several stressful situations as the same time obviously places great demands on a person's resources, but stress can also have cumulative effects. The following case illustrates how stresses that accumulate over time can have long-term negative effects.

Mrs. A. was a 34-year-old woman who came to an outpatient clinic, complaining that the problems of managing her four children, aged 5 through 12, had become intolerable, especially the management of her hyperactive, negativistic 9-year-old son. She found herself either frantically attempting to discipline them or allowing them to do as they pleased while she shut herself up in a room and cried. This situation had distinctly worsened since her husband's death, 11 months earlier. Her husband had been a chronic invalid for five years of their six years of their marriage. Her two older children were by her first husband, who had been discovered to be a bigamist. After this marriage had been annulled, she had a third child out of wedlock and then the fourth child in her second marriage. After her husband's death, she had experienced severely increased economic pressures: she was working a very full schedule and had problems in arranging day care for the children when they were not in school. Except when on her job, she was quite isolated, with few friends and no available relatives. Symptoms of moderate depression, with fears and guilt about impulses to hurt her children, had built up since her husband's death.

—(Wynne, 1975, p. 1615)

The clinical assessment of such a case is complicated. Even though the environmental stress experienced by Mrs. A. was undoubtedly substantial, it is difficult to separate her current distress from her longstanding personality problems and difficult life situation.

In other cases, the multiple stresses in a person's life are easily identified. Someone whose mother and husband have died recently and who has just lost a job and had an automobile accident has suffered a combination of terrible blows. Sometimes some of the blows occur only in a person's thoughts. For example, a man who had recently lost his job and whose son had recently become addicted to heroin heard about a man of about his own age who had recently died of a heart attack. Although he hardly knew the other man, he imagined himself collapsing in the street as the heart-attack victim had done. Although simply hearing about the heart attack would not seem to have been a piercing personal blow, the man began to suffer from an intense fear that he was about to die. In this case, the combination of recent stressful life events and personality factors may have so raised the man's stress level that seemingly minor event brought on an attack of anxiety.

TABLE 5-7

Research has shown that people who have experienced multiple stressors in the recent past are especially susceptible to depression, anxiety, and overreactivity of physiological systems (Cohen, 1988). There is growing reason to believe that mental or physical breakdowns could be predicted if there were a way to qualify how stressful certain life experiences are. For this reason, researchers have sought ways of assessing those experiences. Because recent experiences often exert a more powerful influence and are more easily recalled than those that occurred many years before, efforts have been made to quantify stressful life changes for specific time periods, such as the past year. Table 5-7 contains excerpts from the Life Experiences Survey (Sarason and others, 1978), one of the instruments that have been developed for this purpose.

Even though economics may seem somewhat far removed from psychology, there is growing evidence that economic conditions such as poverty can affect the incidence of stressful life events, which in turn can cause

Assessing Life Stress

Because life experiences seem to be related to susceptibility to physical or psychological breakdown, assessing them might lead to the development of useful predictive tools. Recent experiences often exert powerful influences and are more easily recalled than those that occurred many years before, so several researchers have sought to quantify stressful life changes for specific time periods, such as the past year. Research has shown that people who had many of what they regard as bad or undesirable experiences in the recent past are especially susceptible to abnormal psychological and physical conditions. The following excerpts from the Life Experiences Survey illustrate this assessment approach to stress (Sarason, Johnson, and Siegel, 1978). Note that whether a given event is judged as desirable or undesirable is left up to the individual. Thus, depending on other factors in the person's life, a pregnancy could be judged as desirable or undesirable. People with a large number of life events that they regard as *bad* and as having had a *great effect* on their lives are more likely to experience maladaptive stress reactions. The individual's personality characteristics also help to determine the effects of environmental stressors.

Life Experiences Survey

Listed below are a number of events that may bring about changes in the lives of those who experience them. Rate each event that occurred in your life *during the past year* as *Good* or *Bad* (circle which one applies). Show how much the event affected your life by circling the appropriate statement (no effect—some effect—moderate effect—great effect).

If you have not experienced a particular event in the past year, leave it blank.

Please go through the entire list first, so that you begin to get an idea of the type of events you will be asked to rate.

Event	Type of Event		Effect of Event on Your Life			
1. Minor law violations (traffic tickets, disturbing the peace, etc.)	Good	Bad	no effect	some effect	moderate effect	great effect
2. New job	Good	Bad	no effect	some effect	moderate effect	great effect
3. Change of residence	Good	Bad	no effect	some effect	moderate effect	great effect
4. Being fired from job	Good	Bad	no effect	some effect	moderate effect	great effect
5. Serious injury or illness of close friend	Good	Bad	no effect	some effect	moderate effect	great effect
6. Ending of formal schooling	Good	Bad	no effect	some effect	moderate effect	great effect
7. Breaking up with boyfriend/girlfriend	Good	Bad	no effect	some effect	moderate effect	great effect
8. Failing an important exam	Good	Bad	no effect	some effect	moderate effect	great effect
9. Financial problems concerning school (in danger of not having sufficient money to continue)	Good	Bad	no effect	some effect	moderate effect	great effect
10. Other recent experiences that have had an impact on your life. List each and rate.	Good	Bad	no effect	some effect	moderate effect	great effect

Sarason and others, 1978, pp. 943–946.

health and behavioral problems. A number of studies have shown that low socioeconomic status is associated with a high frequency of stressful events and the learning of inadequate methods for coping with them (Eron and Peterson, 1982). Thus, it is not necessarily socioeconomic status by itself that causes problems, but rather the life events and poor coping skills that are correlated with this status.

Regardless of socioeconomic status, unemployment can cause psychological as well as economic problems. Brenner (1973) has reported that when employment levels decline, admissions to state mental hospitals rise. He also found that economic reverses are correlated with increases in death rates from a variety of conditions, including suicide, homicide, and cirrhosis of the liver, a disorder that is often associated with heavy alcohol use. From demographic data, Brenner has calculated that over a 6-year period a 1-percent rise in unemployment would have the following effects on national statistics.

- 36,887 total additional deaths
- 20,240 additional deaths from cardiovascular diseases
- 495 additional deaths from cirrhosis of the liver
- 920 additional suicides
- 648 additional homicides
- 4,227 additional first admissions to state mental hospitals
- 3,340 additional admissions to state prisons

These physical and physiological effects of unemployment are not necessarily immediate. The entire impact of a rise in unemployment might not be felt for several years after it occurred. People who have multiple stressors in their lives at the time that they lose their jobs run the greatest risk of some sort of breakdown.

Clinical Reactions to Stress

Stress plays a role in most of the conditions that make up abnormal psychology. The three conditions that we will review in this section, while they are dealt with in different ways in DSM-III-R, are all linked to stress arousal and to the resulting clinical symptoms. In addition disorders a recent increase in life stress precedes what is usually a temporary maladaptive reaction. Posttraumatic disorders are often more complicated because of the possibility of delayed and recurring reactions to stress. Dissociative disorders are among the most dramatic and puzzling forms of abnormal behavior and are almost always preceded by an upsurge of stress that the individual cannot handle.

Adjustment Disorder

A person with an **adjustment disorder** is someone who has not adapted well to one or more stressors that have occurred in the previous three months. The stressors might involve a developmental transition (such as marriage, divorce, having a child, or menopause), or they might be situational (such as changing schools, getting a new supervisor at work, or having been socially rejected), or they might be multiple stressors that have accumulated recently. Most of the time a person's maladaptive reactions to these stressors tend to disappear when the stressful circumstances dissipate or when the person learns how to live with new conditions. In the following case, the stressful transition to marriage resulted in an adjustment disorder.

Mark Catton, aged 23, had recently married. He and his wife had known each other for two years at college and were deeply in love. Their getting married seemed a perfectly logical consequence of their affection for each other. The first several weeks after the wedding were wonderful for the couple. They looked forward to their evenings together and often took short trips on the weekend.

One evening at dinner Dorothy talked about a new salesman at her office. She described him as intelligent, handsome, and charming. When Dorothy used the word "charming," something seemed to click inside Mark. He wondered why she had chosen that particular word to describe the new salesman, as well as why she talked so much about someone she had known for only a day. During the next few weeks Dorothy made several additional references to the salesman. Her liking for him was more obvious with each reference. Each time it came up, Mark became increasingly suspicious and depressed. When Dorothy worked until late in the evening twice in one week, his suspiciousness and depression increased. When he confronted her with his suspicion that she was dating the salesman, Dorothy displayed shock and outrage.

During the next few weeks Mark became increasingly depressed. His depression was interrupted only by occasional outbursts of venom directed toward Dorothy. Their sex life soon ceased to exist, and their evenings were filled with silence. The problem reached clinical proportions when Mark began to stay in bed all day. It took great effort for Dorothy to get him to see a psychotherapist, although by this time even Mark knew that something was very wrong.

During his session with the psychotherapist Mark came to see how unrealistic his expectations about marriage were. He also was able for the first time to bring all of his thoughts and feelings out into the open. One recollection about his parents seemed particularly important. He remembered that when he was about 6 or 7 his parents had quarreled a great deal, apparently over his father's suspicion about his mother's activities at home while he was at work. His father had accused his mother of infidelity and had been very nasty. Mark couldn't remember exactly how the situation had been resolved. Although he had not thought about the incident for years, it became very meaningful to him, and discussing it in psychotherapy seemed to help him.

have adjustment disorders.

Bereavement and Grief

Bereavement refers to the loss of someone significant through that person's death. **Grief** is the emotional or affective response to the loss. Table 5–8 lists behavioral and physiological changes frequently observed following the loss of a loved one. These losses are both painful and common. Each year 8 million people in the United States suffer the death of someone in the immediate

---

TABLE 5–8

Behavioral and Physiological Aspects of Bereavement in Adults

Behavioral Changes	Physiological Changes
crying	muscular weakness
agitation, restlessness	sighing
preoccupation with image of	sleep disturbance
the deceased	immunological changes
social withdrawal	endocrine changes
decreased concentration and	cardiovascular changes
attention	decreased body weight
depressed mood	
anxiety	

Based on Hofer, 1984.

---

family. Each year there are 800,000 new widows and widowers, and 400,000 people under age 25 die.

The symptoms of grief are part of a normal recovery process and not a sign of pathology. Nevertheless, grief takes more prolonged, pervasive, and complicated forms than many people realize. These forms vary greatly; there is no uniform and orderly succession of stages through which all grieving must pass. However, certain phrases are observed often enough to be recognized as, if not typical, at least common after the death of a husband, wife, or child. The first reactions are often shock, numbness, bewilderment, and a sense of disbelief—even denial of the reality for a time. This reaction is common even when the death was anticipated. After a few days numbness turns to intense suffering. Grieving people feel empty. They are repeatedly reminded of the person who has died. Waves of crying sweep over them with each reminder; they may have dreams and even hallucinations in which the dead person is still alive.

After this comes a period of despair, as the grieving person slowly accepts the loss. The dominant feelings are sadness and inability to feel pleasure. Tense, restless anxiety may alternate with lethargy and fatigue. Physical symptoms are common—weakness, sleep disturbances, loss of appetite, headaches, back pain, indigestion, shortness of breath, heart palpitations, and even occasional dizziness and nausea (Stroebe and Stroebe, 1987). The bereaved may adopt the mannerisms and symptoms of the deceased. Grief reactions are worst following premature and violent deaths.

Grieving persons may alternate between avoiding reminders of the deceased and cultivating memories. Some desperately seek company, and others withdraw. Sadness is mixed with anger—at doctors who failed, at friends and relatives thought to be unappreciative, even at the dead person for abandoning the living. The motives of people who try to help are sometimes suspected, and grieving persons may alienate their friends by irritability and quarrelsomeness. Most painful of all is self-reproach for having treated the deceased badly or having done too little to prevent the death.

There is evidence that a spouse's recovery from grief is quicker and more complete when the marriage was happy. Isolation is bad for the bereaved, as it is for most people (see Figure 5–5). Grief following bereavement is normal. When the grieving process is abnormal, the individual may suffer various forms of continuing maladjustment, particularly anxiety and depression. Psychotherapy may be needed for persistent anxiety or depression produced by morbid or unresolved grief (Parkes, 1986).

Research is being carried out to better understand the effects of bereavement and the grief process (Zisook, 1987). For example, in one study the effects of bereavement on several thousand men and women in semirural Washington County, Maryland, were investigated (Helsing and others, 1981). The bereaved subjects were compared with still-married individuals who were similar in such factors as age, sex, race, education, religious interests, and number of bathrooms and animals on the premises. The major finding was that bereavement is much harder on men than on women. The overall mortality rate was 26 percent higher for widowers than for married men, compared with only a 3.8 percent difference between the rates for widows and married women. For widowers aged 55 to 64, the mortality rate was al-

FIGURE 5–5
Bereaved people appreciate the visits paid to them by others. Visitors who show acceptance and understanding of the survivor's feelings can provide needed support, reassurance, and comfort. While a conventional expression of sympathy can probably not be avoided, pity is the last thing the bereaved person wants. Pity puts the bereaved person at a distance from, and in an inferior position to, the would-be comforter. It is best to get conventional verbal expressions of sympathy over as quickly as possible and to speak from the heart or not at all.

most 61 percent higher than the rate for married men in the same age group. In men under 55 who remarried (at least half of them did), the death rate was at least 70-percent lower than for those who did not. In men aged 55 to 64, it was 50-percent lower. Death rates for widowers who remarried were even lower than the rates for men in the same age groups who were married throughout the period of the study. Further research will be needed to find out why wives are less affected by the loss of a spouse than husbands. This study did not support the popular idea that the remaining spouse's risk of dying was significantly greater in the early months after bereavement. Only long-term death rates differed for the widowed and still-married subjects.

Research on grief and the failure of some bereaved people to resume a normal life in a reasonable period of time is needed because bereavement is so common and because popular ideas about how people do or should respond to loss may not be correct. There is evidence that the grief process may be more complex than is generally thought to be the case (Wortman, 1987).

Posttraumatic Disorders

Whereas the stressors in adjustment disorder are within the range of common experience, **posttraumatic disorders** involve more extreme experiences (such as disasters) whose effects may extend over a long period. The onset of the clinical condition in posttraumatic disorders varies from soon after the trauma to a long time afterward. These disorders are considered to be acute if the condition begins within 6 months of the trauma and delayed if it begins more than 6 months after the event. The chances of complete recovery are better in the acute form than in the delayed form. Although preexisting psychological difficulties may intensify posttraumatic disorders, many people who develop these disorders do not have a history of psychiatric problems.

A frequent characteristic of posttraumatic disorders is a tendency to reexperience the event. Painful and intrusive recollections and recurrent dreams or nightmares are common. The reexperiencing of a traumatic event may have an aura of unreality about it. When this happens, the person feels emotionally numb or anesthetized, and there is an unstoppable flood of thoughts about the event, along with a feeling of estrangement from the content of the thoughts.

In addition to reexperiencing the stressor, people who are suffering from posttraumatic disorders may show excessive autonomic arousal, hyperalertness, difficulty in concentrating on or completing tasks, and difficulty falling asleep. A symptom that often occurs in children who have experienced trauma is an exaggerated startle response. These symptoms may increase when the

individual is exposed to cues related to the traumatic event (for example, when a victim of an automobile accident sees a car crash in a movie). Preoccupation with the traumatic event may also lead to decreased interest in social relationships, intimacy, and sexuality. Painful guilt feelings are common, as are depression, restlessness, and irritability. In some cases, there may be outbreaks of impulsive behavior, usually of a nonviolent nature (for example, unexplained absences from work), and abuse of alcohol or drugs.

In the following case, there was a short interval between the stressor and the onset of the posttraumatic condition. The case illustrates how denial can be used to blunt the strong feelings aroused by a stressful event.

Harry is a 40-year-old-truck dispatcher. He had worked his way up in a small trucking firm. One night he himself took a run because he was shorthanded. The load was steel pipes carried in an old truck. This improper vehicle had armor between the load bed and the driver's side of the forward compartment but did not fully protect the passenger's side.

Late at night Harry passed an attractive and solitary girl hitchhiking on a lonely stretch of highway. Making an impulsive decision to violate the company rule against passengers of any sort, he picked her up on the grounds that she was a hippy who did not know any better and might be raped.

A short time later, a car veered across the divider line and entered his lane, threatening a head-on collision. He pulled over the shoulder of the road into an initially clear area, but crashed abruptly into a pile of gravel. The pipes shifted, penetrated the cab of the truck on the passenger's side and impaled the girl. Harry crashed into the steering wheel and windshield and was briefly unconscious. He regained consciousness and was met with the grisly sight of his dead companion.

The highway patrol found no identification on the girl, the other car had driven on, and Harry was taken by ambulance to a hospital emergency room. No fractures were found, his lacerations were sutured, and he remained overnight for observation. His wife, who sat with him, found him anxious and dazed that night, talking episodically of the events in a fragmentary and incoherent way so that the story was not clear.

The next day he was released. Against his wife's wishes, he returned to work. From then on, for several days, he continued his regular work as if nothing had happened. There was an immediate session with his superiors and with legal advisors. The result was that he was reprimanded for breaking the rule about passengers but also reassured that,

otherwise, the accident was not his fault and he would not be held responsible. As it happened, the no passenger rule was frequently breached by other drivers, and this was well known throughout the group.

—(Horowitz, 1974, p. 769)

For several days after the accident Harry thought about it occasionally, but he was surprised at how little emotion he felt. However, despite his good performance at work, Harry's wife reported that he thrashed around in his sleep, ground his teeth, and seemed tenser and more irritable than usual. A month after the accident he had a nightmare in which mangled bodies appeared. He awoke in a state of anxiety. During the following days he had recurring, upsetting images of the girl's body. He developed a phobia about driving to and from work, increased his consumption of alcohol, had outbursts of temper at minor frustrations, and began feeling intense guilt about the accident.

In psychotherapy an effort was made to understand the significance of the accident for Harry. Initially Harry resisted describing to the therapist the circumstances surrounding the accident. After this resistance subsided, his strong feelings—the guilt, fears, and anger—emerged and were discussed. Because of complex and defensive motives, Harry could not accept and integrate his traumatic perceptions of the accident. They were stored, but not forgotten. He came to understand that two themes had been most upsetting to him: guilt over his relief at the fact that the girl had been the victim instead of him, as well as guilt over his sexual fantasies about her; and anxiety over the realization that he had come so close to being the victim. Bringing these themes into focus enabled Harry to be more open about himself and to take a problem-solving rather than a defensive stance toward his situation. Psychotherapy enabled him to look at himself in a more realistic way, to feel comfortable doing so within the supportive-therapy situation, and to achieve an improved adaptation.

What happens in posttraumatic stress? In coping with trauma, an individual uses a huge amount of psychological energy to fend off thoughts about it. He or she may feel emotional numbness, which results in loss of interest in social and sexual involvements. Although the event had ended, it is relived daily, and there is an irrational fear that it will happen again. It is this fear that causes hypervigilance and agitation. Intrusive thoughts, images, and dreams may become so preoccupying that the person cannot engage in normal work or love relationships. An example is the case of Mr. C., a violinist who survived a nightclub fire that destroyed the nightclub and resulted in the loss of many lives. Mr. C. functioned well during the fire (he helped rescue people and valuable original musical scores), but 6 months later he could not work: he became anxious whenever he smelled burning meat or smoke, and he had recurrent visions of people tearing and grabbing at others' clothes.

In some cases of maladaptive reactions to overwhelming stress there may be an alternation of intrusive thinking and denial. In the intrusive state, the individual cannot stop thinking frightening thoughts related to the traumatic event. In the denial state, the individual ignores the implications of threats and losses, forgets important problems, and may show a withdrawal of interest in life. Table 5–9 lists symptoms of the intrusive and denial phases of stress disorders.

Posttraumatic stress disorder (PTSD) is now an established psychiatric diagnosis, but it is still a controversial one. Epidemiological evidence suggests that the prevalence of PTSD is 1 percent in the general population and about 3.5 percent in civilians exposed to physical attack and in Vietnam veterans who were not wounded. About 20 percent of wounded veterans show symptoms of PTSD (Helzer and others, 1987). Identifying it can be difficult because the symptoms are so varied; they include recurrent dreams, flashbacks, reenacting the trauma, emotional numbing and estrangement, impaired concentration, sleep disturbances, and an exaggerated startle response.

Certain symptoms may be related to the type of trauma experienced, for example, whether or not the individual played a role in causing the traumatic event (for example, by driving a car recklessly or speeding). Victims of crimes involving violence and humiliation often feel both intensely fearful and ashamed. Parents of homicide victims may have difficulty containing the anger they feel toward the murderer (Ochberg, 1988). Psychotherapy can help victims of traumatic experiences and their loved ones view their victimization objectively

and express powerful emotions that they have not previously expressed. The failure to confront a traumatic event is an important contributor to unhappiness and maladjustment, and the opportunity to tell a sympathetic listener about it can be therapeutic (Pennebaker and Beall, 1986).

Dissociative Disorders

The maladaptive behaviors that arise from dissociative disorders provide a striking contrast to those that arise from posttraumatic stress disorders and adjustment disorders. Stress plays a major role in both, yet the reactions involved appear to be poles apart. Once again we see that similar situations can elicit drastically different responses in people with different dispositions and vulnerabilities.

In posttraumatic stress disorders, individuals cannot get the distressing experiences that they have undergone out of their minds. People with adjustment disorders show milder disturbances and decreased ability to cope, but their behavior clears up when the stressor is removed. The disturbance in adjustment disorders comes from overinvolvement with the stress-causing situations. In contrast, people with dissociative disorders use a variety of dramatic maneuvers to escape from the anxieties and conflicts aroused by stress. Their behavior involves sudden, temporary alterations of consciousness that serve to blot out painful experiences.

Many dissociative disorders appear to begin and end abruptly and are precipitated by stressful experiences. They do not seem to be attributable to organic factors. Although these disorders usually occur after childhood, in most cases there is a history of serious family turmoil. Separation from parents in early childhood and abuse by parents have frequently been reported.

The dissociation often involves feelings of unreality, estrangement, and depersonalization, and sometimes a loss or shift of self-identity. Less dramatic, but somewhat similar, examples of dissociation are commonly observed in normal adults and children. When the first impact of bad news or a catastrophe hits us, we may feel as if everything is suddenly strange, unnatural, and different (estrangement), or as if we are unreal and cannot actually be witnessing or feeling what is going on (depersonalization). Stress can make a person feel stunned or dazed, as if in a dream or in another world. Such feelings of dissociation become abnormal when they become too intense, last too long, or cannot be controlled.

Four conditions classified as dissociative disorders are:

1. Psychogenic amnesia
2. Psychogenic fugue

TABLE 5–9

Symptoms of Intrusive Thinking and Denial in Stress Disorders (Symptoms May Alternate)

Symptoms of Intrusive Thinking

Sleep and dream disturbances
Awareness of ideas and feelings related to the traumatic event
Preoccupation with the event
Compulsive repetitions of actions related to the event

Symptoms of Denial

Selective inattention
Amnesia (complete or partial)
Use of fantasy to counteract real conditions
Withdrawal

Adapted from Horowitz, 1986. Copyright © 1986 by the American Psychological Association. Reprinted by permission of the author.

3. Multiple personality
4. Depersonalization

All of these disorders involve large memory gaps and drastic changes in social roles.

Psychogenic Amnesia

Amnesia, the most common dissociative disorder, involves extensive, but selective, memory losses. Because some memory losses can also be traced to organic changes (for example, head injuries), the word **psychogenic** is used when no organic causes are discernible. The memory losses that are characteristic of amnesia are too extensive to be explained by ordinary forgetfulness. Some people cannot remember anything about their past. Others can no longer recall specific events, people, places, or objects while their memory for other, simultaneously experienced events remains intact. Amnesia is usually precipitated by a physical accident or an emotionally traumatic event such as an intensely painful disappointment.

A young man dressed in work clothes came to the emergency room of a hospital in the city in which he lived with the complaint that he did not know who he was. He seemed dazed, was not intoxicated, and carried no identification. After being kept in the hospital a few days, he woke up one morning in great distress, demanding to know why he was being kept in the hospital and announcing that he had to leave immediately to attend to urgent business.

With the recovery of his memory, the facts related to his amnesia emerged. The day his amnesia began, he had been the driver in an automobile accident that resulted in the death of a pedestrian. Police officers on the scene were convinced that the driver had not been in the wrong; the accident had been the pedestrian's fault. The police told the driver to fill out a routine form and to appear at the coroner's inquest. The man filled out the form at the home of a friend and accidentally left his wallet there. Later after mailing the form, he became dazed and amnesic. He was led to the hospital by a stranger. The amnesia was probably related to the stress of the fatal accident, fear of the inquest, and worry that he might actually have been responsible for the accident.

—(Based on Cameron, 1963, pp. 355–56)

Psychogenic amnesias are seen more often in adolescents and young adults than in children and older people, and occur more often among females than among males. Amnesia was once a favorite plot device in movies, but actually the condition is rare and recovery is usually rapid.

Psychogenic Fugue

Whereas amnesiacs experience simple memory losses, individuals who are going through **psychogenic fugue states** suddenly lose their sense of identity, give up their customary life and habits, and characteristically wander far from home. Such a person sets up a new life in some distant place as a seemingly different person. The fugue state, or amnesic flight, usually ends when he or she abruptly "wakes up," mystified and distressed at being in a strange place under strange circumstances.

Fugues, like amnesia, are often precipitated by intolerable stresses such as marital quarrels, personal rejection, military conflict, and natural disasters. Fugues are usually of brief duration, with complete recovery and little likelihood of recurrence. After "waking up," the person frequently has no recollection of the events that took place during the fugue. The following case illustrates a fugue state with massive amnesia.

Samuel O., a graduate student, impoverished and far from home, was invited to dinner at the home of an instructor whom he had known when they were socioeconomic equals in another town. He accepted the invitation because he was lonely and hungry, but he regretted it at once because his clothes were shabby. He thought, in retrospect, that the instructor had seemed condescending. That evening he left his rooming house in plenty of time for the dinner, but he failed to show up at the instructor's home. Two days later he was picked up by the police in a neighboring state. He could vaguely remember riding a freight train, talking with strangers, and sharing their food, but he had no idea who he was, where he had come from, or where he was going.

Later on, the young man was able to remember the events leading up to the fugue and something of what went on during it. When he started out for the instructor's house, he was still experiencing strong conflict about going there. He was ashamed of his appearance, resentful over the condescension, and afraid to express what he felt and call the dinner off. On his way, he was held up at a grade crossing by a slowly moving freight train. He had a sudden impulse to board the train and get away. When he acted on this impulse, he apparently became amnesic.

—(Based on Easton, 1959, pp. 505–513)

Because dissociative reactions are so difficult to believe, one frequently wonders whether the person is faking. As the following case illustrates, it often is not easy to answer this question.

An enlisted man in the Air Corps had some previous experience as a private pilot. After a disagreement with his wife, he decided to punish her by committing suicide. Choosing the most dramatic method he could

The Ten Faces of Billy

Christene is a loving 3-year-old who likes to draw pictures of flowers and butterflies. David is a withdrawn little boy who bangs his head against the wall when upset. Adelena is a young lesbian. These distinct personalities, along with at least seven others, presented a bizarre puzzle in a Columbus, Ohio, courtroom; they all exist within the same individual—William Milligan, 23, who was accused of rape. Last week, after a brief trial, the ten faces of Billy were found not guilty by reason of insanity.

Milligan's is the second known U.S. case in which a defendant has been acquitted of a major crime because he possessed multiple personalities. The Milligan case started last year when four women were raped last year near the Ohio State campus. An anonymous tip to police—the call might have come from one of Milligan's "personalities"—led to his arrest. During a jailhouse interview, psychologist Dorothy Fuller began routinely by asking if he were William Milligan. "Billy's asleep," came the reply. "'I'm David."

Fuller suspected that Milligan was a multiple personality. One of his two females, the lesbian Adelena, is thought to be the "personality" who committed the rapes. Besides Adelena, little Christene and David, and the core personality Billy, there are:

Arthur, an intellectual who speaks in clipped British phrases. Although most of Milligan's other personalities have taken I.Q. tests (the scores range from 68 to the 130s), Arthur refuses to be tested because it is beneath his dignity.

Ragan, an aggressive male with a Slavic accent who considers himself the others' protector. He threatened to fire the lawyers.

Allen, 18, who plays the drums and is the only personality who smokes.

Danny, 14, and Christopher, 13, both timid and seldom seen.

Tommy, who enlisted in the Navy but was dishonorably discharged after a month. For an interview with his lawyer, Milligan was strapped into a straitjacket. Tommy casually slipped the jacket off in about ten seconds. (Newsweek, December 18, 1978, p. 106)

Since this article appeared, Billy has been confined to a mental health center. If he does win release, he faces a 13-year prison sentence for a previous parole violation. (See Figure 5–6.)

think of, he took off in a large, unattended aircraft and made several passes at the local river, each time pulling up before plunging in. Very soon, all other aircraft were diverted to other cities, and the local control tower was concentrating on trying to persuade him to change his mind. He finally agreed, but then he discovered that although he knew how to take off, he did not know how to land the unfamiliar plane. After some tense interchanges with the control tower, however, he managed to get the plane down. When the welcoming party of military police arrived at the plane, he found himself unable to remember his name or anything about his identity, his present situation, or the events leading up to it.

—(Aldrich, 1966, p. 238)

From the available information we cannot be sure how well the pilot had planned this escapade. Neither can we be confident about whether his memory loss was feigned or real. These gaps illustrate the uncertainties connected with diagnosing dissociative reactions.

Multiple Personality

Multiple personality is the most dramatic of the dissociative disorders. In a multiple-personality reaction an individual assumes alternate personalities, like Dr. Jekyll and Mr. Hyde. Each personality has its own set of memories and typical behaviors. Frequently none of the personalities has any awareness of the others (see Box 5–2). In other cases, there is a one-way amnesia in which personality A is aware of the experiences of personality B while B remains unaware of A.

Multiple personality occurs rarely. Between 1817, when the first case was reported, and 1969, only 90 cases were reported. Since 1970 over 50 additional cases have been described (Boor, 1982). Whether this "epidemic" is a real increase or a reflection of greater interest in the disorder is unknown. Many more female than male multiple personalities have been reported, the ratio being about 4 to 1 (Kluft, 1984).

Clinically, the personalities' behavioral differences and disparate self-concepts seem striking and puzzling.

FIGURE 5–6

William Milligan's art work differed greatly depending on which of his personalities was dominant. Milligan (left) produced the portrait on the right as Christene and the center one as Billy, his core personality.

They may experience themselves as being of different genders, ages, and sexual orientations. They may have separate wardrobes, possessions, interests, and interpersonal styles. Their values, beliefs, and problems may diverge. They may even have different handwritings, handedness, speech patterns, and accents. There seem to be two or more distinctive personalities that alternate in controlling the body. Some, but not necessarily all, of the multiple personalities are unaware of the others.

In the following case, a 38-year-old woman named Margaret B. was admitted to a hospital with paralysis of her legs following a minor car accident that occurred six months earlier.

She reported that until three years before her admission to the hospital she had enjoyed smoking, drinking, visiting nightclubs, and otherwise indulging in parties and social activities. At that point, however, she and her husband, who was an alcoholic, were converted to a small, evangelical religious sect. Her husband achieved control of his drinking, she gave up her prior social indulgences,

and the two of them became completely immersed in the activities of the church.

[The] history revealed that she often "heard a voice telling her to say things and do things," said, "a terrible voice" that sometimes threatened to "take over completely." When it was finally suggested to the patient that she let the voice "take over," she closed her eyes, clenched her fists, and grimaced for a few moments during which she was out of contact with those around her. Suddenly she opened her eyes and one was in the presence of another person. Her name, she said, was "Harriet." Whereas Margaret had been paralyzed, and complained of fatigue, headache and backache, Harriet felt well, and she at once proceeded to walk unaided around the interviewing room. She spoke scornfully of Margaret's religiousness, her invalidism and her puritanical life, professing that she herself liked to drink and "go partying" but that Margaret was always going to church and reading the Bible. "But," she said, "I make her miserable—I impishly and proudly, "I make her miserable—I *make her say and do things she doesn't want to." At length, at the interviewer's suggestion, Harriet reluctantly agreed to "bring Margaret back," and after more grimacing and fist clenching, Margaret reappeared, paralyzed, complaining of her headache and backache, and completely amnesiac for the brief period of Harriet's release from her prison.*

—(Nemiah, 1978, pp. 179–180)

The clash between Margaret B.'s religiosity, on the one hand, and her inclinations to indulge in pleasure, on the other, is a frequent theme in cases of multiple personality. It is noteworthy that as a child Margaret B. had had a playmate, Harriet, to whom she had been very devoted. When they were both 6 years old Harriet had died of an acute infectious disease. Margaret had been deeply upset at her friend's death and wished that she had died in Harriet's place. Perhaps internalizing the image of her dead friend had in some way protected Margaret from prolonged despair and sorrow at her loss. As Margaret grew older, that internalization became the depository for all of her unacceptable impulses and feelings.

Most clinicians think of multiple personality as a psychological adaptation to traumatic experiences in early childhood. These experiences are severe and dramatic; examples are being dangled out of a window or being the victim of sexual sadism. In addition to having experienced harsh trauma in childhood, people with multiple personality seem prone to go into spontaneous hypnotic trances. This temporary defense may become

stabilized into multiple personality when the child faces repeated, overwhelming trauma.

Interest in multiple personality has mushroomed. The International Society for the Study of Multiple Personality was founded in 1984, and many case studies and interpretations of this disorder have appeared in recent years (Braun, 1984) (see Figure 5–7). At the same time, some researchers question whether multiple personality represents anything more than an extreme form of the normal ability to present a variety of distinctive "selves" that are not really separate personalities. An important reason for such disagreements about multiple personality is that cases of this disorder are rare, making it difficult to do good research and to compare cases seen at different times under different circumstances.

Depersonalization

Although DSM-III-R includes **depersonalization** among the dissociative disorders, some clinicians question its inclusion because it does not entail memory disturbances. In depersonalization there is a change in self-perception, and the person's sense of reality is temporarily lost or changed. Someone who is experiencing a state of depersonalization might say, "I feel as though I'm in a dream" or "I feel that I'm doing this mechanically." Frequently the individual has a feeling of not being in complete control of his or her actions, including speech. The onset of depersonalization is usually rapid and causes social or occupational impairment. The state of estrangement from oneself gradually disappears.

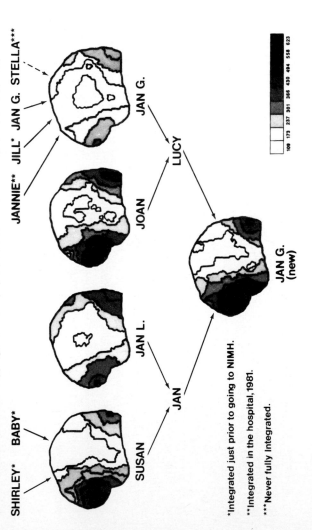

FIGURE 5–7

Evoked-potential recordings of a case of multiple personality. Evoked potentials consist of a short train of large slow brain waves measured by placing electrodes on the scalp. This figure shows different evoked-potential mappings for the multiple personalities of Jan G. (Braun, 1983, p. 89)

*Integrated just prior to going to NIMH.

**Integrated in the hospital, 1981.

***Never fully integrated.

Interpreting Dissociative Disorders

Dissociation seems to represent a process whereby certain mental functions that are ordinarily integrated with other functions presumably operate in a more compartmentalized or automatic way, usually outside the sphere of conscious awareness or memory recall. It might be described as a condition in which information—incoming, stored, or outgoing—is actively deflected from its usual or expected associations. This phenomenon results in alteration of the person's thoughts, feelings, or actions so that information is not associated or integrated with other information as it normally or logically would be.

The dissociative disorders are difficult to explain, for several reasons. Often it is unclear whether a given case involves dissociation or is some sort of psychotic manifestation. Also, it is often difficult to obtain the information needed to draw reasonable conclusions. In the case of Margaret B., one wonders about the stressors that led to Harriet's emergence. How important were the loss of the 6-year-old playmate and the recent changes in Margaret's adult life? In most stress disorders the source of stress is usually easy to identify. In the dissociative disorders, however, the source might not be obvious at all. Because human beings are able to distort their memories, considerable probing is often needed to determine the true nature of the stress.

Dissociative disorders are often discussed in psychodynamic and cognitive terms. These disorders help the individual escape from reality and seem to facilitate the expression of a variety of pent-up emotions. They have been interpreted as attempts to escape from excessive tension, anxiety, and stimulation by separating some parts of the personality from the rest. When there are no indications of a recent experience that might have functioned as a stressor, these perspectives raise questions about earlier stressors that might still have symbolic meaning for the individual. (Margaret's loss of Harriet illustrates this possibility.) In treating dissociative disorders, many clinicians seek to uncover the dissociated memories and to help the individual face then and deal with them more directly. Psychoanalysis, behavior therapy, hypnosis, and videotaped interviews combined with sedative drugs have all been useful for this purpose.

Treating Stress-Related Problems

People often overcome their maladaptive reactions to stress in the course of time, but help from an expert may speed up the process. The clinician has two broad functions: (1) to provide social support for troubled people, and (2) to strengthen their coping skills. Several procedures are used in treating stress-related problems.

Supportive Therapy

It is hard to recover from a stress-related disorder if one is or feels socially isolated. Because most stress reactions involve feelings of inadequacy and isolation, many people can be helped by sympathetic listening and encouragement. Though they use different terms, both psychodynamically and humanistically oriented clinicians emphasize the client–therapist relationship as a means of facilitating adaptive coping. Freudians describe their efforts in this regard as strengthening the client's ego. When the ego is able to manipulate reality more effectively, it is able to handle the id's incessant demands with less stress. The Rogerian therapist's acceptance of clients as they are, coupled with recognition of their strengths and deemphasis of their failings, helps clients feel more positive about themselves and creates a supportive climate. Clients who receive supportive therapy often comment with relief that the therapist did not criticize them either directly or indirectly for their handling of difficult situations. Within a supportive environment clients can relax enough to engage in problem solving and the careful consideration of alternatives that had previously seemed impossible.

Drugs and Sedatives

A variety of anti-anxiety and antidepressive drugs are available to help people who have experienced trauma. While they are not a cure, such drugs can be of considerable value in overcoming panic states and other maladaptive reactions to intense short-term stress. Tranquilizers are often used along with psychological approaches such as supportive therapy.

Relaxation Training

It is possible for people to learn ways of helping themselves deal with stress. It is a well-known fact that people can learn to regulate voluntarily certain effects of the autonomic nervous system. Such regulation, in turn, can affect their emotional state. For example, anxiety can be caused by the sensation of tension that is experienced when muscle fibers are shortened or contracted, as they are during stress. Conversely, tension cannot be present when muscle fibers are lengthened or relaxed. Relaxation training involves the following steps.

1. Focusing attention on a series of specific muscle groups
2. Tensing each group
3. Maintaining tension for 5 to 7 seconds
4. Telling oneself to relax and immediately releasing tension
5. Focusing attention on each muscle group as it relaxes

Relaxation training is used not only as a technique in its own right but also as a basis for other therapies. It is applicable to a wide variety of stress-related problems and can be readily taught both individually and in groups.

Systematic Desensitization

This procedure consists of combining relaxation training and a hierarchy of anxiety-producing stimuli to gradually eliminate the fear of a specific situation. The person learns to maintain the relaxed state while imagining anxiety-associated stimuli from the various stages of the hierarchy. In one study, soldiers with fears of airplanes, open places, and blood were treated with systematic desensitization (Kipper, 1977). The result was a significant reduction in their fears.

Cognitive Modification

Behavioral problems can arise in part because an individual persists in a particular maladaptive line of thought. If someone can be guided to think about a situation in a different, more productive way, adaptive coping may become possible. Cognitive modification involves learning new internal dialogues and new ways of thinking about situations and about oneself. In this sense, cognitive modification is a step toward productive problem solving.

Social Intervention

Some therapists prefer to treat troubled individuals alone, whereas others feel that they can be more helpful if they treat people within their social contexts. Family therapy, in which all members of the family go into treatment together, is based on the latter idea. In some instances the clinical worker might even decide to make one or more home visits to observe the family's interactions in more natural surroundings.

Study Outline

VULNERABILITY AND COPING

1. Whether a situation is stressful or not depends on how the individual appraises it and on his or her ability to deal with it. During **primary appraisal,** individuals interpret a situation as either threatening or harmless. During **secondary appraisal,** they consider the action that is called for and their own resources for coping.
2. **Vulnerability** to stress is reduced by adequate coping skills and social support. There are four types of **behavioral coping,** or what we actually do in reacting to stress: matter-of-fact confronting, anxiety, anger, and defensiveness. **Coping resources** refer to our capability for handling stress. Some stresses may be beyond our ability to cope with them.
3. Stress can be reduced when people know what to expect, have the specific skills needed for stressful situations, and can limit their emotional response. Effective copers know how to probe for information, think constructively, solve problems, behave flexibly, and provide feedback about what tactics work.
4. **Social support** can be defined as the belief that one is loved and valued and that others are available who can be relied on to provide help or understanding if it is necessary. Social support may reduce vulnerability and the possibility of maladaptive behavior. The Social Support Questionnaire provides information on the amount of social support people have and how satisfying it is to them.

STRESS AROUSAL

1. People may react to stress physiologically, psychologically, or behaviorally. Two broad types of stress-arousing conditions are life situations and developmental transitions.
2. Situational stresses can differ in duration, severity, predictability, and suddenness of onset, as well as in the amount of loss of control that they involve. Post-traumatic stress disorders may result from accidents, natural disasters, and military combat.

3. Life transition stresses are associated with stages in development such as birth, puberty, entering college, marriage, career planning, having children, and retirement. Some people adapt to these transitions better than others.

4. Adolescence is a particularly difficult transition. The individual's coping skills are still forming, and the physical changes involved in puberty increase the stress of getting used to new roles and responsibilities. Because of the nature of the changes through which the individual is going, a certain amount of loneliness may be inevitable during adolescence.

5. Old age can be a difficult life transition. The accompanying physical changes and psychological disorders can be stressful. Adaptation to old age is enhanced by economic security, high educational level, social independence, and good health. Major problems are presented by retirement from work, forced relocation, increased dependence on others, and loss of a spouse.

6. Dealing with multiple stressors severely taxes the individual's coping ability. The more stress people experience, the more likely they are to break down either physically or psychologically.

CLINICAL REACTIONS TO STRESS

1. Disorders in which stress is a major causal factor include adjustment disorders, posttraumatic disorders, and dissociative disorders.

2. In **adjustment disorders**, a recent stressful experience has preceded a maladaptive reaction. Prolonged grief reactions to bereavement illustrate the maladaptations seen in adjustment disorders. Most instances of adjustment disorder tend to improve on their own as the stress that precipitated them dissipates. The sign of an adjustment disorder is a reaction that is not proportionate to the circumstances. Other symptoms include depression, anxiety, misbehavior, disturbed sleep patterns, deterioration in performance at work or school, and social withdrawal.

3. **Posttraumatic disorders** involve more extreme types of stress, which may last for a long period. The reaction may be acute or delayed. Posttraumatic disorders involve a recognizable stressor that would be hard for anyone to deal with. They are characterized by recurrent and intrusive recollections of the trauma; psychological numbing and lack of interest in previously significant people and activities; hyperalertness; an exaggerated startle response; and guilt, depression, restlessness, irritability, and substance abuse.

4. People with **dissociative disorders** use a variety of dramatic maneuvers to escape the anxieties and conflicts aroused by stress. Dissociation often involves feelings of unreality, estrangement, and depersonalization, which can go as far as a loss or shift of self-identity.

5. **Amnesia**, the most common dissociative disorder, involves selective memory losses that are too extensive to be explained by ordinary forgetfulness. The condition is rare, and recovery is usually complete.

6. People who are going through **psychogenic fugue states** suddenly give up their customary ways of life and wander far from home. Often they take new identities because they do not remember their old ones. The fugue state ends when the individual "wakes up." Fugues occur in response to intolerable stress; they do not last long and do not usually recur.

7. In **multiple personality** the individual assumes alternate personalities that may or may not be aware of each other. Most clinicians see multiple personality as resulting from traumatic early-childhood experiences.

8. **Depersonalization** is included among the dissociative disorders although no memory disturbances are connected with it. This disorder consists of a change in self-perception and in the person's sense of reality, and it frequently involves a feeling of loss of control.

9. In dissociative disorders certain normally integrated mental functions seem to operate in a more compartmentalized way, usually outside of conscious awareness or memory. It is often unclear whether a given case involves dissociation or is a psychotic manifestation.

TREATING STRESS-RELATED PROBLEMS

1. Stress-related problems can be treated by supportive therapy, which seeks to strengthen clients' self-confidence and thus improve their problem-solving abilities; by drugs and sedatives, which can be valuable in cases of short-term stress; by relaxation training; by cognitive modification, through which individuals may be guided to think in more productive ways; and by social intervention, in which the therapist treats the individual in his or her social context.

CHAPTER 6

Jerome Witkin, *On the R&R*, 1985. Oil on canvas, 84 × 48". Photo courtesy Sherry French Gallery, New York. Courtesy NYNEX, White Plains, New York.

OBJECTIVES FOR CHAPTER SIX:

To learn:

1. The general cognitive and bodily symptoms of anxiety
2. The types and characteristics of anxiety disorders
3. How anxiety disorders are treated

To understand:

1. The influence of the various perspectives in interpreting and treating anxiety disorders

GENERALIZED ANXIETY DISORDER

PANIC DISORDER

PHOBIAS

Simple Phobias

Social Phobias

Agoraphobia

OBSESSIVE COMPULSIVE DISORDER

INTERPRETING AND TREATING ANXIETY DISORDERS

The Psychodynamic Perspective

The Learning Perspective

The Cognitive Perspective

The Biological Perspective

STUDY OUTLINE

CASE A: SUSAN

I wish I could tell you exactly what's the matter. Sometimes I feel like something terrible has just happened when actually nothing has happened at all. Other times I'm expecting the sky to fall down any minute. Most of the time I can't point my finger at something specific. Still, I feel tense and jumpy. The fact is that I am tense and jumpy almost all the time. Sometimes my heart beats so fast, I'm sure it's a heart attack.

Little things can set it off. The other day I thought a supermarket clerk had overcharged me a few cents on an item. She showed me that I was wrong, but that didn't end it. I worried the rest of the day. I kept going over the incident in my mind, feeling terribly embarrassed at having raised the possibility that the clerk had committed an error. The tension was so great, I wasn't sure I'd be able to go to work in the afternoon. That sort of thing is painful to live with.

CASE B: PAUL

It happened without any warning, a sudden wave of terror. My heart was pounding like mad, I couldn't catch my breath, and the ground underfoot seemed unstable. I was sure it was a heart attack. It was the worst experience of my life.

CASE C: SHARON

I can't tell you why I'm afraid of rats. They fill me with terror. Even if I just see the word "rat," my heart starts pounding. I worry about rats in restaurants I go to, in my kitchen cupboard, and anywhere I hear a noise that sounds like a small animal scratching or running.

CASE D: MIKE

Before I come home from work I spend half my time wondering whether a burglar has broken into the

143

The problems described in these four cases are different, but they have one feature in common: the experience of strong anxiety, worry, tension, and discomfort. In Susan's case, which illustrates a **generalized anxiety disorder,** the anxiety is chronic and is felt in a variety of situations. Paul is suffering from a **panic disorder,** in which the anxiety is sudden and overwhelming. People who experience one or more panic attacks worry a great deal about whether and where another attack may take place. Sharon has a **phobic disorder,** in which anxiety is aroused by a specific type of situation, animal, or object. Mike's is an example of an **obsessive–compulsive disorder,** in which thinking certain thoughts and not doing certain things (like checking the lock on the front door) arouse intense anxiety and concern.

Everyone has worries and fears. Freud argued that anxiety can be adaptive if the discomfort that goes with it motivates people to learn new ways of approaching life's challenges. But whether it is adaptive or maladaptive, the discomfort can be intense. This chapter focuses on the serious maladaptive aspects of anxiety, but it is

apartment. As soon as I get home I check every room, under the bed, and in the closets. Before going to sleep I probably check the lock on the front door fifty times. I feel better after each check, but then my concern wells up and I have to go check again.

(a)

(b)

FIGURE 6–1

Anxiety can be experienced under many circumstances and at various levels of intensity. The person in *a* is generally anxious and feels tense and upset even while just watching television or reading a book. The person in *b* is often apprehensive about aspects of life that are not troubling for most people. She is tense about leaving her house to do some shopping. The person in *c* worries all the time about dirt. She cleans the house several times each day and yet feels upset whenever things are in a slight disarray.

(c)

useful to remember that anxiety has many causes and that all people experience it at some time in their lives. It is normal for people to experience anxiety when faced with stressful, threatening situations, but it is abnormal to feel strong, chronic anxiety in the absence of a visible cause.

Surveys of the general population have been conducted in an attempt to assess how widespread various aspects of anxiety are. These surveys suggest that as many as one-third of all adults suffer from nervous complaints, especially anxiety (Lader, 1975). The proportion is lower for males, the economically well off, and the young; it is higher for females, the poor, and the elderly. The clinical workers who probably see the greatest number of anxiety symptoms are physicians in general practice, who often prescribe tranquilizing drugs for anxious patients. One tranquilizer, Valium, has become the most frequently prescribed drug in the United States. The statistics for western Europe are similar (Kounjian, 1981).

The characteristics of anxiety include feelings of uncertainty, helplessness, and physiological arousal. A person who experiences anxiety complains of feeling nervous, tense, jumpy, and irritable (see Figure 6–1). Often he or she has difficulty falling asleep at night. An anxious person becomes fatigued easily and has "butterflies in the stomach," as well as headaches, muscle tension, and difficulty in concentrating. Table 6–1 lists common symptoms of anxiety and self-descriptions given by people with high levels of anxiety.

The experience of intense anxiety may occur after an event has taken place, in anticipation of a future event, or when a person decides to resist a preoccupying idea, change an undesirable aspect of behavior, or approach a fear-arousing stimulus. Although the behaviors observed in anxiety disorders vary widely, they have one thing in common: change and the possibility of change are involved in each of the precipitating situations.

In the previous chapter we discussed one kind of anxiety disorder, the posttraumatic stress disorder, which occurs after an intensely traumatic event such as a serious accident or natural disaster. In this chapter we discuss four types of disorders in which the causes of anxiety usually are not so clear. A generalized anxiety disorder is marked by chronic anxiety over a long period (at least several months). A panic disorder consists of recurrent, sudden anxiety attacks in which the individual experiences intense terror and dread. In phobic disorders, the anxiety has an identifiable cause—for example, being near dogs or having to speak to a group. When the stimulus is not present, the phobic person's tension level is relatively low. In obsessive compulsive disorder, anxiety results from efforts to prevent undesirable outcomes. The individual is plagued with a recurrent need to ward off disaster by thinking about certain ideas and/or performing certain acts.

Symptoms

1. nervousness, jitteriness
2. tension
3. feeling tired
4. dizziness
5. frequency of urination
6. heart palpitations
7. feeling faint
8. breathlessness
9. sweating
10. trembling
11. worry and apprehension
12. sleeplessness
13. difficulty in concentrating
14. vigilance

Self-Descriptions

1. I am often bothered by the thumping of my heart.
2. Little annoyances get on my nerves and irritate me.
3. I often suddenly become scared for no good reason.
4. I worry continuously and that gets me down.
5. I frequently get spells of complete exhaustion and fatigue.
6. It is always hard for me to make up my mind.
7. I always seem to be dreading something.
8. I feel nervous and high-strung all the time.
9. I often feel I can't overcome my difficulties.
10. I feel constantly under strain.

Many clinicians would describe people who are suffering from anxiety disorders as neurotic. In DSM-II, an early version of the classification system that was strongly influenced by the psychodynamic perspective, the word **neurosis** was used to describe disorders marked by anxiety, personal dissatisfaction, and inappropriate (but not psychotic) behavior. These were grouped together because it was thought that they all arose from somewhat similar unconscious mental processes and motivations. Though this view may some day be substantiated, that day has not yet arrived. Because DSM-III-R is designed to classify maladaptive behavior on the basis of observable characteristics rather than theories about its source, it uses the obvious presence of marked anxiety as the criterion for including disorders in this group. In DSM-III-R they are referred to as **anxiety disorders.** Some of the disorders from the former neurosis category in which anxiety is not so openly expressed, such as depressive neurosis and hysterical neurosis, have been placed in other categories. This chapter is restricted to a discussion of disorders in which the individual is abnormally anxious, either generally or under certain circumstances, but still has adequate contact with reality and is rarely incapacitated enough to require institutionalization. The role of anxiety in several other disorders is described in later chapters.

Generalized Anxiety Disorder

Anxiety is usually defined as a diffuse, vague, very unpleasant feeling of fear and apprehension. The anxious person worries a lot, particularly about unknown dangers. In addition, the anxious individual shows combinations of the following symptoms: rapid heart rate, shortness of breath, diarrhea, loss of appetite, fainting, dizziness, sweating, sleeplessness, frequent urination, and tremors. All of these physical symptoms accompany fear as well as anxiety. Frightened people, however, can easily state what they are afraid of. People who suffer from anxiety disorders, on the other hand, are not aware of the reasons for their fear. Thus, even though fear and anxiety involve similar reactions, the cause of worry is readily apparent in the former case but is not at all clear in the latter (see Figure 6–2).

In generalized anxiety disorder, anxiety persists for at least a month (usually much longer) and is not attributable to recent life experiences. The symptoms of generalized anxiety disorder are of four types: motor tension, hyperactivity of the autonomic nervous system, dread of the future and hypervigilance.

1. *Motor tension.* Individuals with this symptom are unable to relax, are keyed up, and are visibly shaky and tense. Strained facial expressions are common, as are furrowed brows and deep sighs. Such individuals are easily startled.

2. *Autonomic reactivity.* In individuals with this symptom, the sympathetic and parasympathetic nervous system seem to be working overtime. There is some combination of sweating, dizziness, pounding or racing heart, hot or cold spells, cold and clammy hands, upset stomach, lightheadedness, frequent urination or defecation, lump in the throat, and high pulse and respiration rates.

3. *Apprehensive feelings about the future.* People with generalized anxiety disorders worry about what the future holds for them, for people close to them, or for their valued possessions.

4. *Hypervigilance.* People who suffer from generalized anxiety adopt a sentry like stance in their approach to life. They constantly scan the environment for

dangers (not necessarily of a physical nature), although they often cannot specify what the dangers might be. This excessive vigilance is related to their hyperaroused state. Because they are always alert to potential threats, they are easily distracted from tasks on which they are working. Their hypervigilance also contributes to difficulty in falling asleep.

Generalized anxiety disorder might best be described as consisting of prolonged, vague, unexplained, but intense fears that do not seem to be attached to any particular object. They resemble normal fears, but there is no actual danger, and in most cases danger is not even imagined to be present. Although anxiety is a factor in many types of disorders, the term *generalized anxiety disorder* is reserved for cases that are not complicated by other problems such as poor contact with reality. While the cause of the anxiety is usually hard to identify, environmental events and recent experiences may play a role. One study found that in a large number of cases of generalized anxiety disorder, the sufferers had experienced important negative and unexpected events in the months before the anxiety reached clinical proportions (Blazer and others, 1987).

Panic Disorder

The indicators of panic disorder are similar to those of generalized anxiety disorder except that they are greatly magnified and usually have a sudden onset. People with panic disorder may not be anxious all the time. Instead, they have unanticipated anxiety attacks that recur after periods (perhaps several days) of normal functioning. Severe palpitations, extreme shortness of breath, chest pains or discomfort, trembling, sweating, dizziness, and a feeling of helplessness mark the panic attacks. The victims fear that they will die, go crazy, or do something uncontrolled, and they report a variety of unusual psychosensory symptoms (see Table 6–2).

TABLE 6–2

Frequently Reported Psychosensory Symptoms Experienced During Panic Attacks

Distortion of light intensity
Distortion of sound intensity
Strange feeling in stomach
Sensations of floating, turning, moving
Feelings of unreality and loss of self-identity

Based on Uhde and others, 1985.

Panic attacks range in length from a few seconds to many hours and even days. They also differ in severity and in the degree of incapacitation involved. In the following case, frequent panic attacks had a definitely incapacitating effect.

A 35-year-old mathematician gave a history of episodic palpitations and faintness over the previous 15 years. There had been periods of remission of up to five years, but in the past year the symptoms had increased and in the last few days the patient had stopped working because of his distress. His chief complaints were that at any time and without warning, he might suddenly feel he was about to faint and fall down, or tremble and experience palpitations, and if standing would cringe and clutch at the nearest wall or chair. If he was driving a car at the time he would pull up at the curbside and wait for the feelings to pass off before he resumed his journey. If it occurred during sexual intercourse with his wife he would immediately separate from her. If it happened while he was lecturing, his thoughts became distracted, he could not concentrate, and he found it difficult to continue. He was becoming afraid of walking alone in the street or of driving his car for fear that the episodes would be triggered by it, and was loath to travel by public transport. Although he felt safer when accompanied, this did not abolish his symptoms. Between attacks the patient did not feel completely well, and a slight tremulousness persisted.

(a)

(b)

FIGURE 6–2
Discomfort marks both fear and worry. In fear, the cause of the discomfort is readily apparent. In the case of anxiety, it is vague. In photograph a, worried family members are waiting for news about the condition of a loved one whose medical condition is critical. In photograph b, a person feels tense and frightened while "enjoying" a good movie.

The attacks could come on at any time of day or night.

The patient had had a happy childhood without nervous symptoms, led an active social life when in remission, and had a contented marriage and vigorous professional life.

—(Marks and Lader, 1973, p. 11)

The term **panic attack** denotes an abrupt surge of intense anxiety rising to a peak that is either cued by particular stimuli (or thinking about them) or occurs without obvious cues (spontaneous and unpredictable). In the former case (which is more common), persons experiencing panic often have persistent phobic fears and the stimuli evoke the fears. People who have panic attacks when evoking stimuli are not present typically do not have phobias as well.

Generalized anxiety and panic disorders run in families and occur twice as often among women as among men. There is no evidence that any specific type of childhood experience predisposes people to these states. Problems often arise in classifying these disorders, because many cases are complicated. Several types of maladaptive behavior may occur simultaneously. Obsessions, compulsions,and phobias might all be observed in a given individual. Severe panic states are sometimes followed by periods of psychotic disor-ganization in which there is a reduced capacity to test reality.

Box 6–1 presents a case of anxiety and panic and classifies it in terms of the DSM-III-R system. A person who has had a panic attack develops anticipatory anxiety: he or she becomes worried and tense, and is afraid that the panic will recur (see Figure 6–3). In some cases, this type of anticipatory anxiety seems to be quite realistic fear.

Drug research has provided an interesting finding that suggests that panic and anticipatory anxiety have different sources. Imipramine, a drug that is used in the treatment of depression, has been shown to prevent the recurrence of panic attacks (Marks, 1987). However, it seems to have no effect on the anticipatory anxiety that panic attacks almost always arouse.

Prior to DSM-III relatively few attempts had been made to identify and compare subgroups of anxiety disorders. Now that attention has been focused on the subgroups, these topics are being investigated more intensively. For example, one group of researchers has compared the patterns of symptoms, family characteristics, type of onset, and clinical course in generalized anxiety disorder and panic disorders (Anderson and others, 1984). Their findings support DSM-III-R's assumption that these conditions are distinct from one another. Table 6–3 compares these disorders with regard to several bodily symptoms. Subjects with generalized anxiety disorder have fewer bodily symptoms than those with panic disorders. Their histories also show an earlier, more gradual onset. A generalized anxiety disorder has a more chronic course and is more likely to have a favorable outcome. Members of families in which a person suffers from a panic disorder tend to have a relatively high percentage of panic episodes. The comparable percentage for family members of those with a generalized anxiety disorder is much lower.

FIGURE 6–3
This experienced professor was suddenly overcome in class with a panic attack—trembling, feeling faint, and having a rapid heart beat. Afterward, he described the experience in this way: "I was certain I was having a heart attack."

TABLE 6–3

Percentages of Patients with Panic Disorder and Generalized Anxiety Disorder Reporting Particular Symptoms

Symptom	Panic Disorder	Generalized Anxiety Disorder
Sweating, flushing	58.3	22.2
Heart palpitations	89.5	61.1
Chest pain	68.8	11.1
Faintness, lightheadedness	52.1	11.1
Blurred vision	31.2	0
Feeling of muscular weakness	47.9	11.1

Based on Anderson and others, 1984.

BOX 6-1
An Anxious, Precise, Demanding Man Seeks Help

Mr. E., 40 years old and recently married, sought clinical help because he was nervous and worried about his health. These lifelong concerns became worse during his courtship and honeymoon.

Mr. E. has trouble falling asleep if the room is too dark or too light, if he has eaten too much or too little, if the sheets are cold or wrinkled, if he forgets his nose spray, or if there is any noise. He fears nightmares, nocturnal asthma attacks, or dying in his sleep. He often awakes in a panicky sweat with nightmares, typically of being chased or suffocated. He worries that his lost sleep is shortening his life and ruining his work efficiency.

Mr. E. had always been anxious and worried. He expects the worst, dreads each time the phone rings lest it be bad news, and suspects that he has a serious illness. He experiences frequent palpitations, shortness of breath, dizziness, and numb fingers and has had numerous physical exams and electrocardiograms. The negative findings do not reassure him as Mr. E. is convinced that his doctors are withholding information, and he is determined to have additional checkups until his condition is diagnosed. He also has gastrointestinal flutters, frequent diarrhea or constipation, and occasional nausea and vomiting. His father died of heart disease and his mother of cancer, and he feels confident that he already has, or soon will have, one or both conditions.

Mr. E. is also extremely anxious about his work. He is a stockbroker responsible for large financial transactions and cannot ever relax his concentration, even on vacations. He has also felt considerable performance anxiety about his recently more active sex life and has suffered from consistent premature ejaculation. There are many specific situations that make him intolerably nervous—waiting in line, sitting in the middle of a row at a movie, riding public transportation, wearing a pair of pants a second time without having them cleaned, having dirty dollar bills, and so forth—but he is able to avoid most of them without great inconvenience. Mr. E. has panic attacks at least every few weeks. They tend to occur whenever something new is expected of him, when he is forced to do one of the things he fears, when he must give a talk, and, at times, for no apparent reason.

Mr. E. is a very precise and demanding man who is difficult to live or work with (or to treat). He is

controlling, self-absorbed, maddeningly fastidious, and meticulous. He did not marry previously because he had very demanding expectations of a woman, and his worries and habits are intolerable to many women. His wife has begun to complain to him, and he is afraid she may leave unless he is able to change quickly. (Frances and Klein, 1982, p. 89)

HOW WOULD DSM-III-R CHARACTERIZE MR. E.?

Because this is a real-life case, it is more complicated than a textbook outline of a disorder. On DSM-III-R's Axis I, Mr. E. might be described in terms of either generalized anxiety disorder or panic disorder. However, because of the definite recurring panic attacks, panic disorder seems the more likely primary diagnosis. Mr. E.'s concerns about being precise and meticulous make obsessive–compulsive personality disorder a reasonable Axis II categorization. Despite Mr. E.'s protestations to the contrary, Axis III would note that he suffers from no apparent physical disorder. The Axis IV rating of psychosocial stress (his recent marriage) would seem to be moderately severe, suggesting a rating of 4. On Axis V, Mr. E. might be described as having a fair level of adaptive functioning in the past year (a rating of 60). Despite his superior work performance, his social and leisure-time difficulties now suggest a decreased level of functioning (50).

Thus, Mr. E. might be classified in this way:

- Axis I: Panic disorder with limited phobic avoidance
- Axis II: Obsessive–compulsive personality disorder
- Axis III: No apparent physical disorders
- Axis IV: Moderate severity of stress (4)
- Axis V: Moderate difficulty in prior functioning (60). Increased difficulty in present functioning (50).

It is important to remember that experienced clinicians might disagree about this classification either because of gaps in what is known about Mr. E. or because of emphasis on different known facts. With additional information, the classification might change. A clinician treating Mr. E. would want to better understand his sexual problems, his conviction that he has cancer or heart disease, and his somatic complaints, for which no bodily cause has been found.

TABLE 6–4

Characteristics of Panic Disorder in Comparison with Generalized Anxiety Disorder

1. Clinical onset is later.
2. The role of heredity seems to be greater.
3. The ratio of women to men is greater.
4. Alcoholism is more common.
5. While depression is common in both, it is unusually more so in panic disorder.

Panic and generalized anxiety disorders differ most clearly in the diffuseness of the anxiety seen in the latter and its focused intensity in the former. But research has shown that they differ in a number of other ways as well. Table 6–4 lists some of them. In addition to investigating the characteristics of panic disorders, researchers are also conducting experiments designed to better understand how the attacks come about. It has been discovered that sodium lactate when administered intravenously to patients with panic disorder will often provoke a panic attack, while this does not happen in normals. There is an active effort in a number of laboratories at the present time to identify the mechanisms by which sodium lactate causes panic attacks (see Figure 6–4).

Phobias

Phobos was the Greek god of fear. His likeness was painted on masks and shields to frighten enemies in battle. The word *phobia*, derived from his name, came to mean fear, panic, dread, or fright. Unlike people who have generalized anxiety disorders, people who have phobias know exactly what they are afraid of. Except for their fears of specific objects, people, and situations, phobic individuals usually do not engage in gross distortions of reality. Nothing physical seems to be wrong with them. However, their fears are out of proportion with reality, seem inexplicable, and are beyond their voluntary control (see Figure 6–5).

One question that inevitably arises in discussions of anxiety is why people spend so much time brooding about vague menaces when there are so many real dangers to worry about. Perhaps the degree of fear we feel about a potentially harmful event is linked not primarily to the degree of threat (in terms of the probability that it will actually happen to us) or even to the amount of injury that we imagine we might sustain if the worst did happen, but to the disturbing quality of the event or situation itself. For example, even though there are three times as many traffic fatalities as there are murders,

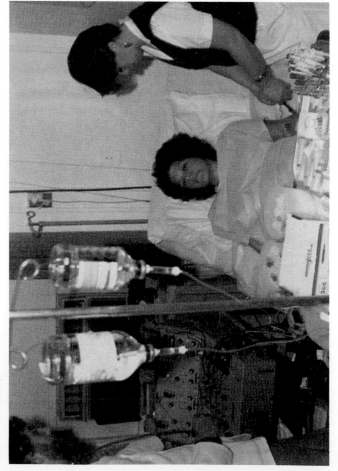

FIGURE 6–4
The calm before the storm. A patient prepares for a sodium lactate infusion as part of a research study. Researchers are trying to determine why an infusion (constant flow) of sodium lactate often results in a panic attack for people prone to panic disorder but does not have this result in normal individuals.

(a)

(b)

FIGURE 6–5

Phobias can cause people to lead restricted lives. Some fears, while strong, do not reach phobic proportions. For instance in photo a, although this man is afraid of heights, he endures the discomfort because he cannot afford to have someone fix a clogged gutter, and to ask his wife to climb the ladder would be humiliating. If he had a true phobia of heights, he would not climb the ladder no matter how costly or humiliating his refusal to do so would be. An effective therapy for conquering phobic fears is shown in photo b. The patient, who has an intense fear of heights, is helped to climb the stairs in the presence of her trusted therapist. For many phobic individuals this type of exposure to a feared situation eventually results in extinction of the irrational fears and the ability to cope with formerly frightening situations.

our thoughts are rarely preoccupied by the danger of an automobile accident. Fear of violent crime, on the other hand, touches many of us. Crucial to the experience of fear is whether people feel that they will be able to respond meaningfully to a situation—that is, whether they will be able to cope.

Phobics do not need the actual presence of the feared object or situation to experience intense tension and discomfort. The following account by a psychiatrist with an airplane phobia shows that simply imagining a phobia-related event can elicit strong psychological and bodily reactions.

I was pampering my neurosis by taking the train to a meeting in Philadelphia. It was a nasty day out, the fog so thick you could see only a few feet ahead of your face, and the train, which had been late in leaving New York, was making up time by hurtling at a great rate across the flat land of New Jersey. As I sat

there comfortably enjoying the ride, I happened to glance at the headlines of a late edition, which one of the passengers who had boarded in New York was reading. "TRAINS CRASH IN FOG," ran the banner headlines, "10 DEAD, MANY INJURED." I reflected on our speed, the dense fog outside, and had a mild, transitory moment of concern that the fog might claim us as victim, too, and then relaxed as I picked up the novel I had been reading. Some minutes later the thought suddenly entered my mind that had I not "chickened out" about flying, I might at that moment be overhead in a plane. At the mere image of sitting up there strapped in by a seat belt, my hands began to sweat, and I felt a kind of nervous uneasiness in my gut. The sensation lasted until I forced myself back to my book and forgot about the imagery.

I must say I found this experience a vivid lesson in the nature of phobias. Here I had reacted with *hardly a flicker of concern to an admittedly small, but real danger of accident, as evidenced by the fog-caused train crash an hour or two earlier; at the same time I had responded to a purely imaginary situation with an unpleasant start of nervousness, experienced both as somatic symptoms and as an inner sense of indescribable dread so characteristic of anxiety. The unreasonableness of the latter was highlighted for me by its contrast with the absence of concern about the speeding train, which if I had worried about it, would have been an apprehension founded on real, external circumstances.*

—(Nemiah, 1985a, p. 895)

The onset of many phobias is so gradual that it is difficult to tell whether there were any specific precipitating factors. In other cases, the apparent time of onset, although not necessarily the cause, can be pinpointed (see Figure 6–6).

I was riding in my husband's car and I suddenly became terrified. I felt as if I would die. I made him turn around and take me home. I ran into the house and suddenly felt safe. I could not understand what had happened. I had never been afraid of cars. The next day it happened again, and it kept getting worse. Finally, just being on the street and seeing a car would bring on a terrible feeling. Now I just stay at home.

—(De Nike and Tiber, 1968, p. 346)

Phobias may begin with a generalized anxiety attack, but the anxiety then becomes crystallized around a particular object or situation (for example, elevators, snakes, or darkness). As long as the feared object or situation can be avoided, the anxiety does not reach disturbing proportions. Some objects of phobias—such as cats, cars, and stairs—are considered aspects of everyday life by most of us. Other objects and situations—snakes, death, and heights are disliked to some extent by most people. However, phobias involve levels of fear that, in addition to being overly intense, interfere with normal living patterns. One study of phobic patients showed that their fears fell into five categories related to (1) separations, (2) animals, (3) bodily mutilation, (4) social situations, and (5) nature (Torgensen, 1979). Table 6–5 gives examples of phobic content that falls into these categories.

Phobias tend to grow progressively broader. For example, one woman had a subway phobia that began with an inability to ride an express train between two fairly distant locations. Gradually the phobia developed

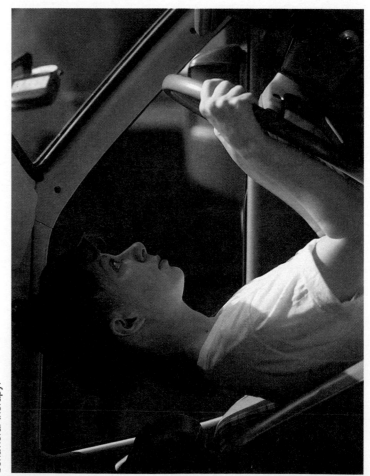

FIGURE 6–6
Phobias are a special maladaptive form of fear that is out of proportion to situational demands, cannot be explained or reasoned away, is beyond voluntary control, and leads to avoidance of the feared situation. One day this woman was suddenly overcome with terror while driving an automobile. Similar experiences in the following weeks contributed to a phobia that required behavioral therapy.

TABLE 6–5

Examples of Five Categories of Phobias

Separation fears
  crowds
  traveling alone
  being alone at home
Animal fears
  mice
  rats
  insects
Mutilation fears
  open wounds
  surgical operations
  blood
Social fears
  eating with strangers
  being watched writing
  being watched working
Nature fears
  mountains
  the ocean
  cliffs, heights

Torgerson, 1979.

until she would have to get off the train at each local stop, wait until her anxiety diminished, get on the next train, get off again at the next stop, and so on, until her destination was reached.

Phobic individuals usually develop ways of reducing their fears. The professor managed to live with his phobia, and the subway rider mentioned earlier was able to get from one place to another. However, the often cumbersome procedures that phobics devise do not eliminate their fear; indeed, the fear seems always to be one step ahead of them. In one sense, phobic individuals who cannot cross the thresholds of certain rooms or cannot work may be as incapacitated as people with severe psychotic symptoms. In another sense, they are more fortunate than people who exhibit free-floating anxiety, since at least their fears are directed toward a specific object, and they can reduce their anxiety by simply avoiding that object.

Phobias, like other forms of maladaptive behavior, do not occur in isolation. They are usually intertwined with a host of other problems. In consequence, it is difficult to estimate their frequency accurately. While mild phobias are common, phobias that are serious enough to be clinically diagnosed occur relatively infrequently. They are the main complaint in perhaps 2 to 3 percent of all clinical cases (Kolb and Brodie, 1982). Phobias do not require hospitalization. Professional treatment, when it is given, is usually carried out on an outpatient basis.

One of the most interesting aspects of phobias is that the stimuli that evoke them are not picked at random. The most common fear-arousing stimuli tend to be animals, objects, or events that presented real dangers in earlier stages of human evolution (McNally, 1987). Although extreme fear of dogs, snakes, and spiders seems maladaptive today, such fear may have been highly adaptive in earlier times. More "modern" phobias are rare. For example, pajama and electric-outlet phobias occur infrequently, even though these objects are often associated with trauma.

Traditionally, phobias have been named by means of Greek prefixes that stand for the object of the fear, as shown in the following examples:

- acrophobia: fear of heights
- agoraphobia: fear of open places and unfamiliar settings
- aquaphobia: fear of water
- claustrophobia: fear of closed places
- xenophobia: fear of strangers

Recently, however, such names have been avoided. People's knowledge of Greek is not what it once was, and in any case, a staggering number of labels would be needed to take account of the great variety of phobias that have been observed. Today, therefore, phobias are grouped into three general categories: simple phobias, social phobias, and agoraphobia.

Simple Phobias

Simple phobias, which are relatively rare, are a miscellaneous category comprising irrational fears that do not fall within the other two categories. Examples of simple phobias are intense fear of particular types of animals (for example, snakes, dogs, or rats) and claustrophobia. Although it is not unusual for people with simple phobias to overcome their fear as a result of a positive experience involving contact with the fear-arousing stimulus, simple phobias tend to be chronic. A variety of therapeutic approaches have been used in treating simple phobias. Procedures that promote association between the fear-arousing stimulus and nonanxiety responses, and at the same time provide information that disconfirms mistaken beliefs about the stimulus (for example, that all dogs are ferocious), often have positive effects.

Social Phobias

Social phobias are characterized by fear and embarrassment in dealings with others. Often the individual's greatest fear is that signs of anxiety such as intense

FIGURE 6-7
People who suffer from social phobias are preoccupied with fears of social scrutiny, criticism, and rejection. They overestimate the likelihood that others will respond to them in these ways. This man is worried about how the people at this party will respond to him. He does not yet have a full-blown social phobia. If he did, he probably would be unable to attend the social gathering.

blushing, tremors of the hand, and a quavering voice will be detected by people with whom he or she comes into contact (see Figure 6-7). Fear of public speaking and of eating in public are frequent complaints of socially phobic individuals. These problems often begin in late childhood or early adolescence.

I sometimes don't get to class because I think the professor might call on me. My fear doesn't have anything to do with being unprepared if he asks me a question, because I'm almost always well prepared. My grades on exams are always near the top of the class. What I keep thinking about is that the professor and all the students will see how red my face gets whenever I have to say something in a group.

Most phobias about interpersonal relationships involve one or more of the following fears: fear of asserting oneself, fear of criticism, fear of making a mistake, and fear of public speaking. People who are afflicted in these ways have much in common. They go through life feeling generally inadequate and have many social and interpersonal difficulties. They attempt to compensate by immersing themselves in school and then in their work, never being really sure of their skills and talents. They dismiss their successes, if any, by saying, "My work isn't really good enough" or "I was just lucky—being in the right place at the right time." They may feel like impostors, fearing that they will be discovered and that the rug will be pulled out from under them.

The incidence of social phobias in two urban populations over a 6-month period ranged from 0.9 to 1.7 percent for men and 1.5 to 2.6 percent for women. These figures are derived from self-reports and screening questionnaires in community surveys. The figures for

TABLE 6-6

Interpersonal Self-Help Techniques for the Social-Phobic Person

1. Respond to anxiety symptoms by approach rather than withdrawal.
2. Greet people properly with eye contact.
3. Listen carefully to people and make a mental list of possible topics of conversation.
4. Show that you want to speak; initiate conversation (asking questions is easier, as it switches attention to the person expected to reply).
5. Speak up without mumbling.
6. Tolerate some silences.
7. Wait for cues from others in deciding where to sit, when to pick up a drink, and what to talk about.
8. Learn to tolerate criticism by introducing controversy deliberately at an appropriate point.

socially phobic people who actually seek clinical help would be lower. Significant depressive symptoms are common in clinical cases of social phobia (Aimes and others, 1983). Table 6-6 lists some hints concerning behavior in interpersonal situations that have been found to be helpful to social phobics (Marks, 1987).

Agoraphobia

The most common phobia is **agoraphobia,** or fear of entering unfamiliar situations. It accounts for 50 to 80 percent of the phobic psychiatric population (Foa and others, 1984). Agoraphobics avoid going into open spaces, traveling, and being in crowds. In severe cases,

BOX 6-2
The Agoraphobic Experience

An agoraphobic person is afraid of being in places or situations from which escape might be difficult or in which help might not be available if incapacitating or embarrassing symptoms developed.

This incident illustrates some of these aspects of agoraphobia.

The woman who lives next door is a very nice person and I like her. One day she asked me if I would like to drive over to a big shopping center that had recently opened about 5 miles from where we live. I didn't know how to tell her that there isn't a chance in the world that I'd go to that shopping center or any other place outside our neighborhood. She must have seen how upset I got, but I was shaking like a leaf even more inside. I imagined myself in the crowd, getting lost, or passing out. I was terrified by the openness of the shopping center and the crowds. I made an excuse this time, but I don't know what I'll say next time. Maybe I'll just have to let her in on my little bit of craziness.

Certain types of thoughts and bodily reactions that are typical of agoraphobia are listed below.

Thoughts
- I am going to choke to death.
- I will hurt someone.
- I am going to act foolish.
- I am going to scream.
- I may loose bowel or bladder control.
- I may vomit.

Bodily Reactions
- heart palpitations
- pressure in chest
- numbness in arms or legs
- nausea
- feeling disoriented or confused
- wobbly or rubber legs
- dizzyness

FIGURE 6–8
Another woman who was also afraid to visit a shopping center near her home sought the help of a clinical psychologist. As part of the therapy, he took her there on a series of trips. She became able to visit a supermarket in the center while the therapist went to another store, and eventually she was able to visit the shopping center on her own.

---

the individual may have an irrational fear of leaving the familiar setting of the home; in the most extreme cases, the victim is unable even to walk down the street (see Box 6–2). Like most other phobias, agoraphobia is more common among women than among men. It often begins in the late teens, although it is also observed in older people. Like other phobias, it waxes and wanes, and it is not uncommon for the object of the fear to

change. Some cases of agoraphobia are preceded by panic attacks marked by intense anxiety. In many cases of agoraphobia seen by clinicians the phobic symptoms are a complication of panic disorder.

People who experience the intense fears that are characteristic of agoraphobia strive to organize their lives in such a way as to minimize exposure to the fear-arousing stimuli. The following account by a professor described a phobia that almost completely confined him to the campus where he taught. The account was published 48 years after his agoraphobia had begun. Only his closest relatives and friends knew of his problem, and he continued as a professor of English at the University of Wisconsin during this time.

Let me assume that I am walking down University Drive by the lake. I am a normal man for the first quarter of a mile; for the next hundred yards I am in a mild state of dread, controllable and controlled; for the next twenty yards in an acute state of dread, yet controlled; for the next ten, in an anguish of terror that hasn't reached the crisis of explosion; and in a half-dozen steps more I am in as fierce a panic of isolation from help and home and of immediate death as a man overboard in mid-Atlantic or on a window-ledge far up in a skyscraper with flames lapping his shoulders. The reader who can't understand why I have not merely whistled or laughed or ordered the phobias off my psychic premises, or who thinks that I must be grossly exaggerating a mere normal discomfort, like the initial dread in the dentist's chair, is not the reader for whom I am writing one line of this book. He belongs among the fools, of whom in my phobic career I have met a goodly number already. I would leave him alone. Let him leave me alone. . . . It is as scientific a fact as any I know that my phobic seizures at their worst approach any limits of terror that the human mind is capable of in the actual presence of death in its most horrible forms. That I have never fainted away or died under them is due to two factors: first, my physical vitality, and second, my skill in devising escapes—psychic surrogates, deflections of attention, or actual retreat to safety—before the exhausting surge has torn me to pieces. But more than once the escape has been at all but the last moment. The fools say nothing ever happened from one of these seizures—so why worry. Nothing ever happened? Well, here is what happens always. First, the seizure happens—as well say nothing happens if a red-hot iron is run down the throat, even though it should miraculously leave no aftereffects. The seizure happens; the acutest agony of the conscious brain happens. Second, the seizure leaves me always far more exposed to phobic seizures for weeks or months; increases my fear of the Fear; and robs me of a goodly part of what little freedom of movement on street and hillside I have. "Nothing ever happened." This means simply that to date I've lived through seizures and continued for fifteen years to teach school, write books, and make jokes at the University Club across the street.

—(Leonard, 1927, pp. 321–323)

Recent research suggests that agoraphobics can be divided into two groups, those with and those without panic attacks. A high percentage of people who experience panic attacks go on to develop agoraphobia unless they are treated early with certain drugs. One theory regarding the panic attack–agoraphobia linkage is that an individual is born with a biological vulnerability to panic attacks. Psychosocial factors, such as a pile-up of stressful life events and upsetting situations, can trigger a panic attack in a vulnerable individual. According to this theory, many patients, unaware of the biological roots of panic attacks, conclude that the situations in which the attacks take place must be the culprit. They become increasingly preoccupied with avoiding such situations and constrict their life styles—often at considerable economic and social expense—in the hope of eluding the attack. One patient confided that she had accumulated hundreds of dollars in fines by parking her car illegally in front of her office rather than face the anxiety associated with walking across the parking lot.

Spontaneous panic attacks, unlike phobia anxiety, can be treated with certain drugs that are effective in treating depression (for example, the tricyclic antidepressants and monoamine oxidase inhibitors). To a significant extent, agoraphobia is a complication of panic attacks that are untreated and therefore are allowed to recur. Antidepressants are effective in suppressing panic but not in reducing anticipatory anxiety and agoraphobia. Behavioral techniques, including graduated exposure to the situation the individual is afraid of, are effective in treating agoraphobia. Some highly motivated agoraphobics are able to carry out this exposure themselves, without the frequent aid of a therapist. The following case illustrates the successful use of this approach.

Ms. A., a 40-year-old woman, had been virtually housebound for 5 years because of classic agoraphobia. In a 1½-hour session, she, her husband, and I delineated her avoidance profile (those places she avoided regularly because they evoked panic) and worked out an exposure-homework program in which she would slowly habituate to one situation after another. I explained how she should keep a diary of her exposure-homework exercises and asked her to mail them to me. This she did regularly. She diligently carried out her exposure program and within weeks was mobile for the first time in years. She kept up her progress for 4 years without seeing me again, but then she had some family difficulties, which depressed her, and quickly relapsed. She saw me once more for an hour and was encouraged to revive her original exposure-homework program. On doing this she recovered her gains, which continued through follow-up for 9 years, when I last heard from her—a gratifying result for 2½ hours of time from a clinician.

—(Marks, 1987, pp. 1163–1164)

Agoraphobics are often clinging and dependent. Studies of the histories of severely impaired agoraphobics have shown that 50 percent of the patients exhibited separation anxiety in childhood, well before the onset of the agoraphobia (Gittelman and Klein, 1984). The association between childhood separation anxiety and agoraphobia is much stronger in women than in men. Because separation anxiety is almost always measured by means of retrospective self-reports, there is a need for longitudinal studies that allow for the observation of subject's behavior in addition to self-reports. Perhaps, in some sense, agoraphobia is a delayed outbreak of childhood separation anxiety.

Obsessive–Compulsive Disorder

A man spends three hours in the bathroom every day, repeatedly washing himself, pursued by the thought that he might pass on a deadly disease to anyone he touches. Another man cannot prevent himself from driving back to reexamine every place on the road where he has hit a bump, because the thought that he has run someone over keeps forcing itself on him. A third man has stopped cooking for fear that he will poison his wife, and has stopped using electrical appliances for fear of causing a fire. A woman feels a recurrent urge to kill her children. Every time a teenage girl is kissed, for several days afterward she is unable to dismiss the thought that she has become pregnant.

All of these people have symptoms of an obsessive–compulsive disorder, they are tyrannized by repetitive acts or thoughts. **Obsessive** people are unable to get an idea out of their minds (for example, they are preoccupied by sexual, aggressive, or religious thoughts); **compulsive** people feel compelled to perform a particular act or series of acts over and over again (for example, repetitive hand washing or stepping on cracks in the sidewalk). History and literature abound with characters who have suffered from obsessions and compulsions (see Figure 6–9).

Obsessions usually involve doubt, hesitation, fear of contamination, or fear of one's own aggression. The most common forms of compulsive behavior are counting, ordering, checking, touching, and washing. A few victims of obsessive–compulsive disorder have purely mental rituals; for example, to ward off the obsessional thought or impulse they might recite a series of magic

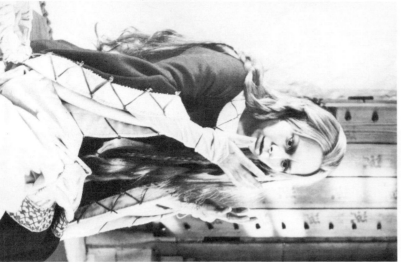

FIGURE 6–9

Shakespeare's Lady Macbeth was haunted by a constant impulse to wash her hands. Eccentric billionaire Howard Hughes, later to become incapacitated by his obsessional symptoms, is shown here during an earlier period when his success was at a peak. This photo was snapped just after Hughes had shattered his own speed record for a flight from Los Angeles to the east coast.

TABLE 6–7

Similarities and Differences between Obsessive–Compulsive Disorders and Phobias

Similarities

1. An identifiable evoking stimulus results in increased anxiety.

2. Efforts are made to avoid or escape from the evoking stimulus.

3. Both disorders respond well to exposure therapy whose basic element is actual or imagined contact with the feared stimulus.

Differences

1. Phobics have persistent worries concerning a central theme, while obsessive–compulsives have more stereotyped repetitive thoughts and actions.

2. The two disorders have different evoking stimuli. Dirt, contagion, or harm to others are common obsessive–compulsive preoccupations, but cause few phobics much difficulty. Rituals are common in obsessive–compulsive disorders, but not in phobias.

3. Obsessive–compulsives usually look less tense and panic stricken when in contact with their evoking stimulus than are phobics.

4. Obsessive–compulsives take longer to feel better after they avoid or escape from their evoking stimulus (e.g., dirt) than is the case for phobics and their evoking stimuli (e.g., spiders).

5. Obsessive–compulsives spend more time thinking about improbable future contacts with the evoking stimulus than do phobics.

Adapted from Marks, 1987.

---

bias fear what might happen to them, whereas victims of obsessive–compulsive disorders fear what they might do. There are mixed cases, however; for example fear of knives might be associated with the obsessional thought that one will hurt someone if one picks up a knife, and fear of elevators might be brought on by a recurrent impulse to push someone down the shaft. An obsessional thought about shouting obscenities during a sermon might lead the victim to avoid attending church, just as a phobia about the sound of church bells would. Normally, the object of a phobia can be avoided while an obsession cannot be, but again there are mixed cases; a dirt phobia may be as intrusive as an obsession, because dirt is everywhere. (See Table 6–7.)

Because of their seemingly senseless character, obsessive–compulsive reactions, like phobias, are extremely intriguing and challenging to clinical workers, researchers, and lay observers. As Figure 6–10 shows, they have also intrigued cartoonists.

The exact incidence of obsessive–compulsive disorder is hard to determine. The victims tend to be secretive about their preoccupations and frequently are able to work effectively in spite of them; consequently, their "problems" are probably underestimated. Obsessive–compulsive disorder is more common among upper-income, somewhat more intelligent individuals. It tends to begin in late adolescence and early adulthood, and males and females are equally likely to suffer from it. A relatively high proportion of obsessive–compulsives—some surveys report up to 50 percent—remain unmarried.

---

words or numbers. About 25 percent of people with an obsessive–compulsive disorder have intrusive thoughts but do not act on them. The rest are both obsessive and compulsive; compulsive behavior without obsessional thoughts is rare.

Compulsive rituals may become elaborate patterns of behavior that include many activities. For example, a man requires that his furniture never be left an inch out of place, and feels a need to dress and undress, brush his teeth, and use the toilet in a precise, unvarying order, all the time doubting whether he has performed this sequence of actions correctly, and often repeating it to make sure. Some theorists believe that compulsive behavior serves to divert attention from obsessive thoughts. In any case, compulsive rituals become a protection against anxiety, and so long as they are practiced correctly, the individual feels safe.

People who suffer from obsessive–compulsive disorder are very cautious. Like victims of phobias and other anxiety disorders, they unreasonably anticipate catastrophe and loss of control. In general, victims of pho-

---

FIGURE 6–10

Ralph seems to have a problem with at least one obsessional thought. (Copyright 1969. Reprinted by permission of *Saturday Review World-Censoni.*)

"AFTER 10 YEARS, RALPH, I SHOULD THINK YOU'D GIVE UP TRYING TO RHYME 'ORANGE!'"

The most common features of obsessive–compulsive disorder are the following:

1. The obsession or compulsion intrudes insistently and persistently into the individual's awareness.
2. A feeling of anxious dread occurs if the thought or act is prevented for some reason.
3. The obsession or compulsion is experienced as foreign to oneself as a psychological being; it is unacceptable and uncontrollable.
4. The individual recognizes the absurdity and irrationality of the obsession or compulsion.
5. The individual feels a need to resist it.

The language used by obsessive–compulsives conveys their exaggerated attention to details, their air of detachment, and the difficulty they have in making a decision:

I seem to be stuck with them—the thoughts, I mean. They seem so unimportant and silly. Why can't I think about things I really want to think about? But I can't stop thinking about trivia like did I lock the garage door when I went to work this morning. I've never not locked it and my wife's home anyway. I get depressed when I realize how much time I waste on nothing.

I feel under such pressure, but I can't make a decision. I write out on 3-by-5 cards all the pros and cons, then I study them, consider all the complications that perhaps might bear on the decision, and then I do it again—but I never seem to be able to make up my mind.

Obsessional thoughts often seem distasteful and shameful. Their content generally involves harming others, causing accidents to occur, swearing, or having abhorrent sexual or religious ideas.

Susan, a quiet 30-year-old college graduate who has held the same responsible job for 8 years, worries that she might put razor blades in other people's food. She refuses to drive a car because she fears she would deliberately smash it into another vehicle. She checks and rechecks the stove. "Off, off, off," she says to herself as she reads the burner switches. But it isn't good enough. She returns again and again, seven or eight times, before she can leave the house.

When she makes coffee at work, she worries that she might have slipped poison into it. She checks her clothing when she leaves work to make sure she hasn't tucked a razor blade into a pocket. She is afraid to hold babies or be around small children. She worries that she might suddenly commit some violent act, such as hurling them to the floor.

She won't shop by herself, afraid that she might slip something into the products on the store shelves. Even when accompanied by her boyfriend, she finds herself needing reassurance. "I was OK, wasn't I?" she asks.

Susan has never put sharp objects in food, hurt a baby, or poisoned coffee.

"All the time I'm doing the checking, part of my mind knows this is ridiculous," says Susan. "But I'm afraid that if I stopped doing the checking, and something really bad happened, I'd feel so guilty that I hadn't checked."

The variety of obsessive–compulsive rituals and thoughts is practically unlimited, but investigators have identified four broad types of preoccupations: (1) checking, (2) cleaning, (3) slowness, and (4) doubting and conscientiousness. The following statements illustrate each type.

CHECKING
• I frequently have to check things (gas or water taps, doors) several times.

CLEANING
• I avoid using public telephones because of possible contamination.

Depending on the situation and the nature of the obsession, the obsessive may feel some pride in his or her unwillingness to make a premature decision, or may feel self-contempt when indecisiveness prevents action and allows others to win acclaim. Only when Charles Darwin faced the possibility of prior publication by a colleague was he able to overcome his obsessive indecisiveness and put *On the Origin of Species* into the hands of a publisher.

Compared with repetitive upsetting ideas, repetitive images are much less common among obsessives. A typical case is the following:

One of the patient's most distressing images consisted of four people lying dead in open coffins in an open grave. Once this image intruded she was unable to continue with her normal activities unless and until she put matters right by having one or more images in which she saw the same four people standing and walking about, seemingly healthy. Although the images appeared for the most part to be spontaneously (i.e., internally) generated, they could be provoked by exposure to violent or aggressive material of one sort or another—books or television programs. The images were extremely distressing and were capable of provoking her to tears in a matter of minutes.

—(Rachman and Hodgson, 1980, p. 257)

• I am often late because I can't seem to get through everything on time.

DOUBTING–CONSCIENTIOUSNESS

• Even when I do something very carefully, I often feel that it is not quite right.

Most of us have had similar feelings. One study compared the preoccupying thoughts of clinically diagnosed obsessives with those of normal individuals. Although the content of the two groups' thoughts showed many similarities, the clinical group's obsessions occurred more frequently, lasted longer, were more intense, and disrupted their lives more than those of the control group (Rachman and de Silva, 1978).

When the compulsive rituals or obsessive thoughts begin to interfere with important routines of daily life, they become significant problems that require professional attention. Their bases frequently are not well understood, but because all of us have had some persistent preoccupations with particular acts and thoughts, their interfering effects can easily be appreciated. Obsessive–compulsive preoccupations—checking details, keeping things clean, and being deliberate—often increase during periods of stress. They can have undesirable effects when speedy decisions or actions are required.

Attempts to find out what obsessive–compulsives are afraid of usually fail. Many clinicians believe that fear of loss of control and the need for structure are at the core of the obsessions and compulsions. Whether the disorder reflects the impact of environmental factors or heredity, its incidence is greater among members of some families than among the general population.

A common feature of psychotic behavior is irrational thought, but an obsessive–compulsive person is not considered to be psychotic since he or she is usually aware of the irrationality. In some cases, however, the border between obsessive–compulsive disorder and true psychosis is imprecise.

Obsessive thoughts and compulsive rituals shade into phobias to the extent that anxiety accompanies the thoughts or rituals and there is avoidance of situations that evoke them. For example, someone who has a washing ritual will try to avoid dirt, much as a person with a dog phobia avoids dogs. Clinical workers often observe that both obsessive–compulsives and phobics have an unusually high incidence of interpersonal problems. The two disorders differ in that the obsessive–compulsive's fear is directed not at the situation itself but, rather, at the consequences of becoming involved with it—for example, having to wash afterwards. Another difference is that obsessive–compulsives develop a more elaborate set of beliefs concerning their preoccupying thoughts and rituals than phobics do about their fears. Cognitions seem to play a larger role in obsession–compulsion than in phobia. This point is illustrated by the case of a 40-year-old man with a checking compulsion.

The other night my wife and I went to the movies. It was torture even though the movie was great. For about an hour before going I couldn't stop thinking about this need I have to check the doorknob in order to make sure it's locked. I had to get out of the car four times to check the doorknob. When I do that sort of thing, my wife tries to be understanding, but I know she is thinking, "How come once isn't enough?" On the way to the theater I kept worrying about whether the door was locked. I would bet I had similar thoughts a hundred times while at the theater. You can't enjoy yourself under those circumstances, can you?

Interpreting and Treating Anxiety Disorders

Whether it is general or specific to certain situations, anxiety is a major component of the disorders dealt with in this chapter. Anxiety and the things that people do to keep it at manageable levels have been looked at from several theoretical perspectives.

The Psychodynamic Perspective

Psychodynamic theorists and many other clinicians believe that the major determinants of anxiety disorders are intrapsychic events and unconscious motivations. They believe that anxiety is an alarm reaction that appears whenever the person is threatened. How an individual adapts to the anxiety alarm depends on its intensity, the cue that evokes it, and the person's characteristic response to alarms. It is normal to experience some overt anxiety; the amount of anxiety and the nature of the threat determine whether an instance of anxiety is normal or pathological.

A distinguishing characteristic of clinical anxiety is that an alarm is frequently sounded in the absence of a consciously recognized source of danger. A danger exists, but its basis is vague or totally hidden from view. A tourist may understandably experience overwhelming anxiety while walking through a jungle. However, some individuals experience the same kind of anxiety in their own living rooms, for no apparent reason. According to the psychodynamic view, their defenses are inadequate to control or contain their anxiety. Figure 6–11 indi-

FIGURE 6–11

From a psychodynamic standpoint, inconsistencies between Snoopy's overt and covert behaviors would be explained in terms of intrapsychic conflicts and attempts to resolve them. (Copyright © 1964 United Features Syndicate, Inc.)

cates that it is possible to develop a defensive posture that effectively masks inner turmoil.

Psychodynamic theorists frequently mention the following as causes of anxiety that reaches clinical proportions: perception of oneself as helpless in coping with environmental pressures, separation or anticipation of abandonment, privation and loss of emotional support as a result of sudden environmental changes, unacceptable or dangerous impulses that are close to breaking into consciousness, and threats or anticipation of disapproval and withdrawal of love.

The psychodynamic view of phobias stems from two fundamental concepts: (1) psychological conflict and (2) unconscious mental processes. From this standpoint the phobic situation or object has symbolic significance; it can be regarded as a stand-in for something else that one is frightened of, something that is completely beyond one's awareness. It represents an unresolved psychological conflict, a holdover from childhood. For example, a child who reaches school age at the same time that her brother is born might be very angry at her mother for sending her to school. She might feel that her mother is getting rid of her so that she can be alone with the new baby all day. On the way to school each day the little girl passes a house where a vicious German shepherd is chained up. The dog becomes associated with her fantasy about her mother's real reason for sending her to school. The girl manages to get through her childhood all right, but in her twenties she develops a phobia about dogs after her mother has expressed strong disapproval of her future husband.

Obsessive thoughts and compulsive rituals may direct attention away from significant, distressing, unconscious thoughts. Psychoanalysts believe that these thoughts often involve aggression and rage that may have first been aroused in the battle for autonomy between the growing child and the mother. When the mother is especially demanding and has unreasonably high expectations about when the child should meet certain developmental challenges (such as toilet training), the child may be forced to bottle up his or her anger. This unacceptable anger expresses itself deviously later in life.

Freud emphasized the roles of several defense mechanisms in the development of obsessive–compulsive disorders. These include isolation, undoing, and reaction formation. Through **isolation,** emotions are separated from a thought or act, which then becomes obsessive or compulsive. However, the emotion is not completely barred from consciousness and constantly threatens to break through the controls that have been imposed upon it. **Undoing** is illustrated by an individual who thinks obsessively, "My father will die" whenever he turns off a light. This thought compels him to turn around, touch the switch, and say, "I take back that thought." The compulsive act could be said to "undo" what he feared might result from the initial obsessive thought, which might be rooted in an underlying aggressive impulse toward the father. **Reaction formation** is illustrated by a mother who compulsively checks her children's rooms dozens of times while they are asleep; she is overly solicitous about her children because of her underlying resentment toward them.

Psychotherapy, the main clinical tool of the psychodynamically oriented clinician, is intended to help people expose and deal with the psychodynamic roots of their maladaptive behaviors. Most psychotherapists believe that such behaviors occur when a person becomes preoccupied with relieving or eliminating anxiety. They feel that by gaining insight into the unconscious roots of anxiety, the person can direct his or her activity toward altering or abandoning unwanted behavior. Chapter 17 reviews some of the major aspects of research on psychotherapy and other therapeutic approaches.

The Learning Perspective

Instead of speaking of symptoms caused by underlying events, learning psychologists speak of acquired responses and response tendencies. They believe that the general principles of learning can be applied to the understanding of all behavior, including anxiety disorders. According to learning theorists, anxiety that reaches clinical proportions is a learned or acquired response, a symptom that has been created by environmental conditions, often within the home.

B. F. Skinner, a leading behaviorist, objects to any references to mental events (thoughts or feelings) as explanations of behavior; he prefers to rely almost exclusively on observable stimulus and response (S and R) variables. Other theorists emphasize S and R variables but have gone one step beyond Skinner in dealing with internal events as well. Dollard and Miller (1950) were among the earliest theorists to broaden the psychology of learning to include mental events. They went so far as to agree with psychodynamic theorists that there is a history behind the development of neurotic behavior and that psychotherapy (the "talking therapy") is the optimum means of modifying it.

If neurotic behavior is learned, it should be unlearned by some combination of the same principles by which it was taught. We believe this to be the case. Psychotherapy establishes a set of conditions by which neurotic habits may be unlearned and nonneurotic habits learned. Therefore, we view the therapist as a kind of teacher and the patient as a learner. In the same way and by the same principles that bad tennis habits can be corrected by a good coach, so bad mental and emotional habits can be corrected by a psychotherapist. There is this difference, however. Whereas only a few people want to play tennis, all the world wants a clear, free, efficient mind.

—(Dollard and Miller, 1950, pp. 7–8)

Learning concepts such as conditioning, reinforcement, and extinction have increasingly been applied to the study of abnormal behavior. Several new, clinically useful techniques, collectively referred to as **behavior therapy** are the most valuable outcomes of these applications. Research using behavior therapy has been directed at discovering the variables that help defuse highly emotional responses.

Exposure Therapies

A common element in most behavior therapies is exposing the client to stimuli that evoke discomfort until he or she becomes used to them. Much research has been carried out in which clients are exposed to feared stimuli and are prevented from making an avoidance or escape response. The client is strongly urged to continue to attend to the anxiety-eliciting stimuli despite the stressful effects that usually accompany this effort.

Exposure therapy has been used in treating both phobic and obsessive–compulsive disorders. A critical element of the treatment is motivating the client to maintain contact with the actual noxious stimuli or with their imagined presence until he or she becomes used to them. This might mean, for example, exposing a compulsive hand washer to dirt until the hand washing no longer occurs, or encouraging such a person to think about dirt, perhaps imagined first as household dust and later as particularly noxious dirt such as vomit or feces. The therapist's task is to identify all components of the

stimulus that evoke an avoidance or escape response and to continue the exposure until the evoked response no longer occurs.

Three types of therapy based on the exposure principle are systematic desensitization, implosive therapy, and in vivo exposure. In **systematic desensitization** a series of fear-arousing stimuli, carefully graded from mild to strongly fearful, are used. Only when a client is comfortable with one level of fear-producing stimuli is the next, slightly stronger stimulus introduced. **Implosive therapy** refers to therapist-controlled exposure to the imaginal re-creation of a complex, high-intensity fear-arousing situation. **In vivo exposure** means that the individual experiences the actual feared situation rather than imagining it under the therapist's direction. In vivo exposure may be conducted gradually, beginning with low levels of stimulus intensity, or rapidly, by exposing the client immediately to high-intensity and prolonged stimulation. This rapid, intense exposure is called **flooding.**

Systematic desensitization, which is used primarily in the treatment of strong fears, is based on conditioning principles. The client is taught to relax and then is presented with a series of stimuli that are graded from low to high according to their capacity to evoke anxiety. The treatment of a death phobia illustrates how systematic desensitization is used. The patient's fears are arranged in a hierarchy, with the items in the hierarchy ranging, in descending order, from human corpses to funeral processions, black clothes, dead dogs, and floral wreaths. The therapy begins with items that are low in the hierarchy, such as seeing a wreath. The therapist tries to teach the client to remain relaxed while imagining or actually seeing a wreath. When the client can maintain a relaxed state consistently, the therapy proceeds with stimuli that are higher in the hierarchy.

A therapist does not try to produce cures overnight with conditioning procedures. Usually, the process of reducing the level of an emotional response to a stimulus that should be neutral is a gradual one. Clinical applications of systematic desensitization have shown that clients who are treated in this way become less upset by previously feared situations and better able to manage their anxiety. It is possible that the most effective part of systematic desensitization is the client's exposure to gradually increasing levels of fear-arousing stimuli under nonthreatening conditions. Individuals who can mentally rehearse being exposed to the upsetting, fear-arousing situations show particularly high levels of improvement.

Implosive therapy is based on the belief that many conditions, including anxiety disorders, are outgrowths of painful prior experiences. For the patient to unlearn them, the original situation must be re-created so that it can be experienced without pain. Therapists who use implosion ask their clients to imagine scenes related to particular personal conflicts and to recreate the anxiety felt in those scenes. The therapist strives to heighten the realism of the re-creation and to help the patient extinguish the anxiety that was created by the original aversive conditions. In addition, the client is helped to adopt more mature forms of behavior.

Implosive therapy uses the methods and ideas of both behavioral and psychodynamic theories. Although it is not uniformly effective in reducing anxiety, research to date suggests that it, like desensitization, can reduce many intense fears.

The term in vivo exposure means that the exposure is carried out in a real-life setting, not simply in the imaginations of the client and the therapist as they sit in the therapist's office. The difference between in vivo exposure and flooding might be compared to the difference between wading into a swimming pool and jumping in at the deep end. For example, an agoraphobic client who experienced intense anxiety anywhere outside her home might be asked to go to a crowded shopping center with the therapist and remain there until her desire to escape disappeared (see Figure 6–1b). Using this procedure, someone with a specific fear can lose it in only three sessions (Marks, 1987).

In the treatment of most anxiety disorders, exposure has produced consistently good results, with improvements lasting for up to several years. The longer the exposure to the critical stimulus, the better the results. How well exposure treatment works depends on the client's motivation and on specific factors in his or her life. For example, when compulsive rituals are triggered by home cues (which is true in many cases), treatment needs to be conducted in the home setting. Failure to improve can usually be traced to failure to comply with treatment instructions, particularly by not seeking exposure to fear-arousing stimuli. In one study, compulsives received in vivo exposure therapy in their homes. The client's task was to avoid responding compulsively when the evoking stimuli were present. Figure 6–12 shows changes in the clients' ratings of their levels of anxiety when exposed to the evoking stimuli. If the client refrained from compulsive behavior in the presence of the stimuli, the level of anxiety decreased immediately after exposure and the decrease was maintained 1 and 6 months later in the presence of the compulsion-evoking stimuli.

An important task for future research is to find out *why* exposure is effective. When a client "gets used to" an upsetting stimulus, what is going on? One possible explanation is that as clients find that they can handle a little exposure to upsetting stimuli and note that their anxiety levels subside, quickly they gain confidence in themselves and develop the courage to persist in their efforts to overcome their problems.

The most effective behavioral technique for treating compulsive rituals is a combination of exposure and

response prevention. The therapist asks the patient to disclose all obsessions and compulsive patterns, and then prohibits them. A compulsive washer, for example, is allowed to become dirty, or even made dirty, and then is ordered not to wash. A typical treatment might allow one 10-minute shower every fifth day. Exposure reduces hypersensitivity to dirt and the associated anxiety; response prevention eventually eliminates the compulsive ritual. Exposure usually has to be done outside the psychotherapist's office, and trained helpers may be needed—wives, husbands, friends, or nurse-therapists. Exposure in fantasy is less effective, but sometimes it is the only possible way—for example, a patient cannot actually run over someone.

Exposure therapy and other behavioral approaches are not highly effective with people who are "pure obsessives," that is, who do not engage in rituals or avoidant behavior. Because depression is a factor in many of these cases, antidepressant drugs are often used in the treatment of obsessions.

Modeling

Another behavioral approach, **modeling**, is often combined with exposure to anxiety-provoking stimuli. While exposure therapies emphasize removing some of the overwhelming emotional response that may inhibit people who have an anxiety disorder, modeling emphasizes *acquiring* behavioral skills and a feeling of compe-

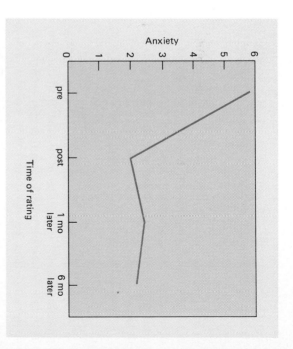

FIGURE 6-12
Changes in rated anxiety before exposure in vivo (pre), immediately afterwards (post), and at 1- and 6-month follow-up points. Reprinted with permission from *Behavior Research and Therapy*, 18, Emmelkamp, R. M. G., van der Helm, M., van Zanten, B. L., and Plochg, I., 1980, p. 65. Treatment of obsessive-compulsive patients: The contribution of self-instructional training to the effectiveness of exposure. (Copyright © 1980, Pergaman Journals, Ltd.)

tence. Modeling creates a stimulus situation in which a fearful person feels safe enough to be able to emit a dreaded response (for example, handling a snake). Observation of models may initially alter only the cognitive component. The observer may have become convinced that it is possible to pick up a snake without ill effects, but watching the model will not immediately rid the observer of the emotional feeling that "snakes are disgusting" or "slimy" or something associated with bad dreams.

The behavioral component of modeling is also important. In addition to acting as a disinhibitor, modeling can function in the acquisition of new skills and response capabilities. This is especially true in **participant modeling,** which is often more effective than modeling alone. In participant modeling, a therapist models a response and then provides corrective feedback as the client performs the same behavior. In addition to the information provided by the modeled behavior, the client receives guidance on his or her own performance. Participant modeling works especially well with complex behaviors, such as those involved in certain social situations.

Modeling plays a role in **guided mastery,** in which the therapist guides the client toward mastery over frightening situations and maladaptive behavior. Guided mastery might involve modeling of adaptive behavior by the therapist, or it might take the form of directions to the client about how to cope with various aspects of a problematic situation. In either case, the guidance helps the client attain a sense of mastery or self-efficacy.

The Cognitive Perspective

The methods developed by behavioral therapists, although they are based on learning principles, have important implications for our understanding of cognitive processes, that is, private or internal processes such as imagery and how we think about ourselves and the world. Therapies like systematic desensitization, exposure, and modeling affect not only clients' behavior but also how they think about themselves. Furthermore, cognitive activity is often a specific step in behavioral therapy; for example, in systematic desensitization the client is asked to visualize, think about, or imagine certain fear-arousing situations. Cognitive rehearsal in combination with exposure in vivo has been used successfully with phobics and obsessive-compulsives. Available evidence suggests that this procedure is highly effective in ultimately reducing anxiety, regardless of whether the client feels relaxed or anxious during exposure.

Modeling can also have an important cognitive element. Someone who overcomes intense fears as a result of a behavioral-therapy program like participant modeling acquires more self-confidence and may begin to think about new ways of behaving in situations that were not covered in the modeling program. The way people think about things often changes when they acquire new response capabilities. These cognitive changes can then lead to important behavioral advances. The term **cognitive behavior therapy** refers to clinical procedures based on principles of learning, such as extinction and reinforcement, that emphasize cognitive behavior.

Cognitive Factors in Maladaptive Behavior

In addition to the increased interest in cognitive aspects of behavior therapy, there has been a rapid increase in the influence of the cognitive perspective on efforts to understand the anxiety disorders. This perspective emphasizes the ways in which certain thoughts and styles of thinking have undesirable effects on behavior. Thoughts that preoccupy people interfere with attention to the task at hand. Worries, daydreams, and ideas that have nothing to do with the task at hand are distracting and reduce behavioral effectiveness. As the cartoon in Figure 6–13 shows, task-irrelevant thoughts can serve as distractors whether we are writing, composing, painting, or carrying out a scientific experiment.

According to cognitive theorists, thinking disturbances that occur only in certain places or in relation to specific problems are the sources of anxiety. These types of thoughts include unrealistic appraisals of situations and consistent overestimation of their dangerous aspects; for example, the *degree* and *likelihood* of harm may both be exaggerated. Thus, a person's train of thought and mental set can be viewed as vulnerability factors that interact with the characteristics of situations. From this point of view, precipitating events (the situation) elicit or magnify an underlying attitude or fear (the vulnerability factor) and give rise to hypervigilance. As this attitude strengthens, danger-related thoughts become more easily activated by less specific, less avoidable situations ("If you look for it, you're sure to find it"). As a result, the anxious individual continually scans internal and external stimuli for danger signals.

An example of this sort of disturbance may be seen in an obsessive person who experiences intense anxiety when having to cross the street and may actually be unable to attempt a crossing. Most people would use the following train of thought.

1. Streets are safe for crossing at green lights or when free of traffic.

2. This street has a green light or is free of traffic.

3. Therefore, this street can be crossed.

FIGURE 6–13
Distractions of the Great. (New Yorker, November 10, 1986, p. 120)

The obsessive person's thinking, on the other hand, might go as follows.

1. Streets are safe for crossing at green lights or when free of traffic.

2. This street has a green light or is free of traffic, but if the light suddenly changes or a car appears unexpectedly . . .

3. Then this street is not safe for me to cross.

Studies of obsessives have revealed unreasonable beliefs and assumptions. Obsessives believe that they (1) should be perfectly competent, (2) must avoid criticism or disapproval, and (3) will be severely punished for their mistakes and imperfections. In addition, at some level they seem to believe that thinking certain thoughts or performing certain rituals will help them avoid the disastrous outcomes they imagine are just around the corner. Obsessive–compulsives make arbitrary rules that they must follow (for example, stepping on every sev-

FIGURE 6–14
The catcher is trying to help the pitcher overcome concern about pitching to a superhitter by encouraging the pitcher to think about the batter in a different way. (From *The Wall Street Journal*—Permission, Cartoon Features Syndicate)

enth crack in the sidewalk). Phobics also make up rules for themselves that are not based in reality (for example, "If I go into an elevator, it might get stuck and I might suffocate"). Unfortunately, these "protective" thoughts and rituals become very intrusive and can interfere with normal activity.

Cognitive Therapy

Cognitive therapists employ a number of techniques. One of these is **cognitive restructuring.** Developed out of the rational–emotive therapy of Albert Ellis, cognitive restructuring calls the client's attention to the unrealistic thoughts that serve as cues for his or her maladaptive behavior. The therapist helps clients review their irrational beliefs and expectations and develop more rational ways of looking at their lives. For example, many people with anxiety disorders are perfectionists who expect too much of themselves and others and become overly emotional when their unattainable goals are not realized. During therapy sessions emphasis is placed on how the irrational things that people say to themselves can affect their emotions and behavior. The baseball player in Figure 6–14 is being advised to do some cognitive restructuring.

By means of cognitive restructuring, people develop more realistic appraisals of themselves and others. For example, when taking an exam a person might think: "This test is hard. Everyone else seems to think it's going to be simple. They all must know a lot more than I do." Such thoughts are likely to lead to a high degree of anxiety. A cognitive therapist would help this client concentrate on a more adaptive type of thought,

such as: "I studied hard. I'll just try to answer one question at a time. If I don't know the answer, I'll go on to the next one. No reason for panic. Even people who do well don't know the answer to every question."

Thought stopping is another cognitive technique. It works on the assumption that a sudden distracting stimulus, such as an unpleasant noise, will serve to terminate obsessional thoughts. The client is asked to get the thought firmly in mind; then the therapist loudly says "Stop!" This sequence—obsessional thought followed by "Stop!"—is repeated several times with the client, rather than the therapist, yelling "Stop!" Finally, the client simply mentally says "Stop!" If it is successful, this procedure provides the client with a specific self-control technique for removing an obsessional thought when it occurs.

A third cognitive technique is **cognitive rehearsal,** through which the client can mentally rehearse adaptive approaches to problematic situations. Cognitive rehearsal is particularly useful for problems that cannot be conveniently simulated in a clinical setting. For example, behavioral rehearsal of social skills by socially phobic individuals requires the presence of a large group of people. However, someone who suffers from a social phobia can imagine being in a group and can mentally rehearse behaviors and internal statements designed to improve his or her interpersonal relationships.

Aaron Beck has developed one of the most influential types of cognitive therapy (Beck and Emery, 1985). He believes that the core psychological problem in anxiety disorders is a vulnerability that grows out of the individual's tendency to devalue his or her problem-solving ability as well as to exaggerate the degree of threat in a problematic situation. Such an individual perceives anxiety-provoking threats to social relationships, freedom, and self-identity.

Beck's cognitive therapy typically consists of five to twenty sessions. A minimal amount of time is spent acquiring background information, searching for the original causes of anxiety, or engaging in unfocused conversation with the patient. Most of the therapy is task-oriented, being devoted to solving problems brought up by the patient. The therapist encourages the patient to talk openly about his or her fears and concerns, and conveys empathy for the patient's anxiety. The Socratic method is used to help the patient become aware of what his or her thoughts are, examine them for cognitive distortions, and substitute more realistic thoughts. Three steps are involved in cognitive therapy: (1) conceptualizing the patient's problem, (2) choosing strategies and tactics to deal with the problem, and (3) assessing the effectiveness of those strategies and tactics.

In a sense, Beck is arguing that each of us has an inner voice. When that voice interferes with our ability to function adequately, the unproductive thoughts that result must be replaced by productive ones. This is done by correcting thinking errors and having the patient work on pertinent homework assignments. Using these techniques, the patient can develop not only improved ways of thinking but also more effective, less anxiety-producing behaviors.

The Biological Perspective

Over the years several different types of reactions have been found to be caused by the individual's biological state. Some of these discoveries have led to the development of medical treatment methods. Although no direct organic cause has been found for most types of anxiety disorders, in view of the findings of physical causation in other conditions it becomes difficult to deny the possibility that there are some links between anxieties and biophysical functioning. People whose nervous systems are particularly sensitive to simulation seem more likely to experience severe anxiety.

Genetic and Environmental Factors

Inbreeding experiments with animals have shown that heredity has a strong influence on such characteristics as timidity, fearfulness, and aggressiveness. Evidence also shows that anxiety disorders tend to run in families. About 15 percent of parents and siblings of people with anxiety disorders are similarly affected (Carey and Gottesman, 1981). Identical or monozygotic twins show more concordance (about 40 percent) for anxiety symptoms than do fraternal or dizygotic twins (about 4 percent). These findings suggest a genetic cause of anxiety; however, the results are not definitive, because the subjects in this type of research not only have identical or similar heredities but usually also live together and thus experience similar environments.

One recent study found children of anxiety-disorder patients to be more anxious and fearful, have more school difficulties, worry more about family members and themselves, and have more somatic complaints than do the children of normal parents (Turner and others, 1987). They also spend more time engaged in solitary activities and are seven times more likely to meet the criteria for an anxiety disorder. Another recent study of 3,798 pairs of adult twins attempted to evaluate the separate effects of genetic and environmental factors in anxiety and depression (Kendler and others, 1986). There was strong evidence of a genetic factor and a statistically significant, but weaker, effect for a family environment factor.

Drug Therapies

Tranquilizing drugs are the most commonly used somatic therapy in the treatment of anxiety. Well over 50 million prescriptions for these substances are filled each year. Although placebo and enthusiasm reactions may account for some of their effectiveness, psychiatrists and other physicians who prescribe tranquilizers have found them valuable in reducing states of great tension. The literature on the behavioral effects of tranquilizers or anti-anxiety drugs suggests that these agents reduce the intensity of responses to stimuli that signal punishment and frustration.

In 1960 a group of drugs called **benzodiazepines** were introduced. They are marketed under trade names like Librium and Valium and are used for the treatment of anxiety, tension, behavioral excitement, and insomnia. Figure 6–15 shows the effect of one dose of a member of this group, diazepam (Valium), on the anxiety experienced when people who were phobic about cats and roaches were exposed to these animals. Similar results were obtained when the dependent measure was how close the person would come to the fear-arousing stimulus. It seems clear that a dose of diazepam made phobics better able to tolerate the animals they were afraid of. One problem with benzodiazepines is their side effects. These include drowsiness, lethargy, motor impairment, and reduced ability to concentrate. The drugs also produce physiological and psychological dependence. Excessive use may lead to undesirable behavior, including disorientation, confusion, rage, and other symptoms that resemble drunkenness.

Several years ago researchers found that benzodiazepines bind to certain receptor sites in the receiving neuron and that the relative potencies of drugs in competing for these binding sites parallel their clinical effects. Receptor sites serve as receiving stations for the brain's nerve cells. They are analogous to locks into which the appropriate chemicals fit like keys. Research has shown that some chemicals open the locks, others

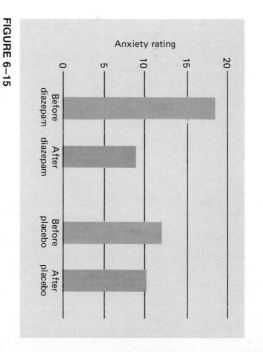

FIGURE 6–15
Subjective anxiety ratings when confronted with phobic stimuli. "After" measures were made 2 hours after the subject took either a pill containing diazepam (Valium) or a placebo. (Adapted from Whitehead, Blackwell, and Robinson, 1978, p. 63)

simply block the "keyhole" so that nothing else can get in, while still others seem to unlock different but related processes. Accordingly, a whole spectrum of drugs has been developed, some of which act as tranquilizers while others block that action and still others produce the opposite effect—anxiety. One anxiety producer that is being used in animal research is a chemical called beta-CCE, a member of a family of substances that are known to have powerful effects on the nervous system.

Efforts to map receptor sites have shed light on the specific sites in the brain that mediate the effects of different types of drugs. One of these mapping efforts has shown that mice that were inbred for "emotionality" had fewer benzodiazepine receptors than "nonemotional" strains of mice (Robertson, 1979). It has also been found that many receptors are specific to certain chemicals. For example, other drugs, such as alcohol and barbiturates, do not bind to the benzodiazepine receptors. Future research will make clearer the mechanism by which anti-anxiety drugs exert their effects, and may give rise to more effective drugs with fewer side effects.

The discovery of receptor sites for anti-anxiety drugs has set off a widespread search for other details of the brain system to which they are a key. Some experts believe that receptor sites are a key to a natural anxiety system and that anti-anxiety drugs act in the same way as natural body substances, perhaps still undiscovered, that keep anxiety under control. One of the exciting questions that are now being investigated is that of what substances produced within the body attach to which types of receptors.

The biggest recent change in the use of drugs to treat anxiety disorders is the increasing use of antidepressants in treating panic and obsessive–compulsive disorders. One group of antidepressants, the tricyclic drugs (imipramine, clomipramine), appear to have therapeutic effects on many people with anxiety disorders (Christensen and others, 1987). There is also evidence that patients with anxiety disorders who receive tricyclic medication may respond more positively to exposure therapy than those treated only with exposure (Roy-Byrne and Katon, 1987).

Evidence that antidepressant drugs are useful in treating anxiety disorders suggests that the relationship between anxiety and depression needs careful study. Cases in which either anxiety or depression receives a DSM-III-R Axis I diagnosis often have features of the other, as well. One study found that all patients in a sample of people diagnosed as depressed also showed anxiety symptoms (Barlow and others, 1986).

Study Outline

1. Although it is normal to experience anxiety occasionally, it is abnormal to feel strong anxiety chronically in the absence of a visible cause. The characteristics of anxiety include feelings of uncertainty, helplessness, and physiological arousal.
2. **Generalized anxiety disorder** is marked by chronic anxiety over a long period. **Panic disorder** consists of recurrent, sudden anxiety attacks leading to feelings of intense terror and dread. In **phobic disorders**, the experience of anxiety is connected to a specific object or situation. In **obsessive–compulsive disorder**, the individual tries to ward off disaster by thinking certain thoughts or performing certain actions.

GENERALIZED ANXIETY DISORDER

1. The physiological responses to fear and anxiety are the same, but in the case of anxiety the cause of worry is not apparent.
2. The symptoms of generalized anxiety disorder are of four main types: motor tension, hyperactivity of the autonomic nervous system, dread of the future, and hypervigilance. The diagnosis of generalized anxiety disorder is reserved for conditions in which the only problem is the presence of prolonged, vague, unexplained, but intense fears that do not seem to be attached to any particular object.

PANIC DISORDER

1. The indicators of panic disorder are similar to those of generalized anxiety disorders except that they are greatly magnified and occur very suddenly. People with this disorder have a variety of unusual psychosensory symptoms. A source of anxiety in panic disorder is **anticipatory anxiety**, or fear of another panic attack.

PHOBIAS

1. A **phobia** is a highly specific fear of certain objects, people, or situations. The fear is out of proportion to reality, inexplicable, and beyond the individual's control. Phobics do not need the presence of the feared object to experience discomfort.

2. There are three general types of phobias. **Simple phobias** are a miscellaneous group of irrational fears that do not fall into the other two categories. **Social phobias** are characterized by fear and embarrassment connected with dealings with other people. **Agoraphobia**, the most common type, is fear of entering unfamiliar situations. Agoraphobia is often a complication of panic attacks.

OBSESSIVE–COMPULSIVE DISORDER

1. **Obsessive** people are preoccupied with recurrent ideas; **compulsive** people feel compelled to perform the same action over and over again. These compulsive rituals become a form of protection against anxiety. The individual recognizes the absurdity and irrationality of the obsession or compulsion and feels a need to resist it, but the feelings of anxiety that accompany resistance are usually overwhelming. Four broad types of obsessive–compulsive preoccupations are checking, cleaning, slowness, and doubting and conscientiousness.

INTERPRETING AND TREATING ANXIETY DISORDERS

1. According to the psychodynamic perspective, the causes of anxiety disorders are intrapsychic events and unconscious motivations. In generalized anxiety and panic disorder, the individual's defenses are inadequate to control or contain anxiety. The psychodynamic view sees the object of a phobia as having symbolic significance, as representing an unresolved psychological conflict. Obsessive–compulsive disorders are viewed as developing out of **isolation**, the separation of emotions from thoughts or actions; **undoing**, or ritual actions that "take back" unacceptable behaving in ways that are opposite to one's thoughts.

2. Learning theorists believe that symptoms of anxiety disorders are learned in the same way that all other behaviors are learned. Whereas Skinner rejects any explanation that refers to internal events, Dollard and Miller include thoughts and feelings in their explanation of how maladaptive behaviors are learned. Therapeutic approaches based on the learning perspective include **exposure therapies** and **modeling**. Three types of exposure therapy are **systematic desensitization**, in which gradually stronger stimuli are introduced; **implosive therapy**, in which the original anxiety-producing situation is re-created in the mind; and **in vivo exposure**, which is carried out in a real-life setting. In vivo exposure may be gradual or may take the form of a rapid, intense exposure called **flooding**. In **modeling**, the patient acquires behavioral skills by watching someone else; in **participant modeling**, the patient then models the desired behavior; in **guided mastery**, the therapist guides the patient toward mastery over frightening situations.

3. Various elements of the cognitive approach can be incorporated in behavioral therapy. According to cognitive theorists, anxiety is a result of faulty, unrealistic, and illogical thoughts and beliefs, especially unrealistic exaggeration of the dangers inherent in a situation. Cognitive techniques that are used to treat anxiety disorders include **cognitive restructuring**, in which the individual recognizes and changes irrational beliefs; **thought stopping**, which helps remove obsessional thoughts; and **cognitive rehearsal**, or mentally rehearsing adaptive approaches to situations.

4. Although no physical cause of anxiety has been found, there are clear associations between anxiety and certain physical functions. The high concordance rate for monozygotic twins may indicate a genetic component. Tranquilizing drugs are the most common biologically oriented treatment for anxiety, although they may produce undesirable side effects. Antidepressants are now being used to treat panic and obsessive–compulsive disorders.

CHAPTER 7

Psychological Factors and Physical Symptoms

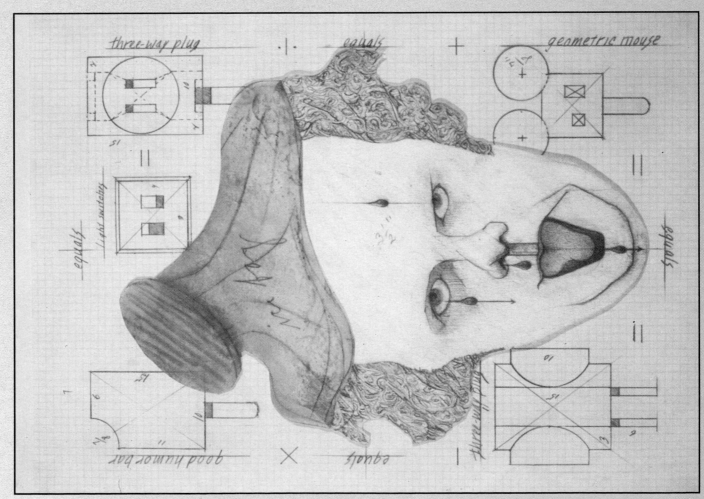

Claes Oldenburg, *Symbolic Self Portrait, Eq.* Collection Moderna Museet, Stockholm, Sweden. Courtesy of the artist.

OBJECTIVES FOR CHAPTER SEVEN:

To learn:

1. What is meant by psychophysiological disorders
2. The names and characteristics of the psychophysiological disorders discussed in this chapter

To understand:

1. How stress may affect the body
2. The role of behavioral medicine and health psychology in disease prevention and recovery from illness
3. The specific ways psychological factors may affect health

*P*erhaps the fact that the Great Depression hit just as she and my father were starting out to raise their family had something to do with it. But no matter. Already as a small child I was aware that in the handling of money my mother was more than simply thrifty; she was downright frugal. Extravagances and luxuries did not exist. She never bought anything, for example, unless she was certain she would use it. And not only use it, but use it to the best purpose and for the longest possible time. The one exception was a new, frilly, never-worn nightgown that she kept in the bottom drawer of the bureau. But even that had its purpose: "In case I should ever have to go into the hospital," she said. And so the nightgown lay there for years, carefully protected in its tissue wrappings.

But one day, many years later, the time came. The nightgown with its now yellowed lace and limp ruffles was taken from its wrappings and my mother entered the hospital, seeking an answer to the mysterious fevers, sweats, and malaise that had plagued her like a flu since autumn. The time was early January, in the deepest darkest days of a cold winter, just before her 69th birthday.

We did not have long to wait for an answer. It came with the finality of a period at the end of a long sentence of strung-out clauses: lymphoma, disseminated, progressive. Privately, her physician told me he was sorry; there was probably only a matter of two or three weeks left, certainly less than even a month.

For days, I agonized over what to do with this information that only I had been told. Should I tell the family? Should I tell my mother? Did she already know? If not, did she suspect? Surely she must after so many months of malaise. Could I talk about it with her? Could I give her any hope?

Could I keep up any hope she might have? Was there in fact any hope?

Some relief came when I realized her birthday was approaching. The nightgown she had saved all those years she now was wearing, but it was hopelessly dated. I resolved to lift her spirits by buying her the handsomest and most expensive matching nightgown and robe I could find. If I could not hope to cure her disease, at least I could make her feel like the prettiest patient in the entire hospital.

For a long time after she unwrapped her birthday present, given early so she would have longer to enjoy it, my mother said nothing. Finally she spoke. "Would you mind," she said, pointing to the wrapping and gown spread across the bed, "returning it to the store? I don't really want it." Then she picked up the newspaper and turned to the last page. "This is what I really want, if you could get that," she said. What she pointed to was a display advertisement of expensive designer summer purses.

My reaction was one of disbelief. Why would my mother, so careful about extravagances, want an expensive summer purse in January, one that she would not possibly use until June? She would not even live until spring, let alone summer. Almost immediately, I was ashamed and appalled at my clumsiness, ignorance, insensitivity; call it what you will. With a shock, I realized she was finally asking me what I thought about her illness. She was, in fact, asking me how long she would live. She was, in fact, asking me if I thought she would live even six months. And she was telling me that if I showed I believed she would live until then, then she would do it. She would not let that expensive purse go unused. That day, I returned the gown and robe and bought the summer purse.

That was many years ago. The purse is worn out and long gone, as are at least half a dozen others. And next week my mother flies to California to celebrate her 83rd birthday. My gift to her? The most expensive designer purse I could find. She'll use it well.

—(McAdams, 1985)

Is this account of a mother's recovery simply a heartwarming anecdote, or does it provide a clue to why some people recover from illness and others do not? Evidence that psychological and social factors play important roles in health and illness—an idea that has intrigued clinical workers for a long time—is increasing. In this chapter we will review existing theories about the relationships among personality, environment, and illness and examine how psychological and social variables operate in health and illness.

First we will focus on a number of conditions that have often been referred to as **psychosomatic** or **psychophysiological disorders**; they are marked by physical complaints and actual tissue damage or impairment. Later in the chapter we will discuss another group of conditions, those that involve physical complaints with no detectable tissue damage or impairment. These conditions have been referred to as **somatoform disorders** because they suggest somatic impairment when there is no evidence that any exists. A third group of conditions that will be dealt with is **factitious disorders**. "Factitious" means not real, genuine, or natural. People with factitious conditions have physical or psychological complaints that appear to be simulated and under their voluntary control. In other words, they seem to be faking.

Many of the disorders covered in this chapter are thought to result from frequent, intense, and prolonged physiological arousal. Whereas some people respond to stress primarily with bizarre thoughts and behavior, others respond primarily with physical symptoms such as cancer and migraine headaches. But while it is known that there are wide differences in individual patterns of physiological, cognitive, and behavioral reactions to stress, the mechanisms behind those patterns remain unclear. Whatever the mechanisms turn out to be, it is now certain that they involve interactions among personal variables (for example, attitudes and physiological patterns) and situational variables (such as past and recent life experiences and social supports). Illness results from multiple factors.

Concepts of Psychological, Social, and Bodily Interactions

Awareness that one's state of mind can influence one's body has a long history. In the eighteenth century Mesmer claimed that he could modify the course of physical symptoms by using his personal "magnetism." In the nineteenth century Charcot pioneered the use of hypnosis in the treatment of bodily complaints, and early in this century Freud applied psychoanalytic concepts to physical symptoms. Freud believed that somatic symptoms had symbolic significance; they represented compromises among forbidden impulses, intrapsychic conflicts, and the need to defend oneself from anxiety.

The Psychosomatic Hypothesis

In the 1930s and 1940s a number of clinicians attempted to integrate Freudian ideas into a growing body of knowledge concerning the bodily aspects of emotional experiences. During this period the **psycho-somatic hypothesis** became popular. According to this hypothesis, bodily symptoms can be caused by a blocking of emotional expression. This idea, in turn, gave rise to the concepts of specificity and organ susceptibility.

Numerous psychoanalytic writers argued for **specificity**: specific emotional conflicts and stresses were thought to be associated with particular physical conditions in vulnerable individuals. Whether these conflicts and stresses resulted in bodily dysfunction depended on the individual's characteristics, including personality profile. For example, it was argued that people who chronically suppress their anger are prone to develop rheumatoid arthritis when they are confronted with situations that arouse anger in most people. It was also argued that many individuals have a particularly weak or susceptible organ (such as the lungs) and that certain stresses evoke unconscious conflicts that result in a specific disorder in that organ. This is known as **organ susceptibility**. Most of the evidence supporting the concepts of specificity and organ susceptibility has come from the observations of psychotherapists, many of whom were psychoanalysts. Only a few laboratory studies were conducted by early psychosomatic theorists, and the number of patients described in clinical reports was small.

More recent research work has focused on how bodily reactions change when people are exposed to various emotion-arousing stimuli. For example, a psychosomatic symptom, such as high blood pressure, can be viewed as a product of the emotional arousal experience when a person is exposed to stress over an extended period. Contemporary research on the psychophysiology of emotions and stress has furthered our understanding of this process. For example, emotional tension has been shown to influence the autonomic nervous system and the endocrine glands. One of the endocrine glands, the adrenal medulla, releases its hormones when the situation calls for "fight or flight." As a result, the rates of breathing and heartbeat and muscle tension increase. These and other bodily changes caused by emotional responses to stress prepare the organism to struggle for survival.

Much of the basic research on the endocrines' responses to stress had used animals as experimental subjects. Experimental studies have dealt with two central questions: (1) How does stress affect endocrine function? and (2) How do different levels of biochemical substances influence bodily functioning and behavior?

Over a number of years Hans Selye subjected a variety of laboratory animals to many kinds of stress. He invariably found that the endocrines spring into action when there are bodily or environmental threats of damage to the organism (Selye, 1976). Selye coined the phrase **general adaptation syndrome** to refer to an organism's pattern of reactions to prolonged stress. This pattern begins with an initial shock or alarm resp[onse] which is followed by a recovery or resistance p[...]. During the alarm phase the adrenal glands show particularly striking changes (see Figure 7–1). They become enlarged and discharge their supply of steroids, a process that causes them to change color from yellow to brown. When Selye's animals were removed from stress, the adrenal glands returned to their normal size and seemed to resume normal functioning, but this recovery was only temporary. After several weeks of renewed stress, the glands again enlarged and lost their store of steroids. Selye found that if the stress is very great and continues for a long time, the animal finally dies from exhaustion.

Not surprisingly, demonstration of the general adaptation syndrome in animals has led to research on its existence in human beings. Studies of professional hockey players and of psychiatric patients appearing at staff conferences found increases in subjects' hormonal secretions during emotional stress that were similar to those found in Selye's animals (Elmadjian, 1963). Be-

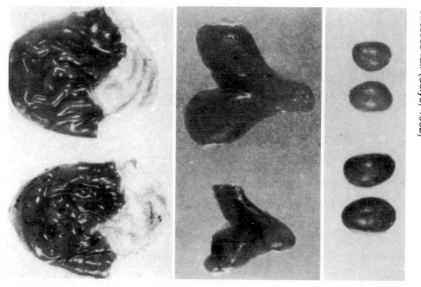

FIGURE 7–1
The organs on the left are those of a normal rat. Those on the right are those of a rat that was exposed to the stress of being forcefully immobilized. Note the marked enlargement and dark discoloration of the adrenals (top), caused by congestion and discharge of fatty-secretion granules; the intense shrinkage of the thymus (middle); and the numerous blood-covered ulcers (bottom) in the stressed rat. (Selye, 1952)

cause of such changes in body functioning, severe and prolonged psychological pressures can cause physical diseases such as high blood pressure and stomach ulcers.

Psychological Factors That Affect Health

Today most researchers who study psychological processes reject simplified ideas of specificity and organ susceptibility in attempting to explain certain physical symptoms. Instead, they look at physical symptoms from an interactional viewpoint: bodily defects may cause psychological problems, and psychological problems may in turn cause bodily defects. When psychological factors are involved in illness, their roles are usually indirect. For example, personality characteristics by themselves may not cause an illness like asthma, but in combination with hypersensitive lungs and certain situational stresses, they may play an important role.

The Biopsychosocial Model

Recently emphasis has been placed on the interaction between psychological states and social and biological variables. According to the **biopsychosocial model**, a person can be regarded as a system with interacting biological, psychological, and social subsystems (Engel, 1977). This model can be illustrated by some of the complex processes involved in brain function. The brain processes both physical and nonphysical inputs (environmental events, ideas); it generates thoughts and behavior; and it regulates bodily functions. At any given moment the brain's circuitry permits simultaneous "programming" of data pertaining to the biological, psychological, and social spheres. The challenge facing researchers is to identify the factors and conditions that play roles in this complex type of information processing.

Biopsychosocial problems often arise when people's lives are disrupted by environmental changes, challenges, and constraints. The word **homeostasis** refers to the mechanism by which the organism mobilizes itself to restore a dynamic equilibrium in the face of these disruptions. At present most researchers and clinicians believe that, for any given individual, a host of variables—physical, psychological, and social—contribute to the phenomenon that we call "getting sick." The idea that illness is due simply to the influence of external agents seems outmoded. While it is true that there are individual differences in the vulnerability of bodily organs to disease, these differences must be considered in light of personality characteristics, environmental factors, and the general condition of the body. The biopsychosocial point of view is not limited to the causes of illness. It is also relevant to prevention and treatment.

If you have a terrible stomachache and someone says, "Don't worry, it's probably psychosomatic," that doesn't help very much. When people use the word "psychosomatic," they often mean, "It's all in your head." This attitude stems from the vague notion that there are two distinct entities—mind and body—that are locked in a struggle for supremacy. Actually, most psychological and physical problems arise from a multitude of interacting factors. When social relationships and environmental events have special personal meaning and evoke strong emotions, a variety of bodily reactions take place. For example, hearing of a loved one's death or going home to spend Christmas with one's family inevitably leads to at least temporary bodily changes.

The connection between psychological factors and physical health is not a one-way street. A psychological state may play a role in one's susceptibility to physical illness, but getting sick also influences one's state of mind. Depression, anxiety, anger, and feelings of hopelessness and helplessness characterize most people who must live with illness and physical incapacity. A physical illness does not have to be catastrophic to have a psychological impact. Anyone who has had the flu, a sprained ankle, or a toothache knows how much psychological damage these relatively minor problems can cause. Of course, the more serious the physical disorder, the greater the likelihood that it will significantly affect the person's thoughts and feelings. Such effects, in turn, compound the effects of the illness.

The scientific recognition that these interactions exist may not seem to be a major discovery. Each of us has felt the psychological letdown that follows the onset of a physical illness. On the other hand, we might reject the less obvious possibility—one that is accepted by many scientists—that our psychological condition plays an important role in creating bodily disturbances. Yet a large body of knowledge suggests that certain personality characteristics may be associated with certain types of physical symptoms—for example, those connected with high blood pressure and heart attacks. Because attitude can affect the speed and extent of recovery from an organic illness, medical researchers are devoting increased attention to the role of psychological complications in physical disorders. It has been estimated that between 25 and 50 percent of patients treated in medical settings have psychological disorders as well as medical ones (see Box 7–1). How specific these associations are and whether they reflect causal (rather than correlational) relationships are explored later in the chapter.

BOX 7-1
Personality and Illness

People's attitudes and beliefs, how their life course becomes organized, and their ability to achieve a reasonably stable sense of who they are and where they are going may influence health. Traits that typify the neurotic person—chronic anxiety, long periods of sadness and pessimism, unremitting tension, incessant hostility—have been found to be associated with asthma, headaches, peptic ulcers, and heart disease (Friedman and Booth-Kewley, 1987). People with these traits are twice as likely as those without them to contract some kind of illness. This means that hostility-like high cholesterol or smoking, may be a serious health hazard. Additional work is needed on the definitions and assessment of the relevant aspects of personality and disease. But there is already good reason to be interested in the possibility of discovering the physiological mechanisms that may link personality and disease (see Figure 7-2).

If maladaptive personality patterns are associated with illness, might changing them weaken the association? That is, if people could be helped to be less anxious, depressed, and hostile would their health status improve? While we do not yet have a definitive answer to this question there are some suggestions that psychotherapy and counseling directed toward achieving desirable personality change does, at least, affect the frequency with which people go to the doctor. In a large study of federal employees covered by a group insurance program, people who began mental-health visits within one year after their chronic disease was diagnosed had lower total yearly medical charges by the third year after that diagnosis than a control group (Schlesinger and others, 1983). The difference in inpatient medical charges for chronic disease patients who had mental-health services compared to those who did not receive them was especially large. Psychotherapy may have helped patients to cooperate better with their medical programs, maintain a more healthful life style, and respond to life in less emotionally upsetting ways.

Psychotherapy can help people enjoy life more and be more effective in their daily living; it can also improve physical health. Research has been pointing at both these conclusions for some time. What is most impressive about these new findings concerns medical costs. All this can be accomplished without spending more health-care dollars over the long run. This means that hospitals can not only improve the quality and appropriateness of their general care for patients with a chronic disease but also may even lower the total costs for these patients by adding outpatient mental-health treatment to disease-specific treatment.

FIGURE 7-2

The individuals in pictures a, b, and c show some of the personality characteristics that are associated with various illnesses. The person in a is anxious and worried; the one in b is sad and depressed; and the person in c is clearly angry. A major task for future research is to find out what there is about these characteristics that is associated with breakdowns in bodily processes.

(a)   (b)   (c)

First we will examine the evidence for general relationships among psychological factors, health, and specific physical disorders.

Stress and Illness

Much abnormal behavior can be viewed as ways of dealing with stress—not good or desirable ways, but ways that become understandable on the basis of two factors: meager or distorted psychological resources and the perceived severity of the situation. Stress is created when individuals face difficult situations and have to ask themselves, "How am I going to handle this one?" or "Can I do it?"

We have observed that stress leads to diverse bodily reactions. The heart, lungs, and digestive, endocrine, and nervous systems, among others, work overtime when people experience stress. When these symptoms are consistently overloaded throughout long periods of a person's life, the likelihood increases that some sort of physical weakness or disturbance will occur. It makes good medical sense, therefore, to study the personal characteristics and aspects of life that go along with strong and persistent stress reactions or might predispose a person to psychological or physical breakdown. Psychological, social, community, and biological factors are each important by themselves, and there is every reason to believe that their joint effects are at least equally as important as their individual effects.

Although they do not usually act alone, certain psychological factors do play roles in physical illnesses. Those factors include the following.

1. Inability to adapt to changes in environmental demands
2. Inability to handle strong feelings and emotions, and to express them realistically
3. Inability to interpret demands, constraints, and opportunities correctly
4. Inability to form rewarding, lasting interpersonal ties, particularly love relationships

There are some indications that an individual's temperament and personality early in life may be predictive of his or her susceptibility to illness decades later. A recent study showed that self-confidence measured in high school students was predictive of physicians' ratings of their health 40 years later (Clausen, 1987). In another study carried out over a period of many years, Rorschach inkblot tests were given routinely to medical students at Johns Hopkins University (Shaffer and others, 1987). At the time of testing, the students were in good health. The researchers developed special ways of rating Rorschach responses in which figures in the inkblots were described as interacting in some way with each other (for example, "Two small children arguing," "Two bears fighting"). The interaction ratings ranged from warm, affectionate, and close ("People kissing") to violent and destructive ("A witch committing a murder").

Twenty to 25 years later the health status of each of the subjects was assessed. Those whose Rorschachs reflected either a relative lack of well-balanced patterns of social relationships—a relatively restricted capacity for emotional relationships or ambivalence about ties to others—were especially prone to develop cancer later in life (As students these physicians had been described as being loners). Interestingly, the Rorschachs of subjects who either were healthy or had cardiovascular disorders tended to be similar to each other but different from those of subjects who developed either cancer or mental disorders. The Rorschachs of the latter two groups tended to be similar. These results suggest the value of exploring the linkages between emotional and social orientations and physiological and biological systems.

Several community and social variables also seem to be implicated in physical functioning. For example, urbanization, poverty, rapid social change, and migration can all have negative effects on health. Occupation, workload, working hours, attitudes toward work, morale, and job performance also can play negative roles. Complicating the picture further are biological factors such as individual differences in body type, hormone levels, and cardiovascular functioning.

Only some of the people who are biologically predisposed to a particular condition actually fall ill. Others seem to have a great capacity to adapt and therefore remain in good health. Psychological contributions to the onset of illness may vary with a number of factors, including age, the particular form of the illness, and what is going on in the person's life. These interacting factors provide a clue to why it is practically impossible to make statements like, "John Jones got pneumonia because he had been working overtime for two months" or "Mary Smith developed ulcers because she is such a nervous person." Many people develop pneumonia without working overtime, and most people can work overtime without becoming sick. Similarly, many people who develop ulcers do not appear to be especially nervous, and most nervous people do not develop ulcers.

As noted earlier, stress stimulates hormonal secretions (particularly those of the pituitary and adrenal glands), activates the autonomic system, brings about biochemical changes, and alters the brain's electrical level. Although all people have these reactions to stress, the strength and pattern of the reactions depend on the nature of the stressful stimulus and the individual's biological characteristics, personality, and life experiences. Recent and past life experiences play important roles in influencing our appraisal of situations and the coping mechanisms we use to deal with stress. Learning that takes place in a social context tends to reinforce or extinguish particular behavioral and physiological reactions.

Longevity

Ever since Ponce de Leon searched in vain for the Fountain of Youth, human beings have been beating their heads against the wall of old age. Evidence that nonbiological factors play roles in longevity is accumulating. Social isolation, sudden loss of a loved one, death of a parent, and chronic loneliness all seem to shorten the life span. Vulnerability to such stresses may be expressed

TABLE 7-1

Predictors of Longevity

Factors in Longevity that Are Wholly or Partly Under Personal Control

1. *Diet.* Too much or too little food reduces longevity. Many people in Western countries would live longer if they are less, particularly foods that are high in fat.
2. *Exercise.* People who are more active and get more exercise are likely to live longer.
3. *Smoking.* The association between cigarette smoking and greater mortality is well documented.
4. *Retirement and work.* Retired people have higher mortality rates than people of the same age who continue to be gainfully employed.
5. *Marital status.* Aged married people have lower mortality rates than elderly people who are not married.
6. *Social activity.* Social activity (for example, belonging to clubs and religious institutions) is modestly correlated with greater longevity.

Less Modifiable Factors in Longevity

1. *Heredity.* There is a positive relationship between the longevity of parents and that of their children.
2. *Sex.* Women live longer than men.
3. *Race.* Up to age 75, blacks have higher mortality rates than whites. After age 75, there is a small difference in favor of blacks.
4. *Intelligence.* Higher intelligence or better mental functioning is associated with greater longevity.
5. *Socioeconomic status.* Education and income levels are strong predictors of longevity.

as anxiety, psychosis, or physical illness. Table 7-1 presents a number of predictors of longevity, only some of which are controllable. In most cases, it is not clear how these variables are related to longevity.

In the United States the mortality rate for all causes of death is higher for certain groups, such as single, divorced, and widowed people. However, knowing that these groups are more vulnerable to fatal illnesses does not tell us much about the mechanism that actually causes the higher rates. Does a love relationship in fact have health-protecting features? There is evidence to support this idea, although longitudinal studies of married and single people are needed to show how personal characteristics influence the course of development, including marriage, illness, and death. Ideally, such research should begin when the subjects are very young. (Early loss of a parent has been related to the subsequent development of various physical illnesses.) In addition, the roles of community factors such as urbanization and neighborliness must be determined. The community, like a loving marital partner, seems to be able to provide social supports that increase an individual's resistance to the negative effects of stress.

It is a well-established fact that women live longer than men (see Table 7-1). However, the cause of this difference is unclear. Probably both genetic and life-style factors play roles. Sex differences in longevity are smaller in nonindustrial than in industrial societies. To a large extent this reflects smaller sex differences in mortality for coronary heart disease in nonindustrial societies. In industrial societies like the United States, higher male mortality rates seem to be related to society's expectations that men will be more aggressive, adventurous, ambitious, and hard-driving than women. If these expectations were changed, would male mortality rates become lower as a result? As more and more women hold jobs and support families, will their mortality rates go up? We do not have definite answers to these questions. Research that compares mortality among men and women who differ in their need to adopt traditional male roles and among women who differ in their conceptions of female roles may clarify this issue.

The term **psychological hardiness** has been used to refer to individuals who are more resistant to stress and less susceptible to illness than most people (Kobasa and others, 1982). People who are psychologically hardy tend to have a strong sense of personal control over their lives, to feel more involved in whatever they are doing, and to be more open to new ideas and change. Future research may show a link not only between psychological hardiness and illness but also between hardiness and longevity.

Behavioral Medicine and Health Psychology

The care of tuberculosis depends more on what the patient has in his head than what he has in his chest.
— (Sir William Osler, 1849, the father of modern medicine)

Although the influence of the mind on the body was well known to ancient healers and has dominated folklore to the present day, until recently the field of medicine has focused almost exclusively on physical causes of bodily illness. New studies strongly indicate that virtually every ill that can befall the body—from the common cold to cancer and heart disease—can be influenced, positively or negatively, by a person's mental state, lifestyle, and social relationships. By unveiling the mechanisms behind these effects, research may point to new ways of preventing and treating disease.

Increasing evidence that psychological factors play a role in health and illness has given impetus to two rapidly developing fields, behavioral medicine and health psychology. **Behavioral medicine** is concerned with ways of improving diagnosis, treatment, and rehabilitation by using psychological techniques that help people adopt healthier ways of living. An important

FIGURE 7–3

Behavioral medicine and health psychology are concerned with reducing the stressfulness of illness and, wherever possible, preventing it. Prevention often involves helping people to make healthful life-style changes. Examples of targets of prevention efforts are smoking, a form of voluntary behavior clearly harmful to health; alcohol abuse, which contributes to cirrhosis of the liver; cancer; injuries from accidents and violence; and overeating and underexercising which contribute to obesity, high blood pressure, and diabetes.

(a)

(b)

(c)

(d)

goal of behavioral medicine is the improvement of service delivery by providers of health care. Researchers in behavioral medicine are particularly concerned with direct patient evaluation and treatment.

The related field of **health psychology** is directed toward the prevention of disease. Health psychologists seek to reduce health risks by changing people's thinking and living habits. Researchers in health psychology tend to be concerned with broader topics, including the acquisition and modification of behavior that influences health or is guided by concerns about health. Health psychologists seek to strengthen behaviors that contribute to good health, such as getting enough exercise, following a balanced diet, and not smoking. As much as 50 percent of mortality from the leading causes of death can be traced to such behaviors. Health psychologists seek to uncover ways of changing behavior and thought so as to maximize health and well-being (see Figure 7–3).

The great need for effective health-promotion techniques is suggested by the facts presented in Table 7–2 showing the results of a national survey of health-related behaviors. If only a small proportion of the people who either are failing to promote their own health or are engaging in activities harmful to their health could be helped to change their behavior, both personal suffering and economic costs would be significantly reduced.

Common to both health psychology and behavioral medicine is a philosophy that emphasizes individual responsibility as a means of maximizing health. According to this view, health is a personal achievement, and people's behavior influences whether they attain it or not. Physical, mental, social, and economic factors all influence health and recovery from illness.

Psychologists who are interested in helping people maintain health and recover from illness employ a variety of techniques to modify behavior that is in itself a

TABLE 7–2

Facts from 1985 National Health Survey

About one-fourth of the adult population was 20 percent or more above desirable body weight.

About one-half of adults had experienced at least a moderate amount of stress in the last 2 weeks.

Forty percent of the population said they exercised or played sports, but only 28 percent were very physically active.

About 30 percent of persons 18 years of age and over smoked cigarettes.

Fifty percent of young mothers, 18 to 24 years of age, with less than 12 years of education had smoked in the year preceding the birth of their last child.

Adapted from Health Promotion and Disease Prevention, 1988.

health problem, to help people stick to prescribed treatment plans that may have unpleasant side effects (such as chemotherapy or a rigid diet), and to help people modify behavior that may increase the risk of disease. An additional focus of behavioral medicine is on modifying the behavior of health care providers in order to improve the delivery of their services—for example, by explaining various possible treatments in clear and nontechnical language.

Behavioral medicine and health psychology are interdisciplinary fields that integrate the behavioral and biomedical sciences. We will illustrate work in these fields with four examples: interpretation of bodily symptoms, the role of information about medical procedures, biofeedback, and psychological interactions with the immune system.

Interpreting Bodily Signals

People go to the doctor when they attend to and are concerned about bodily signals. Their behavior is like that of a driver who does not pay much attention to the sound made by the car engine unless an unusual noise is heard. However, there are significant differences in people's attentiveness to bodily symptoms. Awareness of symptoms depends on psychological processes and is subject to the same perceptual and cognitive rules that govern the perception of external events. People do not appear to be able to perceive highly specific physiological states with great accuracy (Pennebaker, 1982). Furthermore, a person who may be accurate about one bodily system (for example, the digestive system) is no more likely than another to be accurate about another symptom. Rather than basing beliefs about symptoms and sensations on actual physiological states, people often infer their symptoms, emotions, and other external states from their immediate environment. Accuracy in reporting symptoms is most likely when major physiological changes that result in pain have actually taken place.

Physical symptoms can be viewed as problem-solving challenges. Although many cases involve common problems that can be verified objectively, sometimes the physician is unable to substantiate a diagnosis. A number of questions confront the doctor: Is the patient reporting all of the symptoms? Does the patient present symptoms in a way that is misleading? Are the symptoms present all the time or only under certain conditions? Could the reported symptom be an unlabeled emotion? A person who might not be able to express or acknowledge a given emotion may be particularly distressed when emotion-related symptoms appear. From this individual's perspective, the emotion might not seem to be occurring.

The understanding of symptoms is a problem that cuts across a number of psychological and medical disciplines. Changes in bodily functioning are an important aspect of the individual's understanding of the world. Because of the difficulty of measuring various physiological processes, researchers are directing increasing attention to the specific stimulus properties inherent in the physiological signals that are being picked up. They are working on assessment techniques to determine the ways in which people react to various stressors, emotions, and other events on both the physiological and psychological levels.

Using Health-Related Information

The fact that the information we have and the way we interpret it influence our health and our ability to recover from illness was demonstrated by Irving Janis (1958) in a psychological study of recovery from surgery. Janis found that patients who had a moderate amount of fear before an operation made a better recovery than either patients who had little fear or patients who were very much afraid. Janis believes that worry can be constructive and speed recovery, and his findings suggest that a moderate amount of anticipatory fear is necessary for a person to begin the "work of worrying." By mentally rehearsing potentially unpleasant events and gaining information about what to expect, the patient can develop effective ways of coping with postoperative pain and concern about recuperation. Four kinds of information play important roles in patients' responses to illness and treatment.

1. Information about the nature of the illness and the medical reasons for initiating particular treatments
2. Information describing the medical procedures to be carried out, step by step
3. Information about particular sensations (for example, pain or possible side effects of medication)
4. Information about coping strategies can be used in adjusting to the upcoming threat.

Whether or not patients use the information available to them and whether or not they follow medical advice depend on several factors besides the information they get and how it is presented. For instance, people who do not feel that they are in control of their lives may not follow instructions about exercise and medication. Less educated people are more likely than better educated people to break medical appointments and not follow medical advice. Patients who express their con-

cerns to their doctors and receive answers in simple language tend to experience less stress about their physical condition.

Researchers in the area of behavioral medicine are investigating the types of information that are medically useful and the best ways of communicating that information to patients. Without free communication between patients and health care providers, patients' fears stay bottled up and their misconceptions cannot be corrected. Self-help groups made up of patients with similar diagnoses can provide needed social support as well as encourage the communication of information. Films, videotapes, and pamphlets have been used effectively in several community education programs to provide information about health hazards such as smoking and obesity.

Biofeedback

Biofeedback is a technique that is used in behavioral medicine to treat such problems as hypertension, highly volatile blood pressure, and epilepsy (see Figure 7-4). Biofeedback is a way of extending self-control procedures to deal with a variety of physiological behaviors that were formerly thought to be involuntary responses, such as heart rate, blood pressure, and brain waves. Such behaviors were thought to be beyond conscious control until researchers became aware of individuals who apparently are able to control them. One such person, a Yogi practitioner named Swami Rama, was studied intensively at the Menninger Foundation (Green, 1972). Laboratory tests showed that, among other things, Rama was able to speed up and slow down his heart rate at will, to stop his heart from pumping blood for 17 seconds, to cause two areas of his palm a few inches apart to change temperature in opposite directions until their temperature differed by 10 degrees F (the "hot" side of his palm became rosy whereas the "cold" side became ashen), and to produce widely differing brain wave patterns at will.

Rama is not unique, although the extent of his control is startling. Research has shown that humans and animals can learn to control their heart rate, blood pressure, brain waves, and other behaviors. For humans, no external reinforcement of the behavior seems to be necessary. All that is required is that the individual be given information in the form of feedback from the response system in question. Just as we could never learn to shoot a basketball accurately if we did not receive visual feedback and feedback from our muscles, we cannot learn to control our heart rate or brain waves unless we receive some kind of feedback on physiological changes as they occur. The feedback then serves as a reinforcer for change in the desired direction.

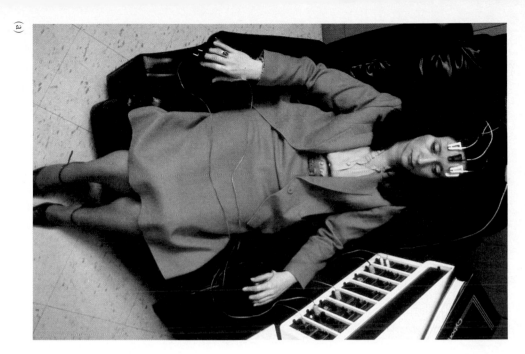

(a)

(b)

FIGURE 7–4

Biofeedback training can help clients control a variety of physiological responses. Photo *a* shows the biofeedback apparatus. Photo *b* shows the video monitor which visually presents the responses as they occur.

Ordinarily we do not get feedback on responses like blood pressure and brain waves, but by precisely measuring physiological events and converting the electronic signals into visual or auditory feedback, we can be made aware of our own physiological responses. This biofeedback process has been used to train people to control the physiological responses of the brain, muscles, and cardiovascular and glandular systems, and has been applied to an enormous variety of clinical problems, including cardiac disorders, high blood pressure, headaches, anxiety, and neuromuscular disorders like cerebral palsy. For example, over half of a large group of headache sufferers benefited significantly from biofeedback training (Blanchard and others, 1982). This positive effect was found for various types of headaches, including migraines.

There is no longer any question that people can learn to control a wide range of bodily functions. However, there are questions about the overall effectiveness of biofeedback, especially when compared to other techniques that are less expensive and time-consuming. There is evidence that skills learned through biofeedback training are lost rather quickly when training stops. As researchers continue to identify the limitations of biofeedback, it becomes more apparent that these techniques are not the cure-all that overenthusiastic proponents initially believed they would be. But it is equally clear that biofeedback can be successfully applied to certain problems. An important goal of current research is to determine how and when biofeedback techniques can be used most effectively to enhance control over physiological and psychological responses.

Psychological Processes and the Immune System

The immune system is the body's surveillance system; it protects the body from disease-causing microorganisms. It is integrated with other physiological processes and is sensitive to changes in the functioning of the central nervous system and the endocrine glands. The immune system regulates susceptibility to cancers, infectious diseases, allergies, and auto-immune disorders (diseases in which cells of the immune system attack the normal tissue). There is increasing evidence that stress and emotional arousal can lower the immune system's resistance to disease.

Animal studies have demonstrated the complex relationship between stress and susceptibility to disease. The effects depend on the age of the animal, its stage in the life cycle, and the timing and duration of the stress. Experimental stressors such as physical restraint, overcrowding, electrical shock, or exposure to a predator have been associated with increased susceptibility to numerous viral illnesses. The induction and rate of growth of tumors in experimental animals have also been altered by such stressors (Locke and others, 1984).

There is evidence that certain early life experiences (for example, daily handling or maternal separation) result in different patterns of cancer susceptibility in rats, with both the nature and the timing of the stressor accounting for significant variability in the response. Another critical factor is the animals' ability to develop an adaptive coping response: exposure to acute *escapable* stress does not influence tumor growth appreciably; however, the identical amount of *uncontrollable* stress markedly exacerbates tumor growth.

Recent research has provided evidence that psychological, behavioral, and environmental factors influence the functioning of the immune system in humans. Immunological consequences of stressors have been observed in such diverse situations as space flight, sleep deprivation, school examinations, bereavement, and depressive states. Not only exposure to multiple or chronic life stressors, but also loneliness, low levels of social support, and poor coping skills seem to lower the effectiveness of a person's immune system (Justice, 1987).

There is evidence that many college students show decreased immune system functioning during exam periods (Jemmott and Locke, 1984; McClelland and others, 1985). This may help explain why they have so many illnesses during these periods. Another example of this relationship is a Canadian study of accountants which was conducted during the 8 weeks preceding the deadline for filing income taxes and 6 months thereafter (Dorian and Garfinkel, 1987). The accountants not only experienced high levels of psychological distress, but they also showed a decline in immune system function at the peak tax-filing periods. Studies like these suggest that high-performance demands may be significantly associated with alterations in the immune system, which, in turn, may increase susceptibility to disease.

from a person suffering from another disorder or none at all. What is becoming increasingly clear, however, is that people—not just cells or organs—have diseases, and that diseases must be studied in the context of people's psychological, social, and cultural environments.

The term **psychophysiological disorder** has traditionally been applied to physical conditions in which psychologically meaningful events are closely related to bodily symptoms. Psychophysiological disorders might be thought of as end products of biopsychosocial processes. A large number of physical problems have been studied from a psychophysiological standpoint. these include disorders of the cardiovascular, respiratory, gastrointestinal, musculoskeletal, and genitourinary systems, as well as the skin. Both clinical data and informal observations suggest the importance of psychological factors in many of these disorders. Consider the following case.

A 38-year-old mother of four children had a 5-year history of attacks of hives, a skin condition characterized by itching, burning, and stinging. During these attacks, areas of her face, trunk, waist, thighs, and arms would swell. There would be swelling even on her tongue and inside her respiratory passages. The attacks initially occurred about once a month, but at the time that she sought help, their frequency was closer to once every 4 or 5 days. Each attack was accompanied by depression and nausea.

An examination in an allergy clinic yielded negative results. After a psychiatrist placed the patient on tranquilizing drugs, the incidence of hives declined markedly. Further study indicated that her attacks usually occurred when she was experiencing intense stress. For example, when she was having marital difficulties and was forced to face the possibility that her husband might leave her, she had an especially severe series of attacks. At one point she felt so overwhelmed by situational stresses that she was hospitalized. During this period she was protected from family tensions, and her hives disappeared completely.

After leaving the hospital the patient entered psychotherapy on a twice-a-week basis. In these sessions she was able to express her frustrations at leading a very restricted life because of her small children's demands and her husband's inability to see why she might need time away from home. Another point that emerged in therapy was the patient's inability to express to her husband how much she needed to have him acknowledge her value as a person, not just as the mother of his children. After several months of therapy, she felt able to tell her husband about her

Psychophysiological Disorders

Recent research on stress, emotions, and social support suggests that the way we live influences our health and longevity. Several groups of physical disorders in which personality and social factors may play a part have been studied over the years. There is no evidence that these conditions are directly attributable to the mental state of the individual or that a person suffering from one of these disorders has a completely different personality

unfulfilled psychological needs as well as her resentment and frustration. At the time that therapy ended, she had been completely free from hives for 4 months.

A major hurdle for the researcher is figuring out how to proceed from relationships that may be at work in a given case to generalizations that could apply to whole groups of people. The most extensive evidence that physical illness is caused by the interaction of psychosocial and biological factors probably comes from the study of cardiovascular disorders.

Cardiovascular Disorders

Every affection of the mind that is attended with either pain or pleasure, hope or fear, is the cause of an agitation whose influence extends to the heart.

—William Harvey, 1628

Written more than 350 years ago, Harvey's allusion to an intimate association between neural factors and the heart received some attention in anecdote and fable, yet was not subjected to systematic scientific inquiry until the second half of the twentieth century. The heart is a highly specialized muscle that pumps blood to the body. The blood flows through the body in an unending loop of blood vessels called the circulatory system. Each day the heart beats 100,000 times, delivering the equivalent of 4,300 gallons of blood to all parts of the body. The arteries provide food and oxygen to the cells, while the veins remove carbon dioxide and waste products. The term **cardiovascular disorders** refers to pathological conditions that are related to the functioning of the heart and blood vessels. There is growing evidence that psychological and social factors play a role in two major cardiovascular disorders: coronary heart disease and hypertension. These conditions have caused over half of all deaths in the United States for more than 40 years.

Coronary Heart Disease

The leading cause of death and disability in the United States is **coronary heart disease** (CHD). One in five Americans develops CHD before his or her sixtieth birthday; of these, 11 percent die suddenly and another 44 percent suffer nonfatal heart attacks. CHD is produced by lesions of the coronary arteries, the arteries that circulate blood within the heart itself. In CHD one or more of the three coronary arteries are partially or totally obstructed by deposits, called **plaques**, that thicken the arterial wall. When the coronary arteries become rigid and narrow as a result of these plaque deposits, the supply of blood to various portions of the heart muscle is temporarily or permanently cut off.

CHD takes a variety of forms. In **angina pectoris,** people suffer from periodic chest pains caused by an insufficient supply of oxygen-rich blood to the heart. The insufficient blood supply is related to plaque buildup (referred to as **atherosclerosis**) in the arteries. A **myocardial infarction**, also caused by an insufficient blood supply to the heart, is more serious than angina pectoris because it involves a more complete curtailment of the heart's blood supply. When people speak of a heart attack, they are usually referring to a myocardial infarction.

A significant factor in heart attacks is stress. From the Stone Age to the present day, human beings have responded to environmental challenges and threats by releasing larger amounts of adrenal and other stress hormones, followed by increases in heart rate and respiration and dilation of the vessels that transport blood to the muscles. Although these responses are adaptive or even life-saving when the threat is a wolf pack, you would do better without them if you are stuck in a traffic jam. In fact, not only are these primitive physiological responses of little help in dealing with most modern-day problems, but they may actually be related to the development of disease.

Stress seems to contribute to coronary disease through the body's general reactions to aversive stimulation. Under arousing conditions, hormonal substances called **catecholamines** are secreted. Two of the catecholamines, **epinephrine** and **norepinephrine,** accelerate the rate of arterial damage and ultimately can lead to heart attacks. Which people are most likely to have heart attacks under high levels of stress, and what steps lead from psychological stress to cardiac damage, are both topics of current research.

Factors that increase the risk of CHD include age (older people are at greater risk), sex (males are at greater risk), cigarette smoking, high blood pressure, high cholesterol level, and diabetes. Some studies have also implicated such factors as obesity, heredity, and lack of physical exercise. These factors may not be causes of CHD; they may simply be correlated with it. Even the most predictive of the risk factors still fails to identify more than half of the new cases of CHD. How these factors are related to the incidence of heart attack in a given individual is not yet known precisely.

Death due to CHD has decreased more than 30 percent in the last 30 years, and recently this decrease has accelerated. Deaths as a result of heart disease have declined from first to third among all causes of death in people between 25 and 44 years of age, but heart disease remains the leading cause of death in people aged 45 and over (Levy and Moskowitz, 1982). Factors that may be contributing to the decline in mortality are improved medical services, the development of coronary care units in hospitals, advances in surgical and medical treatment of CHD, and improved control of blood pressure. Life-style changes, such as less smoking, better eating habits, and increased physical fitness, may also play a role.

Life-Style Patterns. *Life style* refers to a way of life that reflects the values and attitudes of an individual or group. Our jobs, interests, and social relationships show the effects of our life styles.

Twin studies allow the researcher to control for genetic factors and thus highlight the effects of life style and environmental factors. A study conducted in Sweden (Liljefors and Rahe, 1970) provided a unique set of data about the relationship between CHD, personality, and life style. The sample consisted of 32 pairs of identical male twins, 42 to 67 years of age, who were discordant for CHD—that is, only one member of each pair had a heart condition. Virtually all the twins had been raised together at least until their early teens.

The twins' characteristic behavior patterns in four areas—devotion to work, lack of leisure, home problems, and life dissatisfactions—were assessed through interviews. The study's results supported the hypothesis that CHD is related to life style and the experiences (for example, stressful encounters) characteristic of certain life styles. Table 7–3 shows the differences in one twin pair. A more recent study (Kringlen, 1981) has provided further support for this hypothesis.

Studies that compare different cultures and the process of social change also provide evidence concerning the role of life-style factors in disease. In general, low rates of CHD tend to be found in parts of the world where tradition and family ties are strong. Cross-cultural data have provided a broader perspective on the relationship between psychosocial experience and physical breakdown. Japan, for example, has one of the lowest rates of heart disease in the world, while the United States has one of the highest. The rate of death from CHD for Japanese men between the ages of 35 and 64 is 64 per 100,000 population; the comparable figure for American men is 400 per 100,000. Could the nature of life in the United States be responsible for this high mortality rate? A study in which Japanese living in Japan were compared with Japanese-Americans living in Hawaii and California highlights the importance of cultural factors in the development of CHD (Marmot and Syme, 1976). The Japanese living in Japan had the lowest incidence of CHD; the Japanese-Americans living in Hawaii had a somewhat higher rate; and the Japanese-

Americans living in California had the highest frequency of heart disease. Although diet probably accounts for some of these differences, societal and cultural differences also play a substantial role. For example, Japanese-Americans who believed in preserving traditional Japanese culture developed fewer cases of CHD than Japanese-Americans who had strongly accepted American culture.

There are wide regional and cultural differences in a large country like the United States. For example, according to a survey done some years ago, the town of Roseto, Pennsylvania, had a remarkably low death rate, especially from heart attacks. The coronary death rate for men was 100 per 100,000, and the rate for women was almost half that figure (Wolf, 1969). Moreover, residents of Roseto had low rates of several other stress-related disorders, such as stomach ulcers.

These low rates might seem surprising, since both the men and women of Roseto tended to be overweight and their diets contained as much animal fat as those of people in other communities. Their smoking and exercise patterns were not unusual. What seemed to contribute most to the relatively low death rate was the way in which the people lived. Roseto was distinguished from similar communities in that almost all of its residents were of Italian descent. Family relationships were extremely close and supportive, and the town's neighborhoods were very cohesive. Moreover, in Roseto men were the uncontested heads of their families. Personal and family problems tended to be worked out with the help of relatives, friends, and the local priest.

Although Roseto had several stable features, it was, like all American communities, undergoing constant change. Young men and women were marrying non-Italians from other towns. The birth rate was declining, church attendance was down, and people were moving into more modern suburban neighborhoods. Another, more unfortunate trend was also discovered: by the mid-1970s a striking increase in the rate of heart attacks and sudden death could be noticed, particularly among men under 55 (Greenberg, 1978). Apparently social change was weakening Roseto's sources of social and emotional security, with important consequences for the health and longevity of its inhabitants.

Separations from and losses of loved ones often bring about the need for sudden life-style changes and may culminate in a heart attack.

Harry Allen's wife had suffered from lung cancer for many months. Her death came slowly and painfully. For Allen, aged 54, the loss and grief were overwhelming. Everyone knew that the cancer was incurable and that death was approaching. Yet it came as a terrible shock to Allen. Four months before his wife's death, Harry had had a thorough physical

TABLE 7–3

Twin-Pair Members Who Were Discordant for Coronary Heart Disease (CHD)

Twin without CHD	Twin with CHD
Devotion to Work	
The subject has been an auto repairman for the past 33 years. His workday is 8 hours long, and he works less than 5 hours per week overtime. At one time during his life for a 5–10 year period he worked about 8 hours per week overtime.	The subject is an owner of a small fur shop. During his high season he works up to 18 hours per day. The rest of the year he averages 9 hours per day.
Lack of Leisure	
The subject visits friends and family less than once per month. He reads the newspapers and watches TV about once per week. In the summer he rents a "sommarstuga," where he goes once a week. In the winter he goes skiing now and then. He takes a 45-minute lunch break along with a 20-minute coffee break during the day, and he usually relaxes then.	The subject visits friends less than once per month and has a hobby in the summer which he follows at a once-per-week frequency. He reads the newspapers and watches TV frequently. He manages to take regular vacations. The subject's lunch periods are 30 minutes long; he sometimes relaxes then and sometimes does not.
Home Problems	
He was married at 27 years of age. His wife is three years younger than he is. They have three children with one still living at home. He recalls having some arguments with his wife and having had some financial difficulties.	He was married at 33 years of age. His wife is eight years younger than he is. There are two children—both still reside in the home. He generally has had a good home life. He has had considerable economic difficulties.
Life Dissatisfactions	
The subject thinks that neither twin dominated. He had a comfortable childhood and was quite happy with his education. The problems in his marriage he sees as primarily due to his alcohol consumption prior to the last eight years. Since then he has not had much alcohol to drink, primarily because it interfered with his sexual relations. He is quite satisfied with his work.	The subject makes no comment about which twin might have dominated. He recalls a good childhood experience and was satisfied with his level of education. Throughout his working life he has felt constantly rushed and never had enough time for himself. He has had considerable trouble with his creditors in his business and feels he has particular difficulty in being tough enough to collect the money owed him. He feels he has strived a good deal to achieve the luxuries of life and has not succeeded very well.

From Liljefors and Rahe, 1970, pp. 540–541.

examination that included an electrocardiogram. The electrocardiogram as well as the other studies relevant to heart function were completely negative. Yet 2 days after his wife's death Allen collapsed and died of a massive heart attack.

Recent research has explored the role of social losses and social isolation in recovery from heart attacks. In one investigation, 2,320 male survivors of myocardial infarctions were studied to identify factors that were predictive of how long they would live after having had a heart attack (Ruberman and others, 1984). One such factor was education, with the better-educated subjects living longer. Life stress and social isolation, both alone and in combination, also emerged as significant predictors of mortality. Life stress was defined by subjects' reports concerning such problems as job difficulties, divorces and separations, accidents, and criminal victimization. Social isolation was defined in terms of contacts with friends and relatives and membership in social, church, and fraternal organizations.

In Figure 7–5, graphs *a* and *b* show that when the effects of life stress and social isolation were evaluated separately, each of these factors was significantly associated with increased probability of mortality. The risk of death for men who were high in life stress was double the risk for men who were low in life stress. A similar relationship was found when men who where high and low in social isolation were compared. The combined effect of these two factors is shown in graph *c* of Figure 7–5. For men who were high in both life stress and social isolation, the risk of dying was four times greater

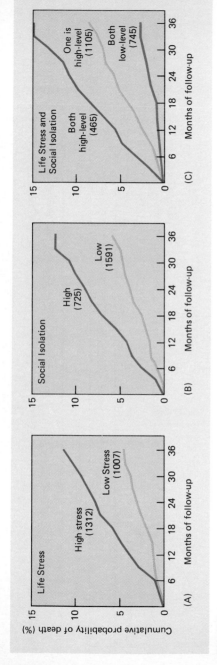

FIGURE 7-5

Cumulative probability of death as a function of number of months that subjects were followed up after myocardial infarction. (Adapted from Ruberman and others, 1984, p. 555. Reprinted by permission of *The New England Journal of Medicine*, 9 (1984), p. 555.

than for men who were low in both life stress and social isolation. The middle line in graph *c* presents the risk of dying for men who were high in either life stress or social isolation.

Personality and Coronary Heart Disease. Might the life-style patterns that are linked with CHD be re-

lated to basic aspects of personality? Is there a heart-attack–prone personality? On the basis of their observations of many heart attack patients, Friedman and Rosenman (1974) concluded that such a personality exists. These people, called **Type A's** (see Figure 7–6), tend to operate under high pressure and to be very demanding both of themselves and of others. Because of these char-

FIGURE 7-6

Type A individuals work rapidly, feel pressured, and frequently try to do two or more things at once. (© 1984 by Sidney Harris–Chicago Magazine)

acteristics, Type A people are believed to run an inordinate risk of suffering heart attacks. The characteristics that seem to typify the Type A person include the following.

1. Talking rapidly and at times explosively
2. Moving, walking, and eating rapidly
3. Becoming unduly irritated at delay (for example, waiting in line)
4. Attempting to schedule more and more in less and less time
5. Feeling vaguely guilty while relaxing
6. Trying to do two things at once.

These characteristics are assessed by means of specially designed questionnaires and interviews. The Type A pattern exists on a continuum, with some people showing more of the characteristics just listed than others. Table 7–4 lists some items from a questionnaire designed to assess the Type A personality.

While the Type A life style has not been proven to cause heart attacks, there are definite links. For example, one study showed that during 8½ years of follow-up, Type A men had more than twice as much heart disease as Type B men (Type B's do not show the Type A behavior pattern and are much less driven) (Rosenman and others, 1975). This difference could not be explained simply in terms of traditional risk factors, such as cigarette smoking, because those factors had been equalized for the two groups. Other research has corroborated that a Type A behavior pattern is a strong predictor of recurring heart attacks.

One type of investigation that may help chart the relationship between personality and CHD and also clarify how known risk factors combine to bring about physical illness is the longitudinal or prospective study. Most clinical problems have been studied retrospectively, that is, after the fact. After someone gets sick, the doctor inquires about past illnesses and experiences that might explain the current problem. More powerful—but also more time-consuming and costly—is the prospective, or before-the-fact, investigation. Such a study gathers information over a relatively long period. Because prospective studies are longitudinal, they can provide a picture of how a person's thinking, behavior, and bodily reactions unfold over time. Depending on the data gathered, this approach permits the researcher to identify interactions between particular personality variables and important life events and the effects of those interactions on the person's health.

An example of a prospective study that points up the strengths and weaknesses of this approach is the Framingham study. A group of 5,127 adult residents of Framingham, Massachusetts, have volunteered to participate in a study on coronary heart disease for the rest of their lives. They have been monitored for the incidence of illness, hospitalization, and death since 1948. Every 2 years each participant is given a physical examination that includes blood tests, electrocardiograms, X rays, and blood pressure readings. Several physical risk factors have been identified by the Framingham study, including elevated blood pressure, cholesterol level, and cigarette smoking. The study has confirmed that weight gains result in elevated blood pressure and thus indirectly increased the risk of coronary heart disease.

A subgroup of 1,674 Framingham participants between the ages of 45 and 77 was assessed for Type A tendencies and then followed up over an 8 year period (Haynes and others, 1980). Women between the ages of 45 and 64 who developed CHD scored significantly higher on the Framingham Type A measure and showed more suppressed hostility (not showing or discussing anger), tension, and anxiety than women who remained free of CHD. Type A women developed twice as much CHD as Type B women. Although working women tended to have higher Type A scores than housewives, being a housewife did not protect Type A women from higher rates of CHD. Figure 7–7a shows that working women under 65 years of age were almost twice as likely to develop CHD if they exhibited Type A rather than Type B behavior. Among housewives in the under 65 age group, CHD incidence among Type A's was almost three times greater than among Type B's. Figure 7–7b shows the association of Type A behavior with CHD incidence among white- and blue-collar men in the 45 to 64 and 65 to 74 age groups. The association was significant only among men holding white-collar jobs.

TABLE 7–4

Questionnaire Items Designed to Reflect Type A Characteristics. The subject's task is to rate each item on a scale ranging from not at all like me to a great deal like me.

1. I don't get upset when I have to wait in line at a store or theater.
2. I usually don't find it necessary to hurry.
3. When I play games, winning is very important to me.
4. I like competing with other people.
5. Second best is not good enough for me.
6. I'm often so busy that I have trouble finding the time for things like a haircut, shopping, and household chores.
7. I often feel like letting someone have it.
8. I get tense at work when I am competing for recognition.

Note: Scoring is reversed for items 1 and 2.

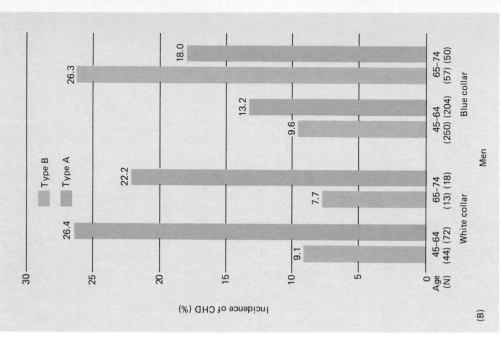

FIGURE 7–7a

Eight-year incidence of coronary heart disease among Framingham working women and housewives with Type A and Type B behavior patterns. (Findings from the Framingham study, adapted from S. G. Haynes, M. Feinleib, T. W. B. Kannel, The relationship of psychological factors to coronary heart disease in the Framingham study, *American Journal of Epidemiology, 111* (1980), pp. 35–58)

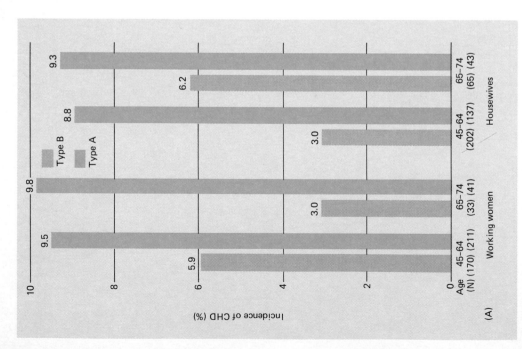

FIGURE 7–7b

Eight-year incidence of coronary heart disease among white-collar and blue-collar Type A and Type B men in the Framingham study. (Adapted from Haynes and others, 1980)

The results of the Framingham study suggest that the Type A behavior pattern operates independently of the usual coronary risk factors (such as blood pressure, age, and weight). The Type A behavior pattern and suppressed anger seem to be important risk factors for CHD in both men and women (Diamond, 1982).

Has a link between the Type A and CHD been proven? Despite many positive results concerning this relationship there have also been some contradictory findings. For example, one study found that Type A men who had had heart attacks were *less* likely than Type Bs to have recurrences (Ragland and Brand, 1988). This unexpected result, as well as other findings not consistent with the Type A formulation, might have been due to methodological aspects of the particular in-

vestigations or to some factor that has not yet been identified (Dimsdale, 1988). In any case, there is good reason to believe that the original Type A–CHD relationship proposed by Friedman and Rosenman needs some revision.

The Type A pattern is, in fact, complex and includes the tendencies to feel under time pressure, be hard-driving, and hostile. The hostility tendency may be the most active Type A ingredient, and there is evidence that people who are hostile, angry, cynical, and suspicious of others have an especially high risk of fatal coronary disease (Barefoot and others, 1987).

Another possible reformulation of the Type A pattern is suggested by evidence that Type As are more physiologically reactive than other people. This excitability might be the most active ingredient (Krantz and Manuck, 1984). Perhaps there are two groups of people, hot and cold reactors, with the cold reactors showing normal cardiovascular responses (blood pressure, heart rate) to stress and hot reactors displaying abnormally intense cardiovascular responses. Hot and cold reactors might not differ in terms of their overt behavior, but the hot reactors might experience steep blood pressure surges under stress. If this proves to be the case, measurements of the Type A pattern by means of questionnaires and interviews may not be as direct a predictor of cardiac disorders as measurements of actual cardiovascular responses under stressful conditions.

The causes of cardiovascular disease are complex, involving behavior patterns superimposed on genetic makeup in response to specific environmental challenges. The particular type of challenge or stress may be of critical importance. For example, the rates of cardiovascular disorders declined in European countries during World War II. It is possible that this was a result of the scarcity of risk-increasing foods such as eggs and richly marbled meats, as well as cigarettes and other risk-increasing commodities. But psychological factors may also have played a role. The fight against the Nazis generated a mutual support system and a group spirit that are not generally found in today's world. Certainly people who lived in war-torn countries suffered great hardship, but in working cohesively against a common enemy, they had clear-cut goals and a sense that they were doing something of great importance. A Dane who was instrumental in smuggling 7,000 Jews out of Denmark under loads of coal in freight cars with false bottoms perhaps described it best. When asked whether such risk taking was stressful, he replied, "Heavens, no. We had to save those people's lives and pulled together to do it. We knew exactly what we had to do, we did it, and we're proud of it" (Eliot and Buell, 1983).

Can the Coronary-Prone Personality Be Modified?

Researchers are now exploring the possibility of reducing the susceptibility to CHD using psychological training (Haaga, 1987). A variety of cognitive and behavioral techniques have been tried with Type As, including self-control training, learning to think about situations in less intense ways, and being attentive to the problems created by personal beliefs that emphasize urgency and the need to gain immediate control over events. Although this work is just beginning, there is some basis for believing that learning to think and act differently exerts a positive influence on the health of Type As. For example, one study found that Type A men who had already had a heart attack were less likely to have another attack if they had participated in a cognitive-behavior counseling program after the first heart attack (Thoresen and others, 1982).

Another group of researchers has tried to help healthy successful Army colonels engage in fewer Type A behaviors (Gill and others, 1985). The colonels participated in a series of counseling sessions that dealt with ways of modifying beliefs and attributions that underlie Type A behavior. They were also given advice on how to avoid potentially stressful situations, and engaged in role plays in which they practiced less highly pressured ways of coping with situations. The findings support the conclusion that the Type A attributes of anger, irritation, and impatience are not necessary aspects of the drive, ambition, creativity, and hard work needed by military leaders. The study showed that the colonels became less prone to Type A behaviors but that their ability to function as leaders was in no way impaired. They actually may have become more effective leaders.

Hypertension

Hypertension is what most people describe as high blood pressure. A blood pressure level that is over 150 (systolic) when the heart contracts and does not fall below 90 (diastolic) when the heart relaxes is usually considered high. High blood pressure indicates that there is resistance to the flow of blood through the cardiovascular system. This places pressure on the arteries and forces the heart to work harder to overcome the resistance. Among younger adults (aged 25 to 44), men have higher blood pressures than women. Among older adults (aged 65 to 74), this pattern is reversed. The blood pressure readings of black adults exceed those of white adults (*Hypertension in Adults*, 1981).

High blood pressure is a major contributor to cardiovascular disorders and is one of the conditions that creates increased risk of heart attacks. Usually it is a silent or symptomless risk because the hypertensive individual might show no observable signs of a medical problem for many years. Hypertension may be the most common chronic disease in the United States today. In addition, borderline systolic blood pressure elevations occur in about 10 percent of people over the age of 20.

Clinical observations indicating that many hypertensives show wide variability in blood pressure readings and seem emotionally on edge much of the time have led to speculation about the causes and treatment of this disorder. Chronic anger and anger suppression (holding anger in) have been identified as particularly important factors (Chesney and Rosenman, 1985) (see Table 7–5). Everybody is exposed to anger-provoking situations. According to one theory, hypertensives experience chronic anger because of their inability to express it or assert themselves in a socially desirable manner. Psychotherapists believe that within the warm acceptance of the psychotherapeutic setting, angry, anx-

TABLE 7-5

The Assessment of Anger

It is important to measure accurately the tendency to become angry and the ways in which people cope with it. If hypertensive people bottle up anger, a way is needed to assess this tendency. Since it can be experienced and expressed in different ways, reliable measures of anger are needed. These are some of the aspects that require assessment together with sample items.

General Anger
It is easy to make me angry.
At times, I feel angry for no specific reason.

Situations that arouse anger
I get angry when I am delayed.
I get angry when I do something stupid.
I get angry when people are unfair.

Anger directed outward (anger out)
When I am angry with someone, I let that person know.

Anger directed inward (anger in)
I harbor grudges that I don't tell anyone about.

Guilt over anger
I feel guilty about expressing my anger.

Based on Siegel, 1985. Courtesy of Hemisphere Publishing Corporation.

Another line of research concerns the relationship between relaxation and blood pressure. If hypertensives could learn how to relax, would their blood pressure levels go down? There is evidence that some reduction in blood pressure can be achieved by teaching relaxation skills to hypertensives. Herbert Benson (1977) has developed relaxation exercises that involve four elements: a repetitive mental device, a passive attitude, decreased muscle tension, and a quiet environment. His approach uses instructions like the following.

Sit quietly in a comfortable position. Close your eyes. Deeply relax all your muscles, beginning at your feet and progressing up to your face. Keep them deeply relaxed.

Breathe through your nose. Become aware of your breathing. As you breathe out, say the word "one" silently to yourself. Continue for 20 minutes. You may open your eyes to check the time, but do not use an alarm. When you have finished, sit quietly for several minutes, at first with closed eyes and later with opened eyes.

Do not worry about whether you are successful in achieving a deep level of relaxation. Maintain a passive attitude and permit relaxation to occur at its own pace. Expect distracting thoughts. When these distracting thoughts occur, ignore them and continue repeating "one."

Practice the technique once or twice daily, but not within two hours after a meal, since the digestive processes seem to interfere with elicitation of anticipated changes.

—(Benson, 1977, p. 153)

This simple method leads to lower blood pressure as well as to the other bodily changes that accompany relaxation. Figure 7–9 shows the types of results that have encouraged clinicians to use relaxation techniques with hypertensives. The figure shows that relaxation led to lower systolic blood pressure during the day and also while the subjects were asleep. There were similar results for diastolic pressure.

Biofeedback, a method that operantly conditions automatic responses, is another promising approach to the treatment of hypertension. It has long been known that automatic responses can be classically conditioned, but it is now clear that operant conditioning of autonomic responses is also possible. Operant procedures are capable of generating highly specific changes in physiological systems that were previously thought to be involuntary. Though some experiments designed to operantly condition autonomic responses have yielded negative results, the overall pattern of the findings is encouraging.

ious people can gain insight into and mastery over their tendency to experience strong emotional reactions. However, firm empirical support for this approach is not yet available.

Some support is emerging for a behavioral approach to hypertension that directs attention to the specific types of situations associated with elevated blood pressure. Lack of competence in dealing with situations that call for assertiveness may be a specific behavioral deficit of many hypertensives. Assertiveness, defined as the ability to stand up for one's rights, express feelings, and avoid mistreatment by others, is a vital interpersonal skill and an indicator of social competence (see Figure 7–8). People who are low in assertiveness tend to be mistreated, fail to express their feelings, and are frequently unable to have their needs met. Natural consequences of these experiences are anger over being pushed around and anxiety about the possibility of exposure to threatening situations in the future. Researchers have been able to show that hypertensives respond positively to behavioral training that involves the modeling and role-playing of appropriate assertiveness. As the social competence of these individuals increases, in many cases their blood pressure declines (Manuck and others, 1985); thus, strengthening the social skills of hypertensives may prove to be of clinical value.

(a)

(b)

FIGURE 7–8

Because people with hypertension may lack skills needed in self-assertion, training programs are being developed to improve their social competence. Examples of situations in which improved social skills might facilitate the coping of hypertensives might be: (a) making an appropriate complaint about service in a restaurant, (b) asking someone for a date, (c) complaining about not getting a seat on a plane for which a reservation had been confirmed.

(c)

Even though both relaxation and biofeedback seem to be effective in reducing blood pressure, some cases will probably require the use of several clinical methods together with psychotherapy aimed at clarify-

ing the conditions that gave rise to the disorder. There is evidence that the combined use of relaxation and biofeedback has particularly good long-term effects on blood pressure (Jacob, Wing, and Shapiro, 1987).

that emotional constrictedness in medical students was related to the incidence of cancer many years later. That study is one of a growing number of efforts to find out whether psychological variables might also be related in some way to the occurrence and growth of cancer and to recovery from the disease.

One emerging hypothesis is that people who have difficulty handling strong feelings are more prone to develop cancers than people who can appropriately ventilate their emotions. In one psychological study of cancer patients, only about 30 percent of the group admitted feeling any discouragement whatever about the future, although many of them had large tumors for which no treatment was available (Plumb and Holland, 1977). In another study, patients with malignant melanoma, a type of cancer, were asked to rate on a scale of 1 to 100 the amount of personal adjustment needed to handle or cope with a serious illness (Rogentine and others, 1979). All of the patients reported that they had made the rating with their melanomas in mind. One year later each patient's clinical status was evaluated. Patients who had low scores (low ratings of the need for adjustment) were clinically worse off at the one-year follow-up than patients with high scores. This result seems consistent with the view that subjects who score low on the scale are using denial or repression of the impact of the disease (lack of concern), whereas those who report a need for more adjustment are more realistic in their appraisal of the illness.

The way people deal with one strong emotion, anger, may be particularly important. In a study to assess the relationship between personality and breast cancer (Greer and Morris, 1975), women were interviewed and took psychological tests the day before undergoing exploratory surgery to determine whether their tumors were malignant. The women whose tumors turned out to be malignant seemed either to express anger too directly or to bottle it up too tightly. The researchers who conducted the psychological interviews and administered the tests could not know whether a given woman's tumor was malignant or benign. They—and the subjects—were "blind" with regard to the outcomes of the operations. Although there were significant differences in anger between the women with malignant and benign tumors, there were no significant differences in other variables, such as intelligence and depression.

Another hypothesis that is being investigated concerns the relationship between depression and cancer. In one study, the MMPI was administered to over 2,000 middle-aged employed men. Two decades later only the MMPI depression score was associated with increased risk of death (Persky and others, 1987; Shekelle and others, 1981). Whether psychological depression can be described as a direct or indirect cause of increased risk of death from cancer was not answered by this study.

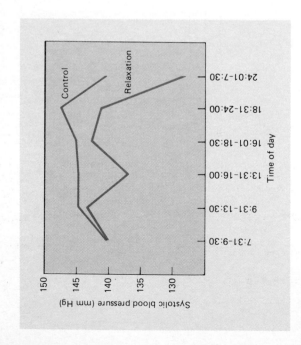

FIGURE 7-9
Systolic blood pressures for hypertensives who were given relaxation training and for an untreated control group. Blood pressure readings were taken during 6 time periods beginning with 7:31 to 9:30 A.M. (Adapted from Agras, Taylor, Kraemer, Allen, and Schneider, *Archives of General Psychiatry*, 37, p. 861. © 1980 American Medical Association)

Antihypertensive medications have also been shown to be effective in reducing blood pressure, but drug treatments have certain drawbacks, including cost, side effects, and difficulty in getting some patients to take the medicines.

Further research is needed to deal with several specific questions. What is it that hypertensives are doing when their blood pressure goes up or down? Might some of the positive effects of relaxation and biofeedback be placebo effects—that is, might lowered blood pressure following relaxation or biofeedback training be due partly to the expectation that the treatment will be effective? Follow-up studies are needed to determine how lasting the results of behavioral procedures are, and comparative studies are needed that evaluate the effectiveness of several treatment methods (biofeedback, psychotherapy, and so on). Behavioral techniques might prove particularly useful in conjunction with antihypertensive drugs in treating high blood pressure.

Cancer

Stress and personality are emerging as two of the most widely studied psychological factors that may contribute to cancer. Animal studies have shown that uncontrollable stress is related to cancer growth (Sklar and Anisman, 1981). Earlier in the chapter we mentioned the Johns Hopkins University prospective study that found

To answer that question we would need more information about the biology of psychological depression and its relationship to the growth of cancer cells.

Though we are a long way from identifying a "cancer-prone personality" or using psychological methods in treating cancers, the increasing attention being given to the relationships between personality and cancer is encouraging (Eysenck, 1987). One of the greatest needs in cancer research is for longitudinal studies that begin before people develop cancer symptoms. Obviously, such studies are difficult to conduct because no one can tell in advance that a person will develop a malignancy. The ideal study would be one in which a large representative sample of apparently healthy people is assessed psychologically and then followed up to determine which individuals develop cancer and whether its incidence can be predicted by psychological data collected before the cancer was identified.

The evidence implicating psychological factors in cancer is still tentative; similar emotional states have been associated with a variety of physical disorders. In much of the available research, methodological limitations make it dangerous to draw firm conclusions. Many studies are characterized by an inadequate or inappropriate control group, vagueness in the definition of psychological factors, use of psychological tests and questionnaires that have been inadequately validated, or dependence on the recollections of patients who already have cancer. Improvements in research methodology may help clarify a number of questions regarding the relationship between psychological factors and cancer.

Headaches

My problem was migraine headaches, which threatened to ruin my career. I had gone to several New York specialists, paying the last one six hundred dollars. . . . "It is the imponderable that causes much illness," said Draper. Draper eventually psychoanalyzed me and helped me discover and understand the stresses and strains that produced the headaches. Once I faced up to them, the migraines disappeared. . . . He was a seminal influence because having discovered that I had been launched in life as a package of fears, he tried to convince me that all fears were illusory.

—(Douglas, 1974, excerpted from p. 177–182)

Few of us would have predicted that the most significant influence in the life of a Supreme Court justice would be that of a psychoanalyst. However, as Justice William O. Douglas' autobiographical account makes clear, his relationship with the psychoanalyst, George

Draper, made a unique contribution to his personal development that was highly valued decades later. The stresses and strains mentioned by Justice Douglas came about because of interactions between his particular personality (his needs, motivations, and concerns) and the situations of his life.

Headaches may be the most commonly reported bodily complaint. Every year an estimated 80 percent of Americans suffer from at least one headache, and 10 to 20 percent go to a physician with headaches as their primary complaint. Headaches also are a major reason given for absenteeism from work or avoidance of other undesired social or personal activities. The majority of headaches are not associated with significant organic disease (Thompson, 1982).

The pain of a headache has three components.

1. Physiological changes (usually either muscular contractions or blood vessel dilation)
2. The subjective experience of pain (aching, distress, fatigue, and so on)
3. Behavior motivated by the pain (for example, pill taking, withdrawal from family and social activities, absence from work).

A number of psychological factors affect the degree of correlation between these three components and the effectiveness of treatment. There are wide differences in people's sensitivity to the physiological changes that signal the beginning of a headache. The experience of pain does not always correspond closely with the actual amount of muscle tension present.

Tension headaches, distinguished by changes in skeletal muscles, are probably the most common form of head pain. The person reports an aching, dull, pressing feeling; the scalp may feel tender if pressed with the hand; and there are persistent sensations of band-like pain or tightness in the head. Tension headaches develop gradually and may last for hours or weeks.

The exact cause of tension headaches is unclear, but they often seem to occur in response to stress. States of prolonged chronic anxiety are common among headache sufferers, and antianxiety drugs are helpful in providing relief. If stress is related to tension headaches, training in how to handle stress should reduce discomfort. Because the experience of stress is such a personal thing, an individual might be helped by achieving a better understanding of the cognitions (specific worries and preoccupations) involved in headaches.

One experiment attempted to accomplish just that (Holroyd and others, 1977). Tension-headache sufferers who seemed organically healthy participated in a cognitive-training program in which it was emphasized that disturbing emotional and behavioral responses are a direct result of maladaptive cognitions. The headache sufferers were encouraged to attribute the cause of their headache to relatively specific cognitions (for example, exaggerating the dangers connected with a specific event). The program also dealt with the cues that trigger tension and anxiety, how anxiety can be dealt with, and the thoughts that precede headaches. Emphasis was placed on the value of monitoring one's own thoughts, being alert for thoughts that arouse strong negative emotions, and replacing them with adaptive ones. For example, when your car will not start in the morning, it is more adaptive to look under the hood or call a taxi than to bang on the steering wheel or burst into tears. The training program directed attention to such questions as "What am I thinking about that induces stress?" and "What are the facts?" Participants were taught to talk to themselves: "Calm down, concentrate on the present—there is no point in catastrophizing."

Tension-headache sufferers who receive this cognitive training were compared with those who did not (see Figure 7–10). The results show that ratings of headache severity were similar for the experimental and control groups at the onset of the experiment. During the training, the experimental group reported that the severity of their headaches declined. This reduction was maintained both immediately after the program had ended and in a later follow-up.

Migraine headaches, the type that brought Justice Douglas to Dr. Draper, are headaches that are localized on one side or on the front of the head. They are severe, tend to recur, and are often accompanied by a variety of somatic symptoms. The throbbing, pulsating pain may last for several hours. Nausea and vomiting are common. In some cases, the dilated cranial artery is visible and tender. The cause of the dilation is not known, and there is usually no permanent structural damage. The cranial arteries of people who suffer from migraines seem to be more responsive than those of other people. Unlike tension headaches, migraines are usually preceded by a sensory, motor, or mood disturbance, called an *aura*. There may be ringing in the ears; tingling, numbness, or weakness of a limb; extreme sensitivity to light; visual blurring; distorted depth perception; nausea; or unaccountable emotional changes. The blood vessels constrict and then dilate. Many migraine sufferers have a family history of such headaches, but whether this is due to heredity or to common living experiences is unclear. Migraine attacks may begin with stressful life changes such as puberty, going to college, or starting a job. A person's migraine attacks are often triggered by particular types of events, moods, and experiences. Table 7–6 lists some migraine triggers.

People with migraines have been described as perfectionist and driving—"I had to get it done," "I was trying to get all these things accomplished"—and the headaches typically occur after the individual has completed a project that is to be evaluated as a success or failure. Some migraine-prone individuals appear outwardly calm and composed, but seem to be hiding anxiety and anger over their inability to achieve perfection.

A published report about a 38-year-old woman with a long history of painful migraines is particularly interesting because it combines features of assertiveness training and cognitive training with an emphasis on personal insight (Lambley, 1976). The patient seemed to have little ability either to assert herself or to express strong feelings like anger. Her treatment consisted of three phases. During Phase A, she and her therapist worked on exercises designed to increase her level of assertiveness. Behavioral rehearsal of self-assertion occupied most of these therapy sessions. During Phase B, the patient's husband agreed to be supportive of her

FIGURE 7–10
Effects on the incidence of tension headache of a training program for coping with stress. (From Holroyd et al., 1977, p. 128)

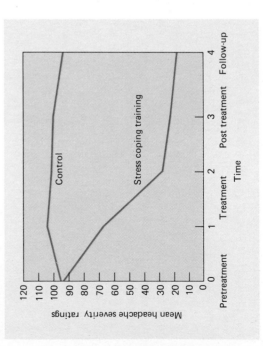

TABLE 7–6

Migraine Triggers

Anxiety, stress, worry
Menstruation
Oral contraceptives
Glare, dazzling lights
Physical exertion
Lack of sleep or excessive sleep
Certain foods and alcoholic beverages
Weather or temperature changes
Pungent odors
Exposure to high altitude

self-assertion at home, and he was taught ways of rein-forcing the desired behavior. During Phase BC, as the husband's cooperation continued, the therapist helped the patient explore the relationship between the migraine headaches and her inhibition of anger and resentment. This period was marked by gains in psychodynamic insight into her difficulty in handling negative emotions. During the therapy the patient recorded the intensity of her headaches on a 5-point scale. Figure 7-11 summarizes the changes that took place during the three phases of therapy and upon follow-up. The assertiveness training did not lead to a decrease in headache intensity, but the husband's reinforcement efforts appeared to bear fruit. The greatest decrease in headache intensity came in Phase BC, which emphasized the patient's acquisition of insight. Nine months later the patient had been completely free of severe attacks for 5 months.

Migraine headaches often respond positively to drugs that constrict the arteries in the scalp. Psychotherapists have observed significant improvement in some people who suffer from chronic headaches, but little or no improvement in people who have migraines only occasionally. Behavior therapy, including relaxation, desensitization, and assertiveness training, helps a significant number of headache suffers. Another helpful technique is biofeedback.

Cluster headaches are often confined to one side of the head with pain that is excruciating, the pain hitting a peak in 3 to 5 minutes and disappearing within an hour. Patients often are pain-free for long periods of time but then experience a series of headaches over several weeks, sometimes several in one day. The headaches often occur at night and wake people from sound sleep. Patients often pace and sometimes bang their heads against the wall in an attempt to quell the pain. Cluster headaches are more common in men.

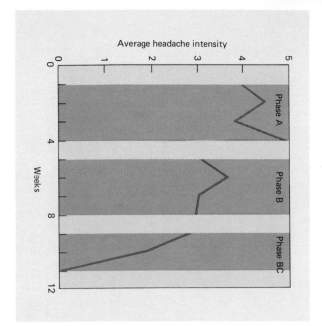

FIGURE 7-11

Average weekly intensity of migraine attacks during therapy. (Based on Lambley, *Journal of Nervous and Mental Disease*, 163 (1976), pp. 61–64, Williams and Wilkins)

Average headache intensity

Weeks

Phase A   Phase B   Phase BC

Allergies

Allergies are a common problem, affecting at least 15 percent of the population. Normally, when an **allergen,** a substance capable of causing an allergic reaction, enters the body, the antibodies produced by the immune system attack it. An allergy is an "abnormal" reaction to an ordinarily harmless substance; it is frequently described as immunity "gone wrong." While most research on allergies is directed toward understanding components of the immune system that are involved in the allergic response, recently there has been interest in the psychological as well as the physical aspects of allergies. One finding of this new line of research is that a person's total stress load, as well as exposure and adaptation to allergens, contributes to allergic reactions. Because asthma is one of the oldest forms of chronic allergy and has been studied most from a psychological standpoint, we will use it to illustrate the contribution of psychological factors to allergic reactions.

Asthma

People who have **asthma** chronically wheeze, cough, and have difficulty breathing. The cause of asthma is unknown, though it appears to be an allergic condition that results in reversible obstruction of the bronchial passages. To the patient, asthma means labored breathing, a feeling of constriction in the chest, gasping, and apprehension. About 30 out of 1,000 people in the United States have asthma.

Asthma patients often report that intense emotional states accompany acute attacks of labored breathing. This is not surprising: one can quickly measure one's emotional state by how easy it is to breathe. It has long been recognized that psychological variables contribute to asthma attacks. According to one theory, asthmatics share a common personality type and similar unconscious conflicts. However, there is little evidence to indicate that asthmatics are psychologically any more deviant than the general population. Another theory holds that characteristic personality features are the result, rather than the cause, of the restricted activities of severe asthmatics.

Although the search for the cause and cure of asthma continues, a number of psychological and situational factors that seem to maintain or worsen asthmatic attacks have been studied successfully. The value of objective study of clinical cases is suggested by an experiment conducted with asthmatic children in Denver (Purcell and others, 1969). Parents of asthmatic children have been described as overcontrolling people who create an emotionally tense home environment. Clinical evidence has indicated that removing the children from the home and placing them in an institutional setting often reduces their asthmatic symptoms. Purcell and his colleagues wished to discover the effects of separating asthmatic children from their families while keeping the environment relatively constant.

The experimental design involved an initial qualification period during which asthmatic symptoms were assessed, a preseparation period, a separation period, and reunion. During the 2-week separation period the child's family lived in a nearby motel or hotel and had no contact with the asthmatic child, who remained within the family home, playing and attending school as usual. A substitute parent cared for the child at home during the separation period. Wheezing declined precipitously during the separation and increased again during reunion (see Figure 7–12). The home environment thus appears to be conducive to asthmatic symptoms, although the psychological mechanism involved is unclear. One possibility is that the breathing obstruction that is characteristic of asthma may be produced by stress-induced activity of the autonomic nervous system, which stimulates mucus secretion, increased blood flow, and constriction of the bronchial tubes. Situational variables and personal vulnerability appear to combine in producing symptoms of asthma.

The importance of psychological factors in the clinical course of asthma is suggested by a recent study of children who died of asthmatic attacks compared to children who did not (Strunk and others, 1985). Especially associated with the deaths were depressive symptoms in the children and conflicts between the children's parents and medical personnel treating the children. The evidence suggested that the psychological features of the cases that resulted in death were not due only to the severity of the disease. More psychological disturbance was noted both in the children who died and in their families.

Gastrointestinal Disorders

Gastrointestinal disorders are abnormalities of the digestive system. The number of television commercials for stomach remedies clearly indicates that many people have trouble with their digestive processes. One such disorder, **diarrhea**, has plagued troops going into battle for as long as wars have been fought. Scientists still do not know exactly how emotional processes are linked to pathological changes in the gastrointestinal tract. There is evidence that anger and hostility increase stomach acidity and that gastric symptoms commonly follow worry, business reverses, family quarrels, and other emotionally disturbing experiences.

Many studies of stress and gastrointestinal disease relate to **ulcers,** which are open sores in the skin or on some mucous membrane such as the lining of the stomach or intestine. Ulcerated tissue disintegrates, and the sores often discharge pus. Peptic ulcers include ulcers in the stomach (gastric ulcers) and in the first part of the small intestine (duodenal ulcers). The incidence of peptic ulcers ebbs and rises. It rose in the 1950s but has declined recently—a seeming paradox if our society is, as many people believe, more stressful now than it was in the past (Murray, 1982).

Cases of peptic ulcer often highlight the interacting roles of a number of relevant variables. The following case of duodenal ulcers in one member of a pair of twins is of particular interest.

John M., an identical twin, developed a series of severe ulcer symptoms, including bleeding, when he was 46 years old. His condition deteriorated to the point where he required hospitalization. He was described as passive, shy, dependent, and anxious. His wife had had several near-psychotic episodes, and John's ulcer symptoms developed about the time she

FIGURE 7–12
Mean daily scores for clinical evidence of wheezing during each period in the Denver asthma study. (Reprinted by permission of Elsevier Science Publishing Co., Inc.; from K. Purcell, K. Brady, H. Schall, J. Muser, L. Molk, N. Gordon, and J. Means, The effect of asthma in children of experimental separation from the family, *Psychosomatic Medicine, 31*, pp. 144–164. Copyright © 1969 by the American Psychosomatic Society, Inc.)

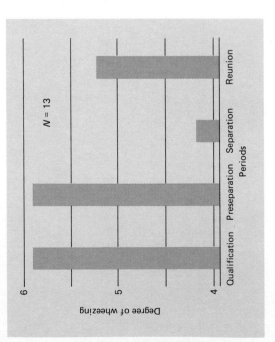

was experiencing a particularly frightening breakdown. She was having an affair with another man and had threatened to kill her children.

John's twin brother Fred was studied because some clinical workers have speculated that psychophysiological disorders may be attributed partly to hereditary features. As in many cases of identical twins, Fred's personality was remarkably similar to John's; he was also shy and dependent. However, he was completely free of ulcer symptoms. The twins had been inseparable until they were 25, when Fred met his future wife; John married three years later. The major difference in the lives of the twins after age 25 was their marriages. Because John, the ulcer victim, had married a disturbed woman, he was forced to live under great tension, which increased his anxiety level. Fred, on the other hand, had married a motherly woman who managed the family affairs dependably. The ulcer-free identical twin had apparently found a psychosocial situation in which his passivity and dependency needs could be gratified, while his brother found only frustration in his marriage.

—(Gotschalk, 1978)

Although John's case does not seem to support a genetic interpretation of duodenal ulcers, the situation is, in fact, equivocal. Ulcers occur mainly in people with high levels of blood pepsinogen (a gastric secretion). Both John and Fred had high blood pepsinogen levels. If they had swapped wives, John might have been cured while Fred got the ulcers. Thus, heredity may be a predisposing factor in ulcer cases, but the level of stress experienced by the individual may determine whether structural damage actually occurs.

In many instances it is impossible to say that psychological stress is the only cause of a physical problem. Yet the high blood pepsinogen levels of both twins and the contrast between their social situations seem consistent with the hypothesis that life experiences contribute to chronic physiological reactions that result in tissue damage. Studies of adolescents have shown that a recent separation or loss is often associated with the onset of peptic ulcers in predisposed individuals (Ackerman and others, 1981).

Somatoform Disorders

So far we have been dealing with psychological and social factors associated with actual diagnosed physical conditions. Many of the bodily complaints that physi-

cians are asked to treat suggest physical pathology, but no actual impairment can be found. Although failure to diagnose a case medically might be due to a doctor's lack of knowledge or to a faulty laboratory test, in a large group of cases psychological rather than physiological factors are responsible for the symptoms. These cases, which do not seem to be produced consciously, are characterized in DSM-III-R as **somatoform disorders.** This category includes both somatization and conversion disorders (to be discussed shortly) and psychogenic pain disorders and hypochondriasis.

Severe prolonged pain either without organic symptoms or greatly in excess of what might be expected to accompany organic symptoms is classified as a **psychogenic pain disorder.** There is often a temporal relationship between the occurrence of an actual, threatened, or fantasized interpersonal loss and complaints of pain. The complaints may be used to evoke social responses, such as attention, from others. **Hypochondriasis** is diagnosed if a person shows an unrealistic fear of disease in spite of reassurance that his or her social or occupational functioning is not impaired. Hypochondriacs have an obsessive preoccupation and concern with the condition of their bodily organs and continually worry about their health (see Figure 7–13). They tend to misunderstand the nature of the significance of physiological activity and to exaggerate symptoms when they occur (Kellner, 1987). This is a physician's account of one of his diary-keeping hypochondriacal patients (Burnside, 1987, p. 1802):

Ask ten doctors about their reaction to patients who come to the office with a diary of their medical problems and eleven will groan.

It takes a fair amount of body focus to make someone want to record it on paper. For some, I guess, it fills empty hours. Maybe it's a way of fighting against other signals that suggest he or she is unimportant. If it's on paper it must be true and it must be significant. Rarely is a diary an aid to bad memory. If anything, folks who record symptoms have extraordinary memories. The importance of the information is inversely proportional to the length of the diary.

Harold Yocum kept the most extensive diary of any patient I have ever seen. Harold was a dapper little guy, standing perhaps five feet four. A local retail clerk, he was always impeccably dressed: sharp creases on his suit trousers (always a suit), carefully knotted ties, handkerchief in the breast pocket just so, highly polished wing tips, carefully clipped nails, and sharply parted hair with the long sweep over the bald spot.

Harold was single and I could never get much social history from him—perhaps he didn't have much social

"THE DOCTOR WILL EXPECT TO HEAR MY SYMPTOMS."

history. He had some college education and had worked as a clerk for many years, but he never chatted about personal activities, friends, or hobbies. Efforts to engage him in such conversation made him uncomfortable, so after a few visits, I stopped trying. Indeed, after a few visits there was no opportunity to try. We had to review the diary. . . . He began to include more and more in his diary—time and dose of medication, general feelings, minor aches and pains, food-stuffs consumed, coffee and cola intake. He even developed his own stress scale and described evacuations in great detail—time, quantity, color.

Soon the volume of material was too much for his spiral-bound notebook and he began to bring in laboriously typed reports.

Somatization Disorder

Somatization disorders are marked by multiple somatic complaints that are recurrent or chronic. This condition is often referred to as *Briquet's syndrome* because a physician by that name described it in detail in 1859. The most common complaints are headaches, fatigue, heart palpitations, fainting spells, nausea, vomiting, abdominal pains, bowel troubles, allergies, and menstrual and sexual problems. With this wide assortment of complaints, it is not surprising that somatizing patients are constantly going to the doctor, changing doctors, and undergoing surgery. Figure 7–14 compares the frequency of major surgical procedures for pa-

tients who were classified as somatizers and for normal controls.

Patients with somatization disorders believe that they are sickly, provide long and detailed histories in support of their belief, and take large quantities of medicines. Almost always, the chronic multiple complaints of somatizers are accompanied by a characteristic personality pattern and by difficulties in social relationships. They share many of the features of histrionic personality disorders, including a self-centered attitude and exaggerated expressions of emotion. Anxiety and depression are common features, as is manipulativeness, which may take the form of suicide threats and attempts. Somatizers impress people as being immature and overly excitable.

The complaints in somatization disorders are usually presented in a dramatic, vague, or exaggerated way. Somatizers tend to use vivid images in describing events and their reactions to them. For example:

- I wake up in the morning stiff as a board.
- My heart felt as if iron bands were being tightened around it.
- I throw up every half hour.
- I can't even take liquids.
- I feel as weak as a cat.
- I really can't take it much longer.

Somatization disorders usually have long medical histories that go back at least to early adulthood. They

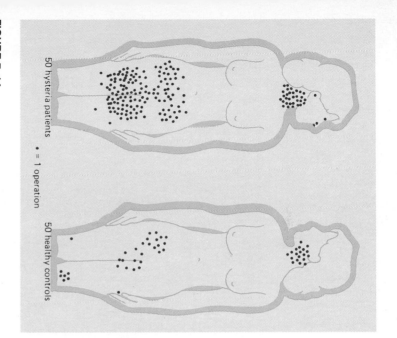

50 hysteria patients • = 1 operation 50 healthy controls

FIGURE 7-14
The complaints of somatizing patients often lead to unnecessary surgery. These two figures compare the number and location of major surgical procedures in 50 somatizing patients and 50 control subjects. Three times as much body tissue was removed from the somatizing patients as from the controls. (Woodruff, Goodwin, and Guze, 1974, p. 67)

seem to occur mainly in women; approximately 1 percent of women have the condition. It is not uncommon for a family to have more than one somatizer. Since people who are classified as having a somatizing disorder tend to be suggestible, the high prevalence of the disorder in certain families may reflect the influence of a somatizing parent (usually the mother) rather than heredity. The vagueness of somatization complaints makes it difficult to do good research on the disorder (for example, the researcher is frequently left to wonder about possible organic causes of the symptoms).

Conversion Disorders

People with **conversion disorders** report that they have lost part or all of some basic bodily function. The disturbance does not seem to be under voluntary control and cannot be explained in terms of the principles of medical science. Paralysis, blindness, deafness, and difficulty in walking are among the symptoms reported by these patients. The onset of symptoms in conversion disorders often follows a stressful experience and may be quite sudden. Psychodynamic theorists believe that the symptom represents an underlying psychological conflict.

Conversion symptoms seem to be naive inventions developed without regard for the actual facts of anatomy. In the case of **glove anesthesia**, for example, the individual may be unable to feel anything on one hand, although the arm has normal sensation. This is anatomically impossible. The sensory nerve supply to this part of the body is organized so that glove anesthesia could not be a result of a neurological disorder.

Although conversion symptoms often seem to appear for no obvious reason, they can frequently be traced to specific precipitating events. Complicating the task of diagnosing conversion disorders is the fact that at times they cannot easily be distinguished from somatically rooted symptoms. One of the characteristic features of conversion disorders has been termed *la belle indifference*. Whereas the individual may experience intense anxiety in other areas of life, his or her lack of concern about what seems to be an incapacitating physical disturbance is remarkable (Ford and Folks, 1985).

Clinical conversion cases usually involve a single disturbance during a given period. Different bodily sites might be affected in subsequent episodes. As mentioned earlier, the episodes tend to follow frustrating or challenging experiences. The symptoms often allow the person to escape from the situation through physical incapacity. When the pressures of these experiences wane, the physical symptoms weaken. Secondary gain may also occur when the person derives something from a physical symptom (such as attention, affection, or a pension) that he or she might not get otherwise.

Because histrionic tendencies and excitability are characteristic of people who have these bodily reactions, their symptoms often tend to be highly dramatic as well as incapacitating. The drama is perhaps most intense in cases of **group hysteria**, outbreaks of conversion symptoms among people who live or work together (see Box 7-2). The mass outbreak of hysteria is a vivid illustration of what social psychologists call group contagion.

Factitious Disorders and Malingering

Although somatoform disorders and problems that have traditionally been described as psychophysiological (for example, asthma and peptic ulcers) are different in a number of respects, they have in common the fact that the individual assumes the role of a patient—someone who receives attention and care. Another group of con-

BOX 7-2
Group Hysteria among Schoolchildren

Two hundred twenty-four elementary-school students assembled in their school auditorium in Norwood, Mass., on the morning of May 21, 1979. The program, a play by the sixth graders honoring their graduation, marked the last formal gathering of the student body for the year. The performance came to an abrupt halt. A sixth-grade boy, a class leader, experienced dizziness, fell from the stage, lacerated his chin, and bled profusely. As a few teachers assisted the boy, several students became ill, and their symptoms began to spread rapidly. First, weakness, dizziness, chills, and faintness developed in four girls and one boy, all sixth graders. Then four more sixth-grade girls complained of the same symptoms. As more and more children became ill, teachers hurriedly dismissed the afflicted students to the auditorium floor and covered them with blankets. Alarmed and bewildered by these events, school officials summoned the fire department. The firemen, suspecting an environmental contaminant, ordered immediate evacuation of the building.

Authorities then moved the stricken children to one area of the school grounds. Sirens of approaching vehicles intensified the chaos. Once police arrived, they directed ambulances to transport the children to a local hospital. Evacuation of the building and isolation of the afflicted students, however, failed to contain the spread of illness; the symptoms struck a new child every few minutes. The illness spread so rapidly that the number of afflicted children exhausted the capacity of the available vehicles. With 34 of the more severely ill already

ditions that are characterized by the same feature is **factitious disorders.** However, in these conditions physical and psychological symptoms are voluntarily self-induced by the patient. They may involve a total fabrication or an exaggeration of a preexisting condition.

In a factitious disorder the only apparent goal is the desire to assume the role of patient. The person often has a history of uncontrollable lying, demands for attention from professional people, and dramatic accounts of vague pains. Classifying a set of symptoms as factitious may be quite difficult. The dramatic way in which the patient presents his or her problems usually arouses suspicion; however, many individuals with this disorder have managed to gather quite a bit of medical information and, as a consequence, may be good enough actors to make their symptoms seem credible. Factitious disorders typically begin during early

adulthood and are often stimulated by hospitalization for a genuine physical problem. Because of their dramatically presented but vague symptoms, individuals with factitious disorders undergo frequent hospitalizations during which unnecessary surgery may be performed. Factitious disorders are more common among men than among women.

The term **Munchausen syndrome** refers to an extreme type of factitious disorder that is marked by repeated, knowing simulation of disease for the sole purpose of obtaining medical attention. A patient with this syndrome may travel great distances to appear at hospitals with dramatic and plausible, yet false, histories that convince physicians and staff members that he or she is suffering from an acute illness. The syndrome is named after Baron von Munchausen, an eighteenth-century German cavalry officer who became legendary for con-

200　　CHAPTER 7　Psychological Factors and Physical Symptoms

hospitalized, the hospital dispatched a team of physicians and nurses to treat another 40 or 50 mildly symptomatic children lying on the lawn. As the physicians examined and reassured these patients, their symptoms began to subside. Within four hours of its precipitous beginning, the epidemic was over. . . .

During the outbreak, rumors spread rapidly throughout the school and the surrounding community. For example, two priests arrived to attend the families and friends of the "deceased" as a result of a rumor that 12 children had died of food poisoning. Another rumor circulated among the students that the boy who lacerated his chin underwent open-heart surgery when hospitalized. Mosquito spray, toxic fumes, gas leaks, water contamination, infectious agents, and psychological influences included some of the causes of the epidemic proffered by both professional and laymen. As the epidemic subsided, the more exaggerated rumors subsided. The cause of the outbreak, however, remained controversial in the community; one segment of the population thought "it was only in their minds," others insisted "it was something harmful in the air." (Small and Nicholi, 1982, p. 721)

Although most instances of group hysteria are treated somewhat like curiosities, the Norwood incident was investigated from a research standpoint. The research had to do with two questions: Were the hysterical symptoms related to events in the current lives of the children? Were the symptoms related to events experienced earlier in their lives?

One of the striking features of the Norwood incident was that the sixth grade had by far the highest number of hysterical cases (most of them girls). The researchers (Small and Nicholi, 1982) found that

1. A few days prior to the epidemic, local newspapers had reported that the school principal, who was re-

spected and admired by both children and parents, would be transferred to another school. Many of the families had become disturbed about his transfer and signed a petition protesting his departure.

2. The epidemic began during the sixth graders' play, which marked their impending graduation and departure from school.

3. The sixth graders had planned a camping trip to follow graduation; those attending would sleep away from home for an entire week, many for the first time.

Thus, the sixth graders experienced or were about to experience the loss of their principal, separation from familiar school surroundings, and an exciting trip that included a new experience for many. Most children take such experiences in their stride. Did other features exist in the backgrounds of the affected children that, within the current climate of loss and change, made them more vulnerable to symptoms of mass hysteria?

By administering questionnaires to parents and children, the researchers were able to make some valuable comparisons between the children who required hospitalization and those who did not. They found that 47 percent of the hospitalized children had lost a parent, whereas only 10 percent of those who were not hospitalized had, and that 74 percent of the hospitalized children had experienced a death in the family, whereas only 39 percent of the nonhospitalized children had had such an experience.

The Norwood epidemic had several characteristics that are typical of group hysteria, particularly psychological stress, which in this case took the form of anticipated loss. In addition, there was a significant link between previous loss and hysterical symptoms. Although this does not prove that early loss causes hysterical symptoms, it does suggest that such loss may be an important vulnerability factor in hysteria.

cocting elaborate lies. Patients with this syndrome tell incredible tales about their medical histories. They also fake symptoms; for example, they may pretend to be in pain, put blood in a urine sample, or manipulate a thermometer to create an impression of fever. Sometimes they go even further, inflicting real injury on themselves by burning, cutting, taking dangerous drugs, or injecting foreign material into their veins. Often they persuade doctors to perform unnecessary surgery. They may spend most of their lives moving from one hospital to another, trying to be admitted. Once in a hospital, they refuse to comply with its rules and make constant demands for attention.

A particularly disturbing variant of Munchausen syndrome is one in which a mother produces symptoms of disease in her child and then presents the child for treatment. The mother's concern may be convincing be-

cause she herself feels a need to be cared for; it is as though she regards the child's body as an extension of her own. The child goes along with the mother because the relationship is so close and intense and the activity so exciting.

Having a factitious disorder is not the same thing as **malingering**. People with factitious disorders simply crave attention and want to be taken care of. Malingerers, on the other hand, seek medical care and hospitalization in order to achieve some specific goal such as compensation, a disability pension, or evasion of the police. Whereas multiple complaints and hospitalizations seem almost a continuous pattern in factitious disorders, malingering often ends abruptly when the patient gets what he or she wants. People with factitious disorders seem incapable of stopping their lying and manufacturing of symptoms, whereas malingering is an entirely conscious process. However, both of these conditions are self-induced, and both increase in response to high levels of stress.

Distinguishing factitious disorder or malingering from other conditions can be difficult. The judgment that a particular symptom is under voluntary control occasionally is made by excluding all other possible causes. Distinguishing between a factitious disorder and malingering also poses problems. When the clinician is not fully aware of the particular purpose for which the malingerer manufactures his or her symptoms, the changes of misdiagnosis increase. An act of malingering might, under certain circumstances, be considered adaptive (for example, when a prisoner of war fakes an illness), but factitious disorders are almost always seen in people with severe, lifelong personality disturbances.

Study Outline

CONCEPTS OF PSYCHOLOGICAL, SOCIAL, AND BODILY INTERACTION

1. During the 1930s and 1940s the **psychosomatic hypothesis,** which held that the blocking of emotional expression could lead to physical symptoms, became popular. Many psychotherapists supported the theory of **specificity,** believing that specific emotional conflicts and stresses were associated with particular physical conditions. Some adhered to the **organ-susceptibility** theory, believing that under stress a person's body would break down at its weakest point.
2. Research has shown that emotional tension influences the autonomic nervous system and the endocrine glands. Hans Selye uses the term **general adaptation syndrome** to describe the pattern of animals' reactions to continued stress. Similar increases in hormone secretions have been found in humans.
3. Contemporary clinicians emphasize the **biopsychosocial model**—they consider illness to be caused by the interaction of psychological states with social and biological variables. Through a mechanism called **homeostasis** the organism mobilizes itself to restore equilibrium in the face of environmental changes, challenges, and constraints.

PSYCHOLOGICAL FACTORS THAT AFFECT HEALTH

1. There is a two-way connection between psychological factors and physical health. Psychological factors that play a role in physical illness include inability to adapt to new situations, inability to handle and express strong emotions, inability to interpret the environment correctly, and inability to form close personal relationships. In addition to temperament and personality, community and social factors, job demands, biological predispositions, and other factors interact to affect physical functioning.
2. Many nonbiological factors affect longevity. They include social isolation, chronic loneliness, and particularly the loss or absence of a loved one. People who are characterized by **psychological hardiness**—have personality characteristics that make them more resistant to stress and less susceptible to illness than those who do not share this trait.

BEHAVIORAL MEDICINE AND HEALTH PSYCHOLOGY

1. **Behavioral medicine** is concerned with helping people adopt more healthful living habits and with improving the delivery of health care. **Health psychology** seeks to prevent disease by strengthening behaviors that contribute to good health.
2. One area in which the behavioral and biomedical sciences are involved is people's awareness of their symptoms and accuracy in reporting them. Another example is the types of information given to patients and the way it is presented.
3. **Biofeedback** is used in behavioral medicine to give people control over functions that were thought to be involuntary, such as blood pressure and heart rate.
4. Animal and other studies have shown that stress, particularly with lack of social support, can lower the immune system's resistance to disease.

PSYCHOPHYSIOLOGICAL DISORDERS

1. The term **psychophysiological disorders** refers to physical conditions in which psychologically meaningful events are closely related to bodily symptoms. They include cardiovascular disorders, cancer, headaches, allergies, gastrointestinal disorders, and rheumatoid arthritis, as well as somatoform disorders, factitious disorders, and malingering.
2. There is growing evidence that psychological and social factors play a role in **coronary heart disease.** A significant factor in heart attacks is stress. Life-style factors, societal and cultural differences, and occupation also play substantial roles, as does separation from or loss of a loved one.

3. Some researchers have concluded that there is a heart attack-prone personality. People with this personality type tend to operate under high pressure and to be very demanding both of themselves and of others. They also show high levels of physiological reactivity.

4. **Hypertension** or high blood pressure has been shown to be associated with prolonged emotional arousal. Relaxation and biofeedback seem to be effective in reducing blood pressure.

5. Stress and personality are among the psychological factors that may contribute to cancer. It is thought that people who have difficulty dealing with strong feelings are more prone to develop cancers than those who vent their emotions. Depression also seems to be associated with cancer.

6. The exact cause of headaches is unclear, but they often seem to occur in response to stress.

7. Chronic allergies such as asthma are often accompanied by intense emotional states. Among the psychological and situational factors that seem to worsen asthmatic attacks are panic and fear.

8. **Gastrointestinal disorders** such as diarrhea and ulcers appear to be caused by a number of interacting factors, including psychological stress. There is also evidence that many victims of rheumatoid arthritis experience significant psychological stress.

9. **Somatoform disorders** are disorders that take the form of bodily complaints without actual physical pa-

thology. They include psychogenic pain disorders, hypochondrias, somatization, and conversion disorders.

10. Severe prolonged pain either without organic symptoms or greatly in excess of what might be expected to accompany organic symptoms is classified as a **psychogenic pain disorder. Hypochondriasis** is diagnosed if a person shows an unrealistic fear of disease in spite of reassurance that his or her functioning is not impaired.

11. **Somatization disorders** are marked by recurrent, chronic somatic complaints that are usually presented in a dramatic, vague, or exaggerated way. The complaints of somatizers tend to be accompanied by a characteristic personality pattern and by difficulties in social relationships.

12. People with **conversion disorders** report that they have lost part or all of some basic bodily function. The disturbance does not seem to be under voluntary control and cannot be explained in terms of the principles of medical science. Conversion episodes tend to follow frustrating or challenging experiences and allow the person to escape from the situation through physical incapacity.

13. **Factitious disorders** are voluntarily self-induced by a person for the sole purpose of assuming the role of patient. **Malingerers,** on the other hand, seek medical care and hospitalization in order to achieve some specific goal such as compensation or a disability pension.

CHAPTER 8

Sexual Variations
and Disorders

Pierre Bonnard, *Man and Woman*, 1900. Oil on canvas, 46 × 28 1/2". Musée National d'Art Moderne, Paris. (Photo: Art Resource)

OBJECTIVES FOR CHAPTER EIGHT:

To learn:

1. The different ways information is gathered about sexual behavior and the kinds of information gathered by each method

2. The types of sexual dysfunctions and the therapeutic approaches used to treat them

3. The varieties of sexual victimization and the effects on the victim

To understand:

1. The range of variations in sexual preference and how they may develop

2. The meaning and implications of gender identity

CHANGING VIEWS OF SEXUAL BEHAVIOR
GATHERING OBJECTIVE INFORMATION ABOUT SEXUAL BEHAVIOR
Surveys
Observational Research
Case Studies
Experimental Findings
SEXUAL VARIATIONS
Homosexuality
Bisexuality
How Sexual Preference Develops
SEXUAL DYSFUNCTION
Types of Sexual Dysfunction
The Treatment of Sexual Dysfunction
The Effectiveness of Sex Therapy
GENDER IDENTITY DISORDER
Childhood Problems of Gender Identity
Transsexualism
THE PARAPHILIAS
Fetishism
Transvestism
Sexual Sadism and Masochism
Autoerotic Asphyxia
Voyeurism
Exhibitionism
Obscene Telephone Calls
Pedophilia
Perspectives on the Paraphilias
Treatment of the Paraphilias
SEXUAL VICTIMIZATION
Child Sexual Abuse
Rape
Response to Victimization
Male Rape Victims
STUDY OUTLINE

In the afternoon, viewers may be titillated with heavy breathing and heavy hissing; at night, stronger allusions to more intimate acts prevail. (Greenberg and others, 1981, p. 88)

Every weekday, 6 hours per day, the three major U.S. television networks present a dozen or more soap operas that are watched by 5 to 10 million people. During each hour of viewing time, petting, intercourse, and other sexual acts are referred to at least twice in the average program. Shorter 20-minute programs have an even higher frequency, averaging 1.5 references during each segment. These sexual references run the gamut from petting to intercourse to rape. Most often, unmarried characters are involved. The cartoon in Figure 8–1 illustrates the content of a typical soap opera.

Surprisingly, even everyday foods like Graham crackers and Kellogg's corn flakes had their origins in sexual concerns (Money, 1984). The Reverend Sylvester Graham, author of "A Lecture to Young Men" (1834), was concerned about the effects of masturbation, sexual fantasies, and lust on health. He developed Graham crackers as the ultimate food to discourage sexual feelings. For similar reasons John H. Kellogg, a prominent abdominal surgeon, developed corn flakes as part of his doctrine of diet, exercise, and abstinence from sex. Kellogg believed so strongly in the healthful effects of sexual abstinence that his own marriage was never consummated. Corn flakes were developed as a food that would extinguish sexual desire. These ideas, which focus on the bad effects of semen loss, especially through masturbation, and of sexual thoughts and fantasies, can be traced all the way back to the ancient Greeks.

cant events in childhood. Although some aspects of his theories continue to be controversial, Freud, more than any other individual, stimulated a rethinking of the role of sexual feelings in development.

Havelock Ellis was another important influence on views about sexuality. Ellis wrote books and articles that focused on the range of sexual behavior that occurred in the lives of ordinary people. He recognized that it was common for both men and women to masturbate, and emphasized the psychological rather than physical causes of many sexual problems. It was Ellis who suggested that objective surveys be taken to find out what happens in ordinary sexual relationships. This useful suggestion was not acted upon until the 1940s.

FIGURE 8–1
Journal of Communication, 31 (Summer 1981), p. 89, Copyright © Arthur Asa Berger.

Changing Views of Sexual Behavior

Although sexual behavior has never ceased to be a topic of great interest to many people, over the centuries ideas about sexuality and sexual deviance have undergone drastic changes. During the fourth century Æ.C. the Greeks regarded sex as a pleasurable part of nature, to be enjoyed with partners of either sex. This open view of sexuality contrasts sharply with the prevailing view during the period between the fall of Rome and the fifteenth century, when church authorities were obsessed with the notion of sex as a sin. During that period many thousands of Europeans were tortured into confessing erotic encounters with the devil, after which they were publicly burned alive. Entire villages in southern Germany and Switzerland were exterminated in this way.

The price that women had to pay to be rescued from this fate was to renounce all sexual or erotic thoughts. By the mid-nineteenth century, the idea of women as morally pure, erotically apathetic, and sexually inert had reached a peak. Women were expected to engage in sexual behavior only as a way of satisfying their husbands and carrying out their obligation to become mothers. Despite these expectations, however, pornography, prostitution, and venereal disease flourished during the nineteenth century.

Some brave souls were willing to risk their professional careers to discuss the role of sexuality in human behavior. One of these individuals, Sigmund Freud, used material gathered from many patients to illustrate the negative effects of a repressive view of sexuality. Freud traced the sexual deviations of adults to signifi-

Gathering Objective Information About Sexual behavior

Scientific information about sexual behavior can be gathered in several ways. Among these are surveys, observation, and experiments.

Surveys

Kinsey's Survey Research

Most of the information about the frequency of different sexual practices comes from survey research. Alfred Kinsey was one of the pioneers in this approach to the study of sexual behavior.

In 1938 Kinsey, a biologist, was asked to take charge of a new course on marriage at Indiana University and to give lectures on the biological aspects of sex and marriage. As he prepared for the course, Kinsey was amazed to find that there were only a few statistical studies on sexual behavior and no scientific data that he could pass on to students when they asked such questions as "Is masturbation harmful?" or "Is homosexuality abnormal?" In his class one night he stated that no one knew the answers to these questions because of a lack of information. He asked whether his students would be willing to submit their case histories so that scientists could discover enough about human sexual behavior to be able to answer some of these questions. They agreed and this was the beginning of several important research studies and ultimately of the Institute for Sex Research at Indiana University.

Kinsey believed that human sexual behavior could be studied objectively. To find out about people's sex lives, he interviewed them about a wide variety of sexual practices. In each interview he asked hundreds of exceedingly personal questions in an accepting and matter-of-fact manner. One of Kinsey's colleagues, the psychologist Wardell Pomeroy, had provided this account of Kinsey's approach to interviewing.

We asked our questions directly without hesitancy or apology. Kinsey correctly pointed out that if we were uncertain or embarrassed in our questioning we could not expect to get anything but a corresponding response. Unlike previous researchers, we did not say "touching yourself" when we meant masturbation, or "relations with other persons" when we meant "sexual intercourse" was intended. "Evasive terms invite dishonest answers," was Kinsey's dictum. We also never asked whether a subject had ever engaged in a particular activity; we assumed that everyone had engaged in everything, and so we began by asking when he had first done it. Thus the subject who might want to deny an experience had a heavier burden placed on him, and since he knew from the way the question was asked that it would not surprise us if he had done it, there seemed little reason to deny it.

—(Pomeroy, 1972, p. 112)

Although change in public attitudes and legal codes rarely comes about because of a single person or event, it would be difficult to overestimate Kinsey's contribution to knowledge about sexual behavior. In addition to promoting scientific research on human sexuality, Kinsey influenced public attitudes (see Figure 8–2) through his objective reporting of results showing that sexual behaviors that had been considered unusual or abnormal were in fact widely practiced. The following letter, one of many that Kinsey received, suggests that many people experience a sense of relief at discovering that their behavior was not as unusual as they had thought.

I am a professional man slightly past middle age and have three grown-up children. I wish that I and others could have read your book years ago. With the exception of homosexualism, for which I have never had the least desire, and extra-marital relations, I believe I have indulged more or less in all of the main class perversions, if they were such, which you describe in your book.

As a result of such episodes I have always felt that I was a moral pervert, a pariah or outcast and thereby developed a degree of inferiority complex which has been a determent [sic] to me in my profession.

Now when I find such a high percentage of others in the same boat, I have been mentally relieved and now can hold my head a bit higher and meet life on a surer basis. I am offering no brief or extenuation for this moot conduct except that the primary urge was more than my inhibitions could withstand. I am

deeply grateful to you for presenting to the world facts that are unquestionable.

—(Pomeroy, 1972, p. 277)

The first Kinsey Report (Kinsey and others, 1948) presented a detailed statistical picture for the sexual behavior of 5,300 American males ranging in age from 10 to 90. Five years later a second report (Kinsey and others, 1953) provided similar information based on interviews with almost 6,000 women. Reports on homosexuality were issued in 1978 and 1981 (Bell and Weinberg, 1978; Bell and others, 1981).

Although there is no question about Kinsey's pioneering contribution in gathering data about sexual practices, some of Kinsey's critics have noted that the sample of people he interviewed was disproportionately white, educated, well off, and midwestern and hence was not really representative of the general population. Kinsey was aware of this problem, but he believed that an effort to obtain a random sample in this highly controversial area was doomed to failure. He tried to compensate for sampling bias by interviewing a large number of subjects (12,000 in the first two studies alone) and using what he called 100-percent sampling, by which he meant that he tried to interview virtually all the members of groups, such as clubs and college classes, that agreed to be interviewed. Although neither of these approaches made his sample more representative, Kinsey's findings have been supported by data collected through other means.

Over the years since Kinsey's surveys, the proportion of college-age males and females reporting that they are sexually active has changed. Not only has there been a great increase in the proportion of members of each sex who report having had intercourse, but the proportion of females has increased much more rapidly than that of males. Before 1970, about twice as many men as women reported having had intercourse. Since 1970, the proportions of men and women have been nearly equal (Darling and others, 1984). Figure 8–3 shows the changes since the beginning of the century in the reports of coital relationships among college-age students.

Another change has been in the increase in and acceptance of oral–genital sexual behavior among college-students. In one survey about oral sex among college women, about two-thirds of the respondents reported that they had experienced it and most reported feeling no guilt about it. The women were just as likely to have performed oral sex as to have received it (Herold and Way, 1983). Kinsey (Kinsey and others, 1953) had found that oral sex was considered more intimate than intercourse and seldom occurred until intercourse had been experienced. Herold and Way (1983) found just the reverse. In their study, two-thirds of the women who were still virgins had experienced oral sex. This

Richard Dellenback

FIGURE 8–2
The Kinsey surveys provided the first scientific view of the variety of sexual behaviors practiced in contemporary life. Probably the most valuable functions of the surveys were making the study of sexual practices respectable and correcting a great deal of guilt-producing misinformation. After the publication of his book on sexual behavior in the human male, Kinsey was invited to address large audiences throughout the country. He is shown here speaking to an overflow crowd at the University of California at Berkeley, 1952. Reprinted by permission of the Kinsey Institute for Research in Sex, Gender, and Reproduction, Inc.

suggests a change in attitudes regarding the level of intimacy represented by oral sex as compared to intercourse. The sequence of oral sex and coitus may be related to religious conviction (Mahoney, 1980). In more religious students, oral sex preceded coitus; in less religious students, the order was reversed. This suggests that vaginal virginity is a concern of highly religious students and that they therefore feel less guilty about oral sex than about coitus.

Other Surveys

Finding a representative sample—one in which the important characteristics of age, educational level, ethnicity, and socioeconomic status match those of the larger population that the investigators would like to study—is always difficult. In a large-scale survey commissioned by the Playboy Foundation in the 1970s (Hunt, 1974), the sample was obtained by randomly selecting phone numbers from telephone book listings in 24 cities. Only

20 percent of the potential respondents agreed to partic-ipate in the survey. Surveys that appear in magazines are even less representative of the general population. They produce large numbers of responses, but the total rep-resents only a tiny proportion of the magazine's reader-ship. Again, therefore, the sample is not representative of the population (Brecher, 1983).

Another way of obtaining data is illustrated by a large study by Blumstein and Schwartz (1983). These investigators recruited couples mainly through newspa-per ads and radio and television announcements that de-scribed the study and asked for volunteers. They sent out about 11,000 questionnaires and obtained a return rate of about 55 percent. In addition to 4,300 married and unmarried heterosexual couples, almost 1,000 gay male couples and nearly 800 lesbian couples completed questionnaires. An example of the results is shown in Figure 8-4. This study has many positive elements: a large, diverse national sample; a research design that al-lowed for comparisons among different types of cou-ples; and a questionnaire that gathered data about nonsexual as well as sexual aspects of relationships. However, this study, too, is not very representative of the general population.

The truthfulness of subjects' answers to any kind of questionnaire is open to question, and this is a par-ticular problem in sensitive areas such as sexual behav-ior. Questionnaires have an advantage over interviews in that the respondent may feel less embarrassed. How-ever, in either case subjects may brag or exaggerate their sexual experiences or not admit to behaviors that they find embarrassing. These possible sources of inaccuracy must be kept in mind when interpreting survey results.

FIGURE 8-3
Percent of college-age males and females who reported having had sexual intercourse. The data are based on selected studies from 1900 to 1980. (Adapted from Darling, Kallen, and Van Dusen, 1984, p. 388)

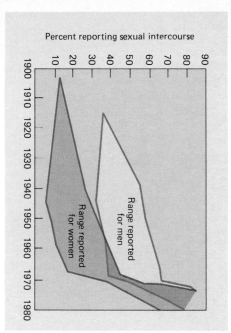

Observational Research

Through the Kinsey study and other surveys, we know a lot more about people's sexual behaviors than we used to. Through observational studies, we know a lot more about the body's responses to those behaviors. The best-known observational studies were carried out by the gynecologist William Masters and the behavior sci-entist Virginia Johnson. Over a 10-year period Masters and Johnson (1966, 1970) studied the sexual responses of 694 men and women under controlled laboratory conditions. They have been largely responsible for giv-ing the laboratory study of human sexual behavior and

FIGURE 8-4
Frequency of sexual intercourse reported by individuals in different types of sexual relationships for varying lengths of time. Adaptation of Fig. 27, p. 196, from *American Couples* by Philip Blumstein, Ph.D., and Pepper Schwartz, Ph.D. Copyright © 1983 by Philip Blumstein, Ph.D., and Pepper W. Schwartz, Ph.D. By permission of William Morrow and Company, Inc.

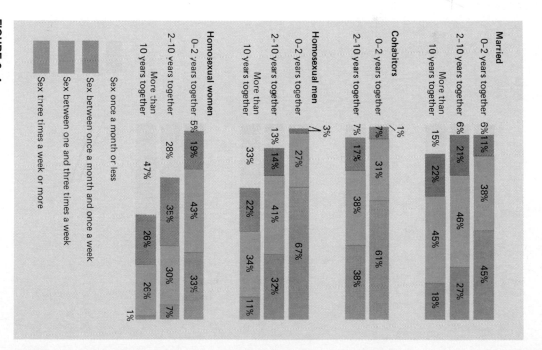

the treatment of sexual dysfunctions scientific credibility and respectability.

In their research Masters and Johnson observed volunteer subjects who engaged in sexual activity to the point of orgasm while sophisticated measuring instruments monitored their bodily reactions. The study monitored more than 10,000 orgasms brought about by masturbation and intercourse. Masters and Johnson carried out much of their research on volunteers from their university community. First, volunteer couples were interviewed to ensure their psychological stability. Before the measurement sessions began, they were asked to have a practice session—to have sexual activity in the laboratory without observers present and without being hooked up to any equipment. Once the actual sessions began, a variety of sexual activities were measured: self-masturbation, genital stimulation by the partner, oral—genital stimulation, and intercourse. Most of the subjects were studied many times to identify variability in their sexual response.

On the basis of their findings, Masters and Johnson described a four-stage pattern of sexual response for both men and women. The initial **excitement** response to sexual stimulation is marked by vaginal lubrication in the female and penile erection in the male. In the male, this is followed by nipple erection, a thickening of the vaginal walls, and a flattening and elevation of the external genitalia. In the male, there is a slight increase in the size and elevation of the testes.

During the second or **plateau** stage, sexual excitement is reflected in increased heart rate, perspiration, and muscle tension. The male's testes increase in size by about 50 percent and are pulled up high in the scrotum. In the female, the tissues surrounding the bottom third of the vagina swell, reducing the diameter of the vaginal opening by up to 50 percent. The clitoris retracts under the hood that covers it.

In the third stage, **orgasm,** that male's penis begins to throb in rhythmic contractions. Semen collects in the urethral bulb, and during ejaculation, contractions of the bulb and penis project the semen out of the penis. In females, orgasm involves rhythmic muscular contractions of the lower third of the vagina and the uterus. Other muscles, such as the anal sphincter, may also contract in a rhythmic fashion. In both males and females, muscles throughout the body contract and there is a temporary state of high physiological arousal.

In males, orgasm is followed by the **resolution** phase, in which physiological arousal decreases rapidly and the organs and tissues return to their normal condition. There is also a short **refractory period** following orgasm during which further arousal is impossible. Females may have two or more successive orgasms before the onset of the resolution phase, and may have no refractory period.

In addition to yielding these insights into the physiological aspects of human sexual behavior, many of Masters and Johnson's findings contradicted popular beliefs about sex. For example, they showed that there are no detectable physiological differences between female orgasms produced through stimulation of the clitoris and those brought about by vaginal stimulation. They also found no significant physiological differences between the sexual responses of heterosexually and homosexually oriented individuals (Masters and Johnson, 1979).

Case Studies

Another way of gaining information about sexual behavior is through case studies. Case studies use an in-depth approach that may require weeks or months of information-gathering. Single case studies are often interesting, but they have limited scientific value. They can be affected not only by lack of accuracy in the subjects' reports but also by bias on the part of researchers, who may selectively seek information that fits their own theoretical perspectives. Despite these problems, case studies provide real-life examples that may add to our understanding of sexual and other behavior. We use case studies throughout this book. Box 8–1 later in the chapter presents two contrasting case studies of the effects of surgical sexual reassignment.

Experimental Findings

Much of the experimental research on sexual behavior has focused on the effects of viewing erotic materials both on sexual arousal and on attitudes toward aggressive behavior. The effects of alcohol on sexual response have also been investigated by a number of researchers.

Although folklore suggests that sexual excitement may be increased by alcohol consumption, experimental findings contradict this notion. In one study (Malatesta and others, 1982), female subjects were given one of four differing amounts of alcohol. Each woman's psychological responses were measured during a period in which she was asked to masturbate while watching erotic videotapes in a private, soundproof room. The more alcohol the woman consumed, the more difficulty she had reaching orgasm and the less physiological response she showed. Figure 8–5a presents some of the findings of this experiment. In an earlier study (Malatesta, 1979), the same experimental procedure was used with men as subjects. Figure 8–5b shows that the results were similar to those for women. In this study, almost half the male subjects were unable to reach orgasm at the two highest alcohol blood levels.

Of special interest in understanding the meaning of data obtained using different research methods is the finding that the women who received the highest dose of alcohol also reported more sexual pleasure and arousal than the other groups. Although it is possible to think of explanations for these contradictory results, the actual cause is not clear. This finding illustrates how survey or other methods relying on reports of behavior and feelings may result in different conclusions than studies based on physiological measures. It is important to consider findings obtained in both ways.

Sexual Variations

Survey research has shown that many individuals have had at least one homosexual experience and that homosexual behaviors are quite common. **Homosexual behavior** is sexual behavior with members of one's own sex. **Homosexuals** are individuals who prefer to engage in sexual activity with members of their own sex over an extended period. Female homosexuality is often called **lesbianism.** Most homosexuals engage in sexual activity only with members of the same sex and are not attracted to members of the opposite sex. However, many homosexuals have heterosexual fantasies and can be sexually aroused by members of the opposite sex. A person's belief that he or she is a homosexual does not depend on actual behavior. Someone with no sexual experience at all may think of himself or herself as a homosexual (Bell and Weinberg, 1978). In recent years the term *gay* has been used by homosexuals to describe their life style because they feel that the term has fewer negative implications than *homosexual*. Individuals who

wish to publicly acknowledge their homosexual orientation usually use the term *gay*.

Bisexual behavior, in which partners of either sex may be preferred at different times, is reported by a small but significant number of survey respondents. **Bisexuals** are sexually attracted to members of either sex and often engage in sexual activity with both men and women.

Kinsey and his co-workers believed that there is a continuum extending from heterosexuality to homosexuality. They used a seven-point rating scale to represent this continuum (see Table 8–1). Kinsey's estimates of the amount of homosexual activity among men were biased by the inclusion of a substantial number of subjects with prison experience. Since it is now known that prisoners have a greater likelihood of homosexual experience than those who have never been in prison, the overall estimates were probably too high. However, his college-educated sample probably yielded accurate esti-

TABLE 8–1

Kinsey's Heterosexual–Homosexual Rating Scale

0	Exclusively heterosexual
1	Predominantly heterosexual; only incidentally homosexual
2	Predominantly heterosexual; more than incidentally homosexual
3	Equally heterosexual and homosexual
4	Predominantly homosexual; more than incidentally heterosexual
5	Predominantly homosexual; only incidentally heterosexual
6	Exclusively homosexual

Adapted from Kinsey, Pomeroy, and Martin, 1948. Reprinted by permission of The Kinsey Institute for Research on Sex, Gender & Reproduction, Inc.

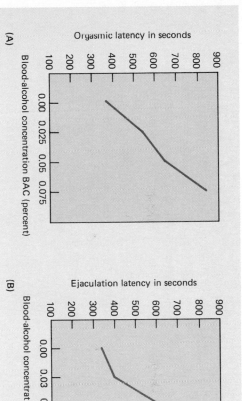

(A) Orgasmic latency in seconds

(B) Ejaculation latency in seconds

FIGURE 8–5

The greater the concentration of alcohol in a person's blood, the less likely he or she is to reach orgasm. Figure 8–5a shows length of time before orgasm for women who had received four different doses of alcohol. Figure 8–5b shows that the pattern for men is similar. (Malatesta and others, 1982, Malatesta, 1979)

mates because that group included few men who had been in prison. Based on this college-educated sample, about 4 percent of men would be classified as predominantly homosexual (rating of 4–6 from Table 8–1) (Gebhard, 1972). About 1.5 percent of all college-educated married men were classified in this group. For unmarried men in this group, 12 percent of the 25-year-olds and 30 percent of those age 30 and above were in this category. Up to one-third of the men reported an occasional homosexual experience usually in adolescence. After age 25 bisexual activities or homosexual fantasies were much less likely among men in general.

Kinsey's data makes clear that females are much less likely to have homosexual experiences than males. Compared to males, only about one-half to one-third as many females were primarily or exclusively homosexual in any age period. Considering the statistics for both males and females, it is fair to say that the number of people who have same-sex erotic experiences is fairly high, 50 percent for males and 20 percent for females, but that the number who are exclusively homosexual is low. Many people called homosexuals because they do not structure their identities and lives around members of the same sex. Kinsey's data are still the best available on the proportion of the population who have some same-sex erotic experience (Pillard and Weinrich, 1986).

One of Kinsey's most surprising findings was that the proportion of males and females with any kind of homosexual experience did not change between 1900 and 1950. In spite of the sexual permissiveness that characterized the 1960s and 1970s, there also seems to have been little change in this proportion since the Kinsey studies. In interpreting the data about homosexual experience, it is important to remember that Kinsey lumped together in a single category such different behaviors as a single incident of mutual masturbation between teenage boys, exploratory caressing of each other's breasts by girls reaching puberty, and frequent oral or anal intercourse by adult males. For many men and women, the homosexual behavior they reported had occurred when they were young, was mainly exploratory, and was brief in duration.

Homosexuality

Kinsey's research showed that homosexual behavior had occurred in one male in three during the late teenage years. However, it cannot be assumed that these adolescents were predominantly homosexual or that they continued either homosexual behaviors or even homosexual orientation into adulthood. The same thing can be said about heterosexual behavior. Its occurrence in adolescence may or may not predict the same kinds of sexual expression in adulthood.

However, there is some evidence that the foundations for homosexual or heterosexual preference can be seen in childhood and adolescence. Homosexual adults are more likely than heterosexuals to report feelings of being different from their peers in childhood, to have had gender-atypical interests, greater sexual interest in other boys, and more intense homosexual fantasies (Green, 1987; Saghir and others, 1973). In the groups studied, homosexual adults reported that the average age of awareness of same-sex attraction was about 13 years and that self-designation as homosexual occurred at about ages 19–21.

Studies of adolescents and young men confirm these findings (Rossler and Deisher, 1972; Remafedi, 1987). Some of the young men had self-labeled themselves as the result of sexual experiences with either men or women, but most of them adopted the self-label as a result of persistent homosexual feelings or attractions. This self-identification often came about over a long period in which they felt extreme emotional turmoil and may have thought about or attempted suicide mainly as a result of concern over their sexual orientation (Remafedi, 1987).

Another type of evidence that supports the findings of development of homosexual identification before adulthood comes from longitudinal studies of boys who were referred to mental-health professionals because of gender-atypical behavior during their preschool years. This behavior included dressing in girl's clothing and preferring female roles in play activities. The majority of the boys for whom these problems were severe can be expected to ultimately develop an adolescent or adult homosexual identity (Green, 1987; Money and Russe, 1979). This suggests that at least for a subgroup of the male homosexual population, adult sexual orientation may be determined early in life.

In summary, then, the evidence on homosexuality suggests that:

1. homosexual activity is not rare in adolescence.
2. there is a subset of adolescents who clearly identify themselves as homosexual.
3. the roots of this sexual orientation may extend back to early childhood.

A Cross-Cultural View

Public attitudes toward homosexuality have changed over time. Homosexual and bisexual behaviors have existed throughout history. Although heterosexual behavior is the preferred pattern in most cultures most of the time, in many societies certain forms of homosexual behavior are accepted or expected. For instance, in a large area of the southern Pacific Ocean stretching from Sumatra through Papua–New Guinea to the island of Melanesia homosexuality has an accepted role in the social institutions of the various tribal peoples (Herdt, 1984). In these groups, cultural tradition says that when males become 9 years old they must leave their families and live in a single long house in the village center. From that time until they are 19 and at the age for marriage they all participate in homosexual activities. After marriage homosexual activity either ceases or occurs only occasionally. Thus, the prescribed male norm in this society is sequential bisexuality. In this culture omission of the homosexual period rather than its inclusion is what is classified as deviant (Money, 1987).

Historically, homosexuality has been condemned by the dominant religions of the Western world; in the eighteenth and nineteenth centuries it was considered an illness. In recent years tolerance of homosexuality has increased. Many cities have enacted ordinances that make discrimination on account of sexual orientation illegal. As one author pointed out, "Homosexuals are being slowly redefined in less value-laden terms as practitioners of an alternative lifestyle, members of a new community" (Altman, 1982, p. 35) (see Figure 8–6). This view may be changing, however, because of concern about the deadly disease known as AIDS (acquired immune deficiency syndrome). AIDS, which can be sexually transmitted, has a high fatality rate, and the number of cases has grown quite rapidly. Because homosexual males, especially those who have many partners, are at a high risk for contracting the virus that may result in AIDS, public attitudes toward homosexuality may shift again.

Psychological Adjustment

Relatively few differences in psychological adjustment have been found between heterosexual and homosexual

FIGURE 8–6
Gay Pride activities provide social support for homosexual individuals by visibly demonstrating their numbers. They also provide a way for homosexuals to publicly state their sexual preferences rather than hide them.

groups. The majority of homosexual individuals are well adjusted and productive people (Saghir and Robins, 1973). In a review of dozens of studies, there was no difference between homosexual and heterosexual groups in the rates of emotional instability or illness. No psychological tests could discriminate between the two groups (Reiss, 1980). Homosexuals, like heterosexuals, may be anxious or depressed and are not always emotionally stable, but homosexuality is not a form of mental illness (Marmor, 1980). In 1973 the American Psychiatric Association removed homosexuality from its list of mental illnesses, and in 1975 the American Psychological Association also took this position. DSM-III-R does not include homosexuality in its list of disorders. Some clinicians believe that maladaptive behavior in homosexuals, when it does occur, is often due to the social stigma attached to homosexuality rather than to something pathological in the nature of homosexuality itself.

Homosexual Life Styles

Just as there is no single personality type or life-style pattern that is characteristic of heterosexuals, there is no single homosexual personality or life-style. The Institute for Sex Research carried on an intensive 10-year study of homosexuals based on a large-scale survey of 1,500 individuals in the San Francisco Bay Area (Bell and Weinberg, 1978; Bell and others, 1981). This survey was the first to investigate how homosexuals differed from each other, not just from heterosexuals. The findings suggested not one but several consistent homosexual life styles:

1. *Close-Coupleds.* Respondents in this category were closely bonded partners whose relationships were similar to those in heterosexual marriages. Close-

coupleds did not seek other partners and reported that they had no regrets about their homosexuality (see Figure 8–7).

2. *Open-Coupleds.* These respondents lived with a special partner but reported themselves to be less happy than close-coupled respondents. They had more outside sexual partners, whom they often picked up by cruising.

3. *Functionals.* This group consisted of "swinging singles" whose lives were organized around sexual experiences. They engaged in frequent cruising, had many friends, and felt that they were well adjusted.

4. *Dysfunctionals.* Respondents in this group were more poorly adjusted than the functionals. They had a large number of partners and a high level of sexual activity, but they saw themselves as sexually unappealing and their lives were marked by distress and conflict.

5. *Asexuals.* These people lacked involvements with others. They had few partners and engaged in little sexual activity. People in this group were less likely than those in other groups to say that they were exclusively homosexual. They were lonely and unhappy.

Few homosexual men and women in this study conformed to society's stereotypes. For example, they were not easily identifiable as homosexuals, and few were completely uninvolved with the opposite sex. One-third of the female and one-fifth of the male homosexuals who were interviewed had been married. One-fourth of the respondents' employers knew that they were homosexuals, as did one-fifth of their neighbors and one-half of their brothers and sisters. Their mothers were the most likely to know.

The sexual problems most frequently mentioned by homosexuals were lack of sexual outlets and the difficulty in finding suitable partners. Homosexual males reported many more sexual partners than female homosexuals did. Many of the men had had hundreds of partners; in contrast, the women tended to have had fewer than ten. Lesbians were more likely to have a relationship resembling a marriage than male homosexuals. Men seem to be more interested in sexual activity, while women emphasized companionship, affection, and emotional support.

This research into the diversity of homosexual behaviors represents a valuable starting point for further inquiries. However, its limitations should be recognized. The subjects may be representative neither of the population as a whole nor of homosexuals in general. The homosexuals in the study were volunteers recruited through public advertising, gay bars, and homosexual organizations. In addition, the homosexual climate in San Francisco is more permissive than in most other communities in the United States. (Homosexuals living in less permissive places report a much higher incidence of social difficulties.) Unskilled and semiskilled people accounted for only 18 percent of the people in the study, and 73 percent of the black male respondents reported having had at least some college education—a much higher percentage than that found in the general population of black males. For these reasons further research is needed before we can decide whether the conclusions from this study correctly describe the entire homosexually oriented population.

Sexual Response

Is the sexual experience of homosexuals different from that of heterosexuals? Yes and no. Masters and Johnson (1979) compared the physiological responses of male and female homosexual and heterosexual couples under laboratory conditions. They found no differences in

FIGURE 8–7
Close-coupled lesbian partners seem to have more satisfying and stable relationships than close-coupled males according to Bell and Weinberg's study of homosexual life styles.

physiological response during sexual activity and orgasm. But they did find that homosexual couples were more leisurely in their sexual activity, communicated more, and were more sensitive to their partners' needs than heterosexual couples.

Bisexuality

The incidence of bisexuality in Western societies is difficult to estimate. Probably about 5 percent of adults are bisexual if bisexuality is defined as sexual activity with both males and females in the past year (Masters and others, 1985). Patterns of bisexuality differ. Sometimes the bisexual individual has a long heterosexual relationship and then a long homosexual relationship. Or the order might be reversed. Sometimes both relationships go on during the same period. One 23-year-old woman described her bisexual experience as follows.

I had been dating a guy I was very friendly with for about a year with a good sexual relationship. Then I suddenly found myself making it with my roommate, who slowly but expertly introduced me to how two women make love. I really enjoyed both kinds of sex and both personal relationships, so I continued them for some while until my graduate school career was over and I moved to a new town.

—(Masters and others, 1985, p. 434)

Some women who are bisexual say that certain emotional needs are best met by men while others are best met by women (Blumstein and Schwartz, 1976).

Bisexuality is most likely to occur under several conditions: during group sex, as a result of sexual experimentation between same-sex friends who are otherwise heterosexual, and when people adopt a philosophy of sexual openness as a sign that they aren't biased against homosexuality (Blumstein and Schwartz, 1977). Bisexual behavior sometimes occurs in situations in which the participants don't think of it as such. Heterosexual individuals may seek same-sex experiences in segregated settings such as prisons, or in isolated military settings (Money and Bohmer, 1980).

Both bisexuals and gays may have conventional heterosexual marriages. This may be due to a desire to have children or to to have a conventional life style. Another reason may be that the person does not begin to experience other sexual feelings until later in life.

Sometimes bisexuals are aware of their attraction to members of the same sex before marriage, but relatively few of them reveal this fact to their prospective spouses (Coleman, 1981/1982). If the spouse later discovers the homosexual relationship, an explosive situation may be created. Husbands seem to feel especially threatened because they tend to see the wife's lesbian preferences as a negative statement about the husband's performance as a lover (Masters and others, 1985).

If bisexuality culminates in a move to a homosexual life style, other problems can arise. A substantial number of active homosexuals are also parents (see Figure 8–8). Being both homosexual and a parent may produce two somewhat conflicting identities.

When I was first coming out I never told anyone that I was a father 'cause I thought I'd be ostracized. But I started telling guys that I'd meet and they were really accepting. And then I gradually realized that it was okay to be gay and a father too. That I could be both. But at first I didn't think I could. I

FIGURE 8–8
These men, photographed at a Gay Freedom Day parade in San Francisco, live openly as both parents and homosexuals. In a less liberal environment they might be denied not only custody but even access to their children.

really thought I'd be rejected. But I wasn't. So now I really feel comfortable being a gay father. And boy is that a good feeling.

—(Bozett, 1981, p. 558)

This double identity may also create problems in the homosexual relationship, especially for partners in close- or open-coupled relationships.

I know of one man who was frightened off by my daughter. He had a bad experience with a father, and in fact the children didn't even live with this guy that this fellow was seeing. But he didn't want to take up anything with me just because of it. (ibid.)

Another man who is coupled has two children who live with him six months each year. During this time the lover is exceedingly resentful of his attention to the children, which creates considerable family conflict. Because of this conflict, the men have temporarily separated.

—(Bozett, 1981, p. 557)

Another problem that sometimes arises is that of child custody. We don't really know how growing up in a household with a homosexual parent (and, in some cases, the parent's lover) can affect a child's development. Although the question has arisen in several court cases, little research on this subject is available.

How Sexual Preference Develops

The Biological Perspective

Animal research has shown that prenatal hormone treatments may play a role in later homosexual behavior patterns. There are a few reports that a prenatal excess or deficiency of sex hormones can also affect human sexual behavior. Females who had experienced an excess of prenatal androgen (hormones that develop secondary sex characteristics in males) were more likely to have a lesbian sexual orientation (Money and Schwartz, 1977). However, treating adults with male or female hormones does not alter their sexual orientation in any way. It is possible, although far from proven, that prenatal hormones could predispose individuals to certain patterns of sexual behavior in adulthood. However, the sexual orientation of the person is also thought to be strongly dependent on socialization after birth (Money, 1987).

The Psychodynamic Perspective

Sigmund Freud believed that all people are innately bisexual. Although psychosexual development usually pro-gresses along a heterosexual course, some circumstances, such as inability to resolve the Oedipus complex, might result in adult homosexual behavior. In general, Freud's view of homosexuality was that it is simply a variation of sexual development. In a letter to a mother who had written to him asking for therapy for her son, he wrote:

Homosexuality is assuredly no advantage, but it is nothing to be ashamed of, no vice, no degradation, it cannot be classified as an illness; we consider it to be a variation of sexual function produced by a certain arrest of sexual development. Many highly respectable individuals of ancient and modern times have been homosexuals, several of the greatest men among them (Plato, Michelangelo, Leonardo de Vinci, etc.). It is a great injustice to persecute homosexuality as a crime, and cruelty too.

—(Freud, 1951, p. 786)

Other psychodynamic theorists have stressed parent–child relationships in explaining homosexuality (Bieber and others, 1962; Marmor, 1980). However, research has suggested that, at least for well-adjusted individuals, the family relationships of homosexuals and heterosexuals do not differ (Bell and others, 1981).

The Behavioral Perspective

The view that homosexuality is primarily a learned phenomenon suggests that pleasant early sexual experiences with members of the same sex or unpleasant experiences with members of the opposite sex can condition sexual thoughts and fantasies. This perspective can also be used to explain why some individuals change their sexual preference as adults. Some investigators have found that individuals who have changed their preference may have had unpleasant heterosexual experiences followed by rewarding homosexual ones (Masters and Johnson, 1979).

What the Data Tell Us

How accurate are the explanations of these theoretical viewpoints? How well do they explain what has been found through research? In general, the answer is not very well. In a large and sophisticated study, Bell, and his co-workers (1981) concluded that neither a psychodynamic nor a behavioral view of homosexuality was supported by the evidence. Their findings include the following.

1. No evidence that parent–child relationships are important in determining sexual preference.

2. No evidence that homosexuality results from atypical experiences with members of the opposite sex during

childhood—experiences such as rape, parental punishment for sex play with members of the opposite sex, seductive behavior by opposite-sex parents, or actual seduction by an older male or female.

The study also provided evidence that sexual preference begins early:

1. Sexual preference is likely to be established by adolescence, even before there is much sexual activity.
2. Sexual feelings of attraction seemed much more important than early sexual activity in the determination of homosexual preference.
3. Adult homosexuals did not lack heterosexual experiences in childhood; however, they did not tend to find these gratifying.
4. Children who did not conform to gender roles in childhood had a somewhat increased probability of homosexual feelings and behavior in adolescence.

Gender nonconformity in childhood means that the person was typically interested in activities that are associated with the opposite sex—for example, playing baseball for girls and playing house for boys. Although gender nonconformity is associated with a higher probability of homosexual orientation, it is not a very accurate clue. At least half the homosexual men in the study were typically masculine in both personal identity and interests while they were growing up, and at least one-fourth of the heterosexual men were nonconforming to male sex roles while growing up. The situation was similar for women. This means that while gender nonconformity in childhood increases the likelihood that the child will be homosexual in adulthood, it does not automatically signal later homosexuality.

Bell and his co-workers conclude that the development of a homosexual preference is probably biologically based. Although their study does not deal with biological data, their findings make that conclusion reasonable. However, as the section on the biological perspective made clear, any biological explanation requires much further research.

Sexual Dysfunction

One of Kinsey's most significant findings was the high incidence of problems of sexual dysfunction. The work of Masters and Johnson and others has supplied information about the causes and treatment of these problems.

Types of Sexual Dysfunction

Problems people encounter in sexual activity may occur in any of four stages of the sexual response. The stages include the following periods.

1. *Appetitive:* the presence of fantasy about sexual activity and a feeling of desire
2. *Excitement:* a period of subjective pleasure and physiological changes, including penile erection in the male and swelling and lubrication of the female genitals
3. *Orgasm:* the peaking of sexual pleasure and the release of sexual tension, as shown by ejaculation in the male and rhythmic muscle contraction in the pelvic area for both male and females
4. *Resolution:* a sense of relaxation and well-being. Men cannot produce an erection or experience orgasm during the resolution period. Women are able to respond almost immediately to additional stimulation.

Sexual problems can occur during any of these stages. In the appetitive stage, physical conditions such as high blood pressure or diabetes can inhibit sexual desire. Some people simply seem to be at the low end of the normal distribution of sexual desire. These problems usually come to the attention of a clinician only when they become a source of concern to the individual or his or her partner.

Sexual problems can also occur at the excitement stage of the cycle (see Table 8–2). The male may fail to attain or hold an erection until the completion of intercourse. This problem is often called **impotence.** In females, a problem at this stage is inability to attain or maintain the swelling-lubrication response until the sex act is completed. This is usually called **frigidity.**

Both males and females may experience problems in the orgasm phase of the sexual-response cycle. In the male, these take the form of premature ejaculation or delayed or absent ejaculation. In the female, they take the form of a delay or absence of orgasm after a normal excitement phase. **Premature ejaculation,** in which the man is unable to inhibit ejaculation long enough for his female partner to experience orgasm through intercourse, is probably the most common type of male sexual dysfunction. The man's failure to control his orgasm often results in his feeling sexually inadequate. Accordingly, from one viewpoint, the male experiences anxiety as he reaches high levels of erotic arousal, and the anxiety triggers the involuntary orgasm.

In **retarded ejaculation,** on the other hand, the ejaculatory response is inhibited. Men with this problem respond to sexual stimuli with erotic feelings and a firm erection, but they are unable to ejaculate. In severe

TABLE 8-2

The Sex Disorder: Where Problem Is Based

Type of Problem	In the Individual	In a Relationship
DESIRE	**For Both Men and Women** low sex drive	**For Both Men and Women** low sex drive aversion habituation or boredom dissatisfaction with frequency desired by partner
EXCITEMENT	**For Men** Erectile dysfunction **For Women** Lubrication dysfunction General lack of arousal	Problems in column 1 may be intrinsic or situational
ORGASM	**For men** Premature ejaculation Retarded ejaculation **For Women** Orgasmic dysfunction	Problems in column 1 may be intrinsic or situational
OTHER	**For Men** Dyspareunia **For Women** Dyspareunia Vaginismus	Problems in column 1 lead to nonconsummation of sexual relationship May be intrinsic or situational

cases, the male may prolong intercourse for a long time, engage in fantasy, and drink, all to no avail. Although physical injuries may be responsible for the problem in some cases, a variety of psychological factors that contribute to the occurrence of retarded ejaculation include ambivalence toward the sexual partner, strongly suppressed anger, and a religious upbringing that engenders sexual guilt.

Psychological and situational factors can be an important cause of inhibited female orgasm. Psychological factors include unresolved conflicts over sexual activity and disturbances in the relationship between the partners. In many cases, however, the explanation is simpler: inadequate stimulation during lovemaking can damage a woman's ability to become sexually responsive. In such cases, the therapist attempts to sensitize both partners to each other's sexual needs, explaining, for example, that a woman is more difficult to arouse than a man. Some women are unable to experience an orgasm without manual stimulation of the clitoris, which has a larger number of sensitive nerve endings than the vagina. This may represent a normal variation in sexual response. Most women do not have an orgasm each time they have intercourse, and about 15 percent of women never have orgasms (Cole, 1985). Not having orgasms can decrease a woman's overall sexual responsiveness as well as leading to depression and a decreased sense of self-esteem. As one 19-year-old college student said,

There's so much talk about orgasms that I've been wondering what's wrong with me, that I don't have them. I used to enjoy sex a lot, but lately it's a bad scene because I just get reminded of problems.

—(Masters and others, 1985, p. 502)

Other problems can also occur that often make sexual intercourse difficult. Both men and women may experience **dyspareunia**, a recurrent or persistent genital pain that occurs before, during, or after intercourse. Women also may be affected by **vaginismus**. This disorder makes intercourse difficult or impossible because of involuntary spasms of the outer portion of the vagina.

Because many cases never come to a clinician's attention, no one knows how prevalent sexual dysfunction is. In a study of 100 couples who had not sought sex therapy, 60 percent of the women reported difficulties in reaching orgasm, and 40 percent of the men reported problems with erection or ejaculation (Frank and others, 1978). Most of these couples described their marriages as at least moderately satisfying.

Because a woman who has problems of this type can still have intercourse while a male who is unable to maintain an erection cannot do so, most of the attention given to problems of excitement has been directed toward those of the male. According to one estimate, half of all American men have experienced at least occasional

episodes in which they could not achieve or maintain an erection (Kaplan, 1974). For this reason, only severe and chronic problems of erection, such as are found in men who have never functioned well, are viewed as serious clinical problems. These dysfunctions may result from psychological or physical causes. One technique that is used in evaluating a man's capacity to have an erection is measurement of changes in penis size during sleep. The ability to have erections during sleep is a clear sign that a man's erectile dysfunction is due to psychological, not physical, causes.

Anxiety stemming from personal conflict or from concern over a physical problem is often an important factor in erectile dysfunction. Physical causes include early undiagnosed diabetes, hormonal imbalances, and the use of narcotics and alcohol. In the past, hidden psychopathology was believed to be the main psychological cause of this type of sexual dysfunction. More recently, however, recognition has been given to **performance anxiety**, in which the man's preoccupation with sexual adequacy ironically interferes with his performance. One 34-year-old man's comment is typical.

After awhile, the problem becomes so predictable that you start to make excuses in advance. It's as though you lose any chance of having sexual pleasure because you become preoccupied with the notion of failure. And that failure hits you right in the gut—you don't feel like much of a man.

—(Masters and others, 1985, p. 502)

Figure 8-9 illustrates the many sources of stress that may interact with biological vulnerabilities to result in problems of sexual performance for men.

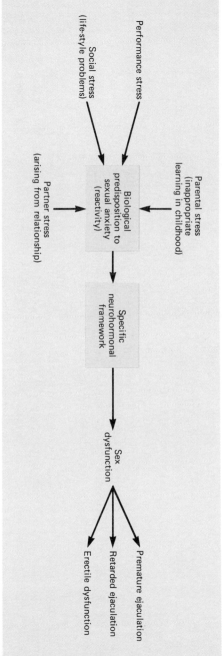

FIGURE 8-9
A variety of types of stress both remote and immediate can contribute to sexual dysfunction in men.
(Cole, 1985, p. 341. Reprinted with permission of the British Journal of Psychiatry.)

The Treatment of Sexual Dysfunction

Since the publication of Masters and Johnson's first two books in 1966 and 1970, sex therapy has emerged as a discipline in its own right. While they recognize that many sexually dysfunctional people are dysfunctional in other areas of their personal and social lives, Masters and Johnson believe that short-term treatment directed primarily at sexual problems can help most people who experience such dysfunctions. They have observed that becoming sexually functional has a positive influence on a person's anxiety level as well as on his or her self-esteem. A man who is anxious but has a good sex life is probably happier than a man who has to deal with a sex problem in addition to anxiety.

Masters and Johnson emphasize the treatment of couples, not just the person who seems to have a problem. This does not mean that the partner is seen as the cause of the difficulty, but rather that both members of the relationship are affected by the problem. The Masters and Johnson approach uses a man and a woman working together as therapists. The therapy program is intensive and takes place daily over a 2-week period. It emphasizes instruction in the sexual needs of both partners, together with exercises in erotic stimulation. Specific homework assignments are given that are designed to help couples become more aware of their own sexual sensations. The therapy procedure includes basic information about the sexual organs and the physiology of the sexual response for clients who lack this information (i.e., most of the people who come for treatment). The presentation of this basic information often has important therapeutic benefits in itself.

Emphasis is also placed on communication, nonverbal as well as verbal, between partners. Because couples who seek treatment typically place lovemaking exclusively under the man's control, sexual intercourse may be attempted only when he indicates that he is interested. The belief of many women that they will be rejected if they are sexually assertive continues to be widespread. In many cases of sexual dysfunction, the most effective treatment may be simply the provision of information about sexual relationships and the encouragement of meaningful communication between sex partners, not complex physical or psychotherapeutic tactics.

Sensate focus is probably the best known of Masters and Johnson's sexual-retraining techniques. The rationale behind sensate focus is that sexually dysfunctional couples have lost the ability to think and feel in a sensual way because of the various stresses and pressures

The Masters and Johnson Approach

they associate with intercourse. They therefore have to be reacquainted with the pleasures of tactile contact. Each partner learns not only that being touched is pleasurable, but that exploring and caressing the partner's body can be exciting and stimulating in itself. The couple is encouraged to engage in sensate focus under conditions that are dissimilar to those associated with the anxieties, frustrations, and resentments of their former lovemaking. Intercourse is prohibited throughout the early stages of treatment because simply banning intercourse can reduce tension in both sexual and nonsexual areas of the relationship. This ban on intercourse was thought by Masters and Johnson to make sensate focus particularly valuable in treating performance anxiety. However, more recently other therapists have suggested that a deemphasis rather than a ban is more helpful to couples (Lipsius, 1987).

The couples technique is especially appropriate in treating premature ejaculation, since this is often more upsetting to the woman than to the man. If premature ejaculation is the problem, the therapists often introduce a method known as the "squeeze technique" that helps recondition the ejaculatory reflex. The woman is taught to apply a firm, grasping pressure on the penis several times during the beginning stages of intercourse. This technique reduces the urgency of the need to ejaculate.

When the couple's problem is related to an orgasmic dysfunction in the woman, the treatment includes an exploratory discussion to identify attitudes that may be influencing the woman's ability to attain orgasm. Then the couple is given a series of graduated homework assignments. If the woman is willing, she begins by exploring her own bodily sensations, stimulating herself by masturbating. As she becomes more comfortable with this technique, her partner begins to participate in the sessions through kissing and tactile stimulation. There is strong emphasis on the woman's clear and assertive communication of her reactions and desires to her partner.

Masters and Johnson have reported very low failure rates of their treatment programs for both heterosexual and homosexual couples. Their findings have been criticized, primarily because their reports are not completely clear on such topics as who is selected and who is rejected for the program and how success and failure are defined (Cole, 1985). Nevertheless, their techniques are far superior to earlier methods of treating sexual disorders.

The Behavioral Approach

Looked at from a behavioral perspective, the Masters and Johnson technique of sensate focus is reminiscent of systematic desensitization in that it leads to the substitution of a pleasurable response for anxiety. Sex therapists often create a sort of hierarchy in which certain parts of the body initially are designated as "out of bounds" and then are gradually included as progress is made. Although orthodox systematic desensitization can be used to eliminate specific anxieties (such as feeling uncomfortable while looking at a man's genitals), the more global sensate focus appears to be appropriate in dealing with the various diffuse anxieties experienced by sexually dysfunctional individuals.

The methods used by Masters and Johnson have been further refined by many behaviorally oriented therapists. For instance, relaxation and modeling may be combined in treating dysfunctional women whose major problem is sexual anxiety. Another behavioral approach to the treatment of interpersonal problems related to sexual performance is described in the following case. Notice the importance of cognitive elements in this treatment plan.

The client was a 24-year-old lawyer who after six months of marriage was upset by his frequent inability to obtain or retain an erection. His history suggested that his mother had been a dominating woman of whom he was fearful and that he was also unwilling to challenge or criticize his wife in any way even though he often felt considerable resentment toward her. He seemed to feel that expressing his feelings was not manly. After several therapeutic sessions directed at his irrational attitudes, he and the therapist composed a carefully worded speech for the client to deliver to his wife.

"Grace, I have something very important and very serious to discuss with you. It concerns you, me, our marriage, and life in general. I want you to please hear me out without interrupting me. . . . I was raised by my mother to bottle up my feelings, especially in relation to women. In thinking over this attitude, I now realize that this is crazy and even dishonest. I feel, for instance, that if I resent the fact that you turn to your father for advice in matters about which I have more knowledge than he, I ought to express my resentment instead of hiding it from you. I feel that when you order me about and treat me like a child, I ought to tell you how I really feel about it instead of acting like an obedient puppy dog. And most important of all, when you go ahead and make plans for me without consulting me, and especially when you yell at me in front of your parents, maybe I should quit acting as if I didn't mind and let you know how strongly I really react inside. What I am getting at is simply that in spite of my love and affection for you, I would really rather be unmarried than be a henpecked husband like my father."

This little monologue was rehearsed several times during a one-hour session until playbacks on a tape recorder convinced the therapist that the client was ready to confront his wife and that he would do so in a forthright and sincere manner. Rehearsal techniques were used in preparing the patient to cope with tears, interruptions, denials, counterallegations, etc. His assignment was then put into effect. The patient reported that his wife "heard me out without interruption. . . . [S]he seemed a little upset, but agreed that I should not withhold or conceal my feelings. I felt incredibly close to her and that night we had very good sex."

—(Lazarus, 1971, pp. 156–157)

The Kaplan Approach

Some therapists believe that behavioral methods are useful for many sexual problems but that other problems require a combination of behavioral approaches with psychodynamically oriented therapy for one or both partners. One of the foremost proponents of this view is Helen Singer Kaplan (1974, 1979). Kaplan, a psychoanalyst, believes that standard sex therapy methods are effective when sexual problems are based on mild and easily diminished anxieties and conflicts. However, there are many individuals whose symptoms are rooted in more profound conflicts. Kaplan thinks that this is especially true in the cases of men and women who lack sexual desire and men who have difficulty maintaining an erection. For these problems Kaplan and her coworkers have developed a lengthened and more individualized treatment program that involves traditional sex therapy and psychodynamically oriented sessions, sometimes with one of the clients and sometimes with both partners. The case of Sam and Susie illustrates Kaplan's approach.

Susie, 28, a housewife, and Sam, 30, a high school principal, had been married four years and have 3-year-old twin sons. The chief complaint was Susie's lack of desire. The couple had a good relationship, each felt in love with the other and they were judged to be good parents. During their marriage they had had intercourse only three times. During the last two years they had had no physical contact because any attempt by Sam to hold or kiss Susie resulted in "hysterics," that is, she had an anxiety attack. The couple were referred to Kaplan after nine months of weekly sessions at a sex therapy clinic had not produced improvement.

The ordinary sensate focusing or pleasuring activities threw Susie into an anxiety state. In addition, when there was any improvement Susie would effectively resist or sabotage the treatment by trying to do too much. For example, if the assignment were to lie next to Sam in bed and hold his hand, she might try to have him caress her breast as well. This would then precipitate her anxious feelings. The therapist discussed this behavior with Susie and gave her the job of controlling the progress of desensitizing her anxiety. She was to select only tasks that were within her comfort-zone, that is, those that produced only tolerable anxiety.

Susie also had a more general problem with fun and pleasure. Whenever she allowed herself to experience them, she developed sharp headaches. As the desensitizing of her phobic avoidance of sexual contact progressed, Susie had a series of dreams about "dead relatives buried in the basement that needed to be removed." A central threatening figure was her deceased father. After discussions with the therapist about Oedipal feelings toward her father and the transfer of some of these feelings to her husband, Susie's father disappeared from her dreams.

After further sessions along with her husband that focused on guilt over pleasure, Susie's pleasure anxiety had decreased, her relationship with her husband was more open, and the couple was having satisfying intercourse at least once per week.

— (adapted from Kaplan, 1979, pp. 73–75)

The Effectiveness of Sex Therapy

Great variations in the success rate for sex therapy have been reported by researchers (Cole, 1985). Successes reported range from 39 to 98 percent. Part of the problem is that the measurement of success is often poorly defined in the research and few follow-up studies are reported so long-term changes are unknown. The particular treatment approach used does not seem to affect the success rate. One study compared Masters and Johnson's technique, a modified technique using only one therapist, and a technique that combined efforts to improve communication with behavioral methods such as relaxation training and contracts (Crowe and others, 1981). All three approaches led to improvement lasting at least one year for couples with problems of impotence, anorgasmia, and loss of sexual interest. There was no difference in effectiveness among the various therapies.

Findings like these suggest that research is needed to determine which therapeutic elements are actually helpful and which elements are unnecessary. For instance, decreasing anxiety about sexual performance has been a focus of many approaches to sex therapy. However, anxiety is a complex construct that has behavioral, cognitive, and physiological aspects. The heightened physiological response that is part of anxiety has been shown to increase, not decrease, sexual response (Beck and Barlow, 1984). However, the cognitive aspects—

for instance, interfering thoughts and problems of focusing attention—have a negative effect on arousal. Such thoughts may increase because of the demand for performance when the partner is clearly aroused. These findings suggest that attempts to decrease the physiological aspects of anxiety may be ineffective or even counterproductive whereas practice in screening out distracting thoughts might be most helpful.

Gender Identity Disorder

Gender identity, a basic feature of personality, refers to an individual's feeling of being male or female. Children become aware that they are male or female at an early age, and once formed, this gender identity is highly resistant to change. Gender identity is different from sexual preference. **Sexual preference** refers to whether a person desires a sexual partner of the same or the opposite sex, it does not refer to the person's sexual self-concept.

Childhood Problems of Gender Identity

In **Gender-Identity Disorder of Childhood**, children who have not yet reached puberty may show considerable distress at being male or female and will express intense desires to be of the opposite sex. For instance a girl may vehemently state her desire to be a boy or even insist that she is a boy. She may refuse to wear ordinary feminine clothing and insist on wearing the clothing typical of males including boys' underwear and other accessories. She may also deny her gender by such behaviors as refusing to urinate while in a sitting position or by the insistence that she either already has or will grow a penis. Boys show the same types of behavior in reverse. In addition to playing with girls' toys and wanting to dress as a girl, a boy may say that he wants to be a woman when he grows up and that his penis and testes are disgusting or that they will disappear as he grows older.

Problems that may relate to gender identity come to clinical attention when parents become concerned because their child's behavior and social relationships are not like those of other children of the same sex and age. For instance, this mother is worried that her son is and will continue to be sexually abnormal.

My boy is showing feminine tendencies and has ever since he was two years old. It started out real cute. His sister had dress-up clothes at her grandparents, and when he got to be about two years old, he'd dress up in these clothes and hats and high heels, and he was just real cute. We thought it was something he'd pass. Now he will be eleven years old this month, and he does this in secret. I just felt like now was the time to investigate it.

—(Green, 1974, p. xxi)

If a young child's behavior is typical of that of children of the opposite sex, it does not always mean that the child has a gender identity problem. Often parents are not aware of how much their own behavior contributes to the behavior of their children. The mother quoted earlier may have encouraged her son to dress in women's clothes by telling him how cute he was then, and at no other time. When this is the case, counseling may be helpful. Parents can be trained to reinforce sex-appropriate behavior in the home—for example, by giving the child special attention or a material reinforcer when he or she is behaving appropriately—and this approach has been found to be effective in helping children acquire new sex roles (Rekers, 1977).

Despite advances in the study of sexual practices, questions frequently arise as to how maladaptive a certain type of behavior is. Children who act out inappropriate sex roles early in their development may drop this behavior as they get older. The 5-year-old tomboy or sissy may simply be going through a phase. However, children who dress in the clothes of the opposite sex and whose play follows the patterns of the other sex, have an increased likelihood of developing a homosexual orientation in adulthood (Money, 1987). A longitudinal study compared boys with extremely feminine interests and behavior in childhood with boys in a control group (Green, 1987). Eleven years later 75 percent of the previously feminine boys were either bisexual or homosexual in fantasy and/or behavior. All but one of the boys in the control group were heterosexual.

Transsexualism

Gender identity in adults can take two forms: **transsexualism** and **nontranssexual gender-identity disorder.** Transsexuals experience an intense desire and need to change their sexual status, including their anatomical structure. In contrast, although adults with nontranssexual gender-identity disorder feel a discomfort and inappropriateness about their assigned sex and often cross-dress, they are not preoccupied with getting rid of their primary and secondary sexual characteristics and acquiring those of the other sex.

Although the number of cases of transsexualism is very small (according to one estimate, only 1 per 100,000 people for females and 1 per 30,000 for males), the behavior has aroused a great deal of curiosity. Scientific interest in transsexualism derives mainly from the light that such cases may shed on the general nature and development of gender identity. When a child's strong desire to be a member of the opposite sex continues into adulthood, transsexualism may result.

The problem begins to surface at puberty, when maturational changes in the body emphasize biological gender. In the follow-up study of feminine boys described in the last section, one boy seemed to have transsexual feelings. Though clinicians agree on the value of studying the lives of transsexuals, the use of medical techniques to bring about bodily changes that conform to the transsexual's gender identity remains controversial.

Changing a male transsexual into a female involves administering female hormones to reduce hair growth and stimulate development of the breasts, removing the male genitals, and creating an artificial vagina. Changing a female into a sexually functioning male is more difficult because the artificially constructed penis cannot become erect by natural means or feel tactile stimulation. In recent years, however, advances in the treatment of primary impotence in men have been applied to transsexual surgery, and an inflation device is sometimes implanted in the penis to make possible artificial erection. The long-term success of this method is still in doubt.

Many of the candidates who apply to clinics for what is called sexual-reassignment surgery show considerable psychological disturbance. In one group of patients who applied to a university gender identity clinic, 92 percent of the males and 60 percent of the females showed other psychological disturbances in addition to problems with sexual identity (Levine, 1980). For this reason, clinicians stress the need to assess each candidate carefully before deciding whether to carry out the medical steps needed for a sex change. After people who are emotionally stable and likely to adjust well to surgery are selected, most reputable centers still require a number of preliminary steps before the surgery is carried out. Because the surgical procedures are irreversible, this degree of caution is needed.

After patients have been selected, they usually are required to spend one or two years prior to the surgery living in the community as a member of the opposite sex. During this period hormone injections are used to alter secondary sex characteristics such as breast size or muscle definition (see Figure 8–10e). This period serves as psychological preparation for life as a member of the other sex and also provides a realistic experience of what that life may be like. Psychotherapy is also often required during the presurgical period. Sometimes clients have what might be called "magical" hopes regarding the surgery. The psychotherapeutic sessions can give them a chance to look at their underlying feelings and perhaps become more comfortable as hetero- or homosexuals.

What happens to those who undergo the surgery? Box 8–1 describes two very different outcomes. In gen-

BOX 8-1

Success and Failure in Transsexual Surgery

Several transsexuals have written about their experiences. One is Jan Morris, whose autobiography is entitled *Conundrum* (1974). James Humphrey Morris was a highly regarded English foreign correspondent. At age 17 he had been an officer in one of Britain's crack cavalry regiments. As a correspondent for *The Times* of London, he covered the successful attempt by Hilary and Tenzing to climb Mount Everest. He covered wars and rebellions the world over and also wrote fifteen books on history and travel. Then James gave way to Jan. Jan Morris refers to her former self as a woman trapped in a man's body.

At age 3 or 4 James Morris realized that he was a girl who had been born into the wrong body. As an adult he enjoyed the company of women but did not

desire to sleep with them. He married at 22, and he and his wife had five children. As middle age neared, he became depressed, had suicidal thoughts, and finally sought a transsexual change. Hormones were used to enlarge his breasts and soften his body to more feminine lines. After surgery to complete the process begun by the hormone pills, Morris divorced his wife. Jan Morris reports that she feels like the person she always wanted to be. (See Figure 8–10a–c.) The children of her former marriage treat her as an aunt.

Not all sex-reassignment surgery is as successful as that of Jan Morris. Some time ago the Princeton alumni weekly carried a memorial notice that included the following description.

(b)

(a)

(c)

FIGURE 8–10

(a) James Morris in 1964. (Courtesy of Jerry Bauer) *(b)* Jan Morris in 1977. (Henry Grossman, *People Weekly* © 1974 Time Inc.) *(c)* A note written by Morris to the authors.

SUSAN F. (NEE WALTER FAW) CANNON '46

He was a courtly southern gentleman. He was soft-spoken and intelligent, one of the few authentic geniuses in our class. He was to many of us a drinking companion, a sympathetic listener, a friend.

Professionally, he did well. He had a severe stuttering problem, so he became a world-class debater at Princeton. He earned a physics degree.

Don Hegstrom, a former graduate and lifelong friend, convinced him that physics, in his context, was dull and he should maybe go for his Ph.D. in the history of science at Harvard. He did.

Walter was a scholar, and a certified intellectual (a label he wore with modesty and grace), a voracious reader, a creative thinker, a historian of national note, a teacher, a poet, an author, an editor ("The Smithsonian Journal of History"), and a curator of the Smithsonian Institution.

Walter Faw Cannon was also Susan Faye Cannon, a fact that she did not recognize until several years ago. Several years ago, Walter publicly proclaimed that he was a female in a male body. And just last year, he had a surgical sex change against the advice of his doctors. Three months before she died, she called and told a classmate that it had been demonstrated conclusively that genetically she had always been a woman. She was very

glad, because she had always suspected it and, in more recent years, known it to be a fact. (Princeton Alumni Weekly, April 5, 1982).

Cannon began discovering his female identity during his undergraduate days at Princeton and during his stint in the U.S. Navy. At the age of 51 Cannon applied to Superior Court in the District of Columbia to change his first name to Faye, his mother's family name, and during the same period he began dressing as a woman. In an interview with the Washington Post, Cannon described his situation. "I don't classify myself as gay, because I don't know what the word means. I define myself as a male woman. Then I know what the words mean" (Levey, 1977, C1).

Cannon's behavior created problems for him in his job at the Smithsonian. In spite of his reputation as a scholar he received a disability retirement in 1979. At the age of 55 he decided to undergo sex-reassignment surgery (see Figure 8–10d and e). Cannon had been a heavy user of painkillers before his surgery because of an arthritic problem. After surgery, her use of these drugs escalated because of the extreme postsurgical pain. In 1981, Susan Cannon was found dead of acute codeine intoxication. It was not clear whether her death was a result of an accidental overdose.

These two cases involving well-educated, successful men who decided in midlife to reconcile their sexual identification with their physical appearance show how hard it is to generalize about the desirability of surgical sex reassignment even for those who clearly seem to be among the small group of true transsexuals.

FIGURE 8–10 (continued)
(d) Walter Cannon before he began receiving hormone treatments. (e) Walter Cannon after receiving hormone treatments and shortly before his sex-reassignment surgery.

Fetishism

Fetishism, a psychological state in which a nonliving object (fetish) serves as a primary source of sexual arousal and consummation, is an example of a sexual deviation that is not usually addressed by the law. Most fetishists are solitary in their activities, although in some cases they commit crimes to acquire their favorite fetishes (often undergarments, boots, or shoes). Some fetishists seek sexual partners with particular characteristics, usually leg amputations or lameness. Fetishists are almost always male, and the fetish varies widely from the clearly erotic (such as an article of women's underwear, especially underwear that has been worn, stained, and not yet laundered) to objects with little apparent connection with sexuality. Fetishism often begins in adolescence.

Rubber fetishes are particularly popular. In England the Mackintosh Society, named for rubberized

FIGURE 8–11
The Seattle "shoe bandit" attacked women on the street and stole a single shoe from each. Here some of the shoes found in his apartment are surveyed by police.

eral, however, the results have been disappointing. During the 1980s several prominent medical centers stopped doing transsexual surgery because the benefits were doubtful (Beatrice, 1985; Masters and others, 1985). In a long-term follow-up in male-to-female transsexuals, only one-third were judged to have a fair or good sexual adjustment (Lindemalm and others, 1986). More than half of the patients were unchanged in social adjustment. Almost one-third considered their sex-reassignment surgery to have been a mistake.

Transsexualism is a prime example of the interactional point of view. Sex is a matter of anatomy and physiology, but gender identity is strongly influenced by psychological, social, and cultural factors. It is likely that there may be a small group of transsexuals for whom sexual-reassignment therapy is an effective treatment. For many more, who are likely to have significant personality problems and other psychopathology, the surgery does not provide an answer to their mental health problems; instead, the problems may worsen. Some individuals become deeply depressed after surgery, while others have transient psychotic episodes (Levine and Lothstein, 1981).

Nontranssexual gender-identity disorder also produces discomfort about one's assigned sex. However, people with this disorder lack the preoccupation for acquiring the sexual organs and other physical characteristics of the opposite sex that is characteristic of transsexuals. Instead they focus on fantasizing that they are of the opposite sex or actually acting out that role through cross-dressing. This cross-dressing differs from that of the transvestites discussed later. Although transvestites obtain sexual gratification from cross-dressing they do not wish to change their sex as people with cross gender disorder do.

The Paraphilias

Not everyone is sexually excited by the same stimuli. Some individuals can gain sexual gratification only from particular objects or situations. Most of these sexual behaviors are tolerated by society if they are practiced in private or with consenting adult partners. The behaviors are likely to cause problems only if others are harmed or if social customs are openly flouted. DSM-III-R classifies these disorders as subcategories of **paraphilia,** which means attraction to the deviant. There are three general classes of paraphilias: (1) preference for the use of a nonhuman object for sexual arousal; (2) repetitive sexual activity with humans that involves real or simulated suffering or humiliation; and (3) repetitive sexual activity with nonconsenting partners.

raincoats, provides reassurance for individuals who feel embarrassed or isolated by their sexual interests. Some rubber fetishists derive sexual excitement merely from wearing rubber garments. Other dress in them or want their partner to wear them during sexual activity because the garments are necessary for them to become sexually aroused. One rubber fetishist describes the role played by rubber boots in his sexual behavior.

I always seem to have been fascinated by rubber boots. I cannot say exactly when the fascination first started, but I must have been very young. Their spell is almost hypnotic and should I see someone walking along with rubber boots, I become very excited and may follow the person for a great distance. I quickly get an erection under such circumstances and I might easily ejaculate. I often will take the boots to bed with me, caress them, kiss them, and ejaculate into them.

—(Epstein, 1965, pp. 515–516)

Fetishism is one of the most puzzling of all forms of sexual behavior. It is chronic, and in some cases the collection of fetishistic objects is the main activity in the individual's life. No one has been able adequately to explain fetishists' sexual attachment to diverse objects. Although theories range from those that stress unconscious motivation to those that hypothesize impaired neural mechanisms such as are found among epileptics, the causes of this unusual type of sexual behavior remain shrouded in mystery (Wise, 1985).

Fetishists do not often seek therapy. In one large London hospital only 60 cases were diagnosed in a 20-year period (Chalkley and Powell, 1983). Of these, about 30 percent were referred by the courts, mainly because of their theft of fetishistic objects (see Figure 8–11). About a third of the patients came for treatment because of anxiety about their fetishistic behavior. About 20 percent came for other reasons and the fetish was identified only after they had begun treatment. Treatment based on learning principles has been applied to fetishism with some success. In aversion therapy, for example, the fetish object is paired, either actually or in fantasy, with an unpleasant stimulus such as electric shock or a sense of overwhelming embarrassment.

Transvestism

A transvestite uses clothing as a sexual stimulant or fetish. **Transvestism** literally means "cross-dressing" (see Figure 8–12). Women are not usually considered to be transvestites, probably because society allows them to dress in most masculine styles. References to cross-dressing can be found throughout history. King Henry III of France cross-dressed publicly and wished to be addressed and treated as a woman. Joan of Arc wore her

FIGURE 8–12
These male transvestites enjoy playing a female role by dressing as women.

hair short and preferred to dress as a man. Most transvestites are heterosexual men who dress in women's clothes, often starting in adolescence. When not cross-dressed, the transvestite usually exhibits masculine behavior and interests.

Although some clinicians have contended that transvestism and transsexualism are basically similar, there are a number of differences between these two conditions. Transsexuals desire to change their genitals and live as members of the opposite sex. They do not experience sexual arousal when cross-dressing. Transvestites, on the other hand, become sexually aroused when cross-dressing but continue to identify themselves as members of their biological sex.

A male transvestite gave this explanation for his behavior in a letter to his wife.

The personal masculine attributes that first attracted you to me are, as you know, an integral part of my personality, just as my transvestism is. It has always been a part of me. . . . We are only make-believe girls, and we know always that we are really men, so don't worry that we are ever dissatisfied with manhood, or want to change forever into a woman. When we are dressed in feminine clothes and attain as close a resemblance as possible to a real girl, we do certainly pretend that we are girls for that short time, but it is a pretense and definitely not a reality.

—(Prince, 1967, pp. 80–81)

An unusual study of a nationwide sample of transvestites provided comprehensive descriptions of their behavior and attitudes (Bentler and Prince, 1969, 1970). Compared with a nontransvestite group, the transvestites were more inhibited in their interpersonal relationships, less involved with other individuals, and more independent. In general, they gave evidence of being less able to seek sympathy, love, and help from others and seemed to be happier when they felt no obligations to others. However, in many areas of personality they did not differ significantly from nontransvestites.

Writers have emphasized several perspectives—psychodynamic processes, conditioning, and biological predisposition—in discussing transvestism. Many clinicians believe that transvestism develops in the context of disturbed parent-child relationships. Others see it as a product of aberrant psychosexual development. Behaviorists see it as a conditioned response that is susceptible to aversion therapy in which dressing in women's clothing is paired with an aversive stimulus. Behavioral training aimed at fostering confidence and adequacy in playing a conventional sex role has also been suggested.

Covert sensitization seems to be particularly useful in treating transvestism and other sexual disorders. In this procedure clients are first asked to imagine as vividly as possible the sexually arousing behavior that they are trying to eradicate, and to follow these thoughts with equally vivid aversion imagery (for example, being discovered and embarrassed). This approach was used for a 31-year-old transvestite, a married police officer who sought help for uncontrollable urges to dress in women's clothing and appear in public. The client had a 16-year history of transvestism that had begun when he was discharged from the Marine Corps. His wife had threatened to divorce him because of his cross-dressing. In treatment, he was asked to form images of deviant sexual scenes as well as aversive images of their undesirable consequences. The following is an example of the material used in the covert sensitization.

You are in your house alone, and you are feeling lonely. You get the urge to put on the clothings, so you enter the bedroom and open the closet. You begin to get aroused as you decide what to wear. As you put on the clothing, you can see the colors and feel the clothing on your hands. You really are turned on as you put on the bra, panties, nylons, wig. You feel like playing with yourself as you apply your makeup, but you can't wait to go out. As you leave the house, you get very excited. You are touching your penis through the panties as you're driving.

And then you hear sirens! The police pull you over, and it's your fellow policemen. They start to laugh and call for other police cars. A crowd is gathering, and they know you're a man. The officers throw you around and take you to the station. The women are disgusted, and the chief will take your gun and badge. You are humiliated, and they call you "sick." Your kids are crying as they return from school because others tease them about having a perverted father. Look what you've done to yourself!

—(Brownell and others, 1977, pp. 1147–1148).

Figure 8–13 shows the average percentages of full erection (measured by penis circumference) during a baseline period, during covert sensitization, and upon follow-up. The figure also shows self-reported changes in sexual arousal to transvestite stimuli. Both the physiological and self-report measures revealed a sizable decrease in sexual arousal. In addition, physiological and

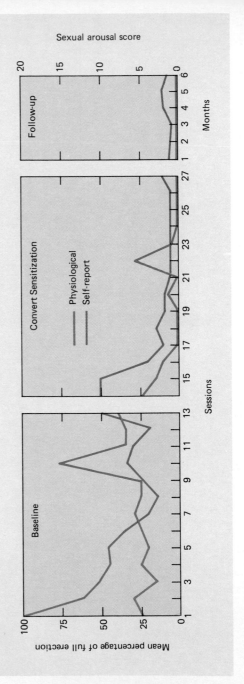

FIGURE 8–13

Mean percentages of full erection and sexual arousal scores (based on actual measurements and self-reports) for a transvestite man during baseline, treatment (covert sensitization), and follow-up periods. (Adapted from K. D. Brownell, S. C. Hayes, and D. H. Barlow. Patterns of appropriate and deviant sexual arousal: The behavioral treatment of multiple sexual deviations. *Journal of Consulting and Clinical Psychology, 45* [1977], pp. 1144–1155, Copyright © 1977 by the American Psychological Association. Adapted by permission of the author.)

self-reported arousal in response to heterosexual stimuli increased. The client, who had received prior treatment for his sexual difficulties, was surprised at the effectiveness of the covert sensitization.

For some transvestites, it is not the clothes themselves that are exciting, but rather the ability to fool the public and be taken for a woman. One transvestite was asked if he would feel happier if social custom allowed people to dress as they wished in public.

"Heavens, no," he smiled. "Merely to be allowed to wear women's clothes in public is nothing. It is the challenge of being so much like a woman that no one knows I'm a man that turns me on. The combination of doing something that I want to, that everyone says is impossible and is forbidden anyway, produces in me an arousal which, because it is in a sexual context, becomes sexual arousal."

—(Gosselin and Wilson, 1980, p. 67)

Sexual Sadism and Masochism

For some people, inflicting or experiencing pain and indignity is linked to sexual gratification. Many people incorporate mildly painful acts—such as biting, nipping, and spanking—into their sexual practices. When both partners enjoy them, these activities can enhance sexual pleasure. However, sadists and masochists often go beyond mild pain and, moreover, cannot enjoy sex any other way. To the **sadist**, achieving orgasm depends on humiliating others or inflicting pain on them. This is often referred to as "discipline." To the **masochist**, sexual satisfaction depends on "bondage"—suffering, humiliation, pain, and ill treatment at the hands of others. Sadism and masochism occur in both heterosexual and homosexual relationships, but, like other sexual deviations, they are poorly understood. Some clinical workers have conjectured that the roots of sadism and masochism are to be found in childhood; others have mentioned possible biological factors. One area that would seem to merit study is the fantasy life of these individuals, for example, the thoughts associated with their sexual activities.

The sexual masochist experiences arousal through his or her own suffering, preferably by being humiliated and beaten. Masochists have fantasies, often beginning in childhood, in which they are bound, tortured, raped, or otherwise abused in ways that they cannot prevent. These fantasies and acts are far more common in males than in females. Five features are found in most cases of sadomasochism: agreement as to which partner is to be dominant and which one submissive, awareness by both partners that they are role playing, the consent of both participants, a sexual context, and a shared understand-

ing by both participants that their behavior is sadomasochistic (Weinberg and others, 1984).

In sadomasochistic relationships the participants agree on the limits beforehand.

My wife and I do play dominance and submission games, and maybe we have the marks to prove it on occasion. But the one playing top dog watches like a hawk to make sure we stop when the other one doesn't like it any more.

Often a signal is set up so that the submissive partner can stop the session at any time if the agreed-upon boundaries are exceeded. One sadomasochistic prostitute explained her approach.

When you have a new client, what I used to do was I used to sit down and I would talk to them first and find out exactly what they wanted. Because sometimes you can get into a session with somebody and get very brutal and that's not what they want. There's heavy dominance and there's light dominance and there's play acting, roles, all different kinds. So the best thing to do is to sit down and talk to somebody first,

—(Weinberg, 1978, p. 29)

When sadomasochism is a person's predominant sexual style, the most common way of reaching other sadomasochistic devotees is the use of ads in sadomasochistic magazines. For example:

Beautiful Dominatrix, 24. A true sophisticate of the bizarre and unusual. I have a well equipped dungeon in my luxurious home. You will submit to prolonged periods of degradation for my pleasure. Toilet servitude a must. I know what you crave and can fulfill your every need.

A very pretty 30-year-old female has fantasies about receiving hand spankings on bare behind. I've never allowed myself to act out any of the fantasies. Is there anyone out there who'd like to correspond with me about their fantasies or experience with spanking?

—(Weinberg and Falk, 1980, pp. 385–386)

As these examples show, the ads contain code messages. "Toilet servitude," for instance, refers to handling feces or being defecated on. Sadomasochistic experiences can also be enhanced by hoods, paddles, enema equipment, adult diapers, and other paraphernalia sold in sex shops. For those who wish to pursue such activities at home, this equipment can now be found in "sex boutiques" in middle-class neighborhoods (see Figure 8–14).

Masochistic needs can also be satisfied without actually inflicting pain. For many couples, the fantasied aspect of violence is most important.

Many of the subjects in one group—for example, the fetishists—had sexual interests that overlapped those in the other groups (see Figure 8–15). Thirty-five percent of any group had all three sets of interests. The biggest overlaps were between fetishists and sadomasochists and between fetishists and transvestites. This research suggests that very often sadomasochism and transvestism are elaborations of an early-learned fetish. Gosselin and Wilson conclude that these sexually variant behaviors are not the deliberate choice of an individual looking for "kicks," but rather a logical, if unfortunate, reaction of a shy, introverted, emotionally sensitive child to a restrictive sexual upbringing.

Sadomasochists may be heterosexual, bisexual, or homosexual in their choice of partners. A questionnaire study showed few differences among these groups (Breslow and others, 1986). In general, subjects in all three groups felt that their sadomasochistic interests were natural ones that were present in childhood. People in all three groups used ads to make contact with others with similar interests. Few subjects in any of the groups reported being sexually abused as children although a sizable minority felt emotionally abused. In general, the homosexual respondents tended to sometimes take the dominant and sometimes the submissive role in their sadomasochistic activities. Heterosexual and bisexual subjects were about equally divided into "predominantly dominant," "predominantly submissive," or "adopting either" roles. Although more men then women seem to be interested in sadomasochism, in one survey using questionnaires placed in a sadomasochistic contact magazine, 40 percent of those who responded were female (Breslow and others, 1985).

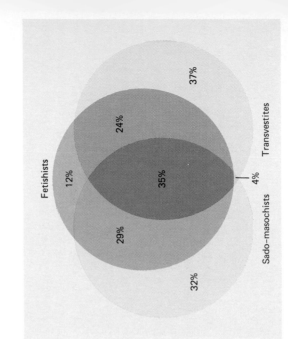

FIGURE 8–15
The overlap of sexual interests among groups of male fetishists, transvestites, and sadomasochists. (Gosselin and Wilson, 1980, p. 167. Copyright © 1980 by Glenn Wilson and Chris Gosselin.)

FIGURE 8–14
The leather clothing, restraints, and whips shown in this sex shop display are attractive to many sadists and masochists.

Of course, he doesn't really hurt me. I mean quite recently he tied me down ready to receive "punishment," then by mistake he kicked my heel with his toe as he walked by. I gave a yelp, and he said "Sorry love—did I hurt you?"

—(Gosselin and Wilson, 1980, pp. 54–55)

My wife believes in discipline. If she gets angry and yells at me, I get an erection. If she ever raises her hand as if to hit me, I get so excited I can't stand it. Actually she has never hit me. When I have fantasies of her hitting or slapping me, my penis becomes erect immediately.

Few studies of fetishists, transvestites, and sadomasochists have been carried out because of the many difficulties involved in obtaining subjects. The results of the studies that have been done so far are hard to interpret because of the unrepresentative samples that investigators are forced to use. Researchers have become very creative in searching for these hard-to-find subjects. For example, one recent study utilized the membership lists of organizations for fetishists, sadomasochists, and transvestites (Gosselin and Wilson, 1980). The subjects, all males, were given the Eysenck Personality Questionnaire (Eysenck and Eysenck, 1975), a paper-and-pencil test that measures extraversion, neuroticism, and psychotism and includes a "lie scale" intended to screen out test takers who do not answer candidly. A questionnaire on life style, sexual characteristics, sexual fantasies, and childhood and adolescent experiences was also included. On the basis of these measures, all three sexually deviant groups were found to be more introverted and more inclined to fantasy than a control group. In the control group, 18 percent of the men could be considered fetishistic on the basis of their sexual fantasies, but only 2 to 5 percent could be called sadomasochistic or had transvestite fantasies.

Autoerotic Asphyxia

Sometimes sadomasochistic needs are satisfied by dangerous **autoerotic practices** or solo sex-related activities. Unintended deaths may result from these practices, but such deaths are rather rare. In the United States an estimated 500 to 1,000 deaths per year result from autoerotic activities (Hazelwood and others, 1983). Little research has been done on this group, but a study of 70 consecutive cases received by the FBI showed that two-thirds of the victims had died while using materials or devices such as ropes, handcuffs, chains, hoods, gags, blindfolds, and belts to physically restrain or mentally humiliate themselves (Hazelwood and others, 1983).

The following is a typical case.

The victim, a 32-year-old married father of three, was discovered dead on his bed by his 11-year-old daughter. The victim was dressed in pantyhose, a lady's sweater, and a brassiere. His hands were restrained to his sides by a soft belt. A sanitary pad was in his mouth and a pink brassiere was wrapped over the mouth and around the head. His scrotum was swollen and exhibited two round areas resembling old cigarette burns. A similar type burn was located on the inner aspect of the left thigh near the scrotum. The cause of death was determined to be accidental asphyxiation. Because of the slack in the belt restraining his wrists, it would have been possible for the victim to slip his feet between his arms, thereby allowing him to remove the gag. Apparently his judgment was impaired due to his asphyxial state.

—(Hazelwood and others, 1981, p. 131)

This victim's sadomasochistic needs apparently led him to inflict burns on his own body as well as to use physical restraints. It seems likely that many individuals who inflict pain on themselves also have sadistic fantasies. Drawings of sadistic fantasies done by a man who ultimately died as a result of his autoerotic practices are shown in Figure 8–16.

Partial asphyxiation is often combined with masturbation to heighten sexual excitement. One person who had engaged in autoerotic asphyxia for many years by hanging himself while cross-dressed provided the following information about this practice in an interview.

He enjoyed the feeling as he lost consciousness and perceived his body going limp. Although he had difficulty expressing the exact nature of the sensation, it appeared that numbness and possibly tingling were part of what he sought, and that a dissociative feeling of watching his body go limp may have played a major role for him. His habit was to use asphyxia as a prelude to masturbation, and he reported that he never ejaculated during asphyxiation. When rushed for time, instead of cross-dressing and hanging himself, he would "give myself a quickie" by applying pressure to both sides of his neck with one hand until losing consciousness.

—(Hazelwood and others, 1983, p. 84)

The majority of autoerotic deaths occur in teenagers and young adult males, although the reported age range is 9 to 77 and a small number of female deaths have been reported (Brody, 1984). Some health professionals believe that parents should be aware of this behavior. As the mother of one victim commented,

FIGURE 8–16
Sketches of sadistic sexual fantasies drawn by a victim of autoerotic asphyxia. Reprinted by permission of the publisher, from *Autoerotic Fatalities* by Robert R. Hazelwood, Park Elliott Dietz, and Ann Wolbert Burgess, Lexington, MA: Lexington Books. D. C. Heath and Company, Copyright © 1983, D. C. Heath and Company.

Yes, I saw the marks, a rashlike redness on his throat—"an allergy," he said. Yes, he did take long showers but all boys do. . . . We saw all the signs . . . and my husband and I ignored them because we had never heard of adolescent sexual asphyxia. . . . After our son died, we called his school and told them what really happened. We begged them to warn other students, but nothing was ever done. The next year, another boy in the school died in exactly the same way.

—(Brody, 1984, p. 20)

Table 8-3 lists some warning signs that may suggest autoerotic asphyxial practices.

Voyeurism

Some sexual variations are not physically harmful but may be upsetting for the victim. One example is **voyeurism**, the impulse to spy on others, usually strangers. The French word "voyeur" means "watcher." The voyeur is subject to an irresistible, repetitive urge to spy on others through windows or doors, in public toilets, in parks, or on beaches, and particularly enjoys watching other people have sex. Like the exhibitionist (to be described shortly), the voyeur or "peeping Tom" is male and achieves sexual gratification from doing something forbidden. Also like the exhibitionist, the voyeur is usually harmless and will run if he is discovered. In some cases, however, usually after feeling intensely stimulated or provoked, the voyeur will let his presence be known—for example, he may exhibit his genitals and ask his victim to touch him or even to masturbate him. Cases have been known in which the voyeur tried to force the victim to have sexual intercourse with him, but such cases are exceptional.

Voyeurism begins in early childhood and usually continues over a long period. Fifty percent of those arrested for voyeurism are later rearrested for similar acts. About one-fourth of the men who are arrested for peeping are married. When voyeuristic acts are related to life stress, the impulse to commit them usually decreases

when the stress dissipates. While voyeurs show few signs of serious mental disorders, they usually have unsatisfying heterosexual relationships.

Exhibitionism

Exhibitionists, who are always males, repeatedly expose their genitals to unsuspecting strangers in public places as a way of experiencing sexual arousal. The exhibitionist does not want to harm anyone; his act of exposure is done for his own sexual gratification. His arousal is apparently heightened by seeing people react with amazement or shock when he unexpectedly shows his penis (see Figure 8–17). Exhibitionists expose their genitals mainly to women and children. One-third of all people arrested for sex offenses are exhibitionists, and about 20 percent of these are arrested more than once.

Exhibitionism can begin between preadolescence and middle age, but it occurs most frequently during the twenties. An exhibitionist has a irresistible, compulsive need to expose his genitals, and he does so despite the anxiety, depression, and shame he feels as a result. Acts of genital exposure often seem to be triggered by feelings of excitement, fear, restlessness, and sexual

FIGURE 8–17
Exhibitionists receive sexual gratification from the shock and alarm expressed by their victims. A response of this kind would provide no sexual gratification.

TABLE 8-3

Signs of Possible Autoerotic Asphyxial Practices

1. Frequently bloodshot eyes
2. Marks on the neck
3. Disoriented or foggy behavior, especially after having gone off alone for awhile
4. Great interest in or possession of ropes, chains, plastic bags, or gas inhalation devices

arousal. When overcome by these feelings, the exhibitionist is driven to find relief. Both psychodynamic and behavioral therapies (particularly aversion therapy) have been tried with exhibitionists. Although both methods seem to achieve some success, the results are unpredictable.

Obscene Telephone Calls

Another way of obtaining sexual gratification with a nonconsenting individual is by making obscene telephone calls. The caller almost always tries to get his victim to give him intimate information, often of a sexual nature, by pretending to be conducting a survey about menstruation, contraception, or sexual practices. In another type of obscene call, the caller masturbates while graphically describing the process to the victim.

Pedophilia

Pedophilia differs from the paraphilias discussed so far. Although it involves the desire for sexual gratification from another nonconsenting human being, in the case of pedophilia that human being is a child. Because of this, pedophilia is considered a much more serious crime than exhibitionism and voyeurism. Pedophiles (who are predominantly male) can be either heterosexual or homosexual, but the odds are two to one that a pedophile is a heterosexual. Girls 8 to 11 years old are the primary targets of pedophiles. In about 90 percent of all cases, the pedophile is someone whom the child knows.

One researcher has classified pedophiles into two groups: fixated and regressed (Groth, 1984). **Fixated pedophiles** begin during adolescence to focus on children as sex objects. They usually remain single and often have their only important sexual relationships with children. **Regressed pedophiles** turn to sexual interest in children only after some serious and negative event in their own lives. These men may be married, and often seem to be seeking a child as a substitute for a woman. They are also likely to have problems of alcohol abuse. Although the two groups may choose either boys or girls or both as their sexual targets, a greater proportion of the children sought by regressed pedophiles are girls.

Pedophilic behavior may take a variety of forms including exposure of the pedophile's sexual body parts to the child; kissing, hugging, and fondling the child in a sexual way; touching sexual parts of the child's body or inducing the child to touch or fondle the pedophile's sexual organs; or attempted or actual intercourse with the child. Later in the chapter we will further discuss sexual victimization of children and ways to prevent it.

Perspectives on the Paraphilias

No single theory has so far been able to explain the development of paraphilic behavior. Each of the perspectives have implications for research in terms of definition of the variant behavior, preferred type of treatment, appropriate treatment goals, and ways of assessing treatment outcome.

The psychodynamic perspective views paraphiliac behavior as a reflection of unresolved conflicts during psychosexual development (Freud, 1969). This view leads to long-term treatment that focuses on changing personality structure and dynamics and also altering overt behavior and sexual fantasies.

The behavioral perspective views sexual variance as something learned by the same rules as more usual sexual behavior—through conditioning, modeling, reinforcement, generalization, and punishment. From this perspective the definition of variant sexual behavior would be based on any personal discomfort of the individual with the behavior and any conflict between this behavior and the rules of society. The treatment which can be as short as one day or much longer is based on understanding the immediate antecedents and consequences of the behavior and on developing alternate forms of sexual arousal. Treatment effectiveness is based on overt behavior as measured by self-monitoring and psychophysiological measures. A broader behavioral view from the social-learning perspective explains the variant behavior as a substitute for deficits in social and sexual functioning, or inability to form a satisfactory marital relationship. The treatment goal is to assist the client to form satisfactory relationships through teaching interpersonal skills. Outcome measures here are client's self-reports of satisfying relationships with significant others as well as of satisfactory sexual relationships.

The biological perspective deals with heredity, prenatal hormonal environment, and a focus on the biological causes of gender identity. The treatment goals include suppression of the variant behaviors and of sexual responsiveness in general and may involve the use of drugs or surgery. The outcome is usually measured in terms of psychophysiological responses as well as sexual activity.

Treatment of the Paraphilias

No one type of treatment seems to be clearly superior for the paraphilias. Much of the research has severe shortcomings and consists of single-subject studies without control subjects. These shortcomings are not surprising when the difficulty of doing research in this area is considered. There is tentative evidence across many studies that behavioral treatment may be effective in reducing or eliminating some paraphiliac sexual behavior and increasing appropriate sexual behavior instead (Kilmann and others, 1982). Many of the therapeutic efforts reported used a variety of behavioral treatments that included aversion therapy. The programs were most effective when they were tailored for the specific problems of the individual paraphiliac. In some cases, especially those concerning exhibitionist and transvestite paraphiliacs, relapses were common and booster sessions were necessary to ensure continued change over time.

As an example of a behavioral technique, covert sensitization was used as a therapy for a 39-year-old married man who had been convicted of sexually molesting his 10-year-old niece (Levin and others, 1977). Before and after the covert sensitization training, the client was shown slides with pictures of young girls and of adult women. Figure 8–18 compares the man's subjective ratings of his sexual arousal by slides of girls and women. His attraction to and anxiety over attraction to slides of women increased dramatically. Although his attraction to young girls decreased only slightly, there was a decrease in the anxiety aroused by them. A physiological measure, magnitude of penile erection, showed the same pattern of changes in attraction.

Biological treatment may be used in combination with other therapies. For instance, trials of the drug **medroxyprogesterone acetate** (MPA) (marketed as Depo-Provera), which temporarily reduces the level of testosterone in the blood, suggest that it may be effective in

reducing compulsive sexual urges. Together with counseling, MPA may help some sex offenders keep their impulses under control. This treatment, which is still highly experimental, does not seem to be effective for sex offenders whose behavior contains a high degree of aggression (Bower, 1981). However, when combined with intensive therapy both in prison and after offenders return to the community, this drug seems to be effective (Groth, 1984).

Sexual Victimization

Some sexual deviations involve a participant who is either unwilling, uninformed, vulnerable, or too young to give legal consent. Among the clearest examples of such deviations are rape and child sexual abuse. When individuals who practice these deviations come into contact with the law, they are usually known as **sex offenders** and are subjected to a variety of treatments as well as to imprisonment. Some cases of rape and child sexual abuse are examples of paraphilias; others are examples of gratification through aggression or, in the case of child sexual abuse, desire for an easily obtainable and easily coerced sexual partner.

Child Sexual Abuse

Cases of actual or suspected child sexual abuse have been in the headlines in recent years. Since 1978 several major surveys have been carried out to determine how frequently child sexual victimization occurs (Painter, 1986). In all these surveys information was gathered from adults about their experience of sexual abuse during their own childhoods. Very different rates were reported in these surveys because they used varying definitions of sexual abuse. Some defined sexual abuse in terms of physical contact ranging from touching or fondling to sexual intercourse or oral–genital or anal–genital contact. Others also included noncontact abuse such as exposure of the offender's genitals or requests for sexual involvement. Partly as a result of these different definitions, and partly as a result of different survey techniques, the rates of abuse reported ranged from about 12 percent to over 50 percent. When these rates are compared with the number of cases reported to social agencies or the police, there is a large difference. Probably only about one-quarter of the cases are actually reported (Finkelhor and Hotaling, 1984). One reason for the low percentage of cases reported is that abuse by family members is usually not made known to the authorities. In one study, 73 percent of the cases were re-

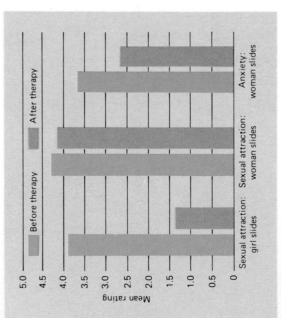

FIGURE 8–18
Changes in a pedophile's ratings of attraction toward girls and toward women, and changes in anxiety toward women before and after therapy. (Levin and others, 1977, p. 907)

ported when the offender was a stranger; when the offender was a family member, no cases were reported. When adults were reporting on their own past experiences, family members were the offenders one-third of the time. But when parents reported on their children's experiences, only 10 percent involved family members (Finkelhor, 1984). This difference also points to an underreporting of child sexual abuse. Of even greater concern, the very acts that may be the most harmful, those carried out by someone with continued access to the child, are the least likely to be reported. Special materials have been developed to help clinicians interview young children to determine whether sexual abuse has occurred. Some of these materials (like those in Figure 8–19) can also be used in play therapy for the treatment of the sexually abused child.

What are the characteristics of families and individuals that may mean a high risk of sexual abuse? Children in step-, foster, and adoptive families seem to be most likely to be victimized (Russell, 1984). Other high-risk groups are children in families where there is marital discord and families in which physical violence and spouse abuse are frequent (Walker, 1984). These groups usually show disruption in family relationships, lack of supervision of children, and focus of attention by the parents on their own concerns rather than on those of the children.

What are the effects of sexual abuse in childhood? In the short term the child may show sexual preoccu-pation including excessive or public masturbation and an unusual interest in sexual organs and sex play. Another likely result is frequent physical complaints and problems such as rashes, vomiting, and headaches, none of which can be explained by medical examination. Some researchers think that at puberty the problems may intensify. What results carry over into adulthood is unclear. Sexual abuse in childhood may result in problems of depression and low self-esteem as well as in sexual difficulties, either avoidance of sexual contact or promiscuity or prostitution (Fromuth, 1986). In a study of college women, a relationship was found between a history of childhood sexual abuse and some measures of adjustment (Fromuth, 1986). However, the degree of family support seemed to account for most of these relationships. An exception was anxiety that took the form of one or more phobias. Even if the family was supportive, the abused group showed more phobic anxiety than the controls. It may be that psychological adjustment is more related to the general family atmosphere than to the specific sexual experience. In contrast to this finding, family support was not protective when adult sexual adjustment was considered. Childhood sexual abuse was related to increased sexual activity, homosexual experiences, and later nonconsensual sex or rape. These relationships existed even when family support was taken into account. Although many people seem to emerge from childhood sexual abuse with no long-term effects, we do not yet have a very good idea

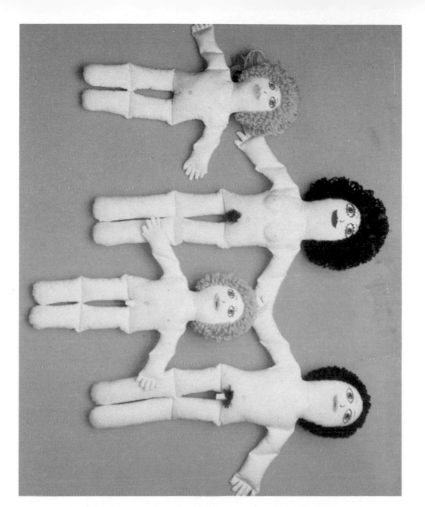

FIGURE 8–19
Anatomically correct dolls such as these can be used to aid in interviewing child victims of sexual abuse, for court testimony and play therapy. The dolls, available in several racial types, have anal, oral, and genital openings, breasts or penises, and pubic hair. They also have movable tongues and fingers to aid in the description of oral molestation or masturbation. (From Real People Dolls, Hylands Anatomical Dolls, Inc., 4455 Torrance Blvd., Suite 310, Torrance, CA 90503).

of how others may be affected. Research studies suggest that the kinds of abuse that appear to be the most damaging are those that involve father figures, genital contact, and force (Browne and Finkelhor, 1986).

As reports of sexual abuse of children have increased, ways to protect children have been investigated. Some information campaigns have concentrated on children's contacts with strangers—for example, "Never get into a car with anyone you don't know," "Never go with someone who says he or she has some candy for you." However, in the majority of reported assaults children are victimized by people they know. To prevent this kind of assault, children need to be taught to recognize signs of trouble and to be assertive enough to report them to a responsible adult. One novel approach is found in a child's picture book called *Private Zones* (Dayee, 1982). The pictures and text are designed to impress on children in simple, nonthreatening language the concept of private zones, who can touch them, what "good" and "bad" touching is, and the importance of communicating an intrusion to a responsible adult. Figure 8–20 shows an illustration from the book along with some of the text.

FIGURE 8–20

Private Zones is designed to inform even very young children about possible trouble signs in adult behavior toward them. The text accompanying this picture reads: This is Tommy! This is Susie! They are going to the beach. They are wearing bathing suits to the beach. Do you know what bathing suits cover? Bathing suits cover special parts of the body called the PRIVATE ZONE. The parts of *your body* your bathing suit covers is *your* PRIVATE ZONE. You have a PRIVATE ZONE. Big people like Mommies and Daddies have PRIVATE ZONES, big kids and small kids that go to school have PRIVATE ZONES. Tommy and Susie have PRIVATE ZONES. Even babies have PRIVATE ZONES.

Rape

Rape, or having sexual intercourse forcibly and without the partner's consent, is a seriously underreported crime. Only about 15 to 20 percent of all forcible rapes are reported to authorities probably because of the emotional trauma experienced by the victim. In the United States, a rape occurs about every 6 minutes (Riesenberg, 1987) (see Figure 8–21). The great majority of convicted rapists are sent to civil prisons for fixed sentences, but some states maintain special treatment facilities for sexual offenders, particularly those who are violent.

Rapes fall into three general categories: power rape, anger rape, and sadistic rape. In a **power rape,** the rapist, who usually feels inadequate and awkward in interpersonal relationships, intimidates the victim with threats of physical harm. In an **anger rape,** the rapist seems to be seeking revenge on women in general and expresses his rage through physical and verbal abuse. He seems to get little or no sexual satisfaction from the rape. The third and rarest type, **sadistic rape,** seems to combine sexuality and aggression and focuses on the suffering of the victim. Rape is not usually motivated by sexual desire and sexual satisfaction seems limited in rape; in one large study, half the rapists had difficulties with erection or ejaculation during the rape itself (Burgess and Baldwin, 1981).

Men between the ages of 20 and 24 are the largest group arrested for rape. The next most-frequent group are 15- to 19-year-old males. Adolescent males aged 12 through 19 account for almost a quarter of the forcible rapes and attempted rapes against all ages of victims (Davis and Leitenberg, 1987).

Date Rape

Many rapes are committed by people who are known to the person who is attacked. Date rape is common according to surveys of university students. About 16 percent of women college students in two different surveys reported that they had been raped by someone they knew or were dating (Sherman, 1985). Eleven percent of the college men in the surveys said they had forced a woman to have intercourse. The typical story was something like what happened to a 20-year-old junior at Carlow College in Pittsburgh.

She met him two years ago at a fraternity party on a neighboring campus. His dashing good looks, she recalls now, coupled with his shy grin and friendly manner made him appear "sweet, but not macho." They talked and danced for hours, and later that evening, he took her in his arms and they kissed.

When he asked if she would like to get something to eat, she agreed. But instead of heading toward a

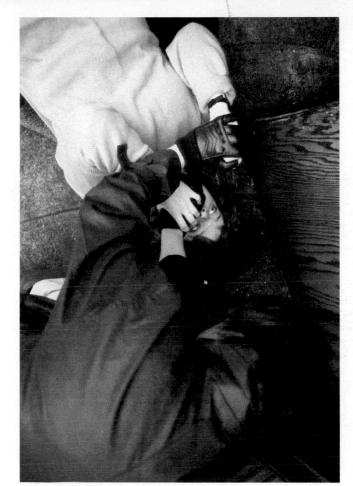

nearly restaurant, he swerved onto a side street, pulled over to the curb and stopped the car. Then he raped her.

—(Sherman, 1985, p. 17)

Research with both high school and college students shows that a sizeable minority of students do not believe that date rape is definitely unacceptable behavior (Mahoney, 1983). The material in Table 8–4 provides information to counter this misperception of the social norm. In a study based on questionnaire responses of college students, those students who were more accepting of date rape were less sure that forcible date rape is really rape, were more traditional in their attitudes toward women, were more self-permissive about premarital sex with friends or acquaintances, and had less knowledge about sex than other students (Fischer, 1986). A measure of acceptance of force in sexual intercourse was found to be correlated with how often college men admitted using force to have intercourse, how much force was used, and with a lower degree of social responsibility and social conscience (Rapaport and Burkart, 1984).

In another research effort, male college students were asked how likely they would be to rape a woman if they could be assured of not being caught. About 35 percent said that there was some likelihood that they would commit rape under such conditions. Men who reported a higher likelihood of committing rape showed greater aggression toward women in a laboratory setting and were also more highly aroused when shown depictions of rape. In fact, their responses closely resem-

bled those of convicted rapists (Malamuth, 1981). These findings suggest that aggression and rape are closely tied together for many individuals and also that the thought of rape does not have completely negative social implications for many young men.

TABLE 8-4

Typical Aspects of Teenage Sexual Assaults and Guidelines for Prevention

The typical teenage sexual assault is committed by a boyfriend or acquaintance and occurs during a date.

Most assaults among teenagers do not involve severe physical violence or the use of a weapon.

The kind of force typically used is verbal pressure.

Most victims are able to prevent an assault from being completed.

Often, drinking or drug use by the offender plays a part in causing the assault.

Although most teenage victims do not have prolonged emotional reactions to sexual assaults, some express fears, depression, and anger years after the experience.

This type of sexual assault can often be prevented by remembering—and following—two simple guidelines:

Everyone has the right to say "no" to unwanted sexual contact.

No one has the right to force sexual contact on another person.

Agton, 1985, p. iii.

The Effects of Rape

One woman in her midtwenties who had been raped agreed to be interviewed about her experience by a medical publication. This is part of her comments.

She told of the chance meeting with a male acquaintance after work one night more than a year ago. As they walked near her home, the man suggested they go into a deserted park and talk for awhile. Once there, he began forcibly fondling her. When she resisted, he threatened to hurt her, pulled off some of her clothing, and raped her.

The victim broke loose, ran out of the park, and began knocking on doors across the street. No one answered; she ran several blocks before spotting a police car. The officers were unable to locate the attacker; they took the victim to a hospital.

What happened at the hospital and afterward? *"I had an examination, and then the police assigned a detective to my case. The next day the rapist was apprehended. At first I didn't want to press charges, because I didn't want to be responsible for sending someone to jail. However, a good friend helped me decide to go ahead with it by saying: You owe it to yourself and a lot of other women."*

You were living with family members at the time. Were they supportive? *"I only told my brother. He said he was sorry it had happened, but that I shouldn't have been out with the guy."*

Did the authorities make you feel awkward because this was an acquaintance rape? *"No, I didn't get that feeling—not at all. The state's attorney did say that it is sometimes more difficult to prosecute [so-called] date rape, but the judge found probable cause at the hearing, and a trial date was set."*

What was your mental state while waiting for the trial? *"I had a lot of depression, a lot of crying, a lot of fear. I began sleeping with a knife beside me in bed. A month after the rape, I decided to seek counseling. As the trial date approached, I had doubts: on the one hand, I just didn't want to deal with it anymore, but, on the other hand, I did want to see it through. A few days before the trial, he [the attacker] pleaded guilty and was given a prison term."*

Did that put an end to your anxiety? *"No, I felt a strong need for counseling. For one thing, I was troubled about developing relationships with men. I recently broke off with a man who was becoming sexually demanding. I know others feel a need for ongoing counseling too; in my group [therapy sessions], there are women whose rape occurred over ten years ago."*

As this anecdote illustrates, the psychological effects of rape can be long lasting. In one study, 36 percent of those raped had not recovered 4 to 6 years after the attack (Bateman, 1986). Generalized feelings of anxiety and fear were higher in the rape victims than in controls no matter how many years had passed since the rape. Estimates are that 80 percent of the rape victim's primary relationships break up within a year of the rape (Riesenberg, 1987). Male partners of female rape victims often show a predictable sequence of behavior (Bateman, 1985). First comes about a week of anger followed by a protective phase. Both of these are accompanied by avoidance of the victim and by anxiety. After about a month the partner becomes depressed and feels guilty, and sexual difficulties with the victim continue. At the end of 3 months of follow-up the partners still felt guilt and depression.

Rape victims need to know what to do and where to go after the rape in order to obtain medical, mental-health, social, and legal services. They also need immediate and follow-up medical care for physical trauma, collection of medicolegal evidence, prevention of venereal disease, and protection against unwanted pregnancy. Rape victims need to be listened to and helped to talk about their experience, as well as to be given basic information and assistance in making decisions about further steps to be taken. An important source of help for rape victims is rape-relief centers where information and psychological support may be obtained (see Figure 8–22).

Response to Victimization

The fears that persist after the experience of rape tend to restrict and control the victim's life. The most prevalent fears are of being alone, of strangers, of going out, and of darkness. Women who have been victims of sudden and violent assaults by strangers are especially likely to remain fearful and depressed for a long time, and they are also more likely to avoid dating for a long period (Ellis and others, 1981).

From the social-learning perspective, a rape is part of an in vivo classical-conditioning situation in which the threat of death or physical damage elicits a strong autonomic arousal, fear. Any stimulus that is present during the rape—darkness, being alone, a man with a particular appearance, being alone—becomes associated with the fear response. These cues then become conditioned stimuli that independently evoke fear and anxiety. Because some of these stimuli are often encountered by the victim in her daily life, she may begin to use avoidance behavior to escape them. This decreases the likelihood that the conditioned fear response will dissipate over time. Behavior therapy offers a way of overcoming these problems. By using both cognitive and behavioral tech-

—(Adapted from Riesenberg, 1987).

—(Sherman, 1985, p. 19)

FIGURE 8-22
Rape-relief centers, often staffed by volunteers, provide immediate support for rape victims as well as information about what medical and legal services to seek and where to find them. These centers attempt to reduce the social stigma that many rape victims experience.

niques, victims can learn to overcome their avoidance behavior and thus extinguish their anxiety (Veronen and Kilpatrick, 1983).

Since an estimated 10 to 20 percent of rape victims have continuing problems of sexual dysfunction several years after the rape, they may also be helped by sex therapy that takes into account anger and resentment toward men, guilt and self-blame, and attitudes toward their partners that may be a residue of the rape. Victims of uncontrollable events such as rape blame themselves for what has happened more than the objective situation suggests is realistic. For instance,

The young woman who was raped after the fraternity party berated herself initially for not picking out some flaw in her assailant's character. She recalls wondering whether her blouse was too low-cut, or whether she had said or done anything to provoke the assault.

Social-psychological research suggests that this self-blame by the victim might be a result of a desire to gain some control over the victimizing experience (Wortman, 1983). The perception that one is a victim and that to have others perceive one as a victim is unpleasant or aversive. Victims react to this aversiveness by evaluating the situation in ways that are self-enhancing (Taylor and others, 1983). Some of these strategies include:

1. minimizing the consequences by making comparisons with others who were less fortunate, or suggesting possible worse outcomes ("I might have been killed").

2. thinking of one's own adjustment to the events as better than most people could attain ("I think I did extremely well under the circumstances. Some people would just fall apart").

3. highlighting the gains from the victimization ("I was happy to find out that I am a very strong person. My life has been made better by this knowledge").

Male Rape Victims

It is likely that even fewer male rapes than female rapes are reported because of the stigma attached to them. Because society expects men to defend themselves rather than to become victims, a male rape victim may be automatically suspected of homosexuality. The response of male rape victims is similar to that of females (Goyer and Eddleman, 1984). Often their life style is temporarily disrupted, they have trouble eating and sleeping, feel depressed, and their sexual activity is negatively affected. They may develop fear of men and are also likely to feel long-lasting anger at the assailant. Rapists sometimes succeed in forcing their male victims to ejaculate, and this is likely to be especially disturbing to the victims. The comments of male rape victims highlight some of these issues.

Even a couple of years after, whenever I'd feel depressed or tired or something, this whole incident would come back to me. I'd think . . . what could I have done to prevent it?

I always thought a guy couldn't get hard if he was scared, and when this guy took me off it really messed up my mind. I thought maybe something was wrong with me. I didn't know what it meant and this really bothered me.

—(Groth and Burgess, 1980, p. 809)

Study Outline

CHANGING VIEWS OF SEXUAL BEHAVIOR

The ancient Greeks regarded sex as a pleasurable part of nature, to be enjoyed with partners of either sex. During the middle ages, however, church authorities were obsessed with the notion of sex as a sin. By the mid-nineteenth century women were expected to be morally pure and sexually inert. This view began to change in the early twentieth century, partly as a result of the writings of Sigmund Freud and Havelock Ellis.

GATHERING OBJECTIVE INFORMATION ABOUT SEXUAL BEHAVIOR

1. Alfred Kinsey pioneered in the gathering of scientific data about sexual behavior. He interviewed people about a wide variety of sexual practices and discovered that sexual behaviors that had been considered unusual or abnormal were in fact widely practiced. He and his co-workers published detailed statistical reports on the sexual behavior of heterosexual and homosexual males and females.

2. Observational studies have provided a great deal of information about the body's responses to sexual stimulation. The best-known observational studies were carried out by William Masters and Virginia Johnson under controlled laboratory conditions. On the basis of their findings, Masters and Johnson described a pattern of sexual response that consists of four stages: excitement, plateau, orgasm, and resolution.

3. Much experimental research on sexual behavior has studied the effects of erotic materials and alcohol on sexual response. The results of this research are contradictory.

SEXUAL VARIATIONS

1. **Homosexual behavior** is sexual behavior with members of one's own sex; **homosexuals** are individuals who prefer to engage in sexual activity with members of their own sex over an extended period. Female homosexuality is often called **lesbianism. Bisexuals** are sexually attracted to members of either sex and often engage in sexual activity with both men and women.

2. Homosexuality is not considered a disorder in DSM-III-R. Types of psychopathology found among homosexuals do not generally differ from those found among heterosexuals. Public attitudes toward homosexuality have tended to redefine homosexuality as an alternative life style, but this view may be changing as a result of the link between homosexuality and the transmission of AIDS.

3. There is no such thing as a homosexual personality or behavior pattern. Homosexuals have been found to have a variety of life styles, ranging from close-coupled to asexual. Male homosexuals report having had many more sexual partners than female homosexuals do.

4. Patterns of bisexuality also differ widely. Bisexuality is most likely to occur during group sex, as a result of sexual experimentation between same-sex friends who are otherwise heterosexual, and when people adopt a philosophy of sexual openness.

5. The role of biological factors in the development of sexual preference is unclear, although a prenatal excess or deficiency of sex hormones may be a factor. So far evidence does not support psychodynamic and behavioral explanations of homosexual preference.

SEXUAL DYSFUNCTION

1. Among the problems that are included in the category of sexual dysfunction are **impotence, frigidity, premature ejaculation,** and **retarded ejaculation.** In addition, many women have difficulty experiencing orgasm or never have orgasms. In **performance anxiety,** the man's preoccupation with sexual adequacy interferes with his performance.

2. Masters and Johnson believe that short-term treatment directed primarily at sexual problems can help most people who experience sexual dysfunction. They emphasize instruction in the sexual needs of both partners, together with exercises in erotic stimulation. Emphasis is also placed on communication between partners.

3. Behavioral approaches to the treatment of sexual dysfunction use such techniques as relaxation training and modeling. Some therapists combine behavioral approaches with psychodynamically oriented therapy. Further research is needed to determine which therapeutic elements are helpful and which are unnecessary.

GENDER-IDENTITY DISORDER

1. **Gender-identity disorder of childhood** occurs before puberty. Children with this disorder reject or deny their assigned gender.

2. **Transsexuals** are adults with disturbed gender identity who have an intense desire to change their anatomical structures to those of the other sex. Many of the candidates who apply for sexual-reassignment surgery are also psychologically disturbed in areas other than gender identity. Adults with **nontranssexual gender-identity disorder** feel their gender assignment is inap-

propriate and often cross-dress, but are not preoccupied with a surgical change in sex.

THE PARAPHILIAS

1. The term **paraphilia** refers to attraction to deviant objects or situations. Paraphilias may involve the use of a nonhuman object for sexual arousal, repetitive sexual activity with humans that involves suffering or humiliation, or repetitive sexual activity with nonconsenting partners.

2. **Fetishism** is a psychological state in which a nonliving object serves as a primary source of sexual arousal and consumption. It is not usually addressed by the law. Most fetishists are solitary in their activities, and the collection of fetishistic objects may be the main activity in their lives.

3. A **transvestite** uses clothing as a sexual stimulant or fetish. Most transvestites are heterosexual men who dress in women's clothes but continue to identify themselves as members of their biological sex. Covert sensitization has been found to be useful in treating this disorder.

4. To the **sadist**, achieving orgasm depends on humiliating others or inflicting pain on them. To the **masochist**, sexual satisfaction depends on suffering, humiliation, pain, and ill treatment at the hands of others. In sadomasochistic relationships the partners agree on the roles each will play and set limits on their activities beforehand. The sexual interests of fetishists, transvestites, and sadomasochists often overlap.

5. Sometimes sadomasochistic needs are satisfied by **autoerotic** practices, or solo sex-related activities. Among these activities is partial asphyxiation combined with masturbation.

6. **Voyeurs** obtain sexual gratification from spying on others, usually strangers, especially as they undress or engage in sexual activity. Voyeurs are usually harmless.

7. **Exhibitionists** repeatedly expose their genitals to unsuspecting strangers in public places as a way of experiencing sexual arousal. Another way of obtaining sexual gratification with a nonconsenting individual is by making obscene telephone calls.

8. **Pedophilia** involves the desire for sexual gratification from a child, often a girl between the ages of 8 and 11. **Fixated pedophiles** begin during adolescence to focus on children as sex objects; **regressed pedophiles** turn to sexual interest in children after a serious and negative event in their own lives.

SEXUAL VICTIMIZATION

1. **Child sexual abuse** may involve touching or fondling or actual intercourse. Some definitions include noncontact abuse such as exposure or asking the child to undress. Child sexual abuse by relatives is probably the most frequent type but is greatly underreported.

2. Short-term effects of child sexual abuse include sexual preoccupation and unexplained physical complaints. Long-term effects may be depression, low self-esteem, and sexual difficulties.

3. **Rape** is having sexual intercourse forcibly and without the partner's consent. In **power rape**, the rapist intimidates the victim with threats of physical harm; in **anger rape**, the rapist seems to be seeking revenge on women in general and expresses his rage through physical and verbal abuse; **sadistic rape** seems to combine sexuality and aggression and focuses on the suffering of the victim.

4. **Date rape**, rape committed by someone known to the person attacked, is common among high school and college students. A sizeable minority of students do not believe forcible date rape really qualifies as rape.

5. The effects of rape include long-lasting fear and anxiety, anger, guilt, and self-blame. Victims may deal with aversive events such as rape by minimizing the consequences through comparisons with other's problems, focusing on their good adjustment to the situation and highlighting personal gains resulting from the victimization.

CHAPTER 9

Personality Disorders

James Kerns, *Cat's Cradle*. Whitney Museum of American Art, New York. Purchased with funds from the Neysa McMein Purchase Award.

OBJECTIVES FOR CHAPTER NINE:

To learn:

1. The three groups of personality disorders and the names and characteristics of the disorders in each group

To understand:

1. The concept of personality disorder
2. Why so little is known about most personality disorders

D r. B., a 41-year-old family practitioner, was getting ready to leave his office at 6 P.M. to rush home and have supper before attending his son's final high school basketball game. The hospital called to inform him that one of his obstetric patients had arrived in Labor and Delivery and was currently showing 5 cm of cervical dilation. He knew that one of his partners was covering obstetrics that night, but he felt compelled to run by the hospital to check her before going home. After checking her, he decided to stay through the delivery, necessitating his missing his son's last game. After the delivery, the physician sat in the locker room and wept. He felt terribly guilt-ridden over missing the game, and as he reflected on the evening, he could not understand why he had not simply handed the case over to his partner. He poignantly stated later that he was not even emotionally attached to this particular patient. His own narcissism had gotten the best of him; i.e., he felt that *he* and *he alone* had to be the one to deliver the baby, as though his partner could not have performed exactly the same function.

—(Gabbard, 1985, p. 2928)

Presumably, most physicians function adequately in conducting their medical practice. Yet as a group, physicians often exhibit a personality style that emphasizes guilt feelings and an exaggerated sense of responsibility (Gabbard, 1985). This style may show itself in both adaptive and maladaptive ways. In one poll of 100 randomly selected physicians, all of them described themselves as "compulsive personalities" (Krakowski,

1982). Twenty percent met all the criteria for Compulsive Personality Disorder and 80 percent came close by meeting three criteria (four are required).

A person's characteristic ways of responding are often referred to as his or her **personality.** Most people's personality styles do not affect their behavior similarly in all situations. Personality styles can be maladaptive if an individual is unable to modify his or her behavior when the environment undergoes significant changes that call for different approaches. If personality characteristics are not flexible enough to allow an individual to respond adaptively to at least an ordinary variety of situations, a personality disorder may be present.

When personality styles become pathological, they can impair an individual's functioning in important situations and can lead to anxiety, feelings of distress, and unhappiness. The point at which a personality style becomes a personality disorder is unclear. **Personality disorders** are longstanding, maladaptive, and inflexible ways of relating to the environment. Such disorders can usually be noticed in childhood or at least by early adolescence, and may continue through adult life. They severely limit an individual's approach to stress-producing situations because his or her characteristic styles of thinking and behavior allow for only a rigid and narrow range of responses. It has been estimated that from 6 to 10 people in every 100 have a personality disorder (Merikangas and Weissman, 1986).

Personality disorders pose problems for people who construct classification systems, as well as for textbook writers and teachers of abnormal psychology. They seem important, and their existence can easily be recognized even by nonprofessional observers, yet little is known about their origins and development. With the exception of the Antisocial Personality Disorder or psychopathic personality (and until recently the Borderline Personality Disorder), very little research has been done on these problems, probably because they often are not dramatic or severely incapacitating and many people who might fall into these categories never seek help in dealing with their problems.

Although the maladaptive behavior that is typical of personality disorders sometimes causes great distress to the people involved, they find it difficult to change the way they think about and respond to situations. The clinical problems are intensified when, as is usually the case, the person does not regard his or her behavior patterns as maladaptive or undesirable even if the unpleasant and counterproductive consequences of those behaviors are obvious to others. As we will see in this chapter, this is perhaps most evident in cases of antisocial personality.

Classifying Personality Disorders

Personality disorders are diagnosed on Axis II of the DSM-III-R. Developmental disorders and mental retardation are also diagnosed on this axis. These three problems have in common a lifetime or near-lifetime duration and stability so that there are not likely to be periods of improvement or change. A diagnosis of personality disorder is made only when a person's inflexible long-lasting behavior pattern or personality style causes important problems in social situations or on the job, or when they result in a high level of personal distress. Table 9–1 lists the different personality disorders and figure 9–1 shows their frequency as well as how that frequency is divided between men and women. Unlike the disorders diagnosed on Axis II, Axis I disorders, called symptom disorders, may come or go. A person often has both a personality disorder and a symptom disorder. The relationship between personality disorders and symptom disorders is unclear, but whatever the relationship it is obviously a close one. Personality disorders may be thought of as vulnerabilities, but each personality disorder is associated with vulnerability to only some of the symptom disorders. For example, schizotypal personalities are thought to be susceptible to schizophrenia, dependent personalities to depression, avoidant personalities to social phobias, and borderline and antisocial personalities to drug and alcohol abuse. While this idea of increased vulnerability has some support, it is not a certainty. Another possibility includes personality disorders as milder forms of symptom disorders. Schizotypal disorder might be a mild form of schizophrenia and borderline disorder might be a form of mood disorder. One additional possibility is that the two groups are not related in cause but each makes the other worse once they are established.

In some instances, the classification statements of Axis II are used to provide information that bears on Axis I. In other instances, a personality disorder referred to on Axis II is the individual's major problem. Many combinations are possible. A person may have a diagnosis on both Axes I and II. Henry A. has psychotic symptoms that call for a diagnosis of schizophrenia. Before the present schizophrenic episode, however, Henry A. had shown several characteristics—odd speech, social isolation, suspiciousness, and hypersensitivity to real or imagined criticism—that had significantly impaired his effectiveness in a variety of situations. because of the different types of behaviors Henry A. shows, he was diagnosed using both Axis I and Axis II:

TABLE 9-1

DSM-III-R Classification of Personality Disorders

A. Odd or eccentric
 1. *Paranoid:* Tense, guarded, suspicious, hold grudges
 2. *Schizoid:* Socially isolated with restricted emotional expression
 3. *Schizotypal:* Peculiarities of thought, appearance, and behavior that are disconcerting to others; emotionally detached and isolated

B. Dramatic, emotional, or erratic
 1. *Antisocial:* Manipulative, exploitive, dishonest, and disloyal, lacking in guilt, habitually breaks social rules, has a childhood history of such behavior and also is often in trouble with the law
 2. *Borderline:* Cannot stand to be alone; intense, unstable moods and personal relationships; chronic anger; drug and alcohol abuse
 3. *Histrionic:* Seductive behavior, needs immediate gratification and constant reassurance, rapidly changing moods, shallow emotions
 4. *Narcissistic:* Self-absorbed, expects special treatment and adulation, envious of attention to others

C. Anxious or fearful
 1. *Avoidant:* Easily hurt and embarrassed, few close friends, sticks to routines to avoid new and possibly stressful experiences
 2. *Dependent:* Wants others to make decisions, needs constant advice and reassurance, fears being abandoned
 3. *Obsessive–compulsive:* Perfectionistic, overconscientious, indecisive, preoccupied with details, stiff, unable to express affection
 4. *Passive aggressive:* Resents demands and suggestions, procrastinates, sulks, "forgets" obligations, or is deliberately inefficient

D. Proposed additional DSM-III-R categories for study
 1. *Sadistic:* Takes pleasure in cruelty and violence, controls others by humiliation and intimidation
 2. *Self-defeating:* Creates situations that are certain to cause disappointment and rejection, feels exploited and mistreated

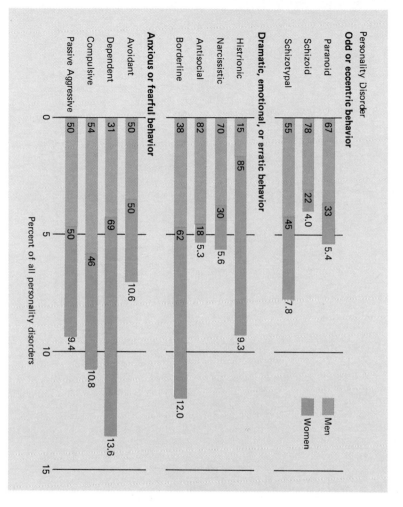

FIGURE 9–1
Not all personality disorders occur with equal frequency and not all affect men and women equally. Each bar shows what percent of all personality disorders are represented by each disorder. The different colored portions of each bar represent the proportion of men and women given this diagnosis. The total does not add up to 100 percent because a few personality disorders do not fit any of these categories. (Data from Millon, 1986)

shared by everyone diagnosed with a particular personality disorder. For instance, for a diagnosis of paranoid personality disorder, any four from a list of seven characteristics must be checked. This means that any two people given this classification might have quite different characteristics.

Personality disorders are grouped into three categories: odd or eccentric behaviors; dramatic, emotional, or erratic behaviors; and fearful or anxious behaviors (see Table 9–1).

- AXIS I: Schizophrenia, paranoid, chronic
- AXIS II: Schizotypal Personality Disorder (premorbid)

Gerry B. Showed similar personality characteristics, but there was no basis for an Axis I diagnosis. Her diagnosis would be as follows.

- AXIS I: _____
- AXIS II: Schizotypal Personality Disorder

A third individual, Deborah C., had characteristics of the same personality disorder that was seen in Henry A. and Gerry B. However, she had additional characteristics that fit another personality disorder. In this case both personality disorders would be diagnosed.

- AXIS I: _____
- AXIS II: Schizotypal Personality Disorder, Borderline Personality Disorder

Personality disorders produce the least reliable diagnoses of any DSM classification. One difficulty in deciding on the appropriateness of an Axis II diagnosis is the unclear boundary between those personality characteristics within normal limits and those that represent disordered behavior. Another problem is that as more research is done using the DSM-III-R criteria, it is clear that some of the categories overlap a great deal with each other. Rather than being separate disorders, they represent different degrees of the same general behaviors. About two-thirds of the patients who meet the criteria for one personality disorder will also meet the criteria for at least one more (Frances and Widiger, 1986). A third problem is that some personality disorders also overlap Axis I categories. For instance, in the study just mentioned, more than half of the individuals who were diagnosed as borderline also had a major affective disorder. If disorders are to be classified into separate types, their criteria should be distinct and mutually exclusive, and the number of ambiguous cases should be relatively few. Some DSM-III-R categories—for example, schizophrenia, the affective disorders, and the organic disorders—are relatively distinct from each other, although there are some fuzzy areas between them. This is not true of personality disorders, many of whose diagnostic criteria overlap.

Some of these problems come about because so little is known about most personality disorders. Another problem stems from the so-called **prototypal approach** used in DSM-III-R. Each disorder has a list of possible characteristics, and if more than a specific number are checked, the diagnosis of that disorder is given. This means that no one of the listed characteristics must be

Odd or Eccentric Behaviors
Paranoid Personality Disorder

People with **paranoid personality disorder** have three outstanding characteristics: unwarranted feelings of suspiciousness and mistrust of other people, hypersensitivity, and restricted emotional response. It is very difficult for such people to have close relationships with others because they are constantly expecting treachery.

A 36-year-old single white male engineer was referred for psychiatric evaluation, with his grudging cooperation, by his project manager. He described his current work situation as very tense because his co-workers had been "ganging up" on him, giving him the most difficult assignments and sometimes removing the crucial information he needed from the relevant files. He said they did this "because they like to see me sweat." He had changed jobs four times in the past 6 years because of similar problems at previous jobs. Aside from his frequent contact with a sibling, the patient was socially isolated. He stated, "I've never trusted people. All they want to do is take advantage of you." He was tense, aloof, and obviously very angry at his co-workers. He was hypervigilant and made several comments indicating that he felt that the interviewer might not "see things my way." There was no evidence of psychosis or depression.

—(Siever and Kendler, 1986, p. 199)

Paranoid individuals rarely seek clinical help. If the situation becomes so difficult that they are forced to seek help (for example, if they find themselves in a situation that requires them to work closely with other people), the therapist's hardest task is to penetrate the barrier of suspiciousness. They are also hypersensitive to criticism, making it especially difficult for them to function in subordinate positions. They have a strong fear of losing independence and the power to shape events. Just the feeling of being in a position of lower rank or lesser power might be intolerable.

For example, one such man could not bring himself to address his superiors at work by the title "Mr." He refused, as he put it, to "crawl" or "jump through the loop." Similarly, he could not bring himself to address his therapist as "Dr." even at their first meeting and used from the outset what he assumed was the therapist's nickname.

—(Shapiro, 1981, p. 138)

People with paranoid personality disorder often seem cold, humorless, devious, and scheming. These characteristics do not promote close, rewarding relationships. Perhaps because people with this kind of personality keep to themselves and rarely become intimate with others, many of their unusual ideas remain unnoticed. Their performance is often impaired, however, because their preoccupation with searching for hidden motives and special meanings limits their ability to consider and understand whole situations. When problems occur, they are often work-related, since work is an area in which interpersonal contacts are difficult to avoid.

Schizoid Personality Disorder

Individuals with **schizoid personality disorder** are reserved, socially withdrawn, and seclusive (see Figure 9–2). They prefer solitary work activities and hobbies and lack the capacity for warm, close relationships. They rarely express their feelings directly. Not only do they have few relationships with others, but they also seem to have little desire for them. In any case, they often have poor social skills, although their speech and behavior patterns are not unusual or eccentric. They also lack

FIGURE 9–2
Spending time alone, withdrawn from others, is typical of people with schizoid personality disorders. They often appear quite detached from life around them.

a sense of humor and seem detached from their environment. Perhaps because of this detachment, males with schizoid personality disorder seldom marry. Females are more likely to marry, possibly by accepting a marriage offer rather than seeking it. When, in her novel *The White Album*, Joan Didion uses the phrase "only marginally engaged in the dailiness of life" (p. 121), she could be describing the detachment of people with schizoid personality disorders.

Although the man in the following example did not complain of social isolation (and schizoid individuals rarely do) his stable solitary existence was a central part of his personality. He also showed a rigidity in his personal life and was not concerned about others' opinions of him as long as they let him alone.

A 46-year-old single white male accountant sought professional consultation on the advice of a colleague because of persistent feelings of dissatisfaction and depression following a change in his work situation. Although he retained his position at his firm, where he had worked for 20 years, many of his more important responsibilities had been shifted to a younger colleague. He had always worked well in a rather autonomous position in the firm but now felt that his daily work routine had been disrupted and he no longer had meaningful tasks to accomplish. It turned out that he had always been socially isolated, with social contacts limited to acquaintances at work, and followed a rather prescribed pattern of reading the newspaper and watching television as his evening recreation. He at times saw a married sister and her family on weekends. This limited life style had been tolerable for him for some time and he appeared *relatively indifferent to the opinions of co-workers as long as he could count on being assigned his quota of accounts. His redefined position left him with less work to do and an unclear role in the firm. He felt as if "the rug had been pulled out from under me." In the consultation, he was a quiet man who although cooperative was difficult to engage affectively. He spoke with little emotion and mumbled at times, exhibiting no sense of attachment to other people in his life, but only to his "way of doing things," which he had great difficulty in changing.*

— (Siever and Kendler, 1986, p. 192)

The emotional responses of schizoid individuals seem rather flat as well as cold. The kinds of frustrations that arouse expressions of anger in most people elicit little observable hostility from these individuals. They often seem vague, self-absorbed, absent-minded, and not very aware of or interested in what is going on around them. Some of these people can support themselves if they find socially isolated jobs. Many of them, however, have problems at work because of the contact with other people that most jobs require. Since schizoid people are not bothered by their lack of personal relationships, they are poor prospects for therapy.

Schizotypal Personality Disorder

People with **schizotypal personality disorders** are characterized by oddities of thinking, perceiving, communicating, and behaving. However, deviations in these areas are never as extreme as those found in cases of full-blown schizophrenia. People with schizotypal personality disorders, like schizoid individuals, are seclusive, emotionally shallow, and socially unskilled, but the speech patterns of the two groups are quite different. People with a schizoid personality disorder have no oddities of speech although they may lack social skills. Those with a schizotypal personality disorder, on the other hand, often are not understood because they either use unusual words and phrases or use common words in unusual ways. They also are likely to express ideas unclearly. At times—usually when they are under stress—their thinking deteriorates and they may express ideas that seem delusional. These cognitive and perceptual characteristics are probably the most important in distinguishing schizotypal personality disorder from borderline and schizoid personality disorders (Widiger and others, 1987).

The behavior of people with a schizotypal personality disorder may, at times, border on the bizarre. Much of the time they seem suspicious, superstitious, and aloof.

Saul, age 28, had had ten years of a variety of therapies but he still felt lonely and isolated, unlovable, undeserving, and unable to experience pleasure. Until he was 12 things seemed fine—he did well in school and made friends. He said, "when I was about 12 years old, I began to get the feeling that I was not like other people . . . , I felt that I was repulsive." He started to keep to himself, and developed a variety of rituals, such as double-checking everything he did. Saul dropped out of college after two years. Shortly afterward his parents sent him to a psychoanalyst; later he saw a behaviorally oriented therapist and also received drugs and went with his parents for family therapy. The only improvement during this long period was during the two times he was admitted to a psychiatric hospital. He functioned very well on the ward, socialized with the other patients, and took a leadership role. Except during these hospitalizations, he continued to be isolated. He spent most of his time alone, refusing even to eat with his parents. He devised various tortures for himself. For example, over a several-year period he starved himself so that he was 40 pounds underweight. Between periods of starvation he would indulge in binge eating and then in self-induced vomiting. Saul read a great deal and had a good vocabulary, but he had an odd manner of speaking that made him sound like a robot. He described himself as a born victim who had no niche in the "fierce competition of the world" and had strong feelings about being repulsive and undeserving. At one point he wrote:

"The feeling that I have as I walk through the world filled with people, wanting so much to be in contact with them and yet always remaining apart, can scarcely be described . . . and worst of all is the knowledge that for me there is no reprieve, that I will have to live in this horrible way all my life on this earth." At one point Saul seemed to improve. He got a job in a bookstore, went with his parents to a family function, and even asked someone for a date. After a series of these systematic attempts to make social contact, he quit his job, spent his time in his bedroom, and resumed binge eating. In a letter to his therapist he wrote that he felt his isolation would never end and that he would be better off dead.

—(Adapted from Spitzer and others, 1983, pp. 55–57)

Saul's self-torture may have been related to depression, but he also had a strange sense of being different from other people. His rituals suggest magical thinking. Many of these characteristics are similar to those of people who have recovered from the psychotic period of a schizophrenic disorder. Schizotypal individuals probably have more than the average risk of an episode of schizophrenia later in life. A 15-year follow-up of patients with schizotypal personality disorder suggests that this category represents a borderline group between health and schizophrenia (McGlashan, 1986). Since many cases of schizophrenia are presumed to have a hereditary, biological component, this would imply that schizotypal individuals share this genetic characteristic.

Dramatic, Emotional, or Erratic Behaviors

The first group of personality disorders is composed of individuals with withdrawn behavior. The second category contains people who seek attention and whose behavior is often highly noticeable and very unpredictable.

Histrionic Personality Disorder

For people with **histrionic personality disorders**, getting the attention of others is a high priority (see Figure 9–3). Their motto might be "All the world's a stage", they often act out a role, such as "the star" or "the victim" as part of an interpersonal relationship. These people strike others as vain and immature and tend to speak in a dramatic, exaggerated, and gushing manner (see Figure 9–4).

This classification is used in cases that are marked by exaggerated expression of emotion, stormy interpersonal relationships, a self-centered attitude, and manipulativeness. The manipulativeness might manifest itself in suicidal gestures, threats, or attempts, as well as in other attention-getting behaviors such as dramatic physical complaints. Histrionic patients often come to the attention of therapists because of a drug overdose or other form of suicide attempt. Therapy for these individuals commonly includes medication (Widiger and Frances, 1985).

Histrionic individuals often react too quickly to situations that require some analysis and thought. They don't always focus their attention long enough to perceive the details of a situation, and as a result they tend to respond with emotionally tinged generalities. When people with histrionic personalities are asked to describe something, they generally respond with impressions rather than facts. For example, a therapist who was taking a case history from a client and had made repeated efforts to get a description of her father reported that the patient "seemed . . . hardly to understand the sort of data I was interested in, and the best she could provide was, 'My father? He was wham-bang! That's all—just wham-bang!'" (Shapiro, 1965, p. 111).

FIGURE 9–3
Attracting attention by their often affected or unusual behavior and dress is typical of those with histrionic personality disorder.

Histrionic individuals often operate on hunches and tend to stop at the obvious. Not only are they suggestible and easily influenced by the opinions of others, but they are also easy to distract. Their attention is easily captured and just as easily turned toward something else. This results in behavior with a scattered quality.

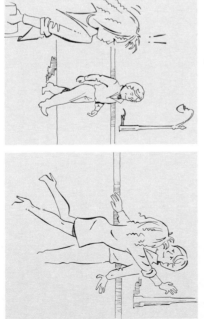

FIGURE 9–4
The speech of those with histrionic personality disorder is characterized by exaggeration and hyperbole. This woman has just seen someone she hardly knows and overreacts by greeting him effusively.

These problems of attention also lead histrionic people to appear incredibly naive about many commonplace things.

A psychoanalyst Anthony Storr (1980), has interpreted histrionic behavior as a pattern that is often adopted by individuals who do not feel able to compete with others on equal terms and believe that no one is paying attention to them. Storr thinks that such people may have been disregarded by their parents as children. Although the child repeatedly tried to get the parents to think of him or her as an individual, those attempts failed. The child then became demanding and resorted to all kinds of dramatic behaviors in order to be noticed. This may help to explain another characteristic of these histrionic individuals, their frequent complaints of poor health, for example, weakness or headaches. The less attention the parents paid to the child, the more the child had to shout or dramatize to get their attention. Histrionic individuals carry these extreme behaviors into adulthood.

Perhaps because of such childhood experience, histrionic people may also feel unlovable and may react to this feeling by trying to make themselves sexually irresistable. Women in particular may dress and behave seductively yet not really desire intimate sexual activity. Women are more likely than men to be diagnosed as histrionic.

Narcissistic Personality Disorder

The word *narcissism* comes from the Greek myth about a young man, Narcissus, who fell in love with his reflection in a pond. Because he could never grasp the image, which he thought was a water nymph, he sorrowed and ultimately died.

DSM-III-R includes several critical factors in its description of **Narcissistic Personality Disorder:** an extreme sense of self-importance and the expectation of special favors, a need for constant attention, fragile self-esteem, and lack of empathy or caring for others (see Figure 9–5). People with a narcissistic personality disorder are often preoccupied with fantasies of unlimited success and brilliance, power, beauty, and ideal love relationships. They may think of their problems as unique and feel that only other equally special people are able to understand them. The case of Robert Graham illustrates many of the characteristics of narcissistic personality disorders.

Graham, a successful 30-year-old actor, contacted a therapist because he was having trouble with a new stage role. In it he had to play a character who was

FIGURE 9–5

Sometimes performers show narcissistic tendencies that may be encouraged by excessive admiration by their fans.

deeply depressed by the death of his wife. As Graham said, he had trouble portraying "a character who was so involved with a woman that his life essentially ended simply because she died."

In his first interview he told the therapist what a good actor he was. "I don't wish to be immodest, but I am uniquely talented." Throughout his life he had been told he was "uniquely cute" and "gifted." He could be charming and entertaining and used these abilities to make other people feel "special" as a way of furthering his career. He seemed to respond to others with a feeling of contempt and remarked that other people were gullible and "easily taken in by experiences."

Graham's relations with women puzzled him. He began dating and had sexual activity early and had romances with a series of women as he grew older. However, in each romance after a short period he would gradually lose interest and usually start an affair with another woman before breaking off with the first. He gave little thought to his former partners after breaking off the relationships. "It is almost as if people are playthings and I need lots and lots of new toys." His account of his life sounded as if he had never grieved or been depressed.

—(Adapted from Spitzer and others, 1983, pp. 71–74)

The category Narcissistic Personality Disorder was introduced because mental-health professionals have seen an increase in cases in which the problem seemed to be excessive self-concern and an inflated sense of one's own importance and uniqueness (see Figure 9–6). In addition, in recent years several psychoanalysts have focused on personal development in the early years of life, the development of the self as a separate entity, and narcissism as an aspect of self-development.

Psychoanalysts ever since Freud have been interested in the idea of narcissism. In Freud's early writings he described narcissism as a developmental stage that occurs very early in life, as soon as the child is able to reliably differentiate him- or herself from the environment. This stage is later replaced by the more mature phase of object love, in which the child is able to "love" in the sense of feeling a relationship with another person (Freud, 1914/1925). Freud later changed his view somewhat and suggested that children often remain at the narcissistic stage because they have been cared for by people who do not love dependably. To protect themselves in this situation, children may turn inward so that they will not be rejected. Freud believed that narcissistic individuals could not profit from psycho-

analysis because they could not form the necessary transference relationship with the therapist.

More recent psychoanalytic theorists have developed some new ideas about narcissism. One of the most influential of these theorists, Otto Kernberg (1970, 1975), has emphasized the unusual degree of self-reference in the narcissist's interaction with other people and the contrast between the narcissist's apparently inflated self-image and his or her unfulfillable need for approval by others. Although this need for praise and approval may make narcissists seem dependent, according to Kernberg they really are unable to depend on anyone because of their deep distrust of others. Like Freud, Kernberg believes that most narcissistic individuals had parents who were cold and indifferent and at the same time were subtly aggressive and spiteful toward their children. Kernberg's views, while they change the emphasis of Freud's ideas, are not a drastic revision of Freudian theory.

Heinz Kohut (1971, 1977), another influential psychoanalyst, suggested a considerably different approach to this disorder. Instead of seeing narcissistic feelings as characteristic of a particular stage of development, Kohut thought of them as an aspect of personality that permeates our lives from childhood through adult life. Narcissism does not fade away by changing to object love but unfolds throughout a person's life-time. It is through this developmental unfolding that the individual gains a sense of self.

R.J. HOLGDBRN, Ph.D.

PROBABLY THE WORLD'S MOST NOTED, MOST ARTICULATE, AND MOST WIDELY RESPECTED AUTHORITY ON THE NARCISSISTIC PERSONALITY

FIGURE 9–6
This sign suggests that Dr. Holgdbrn may have become a specialist in narcissistic personalities from observing his own behavior. (Harley Schwadron)

Kohut believed that in early childhood the normal child feels grandiose or omnipotent and also idealizes his or her parents. Of course, both of these beliefs are unrealistic, and eventually the child discovers that they are false. If parents do not respond to their child's endearing, praiseworthy, and unique qualities, the child may fail to develop a sense of being worthwhile and valued. He or she may continue unsuccessfully to seek such recognition all through life. If the parents are indifferent or rejecting, and not as wonderful as the child fantasizes, the child may grow into an adult who feels depressed and empty. In these terms, the narcissist is engaged in a hopeless search for an idealized parent surrogate. According to Kohut's view, the chief characteristics of a narcissistic disorder are low self-esteem, periodic self-absorption, minor physical complaints, and feelings of emptiness or deadness. Kohut's ideas, although they are very influential, are not reflected as fully in DSM-III-R as those of Freud and Kernberg.

Kernberg believes that traditional psychoanalysis is the most useful approach to the treatment of narcissism, although he thinks that other, more limited therapies can also be useful. Kohut, on the other hand, believed that the therapist must treat the narcissistic disorder before psychoanalysis can be useful. The therapist does this by imagining him- or herself "into the client's skin" rather than concentrating on interpreting the situation objectively. This procedure is intended to develop the client's sense of being understood and appreciated so that the arrested development of the self can be resumed.

The psychoanalytic perspective presumes that the parents of individuals who have narcissistic personalities were unresponsive to their children's needs and were often cold and rejecting. The social-learning perspective has quite an opposite view. It presumes that narcissism is likely to develop if the parents consistently overrate their children and create self-images for them that cannot hold up in the real world. When early childhood is not reflected to the more realistic past and the children are exposed to the more realistic evaluations of others, the clash between the beliefs of importance and talent fostered by the parents and the more realistic responses of outsiders can lead to narcissism (Millon, 1981). Whether either of these viewpoints will be useful in diagnosis and treatment has yet to be determined by research.

Borderline Personality Disorder

Borderline Personality Disorder was first given official recognition as a diagnosis in 1980. Since that time the borderline category has already become so popular that 20 percent of psychiatric patients are given that diagnosis and it is estimated to occur in 3 to 5 percent of the general population (Frances and Widiger, 1986). About two-thirds of those with borderline personality disorder are female. Some writers believe that the fragmentation and change that characterize contemporary American society create problems in maintaining stable relationships and thereby promote borderline pathology.

Identifying Characteristics

People with borderline personality disorder have a number of identifying characteristics (Gunderson and Zanarini, 1987). These include:

1. Intense, unstable personal relationships
2. Repetitive self-destructive behaviors
3. Chronic fears of abandonment
4. Chronic feelings of intense anger, loneliness, and emptiness
5. A wide range of cognitive distortions including undue suspiciousness, feelings of dissociation, and odd types of thinking including superstitiousness and feeling they have a sixth sense about things
6. Impulsive behaviors such as running away, fighting, promiscuity, abuse of drugs, and binge eating that disrupt functioning relationships
7. Unstable social relationships and repeated flight and failure in job situations.

The intense clinging dependency and manipulation that characterize the interpersonal relationships of those with borderline personality disorder make interaction with these people very difficult. They seem to wish for a dependent and exclusive relationship with another person. The dependency is clear to outside observers but vehemently denied by the borderline individual. As a part of this vehement denial comes a need to devalue or discredit the strengths and personal significance of the important others. This often takes the form of extreme anger when the other person sets limits for the relationship, or when a separation is about to occur. In addition to anger, the borderline individual uses manipulative behavior to control relationships. This includes complaints about physical symptoms and self-destructive threats.

Self-destructive behaviors have been called "the behavioral specialty" of those with borderline personality disorder. Table 9–2 shows the frequency of self-destructive acts in one group of borderline individuals. This behavior is designed to call forth a "saving" response from the other person. Overdosing with drugs or wrist-slashing are most common. In recent years se-

TABLE 9-2

The total number of self-destructive acts described by 57 people with borderline personality disorder

Category	Number of Acts	Behavior Pattern
Suicide threats	42	To get attention To cause trouble In rage
Overdose	40	No usual pattern Barbiturates most frequent
Self-mutilation	36	Wrist slashing > body banging >> burning, puncturing, hair removal
Drug abuse	38	Polydrug abuse >> amphetamines, alcohol binges > marijuana
Promiscuity	36	Usually under the influence of drugs or alcohol
Accidents	14	Reckless driving

Adapted from Gunderson, 1984, p. 86.

vere bulimia (an eating disorder discussed in Chapter 15) has become a common self-destructive tactic (Gunderson and Zanarini, 1987).

Self-destructiveness is the characteristic of borderline individuals that generates the most discomfort in those who attempt to help them. The therapists' hope of saving an endangered life is alternately encouraged and then dashed by the client's spiteful efforts at self-destruction. Therapists often experience intense feelings of responsibility for borderline clients. The therapist's initial efforts to be supportive when the client threatens suicide can lead to increased responsibility for the client's life and increased involvement outside of the therapy sessions. Unless the controlling nature of the client's responses are interpreted in the therapy sessions, the situation may become unworkable for the therapist. It is necessary to make the client understand that the therapist cannot be manipulated by threats of suicide and that the client must work to understand these self-destructive urges without acting them out. If this effort is not successful, the threats of self-destruction will recur and the risk to the client will be even greater if the therapist fails to respond on cue. This danger is illustrated by the following example.

A borderline patient periodically rented a motel room and, with a stockpile of pills nearby, would call her therapist's home with an urgent message. He would respond by engaging in long conversations in which he "talked her down." Even as he told her that she

could not count on his always being available, he became more wary of going out evenings without detailed instructions about how he could be reached. One night the patient couldn't reach him due to a bad phone connection. She fatally overdosed from what was probably a miscalculated manipulation.

—(Gunderson, 1984, p. 93)

Their strong need for a relationship leads borderline persons to have chronic and long-lasting fears that the people on whom they are dependent will abandon them. These fears are related to the extreme panic they feel when alone. As a defense against this fear, borderline people are compulsively social. Despite this need for social interaction many of their behaviors are the type that drive people away. These include their intense anger and demandingness, their suspiciousness, and their impulsivity. They deal with stress by being sexually promiscuous, getting into fights, and binge eating and purging.

Marked emotional instability with sudden shifts to anxiety, continued depression, or irritability, which may last only a few hours and never more than a few days, are typical of borderline personality disorder, as is illustrated in the following description by a patient.

"I was alone at home a few months ago; I was frightened! I was trying to get in touch with my boyfriend and I couldn't. . . . He was nowhere to be found. All my friends seemed to be busy that night and I had no one to talk to. . . . I just got more and more nervous and more and more agitated. Finally—bang!—I took out a cigarette and lit it and stuck it into my forearm. I don't know why I did it because I didn't really care for him all that much. I guess I felt I had to do something dramatic."

—(Stone, 1980, p. 400)

Borderline individuals also show disturbance in their concepts of identity: uncertainties about self-image, gender identity, values, loyalties, and goals. They may have chronic feelings of emptiness or boredom and be unable to tolerate being alone. The following anecdote illustrates the behavior of a borderline individual.

A 27-year-old woman was married and had two small children. She had had a stormy adolescence, having been forced into sexual relations with a brother 6 years her senior whom she at first idolized and later feared. Their relationship continued until just before she left home for college, when she told her parents of it. In the ensuing emotional turmoil, she made a gesture of suicide (overdose of aspirin) but was not hospitalized. . . . Outwardly flirtatious, although inwardly shy and ill at ease, she felt *intensely lonely and went through a period of mild alcohol abuse and brief sexual affairs in an effort to cope with her anxiety and sense of inner emptiness. At age 19, she married a classmate and dropped out of school.*

Fairly at ease in the first years of her marriage, she became anxious, bored, and given to fits of sadness and tearfulness after the birth of her second child. Her mood fluctuated widely from hour to hour, day to day, but negative feelings were greatly intensified on the 3 or 4 days before her period. Her husband had grown less attentive as the family expanded, in response to which she became increasingly irritable, provocative, and at times abusive (smashing plates, hurling insults). Her husband began to carry on an extramarital relationship, which she eventually discovered. At that point, she became seriously depressed, lost sleep and appetite, began to abuse alcohol and sedatives, and made several gestures of suicide, including one instance of cutting her wrist. On two occasions she hid for several nights in motels without informing anyone where she was. Each time she took her 8-year-old daughter with her, as though to protect her from the "designs" she imagined her husband had on their elder girl. After the wrist-cutting incident, when she had also left a note

apologizing for being a "failure" as a wife and mother, she was hospitalized. She understood the unrealistic nature of her suspicions, as she explained to the hospital staff, but could not shake off the morbid doubts she experienced.

—(Stone, 1986, p. 210)

Many psychotherapists report that they are seeing an increasing number of borderline patients, and there has been speculation that the proportion of such people in the population is growing. People like Marilyn Monroe, Lawrence of Arabia, Thomas Wolfe, Adolf Hitler, and Zelda Fitzgerald would probably be classified in this category today (see Figure 9–7). Each of them was famous for unpredictable and often extremely changeable behaviors, intolerance of routine and social conventions, periods of desperation, and the many unusual events that characterized his or her life.

Distinguishing Borderlines from Other Groups

The word *borderline* suggests a marginal level of functioning, something that borders on becoming something else. Originally the term borderline was used to describe a marginal or milder form of schizophrenia.

FIGURE 9–7

These famous people—the dictator Adolf Hitler, the actress Marilyn Monroe, the writer Thomas Wolfe—all had personality traits that are similar to those found in people with borderline personality disorders.

Some researchers argue that borderline patients actually represent the boundary between personality disorders and mood disorders. About half of those with borderline personality disorder can also be diagnosed as having a mood disorder. They are also likely to have a family history of mood disorder (Pope and others, 1983). However, people with several other types of personality disorders are equally as likely to be depressed (Shea and others, 1987). An argument against the view that borderline is really a milder form of another disorder is that relatives of a person with borderline personality disorder are ten times as likely to be treated for a borderline or similar disorder themselves as are relatives of schizophrenic or bipolar patients (Loranger and others, 1982).

Another question is whether borderline disorder is really a separate category from other personality disorders, since some researchers have been unable to distinguish it from histrionic personality disorder and antisocial personality disorder (Pope and others, 1983). Figure 9–8 shows the overlapping characteristics between borderline personality disorder and the other personality disorders in the same diagnostic cluster. Overlap may also occur with a personality disorder in another cluster. Sometimes patients who are diagnosed as borderline and those who are diagnosed as schizotypal seem similar. However, the schizotypal and borderline categories have different emphases. The schizotypal category stresses cognitive symptoms: magical thinking, ideas of reference, suspicious thought. The borderline category stresses affective or emotional symptoms: feelings of emotional instability, emptiness, boredom, and inappropriate and intense anger (Gunderson, 1984). Schizotypal individuals are socially isolated; in contrast, borderline individuals cannot stand being alone. Despite these problems of overlap with depression and with other personality disorders, research findings provide support for the borderline personality disorder as a true category of pathologies rather than as a combination of several groups.

Causes and Treatment

Researchers have shown that there may be some genetic factor in borderline disorder. Most of the theories about its cause also focus on a disturbed early relationship between a preborderline child and its parents. There are a variety of descriptions of what this relationship might

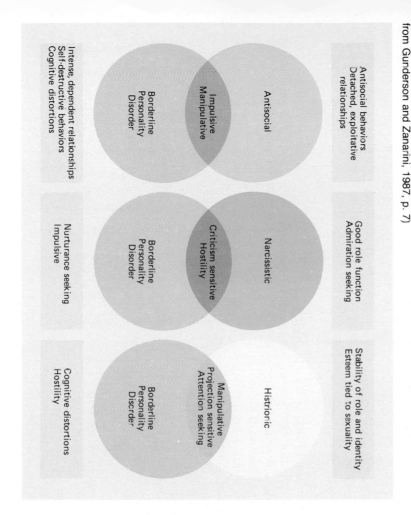

FIGURE 9–8

The borderline personality disorder has some characteristics that overlap with other personality disorders. The similar characteristics are shown in the overlapping circles. Characteristics that distinguish between the two disorders are shown in the boxes above and below each pair. (Adapted from Gunderson and Zanarini, 1987, p. 7)

Antisocial

Impulsive
Manipulative

Borderline
Personality
Disorder

Antisocial behaviors
Detached, exploitative
relationships

Intense, dependent relationships
Self-destructive behaviors
Cognitive distortions

Narcissistic

Criticism sensitive
Hostility

Borderline
Personality
Disorder

Good role function
Admiration seeking

Nurturance seeking
Impulsive

Histrionic

Manipulative
Projection sensitive
Attention seeking

Borderline
Personality
Disorder

Stability of role and identity
Esteem tied to sexuality

Cognitive distortions
Hostility

be like (Gunderson and Zanarini, 1987). Some focus on the attachment experience in early childhood, others on parents who fail to provide adequate attention to the child's own feelings so that he or she never develops an adequate sense of self (Alder and Buie, 1979). Some theorists focus on parental abuse (both sexual and physical) in adolescence as well as divorce, alcoholism, and other stressors (Linehan, 1987). It is clear from all these examples that such stressors in the family often occur and the children do not develop borderline personality disorder. The development of this disorder probably occurs through a combination of neurobiological, early developmental, and later socializing factors.

Treatment

Borderline individuals have been described by Freud and many later writers as unsuitable candidates for psychoanalysis. These writers feared that the unstructured nature of the treatment and its encouragement of fantasy would break down the already unstable self-concepts of such individuals and precipitate them into psychotic breakdowns. However, recent developments in psychoanalysis have provided variations that are considered suitable for the borderline person. Otto Kernberg, for example, believes that most borderline individuals can best be treated in intensive face-to-face psychotherapy sessions at least three times a week over a period of several years. In these sessions the therapist plays a more active structuring role than is usual in classical psychoanalysis. At the beginning the emphasis is on present behavior rather than childhood experiences, and rather than allowing the transference relationship to develop fully, the therapist explicitly describes and discusses the client's apparent distortions of reality—for example, the client's perceptions of the therapist.

Kernberg emphasizes the idea of **splitting,** or failure to integrate the positive and negative experiences that occur between the individual and other people. Splitting is Kernberg's theoretical explanation of the extreme changeability that can be seen in the borderline person's relationships to others. Rather than perceiving another individual as a loving person who sometimes accepts and sometimes rejects—for example, a mother who sometimes hugs and sometimes corrects a young child—the borderline individual shifts back and forth between these contradictory images. Kernberg describes this behavior in one of his patients.

In one session, the patient may experience me as the most helpful, loving, understanding human being and may feel totally relieved and happy, and all the problems solved. Three sessions later, she may berate me as the most ruthless, indifferent, manipulative person she has ever met. Total unhappiness about the treatment, ready to drop it and never come back.
—(Sass, 1982, pp. 14–15)

Long-Term Prospects

It was originally thought that because of their psychoticlike or depressive symptoms, borderline individuals would develop a traditional illness such as schizophrenia or a major mood disorder. However, several follow-up studies show that this rarely happens, instead, borderline personality disorder tends to remain over time (Plakun and others, 1985; Stone and Stone, 1988).

Follow-ups over 10 years or less show that the unstable relationships, poor work performance, and symptom levels usually continue. Long-term follow-up studies show that borderline individuals who have received intensive treatment and are from high socioeconomic levels have a fairly good chance of developing full-time employment. Interpersonal relations also improve after a long unstable period during the young adult years (see Figure 9–9). About a third of these borderline patients eventually marry and establish their own families. However, the range of outcomes is wide and many of those with borderline personality disorder continue to have severe interpersonal and occupational problems. One negative outcome is suicide. Probably 8 to 10 percent of borderline individuals actually kill themselves, although this figure is small compared to the number of suicide attempts. Another frequent negative outcome is alcohol abuse. About one-third of female alcoholics also have the characteristics of borderline personality disorder. Figure 9–10 compares some of the positive and negative outcomes to those found in schizophrenia and major mood disorders.

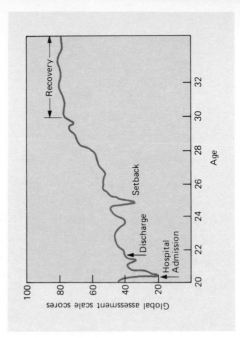

FIGURE 9–9
The typical pattern of adjustment of a patient with borderline personality disorder. (Adapted from Stone and Stone, in press)

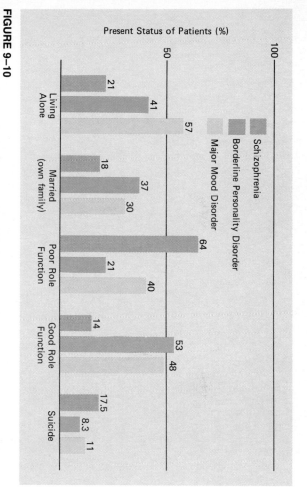

FIGURE 9–10
The long-term outcome for borderline personality disorder is generally better than that for patients with either schizophrenia or major mood disorder. (Adapted from Gunderson and Zanarini, 1987, p. 10)

Present Status of Patients (%)

Schizophrenia
Borderline Personality Disorder
Major Mood Disorder

Living Alone: 21, 41, 57
Married (own family): 18, 37, 30
Poor Role Function: 64, 21, 40
Good Role Function: 14, 53, 48
Suicide: 17.5, 8.3, 11

Antisocial Personality Disorder

Antisocial personality disorder is associated with crime, violence, and delinquency. The essential characteristics of this disorder include a history of continuous and chronic behavior that violates the rights of others, begins before the age of 15, and continues into adult life. In addition, the following characteristics must be present.

1. Age at least 18.

2. Evidence of a conduct disorder before the age of 15, including some of the following behaviors: truancy, school suspension, arrest, running away from home, lying, engaging in sexual intercourse, or using liquor, tobacco, or other nonprescribed drugs unusually early compared to peers, as well as a history of stealing, vandalism, fights, and violation of rules at home or at school.

3. A pattern of irresponsible and antisocial behavior since the age of 15 that includes several of these characteristics: inability to sustain a consistent work record; repeated antisocial acts such as stealing, destroying property, and harassing others; repeated fights or assaults; failure to honor financial obligations; failure to plan ahead; recklessness, especially in driving; mistreatment or neglect of children if a parent; sexual promiscuity; and lack of remorse upon harming others.

Garry Gillmore, whose life is described in Box 9–1, fits this description well.

It is important to distinguish antisocial personality disorder from antisocial behavior or ordinary aggressive behavior. These behaviors would be classified by DSM III-R as **adult antisocial behavior,** one of the DSM categories reserved for behaviors that are not the result of socialization but a disorder based on a core personality problem involving a lack of basic trust in others and an inability to form close relationships (Reid, 1986).

The category of antisocial personality disorder was developed to make the distinction between the effects of personality and socialization on antisocial behavior but so far the effort to separate the two has not been completely successful. Antisocial personality disorder doesn't discriminate well among different types of criminals, at least those who are in prison. In one study, 50 percent of the inmates in two prisons were included in this category (Hare, 1983). Moreover, these criteria are often met by many people who grow up in poor areas. They also leave out many people who appear to be antisocial but were not caught by the police before they were adults (Frances, 1980).

When criminals are divided into groups consisting of those who behave as their peers do and those whose antisocial behavior seems to have other causes, only about one-third of all criminals are included (Hare, 1978). It might be useful to place more emphasis on the personality characteristics of criminals in order to

BOX 9-1

Antisocial Personality Disorder: A Frightening Example

The case of Gary Gillmore illustrates many characteristics of antisocial personality disorder. Gillmore was convicted of two murders and sentenced to death. When he was executed, on January 17, 1977, he was the first person to be put to death in the United States in 11 years. Although he refused to appeal his conviction, several appeals were made on his behalf and his execution was delayed three times. During this period, while newspapers featured stories on his "fight for the right to be executed," he attempted suicide twice.

Gillmore displayed an antisocial personality pattern very early. In spite of his high intelligence, his school grades were poor, he was often truant, and he was repeatedly accused of stealing from his schoolmates. At 14 he was sent to a juvenile center for stealing a car; after his release he was sent to jail several times for burglaries; and at 20 he was sent to the state penitentiary for burglary and robbery. After his release from the penitentiary he spent 2 years in jail for reckless and drunk driving. After this imprisonment he spent 11 years in the state penitentiary for several armed robberies.

Gillmore reported that he had begun drinking at the age of 10 and later had used a variety of illegal drugs—amphetamines, cocaine, and LSD. During his prison stays, he drank when he could and smoked marijuana. He was a talented tattoo artist. Several times he tattooed obscene words and pictures on inmates whom

he disliked. "I thought it was a good way to get back at the snitches. I would tatoo them on their bodies where they could not watch what I was doing. It wasn't until they looked at their tattoo in the mirror that they saw what I had done to them." When he was released from prison in April of 1976, Gillmore went to Utah to work in his uncle's shop. When that job didn't work out, he went on to several others. He met a woman and moved in with her the next day. He said that this was the first time he had ever had a close relationship with anyone. It didn't go smoothly. Her two children irritated him, and he often hit them. His drinking and his tendency to get into fights at parties also caused problems.

Before long Gillmore felt increasingly frustrated. He seemed unable to succeed outside prison. He broke parole by getting drunk, but his parole officer decided not to report him. After an argument with the woman he lived with, he walked into a store and forcibly carried out a stereo, but he dropped it and fled when two security guards attempted to grab him. After a chase by the police, he got away. Again through the intervention of his parole officer, no charges were brought. When he went back to his house, his woman friend ordered him out with a gun.

In July he pulled into a gas station, ordered the attendant to give him all his cash, and then took the attendant into the station restroom and shot him twice in

distinguish those who are capable of feeling guilt, anxiety, loyalty, and empathy from those who are not (Millon, 1981). For instance, the concept of psychopathic personality (to be discussed later) emphasizes the characteristics of lovelessness and guiltlessness.

Conduct Disorder

Antisocial personality disorder, by definition, occurs only in individuals over 18 years of age. Some other classification is necessary for those below that age. The DSM-III-R category **conduct disorder** is used to describe children and adolescents whose behavior problems are more serious than the ordinary mischief and pranks often carried out by young people. This category is used to describe many individuals who are later diagnosed as having an antisocial personality disorder. The term can also be used for adults who do not meet all the criteria for antisocial personality disorders.

The conduct disorders are diagnosed on Axis I, not on Axis II as personality disorders are. Conduct disorder is diagnosed when there is a repetitive pattern of actions over a period of 6 months or more that either violate the basic rights of others or violate social norms or rules appropriate for the patient's age group. Children with conduct disorder may be conforming to a group norm or they may carry out their aggressive activity on a solitary basis. The behaviors that are typical of conduct disorders include purse snatching, mugging, armed robbery, rape, stealing, drug abuse, vandalism, arson, and cruelty to animals and people, as well as truancy, cheating in school or in games, running away from home, and persistent fighting. Figures 9–12a and b illustrate behaviors seen in both disorders.

Because so many behaviors may be included, people who are diagnosed as having a conduct disorder may be quite different from one another.

the head as the man knelt before him. The next morning he walked into a motel.

I went in and told the guy to give me the money. I told him to lay on the floor and then I shot him. I then walked out and was carrying the cash drawer with me. I took the money and threw the cash drawer in a bush and I tried to push the gun in the bush, too. But as I was pushing it in the bush, it went off and that's how come I was shot in the arm. It seems like things have always gone bad for me. It seems like I've always done dumb things that just caused trouble for me. I remember when I was a boy I would feel like I had to do things like sit on a railroad track until just before the train came and then I would dash off. Or I would put my finger over the end of a BB gun and pull the trigger to see if a BB was really in it. Sometimes I would stick my finger in water and then put my finger in a light socket to see if it would really shock me. (Spitzer and others, 1983, p. 68)

Gillmore was evaluated to determine whether he was competent to stand trial. His IQ was found to be 129, in the superior range. His general knowledge was surprisingly good for someone with so little education. He was proud of his vocabulary and read both fiction and news magazines avidly. There was no indication of any organic problems. He reported no bizarre or unusual thoughts except when on drugs. Personality tests revealed no thought or mood disturbances. He slept soundly, had a good appetite, and was not depressed or worried. "I almost never get blue. Though I've made a mess of my life, I never stew about the things I have done."

Gillmore showed the characteristic behaviors of an antisocial personality. He disobeyed rules at home and

FIGURE 9–11
Gary Gillmore.

at school, drank, and used illegal drugs at an early age. By 16 he had been arrested for car theft. While he was in prison he was known for his cruel and violent behavior. He seemed to lack sympathy and felt no guilt. He never had a steady job or a long-lasting relationship.

Ever since his parents could remember, Robbie has been in trouble. For example, when he was a young child he pushed his sister down the stairs and turned the switch on the electric garage door when his 6-year-old cousin was riding his tricycle under it. As he grew older this behavior continued. At 15 Robbie raped his brother. His parents and his teachers were all afraid of him. He never seemed to feel safe whenever he was out of the various institutions to which he had been sent during his adolescence.

Robbie's behavior is impulsive and aggressive. He seems to have no mercy for his victims and attacks people who have been kind to him as readily as strangers or enemies. Although he dislikes being punished or institutionalized, he shows little concern about the harm his behavior has brought about. Consider another example.

Tom lied so plausibly and with such utter equanimity, devised such ingenious alibis or simply denied all responsibility with such convincing appearances of candor that for many years his real career was poorly estimated.... At 14 or 15 years of age, having learned to drive, Tom began to steal automobiles with some regularity. Often his intention seemed less that of theft than of heedless misappropriation. A neighbor or friend of the family, going . . . to where the car was parked . . . would find it missing. Sometimes . . . [Tom] would leave the stolen vehicle within a few blocks . . . of the owner, sometimes out on the road where the gasoline has given out. After he had tried to sell a stolen car,

his father consulted advisors and, on the theory that he might have some specific craving for automobiles, bought one for him as a therapeutic measure. On one occasion while driving [Tom] deliberately parked his own car and . . . stole an inferior model which he left slightly damaged on the outskirts of a village some miles away.

—(Cleckley, 1964, p. 86)

Tom seems to be influenced not by the behavior of those around him but by a desire for excitement. He differs from Robbie in that his actions are focused not on people but on things and hence lack the violence of Robbie's escapades.

In one study, preadolescent children who were in-

stitutionalized for severe conduct disorder differed from other children in the treatment center in several ways (Kazdin and Esveldt-Dawson, 1986). The conduct disorder children were much more likely to have severe problems like arguing and fighting and show a variety of antisocial behaviors such as stealing, cruelty to animals, and destruction of property. They were much less likely than the other institutionalized children to think about killing themselves or to wish to be dead.

There are a number of factors that seem to increase the chances that a child will develop a conduct disorder. These include problems of focusing attention and hyperactive behavior (discussed in Chapter 15) as well as parental rejection, harsh discipline, absence of a father, or having a father with alcohol problems and association with a group of delinquent children. Parents of children with conduct disorder are more likely to have antisocial personality disorder and problems with alcohol than parents in general.

The Disturbed Adolescent

Sometimes an adolescent commits a single dramatic and very damaging act that surprises people who have known him or her for a long time. Such behavior is not viewed as a sign of a conduct disorder because it is not part of a habitual pattern. Violent behavior of this kind seems to be a manifestation of conflict and anxiety. Harry's case is typical.

The police received a call from Harry. He told them that he had come home and found his parents and brother, who was missing. When his body was later found stuffed in a trunk, suspicion finally turned to Harry. At first he seemed an unlikely candidate. He was a first-year student at a prestigious military academy and had been a quiet and somewhat lonely boy in high school. The family had been described as a close one with strong religious beliefs. As the story unfolded, Harry began to appear in a somewhat different light. He wanted to quit school. He hated the hazing the first-year students received. He seemed to have been marked as a loser and was frequently the target of jokes and punishment. His father had refused to allow him to quit school, just as he had earlier refused to allow him to quit Little League baseball even when Harry pleaded. Other students reported that during high school Harry was often teased and mistreated by his classmates.

On the night of the murders, Harry, home for Thanksgiving vacation, apparently felt he could stand the frustration no longer. One way to avoid returning to school was to remove the main obstacle to his quitting—his father.

— (adapted from *New York Times*, November 29, 1976, pp. 1, 31)

Adolescents like Harry are often found to be psychotic or greatly disturbed. There is usually a long-term pattern of turmoil and emotional hurts that have been held beneath the surface. At last some incident, sometimes very minor, triggers violent behavior.

The Psychopath

A subgroup of people who have antisocial personality disorder are what has been called **psychopaths.** Some researchers believe what the DSM-III-R definition of antisocial personality disorder should be narrowed to include only this group. One of the problems in understanding

research findings about antisocial behavior is that the terms *psychopath* and *antisocial behavior* are often used to mean the same thing, yet psychopath differs from the other group. Psychopaths do not seem to behave antisocially merely as a function of learning from their peers in an environment where antisocial behavior is a way of life. Instead, their behavior seems to be a reflection of personality characteristics.

Probably the best definition of a psychopath has been furnished by Hervey Cleckley, whose book *The Mask of Sanity* (1976) has become a classic. Cleckley mentions the following characteristics of psychopaths.

1. Superficial charm and good intelligence
2. Poise, rationality, absence of neurotic anxiety
3. Lack of a sense of personal responsibility
4. Untruthfulness, insincerity, callousness, manipulativeness
5. Antisocial behavior without regret or shame
6. Poor judgment and failure to learn from experience
7. Inability to establish lasting, close relationships with others
8. Lack of insight into personal motivations

These are not characteristics that one either has or does not have. With each of them, it is a matter of degree. It is not surprising, therefore, that estimates of the incidence of antisocial psychopathic personality in the U.S. population range from a few million to 10 million.

It is unusual for a psychopath to begin some activity with the sole purpose of hurting others. What ordinarily happens is that the activity begins without considering its effect on others.

After graduating from high school and having a few dead-end jobs, Bert wanted to go into business for himself. He asked his parents, who had a modest income and some savings for their retirement, to lend him the money he needed to get started. Within 5 months Bert was out of business, his parents' money "lost," as he put it. Several months later, having found a new business opportunity, Bert again pleaded with his parents to borrow the money he needed. They agreed, and again Bert's opportunity fizzled. His parents desperately wanted to help Bert and to believe in him. So great was their need and so successful was Bert in "conning" his parents that they repeatedly helped him engage in activities that were doomed to failure. Bert craved the excitement of going into business for himself, but was able neither to attend to all the details involved in running a business nor to plan ahead. He was magnificent in playing the role of the charming young man on the way up. When he failed, he felt no regrets concerning his failure's _implications for his parents and others who had helpd him._

Researchers have been hampered by the fact that it is so much easier to identify antisocial personalities among individuals who have been convicted of crimes than among the general population. That means that the group on which research is based may not be typical of all people with an antisocial personality disorder. One researcher approached this problem in a unique way (Widom, 1978): she inserted the following ad in a Boston counterculture newspaper.

Wanted: charming, aggressive, carefree people who are impulsively irresponsible but are good at handling people and at looking after number one. Send name, address, phone, and short biography proving how interesting you are to . . .

—(Widom, 1978, p. 72)

The ad drew 73 responses, of which about two-thirds were from males. About one-third of these seemed to meet the criteria for a diagnosis of psychopathic personality. The respondents were interviewed and given a battery of psychological tests. Some of the characteristics of the group are shown in Table 9–3. The researcher concluded that the main difference between her sample and prison samples was that the people who an-

swered her ad and had somehow been able to avoid conviction after arrest or detention by the police. In other respects they seemed very similar to prison inmates.

Perspectives on Antisocial Behavior

Researchers have looked at many aspects of antisocial individuals—their life histories, psychological and physiological functioning, and personality characteristics—in order to understand why these people behave as they do. The biological perspective has yielded a number of interesting findings. There is increasing evidence that heredity may play a role in both criminality and antisocial behavior. Adopted children who were separated at birth from their antisocial parents show more antisocial behavior later in life than control subjects. (Bohman and others, 1982).

How antisocial behavior might be inherited is not yet clear. Researchers have connected habitually violent and antisocial tendencies with the neurochemistry of the body. Impulsive physical violence and aggression in humans is related to very low levels of one of the neurotransmitters, serotonin, and one of its metabolites in the spinal fluid (Virkkunen, 1983). Another idea is that left-handedness and right-brain dominance may somehow be associated with antisocial personality disorder, but so far the evidence is not convincing (Hare and Forth, 1985). Other research has focused on patterns of brain wave activity. For example, some researchers have demonstrated a relationship between one type of electrical brain activity, slow alpha waves, and later antisocial behavior (Mednick and others, 1982). In normal individuals alpha-wave frequency is known to decrease with relaxation and drowsiness and to increase with tension, so the slow alpha waves suggest that some antisocial individuals have a lower than normal arousal level. This may mean that sensory inputs that would be disturbing to most people would not be strong enough to excite antisocial individuals. Such people may crave increased stimulation and may therefore seek out unusual forms of excitement.

The brain wave patterns found in psychopaths have some similarity to the brain wave patterns that occur normally in children and adolescents. This has led to the suggestion that at least one subgroup of psychopaths may have delayed cerebral maturation (Reid, 1986). This fits in with the observation that many psychopaths seem to "burn out" as they grow older. An example of this delayed maturation is shown in the life of Jackroller, a young mugger whose development was studied intensively in the 1920s (Shaw, 1930). Fifty years later, Jackroller told the story of his later life (Jackroller and Snodgress, 1982). He saw what had happened to him as a series of injustices through which he had struggled. He had a history of trouble keeping jobs

TABLE 9-3

Characteristics of Subjects Interviewed by Widom[a]

Characteristic	Percentage of Subjects
Arrest Records:	
Detained	17.9
Arrested as an adult	64.3
Convicted as an adult	17.9
Incarceration:	
As a juvenile	10.7
As an adult	32.1
Psychiatric Hospitalization:	
Hospitalized at some time	21.4
Treated as an outpatient only	46.4
Suicide attempts	28.6
Number with both psychiatric and arrest records	46.4
Parental separation:	
Broken homes	21.4
Divorce	7.1
Parental psychopathology	7.1
Parental alcoholism	17.8

[a]The subjects averaged 25 years of age (from 19 to 47 years old). All except one were white. There were 23 males and 5 females.

and blamed others for most of his difficulties, but he was no longer involved in criminal activity.

Another physiological factor—anxiety—has been studied in antisocial individuals. It had seemed reasonable to assume that people who met the criteria for psychopathic behavior would also show little anxiety compared to other individuals. But this assumption may be true only in a limited sense. Schalling (1978) found that while psychopaths seem to worry less than other people, they nevertheless experience all of the common somatic and muscular indicators of anxiety (high heart rate, shortness of breath, tense muscles). If we divide anxiety into its cognitive part—worry—and its physiological components—the body's responses to fear—antisocial individuals seem to lack the cognitive component of anxiety.

From a cognitive perspective, the study of antisocial behavior focuses on moral development (Kegan, in press.) Just as in the case of psychophysiological factors, the idea of a delay in moral development has been suggested. Between the ages of 7 and 11, normal children can tell when someone else treats them unfairly. If they have been treated unfairly in the past, when an opportunity arises they will "make up" for the past unfairness by striking back when someone else is vulnerable. For example, after being teased for being the shortest player on the peewee basketball team and then growing several inches, instead of feeling empathy for smaller kids the child will think, "Now it's my turn," not, "I'll treat younger kids differently."

A new morality normally begins to develop at about the age of 13. Then children think about the fairness of their own actions rather than concentrating on getting even. Cognitive theorists describe this as the development of the ability to reason in abstract terms and to understand the concept of partnership in relationships. From this point of view, psychopaths are developmentally arrested at the 7- to 11-year-old level because they are not concerned about the effects of their behavior on others.

Treatment Approaches

People with antisocial personality disorder are not usually helped by traditional methods of psychotherapy. Two types of therapeutic programs, either residential or in the community, have reported some success. Effective residential treatment centers force psychopaths to stay for months or years in a program with rigid rules, so that each the psychopath cannot talk his way out (Reid

Both environmental and genetic factors may contribute to the development of antisocial personality disorder. So far no treatment seems effective for severe cases of this disorder; at present most of them are dealt with through the criminal justice system.

and Balis, 1987). In such a situation, the participants initially become depressed because they are forced to face their lack of inner feelings and their inability to establish meaningful relationships with others. The major goals of the entire program are to increase the person's ability to feel emotion, to think constructively about the future, to trust other people, and to develop empathy. The program emphasizes milieu therapy, an approach in which all the staff work together to provide consistent support and long-term stable relationships.

Another type of program has similar goals but is carried out in the community. In Rochester, Minnesota, one of the few such programs, a judge may sentence young male first-offenders, or other men with a good possibility for change, to the program or to prison as an alternate. The offender is required to begin schooling or a job immediately and to return to an unlocked treatment center for the remaining time. Gradually he is given more physical freedom. Throughout the program he is also expected to be responsible for his behavior and that of others in the program. He is also expected to repay his victims for their losses and pay his living expenses. If he fails in the program, his alternate sentence, prison, immediately takes effect. Many people with antisocial personalities find this type of program very stressful. Often as many as 50 percent drop out and return to prison. The rearest rate for people who successfully complete these programs has been significantly lower than the rate for similar people from traditional prison or halfway house settings.

The families of those with antisocial personality disorder often have a difficult time and need understanding and support. They may feel wracked with guilt about how they have "gone wrong" and try repeatedly to get their child to return their love and grow out of the problem. A mental-health professional can help by supporting family members and encouraging them to separate themselves psychologically from their antisocial offspring. This help can also assist them to realize that the situation may never change. For example, they will never be repaid the money they loaned an antisocial child, and helping their child avoid jail by providing bail may do more harm than good.

Anxious or Fearful Behaviors

Disorders in this group have many characteristics in common with the personality disorders described earlier, but they differ from the other personality disorders in that each of these has a prominent component of anxiety or fear.

Avoidant Personality Disorder

The two most outstanding characteristics of **avoidant personality disorder** are extreme sensitivity to rejection or humiliation and low self-esteem. People with this disorder keep away from personal attachments and won't enter into relationships unless the other person provides unusually strong guarantees of uncritical acceptance.

The seclusiveness of avoidant personalities differs from that of people with schizoid personality disorders because avoidant people, unlike schizoids, do want to enter into relationships. The conflict they feel is over wanting affection and, at the same time, doubting their acceptance by others. They cannot seem to rid themselves of the belief that any overtures of friendship will end in pain and disillusion. Some of these feelings come from doubts about their own competence. The primary goal of people in this group is to protect themselves from pain. They are caught between wanting human contact and dreading it. People with avoidant personality disorder seem timid and withdrawn and perhaps also cold and strange to those who have superficial contact with them. However, to those who know them well they appear anxious, mistrustful, and extremely sensitive.

One coping mechanism that those with avoidant personality disorder are likely to use is hypervigilance (Millon, 1986). They continuously assess all their human contacts for signs of deception, humiliation, and negative reactions. As a result, they are able to detect the most minute traces of indifference or annoyance. They literally make mountains out of molehills. This technique of constantly scanning the environment is a self-defeating one, however, because it increases the likelihood that they will pick up just the kind of negative response they expect. In addition, their nervousness can result in making their companions uncomfortable, which can further damage the quality of their relationships with others.

Another maneuver that avoidant personalities use is to narrow their range of activities in order to cut off upsetting stimuli. Someone with an avoidant personality disorder may patronize only a small number of shops and restaurants so as to avoid encountering unfamiliar people or situations, or may even avoid shopping and other everyday activities because they seem too tiring or uncomfortable. Such people may also exaggerate the potential dangers of certain situations; for example, they may refuse to use buses or trains even though others do not doubt their safety. The lives of people with avoidant personality disorders are controlled by fears of looking foolish or being embarrassed or by concern about becoming anxious or crying in public. One unfortunate consequence of this retreat from contact with others and from new experiences is that it gives these individuals more time to be preoccupied with their own thoughts and to relive earlier painful experiences. Thus, a vicious cycle is set up in which the preoccupations make new contacts harder and lead to increased preoccupation.

Avoidant personality disorder was added to the official classification system in 1980. As yet little research has been done that gives insight into its causes or the most effective treatment approaches.

Dependent Personality Disorder

People with **dependent personality disorder** have two basic characteristics. First, they passively allow other people to make all the important decisions in their lives because they lack confidence and feel that they are unable to function independently. Second, to ensure that they will not lose this dependent position, such people subordinate their own needs to the needs and demands of others.

Dependent individuals try to make themselves so pleasing that no one could possibly wish to abandon them. They are self-effacing, ever agreeable, and continually ingratiating. If left on their own, they feel empty, extremely anxious, and unable to function. They may feel anxiety even when the dependent relationship is intact because of the pervasive worry that the dominant figure might be lost in some way—for example, through death or divorce.

Dependent individuls feel that they must act meek and obedient in order to hold onto other people. They also behave affectionately and admiringly toward their protectors. In many cases this may actually be an effective coping technique. The dominant partner will then feel useful, strong, and competent and will want to encourage the relationship. Sometimes, however, things go wrong. The dominant individual may tire of the constant need to demonstrate affection and support and may behave abusively or seek to be rid of the leechlike attachment of the dependent partner. Battered wives are likely to have dependent personalities. They will accept severe physical abuse again and again rather than leave their partners.

As with avoidant personalities, assertiveness training may be useful in treating dependent people. It may be difficult to convince these individuals that their coping styles need to be changed; sometimes a conscious-ness-raising therapy group is used before direct treatment is attempted.

The causes of dependent personality disorders are unclear. One suggestion is that dependent individuals had overprotective parents who made life so easy for their children that they never learned survival skills. Some theorists have suggested that dependent children were insecurely attached to their mothers or other caregivers or did not have close and trusting relationships with others during childhood. So far both of these ideas are interesting but untested hypotheses.

One common way of expressing dependency is through a variety of frequent physical complaints that serve to increase the person's neediness and helplessness. The following case is typical:

A 45-year-old woman came to the clinic because she felt depressed. Tearfully, she complained that her husband does not take her seriously when she tells him of her concern about pains in her neck. She has had 14 children: 10 live at home and 2 have cerebral palsy. Her life has been devoted to her home and family; she rarely goes out, has few friends and has little social life. Her only excursions . . . are to church and to various doctors for care of mild asthma, pains in her neck, and feelings of "depression."

She has been crying daily since her local doctor dismissed her neck pains and advised her to take aspirin for her family effectively, sleeps well, is not bothered by guilt feelings or thoughts of suicide and has had no loss of interest in sex. Her principal focus of concern is her husband's indifference to her somatic complaints and his tendency to laugh them off: She urgently requests medication for her symptoms, but it is to be noted that during a previous visit 4 months earlier with similar complaints she failed to take medication that was prescribed for her.

—(Adapted from Esman, 1986, p. 284)

Obsessive-Compulsive Personality Disorder

Compulsive people have been described as "living machines" (Reich, 1933/1949). As one patient described it, his life was like "a train that was running efficiently, fast, pulling a substantial load, but on a track laid out for it" (Shapiro, 1965, p. 40). An **obsessive-compulsive personality disorder** has several characteristics. One is lack of ability to express many warm and tender emotions. Instead, a person with this disorder seems stiff, formal, and unusually serious. Such an individual is likely to be overly conscientious and inflexible about matters of mortality. Extreme perfectionism is also a problem because it focuses on small details, lists, and rulemaking rather than on getting the job done.

This leads to inability to grasp the "big picture." For instance, in the following example two friends are discussing a house that K is interested in buying. L shows his rigidity in not really listening to what K says but going by his own "rule of house ownership."

K: *So you think I shouldn't buy it?*

L: *Never buy a house with a bad roof. It will cost you its price again in repairs before you're finished.*

K: *But the builder I hired to look it over did say it was in good condition otherwise.*

L: *The roof is only the beginning. First it's the roof and then comes the plumbing and then the plaster.*

K: *Still, those things seem to be all right.*

L: *And, after the plaster, it will be the wiring.*

K: *But the wiring is . . .*

L [*interrupts with calm assurance*]: *It will cost double the price before you're finished.*

—(Shapiro, 1965, p. 25)

This example also illustrates another aspect of compulsive personalities: insistence that their way of doing things be followed, without any awareness of the feelings this creates in other people. K probably really wants to buy the house, and if L's criticisms are, as we suspect, simply evidence of his compulsive personality without any facts attached, K's self-esteem and his positive feelings toward L are not likely to increase as a result of this encounter. People with this disorder focus on rules and neatness and may be disturbed by anything out of place (see Figure 9–13). Excessive concentration on work and productivity is also typical. Even pleasure becomes work.

One such person carefully scheduled his Sundays with certain activities in order to produce "maximum enjoyment." He determinedly set about enjoying himself and became quite upset if anything interfered with his schedule, not merely because he missed the activity, but because his holiday had been spent inefficiently. Another compulsive patient always tried hard, in his social life, to be "spontaneous."

—(Shapiro, 1965, p. 32)

Finally, obsessive-compulsive personality disorder is characterized by indecisiveness. Individuals with this disorder have great difficulty making decisions because they might be wrong. Their inability to make decisions

FIGURE 9–13

Housekeeping routines or other cleaning or straightening rituals occupy a great deal of time for some compulsive people. This person's home library is a source of worry and frustration because of her concern about how to arrange the books. If they are arranged alphabetically by author, then she finds that the different sizes mixed together are visually unpleasing. If she arranges them by size, although they look better, she cannot find a particular book quickly. The result is that she spends a great deal of time both arranging the books and feeling dissatisfied with what she has done.

can be so extreme that they can accomplish relatively little. Pleasure comes from planning a job, not from doing it. The early psychoanalyst Karl Abraham expressed this problem in the following passage.

Pleasure in indexing and classifying . . . in drawing up programmes and regulating work by timesheets . . . is so marked . . . that the forepleasure they get in working out a plan is stronger than their gratification in its execution, so that they often leave it undone.

—(Abraham, 1921/1927, pp. 378, 388)

The term **obsessive–compulsive personality disorder** is similar to **obsessive–compulsive anxiety disorder** (discussed in Chapter 6), but the two disorders are different. People with obsessive–compulsive personality disorder are rigid and restricted in their behavior, but they do not show obsessional thinking that seems to force itself into consciousness, nor do they engage in the kinds of irrational rituals that are performed by people with obsessive compulsive anxiety disorder. People with the anxiety disorder see their behavior as nonadaptive and distressing, but they cannot stop behaving that way. People with a personality disorder, on the other hand, usually exhibit behavior that is rigid and unadaptive but that they feel is under their control.

Someone with an obsessive–compulsive personality disorder usually seeks treatment only when his or her carefully built up life style is threatened. This may happen when a spouse is exasperated and leaves, when a boss decides to fire the difficult employee, or when there is an accumulation of stressful events that make it impossible to carry on as usual. Psychoanalysis or psycho-

dynamic therapy is usually recommended, although it has been suggested that exposure therapy of the kind used in obsessive–compulsive disorder might be useful (Oldham and Frosch, 1986).

Passive Aggressive Personality Disorder

People with **passive aggressive personality disorder** habitually resist demands for adequate performance both on the job and in their social life. Although they have the skills to behave more effectively, they sabotage their accomplishments through procrastination, intentional inefficiency, stubbornness, and "forgetfulness." As the name suggests, people with passive aggressive personalities resent the demands that are made on them, but rather than expressing these feelings directly, they express their anger through passive resistance. For example, if a supervisor comes in at quitting time and requests a complex report by early the next morning, a passive aggressive person would be more likely to mislay some of the needed data than to directly tell the supervisor that the request is unreasonable.

The use of passive aggressive coping mechanisms is not usually an effective way of living, but passive aggressive individuals seem to have no awareness of how their own behavior contributes to the situation. A 30-year follow-up study of a group of college men found that the degree to which passive aggressive behavior was used in early adulthood correlated negatively with good adjustment in middle age (Vaillant, 1976). Perhaps because most passive aggressive individuals do not seek clinical help, this category is one of the least used of those in the personality-disorder group (Frances, in press).

Some therapeutic success with passive aggressive patients has been achieved using the behavioral approach, especially assertiveness training. The problems that may be encountered in using this approach are clearly described in the following case:

Miss Y., a 28-year-old single woman, worked for a management information specialist; she appeared submissive and docile. However, the patient was unable to experience and label the affect of anger, had only vague awareness of the multitude of examples of people infringing upon her life, and generally coped with major deficits in self-assertiveness by a compliant and subservient demeanor. She generally resisted more adequate performance by stubbornness and intentional inefficiency.

The patient responded well to initial attempts to model, role play, and shape new social behaviors. She became more socially at ease and was pleased that she no longer accepted dates with men she didn't like. Whenever she brought up problems with her boss in therapy, however, she became intransigent. She refused to try new behaviors in dealing with him because, as she said, "He doesn't listen, he won't change. No, I couldn't imagine anything helping with him." Attempts by the therapist to coax the patient to try to change her expectations of him, or even to think that the problems with her boss were workable, were to no avail.

The therapist stopped attempting to intervene in the patient's work relationship with the boss, and learning continued in other areas. . . .

The therapist determined that the patient's complaints about her boss were realistic. While backing off from attempting to teach assertive skills directed at the relationship with the boss, the therapist did continue to describe certain assertive ways of handling him, which she might be able to use some day. As therapy helped the patient in other areas of life—with the family, roommate, friends, and social life—the patient became more confident of her ability to express her feelings and negotiate meeting her needs. After a year and a half of therapy, she felt confident enough to look for another job, which she obtained after having ascertained that her new boss was more considerate of his employees.

—(Perry and Flannery, 1982, pp. 168–169)

The behavior of a passive aggressive individual might be compared to a situation that is often found in

child-rearing. The child pushes the parents to the limits of their control and then backs off just in time to prevent retaliation. Like the child, the passive aggressive individual is extremely sensitive to the limits of others and goes that far and no farther. Interacting with a passive aggressive person can be immobilizing because it requires one either to give in or to violate one's own beliefs.

Additional Proposed Categories

Two new categories of personality disorder have been included in the DSM-III-R for research use. Systematic study and clinical use of these categories will determine whether they should be included in the next version of the diagnostic system.

Sadistic Personality Disorder

People with **sadistic personality disorder** show a pervasive pattern of cruel, demanding, and aggressive behavior to other people. This behavior begins at least by early adulthood and is shown in both social and work contacts. It may be a particular problem within the family. This behavior is seldom shown with people of authority but only with those who are not in a good position to fight back. This disorder is different from sexual sadism because the aim of the behavior is not sexual arousal. People with this disorder seem to enjoy the psychological or physical suffering of both people and animals and may torture pets or frighten people by lying to them.

Self-Defeating Personality Disorder

A person with **self-defeating personality disorder** avoids pleasurable experiences and seeks out relationships in which he or she will ultimately suffer. Someone with this disorder makes it impossible for others to help him and will refuse help even when it is both needed and sincerely offered. Any positive personal event, a promotion or any praise from others, may result in feelings of guilt or depression. Another common behavior of those with this disorder is the failure to complete tasks crucial to personal success even though they clearly are able to do so. For example, someone may help others complete an important assignment for a class and then fail to complete his or her own assignment. Initial studies suggest that this personality disorder may be very common.

Treatment of Personality Disorders

Our knowledge of personality disorders is limited because professionals see a restricted sample of people with these disorders. Unless their difficulties become overwhelming, such individuals tend to be satisfied with their behavior, not unhappy the way an anxious or depressed person might be. One important reason for this is that people with personality disorders perceive their difficulties—not their rigid behavior patterns—as the cause of any difficulties they may encounter.

An important thing to remember about personality disorders is that even these individuals, with their rigid coping styles, may behave appropriately or normally some of the time. However, when coping behaviors are called for, each personality disorder is distinguished by the frequency and intensity with which certain behaviors appear. For example, someone with a paranoid personality disorder does not always appear to be suspicious, but he or she is much more likely than most people to be inappropriately suspicious. Many people with personality disorders go through life without ever coming into contact with a mental health professional. However, their rigid response styles often lead them to cope ineffectively with their environment. If the environmental stresses become too great, the response style may become clearly ineffective.

A variety of therapies have been used in treating personality disorders. Most of these disorders are not very responsive to drugs; however, recently there has been an increase in the use of psychoactive drugs—for example, antipsychotic drugs such as Navane; one group of antidepressant drugs, the MAO inhibitors; and lithium. So far the results of drug therapy are not clear (Widiger and Frances, 1985). Behavioral techniques such as assertiveness training and systematic desensitization may be helpful for avoidant and dependent patients (Pilkonis, in press), and assertiveness training is sometimes useful for passive aggressive clients. Although cognitive therapies seem to be appropriate for the deviant cognitive styles, little information on their effectiveness is available. Psychodynamic therapy is used especially for borderline, narcissistic, histrionic, and obsessive–compulsive personality disorders. An intensive milieu therapy that provides clear rules and a stable environment as well as clear penalties for failure to take personal responsibility for behavior is being tried as a way to help those with antisocial personality disorder.

Because personality disorders affect interpersonal relationships, they also tend to elicit certain patterns of behaviors from family members or friends. For this reason any behavior changes that come about through therapy will have an impact on the patterns of these relationships. This means that group or family therapy may be a useful part of the treatment of many individuals with personality disorders (Harbin, 1980). It also means that the therapist must focus the client's attention on the effect of his or her behavior on the behavior of others.

Study Outline

A person's characteristic ways of responding are often referred to as his or her **personality. Personality disorders** are longstanding, maladaptive, and inflexible ways of relating to the environment.

CLASSIFYING PERSONALITY DISORDERS

DSM-III-R uses Axis II for the diagnosis of personality disorders. In some cases, the classification statements of Axis II are used to provide information that bears on the primary diagnosis of Axis I. In others, a personality disorder referred to on Axis II, is the individual's major problem. More than one personality disorder is frequently included in a diagnosis. Personality disorders can be divided into three groups: odd or eccentric behaviors; dramatic, emotional, or erratic behaviors; and fearful or anxious behaviors.

ODD OR ECCENTRIC BEHAVIORS

1. People with **paranoid personality disorder** are characterized by unwarranted feelings of suspiciousness and mistrust of other people, hypersensitivity, and restricted emotional response. It is very difficult for such people to have close relationships with others.
2. Individuals with **schizoid personality disorder** are

reserved, socially withdrawn, and seclusive. They rarely express their feelings directly, lack a sense of humor, and seem detached from their environment.

3. People with **schizotypal personality disorder** are characterized by oddities of thinking, perceiving, communicating, and behaving that are less extreme than those found in cases of schizophrenia. They often are not understood because they use unusual words and phrases or use common words in unusual ways.

DRAMATIC, EMOTIONAL, OR ERRATIC BEHAVIORS

1. People with **histrionic personality disorder** place a high priority on getting the attention of others. This classification is used in cases that are marked by exaggerated expressions of emotion, stormy interpersonal relationships, a self-centered attitude, and manipulativeness. It is possible that such individuals do not feel able to compete with others on equal terms.

2. **Narcissistic personality disorder** is characterized by an extreme sense of self-importance and the expectation of special favors, a need for constant attention, fragile self-esteem, and lack of empathy or caring for others. Narcissistic individuals may have had parents who could not love reliably or were cold and rejecting; or their parents may have consistently overrated them.

3. **Borderline personality disorder** is a relatively new but already frequently used diagnosis. It focuses on instability in such areas as mood, interpersonal relationships, and self-image. Borderline individuals tend to have intense and unstable interpersonal relationships and may use suicide threats to manipulate others. They also show disturbance in their concepts of identity. Long-term follow-up suggests that with intensive treatment a proportion of borderline individuals may improve in their ability to hold jobs and maintain personal relationships.

4. **Antisocial personality disorder** is associated with crime, violence, and delinquency. People with this disorder are at least 18 but had a conduct disorder before the age of 15 and have shown a pattern of irresponsible and antisocial behavior since the age of 15. It is important to distinguish antisocial personality disorder from antisocial behavior that is a result of socialization, or the adapting to the norms of some social groups.

5. Children and adolescents are diagnosed as having a **conduct disorder** when they repeatedly engage in actions that violate the basic rights of others or social norms appropriate for their age group, such as purse snatching, stealing, drug abuse, vandalism, and cruelty to animals and people.

6. The term **psychopath** has been used to refer to a personality type that is characterized by charm, intelligence, poise, insincerity, callousness, manipulativeness, poor judgment, and similar traits. Psychopaths do not particularly intend to harm others, they simply do not consider the implications of their actions.

7. It is possible that heredity may play a part in antisocial behavior, although it is not clear how antisocial behavior might be inherited. Violent and antisocial tendencies have been associated with slower than normal alpha waves. From a cognitive perspective, antisocial behavior results from arrested moral development.

ANXIOUS OR FEARFUL BEHAVIORS

1. The main features of **avoidant personality disorder** is extreme sensitivity to rejection or humiliation and low self-esteem. Individuals with this disorder are likely to be hypervigilant, continuously assessing all their human contacts for signs of deception, humiliation, and negative reactions. They also narrow their range of activities in order to cut off upsetting stimuli.

2. People with **dependent personality disorder** passively allow other people to make all the important decisions in their lives and subordinate their own needs to the needs and demands of others. They are self-effacing, ever agreeable, and continually ingratiating. Another method they frequently use to attract helping behavior is complaints of pain or illness.

3. People with **obsessive–compulsive personality disorder** are characterized by lack of ability to express warm and tender emotions, extreme perfectionism, insistence that their way of doing things be followed, and excessive concentration on work and productivity.

4. People with **passive aggressive personality disorder** habitually resist demands for adequate performance both on the job and in their social life. They seem to have no awareness of how their own behavior contributes to the situations in which they find themselves.

ADDITIONAL PROPOSED CATEGORIES

Two additional categories of personality disorder have been proposed for study in DSM-III-R. They are **sadistic personality disorder** and **self-defeating personality disorder.**

TREATMENT OF PERSONALITY DISORDERS

The treatment of personality disorders is difficult for several reasons. One is that people with these disorders tend to be satisfied with their behavior except in special situations when they are experiencing great stress. Another is that even people with personality disorders may behave appropriately or normally some of the time. Furthermore, knowledge about personality disorders is limited. Nevertheless, such techniques as assertiveness training and systematic desensitization, psychodynamic therapy, and the use of psychoactive drugs may be helpful in specific cases.

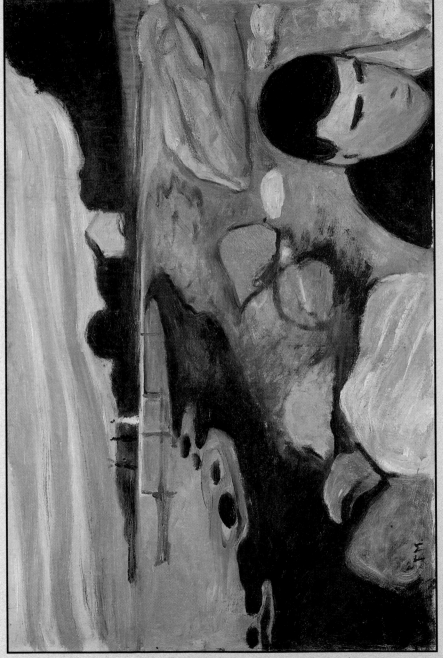

Edvard Munch, *Melancholy (Yellow Boat)*, 1891–92. Oil on canvas. 65.5 × 96 cm. Nasjonalgalleriet, Oslo.

OBJECTIVES FOR CHAPTER TEN:

To learn:
1. The different disorders in which depressed mood is prominant and the differences among them
2. The theories of depression and the treatment approaches used based on each
3. The definition, causes, and treatment of bipolar disorder

To understand:
1. The difference between depressed mood and diagnosable depression
2. The positive and negative features of both the biological and psychological treatments for depression
3. The many reasons why suicide may be considered or attempted

t is difficult to put into words how I felt at that time. I guess my major reaction was one of despair—a despair of ever being human again. I honestly felt subhuman, lower than the lowest vermin. Furthermore, I was self-deprecatory and could not understand why anyone would want to associate with me, let alone love me. I became mistrustful and suspicious of others and was certain that they were checking up on me to prove that I was incompetent myself. . . . I had become increasingly concerned about finances. On one hand, I thought that I was receiving extra money that I didn't deserve and, on the other, I was certain that we were going to wind up in jail. When I received my July salary statement it appeared to me that the total was larger than it should be. This frightened me and I told my wife that we should phone the university immediately and arrange to return the extra money before I got into trouble. Gently, my wife told me that she thought the amount of money was correct and there was nothing to worry about. Of course, she was right. . . . I not ony pondered my current situation but my whole career as well. I was positive that I was a fraud and a phony and that I didn't deserve my Ph.D. I didn't deserve to have tenure; I didn't deserve to be a Full Professor . . . I didn't deserve the research grants I had been awarded; I couldn't understand how I had written books and journal articles that I had and how they had been accepted for publication. I must have conned a lot of people.

—(Endler, 1982, pp. 45–49)

These were the thoughts of a well-known psychologist during a period of severe depression. They illustrate how drastically depression may alter mood and behavior. In contrast, consider the behavior of a well-known writer. He was able to function adequately a good deal of the time, but occasionally manic behavior would break through and his behavior became quite different.

One day a play of his was bought by a film company. He was in Florida when he got the news. He promptly bought himself a new Cadillac and some Chivas Regal and went tearing back to New York. On the way, he was picked up for speeding in a small town in Georgia and thrown into the clink. They allowed him one phone call, and whom did he call? He did not call me [his therapist]; he did not call his wife; he did not even call his mistress. He called the Strategic Air Command to bomb the jail.

—(Kline, 1977, p. 9)

Defining Mood Disorders

The two examples in the preceding section illustrate the range of behavior included in the **mood disorder** category. The essential feature of disorders in this category is that they all reflect a disturbance in mood or emotional reaction that is not due to any other physical or mental disorder. Table 10–1 defines the major categories of mood disorders. Of the two major groups—**depressive disorders** (also called unipolar disorders), and bipolar disorders—the depressive disorders are by far the most common.

Depression

Depressed mood is found in a variety of disorders, so that its mere presence does not mean the person has a mood disorder. The term Depression can refer to a symptom or to a disorder.

Depressed Mood

People use the word *depression* in their everyday language to refer to symptoms. These may be the result of a feeling state, a reaction to a situation, and a person's characteristic style of behavior. The feeling of depression is usually known as "the blues." It may occur in rainy weather, during an annoying cold, or after an argument with a friend. Often an event that is usually expected to be happy ends with such blue feelings. People may experience the blues after holidays such as Christmas or New Year's Day or after moving to a new home. Feelings of depression that are based on these temporary situations usually fade away quickly. Adults who have a major depressive disorder make a sharp distinction between the "black cloud" of depression and the unhappiness they feel when they are not ill (Hamilton, 1982). The novelist Hermann Hesse, who himself suffered from depression, made the difference clear in this description of depression from his novel *Peter Camenzind.*

The first weeks were good and calm. Then by and by the old sadness returned, stayed for days, weeks, and did not dissolve either at work. Who has not felt himself what melancholy is, does not understand this. How shall I describe it? I had the feeling of a dreadful solitude. Between myself and people and life in the city, the squares, the houses and streets was a wide gulf continuously. A major accident happened, important things were reported in the papers—I did not care. Great events were celebrated, the dead buried, markets held, concerts performed—what for? I strolled through . . . the country roads, and around me the meadows kept silent, trees, fields in silent grief, looked at me earnestly and had the desire to tell me something, to approach me, to welcome me. But they were just lying there, unable to say anything, and I understood their suffering and suffered along, for I could not save them.

—(Hesse, 1969)

TABLE 10-1

Mood Disorders

I. Depressive Disorders	
A. Major Depression	One or more major depressive episodes
B. Dysthymia	History of depressed mood a majority of the time
II. Bipolar Disorders	
A. Bipolar Disorder	One or more manic episodes and usually one or more major depressive episodes
B. Cyclothymia	Numerous hypomanic episodes and numerous periods of depressive symptoms
C. Bipolar II	At least one hypomanic episode and one major depressive episode but no manic episode or cyclothymia

Grief and Loss

The term *depression* is also used to describe a sadness that comes from a death in the family. After the death of someone they care deeply about, most survivors experience a depressed mood that is usually called grief. These feelings of depression are entirely normal. In fact, the absence of such emotions might be bad for the person in the long run. Common features of grief include physical distress such as sighing, tightness of the throat, an empty feeling in the abdomen, and a feeling of muscular weakness. In addition, there may be preoccupation with the visual image of the dead person, along with guilt, and hostile reactions. During the process of grieving, the guilt, hostility, feelings of loss, and physical symptoms gradually disappear.

These same symptoms may be the result of any other kind of important loss. For example the breakup of a dating relationship, or divorce or separation, may also bring about these feelings; they are likely to occur even though the person wanted to end the relationship. Other kinds of stressful life events—losing a job, being turned down for a graduate school program, or losing everything in a fire—may bring on feelings of depression. These are not severe enough to be called mood disorders but may be classified as an adjustment disorder with depressed mood (adjustment disorders are discussed in Chapter 5). Severe feelings of depression are also frequent for people who have just had a heart attack or found they have a serious illness. In addition, depressed mood is an important symptom in a variety of other disorders including borderline personality disorder, schizophrenia, and physical changes in the brain such as those seen in Alzheimer's disease. Withdrawal from a variety of drugs including amphetamines, cocaine, and alcohol also is likely to produce symptoms of depression. In such instances, depression is seen as a response or symptom of a life stress or physical change and is not usually considered to reflect a mood disorder.

An example of depressed feelings that does not fall into the category of mood disorder is the following case presenting a short-term response to stress.

A 24-year-old, single, female nursery-school teacher terminated brief psychotherapy after ten sessions. She had entered treatment two weeks after she discovered that the man she had been involved with for four months was married and wanted to stop seeing her. She reacted with bouts of sadness and crying, felt she was falling apart, took a week's sick leave from her job, and had vague thoughts that the future was so bleak that life might not be worth the effort. She felt that she must be in some essential way "flawed"; otherwise she would not have gotten so involved with someone who had no intentions of maintaining a long-term relationship. She felt that others "would have seen it," that only she was "so stupid" as to have been deceived. There were no other signs of a depressive syndrome, such as loss of interest or appetite or trouble concentrating. She responded to mixed support-insight psychotherapy and, toward the end of treatment, began dating a law student whom she met at a local café.

—(Spitzer and others, 1981, p. 261)

The Frequency of Depression

About 6 percent of the U.S. adult population can be expected to experience depression as defined by DSM-III-R criteria in any given 6-month period (Holden, 1986). Of these people 80 percent will never be treated for their depression. Over their lifetimes, one in four women and one in ten men in the United States can expect to experience a major depression.

Depression is a significant problem throughout the world. One longitudinal study kept track of everyone born in Iceland from 1895 to 1897 (Helgason, 1979). There was one chance in eight that at some time before reaching age 75 these Icelanders would develop an affective disorder.

Not only is depression common but its economic cost is high. The cost of treatment for people with depression is more than 2 billion dollars per year in the United States (Stoudemire and others, 1986). If other economic costs are included such as lost productivity and lost income, the total cost is over 16 billion dollars per year.

Risk Factors for Depression

Women are at least twice as likely to have a major depression as men (Nolan-Hoeksema, 1987). Although women are more likely to seek help than men, this does not explain the difference in rate of depression because community surveys of people who have never sought treatment also show a much higher rate for women. Age is another risk factor. The maximum period of risk seems to be the mid- to late twenties.

Being separated or divorced is also a risk factor. These groups have the highest depression rate and married people have the lowest. This is true for both men and women, although women in all marital status categories have a higher risk than men (Leaf and others, 1986). A pile-up of stressful events in a short time period, a family history of depression, and being a young child with a depressed parent also are factors that increase vulnerability to depression (Weissman, 1987).

Another risk factor that has puzzled researchers is the effect of birth cohort. Year of birth affects a person's risk. In recent years the prevalence of depression (the number of people depressed at any one time) and also the incidence (the number of new cases in any given period) seem to be rising among younger people and decreasing among older people (Klerman and others, 1985). These changes have been observed in several large studies both in the United States and in Europe. Figure 10–1 shows these differences in one study.

DEPRESSIVE DISORDER

Even if the depressed feelings are not a part of some other disorder, we still have to answer the question of how to distinguish between the blues or "normal depression" we all feel once in a while and a **depressive disorder** (depression that fits a DSM-III-R criteria). Sadness often is experienced by people who are depressed, but sadness itself is not the same as depression. The thoughts of depressed people contain three key elements of depression. They think of themselves as unworthy or to blame for what has happened, they think they are helpless to change the situation, and they do not think things will be better in the future (Rutter, 1986).

Dysthymia

The milder, less incapacitating form of depressive disorder is **dysthymia**. (The term *dysthymia* comes from the Greek words meaning defective or diseased mood). Dysthymia tends to be chronic, often lasting for years and sometimes is hard to distinguish from a personality disorder.

People with dysthymia tend to be depressed most of the day, more days than not, based on their own description or the description of others. They also have at least several of the following problems: difficulties with eating (either poor appetite or overeating), difficulties with sleeping (either insomnia or sleeping too much), constant feelings of tiredness, difficulty concentrating or making decisions, a low opinion of themselves, and feelings of hopelessness.

Many people with dysthymia never come to the attention of a clinician unless they later develop other problems, usually a major depression. At least one-quarter of the people who develop a major depression have had dysthymia for a long time.

The following case describes a dysthymic woman whose problems with depression have persisted in spite of extensive psychotherapy.

A 28-year-old junior executive had obtained a master's degree in business administration and moved to California a year and a half earlier to begin work

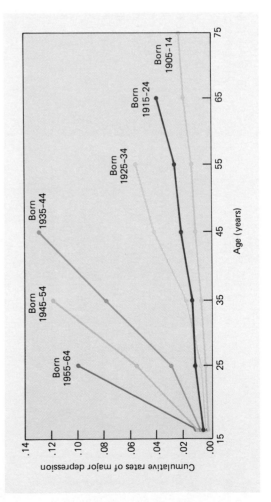

FIGURE 10–1

One risk factor is the historical time period in which a person was born. Cohorts or groups born in each of the 10-year periods since 1935 have an increasing risk of depression just as a result of the period of their birth. (The figure does not show data for those born in the 1965–1974 decade because many of them have as yet not reached the highest risk period. (Adapted from Weissman and others, 1984)

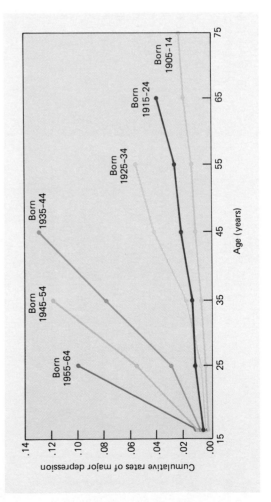

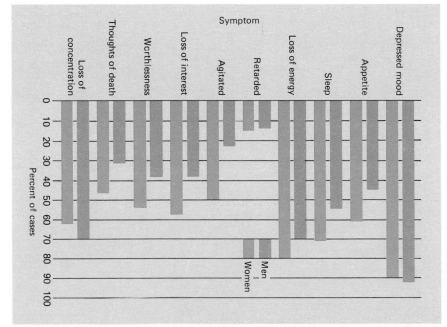

FIGURE 10-2
Some symptoms of depression are experienced by more people than other symptoms are. Men and women also vary in the frequency with which they report different types of symptoms.

Major Depression

A **major depressive episode** is marked by either or both a depressed mood and a loss of interest or pleasure in almost all activities, as well as some of the following problems: marked weight loss or gain when not dieting, constant problems in sleeping, agitated or greatly slowed-down behavior, tiredness, inability to think clearly, feelings of worthlessness, and frequent thoughts about death or suicide. Figure 10–2 shows how frequent some of these characteristics are in men and women who are depressed.

If a person has one or more major depressive episodes but has never had a manic episode, he or she is said to have a **major depression**. The period a depression episode lasts is variable. If it is not treated it may last about 6 months and then the person returns to his or her usual behavior pattern. It is estimated that half of the people who have a major depressive episode will have at least one more in their lifetime. If depression does recur, it is most likely to do so within 2 years. People who have recurrent major depressive episodes have an average of seven of them over their lifetimes (Cancro, 1985). About 15 percent of people with a major depression have some psychotic symptoms, usually delusions (false beliefs about reality). The delusions usually have the quality of despair: "I have an incurable illness and I'm dying," "I am not well because of my sinful behavior." Figure 10–3 shows an artist's version of a characteristic pose of severely depressed people who seem immersed in their own misery. People with major

in a large firm. She complained of being "depressed" about everything: her job, her husband, and her prospects for the future.

She had had extensive psychotherapy previously. Her complaints were of persistent feelings of depressed mood, inferiority, and pessimism, which she claims to have had since she was 16 or 17 years old. Although she did reasonably well in college, she consistently ruminated about those students who were "genuinely intelligent." She dated during college and graduate school, but claimed that she would never go after a guy she thought was "special," always feeling inferior and intimidated. Whenever she saw or met such a man, she acted stiff and aloof, or actually walked away as quickly as possible, only to berate herself afterward and then fantasize about him for many months. She claimed that her therapy had helped, although she still could not remember a time when she didn't feel somewhat depressed.

Just after graduation, she married the man she was going out with at the time primarily because she felt she "needed a husband" for companionship. Shortly after their marriage, the couple started to bicker. She was very critical of his clothes, his job, and his parents; and he, in turn, found her rejecting, controlling, and moody. She began to feel that she had made a mistake in marrying him. Her social life with her husband involves several other couples. The man in these couples is usually a friend of her husband's. She is sure that the women find her uninteresting and unimpressive, and that the people who seem to like her are probably no better off than she.

Recently she has also been having difficulties at work. She is assigned the most menial tasks at the firm and is never given an assignment of importance or responsibility. She admits that she frequently does a "slipshod" job of what is given her, never does more than is required, and never demonstrates any assertiveness or initiative to her supervisors. She views her boss as self-centered, unconcerned, and unfair, but nevertheless admires his success.

— (Spitzer and others, 1981, pp. 10–11)

FIGURE 10–3

In his painting *Depression*, artist Jacob Lawrence has shown the downcast eyes, the drooping head and shoulders, and the shrunken posture of people who are deeply depressed.

depressive disorder are often treated with antidepressant drugs or with electroconvulsive therapy. These types of treatment are described later in the chapter.

The case of Mr. T. S. illustrates a major depressive episode:

Mr. T. S., aged 40, married and father of three children, was hospitalized after a consultation between his family physician and a psychiatrist. In the hospital, if left to his own devices, he would spend most of his time sitting on a chair by the side of his bed, moaning and wringing his hands. His facial expression was one of the deepest dejection, and his eyes were reddened from weeping. At times he would get up and pace the floor heavily. All of his muscles seemed to sag, giving him the appearance of a much older man. If left to himself, he would not eat. He was severely constipated. He tended to ignore his personal appearance and hygiene completely. He had trouble sleeping although appearing to be very fatigued. He blamed himself in the harshest terms for having "ruined his family," and said he did not deserve to live, and he had some incurable disease, the nature of which the doctors were concealing from him.

Mr. T. S., the proprietor of a small business, was a careful, conscientious, and methodical person, very fair in his dealings with others. He placed great emphasis upon routine and was disconcerted by departure from it. He seldom took a vacation, and when he did, he was apt to become restless after a few days, finding it difficult to relax. He was lacking in a sense of humor, although he tried to be a good sport about things.

About three months before his hospitalization, Mr. T.

S. had experienced a minor business reverse. A month later, while he was still trying to cope with this situation, his mother died of a heart attack. He became terribly distressed, appeared to grieve deeply, was restless and agitated, lost his appetite and had trouble sleeping. For a time he strove to carry on his business, but he was quite ineffectual, and had had to turn the management over to an assistant. His self-reproach became increasingly intense and unrealistic. (He spoke of himself as having thrown away the family resources and having caused his mother's death and the impoverishment of his wife and children.) When he began to speak of himself as not deserving to live, his wife had sought medical assistance.

—(Adapted from Hofling, 1968, pp. 360–361)

Theories of Depression

Most researchers think that depression results from an interaction between the person's biological characteristics and psychological vulnerabilities and the occurrence of stressful events or difficult ongoing situations in his or her life (Akiskal, 1985). Despite this view that both characteristics of the person and of the situation are important, each of the perspectives discussed in this book has been used to try to understand the causes of depression and to find effective treatment approaches. As is usually the case, the different theoretical approaches to depression have produced different types of studies and different data, all of which may add to our understanding of the causes and treatment of this complex disorder.

Biological Theories

Biological theories assume that the cause of depression lies either in the genes or in some physiological malfunction that may or may not have an inherited base.

Role of Heredity

The findings of twin studies conducted since the 1930s suggest that hereditary elements figure in some cases of depression. Depression that is part of a bipolar disorder is even more strongly linked to heredity. The younger people are when their first major depression occurs, the more likely it is that their relatives will also experience periods of depression (Weissman and others, 1984). Figure 10–4 illustrates this difference. Relatives of people who had a major depressive episode before they were 20 had an eight-times greater chance of becoming depressed than relatives of normal subjects. Relatives of people who were over 40 when they first had a major depression had little more than the normal risk of depression. This increased risk was found both for relatives of patients who were hospitalized and for relatives of individuals who did not need to be hospitalized (Weissman and others, 1984b).

Although genetic factors seem important in many cases of depression, the exact mechanisms of inheritance of depression is not clear and may even vary from one family to another (Lingjaerde, 1983). It is also obvious that nongenetic factors, either physical or related to a person's environment or relationships, may be required to produce depression even in people with a genetic vulnerability.

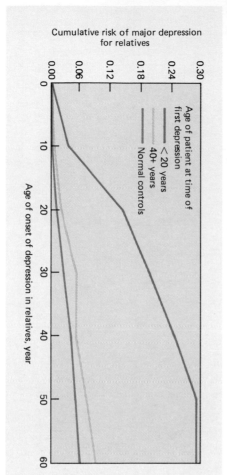

Cumulative risk of major depression for relatives

Age of patient at time of
first depression

— < 20 years
···· 40+ years
— Normal controls

Age of onset of depression in relatives, year

FIGURE 10–4
Cumulative risk of major depression for relatives of depressed people varies according to the age at which the person first becomes depressed. (Weissman and others, 1984, *Archives of General Psychiatry*, 41, p. 1138. Copyright © 1984, American Medical Association)

Biochemical Aspects of Depression

Whatever the mechanism by which the genetic factor is inherited, its influences are biochemical. Depression is probably the result of a lack of certain chemical neurotransmitters at particular sites in the brain. Before discussing these, a brief review of the neuron and how it functions may be helpful.

The basic building blocks of the nervous system are specialized cells called **neurons**—more than 100 billion of them. Each neuron has three main parts: a **cell body** containing the nucleus that regulates the cell's life process, **dendrites**, and an **axon**. The axon branches at its end to form a number of axon terminals, each of which ends in a terminal button.

The neuron can be stimulated either through its dendrites or through its cell body. When the stimulation occurs, an electrical impulse travels along the axon to other neurons, muscles, or glands. To travel from one neuron to another, the impulse must cross the **synapse**, the space or gap between the axon and the dendrites of another neuron. In order to cross this gap, the electrical impulse that travels through the neuron must be changed to a chemical message. The axon terminal buttons contain small **synaptic vesicles** or holding containers for chemicals called **neurotransmitters** that make this transformation possible. When the neurotransmitter molecules are released, they travel across the fluid-filled space between the sending (presynaptic) and receiving (postsynaptic) neurons and bind or attach themselves to specific sites on that neuron's dendrites or cell body. An area on the semiliquid surface of the receiving neuron's membrane precisely matches the shape of the transmitter molecule; the two fit together with the precision of

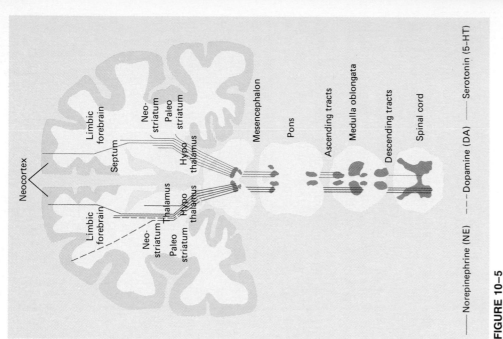

—— Norepinephrine (NE)   - - - Dopamine (DA)   ——— Serotonin (5-HT)

FIGURE 10–5
Pathways of neurons that produce specific neurotransmitters are beginning to be identified. Some of them are shown here. (From *Depression, Manic-Depressive Illness, and Biological Rhythms,* DHHS Pub. No. (ADM) 82-889. National Institute of Mental Health, 1979)

a key in a lock. The chemical reaction between the neurotransmitter molecule and the receptor causes an electrical impulse to travel through the receiving neuron. After the neurotransmitter molecule has fit into its receptor, it is deactivated or shut off so that its action does not continue too long.

Several types of neurotransmitters have been identified. Each neuron synthesizes and stores only one of these types. Most neurotransmitters are breakdown products of the amino acids. Those that are of special interest in the study of the chemical causes of depression have a distinctive amino group in their molecular structure and are called **monoamines.** The most important monoamines are the catecholamines **norepinephrine** (NE) and **dopamine** (DA) and the indoleamine **serotonen** (5HT).

These three monoamine systems (NE, DA, and 5HT) have somewhat different distributions and functions, but all of them originate in the central part of the brain (Lingjaerde, 1983) (see Figure 10–5). All of these systems work in a similar way. Figure 10–6 shows how norepinephrine is generated in the presynaptic terminal and how it facilitates the transfer of the nerve impulse to the postsynaptic terminal of an adjacent neuron. First norepinephrine (NE) is synthesized in the presynaptic terminal in the following way: the amino acid tyrosine is converted to dihydroxyphenylalanine (DOPA) by an enzyme. Then another enzyme converts the DOPA to dopamine (DA). Dopamine is then taken up into storage granules like that shown in Figure 10–6. There it is converted into NE by another enzyme. When an action potential or electrical impulse through the nerve reaches this nerve terminal, NE is released into the synapse. On the postsynaptic nerve terminal there are receptor sites where the molecules of the neurotransmitter can bind. This binding allows the message to be carried from the presynaptic to the postsynaptic cells. In the case of the type of synapse we have been describing, two types of postsynaptic binding sites have been identified for NE. These are named alpha 1 (α_1), and beta (β) adrenergic receptors. The binding of NE to the beta receptors affects an enzyme adenylate cyclase, on the inside surface of the cell membrane. This enzyme stimulates a source of energy in the cell, and this then changes to another messenger compound which stimulates nerve activity. The alpha 1 receptors are thought to work somewhat differently than the beta receptors. Most of the released NE does not make contact with alpha 1 and beta receptors so it is again taken up by the presynaptic nerve terminal and returned to the storage granules. Some of the released NE may be inactivated in a different way by the enzyme monoamine oxydase (MAO). Some of the NE is deactivated by the MAO in the presynaptic terminal. MAO also exists in the synapse. There the synapse MAO and another enzyme catechol-O-methyltransferase

(COMT) chemically alters the NE into several other products. The NE in the synapse has another possible destination; it interacts with alpha 2 (α_2) receptors in the presynaptic terminal. This signals the presynaptic cell to slow down the production and release of NE. It is a kind of feedback mechanism signaling that enough NE is present in the synapse. There may also be some beta receptors in the presynaptic receptors, but not much is known about them. The systems affected by serotonin and dopamine work in a similar fashion.

It may be that people vulnerable to depression have alpha and beta receptors that are extremely sensitive and that the low level of amine production is the body's way of taking care of this problem. One argument in favor of this explanation is that almost all antidepressants gradually produce lowered sensitivity in the receptors (Charney and others, 1981).

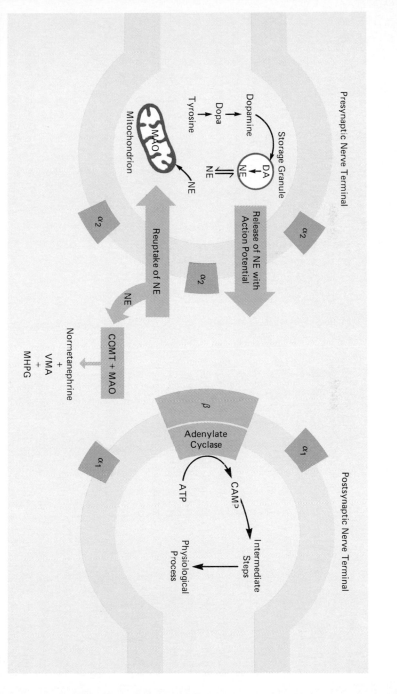

Presynaptic Nerve Terminal

Postsynaptic Nerve Terminal

FIGURE 10–6

This diagram shows pre- and postsynaptic nerve endings that produce and receive norepinephrine in transferring the nerve impulse across the synapse. The text describes the process. DA: dopamine; NE: norepinephrine. Dihydroxyphenylalanine (DOPA) is a precursor of the transmitters DA and NE. The enzymes monoamine oxidase (MAO) and catechol-O-methyltransferase (COMT) are involved in the chemical breakdown of NE. 3-Methoxy-4-hydroxy-phenylglycol (MHPG) and vanillylmandelic acid (VMA) are metabolites in the breakdown of NE. α_1, α_2, and β are receptor sites on the cell membrane. Adenosine triphosphate (ATP) is an energy source for the cell and an earlier form of another chemical involved in neural transmission, cyclic adenosine monophosphate (cAMP). (Adapted from McNeal and Cimbolic, 986, p. 363 Copyright © 1986 by the American Psychological Association. Adapted by permission of author.)

The effect of different antidepressant drugs on the uptake and the metabolism of norepinephrine and serotonin in the brain has helped researchers to understand how chemical neurotransmitters function in their effect on depressed mood. When these drugs are used for a long time there is a decrease in postsynaptic beta-receptor frequency and sensitivity. This decrease in number and in sensitivity also occurs in the alpha 2 presynaptic receptors. Receptor sensitivity for alpha 1 receptors increases after long-term use of antidepressants.

There are several theories of depression that focus on amine function. The **catecholamine theory** of mood disorder suggests that depression is associated with a decrease in levels of brain catecholamines (both NE and DA), but especially NE (Schildkraut and others, 1965). The catecholamine theory was based on the effect of several different drugs on mood. Reserpine, a drug used to treat hypertension (high blood pressure) was known to cause depression in patients who received it. One of the effects of reserpine is the depletion of NE and DA

in the brain. Two types of antidepressant drugs (MAO inhibitors and tricyclics) increase the activity of catecholamines in the brain. MAO inhibitors do this by preventing the breakdown of NE by MAO. The tricyclics block the uptake of the amines and therefore allow the neurotransmitters to continue their effectiveness. Later on other researchers tested the hypothesis by investigating how depression was affected by changing the amount of the amino acid precursors to NE such as DOPA. These attempts did not always support the theory (McNeal and Cimbolic, 1986).

Another theory, the **indolamine theory** of depression, suggested that the neurotransmitter serotonin (5HT) was important in depression (Glassman, 1969). This theory is based on the same general types of evidence as the catecholamine theory and, like it, has not been completely supported. A similar theory has been proposed about the role of another neurotransmitter, acetylcholine (ACh). This theory proposed that increased brain ACh levels were associated with depression and decreased levels with mania (Gershon and Shaw, 1961). The original idea for this theory came from the observation that depression was found in some adults exposed to insecticides potent in an enzyme that inhibits the breakdown of ACh.

Another idea is that depression may be related not to too little or too much activity in the neurotransmitter system, but rather to a failure in the regulation of the system (Siever and Davis, 1985). This means that neurotransmitter activity may be highly variable and may sometimes be an inappropriate response to a situation or to the normal daily cycles of the body. If this idea is correct individuals who are likely to become depressed have some abnormality at a particular point in the system, for instance, lack of sensitivity in the alpha 2 receptors. This is not enough to cause problems under ordinary circumstances, but under stress the system might not function normally.

The Search for Markers of Depression

Since most scientists agree that not all depressions have similar causes, a great deal of effort has been spent on finding subgroups of depressed patients that have similar characteristics. The study of such subgroups should not only make it easier to understand the causes of depression but, even more important, provide clues to the most effective treatment for a particular individual. A major focus of research in this area is the effort to develop a test that could be used to identify various subgroups.

The Dexamethasone Suppression Test. Although the level of hormone activity in depression often is within normal limits, there may be a reduction in the reaction of the hormonal system to different levels of stress or excitation. This is probably due to some problem in the action of the hypothalamus. In an effort to understand this lack of response and to differentiate

among people who seem to have different types of depression, several chemical tests have been developed. One of the most frequently used of these tests is the **Dexamethasone Suppression Test** (DST) (Carroll, 1985). Patients are given the steroid dexamethasone which supresses the production of cortisol, a hormone produced in the cortex of the brain. Normally, dexamethasone suppresses the level of cortisol in the blood for about 24 hours. In some depressed patients, however, the suppression does not last that long (see Figure 10–7).

Although the DST has been enthusiastically accepted by some clinicians, to date research findings have not provided enough evidence to justify its use on a routine basis (APA Task Force, 1987). One problem is that the test does not differentiate between unipolar depression and the depressed phase of bipolar disorders. Many patients whose depressions appear to be biologically related also show no response. Another problem is that the dexamethasone suppressor response has been reported in many other conditions besides depression—for example, alcoholism, schizophrenia, and eating disorders—as well as for normal individuals who were dieting. Thus, the DST cannot be viewed as a clear diagnostic sign.

Another shortcoming of the DST is that it does not discriminate between people who may be helped by antidepressant drugs and those who would not. One possible use is to predict the likelihood of suicide or relapse into depression. If the test does not convert from abnormal to normal suppression when the person seems behaviorally recovered, this may suggest an increased probability of relapse or of a suicide attempt (Targum, 1984).

Scanning Techniques. The development of noninvasive scanning techniques like the PT (positron emission tomography) scan may help investigators under-

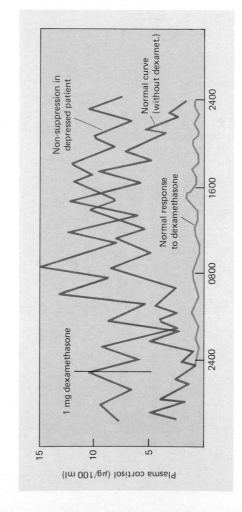

FIGURE 10–7

The dexamethasone suppression test identifies individuals whose hormonal systems do not react in a normal way. In most normal people, a dose of dexamethasone will suppress the secretion of blood cortisol. In some depressed people, however, the blood cortisol level does not decrease over a 24-hour period. (Lingjaerde, 1983, p. 44)

stand the biological changes involved in depression. One advantage of these techniques is their ability to define behavior changes in an objective manner. Figure 10-8 illustrates how scanning techniques can link observed behavioral changes in patients with unipolar disorders to changes in brain activity. A variety of scanning techniques are described in Chapter 13.

Biological Rhythms. Differences in biological rhythms may be a way to identify subgroups of depressed individuals; this approach may also be a way to clarify how biological functioning differs for people who are depressed as compared to those who are not. Regular rhythms in the functioning of living beings have been recognized for a long time. Of these, the 24-hour or circadian rhythms have been studied most. These rhythms can be shown for a large number of biological functions. Some of them, such as body temperature and sleep activity, are usually synchronized so that their peaks occur at the same time. When these rhythms get out of synchrony, other changes occur. For instance, sleep lasts a long time if a person goes to sleep at the top of the body temperature curve. If, instead, the person goes to sleep near the bottom of the temperature curve, sleep lasts a much shorter time. Sleep disturbance is frequent in depressed individuals. They tend to have trouble going to sleep and staying asleep. They also are likely to waken early in the morning and to feel most depressed in the morning. Table 10-2 lists some of the characteristics of sleep of depressed people.

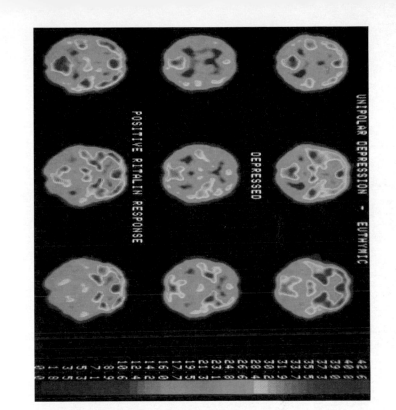

FIGURE 10-8
Three series of PT scans of unipolar depression illustrate how this technique can be used as an objective measure of the changes in biological activity that accompany certain behavior changes. The center row illustrates the decreased glucose metabolism found in a unipolar depressed patient. (The darker the area, the greater the metabolic activity.) The top row shows how the glucose metabolism increases as a patient naturally recovers from a period of depression. The lower row shows a similar increase in glucose metabolism when a test drug improves a patient's behavior. (O. Lingjaerde, 1983, The biochemistry of depression, *Acta Psychiatrica Scandinavica Supplementum*, 302, pp. 36–51. Copyright © 1983 Munksgaard International Publishers Ltd., Copenhagen, Denmark [University of California, Los Angeles])

TABLE 10-2

Major Sleep Disturbances in Depression

Generalization	Findings
Sleep is shallow	Decreased Stage 3 and 4 (Delta) sleep
	Increased Stage 1 sleep
	Greater sensitivity to noises
Sleep is fragmented	Increased awakenings
	Increased stage shifts
	Decreased sleep efficiency
Sleep is short	Decreased total sleep time
	Increased time to fall asleep
	Increased early morning awakening
REM sleep is "intense"	Increased REM density (increased eye movement during REM sleep)
	REM begins sooner after falling asleep
	Increased length and REM density of first REM period
	Increased proportion of REM in first half of night
REM sleep is advanced toward sleep onset	

Campbell and Gillin, 1987, p. 648.

Normal sleep has a number of phases that can be measured by monitoring the electrical impulses of the brain. The one that is of most interest from the standpoint of depression is REM sleep, during which the eyes rapidly move from side to side and brain wave patterns indicate a peak in brain activity. One characteristic in some depressed individuals is a shortened period between falling asleep and the beginning of the first REM period as well as increased length and intensity of the first REM period of the night (Kupfer and others, 1985). This characteristic, together with early wakening, may be due to an advance in temperature rhythm that causes the person to go to sleep nearer to the bottom than to the top of his or her temperature curve (see Figure 10–9).

Originally interest in the REM patterns of depressives was aimed at discovering a way to differentiate among various types of depression. However, the study of REM patterns and their relationship to other biological rhythms may give researchers clues about the biological changes in depression. REM research also has significance for therapy. Depriving depressed individuals of REM sleep can help decrease their depression. This can be done simply by waking the individual whenever REM occurs. This treatment seems to work on the same group of patients who are helped by tricyclic drugs. At least some tricyclic drugs and MAO inhibitors appear to lengthen the cycles in circadian rhythm. The drug **lithium**, which is used primarily to treat bipolar disorders and will be discussed in a later section, also lengthens

the rhythms of the circadian cycle (Wehr and Wirtz-Justice, 1982).

Treatment Based on Biological Theories

The two main drug groups used to treat depression—the tricyclics and the MAO inhibitors (see Table 10–3)—both increase the amount of norepinephrine, but they produce their effects in somewhat different ways. MAO inhibitors retard the breakdown of norepinephrine so that it remains active longer. The tricyclic drugs increase available norepinephrine in another way: they slow its reabsorption by the transmitter neuron and thus keep more of it available in the synapse. Brain imaging using PT scans has shown that antidepressant drugs have their greatest effect in the frontal lobes (Buchsbaum, 1986).

Which group of drugs and which particular drug within a group will be effective is still usually a matter of trial and error on the part of the physician. Usually, one of the tricyclic drugs is preferred because the MAO inhibitors have more potentially dangerous side effects. Use of the MAO inhibitors also requires stricter supervision because when these drugs are taken with foods that contain a substance called tyramine they may produce a toxic reaction and cause blood pressure to rise to a life-threatening level. Because many common foods, including cheese, chocolate, sour cream, and wine contain tyramine, the use of MAO inhibitors requires careful dietary monitoring.

Lithium is used to treat depression that occurs as a part of the mood swings of bipolar disorder. Lithium may change the chemical balance of the body fluids by replacing calcium, magnesium, potassium, and/or sodium or it may slow down the release or increase the absorption of norepinephrine. Whatever the process, it not only seems effective in calming manic behavior but also serves to prevent the depressed phase of the bipolar cycle.

One of the problems in treating a severe episode of depression with either tricyclics or MAO inhibitors is the time lag between their initial use and the first signs of improvement of the patient's mood. Several weeks may go by before any improvement is seen. If there is concern about suicide, a wait of 3 weeks or so may seem too great a risk. In such situations, or if drugs are not effective, electroconvulsive therapy (ECT) may be the treatment used because it produces a more rapid effect. **Electroconvulsive therapy** involves passing a current of between 70 and 130 volts through the patient's head. First an anesthetic and a muscle relaxant are administered. (The muscle relaxant is given to prevent injury from the convulsion caused by the electric charge.) The current is then administered through electrodes placed

FIGURE 10–9
The relationship between duration of sleep and the circadian temperature rhythm. (Adapted from Czeisler and others, *Science, 210*, p. 267. Copyright © 1980 by the AAAS)

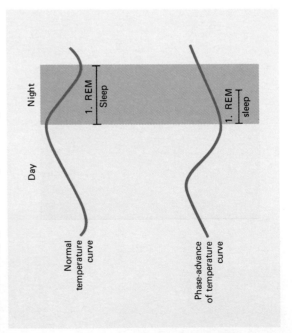

TABLE 10-3

Drugs for Affective Disorders

	Scientific Name	Trade Name	
Antidepressant drugs			
Tricyclics	Imipramine	Tofranil	Used to treat relatively severe depressive symptoms of the unipolar type. Variable effectiveness in moderating symptoms. Slow acting. May take up to 3 weeks before response is seen. Many side effects, some dangerous. MAO inhibitors require restrictions in diet because of serious interactive effects with certain food chemicals.
	Amitriptyline	Elavil	
	Nortriptyline	Aventyl	
	Protriptyline	Vivactil	
Monoamine oxidase (MAO) inhibitors	Isocarboxazid	Marplan	
	Phenelzine	Nardil	
	Tranylcypromine	Parnate	
Antimanic drugs			
Lithium carbonate	Eskalith		Used to treat manic episodes and some severe depressions, especially those that alternate with mania. Effective in reducing or preventing manic episodes but variable with depressions. Many possible side effects if use not closely monitored. High toxic potential.
	Lithane		
	Lithonate		
	Lithotabs		
	Phi-Lithium		

on one or both sides of the head. Placement of the electrodes on one side of the head seems to reduce the chance of memory loss. The electrodes are usually placed on the nondominant side of the brain (for most people, the right side), because that side is believed to be more concerned with nonverbal and emotional behavior as opposed to memory and language functions. Usually a series of 6 to 12 treatments is given.

ECT is very effective in treating severe depression in which there is a great deal of delusional thinking. **Delusions** are incorrect beliefs that are resistant to change despite evidence that disproves them—for example, the idea that others can read your thoughts or that your best friend is plotting to kill you when that is clearly not true. ECT is also effective for some severe depressions that have not responded to tricyclics or MAO inhibitors. It is not effective for mild depressions (dysthymic disorder and adjustment disorder with depressed mood). Despite its effectiveness the use of ECT has brought forth a good deal of controversy (see Table 10-4).

ECT causes many changes. It produces massive discharges of neurons in much of the brain, activates the autonomic nervous system, releases secretions from the endocrine glands, and causes convulsions of many of the muscles. These all cause so many chemical changes in the body that it is difficult to determine which ones have an effect on the depression. It is likely that the seizure activity produces changes in the level of neurotransmitters or changes in the electrical responsiveness of the neuron (Holden, 1985).

ECT can result in memory loss, most of which disappears within a few weeks. The patient's ability to learn and retain information may also be affected for several weeks. Some people who have been treated with ECT report memory lapses several years later. Confusion and memory loss are increased by longer treatments, more frequent treatments, a greater number of

TABLE 10-4

Some Controversies Surrounding Use of Electroconvulsive Therapy (ECT)

Arguments for	Arguments against
1. Theory of ECT based on correcting a malfunctioning neurophysiological mechanism	ECT is not corrective and works to the contrary, causing serious neurological destruction.
2. ECT's immediate effectiveness supported by a large body of well-documented research.	An equally large body of contradictory research can be mentioned, ECT's long-term applicability suffers from a high incidence of relapse.
3. Side effects from ECT are much less than medication in many instances; the side effects are typically transient and dissipate over time.	Side effects are more profound than acknowledged; potential exists for cognitive dysfunction, personality alteration, and permanent organic changes with repeated treatment.
4. ECT is a useful intervention in life-threatening situations such as suicidal intent.	No data exist to defend ECT's utility in life-threatening situations.
5. State regulations regarding voluntary informed consent are too restrictive and legally impede the psychiatrist from administering ECT under certain conditions.	Specific guidelines for ensuring full informed consent are actually inconsistent from state to state and do not necessarily provide the patient with all essential details surrounding treatment effects and outcome.

Reprinted with permission of the authors and publisher from Taylor, J. R., and Carrol, J. L. Current issues in electro-convulsive therapy. *Psychological Reports*, 1987, 60, 747–758, Figure 1.

treatments, and increased strength of electrical stimulation (Taylor and Carrol, 1987). In general, although it may be effective, ECT should be used only after other treatments, usually antidepressant drugs, have been tried. The use of ECT has decreased at least until recently (Thompson and Blaine, 1987). An increase in use has been predicted by some authorities because ECT reduces time in the hospital and therefore also medical costs (Markowitz and others, 1987).

Sometimes ECT can produce dramatic changes in mood. Norman Endler, the psychologist whose description of his own depression (later diagnosed as a bipolar type) appears at the beginning of the chapter, also described his experience with ECT after both tricyclic and MAO-inhibiting drugs had proved ineffective and the depression was still incapacitating him after 5 months. Endler was faced with a choice between ECT and hospitalization; he reluctantly chose ECT.

Dr. Persad met us on the sixth floor at seven-forty-five. He tried to calm me down, and I recall his saying that he had never seen anyone so agitated as I. The prospect of ECT really frightened me.

Beatty [Endler's wife], remained in the waiting area and Dr. Persad and I went into the ECT room. I changed into my pajamas and a nurse took my vital signs [blood pressure, pulse, and temperature]. The nurse and other attendants were friendly and reassuring. I began to feel at ease. The anesthetist arrived and informed me that she was going to give me an injection. I was asked to lie down on a cot and was wheeled into the ECT room proper. It was about eight o'clock. A needle was injected into my arm and I was told to count back from 100. I got about as far as 91. The next thing I knew I was in the recovery room and it was about eight-fifteen. I was slightly groggy and tired but not confused. My memory was not impaired. I certainly knew where I was. Shortly after eight-thirty, I got dressed, went down the hall to fetch Beatty, and she drove me home. At home I enjoyed breakfast and then lay down for a few hours. Late in the morning I got dressed. I felt no pain, no confusion, and no agitation. I felt neither less depressed nor more depressed than I had before the ECT. . . . After about the third or fourth treatment I went up to Dr. Persad's office and spoke to him briefly. He asked me if I had noticed any improvement and to what degree. I believed that I had improved 35 to 40 percent. Dr. Persad believed that the improvement was more likely to be 70 to 75 percent.

—(Endler 1982, pp. 81–83)

After the fifth and sixth treatment Endler went to his office. A colleague who had been helping to manage the psychology department in his absence, was there.

I asked her to remain. She stated that she would be glad to stay as long as I needed her assistance. By early afternoon Kathy looked at me and said "Norm, you are perfectly fine, you do not need me here." She left and I stayed the rest of the day. As of then I resumed the chairmanship full time. A miracle had happened in two weeks. I had gone from feeling like an emotional cripple to feeling well.

—(Endler, 1982, pp. 81–83).

Like many people who have a bipolar disorder, Endler experienced another depression about a year after the first. This time, although the ECT produced improvement and made it possible for him to work effectively, the depressed mood hung on for several months.

Although drug therapy and ECT can be effective, there are still problems with the biological treatment of depression. Choosing the right drug can be a hit-or-miss affair (Stern and others, 1980). The effects these drugs may have after many years of use is also not known. Moreover, some researchers argue that dependence on drugs makes unipolar or bipolar individuals less likely to improve their coping mechanisms and thus increases the chances of their having further affective problems. The attitude of many therapists toward using biological treatment alone is expressed by Silvano Arieti, a well-known psychoanalyst and researcher: "I have never met a patient about whom I could say that his depression came from nowhere and its origin had to be sought exclusively in metabolic disorder" (Arieti and Bemporad, 1978, p. 5).

The Psychodynamic View

The psychological study of depression was begun by Sigmund Freud and Karl Abraham. Both described depression as a complex reaction to loss (Abraham, 1911/1968; Freud, 1917/1957). Depression was the first disorder described by Freud in which the central causal factor was emotion rather than sexual wish. Melancholy, as Freud called it, was grief gone haywire—excessive, drawn out, often unrelated to the environment, and seemingly unjustified. In his major work on depression, *Mourning and Melancholia*, Freud described both normal mourning and depression as responses to the loss of someone or something that was loved. However, in contrast to the mourner, the melancholic suffers "an extraordinary diminution of his ego on a grand scale" (Freud, 1917/

1957, p. 246). Freud believed that a person who is depressed has a strong and punishing conscience or superego. He thought that one reason the conscience becomes so strong is to control the anger and aggressive feelings that otherwise might come forth to hurt others (Freud, 1930).

Why do some individuals react with such extreme irrational grief? Psychodynamic theories emphasize unconscious feelings and reactions to new situations based on what has happened earlier in life. Most psychodynamic formulations focus on the history of relationships between the children and the people on whom they were most dependent as a child, usually their mothers. The disturbance in early childhood relationships might be the actual loss or a feared or fantasized loss of a parental figure. Because it is anxiety-provoking, this early loss is pushed out of awareness but it still exerts its influence. When a symbolically significant event occurs this vulnerability may result in actual depression.

The importance of parental loss has been studied intensively in animal experiments. Research by Harry Harlow and others has tested the effects on infant monkeys of separation from their mothers (Harlow and Suomi, 1974). At first the typical monkey infant shows agitation; this gradually changes to social withdrawal, slow response to stimuli, and slow movement. Eventually the baby assumes a collapsed self-clasping position that suggests behavior of a person who is severely depressed. Separation from their mothers also seems to make monkeys more likely to become depressed later in life if they experience a high level of stress. However, there seem to be personality differences among monkeys that cause some of them to react strongly both to early separation and later stress while others are unaffected (Suomi, 1983).

John Bowlby, a British psychoanalyst, is one of the more prominent theorists who emphasize the importance of loss or separation in childhood to later development. Bowlby thinks that separation of a child from its mother or another important figure during early childhood, whether because of illness, travel, or other reasons, creates feelings of sadness, anger, and continuing anxiety that may affect the individual's emotional relationships in adult life (Bowlby, 1980).

Researchers have provided data that connect the probability of depression in adults with early experiences of loss. For example, the sociologist George Brown found that women who had lost their mothers before the age of 11 were at greater risk of depression than other women (Brown and others, 1977). Although not everyone thinks that early loss has been definitely established as a factor increasing the risk of later depression (Crook and Eliot, 1980), it remains an important part of the psychodynamic perspective.

Often the loss of self-esteem caused by an environmental loss is the most important factor in producing depression. For instance, a middle-aged man became severely depressed after he lost money in the stock market. First he became morose, irritable, dependent, and self-critical. Then he seemed to collapse emotionally.

This severe reaction was better understood when it was learned that this man had dreamed of making a sufficient income from stocks so he could resign from his job, which he detested. Therefore, the loss prevented him from obtaining a future lifestyle that he desperately desired. However, this deeper motive still does not explain this man's change in his estimation of himself, transforming his personality from one of moderate confidence and autonomy to one of self-hatred and childish dependency. This change in self-estimation becomes more understandable when his childhood experience is related. He had been raised by a highly critical father and mother, both of whom preferred his brother. Throughout his maturing years he had been repeatedly told that he could never amount to anything . . . and that he should strive for a secure, if unrewarding, position in life, as this was the best he could hope for. He went into his family's business, where he continued to be devalued and criticized. He managed to hide his hated self from others and also from himself by exploiting his family's wealth and prestigious place in the community, by pursuing certain hobbies so that he became a somewhat pedantic expert, by criticizing his wife and children, and by fantasizing becoming a highly successful entrepreneur. His failure to make money in the stock market revived the dreaded childhood self so that he believed that his parents had been correct in their judgment: he was inadequate and stupid. The loss caused a drastic alteration in his view of himself, which initiated the depressive process.

—(Bemporad, 1983, p. 162)

Psychodynamic therapeutic efforts are aimed at modifying the existing associations between the client's present situation and the client's thoughts and feelings that arise from the past. Long-term psychotherapy is directed at uncovering the unconscious basis of the affective disorder, which is thought to be an unresolved conflict based on childhood experiences. Because such ambitious personality restructuring is not possible in most cases, short-term supportive therapy is often used with depressives to give them an opportunity to express their thoughts and feelings and to encourage them to hope for recovery.

Another type of therapy for depression that stems from the psychodynamic approach is the **interpersonal systems approach** (Gotlib and Colby, 1987). Studies of the childhood of depressed patients show that they are

more likely than nondepressed controls to report parental rejection, abuse, inattention, family discord, and parental emotional disturbance (Digdon and Gotlib, 1985). The systems approach assumes that the whole is greater than the sum of its parts, so that the way a family operates and how it affects its members cannot be understood by looking at each person separately but must take into account how the group interacts. The techniques used in systems therapy are often those that were developed from a behavioral perspective.

A systems therapy approach is illustrated by the case of a young boy who refused to go to school. He and his family had moved to the city 6 months earlier from a small rural community where all their relatives lived nearby. In an initial therapy session the therapist asked the family to act out what had happened the previous morning when Graham stayed home from school.

This enactment was critical in revealing a pattern of interactions that seemed to be strongly involved in the maintenance of Graham's depression. In brief, Mrs. Jones' first comment to Graham that morning was that he looked pale, and she questioned whether or not he was feeling well. Mr. Jones accused his wife of pampering Graham, and stated that he did not look at all pale. Mrs. Jones then felt she had to support her perception and checked Graham's forehead, triumphantly announcing that he felt feverish. Mr. Jones became disgusted and retorted that her coddling Graham was enough to make anyone feverish. As this dialogue escalated, Graham grew increasingly upset and finally broke into tears. Mrs. Jones glared at her husband and retorted, "Now look what you've done." Mr. Jones stomped out of Graham's room in disgust, and Mrs. Jones turned her affection and attention to her son. This scenario offered support for the therapist's preliminary hypothesis of an overly involved mother–son subsystem and a weak marital subsystem.

The therapist probed for further information about how this family was functioning now, as compared to how they had interacted before the move. The ensuing discussion indicated that Mrs. Jones had previously had many of her needs for intimacy and support met through her family of origin. With her primary source of support eliminated by the move, Mrs. Jones turned her attention to her son and had become increasingly involved in his life. Graham had provided an easy opening for this reaction through his mild problems adjusting to the move and difficulties with entering a new school.

—(Gotlib and Colby, 1987, p. 148)

The Behavioral Perspective

Learning theorists assume that depression and lack of reinforcement are related. Peter Lewinsohn and his co-workers have been among the leaders in research on depression from this behavioral perspective. In general, they emphasize that the low rate of behavior output and the feelings of sadness or unhappiness associated with depression are due to a low rate of positive reinforcement and that a major cause of the low rate of positive reinforcement is an actual deficiency in social skills (Lewinsohn and Hoberman, 1982). Further, once people are depressed, then behavior becomes less likable, so a kind of vicious circle is created in which the depression is maintained because acquaintances avoid the depressed person as much as possible and, as a result, further decrease the person's rate of reinforcement (Lewinsohn and Arconad, 1981).

When depressed people find themselves in stressful situations, they tend to cope by delaying (seeking more information before taking any action) and attempting to get emotional support from others. Excessive support seeking may be what makes other people feel uncomfortable and guilty and cause them to try to avoid contact with the depressed person. Depressed people may also make many complaints to elicit sympathy and affection. Although the person who is on the receiving end of this treatment may respond appropriately at first, after a while he or she may begin to be annoyed or frustrated. Even if the depressed person's associates keep on giving support and making reassuring statements, their feelings of frustration may be expressed in nonverbal behaviors or in other ways. Eventually a vicious cycle develops in which the display of symptoms and frustration of the depressed person's companions increase until the companions begin to say things like, "You could get better if you try," "No one has to act like that," and so forth (see Figure 10–10). This, of course, merely serves to worsen an already bad situation. Such feelings, whether expressed or not, are probably one reason why people tend to avoid the company of depressed individuals.

Recent research has suggested that many depressed people are capable of acting differently in different social roles (McNiel and others, 1987). When they meet people casually they may be able to conceal their negative behavior and behave in a socially desirable way. According to this view, it is mainly in long-term relationships, especially marital relationships, that we see the negative actions and negative responses predicted by the behavioral perspective.

A major focus of work on the interaction of depressed people with others is on married couples. The negative attitudes of depressed people and their spouses

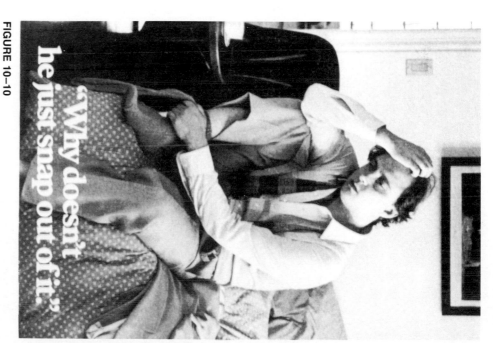

FIGURE 10–10

This poster, part of a campaign to inform the public about the need to seek treatment for depression, portrays a common reaction to the irritating qualities of depressed behavior.

are usually obvious to others. These attitudes influence the spouses' interpretations of their interactions. There is usually both hostility and an attempt to hide negative feelings when disagreements are discussed (Coyne and others, 1987). Depression in one marital partner often seems to cause significant distress or depression in the other partner.

Another characteristic of depressed behavior is negative self-evaluation. Lewinsohn and his co-workers believe that people who are depressed have a negative view of their **self-efficacy** in dealing with situations. This term refers to a person's judgment of his or her own ability to carry out certain courses of action (Bandura, 1977). Depressed people show a bigger difference between their ideas of self-efficacy and their behavioral standards than do people who are not depressed. Lewinsohn's model predicts that this difference is due to a lower perception of self-efficacy rather than to higher standards for behavior, and it has been demonstrated experimentally that this is the case (see Figure 10–11).

client lacks. The plan could include such things as assertiveness training, effective parenting, time management, and relaxation training. This approach is illustrated in the following case.

Alice was a 37-year-old secretary. She was a single parent with two children, a 14-year-old son and a 9-year-old daughter. Alice's initial complaints included having trouble getting things done, lack of concentration, loss of interest in activities, withdrawal from social life, unreliability, fatigue, and headaches. She complained of feeling depressed. After her initial evaluation Alice started working with her therapist. The treatment was to include twelve sessions. In the first half of the treatment Alice used her listing of pleasant and unpleasant events as a starting point for discussion. She identified finances, household chores, parenting, and social activities as her biggest concerns. The therapist helped her prepare a monthly budget and Alice kept a daily log of expenses. Using these techniques made her feel money matters were much less upsetting. Another problem Alice had was her dislike of household chores. She routinely let them pile up and then tried to do them all on the weekend. The therapist helped her organize her chores into small units, pair them with pleasant activities, such as listening to the radio, reward herself for doing them, and assign some of the chores to her children. As a parent, Alice felt totally responsible for any problem her children had; she also had problems disciplining them. The therapist helped Alice to learn to talk calmly to her children about the reasons for her disciplinary actions, to pinpoint their desirable behaviors and reward them with praise, affection, and allowances. Alice also learned to sort out whether it was "my problem, their problem, or our problem" when thinking about her children's difficulties.

—(Lewinsohn and others, 1980, pp. 328–332)

Alice's self-monitoring data (Figure 10–12), showed changes as time went on. The number of pleasant events that she reported increased, the unpleasant events decreased, and her mood improved somewhat. The self-monitoring data for the first 21 days of Alice's treatment were analyzed by a computer program that calculated the correlations between each activity and her mood changes. The results alerted Alice to the relationship of certain events to her mood.

The computer analyses also confirmed Alice's low rate of pleasant activities, especially social activities. The remaining therapy sessions were devoted to this problem. As Alice's daily social interactions increased, the number of pleasant events increased dramatically and the improvement in mood continued. One month later Alice continued to report increased frequency of pleas-

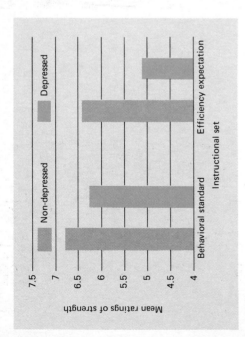

FIGURE 10–11

People who are depressed set their performance standards about as high as nondepressed individuals do, but they have less confidence that they will be able to meet those standards. (R. Kanfer and A. M. Zeiss, 1983, Depression, interpersonal standard setting, and judgments of self-efficacy, *Journal of Abnormal Psychology*, 92, pp. 319–329. Copyright © 1983 by the American Psychological Association. Reprinted by permission of the author)

This suggests that people who are depressed may not try as hard as others would in situations they see as difficult because they have a negative view of their own abilities, not because they set their goals too high (Kanfer and Zeiss, 1983).

Treatment Based on Behavioral Theories

In treating clients who are depressed, Lewinsohn and his co-workers first strive to pinpoint the specific person–environment interactions and events that are related to the depression. One step in doing the initial assessment is to observe the person at home. This accomplishes several things. It alerts the client to the idea that depression is related to interactions with other people and with the environment, and it also gives the therapist a productive and relatively unbiased way of learning about the behavior of the client and others in his or her environment.

Another tool used in this social-learning-based treatment is a list of pleasant and unpleasant events. The client notes how often each event has occurred in his or her life and how pleasant or unpleasant it was (or could be if it had happened), and constructs a tailor-made event list to be used daily. The client also rates his or her mood each day so that both the client and therapist become aware of the relationship between events and the client's mood. A summary of these daily monitorings for one client is shown in Figure 10–12. In addition to this daily monitoring, a specific treatment plan is prepared that includes training in the skills that the

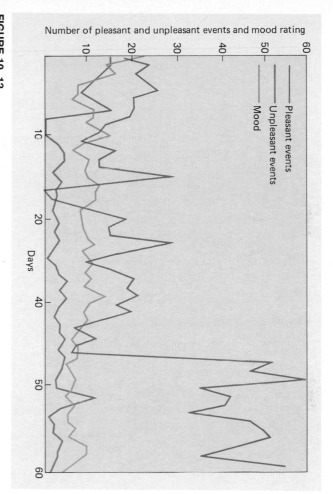

Number of pleasant and unpleasant events and mood rating

— Pleasant events
— Unpleasant events
— Mood

Days

FIGURE 10-12
A record of Alice's daily monitoring of pleasant and unpleasant events and moods. (Lewinsohn and others, 1980, p. 330).

ant events and an improved mood (Lewinsohn and others, 1980).

The Cognitive Perspective

Probably the most influential psychological theories of depression today are derived from the cognitive perspective. The basis for these theories is the idea that the same experience may affect two people very differently. Part of this difference may be due to the way each of them thinks about the event, to what cognitions each has about it. One person who does not receive an expected promotion might think: "I am a worthless person. Everyone thinks poorly of me. If they did not, I would have been selected for the job." A second person in the same situation might think: "R. was chosen for that job I wanted because he had more experience in negotiation. I know I could have done the job, but my qualifications didn't look as impressive on paper."

There are several cognitive theories of depression. They include Beck's cognitive–distortion model, attributional theories such as the learned-helplessness theory of Seligman and his co-workers, theories that emphasize the cognitive aspects of stress, and information-process-

ing theories. Learning-based theories like Lewinsohn's also have a strong cognitive component.

Beck's Cognitive-Distortion Model

Aaron Beck's cognitive-distortion model of depression (Beck, 1967, 1976; Beck and others, 1979) is the most original and influential of the cognitive approaches to depression. Beck argues that depression is primarily a disorder of thinking rather than of mood. He believes that depression can best be described as a **cognitive triad** of negative thoughts about oneself, the situation, and the future. A person who is depressed misinterprets facts in a negative way, focuses on the negative aspects of any situation, and also has pessimistic and hopeless expectations about the future. Table 10-5 illustrates some of these cognitive errors on the part of depressed individuals; Figure 10-13 shows how depressed people tend to emphasize the negative. The cognitions of depressed people differ from the thoughts of people with anxiety disorders (Beck and others, 1987). Those with anxiety as their primary symptom have thoughts that focus on uncertainty and worry about the future. The thoughts of depressed people either focus on negative aspects of the past or reflect a negative outlook on what

TABLE 10-5

Cognitive Errors and the Assumptions from Which They are Derived According to Beck's Cognitive Theory

Cognitive Error	Assumption
1. Overgeneralizing	1. If it is true in one case, it applies to any case that is even slightly similar.
2. Selective abstraction	2. The only events that matter are failures, deprivation, etc. Should measure self by errors, weaknesses, etc.
3. Excessive responsibility (assuming personal causality)	3. I am responsible for all bad things, failures, etc.
4. Assuming temporal causality (predicting without sufficient evidence)	4. If it has been true in the past, then it is always going to be true.
5. Self-references	5. I am the center of everyone's attention, especially of bad performances or personal attributes.
6. "Catastrophizing"	6. Always think of the worst. It is most likely to happen to you.
7. Dichotomous thinking	7. Everything either is one extreme or another (black or white; good or bad).

A. T. Beck (1976), *Cognitive Therapy and the Emotional Disorders.* New York: International Universities Press. Copyright © 1976 by Aaron T. Beck, M.D. Reprinted by permission of the publisher.

the future will bring. The anxious person worries about what might happen and *whether* he or she will be able to deal with it. The depressed person thinks about how terrible the future will be and how he or she will be *unable* to deal with it or improve it.

Beck believes that a person who is depressed blames any misfortune on his or her personal defects. Awareness of these presumed defects becomes so intense that it completely overwhelms any positive self-concepts. Any ambiguous situation is interpreted as evidence of the defect, even if there are more plausible explanations.

A good example is provided by Norman Endler's description of his thoughts during his bout of depression (Endler, 1982). Endler went through a period of fear (not at all based on reality) that his family would desert him and he would be unable to cope with everyday living.

I recall a time during the end of August when I took the subway with my wife. She had gone through the turnstile before I did and I was positive that she was going to desert me. She probably had bad enough of me and my shenanigans and was fed up with my behavior.

—(Endler, 1982, p. 49)

After his recovery from this period of depression, Endler recognized the irrationality of such a thought.

Of course nothing could have been further from the truth. Her kindness and devotion, her concern, compassion, and her love, more than anything else, sustained me during my ordeal. If I had to single out the one person who was most instrumental in my getting better, it would be my wife.

—(Endler, 1982, p. 49)

Beck also thinks that depressed people tend to compare themselves with others, which further lowers their self-esteem. Every encounter with another person becomes the opportunity for a negative self-evaluation. For instance, when talking with others the depressed person thinks: "I'm not a good conversationalist. I'm not as interesting as other people." Beck thinks that the tendency to have these negative cognitions may be related to particular ways of evaluating situations that grow out of childhood experiences. These thought patterns, called **schemata**, affect all the elements of the cognitive triad in later life. A list of the characteristics of these schemata are shown in Table 10–6.

Research findings have also shown that some revisions of Beck's theory are necessary (Hammen, 1985). First, the idea that only those who are depressed distort information needs to be modified. All individuals are biased information processors, although different groups may have different kinds of biases. Second, it may be that distorted thinking causes the depression to continue and intensify in a kind of vicious cycle, but plays no role in beginning the period of depression.

FIGURE 10-13
The cartoonist Roz Chast illustrates the negative focus about the past that is typical of a depressed person.

Research on the outcome or effects of psychotherapy has raised some questions about whether the negative cognitions cause depression. Both cognitive and behavioral therapies can produce a similar improvement in cognition even though the behavioral therapy only focuses on increasing reinforcement through self-initiated positive behavior (Rehm and others, 1987). It is possible that negative thoughts are merely the result of depression, not its causal agent. At present the answer to this question is not clear (Hollon and others, 1987).

Cognitive Therapy for Depression

Beck's therapeutic approach includes pointed but friendly questioning designed to make the depressed person aware of the unrealistic nature of his or her thoughts. Another technique Beck uses is an activity schedule. The client schedules his or her day and then rates each activity on a scale from 0 to 5 for mastery (doing a good job) and pleasure. The following dialog occurred after a severely depressed 38-year-old executive turned in his mastery schedule. One item, "wallpaper kitchen," stood out. This should be an achievement for a severely depressed person, yet the client gave it a 0 for both mastery and pleasure.

THERAPIST: Why didn't you rate wallpapering the kitchen as a mastery experience?
PATIENT: Because the flowers didn't line up.
THERAPIST: You did in fact complete the job?
PATIENT: Yes.
THERAPIST: Your kitchen?
PATIENT: No. I helped a neighbor do his kitchen.
THERAPIST: Did he do most of the work? (Note that the therapist inquires about reasons for feelings of failure that might not be offered spontaneously.)
PATIENT: No. I really did almost all of it. He hadn't wallpapered before.
THERAPIST: Did anything else go wrong? Did you spill the paste all over? Ruin a lot of wallpaper? Leave a big mess?
PATIENT: No, no, the only problem was that the flowers did not line up.
THERAPIST: So, since it was not perfect, you get no credit at all.

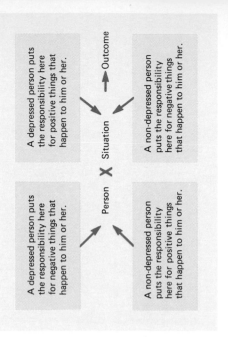

FIGURE 10-14

A comparison of the attribution process in depressed and nondepressed people.

---

ceptance to sheer luck. On the other hand, when one of her articles was rejected (a negative event), she was distressed because she thought the rejection reflected badly on her. Most nondepressed people do the opposite: they accept responsibility for the good in their lives but tend to blame the situation on others when things do not work out. Figure 10–14 illustrates this difference. Attributional models of depression do not claim that attributional style alone is enough to cause depression. These models suggest that attributional style is important only when a person experiences intense or frequent negative events in his or her life (Abramson and others, in press).

Learned Helplessness. People who are depressed seem to feel helpless to control their environment. They think that, no matter what they do, they will be unable to affect the way things turn out. It is possible that such people learn to be helpless as a result of certain situations they have encountered in the past. Martin Seligman (1974, 1975) first popularized this concept, which is termed **learned helplessness.**

Early research on learned helplessness showed that sometimes people feel generally helpless and sometimes they feel helpless only in particular situations. The way a person interprets the situation is important in determining whether or not he or she will feel helpless. On the basis of this research, a revised theory of learned helplessness stresses the importance of the attributions people make in a situation in determining whether they will become depressed in a particular situation (Abramson and others, 1978). According to the revised theory, depression is more likely when people attribute negative qualities to themselves as a result of having experienced situations in which they felt helpless.

There are three dimensions to these feelings of helplessness. The first has to do with whether the person

---

TABLE 10-6

Schemata Used in Beck's Cognitive Theory of Depression

Schemata (silent assumptions)

Consist of spoken, inflexible assumptions or beliefs

Result from past (early) experience

Form basis for screening, discriminating, weighing, and encoding stimuli

Form basis for categorizing, evaluating experiences, and making judgments and distorting actual experience

Determine the content of cognitions formed in situations and the affective response to them

Increase vulnerability to relapse

Beck, 1976.

PATIENT: Well . . . yes. (Note that the irrational belief that "if I don't do everything perfectly, I am useless, inadequate and a failure" is implied by this reasoning. However, the correction of this assumption will be left to a later phase of therapy, when the patient is less depressed. For now, the correction of the cognitive distortion is the objective.)
THERAPIST: Just how far off was the alignment of the flowers?
PATIENT: (holds out fingers about 1/8 in. apart): About that much.
THERAPIST: On each strip of paper?
PATIENT: No . . . on two or three pieces.
THERAPIST: Out of how many?
PATIENT: About 20–25.
THERAPIST: Did anyone else notice it?
PATIENT: No. In fact, my neighbor thought it was great.
THERAPIST: Did your wife see it?
PATIENT: Yeh, she admired the job.
THERAPIST: Could you see the defect when you stood back and looked at the whole wall?
PATIENT: Well . . . not really.
THERAPIST: So you've selectively attended to a real but very small flaw in your effort to wallpaper. Is it logical that such a small defect should entirely cancel the credit you deserve?
PATIENT: Well, it wasn't as good as it should have been.
THERAPIST: If your neighbor had done the same quality job in your kitchen, what would you say?
PATIENT: . . . pretty good job!

—(Beck and others, 1979, pp. 85–86)

Attributional Models of Depression

The term **attribution** is used by social psychologists to refer to the causes a person assigns to things that happen. Beck's cognitive approach predicts that depressed individuals' attributions will be personal—that is, depressed people will blame themselves when anything bad happens. When something good does happen, it is usually attributed to luck. For instance, one woman was not especially pleased when a short story she had written was accepted for publication; she attributed the ac-

sees the problem as **internal** or **external**. People may attribute the situation to their personal inability to control outcomes or they may feel that anyone would have a hard time in the same situation. The second dimension has to do with the **global-specific continuum**. Someone may see a situation as proof that he or she is totally helpless or may see him- or herself as helpless only in a particular situation. The third dimension has to do with whether the situation is viewed as **stable** (chronic) or **unstable** (acute). People may think their helplessness will go on for years, or that it will last only a short time.

The revised learned-helplessness hypothesis suggests that only certain kinds of attributions result in depression. Consider the following situation. Tim has overdrawn his checking account. We could divide his possible attributions as shown in Table 10–7. The revised theory predicts that if Tim's attribution about the cause of failure is stable and global, he is more likely to become depressed than he would if he made other attributions. In this case, if Tim's general style of attribution caused him to explain his unbalanced checkbook in terms of stable global factors, whether internal or external, he would have a high chance of becoming depressed. If his attributions were internal, stable, and global, his depressive thinking would be characterized by loss of self-esteem as well. If he perceived the cause as stable, the feelings of depression would be likely to persist. If he saw the cause as unstable, the depressive reaction would be likely to pass away quickly (Abramson and others, 1978). So far research efforts have shown that either stable or global attributions can produce depression, but internal attributions seem to produce depression only when they are combined with stable and global components (Robins and Block, 1987).

Some people become depressed in certain situations while others do not. The revised learned-helpless-

ness hypothesis assumes that various individuals have different characteristic ways of explaining events and therefore are consistent across situations in the extent to which their causal explanations are internal, stable, and global. This means that for events where no clear cause is apparent, these people are likely to give an explanation that comes from habit rather than from an assessment of the situation. However, not all research data support the view that attributional style is consistent for most people in a variety of situations (Hammen, 1985). The attribution model fits best in situations that have to do with achievement, such as college performance or vocational success. Other kinds of negative events, such as a death or a friend moving away, may call up different sets of attributions from the same person. Another problem for this theory is that only about one-third of depressed people show this attributional style and those that do change their attributional style in periods when they are not depressed (Hamilton and Abramson, 1983). This implies two things. First it suggests that attributions play a role only for a subgroup of depressed people. Second, it raises the question of whether this attributional style is a product or symptom rather than a causal factor in depression.

Life-Stress Models. Having bad experiences can make people unhappy, yet it is clear that many people do not become depressed when negative things happen. The cognitive perspective stresses the importance of a person's **cognitive set** in the interpretation of stressful life events (Paykel, 1979). Some life events may remind a person of important negative experiences in the past. This type of event focuses attention on choices, commitments, and mistakes that have been made and leads to questions about "what life might have been, what it is about, and what it will become" (Brown and Harris,

TABLE 10-7
Examples of Causal Explanations for the Event "My Checking Account Is Overdrawn"

Style	Explanation	
	Internal	External
Stable		
Global	"I'm incapable of doing anything right"	"All institutions chronically make mistakes"
Specific	"I always have trouble figuring my balance"	"This bank has always used antiquated techniques"
Unstable		
Global	"I've had the flu for a few weeks, and I've let everything slide"	"Holiday shopping demands that one throw oneself into it"
Specific	"The one time I didn't enter a check is the one time my account gets overdrawn"	"I'm surprised—my bank has never made an error before"

Peterson and Seligman, 1984, p. 349.

But the attributions of depressed people may be more accurate than these theories predict. Some researchers have found that depressed patients were quite realistic about their own social skills (Lewinsohn and others, 1980). In contrast, other psychiatric patients and control subjects tended to see themselves as more competent than other people saw them. Even more interesting, the realism of the depressed patients' self-perceptions tended to decrease as therapy progressed. In short, as they became less depressed, the patients became less realistic about their effect on others; they deluded themselves more in the same way the nonpatients do. The result of cognitive therapy may be to encourage a normal lack of realism (Sackeim and Wegner, 1986). This fits very well with an observation made by Freud.

"When in his [the depressive's] heightened self-criticism he describes himself as petty, egoistic, dishonest, lacking in independence, one whose sole aim has been to hide the weakness of his own nature, it may be, so far as we know, that he has come pretty near to understanding himself; we only wonder why a man has to be ill before he can be accessible to a truth of this kind.

—(Freud, 1917/1957, p. 246)

The crucial question then becomes, does depression lead people to become more realistic or are realistic people more vulnerable, more likely to become depressed? As yet research has not solved this puzzle.

The Humanistic–Existential Perspective

Whereas psychodynamic theorists emphasize the loss of a loved object as a central cause of depression, existential theorists focus on the loss of self-esteem. The lost object can be real or symbolic—power, social rank, or money—but the loss itself is not as important as the change in an individual's self-assessment as a result of the loss. Many people base their self-concepts on who they are or what they have: I'm the leader of the factory assembly team; I'm the boss; I'm a member of the exclusive city athletic club; I'm the husband of a famous movie star. Identifications of this kind offer external verification of people's worth in their own minds. Thus, in our culture a frequent cause of depression in men is loss of their job. The job represents the man's value in his own eyes. At least until the recent increase in the number of women employed outside the home, a frequent

1978, p. 84). Negative events for which people see themselves as at least partially responsible may be more important than negative events for which there is usually no responsibility, such as death or illness (Hammen and De Mayo, 1982).

An Information-Processing Analysis. The information-processing view of depression attempts to combine ideas of social-learning theory and those of Beck and Seligman with concepts derived from the work of cognitive psychologists interested in learning and memory (Ingram, 1984). The basic idea is that memories are represented by descriptive statements connected by associated linkages. When these linkages are activated beyond certain thresholds, the contents of the system come into conscious awareness in the form of cognitions. But memories are only one set of linkages in the information-processing system. In addition, there may be **primitive emotion nodes** (Bower, 1981). This hypothesis suggests that each specific emotion, such as depression, anger, or joy, is represented by a particular unit or node in memory. Each node connects an autonomic response pattern, the verbal labels used to describe the emotion, a characteristic automatic response pattern, and descriptions of the events that bring forth that particular emotion.

According to this view, the depression unit is activated by the appraisal of a variety of events. Only those losses that are subjectively meaningful will activate the depression node. As time passes after it is activated, the node's level of excitation gradually decreases until it falls below the threshold level. This may explain why depression is usually time-limited and fades without treatment (Lewinsohn and Hoberman, 1982). Depression may last longer if the depression node also has connections to memories of events that have produced depression in the past. For instance, if a person has just lost an important job, this loss will activate the depression node and its network. This means that in addition to the initial depression, the person will begin thinking about past depression experiences. These depressing thoughts continue to activate the depression node and the depression continues.

The results of some experimental work support the information-processing view. People who are depressed recall more of previously presented negatively self-relevant information than people who are not depressed (Derry and Kuiper, 1981). Depressed individuals also give greater attention to negative events, make less accurate attributions about causality, and are less likely to reward and more likely to punish themselves than nondepressed individuals.

Cognitive Accuracy in Depression. Both Beck's theory and the revised learned-helplessness hypothesis stress the inaccuracy of self-perception in depression.

cause of female depression was loss of a mate. This represented not only the loss of a loved person, but also the loss of a major source of prestige, since a woman's social status was traditionally based on her husband's role. Because of the prevailing social norms a woman might be depressed when she could no longer say, "I'm the wife of a successful lawyer," but a man would be less likely to feel a loss of status if he could no longer say, "I'm the husband of a successful lawyer."

Humanistic theorists emphasize the difference between a person's ideal self and his or her perception of the actual state of things. The philosopher Kierkegaard expressed this view very well in the following quotation:

Despair is never ultimately over the external object but always over ourselves. A girl loses her sweetheart and she despairs. It is not over the sweetheart, but over herself-without-the-sweetheart. And so it is with all cases of loss, whether it be the money, power, or social rank. The unbearable loss is not really in itself unbearable. What we cannot bear is being stripped of the external object. We stand denuded and see the intolerable abyss of ourselves.

As Kierkegaard pointed out, depression is likely to result when the difference between the ideal and the real becomes too great for the individual to tolerate.

Contrasting Psychological Theories of Depression

It is sometimes difficult to distinguish clearly how the various psychological theories of depression and the therapies derived from them differ. Learning theories such as Lewinsohn's approach and Beck's cognitive-distortion theory started out quite differently, but as their related therapies developed, many of the techniques used became more similar. The behavioral approach increasingly emphasized social reinforcement and in some cases paid greater attention to cognitive attributions, and Beck included learning-theory techniques like behavioral checklists of events and moods.

The same emphasis on feelings of hopelessness and helplessness is found in the humanistic-existential approach, in which loss of self-esteem and a perceived inability to alter the oppressive demands of society are central ideas. The therapeutic approach of this group is much less structured than the cognitive or learning therapies but somewhat more directive than psychoanalysis. Like the learning and cognitive therapies it is centered on the present rather than on the client's past history, as psychoanalysis is. Existential therapy is essentially a talking therapy and does not use the checklists and specific behavioral observations used in learning and cognitive approaches. Psychodynamic therapists stress cognitive distortions, but they tend to focus not only on how these affect present behavior but also on their origins in the client's earlier life. Interpersonal systems therapy uses many behavioral methods such as role playing and homework assignments, but it also focuses on the dynamic interactions within the family or between marital partners. Cognitive theories are also concerned with a person's past experiences as they generate cognitive schema, but they focus less on the past and more on the distortion. For instance, in the information-processing approach, the linking of stressful events and past memories is clarified for the client.

The thing to remember about the psychological theories and their related therapies is that while they differ in emphasis, some of their basic ideas have become surprisingly similar. It may be that the basic ideas involved in each theory are less important than the way the therapy is carried out. For example, highly structured approaches such as behavioral or cognitive therapies may produce similar results simply because of the depressed person's reaction to the structured approach (Rehm and others, 1987).

An Interactive View

Each of the approaches to depression has something to contribute to understanding and treatment of this disorder. Figure 10-15 shows how biological factors, events in early and present life, and ways of thinking may all interact to produce depression. We do know that some people may be genetically vulnerable or vulnerable because of things such as exposure to harmful substances that pass through the placenta before birth, problems during the birth process, or events after birth.

No one type of therapy is best for unipolar depression. Structured therapies, either cognitive or behavioral, have shown similar results that seemed related to their degree of structure and not to their content (Rehm and others, 1987). Even therapies that differ much more seem to have similar results. A large research project, the Treatment of Depression Collaborative Research Program, was set up to compare the effectiveness of therapy groups employing cognitive therapy; interpersonal therapy, which assumes that some depression is caused by role conflicts, grief, and deficient interpersonal relationships; and drug therapy using a tricyclic antidepressant. The performances of the groups were compared with one another and with a control group. In general the people in the therapy groups improved faster than the controls, but there were no differences in improvement among the groups treated with the different therapies after 16 weeks of treatment (Holden, 1986). These findings suggest that depression may actually be a variety of disorders that have been lumped under one name. It also suggests that because of the

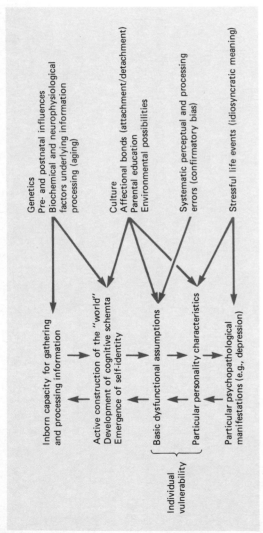

FIGURE 10–15

A theoretical model of the interaction of biological, psychological, and cognitive variables that might produce vulnerability to depression or other disorders. (Perris, 1987, p. 30)

interactive biological and psychological factors in depression, for many people changing any part of the interactive system may result in a lessening of depression.

The Bipolar Disorders

Bipolar disorders, or manic-depressive disorders, are characterized by phases of both depression and mania. Table 10–8 contrasts manic and depressive behavior. The peak incidence of bipolar disorders is during young adulthood. In one study, the average age of bipolar patients when their symptoms were first recognized was 25 (Roy-Byrne and others, 1985). Many people in this group had shown evidence of the disorder as adolescents.

The occurrence of mania is a prerequisite for the diagnosis of bipolar disorder. **Mania** is characterized by a flight of ideas, elevated mood, and increased psychomotor activity. Although mania itself represents an extreme type of behavior, it is probably more useful to describe mania as one extreme on a spectrum of elated behavior. This spectrum includes mood states ranging from normal joy and happiness to extreme and hostile overactivity. A very small number of people may experience one or more periods of mania without ever ex-

TABLE 10-8

Differing Patterns in Manic and Depressive Behavior

	Manic Behavior	**Depressive Behavior**
Emotional characteristics	Elated, euphoric Very sociable Impatient at any hindrance	Gloomy, hopeless Socially withdrawn Irritable
Cognitive characteristics	Racing thoughts, flight of ideas Desire for action Impulsive behavior Talkative Positive self-image Delusions of grandeur	Slowness of thought processes Obsessive worrying Inability to make decisions Negative self-image, self-blame Delusions of guilt and disease
Motor characteristics	Hyperactive Does not become tired Needs less sleep than usual Increased sex drive Fluctuating appetite	Decreased motor activity Tired Difficulty in sleeping Decreased sex drive Decreased appetite

periencing depression (Goodwin and Jamison, 1987). Because this happens so infrequently these people are classified as having a bipolar disorder with the expectation that a period of depression will ultimately occur. Mania can occur from other causes than bipolar disorder. Some drugs can cause people with no history of affective disorders to experience episodes of mania. Drugs that produce this response include steroids, MAO inhibitors and tricyclic drugs used to treat depression, and L-dopa (used to treat Parkinson's disease). Mania can also result from infections, metabolic disturbances, and the growth of tumors. Mania in these cases is considered a symptom of the change in a person's biochemical state and is not classified as a mood disorder.

A variant of bipolar disorder called **Bipolar II** includes no manic episodes but instead at least one episode of hypomania as well as at least one major depressive episode. A **hypomanic episode** occurs when there is a distinct period of elevated, expansive, or irritable mood and other manic behaviors, but social or on-the-job functioning is not greatly impaired and the person does not have to be hospitalized. Bipolar II seems to be a separate type of disorder not a preliminary problem that will later develop into a typical bipolar disorder (Dunner, 1987). Another disorder in this group is **cyclothymia**. In this disorder there is a chronic mood disturbance lasting at least 2 years that includes both hypomanic episodes and frequent mild periods of depressed mood.

People with bipolar disorder usually have episodes of disturbed behavior rather than consistent difficulties. How do people with bipolar disorders behave when they are not in either the depressed or the manic phase? It has often been assumed that even during a period of remission they behave less adaptively than the average person and are more conforming and dependent. This assumption may not be true, at least for individuals receiving lithium treatment. The intellectual functioning of bipolar patients may be less effective during periods of depression or mania, but it improves when the symptoms decrease. Intelligence test scores may actually increase during periods of hypomania (mild manic states) (Clark and others, 1985). The personality test scores of many bipolar individuals return to the normal range between episodes of mania or depression (Lumry and others, 1982). Some researchers believe that artists and writers may have a greater than usual incidence of some milder forms of bipolar disorder (Andreasen, 1973; Jamison, 1983). (See Figure 10-16.)

The periods of depression that occur in bipolar disorder are not any different from the depression that has already been described in this chapter. In a typical bipolar disorder a person will have episodes of both mania and depression and these may tend to recur in a pattern of the person's lifetime. (Figure 10-17 shows

how these patterns may vary.) There are several risk factors that increase the probability of additional episodes (Ambelas and George, 1986).

1. The younger the age at first manic episode
2. The lower the stress of the event associated with the first episode
3. Close family members who have some DSM-III-R disorder.

Manic Episodes

Most episodes of mania occur as part of a bipolar disorder. The very word *manic* conjures up an image of the stereotypical crazy person—the maniac, a stock charac-

FIGURE 10–16
The composer Handel was a very creative person who, if he were alive today, would probably be diagnosed as having a Bipolar II disorder. He was affected by hypomanic states and depression throughout much of his career. One of his most famous works, *Messiah*, was written in such a fury of activity that he completed that lengthy composition in 3 weeks. Only a month later he had completed another major work, *Samson*.

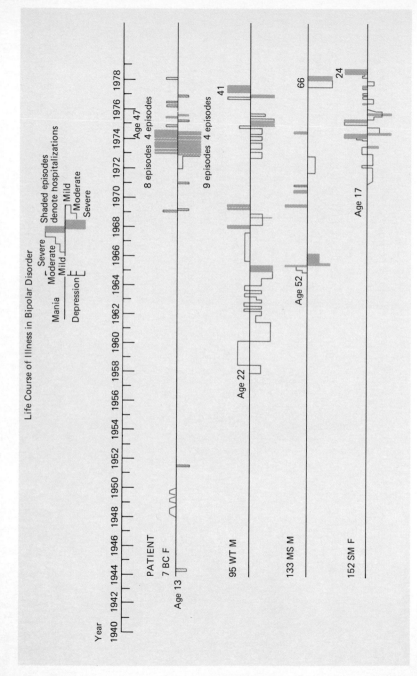

FIGURE 10–17

Manic and depressed episodes for four individuals over time. The shaded areas indicate hospitalizations. The height of each rectangle indicates the severity of the episode; the width of the rectangle shows how long the episode lasted.

ter in many older works of fiction—with frantic behavior, staring eyes, and dramatic gestures. But what is mania really like? The case at the beginning of the chapter illustrates the impairment of judgment and the grandiose ideas that typically accompany mania. Box 10–1 describes the reactions of the child of a bipolar patient to her mother's symptoms. A reaction to a personal experience of mania is described in the following autobiographical account.

First and foremost comes a general sense of intense well-being. I know of course that this sense is illusory and transient, and that my behavior while it persists is so abnormal that I have to be confined, so that a good deal of the gilt is taken off the gingerbread. It is only when I have been free in the manic state that the ecstatic sensations accompanying it have their full effect, but they are apt to produce dire results in the real world, as will be seen. Although, however, the restrictions of confinement are apt at times to produce extreme irritation and even paroxysms of anger, the general sense of well-being, the pleasurable and sometimes ecstatic feeling-tone, remains as a sort of permanent background of all experience during the manic period.

Another, somewhat different account of the first phases of a bipolar illness are given by the psychologist Stuart Sutherland, who experienced acute anxiety and inability to concentrate.

Until I broke down I had always regarded myself as reasonably well-balanced. . . . It never occurred to me that one day my existence would disintegrate within the space of a few hours. For half a year I lived in mental anguish, a prey to obsessive and agonizing thoughts. I had neither interest nor ability to cope with the outside world which formerly I had found so fascinating. I hated myself and I hated others, and so unremitting and painful were my thoughts that I was virtually unable to read: I could not even concentrate sufficiently to peruse the daily paper. For someone accustomed to spending most of the day reading and writing, the complete inability to do either was a singularly refined torture.

There were two aspects of the breakdown that were particularly painful. The onset . . . was marked by levels of physical anxiety that I would not have believed possible. If one is almost involved in a road accident, there is a delay of a second or two and then the pit of the stomach seems to fall out and one's legs

—(Custance, 1952)

BOX 10-1

The Effects of a Bipolar Parent on One Child's Development

The family life of bipolar patients may be extremely stressful. The most severe impact of the bipolar disorder seems to fall on the children. A child with a bipolar parent is more likely to lose that parent either by divorce or suicide than a child in a nonaffected family. In Denmark, a country with excellent treatment facilities, about one in seven of all patients diagnosed as having bipolar disorder ended as a suicide (Joel-Nielsen, 1979). Divorce rates are also higher than average.

Spouses and children almost always prefer that the affected parent be depressed rather than manic. They are constantly alert for signs of mania. Any sign of enthusiasm or liveliness is interpreted in this way and is seen as a threat to family stability (Davenport and others, 1979).

These reactions to her mother's manic and depressive episodes were made by a 30-year-old woman.

My mother went numerous times to a private mental hospital. She was 21 years old when she started, some months after my brother was born. Dr. A. says it is sometimes easier for children to adjust to parents who are psychotic all the time than only part of the time. This is so true—we kids never knew what to believe. Mother was so completely different when she was well. She listened, she was kind, she was generous, she was fun to be with, she never criticized Dad, and she was always at home. But the big problem was the inconsistency, hearing one thing at one period and something quite different at the next. . . .

The inconsistency also does funny things with one's feelings. For instance, when my father got seriously ill and I thought he was going to die, I could not stop laughing. All the time when I was a little girl I would laugh when somebody would get hurt, but what I was really doing was crying on the inside. We seemed to have two sets of everything at that time: two sets of feelings and two sets of thoughts that did not really fit what was actually happening. Life was like a big pretense. . . . We gradually began to learn how to live in our own worlds. Both I and my sister were always looking around for homes outside our own to "adopt" us, and we tried to spend as much time as possible with these families. This helped a great deal, but it also made us realize how differently normal families lived. There was no inconsistency. You could get up in the morning and almost know inside you what was going to happen for the rest of the day. We never knew how any day was going to turn out.

The thing she did when she was sick that bugged me the most was never finishing a job, and even while I was still a child it became an obsession for me that I had to finish what I started. At that time, I felt it was my special duty to clean up after her, collect after her, and finish what she left unfinished. It was like being a slave, and you never questioned it.

When Mother became ill, I always thought that some terrible show was being put on, but she was never ashamed of what she did and what she said. She always felt that she was the greatest and could not be wrong. My brother was so much like her that today he is extremely difficult to live with, and his wife has frequently threatened to leave him. . . .

What effect did all this have on us children? I have already mentioned how fussy I became about tidiness and the need to have everything "just so." But there was also a special danger in my case. Ever since I was small, I have been told that I was just like my mother. I was named after her, and very soon I took to thinking that I was going to be committed when I was 21, like she was. As if it was predetermined, I found myself getting extremely impatient, nervous, muddle-headed, and unable to concentrate. I was sure that they were going to come and haul me away. I felt that I was destined to become exactly like her. . . . I felt as if I were reliving her life. I could not separate her from me inside me. We seemed to be one person inside. (Anthony, 1975, pp. 291–293)

The children of people with bipolar disorder are much more likely than others to develop bipolar disorder themselves. They also show a high rate of unipolar disorder. In one study of 21 families with 37 children among them, 24 percent of the children had been diagnosed with a DSM-III diagnosis, usually some type of mood disorder (LaRoche and others, 1987). Although heredity may be an important factor, stressful family life may also contribute. Lithium treatment may help the affected parent stabilize mood swings but, even with this improvement, treatment for the whole family may be useful. Children of a bipolar parent who develop a disorder are most likely to live in families in which the bipolar parent has frequent episodes of mania or depression (LaRoche and others, 1985).

go like jelly. It was this feeling multiplied a hundredfold that seized me at all hours of the day and night. Sleep was difficult to come by even with the help of sleeping pills, to which I soon resorted. I would awake in terror twenty or thirty times a night.
—(Sutherland, 1977, pp. 1–2)

Environmental factors can sometimes be important in setting off a manic episode. In one study two-thirds of the first manic episodes experienced by patients under study were preceded by a life-related stress of some kind (Ambelas, 1987). Stressful events can also cause a manic episode in people with a past history of manic episodes or bipolar disorder. In one instance when a major hurricane struck Long Island, New York, in 1985, there was a dramatic increase in manic episodes among patients with bipolar disorder who were being treated with lithium (Aronson and Shukla, 1987). All the people who relapsed already had a high level of stress in their lives and most lacked social support from a close, confiding relationship. For each of these people the hurricane had some additional stressful effects. For instance, two people had to move into their parent's homes where there was a high tension level, another person went into a temporary shelter where she knew no one, and yet another wrecked her boyfriend's new car during the storm and their relationship deteriorated. Another stress that can produce manic behavior in vulnerable people is lack of sleep (Wehr and Sack, 1987).

Causes of Bipolar Disorder

The Role of Heredity

There seems to be a strong hereditary factor in bipolar disorders. Overall, the hereditary risk for bipolar disorders is about five times greater than that for unipolar depression (Rice and others, 1987). The overall risk for relatives of people who had their first episode of bipolar disorder at an early age is greater than for others and these relatives also are likely to develop bipolar disorder at an early age.

Several recent studies have located genetic markers for manic depression. A study focused on members of the Old Order Amish, a group living in relative isolation in Lancaster County, Pennsylvania, who are all descended from a small number of ancestors. The researcher found that a dominant gene on the tip of the short arm of chromosome 11 was associated with inherited bipolar disorder (Egeland, 1987). This finding was of special interest because this gene is located near a gene known to be involved in synthesizing the neurotransmitter dopamine, a chemical thought to be involved in bipolar disorder. Two other investigations, one in Israel and one in Belgium, also found genetic markers, but those they found were located on the X chromosome (Baron and others, 1987). The differences in results do not mean that one set of researchers is wrong but rather that similar patterns of behavior can be the result of different genes. This finding that the X chromosome was a carrier made sense of the observation that in bipolar disorder, as in unipolar disorder, women are more frequently affected than men. The risk for the daughter of a bipolar mother is greater than that for a son (LaRoche and others, 1985). (Sons receive a Y chromosome from their father and daughters an X chromosome. Members of both sexes receive an X chromosome from their mother. This means women have a greater chance of inheriting a bipolar X chromosome because they can receive it from either parent.)

One question that has not been settled is whether bipolar and unipolar disorders are genetically related. Some researchers have suggested that the forms of mood disorder differ quantitatively rather than qualitatively; this would mean that different amounts of the same genetically transmitted factor would produce different mood disorders (Gershon and others, 1982). It has been observed that while people who have bipolar disorder have a high rate of relatives with either bipolar or unipolar disorder, in contrast people with unipolar disorder generally have relatives with unipolar but not bipolar disorder (Keller, 1987).

Brain Metabolism

The use of noninvasive methods like PT scans has provided some information about brain metabolism in bipolar disorders. In general, the metabolism rate for glucose increases when a person moves from depression to a more normal state or to mania (see Figure 10–18). It may be that the use of PT scans ultimately will make it possible to distinguish between those with bipolar and unipolar disorders when their initial state is depression. About 6 percent of those who were originally diagnosed as having unipolar depression will later report an episode of mania and be reclassified as having a bipolar disorder (Schlesser and Altschuler, 1983). Identifying the disorder correctly when it begins is important because the most effective treatments for unipolar and bipolar disorders differ. Bipolar individuals are more likely to be helped by lithium and less likely to be helped by tricyclics.

Sleep Studies

Sleep disturbance is often observed as a symptom of depression and of mania. Some researchers have wondered if perhaps the situation might be reversed and the sleep disturbance could be the cause of these disorders. A dramatic but temporary improvement is experienced by almost two-thirds of patients with major depression

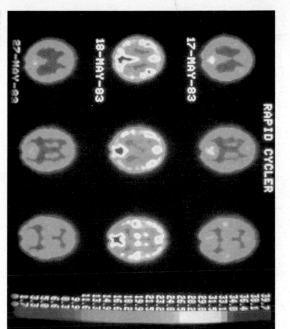

FIGURE 10–18
PT scans of the brain of a bipolar individual who experienced rapid cycles of mania and depression. The top and bottom rows were taken on depressed days and the middle row on a hypomanic day. The colors of the scans correspond to glucose metabolic rates, which are indicated in the color bar on the right. The overall brain metabolic rates for glucose were 36 percent higher on the hypomanic day than the average rates for depressed days, which were within 10 percent of each other. (Drs. Mazziotta, Phelps, et al., UCLA School of Medicine)

if they are kept awake for one night (Wehr and Sack, 1987). The next period of sleep then causes the symptoms of depression to return. Improvements in depression can also come about through waking the patient after only about half the usual sleeping time, or shifting the time of sleep several hours earlier. This approach to treatment may have some practical applications. For example, a physician with a hypomanic temperament and a family history of bipolar illness became depressed. After one night of partial sleep deprivation (sleep from 10 P.M. to 2 A.M. only) he no longer felt depressed. By carrying out this partial deprivation pattern 3 or 4 nights a week for several weeks he continued to avoid depression.

Sleep deprivation can also cause a manic episode in bipolar patients. This has been observed in ordinary life and also produced experimentally. A bipolar patient who was neither depressed nor manic went to an emergency room one evening because of a sore throat. She was kept waiting until five o'clock in the morning, and by then she was so manic that she had to be involuntarily hospitalized. In a study of one night's sleep deprivation of 12 depressed bipolar patients, 9 switched into mania or hypomania during the night or the following day. Six of these remained manic for days or weeks (Wehr and others, 1982). The mechanisms by which sleep produces these antidepressant effects is presently unknown. It may not be the sleep itself that accounts for the change. One possibility is that there is more exposure to light.

Phototherapy

Before an effective treatment for bipolar disorder was known, it was possible to observe the manic and depressed patterns over long periods. Researchers noted that in some cases the pattern was seasonal. Depression appeared in fall and winter and mania or usually hypomanic behavior occurred in spring and summer. Light treatment or **phototherapy** can be an effective treatment for winter depression. In this therapy the depressed person is exposed for 2 to 4 hours per day to very bright light, several times brighter than what is normally used indoors. This treatment produces a rapid improvement in less than a week. However, when the light treatment ends, the deterioration of the person's moods is just as rapid. The effects seem to take place through the eyes, not through the skin, but why this treatment is effective is not known (Wehr and others, 1987). Although studies of sleep deprivation and phototherapy might seem to be focused on the same process because sleep deprivation usually increases exposure to light, the two types of treatment seem to operate independently (Rosenthal and others, 1988). Both these experimental therapies show the important role of biological rhythms in bipolar disorder.

Treatment of Bipolar Disorder

The most effective treatment for bipolar disorder is lithium. It helps about two-thirds of all manic patients and can also help prevent new episodes of either mania or depression (Janicak and Boshes, 1987). Lithium may also be used for someone who is depressed and has had no manic periods if the person has relatives who have had bipolar disorder. Giving antidepressant drugs such as tricyclics or MAO inhibitors may induce manic episodes in such people. Lithium may have dangerous side effects if the amount is not regulated carefully, although the side effects of the antidepressants may be even more serious. One problem with the use of lithium for bipolar disorders is that many patients discontinue the drug against medical advice even though lithium usually does a good job of controlling the symptoms of bipolar disorders. There are several possible reasons why this occurs. One may be that lithium is abandoned when the person is in a low, although not depressed, period in the hope that stopping its use will elevate his or her mood. An even more intriguing reason is unwillingness to give up some of the pleasant cognitive and behavioral changes that come with an elevated mood (Jamison and others, 1980). These include increased sensitivity to the environment, sexual intensity, creativity, and social ease.

Therapists thus must deal with a client's perceptions of the disorder in addition to prescribing an effective medication.

Suicide and Parasuicide

Depressed people often have low self-esteem and feel the future holds no more promise than the past. Such hopelessness is a good predictor of eventual suicide (Beck and others, 1985). The depressed person may not stop at self-condemnation but move from thought to action. Sometimes depressed people threaten suicide, and such threats should always be taken seriously because the best predictor of a suicide attempt is a threat of suicide. Previous suicide attempts are also good predictors; few people kill themselves without some warning. However, sometimes the timing of the suicide is surprising. Many suicides occur when a depressed individual is beginning to recover or has been discharged from a hospital as improved. The writer, Ernest Hemingway, for example, shot and killed himself shortly after he had been released from a hospital after his depression improved.

Suicide is a statistically rare event in the United States; only 13 out of every 100,000 deaths are due to suicide. Yet suicide now ranks ninth among the causes of death in the United States and is responsible for 20,000 to 35,000 deaths per year. Of the total number of people who are clinically depressed, 15 percent will ultimately kill themselves (Fawcett and others, 1987). This rate is about 22 to 36 times higher than the rate for the general population. It is important to remember, however, that a sizeable number of people who commit or attempt suicide are not diagnosed as depressed. Another high-risk group consists of people who have a family history of suicide. There is also a sex difference in suicide rates. Twice as many men as women actually kill themselves, although twice as many women as men attempt suicide. Although very few children commit suicide, suicide threats and attempts are common reasons for therapeutic referrals of children. Since 1949 people born in each successive 5-year period have started with a higher chance of suicide than the preceding group, so it seems likely that the overall rate will continue to increase. For instance between 1950 and 1980 the rate of suicide for men age 20 to 24 had increased from 9 to 27 suicides per 100,000 men in this age bracket.

Suicide and **parasuicide** (suicide attempts that do not end in death) seem to be fundamentally different. People who kill themselves successfully seem to have planned the event carefully. They arrange not to be interrupted and to use effective means. Suicide attempters, on the other hand, may act impulsively, make sure of rescue, and use a method that is slow to take effect or completely ineffective. The main purpose of parasuicides seems to be to manipulate others. Chapter 9 illustrates how people with borderline personality disorder often use suicide threats this way.

There are cultural differences in the way others respond to the act of suicide because different cultures interpret suicide differently. Most Western societies seek to prevent suicide and to interfere with its completion whenever possible. In other cultures, by contrast, it is thought to be an honorable action, perhaps the only acceptable one for a disgraced person.

If the urge to commit suicide is an outgrowth of a profound psychological disturbance, most people would agree that every effort should be made to keep the individual alive so that the problem can be treated. Nevertheless, one may certainly wonder whether there are any circumstances under which no effort should be made to prevent an individual from taking his or her life. What of the aged, the chronically infirm, and the incurably ill who want to terminate what they feel is a hopeless existence? Although the attention of clinical workers is directed primarily toward suicide as an outgrowth of personal problems and feelings of inadequacy and depression, we should bear in mind that there is a broader, more subjective context within which suicide can be considered.

In one study that investigated the influence of the person's situation on others' attitude toward the acceptability of suicide, college students read one of several fictitious scenarios about a man who decided to kill himself. The different scenarios portrayed the man as suffering from depression of different types, severe physical pain or terminal bone cancer. For example, this was one scenario:

John, a 45-year-old factory worker, has been suffering for the past 20 years from severe depression. His doctors believe the depression is likely due to a biochemical disorder of the central nervous system. Despite having received a wide variety of therapies (including drug treatments, psychotherapy, and behavior modification), the depression has gotten worse over time. John feels that the doctors have already done all they can, and he has no hope that his symptoms will be reduced. John is currently experiencing a great deal of psychological pain, and is very upset over the fact that his condition is draining the emotional and financial resources of his family and friends. John feels that the quality of his life now is very poor and will only get worse, and he fears that he will be an increasingly large burden to his loved ones. Despite protests from his family and friends, John has decided to kill himself.

—(Delury, in press)

Students answered a series of evaluative questions about the man and his decision. The evaluations were most favorable when the suicide occurred in response to terminal bone cancer, and least favorable when they described chronic depression.

Many studies have also focused on college student suicide. The young-adult age group has a higher risk of suicide than many other groups. Further, because college students are generally healthy their overall death rate is low. For these reasons suicide is the second-most frequent cause of death among college students. (Accidents are the most frequent cause.)

Although the rate of suicides reported in college health service records is low, ranging from about 1 to 5 per 100,000 students, about 80 percent of the students in a study carried out at three universities reported some feelings of depression, 32 percent had thoughts about suicide, 4.5 percent had attempted suicide at some time, and 1 percent had attempted suicide while in college (Westefeld and Furr, 1987). In general, social problems (love relationships, dating, friends) were most important and family problems came second. Figure 10-19 shows the relative importance of different factors that students reported either made them think about suicide or attempt it.

Causes of Suicide

Ideas about the causes of suicide are divided into two main groups: those that see society as a reason and those that focus on the individual. In a few cases a society literally demands that a person commit suicide. In Japan, for instance, hara-kiri, a ritual suicide, was traditionally an honorable death that atoned for a serious personal failure. Sociologists also point out that in Western society most suicidal people are socially isolated and have few ties with the community. Psychological theories, on the other hand, tend to stress the role of the individual in the decision to commit suicide.

Learning theory emphasizes the importance of suicidal behavior in a person's learned behavioral repertory. Past suicidal behavior and suicide threats, and suicidal behavior on the part of significant people in an individual's environment, all make suicide more likely. Certain reinforcing ideas may also be present—such as revenge, reunion with a deceased partner, or simply peace. The role of modeling in encouraging suicide is discussed in the next section on the effect of the media on suicide.

The psychodynamic perspective is the source of most of the prominent psychological theories in the

clinical literature on suicide. Psychodynamic theories describe suicide as an extreme case of a person's turning hostile or aggressive impulses toward him- or herself. However, this theory is not supported by research findings, which indicate that hostile motives are infrequent in suicide (Linehan, 1981). The absence of a feeling of social support, of being cared about by others, is also important in suicidal feelings and behavior. Feeling needed may also be important. Having a child younger than 18 years of age has been shown to be a protective factor (Fawcett and others, 1987).

A series of negative events beyond the person's control is likely to have occurred during the year before someone makes a suicide attempt. It is likely that several of these events will have occurred close together just before the suicide or parasuicide. A series of psychological losses or **exit events** in which a strong source of social support is removed, seem most likely to precede a suicide attempt. Such an event might be a death, a divorce, or a breakup with a partner. Personality factors probably play a role also. People who behave impulsively or who

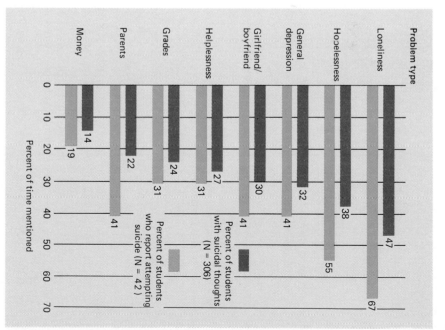

FIGURE 10-19

The percent of the time each of several problem areas was mentioned by students with thoughts about suicide or who reported attempting suicide. (Adapted from Westefeld and Furr, 1987. Copyright © 1987 by the American Psychological Association. Adapted by permission of the authors.)

BOX 10–2

Suicide and the Survivors

Suicide has a strong impact on the families of those who killed themselves and on others who knew them. It is more painful for the family than other kinds of death and often harder to accept or acknowledge. Parents may think of the suicide of their adolescent child as an accidental death. They may also experience strong feelings of guilt and shame that may make normal mourning impossible. Children of a parent who commits suicide are also likely to be seriously disturbed. The surviving parent may claim the suicide was an accident. The child then begins to distrust the parent or doubt the reality of what he or she had observed, or both. Children often feel responsible for a parental suicide or think they should have prevented it. The result of these misperceptions may be a child who is depressed, passive, and self-destructive. Because of the social stigma that surrounds suicide the survivors often avoid talking to others. The suicide of a client is also difficult for a therapist. Often the death is experienced as a personal defeat. Nothing shakes a therapist's confidence more. Again, talking about the situation and one's feelings helps.

In the following paragraphs a wife describes her reactions to her husband's death and a supervising therapist tells us the reaction of one of her students to a client's suicide.

The wife of a university professor and mother of their 12-year-old son, Richard, conveyed some of these feelings of pain, guilt, and anger:

For me the days that followed [her husband's suicide] were full of pain. The questions pounded at me. Why? Why? But shock numbs; somehow I could cope with memorial-service plans. Like a robot, I did what I had to do. People came and went, and I sat for hours without moving much. I remember not taking my clothes off for two days. I didn't want to move or change anything. Talking was an effort. Eating was an effort.

At the end of a week, after the service was over the relatives had left, the real loneliness set in, and the guilt. Each night I dreamed that I was soothing Dick, telling him how much I loved him and still love him, feeling in my dreams that if only he knew, then he would be back and safe. . . . Two months later on the plane as we came home from a Christmas trip to visit Dick's family, Richard said, "I feel like I really miss somebody and I don't even know who." I said, "Don't you think it's Dad?" and the only tears I saw him cry came then. We talk often and he tells me that now he mostly feels mad. "When I start to feel angry or sad," he says, "I try to concentrate really hard on whatever I happen to be doing at the time, like playing ball or riding my bike."

I've found it difficult to be that sensible, to avoid guilt and constant questioning. The notes Dick left said it was his job, that I had nothing to do with what he did. Still, why couldn't I have seen what was happening? Why couldn't I have saved him? He had been the best friend I ever had. I must not have been a good enough friend to him. I wanted

---

abuse alcohol or drugs are more likely to make suicide attempts or successfully kill themselves.

Cognitive theorists suggest that suicide is an example of problem-solving behavior. According to this view, suicide may result from a person's cognitive assessment of the situation as hopeless and of death as a way of getting rid of problems. Parasuicides are often quite rigid in their approach to situations (Shneidman, 1980). For such people, the world appears to be divided into only two parts—good and bad. This recalls the depressed thinking described by cognitive theorists like Beck (1976). This rigidity may include narrow perceptions of situations and of behavioral options.

Suicide and the Media

The possibility of suicide enters the minds of many people. Sometimes hearing about the suicide of someone else, even a stranger, may affect their own behavior. Several different studies have found that suicides increase after a widely publicized story of suicide. In one study the number of suicides by teenagers in the week after the broadcast of a story about suicide rose 13 percent for males and 5 percent for females (Phillips and Carstensen, 1986). The number of suicides for adults rose also but to a very small degree. Even 2 weeks after a story was seen on TV the rate of suicides was still somewhat higher. The more networks that covered a story, the more the increase in suicides. This effect was

304 CHAPTER 10 *Mood Disorders*

not just based on the sensational death of an individual either unknown or famous; general information news stories about suicide had the same effect.

Some people have wondered whether fictional stories about suicide, for example, movies shown on television, would have the same effect. Although at least one study has found that a TV showing of such a movie would increase the suicide rate (Gould and Shaffer, 1986), other researchers studying this effect found no change in the suicide rate (Phillips and Paight, 1987). The reason for this may have nothing to do with whether the content is fictional or not. Instead, it may be a function of the intensity of exposure. Each of the movies was shown only once in each city. The TV news stories that were shown once on only one channel had no effect on the suicide rate either. The increase in sui-

cides was a result of multiple exposure of the stories on each channel and on several channels. This data suggests that it is the frequency of a presentation about suicide, not its format—informational, a true story, or fiction—that determines its effect on the viewers.

The Impact of Suicide on Others

Suicide is a traumatic event for the surviving family members, co-workers, or schoolmates. When a member of a group has committed suicide, group discussion and intervention can sometimes be helpful. For instance, several suicides by high school students prompted a se-

to piece it together; I relived every conversation. But there were no answers, and it didn't fit together. (Kenyon, 1979, p. 17)

The supervising therapist wrote about her student:

S. was an emphatic, intelligent social work student doing second-year internship in the outpatient psychiatric clinic of a university hospital. On arriving at work one day I was told that S.'s client had committed suicide. Shock and disbelief were S.'s first reactions. She did not expect suicide in this particular case. S. began crying; later she felt embarrassed about losing control of herself. All I could do was try to comfort her.

Later that day, as we discussed the matter further, she attempted to pull the pieces of the puzzle together intellectually. Then she would be hit by another wave of remorse and sadness: "Did I do something wrong?" "It can't be real." She also talked about how important life was and felt angry at the client for throwing it all away.

S. was indecisive about whether to go home or to work. On the first day, she experienced extreme swings in mood. She became angry and said that the suicide would not stop her from doing her day's work. She took the death personally: "How could he do this to me?" She felt that other therapists would not have "crumpled" the way she did. Although she was not initially afraid that the clinic staff would be judgmental of her, she was afraid to cry in front of them. Meeting any staff person in the hall occasioned a recall of the suicide and made it very difficult for her to suppress her thoughts and feelings. She felt that as a student she should not have been given the case. She vacillated between wanting and not

wanting people to feel sorry for her. At home that night, she obtained some relief from a spouse who understood how awful she felt.

After Christmas break, S. and I reviewed the case to search for clues to the suicide. She felt relieved when we could not find any. She also discussed the case with the attending psychiatrist who had prescribed medication; the psychiatrist also confirmed that a potential for suicide was not evident in this client's history.

As S. became involved again in the clinic routine, she began to feel better. S. expressed some hostile feelings toward the staff, thinking that they now might be critical of her. Consequently, within the two weeks after S.'s return, I arranged a group meeting with other student interns and staff supervisors to bring the situation out in the open. S. dreaded the meeting but found it useful. It also helped to hear a supervisor detail his own response to a client's suicide.

At this juncture, S. felt that her relationships with clients were different from what they had been. The emphasis now was on herself; she was more concerned about her own feelings than she was about her clients' feelings.

The critical turning point for S. came during a discussion of a current client. Contrary to her usual performance, she had consistently overlooked the client's depression. Finally, she understood her fear of uncovering a depth of feeling that could lead to suicide. Eventually, she was able to help the client recognize and work through the depression. In so doing, a parallel change occurred for S. She began to feel better and once again progress as a therapist. She learned that depression can lift and does not necessarily lead to suicide. (Feldman, 1987, pp. 184–187.)

ries of school meetings for parents and students. Both the signs of potential suicide and various ways of dealing with them were discussed. The program was also designed to help students realize that thoughts about self-destruction occur to most people at one time or another and that there are sources of help for people who have such thoughts. Perhaps one of the best ways to prevent suicide is to demonstrate to the person that someone really cares what happens to him or her. Another type of program focuses more specifically on emotions and on helping survivors express their grief. Box 10–2 illustrates how important expressions of grief can be as well as the devastating impact and guilt felt by survivors. Even in the days immediately after the suicide survivors can be helped by a chance to express their feelings, obtain reassurance, and interpret what happened.

Study Outline

DEFINING MOOD DISORDERS

Mood Disorders reflect a disturbance in emotional reaction not due to any other disorder. The two major groups are **Depressive Disorders** and **Bipolar Disorders.**

DEPRESSION

1. Feeling blue or feeling grief or loss are not the same as a mood disorder. A depression that occurs as a result of an identifiable event is classified as an **adjustment disorder with depressed mood,** not as a mood disorder.

2. Higher risk of depression is related to being female, being age 25–30, being in a recent birth cohort, being separated or divorced, experiencing a series of negative life events, and family history of depression.

DEPRESSIVE DISORDER

1. **Dysthymia** is a chronic form of mild depression. A **major depressive episode** is marked by a depressed mood and/or a loss of pleasure in almost everything as well as a variety of problems including some of these: difficulties in sleeping, eating, changes in activity level and unclarity of thought, and thoughts of suicide. One or more major depressive episodes with no periods of mania is called a **major depression.**

THEORIES OF DEPRESSION

1. Biological theories include genetic inheritance and/or physiological malfunction. At least some depression seems to have a hereditary element. Biochemical mechanisms, especially the malfunction of certain chemical neurotransmitters called monoamines play a major role in depression. The most important of these monoamines for depression are the catecholamines **norepinephrine** (NE) and **dopamine** (DA) and the indoleamine **serotonen** (5HT).

2. Researchers are looking for biochemical markers to

help distinguish different subgroups of depression that may have different causes. Some of the possible markers are chemical responses such as that seen on the **dexamethasone suppression test,** information from **brain scanning techniques,** and differences in **biological rhythm.**

3. The main drug groups that are used to treat depression are the tricyclics and the MAO inhibitors; both increase the amount of norepinephrine in the neurotransmitter system. If drugs are not effective or if it would be dangerous to wait for their effects to become evident, **electro-convulsive therapy** (ECT) may be used. ECT is very effective in treating severe depression, but because of possible hazards, it should be used only after other treatments have been tried.

4. Psychodynamic theories of depression emphasize unconscious feelings and reactions to new situations based on what has happened earlier in life. For example, depression in adults may be related to parental loss or separation in childhood.

5. Psychodynamic therapies focus on modifying the associations between the present and the past. The **interpersonal systems approach** takes into account family interaction and combines psychodynamic ideas with behavioral techniques.

6. Learning theorists assume that depression and lack of reinforcement are related. According to this perspective, a major cause of the low rate of positive reinforcement of depressed individuals is an actual deficiency in social skills. Once people are depressed, their behavior makes them less likable, and this creates a vicious cycle.

7. Treatment based on behavioral theories begins with an assessment of the specific interactions and events that are related to the depression. The client may be asked to list pleasant and unpleasant events and to rate his or her mood each day. In addition, a treatment plan is prepared that includes training in skills such as parenting, time management, and relaxation.

8. Cognitive theories of depression are based on the idea that the same experience may affect two people

very differently because of the different cognitions they have about the event. According to Aaron Beck, depression can best be described as a **cognitive triad** of negative thoughts about oneself, the situation, and the future. Cognitive therapy includes questioning designed to make the depressed person aware of the unrealistic nature of his or her thoughts.

9. Cognitive theorists are concerned with attributions or the causes people assign to what happens. Depressed people attribute negative events to themselves and positive events to luck. People who are depressed seem to feel helpless to control their environment. They may have learned to be helpless as a result of situations they have encountered in the past. This concept is termed **learned helplessness**. A depressed person can feel varying degrees of helplessness depending on whether he or she views a situation as **external** or **internal**, **global** or **specific**, or **stable** (chronic) or **unstable** (acute).

10. The information-processing view of depression attempts to combine social-learning and cognitive approaches to depression. It is based on the idea that memories are represented by linkages associated through content or emotional tone.

11. Existentialist theorists focus on loss of self-esteem as a cause of depression. Humanistic theorists emphasize the difference between a person's ideal self and his or her perception of the actual state of things.

THE BIPOLAR DISORDERS

1. **Bipolar** or manic-depressive **disorders** are characterized by phases of both depression and mania. **Mania** includes mood states ranging from normal joy and happiness to extreme and hostile overactivity. Manic episodes occur far less frequently than depressions. A variant of bipolar disorder, **Bipolar II**, includes at least one major depressive episode and periods of **hypomanic** behavior (elevated mood with relatively unimpaired job cr social functioning). **Cyclothymia** is a chronic disturbance with hypomanic episodes and periods of mildly depressed mood. There is a strong hereditary element in bipolar disorders. Recent work has identified some gene locations associated with increased risk of bipolar disorder. Studies of the effects of sleep deprivation and of exposure to bright light are also helpful in understanding possible causes of manic or depressed behavior in vulnerable people.

2. Lithium has been shown to be effective in treating bipolar disorders.

SUICIDE AND PARASUICIDE

1. The hopelessness that is characteristic of depression sometimes leads to suicide. Among the predictors of suicide are suicide threats and previous suicide attempts.

2. Suicide and **parasuicide** (suicide attempts that do not end in death) seem to be fundamentally different. People who kill themselves successfully arrange not to be interrupted and use effective means. Suicide attempters may act impulsively, make sure they will be rescued, and use a method that is slow to take effect or completely ineffective.

3. Intensive media coverage of suicide, whether it is news accounts or fictional or informational presentations, increases the number of suicide attempts.

Schizophrenic Disorders

To learn:

1. The characteristics of schizophrenic behavior
2. The treatment approaches that are useful

To understand:

1. The historical views of schizophrenia and how they influence present diagnostic criteria
2. The range of possible outcomes after a diagnosis of schizophrenia

"*A*ll of a sudden things weren't going so well. I began to lose control of my life and, most of all, myself. I couldn't concentrate on my school work, I couldn't sleep, and when I did sleep, I had dreams about dying. I was afraid to go to class, imagined that people were talking about me, and on top of that I heard voices. I called my mother in Pittsburgh and asked for advice. She told me to move off campus into an apartment with my sister.

After I moved in with my sister, things got worse. I was afraid to go outside and when I looked out of the window, it seemed that everyone outside was yelling "Kill her, kill her." My sister forced me to go to school. I would go out of the house until I knew she had gone to work; then I would return home. Things continued to get worse. I imagined that I had a foul body odor and I sometimes took up to six showers a day. . . . Things worsened—I couldn't remember a thing. I had a notebook full of reminders telling me what to do on that particular day. I couldn't remember my school work, and I would study from 6 P.M. until 4 A.M., but never had the courage to go to class on the following day. I tried to tell my sister about it, but she didn't understand. She suggested that I see a psychiatrist, but I was afraid to go out of the house to see him.

One day I decided that I couldn't take the trauma anymore so I took an overdose of 35 Darvon pills. At the same moment, a voice inside me said, 'What did you do that for? Now you won't go to heaven.' At that instant I realized that I really didn't want to die, I wanted to live, and I was afraid. So I got on the phone and called the psychiatrist whom my sister had recommended."

After more than a year on medication, first in the hospital and then out, J. decided she was well and stopped both medication and therapy. She got a job but quickly lost it. "My friends and family said I was behaving strangely, but I took no notice. I went out dancing practically every night to make up for the time lost while being afraid . . ."

In the fall she went back to school in Atlanta to finish her senior year. Then she was hospitalized again. "This time things were twice as bad as the first. I no longer heard voices, but the things I saw and dreamed about were far more traumatic. I recall at one point thinking I was Jesus Christ and that I was placed on this earth to bear everyone's sins."

After a month in the hospital J. returned home and received both antipsychotic drugs and psychotherapy as an outpatient. Two years later, still on medication, she was back in college, president of her sorority, "more confident and happy than I have ever been in my life."

—(Adapted from O'Neal, 1984, pp. 109–110).

This young woman seems to have made a good recovery from several schizophrenic episodes. Before they began, she had been functioning at a high level. She was a good student, an officer in her sorority chapter, and president of a campus club, and she had a part-time job and a satisfying relationship with her boyfriend. As we will see later in the chapter, one predictor of improvement from a schizophrenic disorder is the person's level of adjustment before the symptoms appeared.

Not all people who develop schizophrenia experience such a dramatic recovery, even when they continue to use antipsychotic drugs. The following passage, written by the mother of a schizophrenic son, describes a more common pattern.

When Dan first began to suffer from schizophrenia, our family thought it was just a case of teenage blues. We sent him off to college. By the time he began attacking the refrigerator for reading his mind and threatening family members for using the word "right," we had learned to recognize the disease. We have six children. It was a happy family, and I wish I could say it hasn't changed. Our family isn't destroyed, but it is badly damaged.

We did everything we could to be helpful to Dan. We took him weekly to a psychiatrist, and then tried to see that he took his medicine. Whenever he was released from a hospital, we helped him find a job.

We took him around until he found a suitable room in the area, and then once more helped him move his drafting table and other belongings to his new home.

He never took his medicine once he was away from us. Each time he finally began breaking things, and we once more brought the drafting table, suitcases, and sometimes cockroaches back home. Eventually, he would be reaccepted by the hospital, and we sat with heavy hearts while bearing signs of relief. . . . My husband, John, is now 71 and has had two heart attacks. I am 65, in excellent health except for regular unexplainable seizures. . . . There has never been a time when we would be surprised to look out the window and see Dan coming up the driveway.

This was true especially in the year we were testing adult homes, though we continued calling on Dan, taking him out for dinner, and inviting him home for visits. Here is an example of Dan's life during this period:

On August 6, 1981, we drove Dan to Richmond, stopping on the way to buy him a new pair of shoes. Ten days later, John suggested we visit Dan for the day—take him out for dinner and go to a museum. We called to find out Dan was in jail. He had eaten a restaurant meal he couldn't pay for and assaulted a policeman.

The manager of the adult home explained Dan's problem to the police, and they released him, but Dan was not happy to be back at the home. He thought the food was terrible. Dan is a proud man. He wanted to have only the best. He would do anything to eat in restaurants. He sold his new shoes, pawned his watch, ran up a bill in a friendly Vietnamese café, and found new places where he could order a meal only to discover later that he didn't have his billfold. He was constantly asking John to raise his allowance from $20 to $35 a week. Whenever we went to visit him, he would spoil our time together by badgering his father.

[Later, during a period at home,] Dan was getting more and more upset over people "messing with his mind." He finally threatened to kill his younger brother, who moved out to live temporarily with a friend. It wasn't long before Dan was back in the hospital. Though the doctor said there was nothing wrong with him, his lawyer had talked him into volunteering.

While Dan was in the hospital, we once more investigated adult homes, hoping to find one which would please him. By the time he was to be dismissed, we hadn't found anything suitable, and in the end, we presented him with a plan for living at home. He was now 34 years old, and his younger brother, Fred, was away at college, so it would be just the three of us. Here was our proposition:

We welcome you to live at home with us if you take your medicine regularly, eat at meal time, and smoke only in a restricted area. We will give you $30 a week for your expenses, and you will have occasional use of the car after you get your driver's license.

For over a year now, he has been going to the clinic to get his shots. He knows a good thing when he sees it. That $30 never makes it to the end of the week, but if he talks hard enough, he can always get a couple more dollars out of his Dad, who would rather toss him the bills than risk building up his blood pressure.

—(Adapted from Piercey, 1985, pp. 155–157)

Schizophrenic disorders are a prominent part of the category of mental disorders known as psychoses.

A **psychosis** is a disorder that involves alterations of perception, thought, or consciousness. Someone who is psychotic makes incorrect inferences about reality based on these alterations, and believes that the inferences are real and actual. When the person can understand that the inferences are not real but are the products of fantasy or misperception, the psychosis is no longer present.

Many of the psychoses produce the kind of behaviors that were formerly called "madness," "lunacy," or "insanity" in earlier periods. Causal factors have been found for some disorders with these symptoms. The causes may be temporary such as the effect of drugs, reduced availability of oxygen to the brain during high fevers, or extreme vitamin deficiencies, or they may be permanent, for example the consequence of infections such as syphilis. However, a specific cause has not been found for many disorders that produce psychosis. In addition to schizophrenic disorders, these include some manias, certain severe depressions, paranoid states, and brief psychotic reactions. Despite the similarity in psychotic behaviors that result from different causes, there are differences that help to identify the various psychoses (see Table 11–1).

Of all the psychoses, schizophrenic disorders have the most severe impact on people's lives and on the health care system. About 10 in every thousand people (1 percent) of the population will be diagnosed as having a schizophrenic illness at some time in their lives. At any one time, for every 1000 adults in the population, excluding those in psychiatric hospitals, there are approximately 4.6 who have an active schizophrenic disorder and 1.8 people whose schizophrenic disorder is in remission. About half of the entire group are not receiving any treatment, although most of them are in need of mental-health care (von Korff and others, 1985).

The total costs of schizophrenia are high because this disorder tends to occur early in life, from the late teens to early thirties, and also is likely to be chronic or persistent. The cost in the United States has been estimated to be $10 to $20 billion a year in medical care and loss of income (Cancro, 1985). The per-person costs of schizophrenia are also high. Although twelve times as many people in New Zealand had heart attacks as became schizophrenic, the total cost of care for heart attack patients was only one-sixth as high as the cost of care for those with schizophrenic disorders (Hall and others, 1985). The chief reason for this was that those who had heart attacks tended to be older and were less likely to be chronically ill afterward.

TABLE 11-1

Differences among the Acute Psychoses

Type	Behavioral Characteristics
Schizophrenia	Loose associations Flat affect Bizarre delusions Alert, not dazed or confused Aware of time and place
Mania	Hyperactivity Pressured speech Elevated or irritable mood Usually aware of time and place
Organic brain syndrome	Loss of intellectual abilities Poor memory Impaired orientation Possible hallucinations or delusions
Brief reactive psychosis (response to particular conditions or physiological states)	Sudden onset Dramatic array of hallucinations and delusions Visual hallucinations more common than auditory hallucinations Mood tends to be expansive and effervescent Symptoms decline or disappear in a day or two
Psychotic depression	Somatic delusions (e.g., spine being eaten by worms) Hallucinations with negative, critical tone Delusions of guilt and self-reproach Paranoid thinking Biological signs—sleep disturbance, change in appetite, altered sex drive

TABLE 11-2

Differences in the Content of Delusions in Various Severe Disorders

Disorder	Delusion
Paranoid disorder	Delusions of jealousy and persecution
Schizophrenia	Delusions of being controlled; bizarre delusions; sometimes delusions of persecution
Mania	Grandiose delusions
Depression	Delusions of guilt; somatic delusions
Organic brain syndrome	Delusions secondary to perceptual disturbances

SOURCE: Walker and Brodie, 1985, p. 753.

As an example of the high costs of treating schizophrenia, consider the case of the 32-year-old American woman who became ill when she was 14. In 18 years the direct costs for her care in inpatient settings or in community outpatient settings totaled more than $636,000 in 1983 dollars (Moran and others, 1984). This figure did not include costs for outpatient therapy, health care, emergency room care, and social services, or the costs to her parents, who supported her financially when she was not in a hospital or halfway house. In addition to the cost in money, the social and psychological costs of the schizophrenic disorders are tremendous.

Characteristics of Schizophrenic Disorders

The major characteristics of a schizophrenic disorder include the content of thoughts; the form or structure in which thoughts are expressed; perception of the environment; changes in emotional response; an imperfect differentiation between oneself and the environment; and changes in degree of motivation, in relationships, in level of functioning, and in patterns of body movement. The next sections describe each of these aspects of schizophrenic behavior in more detail. When reading them it is important to remember that no single characteristic is always present or is unique to schizophrenia.

Thought Content

A **delusion** is essentially a faulty interpretation of reality that cannot be shaken despite clear evidence to the contrary. Delusions occur in other disorders besides schizophrenia, but in each disorder they have a somewhat different content (See Table 11–2).

Delusions may be expressed in many ways. Some types of delusions occur more often in schizophrenia than in any other type of psychoses. Among these are the belief that the person's thoughts are broadcast from his or her own mind into the external world so that everyone can hear them, the belief that others are either inserting thoughts into the person's mind or removing them, or the belief that the person's thoughts, feelings, and impulses are controlled by some external force. Other kinds of delusions that are typical of schizophrenia but that occur less often include the belief of being persecuted, grandiose thoughts about being an extremely important person, or ideas with a religious

theme. The artist who created the picture in Figure 11–1 expressed some of his delusional thinking through his painting. Another example comes from an author who wrote about a variety of delusions that she had experienced while psychotic. Some of her delusions were somatic—for example, she believed she was able to stop her heart on command. Others were both religious and grandiose. She believed that people were worshipping her as the Madonna and that her child (not yet born) would be the savior of the world (Thelmar, 1932). In the case at the beginning of the chapter, the college student described her belief that she was Jesus Christ.

Delusions can result in violent behavior that harms others. For instance, a mother severed a hand from each of her two daughters with a butcher knife and then chopped off her own hand. She then ran to neighbors and told them that she was John the Baptist and was going to be beheaded (*Seattle Times*, April 1, 1979, p.A13). At other times the behavior, although it is based on delusional thinking, is highly organized and requires immense concentration. For example, for 8 hours a 22-year-old male student performed surgery deep in his abdomen, and carried out the operation in his college dormitory room with a precision that astonished surgeons (Kalin, 1979). He had spent months preparing for the surgery, which, he said, was intended to "denervate his adrenal glands." He had read surgical texts and acquired instruments. Before the operation he sterilized his room, anesthetized himself with barbiturates, donned a sterile mask and gloves, and draped his body in sheets.

Lying supine and looking into strategically placed mirrors to obtain an optimum view, he began by cleansing his abdomen with alcohol. The incision was

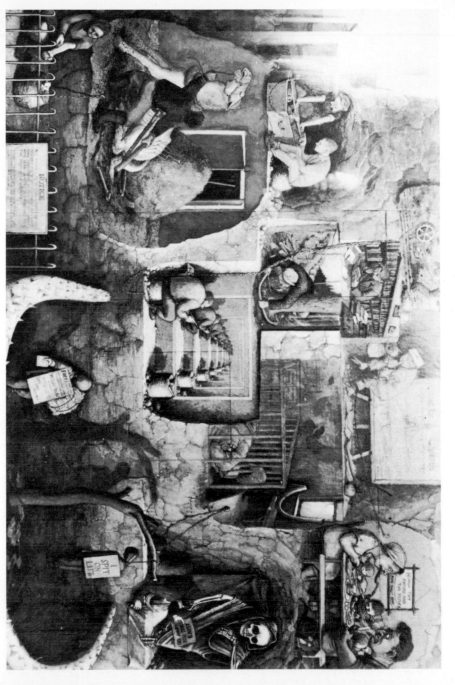

FIGURE 11-1

The artist who created this picture was, at the time, a hospitalized psychiatric patient who was troubled by a variety of tormenting thoughts. Here he represents his negative view of life and some of the topics that were special areas of conflict for him. Talented as an artist, he made painting his vocation after his recovery.

---

made with a scalpel, exposure obtained by retractors, and the dissection carried out with surgical instruments. . . .

After eight hours he had had a minimal blood loss but was unable to obtain adequate exposure to enter the retroperitoneal space because of the unexpected pain in retracting his liver. Exhausted, he bandaged his wound, cleaned up his room, and called the police for transport to the hospital because of a "rupture."

—(Kalin, 1979, p. 2188)

in which the speaker's ideas shift from one topic to another in a way that seems unrelated to everyone else. When the loosening of association is severe the person's speech becomes incomprehensible. An example of loose associations is the answer given by someone with a schizophrenic disorder to the question, "What does this proverb mean, 'Strike while the iron is hot?'"

It could mean (pause) Hercules! (Could you say more?) I saw the movie Hercules. (Yes . . .) And it means don't iron over your hands and don't strike anybody before you cast the first stone.

—(Marengo and others, 1986, p. 498)

The word *autistic* has been used to describe schizophrenic thought patterns. Derived from the Greek word *autos*, meaning self, **autistic thinking** is defined as thinking that is so self-centered that it is fully intelligible only to the person who is doing the thinking. Researchers have found that schizophrenic individuals ask inappropriate questions and get inappropriate answers (Rut-

Form of Thought

Schizophrenia has been frequently referred to as a **formal-thought disorder.** This refers to the structure or organization of thoughts and is different from the thought content problems just described. A frequent type of disordered thought is **loosening of associations**

Women of America, it behooves you one and all to help at this, the most interesting epoch of the World's History, in every way possible, the march of civilization, the march of victory! I will play you Beethoven's Great Symphony with its four fateful opening notes—sol, sol, sol, mi . . . V.V.V. the Day of the Century has dawned

—(R. A. Cohen, 1975, p. 1020)

Schizophrenic individuals may be highly intelligent, not at all confused, and very painstaking in working out logical solutions to problems. However, their thought processes do not lead to conclusions based on reality or universal logic.

Another characteristic of schizophrenic speech is **poverty of content**. This means that even though the speaker talks for quite a while little information is transmitted because what is said is vague, repetitive, stereotyped, and either too abstract or too concrete.

Perception

Hallucinations account for most of the difficulties a person with schizophrenia experiences in perceiving what is going on. **Hallucinations** are projections of internal impulses and experiences onto perceptual images in the external world. Although they may occur in other disorders—for example, during the delirium associated with a high fever or as a result of the effects of drugs or other chemicals on the nervous system—only in schizophrenia do hallucinations occur when the person is in a clear, conscious state. Hallucinations can be associated with any of the senses. In the case at the beginning of the chapter, J. had the hallucination of hearing voices threatening to kill her. This kind of auditory hallucination is the most common type found in schizophrenia. Many schizophrenics report voices making a running commentary on their behavior or speaking directly to them and issuing orders or accusing them of terrible crimes or actions (see Figure 11–2). Hallucinations may also be related to touch. For instance the person may feel burning or tingling sensations. Hallucinations associated with smell, while less common, are also typical. Foul odors are perceived as coming from one's body as a sign of decay and death or of some sexual change. Sometimes hallucinations are visual (see Figure 11–3), or they may be somatic and reflect internal sensations. One account includes the following descriptions.

I saw people whom I had entombed in milk bottles, putrefying, and I was consuming their rotting cadavers.

—(Sechehaye, 1951, pp. 34)

ter, 1985). What seems to be missing is the predictability and the repetitions of meaning that are present in normal speech. This may be the reason that interviewers who talk to someone with a schizophrenic disorder may come away confused about the meaning of what was said.

It is important to remember that not all people with a schizophrenic disorder display peculiar speech. The majority speak coherently most of the time, and peculiar speech is found in other patients about as frequently as it is in schizophrenics (Andreasen and Grove, 1979). To appreciate this point, rate the following examples on a five-point scale from 1, schizophrenic, to 5, normal.

a. Then, I always liked geography. My last teacher in the subject was Professor August A. He was a man with black eyes. I also like black eyes. There are also blue and gray eyes and other sorts, too. I have heard it said that snakes have green eyes. All people have eyes. There are some, too, who are blind. These blind people are led by a boy. It must be terrible not to be able to see. There are people who can't see, and in addition, can't hear. I know some who hear too much. One can hear too much. There are many sick people in Burghölzli; they are called patients. (Bleuler, 1950, p. 17)

b. Yes, of course, the whole thing wasn't my idea. So, I suppose I'd be perfectly happy if he came back and decided to do it all on his own. If I could make two trips myself, I don't see why he can't. (Laffal, 1965, p. 309)

c. Well, I wonder if that part of it can't be—I wonder if that doesn't—let me put it frankly; I wonder if that doesn't have to be continued? Let me put it this way: let us suppose you get the million bucks, and you get the proper way to handle it. You could hold that side? (Gold, 1974, p. 117)

When these excerpts were informally rated by several psychologists, item a was usually rated as schizophrenic. It represents the way people think schizophrenics speak. Item b was rated as normal because it is neither bizarre or obscure. Item c was rated moderately schizophrenic because, while it is not bizarre, it is repetitious, loose, and difficult to follow (Schwartz, 1982). How do these ratings agree with yours? The results may cause you to readjust your ideas about schizophrenics, because b was produced by a patient who was diagnosed as schizophrenic and c is from a conversion by former U. S. President Richard Nixon. Many of Nixon's colleagues produced similar speech (Gold, 1974).

Hard-to-follow speech may also come from people who have been given diagnoses other than schizophrenia. The following excerpt was produced by a hypomaniac patient.

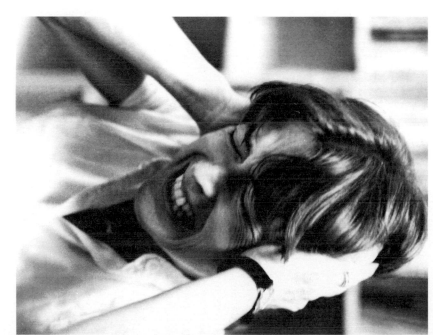

FIGURE 11–2
Some hallucinations are extremely unpleasant. This person hears voices accusing her of horrible crimes that she has not committed.

I was drawing the head of a cat which meanwhile gnawed at my vitals. It was ghastly, intolerable.

—(Ibid., p. 37)

Not all hallucinations are accusatory or unpleasant. Sometimes voices provide comfort and companionship. In a description of his psychotic period, one young adult described both pleasant and unpleasant voices.

The Voices. Testing one, two, testing one. Checking out the circuits: "What hath God wrought. Yip di mina di zonda za da boom di yaidi yoohoo."

By this time the voices had gotten very clear. At first I'd had to strain to hear or understand them. They were soft and working with some pretty tricky codes. Snap-crackle-pops, the sound of the wind with blinking lights and horns for punctuation. In the beginning it seemed mostly nonsense, but as things went along they made more and more sense. Once you hear the voices, you realize they've always been there. It's just a matter of being tuned to them.

The voices weren't much fun in the beginning. But later the voices could be very pleasant. They'd often be the voices of someone I loved, and even if they weren't I could talk too, asking questions about this or that and getting reasonable answers. There were very important messages that had to get through somehow. More orthodox channels like phone and mail had broken down.

—(Adapted from Vonnegut, 1975, pp. 136–137)

Sometimes schizophrenics find these hallucinations so comfortable that they are unwilling to give them up. They serve as protection from the discomforts of reality.

One way to study the perceptions of schizophrenic individuals as they occur is to use a time-sampling method. In one study the patient wore a beeper; when it went off, her task was to record in a notebook what she was experiencing at that time. The patient, Jennifer, was a young woman living in a halfway house after several years of on-and-off hospitalization. At the time of the study she had improved and was considering moving to a cooperative apartment.

FIGURE 11-3
This crayon drawing expresses the artist's perception of his mental illness. Unless he keeps busy, he has visual hallucinations of animals which frighten him greatly.

Her mind was often filled with visualizations of things in her surroundings as though she were looking at them from another place in the room. Frequently the image was also tilted at a 45-degree angle and under the raised side was a black empty space. Sometimes a brightly colored word was suspended in the image. Jennifer realized that these visualizations were distorted but she wasn't surprised or curious about them. Perhaps she had grown used to them.

—Adapted from Hurlburt and Melancon, 1987)

The technique of thought sampling can help us see that perceptual distortions may occur often in everyday schizophrenic thinking. In contrast to the dramatic memories from their period of psychoses by patients who have recovered, the time-sampling technique conveys an idea of just how disabling the disordered perception in schizophrenia may be even when an observer would notice no unusual behavior.

Hallucinations have been investigated from several perspectives (Asaad and Shapiro, 1986). From a biological perspective they have been linked to abnormal brain excitability. PT scans have shown greater biochemical activity in the temporal lobe and auditory areas during auditory hallucinations. The neurotransmitter dopamine may also play a role. From the psychodynamic perspective, hallucinations are thought to represent a breakthrough into consciousness of material from the unconscious. Their content is believed to have psychodynamic meaning such as wish fulfillment, aggressive impulses, or a projection of a critical superego or conscience. Cultural factors are thought to influence the frequency of auditory hallucinations. Another influencing factor is intelligence. From a cognitive perspective, intelligence level may play an important role in auditory hallucinations because these occur more frequently in people with lower intellectual and developmental levels. Perhaps auditory hallucinations represent the best way that less intellectually able people can describe stressful experience (Zigler and Levine, 1983).

Lack of Appropriate Emotion

One of the most common results of schizophrenia is change in emotional expression. This can be either a loss of virtually all signs of emotion or sudden unpredictable outbursts of inappropriate emotional expression. People with a schizophrenic disorder are often described as showing emotional flatness, and this is especially true after the period of acute psychosis has passed. Such people often show a characteristic apathy, and display little emotion no matter what the situation. Talking with someone who behaves this way is very unsatisfactory be- cause it seems that no emotional contact can be made. The person who expresses this lack of affect may also complain that he or she no longer "feels" and cannot experience emotion. Although this flattened affect is a frequent symptom of schizophrenia, it also can occur as a result of taking the antipsychotic drugs that are used to treat many schizophrenic patients.

Sometimes rather than showing flat affect a schizophrenic person may show an inappropriate emotional response. For example he or she may describe a delusion of being tortured and may accompany it by hearty giggles. Another inappropriate emotional response that may occur in schizophrenia is sudden, unpredictable, and seemingly unexplainable outbursts of anger. Whether these inappropriate expressions of emotion are connected to hallucinations and delusions is not known.

Unclear Boundaries of the Self

A person with schizophrenia often has what is called a loss of ego boundaries. This means that the normal feelings a person has of uniqueness, of being a separate individual, and of being in control of his or her own behavior are missing. These feelings may be related to the kinds of delusions that focus on being controlled by others through the insertion or removal of particular thoughts.

Unpredictable Motor Behavior

Just as the emotions expressed during schizophrenia are unpredictable, so is the motor activity. At some times schizophrenic patients may become wildly aggressive and difficult to control, or they may move about constantly, much like a person experiencing a manic episode, stopping only when exhaustion sets in. In contrast, patients may remain motionless in strange postures for many hours, to the point at which circulation is impaired and swelling of body parts such as the feet and ankles occurs.

Motivational Level

Another change that almost always accompanies a schizophrenic disorder is a change in motivation or interest level. This is most likely in the early phases and again in the period after acute psychosis has passed. Parents often notice the first symptoms of what may become a schizophrenic disorder when their child's school grades begin to fall and the child does nothing but sit around listening to music or TV and often retreats to

his or her bedroom and avoids contact with others.

Some people who have experienced a schizophrenic disorder report a slowing down of thought processes. Their thoughts seemed to creep at a snail's pace. One person described her great sense of exhaustion, all concentrated in her head, as if a cogwheel had stuck (Thelmar, 1932). Another person described it this way:

The process of thought is like a chain that has become clogged with muddy oil . . . my mind was moving at the slowest possible rate; the real process of thought entered my consciousness like a slow rhythm or circular movement.

—(Ogden, 1947, pp. 37, 92)

Impaired Interpersonal Functioning

One of the behaviors that is almost always present in schizophrenia in all its phases is social withdrawal and emotional detachment. The schizophrenic patient may be caught up in personal fantasies and inner experiences to the degree that the outer world is excluded. At some times, too, other problems with social interactions arise because the person seems unable to comprehend the most basic social conventions. For example, during at least some phases of the disorder, the schizophrenic person may intrude so much on others' personal space that they become uncomfortable and avoid contact. Such intrusions might involve inserting him or herself into an ongoing interaction with strangers—for example, joining strangers at a lunch table and interacting in an overly familiar way. Another behavior of this kind involves clinging to others or simply standing only inches away when asking a question.

Attention: An Organizing Concept

One way to understand what is going on in behavior that is typical in a schizophrenic disorder is to think about much of it in terms of problems with attention. A review of over 50 autobiographical books and articles by people who had been diagnosed as schizophrenic showed that difficulty in focusing attention and lack of concentration were mentioned more often than any other problem of cognition (Freedman, 1974). For example:

I couldn't read (newspapers) because everything that I read had a large number of associations with it. I mean, I'd just read a headline, and the headline of this item of news would have . . . very much wider associations in my mind. It seemed to start off everything that I read, and everything that I start off caught my attention; seemed to start off, bang-bang-bang, like that, with an enormous number of associations, moving off into things so that it became so difficult for me to deal with, that I couldn't read.

—(Laing, 1967, pp. 51–52)

There are many possible reasons for these attentional problems. One may be that hallucinations compete with actual happenings for attentional focus. Another is that the problems in content of thought may produce distortions in the meaning of what is observed. Another problem might be that disturbance in the sense of self and the anxiety it produces may result in an inability to screen out all the distracting stimuli that normally functioning people ordinarily ignore. These are only a few of many ideas that may explain the kinds of behavior that are common in schizophrenia.

The period when psychotic symptoms first appear is often a time of great anxiety. The case of "J." at the beginning of the chapter illustrates the impact of these anxious feelings. Many people make desperate attempts to control their thinking as they become aware of the onset of psychosis. They often concoct elaborate schemes for character or body building.

It is clear that people who are labeled as schizophrenic do not perceive situations in the same way that most other people do. What is not clear is whether they focus on too many factors in a situation and become confused by too much information, or whether they notice only certain details and thus become incapable of accurately assessing what is happening.

I went to the teacher and said to her, "I am afraid. . . ." She smiled gently at me. But her smile, instead of reassuring me, only increased the anxiety and confusion, for I saw her teeth, white and even in the gleam of the light. Remaining all the while like themselves, soon they monopolized my entire vision as if the whole room were nothing but teeth under a remorseless light. Ghastly fear gripped me.

—U.S. Dept. of Health and Human Services, 1981, p. 2

Diagnostic Criteria

The characteristics of schizophrenic disorder cover a wide range of behaviors, not all of which may occur in any one person. To be diagnosed as having a schizophrenic disorder, a person must show deterioration from his or her previous level of functioning in work, social relations, or self-care. Such a person is likely to be characterized by family and friends as "not the same" as before. Continuous signs of illness must be present for at least 6 months before the diagnosis can be made, and psychotic behavior must be present at some point in the illness. The diagnostic criteria listed in DSM-III-R are shown in Table 11–3.

TABLE 11-3

The DSM-III-R Criteria for Schizophrenia

A. Active phase: At least one of these categories of behavior must occur for at least two weeks:
1. At least two of the following:
   a. Delusions
   b. Hallucinations lasting more than a brief time that may occur through the day for several days or several times a week for several weeks
   c. Incoherent thinking or a marked loosening of associations
   d. Catatonic behavior (a disturbance in motor behavior in which the person may "freeze" into an apparently uncomfortable pose or become extremely overactive)
   e. Lack of changes in affect or grossly inappropriate affect
2. Bizarre delusions such as thought broadcasting or mind control
3. Prominent auditory hallucinations, such as hearing a voice that keeps up a running commentary on one's behavior, or hearing two or more voices talking to each other

B. Level of functioning in work, social relations, and self-care is clearly below the highest level achieved in the past. If the individual is a child, the level of social functioning does not meet that expected for his or her age group.

C. If severe depression or manic behavior is present, it occurred relatively briefly.

D. There must be continuous signs of illness for six months, including at least one week of psychotic symptoms. This period may include phases both before and after the psychotic period and in each case must include at least two of the following behaviors:
1. Marked social isolation or withdrawal
2. Marked impairment in functioning at work or in school
3. Markedly peculiar behavior, for example, collecting garbage or talking to oneself in public
4. Impaired personal hygiene and grooming
5. Blunted, flat, or inappropriate emotional expression
6. Digressive, vague, overelaborate, or circumstantial speech, or poverty of speech content
7. Odd beliefs or magical thinking, for example, being able to see the future, having a sixth sense, believing that "others can feel my feelings"
8. Unusual perceptual experiences, for example, sensing the presence of a force or person not actually present
9. Apathy or lack of initiative

E. No organic factor can be found to explain the disorder.

F. If there is a history of autistic disorder (a developmental disorder discussed in Chapter 16), prominent delusions or hallucinations must also be present before a schizophrenic disorder can be diagnosed. (Adapted from American Psychiatric Association, 1987, pp. 194–195)

A Historical View of Schizophrenic Disorders

Brief descriptions of what today would probably be called schizophrenic disorders are found in the Hindu *Ayur Veda*, which dates from 1400 Æ.Œ., and in the writings of the physician Aretaeus in the first century Æ.Œ. (Kendell, 1983). However, for many centuries descriptions of schizophrenia were much less common and detailed than descriptions of mania. Schizophrenic disorders were not clearly defined until the nineteenth century.

Dementia Praecox

One of the first writers to classify schizophrenia as a distinct disorder was Emil Kraepelin (1856–1926), who called it **dementia praecox**. Kraepelin was the author of the most influential psychiatric textbook of his period. He emphasized that classification depended on the cause of the illness, not just the symptoms observed at a particular time. Kraepelin used the term *dementia praecox* because the onset of the disorder occurred early in life, typically in adolescence. He believed the cause of dementia praecox was irreversible organic deterioration, which would eventually be found to have a specific organic cause and pathology. Based on this belief, he considered recovery from the disorder to be impossible. Despite this idea he noted the great variability in the speed and extent of different individuals' declines and pointed out that there might even be remissions, or periods when the disorder was no longer obvious. In fact, out of 127 cases that Kraepelin studied, 16 seemed to have ended in complete recovery (Kraepelin, 1909, vol. 2, p. 865).

Kraepelin paid no attention to the psychological aspects of schizophrenia; his entire focus was on the symptoms of the underlying deterioration. The person's life history, personality, and experiences with the illness were ignored. When he did mention psychological features, Kraepelin considered them temporary expedients, expecting that findings from microscopes and test tubes would make it possible to investigate the disease objectively.

The Schizophrenias

One of the first people to emphasize the psychological aspects of the disorder was Eugen Bleuler (1857–1939), who was influenced by Freud's work on the neuroses. According to Bleuler, whatever the underlying process might be, many of the symptoms had a psychological cause. Bleuler spoke of "the schizophrenias" instead of using the term *dementia praecox* and broadened the concept of the disorder as well as changing its name. He believed that the symptoms might represent a group of disorders with different causes and outcomes, not a single cause and outcome as Kraepelin had thought. Bleuler noted that although some people with schizophrenic disorders deteriorate, others remain unchanged and some improve. He divided people with schizophrenic symptoms into two groups: chronic and acute. The acute cases had a good chance of recovery. Bleuler also emphasized the role of the environment in schizophrenic disorder. In his view, some individuals might have the potential for developing these disorders, but because particular types of environmental situations did not occur, the disorder remained latent and these people never showed visible signs of schizophrenia.

Bleuler spoke of this group of disorders as characterized by loss of integration of thinking, emotion, and motivation rather than by gradual deterioration. He summed up the primary characteristics of schizophrenic behavior as the "four A's": alterations in affect, alterations in association, ambivalence, and autism. Associated with these changes, in Bleuler's view, were the secondary symptoms of hallucinations and delusions.

Bleuler defined the criteria vaguely so that they could be interpreted in a number of ways. If Bleuler's criteria were used, more people would be considered schizophrenic than when Kraepelin's definition was used. Bleuler's ideas became popular in the United States, but in Europe Kraepelin's ideas continued to dominate. Bleuler's approach led to increased use of the diagnosis of schizophrenia for behaviors that differed greatly both in kind and in severity. To make things worse, Bleuler's diagnostic guidelines were often interpreted more broadly than he had intended. For example, even if the individual had only some of the specified characteristics, the diagnosis of schizophrenia was applied frequently by American-trained clinicians. This meant that the label "schizophrenia" was being used to describe a wide variety of behaviors.

As this more generalized concept of schizophrenia became popular, many people were diagnosed as schizophrenic if they showed even some of the characteristics Bleuler had mentioned. From the 1930s until the 1960s, several important figures in American psychiatry, such as Adolf Meyer and Harry Stack Sullivan, emphasized a broad concept of schizophrenia and psychosis in general, and a concern with the psychodynamics of the behavior and emphasis on interpersonal relationships as causal factors. As a result, emphasis on differential diagnosis—discriminating, for example, between affective disorders and schizophrenia—was thought to be of little importance and the proportion of people who were called schizophrenic increased sharply. For example, in the 1930s about 20 percent of patients at the New York

Psychiatric Institute were diagnosed as schizophrenic. By the 1950s, the figure had reached 80 percent (Kuriansky and others, 1974). In contrast, the proportion of patients diagnosed as schizophrenic at Maudsley Hospital in London, where a Kraepelin-derived definition continued to be used, remained at about 20 percent over a long period.

First-Rank Symptoms

Because such a wide variety of individuals were given the diagnosis of schizophrenia, it became more difficult to do meaningful research on the causes of schizophrenic disorders. One way to deal with this problem was to clarify the definition. Kurt Schneider (1887–1967) was one of the leaders in this effort. Schneider did not deny that Kraepelin's idea of bodily changes was correct, but he believed that since these changes had not been identified, it was important to divide people into types on the basis of their psychological symptoms. Bleuler's four A's seemed too vague to be interpreted reliably; moreover, they had caused people with psychotic symptoms to be grouped with others whose psychoses involved disturbances of thought and perception.

Schneider dealt with this problem by describing a series of **first- and second-rank symptoms.** If first-rank symptoms were present and no organic cause was evident, a diagnosis of schizophrenia was justified. Second-rank symptoms, in Schneider's view, could be found in other psychotic disorders, although if second-rank symptoms occurred with sufficient frequency and in certain combinations, a diagnosis of schizophrenia could still be made without first-rank symptoms. Schneider considered the abnormal inner experiences of the individual to be the most telling characteristics of the illness (see Figure 11–4). His classification system attempted to identify behavioral symptoms that would be readily noticed by an examiner, could be easily agreed upon by several observers, and could occur only in schizophrenia. Those symptoms included one or more of the following: hearing one's voice spoken aloud in one's head; hearing voices that comment on what one is doing at the time; experiences of bodily influence (delusions of passivity); thought withdrawal and other forms of thought interference; thought diffusion; delusional perception; and believing that the feelings or motivation of others are being imposed on one ("made" or "inserted" thoughts or feelings). Table 11–4 lists and illustrates first-rank symptoms. Second-rank symptoms include other forms of hallucinations, confusion, disorders of mood, and emotional blunting.

The first-rank symptoms meet two of Schneider's goals: They are easily noticed and are easy for examiners to agree upon. However, his third goal was not met: Although these signs occur frequently in schizophrenia,

TABLE 11-4

Schneider's First-Rank Symptoms of Schizophrenia

The first-rank symptoms of schizophrenia fall into three groups; special forms of auditory hallucinations, inadequate perception of boundaries between the person and the environment, and normal perceptions with highly personalized delusional interpretation.

1. Auditory hallucinations:
   a. Voices repeating the subject's thought out loud or anticipating the subject's thoughts.

   The voice would repeat almost all the patient's goal-directed thinking—even the most banal thoughts. The patient would think, "I must put the kettle on" and after a pause of not more than one second the voice would say, "I must put the kettle on." It would often say the opposite, "Don't put the kettle on." (Mellor, 1979, p. 16)

   b. Two or more hallucinatory voices discussing or arguing about the subject, referring to him or her in the third person.

   c. Voices commenting on the subject's thoughts or behavior, often as a running commentary.

2. The sensation of alien thoughts being put into the subject's mind by some external agency, or of his or her own thoughts being taken away (thought insertion or withdrawal).

   A 22-year-old woman said, "I am thinking about my mother, and suddenly my thoughts are sucked out of my mind by a phrenological vacuum extractor, and there 's nothing in my mind, it is empty." (Mellor, 1970, pp. 16–17)

3. The sensation that the subject's thinking is no longer confined within his or her own mind but instead is shared by or accessible to others (thought broadcasting).

   A 21-year-old student said, "As I think, my thoughts leave my head on a type of mental ticker-tape. Everyone around has only to pass the tape through their mind and they know my thoughts." (Mellor, 1970, p. 17)

4. The sensation of feelings, impulses, or acts being experienced or carried out under external control, or the sensation of being hypnotized or having become a robot.

   A 23-year-old female patient reported, "I cry, tears roll down my cheeks and I look unhappy, but inside I have a cold anger because they are using me in this way, and it is not me who is unhappy, but they are projecting unhappiness into my brain. They project upon me laughter, for no reason, and you have no idea how terrible it is to laugh and look happy and know it is not you, but their emotions." (ibid.)

5. The experience of being a passive and reluctant recipient of bodily sensations imposed by some external agency.

   A 38-year-old man had jumped from a bedroom window, injuring his right knee which was very painful. He described his physical experience as follows: "The sun-rays are directed by a U.S. army satellite in an intense beam which I can feel entering the center of my knee and then radiating outward causing the pain." (Mellor, 1970, p. 16)

6. Delusional perception—a delusion arising fully fledged from a genuine perception that others would regard as commonplace and unrelated to the content of the delusion.

FIGURE 11–4
This painting, by an artist who had experienced a period of psychosis, seems to represent the kinds of delusional thinking and the feelings of being watched and influenced that Schneider described.

UPI

they are not unique to it. At least one-fourth of patients with bipolar affective disorders also show some of these symptoms (Hoenig, 1984). In addition, the presence or absence of these symptoms does not seem to be related to later functioning and improvement (Silverstein and Harrow, 1981).

The DSM-III-R criteria presented in Table 11–3 represent a kind of amalgam or bonding together of the criteria suggested by the three theorists—Kraepelin, Bleuler, and Schneider. Kraepelin's influence of DSM-III-R can be seen in its emphasis on the course of the disorder over time. However, like Bleuler DSM-III-R does not assume a negative outcome, although it does not require that the behaviors described last over a certain period. It also reflects Kraepelin's approach in its emphasis on the description of behavior in making the diagnosis. Schneider's influence is also clear: DSM-III-R includes several of his signs, such as though broadcasting, thought insertion, and thought withdrawal, in its diagnostic criteria.

Types of Schizophrenia

Traditional and DSM-III-R Subtypes

Kraepelin described three subtypes of schizophrenia or dementia praecox—catatonic, hebephrenic, and paranoid. When Bleuler broadened the description of the disorder, he added a fourth category, simple schizophrenia. These four categories were used for many years. DSM-III-R uses a modification of the traditional types to describe different categories of behavior in the active phase of disorder. These are: paranoid, catatonic, disorganized, and a catchall or undifferentiated group. In addition, there is a residual category for cases in which the psychotic features are no longer prominent.

A person with disorganized schizophrenia shows incoherence in expression, grossly disorganized behavior, and either flat or extremely inappropriate emotional reactions. Such people may show a childish disregard for social conventions and may resist wearing clothes, urinate or defecate at inappropriate times, and eat with their fingers. They behave actively but aimlessly and display emotional responses that are inappropriate to the circumstances. Giggling, silly mannerisms, and inexplicable gestures are common. Usually the long-term outlook for recovery is poor. People with disorganized schizophrenia are likely to have shown symptoms early and to have been poorly adapted even before that time.

Disturbance in motor activity is the major symptom of catatonic schizophrenia. People with this disorder may refuse to speak and remain stiffly immobile or may be extremely agitated. Waxy flexibility is an extreme form of immobility in which the catatonic's arm or leg remains passively in the position in which it is placed. At the opposite extreme, the agitated catatonic shows extreme psychomotor excitement, talking and shouting almost continuously. Patients who experience prolonged catatonic excitement may be very destructive and violent toward others. As with manic excitement, there is a danger of personal injury or collapse due to exhaustion. This form of schizophrenia is now rarely seen, although it was common until 30 or 40 years ago.

The diagnosis that is most often given on first admission to a mental hospital is paranoid schizophrenia. In this form of the disorder none of the behaviors that define the disorganized or catatonic types are present. There is no incoherence, no loose associations, no grossly inappropriate or flat affect, and no unusual patterns of movement. Instead the disorder seems to be primarily in cognitive behavior. It is characterized by delusions and sustained, extreme suspiciousness that are related to a single theme. Since some aspects of intellec-

tual functioning may be unaffected by the delusional thoughts, under certain circumstances paranoid schizophrenics may seem to function relatively well. They also are more likely than the other types to have a good outcome.

The following account was given by a medical student with a Ph.D. in psychology who developed an acute psychotic reaction in which delusions played a prominent role. His case illustrates not only the delusions typical of paranoid schizophrenia but also the acute fright that is felt by someone experiencing the beginning of such a delusional state. During his acute episode, the student had the haunting notion that there was something wrong with him, that he could not breathe, and that he might die. One morning, after an especially fearful, sleepless night, he reported the following experience.

I got up at 7 A.M., depressed, and drove to the hospital. I felt my breathing trouble might be due to an old heart lesion. . . . I decided that I was in heart failure and that people felt I wasn't strong enough to accept this, so they weren't telling me. I looked up heart failure in a textbook and found that the section had been removed, so I concluded that someone had removed it to protect me. I remembered other comments. A friend had talked about a "walkie-talkie," and the thought occurred to me that I might be getting medicine without my knowledge, perhaps by radio. I remembered someone talking about a one-way plane ticket; to me that meant a trip to Houston and a heart operation. I remembered an unusual smell in the lab and thought that might be due to the medicine they were giving me in secret. I began to think I might have a machine inside of me which secreted medicine into my blood steam. . . . A custodian's eyes attracted my attention, they were especially large and piercing. He looked very powerful. He seemed to be "in on it," maybe he was giving me medicine in some way.

Paranoid schizophrenics misinterpret the world around them. Although they are capable of evaluating the situation correctly, they resist the feedback cues that most people use. Well-defined systems of delusional paranoid thinking can also occur in people who in other respects show well-integrated behavior. Such people are diagnosed as having a delusional disorder rather than schizophrenia of the paranoid type (see Box 11–1).

People who formerly would have been diagnosed as simple or borderline schizophrenics—that is, people who have some of the symptoms such as hallucinations and delusions—now are placed in the category of Schizotypal Personality Disorder. The group includes people who exhibit a lifelong pattern of seclusiveness and withdrawal from others. They may show decreasing interest, initiative, and ambition around the time of puberty and

Delusional (Paranoid) Disorders

Everyone engages in paranoid thinking at one time or another. You could probably think of at least one occasion when you have felt that you were being discriminated against or talked about or were suspicious of someone else's motives without adequate proof that such things had actually occurred. We can consider paranoid thinking to be a kind of cognitive style. People vary in how frequently they use it and in how much they let reality influence what they perceive. Paranoid thinking thus can be expressed as a kind of continuum extending from the everyday type to severe delusional thinking that affects all of a person's life (see Figure 11–5).

Illness, drugs, damage to the brain, some effects of aging, and the experience of severe stress can also produce paranoid thinking, but these do not qualify as paranoid disorder or fit on the continuum in Figure 11–5.

Sometimes people who have not thought in this way before suddenly begin to do so. Such varied factors as liver failure, vitamin B$_{12}$ deficiency, hearing loss, brain tumors, syphilis, and a variety of drugs may produce paranoid thinking along with other symptoms. At least 65 different conditions have paranoid features (Manschreck and Petri, 1978).

Paranoid thinking is more common in older people. Often it is caused by social isolation and perhaps by a progressive hearing loss or a loss of vision that makes it harder for the person to verify his or her perceptions of what is actually happening. Sometimes the small strokes or bloodclots in the brain that occur in older people can lead to paranoid symptoms. Another possible cause is atrophy or degeneration of brain tissue. Any of these conditions may produce severe enough maladaptive behavior to require that the person be institutionalized.

A 73-year-old man had lived in the community for years. He was not very sociable but was always thought of as a harmless crank. Then his hearing began to fail and he became afraid that his house

was going to be broken into and all his things stolen. He thought his family was after his money and wanted to get rid of him. As a result, he barricaded himself in his house and refused to see anyone. He was finally hospitalized and given antipsychotic drugs. As a result, his hostile angry behavior decreased but his delusional beliefs were unchanged.

Stress caused by environmental changes can also bring on a temporary episode of paranoid thinking. For example, immigrants experience paranoid disturbances at a much higher rate than native-born citizens. The move to a new place, with all the readjustment involved, usually produces high levels of stress.

After being told by his recruiting officer not to report his bedwetting problem during his induction physical, an 18-year-old enuretic male from the rural South enlisted in the military. The other recruits began to tease him unmercifully with the discovery of his secret soon after the beginning of basic training. He began to believe that his recruiting officer and drill instructor were plotting to murder him so that his bed wetting would remain undiscovered by higher authorities. When he was examined, he exhibited hypersensitivity to criticism, paranoid thinking, and ideas of reference. After two months' hospitalization his delusions cleared. On one-year follow-up, although his social contact was minimal and he remained periodically enuretic, he continued to be free of psychotic thinking while he was living and working on his father's farm. (Adapted from Walker and Brodie, 1985, p. 751)

Paranoid delusions usually fall into one of several categories: the feeling of being persecuted by others,

---

then progressively decrease their attempts at social interaction. (Schizotypal personality disorder is described in Chapter 9.)

A person with schizotypal personality disorder usually comes to the attention of clinicians only if some dramatic life change occurs. Loss of a job or the death or disability of a parent or other caretaker may bring such people into contact with the medical or welfare system because they lack the ability to make it on their own. People with schizotypal personality disorder may be eccentric, but they do not fit the DSM-III-R definition of schizophrenic disorder. They are distinguished primarily by their lifelong inability to function indepen-

dently, even though they are not retarded intellectually. A marked lack of assertiveness prevents them from expressing anger, from making friendly overtures to the people around them, and from having a normal sex life. Marked peculiarities in communication and deviant use of words also may keep others at a distance.

The diagnostic subgroups of schizophrenia listed in DSM-III-R vary in how frequently each occurs and also in expected outcome after the active phase has ended. A problem in evaluating the probable outcome is that over time a person's behavioral picture may change so that his or her classification into one or another of these types may be different at different periods.

FIGURE 11–5
The range of disordered perceptions of reality with paranoid elements.

MILD	MODERATE	SEVERE
Average person Occasional suspicious thoughts	**Paranoid personality disorder** A suspicious cognitive style so strong that it impairs effective behavior. Reality testing is intact.	**Paranoid schizophrenia** Multiple delusions that are likely to be fragmented, accompanied by marked loosening of associations, obvious hallucinations, and other evidence of disorganization. Reality markedly distorted.
Paranoid personality A suspicious cognitive style.	**Delusional (paranoid) disorder** A stable and chronic delusional system. Reality testing is good in all other areas. There are no delusions.	

unwarranted jealousy and suspicion of sexual unfaithfulness by one's lover or mate, the feeling that another person has fallen in love with one when there is no evidence for this, and delusions of illness when none exists. The following descriptions illustrate some of these types.

T.Y. became suspicious that his wife was having an affair with her obstetrician during her pregnancy. The baby did not resemble the father, but he thought it did look like the obstetrician. T.Y. then threatened to kill the physician. After antipsychotic drugs and psychotherapy, his anger and threats of murder disappeared but he continued to believe the child was not his.

B.Z., an accountant, met a famous writer when he came to the accounting firm for advice about his financial planning. Although he was courteous and pleasant, he showed no special attention to her. She became convinced that he was irresistibly attracted to her, and she was soon entirely preoccupied with thoughts about his love and their future life together. Her feelings became so clear that he soon found another accounting firm. Antipsychotic medication was of no help, but after some psychotherapy sessions B.Z. agreed to stop calling the writer and waiting for him in the lobby of his apartment building.

Delusional disorder is rare. It is estimated that it affects only about .03 percent of the population or 3 in every 10,000 people. Although it can occur in young people, it is most likely to appear around ages 40 to 45. Once developed the delusional thinking may remain stable over long periods or it may came and go. Little is known about the causes or the most effective means of treatment of delusional disorder. Antipsychotic medications may be helpful in some crisis situations. Psychotherapy may also be helpful. The most effective way to deal with the delusions seems to be to suggest to the client the ways in which they interfere with his or her goals, rather than attempting to meet them head on. The client can sometimes be taught to recognize and avoid situations that produce or increase the delusions.

Schizophrenic Spectrum Disorders

When the families of schizophrenic individuals are studied, they seem to include more than the expected number of relatives who are somewhat unusual in their behavior. These relatives dress eccentrically, behave in unusual ways, and seem somewhat limited emotionally or somewhat asocial. A greater than anticipated number of relatives of schizophrenics may also show peculiarities in thinking—magical thinking, for instance. Many researchers believe that there may be some genetic relationship between these behaviors and the schizophrenic disorders. They believe that the whole spectrum of disordered behaviors should be investigated together and usually discuss all of these under the label of **schizophrenic spectrum disorders.**

Schizophrenic spectrum disorders include not only these unusual emotional responses and cognitive behaviors but also certain personality disorders. For instance, schizotypal and paranoid personality disorders occur more frequently in the families of people who have schizophrenic disorders (Baron and Risch, 1987). Other disorders that have sometimes been linked to the schizophrenic spectrum are *schizoaffective disorder* (a category

TABLE 11-5

Examples of Negative Symptom Behavior

Poverty of Speech	Flat Affect	Psychomotor retardation
1. Long lapses before replying to questions	1. Avoids looking at interviewer	1. Slowed in movements
2. Restriction of quantity of speech	2. Blank, expressionless face	2. Reduction of voluntary movements
3. Patient fails to answer	3. Reduced emotion shown when emotional material discussed	
4. Speech slowed	4. Apathetic and uninterested	
5. Blocking	5. Monotonous voice	
	6. Low voice, difficult to hear	

NOTE: Items are from the Behavior Rating Inventory of the Psychiatric Assessment Interview.
SOURCE: Adapted from Carpenter and others, 1976. Reprinted with permission from the *British Journal of Psychiatry*.

that includes individuals who show significant depression or manic symptoms along with the development of thought disorder), *atypical psychoses*, and *paranoid disorder* (Kendler and others, 1985). The study of the relationships among these disordered behaviors may provide clues to the causes of schizophrenic behavior.

Positive and Negative Symptoms

Because most authorities agree that schizophrenic behavior can be produced by a variety of causes, there have been many attempts to group together patients with different sets of symptoms in the hope that this will help in identifying possible causes of schizophrenic behavior. At present the most popular division for research use is the distinction between positive and negative symptoms (Crow, 1980). **Positive symptoms** or behavioral excesses include hallucinations, delusions, bizarre behavior, and disordered thinking. Positive symptoms are thought to be a result of problems with the chemical neurotransmitter dopamine. **Negative symptoms** or behavior deficits are such behaviors as poverty of speech and of speech content, flattened affect, apathy, seclusiveness, and impaired attention (see Table 11-5). Patients with positive symptoms often respond well to drug therapies and have a better chance of resuming effective functioning than patients with negative symptoms. People with positive symptoms usually functioned well before the schizophrenic behaviors appeared and these changes in their behavior appeared quickly. The disturbed behaviors tend to come and go, and at times when they are not as obvious the person's social functioning is reasonably effective. Positive symptoms usually respond well to antipsychotic drugs that function by blocking the transmission of the neurotransmitter dopamine. In contrast drugs that increase dopamine transmission, for instance, amphetamine, make the symptoms appear worse. In general, brain scans do not show any structural abnormalities in the brain that are associated with positive symptoms.

Negative symptoms not only are associated with poor functioning after the initial psychotic period but also are related to poor social and educational functioning before hospitalization. Lack of friends and failure to finish high school both increased the risk that negative symptoms would be present when individuals were followed up after their initial hospitalization (Pogue-Geile and Harrow, 1985). This may mean that these early difficulties are influenced by the same factors as the later negative symptoms, or it may simply mean that early deficits in behavior interact with any genetic vulnerability toward schizophrenia that a person may have. Brain scans of people with negative symptoms are likely to show structural brain abnormalities. When negative symptoms are predominant, antipsychotic drugs usually do not produce much improvement. Table 11–6 summarizes the differences between positive and negative symptoms.

Most of the research with positive and negative symptoms has been done with chronic patients, those that have had a schizophrenic disorder over a long period. A more recent study has examined what happens over time to young people who were just experiencing their first schizophrenic episode when they were initially studied; its findings suggest that the relationship between positive and negative symptoms may be more complicated than originally thought (Lindenmayer, and others, 1986). After 2 years both positive and negative symptoms occurred about as frequently as they did originally, but they were not stable over time. Knowledge of who had negative symptoms or positive symptoms in the original episode did not necessarily predict a person's symptom picture 2 years later. Negative symptoms after 2 years were associated with poor functioning and poor outcome, but negative symptoms during the first phase of the disorder were not necessarily related to a later poor outcome. One reason might be that for some people, depression associated with the experience of the

TABLE 11-6

Differences between Positive and Negative Schizophrenia

Characteristic	Positive	Negative
Characteristic symptoms	Delusions, hallucinations	Flattening of affect, poverty of speech
Response to psychoactive drugs	Good	Poor
Outcome	Potentially reversible	Irreversible?
Intellectual impairment	Absent	Sometimes present
Abnormal involuntary movements	Absent	Sometimes present
Postulated pathological process	Increased D₂ dopamine receptors	Cell loss (including peptide-containing interneurons) in temporal lobe structures

Modified from Crow and Johnstone, 1985.
SOURCE: Crow, 1985, p. 481.

initial psychotic symptoms of schizophrenic disorder may have produced a picture of negative symptoms that had a very different meaning than the negative symptoms found in the earlier research with patients who had been ill for a long time. Like other ways of trying to subdivide schizophrenia, the concept of positive and negative symptoms is helpful but needs further refinement.

Outcome Indicators and Long-Term Studies

There are two schools of thought regarding the outcome or prognosis for schizophrenia. One is derived from Kraepelin's original concept of dementia praecox. This view of schizophrenia as a nonreversible deteriorative disorder assumes that the prognosis is negative. The second viewpoint stems from Bleuler's concept of the schizophrenias, which emphasizes the symptoms rather than the course of the disease. From this viewpoint, a certain number and kind of symptoms are necessary for the diagnosis, but the outcome may range from complete recovery to permanent and severe disability.

Information about whether or not there ever is or can be a complete recovery from schizophrenia is very important for individuals who have been diagnosed as having a schizophrenic disorder and for their families. The implications are considerable even for those whose behavior seems to have returned to a preschizophrenic level. These points are dramatically illustrated by a letter written by someone who had earlier been diagnosed as schizophrenic.

A few years ago, during my training in medical school, I was hospitalized at a reputable institution and, at some time during my stay, diagnosed as schizophrenic. Fortunately, I am doing very well now, and am pursuing a career in research on schizophrenia. . . . During the years since my

hospitalization, however, I have often been fraught with profound guilt over my diagnosis of schizophrenia. . . . I felt that for some people I would be forevermore something of a subhuman creature. I grieved and mourned over my loss for several months. . . . Returning to work as a fellow in a department of psychiatry, I was repeatedly in contact with psychiatrists, psychologists, and other mental health professionals. Quite frequently amidst such contacts there were derogatory and slanderous remarks of persons labeled as schizophrenic. Dismayed, I soon had repeated dreams in which I had a brain tumor, dreams that were not in the least bit frightening to me. Having an organic disorder seemed far easier to live with then—preferable to experiencing the full psychological impact of this label of schizophrenia. . . . But I continually have a need to ask myself certain questions. Am I now committed to schizophrenia for life? Or is schizophrenia committed to me?

—(Anonymous, 1977, p. 4)

Predictors of Outcome

Predictions about the outcome of a schizophrenic disorder typically take into account a set of criteria including type of disorder, whether the psychosis appeared suddenly, and level of prepsychotic adjustment. Recently other criteria such as positive and negative symptoms have been added.

Type of Disorder. It is generally assumed that hebephrenics have the poorest chance of recovery. Paranoids and catatonics are thought to have a better prognosis, especially if vivid delusions are present during the initial phase.

Acute Versus Chronic Onset. Cases in which there is a sudden onset, often related to a situation that is seen by others as obviously stressful or traumatic, seem to have the best prognosis. Cases with a gradual onset marked by no outstanding external precipitating event have less likelihood of a positive outcome.

TABLE 11-7

The Five Best Predictors of Level of Functioning after a Particular (Index) Hospitalization for Schizophrenic Disorder

Predictor	Predictive of Good or Poor Prognosis
Impairment of work ability (1 year before index admission)	poor
More advanced age at first hospitalization	good
Poor level of functioning at discharge	poor
Length of occupational disintegration in the 5 years before index admission	poor
A high level of life stress before first signs of psychosis	good

SOURCE: Möller and others, 1982, p. 105.

Premorbid Adjustment. Whether the person's life prior to the appearance of schizophrenia showed adequate school and social adjustment, and whether—if the individual is an adult—he or she demonstrated the ability to be self-supporting are very strongly related to the probable outcome after the period of acute psychosis has passed (Stoffelmayr and others, 1983). If there is a long history of relative deviance, including school difficulties, few friends, and little active dating, the prognosis is poorer. This is especially true if the person has typically been uncommunicative, apathetic, inactive, and accepting of his or her condition.

The person's past level of functioning seems to be a much better predictor of outcome than the severity of the symptoms that appear when the first diagnosis of schizophrenia is made. Table 11–7 summarizes some characteristics that are associated with good or poor outcomes.

Long-term Follow-up Studies

One frequently asked question is, What happens to people who are diagnosed as schizophrenic? Studies that follow individuals over long periods provide important information about the long-term implications of the diagnosis of schizophrenic disorder. However, the definition of schizophrenia has changed over time. Unless we know the particular definition used in the study, the results are hard to interpret. Another drawback of follow-up studies is that, because of their cost, they are often done on the basis of hospital records and the individual is never actually interviewed or personally evaluated.

This introduces a good deal of uncertainty—for example, did all the record keepers use the same definition of level of adaptation?

A long-term study that is of particular interest was done by Manfred Bleuler, Eugen Bleuler's son. This study was one of the first to suggest a good outcome for many individuals who had been hospitalized for schizophrenia. What is important about the study is the amount of personal contact Bleuler had with his former patients. Rather than simply following up or recontacting them after a long time, Bleuler followed his patients' progress closely over a 30-year period (Bleuler, 1972). He found that whatever deterioration occurred happened in the first 5 years of illness. After that the proportions of recovered, improved, and unimproved cases remained fairly constant. Research by a number of other clinicians has supported this finding.

Bleuler's information on the patients he saw during his years of practice suggests that the overall recovery rate has remained constant. However, over many years Bleuler observed changes in the symptom patterns exhibited by his patients. Cases of acute onset followed by severe psychosis became rarer. Moreover, the number of milder chronic conditions seemed to increase and the frequency of severe chronic cases to decrease. Other clinical workers have noted the same trends, as well as a decrease in the frequency of excited catatonic states and an increase in the number of people who have periodic disturbances accompanied by periods of remission. The reason for these changes are not clear; however, this pattern is similar to that found in cross-cultural studies conducted in developing countries in Africa (Cooper and Sartorius, 1977).

In a recently reported study carried out in Vermont (Harding and others, 1987), long-term hospitalized patients who had participated in a comprehensive rehabilitation program and been deinstitutionalized 20 to 30 years earlier were rediagnosed from their records. Those who met the DSM-III criteria for schizophrenia were traced and they or their families were interviewed. Between half and two-thirds of these individuals had recovered or were significantly improved. Figure 11–6 shows how many were functioning at least fairly well in different areas of life.

Although many of these people had made a poor adjustment for at least 5 years after the rehabilitation program, later on many had returned to their previous level of functioning or had even developed further. Some of these, however, functioned well only because they apparently had learned to live with certain symptoms. Some were employed and had good social relationships but still experienced some hallucinations or delusions. Others, who did not work, had nevertheless developed extensive social networks. Because the pa-

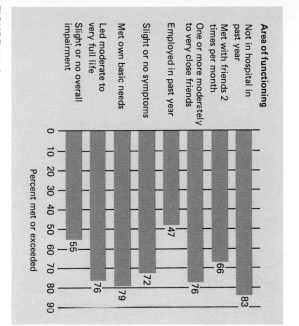

FIGURE 11–6
Many of the long-term patients followed up 30 years after they had left the hospital had at least a marginally adequate level of functioning. The figure shows the percent of the 168 patients who met or exceeded each criterion.

tients in this study had been hospitalized for up to 25 years and were middle aged when the rehabilitation program began, these results suggest that with younger, more recently hospitalized patients the outcome might be even better.

Because the definition of schizophrenia has changed over time and become stricter so that only severe cases and those that persist for some time are now included, it is difficult to evaluate the outcome for many people diagnosed as schizophrenic many years ago. Interpreting the follow-up studies with this reservation in mind it seems reasonable to estimate that one in five patients who meet DSM-III-R criteria for schizophrenia may at least avoid severe and chronic deterioration in behavior (Pfohl and Andreasen, 1986). As people progress through a schizophrenic illness, an ever wider variety of outcomes becomes possible. Not only do symptoms change over time, but predictors of outcome change for the person as the years pass since the disorder first appeared. Even evidence that certain biological factors have a permanent effect on outcome remains scanty (Harding and other 1987).

Therapeutic Approaches

Because the cause or causes of schizophrenic disorders are not well understood, a variety of therapies have been used. Therapies based on the different psychological perspectives are often used together.

Biological Therapies

Perhaps the most universal treatment for schizophrenia today is the use of antipsychotic drugs. For instance, in a survey of practicing psychiatrists in Australia, almost all advocated the use of antipsychotic drugs. However, many also recommended supportive psychotherapy or family or social intervention to accompany the use of drugs (Andrews and others, 1986). The introduction of these drugs in the 1950s revolutionized the hospital treatment of psychotics because the drugs decreased the unusual and hard-to-control behaviors of many patients. This reduced the number of patients who had to be hospitalized for long periods. The exact way in which the antipsychotic drugs work is not clear, although the ways in which they affect the neurotransmitter system are reasonably well understood. What is known about the role of the neurotransmitter system in producing schizophrenic behavior is discussed further in Chapter 12.

In general, people who improve as a result of drug therapy remain on a drug program after being discharged from the hospital. In many of these cases, withdrawal of antipsychotic drugs will be followed by a return of symptoms. For some patients, the drugs appear to have suppressed ongoing psychotic behaviors but do not prevent a new episode (Kane, 1987). Medication also does not affect negative symptoms of apathy and withdrawal (Carpenter and others, 1985). Of those who respond to medication almost one-third relapse within 1 year and half relapse within 2 years (Hogarty and others, 1979). Some people, especially those who have become acutely ill and were adequately adjusted before their illness, seem to recover more completely if drugs are not used. Whether they also should be viewed as a different subgroup within the schizophrenic disorders is not known.

A serious drawback of the use of drug therapies is the potentially irreversible damage to the nervous system that occasionally occurs as a result of overuse of antipsychotic drugs. This damage usually appears in the form of **tardive dyskinesia**, or involuntary movements of the mouth, lips, tongue, legs, or body. The development of tardive dyskinesia is generally related to length of treatment and the amount of drugs given, but at present there is no way to identify people who are at special risk except that the risk seems to increase with age. About 10 to 20 percent of patients in mental hospitals and 40 percent of chronically ill hospitalized and nonhospitalized schizophrenic patients show signs of tardive dyskinesia linked with drug treatment. Because antipsychotic drugs are sometimes given inappropriately or used for too long a time, the risk of these side effects in unnecessarily high for some patients. In 1985, because of these concerns, the American Psychiatric Association issued a warning about the need for "cautious use" of antipsychotic drugs. Emphasis has been given to determining the lowest effective dose and the drugs with the least side effects.

Both because of the risk of tardive dyskinesia and because of the effectiveness of lithium and antidepressants in some cases of mood disorders, accurate diagnosis is becoming even more important. The following case illustrates possible consequences of misdiagnosis.

Mrs. X was referred to a hospital for evaluation of "chronic psychosis." Now age 61, she was first hospitalized at age 40 because of symptoms of withdrawn behavior, inability to function at home, staying in bed, and a marked decrease in speaking to others. Before that hospitalization at 40 she had completed eighth grade, functioned well at home, was happily married, and considered a good mother. For 15 years she was treated with thorazine (an antipsychotic drug). She developed tardive dyskinesia (uncontrolled movements of the lips and tongue) and eventually the thorazine was discontinued. Three months before her present hospitalization she was hospitalized for symptoms of depression. She felt hopeless, wanted to die, had lost her appetite, and had trouble sleeping. [You will recall from Chapter 10 that these are all characteristic symptoms of depression.] Antipsychotic drugs were given, but after two months she was rehospitalized with a severe memory deficit. After her present hospitalization she was given a series of ECT and showed a remarkable improvement. Her family described her as better than she had been in years.

—(Adapted from Ferrell, 1980, p. 3)

It seems likely that Mrs. X's problem should have been diagnosed as an affective disorder from the start. Not only might she have been able to assume her normal family role again with effective treatment for depression, but she might have escaped the disfiguring effects of tardive dyskinesia brought on by antipsychotic medication.

Psychodynamic Therapies

In general, the results of psychotherapy with schizophrenics have not been impressive. Studies comparing the results of psychotherapy with those of drug therapies have indicated that when each is used alone, drug therapy is more effective than psychotherapy alone in shortening the hospital stay and in preventing future re-admissions. However, other types of therapy such as supportive therapy and family therapy may help prevent return to the hospital when combined with drug therapy. These are discussed in more detail later in the section.

One reason for psychotherapy's lack of success may be that psychodynamically oriented therapy provides too much stimulation for some patients, especially chronic patients. A comparison study of day treatment centers found that more professional staff hours and more group therapy programs were associated with less successful treatment programs. Successful outcomes were more likely at centers that had more occupational therapy and a very nonchallenging environment (Linn and others, 1979).

Despite these disadvantages, some psychodynamic therapists, such as Frieda Fromm-Reichmann and Otto Will, were known for their ability to help schizophrenics, even those with very severe symptoms. They worked mainly with people whose disordered behavior was acute rather than chronic. Also, they worked in excellent private hospitals where the general level of therapeutic treatment is high and the therapist can meet with the patient several times a week over a long period.

Behavioral Therapy

It is generally recognized that many chronic schizophrenic patients are deficient in social skills. Many have had this problem throughout life, others are not prepared to make it on their own after a period of acute illness and hospitalization. Social skills training, based on social-learning theory, is often an effective way to improve their quality of life while outside the hospital and to decrease the chances of rehospitalization (Bellack and Mueser, 1986). **Social skills training** includes modeling, role playing, and real-life practice that is focused on teaching new, more adaptive interpersonal behavior. Chronic patients also have inadequate self-care skills. They are often poorly groomed, fail to wash regularly, have poor table manners, and are unable to use public transportation, manage their money, or prepare meals. Behavioral-training methods can focus on the improvement of these skills. Successful transition for patients from the hospital to the community is predicted better by these skills than by the characteristics of behavior at or during hospitalization (Presly and others, 1982).

Behavioral therapy can be effective both in teaching basic survival skills and also in helping a person improve social skills so that he or she can begin to rebuild a network of socially supportive people after discharge from the hospital. The behavioral approach is also useful for teaching job skills which are essential for effective reentry into the community.

Milieu Therapy and Family Efforts

For many patients, the use of antipsychotic drugs has shortened their first hospital stay by shortening the period during which their psychotic symptoms are most evident. This has some very positive effects, since just being hospitalized for a long period, even in the best of institutions, can have negative effects on a person's coping abilities. For that reason, as well as cost factors and concern about civil rights, increased emphasis has been placed on short hospital stays, mainly to begin and assess drug treatment, followed by discharge to aftercare in the community.

The kind of setting to which schizophrenics return and the forms of support available there are crucial to their recovery. One effective source of support can be the patient's family. If the family's attitude toward the patient is judgmental, hostile, and overinvolved, the chances of a relapse are much higher than if the family has a positive attitude (Leff, 1987; Vaughn and Leff, 1976).

Because families may not have a supportive attitude and many patients may not have a family to return to, other kinds of support programs are often provided. These include halfway houses or group homes, day-care facilities, and mental health clinics that provide both treatment and practical help. Some of these supports may be transitional; they help the discharged patient readjust to life in the community. Others are used to help a person who is functioning at a low level stay out of the hospital. Some research suggests that aftercare treatment is most effective for chronic patients who maintain contact with the program on a long-term basis. This suggests that most support programs help people maintain the same level of adaptive behavior they had at the time of their hospital discharge but do not increase their level of performance. Unfortunately, good aftercare programs and sheltered living accommodations are in very short supply.

One effective method that helps prevent relapse and rehospitalization is training of family members. The purpose of such training is to modify critical or controlling attitudes toward the person who has reentered the household after being discharged from the hospital, or to find ways of reducing their face-to-face contact. The kind of behavior that can be modified is illustrated in the following portion of an interview.

He got up one Sunday morning and he sat in the chair and I said, "What's the matter? Don't you feel well?" "No," he said. So I said, "Can I get you a drink?" "No." So I left him. I went back again to see that he was all right. He was still in the same

position. This was nearly an hour later. So I thought, it's not very warm, he must be getting cold. So I went out and got a blanket without asking him and put it on him. "I don't want it," he said. And then I did break down because I thought, well, what the devil can I do for him? And that's when it upset me—when I can't do anything to help him like that.

— (Hooley, 1985, p. 135)

As this example suggests, some relatives may behave in a controlling way because they are concerned about the former patient's welfare, but their behavior may not be pleasing to the patient.

In one study, families who were rated as critical and controlling participated in a social intervention that had three components: (1) educational sessions that explained symptoms, expected behavior, and ways of dealing with individuals who had a schizophrenic disorder; (2) group meetings for relatives that included families who were rated as accepting and uncontrolling; and (3) family sessions in which mental health workers met with the patient and other family members at home to discuss problems and plan effective ways for the family to interact. All of the patients included in the study continued to take antipsychotic drugs throughout the period. At the end of two years the relapse rate for the experimental group was 14 percent compared to 78 percent for a group of control patients on regular medication (Leff and others, 1985).

Emphasis on both behavioral training and aftercare can be effective in preparing people with schizophrenic disorders to leave the hospital and in helping them function in a community setting. One of the most thorough and carefully controlled studies using a behavioral method was carried out by Paul and Lentz (1977). The project began during the patients' hospitalization. Twenty-eight chronic and severely affected schizophrenic patients were assigned to each of two experimental treatments: social-learning focused behavioral therapy and milieu therapy. The behavioral treatment included training in interpersonal skills, work habits, and self-care. **Milieu therapy** refers to therapy in which all staff members or others involved with the patient concentrate on providing a therapeutic environment. There was also a control group of patients from the regular hospital program. The patients were evaluated every 6 months during a 4½-year active treatment period and a 1½-year follow-up. All patients who were discharged were given 26 weeks of aftercare. If they needed rehospitalization, they returned to their original units. At the beginning of the study, more than 90 percent were receiving maintenance doses of medication (i.e., doses intended to keep their condition stable). As the study progressed, drug treatment was discontinued for the majority of the patients without ill effects.

By the end of the 4½ years, over 10 percent of the original social-learning group had been discharged as independently functioning, compared to 7.1 percent of the milieu patients and none of the regular treatment patients. Many other somewhat less improved patients had been placed in the community in sheltered environments; again the social-learning group was superior. Overall more than 95 percent of the social-learning group had at least one 90-day stay in the community compared to less than half of the regular hospital group. These findings are remarkable, because at the beginning of the study all of the patients had been rejected for community placement. One finding from this study that is of particular interest is the important role played by aftercare. The aftercare program originally consisted mainly of drug maintenance. However, because during the 6 months after release, all of the patients experienced a decline in their level of functioning, a consulting service was set up and was maintained for the remainder of the follow-up. The aftercare program was able to reverse the deterioration in the patients' performance after discharge.

Because none of the patients in the study had responded well to drugs in the early stages of their disorder, it may be that they represent a unique group within the general category of schizophrenic disorders. For this reason, the study should not be used to compare drug therapy with the two psychosocial therapies. However, the study does demonstrate that behavioral programs can be effective and that consultation services in an aftercare period are important in preventing deterioration after a return to the stress of life in the community.

Study Outline

Schizophrenic disorders are part of the category of mental disorders known as **psychoses,** which involve alterations of perception, thought, or consciousness. This category also includes some manias, certain severe depressions, paranoid states, and brief psychotic reactions.

CHARACTERISTICS OF SCHIZOPHRENIC DISORDERS

1. The major characteristics include unusual thought content and structure and perceptions of the environment; changes in emotional response; problems in self–other boundaries; and changes in motivations, relationships, level of function, and body movement.
2. The content and structure of schizophrenic thinking differs from normal thought. Loosening of associations, autistic thinking, and poverty of content are characteristic. The content of schizophrenic thought may be based on **delusions,** or faulty interpretations of reality that cannot be shaken despite evidence to the contrary. The structure of thinking is also disorderd.
3. Perceptional differences found in schizophrenia are accounted for mainly by **hallucinations,** or projections of internal impulses onto perceptual images in the external world. Only in schizophrenia do hallucinations occur when the person is in a clear, conscious state. Hallucinations may be auditory, visual, or related to touch or smell. Perception can be studied through thought sampling at specific randomly selected times. Brain scan devices can be used to study hallucinations. These can also be studied from psychodynamic, cognitive, or cultural perspectives.
4. Schizophrenic behavior may be characterized by inappropriate emotions, either by flat affect or emotion that does not fit the situation. **Loss of ego boundaries,** or an unclear sense of the self, is also typical. Sometimes unusual motor behavior can be observed, either frantic activity or rigid motionless posture.
5. Impaired motivation and interpersonal function are typical of schizophrenia. Former patients report that focusing their attention was their greatest problem.
6. To be diagnosed as having a schizophrenic disorder, a person must show deterioration from his or her previous level of functioning in work, social relations, or self-care. Continuous signs of illness must be present for at least six months, and psychotic behavior must be present at some point in the illness.

A HISTORICAL VIEW OF SCHIZOPHRENIC DISORDERS

1. One of the first writers to classify schizophrenia as a distinct disorder was Emil Kraepelin, who called it **dementia praecox.** Kraepelin believed that recovery from the disorder was impossible because it was caused by irreversible organic deterioration.
2. Eugen Bleuler was among the first writers to emphasize the psychological aspects of schizophrenia. He believed that schizophrenic symptoms might represent a group of disorders with different causes and outcomes.

The primary characteristics of schizophrenic behavior could be summed up as the "four A's"; alterations in affect, alterations in associations, ambivalence, and autism.

3. Since Bleuler's criteria were vaguely defined, the diagnosis of schizophrenia began to be used for behaviors that differed greatly. To deal with this problem, Kurt Schneider described a series of **first-** and **second-rank** symptoms. If first-rank symptoms (primarily abnormal inner experiences) were present and no organic cause was evident, a diagnosis of schizophrenia was justified.

TYPES OF SCHIZOPHRENIA

1. DSM-III-R classifies schizophrenic disorders into four categories: disorganized, catatonic, paranoid, and undifferentiated. There is also a residual category for cases in which the psychotic features are no longer prominent. People who have some symptoms of schizophrenia without ever exhibiting psychotic behavior are placed in the category **schizotypal personality disorder.**

2. **Disorganized schizophrenia** is characterized by profuse delusions and hallucinations, grimacing, and gesturing. People with this disorder behave actively but aimlessly and display inappropriate emotional responses.

3. The major symptom of **catatonic schizophrenia** is disturbance in motor activity. People with this disorder may remain stiffly immobile or may be extremely agitated.

4. **Paranoid schizophrenia** is characterized by delusions and sustained, extreme suspiciousness. Paranoid schizophrenics misinterpret the world around them and resist the feedback cues that most people use.

5. **Schizophrenic spectrum disorders** include unusual behaviors, such as eccentric dress, and certain personality disorders. Among the latter are schizotypal and paranoid personality disorders, schizoaffective disorder, atypical psychoses, and paranoid disorder.

POSITIVE AND NEGATIVE SYMPTOMS

1. Recently, researchers have studied subgroups of patients with positive and negative schizophrenic symptoms. **Positive symptoms** are characterized by behavioral excesses such as hallucinations, delusions, bizarre behavior, and disordered thinking. Patients with **negative symptoms** show behavior deficits such as poverty of speech content, apathy, seclusiveness, and impaired attention. In general, patients with positive symptoms are thought to have a better chance of resuming effective functioning than patients with negative symptoms. However, positive or negative symptoms experienced by people in their initial period of psychosis are not good predictors of long-term outcome.

OUTCOME INDICATORS AND LONG-TERM STUDIES

1. Predictions about the outcome of a schizophrenic disorder take into account a set of criteria including type of disorder, whether the psychosis appeared suddenly, and level of prepsychotic adjustment, as well as positive versus negative symptoms. The chances of recovery are greater for paranoids and catatonics, in cases in which there is a sudden onset, and when the individual showed adequate adjustment prior to the appearance of schizophrenia. The severity of the symptoms does not seem to be a good indicator of outcome.

2. Long-term studies of people who have been diagnosed as schizophrenic have found that whatever deterioration occurs happens in the first five years of illness, that there has been an increase in the number of milder chronic conditions, and that rehabilitation programs can have a positive effect on the functioning of deinstitutionalized patients. Probably about 20 percent of patients with a schizophrenic disorder avoid severe and chronic deterioration of behavior.

THERAPEUTIC APPROACHES

1. Perhaps the most universal treatment for schizophrenia is the use of antipsychotic drugs. Many people who improve as a result of drug therapy remain on a drug program after discharge from the hospital. In some cases overuse of drugs causes damage to the nervous system in the form of **tardive dyskinesia,** or involuntary movements of the mouth or other parts of the body.

2. The use of psychotherapy with schizophrenics has not been very successful. However, supportive therapy and family therapy may shorten hospitalization and help prevention readmission.

3. Behavior therapy that focuses on social skills training and basic survival skills can help prevent rehospitalization.

4. **Milieu therapy** involves providing a therapeutic environment by the involvement of all those who deal with the patient. Staff members and family members may be involved.

5. The attitudes of family members can make a difference in a discharged patient's chances of recovery. If the family's attitude is judgmental, hostile, and over-involved, the chances of a relapse are much higher than if the family has a positive attitude. Family members can be trained to modify critical or controlling attitudes.

6. Community support programs include halfway houses or group homes, day-care facilities, and mental health clinics. Such programs seem to be most effective for chronic patients who maintain contact with the program on a long-term basis. The combination of social-learning therapy with consultation services in an after-care period appears to be especially effective.

Henry Moore, *IX Standing Figures*, 1940. Chalk, pen, and watercolor. 10 1/2 × 7″. Tate Gallery, London.

OBJECTIVES FOR CHAPTER TWELVE:

To learn:

1. The general findings about genetic factors in schizophrenia
2. The meaning of assortive mating and the spectrum concept
3. The types of biological and cognitive differences found between patients with schizophrenia and controls

To understand:

1. How genetic vulnerability and family environment may interact
2. Why the search for genetic markers is important
3. The advantages and disadvantages of high risk studies

Genetic Factors

7

he cause of schizophrenic behavior is not known, although it seems likely that schizophrenia is produced by the interaction of vulnerability factors with some kind of environmental stress (Gottesman and others, 1987). This stress may come from disturbed family relationships, but it might also come from many other sources. Schizophrenic behavior has been investigated from many points of view. Experimental manipulation and observational research have both been used in attempts to determine how people who exhibit schizophrenic behavior differ from those who do not. Such factors as heredity, family structure, and biochemistry have been examined. Recently, attempts have been made to find out why some people who have a hereditary risk of schizophrenia develop it while others do not. This is referred to as the high-risk approach. Much current research in these high-risk studies is focused on markers or characteristics that may predict a person's vulnerability to schizophrenic disorders. If these can be identified, they may provide clues to how the disorders come about and how they can be prevented.

The risk of schizophrenia is greater for someone whose relatives have displayed schizophrenic behavior than it is for someone who does not have such relatives. This fact has long been recognized, but it does not definitely establish a hereditary factor in the development of schizophrenia. Merely living with a schizophrenic parent or sibling could create a stressful environment that is conducive to schizophrenic behavior (see Box 12–1). But

BOX 12-1

Growing Up as the Daughter of a Paranoid Schizophrenic

This account illustrates some of the stresses experienced by a child with a schizophrenic parent.

My mother is a paranoid schizophrenic. In the past I was afraid to admit it, but now that I've put it down on paper, I'll be able to say it again and again: Mother, schizophrenic, Mother, paranoid, shame, guilt, Mother, crazy, different, Mother, schizophrenia.

I have been teaching inpatient children on the children's ward of Bellevue Psychiatric Hospital in New York City for 13 years, and yet I'm still wary of revealing the nature of my mother's illness. When I tell my friends about my mother, even psychiatrist friends, I regret my openness and worry that they will find me peculiar. . . .

On the outside our house resembled those of our neighbors, but on the inside it was so different that there was no basis of comparison. Our house was a disaster. Everything was a mess. Nothing matched, furniture was broken, dishes were cracked, and there were coffee rings and cigarette burns clear across our grand piano. I was ashamed of our house. It was impossible to bring friends home. I never knew what my mother might be doing or how she would look.

She was totally unpredictable. At best she was working on a sculpture or practicing the piano, chain smoking and sipping stale coffee, with a dress too ragged to give to charity hanging from her emaciated body. At worst she was screaming at my father, still wearing her nightgown at 6 o'clock in the evening, a wild look on her face. I was never popular as a youngster, and I blamed my lack of popularity on my mother. . . .

Mother was quite interested in music and ballet, and she took me to every ballet and concert in Kansas City. She always looked terrible when she went out, and more than once she arrived at the theatre in her bedroom slippers. I was embarrassed to be seen with her, and before we left home, I would try to convince her to dress properly. She never listened and sometimes became angry, but chic or not, I accompanied her.

I loved music and dance as much as she did. I even gave up Saturday afternoons to stay home with her and listen to the Metropolitan Opera broadcasts, and I loved her most and felt closest to her sitting in front of a gas fire, feeling her bony arm around my shoulders as we listened to the music together. Throughout my childhood I was torn between my bizarre but loving artist–mother and the conventional mothers of my friends. . . .

Trying to make up for my mother's shortcomings was one of the major preoccupations of my early years. I was always cleaning and straightening up the house, vainly hoping to restore order, even as early as age 4, according to one of my aunts. I took care of my brothers, but I bitterly resented the fact that no one took care of me. I felt cheated by having to arrange my own birthday parties, ordering the cake, inviting friends, and choosing the present although I willingly organized parties for my younger brothers. . . .

When I was in high school, Mother and I shared a room with twin beds. When Mother was lying down, she would start to moan as if she were talking in her sleep. "I can't stand that girl. She's evil; she's a bitch. She's just like her father." I was terrorized, but I dared not move. I felt I had to pretend to be asleep, because I didn't want her to know I was listening. I tried to deny the reality of Mother's illness by acknowledging the outbursts. I used to lie in bed, wishing I were dead, believing that I was the worthless girl she was describing. . . . My oldest brother was the target of the same kinds of insults, and we comforted each other. . . .

Next Mother began to insult strangers on the street. She would stop in front of a well-dressed bourgeois of Kansas City, fix her eyes on him for a few seconds, and snap angrily. "What's wrong with you? Why are you looking at me like that? I'm going to tell my lawyer." If my brother or I were with her, we'd be so embarrassed that we'd want to disappear into a crack in the sidewalk. No matter what we did, she wouldn't stop. (Lanquetot, 1984, pp. 467–469)

Family Studies

We know, of course, that relatives share a greater proportion of their genes than unrelated people do and that the closer the relationship, the greater the number of

researchers have struggled with this question for a long time and have established quite clearly that there is a hereditary risk factor in schizophrenia (Deutsch and Davis, 1983). Genetic studies that focus on the hereditary factors in schizophrenia are usually of three main types: family studies, twin studies, and adoption studies.

shared genes. If a disorder is genetically determined, the individuals who are closest in heredity to the diagnosed person (who is often called the *proband* or *index case*) should be at greatest risk of also showing signs of the disorder. Therefore, a common strategy is to compare the prevalence of a disorder in relatives of affected individuals with its prevalence in the general population. Such comparisons are illustrated in Table 12-1. The data in the table show clearly that the more genes two individuals have in common, the higher the risk of the disorder for one when the other has a schizophrenic disorder. Yet this relationship is not a perfect one. Even twin pairs who share the same heredity do not always share the diagnosis of schizophrenia.

Another interesting finding, also shown in Table 12-1, is that the siblings and children of index cases seem to have a higher risk of becoming schizophrenic than the parents of index cases. The reasons for this are not clear, although the same finding has turned up in several studies. The reason may be simply that many schizophrenic individuals do not become parents. Many factors influence whether a person will become a parent. Some of these, such as ability to get and keep a job, form relationships with others, and so on, may tend to be absent in schizophrenic individuals, with the result that they do not have children.

Assortive Mating

One factor that may affect the risk for schizophrenia or other disorders is **assortive mating**. This term refers to the tendency for people to mate with others who are more similar to them than would be the case if their choices were random. Assortive mating occurs for physical traits, psychological traits, and behavior disorders. Table 12-1 shows that the spouses of schizophrenic individuals are more likely than members of the general public to be diagnosed as schizophrenic. This means that their children may get "double doses" of genes associated with disordered behaviors.

Genetic Specificity and the Spectrum Concept

Family studies focus not only on the overall risks for different family relationships but also on exactly how the hereditary mechanisms work. Early in the history of genetic studies of disordered behavior, it was assumed that what people inherited was simply an increased chance of developing some "mental disease." Current knowledge of heredity suggests that various disorders, or at least different groups of disorders, have genetic causes. This is called their **genetic specificity**. In addition to determining specific patterns of heredity for different disorders, family studies provide information about the relationships between schizophrenia and other disorders that may appear in families. If several particular disorders typically occur together in families, this suggests that those disorders may be genetically similar. This is called the **spectrum concept**.

In spite of the fact that schizophrenia includes many different symptom patterns, in general the genetic factors seem to have specificity because these factors do not increase the risk for major mood disorder or delusional disorder (Gottesman and others, 1987). In addition to this specificity, genetic studies provide some support for the idea of a group of related disorders that may have a common genetic base with schizophrenia. All of these disorders, called **schizophrenic spectrum disorders**, include eccentric behavior and disordered and unusual styles of thinking, but they vary in how severely they disrupt a person's functioning. Disorders usually included in the schizophrenic spectrum include schizotypal personality, paranoid personality, and schizoaffective disorders in addition to schizophrenia. (Schizoaffective disorders have characteristics of schizophrenia combined at some times with major depressive or manic behavior.)

In one large study designed to investigate the spectrum concept, the rate of occurrence of mental disorders in relatives of patients who had been hospitalized for schizophrenia was compared with the rate for relatives of surgical patients from the same hospital (Ken-

TABLE 12-1

Risk of Developing Schizophrenic Disorder for Relatives of a Person with This Diagnosis

Relationship to Person with Diagnosis	Risk (percent)
First-degree relatives	
Parent	4.4
Brother or sister (in general)	8.5
With neither parent schizophrenic	8.2
With one parent also schizophrenic	13.8
Dizygotic twin	13.7
Monozygotic twin	46.0
Child (in general)	12.8
Child with other parent also schizophrenic	36.6
Second-degree relatives	
Uncle or aunt	2.0
Nephew or niece	3.5
Grandchild	5.0
Half-brother or half-sister	6.0
Third-degree relatives (first cousin)	2.4
No blood relationship	
Spouse	2.3
General population	0.86

Based on Tsuang and Vandermey, 1980; Gottesman and others (1987).

One environmental variable that can differ even for identical twins is the environment experienced before birth. One study compared 100 pairs of MZ twins in which one member had schizophrenia and the other did not. The schizophrenic twin was twice as likely to have weighed less at birth than the nonschizophrenic twin (Stabenau and Pollin, 1967). The differences in birth weight might have been due to a condition in the mother's uterus that influenced one twin but not the other. For example, one twin may have suffered mild brain damage that predisposed it to develop schizophrenia. The twin who became schizophrenic was also more likely to have had an illness in which the central nervous system was affected. In addition, the schizophrenic twins were described as having been less intelligent and outgoing than the nonschizophrenic twins prior to developing the disorder.

Whatever environmental similarities identical twins experience after birth seem to be created more by behavioral similarities in the twins themselves than by aspects of their environment (Kendler, 1983). In contrast to what might be expected, twins who are reared apart are more similar in personality than twins who are reared together (Farber, 1983). The more contact the twins have, the less similar their personalities seem.

Twins do not occur frequently in the population, and twins who are adopted at or near birth—so that they grow up in clearly different environments—are extremely rare. This means that twin adoption studies base their conclusions on scanty evidence. Even rarer are pairs of twins reared apart in which at least one twin develops a schizophrenic disorder. One researcher found only nine such pairs in her review of all the twin studies that had been done (Farber, 1983). In six of these pairs (67%), both twins had schizophrenic disorders, a rate that is very similar to the rate for monozygotic twins reared together.

In order to put these hereditary factors in perspective, it may help to compare the hereditary risk for schizophrenia with the hereditary risk for other disorders. In general, twin studies show that genetic factors are at least as important in the development of schizophrenic disorders as they are in diabetes, hypertension (high blood pressure), coronary artery disease, and ulcers, all of which have a strong genetic component (Kendler, 1983).

Adoption Studies

Another way of studying the effects of heredity on the development of schizophrenia is through adoption studies. Figure 12–1 shows the influence of both hereditary and environment on an adopted child. The solid arrows represent direct relationships. The influence of genetic

dler and others, 1985). When family groups were compared, 9 percent of the families of schizophrenic patients and less than 1 percent of the families of surgical patients contained at least one other schizophrenic member. Overall, the relatives of the patients with schizophrenic disorders had higher rates of nonaffective psychosis, especially schizophrenia and schizoaffective disorders. This supported the idea of a schizophrenic spectrum of genetically related disorders. Another interesting finding was that although the overall rate of mood disorders was no higher among the relatives of schizophrenic patients than in the control group, relatives of patients who did have these affective disorders were more likely than relatives of control patients to have psychotic symptoms.

Twin Studies

While family studies can give an overall picture of hereditary risks in schizophrenia and the possible genetic relationships among disorders, twin studies provide a way to focus on the environmental factors that contribute to schizophrenic disorders while keeping the hereditary factors constant. This is possible because identical or monozygotic (MZ) twins are produced from the same fertilized egg and therefore have identical heredity. Fraternal or dizygotic (DZ) twins are produced from two fertilized eggs; they have the same genetic relationship as any other brothers and sisters.

Early studies of twins were flawed because there was no convenient method of determining whether the twin pair was of the MZ or DZ type. (Of course, twins of opposite sexes are always DZ.) Now that such a test is available, one source of error has been removed from twin studies. Another problem was that older studies often used only patients who had been hospitalized on a long-term basis. Recent studies are much more sophisticated: they use consecutive admissions to an institution or data from birth registrations to obtain the twins for study. About a dozen major twin studies have been carried out. All show that MZ twins have a greater chance of being concordant for schizophrenia than DZ twins do. (Concordance is a measure of agreement. In this case it means the percent of the time that when one twin was diagnozed as schizophrenic, the other twin would be diagnosed as schizophrenic also.)

In considering a genetic explanation, the fact that there is less than 100-percent concordance for schizophrenia in monozygotic twins cannot be ignored. This finding makes it clear that heredity alone is not enough to produce a schizophrenic disorder, at least in most people. Researchers therefore are focusing on environmental variables that may interact with inherited predispositions.

factors can be assessed by studying the relationship between the biological parents and the adopted child (arrow 1) and holding other things constant. Pre- and postbirth factors and the effects of the adoptive family (arrows 2, 6, and 7) are all environmental factors that can be studied. The indirect relationships shown by the dashed-line arrows are also important. They are potential correlations that could affect the direct outcomes that were shown by arrows 1, 2, 6, and 7. Arrow 3 refers to possible similarities between the behaviors of biological and adoptive parents, and arrow 8 refers to possible similarities in the environment they create. Adoption agencies often place children with adoptive families that are judged similar in intelligence level or socioeconomic position to the biological parents (Scarr, 1981). Arrow 4 refers to possible prebirth or at-birth factors related to the biological mother that might add to the risk status of the adopted child. These could include poor diet, smoking, alcohol or other drug abuse, poor medical care or heightened risk of labor, and delivery problems because of a very young mother. Arrow 5 represents the obvious effects of the environment in the adopted family. By keeping all these factors in mind and controlling for those that are not the variables under investigation, researchers can arrive at a clearer understanding of the role environment and heredity may play in schizophrenia.

There are three basic kinds of adoption studies: those that compare adopted children whose biological

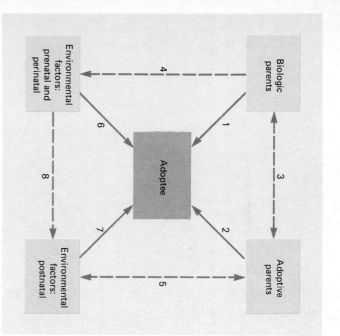

FIGURE 12-1
Possible sources of hereditary and environmental factors that may affect an adopted child. Solid lines show direct relationships. Dashed lines show indirect relationships. The text explains the diagram further. (Cadoret, 1986, p. 53)

parents were diagnosed as schizophrenic with adopted children whose parents did not have this disorder; those that examine the incidence of schizophrenia in the biological and adoptive families of adopted people who became schizophrenic; and those that study the relatively rare individuals who have nonschizophrenic biological parents but whose adoptive parents became schizophrenic.

One of the first large adoption studies ever conducted was reported by a group of Danish and American researchers working in Denmark (Rosenthal and others, 1968, 1975). First the researchers searched the government adoption register of the Copenhagen area to find the names of parents who had given up their children to nonfamily members for adoption. Then they searched the official psychiatric register to see if they could find the names of any of those parents. The records of those who were found were rated, and those that clearly fit a strict definition of schizophrenia were selected. The children who had been given up for adoption by these parents became the index cases. The control group consisted of the adopted children whose parents had no psychiatric history. Three of the 39 index cases and none of the 47 controls were diagnosed as definitely schizophrenic. This high rate (8 percent compared to 0 percent) in the index group points to a hereditary factor. The children of schizophrenic parents also had a higher risk of other schizophrenic spectrum disorders (26 percent compared to 15 percent).

In another kind of adoption study, Kety and his colleagues (1978) took advantage of the comprehensive records kept by the Danish government to locate people who had been adopted and had later become schizophrenic. They compared the frequencies of schizophrenia or other disturbances in the adoptees' biological and adoptive relatives. They also compared these findings with those for relatives of a control group of adoptees who had not been diagnosed as schizophrenic. They found that about twice as many blood relatives as adoptive relatives of schizophrenics had been diagnosed as definitely or possibly schizophrenic. Both rates were higher than those for the control group.

This study also contained an important subsample: half-brothers and half-sisters of the adopted individual who had the same father. Half-siblings share 25 percent of their genes, rather than 50 percent as full siblings do. However, half-siblings with a common father do not share the environment in the uterus before birth (e.g., chemical factor), nor do they share birth traumas and early mothering experience. These paternal half-brother and half-sisters were also found to have a greater risk of schizophrenia and schizophrenic spectrum disorders than the control group. This finding gave increased weight to the importance of genetic factors in schizophrenia. Because the DSM definition of schizophrenia has been narrowed or made more restrictive over time, some of the index cases in these studies would not now be classified as schizophrenic; instead they would be considered to fall within one of the schizophrenic spectrum disorders. Nonetheless, once redefined in this way, the schizophrenic index cases and those now defined as spectrum index cases both had many more relatives with schizophrenic spectrum disorders than the control subjects did (Kendler and Gruenberg, 1984).

A third kind of adoption study is called a **cross-fostering study.** Such a study asks whether children whose biological parents are nonschizophrenic but who are reared by a schizophrenic foster parent are more likely to become schizophrenic than either of two other groups: children with a schizophrenic biological parent or children with nonschizophrenic heredity who are reared by normal individuals. Wender and others (1974) found that it made no difference in the incidence of schizophrenia of the children whether they were reared by schizophrenic or normal adoptive parents. Almost twice as many children with schizophrenic heredity as children without such heredity became schizophrenic in both types of homes. This study suggests that rearing by a schizophrenic adoptive parent does not increase a person's chances of developing schizophrenia.

dicted number of individuals will carry the potential for schizophrenia—they will have the right genetic makeup—but not all of them will become schizophrenic because they are not exposed to significant environmental stress. Another way to explain this difference in predicted and observed frequency is to use the **schizophrenic spectrum view** to broaden the diagnostic criteria to include relatives of schizophrenics who show related disorders.

Polygenic models assume that a number of genes found at specific locations must interact to produce a trait. Many characteristics including height, weight, and skin color, are thought to be influenced by more than one gene. Some models suggest that a limited number of genes and locations are involved. Other polygenic models, called **multifactorial polygenic models,** do not specify the number of gene loci involved in schizophrenia. Instead, they assume that there are many of them

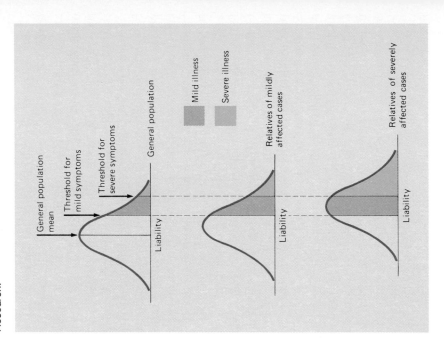

FIGURE 12-2
These distributions show the liability of mild and severe disorders within the schizophrenic spectrum for the general population and for relatives of those with mild and severe disorders. If the liability is greater than the threshold, the disorder can be noted. Relatives of those who are severely affected have a greater risk for both mild and severe diagnoses themselves than the relatives of those who are mildly affected. (Adapted from Baron and Risch, 1987, p. 260. Reprinted with permission from the *Journal of Psychiatric Research.*

A Genetic Model

In studies of heredity, predictions based on theoretical models are compared with the observed frequency of occurrence of various characteristics. If the model is a good one, the agreement between prediction and observation should be close. The two major types of models show the transmission of inherited traits by one gene (monogenic) and by more than one gene (polygenic). A third model involves genetic heterogeneity.

Monogenic models are based on the idea that the genetic transmission that occurs at one locus (the place occupied by a gene pair on a particular chromosome) is all that is necessary to produce a particular characteristic. At any one locus, one gene of the pair may be dominant over the other. That means that the characteristic carried by that dominant gene—say, brown eyes—will be **expressed;** that is, the person will have brown eyes. A recessive trait—for example, blue eyes—will not be expressed unless both members of the gene pair carry the characteristic for blue eyes.

In investigating the genetics of schizophrenia, researchers originally looked for distributions based on a monogenic model, but they did not find them. The number of cases of schizophrenia in relatives of schizophrenics is always less than would be expected by monogenic models. One way of explaining this is to use the concept of **penetrance.** According to this idea, a pre-

and that they are interchangeable. What happens is that genes at all of these loci may have small additive effects on a person's vulnerability to schizophrenia. According to this view, many people have some predisposition to develop schizophrenia. If their predisposition is over a certain threshold, they will develop a schizophrenic disorder; if their liability is below that threshold, they will not (Gottesman and others, 1987). This kind of polygenic model can be expanded to include two different levels of liability. Figure 12-2 illustrates such a model. People to the right of the right-hand threshold would develop a severe form of schizophrenia while those to the left of the left-hand threshold would not be schizophrenic. Those between the two thresholds would develop a mild form of the disorder. Using a complex statistical technique called path analysis, this model seems to predict outcome fairly well for several large sets of data that have been collected to date (McGue and others, 1985; Faraone and Tsuang, 1985).

Genetic theorists tend to favor multifactorial polygenic models of heredity over single major locus models, but some combination of the two cannot yet be ruled out. The varying results from one study to another make it seem likely that schizophrenic disorders are not all based on the same genetic transmission. Figure

12-3 suggests one way of organizing the possible subtypes. The solid lines represent divisions that are generally supported by research findings; the dotted lines represent guesses based on what is currently known.

Genetic Counseling

People seek genetic counseling to learn more about the risk of schizophrenia for themselves, their relatives, or their potential children. This may happen because a relative has been diagnosed as having a schizophrenic disorder or because the individual is thinking of marriage or childbearing. A genetic counselor does not ordinarily give advice but instead presents whatever is known about the risk factors. Because the inheritance of schizophrenia is complex and is not clearly understood at present, a genetic counselor must judge the risks for a particular family on the basis of both theoretical and practical information. Computer programs are available to calculate the exact theoretical risk based on varying combinations of affected and nonaffected relatives. However, because this and other models may not be correct, risk figures can be very inaccurate. Even worse, some individuals may be more vulnerable than

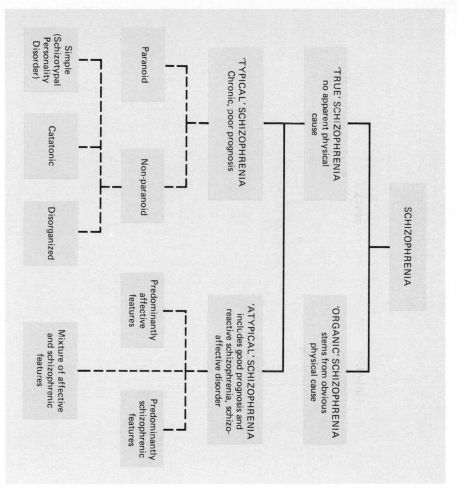

FIGURE 12-3
A model showing one possible division of schizophrenia into genetic types. (From Tsuang and Vandermey, *Genes and the Mind* [Oxford, England: Oxford University Press, 1980]).

others, the amount of risk they bear can vary greatly. The severity of the disorder in the affected relatives, how chronic the behavior is, and the age at which the disorder began all influence vulnerability. If some of those in the family have not yet passed through the age range where the risk of schizophrenia is greatest, they may still have a chance of developing it and thus changing the predictive risk greatly. If work on genetic markers leads to more certain identification of those at greater risk, genetic counseling for schizophrenia can become more precise. Although there is usually minimal risk of schizophrenia developing in a child of a normal parent with a relative who has schizophrenic disorder, the information received from a genetic counselor should be combined with the use of other counseling and therapeutic services (Reveley, 1985).

Vulnerability and Stress Factors

Although this model can be applied to all behavior, in the area of schizophrenia it has been particularly clearly defined by Joseph Zubin (Zubin and others, 1982; Zubin & Spring, 1977). Zubin's hypothesis assumes that schizophrenia is not a permanent disorder but rather a permanent vulnerability to a disorder. Each person has a level of vulnerability to schizophrenia determined by genetic inheritance and prenatal and postnatal physical factors. This level, which may range from no risk to near certainty interacts with stressful events or conditions in a person's life (see Figure 12–4). If the combination exceeds a certain critical level, schizophrenic behavior will occur. Zubin's idea of vulnerability offers one way of understanding why if one identical twin has a schizophrenic disorder, the other twin's chances of also having the disorder is not 100 percent.

According to the traditional biological perspective on schizophrenic disorder, once it occurs in a person, he or she is thought to have the disorder from that time on. Zubin's model has quite a different emphasis. It assumes that when the stressors decrease, the schizophrenic disorder will abate and the person will return to his or her earlier level of functioning (see Figure 12–5).

Manfred Bleuler did a long-term study of patients treated in a large clinic and his findings support Zubin's approach (Bleuler, 1978). About 80 percent of the schizophrenic individuals in Bleuler's' follow-up study had either one or multiple hospitalizations followed by being discharged as improved. About one-third of all former patients were never rehospitalized after their first hospitalization. These findings and those reported in Chapter 11 support the idea that schizophrenia may be an episodic disorder, at least for some people. Most present-day researchers, regardless of whether or not they accept Zubin's statements, would agree that a

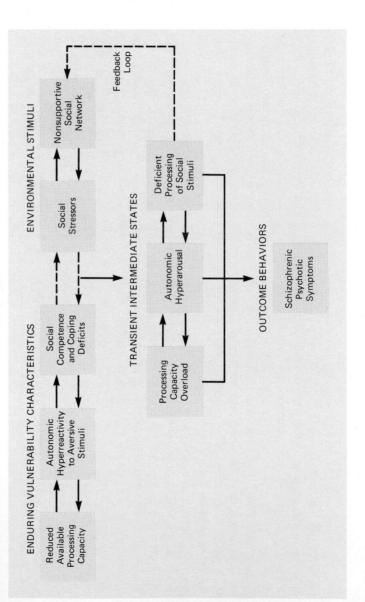

FIGURE 12-4

A model showing how stress and vulnerability may interact in the development of schizophrenic psychotic episodes. (From Nuechterlein and Dawson, 1984, p. 304)

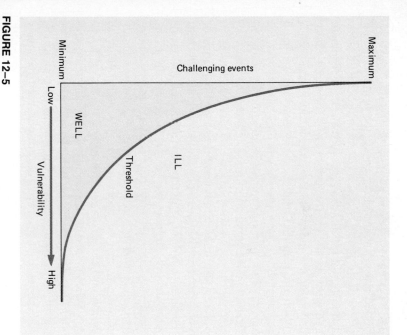

FIGURE 12-5
The relationship between vulnerability and challenging events.
(From Zubin and others, 1982)

schizophrenic disorder is almost always a product of several factors including biological make-up, coping skills, environmental condition, and life events.

An adoption study carried out in Finland supports this point of view (Tienari and others, 1987). The study paired adopted children whose biological mothers were schizophrenic with adopted children whose biological parents were not schizophrenic. First, the researchers collected information about the nearly 20,000 women who had been treated in psychiatric hospitals in Finland at some time during a 10-year period. From this group they found 171 women who had been diagnosed as schizophrenic and who had a child who was adopted by a nonrelative Finnish family before the child was 4 years old. We can appreciate how complex are the tasks required to complete an adoption study by considering the following. First, in this study a large number of cases had to be investigated to determine which of the women in the original sample who were diagnosed as schizophrenic had had a baby and, further, to identify those who had given up the baby for adoption. Fewer than 1 in 100 of the original cases qualified. All that effort had to be expended before the study could even get under way. Some of the other tasks the researchers faced were:

1. Selecting two adopted children as matched controls for each index case

2. Checking the psychiatric histories of the control children's parents

3. Administering structured interviews to all the biological mothers, thus providing a diagnosis with which to compare the diagnosis in the hospital records

4. Interviewing the biological father of each index group member to evaluate whether he had a psychiatric disorder that would add to risk for the child

5. Evaluation of the child-rearing environment of each adoptive family for each index and control child:
   a. Interview with the entire family
   b. Joint interview with both adoptive parents
   c. Psychological testing of adoptive parents together and then also with their adoptive child
   d. Comprehensive test battery for each child and each adoptive parent, separately
   e. Follow-up assessments 5 to 7 years after the initial assessment.

In general the people in the control group are much healthier than those in the index group. Fourteen percent of the control group have a severe psychological disorder compared to 30 percent of the index group.

Data from this Finnish study will not be complete for a long time. One reason is that many of the adopted children have yet to reach or complete the age span of greatest risk for schizophrenia. Figure 12-6 shows percentages for each index-subject age group as they are broken down into different kinds of disorders.

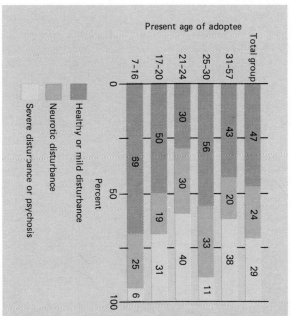

FIGURE 12-6
A comparison of the probability of development of disordered behavior, especially severe psychological disorder, in different age groups of adoptees whose biological mothers were schizophrenic. (Adapted from Tienari and others, 1987, p. 481)

One and one-half percent of the control group have developed a psychotic disorder compared to more than 7 percent of the index group. Most interesting of all is the relationship of psychological problems and environment of adoptive family for the index cases. The study's findings about the index children, shown in Figure 12–7, support the idea that healthy family environment has a protective effect for children who may be at risk for schizophrenia. None of the 49 index children reared in a healthy or only mildly disturbed environment have become psychotic. In comparison, 37 percent of those in a severely disturbed family have developed psychosis or some psychotic characteristics. These findings, although preliminary until the children have all passed the age of maximum risk, support the view that genetically transmitted vulnerability may be necessary for a schizophrenic disorder to occur but that a disturbed family environment may be necessary for that vulnerability to develop into a schizophrenic disorder.

When a person experiences a schizophrenic episode, even if it is clearly brought about by a high stress level resulting from negative environmental conditions, the experience of the psychotic episode itself has many negative implications. Figure 12–8 illustrates the com-

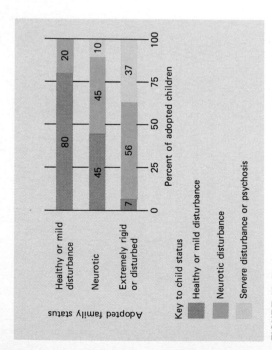

FIGURE 12–7
Whether or not children of schizophrenic mothers develop disturbed behavior seems to depend on the characteristics of their adopted families as well as on heredity. (Adapted from Tienari and others, 1987, p. 483)

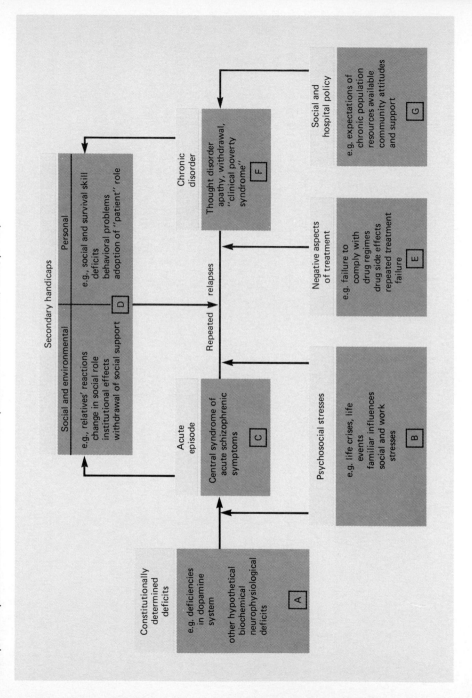

FIGURE 12–8
An interactionist model of schizophrenia showing the many ways in which the consequences of a schizophrenic episode continue to affect the individual. (Marzillier and Birchwood, 1981, p. 142)

342   CHAPTER 12   Causes and Markers of Schizophrenia

plex interactions that may occur after a stressor (B) sets off schizophrenic behavior based on an underlying vulnerability (A). The episode leads to personal and social handicaps (D) that result from the schizophrenic episode. New episodes are likely to occur if there are further psychosocial stresses, or from the added psychosocial handicaps or negative aspects of treatment (B, D, and E). To prevent the disorder from becoming chronic, both hospital treatment policies and social attitudes toward people who have been mentally ill need to be improved.

Although the vulnerability approach includes awareness of biological and environmental interactions, it emphasizes that the disorder is episodic, and that it may come and go in a vulnerable individual depending on the amount of stress in his or her environment.

The vulnerability theory suggests that research efforts in the areas of genetics and psychophysiology can be of great use in pointing out **markers**, or characteristics that can be used to identify vulnerable people. Efforts can then be directed toward helping these individuals avoid the degree of stress that might produce a schizophrenic disorder. This can be done both by providing a supportive environment and by helping vulnerable individuals develop better coping skills so that the unavoidable stressors of life will not affect them so severely. Most of the remainder of this chapter will be devoted to a discussion of the search for markers of vulnerability to schizophrenia.

High-risk Studies and the Search for Markers

One way of studying the causal factors in schizophrenia is to study children beginning in infancy or early childhood and compare the records of those who later become schizophrenic with those who do not. This type of research has several advantages.

1. The subjects can be studied before those who develop disorders have experienced hospitalization and drugs.

2. None of the researchers, relatives, teachers, or subjects know who will become schizophrenic. This removes one potential source of bias in their observations and reports.

3. The information obtained is relatively current when it is gathered. Questions about teenage dating patterns and frequency, for example, are answered more accurately by adolescents than they would be by a 30-year-old schizophrenic patient and his or her 55-year-old mother.

4. The data can be obtained uniformly, not by relying on records from various agencies and individuals working in different ways.

This type of study avoids many problems that arise in dealing with an individual who is already schizophrenic. For example, it is not necessary to rely on the patients' and their families' sometimes faulty and selective memories of past events. This is especially important because once a diagnosis of schizophrenic disorder has been made, everyone in the family may see past events in a different light. Studying the person and his or her family after schizophrenia has developed tells more about the consequences of having a schizophrenic disorder than about its causes. The diagnosis of schizophrenia means that the person has already suffered educational, economic, and social failures and may also have experienced hospitalization and extensive drug therapy. These factors alone may explain many of the differences that researchers find between schizophrenic and control groups.

However, there is one severe problem with longitudinal studies that test people before they become ill and later compare the records for those who develop schizophrenia with those who do not. Since only about 1 percent of the population becomes schizophrenic, many thousands of people would have to be tested in order to be sure that the schizophrenic group would make a large enough sample for useful research. One way to cope with this problem is to do a high-risk study. This means that the researcher selects for study a group that is thought to have a higher potential or risk of schizophrenia than the population in general. One such group consists of children who have at least one schizophrenic parent. The Finnish study described earlier represents a sophisticated high-risk study in which the interaction between environment and heredity can be studied because the subjects were all adopted. Most high-risk studies focus on understanding the differences among children who do and do not develop problems despite the fact that all may have a genetic vulnerability (Mednick and Schulsinger, 1968; Mednick and others, 1984).

A pioneering high-risk study was carried out in Denmark beginning in 1962. Since this study began, many other high-risk studies have been started. Most of the studies are longitudinal and compare children of a schizophrenic parent or parents with children of parents with other psychological disorders and with normal children. However, a study being done at the University of Minnesota is cross-sectional with a short-term follow-up, and compares not only children who are vulnerable because they have schizophrenic parents but also children who are vulnerable because they themselves have engaged in aggressive, bullying behavior or hyperactivity (Garmezy and Devine, 1984). A high-risk study being done at the University of Rochester combines cross-sectional and longitudinal approaches by comparing boys in several age groups at initial testing and over time (Wynn and others, 1987). Some of the results from these studies are presented in Table 12-2.

Another high-risk study with a unique design is being conducted in Israel (Nagler and Mirsky, 1985). This study also compares high-risk children with a schizophrenic parent and matched controls. However, it adds another factor: whether the family lives in a conventional town setting or on a kibbutz, where the children live together and are cared for by a child-care worker. Although kibbutz children visit their parents and eat with them, their parental contacts are much more limited than is usual in a traditional family. One finding of a 15-year follow-up of these individuals is particularly surprising: the only group that showed an increased risk for some mental disorder was the high-risk group who lived on the kibbutz. The reason for this is not clear, but perhaps kibbutz living causes increased stress, for instance, because of lack of privacy, pressure to conform to a common goal, or the greater likelihood that others will know that a person has a schizophrenic parent.

Much research on high-risk subjects has focused on identifying markers for schizophrenia by determining the distinctive early characteristics of children who ultimately become schizophrenic. Table 12-3 lists the characteristics a marker should have to make it useful in detecting genetic biological risk. So far the search for markers suggests several conclusions (Lewine, 1984).

1. A marker, if it exists, may reflect vulnerability to psychosis in general rather than specifically to schizophrenia. When children whose parents have nonschizophrenic psychoses are included, these children also differ from normal controls.

TABLE 12-2

Markers of Increased Risk of Schizophrenia from High-Risk Studies

Childbirth problems—low birthweight and difficult birth
Poor emotional bonding—lack of a close relationship with the mother in the first 3 years of life
Poor motor coordination in infancy
Separation from parents—being raised in an institution or foster home
Intellectual deficits—poor performance on intelligence tests, especially in verbal abilities
Cognitive deficits—distractability and problems in focusing attention
Social deficits—aggressive behavior, anger, abrasiveness
Confusion and hostility in parent-child communication

N. F. Watt (Ed.), *Children at Risk for Schizophrenia: A Longitudinal Perspective.* New York: Cambridge University Press, 1984.

TABLE 12-3

Characteristics Necessary for Useful Markers of Genetic Biological Risk

1. The marker is distributed differently in psychotic than in control populations.
2. The marker is a stable trait rather than a deviation associated with a particular set of temporary circumstances.
3. The marker occurs with higher frequency in family members of identified deviant psychotics than in the general population, and is associated with psychotic spectrum disorder in family members.
4. The marker also occurs at higher frequency in offspring of deviant psychotics before development of psychotic spectrum disease that meets diagnostic criteria.
5. The marker in the offspring is associated with later development of psychotic spectrum disease.
6. Determination of the marker is relatively noninvasive and can be used by a variety of investigators with high reliability

Adapted from Garver, 1987, p. 526.

2. Changes over time, rather than particular traits, may be the most important markers.
3. Among the children in the high-risk group, only some (11 to 14 percent) are clearly deviant.

High-risk studies are making an important contribution to knowledge about schizophrenia. However, they have an important drawback. Since only about 15 percent of all people who become schizophrenic have one or more schizophrenic parents, it may be that the data from these studies apply only to a specific subtype of schizophrenia. As is true of other research carried out on a specific population—such as college students, members of the armed forces, or relatives of hospital patients—it is not clear what general statements can be made from findings based on a particular group. However, because they focus attention on vulnerabilities, the results of high-risk studies may play an important role in the design of prevention programs.

Understanding the Schizophrenic Process

Structural Abnormalities in the Brain

The search for structural abnormalities in the brain that are related to schizophrenia or other disordered behavior has a long history but has produced little in the way of meaningful data. New technology may make this research topic popular again. New scanning techniques make it possible to look at the structure and the function of the living brain without physically intrusive procedures that might harm the patient. More about these scanning techniques is presented in Chapter 13.

One finding that has emerged from the use of scanning techniques is that some schizophrenics have significantly larger **cerebral ventricles** (cavities that contain cerebrospinal fluid) than those found in the brains of nonschizophrenics (see Figure 12–9). The size of the cerebral ventricle in normal individuals is thought to increase with age. When schizophrenic patients are compared with controls of the same age, between one-quarter and one-half of the schizophrenics have significantly larger ventricles than the controls (Weinberger, 1984). This is true both for younger individuals who have a history of intermittent hospitalization and for older and chronic patients who have been hospitalized a long time. In several studies, patients with schizophrenia were found to have larger ventricles than their brothers and sisters, including monozygotic twins of the patients (Andreasen, 1988).

The illustrations in Figure 12–9 are magnetic resonance imaging scans which compare a vertical section of a schizophrenic patient's head with that of a normal

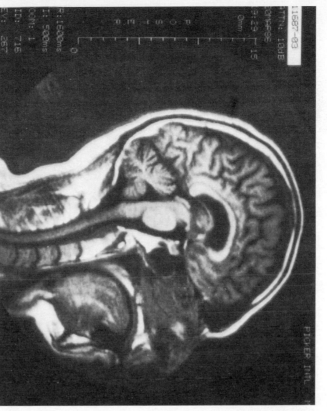

(a)

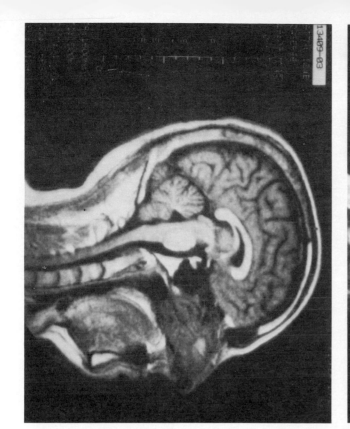

(b)

FIGURE 12–9
These scans produced by a technique called magnetic resonance imaging (MRI) show the enlarged ventricles, decreased volume of the frontal lobes, and widened sulci which are found in some patients with a schizophrenic disorder. (a) MRI scan of a patient with a schizophrenic disorder. (b) A normal control.

individual. Note the enlarged ventricle of the former (the crescent-shaped area in the center) as well as the smaller size of the frontal lobe and the widened sulci or indentations in the surface of the brain. These changes suggest to researchers that at least part of the cause of schizophrenia must date from the early years of life. Likely causes for such changes might be injuries at or before birth, or injuries, infection, or nutritional problems shortly after birth.

Ventricular enlargement may be a biological marker for schizophrenia. It is usually associated with negative symptoms and a poor outcome (Erlenmeyer-Kimling and Cornblatt, 1987) although not all studies agree on this (Farmer and others, 1987). In order to determine what these differences in brain anatomy mean, it will be important to follow high-risk people over time to see when and how these changes in brain anatomy occur in relation to the development of the disorder.

Biochemical Abnormalities in the Brain

There are strong arguments for the assumption that biochemical factors play a role in at least some of the schizophrenias. An impetus to the search for biochemical clues has been provided by the effectiveness of some antipsychotic drugs, which are known to produce certain biochemical changes. However, most earlier research findings that indicate biochemical differences between schizophrenic patients and control individuals have not been confirmed by later studies.

It is not difficult to find organic or biochemical differences between schizophrenics and control subjects. The problem lies in finding an explanation that takes account of all the possible causes of a particular result. Part of the problem is poor experimental design. Often the control group lives under very different conditions than the patient group. For example, many of the people used in earlier studies had been hospitalized for many years, led sedentary lives, ate routine hospital diets, and had been treated with various drugs; they may have been under constant stress, which also has been shown to cause biological changes. The control groups, on the other hand, consisted of college students, hospital nurses, or nonprofessional employees, whose lives obviously differed from those of the patients in many ways. The experimental findings may simply reflect these differences.

Recent developments in technology and the discovery of new neurochemical systems in the body have enabled researchers to take a more sophisticated approach to biological differences than was possible in the past. Instead of being forced to look for the presence of some abnormal substance that is unique to schizophrenics, investigators are now able to look for abnormalities in biochemical *functioning*.

PT Scans

A technology that may provide breakthroughs in the study of chemical activity in the living human brain is the positron emission tomography (PT) scan. This scan shows what is going on chemically inside the brain by recording radiation from a glucoselike substance injected into the individual's bloodstream. The injected material enters the brain and is used by the working brain cells, and the PT scanner records this activity in a series of thin cross sections of the brain. Initial use of this technique with psychiatric patients suggests that the PT scan can be used to distinguish among the brains of control subjects, patients who have been diagnosed as having bipolar disorders, and patients with a diagnosis of schizophrenia (see Figure 12–10). In addition, the PT scan has been used to observe changes in biochemical action in the brain caused by antipsychotic drugs.

One of the findings of research using PT scans is that people who are chronically schizophrenic tend to have a lower level of metabolism in the frontal and temporal lobes of their brains and a somewhat higher flow at the base of the skull than control subjects. When the schizophrenic patients were given psychoactive drugs, their rate of metabolism was similar to that of the control subjects except in the frontal-lobe area (Wolkin and others, 1985).

The Dopamine Hypothesis

Just as neurotransmitters are currently thought to be important in at least some types of affective disorders, biologically oriented research on schizophrenia also stresses the importance of neurotransmitter functioning. In the affective disorders, research has centered on norepinephrine; in schizophrenia, current research focuses on dopamine. The **dopamine hypothesis**, simply stated, says that there is an excess of dopamine at certain synapses in the brain.

Theoretically this could occur in any of three ways:

1. The transmitter neurons could produce too much dopamine.
2. Too much dopamine could remain in the synapses either because it might not break down fast enough or reuptake into the vesicles of the transmitter neuron might not occur fast enough.
3. The receptor neurons might be overactive in their function either because the receptors are too sensitive or there are too many of them.

Currently it is the third explanation, overactive-receptor function, which is best supported by research findings (Black and others, 1988).

The idea that dopamine is involved in schizophrenia comes from two sources. One is the finding that large doses of amphetamine are capable of producing behavior that is very similar to the behavior typical of paranoid schizophrenics in individuals with no history of psychological difficulties. Even more important, low doses of amphetamines make the symptoms of some schizophrenic individuals worse. Biochemically, amphetamines increase the amounts of both the catecholamines, dopamine, and norepinephrine, that are present at the synapse.

The second reason to suspect that dopamine is involved comes from knowledge of the effects of the antipsychotic drugs used to treat schizophrenia. The effectiveness of the drugs in reducing psychotic symptoms is directly related to their effectiveness at binding (or blocking) postsynaptic dopamine receptors (Creese and others, 1976). The story cannot be as simple as this, however, because antipsychotic drugs typically do not produce a quick behavioral improvement; instead, they

produce a gradual improvement over a period of about 6 weeks. This suggests that the biochemistry of schizophrenia is more complicated than the dopamine hypothesis suggests. What appears to happen is that initially the blockage of the dopamine receptor results in feedback that increases the activity of the dopamine neurons in the midbrain. However, after some time the neurons are firing so quickly that their effectiveness is actually decreased (Paul, 1985).

It is possible to measure changes in dopamine activity by measuring the amount of a chemically related product, homovanillic acid, in the blood (Andreasen, 1988). In addition, dopamine receptors can now be identified by PT scans; this may provide another way of investigating the dopamine hypothesis (Sedvall and others, 1986) (see Figure 12–11).

One hypothesis explains the positive and negative symptoms in schizophrenia as well as the findings of both increases and decreases in dopamine. This explanation suggests that schizophrenic disorder may be related to a low level of dopamine activity in the frontal area of the brain which produces negative symptoms. At the same time this low dopamine-activity level might re-

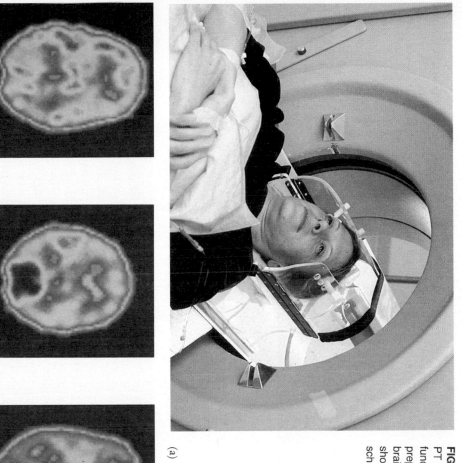
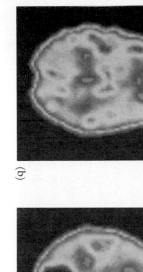
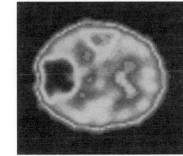

(a)

(b)

(c)

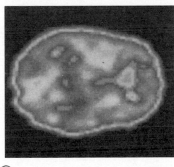

(d)

FIGURE 12-10
PT scan photos show brain metabolism and function. Photo a shows how a patient is prepared for a PT scan. Photo b shows the brain of a normal individual. Photos c and d show PT scans of individuals with schizophrenia and depression, respectively.

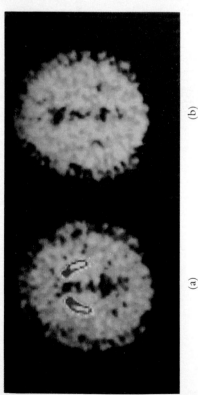

(a)

(b)

FIGURE 12–11

The PT scan makes it possible for researchers to see the effect of various antipsychotic drugs on the D_2 receptors that would ordinarily receive the dopamine after it crossed the synapse. Scan a shows a patient treated with two different drugs that produce a complete blockade of D_2 receptors. Scan b shows the same patient 2 weeks after the drug was discontinued. The receptors are no longer blocked and uptake and binding occur. (Sedvall and others, 1986, p. 999)

sult in increased dopamine activity in the subcortex or limbic area of the brain, which would account for the positive symptoms (Bannon and Roth, 1983).

Psychophysiological Abnormalities

The study of the psychophysiology of behavior concentrates on the relationship between behavior and variations in the functioning of the central and peripheral nervous systems, as well as on the ways in which these systems mediate the responses of other systems (for example, the cardiovascular system). Psychophysiological measurement includes methods of recording and processing bioelectric signals from the surface of the skin.

Psychophysiological responses can be studied using a variety of techniques, including measures of the electrical conductance of the skin, analysis of brain wave patterns by means of an electroencephalograph, and analysis of heart rate by means of an electrocardiograph. Researchers in this area still face many technical problems. For example, some measures of nervous system activity are especially sensitive to the drugs used to treat schizophrenic patients. Since many patients are started on these drugs when they first come to clinical attention, untreated patients are rare. In addition, it is not yet known whether differences in psychophysiological response between schizophrenics and controls are due to the underlying biology of the schizophrenic person or to the effects of being a patient.

Psychophysiological experimentation was formerly very tedious and time-consuming because the responses were recorded as tracings on polygraph paper, which had to be analyzed by hand. Today computers not only can present a complex series of visual or auditory stimuli but can convert the subject's responses from wiggly lines into numbers that can be analyzed using sophisticated computer programs. Under these conditions, re-

search on psychophysiological responses has grown rapidly.

Brain Electrical Activity Mapping

One new technique, brain electrical activity mapping (BEAM), summarizes EEG and evoked electrical potential in the form of color maps (see Figure 12–12). In one study, schizophrenic subjects had more slow wave activity (delta waves), especially in their frontal brain regions, than controls (Morihisa and others, 1983). The greatest difference was found when the subject's eyes were open. These findings are related to PT scan findings of reduced frontal lobe activity in schizophrenic patients and to the lower cerebral blood flow found by some researchers. In addition to the difference in delta waves, research with BEAM has shown increased beta activity in the left rear portion of the brain. This response may be an indication of overarousal. The BEAM technique may provide another way to identify markers of vulnerability to schizophrenia.

The Orienting Response

The **orienting response** is defined by psychophysiological changes that occur when the person notices and is prepared to receive some information from the environment. The frequency and size of the orienting response and the time needed to return to one's normal attention level are the most frequent measures used. Over a series of trials, the size of the orienting response in most people decreases or *habituates*. Most studies of individuals who have been diagnosed as schizophrenic have shown that about half of them are more responsive to stimuli than normal subjects while the other half do not respond. Moreover, among those who do respond, most fail to habituate; that is, their responses stay at an elevated level after many stimulus presentations (Rubens and Lapidus, 1978).

Research using animals suggests that the limbic system controls the orienting response. Researchers

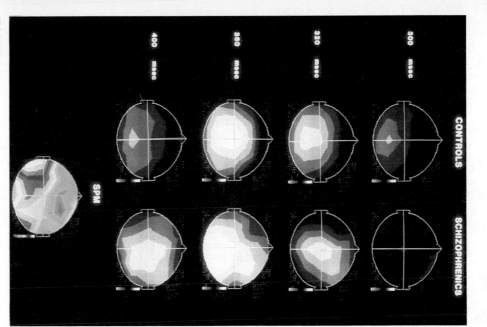

FIGURE 12-12

Brain electrical activity mapping (BEAM) provides a new way of studying electrical activity in the brain. The left column shows the average activity at four time intervals for 10 control (normal) subjects. The right-hand column represents the averaged data of 10 schizophrenic subjects. In all these records, the lowest level of activity is represented by blue, with higher values represented by yellow, red, and white in that order. The single record at the bottom center illustrates the differences between the control and schizophrenic groups. Blue represents the smallest difference and white the greatest.

ent, they are supported by a reasonable amount of research data and clearly deserve further investigation.

Attention

Anyone who has contact with schizophrenics is struck by their attentional deficits. Kraepelin had noted that schizophrenics lose both the inclination and the initiative to keep their attention fixed for any length of time. A great deal of psychophysiological research has focused on understanding these attentional problems.

Eye Movements

One way of studying schizophrenics' responses to external stimulation is through the study of eye movements; in such a visual-tracking task, the person is asked to visually follow a moving target. Two kinds of eye movements have been studied. **Saccadic movements**, which are under voluntary control, are quick jerks with steady fixations. **Smooth-pursuit movements**, which, strictly speaking, are not voluntary, occur when a person tracks a moving target such as a pendulum. Saccadic movements are so complex and sensitive to outside distractions that researchers have been frustrated in trying to study them. Smooth-pursuit movements, however, occur only when a person tracks a slowly moving target, and they cannot be faked. About 85 percent of schizophrenics show abnormal patterns of smooth-pursuit movements (Siever and Coursey, 1985). Figure 12-13 illustrates this difference between normal and schizophrenic individuals. About 50 percent of close relatives of schizophrenics also show this deviant pattern, but only 13 percent of relatives of other types of patients do (Holzman and others, 1984). Deviant tracking patterns also have been shown by people who have bipolar disorders, brain lesions, brain damage, and some drug intoxications. In a study of college students, poor trackers were more likely to receive a diagnosis of schizotypal personality disorder than good trackers. The poor trackers also showed interpersonal difficulties, especially remoteness, and neurological impairment (Siever and Coursey, 1985).

Schizophrenics' deviant tracking patterns can be modified by altering the task conditions, but no matter how the conditions change the schizophrenics' performance is not at the same level as that of controls. Performance on a visual-tracking test is a good marker for vulnerability to schizophrenia (Erlenmeyer-Kimling and Cornblatt, 1987).

The Continuous Performance Test

The Continuous Performance Test (Rosvold and others, 1956) measures sustained visual attention for periods of

have noticed that schizophrenic individuals who give orienting responses show higher-amplitude responses with the right hand than with the left hand. Because of what is known about how the two hemispheres of the brain control behavior, this finding suggests that the problem may lie in the limbic area of the left hemisphere of the brain. This focus on the left-brain hemisphere is supported by data from the intelligence test performance of schizophrenic individuals. Their ability on verbal tests (which is thought to be controlled by the left hemisphere of the brain) is more impaired than their ability on performance tests (which is related to right-hemisphere activity). Although these ideas about left-hemisphere dysfunction are highly speculative at pres-the material. For example, their recall of previously learned information is poor, but their *recognition* of the same information is much better and in some cases may be comparable to or even the same as the performance of a control group. Figure 12–14 shows that even chronic schizophrenic patients who are hospitalized show much less of a difference from control subjects when recognition rather than recall is used as a measure (Calev, 1984).

Studies of long-term memory suggest that the problems of thinking that occur in schizophrenia may not be due only to difficulty in filtering stimuli (as was suggested by the observations of former schizophrenic patients in Chapter 11) or to the problems of attention discussed earlier in this chapter. The problem might also be one of coding the material in the memory system so that it can be found and used again when appropriate (Schwartz, 1982). Some schizophrenic individuals also have problems with short-term memory (George and Neufeld, 1985). These seem to be related to failure to use the kinds of active rehearsal processes that most people use to remember such things as telephone numbers between the time of looking them up and dialing the telephone. In general, however, most cognitive researchers believe that the cognitive deficits of schizophrenics are more likely to occur on the output side in recalling and reproducing the material rather than in originally perceiving it (Grove and Andreasen, 1985).

Research on memory can also help us understand delusions, a form of disturbed thinking that is found most frequently in paranoid schizophrenics. When

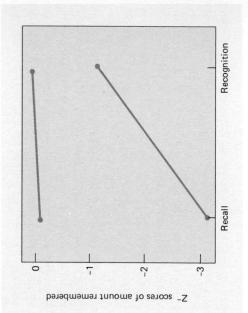

FIGURE 12–14
Mean performance on recall and recognition for 10 schizophrenics and 10 control subjects. (From A. Calev [1984], Recall and recognition in chronic nondemented schizophrenics, *Journal of Abnormal Psychology*, 93, pp. 172–177. Copyright © 1984 by the American Psychological Association. Reprinted by permission of the author)

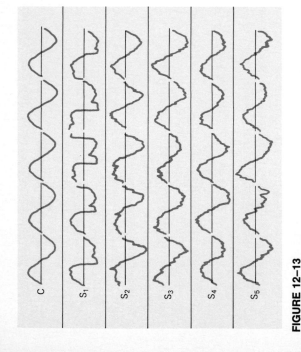

FIGURE 12–13
Samples of visual-tracking performance by a control subject (C) and five patients with schizophrenia (S1–S5). (The target moved back and forth across a 20 degree arc every 2.5 seconds.) (Iacono and Koenig, 1983, p. 39)

up to 20 minutes. The subject is exposed to a series of different stimuli after he or she has been instructed to respond to one particular type of stimulus by pressing a key. Schizophrenic individuals make more errors both by pressing the button for the wrong stimulus and by not pressing the button when it would have been correct to do so. This poor performance may be related to a dysfunction in the ascending reticular system in the brain stem (Mirsky and Bakay Pragay, 1984).

Children of schizophrenic mothers scored more poorly on the Continuous Performance Test than either children of mothers with other disorders or other children in their classrooms (Nuechterlein, 1983). Among children with a schizophrenic parent, those children who scored poorly on measures of attention were most likely to show behavioral difficulties in adulthood that might be early signs of schizophrenia (Cornblatt and Erlenmeyer-Kimling, 1985). It appears that a group of tasks measuring attention may be a useful marker in high-risk groups.

Cognitive Functioning

Memory

People with schizophrenic disorders seem to have a relatively intact network of information in long-term memory. Problems arise when they are asked to recall

paranoid, nonparanoid, and normal control subjects were tested on their processing of information for short- and long-term storage in memory; the normal subjects had the highest scores and the paranoid group the lowest (Broga and Neufeld, 1981). At the same time, although they remembered less of the actual material, the paranoid group was the most likely to draw broad, general conclusions from the material. They seemed to evaluate the situation incorrectly largely because they were depending on their own rigid cognitive system for information instead of processing the new material itself. Paranoid thinking is very similar to a "jump-to-conclusions" response style.

Disordered Thinking

Although schizophrenia is often described as thought disorder, disordered thinking is not unique to schizophrenia. Disordered thinking is part of a continuum that includes normal thinking. In one study, a number of groups were compared by means of tape recordings of their verbalizations on a personality test (the Rorschach) (Solovay and others, 1987). The responses were all rated on a thought disorder index. Although schizophrenics had the highest overall number of thought-disordered responses, all groups showed some examples of disordered thought (see Figure 12–15).

Researchers have attempted to determine whether thought disorder is a permanent trait of people with schizophrenia or whether it is a symptom of acute psychosis. For example, disordered thinking accompanies acute psychotic episodes in mania as well as in schizophrenia. However, some degree of disordered thought

may be a permanent characteristic of people who are schizophrenic and may show up long before other signs of the disorder appear. For instance, in the Danish high-risk study of children of severely schizophrenic mothers, a significantly larger percent of children who later developed one of the schizophrenic spectrum disorders had shown cognitive disturbance when they were tested at age 15 compared to the control subjects (Parnas and others, 1982).

A measure of thought disorder can be useful in assessing the effects of antipsychotic medication. For example, in one study, the responses of schizophrenic patients were evaluated on a thought disorder index before the patients began drug treatment. The results showed that thought disorder as measured by the index dropped dramatically (see Figure 12–16). The maximum effect was reached in about 3 weeks, and then a relatively stable level was maintained. This suggests that the drug was effective in maintaining better cognitive performance, although it is important to note that there was a limit to the effectiveness of the treatment. The level of disordered thinking shown by the schizophrenic patients remained higher than that of nonschizophrenic individuals. Some schizophrenics continue to show bizarre and idiosyncratic speech even after their condition improves (Andreasen and Grove, 1986).

Language

The speech of some schizophrenic individuals is difficult to follow, but this does not seem to be due to their lack of knowledge of grammatical rules. What is perceived as

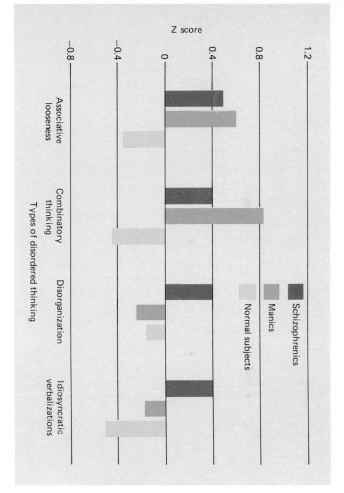

FIGURE 12–15
The frequency of thought-disordered responses of schizophrenic and manic patients were compared with normal subjects. The figure shows how each group differed from the overall mean (0) in each of several aspects of their performance. (The data were transformed for statistical purposes and the results are reported in terms of Z scores). (Adapted from Solovay and others, 1987, p. 17. Archives of General Psychiatry. Copyright © 1987, American Medical Association.)

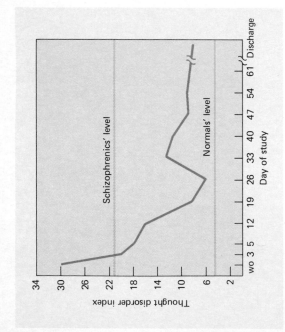

FIGURE 12-16
Mean Thought Disorder Index of 18 schizophrenic patients during their hospital stays. Effects of antipsychotic medications appear quickly and the index reaches a stable level that is higher than the level for normal individuals (W.O. = end of drug-free wash-out period to remove effects of previous medication). (Holzman, 1978, p. 367)

PATIENT: *I cut myself once when I was in the kitchen trying to please David. I was scared for [sic] life because David didn't want me and if David didn't want me then no man would.*

This segment suggests a condensation of two disjointed messages. The right-hand chain of statements describes stress-related thoughts of the type that might lead to suicidal behavior. The left-hand hierarchy seemingly refers to an incident in which the speaker accidently cuts herself. In this context, "I was scared for life" seems to refer to her reaction to seeing that she had accidentally cut herself. The result is a departure from a strict hierarchical ordering of statements, since "no man wants me" and "David doesn't want me" presuppose the "I was scared for life" statement and are referable to the suicide theme, but the statement "I [accidentally] cut myself" is not. This break is represented in Figure 12–17 by a jagged line.

By experimentally studying various aspects of schizophrenics' language, cognitive theorists look for clues to the specific ways in which schizophrenics differ from controls and how conditions can be varied to improve schizophrenics' performance. Through these procedures, they hope to obtain a better understanding of the thought processes that characterize schizophrenia.

abnormal seems to lie in the thought communicated by the speech, not in the language used in the communication. The speech of schizophrenics has been found to differ from the speech of other patient groups and from normals in the way the thoughts are organized. Normal speech has a treelike structure that schizophrenic speech may lack. Read the next two examples and then look at the diagrams in Figure 12–17. The first speech segment was produced by someone hospitalized for depression.

INTERVIEWER: *Can you describe where you live?*

PATIENT: *Yes, I live in Connecticut. We live in a 50-year-old Tudor house. It's a house that's very much a home . . . ah . . . I live there with my husband and son. It's a home where people are drawn to feel comfortable, walk in, let's see . . . a home that is furnished comfortably—not expensive—a home that shows very much my personality.*

The overall message of the above segment is fairly obvious—the woman is extolling the virtues of her house in terms of how it reflects on herself as a person. This message is represented by the tree-shaped plan in Figure 12–17.

The second speech segment was produced by a patient with a schizophrenic disorder.

INTERVIEWER: *Did you ever try to hurt yourself?* (*Interviewer asks about patient's feelings about suicide after being admitted to a psychiatric hospital.*)

Family Relationships

One source of stress that may interact with a person's vulnerability to schizophrenia may be created by profoundly frustrating interpersonal relationships during the early years of life, accompanied by a lack of emotional ties to people. The schizophrenic seems to go through life with no expectation of support and warmth from the social environment. He or she regards other people as uninterested or critical. The drawing shown in Figure 12–18 conveys some of these feelings. Research on high-risk children points to some markers related to family environment that may increase the stress experienced by children.

Family Communication Deviance

Communication deviance refers to the inability of the parent or parents to maintain a shared focus of attention during interactions with another person. Cross-sectional studies have shown that high communication deviance

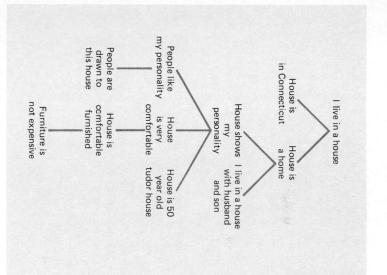

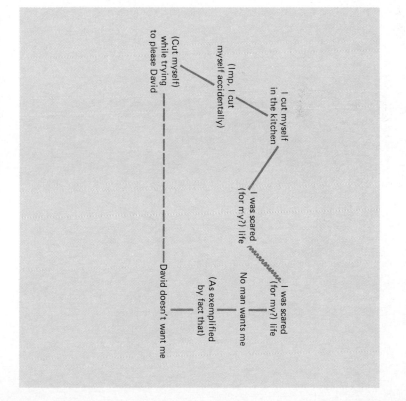

FIGURE 12-17

Hierarchical analyses of speech may provide understanding of schizophrenic thought processes. In the "house is like my personality" segment, certain statements can be located at different sites in the tree depending on how one interprets the communicative intention of the speaker. If "50-year-old Tudor" is metaphorically interpreted as referring to certain human qualities, then this statement is subordinated to the "house shows my personality" statement; otherwise the statement would be subordinated to the superordinate "house" statement. A hierarchical analysis of the "I cut myself" segment interpretations of the text could potentially restore a strict hierarchical structure, but this requires assuming that the speaker disregarded the suicide theme without acknowledging that she changed topic. (Hoffman, Stopek, and Andreasen, 1986; and Hoffman, 1987 *Archives of General Psychiatry*. Copyright © 1986, American Medical Association.

is associated with schizophrenia in the children of such parents (Wynne and others, 1977). However, some of the research on communication deviance has raised questions about the meaning of the findings. The parents' communication problems may be a response to unclear communications from the children.

One way to understand the causes and effects of communication problems is through long-term prospective studies. In the high-risk study carried out at the University of California at Los Angeles, the participating families each contained a mild to moderately disturbed teenage member (Goldstein, 1985). All of the families had contacted the university-based psychological clinic for help. At the time that they were originally seen, the parents were given the Thematic Apperception Test, which was scored for communication deviance. Fifteen years later the children were rediagnosed and grouped according to the original assessment of parental deviance. The number of cases of schizophrenia and schizophrenic spectrum disorders was clearly related to

the earlier assessments of communication deviance (see Figure 12–19). Fifty percent of the children in the families with high communication deviance had a diagnosis in the schizophrenic spectrum, compared to 26 percent in the intermediate families and 9 percent in the low-deviance families.

Expressed Emotion

In addition to how clearly families communicate, the emotional impact of what they communicate is important. **Expressed emotion** is a measure of the attitudes expressed by family members when talking about the person whose behavior is disturbed (Leff and Vaughn, 1985). Table 12–4 lists the categories of expressed emotion that are measured.

Researchers found that patients who returned to families high in negative expressed emotion were not likely to stay out of the hospital as long as patients

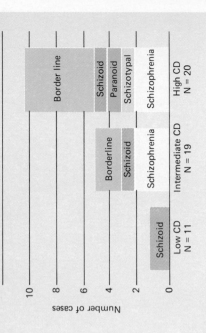

Chart labels: Number of cases; 0, 2, 4, 6, 8, 10; Low CD N = 11 (Schizoid); Intermediate CD N = 19 (Borderline, Schizoid, Schizophrenia); High CD N = 20 (Border line, Schizoid, Paranoid, Schizotypal, Schizophrenia)

FIGURE 12–18
This drawing depicts the isolation felt by a 25-year-old schizophrenic patient.

whose families were less critical. This was true whether or not the patient was also taking antipsychotic drugs (Vaughn and Leff, 1976; Leff and Vaughn, 1981) (see Figure 12–20). Studies carried out in England and Los Angeles produced similar results (Vaughn and others, 1984). Negative expressed emotion includes criticism, hostility, and emotional overinvolvement (exaggerated emotional response to the illness or extreme protectiveness). Relatives who were rated high in negative expressed emotion made remarks like the following.

I always say, "why don't you pick up a book, do a crossword or something like that to keep your mind off it." That's even too much trouble.

I've tried to jolly him out of it and pestered him into doing things. Maybe I've overdone it, I don't know.

He went round the garden 90 times, in the door, back out the door. I said "Have a chair, sit out in the sun." Well, he nearly bit my head off.

—(Hooley, 1985, p. 134)

Relatives who were low in negative expressed emotion were likely to make very different comments.

I know it's better for her to be on her own, to get away from me and try to do things on her own.

Whatever she does suits me.

I just tend to let it go because I know that when she wants to speak she will speak.

—(Ibid.)

As research on expressed emotion has continued several findings have emerged:

1. Expressed emotion in a family may change over time. This means it may be a product both of the degree of upset in the patient and of the family interaction style. Half the families high in negative expressed emotion at the patient's first admission are low one year later. A change from high to low negative expressed emotion in a family is associated with lower relapse rates (Hogarty and others, 1986).

2. There are cultural differences that influence expressed emotion. For instance, relatives in India and Mexican-American relatives in the United States who follow their traditional cultural practices show much lower levels of negative expressed emotion toward their ill relatives than Anglo-Americans in the United States and their relatives in England (Leff and Vaughn, 1985; Jenkins and others, 1986).

3. Expressed-emotion research has implications for patients who do not live with their families. High negative expressed emotion is associated with overstimulating treatment and high expectations in foster

TABLE 12-4

Scales of Expressed Emotion

1. *Critical comments about family members.* Criticisms are rated on the basis of content and/or tone. Remarks are considered to be critical if there is a clear and unambiguous statement that the relative dislikes, disapproves of, or resents a behavior or characteristic. The dissatisfaction is expressed intensely and emphatically; the relative must use phrases such as "It annoys me" or "I don't like it." Vocal aspects of speech such as pitch, speed, inflection, and loudness are used to identify critical tone.

2. *Hostility.* Hostility is rated as present when the patient is attacked for what he or she *is* rather than for what he or she *does*. Negative feeling is generalized in such a way that it is expressed about the person himself or herself rather than about particular behaviors or attributes.

3. *Emotional overinvolvement.* Emotional overinvolvement is rated when there is either an exaggerated emotional response to the patient's illness, marked concern reflected in unusually self-sacrificing and devoted behaviors, or extremely overprotective behaviors.

4. *Warmth.* Ratings of warmth are based on the sympathy, concern, and empathy relatives shown when talking about the patient, the enthusiasm for and interest in the patient's activities, the number of spontaneous expressions of affection, and the tone of voice used when talking about the patient.

5. *Positive remarks.* Positive remarks are statements that express praise, approval, or appreciation of the behavior or personality of the patient.

From Leff and Vaughn (1985). Reprinted with permission from the *British Journal of Psychiatry.*

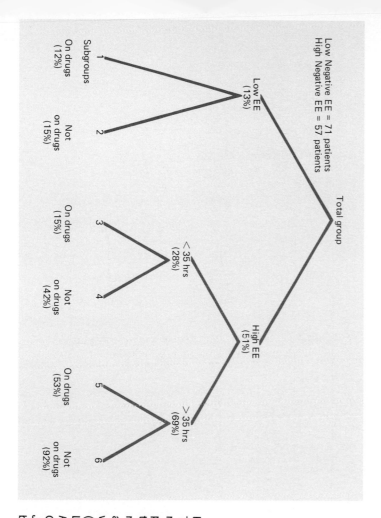

Low Negative EE = 71 patients
High Negative EE = 57 patients

FIGURE 12-20
The relapse rates (after 9 months) of 128 schizophrenic patients grouped by whether their families were high or low in negative expressed emotion (EE) and whether or not the patient was taking antipsychotic drugs. (From C. E. Vaughn and J. P. Leff [1976], *British Journal of Psychiatry, 129,* p. 132. Copyright © 1976 by The British Journal of Psychiatry. Reprinted by permission)

homes and day-treatment centers, and this also leads to high rates of relapse.

Expressed emotion has become a focus for controversy because some people think that the research blames the families for the patient's schizophrenic dis-

order. The research should not be thought of in this way, however. It is true that the early work showed how negative aspects of expressed emotion predict a high relapse rate, and the term "expressed emotion" became an indication of a negative interactive style. More recent work, however, has shown that warmth and positive comments may also help protect *against* relapse (Leff and Vaughn, 1985). In general a high level of emotional expression in a family has been found to help prevent relapse (Spiegel and Wissler, 1986). These findings mean the term must be redefined into its positive and negative components.

Parental Affective Style

Expressed emotion is measured from interviews in which relatives talk about patients. **Parental affective style**, on the other hand, is measured by means of directly observed interactions, in which family members including the patient or client discuss problems that tend to upset the family. Although negative expressed emotion and negative parental affective style may coexist in many individuals, they are not perfectly correlated. Analysis of the interactions of parents and children shows a complex pattern when the affective style of the parent pairs is studied (Valone and others, 1984).

Figure 12–21 shows that when the parents interact with each other, their behavior is modified by this interaction. When one parent was high and one low in negative expressed emotion, the criticisms directed at the child tended to be less harsh. The presence of the parent who was low in expressed emotion seemed to temper the criticisms made by the other parent. Overall, the number of harsh criticisms for this mixed pair did not differ from the number for parents both of whom were low in negative expressed emotion. The adolescent child's manner in reacting to the parent and the kinds

of problems for which the family had come to the clinic also were not related to the parents' expressed emotion levels. This suggests that a parent's level of expressed emotion may be a stable characteristic and not simply a reaction to a child who exhibits problem behaviors.

When both parents were high in expressed emotion, the family interaction was also more emotional (as measured by electrical skin conductance) than when the parents were low or mixed in negative expressed emotion. This arousal was shown not only by both parents but also by the adolescent child, who seemed most aroused when anticipating what the parents' next comments would be. This high level of arousal shows that families with high levels of negative expressed emotion experience a great deal of stress in their interactions.

The Role of the Community

More than 50 studies conducted in Canada, Denmark, Finland, Great Britain, Norway, Sweden, and Taiwan, as well as in the United States, have found that lower-class people are diagnosed as schizophrenic more frequently than people from the middle or upper classes. However, no one has been able to discover why social class is related to schizophrenia. Two theories—social selection and the social-causation or increased-stress theory—have been used to explain the greater incidence of

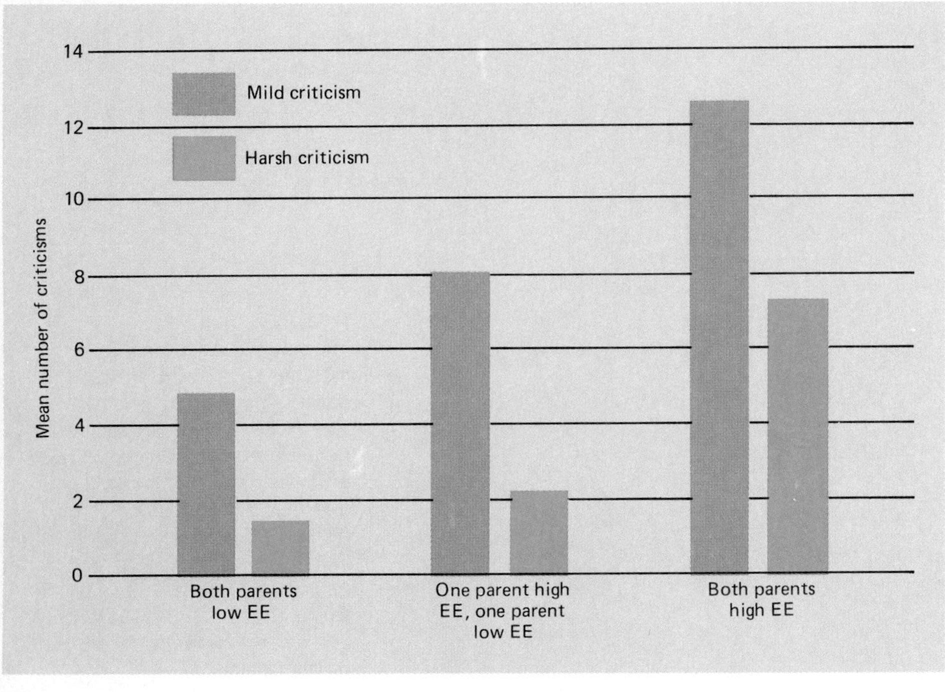

FIGURE 12–21
Expression of affective style by parents grouped by their expressed emotion (EE). (Reprinted with permission from the British Journal of Psychiatry)

schizophrenia among lower-class individuals. The **so-cial-selection theory** assumes that people who cannot make it in society gradually become part of the lower class because of their poor coping skills, in contrast to the idea that people who experience the stress of lower-class living develop poor coping skills. A review of research on the community and interpersonal functioning of people who have had a schizophrenic disorder shows that in at least one subgroup, poor functioning in these areas can be found before the disorder is noticed (Wallace, 1984). Poor functioning also is related to poor outcome after the disorder has been diagnosed. This means that, for at least some people, poor social func-

tioning may be a marker of vulnerability to schizophrenia.

Whereas the social-selection theory points to flaws in the individual as the cause of schizophrenia, an alternative explanation for the greater incidence of schizophrenia in the lower class points to flaws in the society itself. The **increased-stress theory** refers to the amount of stress experienced by people in different socioeconomic classes. Living in areas with high crime rates, run-down housing, and inadequate schools may be more difficult and stressful than living in more affluent areas. At the same time, lower-class people have little money or power to cope with the stresses they encoun-

---

BOX 12-2
Investigating a Single Case from a Variety of Perspectives

Investigation of schizophrenic behavior from several perspectives can help in understanding both the disorder and its symptoms. The case of the Genain sisters illustrates how investigations of heredity, brain anatomy and activity, psychophysiological measures, and family interactions can complement one another.

The sisters, who were identical quadruplets, shared the same heredity (see Figures 12-22 and 12-23). Because the odds for identical quadruplets are one in 16 million births, they became celebrities in their home town. During their childhood, they performed song and dance routines and were so popular that they had a police escort on one early local tour. As they grew older, however, it became clear that they were not developing in a normal way. One sister dropped out of high school. The other three graduated but had trouble holding jobs. During their twenties, all four sisters developed schizophrenic disorders.

Because of the uniqueness of this case (four individuals with identical heredity who all showed schizophrenic behavior could be expected to occur only once in tens of billions of births), a local physician alerted scientists at the National Institute of Mental Health. The sisters came to Washington, D.C., and were hospitalized there for intensive study. During the 3 years that they spent at NIMH, they were examined from a number of perspectives. To protect their privacy, the sisters were given pseudonyms, corresponding to NIMH's initials—Nora, Iris, Myra, and Hester—and the family was given the name Genain, from the Greek words meaning "dire birth."

Several of the quadruplets' family members had histories of psychological problems. Not only was their father's behavior often bizarre, but his brother, his

FIGURE 12-22
The Genain sisters as young children.

mother, and his paternal uncle had each had a nervous breakdown sometime in the past.

Even though they were genetically identical and may all have had the same hereditary risk factor, the sisters' schizophrenia could have been at least partly the result of environmental factors. For example, as is usual in multiple births, they were all small at birth. All of them spent time in incubators and did not go home from the hospital until they were 6 weeks old. They grew up in the glare of publicity and constantly heard comments about their similarity. Their father restricted their interactions with other people by refusing to allow them to

---

BOX 12-2 (CONTINUED)

FIGURE 12-23
The Genain sisters as adults.

play with other children or, later, to take part in school activities or to date.

The girls' father also objected to their stay at NIMH and often threatened to take them out of the hospital. Although he was cooperative and cordial at times, he also had considerable hostility toward people. His wife reported that he had tried to choke her several times and said that she had considered leaving him. At times, he accused his wife of having sexual relationships with his daughters' psychiatrists. During the quadruplets' third year at the hospital, he died.

This report, which reflects the psychodynamic perspective, describes the family relationships in detail:

Mrs. Genain's unfulfilled needs for maternal nurturing found expression in her closeness to Nora. It was the symbiotic tie of mother and infant, one in which the mother does not see the infant as a separate individual but as part of herself. . . . In her adult psychosis, she [Nora] caricatured her mother's friendly facade and stereotyped sweetness. The closeness between them supported a report that Nora was not only her father's "favorite," but her mother's also. The earliest evidence for this was that Nora was always the first of the babies to be burped after feeding.

The most recent evidence was that Nora was the daughter Mrs. Genain took home for trial visits from the hospital, although Iris' adjustment was also appropriate for home visits.

The central role for Myra was the "independent positive." Mrs. Genain identified Myra with her own independent strivings and actions. . . . Myra was the daughter upon whom Mrs. Genain was prone to lean in times of stress, who often strove for the favored position (which in this family was the protected one) with her mother. . . . She tried to live out the role her mother assigned to her of becoming independent, and the dependent–independent conflict became acute for her when she tried to move out on her own.

The central theme of the role Mrs. Genain assigned to Iris was the "repressed" one. She identified in Iris her own feeling that she must put up with anything and in her psychosis, Iris caricatured this aspect of her mother's personality.

Later, when she improved, she made occasional sarcastic remarks to her mother which Mrs. Genain described as being like Iris' prepsychotic behavior and as being hostile to her. . . . In areas that concerned Iris as an individual, e.g., her abilities and appearance, Mrs. Genain was neither concerned nor interested.

The central theme assigned to Hester was the "negative" one. It was as though Hester personified that which Mrs. Genain regarded as undesirable—hostility and sexuality, for example. The perception of these feelings in Hester appeared to have blocked her mother's perception of other human qualities in her. She was the last to be regarded as sick (she had been "bad") and she was not hospitalized before coming to the Clinical Center. Later Mrs. Genain did not even consider a time when Hester might come home for home visits from the hospital. Hester had the end position on the continuum. (adapted from Rosenthal, 1963, pp. 463–465)

Twenty years after the Genains had first been studied at NIMH, they were invited back for a follow-up. During that period Myra had lived the most normal life. She went to business college and later worked as a secretary. She was the only one of the four sisters to marry and have children. Nora was next best in adjustment. She had worked at least 7 years, partly in government training programs. Hester and Iris had each spent more than 15 years in hospitals and had received more antipsychotic drug treatment than either Myra or Nora.

Researchers wondered if scanning techniques, developed after the early study of the sisters, could shed light on the differences in their behavior. The sisters' CT scans appeared normal, but other types of scans showed abnormal patterns. Their PT scans, made when the women were resting, showed activity in the visual areas (see Figure 12-24). Scientists wondered if this was an indication of hallucinations. The PT scans of Myra and Nora, the two sisters who had made the best adjustment, were closer to the normal PT scans than those of the two sisers whose behavior was less adaptive. The Genains also showed much less alpha brain wave activity than is normal. Since alpha waves appear when people relax or let their minds go blank, the low frequency of alpha waves may also suggest hallucinations.

The sisters were also given Computer Electroencephalographic Tomography scans (CET). CET scans show the electrical activity in the brain, in contrast to PT scans, which show chemical activity (see Figure 12-25). All four Genain sisters show low levels of alpha waves on the CET scans compared to a control subject. The correspondence between PT and CET scan patterns both in this case and in general research findings seems fairly close (Buchsbaum and Haier, 1987). Since CET scans are much cheaper and safer for the subject than PT scans, they can be repeated at frequent intervals. These findings, when matched with the sisters' behavioral histories and with the earlier test data, may prove a help in relating specific behaviors with environmental factors and biological functioning.

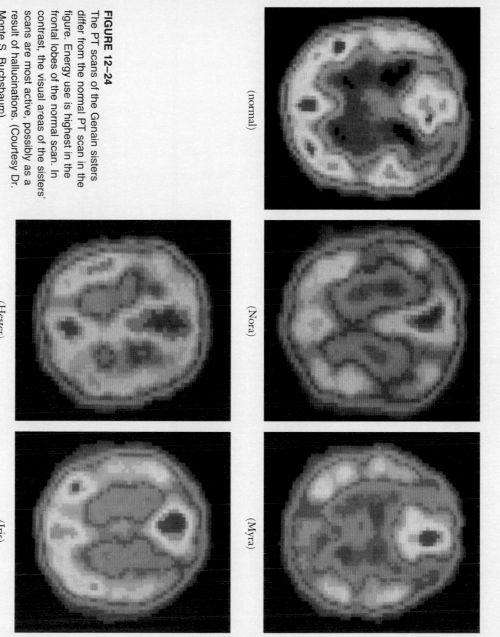

FIGURE 12-24
The PT scans of the Genain sisters differ from the normal PT scan in the figure. Energy use is highest in the frontal lobes of the normal scan. In contrast, the visual areas of the sisters' scans are most active, possibly as a result of hallucinations. (Courtesy Dr. Monte S. Buchsbaum)

(normal)

(Nora)

(Hester)

(Myra)

(Iris)

(normal) (a)

(Nora) (b)

(Hester) (d)

(Myra) (c)

(Iris) (e)

FIGURE 12-25
CET scans of the Genain quadruplets (b–e) show low levels of alpha rhythm compared to the normal map in a. All these scans were made while the subjects were resting with their eyes shut. (Buchsbaum and Haier, 1987 unpaged)

ter. Thus, in a study of schizophrenics and matched controls who lived in conditions of terrible poverty in the slums of San Juan, Puerto Rico, it was found that, although all the participants could be said to live under great stress according to the usual standards, those who were schizophrenic had experienced greater stress than the control group in the period before their symptoms became obvious (Rogler and Hollingshead, 1965).

High density, or the presence of a large number of people in a living unit or neighborhood, has often been thought to be related to psychopathology. However, a recent analysis of the living conditions of people who were admitted for the first time to mental hospitals in Chicago in the years 1960 and 1961 showed that, after differences in socioeconomic status and racial differences were taken into account, most of the cases came from areas where there were both a higher proportion of people living alone and a low population density (Magaziner, 1980).

It may seem that people who are vulnerable to schizophrenia often choose to live alone because they find personal interactions stressful. However, living alone may be a disadvantage in a crisis. People who live alone lack the social interaction and supports that give meaning to life. They also lack input and structure in their daily affairs, and this may lead to withdrawal from others and too much concentration on personal problems (Gove and Hughes, 1980).

This chapter has discussed what is known about schizophrenia, drawing upon research based on a variety of perspectives. Box 12–2 illustrates how focusing on a unique group of people from several perspectives can produce a fuller picture of schizophrenic disorders.

Study Outline

GENETIC FACTORS

1. The more genes two individuals have in common, the higher the risk of a schizophrenic disorder for one when the other has such a disorder. The siblings and children of schizophrenic individuals seem to have a higher risk of becoming schizophrenic than the parents of those individuals. **Assortive mating,** the tendency for people to mate with others similar in physical or psychological traits or behavior disorders, may add to the risk for the children of such a union.

2. **Genetic specificity** means that what is inherited is a particular disorder, not any one of a group of similar disorders. The **spectrum concept** means that several disorders seem to be genetically related. The **schizophrenic spectrum disorders** include schizotypal personality, paranoid personality, and schizoaffective disorder.

3. Twin studies have found that monozygotic twins have a greater chance of being concordant for schizophrenia than dizygotic twins, but the concordance is less than 100 percent. This suggests that environmental variables interact with inherited predispositions to produce schizophrenia.

4. Adoption studies have found that children of schizophrenic parents who are given up for adoption are more likely to develop schizophrenia than adopted children whose biological parents had no psychiatric history.

5. **Monogenic models** are based on the idea that genetic transmission at one locus is all that is necessary to produce a particular characteristic. Such models are not adequate to explain the transmission of schizophrenia. **Polygenic models** assume that a number of genes found at specific locations must interact to produce a trait. **Multifactorial polygenic models** assume that there are many gene loci involved in schizophrenia and that genes at all of these loci may have small additive effects on a person's vulnerability to schizophrenia.

VULNERABILITY AND STRESS FACTORS

1. Joseph Zubin has suggested that every individual has a certain level of vulnerability to schizophrenia, which is determined by genetic inheritance and pre- and postnatal physical factors, interacting with stressful events or conditions in the person's life. If a certain critical level is passed, schizophrenic behavior will occur. In this view, schizophrenia is an episodic disorder; it may come and go depending on the amount of stress in the individual's environment.

2. An adoption study in Finland has demonstrated the protective effect of a healthy family environment for children at risk for schizophrenia.

HIGH-RISK STUDIES AND THE SEARCH FOR MARKERS

1. High-risk studies focus on groups that are thought to have a higher risk of schizophrenia than the general population. One such group consists of children with at least one schizophrenic parent. Studies of such children support a vulnerability view of schizophrenia: They find

that complications at birth and difficult living conditions in childhood are related to the incidence of schizophrenia in children of schizophrenic parents.

2. One focus of high-risk studies is to find markers (for instance, specific behaviors or physiological responses) that may predict which children have the greatest genetic risk.

UNDERSTANDING THE SCHIZOPHRENIC PROCESS

1. Brain scan techniques have shown that some schizophrenics have significantly larger **cerebral ventricles** than nonschizophrenics. Enlarged ventricles have been associated with negative symptoms.

2. Efforts to link schizophrenia with the presence of abnormal substances in the brain have had little success, partly because of poor experimental design. Today researchers are looking for abnormalities in biochemical functioning, aided by the development of new techniques like the PT scan. The **dopamine hypothesis** states that there is an excess of dopamine at certain synapses in the brain. The effectiveness of antipsychotic drugs is related to their effectiveness at blocking postsynaptic dopamine receptors.

3. The study of psychophysiological responses uses such techniques as **brain electrical activity mapping** and measurement of the **orienting response.** This research has found differences between schizophrenic and nonschizophrenic patients that may serve as **markers** of vulnerability to the disorder.

4. The study of schizophrenics' responses to external stimulation focuses on eye movements. Schizophrenic individuals have been found to have more difficulty than normal individuals in tracking a moving target such as a pendulum. They also make more errors on the Continuous Performance Test, which involves responding to specific visual stimuli by pressing a key.

5. Studies of cognitive functioning in schizophrenics have found that people with schizophrenic disorders have difficulty *recalling* material from long-term memory, although they can *recognize* the same information reasonably well. Some schizophrenic individuals also have problems with short-term memory.

6. Although disordered thinking occurs in other disorders besides schizophrenia and to some extent in normal controls, it appears that some degree of disordered thought may be a permanent characteristic of people who are schizophrenic and may show up before other signs of the disorder appear. Disordered thinking can be studied by diagramming patient's verbal responses to see how much the organization of their thoughts differs from the normal tree-like format.

FAMILY RELATIONSHIPS

1. High **communication deviance** (inability to maintain a shared focus of attention during interactions) in parents appears to be associated with schizophrenia in their children. However, the parents' communication problems could be a response to unclear communications from the children.

2. **Expressed emotion,** the attitudes family members express when talking about the person whose behavior is disturbed, can be an important predictor of whether or how soon the person will experience another schizophrenic episode or have to return to a hospital.

3. **Parental affective style** is measured by observing the emotions conveyed in actual family interactions. Negative style for both parents is related to an increased chance of later disorder for the child.

THE ROLE OF THE COMMUNITY

Two theories attempt to explain the greater incidence of schizophrenia in the lower class than in the middle and upper classes. The **social-selection theory** assumes that people with poor coping skills (who are more vulnerable to schizophrenia) gradually become part of the lower class. The **increased-stress theory** holds that living in poor areas may be more stressful than living in more affluent areas (and thus increases vulnerability to schizophrenia).

Brain Disorders and Changes Related to Aging

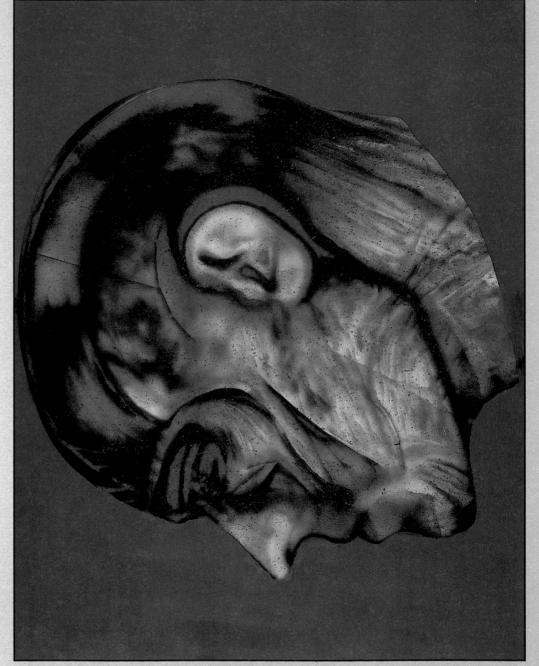

OBJECTIVES FOR CHAPTER THIRTEEN:

To learn:

1. The techniques used to assess brain damage
2. The meaning of delirium and dementia
3. What behavior is typical of Alzheimer's, Huntington's, and Parkinson's diseases and epilepsy and what is known about their causes

To understand:

The meaning of an interactive perspective on brain disorders

*A*nn Martin used to have an enviable memory. Now, at age 58, she forgets recent events and shows poor judgment. (She recently threw out a pair of valuable sterling silver salt and pepper shakers.) Because she can no longer balance her household budget, plan her meals, and take care of herself in other ways, she now lives in a retirement home, even though she is still relatively young. Her condition was diagnosed as Alzheimer's disease, which is caused by physical degeneration in the brain. Alzheimer's disease results in loss of intellectual ability and changes in personality and behavior.

Robert Case had a long history of alcoholism. His drinking binges followed a fairly regular course, as did his drying-out periods. Beginning at about 40 years of age, something new, a progressive memory impairment, entered the picture. Case could easily recall details of his youth and his war experiences, but he had difficulty remembering more recent events. In a recent clinical evaluation, he could not remember the names of five objects for 5 minutes and thought that Richard Nixon was still president of the United States. His memory impairment led to other problems. He would forget that he had left the water running in the sink or bathtub. He became upset at his "stupidity" and sometimes would "fill in" gaps in his memory with details that were untrue. As time passed, he was hospitalized a number of times. When he was admitted, he was usually unable to provide the details of his previous hospitalizations. Robert Case's condition was diagnosed as Korsakoff's syndrome, a type of brain disorder in which an irreversible memory deficit emerges following a history of excessive drinking.

These two cases show both similarities and differences. The main similarity is that the abnormal behaviors from which both individuals are suffering are caused by organic brain disorders. Our knowledge of these conditions is increasing, not only because of new discoveries about how the brain functions but also because of information about the interaction between organic functioning and personal characteristics and environmental variables. The main difference between the two examples is that Martin's condition does not seem to be attributable to external or environmental causes. Case's condition, on the other hand, seems to be directly attributable to the effects of chronic alcoholism.

The Brain: An Interactive Perspective

The brain is an organ, like the kidney, the heart, or the liver, and organs are known to fail because of hereditary factors as well as environmental ones. Yet, to believe that the brain is merely a series of chemical reactions is to remove humans from the responsibility for their actions. In fact, part of the brain is "hard-wired" in advance of birth and part is designed to be plastic and learn from experience.

At one time the prevailing view was that the brain grows through childhood, takes its final shape during adolescence, and then slowly ages. New work shows, however, that each area of the brain develops in unique ways throughout life. While some parts of the brain deteriorate, most brain cells continue to form new connections—a finding cited by some psychoanalysts to refute Freud's contention that, after age 50, people's minds are too rigid for them to benefit much from psychoanalysis. In fact, they say, people in midlife may be more able than they were earlier to benefit from psychotherapy.

Three areas of brain research seem especially pertinent to an understanding of both normal and abnormal behavior.

1. Specifying how the brain grows and maintains itself
2. Identifying the mechanisms by which the brain acquires, stores, and uses information at the cellular and molecular levels, as well as the level of behavior and social interaction
3. Making clear the role played by the brain in monitoring and regulating internal bodily processes.

In the past, people looked for physical causes for

all forms of maladaptive behavior. If people behaved in odd ways, it was because there was something physically wrong with them. People could be "born criminals" or have "bad blood." Then scientists became aware of the psychological and social causes of behavioral problems. Physical explanations came to be seen as inadequate and even as somewhat simple-minded. Today, however, psychologists are developing a more complete picture of how intertwined the psychological, social, and physical domains of human life are.

We learn social skills, interact with others, and acquire personal attitudes within a framework of physical development. Human functioning is influenced by organic events that occur during intrauterine life, the birth process, and the long period of development outside the uterus. The brain may become damaged suddenly, for example, when a person has a stroke or receives a head injury in an accident (see Figure 13–1). In other cases certain diseases cause slow deterioration in the brain. These changes in the brain's physical nature, whether they happen quickly or slowly, and whether they involve large or small areas, are often the cause of unusual behavior. Damage to the brain can lead to a wide variety of behavioral problems, depending on what part of the brain is affected and how much of it is damaged.

What is known today about brain disorders is consistent with what we have already said about the interaction among personal and environmental factors, vulnerability, and stress. It would simplify the lives of clinicians and researchers if they could assume that certain types of maladaptation are due to personal variables and others to situational pressures. Unfortunately, such an assumption would be incorrect. Behavior is a joint product of individual differences and environmental variables. The particular mix of these variables determines how people act and what they think about. There is no standard type of psychological effect for each type and degree of brain defect.

Vulnerability To Brain Disorders

The same amount of brain damage or deterioration can have varying effects, depending on the affected individual's personality and abilities and the social supports available to cushion the organic blow. Thus, there are many cases in which the psychological and behavioral effects of brain injuries and tumors do not conform to what would be expected on the basis of the amount of brain damage suffered.

(a)

(b)

FIGURE 13-1
Automobile accidents often cause head injuries that affect the victim's mental functioning. This person sustained a head injury in a car crash (a). The injury resulted in large and permanent losses in ability to attend to stimuli, concentrate, and solve different kinds of problems, even simple things such as counting out correct bus fare (b).

The following are among the factors that influence vulnerability to brain damage and brain disorders:

1. *Age.* The age at which a brain condition develops can have both long- and short-term effects. Although in some instances an infant brain is better able to compensate for an injury than an adult brain, the infant brain may also be more susceptible to a variety of pathological conditions. Many behavioral deficits that are caused by damage to the brain in infancy are not noticed until considerably later.

2. *Social support.* The presence of caring, accepting people on whom the individual can rely usually eases adjustment to a brain condition. Social isolation, on the other hand, increases cognitive deficits and, thus, abnormal behavior.

3. *Stress.* The greater the stress, the greater both the cognitive and behavioral deficits will be. Elderly people with chronic brain conditions often show marked deterioration following a piling up of stressful life events such as retirement or the death of a spouse.

4. *Personality factors.* It is a common clinical observation that some people react with intense anxiety, feelings of depersonalization, paranoid thinking, defensive-

ness, and hallucinations to any condition that causes even mild clouding of consciousness and impairment of cognitive and perceptual functioning.

5. *Physical condition.* The site of brain disorder, the rate of onset of the disorder, and the duration of the disorder all influence the clinical picture. In addition, the individual's general level of health plays a role in his or her adjustment.

An individual's psychological state and social relationships at the onset of an organic condition can influence the impact of the condition on his or her behavior. A person with a stable personality usually responds differently, and more adaptively, to treatment than someone in the throes of marital turmoil or financial reversal. When personal problems complicate an organic condition, both medical and psychological treatment may be necessary. In addition to its personal effects, impairment of brain function has a profound influence on interpersonal relationships. For example, people with epilepsy suffer from undesirable social consequences as well as from the seizures themselves.

Because determining the presence and extent of brain damage is complicated by the need to isolate its effects from those caused by personal and social factors, clinicians must avoid overly simple diagnoses. Clearly, a person who is noticeably disoriented, has trouble solving problems, and displays shallow or very changeable moods and emotions is suffering from some sort of behavioral problem. But the primary aspects of the diagnosis—an estimate of the roles played by organic damage, personality, and life stress in causing the disturbance—are not so easily determined.

psychological tests are used to assess impairment in such areas as awareness of and responsiveness to sensory stimulation, ability to understand verbal communication and to express oneself, and emotional expression. Neuropsychological testing is sensitive to impaired functioning of various regions of the brain.

Brain Imaging

Progress in constructing tests to measure disturbances in various regions of the brain has been limited by the lack of direct information about what actually goes on in the brain. As we saw in Chapter 12, new technology using a variety of brain-imaging techniques is rapidly changing this situation. This technology contributes to clarifying the relationship between damage to specific regions of the brain and its effects on psychological functioning.

The CT scan provides films that show where injuries, deterioration, or enlargement occurred. The PT scan allows researchers to visualize the activity of different parts of the human brain. A PT scan is a color or black-and-white reconstruction of x-ray pictures that show patterns of glucose utilization—an index of brain activity—in different parts of the brain. Much as weather maps show various levels of rainfall, a PT scan shows the levels of glucose metabolism in different parts of the brain as they vary with the person's mental state and behavior. The PT scan enables scientists to study biochemical changes in the brain that could never be charted before. Whereas the CT scan shows the brain's anatomy, the PT scan reveals the varying strength of biochemical processes that occur in different areas of the brain.

A new technique, magnetic resonance imaging (MRI), has recently been developed to diagnose a wide range of disorders from coma to schizophrenia (Council of Scientific Affairs, 1987). Using arrays of sensitive detectors placed over the head, researchers are able to locate and measure precise sites of neural activity deep within the brain's furrows and creases (see Figure 13–2).

Both the CT and the MRI provide visualizations of brain anatomy and possible structural abnormalities. Unlike the CT, which is limited to imaging brain regions in a transverse plane, the MRI can image in all planes. The MRI technique offers advantages over the CT scan because of its improved precision of visualization. The PT scan is the most elegant of the available imaging techniques because of its sensitivity and flexibility, and its ability to measure regional cerebral blood flow. The PT permits the assessment of metabolic activity and the measurement of neurotransmitter function (Andreasen, 1988).

Assessing Brain Damage

A variety of procedures are used in assessing the extent of damage or deterioration of the brain. In addition to a general physical evaluation, clinical tests may include a mental-status examination, neuropsychological testing, and both traditional x-rays and newer radiological techniques such as PT and CT scans that provide information on the brain's soft tissues and chemical activity.

The **mental-status examination** consists of an interview, which is useful for clinical observation as well as for any statements the individual might make. The mental-status examination is often supplemented by psychological testing and a neurological examination. Clinicians use the mental-status examination to elicit the following information.

1. Level of consciousness. How aware is the individual of what is going on?
2. General appearance (behavior, dress, cooperation).
3. Attention span.
4. Orientation with regard to time and place.
5. Short-term memory (events of past life or common knowledge).
6. Language (spontaneous speech, comprehension, repetition, reading, writing).
7. Stream of thought. (Do the individual's ideas fit together logically?)
8. Mood.
9. Judgment and insight.

Neurologists, or physicians who specialize in diseases of the nervous system, use various techniques to assess brain damage and its cause. **Neuropsychology** is a relatively new branch of psychology that deals with relationships between behavior and the condition of the brain. Clinical neuropsychologists are particularly interested in the effects of brain lesions on behavior. Neuro-

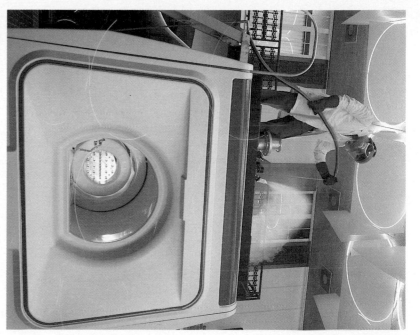

FIGURE 13-2

Magnetic resonance imaging (MRI) is used to map the changing contour of magnetic fields around the head. This permits calculation of the precise location—in three dimensions—of electrical activity within the brain. Researchers have played tones of different pitches and used magnetic sensors to track the resulting electrical signals in the auditory center of the brain. As the tones change, the location of the brain activity moves. Thus the brain appears to contain a "tone map," in which particular bunches of neurons handle sounds of different pitches.

The future of neuromagnetism is closely bound to the future of superconducting materials. Superconductors, carrying electric current with perfect efficiency, form the heart of the advanced sensors that make it possible to detect very weak magnetic fields. The sensors are known as "squids," or superconducting quantum interference devices. They are sensitive enough to measure ghostly fields with barely a billionth of the strength of the earth's own magnetic field, the force that turns compass needles. That, in turn, is a thousandth of the strength of a small bar magnet.

Organic Mental Disorders

Many of the organic mental disorders are basically physical disorders that have psychological symptoms associated with them. Because DSM-III-R uses Axis III to describe physical disorders and conditions, many of the traditional names have disappeared from the two main axes (Axis I and II) of the psychiatric diagnostic system. The classification scheme used in Axis III of DSM-III-R puts emphasis on the clusters of symptoms that accompany brain damage. A **syndrome** is a group of symptoms that tend to appear together. Clusters of psychological and behavioral symptoms that are connected

with temporary or permanent brain dysfunction are called **organic brain syndromes.** Cognitive loss is generally thought to be the hallmark of these organic brain syndromes. This loss can affect perception, memory, imagination, thought processing, problem-solving skills, and judgment. Of these, the most common syndromes are delirium, dementia, intoxication, and withdrawal. Delirium and dementia are emphasized in this chapter; intoxication and withdrawal are discussed in Chapter 14.

Organic brain syndromes are most often marked by delirium (which affects the person's state of consciousness or attention) or by dementia (which causes loss of intellectual ability), or by a combination of both. Delirium is often a short-term condition that is reversible, whereas dementia generally implies a nonreversible and often progressive condition. People with organic brain syndromes are likely to die earlier than people in the general population, especially if they are under 40 years of age (Black and others, 1985).

Delirium

Delirium is marked by relatively global cognitive impairment, disorientation, and confusion. In delirium, an individual has difficulty mobilizing, focusing, shifting, and sustaining attention. A wide and changeable range of strong emotions that do not seem related to environmental events may be evident. The presence of two or more of the following symptoms permits diagnosis of this condition.

1. Perceptual disturbances (for example, misinterpreting what is happening in a situation)

2. Incoherent speech

3. Insomnia or daytime sleepiness

4. Increased or decreased psychomotor activity (for example, hyperactivity)

5. Disorientation and memory impairment.

Delirium can occur as a result of either an acute or a chronic brain condition. There are four general organic causes of delirium:

1. Brain disease (for example, an infection or tumor)

2. A disease or infection in another part of the body that affects the brain (for example, a metabolic condition)

3. Intoxication (for example, with drugs)

4. Withdrawal from a substance to which an individual is addicted (for example, alcohol).

Delirium generally accompanies some other serious physical problem; about 10 percent of hospitalized medical and surgical patients become delirious (Lipowski, 1987). A person who is hospitalized after a heart attack may become delirious because the amount of oxygen supplied to the brain may depend on whether the patient is sitting up or lying down. Inadequate excretion of body wastes can also cause delirium. For example, if the kidneys fail to function, the toxins that are usually filtered out by the kidneys will accumulate in the bloodstream and the blood will have less room for oxygen. As a result of such physical disturbances, the brain begins to starve for oxygen, and symptoms of delirium may occur. The symptoms generally disappear shortly after the condition that led to their appearance has been corrected.

Psychological stress, sleep and sensory deprivation, prolonged immobilization, and severe fatigue are likely to contribute to the onset of delirium and to increase its severity. It is believed that a general derangement of brain metabolism coupled with an imbalance in the neurotransmitters underlies all cases of delirium. Delirium can also take place because of intoxication or the sudden withdrawal of alcohol or other drugs.

Although every person has the potential to develop delirium, there appear to be wide variations in susceptibility. Some people become delirious in response to metabolic changes or medications that do not produce delirium in others, whereas others fail to become delirious under metabolic conditions that are likely to produce delirium in most people. The incidence of delirium is highest among old people. It is not known to what extent this is a function of age itself rather than the frequency of organic brain disease and systemic disease in old age.

Patients with organic brain lesions are especially liable to develop delirium, as are people with long histories of alcohol or drug addiction. Delirium is frequent following surgery, either immediately or after a lucid period of several days, and seems to be due to the physical stress of the surgery itself and to the psychological stress of the surgery and the postoperative period. In a sense, delirium is a threshold phenomenon; that is, each individual probably has a specific threshold for this condition. Preexisting brain damage, addiction, and certain chronic medical disorders probably bring people close to this threshold even if they do not exceed it; relatively small metabolic changes may then push the patient over the threshold.

Delirium Tremens

One of the most dramatic examples of delirium can be seen in an acute brain condition called **delirium tremens** (or "the DTs?") that may sometimes result from excessive alcohol consumption. People with the Dts may be unable to follow directions like "stick out your tongue" or to attend to events going on around them. In addition to delirium, the DTs are characterized by tremors and visual hallucinations that result in a state of terror. The following excerpt from *Huckleberry Finn* is a vivid description of the DTs.

I don't know how long I was asleep, but all of a sudden there was an awful scream and I was up. There was Pap looking wild, and skipping around every which way and yelling about snakes. He said they was crawling up his legs; and then he would give a jump and scream, and say one had bit him on the cheek—but I couldn't see no snakes. He started running round and round the cabin, hollering,

"Take him off, take him off; he's biting me on the neck." I never see a man look so wild in the eyes. Pretty soon he was all fagged out, and fell down panting; then he rolled over and over wonderful fast, kicking things every which way, striking and grabbing at the air with his hands, and screaming and saying there was devils a-hold of him. He wore out by and by, and laid still awhile, moaning. Then he laid stiller, and didn't make a sound. I could hear the owls and wolves away off in the woods, and it seemed terrible still. He was lying over by the corner. By and by he raised up part way and listened, with his head to one side. He says, very low: "Tramp-tramp-tramp; they're coming after me but I won't go. Oh, they're here, don't touch me—don't! Hands off—they're cold; let go. Oh, let a poor devil alone." Then he went down on all fours and crawled off, begging them to let him alone, and he rolled himself up in his blanket and wallowed in under the old pine table, still a-begging; and then he went to crying. I could hear him through the blanket.

—(Clemens, 1923)

The symptoms of delirium tremens usually are not evident until after the person has stopped drinking. Several aspects of the mechanism that causes its symptoms are not well understood, but the DTs seem to be due to the prolonged interference of alcohol with the metabolism of neurons. The condition occurs in about 5 percent of alcoholics. Regardless of the cause (alcohol, infection, and so on), diffuse slowing of brainwave patterns is a regular finding.

Delirium tremens can last for a week or longer and must be treated in a hospital. During an episode of the DTs, the patient's physical condition deteriorates and he or she becomes highly susceptible to infections. Tranquilizing drugs and a quiet and orderly environment are essential, since even routine conversations among hospital personnel may frighten the patient and heighten his or her hallucinatory experiences. Renewed ability to sleep and rest usually indicates that an episode of DTs is coming to an end. However, recovery depends on restoration of metabolic equilibrium. In some cases equilibrium cannot be restored and death occurs.

Dementia

The essential feature of **brain deterioration**, or **dementia**, is a gradual loss of intellectual abilities that is sufficient to interfere with social or occupational functioning. Memory impairment, decline in ability to exercise good judgment and engage in abstract thinking, loss of self-control, and personality changes also occur. Dementia may be progressive, static, or even reversible if an effective treatment is available. Because individuals with dementia are not able to think clearly and often have difficulty making rational judgments, they are particularly vulnerable to physical, psychological, and social stress. Demented individuals are more likely than other people to experience delirium (see Figure 13–3).

The onset of dementia is gradual, and the course of the disorder is insidious. The term **senile dementia** is often used to refer to the condition when it occurs in people over 65. Autopsies show that most senile dementias have the characteristics of **Alzheimer's disease** which will be discussed later in the chapter. If dementia occurs in younger individuals, it is termed **presenile dementia**. In people with this condition there is a progressive atrophy (degeneration) of brain tissue, and their brainwave patterns are almost invariably abnormal. The individual becomes increasingly subject to lapses of memory, poor judgment, and disorientation. Deterioration in personal habits is common, and behavior may

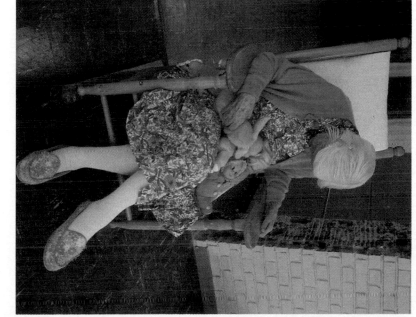

FIGURE 13–3

Dementia was not a major public health concern prior to the twentieth century because few people lived beyond the age of 75 years and dementia is largely a problem associated with advanced age. Today, more than 50 percent of the entire U.S. population reaches age 75 years and 25 percent live to be 85. The U.S. Census Bureau estimates that by the year 2000 there will be 35 million persons older than 65 years and that by the year 2050 this number will rise to 67 million. A large number of older people in nursing homes have some degree of dementia. The economic impact of dementia is great, running into the billions of dollars each year.

become unpredictable and impulsive. Because the person often remembers past events better than recent ones, he or she seems to live in the past much of the time.

The rate at which behavior is affected and the manner in which it changes are influenced by many factors, not the least of which is the individual's reaction to the physical and psychological deterioration. A sizable percentage of senile people undergo profound personality changes. Reconstruction of their earlier personalities usually uncovers the presence of maladaptive behavior patterns before the onset of senility, including actual and severe psychotic or neurotic reaction patterns or more likely, tendencies in those directions. These tendencies are made worse by the onset of senility, but they are not caused by it. Over half of the cases that are diagnosed as senile dementia show various combinations of agitation, paranoid and schizophreniclike reactions, and depression. One common symptom is **confabulation:** when faced with loss of particular memories, the individual fills in memory gaps with detailed, but inaccurate, accounts of his or her activities. The case described at the beginning of the chapter illustrates this tendency.

The following case describes symptoms that are often seen in primary degenerative dementia. These include a progressive memory deficit, at first for recent events but later for remote ones, along with narrowing of interests, loss of initiative, sluggishness of thought, apathy, irritability, and restlessness at night.

A talented artist was referred by his wife; he had become anxious and mildly depressed when his first symptoms emerged. In many respects he was very fortunate. At the age of 65 he had achieved a national, even international, reputation as an illustrator . . . [he] had devised a special process used to produce color covers and prints. . . . Recognition of his work gained him election to one of the distinguished clubs of artists in the city.

There had been some beginning failure in his memory. He complained of some difficulty in the use of his hands and arms, a clumsiness and lack of precision that did not exist before. When first seen, he advised that his father had become senile . . . and had had a slowly progressive course of increasing mental impairment, which the patient feared for himself, abhorring the thought. He was accompanied on his first visit by his wife, who had been his model. They had been married 30 years and had two daughters, both married.

She declared that at home he had become critical and querulous. He seemed to avoid going out to meet his artist friends. Furthermore, in contrast to his usual self-assurance at his work he seemed anxious and

upset when requested to take on a new contract. His concern over his abilities, his doubts, and even refusal of work were reflected in his relations with his wife. [Over the succeeding months it was learned that she had commenced to drink and did not seem as interested in the care of the house.] Also, he said his daughters were hounding him. Although he was able to talk most interestingly of his past work and life, it was clear that he had difficulty in recalling his earlier visits with his physician, when they occurred, or what had been discussed. The course was slowly progressive. As time went on, the tension and near panic he felt over inability to perform, on the recognition of his slowly progressive impairment of perception and skill, accompanied by much anxiety in meeting his business and social acquaintances, continued to increase. . . .

The failure in this mental functioning proceeded slowly. Periods of disorientation were first noticed at night when he arose to go to the bathroom. Some six years after onset he became seriously disturbed, had the delusion that men were attempting to kill him, and hallucinated voices. . . . He would talk to [his wife] of planning a Christmas card, but would forget that his daughters were married. His death, in a local general hospital, occurred quickly from cardiac arrest seven years after he was first seen.

—(Kolb and Brodie, 1982, pp. 238–239)

The Aging Process

For many years most of the problems of older people were lumped together under the heading of senile disorders. We now know that several different types of psychological and behavioral problems occur among old people. The elderly are vulnerable to serious consequences of brain changes such as senile dementia as well as certain other psychological conditions in which the role of organic factors is much less clear-cut. For example, depressive episodes increase in both frequency and depth in the later years of life. Transient depressions, which usually are without suicidal risk or intolerable distress, may occur in 30 percent or more of elderly people. Depression is likely to be provoked by the beginning of an illness or disability, but given time, most people adjust to these changes in their health status. The majority of severe depressions in old age are relapses, although new cases may occur even after the age of 75. Paranoid and hypochondriacal disorders are also common in older people.

Overall, the major clinical challenge facing the elderly is the greater likelihood of disorders in which there is brain degeneration. However, the problems of the elderly also reflect a number of other psychological

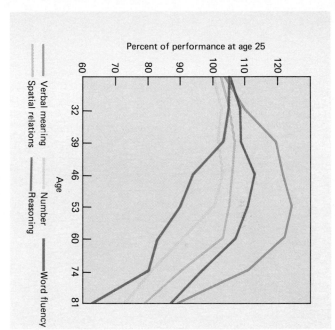

FIGURE 13–4
Performance on a variety of tasks used to measure intelligence is shown as a percent of performance at age 25. (Adapted from data presented by Schaie, 1983, p. 114) The later years of life are marked by gradual, irreversible physical decline and by psychological and social changes. However, there is ample evidence that social stimulation, interest in meaningful activities, and feeling that one is needed by other people prolong the ability to lead a happy, productive life.

One of the few longitude studies of the relationship between age and intellectual functioning is the Seattle Longitudinal Study. The original subjects, who ranged in age from 18 to 67, have now been tested 4 times over a 21-year period. The results have given a reasonably good picture of longitudinal change in cognitive abilities. The data show that there are only small changes in the kinds of abilities measured by intelligence tests before the age of 60, and no reliable decrease can be shown in these abilities before the age of 74. Although there is some decrease in measured ability beginning in the late 60s, it is not until age 81 that the average person falls below the middle range of performance for young adults. The data from the Seattle Longitudinal Study also suggest that there are very great individual differences in intellectual change throughout adulthood.

---

problems that often accompany increased age. These problems seem to be outgrowths of personal insecurities evoked by such life changes as having to live alone or being supported by others. With advancing age, the social niche in which the individual lives often changes drastically. At the same time, physiological changes may create additional stress as the person seeks to maintain self-esteem and competent, satisfying interactions. It would not be an exaggeration to say that the daily stresses the elderly have to cope with are so numerous and so severe that they would probably tax the coping resources of young adults.

Three points need to be kept in mind about the elderly. One is that there are many examples of successful old people—people who are active, feel that they have something to offer, and make contributions to their families and communities (see Figure 13–4). These people may suffer the physical declines that are frequent among the elderly, but they have found ways to work around them. A second point is that there is every reason to believe that most people can adapt successfully to the developmental transitions they encounter throughout life. Through public-education programs, society could do a much better job of preparing people for these changes. The third point is that there has been an unfortunate clinical neglect of older people. This is particularly true with regard to their psychological needs. Counseling and psychotherapy for the aged have often been dismissed as a waste of time. Yet many older people need opportunities to express their reactions to the variety of problems they face and to receive the support and advice of trusted clinicians.

Alzheimer's Disease

Alzheimer's disease is an insidious, heartbreaking malady that is associated with advancing age. Its memory lapses, confusion, and dementia inevitably get worse. People with Alzheimer's disease forget how to cook, go on wild spending sprees, lose the ability to balance their checkbooks and count change, and forget how to drive a car. Nearly total bodily and behavioral deterioration is typical in its final stages (see Figure 13–5).

By far the leading cause of mental deterioration among the elderly, Alzheimer's disease affects between 5 and 10 percent of all people over 65. In one family out of three, one parent will die of the disease. The disease tends to run in families and to be more frequent among females than among males. Because most Alzheimer's patients must eventually be placed in institutions, the disease (which has an average duration of about 7 years) places tremendous demands on the nation's health-care resources. Alzheimer's victims constitute 50 to 60 percent of the 1.3 million people in nursing homes, accounting for more than half of the over $25 billion spent annually on nursing home care. The disease will become more common and take an even greater toll as the average age of the U.S. population continues to increase.

Alzheimer's disease is also the most common form of presenile dementia. In these cases also, it usually causes gradual intellectual deterioration with growing lapses of memory (see Table 13–1). The progressive destruction of nervous tissue leads to slurring of speech,

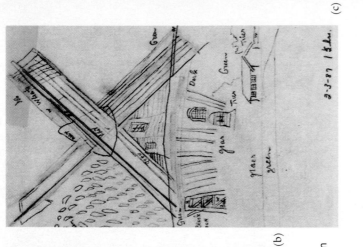

FIGURE 13-5

Alzheimer's disease destroys minds, but there have been few opportunities to study the disorder's impact on artistic creativity, one of the highest expressions of the human mind. These paintings and the sketch were created by an artist who began to show signs of Alzheimer's disease in his late sixties. When examined at the age of 74, he could not remember words 3 minutes after they were addressed to him. He was able to copy complex abstract figures, but his artistic ability had deteriorated.

A painting (a) completed at the time behavioral changes were first apparent shows good perspective, color sense, and attention to detail. A second (b), done seven years later, shows deterioration of all of these qualities, but retains some artistry. In a third picture (c), a sketch of the same subject done 2 years after that, the artist could only copy gross details from previous paintings. Testing over several years indicated that he first lost motivation, memory, and organizational ability, while visual perception and the physical ability to draw lasted longer.

involuntary movements of arms and legs, and in some cases, seizures. When the disease manifests itself primarily in the intellectual sphere, the individual may experience great anxiety about the deterioration of his or her abilities. It is not yet known why the neural degeneration that is fairly common among old people occurs in some people who are much younger.

Research and experience with the increasing number of Alzheimers' patients have increased knowledge of the symptoms of the disease and ways of helping victims adjust. Box 13–1 summarizes current knowledge in these two areas.

Research Directions. Alzheimer's disease was first identified in 1906 by a German physician, Alois Alzheimer. His patient, a 51-year-old woman, suffered loss of memory, disorientation, and later, severe dementia. After her death, Alzheimer performed an autopsy on her brain and found the two distinctive characteristics of the disease: tangled clumps of nerve cells and patches of disintegrated nerve-cell branches. Because Alzheimer's patients were relatively young, the disease was thought to

TABLE 13-1

Phases in the Cognitive Decline Accompanying Alzheimer's Disease

Phase	Examples
1. Complaints of memory deficit	Forgetting names that one formerly knew well
2. Increased cognitive decline and signs of confusion	Losing or misplacing an object of value
3. Moderately severe cognitive decline and intensified confusion (early dementia)	Inability to recall major aspects of one's life, such as the names of close family members
4. Severe cognitive decline and confusion (middle dementia)	Largely unaware of all recent events and experiences
5. Very severe cognitive decline and confusion (late dementia)	Loss of all verbal abilities, need for assistance in eating and toileting

Based on Reisberg, 1985.

be a disease of middle age; similar symptoms in elderly people were regarded as a natural consequence of aging. Today this view has been discarded. Nerve cells that resemble those noticed by Alzheimer have been found to contain two abnormal rigid structures called *plaques* and *tangles*. The greater the number of plaques and tangles, the more severe the intellectual disability of the patient. Thus, dementias of the Alzheimer's type seem to involve a specific pathological process rather than being a normal consequence of aging.

Neurochemicals. The cause of the degenerative process is not yet known, but recent research gives reason to believe that it may be discovered in the foreseeable future. Research to date has shown that there is a loss of neurons, especially in the frontal and temporal lobes of the cerebral cortex. Other clues to understanding the disorder are being provided by research on the chemical messengers in the affected parts of the brain (Coyle and others, 1983). *Acetylcholine*, a chemical that nerves in the brain use to signal to one another is known to be in-

BOX 13-1
Helping the Person with Alzheimer's Disease

Table 13-2 shows the frequencies with which various symptoms occur as the disease progresses. Caretakers of Alzheimer's patients need to be familiar with both the symptoms of the disease and ways to deal with them. A basic ground rule for Alzheimer's patients is: take nothing for granted. Many different personal characteristics, abilities, and behaviors surface when caring for Alzheimer's patients. While no one patient will be like another, certain types of behaviors appear with a greater frequency than others. The following overview will present some of the most common behavioral concerns and coping strategies useful to caretaking family members.

SYMPTOM

1. *Depression*
Unhappiness and withdrawal are common in Alzheimer's disease patients.

2. *Hostility, Belligerence, and Aggression*
Alzheimer's patients can be selfish and hostile.

3. *Disorientation*
The Alzheimer's patient will become increasingly confused about people, places and time.

4. *Wandering*
Wandering and restlessness are common problems.

5. *Anxiety and Suspiciousness*
Worries and paranoid thinking occur in many cases.

COPING STRATEGY

1. Caregivers can try to increase activities that the patient formerly enjoyed and can still manage. Try to involve them in such activities, perhaps with another family member or a friend. Talk with them; reminisce about family, friends, and activities.

2. Confronting the situation head-on and trying to reason with Alzheimer's patients will not work. Being reassuring and calm may help to reduce the hostility. Trying to distract the person with questions about the problem and gradually moving their attention to something else may also help.

3. Labeling items can help, or color coding rooms such as the bathroom or bedroom, can alleviate some problems in the early stages of the disease. Talking in a calm voice, and reassuring them of where they are and who they are with, may help ease their feelings of being lost and alone.

4. Walking and other physical exercises may help alleviate such problems. Keeping the household free of clutter is a major consideration so that there is not added confusion or harm to the person as they wander through what was once a familiar environment. Identification bracelets and safety locks are other useful devises for those individuals who are given to wandering.

5. Patient fears and anxieties cannot really be dealt with in a rational and normal manner. Identifying what is frightening the patient may be helpful, but directly confronting and telling the patient there is nothing to their concerns will not work. It is often useful to develop calming answers to the situation that is frightening and then distract the patient to another subject.

BOX 13–1 (CONTINUED)

FIGURE 13–6
Persons with Alzheimer's disease become progressively more disoriented, tend to wander, and get lost.

FIGURE 13–7
Alzheimer's disease has a profound effect, not only on the person who develops it, but also on the lives of all the members of the family. In this home reminder signs are used to lessen the memory problems Alzheimer's disease creates.

volved in learning and memory. There is some evidence that an acetylcholine deficiency might contribute to the learning and memory deficits of senility. Autopsy of the brains of patients who have died shows that *choline ace-tylcholine transferase,* an enzyme that forms acetylcholine, is greatly reduced in the cerebral cortex and hippocampus regions of the brains of patients dying with senile dementia. It appears that impairment in acetylcholine production is a fundamental and relatively specific defect in the brains of patients with Alzheimer's dementia. Accordingly, one focus of current research is the development of drugs that will increase the formation of acetylcholine, prevent its destruction, or directly stimulate the acetylcholine receptors.

Genes. Another focus is the genetics of the disease. Half the immediate family members of patients with Alzheimer's disease may develop the devastating mental disorder if they live into their nineties. There is growing evidence that Alzheimer's disease is a hereditary disease, governed by a gene or genes that cause damage to the

patient's brain late in life. The identity and function of the suspected gene are unknown. The risk of developing Alzheimer's is four to five times as great among close relatives of patients as it is in the general population.

The disease has been linked to abnormalities on chromosome 21, but no specific gene has yet been proved to be a factor in the disease. Chromosome 21 has been identified as the location of the gene for a protein that is found in the characteristic clumps and plaques of a substance called amyloid, which is found in the brains of most Alzheimer's patients. But it is not known whether amyloid is a cause or an effect of the mind-destroying disease process (Mozar and others, 1987).

Gene mapping is a valuable technique in determining the contribution of genetic factors to disorders, such as Alzheimer's disease. There are basically two kinds of gene maps: genetic linkage maps and physical maps.

Genetic linkage maps are constructed by studying family histories and measuring the frequency with which two traits are inherited together, or linked. If two

TABLE 13-2

Percentages of Alzheimer's Disease Patients at Three Levels of Severity Showing Specific Problems

Type of Problem	Mild	Moderate	Severe	Total Sample
Restlessness	60%	40%	50%	45%
Suspiciousness	20%	24%	29%	24%
Falling	20%	33%	29%	28%
Hallucinations	10%	24%	30%	21%
Wandering	18%	22%	50%	26%
Agitation	10%	27%	38%	24%
Hygiene	8%	24%	71%	28%
Incontinence	5%	16%	30%	16%

genes for different traits are often inherited together, they are usually located near each other on the same chromosome. If they are never inherited together, they are probably distant from each other or perhaps even on different chromosomes. In this way, knowing the location of only one gene can help locate other, nearby genes.

Physical maps, on the other hands, chart distances between physical landmarks on the genes. These landmarks could be dark bands that are visible under a microscope. Using recent advances in molecular biology, they could be sites where certain enzymes act to break the chromosomes into smaller pieces. With a detailed physical map, one could figure out the actual distance. To date, only about 400 of the approximately 100,000 or so human genes have been located.

Alzheimer's disease would be far easier to treat and detect if its cause were known. The fact that the disease often occurs in several members of the same family suggests that a genetic factor is at work. Screening for hereditary influences might reveal genetic markers, and it might be possible to identify environmental factors that influence the age of onset and the progress of the disease.

Little progress has been made in the treatment of Alzheimer's disease since Alzheimer's day, and even diagnosis remains difficult. The only way to be absolutely certain that a patient has the disorder is to examine the brain after death. While the patient is alive, the diagnosis must be arrived at by a careful process of elimination. Through brain imaging and other tests, it is possible to determine that the patient has not suffered a series of small strokes and does not have Parkinson's disease, a brain tumor, depression, an adverse drug reaction, or any other disorder that can cause dementia (see Figure 13–8).

Although much remains to be discovered about this disease, two critical crossroads reached in the ap-

proach to treatment for Alzheimer's disease were (1) the recognition of Alzheimer's disease as a disorder distinct from the normal aging process, and (2) the realization that in developing therapeutic and social interventions for a major illness or disability the concept of care can be as important as that of cure.

The Family. In addition to searching for the causes of Alzheimer's disease, researchers are attempting to find ways of treating not only the patient but caregivers as well. Those who care for people with Alzheimer's disease often experience severe stress. Marian Roach (1983) has provided the following description of her reactions and those of her sister, Margaret, to their mother's deterioration as a result of Alzheimer's disease.

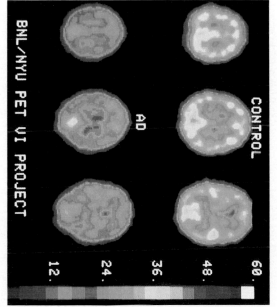

FIGURE 13–8
These PT scans show the characteristic lower glucose metabolism seen in the brain of an Alzheimer's patient (bottom) compared to that of an age- and sex-matched control (top).

BNL/NYU PET VI PROJECT

CONTROL

AD

60. 48. 36. 24. 12.

I noticed that she had stopped taking phone messages. One friend said she sounded "jealous and hostile." She would abruptly hang up on people. She became obsessed with the plumbing: She would look under the sinks and start to take apart the pipes, convinced there was a drip. She would walk away in the middle of conversation. She became repetitive, depressed. (p. 23)

As the deterioration continued, the pressures and emotional strain worsened.

Margaret and I have no relatives but my mother. The decisions we make are made together. Margaret works until 11 at night and on weekends. We have a young woman who lives in the house from Monday through Friday. Another woman comes on Friday and Saturday nights. Yet another takes my mother out—for rides or to the movies—three afternoons a week. But the burden of care is on my patient sister, who manages the schedules and sees my mother daily. I work during the day. I am with my mother on Sundays.

As I have gotten to know this disease, I have felt ashamed at my own embarrassment. I find myself explaining her condition to people, to excuse her behavior. Sometimes I do this in front of her and, for an instant, my mother will look terribly embarrassed. I see it in her face and I feel very unlike a daughter. I feel like a traitor. And then she will forget my explanation of her "memory problem," and her questions and repetitions, along with my embarrassment, will continue. Alzheimer's victims are likely to say or do anything during the stages just before they can do literally nothing for themselves. It is difficult to know what to expect. The anticipation is sometimes the worst part.

I sometimes dread the weekends. I try not to cry in front of Margaret, who tries not to cry in front of me. Margaret and I have discussed the possibility of our contracting the disease. If I get it, I have said that I'd want Margaret to kill me; she has said the same. (p. 31)

Research on the aspects of caring for Alzheimer's victims that are particularly stressful for people like Marian and Margaret Roach has shown that the sense of lack of control over what will happen next is of great importance (Pagel and others, 1985). In addition, caregivers feel isolated, unable to deal effectively with the continuing stress, and confused about their own reactions. Support groups and group therapy can be valuable in allowing family members to express their feelings, particularly those that they consider unacceptable (for example, anger and disappointment). The opportunity to compare their experiences with those of other

people who are going through the same trial often makes them aware that such feelings are normal and understandable.

Pick's Disease

Pick's disease is much less common than Alzheimer's disease. Whereas the risk of Alzheimer's disease increases steadily through adult life, Pick's disease is most likely to develop between the ages of 60 and 70. After that period the risk decreases (Heston and Mastri, 1982). Its symptoms are so similar to those of Alzheimer's disease that it takes an autopsy to tell the two disorders apart. People who have died from Pick's disease show a characteristic form of brain atrophy. Among people over age 40, 24 out of 100,000 can be expected to die of the disease. There appears to be a strong genetic factor, and men are at greater risk of developing the disease than women (Heston and others, 1987).

There are no known cures for any of the senile and presenile dementias. Their treatment consists mainly of emotional support and sedative drugs. Efforts are made to structure the individual's life so that his or her days are uncomplicated and routinized so as to avoid pressure and tension. Various types of biophysical treatments (for instance, the use of cerebral stimulants, vitamins, and inhalation of oxygen) have been tried. Although research on these treatments continues, no cure for dementia has yet been found.

Multi-Infarct Dementia

Another less common dementia, which is more likely to occur after age 65 than before, is **multi-infarct dementia.** This disorder is caused by a series of minor strokes that occur at different times. The onset is abrupt and the course of the disorder is fluctuating rather than uniformly progressive. The pattern of deficits is "patchy," depending on which areas of the brain have been destroyed. As the condition worsens, the relatively intact areas of intellectual functioning decrease and there is increased disturbance in several functions, including memory, abstract thinking, judgment, and impulse control. Hypertension may be a major factor in multi-infarct dementia. Controlling high blood pressure helps prevent this type of dementia and reduces the likelihood of minor strokes when multi-infarct dementia is already present.

Other Organic Brain Syndromes

Other organic brain syndromes that are discussed in DSM-III-R not only are less common than delirium and dementia but also do not involve as great a change in overall functioning. In an **amnestic syndrome,** for in-

TABLE 13-4

stance, there is a memory disturbance marked by inability to learn new material or recall information acquired in the past. Table 13-3 describes the three main diagnostic features of amnestic syndromes.

Amnestic syndromes are marked by neither the confusion and clouding of consciousness seen in delirium nor the general loss of intellectual abilities seen in dementia. The most common forms of amnestic syndrome result from thiamine deficiency and chronic alcohol use. The syndrome may also follow head injuries, surgery, or anything else that interferes with the flow of blood through the brain. The treatment depends entirely on the cause; no specific treatment is available for most of the disorders that cause this condition.

The diagnosis of **organic delusional syndrome** applies when there are delusions that seem to be attributable to an organic process. Intellectual impairment is absent or slight, and the confusion of delirium is absent. A number of substances discussed in Chapter 14 (for example, amphetamines, cannabis, and psychedelics) may cause this syndrome.

Organic hallucinosis refers to a syndrome that is characterized by recurrent or persistent hallucinations experienced in a state of clear awareness. This diagnosis is used when an organic factor is believed to be involved. Use of psychedelics is a common cause of this syndrome. The types of hallucinations manifested are often related to the substance involved. For example, alcohol tends to induce auditory hallucinations.

The **organic affective syndrome** features an abnormal mood, either depressive or manic, that is judged to be a consequence of a brain disorder rather than a personal response to an event or situation. The syndrome is often caused by toxic or metabolic factors. Disorders of the endocrine system can also play a role.

The **organic anxiety syndrome** is marked by recurrent panic attacks or generalized anxiety. This diagnosis is made when there is evidence from the patient's medical history, physical examination, or laboratory tests that a specific organic factor is causally related to the disturbance.

In an **organic personality syndrome** there are changes is the person's motivation, emotions, and im-

pulse control. He or she may seem uncharacteristically apathetic, irritable, or euphoric. As with the other syndromes, the diagnosis of organic personality syndrome is used when an organic factor is believed to be involved in the personality change. Structural damage to the brain—caused, for example, by a tumor or head injury—is common in this syndrome. Table 13-4 describes the diagnostic criteria for organic personality syndrome. The clinical picture depends to a great extent on the size and location of the brain lesion. The syndrome is more likely to be diagnosed in people who are over 50 years of age, who have no history of mental disorder, and in whom a personality change takes place abruptly over a relatively short period.

Brain Disorders with a Variety of Causes

To illustrate the range of problems that produce symptoms of organic brain disorder, we will discuss a number of additional disorders that alter behavior, emotions, and cognitive functioning. These include disorders that are related to heredity, to the lack of a particular neurotransmitter, to infection, to a nutritional deficiency, or to brain damage caused by outside forces, the growth of a tumor within the brain, or cerebrovascular problems.

Huntington's Disease: A Genetically Based Disorder

Huntington's disease, or **Huntington's chorea,** is a rare hereditary disorder that is transmitted by a single dominant gene and is characterized by progressive degeneration of brain tissue. It can begin at any time from childhood to late in life, but most commonly the onset

---

TABLE 13-3

Diagnostic Features of Amnestic Syndrome

1. *Anterograde amnesia*—impaired ability to learn, retain, and reproduce new information.
2. *Retrograde amnesia*—impaired ability to recall memories that were established prior to the onset of the disorder.
3. *Confabulation*—expression of inaccurate and at times inappropriate answers to straightforward and simple questions.

Feature	Examples
1. Emotional instability	Temper outbursts, sudden crying
2. Impaired impulse control	Poor social judgment, shoplifting
3. Marked apathy and indifference	No interest in usual hobbies
4. Paranoid thinking	Extreme suspiciousness

occurs between the ages of 30 and 50. The offspring of affected fathers often experience the disorder at an earlier age than their fathers did. Four types of symptoms are observed in Huntington's disease: dementia, irritability and apathy, depression, and hallucinations and delusions. In addition, there are choreiform movements—involuntary, spasmodic jerking and twisting movements of the neck, trunk, and extremities, and much facial grimacing. (The word *chorea* refers to these movements.)

The psychological and behavioral symptoms of Huntington's disease are even more devastating than the physical ones. As the disease develops, the person experiences increasing difficulty in memory storage and retrieval. There is also evidence that intelligence test scores get progressively lower in the period just before the appearance of the characteristic choreiform movements. This suggests that the gene for Huntington's disease does not suddenly "turn on" at the time that the involuntary movements appear.

Impulsiveness in behavior and paranoid and depressive thinking are likely to occur as the disorder progresses and family life becomes disrupted. It is not clear whether these behavioral components of Huntington's disease are organically caused or whether they are psychological reactions to physical deterioration. Recently it has become known that people with Huntington's disease have a deficiency of one neurotransmitter, GABA (gamma-amino-butyric-acid).

The disorder usually begins in middle life, although the onset can occur much earlier. The folksinger and composer Woody Guthrie died in 1967 after suffering from Huntington's disease for 13 years. As a result of a misdiagnosis, Guthrie had been considered an alcoholic and had been placed in a series of mental hospitals for years before the correct diagnosis was made. Guthrie had eight children, one of whom has already died of Huntington's disease.

Since the disease is inherited through a single dominant gene, each child of an affected parent has a 50-percent chance of inheriting the disorder. There is no skipping of generations, and until recently there has been no way of distinguishing carriers of the gene from noncarriers until the symptoms appear. The fact that Huntington's disease does not manifest itself until the middle decades of life means that members of a family that might be affected by it must spend their childhood, adolescence, and early adult years not knowing whether they will develop the disorder or not.

In the San Luis region of Venezuela, the prevalence of Huntington's disease is 700 times higher than in the United States. Within a population of about 3,000, about 150 people have been stricken by the disease and 1,500 more have a substantial risk of developing it. This is because San Luis is the home of a handful of families with many affected members. By far the largest of these families is the Soto family, which has the highest known concentration of Huntington's disease of any family in the world. This is bad news for the Soto family but good news for science. By carefully studying the blood of Iris del Valle Soto and other members of her extended family of almost 4,000 people covering eight generations, researchers achieved a startling breakthrough. They pinpointed the location in the specific chromosome pair (chromosome pair 4) at which the gene for Huntington's disease is located (Wexler and others, 1985). This was an important first step toward developing a diagnostic test for the disease and perhaps, eventually, a treatment. The diagnostic genetic test is now being used at several clinical centers throughout the country on an experimental basis. It is important to determine how people at risk respond to the opportunity to be tested, if they are willing to be tested, and how they react to the test results. The knowledge that they were certainly going to develop this disease at some time in the future would be extremely stressful to most people. On the other hand, if the test results were negative, children of a parent with Huntington's disease would be relieved of a terrible worry that they might develop the disease and pass it on to any children of their own.

Genetic Counseling

As noted in Chapter 12, the purpose of **genetic counseling** is to alleviate problems related to the occurrence or possible recurrence of a genetically influenced mental disorder. Twin, adoption, and family studies have shown that these disorders include schizophrenia, affective disorders, presenile dementias, and alcoholism. The most obvious use of genetic counseling is to help a couple decide whether they want to have children when a serious mental illness appears to run in one of their families. A genetic counselor may also relieve parents' anxiety about the future health of already born children by providing reliable information or clarifying a diagnosis of mental disorder through analysis of the family's history. The counselor may also talk to unaffected family members about their fears of developing the illness, and may give advice about how and when to inform children that they are at risk.

Genetic counseling involves seven steps: (1) diagnosis of any symptoms currently present; (2) taking a family history; (3) establishing the risk of mental illness; (4) evaluating the needs of the client; (5) weighing burden, risk, and benefit; (6) forming a plan of action; and (7) follow-up. Every possible source of information is used. In uncertain cases the counselor may abstain from risk analysis rather than offer estimates that might be inaccurate.

In the case of Huntington's disease, the counselor can calculate exact risk figures based on current knowledge of genetics. The counselor must bear in mind whether the mental health of living children is in question, whether future childbearing is a concern, whether the client understands the meaning of the diagnosis, and so on. He or she must take into account the genetic relationship between the client and the ill relative. Intelligence, compassion, confidence, candor, and flexibility are important qualities in a counselor, especially when the client is deciding whether to have a child.

Parkinson's Disease: A Neurotransmitter Deficit

Like Huntington's disease, **Parkinson's disease** is progressive and may begin by the age of 50. Its symptoms include tremor, rigidity, an expressionless, masklike facial appearance, and loss of vocal power. A person with Parkinson's disease typically exhibits social withdrawal, reduced intellectual ability, and rigidity in coping with his or her problems. Most Parkinson's patients seem emotionally overcontrolled. It is difficult to determine how much of the behavioral maladaptation associated with Parkinson's disease is due to organic processes and how much is due to the patient's psychological reaction to them.

There is evidence that the brains of Parkinson's patients are deficient in dopamine. Unlike the dementias discussed so far, this disorder can be treated. A drug called L-dopa is used to relieve some of the symptoms. One study found the Parkinson's patients treated with L-dopa showed clinical improvement that persisted over a 10 year period (Bauer and others, 1982).

Recently, surgeons have carried out tissue implantations into the human brain as a possible way of relieving Parkinson symptoms. In one case, the right adrenal gland was removed from a 35-year-old man suffering from Parkinson's disease and part of the gland—the medulla—was transplanted to the patient's brain. The hope was that the adrenal tissue would manufacture needed dopamine. A beneficial effect has been found for this procedure; the degree of incapacity for some patients is reduced. However, they are not cured and still require medication (Lewin, 1988). The idea of the implantations makes sense and researchers are continuing to study the procedure for both Parkinson's disease and Huntington's disease.

General Paresis: An Infectious Disease

Infectious disorders often have an acute onset, although the possibility of slow-acting viral infections should not be ruled out. The central nervous system often is more susceptible to bodily infections than other tissues of the body. Some of these infections do not last long, and successful treatments have been worked out for many of them. If left untreated, however, some infections can lead to irreversible brain disorders.

Untreated **syphilitic infections** are an example of this type of condition. If syphilis is diagnosed before its terminal stages, it can be treated with drugs, usually penicillin. The aim of the drugs is to return the cerebrospinal fluid to normal, which may require many months. These drugs may cure the patient, but the degree of improvement depends on how many neurons were destroyed before the treatment began. When the destruction is great, losses in intellectual functioning cannot be restored. Another factor that influences recovery is the individual's preinfection personality. The kind of deterioration that occurs depends partly on lifelong personality characteristics. The more stable the personality, the greater the chance of recovery.

One of the results of untreated syphilis in its late stage is **general paresis**, or **dementia paralytica**, a progressive deterioration in psychological and motor functioning that results in paralysis, psychosis, and death. Among the symptoms of general paresis are loss of cognitive functions, slurring of speech, tremors of the tongue and lips, and poor motor coordination. These symptoms are progressive and eventually lead to a helpless condition. Before the cause and treatment of syphilis were discovered, patients with general paresis represented between one-tenth and one-third of all admissions to mental hospitals.

Because of the negative relationship between the degree of possible improvement and the extent of irreversible brain damage, prompt diagnosis and medical treatment of syphilitic infections is clearly the best approach to reducing the incidence of general paresis.

Pellagra and Korsakoff's Syndrome: Nutritional Deficiencies

Vitamin and other nutritional deficiencies can affect the nervous system. For example, **pellagra** is a reversible disease that is caused by a deficiency of the vitamin niacin (nicotinic acid) or its derivatives. The deficiency affects cells in the area of the cerebral cortex that controls body movement and in other parts of the brain. There are a variety of symptoms, including a skin disorder (the skin looks as if it had been severely sunburned), diarrhea, and psychological deterioration. The signs of psychological impairment are similar to those of anxiety disorders and depression: anxiety, irritability, loss of recent memory, and difficulty in concentration. Untreated cases may manifest delirium, hallucinations, and a variety of psychotic behaviors.

The incidence of pellagra has declined sharply in the United States as a result of improved diet, but it is still common in many underdeveloped countries. Chronic alcoholics who have poorly balanced diets may show symptoms of pellagra. On the basis of behavior alone, it is difficult to distinguish between pellagra and conditions like anxiety or schizophrenia, but when a niacin deficiency is suspected (usually on the basis of skin and digestive symptoms), diagnosis is relatively simple. Except in very severe cases, nutritional therapy is highly effective. The individual is placed on a protein-rich diet that is also rich in vitamins (niacin, thiamine, and vitamin B complex). Mild cases improve noticeably within 48 hours.

Nutritional deficiencies sometimes combine with toxic substances to produce substantial and irreversible damage to brain tissue. **Korsakoff's syndrome,** which occurs in some chronic alcoholics, results from a combination of alcoholism and vitamin B_1 (thiamine) deficiency. Recent and past memories are lost, and the person seems unable to form new memories. In addition, there are perceptual deficits, loss of initiative, and confabulation. Delirium tremens frequently is part of the patient's medical history. The longer the vitamin deficiency has persisted, the less responsive the individual will be to vitamin therapy.

Brain Injuries and Tumors

Head injuries and intracranial growths (brain tumors) can lead to both acute and chronic disorders (see Figure 13–9). In many cases it is difficult to determine the extent to which abnormal behavior is a result of damage and how much represents a lifelong behavior pattern or simply a reaction to knowledge of the injury. These factors can interact in many ways. A startling or traumatic event, whether or not it involves physical injury, usually has some specific and symbolic significance for the individual. The term **traumatic neurosis** has been used to describe reactions that follow such as event. A blow to the head that caused little physical damage might be exploited by the injured person, as in some hysterical disorders. The reaction may be reinforced by secondary gains, such as sympathy or permission to quit one's job. Table 13–5 lists some of the factors that influence the effects of a brain injury.

Brain injuries are usually classified into three groups: **concussions,** or transient states that momentarily change the physical condition of the brain but do not cause structural damage; **contusions,** in which diffuse, fine structural damage—for example, the rupturing of tiny blood vessels—takes place; and **lacerations,** which involve major tears or ruptures in the brain tissue.

Although a concussion might include a temporary

FIGURE 13–9

On Christmas Day, 1985, James McDonnell came home to his wife in Larchmont, New York, after 14 years of amnesia. He had lost his memory after suffering head injuries in two automobile accidents, had gone to Philadelphia, and had found a job in a restaurant. McDonnell said that his memory had returned on Christmas Eve when he bumped his head.

loss of consciousness, the person can be expected to recover completely within 24 to 48 hours. Sometimes it is difficult to diagnose precisely the extent of brain injury and its potential effect on brain functioning. A variety of tests and observations are used to analyze each case, including x-ray evidence of skull fracture, a brain scan to determine tissue damage, a test for blood in the spinal fluid, and observation of symptoms such as bleeding from the skull orifices (for example, the ears), throbbing headaches, prolonged loss of consciousness, and sluggish cognitive behavior. Head injuries can lead to highly specific losses in motor or cognitive functioning, with the extent of the loss depending on the kind of

TABLE 13-5

Factors that Influence the Effects of a Brain Injury

1. Age
2. Site of injury
3. Extent of damage
4. Emotional reactions to resulting physical and mental deficits
5. Personality and social competence
6. Social support available after injury

injury and where it is located. Although perhaps 1.5 million people suffer head injuries in automobile accidents each year, less than 1 percent of first admissions to mental hospitals are attributable to head injuries.

Sometimes the brain is injured not by an accident or a blow but by pressure inside the skull, perhaps from a tumor. In such cases the speed with which the intruding body develops also influences the amount of loss. A tumor might grow slowly for a long time before there is evidence of intracranial pressure or behavioral change (see Box 13–2). A good prognosis in cases of brain injury or tumor depends on how early and how accurately the condition is diagnosed and whether a treatment for the condition exists.

In some cases in which there is known physical damage, only minor behavioral deficits develop. Apparently some people adapt to minor brain damage better than others. Thus, while brain damage can cause maladaptive behavior, the opposite can occur: an individual can respond maladaptively to the knowledge of having a damaged brain. Furthermore, any type of major injury or traumatic condition might set off a maladaptive psychological reaction such as a psychosis. **Posttraumatic psychoses** are similar to other psychoses. They involve confusion, delirium, and temporary catatonic, manic, or depressive reactions. A posttraumatic psychosis might develop abruptly when a person begins to regain consciousness after receiving a head injury.

Unfortunately, it is usually unclear whether a latent psychosis existed before the traumatic event occurred. The patient cannot, of course, remember the period of unconsciousness following brain trauma, and recollections of the confused state that occurs just after regaining consciousness usually are hazy. In addition, there may be amnesia (loss of memory) for some time prior to the injury. Even after relatively minor injuries, many patients complain of headaches, dizziness, fatigue, lack of concentration, and anxiety. In most cases these complaints are of short duration.

Tumors produce a variety of physiological and psychological changes because their presence causes a rise in intracranial pressure or interferes with the blood supply to the brain. Their symptoms depend on their location in the brain. For example, tumors growing in or near the frontal lobe frequently lead to a gradual onset of mental changes, but again, the symptoms depend on the site of the tumor. One group of people with frontal-lobe tumors may become exuberant and euphoric; their conversation is punctuated by laughter and jokes. Another group may show general apathy and slowness in responding.

Memory disorders are very common in people with cerebral tumors and are often the first noticeable indication that a problem exists. The nature of the memory impairment varies widely. For example, people

with left-hemisphere lesions may have difficulty with material that they hear, but they may be able to cope with the same material if they can see it. Researchers are investigating the degree to which training in attentional and cognitive skills can aid in the rehabilitation of brain-damaged individuals (Gummow and others, 1983).

Early in their development some brain tumors result in changes that neurologists can assess. However, in the absence of other evidence to suggest the presence of a tumor, personality and behavioral changes often result in misdiagnosis and are attributed to nonorganic factors. The role of organic factors may become evident later. For example, the composer George Gershwin underwent psychoanalysis because he suffered severe headaches. It was not until shortly before his death that the diagnosis of a brain tumor was made.

Epilepsy: Multiple Causal Factors

Epilepsy has inspired awe, fear, a sense of mystery, and puzzlement throughout history. The Greek physician Hippocrates argued that epilepsy was a naturally caused disease, but for most of modern history it was seen as a sign of demonic possession. Many famous people including Julius Caesar, the elder William Pitt, and Fyodor Dostoyevsky, were epileptics. Dostoyevsky, one of the word's great novelists, suffered from epileptic seizures. His first attack came while he was in prison in Siberia. He believed that the agony of living in chains, the stench, and hard labor had precipitated the seizures, which persisted for years even after he was permitted to leave the prison.

The illness of Vincent van Gogh (1853–1890) is an example of the complex mental changes associated with epilepsy. Van Gogh, the son of a Dutch preacher, was the product of a difficult birth. As a child he was unruly and required special schooling. Later he failed as an art dealer, a teacher, and a preacher. He described himself as "a man of passion, capable and prone to undertake more or less foolish things which I happen to repent more or less." Shunned by the few women he loved, he pursued his mission as an evangelist to a miserably poor mining district with such extreme devotion that he was dismissed by the church. Only then, at the age of 27, did he begin his career as a painter—a career that he pursued with singular intensity for the last 10 years of his short life.

Beginning in his midtwenties, Van Gogh suffered from peculiar sensations in his stomach, episodes of terror, and lapses of consciousness. The illness may have been precipitated partly by the use of absinthe, an alcoholic drink that heightens susceptibility to epileptic ep-

BOX 13–2

Mass Killer with Malignant Brain Tumor

The behavioral effects of brain injuries and tumors are often puzzling and sometimes dramatic. For example, the evening of July 31, 1966, Charles Whitman, a student at the University of Texas, wrote the following note.

I don't really understand myself these days. I am supposed to be an average, reasonable, and intelligent young man. However, lately (I can't recall when it started) I have been the victim of many unusual and irrational thoughts. These thoughts constantly recur, and it requires a tremendous mental effort to concentrate on useful and progressive tasks. In March when my parents made a physical break I noticed a great deal of stress. I consulted Dr. Cochran at the University Health Center and asked him to recommend someone that I could consult with about some psychiatric disorders I felt I had. I talked with a doctor once for about two hours and tried to convey to him my fears that I felt overcome by overwhelming violent impulses. After one session I never saw the doctor again, and since then I have been fighting my mental turmoil alone, and seemingly to no avail. After my death I wish that an autopsy would be performed on me to see if there is any visible physical disorder. I have had some tremendous headaches in the past and have consumed two large bottles of Excedrin in the past three months. (UPI)

Later that night Whitman killed his wife and his mother. The next morning he went to the tower on the university campus with a high-powered hunting rifle and opened fire. Ninety minutes later he was shot to death, but by that time he had shot 38 people, killing 14, and had even managed to hit an airplane (see Figure 13–10).

Because of the shocking nature of this incident, it attracted widespread attention. There were many attempts to explain Whitman's murderous acts. The letter that Whitman had written provided a number of clues. It referred to intense headaches, and a postmortem examination revealed a highly malignant tumor in a region of the brain that is known to be involved in aggressive behavior. Some experts suggested that Whitman's actions had been caused by brain damage. Others viewed them as products of the "unusual and irrational thoughts" to which he referred in his letter. A study of Whitman's life revealed that he had had many positive experiences with guns, and some authorities on violent behavior pointed to these experiences as a possible causal factor. Still others cited Whitman's reference to "overwhelming violent impulses" and suggested that those impulses had been bottled up for many years and had finally exploded into action because of the recent life stresses described in his letter.

We cannot be certain which of these potential causes was most important. Perhaps all of them contributed to his actions to varying degrees. The Whitman case dramatically illustrates the many perspectives from which a single act can be viewed and explained.

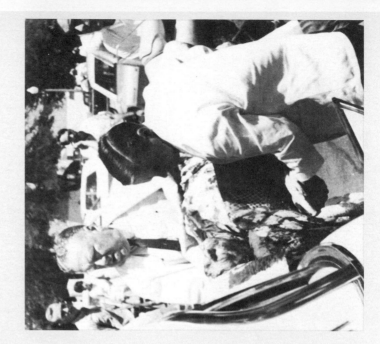

FIGURE 13–10
Charles Whitman, shown here in a college photo, killed his wife, mother, and 14 strangers who were hit by bullets he sprayed from a perch high in the tower of the administration building at the University of Texas.

isodes. He underwent unpredictable mood shifts—"at-tacks of melancholy" alternating with ecstatic states or "indescribable anguish." He became argumentative and reclusive. He lost sexual interest, fell victim to violent rages, and complained of poor circulation and a weak stomach. After an outburst of anger at a friend, he cut off an earlobe and was hospitalized in an acute halluci-natory psychotic state. He had no memory of the events preceding his hospitalization. Although he never suf-fered major seizures, the attending physicians correctly diagnosed him as epileptic. Two weeks after entering the hospital, he had already recovered enough to paint his serene "Self-Portrait with Bandaged Ear and Pipe" (see Figure 13–11). But there were further psychotic episodes, often provoked by drinking bouts, and he re-mained in an asylum for a full year. A few months after his release, although he apparently was no longer suffer-ing from either psychosis or lapses of consciousness, he committed suicide.

It was the English neurologist Hughlings Jackson who first accounted for epileptic seizures in terms of brain lesions. He believed that the seizures resulted from excessive discharging by nerve cells in the gray matter of the brain and that irritation of specific areas of the brain caused the particular symptoms manifested by epileptics. However, many questions remain. The causes of the brain lesions found in epilepsy are not

FIGURE 13–11
Van Gogh's "Self-portrait with Bandaged Ear and Pipe."

clear; moreover, brain lesions are not the only cause of epilepsy.

Most forms of epilepsy are not believed to be hereditary, but there seems to be a predisposition toward epilepsy in some families. Although it is diffi-cult to give a precise estimate, perhaps half of all cases of epilepsy may be preventable because they result from head injuries at birth, infectious diseases of child-hood, or brain infections and injuries later in life. The clinical problem of epilepsy is particularly challenging because its solution usually requires establishing the particular combination of causes at work in a given case.

Current epidemiological research shows that the incidence of epilepsy varies from one country to another. In the United States, repeated sponta-neous seizures occur in 0.5 to 1.0 percent of the pop-ulation. The disease is more common in less affluent countries because minor or moderate central nervous system infection and trauma are more likely to be neglected.

Epilepsy is best looked at as a group of related disorders rather than as a single disorder. **Acquired** or **symptomatic epilepsy** refers to seizures for which the cause is known. The causes include brain infections, head wounds, metabolic disorders, and tumors. Many other forms of epilepsy have no apparent cause.

Grand Mal and Petit Mal Seizures

An epileptic seizure is a result of transient electrical in-stability of some cells in the brain, which sometimes triggers an "electrical storm" that spreads through part or all of the brain. This culminates in a seizure, which can take one of many forms. Many epileptics have only one type of seizure, but a sizable minority experience two or more types. The major types include grand mal and petit mal seizures and psychomotor epilepsy. The brainwave patterns that are characteristic of each type are shown in Figure 13–12.

The most severe form of epileptic disorder is the **grand mal seizure**, which typically lasts from 2 to 5 minutes. This type of attack leaves a painful impression on anyone who witnesses it. The victim of a grand mal seizure displays a set of very striking symptoms. The sei-zure often begins with a cry, followed by loss of con-sciousness, falling to the floor, and extreme spasms. These uncontrollable spasms can cause serious harm to the victim. Among the greatest dangers are head injuries and severe biting of the tongue or mouth. The muscular movements of a grand mal seizure are usually preceded by an *aura*, in which the individual experiences a clouded state of consciousness, including feelings of un-reality and depersonalization (feelings of strangeness about oneself). The aura may last only a few seconds, but it is often remembered very vividly.

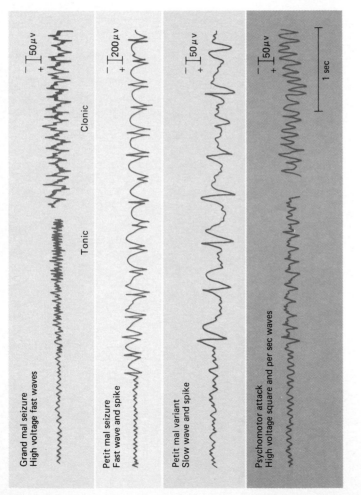

Grand mal seizure
High voltage fast waves

$-\left[\begin{array}{l} 50\,\mu v \\ + \end{array}\right.$

Tonic

Clonic

Petit mal seizure
Fast wave and spike

$-\left[\begin{array}{l} 200\,\mu v \\ + \end{array}\right.$

Petit mal variant
Slow wave and spike

$-\left[\begin{array}{l} 50\,\mu v \\ + \end{array}\right.$

Psychomotor attack
High voltage square and per sec waves

$-\left[\begin{array}{l} 50\,\mu v \\ + \end{array}\right.$

1 sec

FIGURE 13–12
EEG patterns of various types of epileptic seizures. (Gibbs, Gibbs, and Lennox, 1939, p. 1112)

Following the aura, the *tonic phase* of the seizure begins. The body is in an extended position, the eyes remain open, the pupils are dilated, and the corneal and light reflexes are absent. The tonic phase lasts for 15 to 30 seconds and is followed by the *clonic phase*, during which the body alternates between marked muscular rigidity and relaxation. Bladder and bowel control may be lost. Following the convulsive part of a grand mal seizure, there may be a deep sleep that lasts for an hour or two. As the victim regains consciousness, he or she may be bewildered and amnesic. While some grand mal epileptics have daily attacks, cases have been reported in which there were only a few seizures in an entire lifetime.

In the **petit mal seizure** which is particularly common in children, there is no convulsion. Rather, there is a lapse of consciousness characterized by blank staring and lack of responsiveness lasting up to about half a minute. The individual usually does not lose consciousness. These seizures may occur many times a day.

Petit mal attacks may be difficult to identify unless the person is known to be epileptic or an attack is actually observed. They commonly start in early childhood. Some children have so many attacks daily that they have difficulty attending to what is going on around them. Most petit mal attacks result from disturbances in subcortical brain structures, although the cause of these disturbances is usually unknown.

Psychomotor Epilepsy

In **psychomotor epilepsy**, a type that includes 15 percent of epilepsy cases and is rarely seen in children, the patient retains control of his or her motor functioning but loses the ability to exercise good judgment in carrying out activities. During a psychomotor attack, the individual is in a kind of trance and carries out movements that may be repetitive and highly organized but are in fact semiautomatic. Psychomotor seizures may resemble those of petit mal epilepsy, but they last longer (up to 2 minutes), involve muscle movements related to chewing and speech, and show more clouding of consciousness. The occasional visual hallucinations and the confused state that characterize psychomotor epilepsy are similar to some symptoms of psychosis.

In some cases fear, terror, rage, and depression are among the emotional side effects of psychomotor seizures. These outbursts of emotion come on suddenly. They are apparently automatic and unpremeditated, and they cannot be recalled later. Another feature of this syndrome is inability to shift attention to new objects and situations. There is some evidence suggesting that this syndrome may be associated with temporal lobe lesions; hence, it is referred to as **temporal lobe epilepsy.**

Psychological Factors

Over the years there has been much conjecture about the role of psychological factors in epilepsy. Are epileptics helpless victims of their condition, or is it possible that the disease is part of their psychological adjustment to some other aspect of their lives? Clinicians have observed that epileptics' seizures tend to become more frequent when they are confronted with challenges and problems they do not feel competent to handle.

From a psychological point of view, the disease often creates overwhelming stress for epileptics and their families. Much of this stress is related to lack of knowledge about epilepsy, its causes, and its treatment. Other important factors are the role of general life stresses in bringing on seizures and the effect of the stress caused by the ever-present possibility of a seizure, the need to lead a somewhat restricted life, and the stigma that attaches itself to people who are known to be epileptic.

There is increasing recognition of the developmental problems posed by epilepsy. For example, approximately 60 percent of all epileptics experience their first seizure before they are 10 years old. This represents a major handicap during a formative period of physical and psychological growth. Kurt Eichenwald (1987), who has epilepsy, has described some of his college experiences.

My staring spells—periods of a few seconds of mental absence—had been going on for as long as I could remember. Although I mentioned them to my doctor and my parents occasionally, the events did not seem significant.

Then, in my first semester at college, I was horsing around in the dorm with my roommates, and I fell, hitting my head against a chair. I had a concussion. No one to this day knows if the concussion affected my seizures, but the staring spells soon increased in frequency and severity. I learned they were different from other people's passing moments of distraction.

I remember once, in the dining hall, suddenly realizing everyone was looking at me. My lap was wet. I thought someone had thrown something at me. In fact, I had begun to stare while holding a glass of Coca-Cola in my hand. It had fallen in between my legs and shattered. (p. 30)

Later, he began having more major seizures.

I experience what is called an "aura" as random brain cells start to fire. I feel a sense of separation. My head throbs, and I see a flash of lights. Even today, I am not sure of the order of these feelings or the amount of time separating them.

As the electrical firestorm sweeps across my brain, I lose consciousness and fall to the ground. The muscles in my body tighten up and my jaw clenches, the teeth possibly biting and bloodying my lips, tongue or cheek. My body jerks for a period, usually for less than a minute. During that time, I often get excessive amounts of saliva in my mouth, creating a froth. My breathing becomes irregular, sometimes even stopping. I also can become incontinent.

The convulsion ends, and I fall into a deep, though brief, sleep. As I wake up, another seizure can be triggered, starting the process again.

While unconscious, I do not respond to pain, such as the injection of needles. I have awakened half-frozen in a snowdrift but unaware, until my waking, of the cold.

When fully awake, I am very confused and panicked. Often, it takes time for me to realize where I am. I am unsure where I am, who is with me or even what day it is. My speech is broken, and I stutter horribly, so that I am unable to ask questions except of the most patient observers. (p. 31)

Treatment of Epilepsy

There are three major ways to treat epilepsy: drugs, surgery, and psychological management. Certain drugs, such as Dilantin and phenobarbitol, can reduce the frequency and severity of seizures. Unfortunately, there is considerable variation in the way people react to these drugs. The only way to establish the optimal dosage is through trial and error. In some cases the epileptic may use substances (e.g., alcohol) that interfere with the effectiveness of anticonvulsive drugs.

If the seizures are a result of some identifiable structural defect and drugs either are not effective or have strong side effects, surgical intervention may be considered. The seizures of temporal lobe epilepsy are especially difficult to control by means of medication, but some studies have reported successful results following removal of parts of the temporal lobe. Because brain surgery entails obvious risks, it is used only when it is clear that some abnormality of brain tissue is causing the seizures. However, because the brain is such a complex structure, it is not always possible to be absolutely certain where the abnormality is. In some cases diagnosed as temporal lobe epilepsy, the temporal lobe has been removed and has been found to have no lesions. For this reason, surgery is seen as a treatment of last resort, to be attempted only after drugs and psychological approaches have failed.

A variety of psychological methods have been used in treating epileptics. Operant conditioning procedures have been tried successfully with some epileptics who cannot be helped by medication. For example, epileptic children have been rewarded with attention and care following seizure-free periods. After a seizure occurs, these reinforcers are withdrawn or reduced in strength. Avoiding or changing certain cognitive cues can also be helpful because it is known that the aura preceding a grand mal seizure can be induced by thinking certain thoughts. Epileptics who have this form of the disorder can be trained to direct their attention to pleasant thoughts when they feel an aura coming on. Desensitization and relaxation training have been found to be helpful in reducing the frequency of epileptic attacks. Biofeedback, in which patients receive visual or auditory information about their brainwave patterns, can also be an effective treatment.

Many epileptics need help to cope with their condition. Because the disorder frequently begins before adulthood, the emotional responses of the epileptic's family must also be dealt with. Often the patient and the family see epilepsy as a kind of disgrace and react to it with shame and guilt. Because an atmosphere of emotional tension and frustration can increase the severity of an epileptic's seizures, psychotherapy and counseling are frequently recommended both for the victim and for members of his or her family. Many people still see epilepsy as frightening and mysterious. As a result of such attitudes, an epileptic often feels socially stigmatized. Organizations like the Epilepsy Foundation work to provide information about epilepsy and to decrease occupational, social, and legal discrimination against epileptics. They publicize facts like the following.

1. Epileptics have the same intellectual capabilities as the general population.
2. Between seizures an epileptic suffers no disturbance in psychological function.
3. Most cases of epilepsy (about 80 percent) can be controlled with anticonvulsive drugs.
4. The genetic factor in epilepsy is probably no greater than in many other common diseases. A person with epilepsy who marries a nonepileptic may expect a 2-percent risk of having a child who also has the disorder. In many cases the risk is even less, especially if the epilepsy is associated with a birth injury or later accident or infection.

Cerebrovascular Accidents: Blockage of Blood Supply

Cerebrovascular accidents (CVAs), or strokes, are blockages or ruptures of the blood vessels in the cerebrum. When these blood vessels break or are blocked by a clot, a portion of the brain is deprived of its supply of oxygen and blood. Extensive damage to the brain and obvious changes in behavior may result. When the affected blood vessels are small and the interference with blood flow is temporary, the symptoms are milder—perhaps only confusion, unsteadiness, and excessive emotionality. Some of the behavioral effects of a stroke may be similar to the dementia that occurs in cases of brain deterioration. However, the symptoms of stroke characteristically have an abrupt onset.

Eric Hodgins, an editor and author, suffered a severe stroke that resulted in **aphasia**, a disturbance in the ability to use words, and paralysis of the left side of his body. He recovered from the aphasia. His account of his stroke vividly portrays the psychological as well as the physical side of the stroke experience.

The first thing to be said about it, is that it is like nothing else on earth. . . . The victim–patient is confused, or stunned, or shocked, or unconscious. Whatever his state he is not in good condition to give any fellow layman a clear and coherent account of what happened. Perhaps he can talk—perhaps not. Even with speech, he can't say "It hurts?"—because it probably doesn't. So, stroke exists in no focal plane the uninitiated layman can understand or recognize, or on which he can practice his own brand of differential diagnosis. Thus, as with the traffic accident, a variable period of total confusion elapses after the stroke has struck before the cry goes up, "Somebody get a doctor!" . . .

Unlike other patient types I can think of, the stroke patient goes to the hospital with profound relief, and gladly. Although he is probably not in pain, he is in considerable fear—more than he can express. Something has gone very, very wrong, but "Somebody will fix it": this child-like phrase describes the depth of the patient's need for support and reassurance . . .

In my own case I found it both depressing and infuriating that I encountered no physician with the willingness or capacity to say, as my acute symptoms subsided, "I freely concede you are in a jam—in fact, in several jams. I have no ready-made solutions—but I will help you think your way out of your jams, because I conceive it part of my job, my medical job." Perhaps it is a contentious suggestion that medicine should reach this far out from its examination rooms and its prescription pads to help the stroke patient. But in that case, whose job is it? (Eisenson, 1973, pp. 204–207)

Strokes are the third-ranking cause of death after heart attacks and cancer. There are approximately 500,000 new strokes and 200,000 deaths due to strokes in the United States each year. Over 80 percent of these involve people over the age of 65. In addition to age, high blood pressure plays a major role in strokes. The single most important way in which strokes can be prevented is through the treatment and control of high blood pressure. Many clinicians have observed that strokes occur especially often in people who live pressured lives. However, it is not clear why these people tend to have their strokes while they are relaxing or vacationing.

An Integrative Approach to Brain Disorders

Because the conditions discussed in this chapter involve actual organic defects, it is tempting to see them as purely medical problems. Why do we consider brain disorders to be different from other organic problems, such as broken arms or gallstones? A physical defect lies at the root of all of these conditions, but the brain has a complex effect on our behavior as well as on our body. This effect is not as clear and predictable as the effects of damage to other parts of the body. Once a broken arm has been set and healed, the person can return to the condition he or she was in before the accident. This is not the case with brain injuries, and it is for this reason that they are of interest to psychologists.

To comprehend the effects of a brain injury on behavior, we require information about the person's life history, personality, and environmental and biophysical factors. Purely physical conditions such as broken arms can be treated successfully without such data. Although brain disorders can be treated medically, psychodynamic, learning, cognitive, and community concepts are also important. Thus, from both the scientific and clinical standpoints, the most fruitful approach to brain disorders is one that integrates knowledge from these diverse fields.

From a psychodynamic perspective, although certain forms of maladaptive behavior may be organically caused, the way people respond to their condition involves psychological factors such as personality, earlier experience and ways of coping. For example, the more outgoing a person is, the greater the likelihood of improvement in his or her condition. Many cases of brain disorder indicate that an individual's personality at the time of the organic damage has an effect on the degree and form of his or her behavioral deterioration. For example, the content of hallucinations and the ease with which they are expressed depend on personality characteristics.

Behavioral psychologists are less interested in the effects of personality and experience than psychologists who emphasize other perspectives. They focus on people's ability to adapt to even the most drastic situations. Teaching new responses to compensate for those that have been lost is seen as more important for adjustment than simply helping people accept their new lot in life. Moreover, the way people respond to such training can

provide more relevant information about their present psychological state that an examination of their personality before the illness occurred. Because of their emphasis on revising people's maladaptive responses as quickly as possible, behavioral psychologists have a major contribution to make in the treatment of organic brain disorders.

Cognitively oriented psychologists have contributed a variety of techniques to help people in the early stages of dementia deal with the deterioration in their abilities. Memory-aiding techniques such as list making are practical examples. Cognitive techniques are also useful in countering the depression that often accompanies the development of physical problems and declining intellectual competence.

Damage to the brain and central nervous system would not seem to be a condition that is influenced by community variables. Yet, from all indications, central nervous system dysfunction is not randomly distributed. Cases of brain damage are highly concentrated in the poor white and black segments of the population. Such problems seem to be most prevalent among black children of lower socioeconomic status. This is true for sociological, not biological, reasons. Black infants are not biologically inferior at the moment of conception, but they may become so shortly thereafter. Inadequate nutrition and prenatal care result in complications of pregnancy, which take their toll in high rates of premature births and congenital defects. These abnormalities include neurological damage that results in impaired intellectual functioning and in behavioral difficulties such as hyperactivity and short attention span. No single complication of pregnancy is more clearly associated with a wide range of neurological dysfunctions than premature birth. For these reasons, those who focus on the community perspective emphasize the prevention of brain disorders through preventive medical care, especially good prenatal care.

The stigma attached to many of the behavioral maladaptations stemming from brain damage often makes the situation worse. People tend to avoid and isolate individuals who are markedly deviant. The behavior of old people provides one of the clearest illustrations of the effects of this social rejection. Mild brain deterioration in a socially rejected older person may lead to greater behavioral maladaptation than moderate deterioration in a person who lives in a friendlier, more accepting environment. From the community perspective, changing people's attitudes toward those who behave differently because of brain disorders can sometimes lessen the behavioral effects of these biological changes.

THE BRAIN: AN INTERACTIVE PERSPECTIVE

The brain develops throughout life. While some parts of the brain deteriorate, other cells continue to form new connections. What is known about brain development is consistent with what has been said earlier about interactions among personal and environmental factors, vulnerability, and stress.

VULNERABILITY TO BRAIN DISORDERS

In the past, people looked for physical causes for all forms of maladaptive behavior. Today, psychologists believe that the psychological, social, and physical domains of human life are intertwined. Behavior is thought to be a joint product of individual differences and environmental variables. Among the factors that influence vulnerability to brain disorders are age, social support, stress, personality factors, and physical condition.

ASSESSING BRAIN DAMAGE

The procedures used in assessing brain damage include a mental-status examination, neuropsychological testing, and radiological techniques. The **mental-status examination** provides information about the patient's level of consciousness, attention span, short-term memory, and the like. Neuropsychological tests are used to assess impairment in such areas as awareness of and responsiveness to sensory stimulation. Brain imaging is used to assess injuries or deterioration in specific regions of the brain and to visualize brain function.

ORGANIC MENTAL DISORDERS

1. Clusters of psychological and behavioral symptoms that are connected with temporary or permanent brain dysfunction are called **organic brain syndromes.** Of these, the most common are delirium, dementia, intoxication, and withdrawal.
2. **Delirium** is characterized by relatively global cognitive impairment, disorientation, and confusion. It generally accompanies another serious physical problem. **Delirium tremens** is an acute brain condition that sometimes results from excessive alcohol consumption.
3. Brain deterioration, or **dementia,** is a gradual loss of intellectual abilities that is sufficient to interfere with social or occupational functioning. The term **senile dementia** is often used to refer to the condition when it occurs in people over 65. In younger individuals it is termed **presenile dementia.** A common symptom is

confabulation, or filling in memory gaps with detailed, but inaccurate, information.
4. While brain deterioration increases with advancing years, many people seem to age successfully. Certain conditions, such as depression, paranoid thinking, and hypochondriasis increase in older people.
5. **Alzheimer's disease** is a disorder associated with advancing age. It is characterized by memory lapses, confusion, and dementia, and has an average duration of about seven years. The nerve cells of Alzheimer's victims contain abnormal rigid structures called plaques and tangles. There is also evidence of neurotransmitter deficiencies and genetic abnormalities in patients with Alzheimer's disease.
6. **Pick's disease** is similar to Alzheimer's disease except that it is most likely to develop in the sixth decade and involves a form of brain atrophy.
7. **Multi-infarct dementia** is caused by a series of minor strokes that occur at different times and cause disturbances in memory, abstract thinking, judgment, and impulse control.
8. Other organic brain syndromes include **amnestic syndrome,** which is characterized by severe memory disturbance; **organic delusional syndrome,** in which there are organically caused delusions; **organic hallucinosis,** or hallucinations caused by an organic factor; **organic affective syndrome,** in which an abnormal mood is caused by a brain disorder; **organic anxiety syndrome;** and **organic personality syndrome,** which refers to personality changes that appear to be caused by an organic factor.

BRAIN DISORDERS WITH A VARIETY OF CAUSES

1. **Huntington's disease** is a rare hereditary disorder that is characterized by progressive degeneration of brain tissue. The symptoms include dementia, irritability and apathy, depression, and hallucinations and delusions. In addition, there are **choreiform movements,** or involuntary, spasmodic jerking and twisting movements. The disease is inherited through a single dominant gene. A diagnostic test is being developed to predict who will develop the disease.
2. **Parkinson's disease** is a progressive disorder that is characterized by tremor, rigidity, and loss of vocal power. It is believed to be caused by an acquired defect in the brain mechanism. Some of the symptoms can be relieved by the use of the drug L-dopa.
3. Infectious disorders such as **syphilis** can lead to **gen-**

eral paresis or **dementia paralytica,** a progressive deterioration in psychological and motor functioning that results in paralysis, psychosis, and death. Prompt diagnosis and treatment is the best approach to reducing the incidence of this condition.

4. Vitamin and other nutritional deficiencies can affect the nervous system. **Pellagra** is caused by a deficiency of niacin; **Korsakoff's syndrome** results from a combination of alcoholism and thiamine deficiency.

5. Brain injuries can be classified into three groups: **concussions, contusions,** and **lacerations.** Such injuries can lead to specific losses in motor or cognitive functioning, as well as psychological reactions. Tumors in the brain can also produce behavioral changes. **Post-traumatic psychoses** involve confusion, delirium, and temporary catatonic, manic, or depressive reactions.

6. **Epilepsy** refers to a group of disorders involving seizures caused by transient electrical instability of some cells in the brain. The most severe form of epileptic disorder is the **grand mal seizure,** which includes loss of consciousness and extreme spasms. In a **petit mal seizure** there is a lapse of consciousness but no convulsion. **Psychomotor** or **temporal lobe epilepsy** is a trancelike state in which the individual carries out repetitive, semi-automatic movements. It is possible that psychological as well as organic factors play a role in epilepsy.

7. The methods used to treat epilepsy are drugs (e.g., Dilantin and phenobarbital), surgery, and psychological management. Surgery consists of removal of parts of the temporal lobe and is attempted only after drugs and psychological approaches have failed.

8. **Cerebrovascular accidents,** or **strokes,** are blockages or ruptures of the blood vessels in the cerebrum. They can cause extensive damage to the brain and obvious changes in behavior. In some cases the effects are similar to those of dementia.

AN INTEGRATIVE APPROACH TO BRAIN DISORDERS

Brain disorders can be treated psychologically as well as medically. Psychodynamic approaches emphasize the role of personality in people's responses to organic conditions. Behavioral psychologists focus on teaching new responses to compensate for those that have been lost. The cognitive perspective has contributed techniques to help people deal with declining intellectual competence.

CHAPTER 14

Addictive Disorders

Miquel Barceló, *Untitled*, 1983. Oil and collage on paper, 59 × 95". Courtesy Thomas Segal Gallery, Boston.

OBJECTIVES FOR CHAPTER FOURTEEN:

To learn:

1. The meaning of substance dependence, tolerance, withdrawal, and relapse prevention
2. The characteristics and effects of the drugs discussed in this chapter

To understand:

How the perspectives influence the treatment of alcohol dependence

7

he gentleman in the corner had been regarded as a true American success, lanky and deep-voiced, brilliant and beloved, the master of all he surveyed. Now, he gazed out defiantly, as if still on the summit, too high to see the cat feces at his feet or the unopened mail or the mirror that would have told him he was master of nothing but his own delusions.

Those who were to thrust the mirror in front of the 62-year-old man, whom I will call James B., were his daughter Isabel, myself, and three of the friends who loved him best.

If James B. had denied his problem, so had we. He had been depressed over the death of his wife and the loss of his architectural business He had been presenting different excuses to each of us for his growing isolation. He had kept us at bay by clever use of the telephone, until it was cut off for nonpayment of a bill he had never opened.

Yet at last we had gathered into a crisis intervention team and surprised him, hung over, before he could perfect his alibis . . . .

"Daddy, we are here because we love you." Isabel's voice wavered, but the 9-month-old baby on her knee stared at her grandfather unblinkingly. James B., very gingerly, poured out coffee. "I can understand your concern," he said. He had thrown on a shirt—even a tie—but below his bathrobe, his thin, red legs had the look of arms flung down in defeat. "I've had this local flu. I've been going to my doctor for shots every day."

"I checked with your doctor, Daddy, and he hasn't seen you for two years. We think your disease is alcoholism."

All of James B.'s roles now seemed to collide and fall away, revealing the obsession which shone in

tal disorders are characterized by actual organic impairment resulting from ingestion of psychoactive substances (for example, physiological changes in the brain). **Psychoactive substance use disorders** involve maladaptive behavior that goes along with more or less regular use of psychoactive substances. The former type is used to characterize the direct acute or chronic effects of psychoactive substances on the central nervous system. The latter relates to the impaired control of psychoactive substance use and refers to behavioral and psychological changes that would be considered undesirable in almost any subculture—for example, impaired social or occupational performance, inability to stop taking the substance, and development of physiological or psychological symptoms if its use is discontinued.

People who use psychoactive substances may have periods of intoxication or withdrawal symptoms. **Intoxication** leads to a substance-specific syndrome that follows recent ingestion of the psychoactive substance. The syndrome includes various types of maladaptive behavior, such as belligerence and poor judgment. In **withdrawal**, a substance-specific syndrome follows cessation of or reduction in intake of a psychoactive substance that was previously used regularly to induce a state of intoxication. A generalized reduction in goal-directed behavior (for example, going to school or work), together with cognitive deficits (such as inability to concentrate), is a common consequence of prolonged heavy use of a psychoactive substance. There may also be **flashbacks** in which the person reexperiences one or more of the perceptual symptoms, such as hallucinations, that were originally experienced while intoxicated.

Some mood- and behavior-modifying substances have medical uses. Physicians prescribe these substances to reduce pain, relieve tension, or aid in limiting food intake by suppressing appetite. Although the use of these substances is common in many cultural groups, there are some subcultural differences. Some religious groups, such as Moslems, frown on the use of alcohol. Mormons are expected to avoid not only alcohol but also coffee, tea, and other products that contain caffeine. On the other hand, some subcultural groups not only use alcohol but view the use of illegal substances such as marijuana or cocaine as a legitimate recreational activity.

Throughout history people have used a variety of substances to modify their moods and behavior. The use of some substances has become so common that it is considered normal and even appropriate; examples include champagne toasts for the New Year and a cigar for the new baby. A majority of adults use alcohol as a recreational drink; many individuals, from children to elderly people, use caffeine in the form of coffee, tea, or cola drinks as a stimulant; and a great many teenagers and adults use nicotine in the form of cigarettes.

---

his eyes like unrequited love. "That's preposterous! My problems have nothing to do with alcohol."

Mel, his former business partner, said he had watched the most brilliant man he had ever known become addled into dull predictability. George, his former chess opponent, blushed and said that James B. had begun to cheat at the game. Lisa, his former lover, tremulously said she was going to marry a man she didn't love because the one she did had not preferred her to the bottle. I reminded him of the stars, and all of the people, including my baby and Isabel's, who could still learn from him.

Coached about the new science of alcohol and the liver, we tried to convince James B. that there was no shame in being an alcoholic.

"Look, can't you understand?" James B. said. "I'm sick, yes; depressed, yes; getting old, yes. But that's all."

"Jim," Mel said, in a voice that resonated with the tension we all felt, "it sounds like you would rather be anything at all than an alcoholic."

After 14 hours of this scenario, some of us began to question whether he really was an alcoholic. Maybe it was some other illness. Then he let spill a few words. "Geez, if I couldn't go down to the pub for a few, I think I'd go nuts!"

"Aaah," Isabel said. "You just admitted it." She put the baby on her father's knee. "Look at your granddaughter. This is your immortality, Daddy, and she needs you. Please don't die. Please choose life, for us."

James B. put his face, the color of gravel, in his hands. No one spoke. When he looked up, he said he would go to a local hospital. (Franks, 1985, p. 48. Copyright © 1985 by the New York Times Company. Reprinted by permission.)

Alcohol is one of a group of substances that have ruined the lives of countless numbers of people. Although there are many differences among them, all of these substances are **psychoactive; that is, they affect thought, emotions, and behavior.** As the case of James B. shows, they are capable of causing serious physical symptoms. This case also illustrates the tendency of abusers to deny that the substance they are using excessively is a major factor in their problems.

DSM-III-R distinguishes between two categories of disorders stemming from the use of psychoactive substances. **Psychoactive substance-induced organic men-**

Substance Dependence

In order to justify the diagnosis of a **psychoactive substance use disorder**, the impairment in functioning that results from the substance use must be severe and long-lasting. Some of the symptoms must continue for at least a month or they must occur frequently for a period of at least 6 months. Getting drunk at the company New Year's Eve party would not qualify; neither would a single drunken binge after a family quarrel. Instead, there must be significant, ongoing maladaptive behavior that interferes with social functioning or effectiveness on the job and continues even though the person knows that use of the substance is having important negative consequences.

Another characteristic of substance dependence is that when not actually using the substance, the person spends a lot of time looking forward to using it and devotes a great deal of effort to making it available. For example, an office worker might have a three-martini lunch and keep the glow going by nipping at a bottle he keeps hidden in his desk. He would be unable to restrict his use of alcohol to certain times of the day, such as after working hours, even though his accuracy in preparing reports had slipped and he had received several warnings from the boss. A factory worker might know that her safety depended on being alert around a drill press, yet she might still drink on the job. A retired engineer might continue to drink even though he knew that the resultant damage to his liver was creating a life-threatening situation. All of these examples involve alcohol, but we could have substituted marijuana, heroin, or Valium. The critical factor is not the particular substance used but its effects on the person's life.

Physiological dependence on a substance can be shown in one of two ways: tolerance or withdrawal. Withdrawal refers to a particular set of physical symptoms that occur when a person stops or cuts down on the use of a psychoactive substance. The physical reaction that occurs when the use of heroin is stopped is probably the best-known form of withdrawal. **Tolerance** means that the person has to use more and more of a substance to get the same effect, or that the same-sized dose has progressively less effect as time goes by. For example, the pain-reducing power of morphine decreases if the drug is given over a long period. As alcoholics consume increasing amounts of alcohol, their cell membranes are altered so that less and less of the alcohol permeates the membranes. If less alcohol is actually penetrating cell membranes, an alcoholic may have less alcohol in his or her brain than a normal person with the same blood level of alcohol would. This is interesting in view of the fact that some alcoholics can perform well after consuming an amount of alcohol that would put a nonalcoholic into a coma.

Table 14–1 lists the criteria of dependence on psychoactive substances. The substances that can produce physiological dependence include alcohol, amphetamines, barbiturates, opioids, and tobacco. Four types of substances are related to psychological dependence only (i.e., have never been shown to produce physiological dependence). They are cannabis, cocaine, psychedelics, and PCP. Table 14–9 gives more information about these substances.

Psychologists are interested in substance dependence because a person's response to drugs seems to be due to a combination of physiological and psychological factors. Some people can control their use of many of these substances; others seem unable to do so. Some individuals who are addicted have severe withdrawal symptoms; others do not. The effects that drugs produce also differ from one user to another.

TABLE 14-1

Criteria of Dependence on Psychoactive Substances

1. The repeated (unsuccessful) effort to cut down or control substance abuse;
2. The frequent intoxication or impairment by substance use when one is expected to fulfill social or occupational obligations (for example, absence from work because of being hung over or high, going to work high, driving when drunk);
3. The need for increased amounts of the substance in order to achieve intoxication or the desired effect, or experiencing diminished effect with continued use of the same amount of the substance (tolerance);
4. The experiencing of a substance-specific syndrome following cessation or reduction of intake of the substance (withdrawal);
5. The frequent preoccupation with seeking or taking the substance;
6. The relinquishing of some important social, occupational, or recreational activity in order to seek or take the substance;
7. The frequent use of a psychoactive substance to relieve or avoid withdrawal symptoms (for example, taking a drink to relieve morning shakes);
8. The frequent use of the substance in larger doses or over a longer period;
9. The continuation of substance use despite a physical or mental disorder, or despite a significant social problem that the individual knows is made worse by the use of the substance;
10. The presence of a mental or physical disorder or condition that is usually a complication of prolonged substance use.

Based on Millman, 1986

Probably both the personality and physiological characteristics of the user and the environment or setting in which the substance is used influence the reaction observed. This is another case in which the interaction between the person and the situation, which has been referred to so often throughout the book, is important in understanding individual behavior. However, although these individual characteristics have a major influence on a person's response to a mood- or behavior-modifying substance, such substances do have certain general effects that are experienced by most people who use them.

Alcohol

What Is Alcohol?

Alcohol is a chemical compound known as ethyl alcohol or ethanol. Other kinds of alcohol are isopropyl alcohol (rubbing alcohol) and methyl alcohol (wood alcohol). Only ethanol is safe for human consumption. Manufactured by two methods, distillation (hard liquors) or fermentation (beer and wine), alcohol has been known for at least ten thousand years. The oldest of all archaeological records contain reference to its use.

The ethanol contained in beer, wine, or hard liquor is the same drug. The only difference is in the amount of alcohol as a percentage of total volume. In beer and wine, the percentage usually varies from 3 to 14 percent. In hard liquor, or spirits as they are sometimes called, the percentage varies from 40 percent (80 proof) to 75 percent (150 proof). The amount of pure ethanol is generally about the same in a one-and-one-half ounce shot of whiskey (or other hard liquor), a six-ounce glass of wine, or a twelve-ounce bottle of beer.

In the short term, alcohol acts on the central nervous system, the brain and spinal cord, as a "blocker" of messages transmitted from one nerve cell to the next. It first affects the frontal lobes of the brain, the seat of inhibitions, reasoning powers, memory, and judgment. After continued consumption, it next affects the cerebellum, the seat of motor muscle control, balance, and the senses (touch, hearing, sight, smell, and taste). Finally, it affects the medulla and spinal cord, the seat of involuntary functions such as breathing, heart rate, and body temperature control. If enough alcohol is consumed, to the point of a blood/alcohol level of .50 percent or more, the involuntary function system can shut down and the person dies from acute alcohol poisoning.

Alcohol Abuse

Negative effects of overuse of alcohol have been considered a serious problem for many years. About 70 percent of adults in America drink alcohol on occasion; 12 percent of them are heavy drinkers, people who drink almost every day and become intoxicated several times a month. More men than women are heavy drinkers. For both men and women, the prevalence of drinking is highest and abstention is lowest in the 21- to 34-year age range (Goodwin, 1985; Helzer, 1987). Table 14–2 provides estimates of the percent of alcohol in the blood as a function of amount of alcohol consumed and body weight. Box 14–1 summarizes information about some of the many areas of life and segments of the population that are adversely affected by alcohol intake.

Abuse of alcohol or other psychoactive substances means using them in a way that has negative effects on a person's life. Alcohol abuse shows several typical patterns: regular daily intake of a large amount, regular heavy drinking confined to weekends, and unpredictable binge drinking (long periods without alcohol interrupted by episodes of heavy drinking lasting for weeks or months). Alcohol abuse is often referred to as **problem drinking.** Problem drinking should not be viewed as a step on the way to alcoholism, though some individuals do progress from one to the other. Alcohol dependence or addiction is referred to as **alcoholism.** Alcoholism is something quite different. Figure 14–2 shows the change to solitary drinking behavior typical of alcoholism.

My alcoholism took years to develop into a chronic affliction, and during much of that time I went to bars after work, one of the guys. The delusion was gradually reinforced by gravitation. I mingled more and more with other persistent drinkers who took longer and longer to call for their bar tabs. Most of us were actually alcoholics in varying stages of development. The nonalcoholics had long ago selected themselves out. Those of us who remained agreed that we were "normal." Unhappy, but normal.

Alcoholic perceptions are like that, in a hundred insidious and distorting ways. All of them are aimed at protecting a drunkard's notion that he is possessed of free will. My drinking buddies and I agreed that we did not have a drinking problem. Everything in our increasingly narrow world, though, was a problem that required drinking: the wife, the kids, the boss, the government. In dingy watering holes from which everyone with a healthy life to lead had gone home, we conspired to overlook the obvious, that our bodily cells were addicted, and our minds were along for the ride.

TABLE 14-2

Are You Drunk?

This table shows the estimated percent of alcohol in the blood according to body weight and the number of drinks consumed. One drink equals one ounce of 100-proof alcohol, a 4-ounce glass of wine, or a 12-ounce bottle of beer. Alcohol in the blood decreases over time. To calculate how much time decreases blood-alcohol level, subtract .015 for each hour that has passed since the first drink.

PERCENT ALCOHOL IN BLOOD

Body Weight	Drinks						Blood alcohol percent	Interpreting the Results Intoxicated?
	1	2	3	4	5	6		
100 lbs.	.038	.075	.113	.150	.188	.225	.000 to .050%	No
120	.031	.063	.094	.125	.156	.188	.050 to .100	Maybe[a]
140	.027	.054	.080	.107	.134	.161	.100 to .150	Probably
160	.023	.047	.070	.094	.117	.141	.150 and above	Yes
180	.021	.042	.063	.083	.104	.125		
200	.019	.038	.056	.075	.094	.113		
220	.017	.034	.051	.068	.085	.102		
240	.016	.031	.047	.063	.078	.094		

[a]In most states, .100 is proof of illegal intoxication.
SOURCE: Government of the District of Columbia.

BOX 14-1
The Scope of the Alcohol Problem

- Alcohol is a factor in nearly half of all accidental deaths, suicides, and homicides, including 42 percent of all deaths from motor vehicle accidents.

- An estimated 18 million adults 18 years and older in the United States currently experience problems as a result of alcohol use.

- Alcohol can cause functional changes in heart tissue even in young adults, and is associated with many cancers, damage to other vital organs, diminished immunity to disease, and many other health problems.

- Alcohol is twice as popular among college students as the next leading drug, marijuana, and more than five times as popular as cocaine.

- Drinking differences between boys and girls are diminishing. The number of young female drinkers has been increasing more rapidly, and girls also tend to experiment more with alcohol.

- Two-thirds of the adult U.S. population drink; however, the 10 percent of these (6.5 percent of the total adult population) who drink most heavily drink half of the total amount of alcohol consumed.

FIGURE 14-1

FIGURE 14–2
At first, many heavy alcohol users drink in bars or other social situations. As alcoholism worsens, drinking becomes more solitary and nightmarish.

Inexorably, the need for alcohol grew, while the lies wore thin. As my alcoholism accelerated, I abandoned most drinking partners and joined the ranks of solitary topers bellied up to countless bars. I lost any sense at all of what would happen after I started drinking; I became completely unpredictable. Sometimes I would go home after a couple of drinks (there was usually more booze there). More often, I would join the lineup of other alcoholics at the bar telephone stalls, fumbling with worn-out excuses about unexpected visitors and urgent business meetings. Sometimes I would simply hole up in my office with a bottle after everyone else had gone home. Most frightening of all, I began to suffer alcoholic blackouts during drinking episodes. I would swim back into consciousness with no recollection of where I had been or what I had done. Once, I came to late at night on a downtown city street with my suit trousers slashed down one side by a razor.

Many college administrators feel that the use of alcohol and other drugs on their campuses is increasing. As a result many schools have established programs to educate students about the effects of alcohol. Table 14–3 shows the results of a survey of college deans concerning alcohol use and abuse on their campuses. The excessive use of alcohol by many high school students is also considered a major problem. A recent survey in New York state found that 27 percent of secondary school students drink more than moderately (see Table 14–4). Evidence that substance use begins at early grade levels suggests that intervention efforts should begin prior to junior high school, perhaps as early as the fourth or fifth grade (Keyes and Block, 1984).

Alcohol and Health

Alcoholism is one of the most common mental disorders in the United States, and abuse of alcohol is strongly associated with increased risk of dying. Table 14–5 describes the negative effects of alcohol on various bodily organs and systems. People who drink heavily even on occasion face an increased risk of death associated with accidents, especially those caused by drunken driving. This is because alcohol acts like a general anesthetic, thereby impairing driving skills. Drivers aged 16 to 24 have the highest rate of alcohol-related crashes. Figure 14–3 shows the relationship between blood alcohol concentration and the probability that the person will cause a fatal automobile accident.

Research data show that alcohol is also involved in a high percentage of nontraffic accidents: almost 50 percent of people who died from falls had been drinking; 52 percent of the fires that led to adult deaths involved alcohol; and 50 to 68 percent of drowning victims had been drinking (*Alcohol and Health*, 1987).

Highway accidents in which alcohol is involved are the primary cause of death for young people. After 18-year-olds received the right to vote in 1971, the legal drinking age was lowered in many states. Studies of auto accident statistics from these states produced convincing evidence that the age reduction had resulted in

TABLE 14-3

Alcohol Use among College Students as Reported by College Deans

Percent of students who drink:	
Excessively[a]	16.1
Socially[b]	52.1
Experimentally[c]	26.3
Not at all	24.7
Percent of students needing treatment for alcohol abuse	5.6
Percent of students leaving college because of alcohol	2.3
Percent of institutions reporting increases in the last five years:	
In excessive drinking by students	35.9
In student use of marijuana	17.1
In student use of cocaine	40.9
In faculty and staff use of alcohol	22.1
In number of students seeking help for alcohol abuse	44.2
Percentage of institutions reporting increases in alcohol-related problems in the last five years:	
Bad hangovers	21.0
Drinking before or while driving	23.8
Drinking before class	15.5
Missing class	22.1
Getting lower grades	23.8
Fighting	26.5
Damaging property	29.8
Loss of memory	19.9
Doing something later regretted	24.3

[a] Occasional to frequent drinking resulting in intoxication.

[b] Drinking in social settings and usually in moderation, as a secondary reason rather than main reason for the occasion.

[c] Infrequent drinking that may include such first-time experiences as patronizing a bar, drinking to the point of intoxication, or getting sick.

SOURCE: 1982 Chronicle of Higher Education Survey from John Minter Associates, *New York Times*, August 22, 1982, p. 20E. Copyright © 1982 by the New York Times Company. Reprinted by permission.

TABLE 14-4

Drinking Rates Among Secondary School Students in New York State (N = 1,542,000).

Drinking Classification	Percent
Abstainers	27%
Infrequent drinkers	14
Light drinkers	16
Moderate drinkers	14
Moderate/heavy drinkers[a]	14
Heavy drinkers[a]	13

[a] Heavy drinkers drank a very large amount once a week, moderate/heavy drinkers drank a large amount once a week.

SOURCE: Barnes, 1984.

an increased proportion of auto crashes and fatalities involving youthful drivers. Since 1976, therefore, many states have raised the drinking age. In the 12 months after Michigan raised the drinking age, accidents resulting in death or injury among 18- to 20-year-olds dropped by 28 percent.

Alcohol may also have some beneficial effects. Moderate use of alcohol (2 ounces, or two drinks, per day) may lessen the chances of a heart attack (Hennekens and others, 1979). It is not clear why this should be the case, but researchers have suggested a number of possibilities. Alcohol may reduce psychological stress, or it may promote the formation of substances that help prevent or remove the plaque that can clog the coronary arteries. Some researchers worry that announcing positive effects of alcohol use will be interpreted as a suggestion that drinking is desirable for everyone. They point out that it is premature to recommend alcohol as a heart-attack preventive. A moderate amount for one person may be too much for another because of individual differences in tolerance for alcohol.

When alcohol is abused extensively, brain damage can result. For example, CT scans of young chronic alcoholics showed reductions in the density of their left brain hemispheres compared to those of nonalcoholic

TABLE 14-5

The Effects of Alcohol on the Body

Bodily Organ or System	Effect
Brain	Brain cells are altered, and many die. Memory formation is blocked. Senses are dulled. Physical coordination is impaired.
Stomach and Intestines	Alcohol can trigger bleeding and can cause cancer.
Heart	Deterioration of the heart muscle can occur.
Immune System	Infection-fighting cells are prevented from functioning properly. Risk of bacterial disease is increased.
Reproduction	In men: hormone levels change, causing lower sex drive and enlarged breasts. In women: menstrual cycles become irregular and ovaries malfunction.

individuals (Golden and others, 1981). Brain dysfunction is present in from 50 to 70 percent of detoxified alcoholics at the beginning of treatment. Certain cognitive abilities of people who use alcohol only moderately in social situations have been found to be impaired even 24 hours after they last used alcohol (Eckhardt and others, 1981).

One of the most dramatic findings concerning the effects of alcohol has been the identification of **fetal alcohol syndrome.** This syndrome, which produces mental retardation and a number of physical malformations, results from heavy use of alcohol by pregnant women. Even light to moderate alcohol use is now thought to have negative effects on the unborn child. (Fetal alcohol syndrome is discussed in Chapter 16.)

Perspectives on Alcohol Abuse

The Biological View

Ingestion of alcohol is associated with numerous behavioral, biophysical, and psychological changes. After the first drink, the average person experiences a lessening of anxiety. As more alcohol is consumed, the depressant action of alcohol effects brain functions. The individual staggers, and his or her mood becomes markedly unstable. Sensory perception is seriously impaired.

Influenced by evidence that heavy drinking leads to a variety of bodily changes, writers have often characterized alcoholism itself as a disease. E. M. Jellinek (1960), often referred to as the father of the modern study of alcoholism, believed that alcoholism is a permanent and irreversible condition and that alcoholics are essentially different from nonalcoholics. Alcoholics, he contended, experience an irresistible physical craving for alcohol. Satisfaction of this craving leads to loss of control as a result of increasing physical dependence on alcohol. Alcoholic individuals feel compelled to continue drinking even after ingesting only a small amount of alcohol. Jellinek believed that the only way alcoholics can return to a normal life is through complete abstinence.

Some of Jellinek's ideas have been questioned on the basis of research findings that seem inconsistent with them. However, Jellinek's disease concept of alcoholism has succeeded in changing people's attitude toward alcoholics from one of condemnation and blame to one of concern. In addition, it has focused researcher's attention on the biological aspects of alcohol abuse.

Genetic Factors in Susceptibility to Alcohol. Studies using animals have shown that it is possible to breed strains of mice or rats that differ in their metabolism of alcohol. Some of these strains prefer diluted al-

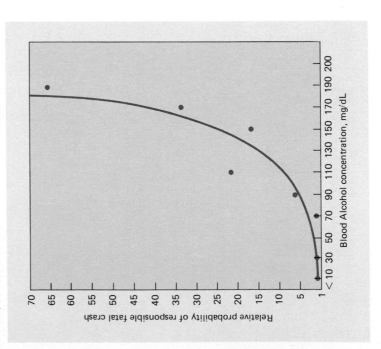

FIGURE 14-3
The relative probability of being responsible for a fatal crash rises with rising blood alcohol concentrations. (Council on Scientific Affairs, American Medical Association, 1986, p. 523).

cohol solutions to water, while others avoid alcohol at all costs. It has been demonstrated many times that alcoholics are about four times more likely to be alcoholic than are sons of nonalcoholics. This is true even when children are adopted and have no exposure to their biological parents after the first few weeks of life (Goodwin, 1986; Schuckit, 1987).

Evidence for genetic predisposition to alcoholism is growing, and it is now widely accepted by researchers in the field that alcoholism can result from the interaction of heredity and environment. Possibly characteristic brain electrical patterns have been found in subjects who are not alcoholic but are judged to be at risk of alcoholism because alcoholism exists among their first-degree relatives.

Studies of individuals who had a biological parent with alcoholism but were removed from the alcoholic environment through adoption at an early age have allowed assessment of the relative contributions of genetic and environmental factors in the genesis of alcoholism. Such studies have identified two types of genetic predisposition to alcoholism, male-limited and milieu-limited (Cloninger and others, 1981).

- Male-limited susceptibility occurs only in males, is highly heritable, gives rise to severe early-onset alcoholism often requiring extensive treatment, and is associated with serious lawbreaking.

- Milieu-limited susceptibility, found to occur in both sexes, is perhaps involved in most cases of alcoholism. This type of hereditary alcoholism has a late onset, is usually not as severe as male-limited alcoholism, and is not associated with the legal system. Milieu-limited susceptibility requires environmental provocation to become expressed as alcoholism, but environmental provocation does not mean that there must be alcoholism in the adoptive parents. The only significant parental factor found associated with this type of alcoholism in the adoptees was low socioeconomic status of the adoptive father.

Knowledge that alcoholism has both genetic and environmental components can have important practical applications. Prevention of alcohol abuse and alcoholism would certainly be an important application of this new and growing knowledge. If reliable biological indicators of a predisposition toward alcoholism can be found, individuals who have those indicators can know the risks they face and can make informed choices about drinking.

Another practical application is improved treatment. It is already clear that alcoholism is not a single disease entity. By clarifying the nature of various subcategories of alcoholism, genetic studies can point the way to more specific and effective therapies based on the genetic uniqueness of individuals.

Genetic molecular variations in alcohol-metabolizing enzymes are a major area of research on the heredity of alcoholism because a mutation that produces a slight alteration in the molecular structure of these enzymes could be expected to have a pronounced effect on their ability to remove alcohol from the body. Many investigators believe that such studies have the potential of explaining fundamental mechanisms of alcoholism and of identifying genetic markers of susceptibility.

Sensitivity to Alcohol. Individual sensitivity to the effects of alcohol varies greatly. Some people can remain conscious after drinking a quantity of alcohol that would cause others to "pass out," become comatose, or even die. Others are so sensitive to alcohol that just one or two drinks can produce acute discomfort accompanied by facial flushing, elevated skin temperature, and a rapid pulse. These individual variations are probably due to differences in the ability to metabolize alcohol, to innate differences in the central nervous system's sensitivity to alcohol, or to differences in the capacity to adapt rapidly to the presence of alcohol (acute tolerance).

A major area of study is the comparison of alcohol metabolism in different races (*Alcoholism: An inherited disease*, 1985). There is evidence of a high prevalence of sensitivity to alcohol among people of Oriental derivation (Chinese, Japanese, Koreans, Native Americans, and Eskimos). Signs of sensitivity—rapid facial flushing, elevated skin temperature, and increased pulse rate—after consuming moderate amounts of alcohol appear to be common among these groups but are seen in only 5 percent of Caucasians. Recent studies suggest that these differences are based on genetic variations in the enzymes involved in alcohol metabolism.

Another important area of research on susceptibility to alcohol is the role of neurochemical and neurophysiological factors. Alcohol affects every system of the body, but its greatest, most immediate, and most visible effects are on the central nervous system. The chemical processes involved in the transmission of neural impulses are carried out at the synapse by neurotransmitters that are released from the axon and join with specific receptors in the dendrites of nearby neurons. (Figure 3–3 illustrates this process.) The propagation of an electrical signal along a nerve cell is based on the movement of sodium and potassium ions back and forth through the membrane that encloses the cell.

All the complex features of the self—thoughts, emotions, actions—are based on these chemical and electrical processes, which occur in billions of nerve cells at any instant. Several features of this system could be involved in inherited predisposition to alcoholism. Alcohol interfere with numerous processes involved in nerve cell function, and if there is inherited variation in these processes it could result in either neurochemical vulnerability or resistance to alcoholism. Among the leading neurochemical hypotheses are the following.

- Individuals who are predisposed toward alcoholism might have nerve cell membranes that are less sensitive to the permeability-altering effects of alcohol, which would affect the movement of sodium and potassium ions and the propagation of nerve impulses.

- Predisposition toward alcoholism might be based on inherited variations in the sensitivity of certain enzymes to inhibition by alcohol. This also would affect the transmission of nerve impulses, which depend on the enzyme's regulation of the flow of ions through the nerve cell membrane.

- Predisposition toward alcoholism may be based on inherited variations in the neurotransmitter release and uptake systems involved in the chemical propagation of nerve impulses between nerve cells.

- People who are predisposed to alcoholism may produce abnormal amounts of certain morphinelike compounds that may be involved in alcohol addiction.

- Predisposition toward alcoholism may be based on inherited variations in the brain's neurochemical mechanisms for reinforcing certain behaviors.

The Psychodynamic View

Psychodynamic theorists often describe the typical person who develops an alcohol problem as an **oral-dependent personality.** They believe that such a person's basic need for oral gratification was not satisfied early in life. This lack of satisfaction resulted in the development of an individual who is driven to secure oral satisfaction through such devices as drinking, smoking, and eating, and whose personality is characterized by self-doubt, passivity, and dependence.

Although there is no conclusive evidence that personality factors are involved in the development of alcoholism, a study reported by Jones (1981) demonstrated a consistent set of personality attributes among some alcoholics. The study drew upon data from a longitudinal research project that had begun when the subjects were 10½ years old. In middle age the subjects were interviewed about their drinking patterns. Jones found that as adults, male problem drinkers were likely to be described as relatively hostile, submissive, socially unsuccessful, and anxious. In general, these men had been rated as rather extroverted in adolescence. However, at that time they also described themselves as having less satisfactory social relationships and greater feelings of inferiority than other males in the study. Jones

believed that these men were rather impulsive and unsure of themselves in adolescence and that they had difficulty forming deeper, more lasting friendships. Additional longitudinal studies are needed to clarify the roles of personality and psychodynamic factors in alcohol use.

Learning Factors

Some people drink as a way of coping with problems of living. They learn this behavior through reinforcement (being accepted by friends who value drinking), modeling (seeing others "solve" their problems with alcohol), and other learning mechanisms. Short-term use of alcohol may be reinforcing for many people because of the pleasurable feeling of relaxation it produces. But since drinking is not an effective coping mechanism, their life situation does not improve. Feeling even less able to cope constructively, they increase their maladaptive coping behavior.

It is also possible that alcohol is sought for its short-term excitatory actions and is reinforcing because it makes people "feel good." Like all psychological phenomena, reinforcement has underlying neurochemical mechanisms. Most researchers agree that alcohol is a reinforcer, that its reinforcement arises from specific mechanisms within the brain, and that these mechanisms, which constitute the brain's reward system, are probably located in a specific cluster of nerve cells.

Several studies have implicated certain neurochemicals in the reinforcing properties of alcohol. Alcohol may make many people "feel good" because it alters the levels of dopamine and norepinephrine, as well as opioid peptides, in a specific brain region. Subjectively, these neurochemical changes are experienced as excitation, and because that experience can be pleasurable, both people and animals will seek alcohol again (*Alcoholism: An Inherited Disease,* 1985).

Cognitive Factors

Behavior is influenced by expectations about the consequences of behaving in a particular way as well as by what actually does happen (Wilson, 1987). Behavior thus can be shaped and maintained by cognitive appraisals of what has happened and what is likely to happen. A problem drinker learns to expect positive effects from drinking and interprets the experience in that way, despite the fact that the predominant quality of the actual experience is negative.

The importance of expectancy is illustrated by an experiment reported by Marlatt and others (1973). These investigators used a taste-rating task to determine whether drinking rates are affected by the actual presence of alcohol or merely by the expectancy of alcohol. The taste-rating task was an unobtrusive measure of drinking because the person's attention was focused on

FIGURE 14–4

Behavioral Alcohol Research Laboratory (BARLAB), a University of Washington research facility, is designed for direct observation of drinking behavior in a seminaturalistic setting.

the taste of the drinks. The drinks used were vodka and tonic, and tonic alone. The subjects were permitted to drink as much of the beverages as they wished in the time allotted. The researchers found that the only significant determinant of the amount of alcohol consumed was the subjects' expectations regarding what they were drinking; those who expected alcohol drank more. This finding supports a cognitive interpretation of drinking. (Later in the chapter we discuss the applications of this cognitive perspective to therapy for problem drinkers.) Figure 14–4 shows a naturalistic setting for experiments on drinking behavior.

There is evidence that a person's belief about the alcohol content of a drink, regardless of its actual content, can be a significant determiner not only of alcohol consumption but also of various behaviors that may accompany or result from drinking such as depression, delay of gratification, social anxiety, and sexual responsiveness in men. This evidence comes from studies using the *balanced placebo design*, in which half of the subjects are given a drink containing alcohol and half are given a nonalcoholic beverage. By varying both drink content and expectancy set, this design permits joint and separate evaluation of the behavioral consequences of a subject's belief that he or she has consumed alcohol and the consequences of actual alcohol consumption.

Social and Community Factors

The problem of excessive use of alcohol has sociocultural as well as psychological dimensions. The values and customs of the community influence attitudes to-

ward drinking. In the past, problems of alcohol use were extremely frequent among certain ethnic groups, such as the Irish and Swedish, relatively infrequent for Italians, and particularly infrequent for Jews. Today, however, alcoholism is decreasing among Irish- and Swedish-Americans but rising among second- and third-generation Italian-Americans and Jews. Changing social customs within the cultural group seem to be a significant factor in these patterns of alcohol consumption.

Rates of alcoholism are low in groups in which the drinking customs, values, and sanctions are well known, agreed to by all, and consistent with the rest of the culture (see Figure 14–5). Among the sociocultural conditions that minimize alcohol problems are the following.

1. Exposure of children to alcohol at an early age in a strong family or religious setting. The alcoholic beverage is served in diluted form (wine as opposed to distilled spirits, for example) and in small quantities.

2. The beverage is considered a food and is served mainly at meals.

3. Drinking is not considered either a virtue—for example, a proof of manhood or virility—or a sin.

4. Abstinence is socially acceptable but excessive drinking or drunkenness is not.

A variety of social and interpersonal factors also influence alcohol consumption. These include the level of stress in the community and in the individual's personal life. Among the personal factors are friendships,

(a)

(b)

FIGURE 14–5
The context in which alcoholic beverages are consumed is an important factor in alcoholism. Drinking wine at family gatherings, like this Jewish Passover ceremony (a), is much less likely to lead to problem drinking than drinking in situations in which there is pressure for the individual to "excel at drinking" (b).

family situation, and employment and financial status (Linsky and others, 1985).

Treatment

The first step in treating an addicted alcohol user is usually detoxification, or "drying out." Physiological withdrawal symptoms often begin 6 to 24 hours after heavy drinking has stopped, although they can occur when alcoholics simply reduce their intake of alcohol. Withdrawal signs can include tremors, delirium, sweating, confusion, increased blood pressure, and agitation. There is no established sobering agent—nothing that counteracts the effects of alcohol or speeds its breakdown and passage out of the body. Many alcoholics can withdraw on their own, but some are so severely dependent that they have to be detoxified—supervised as they go through a gradual withdrawal. Once detoxification is complete, insomnia, depression, and anxiety may persist for weeks or months. However, these usually receive no treatment after the detoxification period has ended.

Most recovery from alcoholism is not the result of treatment. Probably no more than 10 percent of alcohol

TABLE 14-6

Determining Extent of Drinking Problem and Alcoholic's Willingness to Admit the Problem—The Initial Steps in Treatment Planning

It is not necessarily useful simply to ask how much a person drinks, because the response is likely to be vague and may be influenced by denial. One of the best ways of determining the extent of denial of the symptoms is a series of questions that can be addressed to alcoholics. Some helpful questions about drinking patterns or habits are the following:

Do you sometimes drink heavily after a disappointment or quarrel?
Do you always drink more heavily when you feel under pressure?
Are you drinking more often without eating?
Do you try to sneak in extra drinks on social occasions?
Have you attempted various ways to control your drinking?
Have you failed to keep promises to yourself to cut down?
Do you avoid your family and close friends while drinking?

Useful questions about feelings include:

Do you feel guilty about your drinking?
Do you want to go on drinking when your friends have had enough?
Do you often regret what you have said or done while drinking?
Do you feel uncomfortable if alcohol is not available in certain situations?
Are you annoyed by the way others talk about your drinking?

If friends or family members can be interviewed these are questions that might be addressed to them:

Does this person's drinking ever worry or embarrass you?
Does it spoil family holidays?
Does it create a tense atmosphere?
Do you lie to conceal it?
Does he or she try to justify the drinking or avoid discussion of it?
Do you or your children fear physical or verbal assault from this person when he or she is drinking?
Does this person become remorseful and apologize after a drinking episode?
Do others talk about this person's drinking?

abusers are ever treated at all, but as many as 40 percent recover on their own. Alcoholics with a stable job and family life have the best chance; age, sex and the duration of alcohol abuse matter less. An important step in overcoming alcoholism is the alcoholic's acknowledgment of the disorder. Alcohol abusers, feeling ashamed and guilty, often refuse to admit the problem to themselves and try to conceal it from their families and friends, who in turn may avoid acknowledging it for fear of being intrusive or having to take responsibility. It is valuable in clinical interviews to determine the patient's willingness to admit the seriousness of his or her drinking problem (see Table 14–6).

Denial and obliviousness are not the only sources of misunderstanding. In a society that has so many heavy drinkers, it is not always easy to decide when a drinking problem has become so serious that special help is needed. Alcoholism can be hard to observe day by day, even if it's easily recognizable over a period of years. Patterns of abuse through a lifetime are variable. The symptoms come and go. Alcoholics are not always drinking uncontrollably; some drink only on weekends,

and many succeed in remaining abstinent or nearly abstinent for months at a time. In the following sections we describe several treatment programs for problem drinkers and detoxified alcoholics.

The Biological Approach

Earlier in the chapter we mentioned that biological theories regarding susceptibility to alcohol might someday lead to effective physical therapies for alcoholism. Such therapies have not yet been developed, but one outgrowth of the view that alcoholism is a disease, caused perhaps by an allergy or physiological sensitivity to alcohol, is the belief that the alcoholic needs to avoid alcoholic beverages completely. According to the disease model, losing control of drinking is an involuntary manifestation of an internal addictive disorder. If one drink is enough to set off a drinking binge in alcoholics who want to rehabilitate themselves, that drink must not be taken. Because Alcoholics Anonymous (AA) attempts to help the alcoholic resist taking that one drink, the AA program is widely recommended by adherents of the

The Psychodynamic Approach

Clinicians who take a psychodynamic perspective advocate psychotherapy for alcoholics. Although there have been some encouraging clinical reports on the usefulness of psychotherapy, research on the topic has not yet produced definitive conclusions. Most studies of psychotherapy with alcoholics are not comparable with respect to such important variables as the setting in which the treatment was applied, the duration of the therapy, and the criteria by which the therapy was evaluated.

The use of psychotherapy to help people with alcohol problems may be limited by the fact that they often need help at odd hours in their efforts to stay sober. The low self-esteem of some overusers of alcohol may be even further lowered by having to depend on people who do not have an alcohol problem.

In the past, psychotherapists believed that alcoholism is merely a symptom of underlying psychological difficulties. The logical conclusion was that such patients would improve in regard to their drinking, if insight seeking was successful. Today, it is widely recognized that psychotherapeutic exploration for someone who is still drinking not only provides very little benefit but may be barely remembered from one session to the next.

The Learning Approach

Aversive conditioning is based on the principles of classical conditioning. If a glass of alcohol (conditioned stimulus) regularly precedes an aversive stimulus such as a nausea-producing drug (unconditioned stimulus), the alcohol will eventually elicit some part of the unconditioned response—in this case, vomiting. Once the unpleasant response has been conditioned to alcohol, the habit of avoiding alcohol will be established through operant conditioning. The response of abstinence is strengthened because it reduces the unpleasant feeling (nausea) that the conditioning situation has associated with alcohol. Electric shock is sometimes used in place of nausea-producing drugs in this procedure, but it seems to be less effective. Aversive-conditioning approaches often require "booster sessions" because the threat of an unpleasant reaction tends to weaken over time. Long-term follow-up studies are needed to establish the success rate of aversive conditioning.

Another learning approach, **covert sensitization**, uses aversive images and fantasies rather than actual shocks and chemicals. Alcoholic patients are told that they can eliminate their "faulty habit" by associating it with unpleasant stimuli. They are instructed to close their eyes and imagine that they are about to drink an alcoholic beverage. They are then taught to imagine the sensations of nausea and vomiting. If it is repeated often enough, the association between nausea and the sight,

---

disease model. It is the most widely used group treatment for alcoholism.

The basic strategy of AA is known as the Twelve Steps. Recovering alcoholics must admit their powerlessness over alcohol and seek help from a higher power, which can be understood in any way an individual member chooses. Members are urged to pray or meditate to get in touch with that power. They are asked to make a "moral inventory," confess the wrongs they have done, beg forgiveness, make amends, and carry the message to other alcoholics. AA takes the position that anyone who has once been an alcoholic is always an alcoholic; the disease can be arrested but vulnerability is permanent.

The most famous AA slogans are "It's the first drink that gets you drunk," which states the goal of abstinence, and "One day at a time," which places present action before long-term planning and dreaming. AA members are told that alcohol is the source of their problems but that they nevertheless must assume responsibility for their own recovery. They must also resolve to devote themselves to helping others in need without regard to personal prestige or material gain.

One study estimated that of the alcoholics who stay in AA, about half are abstinent after 2 years, 15 percent drink lightly to moderately, and at least 13 percent drink abusively. Because 21 percent could not be traced after two years, the number of failures may be higher (Alford, 1980). These figures are somewhat difficult to interpret because many alcoholics drop out of the program, presumably as failures, yet are not counted in the statistics. However, a comprehensive review of research on the topic supports the conclusion that AA is an effective source of help for many alcoholics (Leach, 1973). One of AA's most important rehabilitative ingredients is the social support it provides for members. Members know that they can call upon fellow members at any time for aid in resisting the temptations of alcohol. Although AA may not be the right approach for every alcoholic, for those who find it congenial it can be a valuable source of support, belongingness, and security.

Another biological approach to alcohol problems is the use of disulfiram to alter the body's response to alcohol. Disulfiram is a drug that causes extreme and sometimes violent discomfort (nausea, vomiting, cold sweats) when a person drinks alcohol within 12 hours of taking it. Since disulfiram is self-administered, the success of this technique depends on the individual's motivation to reduce or eliminate drinking. If the person wants to drink, disulfiram therapy will fail. It may be useful, however, as part of a therapeutic approach that also deals with motivations or situational cues that lead to alcohol use (Council on Scientific Affairs, 1987; Fuller and others, 1986).

smell, and taste of alcohol is presumed to establish a conditioned aversion to alcohol.

The Cognitive Approach

In the cognitive approach, clients are oriented toward monitoring their own behavior by noting the situational and environmental antecedents and consequences of heavy drinking. Their past learning in relation to drinking is reviewed, and their expectations about the effects of alcohol are discussed. Participants in controlled-drinking programs are encouraged to ask themselves questions like the following.

- At what places am I most likely to overdrink?
- With which people am I most likely to overdrink?
- When am I most likely to overdrink?
- How do I feel emotionally just before I begin to overdrink?

Special emphasis is placed on drinking as a response to stress. This approach makes sense, since a high percentage of people with alcohol problems report that their heavy drinking often begins when they are faced with unpleasant, frustrating, or challenging situations. Improved problem-solving skills, particularly in the area of interpersonal relationships, learning how to anticipate and plan for stressful experiences, and acquiring the ability to say "No, thanks" when offered a drink have been shown to have therapeutic value for alcoholics (Marlatt and Gordon, 1985).

One reason that learning approaches may not be effective is that the short-term effects of alcohol often are positively reinforcing. Only the effects of overconsumption ending in intoxication, dangerous or socially frowned-upon behavior, or a period of binge drinking have negative-reinforcement properties. The cognitive perspective deals with this problem by focusing the client's thoughts on the consequences of the drinking behavior as well as on the specific situations in which drinking is most likely to appear tempting. The client and the therapist work together to develop cognitive coping techniques to deal with these situations.

Relapse Prevention. While the goal of therapeutic efforts is to help alcoholics stop drinking, maintaining sobriety over the long term is also of great importance. Alcoholics who undergo treatment have a high relapse rate. Many go through treatment a number of times or through a number of treatments and still relapse into uncontrolled drinking.

For those who view alcoholism as a disease, a relapse is a failure that the victim is powerless to control. From the cognitive viewpoint, a relapse is a slip or error. Such a lapse might be prevented in the future by strengthening the person's coping skills. The cognitive approach views a relapse as a fork in the road. One fork leads back to the abusing behavior, the other toward the goal of positive change. Figure 14–6 describes the cognitive–behavioral approach to the relapse process.

Relapse-prevention programs combine a cognitive approach with a variety of treatment procedures designed to change the individual's drinking pattern (Marlatt and Gordon, 1985). The programs are equally useful whether the goal is abstinence or controlled drinking. The only requirement is that the client make a voluntary decision to change. The relapse-prevention approach assumes that the person experiences a sense of control over his or her behavior as long as the treatment program continues. If the person encounters a high-risk situation, this sense of control is threatened and a relapse is likely. High-risk situations include negative moods such as frustration, anger, or depression; interpersonal conflicts such as an argument with an employer or family member; and social pressure to indulge in drinking (see Figure 14–7). If the person is able to make an effective coping response—for example, behaving assertively when friends suggest "just one drink"—the probability of a relapse decreases.

An important factor in relapses is the **abstinence-violation effect.** When a relapse occurs, the individual

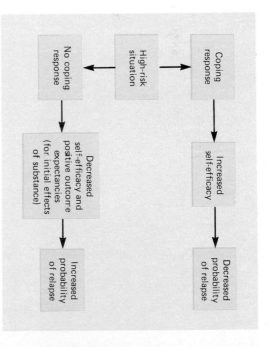

FIGURE 14-6

A cognitive–behavioral analysis of the relapse process begins with exposure to a high-risk situation. A high-risk situation is any situation that arouses stress, negative emotions, strong urges and temptations, interpersonal conflict. Having a coping response increases the sense of self-efficacy (feeling that one is in control) and decreases the probability of relapse. Not having a coping response decreases self-efficacy (and heightens the feeling of not being in control) and, together with positive expectations about the favorable effects of the substance, increases the probability of relapse.

(a)

(b)

FIGURE 14-7

Increased stress and the feeling of not being in control in a problematic situation increases the risk of relapse. The person in a is insecure and feels social pressure to join friends in drinking. The person in b has heard that because of a business slowdown her job might be eliminated and has reacted by starting to drink.

has two kinds of cognitive and emotional responses. One is conflict and guilt; the other is self-blame. An alcoholic who breaks abstinence for the first time may continue to drink after the lapse in order to relieve the conflict and guilt related to the first drink. The individual may also reduce the conflict between the drinking behavior and the goal of avoiding relapses by thinking: "This just proves I'm an alcoholic. I can't control my drinking once I start it." Rather than attributing the lapse to the difficult situation, people who use these cognitions are likely to blame themselves for lack of willpower or inability to resist temptation. Such thoughts increase the probability that a single drink may snowball into a full-strength alcoholic binge and a total relapse.

In addition to viewing any slip into drinking as a lapse and not necessarily a relapse, one of the primary goals of the relapse-prevention program is to train the individual to recognize the early-warning signals that may precede a relapse and to plan and carry out a series of intervention or coping strategies before it is too late to do anything about it. The relapse-prevention technique holds promise not only for alcohol abuse but also for drug use, smoking, and other problems of self-control such as dieting. Its main ingredients—identifying high-risk situations and learning pertinent coping and behavioral skills—are applicable to many types of situations. There is a need for research that explores its short-and long-term effects and its limitations (Brownell and others, 1986).

Abstinence versus Controlled Drinking. A sometimes intense and angry dispute about the necessity for abstinence began in the 1960s when studies reported

that some former alcoholics could continue to drink moderately. Most advocates of controlled drinking are behavioral or cognitive–behavioral therapists who see alcohol abuse as a bad habit or a personal or social problem. Defenders of abstinence, including Alcoholics Anonymous and many medical and mental health professionals, believe that loss of control is inevitable for an alcoholic once drinking starts. They tend to regard alcoholism as a disease whose progress can be arrested only by removing the poison that causes it.

Critics of the disease approach argue that while abstinence can work well for some individuals, it is very hard to live up to; moreover, recovery from alcoholism may not require such a drastic step. One study that suggested that alcohol abusers can recover without abstinence is known as the Rand study (Polich and others, 1980). Over 900 individuals with severe alcohol problems were studied for four years after they had been admitted to one of eight federal alcoholism treatment centers. The researchers found that at the end of four years almost half of the subjects were either abstaining from alcohol or drinking in a controlled manner. One of the most interesting findings was that alcoholics over age 40 who were highly dependent on alcohol when they were admitted to the program had lower relapse rates when they abstained completely. In contrast, those under 40 who had low levels of dependence when they entered the program were less likely to relapse if they practiced controlled drinking rather than abstinence.

Another longitudinal study also found that some alcohol abusers can return to drinking on a controlled basis without abusing alcohol (Vaillant and Milofsky, 1982). However, subjects who were alcohol dependent and/or had many alcohol-related problems generally achieved successful results only if they became abstinent (see Figure 14–8).

These findings suggest that there may be two groups of alcohol abusers. Some can successfully resume drinking on a controlled basis. Others must abstain entirely if they are to cope with their alcohol problem. Both studies show that level of abuse before treatment plays an important role in the success of various treatment strategies. However, most researchers in this area would agree that the success rates of treatment procedures are not high enough.

Further research on such issues as the value of abstinence versus controlled drinking needs to be sufficiently complex to take account, not only of subjects' drinking histories, but also of motivations and expectations about what would constitute success in coping with their drinking problems (Miller, 1985; Peele, 1984, 1985). For example, how much does abstinence change the life of an alcoholic? Alcoholics in the first few years of abstinence have been compared with returning prisoners of war. Their world is unfamiliar, because they have been living in an environment created by alcohol. Feelings that have been blunted or suppressed come back to trouble them. They have lost a great deal of time and must start where they left off. Being sober, like being free after imprisonment, entails new responsibilities. Thus alcoholics in the early stages of abstinence often suffer from anxiety and depression and may find it difficult to hold a job or preserve a marriage. The resolution of these problems comes when

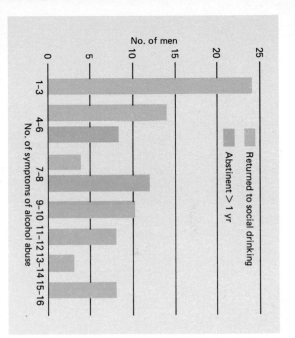

FIGURE 14-8
A return to controlled social drinking has a greater chance of success if the person has only a few symptoms of alcohol abuse. Only four men who had six or more problems were able to return to social drinking. Most of these multiproblem people who did not resume alcohol abuse eventually became abstinent. (Vaillant and Milofsky, 1982, p. 129)

they establish new personal relationships, rebuild old ones, and begin to develop confidence in their power to control their lives.

Preventing Alcohol Abuse

Although there has been much research related to the treatment of alcoholism, differences of opinion exist among experts concerning which treatments are particularly effective. One difficulty in interpreting the available evidence is that many people (perhaps over 50 percent) who enter alcohol treatment programs drop out of them, and no one knows what happens to the dropouts. Studies comparing inpatient and outpatient programs have produced conflicting results (Miller and Hester, 1986). It is becoming clear that much treatment research has failed to find differential effectiveness because different types of patients have been lumped together in study populations. Despite conflicting findings concerning treatment programs, a picture of which alcohol abusers are likely to do well, regardless of the treatment, is emerging: people with jobs, stable relationships, minimal psychopathology, no history of past treatment failures, and minimal involvement with other drugs.

Research on treatment for alcoholism is improving and should yield practically applicable results. Preventing alcohol abuse, however, would obviously be better than having to treat it. Unfortunately, less is known about prevention than about treatment (see Box 14–2). According to some studies, taxes that raise the price of alcohol and therefore reduce a society's total consumption have a more than proportionate effect on serious alcohol abuse. There are usually fewer alcohol problems in countries where the price of alcohol is high relative to the average income. It is less clear whether merely limiting alcohol advertising is effective.

Sometimes authorities believe that alcohol abuse would become rare if people were taught how to drink from an early age. This preventive behavioral approach emphasizes taking alcohol only with food, only at certain times of day, and only to celebrate rather than to escape. Binge drinking and drunkenness should be subject to strong social disapproval. It should be made very clear when drinking is appropriate and what the informal penalties are for inappropriate drinking; weak, vague, and ambiguous rules and sanctions promote uncontrolled alcohol use. This kind of customary restraint is historically well-established in some cultures and ethnic groups, but difficult to impose through public policy. People tend to resist any official demand for more restraint than their entrenched attitudes already endorse. There is also the question of which comes first—ability to drink safely and moderately, or effective customary

BOX 14–2

Television and Alcohol Use

The prevention of alcohol-related problems should be a broad effort encompassing a range of strategies. Adults and children watch television several hours each day. How does the depiction of alcohol's use on TV influence the public's concept of how much drinking is acceptable or desirable (see Figure 14–9)? There is ample evidence of the influential role the mass media play in influencing behavioral patterns and life styles in general and alcohol usage in particular (Gerstein, 1984). If some of the following suggestions were adopted by the producers of television shows, they might contribute to the prevention of alcohol consumption levels that are self-defeating and that pose community problems.

1. Try not to glamorize the drinking or serving of alcohol as a sophisticated or an adult pursuit.

2. Avoid showing the use of alcohol in those cases in which another beverage might be easily and fittingly substituted.

3. Try not to show drinking alcohol as an activity that is so "normal" that everyone must indulge. Allow characters a chance to refuse an alcoholic drink by including nonalcoholic alternatives.

4. Try not to show excessive drinking without consequences or with only pleasant consequences.

5. Demonstrate that there are no miraculous recoveries from alcoholism; normally it is a most difficult task.

6. Don't associate drinking alcohol with "macho" pursuits in such a way that heavy drinking is a requirement for proving one's self as a man.

7. Portray the reaction of others to heavy alcohol drinking, especially when it may be a criticism.

FIGURE 14–9
What adults and children see on television serves as a model for their behavior. Scenes such as these contribute to social norms concerning what constitutes acceptable and desirable behavior. If viewers are exposed on TV to unrealistically high levels of heavy drinking, they might come to identify with the heavy TV drinkers and increase their own consumption levels. Changing the way in which alcohol consumption is portrayed on television and in the movies might contribute to the prevention of alcoholism.

restraints. It may be the absence of alcohol abuse that explains the survival of these customs, rather than the other way around.

Other Drugs

Strictly speaking, alcohol is a drug—it is a chemical substance that leads to physiological and psychological changes when ingested. But for most people the word *drugs* means pills, powders, and pot. Psychoactive drugs may be classified into several groups: barbiturates and tranquilizers, the opioids, cocaine, amphetamines, psychedelics, phencyclidine (PCP), marijuana, and nicotine.

Barbiturates and Tranquilizers

Barbiturates (such as phenobarbitol) and tranquilizers (such as Valium) are grouped together because they both have a depressing effect on the central nervous system. They probably do this by interfering with synaptic transmission. Either they inhibit the secretion of excitatory neurotransmitters or they cause the release of inhibitory transmitter substances. Both types of drugs reduce anxiety and insomnia and affect a wide range of bodily functions. They are both very popular. Each year Americans consume over 300 tons of barbiturates; tranquilizers are an even bigger business.

Barbiturates, or derivatives of barbituric acid, are prescribed by physicians for relief of anxiety or to prevent convulsions. Illicit use of barbiturates often occurs in conjunction with the use of other drugs, notably alcohol and heroin. Mild doses of barbiturates are effective as sleeping pills, although they may actually cause sleep disorders if used over a long period. Higher doses, such as those used by addicted individuals, trigger an initial period of excitement that is followed by slurred speech, loss of coordination, severe depression, and impairment of thinking and memory.

The body quickly develops a tolerance for many of the effects of barbiturates and tranquilizers. As tolerance develops, the amount of the substance needed to maintain the same level of intoxication is increased. The margin between an intoxicating dose and a fatal one also becomes smaller (see Figure 14–10). These drugs can cause both physical and psychological dependence. After addiction has developed, sudden abstinence can cause withdrawal symptoms including delirium, convulsions, and death. People who are addicted to barbiturates often eat the drugs like candy during the day and take a massive dose at bedtime.

There are three types of barbiturate abuse.

1. *Chronic intoxication*, in which people obtain prescriptions, often from more than one physician. Initially they seek barbiturates to reduce insomnia and anxiety. Chronic use leads to slurred speech and decreased effectiveness on the job.

2. *Episodic intoxication*, in which young adults take barbiturates to produce a "high" or state of well-being.

3. *Intravenous injections*, in which the drug is injected, often in combination with other drugs (such as heroin). Intravenous use produces a "rush" of pleasant, warm, drowsy feelings. Many complications are associated with prolonged use of the drug in this manner.

Barbiturates in home medicine cabinets are second only to aspirin as a cause of childhood death from accidental drug overdose. They are second to alcohol as a cause of lethal accidents in adults, and they are the drugs that are most commonly taken with suicidal intent. Relapses are common among barbiturate users because the drug is an easy way of escaping tension, anxiety, and feelings of inadequacy.

Some **tranquilizers** act like barbiturates, while others act quite differently. Overuse of tranquilizers is common. They are frequently prescribed to reduce anxiety, and perhaps half a million Americans use them for nonmedical purposes. As with barbiturates, the body develops a tolerance to many tranquilizers. Physical and psychological dependence and serious withdrawal symptoms may occur. Apparently unaware that they are add-

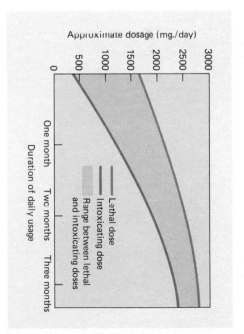

FIGURE 14-10
The relative relationship between lethal and intoxicating doses of short-acting barbiturates in the blood changes as tolerance develops. (Dosages are only approximate because of individual differences in tolerance to the drug and patterns of use.) (Adapted from Wesson and Smith, 1977, p. 35)

ictive or that they can cause death, many people use tranquilizers freely. The undesirable effects of these substances increase when they are used in combination with alcohol and other drugs. Tranquilizers are involved in about one-quarter of all drug-related deaths (Vischi and others, 1980).

Valium is a member of the *benzodiazepine* group of tranquilizers. Drugs in this group produce less euphoria than other tranquilizing drugs, so the risk of dependence and abuse is relatively low. Nevertheless, tolerance and withdrawal can develop.

The Opioids

The word **opioid** describes all drugs with morphine-like effects. These drugs bind to and act upon opioid receptor sites in the brain. The opioids include a variety of substances, some of which occur naturally while others are synthetic.

Natural Opioids

Several forms of opioids that resemble opium and heroin in their effects are manufactured by the brain and the pituitary gland. These substances, called **endorphins**, can also be made artificially for experimental use. Research using these endorphins may provide insights into the mechanisms of pain, pleasure, emotion, and perception. There is already some evidence that when individuals suffering from chronic spinal pain are treated effectively with acupuncture, endorphins are released into the spinal fluid. The endorphin levels seem to peak at the moments when the pain-relieving effects of the acupuncture are most pronounced.

Study of the endorphins has led to the mapping of the entire opioid-receptor system. The nerves of the brain and spinal cord have been found to contain specific sites to which opioids must bind in order to produce their effects. Morphine and similar drugs block pain signals to the brain because they fit into these sites like a key into a lock.

Work on the possibility that drug addiction may yield to endorphin therapy has begun in several laboratories. Some scientists suspect that addiction is a deficiency disease: The addict's craving for and dependence on opioids may be caused by chronic underproduction of natural endorphins. If this is the case, it may be possible to use synthesized endorphins to correct the underlying cause of addiction. Two possibilities might account for endorphin deficiencies. One is that the opioids themselves suppress endorphin production; the other is that some people have a genetically caused deficiency in endorphin production.

While the endorphins have been isolated and examined directly by biochemists, behavioral researchers have been able to study their action either by injecting endorphins into subjects and observing their analgesic (pain-killing) effects or by injecting a drug called *naloxone*, which blocks the effects of the endorphin. If a procedure produces analgesia when naloxone is not used but does not affect pain when naloxone is present, there is indirect evidence that endorphins mediate the pain-reducing effects of the procedure. For example, research done in China has shown that injections of naloxone greatly reduce the analgesic effects of acupuncture.

The Opiates

The word **opiate** refers only to drugs of this type that are derived from the juice of the opium poppy, *Papaver somniferum*. Archaeologists think that the opium poppy's seemingly miraculous powers were first discovered by Neolithic farmers on the eastern shores of the Mediterranean Sea. This knowledge spread from Asia Minor across the ancient world. In the seventeenth century opium was praised by a prominent physician as God's greatest gift to humanity for the relief of its sufferings.

In 1804 the most important active ingredient of opium, **morphine**, was identified. Physicians applauded it as a painkiller of known reliability. Opium and its derivatives were also used to treat coughs, diarrhea, fever, epilepsy, melancholy, diabetes, skin ulcers, constipation, and a variety of other ills well into the 1800s. Many people became addicted to opium and its derivatives after it was given to them for medicinal purposes; the nineteenth-century English writers Thomas De Quincy and Samuel Coleridge are examples. Opium derivatives were popular as home remedies, and until the 1860s there were few restrictions on who might sell or purchase them. One of the largest abuses of the drug was to sedate infants. Working mothers and women who tended babies for pay used these home remedies to keep infants sleepy and calm. By the late 1800s many physicians were becoming concerned about the problem of opium addiction.

Just as morphine was at first considered a safe substitute for opium, **heroin**, which was produced for the first time in 1874 by boiling morphine in acetic acid, was at first hailed as a safe and effective substitute for morphine. This soon proved to be horribly untrue, and today heroin is involved in over 90 percent of narcotic-addiction cases.

Heroin can be injected, smoked, or inhaled. Heroin addicts go through a characteristic sequence of experiences. After the drug is injected, the user feels a "rush" or "flash" as the nervous system reacts to its presence. Addicts describe the rush as an extraordinarily pleasurable sensation, one that is similar in many ways to sexual orgasm, only more intense and involving the whole body. Following the rush, the user experiences the "nods," a lingering state of euphoric bliss. Fatigue, tension, and anxiety fade away. Feelings of inadequacy are replaced by relaxed contentment. One young addict reported that after experiencing his first heroin high he had exclaimed to himself: "Why didn't they tell me such wonderful feelings existed?" A significant number of heroin addicts have stated that unless the world could provide them with a feeling to compensate for the loss of the high, they would never be able to give up heroin.

The Effects of Opioids

The term **opioid** refers to any natural or synthetic substance that acts on the body in a way that is similar to the action of derivatives of the opium poppy. Opioids have both sedative (sleep-inducing) and analgesic (pain-relieving) effects. The opioids are sometimes called **narcotics**, but because this term is used differently by those who study drugs and by the legal system, it does not always have the same meaning to law enforcement personnel, laypeople, physicians, and scientists.

The opioids cause mood changes, sleepiness, mental clouding, constipation, and slowing of the activity of the brain's respiratory center. An overdose may cause death due to cessation of breathing. The withdrawal reaction can be severe and is manifested by sweating, muscle pains, nausea, vomiting, diarrhea, and other symptoms that may last for 2 or 3 days; less severe symptoms may persist for 4 to 6 months. Heroin use is likely to be associated with serious deterioration of the individual's social life and family relations.

Many American service personnel in Vietnam became users of opium products, especially heroin (see Figure 14–11). But only a relatively small number of these individuals continued to use the drugs after they returned to the United States. This was true whether they had become physically dependent on the drugs or not; whether they had injected, smoked, or "snorted" them; and whether they had been in a detoxification program or not. The amount of heroin they had used in Vietnam, their ethnic background, and their social class had little bearing on whether they continued to use drugs after returning to the United States. Behavior before entering the military was the best predictor of continued drug use after discharge. Veterans who continued to use drugs had not finished high school, had a criminal record, or had used a combination of addictive drugs while in Vietnam.

Causes of Opioid Addiction

The finding that many veterans who used opiates in Vietnam were able to abstain upon returning home stimulated interest in the idea that controlled use of at least some addictive substances is possible for some people. Additional support for this view was provided by reports of people who have used opioids in a controlled manner for long periods. Although some users require

FIGURE 14–11

A GI in Vietnam holds an empty vial of heroin against his nose. In 1970, more than 11,000 service personnel in Vietnam were apprehended for drug use. For each individual caught, it is estimated that five escaped detection.

drugs in increasingly large dosages every day, other daily users seem able to limit their intake. Perhaps the reason that controlled use of opioids has received relatively little attention is that people who are able to achieve such use do not come to the attention of clinicians. In any case, a better understanding of the process of opioid addiction is necessary so that effective social policies—for example, drug use laws and treatment procedures—can be formulated.

At present there are two competing views of opioid addiction: the exposure orientation and the adaptive orientation. According to the **exposure orientation**, the cause of addiction is simply exposure to opioids. When a person experiences stress, endorphins are secreted and produce a stress-induced analgesia (increased tolerance for pain). Some researchers have suggested that use of heroin and other opioids may cause a long-term breakdown in the biochemical system that synthesizes the endorphins (Jaffee, 1985). According to this view, an addict continues to use opioids because drug use has broken down the body's normal pain-relief system. It is also thought that opioid drugs are reinforc-

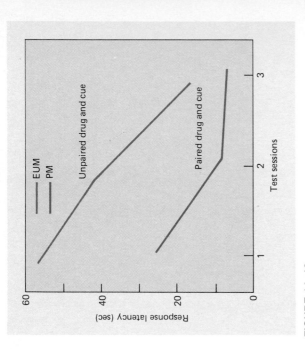

FIGURE 14-12
Rats' sensitivity to pain after a morphine injection differs depending on whether earlier morphine injections were given in the same or different surroundings.

ing because they postpone painful withdrawal symptoms. This view does not explain the Vietnam experience, nor does it explain why some addicts have severe withdrawal symptoms while others do not. Moreover, some people become seriously addicted to drugs that do not produce severe withdrawal symptoms, such as nicotine and coffee.

The **adaptive orientation** is an interactional one in which both the person and the situation are considered to be important factors in the development of addiction: People's characteristics (their expectations, worries, etc.) and the situations they face in life, particularly those that create stress, jointly influence their need for and reactions to drugs. The available evidence is consistent with this interpretation. This view can explain why some military personnel could so easily leave heavy drug use behind when they returned to the United States. In Vietnam, they were faced with strange people and places, boredom, danger, feelings of helplessness, and other emotions and situations that made their coping mechanisms appear inadequate. Once they had returned home, the situational cues that were related to a craving for opioids were absent.

Animal experiments also support the interactional view. In one such experiment rats were individually housed in translucent cages. Each cage was kept in an unlighted drawer of a filing cabinet with air supplied by a relatively noisy ventilating fan. For one group the drawer was opened in a lighted room and the fan turned off. This procedure was the conditioned stimulus (CS). While the drawer was open the rats were injected with morphine (the unconditioned stimulus or UCS). In the other group the CS and UCS were not paired. The morphine was injected while the drawer was opened quickly in a dimly lit room with the fan still on. Then four hours later the drawer was opened in a lighted room with the fan turned off. After 15 of these daily trials all the rats were given three test sessions. They were injected with morphine (the UCS) paired with the CS; 45 minutes later they were tested for response to pain. The rats that were in new situations (that is, had not previously had the CS and the UCS paired) were slower to develop tolerance (Siegel and others, 1981) (see Figure 14-12). This experiment demonstrates that, regardless of the physical effects of a drug, experiences with the drug itself and with an environment related to its administration are important factors in the effectiveness of the drug. The results support an interactive view of addiction.

Both groups of rats showed increasingly short response times over the three test sessions. This indicated that the injection was having less effect (they were becoming drug tolerant). However, tolerance developed at different rates in the two groups. The rats that were in new situations (that is, had not previously had the CS and the UCS paired) were slower to develop tolerance (Siegel and others, 1981) (see Figure 14-12). This experiment demonstrates that, regardless of the physical effects of a drug, experiences with the drug itself and with an environment related to its administration are important factors in the effectiveness of the drug. The results support an interactive view of addiction.

Clinicians do not agree on how opioid addiction

should be treated. Since the nineteenth century treatment has consisted primarily of hospitalization for withdrawal from the drug. Aside from being expensive, hospitalization generally seems to be ineffective, although positive findings have been reported in a 20-year follow-up study of hospitalized addicts (Vaillant, 1973). Although 23 percent had died (mostly from unnatural causes) and 25 percent were still known to be using drugs, somewhat more than one-third had achieved stable abstinence, mainly as a result of strict supervision after discharge from the hospital.

One recurring finding of research on opioid addicts is that they frequently have severe personality problems (Kosten and Rounsaville, 1986). They suffer particularly from depression and their suicide rate is thought to be five times the average. Depression often continues after withdrawal and even becomes worse. Some authorities believe that the drugs cause depression, and others think that more often depression—or at least a vulnerability to depressive symptoms under stress—leads to opioid abuse when the drugs are available. Depression in addicts may have been overestimated, since there is some evidence that the ones who seek treatment are more depressed than those who do not.

Treatment for Opioid Dependence

Methadone maintenance is the most widely used treatment for opioid addicts. Methadone is a synthetic substance whose action is pharmacologically similar to that of other opioids, including heroin; however, methadone's effects last from 24 to 48 hours rather than 6 to 12. When taken orally in constant doses, methadone does not produce the intense euphoria that is produced by heroin. Its withdrawal effects are also less intense (though somewhat more prolonged) than those of heroin, and their appearance is delayed. In sufficient doses methadone blocks the action of heroin so that the dependent person does not experience its euphoric effect. At lower doses it will not block heroin's effects but will suppress "heroin hunger." While the biochemical and physiological properties of methadone are not fully understood, it apparently blocks all the ordinary effects of morphinelike drugs by competing with them at receptor sites in the central nervous system. Through the use of methadone, the craving for heroin is relieved. Methadone prevents withdrawal and allows a heroin-dependent person to function in society.

Methadone-maintenance programs seem suitable to a wide range of opioid-dependent individuals, and since they can be carried out on an outpatient basis, they cost less than institutional treatment. However, despite its relative effectiveness methadone maintenance is not universally supported. Critics claim that it does not really cure addicts but merely transfers their dependence from one drug to another.

Detoxification—controlled and supervised withdrawal—is the first step for all patients not assigned to methadone maintenance. It is usually attempted, for example, with any patient who is in treatment for the first time or has been dependent on opioids for no more than a year or two. Hospitalization may be convenient but is not necessary. It is now standard practice to substitute oral methadone for whatever drug the patient is taking and then gradually to lower the dose to zero over a period of a week or two. Clonidine, a nonopiate drug originally marketed to lower blood pressure, has proved to be effective in easing withdrawal because it acts at some of the same nerve endings as opioids.

Dealing with drug addicts and with the traffic in illegal drugs is a major problem in many countries. The British tried to control heroin abuse through a system of outpatient drug-dependence clinics. These clinics gave addicts daily maintenance doses not only of methadone but even of heroin and cocaine. By providing a legal daily maintenance dose, the clinics hoped to draw the addicts into contact with the helping system and make it unnecessary for them to support their habit through crime. The ultimate goal was to gradually wean addicts from the drugs if possible, or at least to stabilize them on a fixed dose of heroin or methadone in a lifetime program. In a 10-year follow-up study of the effectiveness of the system, investigators found that 40 percent of a group of addicts who had attended the clinics in 1969 were still attending a clinic and receiving heroin or methadone (Wille, 1981). The majority of these continuing users had been socially stable for at least 10 years. Most of them were employed and were not currently in trouble with the law. Of the group who were no longer attending the clinics, at least half had become abstinent.

There are few follow-up studies from other countries with which these data may be compared. However, the data that exist suggest that the British program was at least as effective as approaches used in other countries (Jaffee, 1985). Moral objections to the government's providing heroin and cocaine for addicts has been a constant threat to the existence of the British program as more than a methadone-maintenance plan (see Figure 14–13).

Is abstinence the solution to the addict's problems? A recent study suggests that merely abstaining from opioids has disappointingly little effect on the other medical, emotional, and social problems of addicts (Kosten and others, 1987). The subjects of the study were 150 patients who applied for treatment at an addiction clinic. Three-fourths were men, and they had used opioids for an average of 10 years. Two-and-a-half years later the researchers interviewed most of them again. Some were now abstinent, and some were using even more opioids than before; most were in-between.

All their problems had, on the average, improved, and drug abuse had improved most. But neither at the time the addicts were admitted to the clinic nor at the follow-up interview was the level of drug abuse correlated with any other problems except legal difficulties. The percentage of time spent drug-free during the period of the study was also unrelated to any other aspect of the outcome. The severity of a patient's drug problem at the time of admission to the clinic was not even related to its severity after 2.5 years, although it was weakly correlated with psychological problems at the follow-up. The severity of medical, family, and psychological problems at the time of the follow-up depended mainly on how serious those problems were to begin with.

The authors concluded that addicts need family therapy, psychotherapy for depression, vocational counseling, and other types of treatment at least as much as they need help in achieving abstinence. Psychodynamically and cognitively oriented therapies have been found to be helpful with opioid addicts, particularly those with longstanding addictions and severe psychiatric disorders (Woody and others, 1986).

Cocaine

Sigmund Freud described the effects of cocaine in this way. He had become interested in the drug because of its pain-relieving properties. After a short time (10–20 minutes), he feels as though he had been raised to full height of intellectual and bodily vigor, in a state

FIGURE 14–13
A drug dependence clinic in England.

of euphoria, which is distinguished from the euphoria after consumption of alcohol by the absence of any feeling of alteration. . . . One can perform mental and physical work with great endurance, and the otherwise urgent needs of rest, food, and sleep are thrust aside, as it were. During the first hours after cocaine, it is even impossible to fall asleep. This effect of the alkaloid gradually fades away after the aforesaid time, and is not followed by any depression. . . . I could not fail to note, however, that the individual disposition plays a major role in the effects of cocaine, perhaps a more important role than with other alkaloids. The subjective phenomena after ingesting of coca differ from person to person, and only few persons experience, like myself, a pure euphoria without alteration. Others already experience a slight intoxication, hyperkinesia, and talkativeness after the same amount of cocaine, while still others have no subjective symptoms of the effects of coca at all.

—(Freud, 1936)

Cocaine is the main active drug in the leaves of the coca bush which grows on the eastern slopes of the Andes Mountains in South America. The Indians of Peru and Bolivia have used its leaves for centuries to increase endurance and decrease hunger so that they can cope better with the rigors of their economically marginal, high-altitude existence. In 1860 cocaine was isolated and purified. Whereas the opioids are "downers" that quiet the body's responses, **cocaine** is an "upper"

that increases heart rate, raises blood pressure and body temperature, and decreases appetite. Cocaine puts the body in an emergency state in much the same way that a rush of adrenaline would in a stressful situation. Although it is not clear how cocaine produces this effect, it is likely that it is produced by the release of large amounts of dopamine in the brain. Cocaine also affects at least three parts of the brain itself: the cerebral cortex, which governs reasoning and memory; the hypothalamus, which controls appetite, body temperature, sleep, and emotions such as fear and anger; and the cerebellum, which regulates motor activities such as walking and balance.

Like heroin, cocaine initially had a positive, even benign image. Freud, who periodically used cocaine himself, recommended it for use in treating depression and other conditions, including morphine withdrawal. Its use as a local anesthetic led to the discovery of synthetic substitutes with low toxicity, while its use in treating morphine withdrawal indirectly led to self-administration of the drug. From about 1880 to 1900 cocaine was actually an ingredient in some popular brands of soda pop.

Cocaine can be "snorted" or sniffed, smoked (often in a water pipe), or injected directly. Today cocaine is the drug of choice for many conventional and often upwardly mobile citizens—young professionals, executives, politicians—and is used rather openly in spite of its illegal status (see Figure 14–14). It produces feelings of wittiness and hyperalertness and is often praised by users as being almost risk free: no hangovers like those

FIGURE 14-14
Middle-class New Yorkers openly snort cocaine at a party.

produced by alcohol, no injection scars like those caused by heroin use, and no lung cancer, which is associated with use of marijuana and tobacco. Unfortunately, its action is more complex and less benign than most users believe. Table 14–7 lists the effects of cocaine use.

High doses or repeated use of cocaine can produce a state resembling mania, with impaired judgment, incessant rambling talk, hyperactivity, and paranoia that may lead to violence or accidents. There is also an acute anxiety reaction that is sometimes severe enough to be called panic. Serious acute physical reactions are also possible. By constricting blood vessels and increasing

TABLE 14-7

Effects of Cocaine[a]

1. Euphoria
2. Increased energy
3. Enhanced mental acuity and alertness
4. Increased sensory awareness (sexual, auditory, visual)
5. Decreased appetite
6. Decreased need for sleep
7. Increased self-confidence
8. Delusions
9. Constricted blood vessels and increased heart rate
10. Convulsions

[a]The effects depend on dosage and degree of habitual use.

the heart rate, cocaine can produce cardiac symptoms, including irregular heartbeat, angina, and myocardial infarction. High doses may also cause nausea, headache, cold sweats, tremors, and fast, irregular, shallow breathing. People who have high blood pressure or damaged arteries may suffer strokes as a result of cocaine use. Death usually results from convulsions followed by paralysis of the brain centers controlling respiration, followed by cardiac arrest; in serious cases an acute overdose must be treated with oxygen and anticonvulsant drugs. A common cause of death is intravenous injection of a "speedball"—a combination of heroin and cocaine.

Cocaine presents serious problems when it is taken habitually in large doses. As long as only a limited quantity is consumed, cocaine can be taken daily for years with no apparent ill effects. But since it is one of the most powerful drug reinforcers, desire for it is hard to control. A damaging habit usually develops over a period of several months to several years. Compulsive users cannot turn the drug down; they think about it constantly, dream about it, spend all their savings on it, and borrow, steal, or deal to pay for it.

Short-term tolerance for cocaine develops very fast with repeated doses during a single session; users often say that they never quite recapture the euphoria of the first snort. After months of use, long-term tolerance may also develop, although this happens less strikingly and consistently.

Whether cocaine can be said to produce a withdrawal reaction depends partly on definitions. It does not cause physiological addiction like that associated with alcohol, sedatives, and opioids, in which the central nervous system becomes hyperexcitable when deprived of the drug. Therefore, abstinence does not usually result in acute physical discomfort. A common pattern of cocaine abuse consists of binges or runs followed by crashes. A week-long run produces extreme acute tolerance and exhaustion from lack of food and sleep. The user becomes agitated and depressed, and then falls into several days of severe depression, excessive sleep, overeating, and sometimes chills, tremors, or muscle pains.

The crash is more like a hangover than an alcohol or opioid withdrawal reaction; during the acute phase there is no desire for cocaine. Afterward the abuser may go through a period of unhappiness and lethargy that stimulates further craving. Even many months or years later, a passing but intense craving can reemerge, especially when certain moods or situations have come to evoke a conditioned response.

Cocaine use is increasing rapidly in the United States. A survey in 1985 showed that close to 6 million people in the United States were using cocaine (*National Household Survey on Drugs*, 1985). Among young adults between the ages of 18 and 25, 28 percent have used it. Emergency-room admissions associated with cocaine use tripled between 1981 and 1984. Today cocaine is the most frequently used drug after marijuana. Crack, a potent form of cocaine that is smoked rather than sniffed, produces especially strong craving. Some users say they become slaves to crack in just days or weeks.

Why is crack addictive? Probably because it alters brain chemistry and moods in the same way as cocaine powder. But it does so more rapidly and intensely, producing not only a higher "high" but also a deeper "crash" that leaves the user desperate for more. Researchers are zeroing in on how cocaine produces euphoria and the depression and craving that result from chronic use. The drug interferes with the normal functioning of neurotransmitters, chemicals that activate nerves in an area of the brain associated with pleasurable feelings.

Treating Cocaine Dependence

The cocaine dependent person must first become convinced that treatment is necessary. As in all types of drug and alcohol dependence, more or less subtle forms of denial are common; for example, abusers may want relief for some of the side effects without giving up the habit itself. Sometimes they are induced to come in for treatment only by pressure from family members, employers, or the law. People seek treatment at different stages of dependency, and the severity of the symptoms varies greatly.

Sometimes cocaine users can help themselves. One way of doing so is through aversive conditioning. The user resolves not to use cocaine at certain times and places, with explicit self-imposed penalties if the promise is broken. Contingency contracting is a variant of this technique that requires the cooperation of a professional. The cocaine abuser deposits a letter with a psychotherapist that is to be sent if a sample of the client's urine reveals evidence of cocaine use or a sample is not produced for inspection. The letter contains an admission that is likely to be embarrassing or damaging either professionally or financially. Since the penalty is severe and public, the motivation to fulfill the contract is strong. Unfortunately, many people who are offered contingency contracts decline, and almost all who decline eventually drop out of treatment or resume cocaine use. Possibly abusers who refuse contingency contracts have more serious problems, while those who sign such contracts are already prepared to give up the drug anyway.

Psychotherapy alone rarely solves drug problems, but it can be an important part of treatment. Supportive psychotherapy is a relationship with a sympathetic professional who provides comfort and encourages the abuser to stay away from sources of cocaine. Interpretive or exploratory psychotherapy can help abusers understand what functions cocaine has been fulfilling in their lives and find other ways of coping.

Many cocaine users have also joined mutual-help groups: Alcoholics Anonymous, Cocaine Anonymous, and Narcotics Anonymous. All of these programs use more or less the same approach: they encourage their members to confide in others who have the same problem, to share their feelings, to make a resolution to overcome dependency, and to support the resolutions of other members. Members admit their powerlessness to control their drug use and seek help from a higher power while taking a "moral inventory" of themselves and pledging abstinence one day at a time.

Amphetamines

Amphetamines, like cocaine, are potent psychomotor stimulants. Various drugs in this group are called speed, crystal, pep pills, bennies, meth, and many other names, depending on the specific active agent. Despite their dissimilar chemical structures, amphetamines and cocaine have many similar properties. They both probably act by influencing the norepinephrine and dopamine receptor systems. Antipsychotic drugs block not only the dopamine receptors but some of the norepinephrine receptors as well. If antipsychotics are given prior to amphetamine or cocaine use, most of the behavioral effects of these two drugs are inhibited.

Moderate amphetamine use results in increased wakefulness, alertness, and elevation of mood. Psychomotor performance is improved temporarily, but the improvement may be followed by a compensatory rebound or letdown in which the user feels fatigued, less alert, and somewhat depressed.

The medical uses of amphetamines include suppression of appetite and improvement of mood in mild depressions. Amphetamines are also helpful in treating certain neurological and behavioral disorders. College students who use amphetamines when "cramming" for exams not only notice increased energy and tolerance for sleeplessness but also increased productivity on the next day's exam. Although this may be useful at times, even the "improved" performance may not be truly better. Many students have the disillusioning experience of looking at their wondrous performance later and finding it to be of poor quality. The drug impaired their critical thinking at the same time that it increased their output.

High doses of amphetamines have significant effects on the central nervous system and the cardiovascular system; they lead to nervousness, headache, dizziness, agitation, apprehensions, confusion, palpitations, and elevated blood pressure. Regular use of large amounts leads to greater tolerance for the drug and increased intolerance for being without it. Users become malnourished, exhausted, careless, and indifferent to normal responsibilities. Often their thinking is characterized by a paranoia that may develop into a full-blown psychosis accompanied by hallucinations. Withdrawal symptoms, if they occur, are mild compared with those that often accompany cessation of opioid use; they also differ qualitatively. Since tolerance for amphetamines develops rapidly, many users inject it into a vein to obtain more intense effects. This high-dose, long-term use of amphetamines is dangerous and self-destructive. Since the initial effects are stimulating and pleasant, unwary individuals often proceed to higher doses and eventually to a state of dependence. Aversive conditioning and token economies have been used with some success in treating amphetamine addicts.

Psychedelics

Psychedelics or hallucinogens act on the central nervous system to produce alteration of consciousness. They change the user's perceptions of both the internal and the external world. There is usually sensory displacement, which can drastically alter color perception and hearing. Auditory, visual, and tactile hallucinations accompany the experience, along with a changed perception of self. Among the natural psychedelic substances are mescaline, psilocybin, and dimethyl tryptamine (DMT). Synthetic psychedelics include diethyltryptamine, STP, and dilysergic acid diethylamide (LSD).

In many cultures psychedelics have been used for hundreds of years. Mescaline, which is derived from the peyote cactus, and psilocybin, which is obtained from "magic mushrooms," are used for religious ceremonies by Indians in Mexico and Central America. West Africans and Congolese have traditionally chewed the ibogaine root, which contains tryptamine, to "release the gods." In the 1950s and 1960s extensive research was conducted on the biochemical, psychological, and therapeutic effects of such drugs. At the same time, some people became interested in the psychedelics as a way of obtaining religious insight. Timothy Leary and others who promoted this view touched off a craze for psychedelics among college students.

LSD (popularly called "acid") is a colorless, odorless, and tasteless material. Effects are produced by as little as 50 micrograms (a microgram is a millionth of a gram), an amount that in pure form would not be visible to the naked eye. No legally manufactured LSD is available to the general public, and the output of illegal, often amateur, laboratories is rarely pure LSD.

The immediate effects of LSD usually last about 8 to 12 hours. The mechanism of its action is not well understood, but it is known to stimulate the sympathetic nervous system and to produce physiological changes like those seen in a person who is aroused, excited, or under stress. The most common subjective effects are euphoria, quick shifts from one mood to another, and altered awareness of the color, size, and shape of stimuli. Time perception is so altered that minutes may seem like hours. Bizarre sensations may be experienced, frequently including feelings of separation or disintegration of some part of the body. The user is usually aware that these effects are due to the drug and are not "out there." Some users experience bewilderment, disorganization, personal and sexual identity confusion, and fears of losing control. They may experience intense emotions that they cannot label. In fact, one of the most unfortunate effects of LSD is the feeling of being overwhelmed by confusing emotions that cannot be sorted out because they are going by so fast. For example:

A 25-year-old woman used some LSD because a friend had had a number of "great" LSD experiences and convinced her that it would make her less inhibited sexually. About a half hour after ingesting the LSD, she became confused and disoriented. The walls, floor, and ceiling became wavy, "as if an earthquake were taking place." She became panicky

LSD sometimes produces extreme anxiety or panic reactions. Such "bad trips" are generally short-lived and can often be modified by supportive reassurance. Bad trips may be terminated by appropriate medication and occasionally by hospitalization. The most serious effects of LSD are paranoid symptoms (feelings of being followed, spied on, or persecuted), psychosis resembling that found in schizophrenia, and severe depression that occasionally leads to suicide attempts. Negative effects of a large dose of LSD may persist for months, require long hospitalization, and resist the usual forms of treatment. The frequency of such reactions is difficult to determine but is probably less than 1 percent. When such problems arise, it is often difficult to separate the effects of LSD from those of prior drug use, personality characteristics, and a variety of other factors.

A more common effect of LSD use is "flashbacks": spontaneous recurrences of parts of the LSD experience long after the action of the drug has ceased. Such recurrences can take place in the first few weeks and have been reported as long as 2 years following the last dose of the drug. It is not clear why these flashbacks occur. One possibility is that LSD causes biochemical changes in the body that last long after drug use. The aftereffects may have serious consequences if they occur in situations that require attentive thinking and decision making.

Most of the hallucinogens are fairly easy to produce chemically, and their use spread rapidly in the 1960s despite widespread reports of severe drug reactions, including homicide, suicide, and acute panic attacks. It is likely that many users thought these reports were propaganda to discourage drug use. LSD use declined in the early 1970s, perhaps in part because of reports of genetic damage to users and to their offspring.

Treatment for abuse of psychedelics depends on the severity of the reaction. Severely affected people must have medical attention to prevent cardiovascular or respiratory collapse. If psychotic behavior is present, antipsychotic drugs of the type used to treat schizophrenia may be helpful, although about 10 percent of acutely psychotic drug users never recover. Psychologically based therapy, particularly group psychotherapy and supportive drug-free groups, can be helpful because users of psychedelic drugs often have feelings of low self-worth and use the drugs to improve their relationships with other people. Many of these abusers need help with their social responses so that they can substitute reinforcing social experiences for the reinforcement they get from drugs.

Phencyclidine (PCP)

PCP (phencyclidine) is most often called "angel dust." It was first developed as an anesthetic in the 1950s. However, it was taken off the market for human use because it sometimes caused hallucinations. It is available in a number of forms. It can be a pure, white crystallike powder, or a tablet or capsule. It also can be swallowed, smoked, sniffed, or injected. PCP is sometimes sprinkled on marijuana or parsley and smoked.

Although PCP is illegal, it is easily manufactured. Users can never be sure what they are buying since it is manufactured illegally. Sometimes it may not even be PCP, but a lethal by-product of the drug.

The effects of PCP depend on how much is taken, the way it is used, and the individual. Effects include increased heart rate and blood pressure, flushing, sweating, dizziness, and numbness. When large doses are taken, effects include drowsiness, convulsions, and coma. Taking large amounts of PCP can also cause death from repeated convulsions, heart and lung failure, or ruptured blood vessels in the brain.

PCP is classified as a dissociative anesthetic. It may cause hallucinations, but it also makes the individual feel dissociated or apart from the environment. In small doses, it produces insensitivity to pain; in large doses, it produces a comalike state and blank stare. People who take larger doses feel as if they are being bombarded by stimuli. They may lose the ability to test reality and suffer severe intellectual and emotional disorganization. PCP users sometimes develop severe depression or a severe psychotic state that is not easily reversible. Whether these outcomes are a result of the drug alone or of underlying personality characteristics is not clear. Table 14–8 shows the effects of PCP at different dosage levels.

Marijuana

The cannabis plant has been harvested throughout history for its fibers, oils, and psychoactive resin. **Marijuana**, which consists of the dried leaves and flower tops of the plant, is the form in which it is most often used in the United States. The solidified resin, called **hashish** (or, colloquially, hash), can also be used to produce psychoactive effects.

TABLE 14-8

Dose-Related Effects of PCP

Low to moderate dose (5 mg)
Blank stare
Assaultive, agitated behavior
Increased blood pressure

Moderate to high dose (20 mg or greater)
Coma
Unresponsive stare (eyes fixed open)
Muscle rigidity
Slowing of EEG brain waves

High to extremely high dose (up to 500 mg)
Prolonged coma
Seizures

Based on Young, Lawson, and Gacono, 1987. Reprinted by courtesy of Marcel Dekker, Inc.

One out of every five Americans has used marijuana at least once, in spite of the fact that it is classified as an illegal substance and its cultivation, possession, distribution, and use are prohibited. Despite these prohibitions and the controversy over its safety, the use of marijuana increased sharply during the 1960s and 1970s. Its use has been declining ever since (Millman, 1986).

Marijuana is not pharmacologically a narcotic, although it has been legally classified as one since 1937. The mechanism of its action is not well understood, but its more common effects have been identified. (Table 14–9 compares the properties of marijuana with those of other drugs.) An important advance was the isolation of the major active ingredient in marijuana, THC (delta-9-tetrahydrocannabinol). Only barely detectable concentrations of THC are present in the brain of a rat after one dose. But with repeated administration THC and the products of its metabolism gradually build up and are detectable as long as 8 days after the administration of a single dose.

THC can be taken by either eating or smoking parts of the cannabis plant. Smoking is the fastest way to feel the drug's effects. When the smoke is inhaled, it is spread across the surface of the lungs, quickly absorbed into the bloodstream, and carried to the brain in a few seconds. When THC is eaten, the chemical enters the bloodstream from the digestive system and is carried to the liver. There enzymes break it down into other substances, which are carried to the brain by the circulatory system.

The psychological effects of marijuana use are illustrated in the following descriptions.

Usually the first puff doesn't affect me, but the second brings a slight feeling of dizziness and I get a real "buzz" on the third. By this I mean a sudden wave of something akin to dizziness hits me. It's difficult to describe. The best idea I can give is to say that for a moment the whole room, people, and sounds recede into the distance and I feel as if my mind contracted for an instant. When it has passed I feel "normal" but a bit "airy-fairy."

The first time I smoked I had the feeling of being entirely outside of my body, hovering above it and as it was lying on the bed, I was exceptionally conscious of my body for part of the time, realizing how, and feeling how, each individual part was working.

—(Berke and Hernton, 1974, pp. 96, 97)

Marijuana became popular as a recreational drug partly because it is cheap and readily available but also because many people believe that when used in moderation it is not a risk to physical or mental health. Despite this widespread attitude, the federal government has conducted a vigorous and costly campaign to prevent the entry of marijuana into the country. As a result, a great deal of marijuana is grown illegally in the United States and Canada. Several authoritative reports have been issued on the effects of marijuana on health, but scientific controversy and public confusion still exist as to whether marijuana should be legalized or whether the laws against it should be strengthened.

In the early 1980s a committee of the National Academy of Science was asked to make a critical review of current knowledge about the effects of marijuana on health (National Academy of Sciences, 1982). The committee's report concluded that marijuana has a variety of effects, some of which are harmful to human health. Marijuana use causes changes in the heart and circulation that are similar to those caused by stress. These changes might be a threat for individuals with high blood pressure or heart disease. Marijuana smoke causes changes in the lungs that may lead to respiratory problems, but cancer-producing agents in marijuana smoke are even more of a problem. Marijuana smoke contains about 50 percent more carcinogens than tobacco smoke.

In males, marijuana suppresses the production of male hormones, decreases the size and weight of the prostate gland and testes, and inhibits sperm production, although these effects appear to be reversible. Such specific effects have not been found for non-pregnant women. In pregnant women, however, THC crosses the placental barrier and may harm the unborn child. It can also be secreted in breast milk, thereby affecting nursing infants. Various studies have shown that marijuana blocks ovulation and can cause birth defects in animals. The belief that marijuana use is associated with chromosome breaks, which are thought to be indicators of genetic damage, does not appear to be correct. Contra-

TABLE 14-9

Drugs: Characteristics and Effects

	Typical Effects	Effects of Overdose	Tolerance/Dependence
Depressants			
Alcohol	Biphasic: tension reduction "high," followed by depressed physical and psychological functioning	Disorientation, loss of consciousness, death at extremely high blood-alcohol levels	Tolerance; physical and psychological dependence; withdrawal symptoms
Barbiturates Tranquilizers	Depressed reflexes and impaired motor functioning, tension reduction	Shallow respiration, clammy skin, dilated pupils, weak and rapid pulse, coma, possible death	Tolerance; high psychological and physical dependence on barbiturates, low to moderate physical dependence on such tranquilizers as Valium, although high psychological dependence; withdrawal symptoms
Stimulants			
Amphetamines Cocaine Caffeine Nicotine	Increased alertness, excitation, euphoria, increased pulse rate and blood pressure, sleeplessness	For amphetamine and cocaine: agitation, and with chronic high doses, hallucinations (e.g., "cocaine bugs"), paranoid delusions, convulsions, death	For amphetamine and cocaine: tolerance; psychological but probably not physical dependence
		For caffeine and nicotine: restlessness, insomnia, rambling thoughts, heart arrythmia, possible circulatory failure. For nicotine: increased blood pressure	For caffeine and nicotine: tolerance; physical and psychological dependence; withdrawal symptoms
Opioids			
Opium Morphine Heroin	Euphoria, drowsiness, "rush" of pleasure, little impairment of psychological functions	Slow, shallow breathing, clammy skin, nausea, vomiting, pinpoint pupils, convulsions, coma, possible death	High tolerance; physical and psychological dependence; severe withdrawal symptoms
Psychedelics and PCP			
LSD PCP (dissociative anesthetic)	Illusions, hallucinations, distortions in time perception, loss of contact with reality	Psychotic reactions, particularly with PCP; possible death with PCP	No physical dependence for LSD, degree unknown for PCP; psychological dependence for PCP, degree unknown for LSD
Marijuana			
	Euphoria, relaxed inhibitions, increased appetite, possible disorientation	Fatigue, disoriented behavior, possible psychosis	Psychological dependence

dictory evidence exists as to whether the drug causes atrophy or other gross changes in the brain.

One area in which definite conclusions about marijuana use have been reached is its effects on the functioning of the brain and nervous system. Marijuana impairs motor coordination and perception and makes driving and machine operation more hazardous. It also impairs short-term memory and slows learning. One particularly important point is that the impairment lasts for 4 to 8 hours after the feeling of intoxication is over. This means that behavior may be affected even when the user is no longer aware of the presence of the drug.

One positive aspect of marijuana and its chemical derivatives is its therapeutic potential. Evidence suggests that marijuana is useful in the treatment of glaucoma, an eye disorder that may cause blindness, and that it helps control the severe nausea and vomiting that accompany chemotherapy for cancer. It may also be useful in treating asthma and certain types of epileptic seizures. However, the stress it puts on the cardiovascular system may make marijuana an inappropriate drug for treating older people.

Government agencies are reluctant to legalize the sale and use of marijuana because of vocal public opposition. Some opponents argue that the most potent deterrent of marijuana use is the possibility of arrest and imprisonment. However, while enforcement of marijuana laws is a major drain on the resources of the criminal justice system, it does not seem to be effective. Some people have proposed licensing the sale of marijuana, as is done with alcohol, and writing laws regulating its potency. Endangering the lives or well-being of others—for example, by operating a motor vehicle while intoxicated—would be penalized, but safe recreational use would not be illegal. Other writers have suggested eliminating criminal penalties for users but not for sellers of marijuana. These proposals reflect the trend toward increasing acceptance of marijuana use.

Peer pressure is the strongest factor influencing adolescents toward marijuana use. Marijuana use by high school students appears to have peaked in 1978 and has declined significantly since then, perhaps because the fashion shifted toward alcohol. Because of the prevalence of its use and the public controversy about whether it should be decriminalized, over 20 percent of the states have dropped criminal penalties for minor marijuana offenses in the last few years. Several other states permit the use of marijuana for certain medical purposes.

There is a great need to base laws and social policies concerning marijuana and other drugs on facts rather than on opinions and fears. Laboratory research and studies of the longer-term effects of drugs and therapies are a first step toward providing the facts.

Nicotine

I can quit smoking if I wish; I've done it a thousand times.

—Mark Twain

Nicotine use is believed to be physically hazardous, not only by professionals but by many smokers themselves (see Figure 14–15). Despite this knowledge, many people continue smoking; some experience psychological distress in the form of anxiety and guilt because they cannot stop smoking. The difficulty of giving up tobacco use on a long-term basis may be due to the unpleasant nature of the withdrawal experience, the importance of social or environmental cues, and the highly overlearned nature of the habit (the pack-a-day smoker is reinforced by the rapid effects of nicotine in each of about 75,000 puffs per year). Withdrawal symptoms—irritability, anxiety, headache, and difficulty in concentrating—do not occur in all smokers, but in some heavy smokers withdrawal symptoms can be detected within 2 hours after the last cigarette. Since many smokers use cigarettes as a way of coping with stress, it is not clear whether these symptoms are related to the withdrawal of nicotine or whether some of them may be related to psychological characteristics that helped start the addictive behavior. Tobacco withdrawal is also associated with a number of physiological changes, including decreased heart rate and blood pressure, and with impaired performance on tasks that require vigilance.

Most professionals agree that addiction to cigarette smoking is hard to overcome on a long-term basis. The results of one survey of therapeutic success are shown in Figure 14–16. Although these data were gathered some time ago, they remain accurate. When these data are combined with data for people who attempt to stop smoking on their own, the picture is brighter. Of the latter group, from half to two-thirds eventually succeed (Schachter, 1982; U.S. Department of Health, Education and Welfare, 1979).

Therapeutic efforts to help people stop smoking take several forms. Some of these efforts use the biological perspective. From this viewpoint, the problem is not so much that smoking calms the nerves as that nonsmoking sets up the negative reinforcement of withdrawal symptoms, which can be ended by having another cigarette. By resuming the use of cigarettes, the individual is attempting to regulate the nicotine level in his or her body. This may have important physiological effects because nicotine stimulates the release of *central peptides*, hormones that have a powerful effect on key mental and physical functions. This suggests that smokers who are heavily dependent but want to quit smoking may require, on a temporary basis, some pharmacologi-

FIGURE 14–15
"Phil suddenly decided to give up everything that was bad for him—no more smoking, drinking, or junk food—and he feels absolutely *terrific!*" (Drawing by Handelsman, © 1985 The New Yorker Magazine, Inc.)

cal substitute for the nicotine they are deriving from cigarettes.

In 1984 nicotine-containing chewing gum was approved by the Food and Drug Administration for prescription use in the United States. The gum was developed to ease withdrawal from tobacco by providing both an alternate source of nicotine and a substitute oral activity. Nicotine gum probably does not give the same positive pleasure as smoking a cigarette because nicotine is absorbed more slowly through the lining of the mouth than through the lungs. However, the gum may enable a smoker to break the habit in two stages. First the smoker can focus on overcoming the behavioral and psychological components of tobacco dependence without having to cope with nicotine withdrawal at the same time. Linked with each smoker's puffing habits are the many other actions involved in handling cigarettes and responding to cues that call for lighting up. Once these behavior patterns are controlled, withdrawal from the nicotine gum might be accomplished more easily.

Because smoking is a complex behavior, all components of that behavior need to be addressed in helping a person stop smoking. The gum may be more effective when used as part of a smoking cessation program or with counseling. Some clinicians feel that without a treatment that is capable of reducing withdrawal symptoms, therapists become drained by having to provide constant encouragement and support to help their clients tolerate withdrawal. The rapid and tangible effects of the nicotine gum in relieving withdrawal symptoms may be a boost to the morale and confidence of both the client and the therapist (Grabowski, 1985).

Research is needed to evaluate the effects of nicotine gum by itself and in combination with other factors. For example, one recent experiment evaluated the gum using a balanced placebo design (Gottlieb, 1985). An advantage of this design is that it permits an answer to the question, what is the effect of receiving a drug alone and in combination with the subject's expectancies about the drug's effects? Gottlieb found that nico-

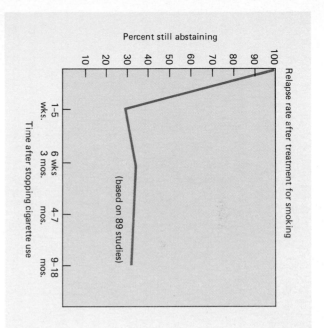

FIGURE 14-16
The relationship between relapse rates and time after stopping cigarette use. (Adapted from Hunt, W. A. and Bespalec, D. A. An evaluation of current methods of modifying smoking behavior, *Journal of Clinical Psychology*, 1974, 30, 430–438. (c) 1974, Clinical Psychology Publishing Co.) (Reprinted with permission)

tine gum helped people stop smoking, but he also found that its effects were weaker than those of smokers' positive expectancies. Many smokers who were given a placebo but were told that it was nicotine gum showed a strong positive effect. Thus, cognitive factors are an important influence on the success of efforts to stop smoking.

One cognitive approach to smoking involves a training program in which smokers are helped to identify the situation in which they are most likely to smoke. They then learn cognitive coping techniques as alternatives to smoking and use self-reinforcement when they are successful in resisting the temptation to smoke.

Cognitive methods seem to be effective for many ex-smokers. One study assessed the way callers to a relapse-counseling hotline described how they dealt with the temptation to smoke (Shiffman, 1982). The relapse crises were usually brought on by situational factors: ci-

ther positive feeling states related to other smokers, eating, or alcohol consumption, or (more frequently) negative feelings, especially anxiety, anger, and depression. Ex-smokers who performed any coping response in these situations were more likely to avoid a relapse. Behavioral responses such as getting up and leaving the situation were useful, but a combination of behavioral and cognitive coping responses worked best, especially in situations involving alcohol. Cognitive coping consisted of such things as reviewing the reasons for not smoking.

Some behavioral methods combine aversive stimuli, such as mild electric shock, with smoking. In another technique, **rapid smoking**, the subject smokes cigarettes at such a high frequency that the desire to smoke decreases. However, rapid smoking can increase blood pressure significantly. Research on this technique indicates that it causes a substantial short-term decrease in smoking behavior but that after a while smokers are likely to return to their previous behavior. The long-term effectiveness of this technique might be enhanced if it were used as part of a multicomponent program with cognitive elements like those mentioned earlier (Lowe, 1985).

Substance dependence continues to be a major problem throughout the world. Recent developments in the study of pain regulators and pain receptors in the body are providing some valuable clues, particularly in the area of opioid abuse. Information about the health consequences of using some substances—for example, marijuana and tobacco—have decreased their overall use. Some therapeutic procedures, especially those that emphasize cognitive techniques for relapse prevention, show promise as treatments for alcohol and tobacco abuse. Still unanswered, however, is the question of whether social policy should be changed—for example, to decriminalize marijuana or provide maintenance doses for heroin addicts in government clinics. In part because of lack of knowledge about the consequences of these actions—such as whether they would increase or decrease use of the substance—and in part because of philosophical differences among citizens, lawmakers, and scientists, these policy issues seem likely to remain unresolved.

Study Outline

In **psychoactive substance-induced organic mental disorders** actual organic impairment results from use of psychoactive substances. In **psychoactive substance use disorders** the focus is on the maladaptive behavior re-lated to regular use of psychoactive substances. People who use these substances may have periods of intoxication or withdrawal. **Intoxication** leads to a substance-specific syndrome that includes various types of maladaptive behavior. In **withdrawal,** a substance-specific syndrome follows reduction of intake of a psychoactive substance that was previously used regularly.

SUBSTANCE DEPENDENCE

In **substance dependence,** significant, ongoing maladaptive behavior occurs as a result of use of the substance, interfering with social functioning or effectiveness on the job and extending over a period of at least a month or recurring over at least a 6-month period. Physiological dependence can be shown by tolerance or withdrawal. **Tolerance,** means that the person has to use increasing amounts of the drug to feel the same effect. **Withdrawal** means that certain physical symptoms occur if the use of the substance is decreased or stopped.

ALCOHOL

1. Abuse of alcohol or other psychoactive substances means that their use has negative effects on a person's life. Alcohol abuse is often referred to as **problem drinking,** while alcohol dependence or addiction is referred to as **alcoholism.** Problems with alcohol are strongly associated with increased risk of dying in an accident, especially one caused by drunken driving. Other health risks associated with overuse of alcohol are high blood pressure, cancer, and cirrhosis of the liver. Extensive abuse can cause brain damage.
2. From a biological perspective, alcoholism is a permanent, irreversible condition in which the individual experiences an irresistible physical craving for alcohol. The only treatment that can succeed, in this view, is complete abstinence. Some research findings indicate a genetic basis for alcohol problems, perhaps expressed in alterations of certain neurobehavioral functions. However, it is clear that environmental factors are also involved.
3. According to psychodynamic theorists, a person with an alcohol problem has an **oral-dependent personality** as a result of lack of satisfaction of the need for oral gratification in childhood. There is no conclusive evidence that personality factors are involved in the development of alcoholism.
4. Learning theorists point out that some people drink as a way of coping with problems of living. This behavior is learned through reinforcement, modeling, and other learning mechanisms.
5. Cognitive theorists emphasize the effects of expectancy on the behavior of people who consume alcohol. There is evidence that a person's belief about the alcohol content of a drink can be a significant determiner of such behaviors as depression, delay of gratification, and social anxiety.
6. The biological approach to the treatment of alcoholics calls for complete abstinence from alcohol. This approach is used by Alcoholics Anonymous, a self-help program for alcoholics that emphasizes the need for spiritual awakening. Another biological approach is the use of disulfiram, a drug that causes extreme discomfort when a person drinks alcohol after taking it.
7. Psychotherapy is sometimes useful in treating alcoholics, but there are no definitive conclusions on the subject. Learning techniques such as aversive conditioning and covert sensitization have been used with some success, as have cognitive techniques in which clients are oriented toward monitoring their own behavior in relation to alcohol use.
8. **Relapse-prevention programs** combine a cognitive approach with a variety of treatment procedures designed to change the individual's drinking pattern. They help the alcoholic identify high-risk situations and learn pertinent coping and behavioral skills.
9. Preventing alcohol abuse is better than treating it. There is a need for research on ways to prevent excessive use of alcohol. Social influences, such as the mass media, are a potentially powerful tool in prevention efforts.

OTHER DRUGS

1. **Barbiturates** are derivatives of barbituric acid that trigger an initial period of excitement followed by slurred speech, loss of coordination, severe depression, and impairment of thinking and memory. Some **tranquilizers** act like barbiturates and can cause physical and psychological dependence and serious withdrawal symptoms.
2. The **opioids** (sometimes called **narcotics**) include both naturally occurring and synthetic substances. Several forms of opioids, known as **endorphins,** are manufactured by the brain and the pituitary gland. **Opiates** are opioids that are derived from the juice of the opium poppy. Their most important active ingredient is **morphine,** which is used primarily as a painkiller. **Heroin** was originally used as a substitute for morphine, but today it is involved in the vast majority of narcotic-addiction cases.
3. The opioids cause mood changes, sleepiness, mental clouding, and other physical effects. An overdose may cause death due to cessation of breathing. Withdrawal symptoms include sweating, muscle pains, nausea, vomiting, and diarrhea.
4. According to the **exposure orientation,** the cause of opioid addiction is exposure to the drugs. The **adaptive orientation** considers both the person and the situation to be important factors in the development of addiction. The available evidence is consistent with the latter orientation. The most widely used treatment for opioid addicts is **methadone maintenance,** which involves substituting another drug that does not produce the euphoria that accompanies heroin use but relieves the craving for heroin.

5. **Cocaine** is derived from the leaves of the coca bush. Its effects include increased heart rate, blood pressure, and body temperature and decreased appetite, together with feelings of wittiness and hyperalertness. High doses can produce a state resembling mania and sometimes cause strokes. Since cocaine is one of the most powerful drug reinforcers, desire for it is hard to control. Treatment of cocaine abuse requires that the abuser be convinced that treatment is necessary.

6. **Amphetamines** are potent psychomotor stimulants whose use results in increased wakefulness, alertness, and elevation of mood. High doses lead to nervousness, headache, dizziness, agitation, and other symptoms. Regular use of large amounts causes users to become malnourished, exhausted, careless, and indifferent to normal responsibilities.

7. **Psychedelics** or **hallucinogens** act on the central nervous system to produce alteration of consciousness. They change the user's perceptions of both the internal and the external world. The most frequently used psychedelic drug is LSD (d-lysergic acid diethylamide). Treatment for abuse of psychedelics depends on the severity of the reaction; severely affected people must have med-

ical attention to prevent cardiovascular or respiratory collapse.

8. **Phencyclidine** or PCP is a dissociative anesthetic that causes the user to feel dissociated from the environment. Users sometimes lose the ability to test reality and suffer severe intellectual and emotional disorganization. Many PCP deaths are not due to overdose but are direct results of homicide, suicide, or accidents.

9. **Marijuana,** the dried leaves and flower tops of the cannabis plant, is the most commonly used illegal drug in the United States. It is not pharmacologically a narcotic, although it has similar psychological effects. The effects of marijuana use on health are unclear, but there is no doubt that it impairs motor coordination and perception, short-term memory, and learning.

10. **Nicotine** is contained in tobacco smoke. Smoking is believed to be physically hazardous; however, it is extremely difficult for users to give up the habit. Therapeutic efforts to help people stop smoking take several forms, including the substitution of nicotine gum, the use of cognitive techniques, and **rapid smoking,** in which the subject smokes cigarettes at such a high frequency that the desire to smoke decreases.

CHAPTER 15

Maladaptive Behaviors of Childhood and Adolescence

Lee N. Smith, *The Last Stand*, 1984. Oil on canvas with construction. 91 × 75". Courtesy D. W. Gallery, Dallas.

OBJECTIVES FOR CHAPTER FIFTEEN:

To learn:

The names, characteristics, and treatment approaches for childhood and adolescent disorders that lead to maladaptive behavior

To understand:

1. How disorders in childhood and adolescence differ from those in adulthood
2. The unique aspects of therapy for children and adolescents

A t three years of age, Anna was a quiet child. She spent a great deal of her time sucking her thumb and hugging a teddy bear that was almost without fur as a result of constant loving. When her mother went into the bedroom to make the beds, Anna followed. The same things happened when her mother went to the telephone or took the wash out of the washing machine. She cried every day when her mother left her at the day-care center. The teachers there reported much the same behavior that she showed at home. At Anna's age her older sister had been a whirlwind of activity and spent her time playing with blocks or riding her trike. Anna's mother wondered whether she should worry about Anna's behavior.

Children's behavior can vary greatly. Deciding to do something about unwanted behavior in a child can be much more agonizing than making a similar decision about an adult. Parents often feel responsible for everything their children do, and they feel especially guilty about admitting that their child has a problem that is serious enough to require professional help. When parents or others intervene, they may make things worse by emphasizing a problem that might disappear if it were ignored. On the other hand, many behavioral problems are easier to treat in children, since their behavior patterns and interaction styles have not yet become firmly established.

Even more important, behavioral problems sometimes interfere with a child's development by delaying the learning of all kinds of school and social skills. Moreover, many children with psychological problems

The Scope of the Problem

In the United States today, 6 million or more children between the ages of 5 and 19 have psychological problems that are severe enough to interfere with their learning in school and to require some kind of professional contact. At least 13 percent of all children in the United States have severe psychological problems. In some groups the rate of problem behavior is even higher. For example, children who come from homes where there is child abuse have a high rate of psychological problems (Erickson and Egeland, 1987) (see Box 15–1). For many of these children, their problems will extend into adulthood.

Efforts to help troubled youngsters are often dissatisfying for several reasons. Lack of understanding of the nature of childhood disorders and their causes is one important factor. For example, it is not known whether some disorders of childhood, such as psychoses, depression, and anxiety disorders, are extensions of the adult categories or whether they have different causes. One piece of evidence that suggests that many childhood disorders are distinct from their adult versions is the difference in the sex ratios in these disorders for children and adults. In childhood, boys are affected more often than girls in almost all categories. Beginning in adolescence, however, affective disorders and anxiety disorders are more frequent in women, and there is no sex difference in schizophrenic disorders (Rutter and Garmezy, 1983).

Some maladaptive behavior in childhood results from the fact that in the normal course of things children do not all develop at the same rate. Children who develop later than their age-mates often carry feelings of inadequacy and inferiority into adulthood. Personalities of children who are late in maturing physically may be permanently affected. Problems can also result from lateness in acquiring cognitive skills. Children who are unable to master academic work when their classmates are ready for it are at a serious disadvantage both in school and in later life, even if they catch up afterward (see Figure 15–3).

are brought to the attention of mental-health workers only when some crisis occurs. By then the problem may be difficult to treat because it has become so severe that the child had been labeled as a "problem." Children like Anna are less likely to be referred for problem behavior than children who are extremely active, damage property or belongings, or who in other ways make life difficult for those around them.

Normal or healthy development comes about through a series of interlocking social, emotional, and cognitive competencies. Competencies at one developmental period not only help the child adapt to the environment, but also help prepare the way for new competencies in the next period. These developing competencies also integrate the old ones into new patterns of functioning. Pathological development on the other hand may be thought of as a lack of growth and integration of these competencies (Ciechetti, 1987). Because of the important role early competencies play in later ones, an early disturbance may ultimately result in the emergence of a much larger disturbance some years later.

Because of the interlocking aspects of development as time goes on, attention should be paid to unusual patterns of childhood behavior whether these are hard to live with or not. Antisocial and acting-out behavior and severe reading problems in children are often correlated with adult disorders. On the other hand, such childhood problems as shyness, fears, tics, nervousness, hypersensitivity, speech defects, and anxiety reactions may leave few discernible effects on later development, although adults who had these problems in childhood may be described as at least mildly maladjusted compared to the average person (Rutter and Hersov, 1985).

Psychological disorders that affect children run the gamut from extremely serious to the rather minor. Some of these are unique to childhood, whereas others may be experienced by both children and adults. Some disorders, such as depression and schizophrenia, include behaviors that would be abnormal at any developmental stage. Others, such as phobias of early childhood, represent exaggerations of normal developmental trends. These disorders can affect the child's mood (as in anxiety disorders or depression) or behavior (as in hyperactivity or conduct disorders). They can also produce physical symptoms, as in eating disorders like anorexia nervosa or bulimia nervosa. In addition, there are more severe disorders, such as mental retardation and autism, in which the child does not develop normally over a long period and the outlook for significant change is poor. These severe developmental disorders are discussed in Chapter 16.

Disruptive Behaviors

Two kinds of children who behave disruptively are of special concern to adults: children who do not pay attention and seem exceptionally active, and children who behave aggressively, break rules, and cause significant

BOX 15-1

Effects of Child Abuse and Neglect

Parents who neglect their children may fail to provide food, clothing, warmth, a clean environment, and the supervision necessary to keep the child safe. Or they may provide these things but express no interest in their children and fail to interact with them more than is absolutely necessary. Abusive parents, on the other hand, may use severe physical punishment and even permanently harm their children, or they may use psychological forms of abuse that leave their children feeling like innately bad people who are unworthy of love. Neglected children show the effects of lack of parental stimulation. They talk less and make fewer social responses. In addition, they engage in little exploratory or inquisitive behavior. They also are likely to be depressed.

Child abuse can leave both psychological and physical scars. Physically abused children are often seriously damaged. Many suffer neurological damage, and one-third of these have problems that are severe enough to handicap them in everyday life (Martin, 1976). Children who have been physically abused tend to be deficient in motor skills such as those involved in running, skipping, or riding a tricycle. This may be caused by their fear of exploring and taking risks, but poor motor development has been noted as early as 4 months of age, so lack of exploratory behavior is not a complete answer. Abused children also show delayed development of speech and language. Preschool children may be abused for talking, so they simply don't practice speaking. Instead, much of their communication is nonverbal.

The IQs of abused children are lower than might be expected (Salter and others, 1985). The delay in their cognitive development might be due to the unpredictable and dangerous environment in which such children live. Instead of concentrating on learning, they are anxious, preoccupied by fantasy, and concerned with ways of surviving. Fear of failure and difficulty in paying attention to instructions seem to handicap abused children in testing situations.

For abused children, the world is an unpredictable and hateful place. The adults they live with may be hostile and impatient and can become violent without warning. These children must be prepared to anticipate and meet the needs of their parents and are constantly afraid of harsh punishment and verbal abuse. As a result, the children look unhappy and take little pleasure in their surroundings. They may have sleep disturbances, wet their beds, be apathetic, fearful, or phobic, and underachieve in school. They are also likely to be depressed, to have low self-esteem, and to think of themselves as innately bad (Gelardo and Sanford, 1987).

Much research on child abuse and neglect has lumped both kinds of parents together. However, although they overlap somewhat, these two groups differ in important respects. In one study, abusive, neglectful, and control-group mothers were observed in their homes for 90 minutes on each of 3 consecutive days (Bousha and Twentyman, 1984). The abusive mothers showed the highest rates of physical and verbal aggression and neglectful mothers the lowest rate of interaction. Figure 15–1 shows some of the differences among the three groups of mothers. The children of these mothers also behaved differently (see Figure 15–2). The control children showed less aggressive verbal and physical behavior and more initiations of social behavior than either of the other two groups. The neglected children initiated very little social behavior.

Some researchers have wondered whether the cognitions of the two types of mothers differ when they evaluate situations involving their children. In one study, mothers were shown several sets of pictures (Larrance and Twentyman, 1983). Each set of pictures showed both the mother's own child and a similar child engaging in some activity. In one example, the result is the result of the activity. In one example, the result is crayon marks on the wall. Other sets portrayed a good outcome, such as a completed puzzle or a prize for winning a game. In all the pictures the children's faces were hidden so that the mothers could not see their expressions.

The results showed that both the abusing and the neglectful mothers had more negative expectations regarding their own children's behavior than the control mothers did. If the results were bad, they blamed their children, believed that they had acted intentionally to annoy them, and did not look at situations cues in evaluating the children's behavior.

Research on child abuse and neglect suggests that parents who behave in this way may follow a four-stage pattern (Twentyman and others, in press):

1. The parent has unrealistic expectations for the child.

2. The child acts in a way that does not confirm these expectations.

3. The parent misattributes the child's actions to intentional and negative motivations.

4. The parent overreacts and excessively punishes the child.

Child abuse and neglect may have implications for the child's development, behavior, and mental health both in childhood and as an adult. Researchers are beginning to try to understand the behaviors and thoughts that lead to abuse and to devise ways of helping abused and neglected children and their parents.

BOX 15–1 (CONTINUED)

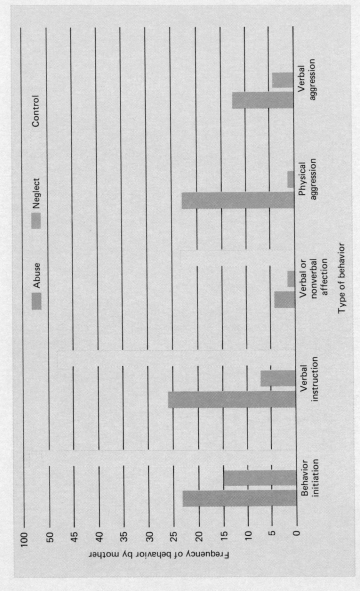

FIGURE 15–1
Frequency of different types of behaviors of abusive, neglectful, and control-group mothers when interacting with their children. (Adapted from Bousha and Twentyman, 1984, p. 110)

FIGURE 15–2
Frequency of different types of behaviors by children when they interacted with their mothers who were abusive, neglectful, or from a control group. (Adapted from Bousha and Twentyman, 1984, p. 110)

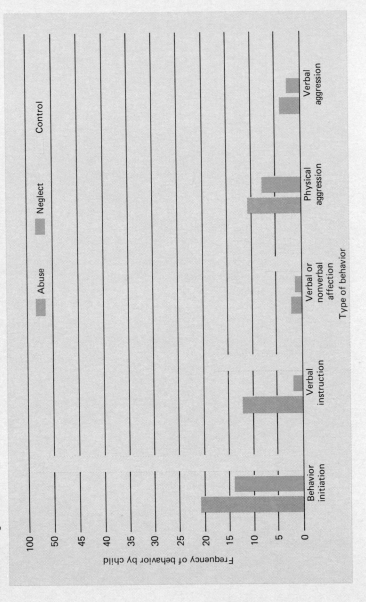

harm to other people and their property. The first type is diagnosed as having attention-deficit hyperactivity disorder (ADHD) while the latter group have conduct disorder.

Many times both conduct disorder and ADHD occur together, but there are some distinctions between them. Children who are diagnosed as hyperactive are almost always male; this is not as true in conduct disorder, although in this second category boys are still the majority. Children with ADHD also show cognitive impairment, impulsivity, and poor school achievement. Children with conduct disorder have fewer distinctive characteristics as a group. They differ from other children primarily because of their disregard for other people and their degree of hostility (Werry and others, 1987).

Attention-Deficit Hyperactivity Disorder

Children vary in their degree of motor activity. Most children may seem overactive to adults, but some children never seem to stop moving. During their preschool years they run, climb, and crawl incessantly and without apparent purpose. As they become older, they show a marked inability to sit still and they have a tendency to fidget excessively. An observer would conclude that they are more active than the average child and that their activity has a purposeless, random quality.

FIGURE 15-3
Learning to write requires a certain degree of coordination and cognitive skill. Children develop these skills at different rates. Those who develop them later than average often are at a disadvantage in kindergarten and in later school years.

Restless behavior of students is a major complaint from school personnel. When teachers rate children in their school classes, they classify 10 percent of all boys and 1 percent of all girls as hyperactive (Lambert and others, 1978). Some of these children may not be considered hyperactive by their parents or by mental-health professionals. The structure of classroom activities or the frustrations encountered in learning may cause these children to behave with less control or may make their activity levels more noticeable while they are in school. Nevertheless, such hyperactive behavior is the most frequent reason why children are referred to mental-health facilities (Ross and Ross, 1982). Many overactive children do not only have trouble getting along with their teachers, but with other children as well. When students are asked to name classmates whom they do not prefer as work or play partners, the names of overactive children tend to be very high on their lists (Pelham and Bender, 1982)

Behavioral Characteristics

In contrast to these overactive children, children who have **Attention-Deficit Hyperactivity Disorder** (ADHD) show degrees of impulsivity, hyperactivity, and inattention that are inappropriate for their developmental level. Children with this disorder usually have some disturbance in each of these three areas of behavior although the amount of disturbance in each area may not be the same. **Impulsiveness** is shown by acting out of turn, starting a task without looking at the directions, and interrupting when others are talking. Another way impulsiveness manifests itself is in accident-prone behavior or doing dangerous things without thinking about the consequences. **Hyperactivity** includes jumping around, fidgeting, constantly manipulating or fiddling with objects, excessive twisting and wiggling when sitting down, and an inability to remain seated. **Inattention** is shown by a failure to follow through on tasks, frequent shifts from one activity to another, and failure to follow rules and to listen to what others say. About half the time ADHD develops before age 4. At least three times as many boys as girls in the general population fit this description. Of children brought to clinics because of these behaviors, boys outnumber girls by as many as nine to one.

Children who are classified in the ADHD category have more serious problems than children who are merely very active. They may have deficiencies in visual and auditory discrimination, reading, writing, and language development. Children who have this disorder are likely to fail not only in school but also in social situations, both outcomes that cause them to have a low opinion of themselves. As a result, they make few friends and are likely to develop various physical complaints as well as emotional problems, especially depression (Ross and Ross, 1982).

In a study comparing the behavior of such hyperactive boys and their nonhyperactive brothers, mothers were asked to rate the severity of various behavior problems in both sons (Tarver-Behring and others, 1985). For all the behaviors rated, the hyperactive sons created more severe problems (see Figure 15–4). This was especially true in interpersonal situations involving play with other children or when the mother's attention was focused on other things such as talking on the phone, entertaining visitors, taking the child to public places, or driving.

In order to see whether the mothers played a role in creating the hyperactive behavior by interacting differently with their two sons, the mothers were observed alone with each son in two kinds of situations: free play and a series of structured tasks. During free play the hyperactive boys were less likely than their brothers to answer their mothers' questions and were more likely to be distracted. Their behaviors differed in the same way during the structured task; in addition, the hyperactive sons were less likely to follow instructions from their mothers. In this study, the mothers' behavior toward their two sons did not differ, but it is likely that over time the hyperactive sons' lack of responsiveness might lead their mothers to interact with them less.

Children with hyperactive behavior experience difficulty in social interaction in school as well as at home. In both situations, others feel under pressure as a result of their behavior. Teachers are more intense and controlling with hyperactive boys than with their peers. The presence of such a child seems to alter the teacher's be-

havior for the whole class (Whalen and Henker, 1985). In classrooms with a hyperactive child, the rate of the teacher's negative interactions with the other children in the class also increases.

Hyperactive boys have social difficulties with their peers as well as with parents and teachers. Parents often report that their hyperactive children have no friends or get along only with children several years younger than they are. One reason for this is that hyperactive children have deficits both in their social knowledge and in their performance of socially skilled behaviors (Grenell and others, 1987). These deficits do not carry over into all behaviors. The biggest problem for these children comes when they need to maintain an already established relationship. When conflict arises they are less friendly, more impulsive, and more assertive toward the other child. They have difficulty in following the rules in games or in cooperating on joint projects.

In some kinds of interactions hyperactive children's behavior is as socially skilled as that of normal children. In order to be able to help hyperactive children improve their social performance we need to know more about specific deficits associated with this disorder. One research project that dealt with this question took place at summer camp. Pairs of boys, one hyperactive and one a control, played a game. Each time one boy played the role of an astronaut and the other of mission control (Whalen and Henker, 1985). The astronaut was to be the follower, to listen carefully to mission control messages, comply with instructions, and give appropriate feedback. Mission control was the leader who conveyed the needed information and guided the astronaut. Each boy played the game twice in each role, each time with a different partner. The most interesting finding was that unlike the normal boys, the ADHD boys seemed not to benefit from the opportunity to observe another boy in the more difficult role of mission control before playing the role themselves (see Figure 15–5). This difference in ability to learn vicariously in a situation may be related to the poorer social skills demonstrated by hyperactive children.

Long-Term Effects

Children who are hyperactive may improve as they grow older. Ten years after their diagnosis with ADHD the behavior of only about one-third of male adolescents still meets the criteria for the disorder (Gittelman and others, 1985). Adolescents in this group had at least a 50-percent chance of developing a conduct disorder. This often means trouble with the law; up to half of all adolescents who have ADHD end up in court for theft or truancy (*Harvard Mental Health Letter*, 1985). These problems are likely to continue when they become adults.

FIGURE 15–4

Mean rating of severity of child behavior problems in 14 situations from the Home Situations Questionnaire as completed by mothers for both their hyperactive and nonhyperactive sons. (Tarver-Behring and others, 1985, p. 207)

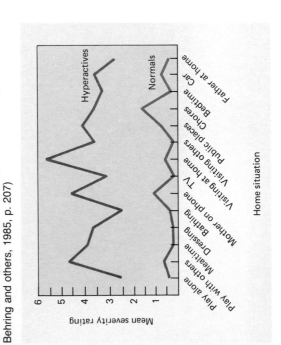

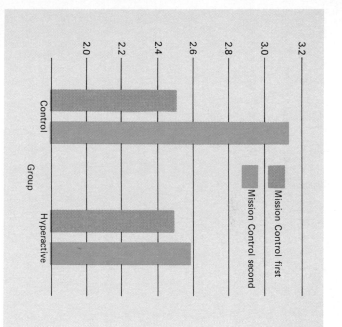

FIGURE 15–5
Communicative efficiency of hyperactive and comparison boys when serving as mission control during the first versus the second game. When they repeated a game about space travel, hyperactive boys showed less change in their behavior after they had a chance to observe another boy play the role of mission control than the control boys did. (Whalen and Henker, 1985, p. 469)

For those who continue to show ADHD behavior in adulthood there is a high probability of trouble with the law and of drug abuse compared to that for comparable people who did not show ADHD behavior in childhood. At least one researcher has also found that hyperactive children have a greater than average change of having an antisocial personality disorder when they become adults (Weiss and others, 1985).

Possible Causes

The causes of attention-deficit hyperactivity disorder are unknown. Children who have this disorder appear to have all the "basic equipment" needed to develop and function adequately. Neither their family climates or other environment nor their early childhood experiences appear different from those of their peers.

Most children who have the disorder show no evidence of actual brain damage. Complications during pregnancy or birth and illnesses of early infancy have been found to be associated with hyperactive behavior, but the relationship is not strong enough to be used in predicting future school or behavior problems (Hartsough and Lambert, 1985). Another possible cause may be hereditary. Often the father of an ADHD child also had a troubled childhood, was a school dropout, and remains restless and short-tempered. In addition, some researchers have found high rates of antisocial personality disorder in male relatives and histrionic personality disorder in female relatives (Ric and Ric, 1980). Another possibility is that the disorder may be a result of a deficiency of neurotransmitters such as dopamine or norepinephrine.

Treatment

Stimulants and Other Medications. By far the most common treatment for hyperactive children is the use of psychostimulant drugs like methylphenidate (Ritalin) or dextroamphetamine (Dexedrine). A large number of studies show that these drugs have positive short-term effects: many children show improved behavior and a decreased disruptiveness in the classroom although their school performance may not change much. On the other hand, extensive reliance on drugs may also reduce the interest of parents and teachers in finding other ways to help. Stimulant drugs often are tried without first focusing on parent counseling or school consultation. Because there is no clear evidence that stimulants are effective in the long term or even that they are effective in the short term, these psychological interventions should be tried first.

Stimulants have some side effects that may cause problems if they are used over a long period. They may cause insomnia, headaches, nausea, and tearfulness. Some children also develop incessant talking or explosive outbursts of rage when they are treated with these psychostimulants. In some cases the drugs depress the appetite so that weight gain is below normal. Dextroamphetamine may also suppress growth and decrease the child's adult height by as much as one and one-half inches. It is also difficult to predict how long the improvement produced by the drugs will last. In many cases change in behavior may last only as long as the medication is being taken. As the effect of each dose wears off, the child's behavior returns to its premedication baseline rather quickly. In one study, deterioration of behavior was serious enough to require renewed use of medication in almost all cases (Abikoff and Gittelman, 1984).

About 30 to 40 percent of children who use stimulant medication do not improve or have unpleasant side effects (Whalen and others, 1985). Many parents refuse stimulant therapy for their children, while others discontinue it prematurely, often because the children dislike taking the drugs (Brown and others, 1984). These problems, together with the growing awareness that attention-deficit hyperactivity disorders may have lifelong effects, have encouraged researchers to look at other therapeutic possibilities.

One problem that occurs with the use of these stimulant drugs is that the medication, rather than any personal action, may be seen as the sole reason for any changes in the child's behavior. As a result, the child may feel no responsibility for his or her behavior. Social psychologists might see this as a demonstration of attribution theory, which emphasizes the importance of self-statements about cause on the behavior that follows. The importance of attribution can be seen in the following example, in which stimulant therapy for a 9-year-old boy was terminated:

The result was marked behavioral deterioration accompanied by such spontaneous attributional statements as "My pills help me get done with the work" and "I get angry without my pill." After four days, Tom was given pills again, but this time they were placebos. Even so, task attention and productivity returned to high levels, and the teacher attempted "reattribution therapy" by emphasizing that Tom, not the pills, was controlling his behavior. When he was allowed to earn his way off medication by finishing his work four days in a row, Tom met this criterion and continued to perform well in the classroom with neither medication nor placebo.

—(Whalen and others, 1985, p. 404)

Another approach to drug therapy in the treatment of ADHD is the use of imipramine and other tricyclic antidepressants. In general, stimulant drugs are preferred because they seem more effective and because they have fewer negative side effects. However, there may be a subgroup of hyperactive children who are also anxious or depressed in addition to their hyperactivity who respond better to imipramine (Pliszka, 1987).

Behavioral Approaches. Behavioral treatments have been used alone or in combination with medications. Behavioral therapy can be effective in the short term when the behaviors and their setting are specifically targeted. However, behavior modification based on continuous reinforcement can have the same negative effect on children's perceptions of self-efficacy as medication does (Horn and others, 1983).

One reason for the appeal of cognitive–behavioral therapy in contrast to a straightforward behavior modification–reinforcement approach is that it gives children the message that they can control their own behavior. Researchers have used cognitive–behavioral therapy as a way to enhance the effectiveness of treatment and also to increase the transfer of adaptive behavior to other areas. So far, this approach seems promising, judging from the results of some individual case studies although it is important that the child not be made to feel responsible for more change than he or she is likely to be able to accomplish.

Generally, cognitive behavior therapy has shown greatest effects in improving academic achievement rather than social behavior. One intensive cognitive-be-

havior modification program has produced changes in cognitive style, academic achievement, and intelligence test scores, and also in parent and teacher ratings of the child's behavior (Kirby and Khazindar, 1985). The combination of cognitive–behavioral therapy and stimulant therapy is a promising treatment approach. For instance in one study short-term measures showed that such a combined treatment produces performance in ADHD children that is very similar to that of the normal control group. The two treatments seemed to have an additive effect, that is, the combined treatment group was superior in result to either of the two treatments alone (Gittelman-Klein and others, 1980). However, other studies have shown that behavioral therapy does not add to the benefit of stimulant therapy.

Other Approaches. Another approach to the treatment of ADHD is based on the theory that hyperactivity is caused by too much sugar in the diet (Varley, 1984) or by hypersensitivity to certain food additives (Feingold, 1975). These ideas have adherents among many parents and some professionals, but so far research has not provided sufficient evidence to support them (Milich and others, 1986). Sugar and chemical additives used in food dyes may have negative effects on learning in a subgroup of hyperactive children who are especially sensitive to those chemicals (Milich and others, 1986). However, until such findings are repeated and better understood, the question of chemical causes of hyperactive behavior remains open.

Conduct Disorder

Children and adolescents who are classified in the category of conduct disorder go far beyond the pranks and mischief that are characteristic of their age group. Their behavior seriously violates the basic rights of others or the major rules of society. Children who have conduct disorders are often truant and may lie, steal, run away from home, and molest animals and other people. They may begin voluntary sexual activity very early and regularly use illegal drugs. Conduct disorders may occur mainly during group activity with peers or when a single child makes an unprovoked attack on animals or people. Up to half of all children with conduct disorders are also considered hyperactive (Rutter and Garmezy, 1983).

Defining Conduct Disorder. The category of **conduct disorder** includes varied types of individuals but experts do not agree on how this category can be meaningfully subdivided. A study of data from three long-term longitudinal studies suggests that all of these behaviors may be part of a single group (Robins and Ratcliff, 1980). Although specific types of deviant behavior in children can be used to predict later deviance, the overall childhood deviance measure is the best predictor of deviance in adults. Many studies have shown that children who engage in antisocial behaviors, except for some minor sex offenders, do not behave in very specialized ways and that little is gained by dividing them into subgroups (Rutter and Giller, 1984).

It is clear, however, that there are important differences between occasional minor delinquency, which is common, especially among inner-city boys, and persistent antisocial behavior that causes severe harm to the victim. Conduct disorder should not be confused with socialized delinquency, which ordinarily tends to increase from about age 8 to about age 19 or 20 and then decreases. In conduct disorder there is remarkable consistency over time.

The long-term outcome for conduct disorder is clearly worse than for emotional disorders. Children who engage in antisocial behavior and hyperactivity are much more likely to engage later in criminal behavior, become alcoholic, or develop a personality disorder in adult life than are children with purely emotional disorders (Rutter and Garmezy, 1983).

Many children and adolescents who have a conduct disorder also are emotionally disturbed. They are especially likely to be depressed (Rutter, 1984). Children with social problems whose peers think of them negatively, tend to feel good about aggressive solutions to problems (Asarnow and Callan, 1985). They rate other trouble-causing peers as "fun to be with." Responses like these suggest that the children involved lack the skills to become popular with most of their peers. One way of dealing with this skill deficit is preschool education.

Treatment. Probably the most effective treatment for conduct disorder is prevention. This involves helping children to develop skills that will give them success experiences both now as youngsters and as they grow older. In a project that was designed to enhance preschool children's cognitive development, a follow-up study was carried out on two groups of adolescents, half of whom had attended preschool as children and half who had not (Schweinhart and Weikart, 1980). Although the intelligence test scores of children who had been in the preschool group did not differ from those of children in the control group, their motivation and achievement in school and their classroom behavior were superior to those of the controls. Even more important in terms of the treatment of conduct disorders, their self-reports of delinquent behavior were much lower than that reported by the controls. This suggests that skill building may be an important tool for modifying aggressive behavior that is typical of conduct disorder.

For skill building to be helpful, the way the child customarily evaluates situations must be taken into account. One interesting difference between aggressive and nonaggressive children is that the former show more bias in interpreting the causes of social interactions (Milich and Dodge, 1984). In situations in which the cause was not obvious—for example, being hit on the back with a ball—aggressive children are more likely to interpret the act as hostile. Sometimes this response may be caused by past experiences. For example, a psychologist reported the following incident:

I was treating an aggressive adolescent boy named Rocky twice per week on a long-term basis. We had built a good, warm relationship. One day I saw Rocky in the hallway and approached him from behind as he talked to a peer. I touched him on the shoulder and began to say hello when he turned around and impulsively punched me in the jaw. As soon as he realized whom he had hit, he apologized profusely saying that he thought I must have been another patient on the ward. It was painfully clear to me that Rocky had been perceptually ready to perceive an attack from another.

—(Dodge, 1985, p. 93)

One study compared aggressive and nonaggressive boys who were chosen on the basis of ratings by teachers and fellow students. The boys read a series of brief stories like the following:

Let's imagine that you are sitting in the lunchroom at school, eating your lunch with a bunch of kids from your classroom. You look up and see _____ (the name of a boy in the subject's peer group) walking toward your table with his lunch tray. You look back at your table and begin eating. The next thing you know, _____'s lunch tray has spilled all over your back. The other kids laugh, and your back is all wet. Now, how do you think that might have happened? What would you do if this really happened?

—(Dodge, 1985, p. 78)

The boys were then asked what the peer's intention was and what they would do to retaliate. The aggressive subjects made hostile attributions 50 percent more frequently than the nonaggressive boys did; in addition, they were more likely to say they would retaliate. The hostile attributions were clearly responsible for this increased tendency toward retaliation. This difference in attributional bias also occurs in real life.

One way of dealing with these aggressive responses might be to devise interventions that aim at debiasing perceptions. For instance, the child might be taught to use "think-aloud" procedures like the following:

Uh oh, my pencil is missing. There, I see that Ronald has it. Now before I go and get it back, let me think about what happened. I'll do it out loud, like my skills leader has told me. Let's see, first I'll say to myself "What happened?" Well, I lost my pencil and Ronald has it. Ronald could have stolen it. Or maybe he just found it and was using it. Or maybe he doesn't know that it is mine. I wonder what Ronald is thinking. I guess I could ask him. I'm not sure which of these is right, but I don't want to get into a fight. I'd rather stay friends with Ronald, because we play basketball together. So I'll give him the benefit of the doubt. Maybe he just found it. I'll go ask him to return it.

—(Dodge, 1985, p. 101)

For this kind of approach to be effective, the child must have a warm working relationship with a clinician or some other person with whom he or she can have a series of positive social encounters. The positive encounter must happen over and over again to demonstrate to the child that his or her initial negative expectations were not accurate. Even then it may be difficult for the child to generalize the experience to other people, especially peers.

Emotional Disturbances

Emotional disturbances and the disruptive behavioral disorders discussed earlier in this chapter are two quite different kinds of problems. Childhood emotional disorders occur about equally in boys and girls, although they tend to be somewhat more frequent in girls. In contrast, disruptive behavior disorders are much more frequent in boys. Behavioral disorders are also quite strongly related to problems in reading and to school achievement. This is not true of emotional disorders.

In general, emotional disorders respond better to treatment and are less likely to continue into adolescence and adulthood than childhood behavior disorders. Only about one-third of children with emotional disorders still have those disorders four or five years later (Richman and others, 1982).

The emotional disorders that are most common in children include several kinds of anxiety disorders—separation anxiety, generalized anxiety, phobias, obsessive compulsive disorders—and depression. As children grow older, anxiety symptoms may decrease. However, children who are very high in anxiety, although they may no longer have an anxiety disorder, seldom move to the low end of the anxiety scale. Depression becomes more frequent in adolescence and tends to overlap with behavioral disorders, especially conduct disorders (Rutter and Garmezy, 1983).

Specific fears often reported by young children become fewer as children grow older. There are also changes in many fear patterns that seem to be related to the child's developmental progress. Some fears occur so frequently in infancy that they are not considered abnormal. These include fear of noises, falling, and strange objects or people. Such fears reach a peak about the age of 2 and usually decline rapidly after that.

When children are very young, their level of cognitive functioning does not always allow them to make sense of the world. Research in child development has shown that children's logic is not the same as that of adults. For example, young infants do not seem to recognize that when objects or people are out of sight, they still exist. Probably for this reason, young children are often afraid when their caretakers leave the room. After infancy other fears develop, but usually are intense only during the preschool years. Fear of the dark and fear of animals are examples.

As children grow older, they acquire the ability to continue to think of the past and anticipate the future. When this happens, their fears are likely to change. Instead of being afraid of what is happening in a given situation, children begin to anticipate and to worry about what may happen.

Anxiety Disorders of Childhood

Anxiety in children takes many forms. Some children are preoccupied with thoughts about terrible (and unlikely) things that might happen to them or their families; other show a general social anxiety in which they shrink from contact with people or even refuse to speak for long periods. Still others have phobias, or unrealistic fears of specific objects or places, that may greatly interfere with their everyday living. Some children develop obsessive compulsive behaviors. In this section, we describe several of these problems. Some are unique to children, and others occur in adults as well.

Fears and Phobias

Most children's fears disappear as they grow older, even without treatment. On the other hand, some children's fears are intense and disturbing and are appropriate objects of professional concern even if they may disappear spontaneously later. To appreciate the impact of a childhood phobia on the child and his or her family, imagine Cindy, who has an unreasonable fear of dogs. She will not go out to play even in her own fenced yard because a dog might come near. She is unable to walk to school or go on errands, so she must be chauffeured everywhere.

Animal phobias and other fears that continue beyond the age at which they normally would disappear can usually be treated effectively using some kind of behavioral approach such as systematic desensitization or modeling (see Figure 15–6). At the beginning of therapy the fearful child observes another child or adult interacting in the feared situation. Then, after a number of sessions, the fearful child is encouraged to approach the feared object gradually until finally he or she interacts with it as the model does. This adaptation of social-learning theory, stimulated by the work of Albert Bandura and others (Bandura and Menlove, 1968), is often used successfully in treating frequently occurring fears.

Modeling of a somewhat different sort (**symbolic modeling**) can be used to prepare children for frightening and unfamiliar situations such as surgical and dental procedures. This procedure typically uses a realistic film that shows the child what to expect. Studies have shown that symbolic modeling may be an effective aid in reducing anxiety (Melamed and Bush, 1986).

Psychodynamic and learning theorists have very different views of phobias. The case of Little Hans is one of the most famous examples of a phobic disorder. Compare Freud's description of the case of Little Hans (Freud, 1909/1950) with later explanations of the same case by behaviorally oriented theorists.

When he was 5 years old, Hans refused to go out into the street because he was afraid of horses. He was especially fearful that the horses might bite him. Because of the increasingly constrictive life that his phobia forced him to lead (horse-drawn vehicles were the automobiles of that era), Hans' father discussed the case with Freud. The father interpreted Hans'

FIGURE 15–6
Modeling is often used in treating phobic behavior. After seeing that no unpleasant results occur when another child pets a dog, a child who is fearful of dogs may be able to make an approach.

phobia as being due to a "nervous disorder." Freud had only indirect contact with the boy; Hans' treatment was carried out by his father.

Hans' father had often played "horsie" with him, and Freud believed that horses' bridles reminded Hans of his father's dark mustache. Freud thought that Hans harbored aggressive fantasies and thoughts toward his father because he was the boy's only rival for his mother's love. At the same time, Hans loved his father. In his fantasies Hans expected retaliation from his father for the primitive hostility he felt toward him. To avoid this fantasied punishment, Hans "forgot about" his aggressive feelings and shifted his fantasies of retaliation onto horses. This resulted in the fear that horses would bite him. From one point of view, this was a convenient resolution of the conflict because Hans could avoid horses more easily than he could avoid his father.

Freud portrayed Little Hans as presenting a classic conflict of love and hatred directed toward the same person. He maintained that Hans dealt with the conflict through repression of his ambivalent and incestuous impulses, together with the mechanism of displacement. Apparently as a result of the therapy, Hans recovered from his phobia.

A number of behaviorally oriented theorists reviewed the case of Little Hans and argued that Hans' behavior was simply an instance of classical conditioning (Bandura, 1969; Wolpe and Rachman, 1960). They noticed that three major elements seemed to be present whenever Hans had a phobic response: a large horse, a

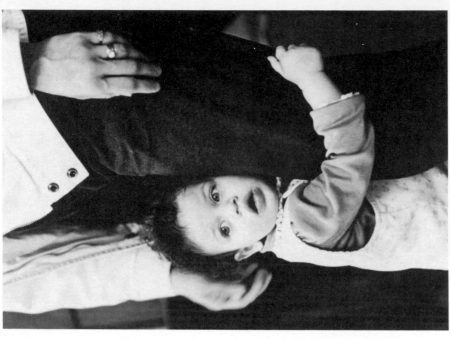

heavily loaded transport vehicle, and a high travel speed for both horse and vehicle. Freud had noted that Hans became afraid of horses after he was frightened by a serious accident involving a horse. The behavioral theorists believed that this experience rather than displaced hostility toward his father, was the cause of Little Hans' reactions. They argued that Little Hans underwent a classical-conditioning process when he saw the accident, and that this was the cause of his continued fear of horses.

It is clear that the perspective from which the phobia is viewed is important in determining both the cause of its development and the kind of therapy used. A psychodynamically oriented clinician would help a phobic child identify the feelings that may have aroused the phobic reaction. A behaviorally oriented clinician would concentrate on helping the child tolerate the feared object by exposing him or her to the fear-producing situation. A cognitive therapist would be interested in the history of the fear, at least in order to determine what thoughts the feared stimulus evokes. Cognitive therapy would teach the child to be aware of the irrationality of these thoughts and help him or her substitute more adaptive ways of thinking in the phobic situation.

Separation Anxiety Disorder

Another disorder that occurs mainly in childhood is **separation anxiety disorder.** Children with this disorder show excessive anxiety or even panic when they are not with major attachment figures, usually parents, or in familiar surroundings. Such children may be unable to stay in rooms by themselves and may refuse to go to school or visit friends' homes. When such children are asked why they are afraid, they may express fear of getting lost and never finding their parents again. Or they may have greatly exaggerated fears of animals, monsters, kidnappers, muggers, and of accidents or illness that may strike them or their parents. Very often such children complain of nausea, headaches, abdominal pains, or rapid heart rate. Sometimes, especially in older children, anxiety or panic is anticipated and seen when the time for the separation approaches.

In early childhood all children experience some separation anxiety (see Figure 15–7). This normal developmental stage is different from the excessive reaction to separation in the separation anxiety disorder. Another important point to remember is that to meet the DSM-III-R criteria for this diagnoses, the disturbed behavior must last for at least 2 weeks.

Children with separation anxiety disorder often have trouble going to sleep and insist that someone stay with them until they do fall asleep. Another way children express this anxiety is by waking during the night and getting into bed with a parent or sibling. Although

FIGURE 15–7
For the period beginning before an infant's first birthday and extending for about 18 months, most children experience distress when they are about to be separated from a parent. This desire to stay in contact with the attachment figure may have biological roots. Through natural selection, infants of all species who stayed close to their mothers were more likely to survive.

these children may have no interpersonal difficulties when separation is not an issue, if they are away from home they may be extremely homesick and miserable or even panic. Under such circumstances they withdraw from social activity and are unable to concentrate on work or play.

Many times separation anxiety disorder develops after the child experiences some life stress. This could be a loss by death of a relative or pet or a threatened loss such as a serious illness in the family. Moving to a new neighborhood or a new school also may help precipitate this disorder. Why some children have this reaction to stress and others don't isn't clear. Neglected children are not likely to develop separation anxiety disorder; instead, children with this disorder are likely to come from families that are caring and close knit. Some tendency to experience separation anxiety may run in families: it seems to be more common in close biological relatives of children with the disorder than in the general population.

It may be that children who develop a separation disorder have experienced some difficulties during the attachment process that many theorists believe takes place in the first two years of the child's life. The establishment of a secure attachment is considered important in preventing later psychological disorders, especially depression (Bowlby, 1980). Research on children who are securely attached shows that as they grow older they become more independent and better able to form good social relationships than other children.

Generalized Anxiety

Some children are anxious primarily in a situation where they anticipate or experience separation. Other children seem to be more generally anxious and to worry excessively and have unrealistic fears most of the time. Figure 15–8 illustrates some of the thoughts a child like this may have. Children who have such excessive worries for 6 months or longer are classified by DSM-III-R as having an **overanxious disorder.** Children with this disorder tend to worry a great deal about upcoming events such as routine visits to the doctor or school examina-

tions. Even routine events such as keeping appointments and deadlines are sources of considerable worry and preoccupation for them. Such children usually have a poor self-concept and worry a great deal about social acceptance and other types of social evaluation. Children with overanxious disorder often have a variety of physical complaints such as headaches or stomachaches for which no physical cause can be found. Children who are the oldest in small families and those who have families that put a focus on achievement are especially likely to develop this disorder. The child's mother is also more likely than average to have an anxiety disorder herself.

Figure 15–8 suggests that this child heard all these warnings and gradually made them part of her own thinking. Children who are excessively anxious in early life are more likely than others to develop some kind of anxiety disorder, either generalized anxiety or a phobic disorder, in their adult lives.

Obsessive-Compulsive Disorders

Many children engage in mild rituals and obsessions as part of their normal development. Bedtime and dressing rituals are common in toddlers, preschool children, and younger grade school children. Compulsions, such as

FIGURE 15–8
Sometimes worries of an anxious child seem like a replay of all the worries and concerns they may have heard from anxious parents.

trivial motor acts, are also common. A young child may stroke his or her blanket continuously before falling asleep or may suck his or her thumb only at bedtime. Even children's games reflect these rituals. Children often feel compelled to avoid certain objects, such as sidewalk cracks, or to chant rhymes or songs in a repetitive fashion. Such behaviors rarely are maladaptive in childhood. Sometimes, however, they develop into more disruptive **obsessive-compulsive** and **ritualistic** behaviors that require treatment. In the following case a behavioral approach was used successfully:

Byron was a 5-year-old child who had an obsessive compulsive fascination with electrical devices. He also had a ritual of being unable to sleep except in his parents' bed and a negativistic attitude, which was expressed in a refusal to follow his parents' instructions.

He roamed through the house turning lights on and off and staring at them and unplugging the refrigerator and other appliances. At the grocery store, he cut off power to the meat counter. At neighbors' houses, he unscrewed lightbulbs, dismantled lamps, and unplugged clocks and other appliances. In the evening, it sometimes took his parents two or three hours to get him to bed. The evening was punctuated by requests for water for his thirst and cookies for his hunger. During the night, he continued to get up and would lie down between his parents in their bed. Despite their efforts to remove him, he was usually found asleep there the next morning.

Byron's parents were taught how to make his maladaptive behaviors less rewarding and how to reward his adaptive behaviors. They were instructed to stop all attempts to spank him, reason with him, or attempt to understand his behavior. They were to meet all his requests for food prior to bedtime. If he stayed in bed all night, he would receive eight tokens in the morning. These tokens could then be exchanged on a daily basis for activities such as snacks, watching TV, or visiting friends. If Byron did get into his parents' bed, they were to pretend to be asleep and make it uncomfortable for him by taking up more room themselves. If this failed, his mother was to lead him matter-of-factly back to bed.

When Byron played with switches, he was required to pay half the tokens in his account for each episode, and in addition his parents were instructed to put him in his room for a 30-minute time period. Since he gained tokens during the day only by following instructions, this meant he lost his opportunity to earn tokens. Within 3 or 4 weeks of behavior therapy,

Byron began to develop friendships with other children and, since his obsession with electrical items was controlled, he was again invited into their homes. He stopped sleeping with his parents, and slept in his bed instead.

—(Adapted from Ayllon and others, 1977, p. 316–321)

Figures 15–9 illustrates the dramatic improvement that behavior therapy produced in Byron's behavior.

Despite the success of therapy in Byron's case, in general the outlook for children who engage in severe obsessive-compulsive behavior is not promising; about 50 percent do not make a substantial recovery (Elkins and others, 1980). They spend most of their day in rituals and obsessive thoughts, and this severely restricts their functioning. Fortunately, such a severe degree of obsessive-compulsive behavior in childhood is rare. It involves less than 1 percent of all children who come to the attention of mental-health professionals (Rapoport and others, 1981). Two such cases, adolescent patients who were hospitalized because of the severity of their problems, are described in the following excerpt:

Patient A was a 14-year-old boy who began washing eight to ten times a day after his family moved to a new neighborhood when he was 4. After that, he had only occasional episodes until about two years ago, when he began washing excessively because of fear of sperm on his body. He also had obsessive thoughts of death and compulsively checked light switches. He had been treated both by psychotherapy and with antipsychotic drugs. At school, he was quiet and

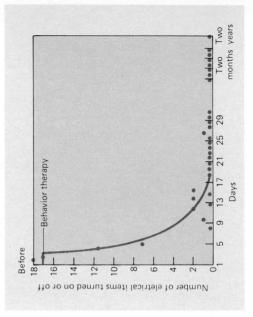

FIGURE 15–9
The number of electrical items turned on or off by Byron before, during, and at the end of behavior therapy, and at follow-ups 2 months and 2 years later. (Ayllon, Garber, and Allison, 1977)

FIGURE 15–10
Although adults seldom think of children as depressed, many children describe their own thoughts in ways that would suggest depression in adults. This adolescent could be thinking about whether she should go home to watch TV, but she might also be thinking that she doesn't know how to do anything or that no one cares about her or that she wishes she were dead.

unaggressive, participated in many activities, and was a good student. His parents had a mutually supportive relationship and were of middle class in socioeconomic status. All his siblings were well; however, his father was mildly depressed.

Patient B was also 14 years old. For the last 2 years, she had washed herself excessively, and was preoccupied by number rituals, such as the compulsion to perform all her daily acts in multiples of six. Until her symptoms developed, she had no obsessive traits, was a good student and had many friends. She had been treated by psychotherapy for 1 year. Her symptoms began suddenly at a time when her father's business failed. Both parents, of middle class socioeconomic status, were alcoholic.

—(Adapted from Rapoport and others, 1981, p. 1548)

These adolescents were among nine children who were studied by Judith Rapoport and her co-workers. Although none of the children could function effectively because of the severity of their obsessive-compulsive problems, none showed any signs of disordered thinking and all were able to discuss their problems sensibly. All of the children showed some depressive symptoms. Only three met the criteria for major depressive disorder at the time of hospitalization, but all would have met those criteria at some time in the past. Before their symptoms began, their development had not been particularly unusual. In general, they were good, but not outstanding students, and they seemed somewhat timid, although they were not excessively withdrawn.

Depression in Children and Adolescents

Childhood is often pictured as a happy time with little responsibility, much play, and infinite enjoyment. Why is it, then, that many children often think such thoughts as: "I'm dumb, ugly, and stupid," "I wish I were dead," and "You don't love me" (see Figure 15–10).

Frequency of Mood Disorders

Many children often feel sad or depressed. In one large group of families who participated in a family health plan, more than 17 percent of the children showed clinically significant evidence of sadness or depression (Kashani and Simonds, 1979). Although less than 2 percent of these sad children met the criteria for affective disorders, they were significantly different from children who were not sad. They had more physical complaints, were more likely to be overactive, had lower self-esteem, and were more likely to be involved in fights and to refuse to go to school. In another study, about 10 to 12 percent of the 10-year-olds in a school district population were described by parents and teachers as often appearing miserable, unhappy, tearful, or distressed. When the children were interviewed, their responses created the same impression (Rutter and others, 1981).

Depression is frequent among children who come to clinical attention. Between 30 to 60 percent of child mental-health outpatients meet the criteria for depression (Weller and Weller, 1985). Depression in childhood may also be relatively long lasting. In one study of children 8 to 13 years old (Kovacs, 1985), it took 1.5 years before 92 percent of children who met the criteria for major depressive disorder (see Chapter 10)

sified as having a bipolar disorder (Strober and Carlson, 1982).

Long-Term Patterns

Depression in childhood can be relatively brief or follow a reoccurring or long-lasting pattern. Some children experience depression through a large part of their lives. In one longitudinal study, several children showed differing but long-continuing patterns of depression (Chess and others, 1983).

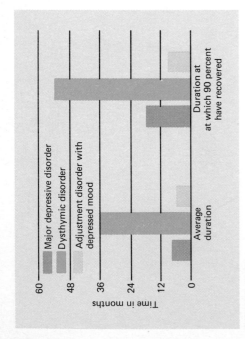

FIGURE 15–11
Duration of depressive disorders in children. (Data from Kovacs, 1985)

had recovered (see Figure 15–11). The chances of an other occurrence of depression were also high. Seventy-two percent of these children had a second episode within 5 years.

Children in the study who had a dysthymic disorder (chronic depressed or irritable mood) had a longer period of depression. On the average, they had the symptoms for 3 years, and at the end of 6.5 years 89 percent had recovered. Some of these children had become depressed by the time they were 6 years old. During the period when the children had the dysthymic symptoms, their risk of developing a major depressive disorder was also quite high.

Least severely affected were school-age children who had adjustment disorders with depressed mood. After 9 months, 90 percent of these children had recovered. None of the group developed a more severe depressive disorder. In this study, boys and girls had equal rates of depression, although many studies have found depression to be more common in boys before puberty.

Changes in Adolescence

Major changes in mood disorders seem to take place in adolescence (Rutter, 1984). There is a large shift in the sex ratio—during adolescence mood disorders become much more common in girls than in boys. Mood disorders also become generally more common in adolescence. In one study about 1 out of 9 children had depressive feelings before adolescence and 2 out of 5 had them after adolescence (Rutter, 1980). The higher incidence of depression seems to be related to puberty rather than simply to age. After puberty other mood disorders may also occur. Hypomania, a disorder in which there is an unusual elevation of mood, and bipolar disorders begin to be seen in this period. One study found about 25 percent of adolescents with primary major depression also had manic episodes and were reclas-

At 8 years of age, Harold had been having behavioral problems for a year. He disliked school, was shy, and had few friends. He was moody, quiet, and afraid of new situations. Because there had been several problems in his life—his parents had separated when he was 6 and his mother had been briefly hospitalized for severe depression—it was unclear whether his depression was due to these events or to other causes. Things improved, but at 12 Harold became depressed again and disliked school intensely. At 17 he reported that he could "step into an unhappy mood for no apparent reason" and then would feel tired and irritable and would avoid people. Shortly after this he became severely depressed for about two weeks and was treated with antidepressant drugs. At 22 he had moved to his own apartment. He made some money mopping floors but was basically supported by his mother. He spent most of his time practicing music—he had taught himself to play the piano, banjo, and guitar. He summarized his existence as going from "slow deadness to acute crisis" and described recurrent depressions at ages 9, 15, 18, and 19, each of which lasted months even when treated with antidepressant drugs.
—(Adapted from Chess and others, 1983, pp. 413–414)

Sylvia's depression was not noted until she was 21, after months of an intense obsessive preoccupation that her skin and hair were terribly ugly, which was not true. She threatened to drop out of college, and although she had top grades and was attending a top-level school she had changed colleges twice. She was hospitalized briefly and for the next year made many suicidal threats and a few suicidal attempts and then gradually improved.

During her therapy sessions she reported that she had been depressed even as far back as age 8 and had always covered it over with a veneer of cheerfulness and friendliness. This was substantiated by some poems she had written from ages 12 to 15 which were filled with melancholy and hopelessness. She did not report any life events that could explain the cause of her depression, although she did have several family members who had been depressed.
—(Adapted from Chess and others, 1983, p. 415)

The researchers concluded that the reasons for these long-continued depression patterns did not seem to be related to the child's early temperament, to the way the parents and child interacted, or to the stresses in the environment. They thought that the basic cause of this type of depression was probably biological. This conclusion is supported by evidence that relatives of children who are depressed have a greater risk of depression than of some other disorders (see Figure 15–12).

Although some childhood depressions seem to have a biological base and there is evidence of a genetic component, exactly what is inherited is not clear. The role of stress and vulnerability in many cases of depression is an interactive one. Bowlby's (1980) research on the attachment of mothers and infants suggests that an insecure mother–child relationship early in life, the child's perception that he or she is not loved, and loss of a parent during childhood, may all cause depression in childhood. The following case shows how these feelings of loss can arise from events other than parental death or divorce.

Michael, who had been seen for some time, was displeased with himself and withdrawn from other people. He suddenly told the therapist about a repetitive dream. "I have this dream coming up all the time. Ever since I have been little it has come up." Michael had been born to an unmarried mother. His father had deserted her before Michael's birth. After 5 years, during which she and Michael lived alone together, she had married. The family now consisted of two parents and six children. Suddenly Michael had a real family, although he had "lost" his exclusive relationship to his mother. In reporting his dream, he said:

"In the dream, I have money, a lot of money, and I lose my money. Well, I don't lose it, but I give it to my mother for her to keep, and then when I ask her for it because I want to buy something for myself she tells me that she has already given it to somebody else, that she has given it to my brothers and sisters, and they have spent it. . . . And this dream comes up over and over." He said he had this dream almost every month. Once he related that dream and cried, the depression began to become very obvious. Nobody had mentioned the word depression before, but when we looked back we could see that he was struggling with depressive affect most of the time, and after he related his dream, it became manifest.

—(Adapted from Anthony, 1977, pp. 63, 64)

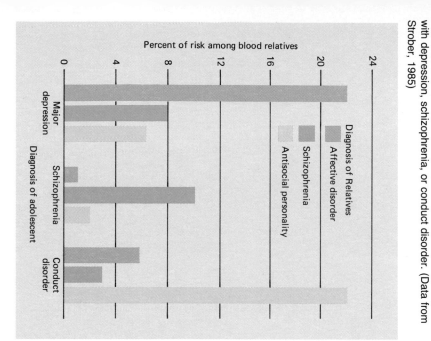

Percent of risk among blood relatives

Diagnosis of Relatives
Affective disorder
Schizophrenia
Antisocial personality

Major depression

Schizophrenia

Conduct disorder

Diagnosis of adolescent

FIGURE 15–12
Risk for psychiatric illness among blood relatives of adolescents with depression, schizophrenia, or conduct disorder. (Data from Strober, 1985)

Suicidal Behavior in Childhood and Adolescence

Thoughts of suicide and even suicide attempts do occur in young children. In one group of children between the ages of 6 and 12 who were seen at a mental-health outpatient clinic, more than one-third had thought about suicide or had threatened or attempted suicide (Pfeffer and others, 1980). The suicide methods tried or considered included jumping from high places, hanging themselves, running in front of cars, stabbing themselves, and swallowing pills. Negative perception of family environment is one of the strongest predictors of suicide, of suicidal attempts, and of suicidal thoughts among depressed children (Kranz and Moos, 1987). Suicidal children see their family environment as unsupportive, stressful, and high in conflict.

Not all children who kill themselves are depressed. Children who are angry or have personality disorders and problems of impulse control also are likely to kill themselves. Feelings of hopelessness may also increase the probability of suicide.

Rates of suicide and parasuicide increase sharply during adolescence. Younger children do kill themselves, but suicide before age 10 is rare. From ages 10 to 14 the rate of suicide increases a hundredfold, and between age 15 and 19 there is an additional tenfold increase. In the United States a teenager tries to commit suicide every 1.1 seconds. Every 80 seconds, a teenager succeeds (Federal Centers for Disease Control, 1987). Suicide among teenagers has increased sharply in recent years and is now the second-most likely cause of death

TABLE 15-1

Behaviors that Are Characteristic of Depressed Children 4 to 11 Years of Age

Complains of loneliness
Fears he/she might think or do something bad
Feels he/she has to be perfect
Feels or complains that no one loves him/her
Feels others are out to get him/her
Feels too guilty
Feels worthless or inferior
Self-conscious or easily embarrassed
Sulks a lot
Too fearful or anxious
Unhappy, sad, or depressed
Worrying

SOURCE: Achenbach and Edelbrock, 1983.

among this group. Figure 15–13 shows that increase in successes for 15- to 19-year-olds. A number of possible factors for this increase have been suggested including changes in family structure, an increase in alcohol and substance abuse, and pessimism about the future including a look of personal opportunities in adulthood as well as the threat of nuclear war. Each of these has some data to support it (Simmons, 1987). For example, teenagers who attempt suicide are likely to come from families that are violent and often in the process of breaking apart (National Center for Health Statistics, 1984). Drug use also may play a role. More than half of the adolescent suicides in one study have received a primary diagnosis of substance abuse (Murphy and others, 1986). Another explanation for the increased rate lies in the idea that if there are more people in a particular cohort group, as has been the case with adolescents during most of this period, there is more competition for jobs and health services and also for teacher attention and academic honors. This idea can be tested because the number of teenagers in the population is now declining and will continue to do so until the mid-1990s. If the model is correct, teenage suicide should also level off (Archives of General Psychiatry, 1986).

Evaluation and Treatment of Childhood Depression

Depression is hardest to assess in very young children, since they have difficulty describing their emotional state. While fear can be inferred from behavior, facial expressions, and physiological responses, depression is harder to assess because of the importance of its cognitive components. Some of the characteristics of depressed children are shown in Table 15–1. When a child is thought to be depressed, the first step is to establish whether that diagnosis fits. One way to do this is by relying on information from the parents about developmental history, present behavior, and functioning in the family. The teacher can add information about school behavior and performance. However, even in adolescents whose cognitive development should allow them to communicate these feelings, many parents and teachers fail to note depression until the symptoms become quite severe (Rutter and Garmezy, 1983). Agreement among the reports of parents, teachers, and the child about a variety of emotional problems is greater for 6- to 11-year-olds than for adolescents (Achenbach and others, 1987).

A structured interview with the parents and also an interview with the child is one way to get information. One approach is to use an adaptation of an interview used to diagnose depressed adults. A child's version of the Schedule for Affective Disorders and Schizophrenia (Kiddie SADS) has been shown to measure depression in children reliably although not as well as in adults (Chambers and others, 1985). Another less expensive way of getting information about depression in childhood is to use a questionnaire. One measure frequently used is the Children's Depression Inventory (Kovacs and Beck, 1977). Questionnaires of this type provide the opportunity to screen children for depression.

The traditional approach to treating depressed children has been psychodynamically oriented therapy. More recently, behavioral therapy and family therapy have also been frequent choices. Behavioral therapy is often oriented toward helping the child learn social skills or assertive behavior. In many cases researchers have found that depressed children have depressed parents; this suggests that they have learned to cope with stress in the same way that their depressed parents do. One way to provide models of nondepressed coping styles is through therapy in which the therapist models effective behavior for the child (Petti, 1981).

A reason to involve the parents and employ some

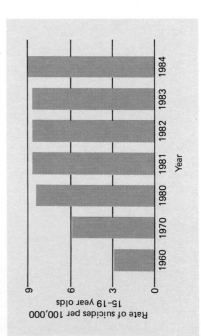

FIGURE 15-13
The role of suicide for 15 to 19-year-olds has tripled in the last quarter-century. (National Center for Health Statistics, 1987)

type of family therapy is that many children who are depressed and who may think about or attempt suicide also think of their families as high in conflict and low in control (Asarnow and others, 1987). Working with the entire family seems very important. One research question that needs to be answered is whether other family members share this perception of the family climate.

Cognitive therapy with the children is also appropriate because of the evidence that depressed children feel incompetent and that these cognitions relate in rather specific ways to the depressed state rather than simply reflecting a general disruption and disturbance (Weisz and others, 1987) or reflecting reality of performance in academic, social, and athletic activities (Asarnow and others, 1987).

The cognitive perspective suggests that another possible contributing factor to depression in both children and adults is beliefs about their own helplessness. In one study of 8- to 17-year-olds from several outpatient clinics, these depressed adolescents and preadolescents had strong beliefs in their own incompetence (Weisz and others, 1987). The depression did not seem to be related to their perception of a lack of connection between their behavior and the outcome. In other words, unlike what is sometimes seen in adults, these children did not view what happened to them as a lack of available reinforcement. Instead, as do some other depressed adults, they believed the lack of reinforcement occurred because they deserved none.

Antidepressant drugs are used to treat depression in children and adolescents as well as in adults. Tricyclic medication is as readily prescribed for adolescents as it is for adults. Among younger children, only those who are severely depressed seem to respond to tricyclics in the same way that adults do (Toolan, 1981). Because of the lack of information about the effects of such drugs during these crucial years of physical and cognitive development, most clinicians use them with great care.

Problems with Physical Symptoms

Childhood and adolescent disorders with physical symptoms include movement disorders (rapid, involuntary movements or voluntary stereotyped movements such as rocking of the entire body), as well as stuttering, bedwetting, sleepwalking, and eating disorders. Among the eating disorders that occur in childhood and adolescence are **pica**, in which the child persistently eats nonfood substances such as paint, string, leaves, or pebbles; **rumination disorder of infancy**, in which the infant regurgitates partially digested food; **anorexia nervosa**, in which adolescents become preoccupied with "feeling fat" and may diet until they die from malnutrition; and **bulimia nervosa** or binge eating that is often followed by purging through self-induced vomiting or the use of large doses of laxatives or diuretics. The two disorders that we discuss in this section, anorexia nervosa and bulimia nervosa, are especially prevalent throughout adolescence as well as young adulthood, and are more likely to be found in females than in males.

Anorexia Nervosa

Although anorexia nervosa has been recognized since the late 1700s and was given its present name in 1874, only recently have its psychological features become a subject of clinical interest. For many years medical opinion held that anorexia nervosa was a result of an endocrine disturbance, and the possibility remains that the condition is due to a disorder of the hypothalamus. (Certain hypothalamic tumors are know to give rise to a distaste for food.)

Characteristics of Anorexics

Although the term **anorexia nervosa** means nervous loss of appetite, researchers have found that anorexics are indeed hungry. They have both physiological and cognitive feelings of hunger, together with a strong preoccupation with food. Anorexics are likely to discuss recipes and cook elaborate meals for their families or friends, but somehow they never have time to eat what they prepare. If they do eat with others, most of the time is spent cutting food into tiny pieces and moving it around on the plate. If they actually eat, it is usually when they are alone.

Research on starvation has shown that when people are starving, for whatever reason, as long as they eat more than 200 calories a day they will experience hunger. If the consequences of starvation are so unpleasant, why do anorexics find reinforcement in partially starving themselves? There are some basic differences between anorexics and people who starve involuntarily (see Table 15-2).

People with anorexia nervosa have a intense fear of becoming fat even when they are obviously underweight. They claim to "feel fat." To be considered anorexic, a person must refuse to eat to such an extent that his or her body weight is at least 15-percent below the normal level, or fail to gain weight during a period of growth so that his or her body weight is 15-percent below what would be expected. For women, the weight loss must be great enough to result in the absence of at least three consecutive menstrual cycles.

Anorexia is most common in middle- and upper-class adolescent females. The first case of anorexia in a black female was not reported until relatively recently

TABLE 15-2

Comparison of Psychological and Behavioral Changes in Starvation and Anorexia Nervosa

Mood or Feeling State

Starvation: Lack of initiative; quarrelsome; indecisive; loss of concern about physical appearance

Anorexia nervosa: High initiative; strong-willed; pride in personal appearance; frequent periods of feeling exuberant

Mental Content

Starvation: Thinking, dreaming, and daydreaming about eating food

Anorexia nervosa: Same as in starvation, but preoccupation with thoughts of gaining weight continues after eating resumes

Activity Level

Starvation: Fatigue, avoidance of physical exertion

Anorexia nervosa: Seemingly inexhaustible energy; physical exercise sought; overactivity

Sexual Activity

Starvation: Decrease in sexual fantasies, feelings of interest; inability to maintain erection (males); cessation of menstruation (females)

Anorexia nervosa: Same

SOURCE: Adapted from Casper and Davis, 1977, pp. 977–978.

Garfinkel, 1980). For ballet dancers, the more competitive their ballet school, the more likely they are to be anorexic.

Other Factors. Only one in every 100 to 150 teenage girls age 15 and over becomes anorexic, and the rate is even lower for younger girls. This suggests that other factors besides sociocultural pressures play a role in the development of anorexia.

In their attempts to understand this disorder, researchers have divided anorexics into subgroups: those who were thin primarily because of restricted food intake (the restrictor group) and those who, in addition to restricting food intake, used vomiting and purging with laxatives to control their weight (the bulimic anorexia group). (Not all bulimics are anorexic. Some are of average weight and use purging only to compensate for the extremely high calorie intake during binges.) There are a number of differences between the two

FIGURE 15-14
Cultural pressures encourage the idea that thinness, beauty, and desirability are all part of a package. This photo of a fashion model illustrates the slender ideal.

(Jones and others, 1980). Anorexia nervosa is also found in men, but it is much rarer. In a study conducted at a large hospital over a 20-year period, only 9 percent of the patients diagnosed as anorexic were men (Crisp and Burns, 1983).

Causes of Anorexia

Sociocultural Pressures. The incidence of anorexia appears to be increasing, perhaps as a result of sociocultural pressures (see Figure 15–14). The "ideal" weight for females has decreased in recent years. For example, a team of researchers found that the average bust and hip measurements of models in *Playboy* magazine centerfolds decreased over a 20-year period (Garner and others, 1980). They also found that the average weight of contestants in the Miss America pageant had decreased over the same period. Meanwhile the discrepancy between ideal and reality increased because the average weight of American women under 30 increased by 5 pounds. The same cultural pressures can be seen in occupational groups where thinness is especially desirable. Female ballet dancers and models are more likely to be anorexic than other women of their age (Garner and

subgroups: those in the bulimic anorexic group are more likely than those in the restrictor group to abuse alcohol or drugs and to have other problems of impulse control, such as stealing (Leon and Phelan, 1984). The families of the bulimic anorexics are less stable, have more parental discord and physical health problems, and have experienced more negative events in the recent past. These families of bulimic anorexics have much higher rates of mood disorders and substance abuse disorders than the families of restrictors (Kog and Vandereycken, 1985). Thus, it is possible that genetic factors play a role in the development of anorexic disorders.

Consequences of Anorexic Behavior

Anorexia disturbs the body's functioning in many ways including retarded bone growth, anemia, dry skin, low body temperature and basal metabolism rate, slow heart rate, and lack of tolerance for cold (Rock and Yager, 1987). Anorexia results in a least a temporary absence of menstrual periods. In addition, a number of physiological changes are likely to accompany anorexia, especially if there is vomiting. One of these, a low level of serum potassium, may cause cardiac arrhythmia, a tendency toward changes in heart rate that can result in death (see Figure 15–15).

Some researchers believe that these changes may be due to malfunctioning of the hypothalamus (Halmi and others, 1983). The hypothalamus controls the body's water balance, maintenance of body temperature, secretion of the endocrine glands, and fat metabolism. It is not clear whether the hypothalamic changes occur before the anorexic behavior begins or as a result of changes in eating behavior. This hypothalamic malfunction may also be related to impairment in dopamine regulation and, thus, to the development of depression. Both types of anorexics show obsessive preoccupations and feel a great deal of stress. Test results from the MMPI also indicate that anorexics are likely to be depressed (Leon and others, 1985) and this depression is likely to continue even after successful treatment for their weight problem (Toner and others, 1986).

The long-term outcome for both restricting and bulimic anorexic groups is much the same when either anorexic symptoms or social functioning is considered (see Figure 15–16). The only differences were that the bulimic group was more likely to have a substance abuse disorder than the restricting group. Both groups were much more likely than a matched comparison group to have had an affective or anxiety disorder sometime in their lives (Toner and others, 1986). Depression seems to be a continuing problem for anorexic patients. A long-term follow-up study of 151 former anorexia patients found that 9 had died an average of 7 years after their first medical contact with anorexia, 7 of them by suicide (Tolstrup and others, 1985).

FIGURE 15–15
Karen Carpenter, shown here with her brother, died from a heart attack in her early thirties. Physicians thought the recording star's long battle with anorexia nervosa was an important factor in her death.

Therapy for Anorexia

The two major therapeutic approaches used in treating anorexia are behavioral methods and family therapy; these approaches are often used together and combined with nutrition management. In behavioral programs hospital privileges are made dependent on weight gain. While this technique often leads to increases in body weight, it has some negative features. If the weight gain

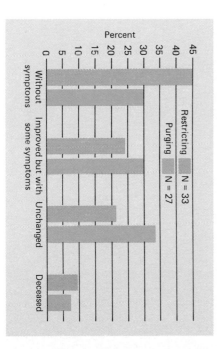

FIGURE 15–16
Groups of anorexic individuals who restrict their food intake and those that use purging for weight control show little difference in outcome after treatment. (Adapted from Toner, Garfinkel, and Garner, 1986, p. 526)

required is too great (some programs have required a half-pound gain per day), patients may develop bulimia and use laxatives and vomiting as a method of weight control (Leon and Phelan, 1984). They are also likely to show poor social adjustment.

Cognitive–behavioral approaches to anorexia have also been tried. These focus on the faulty thinking that seems to contribute to the faulty body image of some anorexics. Cognition interventions are usually combined with other approaches. Nutritional counseling is usually included as well. Emphasis is placed on establishing normal eating patterns.

Because behavioral therapy has met with limited long-term success, some researchers have focused on family therapy, especially for younger anorexics. One family therapist who has taken a special interest in anorexic adolescents is Salvador Minuchin (Minuchin and others, 1978). Minuchin has found predominant characteristics in families with an anorexic child: enmeshment, overprotectiveness, rigidity, and lack of conflict resolution. The enmeshed family is one in which no one can be an individual or have a separate identity and the insistence on togetherness results in the lack of privacy. Family members are overprotective; they frequently express concern for each other's welfare and respond protectively to the least sign of distress. Families of anorexics also tend to be very rigid and to resist change. They have what amounts to a storybook image of themselves, and the growth of individuality in an adolescent child is a threat to this picture of perfection. Tolerance for conflict is also extremely low in these families. Some deny that any differences exist among their members, others deal with differences by shifting conversation to other topics. When such tactics are used, conflicts within the family are not resolved. Instead, natural differences accumulate and stress builds up.

Minuchin and his co-workers followed most of their first 50 anorexic cases for at least 2.5 years after treatment began. They reported a recovery rate of 86 percent, with recovery defined as no symptom of eating disturbance or psychosocial difficulty at home, at school, or with peers (Minuchin and others, 1978). This study focused on young girls (average age 14) who had very recently begun to show anorexic symptoms. It is possible that this high recovery rate might not occur with older anorexics with more established eating (or noneating) habits.

Bulimia Nervosa

In bulimia nervosa, or binge eating, the person is aware of his or her abnormal eating patterns, afraid of being unable to stop eating, and likely to be depressed and self-critical about this behavior. In bulimia, binge eating occurs at least twice a week for at least 3 months and is often accompanied by laxative use, self-induced vomiting, or rigorous dieting in order to compensate for the binge behavior. Many anorexic patients have symptoms of bulimia; they are called bulimic anorexics or purging anorexics. But other people are bulimic without being very thin. Bulimics may be of average or above-average weight. Some researchers have suggested that bulimia is a type of depression and should be classified as an affective disorder. As of now the evidence does not uphold this view (Hinz and Williamson, 1987). So far all that can be said is that bulimia, like many other chronic disorders, is often accompanied by depression.

The Binge–Purge Cycle

Binge eaters are generally on some sort of weight-reduction diet, and the binge represents their falling "off the wagon." They may binge only at certain times rather than continuously, and many hide food and eat in secret. They may consume prodigious amounts of food during one of these binges. Between 2000 and 5000 calories are usually consumed per binge, up to twice as many calories as most people consume in a day (Johnson and others, 1983). Most binge eaters consume easily prepared, high-calorie foods such as chips, fast food, bread, and sweets, and many focus their binges on particular foods (Mizes, 1985). Binges often occur while the person is at home alone watching TV or browsing through a magazine, or in a car or fast-food restaurant. If food runs out during a binge, the bulimic may rush out to buy more. Bulimics tends to eat in an unsystematic manner; they binge, do not eat for a day, and then binge again.

Binging is quite common among college women, but clinically significant bulimic behavior is not (see Figure 15–17). Even when the criteria for bulimic behavior are met, the condition may not be long lasting (Drewnowski and others, 1987). Even though bulimia is sometimes described as an epidemic on college campuses, that is not true unless one is referring to self-reported overeating with or without occasional purging. Although two-thirds of college women report eating binges, these are not as severe or frequent as those of bulimics and are not usually accompanied by self-induced vomiting or the use of laxatives. Only 1.3 percent of college women can be classified as bulimic (Schotte and Stunkard, 1987).

Attempts to explain bulimia have focused on the role of negative cognitive/emotional states in bringing on binge episodes. Pressure at work or school and problems with personal relationships often precede binges, and most bulimics feel anxious, depressed, and somewhat guilty before a binge. They also report that their binges are prompted by contact with certain people, most frequently their mothers but sometimes their boyfriends, fathers, and sisters (Carrol and Leon, 1981).

FIGURE 15-17
Cumulative binge and binge–vomit or purge frequencies for university students show that bulimia is not common but binge eating occurs more frequently. (Adapted from Schotte and Stunkard, 1987. Journal of the American Medical Association. Copyright © 1987, American Medical Association.)

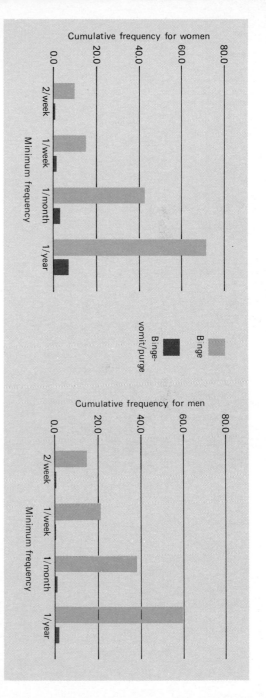

Consequences of the Binge–Purge Cycle

During their binges most bulimics feel immediate relief from anxiety and depression. Bulimics may be using binges or on preventing purging. Many of the studies that have been reported deal with single subjects, so a clear picture of the general process is lacking. Relaxation training seems to be helpful in preventing the binge binging as a means of coping with stress. If this is the case, teaching them alternative coping skills should be an important part of therapy.

In the postbinge period most bulimics feel disgust and anger at their lack of self-control, guilt over having eaten "forbidden" foods that violate their strict and unrealistic diet standards, and depression at their inability to stop binging. These negative postbinge feelings are thought to serve as a cue for purging which undoes the eating act and leads to a decrease in negative feelings (Rosen and Leitenberg, 1982). Postbinge purging in the form of vomiting has been reported by over 90 percent of bulimics (Mizes, 1985). Purging alone often is not enough to produce a better mood, however. In one study, 70 percent of bulimic individuals reported thoughts about suicide at the conclusion of the binge–purge cycle (Abraham and Beaumont, 1982). This negative state can serve as a precipitating factor for another cycle.

Bulimia is not just an eating problem. It is associated with poor overall adjustment (Johnson and Berndt, 1983). This means that not only do bulimics have poor skills for coping with depression and anxiety but they also experience these feelings unusually strongly. In addition to the psychological consequences of anxiety, depression, and guilt, the binge–purge cycle can also have distressing physical results. The most serious of these are due to the potassium imbalance from frequent vomiting, which can lead to muscle weakness and also to heart problems. Vomiting can also damage the esophagus and increase tooth decay and damage to tooth enamel.

Treatment of Bulimia

Treatment of bulimia can be focused either on preventing purging. Many of the studies that have been reported deal with single subjects, so a clear picture of the general process is lacking. Relaxation training seems to be helpful in preventing the binge from starting (Mizes and Fleece, 1984). Treatment to prevent purging involves exposure and response prevention. For instance, in one study, subjects were asked to eat until a strong urge to vomit occurred (Leitenberg and others, 1983). While they were eating, the therapist focused subjects' attention on negative thoughts about feeling full, fat, ugly, and rejected. The therapist also helped them focus on three positive thoughts: (1) the postbinge anxiety would decrease and not be as unpleasant as they feared. After physical sensations after eating were abnormal and could be relieved without vomiting; (2) the strict diets they set for themselves were unrealistic and set them up to "blow it" and binge; (3) the postbinge anxiety would decrease and not be as unpleasant as they feared. After an hour until they felt sure they were not going to eating, the patients stayed with the therapist for at least vomit. Four of the five patients treated either stopped an hour until they felt sure they were not going to vomiting or showed a definite improvement. One patient showed no change.

Antidepressant drugs are also used to treat bulimia. In some cases these are initially helpful in reducing the race of binging, but relapses may occur when the medication is stopped. In some cases binges occur even when the drug therapy is continued (Stewart and others, 1984).

Bulimia may be related to mood disorders, as is suggested by the higher incidence of both mood disorders and alcoholism in relatives of bulimic individuals. However, other psychological factors may also contribute to bulimic behavior. It seems likely that certain personality factors that may be genetically determined make some people more vulnerable to family and social experiences that have a negative effect on self-esteem and feelings of self-efficacy (Strober and Humphrey, 1987). Therefore, a behavioral treatment may be more effective than the use of antidepressant drugs in enhancing coping skills and thereby preventing relapse. Research programs for the treatment of bulimics are quite structured and focus on eating behavior. In general, such treatment has been successful (Mitchell and Eckhart, 1987).

Therapy with Children and Adolescents

Many times the most effective approach to therapy with young children is to work with the parent instead of the child. This type of therapy may have several purposes:

1. Help the parent to understand the way children develop and the kinds of behavior typical of different ages.

2. Show the parent adaptive ways to deal with the child, for instance, how to play with a young child or how to use constructive methods of motivation rather than harsh discipline.

3. Suggest ways to improve family interactions that may be causing stress for the parents or the child or both.

When therapy focused on the child seems the most appropriate, several differences between therapy for children and for adults must be considered:

1. Children rarely initiate treatment for themselves and typically do not understand the purpose of mental-health services. Therefore, some children actively resist being taken for treatment.

2. Not only must the child's parents initiate, continue, and finance treatment, but they usually must modify their own behavior in certain respects.

3. Often children are referred for therapy because they are deviating from the normal pattern of development. This means therapy must be at least partly directed toward attaining those norms if that is possible.

Many therapies that are used with adults have been adapted for use with children, and some methods that are uniquely suited to young children have been developed as well. Play therapy, storytelling techniques, and parent-administered behavior-modification programs are examples of therapies specially tailored for children. Until behavioral therapy became popular,

much therapy for children was psychoanalytic in its orientation.

Play Therapy

Because young children's limited verbal skills made traditional talking therapy inappropriate (see Figure 15–18), many therapists began using play therapy. They met with the child in a playroom and used the child's play activities or play interactions between the child and the therapist as a therapeutic vehicle (see Figure 15–19). Psychodynamically trained therapists use play as a substitute for the free-association approach they use with adults. Nondirective therapists use play to help the child act out his or her feelings, face them, and learn to control them.

The following example illustrates the nondirective approach:

Joann, age 6, comes into the playroom and begins to play with the clay. This is her fourth play therapy session. She is usually very quiet and does very little talking. Every time she comes in she plays with the clay and makes the same thing—a figure of a man carrying a cane. Each time, after she is finished, awful things happen to him. He is punched full of holes, beaten with a stick, run over by the toy truck, buried under a pile of blocks. The fourth time the clay figure emerges, the therapist says, "Here comes that man again."

JOANN: *Yes. (Her voice is tense, determined.)*
THERAPIST: *The man with the cane?*
JOANN: *Yes. (She begins to punch him full of holes.)*
THERAPIST: *You're putting holes in the clay man.*
JOANN: *Stab! Stab! Stab!*

FIGURE 15–18
Traditional psychodynamic therapy is not appropriate for young children. (From Roche Report: *Frontiers of Psychiatry*, April 1, 1982, p. 11)

"So tell me, when did you first notice you were having trouble coping with life's little ups and downs?"

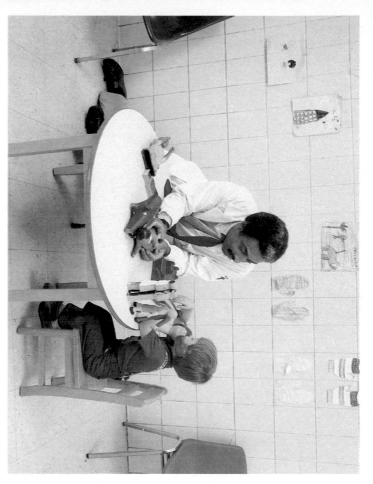

FIGURE 15-19
Children often communicate better through play than through speech. Play therapy is designed to take advantage of this fact and to give children a symbolic way to express their fears, aggressions, and insecurities.

THERAPIST: *You're stabbing him.*
JOANN (*in small voice*): *Ouch. You hurt me.* (*Voice changing*) *I don't care. I want to hurt you.*
THERAPIST: *The clay man is crying because he is hurt.*

JOANN (*interrupting*): *I want to hurt him.*
THERAPIST: *You want to hurt him.*
JOANN (*emphatically*): *I don't like him.*
THERAPIST: *You don't like him.*
JOANN: *I don't like him. I hate him. Look. This hole went clear through him. It went in his front and out his back.*
THERAPIST: *He gets holes punched clear through him. You fixed him.*
JOANN: *Yes. I'll tear his head off.*
THERAPIST: *You'll even tear his head off?*
JOANN: *I know, I know. I'll put him clear down in the bottom of the jar and then I'll put the clay in on top of him and he'll smother.* (*She tears him into little pieces and gouges her thumb through the clay and carefully puts the pieces down in the bottom of the jar and then covers it with all the rest of the clay*).
THERAPIST: *You tore him into little pieces and buried him in the bottom of the jar. Joann nods— and smiles at the therapist. Then she goes over to the baby doll, pretends to feed it, holds it tenderly in her arms, puts it in bed, sets the table, and plays house very quietly.*

This was the pattern of Joann's behavior while in the playroom. She always made the clay man, tore him up, got rid of him, and then played with the baby doll. This continued through the seventh interview, and then she stopped making the clay man. She sometimes played with the clay, but made cats or toy dishes or candles. She was very fond of the doll and continued with this play.

— (Axline, 1947, pp. 179–180)

In the course of the therapy, Joann's nervous, tense, withdrawn behavior greatly improved. The therapist later learned that Joann's mother, who had been a widow for three years, was considering remarriage to a man who limped and carried a cane. Expressing her feelings without discussing them had apparently enabled Joann to accept her mother's marriage plans.

Note that the therapist offered no interpretations. Simply being able to express these negative thoughts in the presence of an accepting adult seemed beneficial to Joann. A psychodynamically oriented therapist might have handled this situation differently. Using the play behavior as a base, the therapist might have interpreted the behavior to the child. For example, when Joann stabbed the clay man, a psychodynamically oriented therapist might have begun by saying, "You're angry with the man. You want to hurt him." Eventually, after many play-therapy sessions, Joann would have come to understand why she felt as angry as she did about her mother's proposed marriage.

Cognitive and Behavior Therapies

Cognitive therapy, which has a behavioral rather than a psychodynamic orientation, is becoming increasingly popular in work with children and adolescents. In this chapter it is illustrated by some of the interventions for hyperactivity and for bulimia.

Probably the most often-used treatments for children involve behavioral methods of various kinds. One example can be seen in the following case:

Valerie, an 8-year-old girl from a low-income area, started to miss school in the second grade and in third grade the problem became worse. Whenever her mother attempted to take her to school, Valerie threw a temper tantrum or said she felt sick, so her mother left her at the neighbor's. The therapists concluded that Val was getting reinforcement for staying away from school. By staying home, she gained extra contact with her mother and fun at the neighbor's house while her mother was at work. Some of the things Val liked most—chewing gum, ice cream, soda pop, and having her cousin stay all night—were combined as reinforcers to reward Val for going to school. Her mother no longer took Val to the neighbor's. Instead she reinforced Val by leaving home early before the children left for school and meeting her at the school door each morning, and by giving her candy when she returned from school and special treats when she had completed a week of school attendance. She also ignored Val's complaints of illness. The effect of this treatment on Val's school attendance is shown in a graph (see Figure 15–20). In addition, Val's grade-point average changed from C's before the treatment to A's and B's.

— (Adapted from Ayllon and others, 1970).

A unique aspect of behavioral therapy for children is that one or both parents can be trained as "therapists" so that behavior modification can be carried out at home. The case of Valerie, and that of Byron described earlier, are examples of therapy in which parents carried out the actual treatment. Although in many cases a clinician must plan the behavioral interventions and train the parents to carry them out, in some instances, particularly for less severe but still disruptive behaviors, group training sessions can be used to teach parents how to develop successful home treatment programs.

Family Therapy

In the **family systems** approach to therapy the basic idea is that it is the system of family interaction, not one individual, that is disturbed. Even though one person is usually identified as the member with the problem, that person's symptoms are a reflection of a disturbance in a larger family unit. For example, a hyperactive boy was referred for treatment. Although he was labeled as the problem, a look at the family showed the problem was much greater.

In this family the husband and wife did not get along. The husband spent all his time caring for his own dependent parents. He felt burdened by his wife and 3 children and felt no one looked after his needs. The wife felt neglected and uncared for and got satisfaction from the antics of her youngest child, the hyperactive boy. The other two older children who were well behaved seemed excessively mature in their actions. The problems in this interconnected system could be seen by looking at any of the members, not just at the young boy labeled as hyperactive.

—(Andolphi and others, 1983)

Family therapy has much in common with the psychodynamic approach because it often focuses on the meanings behind the behavior of each of the family members.

Results of Therapy

The results of therapy with children are about the same as those of therapy with adults. This means that treated children experience outcomes about two-thirds of a standard deviation better than those experienced by untreated children. This conclusion and others comes from an analysis of 75 studies of the effectiveness of therapy for children (Casey and Berman, 1985). As in therapy with adults, the largest effect of therapy with children was on measures of fear and anxiety. Unlike adults, however, children tended to show relatively little change in self-esteem, overall adjustment, and social adjustment.

Reports of the effects of therapy from parents and therapists have been encouraging. In contrast, reports from teachers and classmates seem more restrained. Another indicator of therapeutic outcome shows up when children's behavior changes are compared with their self-reports. Although their actual performance is often better, positive self-reports from the children are rare. One reason for this may be that children have difficulty engaging in introspection, or thinking about how they see themselves.

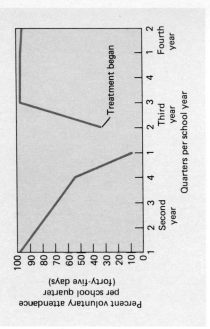

FIGURE 15–20
Valerie's voluntary school attendance. The behavioral intervention (including positive reinforcement) was initiated during the second quarter of the third year of school. (Ayllon and others, 1970, p. 135)

Study Outline

THE SCOPE OF THE PROBLEM

Six million or more children in the United States have psychological problems that are severe enough to interfere with their learning in school and require professional contact. Many more boys than girls are brought for evaluation or treatment of psychological problems during childhood.

DISRUPTIVE BEHAVIORS

1. Restless behavior of students is a major complaint of school personnel, but some children who are considered hyperactive by teachers may not be classified as such by mental-health professionals. Children with **attention-deficit hyperactivity disorder** (ADHD) have problems of impulsiveness, hyperactivity, and inattention. They usually have difficulties both in school and in social interactions. The most common treatment for this disorder is the use of psychostimulant drugs, but cognitive—behavioral techniques are also used. If ADHD problems continue into adolescence or adulthood, a conduct disorder often accompanies them.

2. Children with **conduct disorder** engage in behaviors that seriously violate the basic rights of others or the major rules of society. Children with conduct disorders often engage in criminal behavior, become alcoholic, or develop personality disorders as adults. Prevention through skill building may be the most effective treatment.

EMOTIONAL DISTURBANCES

1. Children's emotional disturbances, both anxiety disorders and depression, are less likely to continue into adulthood than are behavior disorders.

2. Children's excessive fears and phobias can often be treated effectively with behavioral techniques.

3. Children with **separation anxiety disorder** show excessive anxiety when they are not with major attachment figures or in familiar surroundings.

4. Children who have an **overanxious disorder** have excessive worries for 6 months or longer. They also often have a variety of physical complaints.

5. Children sometimes develop **obsessive-compulsive** and **ritualistic** behaviors that require treatment. These disorders are rare and are difficult to treat successfully.

6. Depression is frequent among children who come to clinical attention. Childhood depression is more common in boys than in girls and may be relatively long-lasting. Some children who are depressed continue to have periods of depression later in life. During adolescence mood disorders become more common in girls than in boys and may take the form of hypomania or bipolar disorder. Mood disorders become more common in adolescence, as do suicide and parasuicide.

7. Some researchers believe that the basic cause of childhood depression is biological, and there is evidence of a genetic component. Stress appears to be interact with vulnerability to produce depression.

PROBLEMS WITH PHYSICAL SYMPTOMS

1. **Anorexia nervosa** means nervous loss of appetite, but anorexics have both physiological and cognitive feelings of hunger and a preoccupation with food. People with this disorder have an intense fear of becoming fat even when they are obviously underweight. Sociocultural pressures may have contributed to the increase in the incidence of anorexia in recent decades.

2. Some anorexics stay thin by restricting food intake. Others combine food restriction with periodic binges and purges. Anorexia is related to depressed mood and has effects on the body, including retarded bone growth, anemia, dry skin, low body temperature, and others. Many anorexics recover when treated with a combination of behavioral methods and family therapy.

3. In **bulimia nervosa**, binge eating occurs at least twice a week for at least 3 months and is often accompanied by laxative use, self-induced vomiting, or rigorous dieting. Binge episodes appear to be brought on by negative cognitive/emotional states such as pressure at work or school and problems with personal relationships. Negative feelings after the binge are thought to serve as a cue for purging to "undo" the effects of the binge.

4. Treatment of bulimia can be focused either on preventing binges or on preventing purging. Relaxation training may help prevent binges, while treatment to prevent purging involves exposure and response prevention. Bulimia is associated with poor overall adjustment, especially poor skills for coping with anxiety and depression.

THERAPY WITH CHILDREN AND ADOLESCENTS

1. Sometimes the most effective therapeutic approach to children's psychological problems is to work with the parent rather than the child.

2. Many therapies that are used with adults have been adapted for use with children, and other methods have been developed specifically for use with young children: play therapy and behavior-modification programs. A unique aspect of behavioral therapy for children is parents can be trained to carry out interventions at home.

3. Another approach is to work with the family as a whole. **Family systems therapy** is based on the idea that a child's maladaptive symptoms reflect a disturbance in the entire family unit.

CHAPTER 16

Developmental Disorders

To learn:

1. Behavioral characteristics, possible causes, and treatment approaches to autism

2. Possible causes of retardation, how it is classified, and behavioral characteristics typical of each type

To understand:

Impact of developmental disorders on the person affected and on other family members.

*P*eter nursed eagerly, sat and walked at the expected ages. Yet some of his behavior made us vaguely uneasy. He never put anything in his mouth.

Not his fingers nor his toys—nothing. More troubling was the fact that Peter didn't look at us, or smile, and wouldn't play the games that seemed as much a part of babyhood as diapers. While he didn't cry, he rarely laughed, and when he did, it was at things that didn't seem funny to us. He didn't cuddle, but sat upright in my lap, even when I rocked him. But children differ and we were content to let Peter be himself. We thought it hilarious when my brother, visiting us when Peter was 8 months old, observed that "that kid has no social instincts, whatsoever." Although Peter was a first child, he was not isolated. I frequently put him in his playpen in front of the house, where the school children stopped to play with him as they passed. He ignored them too. . . .

Peter's babbling had not turned into speech by the time he was 3. His play was solitary and repetitious. He tore paper into long thin strips, bushel baskets of it every day. He spun the lids from canning jars and became upset if we tried to divert him. Only rarely could I catch his eye, and then saw his focus change from me to the reflection in my glasses. It was like trying to pick up mercury with chopsticks.

—(Eberhardy, 1967, pp. 257–258)

Peter's case is an example of one of the serious developmental disorders, known as autistic disorder. Autistic disorder (autism) and mental retardation are two developmental disorders that have an overall effect on children's patterns of development. Other developmental disorders are more specific: they affect speech (stuttering or difficulties in pronunciation), academic skills (reading disorder, expressive-writing disorder, or arithmetic disorder), or motor skills (coordination disorder). However, none of these disorders has as great an impact on other children and their families as autism and mental retardation (see Box 16–1). This chapter is devoted to these two major developmental disorders.

Autistic Disorder

Autistic disorder occurs in 2 to 4 children out of every 10,000 under the age of 15. Boys are three to four times as likely to be autistic as girls (Campbell and Green, 1985). Autism is not common, but its effects are devastating.

BOX 16–1
How Families Adapt to Retarded Children

From the parents' point of view, the birth of a mentally retarded child is a stressful and often tragic event. For nine months they have looked forward to the arrival of a healthy, normal child. When those expectations are shattered, they often go through a grieving process similar to that following the death of a family member. In the past, many professionals emphasized the parents' need for help until they could accept the situation. They viewed the process as time limited. One parent of a retarded child comments on this view.

Parents of retarded people, the theorists tell us, learn to live with their children's handicaps. They go through stages of reaction, moving through shock, guilt, and rejection to the promised land of acceptance and adjustment.

My own experience as the father of a retarded child did not fit this pattern. Instead, it convinced me that most people seriously misunderstand a parent's response to this situation. The standard view does not reflect the reality of parents' experience or lead to helpful conclusions.

Professionals could help parents more—and they would be more realistic—if they discarded their ideas about stages and progress. They could then begin to understand something about the deep, lasting changes that life with a retarded son or daughter brings to parents. And they could begin to see that the negative feelings—the shock, the guilt, and the bitterness—never disappear but stay on as a part of the parent's emotional life.

Most parents, I believe, never fully resolve the complexity of feelings about their child's retardation. They don't "adjust to" or "accept" that fact, at least not in the way psychology books describe it. (Searl, 1978, p. 27).

Many parents of retarded children retain some optimism about their child's future progress while the child is still young. For example, they may overestimate the child's learning potential and underestimate problems in

learning. This is illustrated by the observation that parents of young children are more supportive of the concept of mainstreaming (combining children of all abilities into one school program) than parents of older children, who see a greater need for special education programs (Suelzle and Keenan, 1981). In general, just as the grieving process goes on over a lifetime, the parents' acceptance of the severity of their child's disability is not steady and gradual. Instead, problems of acceptance flare up acutely at particular stages in the child's development.

Families of retarded children go through a series of crises as the child reaches various developmental stages. In one survey, three-quarters of the parents described life with their retarded child as a series of ups and progressively greater downs. Only one-quarter described their grief as being healed by time (Wikler and others,1981). The parents were asked to evaluate the extent to which they were upset at a number of points, including early events such as the time of diagnosis, the time for walking and talking, and decisions on school placement, and later events such as the onset of puberty, the twenty-first birthday, and discussion and decisions about the care of the child after the parents' death.

When the parents' responses were compared with the predictions of social workers, the results showed that the social workers tended to overestimate the extent to which the parents' were upset over the earlier experiences and to underestimate the extent to which they were upset over the later experiences. For example, the social workers overestimated the extent to which parents were upset at the times when the child would normally have been expected to walk, when the child entered a special-education class rather than the regular school program, and when younger siblings surpassed the retarded child in functioning. They markedly underestimated how upsetting the child's twenty-first birthday was to the parents.

The unmet needs of parents seem to form a U-shaped curve. These needs are high among parents of preschoolers, drop off when the children enter some kind of school program, and rise again, even beyond

Characteristics of Autistic Behavior

Children with **autistic disorder** show several kinds of impairment—in social relationships, communication, and activities (see Figure 16–2). Their social interactions are highly unusual. In general, such children have a noticeable lack of awareness of the existence or feelings of others. They may treat people as though they are objects and are likely to have no empathy for the feelings of others. They do not seek out an adult for comfort if they are hurt or upset. They don't like to be held and they avoid eye contact. Autistic children prefer solitary play and have a poor understanding of social conventions. Even as young children, autistic children do not enjoy the usual parent–child kiss-and-cuddle routines. They do not wave good-by or play peek-a-

the original levels, when the children become young adults.

Periods of transition in the children's lives are also associated with increased family stress. Both entry into adolescence and to young adulthood seem particularly stressful. Figure 16–1 shows the stress levels of families with retarded children of different ages. Two samplings 2 years apart showed similar findings.

In the past, parents of severely retarded children were urged to institutionalize such children shortly after birth, before they had had a chance to become attached to them. More recently, they have been urged to care for their children at home. However, the presence of a retarded child puts great stress on a family. Parents report a sense of loss and hopelessness, a decrease in self-esteem, and increases in shame, guilt, and marital disharmony (Lobato, 1983). The father of one autistic and retarded child wrote movingly in his diary about the stresses that his son's problems imposed on him and his wife, Foumi.

> *I notice that I have become more distrustful of Foumi, have lost some of my faith in her, so necessary for our marriage, or any marriage, because she has borne me Noah. Even though genetically, I suspect, it is I who am the wreck. But worse than cheating or mutual suspicion when it comes to unfixing the mystique that glues a marriage, I guess, is to have a disturbed kid. At first I thought it would draw us closer together, necessarily cement our relationship. Now Foumi and I have to be wary that it doesn't draw us apart. We have to be intelligent enough to realize there is a strain on any marriage whenever a baby is sick. And we always have a sick baby.*
> (Greenfeld, 1970, pp. 66–67)

Very little research has been done on how parents cope with these stresses. A study of parents whose children were in a preschool program found that some parents, especially those who were younger and less well educated, used religion as a coping device (Friedrich and others, 1986). These parents believed that "God specifically chose me to be the parent of this special child." This belief appeared to give them comfort and increase their feeling that things were under control. Another group of parents believed that they were in control of their lives and could deal with the situation. These parents tended to be older and better educated. The results of this study suggest that the belief that someone or some force is in control can be helpful in

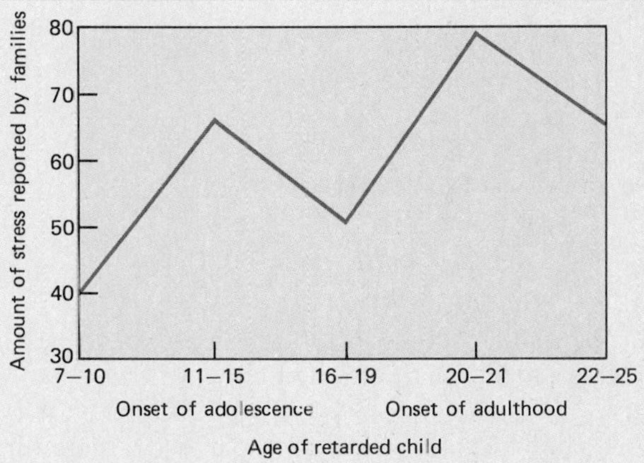

FIGURE 16–1
The amount of stress reported by families of retarded children varies with the age of the children. Developmental transitions seem to produce especially high levels of stress. (Wikler, 1986, p. 705)

withstanding the stress of having a retarded child. These feelings could be enhanced through support groups formed by the families themselves. Such groups could not only provide emotional support but increase feelings of control by sharing advice about parenting techniques and information about the availability of community facilities.

The brothers and sisters of retarded children may also be affected by the child's presence. Again, there has not been much research on these effects. What we do know suggests that the parents of a retarded child often place increased demands on their other children. They are expected to care for the retarded child and to subordinate their needs to those of their sibling. Their parents expect more of them and at the same time often have less time and attention to give them. These children sometimes feel pressure to excel in order to "make up" for their retarded sibling.

Much of the research on the effects of a retarded child on other family members was done some years ago, when many children were institutionalized, and in many cases there were no control groups. This is an area where more facts are needed. What is known at present is that, not surprisingly, the parents' attitudes toward the retarded child and their ways of dealing with the situation have an important effect on their other children's adjustment (Brody and Stoneman, 1984).

half of all autistic children do not develop speech at all. Even their babbling as infants is not intended as communication. If they do learn to talk, their speech is likely to be unusual. For instance, they may simply repeat what is said to them (**echolalia**) or repeat commercials they have heard on television. They also tend to reverse "you" and "I"; thus, when asking for a drink they might say "You want a drink" instead of "I want a drink." In addition, their tone of voice may be unusual—singsong or monotonous.

Autistic children have a very narrow range of interests and activities; they may spend a great deal of time spinning objects, flicking their fingers, or twisting or rocking their bodies (see Figure 16–3). Sameness and routine are very important. Moving a piece of furniture or changing the daily routine in any way can be terribly distressing to an autistic child.

As they grow older, autistic children may spend their time repetitively feeling or smelling objects or lining up items in a row. Bus timetables and the like may be fascinating to them and they sometimes spend hours studying such items. Because autistic children have a tremendous drive to carry out these fixations, the channeling of this behavior into somewhat similar productive activities has been suggested as a therapeutic approach by one woman who has successfully overcome most of her autistic symptoms (Grandin, 1987).

boo. As toddlers, they do not follow their parents around the house or run to meet them when they come home.

Communication impairment is even more dramatic than impaired social behavior in autism. About

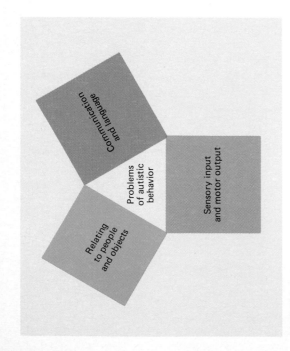

FIGURE 16–2
Problem areas of autistic behavior.

FIGURE 16–3
Autistic children perform many strange-appearing ritualistic behaviors such as repetitive body rocking and finger-flicking.

Prospects for Change

As with other children, the intelligence test scores of autistic children predict their school achievement, later occupations, and social status. One key predictor of later outcome is whether the child has developed fairly good language skills by the age of 5.

A follow-up study of children diagnosed as autistic at a Canadian regional research center several years earlier showed that more than half the children were being cared for in institutions, that most had experienced a persistence of symptoms, and that few were living independently or were capable of holding a job (Wolf and Goldberg, 1986). About 90 percent of the group was mentally retarded.

A few autistic children who have made a good adjustment later in life have written about their experiences and provided some insight into what it must feel like to be autistic.

Tony was referred to a children's clinic when he was 26 months old. He did not speak at all and he did not seem to respond to his parents or the clinic staff in the way a young child might be expected to do; instead he ignored their approaches. His parents said he had always seemed stiff and hard to hold, he never smiled back at them, and he spent most of his time spinning objects or watching his hands as he moved his fingers.

Tony spent several years in a therapeutic nursery school and by age 3 had learned to communicate although he was severely echolalic. By the time he was 6 his intelligence test score was just slightly below average. During high school he was very aware of his feelings of being different. He quit high school in 10th grade and joined the army but was quickly discharged for fighting. Then he worked as an assembler in a manufacturing plant. He tried to get a girlfriend, but had been unsuccessful. He said he has difficulties with anxiety, periodic overuse of alcohol, and unusual sensory experiences. This is a portion of what Tony wrote about himself:

"In school I learned some things very quickly but others were beyond learning comprehension. I used to disrupt the whole class and love to drive the teachers nuts. When I first started talking—5 years old—I started talking about an incident that happened a year before. I was obsessed with certain things and played in my own way. I make things with Garbage or Junk and Play with them. I like mechanical Battery Power toys or electronic toys. . . . IN tenth grade I quit school and worked washing cars and work(ed) many other Jobs too. I was very depressed and Hyper at work. I got along with my boss at all

my Jobs. I tend to get lazy and had trouble getting along with other people. So in (an) effort to keep my Jobs I avoided many people. I found It a lot easyer to get along with older people and FEARED People my age because of school. I went into the army and got in lots of Fights with people. So I got discarged (discharged). I also have great Troubl(l)e getting thing(s) organized and massunderstand almost everything.

"And had and still have some mental blocks and great difficulty paying attention and listening to people and was verry eas(i)ly distracted. I demanded to be amused by people and got board verry eas(i)ly and cant deal with stress. And had great difficulty fulfilling obligations. I would bear electronic Noises and have quick siezions (seizures) in bed and many other phh(y)sical problems. Often I have to be Force to get things done and (was) verry uncoordinated. And was verry Nervous about everything. And Feared People and Social Activity Greatly . . . I never got Fired from a job. My problems havn't changed at ALL from early childhood. I was Just able to Function. And it still (is) the same today."

— (Volkmar and Cohen, 1985)

Another person who was autistic in childhood but was above average in intelligence had fewer difficulties than Tony but still has some characteristics of autism:

I am now 36 years old and work as a consultant, designing livestock facilities for feedlots, ranches, and meat plants throughout the U.S. and abroad. I have also authored articles in both national and international livestock publications. At the present time I am doing research on animal behavior and neurophysiology and working on my doctorate in animal science at the University of Illinois. . . .

At the age of 1-1/2 to 3 I had many of the standard autistic behaviors such as fixation on spinning objects, refusing to be touched or held, preferring to be alone, destructive behavior, temper tantrums, inability to speak, sensitivity to sudden noises, appearance of deafness, and an intense interest in odors. . . .

At the age of 3 to 3-1/2 my behavior greatly improved, but I did not learn to speak until 3-1/2. At the age of 3 to 4 my behavior was more normal until I became tired. When I became tired, bouts of impulsive behavior would return. . . .

In college I was on the Dean's honor list, but getting through the foreign language requirement was difficult. I scraped by with Ds and Cs. Learning sequential things such as math was also very hard. My mind is completely visual and spatial work such as drawing is easy. I taught myself drafting in six months. I have designed big steel and concrete cattle facilities, but remembering a phone number or adding up numbers in my head is still difficult. I have to write them down. Every piece of information I have memorized is visual. If I have to remember an abstract concept I "see" the page of the book or my notes in my mind and "read" information from it. Melodies are the only things I can memorize without a visual image. I remember very little that I hear unless it is emotionally arousing or I can form a visual image. In class I take careful notes, because I would forget the auditory material. When I think about abstract concepts such as human relationships I use visual similes. For example, relationships between people are like a glass sliding door. The door must be opened gently, if it is kicked it may shatter. If I had to learn a foreign language, I would have to do it by reading, and make it visual

— (Grandin, 1984, pp. 144–145).

Successful adjustment is achieved by only a small proportion of autistic children. More typical is the case of Bruce:

During his preschool years he was involved in extensive therapy but he remained mute, bizarre, and socially isolated. During Bruce's school years no special program was available, so his mother took special courses to prepare herself to teach him. Through her efforts he learned about 100 words. He never used them voluntarily and relied on simple signs for communication.

At 20 Bruce is physically healthy. He remains mute, but does use signs to express his wishes. As a child, he had unusual skill at assembling puzzle pieces. He still has this ability which helps him in his prevocational training. If left alone he still rocks his body for hours and twirls objects in front of his face, much as he did when he was a preschooler.

— Adapted from Cohen and others, 1978, pp. 68–69)

Therapy

Behavior-modification programs have often been used with children who are severely autistic. These programs have shown promise in improving such children's language and self-help skills, which, in turn, improve their chances for social adjustment.

At the beginning of a behavior-modification program, it may take 15 to 30 minutes to get a correct response from the child, even for simple tasks such as looking at the instructor on command. Once the child can consistently follow simple commands, he or she may be asked to perform imitative behavior, first by following visual instructions (such as raising an arm when the instructor does) and then by following verbal instructions (such as raising an arm when the instructor asks for that movement). The entire program takes several hours a day for months at a time. For this reason, at least one parent is trained to work with the child between visits to a professional. As the child progresses, the parent takes over a great deal of the training.

Although they help autistic children with specific skills, behavioral approaches to autism have often met with limited success (Franks, 1985). One of the biggest problems is the child's inability to generalize the responses that have been learned to other situations.

One follow-up study of children who had participated in intensive behavioral training suggests that this type of treatment may be effective for a subgroup of autistic children (Lovaas, 1987). As preschoolers, the children were treated by trained therapists for 40 hours a week for at least 2 years. Their parents were also trained in the treatment procedures so that they could continue the treatment during all the child's waking hours. During the treatment each child's behavioral deficiencies were specifically targeted and special programs to accelerate development of each behavior were developed. Some of these are shown in Figure 16–4. The treatment procedure dealt with high rates of aggressive and self-stimulation behaviors in a graded series of methods. First these behaviors were ignored. If that did not reduce them a "time-out" procedure was used in which the activity was interrupted until the child's objectionable behaviors ceased. More acceptable forms of behavior were shaped as replacements. Finally, if these methods were ineffective, the therapist said "no" very loudly or gave the child a slap on the thigh while the undesirable behavior was going on. Despite a general reluctance to use physically aversive behavior, work on the project showed that this was an essential element in producing behavior change. Children who improved in the program were placed in regular preschool and primary school programs. The rate of improvement in the intensive therapy group was compared to that for a similar group of children who were given the same type of therapy only 10 hours a week and to that of a group treated in other programs. A comparison of the groups is shown in Figure 16–5. The results of this project suggest that intensive behavioral training may allow a subgroup of autistic children to reach an average level of functioning, and that this approach is superior to less intensive training and to the usual therapies that autistic children may receive.

Research on Autistic Disorder

Autism was first described by Leo Kanner, a child psychiatrist, in 1943. Kanner presented cases of children who exhibited a unique pattern of behavior in which

(a)

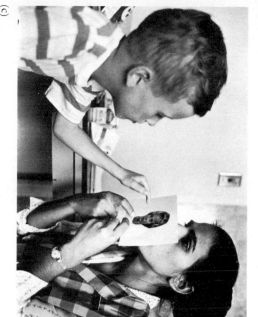

(b)

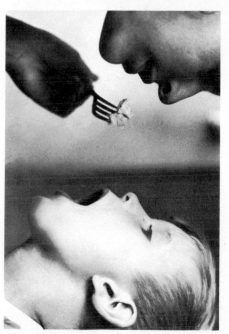

(c)

(d)

FIGURE 16–4
Autistic children receive special learning programs. (a) The therapist is hand-prompting a mute child to make the "wh" sound. (b) The therapist is using food as a reinforcer for attending to him and making eye contact. (c) The therapist is teaching a child to identify parts of the face from a picture after he has learned to name the parts from his face and hers. She uses verbal reinforcement. (d) Autistic children have difficulty playing with other children. The therapist is using food to reinforce joint play activity.

they were unable to relate in an ordinary way to people and situations from the beginning of life. In addition to this "extreme autistic aloneness," he stressed the children's "obsessive desire for the maintenance of sameness." Kanner thought of autism as a child psychosis and believed that most autistic children were basically very intelligent.

We now know that in the majority of cases autism is connected with global mental retardation. Although research on autism usually groups all autistic children together, such children seem to fall into at least two groups: those who are normal or near normal in intelligence and those who function at a retarded level (Prior, 1984). One important area for future research is the separate study of these two groups, which may be very different despite the similarities in their social functioning.

The Cognitive Perspective

A cognitive deficit seems to be central to autism. Most autistic children can see and hear normally, but they re-

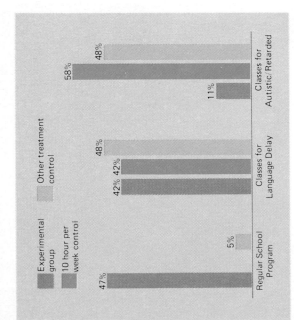

FIGURE 16-5
School placement at second grade for autistic children who were treated with an intensive behavioral therapy intervention during their preschool years compared to school placement of control groups. (Data from Lovaas, 1987. Copyright © 1987 by the American Psychological Association. Reprinted by permission of the author.)

Experimental group / Other treatment control / 10 hour per week control

Regular School Program: 47%, 42%, 5%
Classes for Language Delay: 42%, 48%, 42%, 11%
Classes for Autistic/Retarded: 58%, 48%

spond to sensory input in a distorted way. From a very early age they are either under- or overresponsive to all kinds of stimuli. Often both ways of responding can be seen in the same person. Some of the perceptual disturbances of autistic children seem to decrease with age, especially if the child responds well to treatment for the overall disorder, but there seems to be no doubt that early cognitive development in autistic children is abnormal.

The most universal symptom of autistic disorder is language disturbance. More than half of all autistic children remain mute, and for those who do speak, specific aspects of language disorder remain. The "I" and "you" reversal is characteristic of autistic speech. Another characteristic is **echolalia** in which the child simply echoes or repeats all or part of what has been said to him or her. Both the language and manner of speaking of autistic children seems mechanical and monotonous.

Autistic children have problems with the social aspects of language, too. Even those who function well have difficulty initiating conversations or maintaining them. The usual kinds of expressions people use for these things "Speaking of" or "By the way" don't seem to be easy for autistic people to use. They also have trouble in social situations because they seem generally oblivious of their impact on others.

Another indication of the cognitive difficulties of autistic children is their lack of development of symbolic play (Konstantareas, 1986). Using a stick for a horse or a big box for a playhouse are examples of symbolic play,

which usually develops in normal children by about 21 months of age and becomes elaborated as they grow older. At least half of autistic children show a complete absence of symbolic play.

The cognitive problems of autistic children don't seem to be a function of poor memory. Autistic children's short-term recall is not deficient. For instance, when asked to repeat strings of words, autistic children can repeat random meaningless strings as well as they could meaningful sentences. In general, research on cognition suggests that, while their basic input and simple memory may not be impaired, autistic individuals have a problem with higher-level cognitive processing in which stimuli are organized by meaning. Autistic children have more problems with symbolic thought than with real-life examples. For instance, one group did better at puzzles that required thinking about alternatives if the material they used was three-dimensional (colored wooden shapes) instead of two-dimensional (line drawings) (Prior and McGillivray, 1980). These cognitive deficiencies are probably related to the absence of symbolic or representational play in autistic children (Wulff, 1985).

The Biological Perspective

Because of the pattern of cognitive disabilities in autism, researchers have focused on problems in the left hemisphere of the brain, where language and symbolic material are assumed to be processed.

The cognitive problems, especially the language problems, of autistic children seem different from those that occur in either left-hemisphere or bilateral damage to the brain. It has been suggested that these problems are caused by early damage to the limbic system, which then affects other parts of the nervous system (Prior, 1984). Another possibility is that the symptoms of autism can be explained in terms of a dysfunction of behavioral systems in the brain stem that is further distorted by the functioning of the midbrain and the cortex (Ornitz, 1985).

Some kind of brain pathology seems likely in autistic individuals, since at least one-fifth of autistic children develop epileptic seizures in adolescence (Deykin and MacMahon, 1979). The risk of seizures is much greater for those who are severely retarded than for those who are not. Some kind of brain injury at or after birth is also a possibility. In a study of 17 sets of identical twins in which only one of each twin pair was autistic, 12 of the affected twins probably had experienced brain damage (for example, from convulsions shortly after birth) (Folstein and Rutter, 1977).

So far there have been no specific findings in either brain anatomy or brain biochemistry that differentiate autistic individuals from other groups (Rumsey and others, 1985). PT scans of a group of autistic adults show a higher rate of glucose metabolisim than that found in a group of normal subjects, but there is a large overlap between the two groups. Differences in neurotransmitter activity has also been investigated with conflicting results (Yuwiler and Freedman, 1987).

Some researchers have wondered about the possibility that there is a hereditary factor in autism. Autism is a rare disorder, and autistic individuals rarely marry and have children. Hence, a family history of autism would not be expected. However, research has turned up some findings that suggest a genetic link. Two percent of the brothers and sisters of autistic children are also autistic. Although this percent is low, it is 50 times greater than would be expected by chance (Rutter, 1967). Moreover, a family history of delayed speech is much more common in families of a child who is autistic (25 percent of all of the families) than in the average family (Bartak and others, 1975). Another clue comes from the finding that when one of a set of twins was autistic the probability that the other twin would also be autistic was greatly affected by whether the twins were monozygotic or dizygotic (see Figure 16–6). Knowledge about the genetics of autism suggests that what is inherited is probably not autism but some general tendency to have language or cognitive abnormalities (Rutter and Garmezy, 1983).

It has also been suggested that the parents of autistic children share HLA antigens (human leukocyte antigens). Antigens are substances that stimulate the production of antibodies in the blood. The antibodies are blood proteins that are generated by the immune system and protect a person against specific microorganisms or toxins in the blood. When antigens of the parents are the same, this may increase the likelihood that

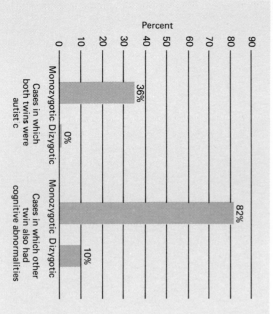

FIGURE 16–6
Differences between monozygotic and dizygotic twin pairs in which at least one twin is autistic.

the unborn child will be attacked by its mother's immune system (Stubbs and others, 1985). A finding supporting this idea is that mothers of autistic children report a greater frequency of both spontaneous abortions and bleeding during pregnancy; these may be due in part to immune system attacks. Although this idea is still somewhat speculative, comparison of HLA antigen samples from parents of autistic children with samples from parents who did not have an autistic child showed the predicted differences. Seventy-five percent of the parents of autistic children shared antigens, but only 25 percent of the control parents did so.

Another area of research focuses on whether prenatal illness of the mother or other prenatal, birth-injury, or postnatal factors are related to autism. So far there has been a variety of findings about these relationships, but no single variable accounts for a large proportion of cases of autism or distinguish between autistic children and controls (Tsai, 1987).

Autism versus Childhood Schizophrenia

Although autism was originally thought of as a psychosis, it is now considered to be a developmental disorder. However, psychosis can occur in children, and some childhood psychosis may be the same disorder as schizophrenia in adults. Childhood schizophrenia is even rarer than autism and much rarer than schizophrenia in adulthood. It is not clear whether schizophrenia that occurs before age 15 has the same consequences and outcome as schizophrenia in adulthood; however, the symptoms are similar and include hallucinations, bizarre fantasies, ideas of being controlled by others, and paranoid ideas (Beitchman, 1983).

MENTAL RETARDATION

Mental retardation means a significantly below-average level of intellectual functioning as measured by an individually administered intelligence test. To be classified as mentally retarded, a person's social as well as intellectual functioning must be impaired (see Figure 16–7).

Mental retardation is regarded as a chronic, irreversible condition that begins before the age of 18. If intellectual functioning drops to retarded levels after age 18, the problem is classified as a dementia rather than mental retardation.

Although many children with autistic disorder are also retarded, there are several differences between autism and retardation.

Mild Retardation: Alice is 16 and has been in special classes since preschool. She can feed and dress herself well, but she needs help in deciding on appropriate clothes to wear. She can write simple letters and use the telephone. She can carry on an ordinary conversation, but she does not seem aware of important current events and is unable to talk or write about abstractions. She rides a bicycle and seems well coordinated. She can find her way around her neighborhood but can't go farther without aid. She can cook simple meals and go shopping for specific items by herself.

Moderate Retardation: Bob, age 17, has been in a special-educational program since he was 6. He can dress himself but needs to be checked over to be sure he is completely dressed before going out. He can go to a nearby store by himself but cannot tell if he has been given the correct change. He cannot take buses alone. In his group home he makes his bed, helps set the table, and sweeps the floor. He works in a sheltered workshop stuffing envelopes. His speech is barely understandable, but he responds to directions and requests.

Severe Retardation: Jason, age 21, has been in educational programs since he was 6. He can feed himself with a spoon and can dress himself if the clothing is not too difficult to get on. He gets lost if he goes more than a block from home. He can talk, but his speech is repetitive and his vocabulary small. He enjoys going to the store with others but has no concept of making purchases. He cannot select three objects from a group. Jason has been enrolled in two different shelter workshop programs but has been unable to learn the job routine.

Profound Retardation: Peggy is 30. She has been slow in development since birth and has been in a special educational program since preschool. She cannot dress herself completely. She can use a spoon but not a knife and fork. She does not interact much with other people except by smiling or laughing; she does not talk. She can respond to simple commands like "Come here" and to her name. She spends a great deal of time rocking her body back and forth. Although she likes TV, she pays attention for only brief periods and seems to be watching only the movements.

Mental retardation has many causes, but these may be grouped into two general categories: psychosocial reasons and nonenvironmental factors. Retarded children who are also **psychosocially disadvantaged** may show no specific disabilities but may resemble their parents in intellectual achievement. They are likely to experience little intellectual stimulation in their environment, receive poor medical care, and have unhealthful

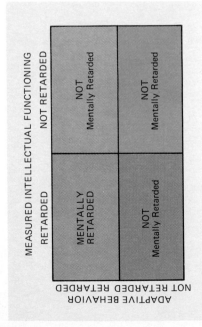

FIGURE 16-7
Only people who are significantly below average in both intellectual functioning and adaptive behavior are classified as mentally retarded.

1. Retarded children may have a cognitive development that is equal to their social development. In autism the child's social development is always lower than the cognitive development.

2. Retarded children show delays in language but autistic children show severe language deficits and more language deviance.

3. Self-stimulation, preoccupation by visual and auditory stimuli, and bizarre behaviors like spinning objects and flapping and twirling the body are common in autism but not in retardation.

4. Retarded children are motivated to please adults, but autistic children are not concerned about their impact on others.

Degrees of Mental Retardation

There are four categories of mental retardation based on intelligence-test scores: *mild, moderate, severe,* and *profound* (see Table 16–1). The following cases illustrate these categories and Table 16–2 summarizes the characteristics of each group.

TABLE 16-1

Levels of Mental Retardation

	IQ	Percent of All Retardation
Mild mental retardation	50–70	85%
Moderate mental retardation	35–49	10%
Severe mental retardation	20–34	4%
Profound mental retardation	Below 20	Less than 1%

TABLE 16-2

Behavior of Retarded Individuals at Various Stages of Development[1]

Level of Retardation	Highest Level of Adaptive Behavior		
	3 Years of Age	9 Years of Age	15 Years of Age and Over
Profound	Drinks from a cup with help, sits unsupported or pulls self up, imitates sounds, repeats Ma-Ma. Indicates knowing familiar people and interacts with them nonverbally.	Tried to feed self but spills, can pull off pants and socks, walks alone, uses 4–10 words, may play with others briefly.	Feeds self, can dress except for small buttons and zippers; toilet trained but may have accidents. Can climb steps and throw a ball. Vocabulary of up to 300–400 words and uses grammatically correct sentences or if nonverbal may use gestures for communication. Understands simple questions and directions. Participates in simple group games.
Severe	Feed self with finger foods. Can remove clothes, but often does so inappropriately, stands alone or walks unsteadily. Says 1 or 2 words, plays "patty cake" or with toys.	Feeds self with spoon. May be messy. Drinks unassisted. May indicate need for toilet, runs and jumps. Speaks 2–3 word sentences. Interacts with others in simple play.	Feeds self adequately with spoon and fork, can dress with zippers and buttons, is toilet trained. Can run, go up and down stairs alternating feet. May communicate in complex sentences, participates in group activities, does simple tasks and errands.
Moderate	Tries to feed self but spills, can pull off pants and socks, walks alone, uses 4–10 words, may play with others briefly.	Feeds self, can dress except for small buttons and zippers, toilet trained but may have accidents. Can climb steps and throw a ball. Vocabulary of up to 300–400 words and uses grammatically correct sentences or if nonverbal may use gestures for communication. Understands simple questions and directions. Participates in simple group games.	Feeds, bathes, and dresses self. Selects daily clothing, can wash and iron own clothes, good body control, can carry on simple conversation and can interact cooperatively with others. Can go on errand without a list. Can assume responsibility for simple household tasks.
Mild	Feeds self with spoon. May be messy. Drinks unassisted. May indicate need for toilet, runs and jumps. Speaks 2–3 word sentences. Interacts with others in simple play.	Feeds self adequately with spoon and fork, can dress with zippers and buttons, is toilet trained. Can run, go up and down stairs alternating feet. May communicate in complex sentences, participates in group activities, does simple tasks and errands.	Cares for own personal grooming, sometimes with reminders. Can go around own neighborhood easily. Carries on everyday conversation. Writes simple letters and uses telephone. Can go shopping, prepare simple meals and initiate most of own activities.

[1]Areas of the same color describe identical behavior. This illustrates how the same behaviors appear at different ages depending on the level of retardation.

diets and living conditions. Thus, their heredity and/or environmental experiences may cause their intelligence test scores to fall in the lower end of the distribution.

For a long time it has been thought that most mild mental retardation was usually explained by this combination of heredity and environmental conditions. In contrast, lower intelligence scores—those in moderate, severe, and profound retardation levels were thought to be the result of some kind of pathology— disease, injury, chromosomal abnormality, or specific genetic disorder. Modern epidemiological research has cast doubt on this theory. Studies of the Swedish population show that at least half and often a much greater proportion of mildly retarded people in the population had some chromosomal defect, specific genetic disease, or retardation that was associated with some specific pre- or postnatal disease or injury (Akesson, 1986). This suggests that such factors play a role at all levels of re-

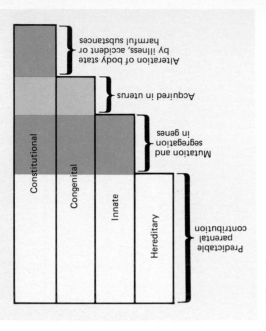

FIGURE 16–9
Definitions of nonenvironmental contributors to psychopathology.

tardation. However, it is also true that compared to people in other retarded groups those in the mildly retarded group are more likely to have family members who also fall in the mildly retarded category. For instance, the IQ scores of the brothers and sisters of one group of retarded children were measured. None of the siblings of the severely retarded children were retarded, but 20 percent of the siblings of mildly retarded children were also retarded (see Figure 16–8). These findings indicate that although there is some overlap, mild and severe cases of mental retardation probably have different causes.

Biological Causes

Whenever nonenvironmental causes of retardation are discussed, a number of overlapping terms are used. Figure 16–9 explains the differences among these terms. The predictable gene-based qualities that are transmitted from the parents to the children are **hereditary.** However, some of the genes available at the moment of conception are not quite like those of either parent and are called **mutants.** In addition, in polygenic disorders such as schizophrenia, each nonaffected parent may contribute enough pathologically related genes so that together these genes move the child over the threshold from nondisordered to disordered.

Disorders caused by mutations, superthreshold doses of affected genes, and disorders caused by predictable parental contribution are all referred to as **innate.** In addition, certain disorders can be acquired in the uterus, for example, as a result of chemical substances passed to the child through the mother's placenta. These factors, together with the innate factors mentioned above, make up what are called **congenital** factors. **Constitutional** factors include both innate and congenital factors and also factors that are due to illness or injury after birth.

FIGURE 16–8
IQ distribution for siblings of severely retarded (IQ less than 50) and mildly retarded (IQ 50–69) white children. (Nichols, 1984, p. 163)

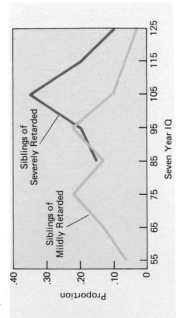

Hereditary Disorders

Some disorders are caused by specific genes that have been identified. If the disorder is caused by a dominant gene, only one gene of that particular gene pair needs to be affected to produce the disorder. In contrast, in recessive disorders, both members of the gene pair must be affected.

Disorders Caused by Specific Dominant Genes

The number of known dominant genes that cause severe retardation is small because people who are affected by these disorders do not usually have children. Often a mutation, or spontaneous variation in a gene, seems to be responsible for the first case of a dominant gene disorder recognized in a family. In many of these disorders the symptoms do not become apparent immediately after birth. An example of such a disorder is **tuberous sclerosis.** In addition to severe retardation and seizures, this condition produces small fibrous tumors, often beside the nose, as well as internal tumors and skin abnormalities. The seizures may not begin until the child is 3, and the tumors may not appear until several years later. In some mild cases the tumors appear but retardation may be minimal or absent.

Disorders Caused by Specific Recessive Genes

A parent may carry only one recessive gene in a particular gene pair without showing symptoms of the problem transmitted by the gene. If both parents carry the same recessive gene, one in four of their children may be affected by the problem and two in four may become carriers like their parents. Many of these inherited problems involve disorders of the metabolism, or the way the body utilizes various chemicals.

Phenylketonuria (PKU) is a disorder in which the body is unable to oxidize the chemical phenylalanine, which therefore accumulates in the body. If this accumulation is allowed to continue, severe mental retardation may result. Very few untreated PKU victims have IQs above 50. If treatment, which involves a restrictive diet, is started early, most of these changes can be prevented, although earlier damage cannot be reversed. Children who received treatment at an early age are usually in the normal range on intelligence tests and neurological examinations, although they score lower on intelligence tests than their siblings did at comparable ages.

Newborn infants can be tested for PKU although, because only 1 in 17,000 children has PKU, the costs of such testing are high per case actually identified. However, the costs of caring for the retarded are also high. In one program the saving from detecting and treating each infant with PKU and thus preventing retardation was over $200,000 (Barden and others, 1984).

Before treatment for PKU was developed most people who had PKU did not reproduce. Now that treatment has saved them from retardation, PKU women are more likely to have children and these children are likely to be retarded. The retardation does not arise from a particular pair of recessive genes but instead comes from the environmental characteristics within the mother's uterus. A high phenylalanine level in the uterus is almost certain to result in severe fetal brain damage. This problem may be avoided or the risk decreased if the PKU mother follows the special diet designed to control blood phenylalanine level.

A lifelong adherence to this diet may be a good idea. It had been thought that children with PKU could go off their special diet when they became adults, but it is now known that change to a normal diet has negative long-term effects (Matthews and others, 1986). Adults who go off the diet may develop problems with short-term memory, coordination, and ability to concentrate. Based on this research, teaching dietary management beginning in early childhood can prevent retardation in the next generation (see Figure 16-10a and b).

Tay-Sachs disease, another inherited metabolic disorder, is inevitably fatal. This condition, which is

FIGURE 16-10a and b.
Young children with PKU can be taught how to select foods low in protein and phenylalanine (phe) that are safe for them to eat. Figure 16-10a shows a page from a parents' manual that illustrates a teaching game. Figure 16-10b shows a page from a pamphlet that parents can leave with a babysitter to explain what foods are safe. (Adapted from Trahms and others, 1987).

FISHING for FRUIT

For ages 2 1/2 to 6 years

Objective: To learn the names of fruit (and other foods) and to recognize them as yes or no foods.

Materials: One small magnet, stick or dowel about two feet long, magazines, cardboard, scissors, paperclips and a string about three feet long.

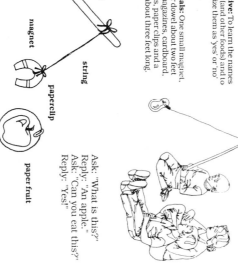

stick

string

magnet

paperclip

paper fruit

Ask: "What is this?"
Reply: "An apple."
Ask: "Can you eat this?"
Reply: "Yes!"

(a)

Method: Cut pictures of fruit from magazines and paste on cardboard. Cut the cardboard to fit the shape of the fruit. Put a paperclip on each item of fruit. Tie the string to one end of the stick, at the other tie a small magnet.

Put the pictures in a big pan or bathtub and have the child 'fish' for the fruit. Other foods can be included in this game, too.

(b) what if the child is extra hungry?

There are foods this child can eat that contain very little or no protein and phe. They are called "free foods" and may be used as needed to satisfy hunger. Some free foods are:

apples, apple juice.

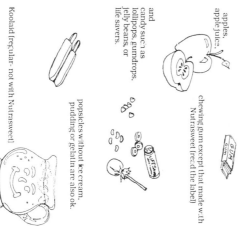

chewing gum except that made with Nutrasweet (red the label)

and candy such as lollipops, gumdrops, jelly beans, or life savers.

popsicles without ice cream, pudding or gelatin are also ok.

Koolaid (regular- not with Nutrasweet).

Tell mom and dad what you gave their child. Remember, they must know exactly what their child eats.

caused by a recessive gene, occurs most often in Ashkenazi Jews whose ancestors came from a small area in Eastern Europe. It causes progressive degeneration of the nervous system, degeneration of the brain, and death, usually before the age of 4.

Disorders Carried by the Sex Cells

Every person has one chromosome pair that determines his or her sex. A woman has a pair of X chromosomes, one inherited from each parent. A man has one X chromosome inherited from his mother and one Y chromosome inherited from his father. If an abnormality occurs in this chromosome pair, called the sex cells, it does not always produce defects as severe as those produced by abnormalities in the nonsex chromosomes or **autosomes**. When an abnormality affects the **autosomes,** mental retardation is almost always present.

One abnormality of the sex cells is called **Fragile X Syndrome.** It is the second-most common identifiable cause of mental retardation in males. The most common is Down syndrome, which we will discuss in the next section. Fragile X syndrome is estimated to account for up to 10 percent of all mental retardation (Rogers and Simensen, 1987). This syndrome usually results in severe to profound retardation, although some of those affected are only mildly retarded. Autistic behaviors and speech problems are often seen in people who have Fragile X syndrome (Brown and others,

1986; Hanson and others, 1986). Men who have this syndrome are more likely than women to be severely retarded. Because the Fragile X syndrome is transmitted through the X chromosome, men must inherit the disease from their mothers. If only one of a woman's X chromosomes is affected by the Fragile X syndrome the woman may or may not be retarded herself, but she may be a carrier who can transmit the problem to her children. In four generations of one family that was studied the great grandmother was a carrier of the disorder (see Figure 16–11). In the 40 people who were in the next three generations of her family, there were 7 men with Fragile X syndrome, 6 women who were carriers and passed the disorder on to their children, and 9 other women who were potential carriers but who had not yet given birth to a child with the syndrome. Several of these female carriers were at least mildly retarded.

Disorders Due to Mutation

More than half of the children who are severely or profoundly retarded have genetic disorders that are not transmitted directly through specific dominant or recessive genes. About one-third have single-gene mutations and most of the remainder have chromosomal abnormalities. **Chromosomal abnormality** actually occurs in about 10 percent of all conceptions. However, since most of these abnormal fetuses are naturally aborted

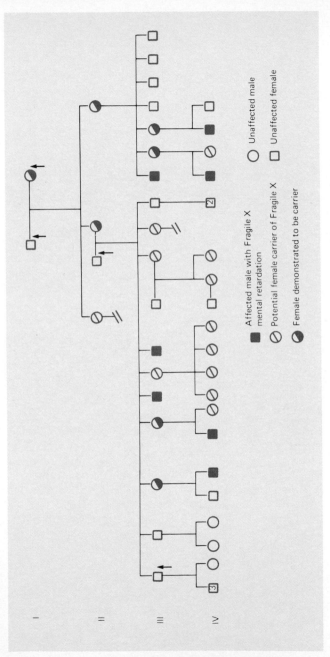

FIGURE 16–11
A partial family tree showing the inheritance of Fragile X syndrome over four generations. (Adapted from Saul, R. A., Stevenson, R. I., Simensen, R. J., Wilkes, G., Alexander, W., and Taylor, H.: Fragile X Syndrome in South Carolina, in the *Journal of the South Carolina Medical Association,* 78, p. 476, 1982.)

through miscarriage; only about 1.5 percent of all newborns have such a problem.

Down Syndrome

The most frequent chromosomal abnormality is **Down syndrome**, which occurs about once in every 800 births.

Characteristics of Down Syndrome.
Children who are affected by Down syndrome have many characteristic physical features that make this disorder easy to recognize. Some of the most striking physical features are a flat face and a small nose, eyes that appear to slant upward because of small folds of skin at the inside corners, slightly protruding lips and tongue, small ears, and small square hands with short fingers and a curved fifth finger. Children with Down syndrome tend to be shorter than average, with especially short arms and legs in proportion to their bodies. They also are likely to be somewhat obese in childhood and adolescence. In addition to being retarded, such a child is likely to have a congenital heart abnormality.

Children with Down syndrome have about a 99-percent chance of being retarded. There is considerable variability in the level of retardation, which may range from mild to severe. In general, Down children seem especially weak in tactile perception, higher-level abstraction and reasoning, and auditory perception.

Programs to provide increased stimulation to very young Down syndrome children have attempted to modify the typical downward trend of developmental progress. Intervention often begins a few days after birth with physical-therapy programs. Programs for young children provide a variety of activities to help develop both physical and cognitive skills (see Figure 16–12). Parents are also trained to take part in activities to stimulate their children.

As infants, Down syndrome children explore their environment in the same ways that other children do (MacTurk and others, 1985). During the preschool period, their development, although slower than that of nonhandicapped children, seems to follow a similar pattern. One difference is that these children show less exploration behavior and are not as active in investigating their surroundings. Through their childhood and adolescence, Down syndrome children have poorer muscle tone and coordination than other children (Morris and others, 1982). As a result, they are less active, carry out tasks more slowly, and have poorer balance than other children (Kanimura and Kusano, 1981). As Down syndrome children reach school age their delays in physical and cognitive development begin to cause more problems (Hartley, 1986). Deficits in short-term memory often mean that information overload occurs and this can result in poor performance. Auditory memory is espe-

cially poor, making the child less able to learn from verbal information (Varnhagen and others, 1987). Other problems of Down children which can be major hindrances in pursuing a normal life are inability to comprehend instructions, to pay attention to several things at once, and to express clearly what they are thinking or what they need. Often even older Down syndrome children use a kind of telegraphic speech in which connecting words like "and" or "but" and other words such as prepositions and adverbs are missing. Such a teenager might say "Cat. Jump. Roof. Tree," instead of "The cat jumped off the roof and into the tree." Because Down syndrome children often learn better by seeing material rather than hearing it, some researchers have tried using computers to improve this telegraphic speech (see Figure 16–13). Teenagers were able to improve their language structure by using special computers that read back what they wrote. One boy, who before the project could only describe his father who had recently died by saying, "Dad. Talk. Down. Boom," was able to write: "My father and I went to his office. We would eat lunch and drink Diet 7-Up. I love you, Dad" (Kolata, 1987). Such efforts cannot cure the retardation of Down syndrome people, but can help them function more effectively.

The average adolescent or adult with Down syndrome has the abilities of a young child. Mental development for people with Down syndrome can continue into their thirties and forties if they are in a stimulating environment (Berry and others, 1984). However, for many such people aging appears to occur early and brings with it a decrease in cognitive abilities. This may occur because their brains contain fewer neurons than the average, with the result that the normal loss of neurons with aging affects them with unusual severity. Re-

FIGURE 16–12
Enrichment activities for young Down syndrome children may help them achieve far more as they grow older than would have been previously expected.

searchers have discovered that the brains of young adults with Down syndrome tend to show plaques and tangles that appear similar although not identical to those found in Alzheimer's disease (see Figure 16–14). As in Alzheimer's disease, these changes seem to be concentrated in the hippocampus, the area of the brain that plays a selective role in learning and memory. About 25 to 40 percent of Down syndrome adults actually become demented, that is, lose their memories and the ability to care for themselves.

Causes of Down Syndrome.   In most cases Down syndrome results from the presence of an extra chromosome: there are three number-21 chromosomes instead of the usual two. For this reason, Down syndrome is also called **trisomy 21** (Figure 16–15a). The trisomy usually results from a mistake in the cell division of either the egg or the sperm and occurs by accident. In a

FIGURE 16–13

The use of computers may be a way to help Down syndrome adolescents overcome some of their problems in expressing their thoughts. Here, Christine, a 13-year-old, is using a computer to write more eloquently about her thoughts than she can say them. She wrote the poetic statement, "I like God's finest whispers."

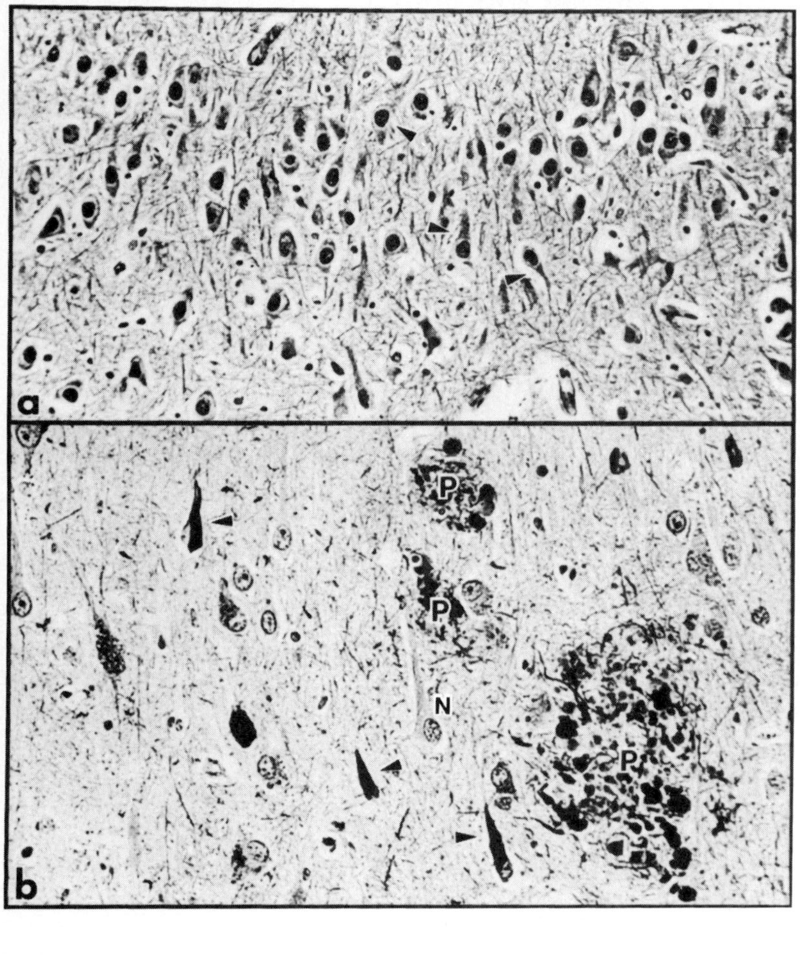

FIGURE 16–14

Almost all adults with Down syndrome who live to be 30 or older develop brain lesions like those seen in patients with Alzheimer's disease. Only a minority of the Down syndrome group become demented as Alzheimer's patients do. Photo (a) shows brain tissue from a normal adult. The neurons are marked with arrows. Photo (b) shows brain tissue from an adult with Down syndrome. Arrows show neurons with neurofibrillary tangles. Plaques are marked with a P and normal neurons with an N.

few cases Down syndrome is produced by the process of translocation. **Translocation** occurs when a chromosome breaks off and attaches itself to a different chromosome (see Figure 16-15b). A parent can carry a translocation without showing symptoms of Down syndrome because the correct amount of genetic material is there even though it is out of place. But if the parent passes on both the normal chromosome 21 and the translocated parts of chromosome 21 to a child, the child will end up with too much genetic material for chromosome 21 just as in the case of the trisomy 21

process. Mosaicism is another, very rare, cause of Down syndrome. **Mosaicism** means that not all the cells in a person's body have the same chromosome count. For example, some cells might have 46 chromosomes and some cells 47. Mosaicism is not transmitted from a parent, instead it results from an error in cell division in the fertilized egg. Infants who have mosaic Down syndrome may have only some of the characteristic features of the disorder because only some of their cells have an abnormal number of chromosomes.

The risk of having a child with Down syndrome

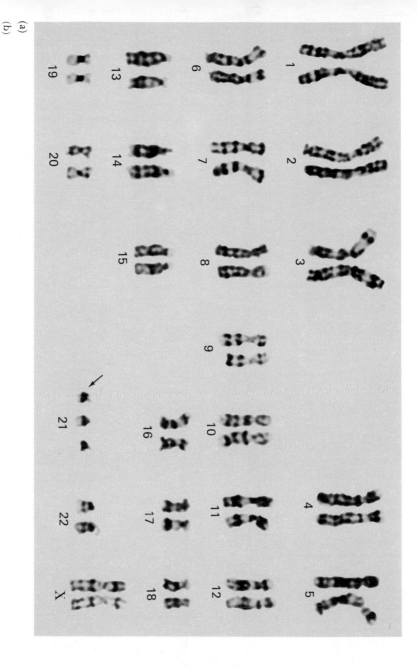

(a)

(b)

FIGURE 16-15a and b.
Chromosomal abnormalities are detected with relatively high frequency. Many human fetuses abort spontaneously because of chromosomal abnormalities. The most common abnormality in children who are born alive is trisomy 21, which causes Down syndrome. In more than 95 percent of Down syndrome cases there are 47 chromosomes, with 3, rather than 2, twenty-first chromosomes. In a few other cases there are only 46 chromosomes but one member of the number 21 chromosome pair is defective. Photo 16-15a shows the chromosomal analysis of a girl with Down syndrome. Trisomic chromosome 21 is indicated by the arrow. The drawing in Figure 16-15b illustrates the process by which a chromosome translocation takes place. This "translocation chromosome" has been formed by the breaking and rejoining of chromosomes 14 and 21 (with loss of the little pieces). (Adapted from Facts about Down Syndrome, U.S. Dept. of Health & Human Services, 1984)

The chances of giving birth to a child with Down syndrome increases dramatically with the age at which a woman becomes pregnant (see Figure 16-16). It is not clear why age of the mother has this effect. It might be that since women are born with all the **oocytes** (eggs) they will ever have, the eggs of an older mother may have passed their prime because of aging. Another possibility is that the eggs have been damaged over the years by such influences as medication, radiation, or other harmful substances in the environment. It was thought that the age of the mother was the only important factor. Recently, however, researchers have demonstrated that in about 25 percent of the cases the father is the source of the extra chromosome. Since older fathers also seem to increase the child's risk for other genetic disorders, researchers are now looking at what factors related to the father's age might produce Down syndrome. Because men's supply of sperm is renewed continually unlike women's egg supply, the answer does not seem to be in the aging of the genetic material itself.

Amniocentesis

In addition to Down syndrome, there are other trisomies that are related to retardation: **trisomy 13** and **trisomy 18**. These conditions, which are much rarer than Down syndrome, cause more severe retardation and a shorter life expectancy. The parents of an infant with any of these trisomies face an increased risk of trisomy in future pregnancies.

Help is available for parents who believe their unborn child is at risk for trisomy or a disorder caused by dominant or recessive genes. For a number of years **sonograms** or **ultrasound scans,** which shows the fetus on a TV screen, and **amniocentesis,** an analysis of the am-

niotic fluid inside the amniotic sac surrounding the infant, have helped to detect the presence of Down syndrome and other genetic defects including some inherited disorders (see Figure 16-17). Amniocentesis cannot be used until about the fourth month of pregnancy and the cells must be cultured for 2 weeks after the test, so the pregnancy is well advanced before the result is known. This means that if the tests show a defect in the fetus and the parents decide on an abortion, the advanced pregnancy makes this procedure physically and emotionally difficult.

Amniocentesis may be suggested if the risk of a retarded or otherwise genetically damaged child is high—for example, if the mother is over 35 or if there is another child with genetic problems in the family. The results, together with information about the parents' genetic history, are used to counsel parents regarding the probable outcome of the pregnancy. Given this knowledge, the prospective parents can decide to terminate the pregnancy, or they can prepare themselves for the birth of a child with a specific problem. In the majority of cases the procedure reveals that the fetus does not have the defect, and the parents are spared months of needless anxiety.

A newly developed procedure, **chorionic villus sampling** is an alternative to amniocentesis and can be performed after only 9 weeks of pregnancy. In this test, cells are taken from the hairlike projections (**villi**) on the gestational sac that surrounds the fetus early in pregnancy (see Figure 16-18). Test results are available in only a few days. Both amniocentesis and chorionic villi sampling can be carried out by using a needle inserted in the pregnant woman's abdomen, or the chorionic test can be done with a tube inserted into the cervix. One danger of amniocentesis has been that between one-half and 1 percent of the tests are followed by a miscarriage, so their use involves some risk to the infant. The chorionic test may have a larger miscarriage rate, about 1.9 percent. However, miscarriages also occur naturally as pregnancy progresses so some part of this increased risk might be explained by a miscarriage which would have occurred even if the chorionic procedure had not been used.

Another new test, the **alpha-feroprotein** test, requires only a blood sample at the end of the fourth month of pregnancy. It can indicate not only possible genetic disorders such as Down syndrome but also neural tube defects such as **anencephaly,** in which the baby is born with a rudimentary brain or no brain at all, and **spina bifida** in which a portion of the spine does not close and the nerve column is exposed. The bodies of children with spina bifida are partially paralyzed. The degree of paralysis depends on how high up on the spine the nerves are exposed. The alpha-feroprotein blood test is not conclusive, so if the test is positive the

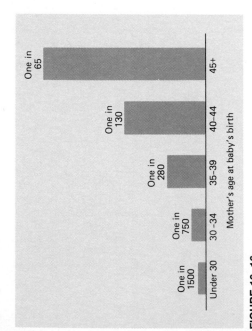

FIGURE 16-16
The chances of giving birth to a child with Down syndrome increases as the mother's age increases. (Smith and Wilson, 1973, p. 17)

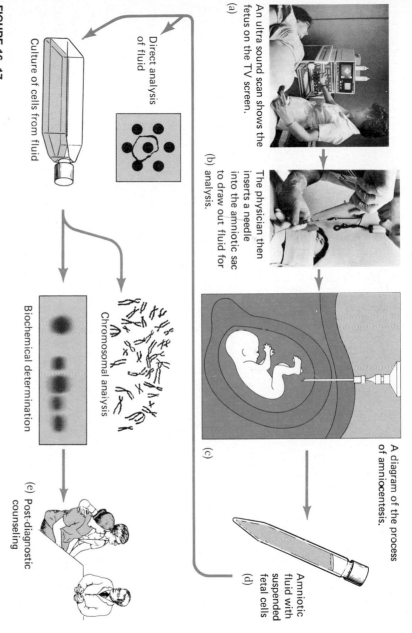

(a) An ultra sound scan shows the fetus on the TV screen.

(b) The physician then inserts a needle into the amniotic sac to draw out fluid for analysis.

(c) A diagram of the process of amniocentesis.

(d) Amniotic fluid with suspended fetal cells

Direct analysis of fluid

Culture of cells from fluid

Biochemical determination

Chromosomal analysis

(e) Post-diagnostic counseling

FIGURE 16–17

The process of amniocentesis: (a) An ultrasound scan shows the fetus on the TV screen. (b) The physician then inserts a needle into the amniotic sac to draw out fluid for analysis. (c) A diagram of the process of amniocentesis. (d) Amniotic fluid with suspended fetal cells; direct analysis of fluid; culture of cells from fluid; chromosomal analysis; biochemical determination. (e) Postdiagnostic counseling.

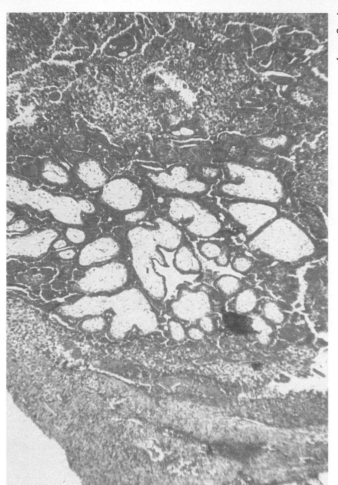

FIGURE 16–18

Sampling the chorionic villi is a technique that can detect some genetic disorders early in pregnancy.

pregnant woman needs a sonogram and perhaps an amniocentesis as well.

Although these tests can save heartbreak for parents if a defect is detected, they may cause an unneeded risk for the fetus if the test shows no disorder to be present. They may also pose a difficult decision for couples who do not believe in abortion. The use of these tests is growing rapidly, however, in part because of fears by physicians of legal liability if the tests are not offered and the child has a birth defect.

Disorders Caused by Prenatal Environment

The environment in which the fetus lives before birth is a frequent cause of below-average intellectual functioning. In fact, mental retardation of prenatal origin is the most common of all birth defects. Prenatal factors that have been linked to mental retardation include maternal infections, blood incompatibilities and chronic maternal conditions, chemicals in the fetal environment, radiation, malnutrition, the age of the parents, and maternal stress.

Maternal Infections

The placental sac surrounding the unborn infant acts as a barrier that prevents many infections from being transferred from the mother to the fetus, but a number of viruses may cross this barrier. Three viruses that are known to cause congenital malformations are **rubella virus** (German measles), **cytomegalovirus,** and **herpes virus hominus (herpes simplex).**

About half of all fetuses whose mothers contract rubella in the first 3 months of pregnancy are also infected. The virus destroys cells and may interfere with the fetal blood supply. In one group of children of mothers who had rubella, about one-third were retarded (Chess, 1978). Retardation can also result if the mother had a bacterial infection such as syphilis or a chronic viral illness like herpes. Syphilis in the mother causes miscarriages and stillbirths as well as mental retardation, blindness, deafness, and other birth defects. Herpes infections in adults and older children are usually quite mild, but in a fetus or newborn child the same virus can cause widespread infection that can result in death. Although the herpes virus can pass through the placenta and infect the fetus, the most common way in which herpes is passed from mother to child is through direct contact during the birth process.

Rubella can be controlled by a general vaccination program. Syphilis can be treated with penicillin, preferably given to the mother, although damage may still oc-

cur if treatment is not begun as soon as the infection is discovered. Herpes simplex has no known cure, but since the child is usually infected by contact with the virus during the birth process, Caesarean section may avoid this contact and lower the risk of infection to the child.

Blood Incompatibilities and Chronic Maternal Conditions

Sometimes biochemical substances in the fetus cause the mother to develop an antibody response to the baby. These antibodies may damage fetal tissues in much the same way that people reject organ transplants. Incompatibility of several different blood factors may have this result. The most familiar is **Rh incompatibility.** This occurs if the child has Rh-positive blood, inherited from the father, while the mother has Rh-negative blood. If the Rh-negative mother has previously been sensitized to Rh-positive blood, either by a blood transfusion or as a result of an earlier pregnancy, she will produce antibodies against the baby's Rh-positive cells. The production of Rh-positive antibodies can be prevented by means of an injection that destroys the Rh-positive cells in the mother's blood prior to her new pregnancy.

Some chronic medical conditions in the mother may also cause retardation in the fetus. Hypertension (high blood pressure) and diabetes are examples of chronic disorders that may interfere with fetal nutrition and lead to brain damage.

Drugs

Drugs taken by the mother can pass through the placenta to the fetus. The average pregnant woman probably uses at least four drugs during pregnancy, including aspirin, tranquilizers, antihistamines, and other popular medications. Even mild tranquilizers such as Librium are associated with an increase in the rate of serious fetal malformations. In addition, chemicals in the air, food, and water may affect the child before birth.

Children born to mothers who are chronic alcoholics often exhibit **fetal alcohol syndrome,** a specific set of characteristics that includes mental retardation (see Figure 16–19). About 40 percent of the children born to alcoholic mothers have serious abnormalities (Jones and others, 1974). Frequently the children are small in weight and height and have unusual facial features such as small eye slits, a flattened nasal bridge, and malformed ears. Smaller-than-average head size is also common. Many of these children are moderately retarded, and as they grow older their intellectual performance decreases further. At age 7 they perform more poorly, compared to children of the same age, than they did at 4.

FIGURE 16–19

This 6-year-old child shows the physical characteristics of fetal alcohol syndrome. Although from early infancy he has lived in a foster home that provides a high level of care, his intellectual development is at the moderately retarded level.

Two out of every 1,000 babies born alive have fetal alcohol syndrome, and 3 others show some characteristics of it (Hanson and others, 1978). This is probably a significant underestimate of the number of children whose development is affected by alcohol. For example, although most children born to alcoholic mothers do not show physical signs of the fetal alcohol syndrome, one study showed that 44 percent of these children had IQs below 79, compared to 11 percent of a control group (Jones and others, 1974). Because the controls were matched to the experimental group in socioeconomic status, age, and other factors, the mothers of the children in both groups were mainly high-risk women. This probably explains the unusually high frequency of lower-IQ children among the controls.

In recent years alcohol use during pregnancy has become recognized as an important cause of retardation. Even women who drink moderately during pregnancy may have children who are affected to some degree. So far no safe limits of alcohol use during pregnancy have been established.

Problems at and after Birth

Certain conditions occurring at birth are known to increase the probability of mental retardation, although these are not nearly as frequent causes of retardation as

some of the prenatal causes. Two of the most common birth complications are asphyxia and prematurity. Some infants do not get enough oxygen during or before the birth process. If death does not result from this asphyxia, seizures, retardation, and other problems are likely to occur. Premature infants usually are low in birth weight. When a child weighs 3 pounds or less at birth, the risk of retardation as well as health problems becomes much greater. Because adolescents often give birth to small infants and—especially in the case of unmarried mothers—often do not have adequate medical care, their infants are at high risk for retardation and other problems. For this reason alone, the increase in pregnancies among adolescent girls should be viewed with concern.

Damage to the central nervous system after birth can also cause retardation. Among the causes of such damage are infections, blows to the head, tumors, asphyxiation, and poisons. Some poisonous substances damage the brain cells by depriving them of oxygen. Carbon monoxide, barbiturates, and cyanide work in this way. Other poisons damage specific sites in the brain. Of these, lead, arsenic, and mercury are the most common.

Severe meningitis or encephalitis, which sometimes develops as a complication of mumps, measles, or chicken pox, can cause inflammation of the brain and the surrounding tissue. Often this results in retardation, seizures, or both. Some ear and blood infections can also damage brain tissues. Probably the most frequent causes of head injury are automobile accidents and child abuse. In an English institution for the retarded, researchers found that 11 percent of the children were handicapped because of brain damage associated with abuse (Buchanan and Oliver, 1977).

Psychosocial Disadvantage

About three-quarters of all retarded people are in the mildly retarded category. In many of these cases there are no obvious causal factors like the ones just discussed. However, careful epidemiological study often points to some contributing biological factors (Akesson, 1986). In many instances, these mildly retarded individuals cannot be singled out on the basis of their appearance, and often they are not identified as retarded until the early years of school. A very large number of children in this group come from families of low socioeconomic status. Because in many cases their parents' IQs also fall in the mildly retarded range, the question is often asked whether heredity is the predominant factor in their retardation.

The Role of Heredity

There have been a number of investigations into the hereditary and environmental aspects of intelligence. In one study, the researchers were interested in whether the social class of a child's adoptive family or the IQ of his or her biological parent was the better predictor of the child's intelligence (Scarr and Weinberg, 1978). They studied adopted and biologically related adolescents in families ranging from working class to upper middle class. The intelligence-test scores of the biological parent–child pairs were significantly more similar than those of the adoptive parent–child pairs. When children in a family were compared at age 18, the adopted siblings hardly resembled each other at all in intelligence, whereas biological siblings did resemble each other. The adopted children's average IQ was 106. This is higher than the average of 100 estimated for the adopted children's biological mothers but below the average of 112 for the children born into the adoptive family. Thus, at least in the socioeconomic range studied, "intellectual differences in the children at the end of the child rearing period have little to do with environmental differences among families" (Scarr and Weinberg, 1978, p. 691). In interpreting the results of this study, it is important to remember that most of the children in the study were adopted into homes that were superior in child-rearing skills. If some homes had provided extremely negative environments, a stronger environmental effect might have been noted.

Environment has been referred to by some as a threshold variable (Jensen, 1969), meaning that once a certain minimal quality of environment has been reached, further environmental stimulation is unimportant when compared to inherited capability. To put it another way, heredity provides a range of possibilities for the developing child, but the child's level of achievement within that rather wide range might be attributable to the environment in which he or she grows up. The results of many studies show that between 50 and 80 percent of the variation in intelligence factors is due to inheritance and the remainder to environmental influences (Zigler and others, 1984).

Effects of Environmental Change

Some investigators have tried to manipulate the environment to determine the effect on children who are thought to have low intellectual potential. In a program carried out in North Carolina, pregnant women with IQs averaging 80 were recruited for study (Ramey and Haskins, 1981). After their babies' births, half of the infants were cared for during the day at an educational day-care center and half were reared at home by their mothers. Both groups of children received medical care and dietary supplements, and their families were given social services if they requested them.

At the age of 3, the experimental children had significantly higher IQs than the control group. This difference seemed to be due to a decline in IQs of the control infants during the 12- to 18-month period. By the time the children were 5 years old, 39 percent of the control group had IQs below 85, whereas only 11 percent of the experimental group had IQs in this range. This study suggests that educational day care beginning before 3 months of age results in normal intellectual development, at least until the age of 5, for children of high-risk families.

Whether interventions that enrich the environment of economically deprived children who are at risk for retardation have a long-term effect on their intellectual performance is still an open question. Some investigators believe that interventions that begin in the very early years of life are most likely to succeed. Others believe that the early period of life is not uniquely critical and that later interventions also have a good chance of success (Clarke and Clarke, 1979). Most investigators would agree that work with the parents of young children, as well as with the children themselves, enhances the success potential for any program.

Typically, intervention programs produce improved scores during and immediately after the program. The same effect can be seen in the increased intelligence-test scores of culturally deprived children after their first year in school. However, in both cases these at-risk children seem to lose their early gains, and in later grades their performance worsens compared to that of other children. This change might be a function of the changing demands of school programs as children grow older. In the higher grades greater emphasis is placed on abstract thinking. This is also true of the content of intelligence-test questions aimed at older children. Perhaps many of these at-risk children are deficient in the ability to think abstractly. On the other hand, perhaps the special help in cognitive skills that the children obtained in the program was not complete enough to enable them to use those skills independently or to apply them to more complex levels of problem solving. This area of research is filled with many unanswered questions.

Cognitive Functioning in Retardation

In the past, retarded people were usually institutionalized for life. However, as more has been learned about their capabilities and institutionalization has become less popular, a variety of training programs has been developed to help retarded people live more independent lives.

Identification of Retardation

People who are profoundly, severely, or moderately retarded are often identified soon after birth. Such individuals are more likely than the average person to have multiple, easily identifiable physical abnormalities or poor responsiveness at birth, or to have seizures or speech or hearing disorders later. In some cases screening programs may prevent the development of retardation by identifying those at risk. For instance, many states require testing to detect PKU in newborns.

In contrast, most children who are mildly retarded, because they appear physically similar to other children and may have social or manual skills that partially mask their inability to handle intellectual tasks, may not be identified as retarded until they have been in school for several years, or even remain unidentified throughout their entire school careers. One study of a large number of school children found that almost 5 percent had intelligence-test scores that classified them as retarded and almost 10 percent had IQs below 80. Despite this fact, none had been referred for suspected learning problems (Mercer, 1971).

Even those who are labeled mildly retarded while in school are able to fade into the general public as they grow older. As adults, these people can function adequately because the emphasis on intellectual attainment that is characteristic of the school years has been replaced by a need for other skills on the job.

Developmental and Difference Models

Understanding differences in learning abilities is important not only from a theoretical standpoint but also in developing efficient teaching methods for use with retarded children and adults. Two basic models are used to describe the intellectual functioning of retarded individuals: the developmental model and the difference model (Detterman, 1987).

The **developmental model** assumes that the process of cognitive development is no different, at least for mildly retarded people, than it is for people with higher IQ scores. This theory stems from Jean Piaget's idea of cognitive development as a process in which stages occur in a fixed order but are attained at different rates. The thing that distinguishes mentally retarded people from others is that they progress more slowly through the stages and do not attain the higher stages. From this viewpoint, two people at the same developmental level would be able to handle a problem in the same way whether their chronological age was 3 or 16. Sometimes developmental level is referred to as mental age and contrasted with actual or chronological age.

Some research findings support this idea. Work with retarded children has shown a correspondence between Piaget's stages of cognitive development and the classifications of retardation: a severely retarded adult performs at Piaget's lowest level, the sensorimotor stage; a moderately retarded adult performs at the preoperational level; and so on (Inhelder, 1969). Retarded children also show a fixation or slowing down of cognitive development as they grow older.

The **difference model** of development, on the other hand, suggests that the cognitive functioning of retarded people differs from that of normal individuals in other ways besides rate of development and level attained. Children whose retardation is related to an identifiable defect such as an extra chromosome appear to differ in the structure of their intelligence from children whose retardation is familial. They are likely to show specific areas of poor intellectual performance rather than a generally lower level of intelligence (Weisz and others, 1982).

The developmental and difference models have important implications for the teaching of mildly retarded children. Should unique educational methods be used because of differences in cognitive processes between normal and retarded children, or can the methods and materials used in regular teaching programs, elaborated and presented more slowly, be used to teach retarded children? So far we do not have a clear answer to this question.

Public Educational Programs

School programs for the retarded have changed greatly over the last 20 years. Special classes have been established for severely and moderately retarded students who previously were totally excluded from school programs, and many slow-learner classes for mildly retarded children have been abolished. The children from such classes have been "mainstreamed," or integrated into regular classes. Both these changes have come about as a result of court decisions in cases dealing with the civil rights of the retarded.

The Education for All Handicapped Children Act of 1975 required public schools to provide free appropriate education to all handicapped children. Because of this law and recent court decisions, school districts are obligated to provide training for severely and profoundly retarded children. Such programs concentrate on basic communication and social skills. Although it is too early to assess whether they improve the child's performance, these programs do seem to prevent many severely and profoundly retarded children from being institutionalized in early childhood. Instead, a large number are now cared for at home, sometimes through adolescence or longer.

School classes for slow learners have been affected by a series of legal decisions, beginning with the *Brown v. Board of Education* case of 1954. In that decision, which marked the end of legally segregated schools and had been criticized as offering poor education. Although students were usually placed in classes for slow learners on the basis of intelligence tests, a high proportion of those students were from minority groups. Critics argued that intelligence tests were unfair to lower-class or minority children because they were heavily loaded with socially and culturally biased items. These items would be familiar to middle-class children but might not be part of the experience of a child from a lower-class or minority family. Pressure to place mildly retarded children in regular classrooms has also come from laws requiring the "least restrictive" placement possible for any given child. There is growing movement to avoid identifying and labeling children as retarded because of concern that such labels may stigmatize them. For minority children in particular, it is feared that such labels may be a result of test bias rather than valid estimates of their abilities.

Education in a mainstreamed or regular class is believed to be desirable for retarded children because exposure to normal role models and the absence of labeling might help them improve their achievement level and social adjustment. So far, however, this belief has not been supported by research findings. There seems to be little difference in performance between children who have been mainstreamed and those who have been placed in special classes. In one large study, both groups scored in the lowest 1 percent on standardized tests of reading and arithmetic (Kaufman and others, 1982). Nor does mainstreaming by itself improve the social status of a retarded child. In a study of more than 300 mainstreamed classrooms, the students were asked to rate each other's behavior. The mean rating for the retarded children was one standard deviation below that for their nonretarded classmates (Gottlieb and others, 1978). The basis of the ratings was not the label "retarded" but the behavior of the retarded children.

New Approaches to Intelligence Testing

In response to legal pressures and the efforts of parents and civil rights groups, many schools have given up the use of intelligence testing in assigning students to

classes. Yet because intelligence testing is important for some purposes, several new approaches to such testing have been developed. The most promising of these is the Kaufman Assessment Battery (K-ABC) (Kaufman and Kaufman, 1983). This test, discussed in Chapter 4, attempts to combine traditional intelligence-test tasks with recently developed cognitive tasks in order to measure abilities that are relatively unaffected by cultural and environmental factors. Some sample items are shown in Figure 4–4. One of the purposes for which the K-ABC was constructed was to aid in the diagnosis of specific cognitive deficits so that teachers could concentrate on those deficits. This approach to teaching mildly retarded children was pioneered in Israel and the United States by Reuven Feuerstein (Feuerstein and others, 1980). Although Feuerstein's ideas have stimulated teachers and others to work to improve their teaching of retarded students, many researchers question whether improvement in specific cognitive skills affects overall classroom performance (Bradley, 1983).

Another test, the System of Multicultural Pluralistic Assessment (SOMPA) (Lewis and Mercer, 1978), includes a traditional children's intelligence test, the Wechsler Intelligence Test for Children (WISC), but also gathers information about the child's health and social competence and information about his or her social and economic background. This information is used to construct a measure of estimated learning potential (ELP). The ELP is not a measure of innate intelligence, instead it provides an estimate of how much a child can profit from some type of school program (Anastasi, 1988).

So far neither of these test batteries or others that have been developed seem to have solved the problem of test bias. However, the K-ABC has prompted a flood of research that may be useful in providing better tests for use in making both educational and clinical decisions (Kamphaus and Reynolds, 1984).

Deinstitutionalization

Emphasis on normalizing the lives of the retarded has increased in recent years. Changes in the law have required that even severely retarded individuals receive the least restrictive care possible. As a result, many people who have been in institutions for many years have been discharged and have returned to the community. Young children who formerly would have been sent to institutions often live at home and attend special school programs that include job training. Currently less than 19 percent of all mentally retarded people live in institutions.

Deinstitutionalization can have a major impact not only on retarded individuals but on their families as well. In one case residents of a large institution were moved into small community-based living groups because of a court order (Latib and others, 1984). Initially most of their families opposed deinstitutionalization. Many of them had made the decision to institutionalize

their relatives many years earlier, often under great stress. In general, they believed that their relatives had reached their highest level of development and had little chance of learning new skills. They thought they were adequately cared for and worried that they would not be protected in small residential settings. They also wondered how long funding would be available for community-based homes. Before the move, the families were surveyed about their expectations. Six months later they were interviewed again. Figure 16-20 shows the results. These results ware especially impressive in view of the fact that the families' initial expectations were so negative.

For retarded individuals who are discharged from large institutions, several kinds of living arrangements are possible. The most frequent choice is a group home for up to 15 residents. Other possibilities are a return to the retarded person's own family or to a foster home, or, less frequently, a move to a medium-sized institution or a nursing home (Craig and McCarver, 1984).

Group homes for the retarded function both as a permanent home for those who are unable to live independently and as a transition point for those who are learning living skills that will help them live on their own (see Figure 16-21). Staff members work to broaden the resident's experiences—for example, by taking them on excursions. One problem in opening new group homes is the opposition of potential neighbors. Once the home is established, the opposition generally decreases and the neighbors' unrealistic fears about crime, property values, and quality of life dissipate (Okolo and Guskin, 1984).

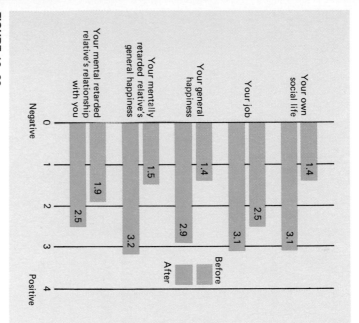

FIGURE 16-20
Expected and actually perceived changes in family life after deinstitutionalization of a family member. (Adapted from Latib and others, 1984, p. 81.)

Your own social life — 1.4 · 3.1

Your job — 2.5 · 3.1

Your general happiness — 1.4 · 2.9

Your mentally retarded relative's general happiness — 1.5 · 3.2

Your mental retarded relative's relationship with you — 1.9 · 2.5

Negative 0 · 1 · 2 · 3 · 4 Positive

After / Before

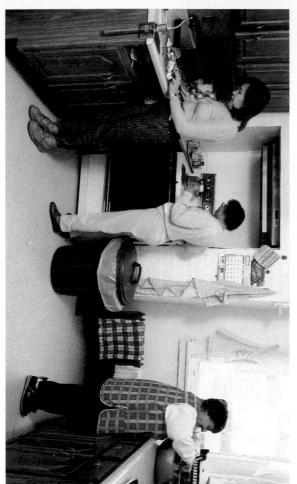

FIGURE 16-21
In addition to providing shelter, group homes are a place where retarded adolescents and adults learn valuable homemaking and self-management skills.

Carolyn has lived in a community residence for three years after moving from her family home at the age of 28. She lives with four other women residents who rent and maintain a six-bedroom house in a residential area. They essentially run the house in an independent manner and have their own rooms and housekeeping responsibilities. There is a counselor-advocate available for assistance whenever needed. Carolyn had been working in a sheltered workshop for two years and now has a job assisting in a thrift store. She works full time and handles her money herself. She has contact with friends outside the home and uses public transportation to visit them. Carolyn feels she is about ready to live on her own, possibly with another resident of the facility.

—(O'Connor, 1976, p. 48)

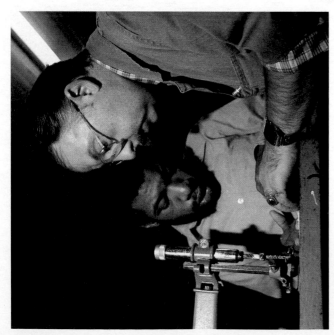

FIGURE 16–22
A sheltered workshop offers both a place to learn job skills and a working environment for people who cannot compete for jobs on an equal basis.

An important part of community-living programs is the job training offered to residents through sheltered workshops or special training programs (see Figure 16–22). The women described in the following excerpts illustrate how such programs enhance the lives of retarded individuals.

Linda had been in an institution for nearly 17 years before coming to the Community Residential Facility just two years ago. At 25, she has an estimated IQ of 21 and is physically handicapped. The home she lives in is near a large city and is a contemporary family house which has very homey and personalized living areas. Linda's home responsibilities include making her own bed and cleaning her own room; occasionally she helps clean the rest of the house and helps with the gardening. Linda works in a sheltered workshop doing piecework and other small jobs such as collating, assembling, and stapling, and she has been working for over one year. For working a half-day, two days per week, she earns over $20, which she puts into an account for clothing and recreation. Thirty hours a week, Linda attends an adult education class where she learns basic living skills. Linda gets along very well with other residents, but the facility operator doubts she will ever be able to live without supervised care.

—(O'Connor, 1976, pp. 46–47)

Vocational and Social Skills Training

Knowledge and use of appropriate vocational and social skills are key factors in success both in competitive job environments and in sheltered workshops. Skills training through modeling has been found to be more effective than coaching in the same skills. In one study, several problem situations were modeled so that prospective workers could learn to identify both problem behaviors and appropriate ways of dealing with such situations (LaGreca and others, 1983).

You come to work in the morning and can't find one of the materials you need to do your job (for example, the napkins). Inappropriate solution: walk around, talking to co-workers; sit at table and do nothing. Appropriate solution: request help from supervisor politely.

You are working in the morning and the person working next to you is being very loud, talking and laughing. You are finding it hard to concentrate on your work because of the noise. Inappropriate solution: yell at co-worker to "shut up"; throw something at co-worker; insult co-worker; threaten co-worker. Appropriate solution: politely request quiet behavior; ignore co-worker.

—(LaGreca and others, 1983, p. 272)

The effectiveness of modeling is shown by a comparison with both a coaching group and a control group. After 7 weeks on the job only 1 of the 11 people in the modeling group had been fired. Half of the coaching group had been fired; in the control group, 10 had been fired and only 2 were still on the job.

Another important aspect of retarded people's lives is a supportive network of people. One way to increase the amount of support available is to help the individual learn social skills. Another is to make sure that decisions about living and working conditions take friendships into account. If friendship networks are kept in mind when residents of facilities for the retarded have to be relocated, the outcome is likely to be much better. In one study, residents who had moved to a new home with chosen friends were more sociable several years later than residents who had been separated from friends (Romer and Heller, 1983). They were also better able to care for themselves.

While mentally retarded individuals are being integrated into the community, they are vulnerable to personal, sexual, and financial exploitation. One source of this problem is the tendency of the retarded to answer "yes" to all questions, regardless of content. This tendency can be measured using the reverse-question technique: Within the same interview two opposite questions are asked, such as "Are you usually happy?" and "Are you usually sad?" In one study, almost half of the retarded people interviewed answered "yes" to both questions (Sigelman and others, 1981). This tendency to say "yes" is correlated with IQ: the lower a person's IQ, the greater the tendency to agree. Such readiness to agree clearly can have negative consequences. For one thing, it means that retarded people are likely to agree to inappropriate or unfair requests.

One way to prevent exploitation of retarded individuals is to pay special attention to teaching them what is expected of a person and how to say "no" (Schilling and Schinke, 1984). For example, participants in a training program for food service workers were taught how to handle their earnings and how to say "no" to people who asked to borrow money. Another problem area is sexual behavior. Training programs have taught retarded people how to recognize and escape from sexually exploitive situations. Mentally retarded individuals also need to be trained to understand what society views as appropriate sexual behavior and to avoid such acts as public masturbation and inappropriate sexual approaches to others.

Psychological Problems

Retarded individuals are likely to experience psychological problems as well as intellectual retardation. In one study, up to 40 percent of retarded children were rated by their parents or teachers as psychologically disturbed (Rutter and others, 1970). Severely retarded children exhibit an even higher rate of disturbance: nearly half may be diagnosed as having a behavior disorder. The same types of disorders are seen in retarded children as in nonretarded children, although the frequencies of different types of disorders differ in the two groups. Those who are severely retarded are more likely to have a psychosis or to be hyperactive and less likely to have a conduct disorder (Rutter and others, 1975). This difference is probably explained by the likelihood that severely retarded children also have central nervous system damage.

Retarded children living with their parents may have more problems during adolescence than nonretarded children do. Mildly retarded adolescents in particular may experience a "friendship void." They tend to be socially isolated. Most of their contacts with others are at school, not in social activities. If they do have social interactions, these tend to be with younger children, not those of the same age (Brier, 1986). In one study, 84 percent of retarded children developed emotional or behavioral problems during adolescence (Zetlin and Turner, 1985). These included temper tantrums, violent or destructive behavior, and for some, use of drugs and alcohol, and for other an increase in withdrawal behavior. Many of these problems seemed to be related to the young people's growing awareness of the gap between themselves and other teenagers in terms of expectations for the future and ability to be independent. The retarded adolescents' desire for dating relationships was another source of problems. When these young people became adults, only one-third were still in conflict with their parents. The rest either had adjusted to dependence on their parents or had been able to establish fairly independent life styles that gave them satisfaction.

Retarded individuals often have a low opinion of themselves. When they live in the community this problem becomes more severe because there are more opportunities for comparisons with nonretarded people. In one study, retarded individuals living in an institution were more likely to rate themselves as smart and attractive than retarded people living in a community setting. Since the intellectual level of those in the institution was lower and the rated attractiveness no different, the community group's exposure to and self-comparisons with nonretarded individuals probably accounted for the difference (Gibbons, 1985).

The kinds of problems these adolescents and adults face can be helped by psychotherapy. Family therapy is often used, especially for adolescents. Individual psychotherapy can be useful in the same way that it may be helpful for nonretarded adolescents. Social-skills training and job preparation also contribute to adjustment. Such techniques have helped many retarded people to adjust well, marry, and live semiindependent lives (see Figure 16–23).

FIGURE 16–23
This photo shows Victor, 30, and Kathy, 29, after they had announced their marriage plans. A few years ago such an announcement would have been almost unthinkable because both Kathy and Victor are retarded.

Study Outline

AUTISTIC DISORDERS

1. Children with an **autistic disorder** show impairment in social relationships, communication, and activities. They have a noticeable lack of awareness of the existence or feelings of others. They have a very narrow range of interests and activities, and about half do not develop speech at all.

2. In adulthood about two-thirds of autistic individuals are severely handicapped, but some are able to make a good adjustment to life in the community. A key predictor of later progress is development of language skills by age 5. Intensive behavioral training early in life has been the most effective therapeutic approach.

3. In the majority of cases autism is connected with global mental retardation. Autistic children seem to have a cognitive deficit, especially in relation to language and comprehension. These problems may be caused by early damage to the limbic system or a dysfunction of behavioral systems in the brain stem. There is also some evidence of a hereditary factor that involves a general tendency toward cognitive abnormalities.

MENTAL RETARDATION

1. **Mental retardation** means a significantly below-average level of intellectual functioning as measured by an individually administered intelligence test. There are four categories of mental retardation based on intelligence-test scores: **mild, moderate, severe,** and **profound.**

2. The causes of mental retardation can be grouped into two general categories. Children who are **psychosocially disadvantaged** may show no specific disabilities but may have low intelligence-test scores because of their hereditary and/or environmental experiences. Other children are retarded as a result of disease, injury, chromosomal abnormality, or a specific genetic disorder.

3. Some cases of retardation are caused by specific dominant genes and some by specific recessive genes. The latter often cause disorders of metabolism such as **phenylketonuria. Fragile X syndrome,** a disorder transmitted through the female sex chromosome, is the second-most frequent cause of retardation in men.

Many other cases of retardation are due to **chromosomal abnormalities.** The most frequently occurring of these is **Down syndrome,** which usually results from the presence of an extra number-21 chromosome. Children with Down syndrome have many characteristic physical features and show considerable variability in level of retardation. Several diagnostic techniques, **ultrasound, amniocentesis, chorionic villus sampling,** and an **alpha-feroprotein test** can detect genetic disorders in the fetus.

4. Mental retardation can be caused by a variety of prenatal environmental factors. Among these are maternal infections (e.g., by the rubella or herpes virus), blood incompatibilities (especially **Rh incompatibility**), and drugs taken by the mother. **Fetal alcohol syndrome** produced by alcohol use during pregnancy is an important cause of retardation. Mental retardation can also be caused by problems at birth and after birth, such as damage to the central nervous system or inflammation of the brain due to meningitis or encephalitis.

5. In the many cases of mild retardation there are no obvious causal factors, although careful investigation may suggest disease or injury may play a role. A large number of children in this group come from families of low socioeconomic status. An important factor in the intellectual potential of the individual is heredity, but environmental stimulation can make a difference in whether a person reaches his or her full potential. Changes in environment have been shown to affect IQ, but it is not clear whether such changes have a long-term effect on intellectual performance.

6. The **developmental model** of retardation assumes that the process of cognitive development is no different for retarded people than it is for people with higher IQs, but that it occurs more slowly. The **difference model** suggests that the cognitive functioning of retarded people differs in specific ways from that of normal individuals.

7. In recent years many retarded children have been "mainstreamed," or placed in regular public school classrooms, as a result of court decisions dealing with the civil rights of the retarded. The results to date suggest that mainstreaming does not improve a child's achievement level or social adjustment. Methods of intelligence testing have been developed that attempt to decrease the influences of cultural factors on test scores.

8. Efforts to normalize the lives of the retarded have also led to the discharge of many retarded people from institutions. Deinstitutionalized individuals may live with their own family, in group homes, in a foster home, or in a medium-sized institution or a nursing home. Job training is an important part of community-living programs.

9. Modeling is often used to teach vocational and social skills to retarded people. Special training is required to teach them ways of avoiding sexual and financial exploitation.

10. Retarded individuals are likely to experience psychological problems as well as intellectual retardation. This is especially true of adolescents living with their parents and adults living in the community. These problems can be helped by psychotherapy.

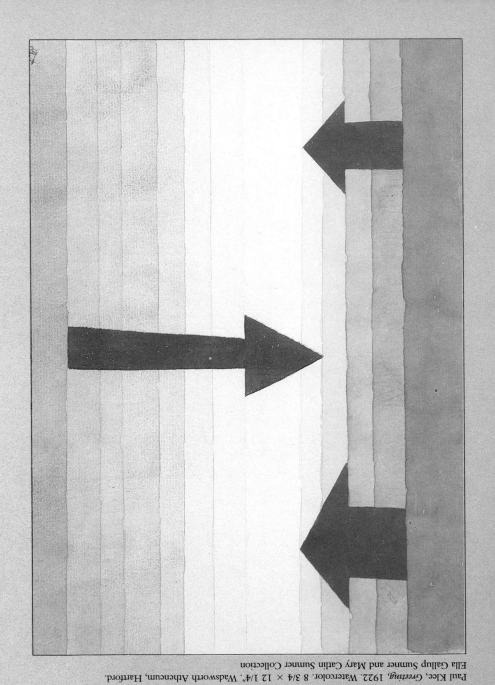

Paul Klee, *Greeting*, 1922. Watercolor, 8 3/4 × 12 1/4". Wadsworth Atheneum, Hartford.
Ella Gallup Sumner and Mary Catlin Sumner Collection

OBJECTIVES FOR CHAPTER SEVENTEEN:

To learn:

1. Which therapeutic approaches are used by those influenced by each of the perspectives

2. The specific techniques used in each therapeutic approach

To understand:

1. What researchers need to consider when they wish to compare therapy techniques

2. The pros and cons of hospitalization and deinstitutionalization

B etty Rouse, housewife and mother of three adolescent children, had been in psychotherapy for two years. She had sought therapy because she felt herself to be an unhappy, inadequate person, who, as she put it, "was not good for much besides cooking dinner and chauffeuring the kids around to Scout meetings."

During the first several months of therapy, she talked mainly about herself. As time passed, however, her husband Fred was mentioned with increasing frequency and strong emotion. By the end of therapy, Betty concluded that, while many of her problems were of her own making, Fred had consistently made them worse by showing that he saw her as "just a housewife and mother," not as someone who was admirable for her own sake. After trying fruitlessly to talk with Fred about how he always belittled her, Betty concluded that her self-esteem was more important to her than she had ever realized and that Fred would only hinder its strengthening. With great pain and guilt, mainly because of the effect it might have on the children, Betty decided to get a job, live apart from Fred, and eventually get a divorce. She hoped one day to meet a man who would both love her and value her as a person.

Was the outcome of Betty Rouse's psychotherapy good or bad? The answer depends on a number of things, including her past life and our own values. Therapy situations involve a special relationship between a professional clinician and a person with a problem. Therapy is difficult to do and hard to evaluate because each person's problem is unique and because the various therapeutic approaches differ greatly. Would the outcome of Betty Rouse's therapy have been different if she had been seeing a behavior therapist, a biologically oriented psychiatrist, or a family therapist? So many factors are involved that we cannot answer this question, but it is possible to make comparisons among the therapeutic approaches used for different types of cases.

It is important to keep in mind the similarities as well as the differences among the various therapeutic approaches. All therapeutic relationships are aimed at providing clients with certain ingredients that are missing from their lives. Regardless of their therapeutic orientation, all clinicians must deal with the patient's demoralized state and with his or her expectation of receiving help. All therapists must attempt to form some sort of supportive therapeutic relationship. All clinicians must communicate their views of the problems that have been presented, and possible solutions to those problems must be devised.

In preceding chapters we have described major therapeutic approaches to specific types of maladaptive behavior. We have discussed the "talking therapies," such as psychoanalysis and client-centered counseling, in which conversations between the client and the therapist are the vehicle for achieving change; cognitive–behavioral therapies, such as systematic desensitization and token economies, which involve applications of learning and cognitive principles in specially structured clinical situations; and somatic therapies, such as the use of antipsychotic, antidepressive, or tranquilizing drugs and electro-convulsive treatments, which are aimed at achieving behavior change through physical means.

Although we have talked about these approaches in relation to specific disorders, it is useful to summarize what we know about the various therapeutic methods in general. Reviewing these methods toward the end of the book will highlight how much we have learned along the way and also lay the groundwork for a discussion of how different therapies can be evaluated and compared. Do most or all of the different therapeutic approaches have common elements? Is a particular therapy effective for certain types of problems but not for others? What gaps exist in current knowledge about therapies and their rates of success?

Psychotherapy

All forms of psychotherapy involve interchanges between a client and a therapist. These interchanges, which are nonverbal as well as verbal, are aimed at understanding what is on the client's mind. This under-standing is then used as a basis for efforts to change the client's maladaptive ways of thinking, reacting to situations, and relating to others.

Most psychotherapists adhere to some type of psychodynamic or cognitive theory. Psychodynamic orientations emphasize the role of unconscious conflict in causing personal problems, whereas cognitive orientations emphasize the role of unrealistic or irrational thinking. Many psychotherapists utilize both psychodynamic and cognitive concepts in working with clients.

In the course of their work, and regardless of their theoretical orientations, psychotherapists, must perform three tasks: (1) listen, (2) understand, and (3) respond. The therapist listens to the patient in order to find out about his or her preoccupations, worries, and concerns. Listening serves two functions: it lets the therapist hear about topics that the client brings up spontaneously and it provides information that is pertinent to the therapist's hypotheses about the client's problems. Listening provides a basis for the therapist's understanding of the client's self-concept and view of the world.

Through listening and understanding, the therapist becomes able to respond. The response might be a question aimed at eliciting more information, or it might be a comment. The comment might be an interpretation of what has been going on in the session or in the client's interpersonal relationships. Those relationships are of three types.

1. Current in-treatment relationships
2. Current out-of-treatment relationships
3. Past relationships

Current in-treatment relationships have to do with what is going on between the therapist and the client. (Do they like each other? Is there tension between them?) Current out-of-treatment relationships involve significant others such as the client's spouse, friend, or employer. (Is the patient experiencing less tension at work? Are there opportunities for good social relationships?) Psychodynamically oriented therapists in particular attempt to explore past relationships in order to uncover clues to the causes of current difficulties. (Are current difficulties with friends consistent with or a continuation of undesirable relationships in early childhood?)

Therapists are interested in determining the degree to which these three types of relationships may be related; for example, are conflicts between the client and the therapist similar to the client's earlier conflicts with parents or current conflicts between the client and a spouse or friend? In addition to searching for continuities in interpersonal relationships, the therapist is attentive to themes that recur over several sessions. How similar is the way the client and the therapist relate to each other in the twentieth session to the way they related during their first therapeutic meeting? Are similar or different emotions and motives expressed as the therapy progresses?

Psychoanalysis and Psychodynamic Therapy

Psychoanalysis is a specific subtype of psychodynamic therapy. Because psychoanalysis takes a long time and is expensive, only a small fraction of the people who desire it can experience it. However, psychoanalytic concepts and techniques are widely used by nonpsychoanalytic therapists.

Before they can analyze others, psychoanalysts must undergo analysis themselves. The number of analytic interviews included in a psychoanalyst's training can range from fewer than 200 sessions to about 2000. On the average, most analyses, whether they are conducted for training or therapeutic reasons, require between 2 and 5 years. The American Psychoanalytic Association recommends at least four analytic sessions each week. Over the years, the total number of sessions in a typical psychoanalysis has increased (see Figure 17–1).

Psychoanalysis makes extensive use of **free association**, in which the client expresses thoughts and feelings in as free and uninhibited a manner as possible. This results in a natural flow of ideas unencumbered by interruptions or explanations. One psychologist has pro-

FIGURE 17–1
Psychoanalysis usually involves 3 to 5 sessions per week for several years.

vided the following description of free association as it occurred in his own psychoanalysis.

I learned to be profoundly impressed with my unconscious. Some hours seemed to be little short of miraculous. Without any plan or preparation on my part, my free associations would apparently adopt a theme, which might also be the theme of a dream the preceding night. Many times it was possible to connect this theme with certain experiences of that day or of the day before, experiences with emotional content and which, not being wholly resolved, had left a residue of tension. The remarkable thing was the way in which my free associations would weave in and around this theme, coming back to it again and again, instead of just flitting on and on like a butterfly from one theme to another. I gained the impression that the episode of the day before pertained to deep-seated grievances going way back to early childhood and infancy—wrongs which had never been completely resolved; and that my associations were like outcroppings of rock which reveal the possibility of a continuity of structure between the surface exposure and submerged strata.

—(Symonds, 1940, p. 14)

The examination of dreams and fantasies is also important in psychoanalysis. Although the following example is not drawn from a psychoanalytic session, it illustrates the therapeutic use of fantasy material.

A 26-year-old patient reported that he was feeling rejected by his fiancee although she had done nothing

that insight enabled her to see herself in relation to her husband in a new way.

Whereas in principle the agenda of a psychoanalytic session is determined by the free associations of the patient, psychodynamically oriented psychotherapy usually focuses on a fairly specific problem or group of problems rather than on a general reshaping of the personality. Many people seek clinical help because of something that has happened to them. Stressful situations often call for readjustments in an individual's life, and the therapist helps by listening, supporting, and clarifying.

The principles and mechanisms that operate in psychoanalysis are believed also to play a role in psychotherapy. One of the most important of these is the relationship between the person seeking help and the helper. Freud noticed that his patients' attitudes toward him changed as their analysis proceeded. He also noticed that his own attitudes toward his patients changed. As the relationship between patient and therapist develops, it comes to involve feelings and patterns of behavior that originally were experienced earlier in life, often in relation to significant figures of one's childhood. For example, during psychotherapy feelings toward one's father may be transferred to the therapist.

A key aspect of psychoanalysis is the use of this **transference** as a vehicle for resolving interpersonal conflicts and revealing the meaning of anxiety. In **positive transference,** the patient feels predominantly friendly and affectionate toward the analyst. However, in **negative transference** hostility predominates. **Countertransference** refers to the therapist's emotional reactions to his or her patients. Psychoanalysts must be analyzed themselves because of the belief that their self-insight will reduce the occurrence of countertransference reactions.

The case of Bill Jenkins, a 40-year-old construction supervisor who sought psychotherapy because of the increasing number of arguments he was having with his wife, provides an example of transference.

During the first twenty sessions be described in detail to the therapist frustrations connected with his marital and work situations. In these sessions, he never referred to any thoughts he might have had about the therapist. In the twenty-first session, Jenkins noticed a small crack in one of the walls of the therapist's office. He said to the therapist: "It looks like the construction company that put up that wall didn't do a very good job." After several uncomfortable pauses, he went on, "You know, Doc, I feel embarrassed saying this but somehow I keep feeling sorry for you, feeling like, in a way, you've been a loser. Like that lousy construction job over there (pointing to the crack in the wall). Some of

to justify his reaction. He then reported that the feeling bad started the previous day when he had been at a picnic with his fiancee and his best friend. Although his fiancee and his friend had been attentive to him, be felt uncomfortable. He then recalled that during the picnic he had experienced the following daydream. *"Jane (his fiancee) and Bob (his friend) began to look at each other in a loving way. They passed signals back and forth of getting rid of me. They arranged to get together later that night. I got the old feeling of being rejected—wanting to be in but kept out and not wanted. They sneaked off at night and necked and had bad sex. Then they told me about it and I gave her up although I felt a deep loss at the same time."* After having experienced this fantasy, he had felt rejected by his fiancee even though in reality she continued to be very affectionate to him.

After recounting the fantasy in the therapeutic hour, the patient had a stream of associations. "I feel sad and low, almost as though she actually was unfaithful. Bob reminds me of competing with my brother. I was always second fiddle to him. . . . I never made it up to his level. I was always losing out. . . . He was always better than me. Everybody liked him more than me."

The patient was then able to view his unpleasant reaction at the picnic as analogous to his early pattern of expecting to be pushed to one side by his brother. He visualized Bob's displacing him as his brother had previously triumphed over him. It became clear to him that his current reactions of jealousy and vulnerability were not justified on the basis of the reality situation. With this realization, his feelings of estrangement from his fiancee disappeared.
—(Beck, 1970, pp. 6–7)

In the course of telling the therapist about a fantasy, the client may acquire some insight into the relationship between his or her early experiences and a current tendency to distort reality. **Insight,** or understanding of one's inner life, is a goal of most psychotherapies.

After months of talking about her husband as a demanding, overbearing man who was always gloomy, Rose Francis, aged 50, remarked to her therapist: "You know, I guess I really don't like him." There was a tone of wonder and surprise in her voice when she said this. After recognizing her strong negative feelings toward her husband, Mrs. Francis found it possible to identify and sympathize with some of her husband's worries and concerns. She became better able to see the world through his eyes. Being able to say out loud "You know, I guess I really don't like him" made her more aware of just how angry she felt toward her husband. Somehow those construction guys are pretty smart fellows who don't mind taking advantage of innocent people."

The characteristic Jenkins was attributing to the therapist (being a loser) could not have been based on facts available to him because Jenkins knew little about the therapist's background. What he said was the first outward expression of his developing relationship with and fantasies concerning the therapist. In subsequent sessions, Jenkins himself observed the similarity between his pictures of the therapist and his father, who was an alcoholic and a "loser." At one point he said, "It doesn't make sense, does it, for me to see you as being like my father?"

In asking that question, Jenkins showed insight and came close to making an interpretation of his behavior toward the therapist (seeing him as a loser like his father). Interpretations of behavior that arise during psychotherapy sessions may be made by either the therapist or the client. Many people go into psychotherapy expecting to be told what is wrong with them and what to do about it, but psychotherapists usually limit their intervention to making interpretations. Actually, most therapists prefer that clients evolve their own interpretations and achieve self-understanding with the help of the therapist. But many therapists will offer interpretations when they seem especially appropriate and the client seems unable to make or express them. Through these interpretations, therapists seek to expose areas of conflict, portions of which have been unconscious, and to help the client understand past psychological events. During therapy, individuals may be confronted with an interpretation that they have an interest in not acknowledging. They may become irritated with the person who has confronted them, and in an effort to protect themselves they may try to think of more acceptable, but incorrect, explanations for their behavior. Psychoanalytic treatment is aimed at helping the client place his or her motivations in perspective and redirect their influence on everyday life.

In psychoanalysis, transference and countertransference reactions are ultimately dealt with. In other forms of psychotherapy, interpretations of these processes might be less important than dealing with the pressing problems in the client's day-to-day life. This does not mean that transference and countertransference do not occur or that the therapist doesn't think they are important. It means that the therapist has decided to give the highest priority to the problems that the client feels are most crucial. In some cases psychotherapists wish that they could explore certain aspects of the client's thinking but conclude that the client isn't ready to engage in such exploration.

In the initial stages of psychotherapy, tentative answers must be sought to a number of questions:

- Why did the client come to me?
- What are the pressing problems from the point of view of the client?
- What underlying problems is the client not aware of?
- Will it be possible to help the client explore these underlying problems?

The answers to these questions help the therapist set objectives and decide on tactics for later stages of therapy. Clients often feel that as a result of their therapy experience they are able to see themselves, their past lives, and the people in their lives in a more objective light. Identifying the subjective reactions of both clients and therapists to what goes on in therapy sessions is an important research task.

Illustrative of how this task can be approached is the study of "good" and "poor" psychotherapy sessions, sessions that either the therapist or the client or both feel were particularly valuable. For example, Hoyt and others (1983) had psychotherapists and independent observers rate the quality of therapy sessions. The ratings were then related to what had gone on in the sessions. One finding was that therapists and independent observers often disagreed about the relationship between specific occurrences in the sessions and their degree of "goodness" or "badness." Therapists seemed to believe that a session was not particularly "good" if the client seemed resistant or difficult to relate to. On the other hand, outside observers often felt that a session was productive if the client was difficult and the therapist had to take a more active role as a result. Table 17-1 lists factors that independent observers rated as contributing to either "good" or "bad" sessions.

TABLE 17-1

Factors Contributing to "Good" and "Bad" Psychotherapy Sessions as Rated by Independent Observers

Factors Contributing to "Good" Sessions

1. The patient was encouraged to express thoughts and feelings.
2. The meaning of the patient's behavior was discussed.
3. The patient's avoidance of painful material was discussed.
4. The patient's responsibility for what went on in the session was discussed.

Factors Contributing to "Poor" Sessions

1. There were long silences.
2. The therapist used humor in discussing topics.

Adapted from Hoyt and others, 1983. The Journal of Nervous and Mental Disease. Copyright © 1983 by Williams and Wilkins.

Hypnosis

Hypnosis is used for a variety of purposes: to suggest specific changes in thinking or behavior, as an aid in psychotherapy (for example, to help a client overcome anxiety or deal with upsetting ideas), and to enhance relaxation. Although the technique has been used clinically for years, research on hypnosis is in its infancy. There is considerable controversy over what hypnosis actually is and whether it really involves a special trance-like state. Because of its success in inducing states that appear to involve relaxation, it has aroused the interest of behavior therapists as well as psychotherapists.

It is now known that hypnosis is an altered state of consciousness—not sleep, but an intense alertness in which the mind can screen out extraneous matters and focus on particular details. The hypnotic trance is characterized by extreme relaxation and heightened susceptibility to suggestion. It allows people to suspend logical reasoning and draw upon psychological strengths that they do not normally command voluntarily. The focused concentration and heightened suggestibility of the trance state help the individual accept the therapist's directions and come to grips with problems more rapidly. When used with people who are suffering from great pain, hypnosis seems to mask the discomfort. The person still "feels" the pain at some level, but conscious awareness is blocked. Just how the trance state enables one to "disconnect" pain from awareness is not known.

Hypnotists typically begin their sessions by asking subjects to stare at an object, suggesting in a soothing voice that their eyelids are becoming heavy, that they are relaxing and becoming hypnotized, and that they will find it easy to comply with the hypnotist's suggestions (see Figure 17–2). In experimental settings this "hypnotic induction" typically lasts for about 15 minutes. If the subjects are willing to be hypnotized, they appear relaxed and drowsy and become responsive to test suggestions from the hypnotist. Afterward they report changes in bodily sensations and claim that they have been hypnotized. People who are susceptible to hypnosis have beliefs and expectations that motivate them to adopt the hypnotic role. They usually have better than average ability to focus attention as well as a vivid imagination.

Humanistic and Existential Therapies

Several forms of psychotherapy either disagree with the assumptions of psychodynamic theory or modify them in certain ways. The neo-Freudians accept most psychodynamic principles but reject the emphasis placed by psychoanalytic theory on instinctual unconscious impulses. **Humanistic therapies** emphasize people's desire to achieve self-respect. Existential therapists, whose view-

FIGURE 17–2
A hypnotist can produce a relaxed and suggestible state in subjects willing to be hypnotized.

points often overlap those of humanistic therapists, emphasize the need to confront basic questions of existence, such as: What is the meaning of my life? Am I hiding from myself?

Client-Centered Therapy

Carl Rogers, the founder of **client-centered therapy**, saw the individual as seeking personal growth but needing the support of an appreciative, accepting therapist. The therapist is a nondirective facilitator who encourages the client's self-exploration and efforts to achieve greater maturity and self-confidence. Whereas in psychoanalysis the therapeutic relationship—transference and countertransference—and the analyst's interpretations help clients solve personal problems, in client-centered therapy a nonjudgmental therapist facilitates the process of self-understanding by serving as a mirror for the client.

As a group, client-centered therapists have been among the leaders in research about what actually goes on in psychotherapy. Rogers saw psychotherapy as a growth process and encouraged objective study of the events that occur as therapy progresses. He recognized that people's ideas and ways of looking at the world influence their emotional lives.

The client-centered therapist believes that perceptions and cognitions determine whether an individual has warm, positive interpersonal relationships or strained relationships that stir up unpleasant emotions. As the client restructures his or her view of the world, troubling emotions such as anxiety and anger become less potent. For example:

When I started coming here, I saw my problem as anger—toward other people as well as myself. There were times I felt like a seething inferno. You sat there as I ranted and raved and I really appreciated the fact that you listened so attentively to everything I said. Sometimes you would reflect back to me what I had just said, sometimes you would just ask a question about a comment I had made. I don't really know how it happened but I began thinking about why I get so angry at home. Then a lot of things fell into place. I was angry because I was doing things I didn't want to do. I was doing those things out of guilt and obligation. Why should I think I had to be nice to people I can't stand? When I finally realized that I didn't have to do certain things, I became more spontaneous and less angry.

Client-centered therapists believe that people are basically good and that no feelings are intrinsically destructive. What appear to be destructive feelings reflect externally imposed distortions that resemble the contortions of a plant trying to grow under a brick. For Rog-

ers, therapy is present-oriented and existential. Labels and diagnoses are not useful. What is needed is **unconditional positive regard**, reflected in the therapist's nonjudgmental, empathetic listening. Whereas a behavior therapist would concentrate on getting clients to change their behavior, a Rogerian therapist would concentrate on supplying an environment in which the client feels free to express thoughts and feelings. The Rogerian therapist assumes that unconditional positive regard will increase the client's self-acceptance and self-knowledge, which, in turn, will lead the client to change his or her behavior.

Existential Therapy

Existential therapies also emphasize the present and the need to recognize the uniqueness of each client. Existential therapists work as partners with their clients. Many combine humanistic and psychodynamic approaches in dealing with anxiety, its causes, and the defenses that the client erects to cope with it. In this sense the existential approach is a therapeutic hybrid.

The emphasis of existential therapy is on helping clients come to terms with basic issues concerning the meaning and direction of their lives and the choices by which they shape their own destinies. Like the majority of clinicians who see nonhospitalized clients, most existential therapists work with people who are troubled by anxiety and depression. Existential therapists see their primary role as helping lonely people make constructive choices and become confident enough to fulfill their unique selves rather than repressing or distorting their experiences.

Gestalt Therapy

Gestalt therapy focuses on clients' perceptions of themselves and the world. It is based on the recognition that people unconsciously organize their perceptions as a *Gestalt*: a meaningful, integrated whole. A Gestalt therapist uses a variety of techniques, including role playing, in an effort to stimulate the client to express strong emotions.

Fritz Perls, the founder of Gestalt therapy, stressed the relationships among distorted perceptions, motivations, and emotions. Perls's therapy was a function of his personality. He could be inspiring and manipulative, perceptive and hostile. He says in his autobiography, "I believe I am the best therapist for any type of neurosis in the States, maybe in the world. . . . At the same time I have to admit that I cannot work successfully with everybody" (Perls, 1969). Unlike most humanistic therapists, who stress the importance of unconditional positive regard for the client, Perls believed that the therapist's main task was to frustrate the client, to make him or her angry enough to fight out conflicts with authority and thereby develop enhanced feelings of self-worth. Perls believed that instead of trying to reconstruct the history of the client's relationships with others, the therapist should stress the client's moment-to-moment experiences as each session progresses.

Gestalt therapists believe that anxiety and personality disorders arise when people dissociate parts of themselves, particularly their need for personal gratification, from awareness. Because dreams often contain clues to dissociated parts of the self, Gestalt therapists encourage discussion and acting out of dreams.

The Cognitive Psychotherapies

The cognitive psychotherapies seek to correct misconceptions that contribute to maladjustment, defeat, and unhappiness. Imagine someone who, as a result of the vicissitudes of life, develops a faulty belief to the effect that "no one could possibly like me if I reveal my true self." Such people are likely to spend time endlessly avoiding others, avoiding spontaneous behavior, and eating their hearts out in loneliness. Another set of circumstances may convince someone that a series of incidents of "bad luck" mean that whatever happens next is likely to be disastrous. Thereupon the individual becomes fearful of the immediate future. Or, after many frustrations and conflicts, a person becomes so anxious that he or she is convinced that a "nervous breakdown" is imminent. The person then tries to avoid all stress even though the best approach would probably be subjection to normal stresses since success in handling them would provide the only convincing evidence of mental well-being.

Since opinions, beliefs, or conceptions are ordinarily formed on the basis of evidence, adequate or inadequate, we can also assume that beliefs are modified by evidence, adequate or inadequate. Thus, in order to modify their misconceptions clients must review the evidence in some way. Psychotherapy may, in fact, provide one of the few situations in which individuals are encouraged to think somewhat systematically about their beliefs, particularly their beliefs about themselves. A number of psychotherapeutic approaches share the assumption that maladaptive behavior is a product of unrealistic perceptions and conditions. The various cognitive therapies use different tactics in redirecting the way people see and interpret their experiences, but they all generally reject the Freudian emphasis on the powerful role of unconscious drives.

An early cognitive approach to therapy was developed by George Kelly. Kelly's (1955) **psychology of personal constructs** led him to ask clients to examine the roles they played in interacting with others and the assumptions underlying those roles. In his **fixed-role therapy** Kelly encouraged his clients to practice new roles and relationships. Kelly saw people as problem-solvers whose faulty beliefs and assumptions often lead to undesirable solutions to the problems of living. According to Kelly, by discussing the client's personal constructs and social roles, the therapist helps the client question and reevaluate aspects of his or her life that arouse anxiety.

Another clinical approach based on cognitive theory is Albert Ellis's **rational-emotive therapy.** Ellis (1970) believes that self-defeating thinking is at the root of maladaptive behavior. Such thinking is based on arbitrary, inaccurate assumptions about oneself and others. It is often marked by a preoccupation with "musts": "I *must* always be friendly to people," "I *must* not disappoint my parents," "I *must* be a big success." In rational-emotive therapy these musts are seen as causes of emotional arousal, which, if maintained at too high a level for too long a time, causes psychological and physical wearing down. Most of these and other self-defeating musts were pounded into our heads as children, and we tend to accept them without question. Thus, rational-emotive therapy has two goals: to get people to question these fundamental, but mistaken, beliefs, and then to exchange them for more constructive ones.

During the course of therapy the cognitive therapist actually demonstrates the ways in which unrealistic self-verbalizations can create or worsen emotional problems. The therapist also actively questions and contradicts faulty, unreasonable assumptions by the client and suggests alternative ways of thinking. Role playing is often used, with the therapist demonstrating the behavioral consequences of different types of beliefs.

Aaron Beck's (1976) cognitive therapy is also directed toward the thoughts that underlie intense, persistent emotional reactions. Beck's technique involves frequent, gentle questioning of the client about the basis for what he or she is saying. Beck speaks of "automatic thoughts" that seem to arise by themselves, without reasoning. These thoughts are accepted as valid even though they are not the products of rational consideration of alternatives. Children who simply accept their parents' values without questioning them are engaging in automatic thought. According to Beck, therapy should be aimed at terminating automatic thinking and replacing it with thoughts that result from rational consideration of alternatives.

Beck's cognitive therapy has been used with various forms of maladaptive behavior, but he has specialized in work with depressed people. In this work, emphasis is placed on the irrational ideas that contribute to feelings of depression and thoughts of suicide.

Cognitive–Behavioral Therapies

Whereas in traditional psychotherapy conversations between the client and the therapist are the primary vehicle for achieving clinical improvement, most cognitive–behavioral therapies rely heavily on a growing number of other techniques such as modeling and role playing. These clinical approaches began as **behavior therapy**. In contrast to the various psychotherapies, the roots of behavior therapy can be found in operant and classical conditioning; cognitive and psychodynamic events were intentionally ignored. The operant elements led to techniques for directly changing behavior, an approach that came to be known as **behavior modification.** The classical-conditioning elements led to a variety of techniques, notably systematic desensitization, that are used to reduce people's fear of specific objects or situations. Table 17–2 lists core characteristics of behavior therapy.

In recent years increased recognition has been given to the simultaneous influences of environmental manipulations, such as those used in behavior modification programs, and cognitive processes. Cognitive–behavioral interventions aim to correct people's misconceptions, strengthen their coping skills and feelings of control over their own lives, and facilitate constructive self-talk. Whereas cognitive therapists like Ellis and Beck use the conversational format of psychotherapy, clinicians who use cognitive–behavioral therapies are more likely to use structured training sessions that require the client to practice prescribed exercises.

TABLE 17-2
Core Characteristics of Behavior Therapy

1. Most abnormal behavior is acquired and maintained according to the same principles as normal behavior.
2. Most abnormal behavior can be modified through the application of social-learning principles.
3. The current determinants of behavior must be assessed.
4. People are best described by what they think, feel, and do in specific life situations.
5. Treatment methods are precisely specified and objectively evaluated.
6. Treatment outcome is evaluated in terms of generalization to the real-life setting and its maintenance over time.
7. Treatment strategies are individually tailored to different problems in different individuals.
8. Extensive use is made of psychological assistants, such as parents and teachers, to modify problem behavior in the settings in which it occurs.

Based on O'Leary and Wilson, 1987.

There is growing evidence that cognitive–behavioral training can be quite effective in helping people overcome fears and inhibitions and increase their coping skills. While the mechanism by which this training leads to improvements in behavior has not been completely described, an important factor seems to be the client's sense of self-efficacy, that is, the client's belief that he or she is effective at carrying out tasks. Feelings of self-efficacy increase when individuals acquire new skills, and this encourages them to strengthen their skills even further.

Efficacy expectations refer to the belief that one is able to execute successfully the behavior required to produce a particular outcome. If people possess the necessary skills and there are adequate incentives, efficacy expectations can be major determinants of whether coping behavior will be initiated, how much effort will be expended, and how long that behavior will be sustained in the face of stress-arousing circumstances. Efficacy expectations may be altered through performance accomplishments, vicarious experiences, verbal persuasion, and emotional arousal. Of these, performance accomplishments have the most positive effect on efficacy expectations (Bandura, 1982, 1986). It seems possible that efficacy expectations are among the most important contributors to behavioral change (see Figure 17–3).

Relaxation Training

Relaxation training often helps people who are tense and generally anxious. In one approach, emphasis is placed on learning to contrast muscular tension with muscular relaxation. In another, meditation procedures are employed. In yet another method, known as autogenic training, self-suggestion is the key ingredient.

Muscular Relaxation

Muscular relaxation involves tensing and then relaxing various muscle groups. The individual is encouraged to note the differences between feeling tense and feeling relaxed. Relaxation training is used in many methods of natural childbirth and in yoga. People who have difficulty falling asleep often find that relaxation exercises help them get to sleep more quickly. At first individuals use relaxation exercises mainly in the therapy situation. But as their ability to relax themselves in stressful situations improves, they are encouraged to relax themselves in everyday life. Instructions like the following are used in muscular relaxation training.

All right, lean back comfortably in the chair. Place both hands on your thighs or in your lap. Now, close your eyes and follow my instructions. First of all, I

calm. Now move down to the shoulders and just relax the shoulders completely, letting them droop, go completely at rest, become completely tranquil, completely limp. And then move down the shoulders to the arms . . . down to the elbows . . . and from there down the forearms to the wrists . . . hands and fingers; relaxing all of these muscles and letting the arms dangle from the frame of your body; letting them hang completely limp. And now move down to the chest. Take a deep breath and, as you exhale, relax every muscle in the chest. Let all the muscles there go completely limp and relax; let all the pressure and all the tightness go out of that area of your body and let the muscles relax completely. Now move down to the stomach. Relax all of the muscles of the stomach; without any pressure or any tension in any of the musculature of the midsection of your body. Now go up and down the spine. Go up one side and down the other, relaxing every muscle in the back. Become completely at rest and completely relaxed. And now move down to the waist . . . and buttocks . . . down to the thighs . . . knees . . . calves of your legs . . . ankles, feet, and toes, relaxing every muscle; letting them become completely limp and completely relaxed. With each breath you may relax just a little bit more and become completely calm, completely tranquil.

—Walker, Hedberg, Clement, and Wright, 1981, pp. 66–67)

FIGURE 17-3
Efficacy expectations influence an individual's performance. These two individuals both know that being outgoing and cheerful contributes to the enjoyment of social relationships. Yet the unfavorable efficacy expectations of the person in photo *a* contribute to ineffective social behavior, whereas the favorable expectations of the one in photo *b* contribute to effectiveness and a feeling of being at ease.

want you to relax the muscles of the forehead and the scalp. Just consciously think about your forehead and scalp and begin to relax those muscles. Let all of the muscles in that area go completely limp, become completely tranquil, and become completely at rest. Smooth all the wrinkles out of the forehead and relax the muscles of the forehead and scalp. Now move down to the facial muscles and relax all of the muscles of the face, just letting all of the tension go out of those muscles; letting them become completely limp; letting all the flesh and all of the muscles of the face just relax completely without any pressure or any tension. Relax the tongue, the lips, the cheeks, and the jaws, without any pressure in any of those muscles. Now, move down to the neck and relax all the muscles in the neck, letting them go completely limp, becoming completely relaxed . . . completely

Meditation

In relaxation training using meditation procedures, the individual learns to concentrate on a thought, a sensation, a word, an object, or some mental state. Some techniques are very active and require that the person make a strenuous effort to focus on a specific thing. Certain yoga techniques, for example, require that the practitioner maintain specific postures and deliberately control his or her breathing or other bodily functions. Other meditation techniques, such as transcendental meditation (TM), are passive approaches. Practitioners simply remain in a quiet atmosphere and make a relaxed attempt to achieve a state of inner peace. The individual concentrates on a *mantra* (a specially selected word) and tries, but does not strain, to exclude all other thoughts. Most passive techniques are practiced for 20-minute periods each day, once in the morning and again before dinner.

Autogenic Training

Strictly speaking, autogenic training is not exclusively a relaxation technique. Rather than training people to achieve a state of low arousal, autogenic training aims at a state of psychophysiological equilibrium. Although this often involves decreasing physiological arousal, autogenic training does not try to produce complete relaxation. The autogenic method teaches the individual to assume an attitude of "passive concentration" on a series of "formulas," or self-suggestions, pertaining to various physical, emotional, and mental sensations. The following are standard formulas (one limb at a time for those related to the limbs).

1. My arms are heavy.
2. My legs are heavy.
3. My arms are warm.
4. My legs are warm.
5. My forehead is cool.
6. My heartbeat is calm and regular.

The individual is encouraged to imagine feelings, sensations, or scenes that may make the sensation more vivid, but is warned not to *try* to make the sensation occur. Concentration on the formula must remain a passive experience, whether or not the sensation is perceived.

There is evidence that progressive relaxation has greater effects on the muscles whereas autogenic training has greater effects on the autonomic nervous system (Lehrer and Woolfolk, 1984). Relaxation therapies appear to be helpful for a variety of psychosomatic disorders, particularly tension headaches and migraine headaches. However, they usually are not sufficient by themselves. Life styles, social environments, and views of the world can create or compound people's problems in living. Such factors as the quality and nature of available social support and the individual's goals, attitudes, and values often must be dealt with. Table 17-3 lists a number of factors that bear on the advisability of using relaxation techniques in a given case.

Research on relaxation skills requires answers to two questions: Has the individual learned the relaxation skill? Does use of the skill lead to beneficial clinical results? Obviously, if the skills were never learned, there

TABLE 17-3

Factors in Successful Use of Relaxation Training

1. The individual's problems do not have an organic basis.
2. The individual is not psychotic, depressed, or subject to panic attacks.
3. The individual is able to assume responsibility for active participation in treatment, with special emphasis on home practice.
4. Family members are cooperative with and supportive of the individual's treatment.
5. The individual has reasonable expectations (i.e., does not expect a miracle).

would be little reason to expect positive results from relaxation training. Appropriate control groups are needed to provide an adequate basis for judging the effectiveness of the training. There is also a need for studies that explore the effectiveness of relaxation training both alone and in combination with other types of therapy.

Systematic Desensitization

Systematic desensitization combines behavioral training (muscular relaxation) with cognitive activity. It begins with the induction of a relaxed state. While the person is relaxed, he or she imagines scenes that are related to his or her specific fear. Desensitization begins with scenes or images that are only mildly fear arousing. The individual is encouraged to concentrate on perpetuating the relaxed state while imagining those situations. Once the person is able to remain relaxed, progressively more upsetting scenes are imagined.

The theory behind systematic desensitization is that the relaxation response competes with previously learned anxiety responses, such as fears and phobias. (Other responses, such as eating, sexual arousal, or animated conversation, might also compete with anxiety-arousing thoughts.) Research has shown that practicing relaxation when the fear-arousing stimulus is actually present (*in vivo* desensitization) yields superior results to simply imagining the stimulus. Desensitization works best with people who habitually show noticeable increases in physiological arousal (e.g., accelerated heart rate, moist palms) when exposed to the fear-arousing stimulus.

Exposure Therapies

Exposure therapies are based on the principle that continued exposure to anxiety-provoking stimuli (for example, exposing a person who is afraid of dirt or dirty objects) will decrease anxiety. **Exposure** consists of a gradual approach to an anxiety-provoking situation. Under such conditions the distress experienced in the situation is kept at a relatively low level.

Exposure to fear-arousing situations is one of the most effective ways of overcoming fear. However, there are positive results only if clients are willing to expose themselves to the situations they are afraid of. Although **in vivo exposure** (actually being in the situation) usually works best, **fantasized exposure** (thinking about being in the situation) is also effective. Exposure treatment is appropriate for many unpleasant or disadvantageous emotional responses. If the treatment is effective, improvement can usually be observed within five or six sessions.

You are standing behind a one-way mirror. You see a bare room except for two single beds with clothes on them. One bed has male clothes on it and the other has female clothes on it. Straight ahead at the other end of the room, you see a door open and a naked man about your age walks into the room. He walks toward the beds which are next to each other about four feet apart. He starts to go toward the bed with the female clothes on it. He looks at the clothes; suddenly you can see a painful expression on his face. He sits down on the bed. Now he starts to sweat and looks sick. He reaches for a bra and he starts to gag. As he puts the bra on he starts to vomit all over the clothes and on himself. He groans in agony as he doubles over and falls down to the ground. He is lying with the bra on and wallowing in vomit.

—Cautela, 1985, p. 93)

A covert modeling scene was then presented in which the model puts on the male clothes and looks happy.

In general, covert modeling involves constructing scenes or situations in which the client can picture the behavior that is to be changed. Although this is a relatively new technique and requires more research, available evidence suggests that it is a promising clinical tool (Kazdin and Mascitelli, 1982).

Like other cognitive and behavioral therapies, modeling is often combined with other approaches. For example, while reinforcing adaptive overt behavior, the therapist might help the client acquire more realistic ideas about problem areas. In treating a complex problem such as intense anger in a child, the therapist might: (1) teach the parents to be more effective in reacting to temper tantrums (modeling might be used to accomplish this); (2) help the child identify the situations and thoughts that evoke the tantrums; (3) model cognitive and behavioral responses to stress and frustration that are more effective than anger; and (4) use guided rehearsal and praise to strengthen the child's adaptive behavior.

Assertiveness Training

Assertiveness training is specifically designed to enhance the interpersonal skills one needs to stand up for one's rights, such as refusing unwanted requests, expressing opinions, and making requests. Assertiveness training is preceded by a careful assessment of the client's responses in certain types of situations. The assessment is designed to answer these questions: What situations are of concern to the client? What does the client typically do in these situations? What are the personal and environmental blocks to more assertiveness in these situations?

Lack of assertive behavior is often related to deficits in social skills or to interfering emotional reactions

Flooding is a form of exposure therapy in which the client is exposed to a flood of fear-arousing stimuli that is not terminated simply because the client experiences a high level of tension. In flooding, the clinical session is saturated with frightening thoughts and images in the hope that emotional responses to them will be extinguished through burnout. If this happens, **extinction** is said to have occurred.

In **implosive therapy** the client experiences higher and higher levels of anxiety through imaginal presentation of scenes depicting behavior and situations that he or she has strenuously avoided in the past. The imagery used in treatment is intended to represent conflict areas that are thought to be the source of the avoidance behavior. Implosion is based on the therapist's interpretation of the psychodynamics underlying the avoidance behavior. The imaginal material used in implosion therapy tends to be much more intense than that used in flooding.

Modeling

Often people are unaware that habit controls much of their behavior. Through **modeling,** they can be shown that there are other ways of doing things. Although modeling can take place when an individual observes someone demonstrating specific social skills, it also occurs informally, for example, when children imitate the heroes of television shows. In clinical applications of modeling, demonstrations by models are often combined with **guided rehearsals,** in which the individual is encouraged to imitate the behavior of the model with the model helping whenever necessary. When people imitate the adaptive behavior of models, their new responses are strengthened by positive reinforcement. The success of a modeling program depends on several factors.

1. How carefully the observer attends to the modeled behavior.
2. How well what was observed is retained.
3. The observer's ability to reproduce the modeled behavior.
4. How motivated the observer is to use the modeled behavior.

Live modeling involves direct observation of a model. **Symbolic modeling** refers to observation of a model who is presented indirectly through film, video or audio tape, or printed word. **Covert modeling** is a logical extension of symbolic modeling in which the individual is asked to imagine observing a model and a particular consequence. For example, a male cross-dresser was asked to imagine the following scene.

(a)

(b)

(c)

FIGURE 17-4
Modeling can be an effective technique in assertiveness training. In this series of photos, (a) the therapist demonstrates an introduction for a shy client, (b) the client practices with others, and (c) the client uses her new skills in the stress-producing setting of a job interview.

and thoughts. If appropriate behaviors are available but are not performed because of anxiety, the focus may be on enhancing the client's anxiety management skills. Modeling and behavioral rehearsal play important roles in assertiveness training programs (see Figure 17–4). Positive feedback is offered after each rehearsal, and prompting is provided when needed. Homework as-signments are used if, as is desirable, the client agrees to carry out tasks that require assertiveness outside the training sessions. If the assertiveness deficits extend over a broad range of social behaviors, a number of training sessions may be needed. However, if the problem is fairly specific, a few sessions may be sufficient.

Paradoxical Intention

Paradoxical intention is a technique in which the therapist instructs the client to perform behaviors that appear to be in opposition to the client's therapeutic goal. For example, an individual who complains of inability to fall asleep within a satisfactory interval might be asked to remain awake as long as possible. An agoraphobic who cannot go into crowded places for fear of suffering severe heart palpitations might be instructed to go into crowded places and try to become anxious. Paradoxical intention is a relatively new technique that requires more research. It is not yet clear when it is appropriate or why it seems to be effective in particular cases. Perhaps it is effective because it requires the client to maintain the very behavior that he or she seeks to change under conditions that cannot support continuation of that behavior. Exposure to anxiety-provoking situations is an element of paradoxical intention and may contribute to its effectiveness.

Behavior Modification

Operant methods use schedules of reinforcement and shaping to gradually achieve a desired response. Special prompts might be employed to highlight a situation that calls for a particular response. **Fading** refers to gradual elimination of these special cues when they are no longer needed. Positive reinforcers (such as praise or money) are used to strengthen desired responses. The token economy is one of the most common applications of operant principles to modify maladaptive behavior. Extinction procedures and punishment might be used to eliminate undesirable responses. When punishment is employed to eliminate a response, it is a good idea to positively reinforce an alternative, more desirable, response at the same time.

Reinforcement and cognitive approaches may be combined in some cases. For example, both environmental and cognitive factors usually play important roles in therapy for depressed people. A depressed person might be helped to do things that lead to positive reinforcement from others. At the same time, the therapist would help the individual become aware of and change internal events, such as negative self-statements, that enhance his or her feelings of pessimism and worthlessness. Simultaneously strengthening social skills and

FIGURE 17–5
Members of a therapy group have opportunities to learn and gather support from other members and from the therapist.

modifying thoughts and attitudes can be a very valuable therapeutic approach.

Another major development of recent years is the use of biofeedback procedures in which the individual is reinforced whenever a designated change in bodily functioning takes place. Through biofeedback the individual becomes better able to control internal processes, such as body temperature and heart rate, that are related to maladaptation.

Group Therapy

Group approaches to psychotherapy are used not only because they are less costly but because many clinicians believe that therapy can be at least as effective with groups as it is with individuals. One appealing feature of group psychotherapy is that clients can learn both by observing other group members' adaptive and maladaptive attempts to solve personal problems and by comparing their own relationship with the therapist with those of the other members (see Figure 17–5).

Group therapy is usually seen as a means of broadening the application of psychotherapeutic concepts. Some advocates of group psychotherapy believe it may actually produce better results than individual therapy. There is evidence that groups are particularly effective when they give participants opportunities to acquire new social skills through modeling (Curran and Monti, 1982). Opportunities to rehearse or practice these skills in the group increase the chances that the participants will actually use their newly acquired skills in everyday

life. The following are among the most frequently observed features of group therapy:

1. *Self-disclosure*—the opportunity to tell the group about one's personal problems and concerns.

2. *Acceptance and support*—feeling a sense of belongingness and being valued by the group members.

3. *Norm clarification*—learning that one's problems are neither unique nor more serious than is true for other group members.

4. *Social learning*—being able to relate constructively and adaptively within the group.

5. *Vicarious learning*—learning about oneself through the observation of other group members, including the therapist.

6. *Self-understanding*—finding out about one's behavior in the group setting and the motivations contributing to the behavior.

Group therapy provides an opportunity for members to observe how their behavior affects other people and to receive personally relevant feedback. To maximize the likelihood that this will happen, group therapists often emphasize not only what members reveal about themselves, but also how the others react to what is said in the group setting.

John, who had been in the group for approximately six months, reported to the group that he had had an extremely upsetting fight with his girlfriend that had resulted in the rupture of their relationship. He and she were coming home from a Hawaiian vacation trip between Christmas and New Year's. It had been a very good trip, during which they had deeply enjoyed each other's company. Yet John noticed that his girlfriend had grown silent and tearful on the way home. Upon inquiring he learned that she did not wish to talk; she stated she was having some problems around the holidays, and needed some time and space to think about them. John guessed from previous conversations that she was troubled by her feelings surrounding her ex-husband (she had been divorced for only four months) and as he grew annoyed and demanded more information from her. (Before they started dating he had carefully and closely questioned her about her relationship with her ex-husband, and she had reassured him that that was no longer an issue for her. John now felt that she had lied and he became more indignant and intrusive.) The situation—her withdrawal and his demands—escalated until John raised the question of whether or not they should continue their relationship. After they returned to their homes, he gathered up all the Christmas presents she had given him and left them on her doorstep with a note stating that it was better if they ended their relationship. The next day he thought better of it and tried calling her, but she refused to speak to him. He then tried to force his way into her house using his key; she became frightened and called the police.

—(Yalom, 1986, p. 707)

How did what John said, and the way that he said it, affect the other members? His account of the incident was biased by his personal involvement in the incident and his strong emotions. All four of the women in the group expressed feelings suggesting that what John said had frightened them. One woman said that John appeared very impatient in most group sessions. Two women said that John frequently seemed angry. The fourth woman mentioned that John frightened her and she preferred not to sit next to him. Another group member observed that John had on more than one occasion commented on the "petty grievances of other members." Yet another mentioned that John lacked empathy for the problems and limitations of other people. Interestingly, John commented that he tended to present a "strong front" to the group, by which he meant he did not admit to weaknesses and failings. All of these contributions of members following John's account focused attention on the "here and now," how the group members were affecting each other.

Cognitive–Behavioral Group Therapy

Although group therapy has traditionally been carried out from a psychodynamic perspective, cognitive and behavioral therapists are developing their own group techniques. The focus of cognitive–behavioral group therapy is on increasing the skills and comfort of people in social situations. Group members role-play specific social situations that they find difficult. The themes of particular sessions are often programmed by the therapist from prior knowledge of the members' problems. The therapist may model alternative ways of handling these situations. The role playing is accompanied by social reinforcement and feedback, and homework tasks are assigned. Other techniques are used as well, including graded task assignments, examination of specific types of distortions that may arise in social interactions (such as overgeneralization and catastrophizing), and discussion of types of cognitions that have negative and positive influences in group situations.

Cognitive–behavioral group therapy is more highly structured than group therapy conducted along psychodynamic lines. Although it is a relatively new approach, group members not only seem to value the task-oriented sessions but also exhibit improved behavior. (Falloon, 1981; Steuer and others, 1984).

From a psychodynamic point of view, group psychotherapy represents an opportunity to deal with transference in a social situation and to compare one's attitude toward participation in a group with those of other group members. The group is often seen as an extension of the family. For example, a frequent topic that arises in group therapy is the competition of group members for the therapist's attention. A psychoanalyst might see echoes of the members' relationships to parents and siblings in their performances in the group. A cognitively oriented clinician, on the other hand, would be interested primarily in the often irrational ideas of group members concerning what goes on, or should go on, in social situations. Client-centered therapists see the therapist's role in groups as basically the same as in individual counseling; in both situations the therapist is a facilitator of personal growth. Cognitive–behavioral therapists are increasingly using techniques such as modeling and behavior rehearsal in groups.

Family Therapy

Sometimes therapy focuses on individuals who already constitute a group. Two examples are family therapy and marital therapy.

Family therapy is based on the idea that many problems both arise from family behavior patterns and are affected by them. It often is recommended when one member of a family, usually a child, is referred to a mental-health professional. If maladaptive interactions with other members of the family are suspected as part of the problem, one of the most effective ways that a therapist can help the child is to work with all the family mem-

FIGURE 17–6
During this family-therapy session the therapist observes how the members of the family interact. In this photo the therapist is using what has just been said by a family member to help the others see how one person's behavior affects other members of the family.

can be triggered by a child's attempt to handle a phase that is still a source of conflict for one of the parents. Facilitating the family's transition from one developmental phase to another is the basic goal of the family therapist.

Family therapists report distinct patterns of family symptoms. In some cases, each partner in a marriage demands too much of the same thing from the other: service, protection, care, and so forth. In other cases, they compound each other's problems by complementing each other. One partner takes charge and the other becomes incompetent: an overbearing and emotionally distant husband has a "hysterical" wife whose erratic behavior makes him still more overbearing; a strong, angry wife has a passive, alcoholic husband who is a suitable object of her anger, and that anger makes him even more passive; the husband of a depressed and hypochondriacal woman needs to be a healer and savior. Often family therapy aims to reveal what is hidden: the passive partner's suppressed anger, the savior's feelings of helplessness.

A related idea is that of unconscious or unacknowledged roles. Roles in the drama of family life, assumed perhaps out of loyalty or a need for belonging, may become destructive yet hard to abandon because they help to maintain the family. For example, a child who becomes "parentified" because of a mother's or father's incapacity is likely to play this adult role poorly, using authority too harshly or making it a vehicle of rivalry with younger brothers and sisters. Another child may be assigned the role of bad boy so that one of the parents can play disciplinarian. Such roles must be openly recognized and the assignments altered if the family is to become more healthy. The family members often develop an unspoken family mythology that has important effects on all family members. The mythology may be something like, "John is the stupid one," "Father can't work." These myths are especially likely to create conflict when they are incompatible with family ideals or are not accepted by all members of the family. Therapists often find that bringing the myths out in the open in family discussion is helpful in focusing on the problems these distorted role assignments create.

The Family as a System

If any single idea could be said to guide family therapy, it is probably the notion of a family system. Human life can be organized hierarchically into systems of varying size and complexity: the individual, the family, the society, the culture. The family is seen as a self-maintaining system which, like the human body, has feedback mechanisms that preserve its identity and integrity by restoring homeostasis—the internal status quo—after a disturbance. A change in one part of the family system thus is often compensated elsewhere. Families have

bers together (see Figure 17–6). The following are some of the core problems with which family therapy deals:

1. Inability to resolve conflicts, make decisions, or solve problems

2. Chaotic organization and lack of agreed-upon responsibilities

3. Too rigid an organization resulting in an inability to respond to changing circumstances and stress

4. Overcloseness to the point that individual family members may lose any sense of individuality

5. Lack of emotional ties and communication among family members

6. Failure of the parents to agree on child-rearing practices.

Instead of treating family members individually, the therapist encourages the family to work as a group, dealing together with their attitudes and feelings toward one another and their resistance to cooperation and sharing. Family therapy often provides a valuable forum for airing hostilities, reviewing emotional ties, and dealing with crises. Every family must pass through a series of stages, each of which is potentially a crisis—changes in behavior are required, relationships shift, and everyone feels pressured and disorganized. Behavioral problems often arise when the life cycle of the family is interrupted. It is not the task of the child, alone, to get through the changes brought by stages of development such as becoming an adolescent or going to college. It is a job for the whole family, with implications for each member. Maladaptive behavior in the family as a whole

mechanisms for adapting to changed circumstances, and, like individuals, they have biologically and socially determined states of development.

A family that functions poorly cannot adjust to change because its mechanisms are either inflexible or ineffectual. The family's daily habits and internal communication—its transactional patterns, as they are called—harm its individual members. The pathology is in the system as a whole. Individual disorders not only serve as a source of protection and power for the disturbed person but may also preserve the family system and act as a distorted means of communication within that system. They fulfill the same function that neurotic symptoms are said to fulfill for individuals in psychodynamic theory.

Some families are highly interdependent; everyone in them is overresponsive to everyone else. They develop habits of intimate quarreling and complaining that become difficult to change. In other families, the family members have little mutual contact or concern; their boundaries are rigid. Family systems that are too closely knit, or enmeshed, respond too intensely to change; every disturbance may turn into a crisis. Systems in which the family members are distant, or disengaged, do not respond strongly enough; serious problems are ignored and issues are avoided.

In family therapy, the main concern is with processes rather than sources and forces. Systems theory defines influences as mutual and causality as circular, so family therapists tend to avoid blaming and attributing causes—although there are exceptions to this as to every other generalization about the field. The symptoms of a defective family system are said to take different forms in different members of the system. A husband and wife, for example, may seem to have very different personalities, but this may be due not to their intrinsic characteristics as individuals but rather to their functions within that system. For this reason, family therapists often make limited use of ordinary psychiatric diagnoses, which describe individual pathology, and diagnose family situations instead.

Marital Therapy

Marital therapy can be viewed as a subtype of family therapy. The overlap is seen in the couple who battle about how to handle their 6-year-old son, who sets fires: the wife blames the husband's permissiveness, he blames her strictness, and both see the child as the one needing treatment. To the therapist, the problem is the parental pulling and hauling for control over the child, and the child's fire-setting is a search for clarification. The therapist points this out and coaches the parents in making changes in the rules by which they operate. Those changes may not be directed at individual feelings, yet such therapy, usually short-term, often yields personality changes as the problem and its accompanying stress disappear.

Couples frequently seek marital therapy because one or both of the partners believe that the relationship is troubled or are contemplating ending it through divorce or separation. By seeing the therapist together, the partners can more easily identify problems and alter the ways in which they relate to each other. The main advantage of couple's therapy is that the therapist, as an impartial observer, can actually witness the couple's interactions rather than hearing about them in a secondhand and perhaps one-sided report. Both family and couples therapy can be carried out from one of several perspectives. Family therapy is likely to include behavioral or psychodynamic approaches. Couple's therapy often utilizes a cognitive focus as well. Regardless of the type of marital therapy practiced, a current trend is to focus attention on specific relevant issues such as helping the couple increase communication, express feelings, help each other, and enjoy shared experiences.

Psychodrama

Although most group therapy is essentially an expanded, more complicated, and more realistic version of individual therapy, a number of approaches have been designed especially for groups. One of these is **psychodrama**, which was created by Jacob Moreno in the 1920s. Moreno led impromptu activity groups of children in the public gardens of Vienna. He noticed that when the children were encouraged to act out stories instead of merely reading or listening to them, they often displayed unexpected depths of feeling and understanding. He later experimented with a form of theater, the "theater of spontaneity," in which players were encouraged to draw upon their inner resources in creating the dramatic action rather than following a script.

In psychodrama a group of individuals assembles under the leadership of a therapist (often called the director). The group enacts events of emotional significance in order to resolve conflicts and release members from inhibitions that limit their capacity for spontaneous and creative activity, particularly social activity. Behavior therapists use role playing to give clients practice in new social skills, but in psychodrama role playing tends to be more spontaneous and oriented toward expressing strongly felt emotions (see Figure 17–7).

Moreno saw psychodrama as a vehicle for expressing strong emotions, acquiring insight into one's own behavior, and realistically evaluating the behavior of others. Psychodrama is a directive treatment in that the therapist controls the mechanics of the therapy situation. However, it is nondirective in that the emotional content of sessions arises spontaneously from the activities of the participants.

Research on the Psychological Therapies

Many groups have a stake in the evaluation of therapeutic effectiveness. Patients, their families, therapists, researchers, insurance companies, legislators, and planners of mental-health services all want to know which therapy is most effective. Given the number of psychological therapies, it is obvious that researchers who study these areas have their work cut out for them. Obtaining information about therapeutic effectiveness is not easy for a number of reasons. For example, therapists differ in their ability to carry out particular therapies. Furthermore, some therapies may be more effective with certain types of patients than others. Psychological therapy is not a unitary process applied to a unitary problem. Research on therapy is improving because studies are becoming more complex and incorporating more relevant factors into their research designs. Some of the practical differences between laboratory experiments and research on psychotherapy are summarized in Table 17–4.

Comparison of a particular therapy with a control condition is useful, but studies that compare the effectiveness of several treatment approaches for similar groups of clients are even more significant. Most clinicians agree that the same therapy will have varying effects on different types of patients. There is a need for experiments in which the independent variable is a specific therapeutic procedure (such as group therapy and systematic desensitization) and the dependent variable is some aspect of behavior (such as frequency of suicidal thoughts).

Before a research project is carried out, there must be agreement on how to measure the results. For example, suppose a researcher intends to assess the effectiveness of different therapies designed to reduce the tendency to hallucinate. One way to measure the dependent variable would be to count the number of times people report having hallucinatory experiences. But people might have hallucinations that they did not report, or might make up such experiences just to have something to report. Thus, whereas some clinicians might contend that frequency of reported hallucinations is a reasonable index of the general tendency to hallucinate, others might not be satisfied with this conclusion.

In any research, all groups of subjects must be as similar or equal as possible before the experiment begins. The therapists in the various groups should also be comparable. Many other factors must also be controlled. For instance, suppose the staff on the ward of a mental hospital believe that their program is a significant therapeutic innovation. Their enthusiasm for the program might, *by itself*, influence the patients in their care. Ac-

FIGURE 17–7
Acting out emotionally significant events can help people deal with strong emotions that they may have been afraid to acknowledge.

Integration of Therapeutic Approaches

When therapists who base their techniques on different perspectives discuss their work, there are inevitable differences of opinion. The issues that separate the various schools of thought seem substantial. Should therapists actively direct patients toward behavioral change, or should they focus on the development of insight? Should therapy delve into the past or examine the present? Should its duration be long or short? Despite the different ways in which these questions are answered, there is evidence of a movement toward the integration of therapeutic approaches. "Talking therapies," such as psychoanalytically oriented psychotherapy, are placing more emphasis on the need of patients to take responsibility for themselves and develop self-mastery. Behavioral therapies are giving increased attention to the cognitive underpinnings of behavioral change. Often this means helping patients acquire insight into their misconceptions about themselves and their social relationships. Many cognitive–behavioral therapists relay heavily on imagery as a means of achieving therapeutic goals. The use of imagery for treatment purposes clearly acknowledges the potentially crucial role of private events.

There is growing evidence that performance-based therapies, in which individuals actually deal with problematic situations, can be very effective. However, cognitive processes, such as insight, may play an important role in helping people develop more adaptive performance orientations to their problems of living. As more therapists attend to the relative roles of cognition, emotion, and behavior, steps toward greater integration of therapeutic approaches are becoming noticeable.

TABLE 17-4
Differences Between Experimental Laboratory Studies and Therapy

Factor	Laboratory Study	Psychotherapy
1. Independent variables	Usually quite clearly defined	Complex, often difficult to define clearly
2. Dependent variables	Usually quite clearly defined	Often involve complex set of responses that change over time
3. Experimental situation	Well-controlled	Not possible to eliminate unexpected events
4. Other situations	Researchers usually not concerned about what happens outside experimental situation	Therapist is interested in what happens outside therapy situation

tually, there is evidence that such an **enthusiasm effect** operates in a variety of situations, including hospitals, schools, and private consulting rooms.

Most studies of therapy techniques compare a group of people who receive treatment with one or two groups of people who do not. But such comparisons do not show how individuals within the groups are affected by specific aspects of the treatment. Clinicians also need to know how changes in the client's behavior are related to what the clinician does or says. Some behavior therapists see single-subject research, which is described in Box 17-1, as an important source of information.

Outcome Studies

There are disagreements about the relative effectiveness of the different psychological therapies. In evaluating psychotherapy a common procedure has been to compare two groups, one that is treated clinically and one that is not. Researchers with different criteria and expectations have obtained different results in such comparisons. For example, after reviewing the literature, Eysenck (1952, 1961) concluded that psychotherapy was an ineffective clinical method. He argued that many apparent successes could be explained by **spontaneous remissions**, in which the client's symptoms would have disappeared in time with or without treatment. Bergin and Lambert (1978) found that psychotherapy had an effect but that the effect was not necessarily positive. Some patients actually seemed to deteriorate because of psychotherapy.

One of the most important questions in outcome studies is what the criteria for improvement should be. Table 17-5 organizes a number of ways of thinking about outcome measures. Which are more important, changes in how the client feels and behaves, or changes in what he or she thinks about? Would the opinions of

the client's family or co-workers be helpful in evaluating improvement? How important is the therapist's evaluation of the outcome? Sometimes the therapist and the client don't agree. Anthony Storr, a British psychoanalyst, gives this example of what he had considered an "unsuccessful" case:

Some time ago I had a letter from a man whom I had treated some twenty-five years previously asking whether I would see, or at any rate advise treatment for, his daughter. He assumed, wrongly, that I would not remember him, and, in the course of his letter, wrote as follows: "I can quite truthfully say that six months of your patient listening to my woes made a most important contribution to my life style. Although my transvestism was not cured, my approach to life and to other people was re-oriented and for that I am most grateful. It is part of my life that I have never forgotten."

TABLE 17-5
Important Dimensions of Therapy Outcome Measures

Dimensions

Focus of measures	Emotions Thoughts Behaviors
Possible processes	Evaluation Description Observation
Possible sources of data	Self-report Therapist rating Relevant-other rating Trained observation by others Trained self-monitoring Instrumental behavior

The three dimensions may be combined in many ways, but all combinations may not yield similar results.

BOX 17-1
Single-Subject Research

Single-subject research differs in an important respect from the traditional case study. Although case studies may provide insights about treatment, they generally rely on anecdotal information and impressions, which may be misleading. In single-subject studies, on the other hand, behavior is observed directly, either in the actual problem situation or in a simulated laboratory environment. The behavior is also measured continuously, before, during, and in some cases after treatment. Immediate information about whether the treatment is having the desired effects can be obtained. This allows the therapist to make decisions about the treatment while it is going on.

The most common test of the effect of a clinical procedure with a single client involves the A-B-A-B research design. This design is used most often to determine whether operant-conditioning procedures are effective in bringing about behavioral changes. It consists of obtaining a baseline measure of the target behavior (A), instituting reinforcement-contingency procedures (B), removing the contingency so that the conditions that were present during the baseline period are reinstated (A), and reintroducing the phase-B contingency (B). This repeated-measures design is a very powerful method for isolating the conditions that control behavior.

An A-B-A-B design was used in operant therapy with a 19-year-old man who had been admitted to a hospital with complaints of pain in the lower back, hips, and both legs, and great difficulty in walking, sitting, and standing. An exhaustive medical study determined that his symptoms were unrelated to physical causes, and the case was diagnosed as a psychological disorder.

The operant therapy consisted of visits by a young assistant to the patient's room three times daily. During these visits the assistant spent approximately 10 minutes talking to the patient about topics unrelated to his walking. During an initial 3-day period she encouraged him to walk but provided him with no reinforcement for doing so. During the next 3-day sequence she instructed the patient to walk and reinforced him when this happened. Reinforcement consisted of comments such as "Good," "That's great," and "You're doing fine," accompanied by attention, friendliness, and smiling. Reinforcements were not given during the following 3-day period, but they were reinstituted during the final 3 days of the experimental therapeutic program.

Figure 17-8 summarizes the results of the program. During the instruction period there was no increase in walking. The addition of reinforcement resulted in increased walking. When reinforcing contingencies are discontinued, there is usually a decrement in the target behavior. In this case, contrary to what might be expected, improvement continued during the period when no reinforcement was given. Uncontrolled and unscheduled reinforcement by other patients may have contributed to this continued improvement. The great-

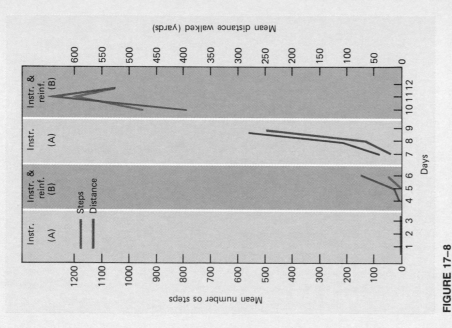

FIGURE 17-8

The chart shows changes in walking behavior during the four conditions of the repeated-measures design. Mean number of steps and distance are shown as a function of instructions and reinforcements.

est improvement occurred during the final phase of the program.

Single-subject A-B-A-B designs are useful in monitoring a particular type of behavior (such as temper tantrums or inappropriate verbal responses) over time. Effective treatment strategies can be developed by adding therapeutic components to facilitate behavior change in a cumulative manner. This process is greatly aided by the continual, ongoing assessment of treatment outcome. A limitation of single-subject research designs is that it may be difficult to control such factors as the occurrence of reinforcement during noncontingent periods. It is also difficult to know whether the findings can be generalized until the same procedures are carried out with many clients. Yet for clinicians and researchers who are interested in behavioral measurements and the specifics of cause and effect relationships, single-subject designs are an effective tool.

Looked at from one point of view, my treatment of this man was a failure. His major symptom, the complaint which drove him to seek my help, was not abolished. And yet I think it is clear that he did get something from his short period of psychotherapy which was of considerable value to him. A man does not write to a psychotherapist asking him to see his daughter, twenty-five years after his own treatment was over, using the terms employed in this letter, unless he believes that what happened during his period of treatment was important.

—(Storr, 1980, p. 146)

If all the measures of improvement do not agree, which is most important? How can we compare studies that use different outcome measures to evaluate the effectiveness of various therapies? Clearly, although outcome research is progressing in sophistication, many of the important questions will be difficult to answer. Personal accounts of experiences in psychotherapy provide researchers with hypotheses for future research. Identifying the elements of personal growth and the factors that foster it will contribute to the development of better formal and informal therapies. In this regard, the observations of people who have had successful therapy can be enlightening. Box 17-2 contains comments about psychotherapy by two clients who were asked to evaluate their experiences.

It is not unusual for clients to see themselves as cured while their therapists see them as unimproved or

BOX 17-2
Two Clients Comment on Their Psychotherapy Experiences

Sandra L. Harris, a prominent clinical psychologist, has described how she felt the impact of her psychotherapy experience long after its completion.

A friend died recently. I am still assimilating the loss and taking stock of all that he meant. Jim was no ordinary friend. He was my therapist some twenty years ago and a central figure in my transition from adolescence to adulthood. He had an important influence on my decision to become a clinical psychologist. Although we saw each other rarely in the intervening years, the fact of his existence remained a tangible, if peripheral, fact to me.

His death has led me once again to reflect on what it is that matters in therapy and how enduring changes are wrought. When I think about the girl I was in my freshman year at the University of Maryland, and the young woman I was when I graduated four years later, it is clear that it was not only the issues Jim and I discussed, but how we talked that made the difference. The intangibles of trust, respect, and caring were at least as important as the active problem solving which transpired in our weekly meetings. It was not a dramatic transformation, rather it was a slight shifting of a path by a few degrees on the compass. Over the years that shift has had a cumulative effect and I walk a very different road than I would have without him. (Harris, 1981, p. 3)

Another woman, whose problems were much more serious, described the role her psychotherapist has played in her personal growth during her treatment for a schizophrenic disorder.

For a patient and therapist to work together so closely for so many years, they must establish a bond that is professional, certainly, but also based on the commonality of humanness that exists between two people. I had drawn so far inside myself and so far away from the world, I had to be shown not only that the world was safe but also that I belonged to it, that I was in fact a person. This grew from years of our working together to develop mutual respect and acceptance and a forum of understanding, in which I believed that he had the capacity to comprehend what I said and that I had the potential to be understood.

The question of whether the fragile ego of the schizophrenic patient can withstand the rigors of intensive therapy seems to me an unfortunate hindrance to the willingness of psychiatrists to attempt psychotherapy with schizophrenic individuals. A fragile ego left alone remains fragile. It seems there must be some balance that can be achieved so that schizophrenic patients can receive the benefits of psychotherapy with therapists who are sensitive to their special needs and can help their egos emerge, little by little. Medication or superficial support alone is not a substitute for the feeling that one is understood by another human being. For me, the greatest gift came the day that I realized that my therapist really had stood by me for years and that he would continue to stand by me and to help me achieve what I wanted to achieve. With that realization my viability as a person began to grow. I do not profess to be cured—I still feel the pain, fear, and frustration of my illness. I know I have a long road ahead of me, but I can honestly say that I am no longer without hope. (A Recovering Patient, 1968, p. 68)

even as being worse. Studies of improvement therefore should include three independent measures: the client's evaluation of the progress made; the therapist's evaluation; and the judgments of people who know the client well, such as family members and friends.

Another approach to evaluating the effectiveness of therapy is to assess the resultant behavior change. Although one of the goals of psychotherapy is enhancement of the client's self-awareness and insight, most people would consider therapy a failure if the person's behavior remained the same. It is not enough to be a source of insight.

Changes in overt behavior are easier to describe and assess objectively than changes in attitudes, feelings, and beliefs. But questions remain. To what degree should behavioral change be used as a criterion? Who should determine the kinds and amounts of change desired? How lasting should the change be? How longstanding and disabling has the patient's condition been? It seems reasonable that criteria for success should be related to the difficulty of the hurdle to be overcome. Implicit in this conclusion is the recognition that criteria that are appropriate in one case may be inappropriate in others.

Comparing Therapies

There is growing support for the conclusion that psychological therapies are worthwhile for many people. But are the different therapeutic approaches equally effective? In one widely cited comparative study (Sloane and others, 1975), the subjects were college students who had applied for treatment—mostly for anxiety and personality disorders—at a psychiatric outpatient clinic. The goal of the study was to compare the relative effectiveness of behavioral therapy (desensitization, assertiveness training, and so on) and more traditional, short-term, psychodynamically oriented therapy. In addition to these two groups, there was a control group whose members were told that they would have to wait about 4 months to receive treatment.

The clients were followed up 4 and 12 months after completing therapy. The measures used in the treatment comparisons were derived from interviews with the clients at these times, from the clients' ratings of their own improvement, and from improvement ratings made by an independent assessor. At 4 months, the psychotherapy and behavioral-therapy groups had improved equally, and significantly more than the waiting-list group. At the 1-year follow-up, the behavioral-therapy clients, but not the psychotherapy group, showed some significant improvement with regard to the problems that had led them to seek therapy. However, there were no significant differences between the two groups

with regard to social adjustment. The 1-year follow-up results were complicated by the fact that some of the clients continued to receive treatment even though the therapy sessions were supposed to end after 4 months. The researchers concluded that their study provided no clear evidence that behavioral therapy was superior to psychotherapy.

The same researchers reported an interesting additional set of comparisons for some of the subjects in their treatment study (Sloane and others, 1977). One year after beginning treatment, the subjects were mailed questionnaires in which they were asked to rate the importance of 32 factors in the success of their treatment. What was most striking about their responses was the similarity between the psychotherapy and behavioral-therapy groups. Both groups emphasized the importance of gaining insight into one's problems, the client–therapist relationship, the opportunity to give vent to emotions, a sense of trust in the therapist, and the development of confidence. Thus, even though the two treatment approaches are based on different assumptions and use different methods, they were described similarly by the clients. This similarity held both for the sample as a whole and for subgroups of clients who were judged to have responded most positively to the treatments offered them.

In a more recent project, researchers analyzed four studies on the outcome of psychotherapy and concluded that who performs the therapy matters much more than what kind of therapy it is (Luborsky and others, 1986). The studies were conducted at Johns Hopkins University, the University of Pennsylvania, the University of Pittsburgh, and McGill University. Altogether, 25 therapists and 240 patients were involved. In three studies, the patients were average psychiatric outpatients; in the Pennsylvania study, they were heroin addicts taking methadone. The techniques included individual psychodynamic psychotherapy, cognitive–behavioral therapy, and group therapy, all in various combinations and for varying lengths of time. Among the many measures of outcome were judgments of improvement by both patients and therapists and ratings of interpersonal behavior, social adjustment, depression, severity of addiction, and other symptoms.

In all four studies some therapists had a significantly higher success rate than others. Differences among therapists were much greater than differences among therapies in producing a favorable outcome. There was little evidence to show that any individual therapist did better with a particular kind of patient. The researchers suggested that more might be learned about how psychotherapy works by studying the most effective therapists than by comparing different forms of treatment.

There is growing evidence that the various psychological approaches to treating cases that do not involve extreme psychopathology are often effective. However, one should not conclude that it makes no difference which techniques are employed in clinical work. There is a need for more information on which treatments are especially effective with particular problems, and on the similarities and differences in the techniques and results of psychological therapies (Garfield and Bergin, 1986).

Psychological therapies have been less successful with serious conditions such as schizophrenia, some types of affective disorders, alcoholism, and drug abuse. However, psychological therapies can play an important role in treating some of these conditions when used in combination with somatic methods like drug therapy and ECT. The value of the psychological component of these combinations frequently lies in helping the patient deal realistically with problems of day-to-day living. For example, social-skills training has been used effectively to help psychotic individuals taking antipsychotic drugs to adjust better to hospital or community settings. Perhaps as more is learned about the distinctive features of particular therapies, it will be possible to combine them in ways that are optimal for clients (see Figure 17–9).

Evaluating the effectiveness of therapeutic efforts requires carefully planned large-scale projects. Conclusions about the relative effectiveness of these different techniques cannot be drawn from research that is too limited in scope or methodologically weak. We noted earlier that there is no best index of clinical outcome. That being the case, research studies should conclude several measures of outcome, such as clients' self-reports and behavioral measures gathered before and after therapy, as well as expert judgments of clinical progress. There might be significant differences between therapeutic approaches to specific problems with respect to some outcome measures but not others. Furthermore, a therapeutic procedure may be valuable even if it doesn't bring about a complete cure. A person who is less anxious after therapy will be grateful for that benefit despite the failure to achieve a total release from anxiety.

An example of the kind of large-scale project needed to compare different therapeutic approaches is a study of 250 patients who were either moderately or severely depressed (Klerman, 1987). The patients were divided at random into three groups: the first and second groups were treated with one of two types of brief psychotherapy, designed to last 16 weeks, while the third group was given the drug imipramine. Another control group of patients got harmless pills plus weekly supportive consultations with a psychiatrist. While 50 to 60 percent of the patients who received either the psychotherapeutic treatments or the drug reached "full recovery" with no serious symptoms, fewer than 30 percent of those in the control group reached full recovery.

The new findings strengthen earlier research that suggests that some forms of psychotherapy are as effective as drugs in treating depression. They are also in accord with other research showing that the effects of behavior therapy and antidepressant drugs are similar (Christensen and others, 1987).

Arguments over the effectiveness of therapeutic programs can be expected to continue for several reasons: people's problems, expectations, and the extent to which their lives can be changed vary; therapists use different methods and have different expectations; and there are no uniform criteria for judging therapeutic effectiveness. Many people are helped by therapy, but some get worse. Even though psychological therapies are not for everyone, they seem to help a sizable number of people sort out their problems and develop new ways of handling stress and the challenges of life.

Meta-Analysis

Recently the technique known as **meta-analysis** has been used in research on therapeutic outcome. Smith, Glass, and Miller (1980) pioneered this technique in their comprehensive review of the research literature. Their results led them to conclude that the average client receiving therapy was generally better off in a measurable way than 75 percent of people who receive no treatment, and was also better off with respect to the alleviation of fear and anxiety than 83 percent of untreated controls. Whether meta-analysis, a way of quan-

FIGURE 17–9
Treating abnormal behavior often requires the therapist to combine different therapeutic procedures to create the best treatment for a given client. (From *The Wall Street Journal*, permission Cartoon Features Syndicate)

The Ingredients of Effective Therapy

There is evidence that therapeutic effectiveness may be more closely related to therapists' personalities than to their theories. This suggests that we need to increase our understanding of what clients and therapists do during therapy sessions and how they react to one another. The therapeutic situation merits investigation, regardless of its measurable results, because each contact between a client and a therapist involves a unique interpersonal experience composed of complex events. This is true not only in traditional psychotherapy but in the newer behavioral and cognitive therapies as well.

Research on the nature of psychological therapies has explored the characteristics, attitudes, and behavior of the client and therapist in addition to the therapeutic technique used. What goes on in therapy sessions can be characterized in terms of the operation of two sets of factors. **Technique factors** are the procedures employed by the therapist, which may or may not match the descriptions of those procedures found in books and manuals. **Interpersonal factors** refer to the social chemistry of the relationship between the therapist and the client. To minimize the effects of individual differences among therapists, Freud struggled hard to establish technique factors as the single most important therapeutic influence in psychoanalysis. More recently, behavioral theorists have also emphasized the need to specify the procedures they employ. While it would be convenient if technique factors were the only ingredients in therapy, interpersonal factors not only are important but can be decisive in influencing the outcome.

An example of the importance of interpersonal factors is provided by a study that included groups of trained and untrained therapists (Strupp and Hadley, 1979). One group consisted of experienced professional psychotherapists; the other group of Vanderbilt University professors who were selected on the basis of their widely recognized interest in their students, their accessibility, and their willingness to listen and help students solve personal problems. None of the professors had worked in the field of psychology or in any other "helping" profession. The subjects were college students, most of whom complained of anxiety. Each student was assigned to either a professional or a nonprofessional therapist. A third group of subjects constituted a control group. Each control subject went through an assessment procedure, but the start of therapy was delayed.

The study found no significant differences that could be attributed to the type of therapist to which a given client had been assigned. Clients who were treated by either psychotherapists or professors showed more improvement than the control subjects. The measures of

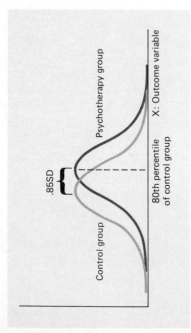

FIGURE 17–10

Meta-analysis involves the statistical combination of many separate and often very different studies. This figure illustrates the general findings of an analysis that combined 475 controlled studies of therapeutic effectiveness. The average person in the treated group was 0.85 standard deviations above the mean for the control group on the measures used to evaluate therapeutic outcome. This difference is a large one when compared to the effects of many experimental interventions used in psychology or education. For example, cutting the size of a school class in half causes an increase in achievement of 0.15 standard deviation units. The effect of 9 months of instruction in reading is an improvement in reading skills of 0.67 standard deviation units. (Smith and others, 1980, p. 88)

tifying outcome measures so that they can be combined over many studies, is the best way to answer questions about therapeutic effectiveness is still being debated.

Meta-analysis involves (1) grouping studies in which treatment conditions have been compared with an untreated control condition on one or more measures of outcome; (2) statistically determining the therapeutic factors on different groups using the available measures; and (3) averaging the sizes of the effects across the studies that the researcher wants to compare. In this way groups receiving psychotherapy can be compared with untreated control groups and groups receiving other therapeutic approaches, such as systematic desensitization and behavior modification. Figure 17–10 provides an example of a meta-analysis of 475 studies of the effects of psychotherapy.

The number of meta-analytic studies is increasing, and so is their complexity. Greater complexity is needed, in part, because researchers do not want to be criticized for mixing apples and oranges. The results of meta-analysis are harder to interpret if the effect sizes from fundamentally different types of studies are lumped together. Perhaps the sharpest criticism of meta-analysis is that comparisons of studies that are methodologically weak can add little to an ultimate evaluation of therapeutic effects. On the other hand, meta-analysis of tighter, more homogeneous studies could prove very enlightening (Kendall and Maruyama, 1985; Strube and others, 1985).

change included the students' own ratings, judgments by independent experts, MMPI scores, and clinicians' evaluations of their clients' progress. Favorable outcomes were most prevalent among clients whose therapists actively provided them with information, encouragement, and opinions. The therapists whose clients improved were those who made special efforts to facilitate the discussion of problems, focused on the here and now rather than on early-childhood experiences, and encouraged the client to seek new social activities. Thus, the personal qualities of the therapist clearly are a very important factor in therapeutic process.

If psychological therapies are effective in treating specific clinical problems, an important question is, Which events in therapy sessions are the active ingredi-

(c)

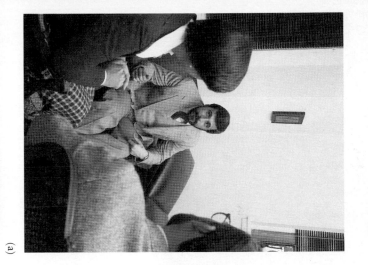

(a)

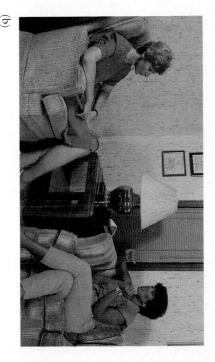

(b)

FIGURE 17-11
There is evidence that what goes on early in the patient-therapist relationship may be an important predictor of outcome. Although a patient who has an early negative reaction to his or her therapist may eventually be able to work productively with the therapist, a successful therapeutic outcome is more likely if the reaction is warm and positive (Frances, and others, 1985). One factor in positive or negative reactions to the therapy situation is the patient's first impression of the therapist. Which of these therapists would you prefer to go to? Rank order your preferences and think about the basis for the rank ordering.

ents, the ones that actually bring about change? Evidence from studies like the one just described suggests that the active ingredients might be interpersonal factors and not the therapeutic process as usually described in textbooks. The following characteristics of therapists may influence the process of personality change and, thus, the outcome of therapy: warmth, friendliness, genuineness, interpersonal style, beliefs, values, and prejudices. In addition to the therapist's personality, his or her age, sex, and socioeconomic background may also play a role in the therapeutic process (see Figure 17-11). The means by which therapists' characteristics are communicated to the public include the therapist's appearance and his or her verbal and nonverbal behavior.

Improving the Design of Psychotherapy Research

We have seen that in addition to technique factors such as the type of therapy practiced by the clinician, researchers must consider client and therapist factors and the tone or quality of the therapeutic relationship. Table 17-6 summarizes the research and clinical questions raised by these factors. The design of therapy research will improve as these questions stimulate methodological advances.

A number of clues are already available to permit the strengthening of research designs. These pertain to sample size, patient specificity, treatment specificity, and outcome measures.

TABLE 17-6

Questions Raised by Client, Therapist, and Relationship Factors

1. Client factors	What role do the personal characteristics of clients play in the outcome of therapy? Among the factors that often play important roles are the attitudes of clients toward therapy, their educational and socioeconomic levels, their levels of psychological distress, the social supports available to them in their environment, and the nature of the problem for which they are seeking help.
2. Therapist factors	What contributions do the characteristics of the therapist make to the process of therapy and its outcome? Among the important therapist variables are training, experience, clinical orientation, and personal qualities. The therapist's sex, age, ethnicity, and cultural background may also play important roles.
3. The therapeutic relationship	Does the therapist–client relationship make a difference? Available evidence suggests that the psychological chemistry that takes place when a therapist with a particular personality meets a client with a particular personality is an important factor in several types of therapy. Although therapist–client relationships have been explored more deeply in psychotherapy, there is evidence that they are also very important in other forms of therapy.

1. *Sample size.* Because of the need to incorporate a large number of factors in the design of therapy research, large enough sample sizes are needed to allow for appropriate statistical analyses and justifiable inferences from results.

2. *Patient specificity.* Firm conclusions are more likely if subjects are relatively homogeneous in terms of factors that are not the target of the treatment intervention. So many factors may influence outcome that it is important to control as many extraneous variables as possible.

3. *Treatment specificity.* The more clearly defined the treatment or treatments, the more likely it is that reasonable inferences can be drawn from the research. This requires careful specification of the therapeutic techniques used in the research.

4. *Outcome measures.* The more relevant the outcome measures are to the type of case being treated, the more useful the study will be. For example, since obsessive–compulsives rarely hallucinate, there would be little value in using the frequency of hallucinations as an outcome variable. A more useful variable would be the frequency of obsessive thoughts and compulsive behaviors.

Control and Comparison Groups

Control and comparison groups are needed in therapy studies because many influences beyond those that are of special interest to the researcher may be at work during the period covered by therapeutic intervention. Without adequate control or comparison groups, researchers cannot rule out the possibility of alternative explanations such as spontaneous remission.

No single control group is appropriate for testing all hypotheses. The control group or groups for a particular study must be chosen on the basis of the particular question under investigation. Table 17–7 describes some types of control groups that have been used in

therapy outcome research. The type of control group or groups used in a given study depends on the number of subjects available and on the nature of the setting in which the research is carried out.

Biological Therapies

In Chapter 3 we discussed the biological orientation to maladaptive behavior and the therapies that have been generated by this point of view. The most widely used biological therapies today are **electro-convulsive therapy (ECT)** and a growing variety of drugs that influence psychological functioning.

Electro-Convulsive Therapy

Although ECT is still an important biological therapy, its use has declined in the past 20 years. ECT is particularly effective in treating cases of severe depression in which rapid recovery is essential (for example, where a suicide attempt seems likely). It is also effective in treating acute mania and, to a lesser extent, catatonic states and some forms of schizophrenia. Available evidence suggests that ECT is a relatively safe procedure, particularly when used with anesthetics and muscle relaxants that substantially lessen the traumatic effects of the treatment. Risks are further reduced by applying the electric current to only one side of the head. However, there is concern about the cognitive consequences of passing an electric current through a person's head. The major risk is memory loss, although this can be reduced by using ECT on the nondominant side of the brain and in the lowest possible dose.

Even though it has been used for many years, the mechanism by which ECT works is not yet clear. It is

TABLE 17-7

Types of Control Groups in Therapy Outcome Research

Untreated controls	A group that theoretically receives no treatment. No-treatment control groups are ethically questionable if the subjects are people who have come to a clinic seeking help for personal problems.
Dropout/wait-list controls	People who request treatment and either do not attend sessions or are offered treatment but only after a waiting period.
Attention-placebo controls	Patients who see a therapist on the same schedule but receive a presumably inactive treatment.
Crossover controls	For a set period, one group serves as the control while the other receives treatment; then the conditions are reversed.
Patients as own controls	Changes in a patient's behavior during a baseline period of no treatment are contrasted with behavioral changes occurring after treatment (see Box 17-1).

Based on Schacht and Strupp, 1985.

thought that the active ingredients in ECT are the electrical-biochemical events that follow the seizures triggered by the electrical impulses. The lack of precise knowledge about how ECT works, together with its occasional adverse effects and the availability of effective drugs, has contributed to the decline in its use.

A psychiatrist who was treated with ECT has described its positive effects on him.

After the first treatment in both series, I felt a blunting of the acute sadness of the depression. Whereas before treatment I became tearful with very little provocation, and felt intensely sad out of all proportion to the stimulus. After one single treatment I was no longer crushed by any chance sadness. The troublesome symptom of irritability also subsided early in the course of treatment. Before treatment, I was very easily irritated by trifles and expressed, on more than one occasion, an irrational belief that people were doing stupid things intentionally to annoy me. I hope that this account will help to dispel the erroneous belief that ECT is a terrifying form of treatment, crippling in its effects on the memory and in other ways. The technique today is so refined that the patient suffers a minimum of discomfort, and the therapeutic benefits are so great in those cases when it is indicated that it is a great pity to withhold it from mistaken ideas of kindness to the patient.

—(Anonymous, 1965, pp. 365–367)

A clinician who is considering the use of ECT must perform a risk-benefit analysis. On the benefit side is the likelihood of rapid improvement and, for depressives, the reduced likelihood of death due to suicide. On the risk side, however, are the possibility of death in the course of receiving ECT (this risk is low, with an incidence of about one in 10,000 treatments), the chance of memory impairment (which is short-term and becomes less noticeable with time), and the risk of spontaneous seizures (which are infrequent). In weighing the advantages against the risks, clinicians might reasonably consider ECT when there is severe depression or a pos-

sibility of suicide, or when drugs and other therapies are ineffective or seem inappropriate.

Drug Therapies

Many drugs have been used clinically and in research. They fall into three broad categories based on whether they are used with people who are depressed, schizophrenic, or anxious. The drugs that are used in the treatment of depression include the tricyclics, monoamine oxidase inhibitors (MAO inhibitors), stimulants, and more recently, lithium. The neuroleptics, particularly the phenothiazines, are used with schizophrenics. Anxiolytic drugs (minor tranquilizers) are used to treat people who are suffering from anxiety. These drugs include benzodiazepines such as diazepam (Valium).

There are many unanswered questions about these drugs. Even though their safety has improved over the years, a number of risks must still be considered, including the risk of physical and psychological side effects. An extreme example of a psychological side effect is the vegetablelike state into which some patients sink when they have taken some of these drugs. Depending on the drug employed, other side effects may include drowsiness, confusion, nightmares, poor appetite, insomnia, blurred vision, and heart palpitations. On balance, however, the psychoactive drugs have helped many people live normal or almost normal lives.

Like those of psychological therapies, the effects of drug therapy are not always predictable. Factors such as age, sex, and genetic background can influence a person's response to a drug. The effectiveness of a particular drug may also depend on how it is metabolized, whether the patient takes it as prescribed, and whether other drugs are being taken at the same time.

Drug Research

Physicians who prescribe drugs want to maximize their therapeutic effects and minimize their undesirable consequences. These goals require the use of carefully designed research procedures. First, extensive preliminary research is done to study the effects of varying doses of a drug on laboratory animals. If these tests suggest that the drug is effective and does not have harmful side effects, the drug is administered to human beings under carefully controlled conditions. If these results are also positive, the drug may be approved for large-scale clinical trials and scientifically compared with other treatment methods. If it passes these tests successfully, it may be approved for use in clinical practice.

Clinical Trials. Clinical trials involving drugs and other therapeutic procedures can be complex and costly, and may extend over many years. They often include samples of subjects located throughout the country and even the world. The following are some of the steps in a clinical trial.

1. Planning the research design and statistical analyses.
2. Deciding on the dependent measures to be used in evaluating the trial.
3. Organizing procedures for gathering data.
4. Assigning subjects to treatments.
5. Assuring that clinical personnel are "blind" to the assigned treatment whenever possible.

In the course of conducting clinical trials, scientists must be careful to rule out alternative explanations for the results they get. In addition to the enthusiasm effect discussed earlier, researchers have to be aware of **placebo effects.** A placebo (often referred to as a "sugar pill") is an inactive substance that has no pharmacological effects but under certain conditions may produce noticeable improvements in patients (see Figure 17–12). When a placebo is effective, it is because it has some of the same suggestive properties as a real treatment. Physicians know that the confidence with which they prescribe given medicines can influence their patients' reactions. Suggestible patients often show great improvement if a drug, even a chemically inactive one, is presented to them as a "wonder drug."

It might seem sufficient to evaluate the effectiveness of drugs by comparing placebo groups with groups that are given chemically potent drugs. Actually, this is not the case, because the knowledge of which patients have received active substances and which ones have not can have a considerable influence on a physician's behavior or evaluations. Thus, the double-blind method is used to ensure that none of the participants knows whether the drug given to a particular patient is active or inert.

Comparative Studies. When we reviewed the psychological therapies, we mentioned the need to compare

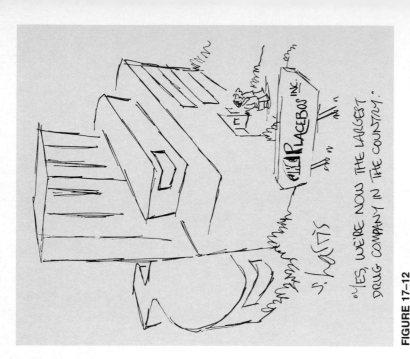

"YES, WE'RE NOW THE LARGEST DRUG COMPANY IN THE COUNTRY."

FIGURE 17–12
Cartoon by Sidney Harris in *Current Contents* (Institute for Scientific Information, 3501 Market St., Philadelphia, PA 19104).

different approaches in order to identify the ones that are likely to be most effective in treating particular disorders. We also gave examples of research comparing psychological and drug therapies. An example of a comparative study involving more than one biological treatment approach is one that was carried out over several years at California's Camarillo State Hospital (May, 1968). The subjects were 228 schizophrenic patients who had been admitted to the hospital for the first time. These men and women had not had extensive clinical care before they were hospitalized. Clinical psychiatrists agreed that the patients were about average in terms of their prospects for recovery.

Each patient was assigned to one of five treatment groups. After a treatment period of 6 to 12 months, the patients were categorized on the basis of whether they were discharged from the hospital because of improvement or whether they were judged to be unresponsive to therapy. Before and after treatment each patient was given a comprehensive multidisciplinary evaluation by psychiatrists, psychologists, nurses, and social workers. The five conditions in the experiment were as follows.

1. *Milieu therapy.* Patients in this group received basic ward care at a level that was judged to be good to superior for a public hospital. The patients received nursing care, hydrotherapy, and occupational, industrial, and recreational therapies. Nurses conducted

weekly community ward meetings, and a social worker was assigned to each patient.

2. *Electro-convulsive therapy (ECT)*. These patients were given ECT three times a week. (The frequency was decreased if the patient showed severe confusion or memory loss.) The average number of treatments was 19 for males and 25 for females.

3. *Drug therapy*. These patients were given antipsychotic drugs (either trifluoperazine or chlorpromazine).

4. *Individual psychotherapy*. Patients in this group received support therapy aimed at fostering a better awareness of reality. This therapy varied according to the characteristics of the patient and the therapist. Relatively little emphasis was placed on in-depth interpretation; the primary focus was on working through the patient's current problems. The number of interviews ranged from 12 to 106.

5. *Individual psychotherapy plus drug therapy*. Each patient in this group received both psychotherapy and a drug.

One measure of the success of a hospital program is its discharge rate. In the Camarillo study, not all of the subjects showed sufficient improvement to allow release. Considering only those who were successfully released, we find that the drug-alone, ECT, and psychotherapy-plus-drug groups had mean hospital stays of 130, 135, and 138 days, respectively. The average stay of the psychotherapy-alone group was 185 days, while the average for the milieu group was 163 days. Among the unimproved patients, the psychotherapists persisted much longer before giving up than clinicians using other forms of treatment. When both successfully and unsuccessfully treated cases were combined, the drug-alone treatment was highly superior in shortening hospital stay. Only two drug-alone patients were not improved enough to be discharged.

In the Camarillo study, the drug-alone and psychotherapy-plus-drug approaches provided the best treatments for the average schizophrenic admitted to that state hospital. There were no substantial differences in effectiveness between these two groups. ECT was less effective than either the drug alone or psychotherapy plus drug treatments. Least effective of all were the psychotherapy and milieu approaches. A follow-up carried out several years after completion of the research suggested that the same pattern of results had persisted (May and others, 1981).

Even though the Camarillo project appears to argue strongly for the use of antipsychotic drugs with schizophrenics, not all of the results can be interpreted so readily. Psychotherapy alone may indeed be ineffective with hospitalized schizophrenics; however, its ineffectiveness may have been due to the particular forms or styles of psychotherapy used at Camarillo. Or perhaps the frequency of the psychotherapeutic sessions was too low. One uncontrolled factor was the variability of the approaches used by the psychotherapists. Perhaps it is significant that patients in the psychotherapy-alone condition had fewer, but longer, contacts with their doctors than patients in the other conditions. The apparent failure of the psychotherapy and milieu conditions may have been due to failures of the particular methods used at Camarillo and not to inherent weaknesses in these approaches.

A methodological weakness of the Camarillo study is the fact that it could not use a blind or double-blind technique. Thus, there is a limit to the extent to which the results can be generalized. Nevertheless, the results provide a practical basis for using drugs to improve the functioning of schizophrenics, together with a caution against assuming that psychotherapeutic and milieu approaches are always effective. Recent evidence suggests that although psychotherapy without drugs may not yield favorable results within the hospital, the picture is different after patients have been discharged. Psychotherapy seems to play a positive role after discharge (Davis, 1985). Perhaps the main effect of drugs is to alleviate symptoms and disordered thought while psychological interventions improve the patients' interpersonal functioning so that they are more likely to stay out of the hospital.

Hospitalization

Serious physical illness may require hospitalization not only because the hospital provides round-the-clock care but also because it can offer all the complex therapies that a patient might need. Some comprehensive mental hospitals provide an enriched program of therapies. Patients at expensive private hospitals may receive psychotherapy, drug therapy, and active social, educational, and recreational programs. The budgets of most state hospitals do not permit such varied fare. As a result, many patients in state hospitals receive drugs but few psychological therapies, and live in a relatively impoverished, unstimulating social environment. This is unfortunate because a hospital can be a place that helps a person cope with a crisis and experience personal growth.

No matter what kind of hospital is available, the major reasons for psychiatric hospitalization are as follows:

1. Thought or behavior that poses a threat to self or others.

2. Thought or behavior that is intolerable to members of the patient's community.

3. Failure of outpatient treatment and the hope that inpatient treatment will reverse the process.

4. A treatment procedure that requires a degree of control that is possible only in a hospital.

5. Withdrawal from alcohol or drugs.

6. Physical illness that is complicated by a mental disorder that requires continuous care.

Researchers have studied the kinds of hospital activities that are helpful to patients when they are not in an acute phase of their disorder. One experiment compared a fairly traditional mental-hospital routine with a routine based on social-learning principles (Paul and Lentz, 1977). Under the traditional routine, patients spent 6 percent of their time taking drugs, 4.9 percent in classes and meetings, and 63.4 percent in unstructured activities. This last percentage represents a great deal of boredom and a waste of therapeutic opportunities. Under the social-learning routine, however, 58.9 percent of the patients' time was devoted to classes, meetings, and structured activities. Only 11.6 percent of their time was spent in unstructured activities. The ward employed a token economy to motivate the patients to engage in productive behavior. A comparison of the effects of the two approaches showed that the social-learning group had a significantly higher percentage of discharges to the community than the traditional group. However, regardless of the treatment used, only a small percentage of the patients were able to function in a self-supporting way.

A striking example of the positive effects of the social-learning program can be seen in the following case.

Thelma, a 42-year-old single woman, had lived continuously in mental institutions for more than half of her adult life. Before she was hospitalized, she lived in her sister's home, where she served as an unpaid housekeeper and babysitter. Upon entering the program, Thelma was generally less withdrawn than most other patients in the project, but she was badly groomed and regularly displayed a variety of intermittent "crazy" mannerisms. Hospital staff characterized her behavior with others as "nagging, tattling, complaining, and lying," and noted her marked stammering and facial grimaces.

Thelma's response to treatment was remarkable. Eleven weeks after treatment began, she was performing well in all areas of functioning, including interpersonal skills, and was indistinguishable from normal on 90 to 100 percent of all hourly observations. She was admitted to a prerelease group and was taught alternative means of expressing her concerns, methods for establishing friendships, techniques for pacing speech to overcome stammers and grimaces, as well as vocational and money management skills. She was released within 30 weeks, having "dramatically improved from the obnoxious patient who had entered the program to a pleasant socially appropriate woman."

Since her relatives would have nothing to do with her and even made an attempt to keep her institutionalized, a woman who hired Thelma as a live-in domestic and babysitter agreed to act as her sponsor upon her release. This job did not last because of turmoil in the employer's family. Nevertheless, Thelma continued to find employment, living quarters, and friends on her own, and became exceptionally active socially. By the time the project ended, Thelma had supported herself over five years and showed no indication of any need for reinstitutionalization in the future.

—(Science Reports, 1981, pp. 6–7)

Research on the process of resocialization may contribute answers to such questions as, What steps could help chronic patients adjust successfully to the community? Gordon Paul (1969) has suggested ten steps that mental hospitals might take to provide greater happiness and effectiveness among patients, higher morale among staff members, and a more positive social-rehabilitation role for the institution.

1. *Emphasize a "resident" rather than "patient" status through informal dress of staff; open channels of communication in all directions, and broad (but clear) authority structure.*

2. *Make clear, through a set of rules and attitudes, that the residents are responsible human beings; are expected to follow certain minimal rules of group living; and are expected to do their share in participating in self-care, work, recreational, and social activities.*

3. *Utilize step systems which gradually increase the expectations placed on the residents in terms of their degree of independence and level of responsibility, with community return emphasized from the outset.*

4. *Encourage social interactions and skills and provide a range of activities as well as regular large and small group meetings.*

5. *Emphasize clarity of communication, with concrete instruction in appropriate behavior and focus on utilitarian "action" rather than "explanation."*

6. *Provide opportunity to practice vocational and housekeeping skills, with feedback, and specific training in marketable skills when needed.*

7. *Reacquaint residents with the "outside world" by exposing them to the community and bringing in community volunteers for discussions.*

8. *Identify the specific unique areas for change and support in concrete terms for each individual.*

9. *Prepare residents and significant-others to live in mutually supportive ways in the community through pre-release training and scheduled aftercare.*

10. *When no significant-other exists, train and release residents in groups of 2–3 as a "family" to provide significant-others for one another.*

—(Paul, 1969, p. 91)

The effectiveness of a hospital depends on the needs of its residents, the quality and scope of its programs, and the community and family resources available to the patient. Because of variations in all of these areas, it is not surprising that there are strong differences of opinion about the effectiveness of hospitalization. When all factors are considered, it seems reasonable to conclude that some severely disturbed people can benefit from life in a socially active, therapeutic hospital. The precise percentage of currently institutionalized individuals who might benefit from this experience is very difficult to estimate.

If a ward is run mainly to satisfy the staff, or if a latent goal of the hospital is to maintain order and stability in the institution, the patients get the message. No therapy takes place because patients' behavior is aimed at minimizing conflict with the system and disruption of routine.

An unfortunate hospitalization is a special kind of experience whose mark may be visible long after its completion. It can increase patients' sense that they bear a stigma and make it easy for them to acquire "sick roles"—that is, to come to see themselves as sick people who will always have to be taken care of. It can also lead to a weakening of social and work skills. When these things happen, patients become less able to function in the community.

When complete hospitalization is not required, partial hospitalization may be employed (Rosie, 1987). This may include either day or night hospitalization and, perhaps, evening and weekend care in the hospital.

Day hospitals are used to provide treatment for patients who can live at home but need the structure and social interaction available in the treatment center. Day hospitals also allow members of the patients' families to function more normally because they can carry on their usual activities during the day. Day hospitals often concentrate on teaching social and interpersonal behaviors as well as helping patients learn practical skills such as how to use the bus system or a pay telephone. They may also include training in basic work skills so that patients can get jobs in sheltered workshops that will provide the satisfaction of doing useful work and some payment as well.

Evening, night, and weekend programs are designed primarily to help hospitalized patients make the transition from the hospital to the community. Such programs are especially useful for people who are able to return to their jobs, schools, or training programs but do not have adequate family or social supports to go from inpatient to outpatient status without a partially protected transition period. The concept of night hospitals has gained some acceptance, but relatively few such hospitals have been established on a formal basis.

Over the past few decades hospitalizations have become less frequent while the use of outpatient services has mushroomed. Patients are being discharged after shorter periods of hospitalization, largely because of the effectiveness of psychoactive drugs and an increase in efforts to return patients to the community as quickly as possible. This **deinstitutionalization** process can be a boon to personal development if the individual has a good place to live, sufficient social support, and supervision when needed. Unfortunately, many people who have been discharged from mental hospitals live in furnished rooms in undesirable neighborhoods, are socially isolated, and receive little professional help beyond brief contacts with physicians who prescribe antipsychotic drugs.

The lack of adequate care in the community for chronic mental patients has contributed to the large numbers of homeless people in American cities (see Figure 17–13). Thousands of deinstitutionalized people have nowhere to live. They wander about city centers, sleep where they can, and carry their belongings with them. While the problem of homelessness is complex, the "dumping" of deinstitutionalized people on a community only contributes to human misery.

FIGURE 17-13
The "dumping" of chronic mental patients on communities with inadequate clinical and rehabilitation programs contributes to the problem of homelessness.

Study Outline

PSYCHOTHERAPY

1. All forms of psychotherapy involve interchanges between a client and a therapist that are aimed at understanding what is on the client's mind. This understanding is used as a basis for efforts to change the client's maladaptive ways of thinking, reacting to situations, and relating to others.

2. **Psychoanalysis** is a subtype of psychodynamic therapy that makes extensive use of **free association,** in which the client expresses thoughts and feelings in as free and uninhibited a manner as possible. The examination of dreams and fantasies is also important in psychoanalysis. The goal is to help the client gain **insight** into the relationship between his or her early experiences and a current tendency to distort reality.

3. A key aspect of psychoanalysis is the use of **transference** as a vehicle for resolving interpersonal conflicts and revealing the meaning of anxiety. In **positive transference,** the patient feels predominantly friendly toward the analyst; in **negative transference,** hostility predominates. **Countertransference** refers to the therapist's emotional reactions to the patient.

4. **Humanistic therapies** emphasize people's desire to achieve self-respect. In **client-centered therapy** the individual is seen as seeking personal growth but needing the support of an appreciative, accepting therapist. This form of therapy emphasizes **unconditional positive regard** for the client.

5. **Existential therapies** also focus on the present and stress the uniqueness of each client. Their emphasis is on helping clients come to terms with basic issues concerning the meaning of their lives and the choices by which they shape their own destinies.

6. **Gestalt therapy** focuses on clients' perceptions of themselves and the world. It is based on the recognition that people organize their perceptions as a meaningful, integrated whole.

7. The **cognitive psychotherapies** seek to correct misconceptions that contribute to maladjustment, defeat, and unhappiness. George Kelly's **psychology of personal constructs** led him to ask clients to examine the roles they play in interacting with others and the assumptions underlying those roles. Albert Ellis' **rational–emotive therapy** is based on the belief that self-defeating thinking is at the root of maladaptive behavior. Aaron Beck's approach to therapy involves fre-

quent, gentle questioning of the client about the basis for what he or she is saying. It is aimed at eliminating thoughts that are not products of rational consideration of alternatives.

COGNITIVE–BEHAVIORAL THERAPIES

1. **Behavioral therapy** has shown rapid development in recent years. **Behavior modification** consists of using environmental manipulations to directly change behavior. This approach has increasingly been combined with cognitive processes designed to help people correct their misconceptions, strengthen their coping skills, and facilitate constructive self-talk.

2. **Relaxation training** uses a variety of techniques, including **muscular relaxation, meditation,** and **autogenic training.** In the latter technique the individual is taught to assume an attitude of passive concentration on a series of physical, emotional, and mental sensations.

3. **Systematic desensitization** combines behavioral training with cognitive activity. The patient is induced to relax and then exposed to scenes or images that are progressively more fear arousing.

4. **Exposure therapies** are based on the principle that continued exposure to anxiety-provoking stimuli will decrease anxiety. **In vivo exposure** (actually being in the situation) works best, but **fantasized exposure** is also effective. In **flooding,** the client is exposed to a flood of fear-arousing stimuli. In **implosive therapy,** the client experiences higher and higher levels of anxiety through imaginal presentation of scenes depicting situations that have been avoided in the past.

5. Through **modeling,** clients can be shown that there are alternative ways of doing things. Demonstrations by models are often combined with **guided rehearsals,** in which the individual is encouraged to imitate the behavior of the model. **Live modeling** involves direct observation of a model; **symbolic modeling** refers to observation of a model presented through film or another medium. In **covert modeling,** the client is asked to imagine observing a model and a particular consequence.

6. **Assertiveness training** is designed to enhance the interpersonal skills one needs to stand up for one's rights.

7. **Paradoxical intention** is a technique in which the therapist instructs the client to perform behaviors that

appear to be in opposition to the client's therapeutic goal.

GROUP THERAPY

1. In **group therapy**, clients can learn both by observing other group members' attempts to solve their problems and by comparing their relationship with the therapist with those of other members.

2. The focus of **cognitive–behavioral group therapy** is on increasing the skills and comfort of people in social situations. Group members role-play situations that they find difficult, and the therapist may model alternative ways of handling those situations.

3. **Family therapy** is a specialized clinical approach that is used in treating family groups. The family is often conceived as a system that is malfunctioning. The therapist's task is to identify the areas of malfunction and help the family deal with them in an effective manner.

4. **Marital therapy** can be viewed as a subtype of family therapy in which the therapist helps the couple alter the ways in which they relate to each other.

5. **Psychodrama** is an approach that was designed especially for groups. In this technique a group of individuals led by a therapist enacts events of emotional significance in order to resolve conflicts and release members from inhibitions.

RESEARCH ON THE PSYCHOLOGICAL THERAPIES

1. In research on the effectiveness of psychological therapies, all groups of subjects must be as similar or equal as possible before the experiment begins. The planning of therapy-outcome studies requires careful attention to the criteria of improvement that should be employed.

2. Comparative studies have found that psychological therapies are most useful in treating milder, nonpsychotic disorders. Behavioral and cognitive–behavioral therapies are especially effective in treating anxiety disorders. Psychological therapies have been less successful with serious conditions such as schizophrenia, but can play an important role when used in combination with drug therapy or electro-convulsive therapy. Both psychological and drug therapies have been used successfully with depressed patients.

3. Recently the technique known as **meta-analysis** has been used in research on therapeutic outcomes. This involves grouping studies in which treatment conditions have been compared with an untreated control condition, statistically determining the therapeutic effects on different groups, and averaging the sizes of the effects across the studies to be compared.

4. Studies of what actually goes on in therapy sessions have focused on **technique factors**, or the procedures employed by the therapist, and **interpersonal factors,**

or the relationship between the therapist and the client. Such studies have found that the personal qualities of the therapist are a very important factor in the therapeutic process.

BIOLOGICAL THERAPIES

1. The use of **electro-convulsive therapy** has declined in the past 20 years because it is not clear exactly how it works and because it occasionally has adverse effects. It might reasonably be used when there is severe depression or a possibility of suicide, or when drugs and other therapies are ineffective.

2. Drugs are frequently used in treating people who are depressed, schizophrenic, or anxious. The safety of these drugs has improved, but their use still entails the risk of physical and psychological side effects. In addition, their effects are not always predictable.

3. **Clinical trials** of new drugs can be complex and costly, and may extend over many years and include samples of subjects at many locations. In conducting such trials, scientists must rule out alternative explanations for the results they get. To avoid the **placebo effect,** in which patients show great improvement because they believe in the effectiveness of a drug, the double-blind method is used.

4. There have been few well-controlled comparative studies of biological therapies. The available evidence suggests that antipsychotic drugs are the least expensive form of effective treatment for schizophrenia. It appears that although psychotherapy without drugs may not yield favorable results in a hospital setting, psychotherapy can play a positive role after discharge for schizophrenic patients.

HOSPITALIZATION

1. Psychiatric hospitalization is appropriate in cases in which the patient's thought or behavior poses a threat to self or others or the patient requires a treatment procedure that is possible only in a hospital. When completed hospitalization is not required, partial hospitalization may be employed.

2. Research on hospital activities has found that hospital routines based on social-learning principles can result in a significantly higher percentage of discharges to the community than traditional mental-hospital routines.

3. Over the past few decades hospitalizations have become less frequent and there has been an increase in efforts to return patients to the community as quickly as possible. **Deinstitutionalization** can enhance personal development if the individual has a good place to live, sufficient social support, and supervision when needed. Because of insufficient clinical and rehabilitation facilities, many cities have had big increases in the number of homeless people with chronic mental problems.

Society's Response to Maladaptive Behavior

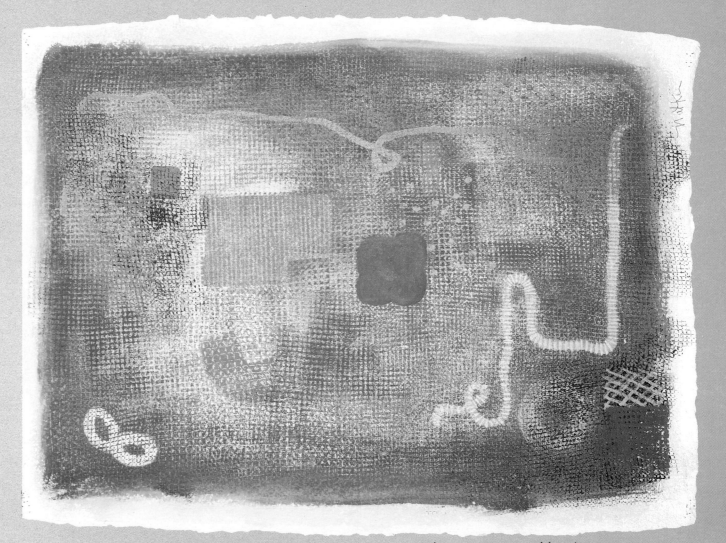

Robert Natkin: Untitled, 1974. Acrylic on paper 22 × 30″. Credit: Courtesy the artist.

To learn:

1. The meaning of primary, secondary, and tertiary prevention
2. The kinds of problems for which each type of prevention is used
3. Ways in which each type of prevention may be applied

To understand:

1. The pros and cons of commitment and of deinstitutionalization
2. The concept of the insanity defense and the problems that arise from its use
3. The ethical and legal questions in treating those who have any type of psychological problem

*A*nn Jackson had taught at Buchanan High School for eight years. She was 33 years old, still had some ideals, and had a reputation among both students and faculty of being a nice person. She was also a discouraged person who too often felt she wasn't able to reach several of her students. One who fell into this group was 16-year-old Bill Hadley. Bill paid little attention in class, did not complete assignments, and frequently did not show up at all. But what worried Ann Jackson the most was what she knew about Bill's activities outside class. Other students were afraid of him because of his imposing size, his bullying attitude, and his history of antisocial behavior. He had had numerous contacts with the police for a variety of reasons. He had been accused of puncturing the tires of a dozen cars parked along a street, extorting money from other students, and shoplifting at neighborhood stores. The most serious offense was a severe beating Bill had given to another student. According to those present at the fight, Bill was in such an uncontrollable rage that he couldn't stop hitting and kicking the other student even though it was evident that the student was helpless and in pain, and he started fighting with the spectators when they intervened. Ann Jackson couldn't get Bill out of her mind. She continually worried about what was going to happen to him.

Small problems have a way of becoming big problems if nothing is done about them. Ann Jackson wished that something could be done to redirect Bill Hadley's life while he was still young, but she didn't know what

Situation-Focused and Competency-Focused Prevention

Throughout this book we have considered methods of assessing, treating, and caring for individuals with behavior problems, but we have only briefly mentioned the possibility that the actual occurrence of maladaptive behavior in the population can be reduced. This is the focus of prevention.

Prevention can be approached from two perspectives. **Situation-focused prevention** is aimed at reducing or eliminating the environmental causes of disordered behavior, while **competency-focused prevention** is concerned with enhancing people's ability to cope with conditions that might lead to maladaptive behaviors. Situation-focused approaches seek to change the environment, for example, by making it less stressful. Competency-focused approaches seek to strengthen people's coping skills so as to make them more resistant should various types of stress-arousing situations arise (Cowen, 1985).

Divorce is an example of a common stress-arousing situation. Its occurrence has increased dramatically over the last several decades and has resulted in changes in life styles and in the environments in which children are brought up. (Nearly half of all children can expect to spend some time—an average of about 6 years—living in a single-parent family.) Divorce and parental discord are related to impaired functioning and social behavior in children. Divorced people are likely to be overrepresented among people who make suicide attempts, become alcoholics, go through periods of depression, and seek help from mental-health professionals.

There is a need for programs that can reduce the likelihood of maladjustment in divorced couples and their children. Preventive work related to this problem is just getting under way. An example is a program for newly separated individuals that provided the participants with psychological support and special training over a 6-month period after the separation (Bloom and others, 1982). Staff members made themselves available to participants when advice and counseling were needed. Training was provided in such practical areas as how to find employment, change jobs, and deal with child-rearing problems. Compared with newly separated people who did not participate in the program, the participants experienced less anxiety, fatigue, and physical illness, along with improved coping ability. There was some evidence that the intervention program was more effective for women than for men. Participants' com-

---

she, the school, or the community could do now or what could have been done earlier to prevent Bill's current unhappiness, anger, and counterproductive behavior.

Many well-meaning and intelligent people feel helpless when confronted with obvious mental distress in another individual. At the same time, everyday life is full of examples of people who are able to either help people in distress or help prevent distress from occurring. In the following example an exceptionally effective young college graduate was found to have had a chaotic, stress-inducing family life. Yet an informal relationship with a neighboring family gave him valuable opportunities for personal growth.

He came from an extremely disturbed home setting in which every member of his family except himself had been hospitalized for severe mental illness; and yet he had graduated from a renowned university with honors, had starred on the football team, and was unusually popular. During his government training he was held in the highest esteem by staff members and was rated as best liked and most likely to succeed by his peers.

In examining this young man's history we discovered that during his elementary school years he had essentially adopted a neighborhood family as his own and spent endless hours with them. Certain characteristics of this family appear most significant. They were a helping family in the sense that love emanated from them and was freely available to all. Of special significance for the fellow under consideration was his relationship with a boy in the family, a year older than he, who formed for him a positive role model with whom he closely identified and whom he followed to his considerable satisfaction.

An even more crucial factor was his relationship with the mother in this family, who became his guide, counselor, and chief source of emotional nurturance. His reports indicate that while this relationship was intense, it was not symbiotic, and seemed to foster his independence and self-development. Although there are probably few like her, she represents a dimension of socially indigenous therapy that may be more significant than is usually recognized. Her home became a neighborhood gathering place. It might be characterized as an informal therapy agency, a kitchen clinic.

—(Bergin and Lambert, 1978, pp. 149–150)

In this chapter we discuss the role played by society in dealing with deviance and preventing problems of living.

ments after the program ended suggested that their knowledge that interested people and special services were available if needed may have been the most powerful ingredient in the program. Future research will be needed to determine the long-term effects on both parents and children of programs that are designed to reduce the traumatic effects of an inevitably distressing situation.

The program just described was activated only after the participants had already taken steps toward divorce. A competency-focused approach might aim to strengthen skills that are important in interpersonal relationships, particularly with one's spouse, long before thoughts of divorce might arise. The idea behind such an effort would be to increase coping skills and thereby enable couples to handle the stresses of marriage in more effective ways. Research on this type of preventive intervention is under way (Barker and Lemle, 1984). For example, Markman and his colleagues (1983) are seeking to strengthen skills that seem to help couples weather the stresses that challenge a marriage. Their program emphasizes communication skills. For example, the couples are taught to focus on one topic at a time and to make their concerns and irritations clear, as in "I may seem angry because I had a bad day at work." They are also trained to "stop the action" until the partners cool down when repetitive cycles of conflict begin. One

of the major signs of distress in a couple is escalating hostility, often in the form of nagging that provokes an angry response.

Early-education programs also illustrate competency-focused prevention. Their aim is to prevent or reduce problems in subsequent years. One project began with the frequent observation that maladapted children (and adults) tend to have weak interpersonal cognitive problem-solving skills (Shure and Spivack, 1982, 1987). These skills include the ability to identify problems and feelings (in oneself and others), to think of alternative solutions to a problem, to see relationships between alternative approaches and the achievement of goals, and to appreciate the consequences of one's actions. Interpersonal problem-solving skills can be thought of as mediating effective behavioral adjustment as well as fostering academic competence (see Figure 18–1).

The following is an excerpt from one of the lessons used by Spivack and his co-workers in teaching young children to be more sensitive to their feelings and those of others.

Now this is just a game. *Have each child hold a toy previously used from trinket box.* Peter, you snatch Kevin's toy from him.

Kevin, how do you feel about that? *Kevin responds.*

FIGURE 18–1

Children often act directly—when they want something they take it or they express displeasure by hitting another child. Cognitive games of the kind used by Spivack, Platt, and Shure attempt to create greater empathy with others and in this way change the self-centered aggressive behavior often seen in childhood.

Peter, no let him have it back.

Now, how do you feel, Kevin? *After child answers, repeat with other pairs.*

Use a picture of a firetruck. Larry, how would going for a ride on this firetruck make you feel? *Let child respond.*

Let's pretend that a man came and drove the truck away and you could NOT have a ride. How would you feel now? *Same child responds.*

Now let's pretend he came back and said, "Okay, now you can go for a ride." How would that make you feel? *Same child responds.*

Use a picture of a ball. How do you think Steven might feel if we let him play with this ball? *Group answers.*

Maybe he would feel happy and maybe he would not feel happy. Let's find out. How can we find out? *Encourage children to ask.*

Let's pretend someone came along and threw the ball out the window so Steven could not play with it anymore. Now how do you think Steven might feel?

He might feel sad or he might feel mad. How can we find out?

Encourage children to ask.

—(Spivack and others, 1976, pp. 183–184)

These researchers found that behavioral adjustment was positively influenced by training in cognitive and social skills. This positive effect was greatest for children who originally seemed most maladjusted, and positive results were still evident a year later. In a related project inner-city mothers who were given training in interpersonal cognitive problem-solving skills were able to pass their training on to their children. Research with older children and adults supports the idea that the skills involved in academic and social effectiveness are learnable. Furthermore, it has been shown that improved teacher training—for example, teaching them to reinforce students' adaptive behavior—contributes to a more productive learning environment in the classroom.

society does not seem willing or able to take the needed steps.

Prevention can take place on three levels. **Primary prevention** is concerned with the reduction of new cases of mental or physical disorder in a given population. Scientific information about cause and effect is very important in primary prevention. For example, knowledge of the possibility of harm to the unborn child has persuaded many women not to smoke or drink during pregnancy. Physicians are much more careful about prescribing medication for pregnant women because of information linking even seemingly harmless drugs with birth defects. Psychologists are conducting research on ways to discourage children from beginning to smoke cigarettes (Flay and others, 1985). Another example of primary prevention is premarital counseling. Marital problems and divorce are highly correlated with maladaptive behavior. Premarital counseling is aimed at encouraging couples to anticipate any problems and to develop ways of coping with them before marriage.

The aim of **secondary prevention** is to reduce the duration, intensity, and disability of an existing abnormal condition. For example, if a child with phenylketonuria (PKU) is identified early, a special diet can prevent serious retardation. Enrichment programs for infants from homes where little stimulation is available can improve children's intellectual functioning and their level of achievement in school.

Whereas secondary prevention refers to the diagnosis and treatment of disorders as soon as possible, **tertiary prevention** is aimed at reducing the impairment that may result from a given disorder or event. This is achieved through rehabilitation and resocialization. For example, behavioral therapy for a hyperactive child may help him or her become more attentive in school and more accepted by other children. Counseling or group therapy after a traumatic event such as the death of a spouse or a rape may provide the social supports that reduce a person's vulnerability to stress.

Preventive measures have been developed in many cases in which biophysical factors are known to cause maladaptive behavior. However, the effects of detrimental social factors have frequently been ignored or neglected. It is much easier to detect and control the effects of an enzyme deficiency in newborn infants than it is to detect and control the pervasive influence of poverty and racism. But ignoring these causes and correlates of maladaptive behavior will not decrease their influence.

Types Of Prevention

If we all know that an ounce of prevention is worth a pound of cure, why aren't preventive measures more common? In some cases it is not clear what steps are needed to achieve the goal of prevention, and in others

When prevention methods are successful, risk factors that lead to abnormal behavior are reduced or eliminated. In general, priority in efforts to achieve prevention is given to serious conditions that have high rates of incidence, and for which effective methods are available. For example, one of the most serious and prevalent maladaptive behaviors of childhood is juvenile delinquency. Delinquent behavior seems to have many causes, ranging from poor living conditions to a psychopathic or antisocial personality disorder to psychosis. It is sobering to realize that one out of nine children will be referred to juvenile court for an act of delinquency before his or her eighteenth birthday and that perhaps one-third of all cases of delinquency involve repeat offenders.

Obviously, not all delinquents are arrested for their crimes. Thus, when juveniles are asked about their delinquent activities, the percentage of young people who have been involved in delinquency becomes even higher. Some of the following conditions have also been identified with delinquency.

1. Poor physical and economic conditions in the home and neighborhood.
2. Rejection or lack of security at home.
3. Exposure to antisocial role models within or outside the home, and antisocial pressures from peer-group relationships.

(a)

(b)

(c)

FIGURE 18-2

Primary and secondary prevention of delinquency can take many forms. (a) Sometimes an interested adult can serve as a role model. Both the skills learned and the feeling that someone cares can be important in the primary prevention of delinquency. (b) Sometimes goals can be achieved by cognitive coping strategies that help a person resist peer pressure for delinquent behavior. (c) Family therapy can often be affective for secondary prevention of delinquent behavior.

4. Lack of support for social achievement in school.
5. The expectation of hostility on the part of others.

Juvenile delinquency can be approached at different levels of prevention. Primary prevention often takes the form of programs aimed at improving living conditions and school achievement. Sometimes primary prevention comes about more informally. There is some evidence that if children growing up in high-crime areas have a positive figure to copy or model themselves after, their behavior may be more influenced by that person than by their antisocial peers. The value of a model is shown in the following example.

Caesar and Richard are two brothers who lived in a high-crime community. Neither has become delinquent. Talking with them gives us some clues to why this is so. Caesar has had one year of community college. He quit because he had to support the family, but at present he is unemployed. He spends his time with gang members but does not participate in their antisocial activities. He thinks he is able to do this because the others admire him for his skill at restoring old cars (see Figure 18–2a). This admiration makes it possible for him to know them without participating in their activities, to dress differently, and to see himself as a potentially achieving person who will contribute to the community. Caesar attributes his goals and behavior to his efforts to be like an older, retired gang member, Hood.

Hood's been through it all. He's lived here all his life—he's done time—he's been a user but now he's clean. He is harassed by the cops so much that he had to get a letter from a judge saying that he was clean and that he should be left alone. He helps all of us in the barrio. He tells it like it really is, takes us to the ball game, helps raise money for bail, whatever. He does it all for nothing. Not even teachers and counselors work for nothing.

—(Aiken and others, 1977, p. 217)

Richard, a younger boy, thinks Caesar, his older brother, was instrumental in the development of his own prosocial behavior.

My mother told my brother when my father left that he was responsible for me, she wasn't. My brother counseled me, looked out for me, and told me what to do. He told me never to steal—that if I wanted something to come to him and he'd try to get it for me or see if I could earn it. If my brother thought that I was getting into trouble, he would probably kick my butt.

—(Aiken and others, 1977, p. 217)

Richard is classified as a slow learner in school and has problems in math and reading. But he has learned how to repair bicycles and sees this as a way to gain status in the community.

Some adolescents develop their own cognitive mechanisms to help them resist peer pressure. Linda Carmichael, who lived in a Chicago tenement inhabited by winos, junkies, and petty hustlers, went to college. Linda wants to get out of the ghetto (see Figure 18–2b). This is how she described the cognitions that helped her keep on her track when her peers sneered and when she "wanted to be out partying and goofing off like everyone else": "I'd start thinking about all those people on the street with nothing to look forward to and where would I be without school. That kept me going" (Goldman and Williams, 1978, p. 34)

Secondary prevention progams concentrate on young people who have shown early signs of delinquency. An example of this approach is a project aimed at rehabilitating predelinquent boys in a homelike setting (Kirigin and others, 1982). This project focuses not only on teaching social and vocational skills but also on helping boys to behave less impulsively. The project has been carried out at Achievement Place, a group home in Lawrence, Kansas, for 12- to 14-year-old boys who have committed minor nonviolent offenses (such as theft or truancy) but seem to be on the road to more serious crimes. House-parents at Achievement Place

identify target behaviors and employ token reinforcement systems to strengthen prosocial tendencies. The emphasis is on social and academic skills as well as on self-care.

Sometimes changing delinquent behavior might be classified as tertiary prevention. For example, the youth might be involved in seriously maladaptive behavior. For instance, a 14-year-old boy was referred to a therapist by the court because he had set several large grass fires that had endangered houses. He could not explain his behavior, and neither could his parents since he had always behaved responsibly at home.

The boy's family was seen for six family-therapy sessions (see Figure 18–2c). These sessions revealed that the family could not discuss problems openly but tended to communicate nonverbally. Several recent family crises had caused tension. The father seemed to handle his unhappiness by withdrawing from the family into club activities. The son seemed to express his anger at family problems by setting fires. Once they began to meet in therapy sessions and these problems became evident, all of the family members were able to change their behavior. One year later there had been no more fire-setting (Eisler, 1972).

At all levels of prevention, the problems of delinquency and the therapeutic treatment of delinquents are far from solved. The number of delinquents who go on to commit more antisocial acts is high. Different approaches work best with different types of cases, but as yet all methods produce more misses than hits. Understanding delinquency requires a better grasp of the variables involved in the interaction between the person and the situation.

Sites of Prevention

In this chapter we are especially interested in research that is relevant to the prevention of maladaptive behavior. Where data are lacking, we speculate about the use of social experimentation. We do not attempt a comprehensive analysis of all the components of a complex social structure; instead, we direct our attention toward three areas that definitely affect the growth and development of children and adults: the family, the school, and the community.

The Family

Parents are important because of the genes they contribute and the environment they provide for their children. This environment begins in the uterus during the 9 months before birth. Whatever can improve prenatal care and thus reduce the incidence of premature birth and other foreseeable difficulties might help reduce several types of problems, such as low intelligence. Improved prenatal and neonatal care can be expected to reduce brain damage, which, among other conditions, is related to certain types of epilepsy.

From the standpoint of prevention, the family is important because much of the child's earliest learning and development takes place within the family setting. Parents' ideas about child-rearing and the growing-up process make important contributions to the day-to-day environment of children (see Figure 18–3).

One of the most common observations of clinicians who specialize in treating childhood disorders is that treating the child is not enough. The parents are usually part of the problem. The following are some extreme examples: Children of psychotic parents are slow in de-

WHAT WENT WRONG?

Never owned dog?

Did not learn to play a musical instrument?

Had strange middle name? Johnny Xerxes Miller

Too much fruit salad in early life?

FIGURE 18–3
Some well-intentioned, overly conscientious parents worry too much about what children need early in life to lay the groundwork for a good life later. On the other hand, there are parents who do not devote enough attention to their children's needs. (New Yorker, October 5, 1987, p. 48)

veloping speech and bladder control, have more eating and sleeping problems, and are more likely to be delinquent than other children. Alcoholic parents have a disproportionately large number of hyperactive children, and alcoholic mothers are overrepresented among mothers of babies with low birthweight and low IQs. There is also a relationship between criminality in parents and delinquency in their children. Children who have been physically abused, malnourished, and neglected by their parents are more prone to various forms of maladaption than other children. Under certain circumstances even "normal" parents—that is, parents who are not obviously disturbed—can have negative effects on their children's development.

Child Abuse

Parental failure is most blatant when parents physically harm their children. There are varying estimates of the number of children who are physically mistreated in the United States each year. It is difficult to make such an estimate, because **child abuse** varies in degree and is often hidden from view by embarrassed and ashamed parents. But thousands of children, many under 3 years of age, are seriously—often fatally—mistreated each year. When emotional abuse is included as well as physical abuse, the figure becomes much larger. A sizable percentage of abuse cases involve sexual assault.

Abusive parents tend to be less intelligent and more aggressive, impulsive, immature, self-centered, tense, and self-critical than nonabusive parents. They are more likely to have been abused themselves as children; thus, child abuse is a vicious cycle. Table 18–1 lists family characteristics often associated with child abuse. Complicating the situation is the fact that despite the frequent and severe abuse by their parents, many children are deeply attached to them and resist efforts to remove them from their homes.

The physical and psychological damage done to children by abusive parents can be observed immediately.

The blond-haired boy was curled unresponsive in the fetal position in a crib that was wheeled into the courtroom. Doctors recited the abuse the child had endured: a beating which caused gangrene and permanent brain damage; and having the words "I cry" burned into his back with a cigarette.

Often less observable are the long-term effects. The following report describes Rick, a 26-year-old college junior who sought psychotherapy. The case is interesting because it suggests how problems of adult life may be related to the experience of childhood abuse. Rick seemed to be able to function effectively. Unfor-

TABLE 18-1

Characteristics of Abusing Families

Parents' Histories

Experience of abuse or neglect
Lack of affection from parents
Large families
Married as teenagers

Current Family Situation

Socially isolated, parents lack social support
Marital discord
Parental impulsivity
Parental retardation or illiteracy
Stressful living conditions (e.g., inadequate housing)

Parents' Approach to Child-Rearing

Infrequent praise of children
Strict demands on child
Low level of child supervision
Early toilet training
Maternal dislike of caretaking
Parental disagreements over child-rearing practices

Based on Nietzel and Himelein, 1986.

---

tunately, many victims of child abuse do not turn out so well.

When he was two months old, he was hospitalized in traction with multiple broken bones in his legs, hips, and rib area. His mother had claimed that he had fallen from her lap to the floor, an impossible story in view of the extent of the injury. He remained immobilized in the hospital for six months. Then he was sent home in a partial body cast, and two weeks later he returned to the hospital with a similar set of fractures and put back in traction. This time the doctor suggested to his father that Rick should be placed in a foster home or his mother should be admitted to a mental hospital. The father refused and Rick returned home. Three times during the next four years Rick's father took him to the doctor when he appeared sick and the doctor diagnosed starvation, saying the child clearly wasn't being fed. These events are known to Rick through his father, his father's relatives, and his family physician. Rick himself has only one memory before age 10—that is of at age 7 playing with his grandfather whom he saw only a few times in his life. From the time Rick can remember, his mother totally ignored him, never talked to him or fed him, nor did she strike him

---

again. His only sibling is a brother 16 months older than Rick, who suffered similar malnutrition but no violent injuries. Rick recalls believing his brother was the mother's favorite because he can recall her fixing the brother a meal once, which he claims she never did for him.

Rick's presenting complaints were anxiety during tests (although he does quite well on them) and a recurring nightmare which he had no insight into although it was found to be strikingly transparent: He is driving along in a car and passes a terribly injured man in a ditch—the injury varies, most commonly his leg is cut off. He drives into a nearby town and approaches people asking them to help the man in the ditch, and each one gives him an excuse why they cannot. A feeling of horror surfaces, not upon first seeing the man but when he realizes no one will help. At this point Rick awakens.
— (Barrett and Fine, 1980, p. 290)

Rick's nightmares suggest that he is still reliving his childhood situation, in which he was helpless and no one would help him.

An abusive parent is usually a very troubled person who seems to be a victim of uncontrollable impulses and frustrations. The following is an excerpt from a group therapy session in which the participants were mothers who had abused their children.

MOTHER 1: I was just at my breaking point and I knew if I didn't get help somewhere, it would just go on and on and end up a vicious circle. I think that everyone who has had this problem at one time has thought "my goodness, I must be the only person in the world that feels this way." And when I found out that I wasn't, that was a load off my mind.

THERAPIST: Feels what way?

MOTHER 1: Desperation with their children. Not knowing how to cope. Afraid that you would just lose control completely and knock their head off, you know. I think we were all brought up to believe that women are supposed to have children and they're supposed to have the mother-instinct and if you don't have it, there is something definitely wrong. And I think it took this group to make me realize that women just aren't born with the mothering instinct . . . that has helped me.

ANOTHER MOTHER: If you're going to pound your child, the best thing to do is separate yourself from your child.

MOTHER 1: That's fine to say, but what if you're like me and you can go on beautifully for a month, two months, three months and all of a sudden like last week I was feeling just fine and I cleaned house like I do every Monday . . . I got all them damn floors waxed and _____ wakes up from her nap and she couldn't get her body shirt undone so she got all upset and she wet all over my new waxed floor. And I just went berserk and I threw her around like she had killed somebody, because right at that moment I just snapped, I didn't feel it coming. I was fine, everything was hunky-dory, nothing was wrong, I wasn't in a bad mood, there was no warning . . .

This type of behavior is typical of abusive parents. Behavioral training in impulse control and coping skills can be helpful for parents who want to change their behavior. Numerous kinds of preventive programs have been attempted. These include parental education and the use of parents as therapists. A promising mutual-aid approach is Parents Anonymous (PA), and organization that is concerned with the problems of parents who abuse their children.

An example of preventive research on abuse is a study in which abusing parents received training in parenting skills (Wolfe and others, 1981). The parents' training consisted of reading about effective parenting techniques, observing modeled demonstrations of how to handle common child-rearing problems, and learning relaxation and other coping skills. In addition, project staff members made weekly home visits to help the parents implement what they had learned. When parents who participated in this program were compared with a control group of abusers, the parents in the special program showed significant improvement in parenting skills. A follow-up showed that none of the specially treated abusers harmed their children during the year after their participation in the program. This study suggests that effective child management skills can be taught to abusive parents with a relatively small investment of time and labor.

Spouse Abuse

"To have and to hold . . . to love and to cherish . . ." This sentiment reflects the feelings of most people toward marriage—but these feelings are not shared by everyone. In the 1970s, largely as a result of the women's movement, attention was drawn to the plight of abused women—those who are browbeaten psychologically as well as those who are physically assaulted—who cower in bedrooms and kitchens, are patched up in emergency rooms, and, not infrequently, are beaten, shot, or stabbed to death in their own living rooms.

A woman who has been abused over a long period is afraid. Fear might be a woman's first and most immediate feeling during or after a beating, but other negative feelings may surface when she is not in physical danger. The abused woman is likely to develop doubts about herself. She might wonder whether she is justified in fearing for her life and calling herself an "abused wife." Most likely, however, a woman who thinks or feels that she is being abused is probably correct.

An abused woman may also feel guilty, even though she has done nothing wrong. An abused wife may feel responsible for her husband's violence because she believes she may have provoked him in some way. She then places the shame and blame on herself instead of on her abuser. Along with the feelings of being a failure, both as a woman and in her marriage, may come a real feeling of being trapped and powerless.

A wife abuser tends to be filled with anger, resentment, suspicion, and tension. He also, underneath all his aggressive behavior, can be insecure and feel like a loser. He may use violence to give vent to the bad feelings he has about himself or his lot in life. Home is one place where he can express those feelings without punishment to himself. If he were angry with his boss and struck him, he would pay the price; but all too often he gets away without any penalty when he beats his wife. One study found that compared with nonabusive husbands, abusive husbands were less assertive in social relationships than their wives, more likely to have been abused as children and more likely to have witnessed spouse abuse between their own parents (Rosenbaum and O'Leary, 1981).

Efforts to help abused spouses include not only emergency care, safety, and shelter but also long-range planning. Because abused spouses need to develop better feelings about themselves—that is, change their self-image—they need to strengthen their self-related positive cognitions. Counseling often emphasizes the following types of self-statements:

- ☐ I am not to blame for being beaten and abused.
- ☐ I am not the cause of another person's violent behavior.
- ☐ I do not have to take it.
- ☐ I deserve to be treated with respect.
- ☐ I do have power over my own life.
- ☐ I can use my power to take good care of myself.
- ☐ I can make changes in my life if I want to.
- ☐ I am not alone. I can ask others to help me.
- ☐ I deserve to make my own life safe and happy.

The three types of prevention can all be applied to spouse abuse. Premarital counseling illustrates primary prevention; marital counseling to reduce discord illustrates secondary prevention; and providing abused spouses with safety, shelter, and counseling illustrates tertiary prevention.

Effects of Divorce on Children

When we mentioned divorce earlier in the chapter, most of the emphasis was on minimizing maladjustment in the couple. There is also a sizable literature on the negative effects of divorce on children, and growing evidence that these effects can be reduced by taking certain preventive steps.

Each year about a million American children experience the disruption of their homes by the separation or divorce of their parents. It is estimated that by the end of the 1980s nearly one-third of all children in the United States will have experienced parental divorce. Despite its frequency, from a cultural standpoint divorce is still considered to be an unusual event with many negative implications for the people involved. It is also one of the most stressful and disorganizing events that may occur in a person's life, one for which most people, both children and adults, are not psychologically prepared.

The degree to which divorce is upsetting to children has been recognized for a long time. Children of divorced parents show up much more frequently in psychiatric outpatient clinic populations than their proportion in the population would predict. Even children in nonclinical samples are likely to exhibit dramatic divorce-related changes in play behavior and relationships with others (Hetherington and others, 1979; Wallerstein, 1986). Not only do children have to deal with their own stress, but they must cope with parents who are also experiencing high levels of stress and whose own physical and emotional health may have significantly deteriorated (see Figure 18–4). The clinical experience of many therapists and counselors has provided some ideas that may help parents soften the blow of divorce for their children.

1. *Tell the children ahead of time.* This lets them prepare for one parent's moving out.

2. *Tell the children the reasons that the decision was made.* This helps prevent children's frequent belief that they were the cause of the breakup. Make the explanation brief but honest and suitable for the age of the child.

3. *Emphasize that the divorce is a permanent decision.* Many children harbor the belief that their parents will eventually get back together.

4. *Explain what changes there will be in the child's life.* These may include moving, a new school, and much less money to spend. Emphasize the positive challenge of adapting to the new situation.

5. *Let the children be free to express their anger.* This is an effective way to prevent long-term problems. At the same time, the parents should avoid using their children as a dumping ground for their own sense of anger or despair. Instead, they should share their negative feelings with an adult friend or with a therapist or counselor.

6. *Avoid forcing the child to choose between the parents or to take sides.* Custody and visitation rights that are fair to both parents should be agreed upon. Both parents should make continued contact with the children a high priority.

Parents as Therapists

While parents sometimes fail to help their children develop optimally, there are numerous instances in which they play very positive roles. For example, there is growing evidence that parents can be trained to respond therapeutically to their children's behavioral problems (Moreland and others, 1982). The main techniques for bringing this about are modeling, behavioral rehearsal, and reinforcement (see Figure 18–5).

Many demonstrations of the use of parents as therapists have focused on extreme forms of behavior such as autism and some forms of mental retardation. Parents of autistic children have been taught to observe behavior, to identify responses that need to be strengthened or weakened, and to use reinforcers skillfully. The following is an interchange between a mother and a psychologist who was training her to deal more effectively with her 6-year-old son Dorian. The mother had already learned several principles of behavioral therapy in preparation for her conference with the psychologist. She had listed the behaviors that she felt Dorian had to learn, as well as a number of points that she and her husband would have to learn simultaneously.

MRS. COOPER: *We would like Dorian to respond to instructions in various arts and crafts activities which would eventually lead to his learning of reading, writing, numbers, colors, and appropriate behavior in the classroom. In order to achieve this broad objective, he has to learn the following. The following are most of his problems. . . .*

a) The proper use of objects, such as crayons, paste, paper, pencils, and books.

b) Sit still and pay attention. (They are not necessarily in that order. That is how they came to my mind.)

c) Focus his vision on what we point out.

d) He has to perceive the whole picture rather than focusing or fixating on a small part of it. (Perception, I feel, is somewhat of a problem.)

e) I would like him to learn to take pride and enjoy his success. Pride in his own achievement will, I hope,

(a)

(b)

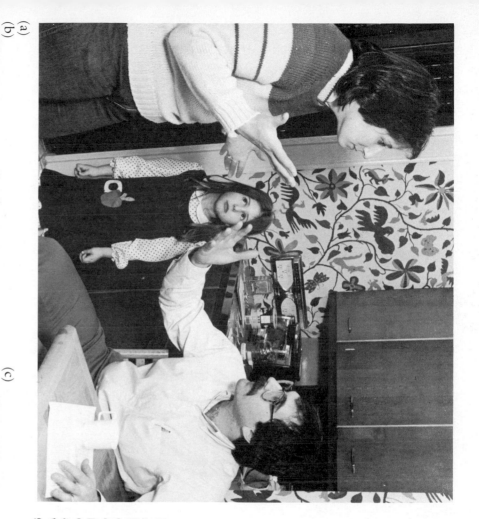

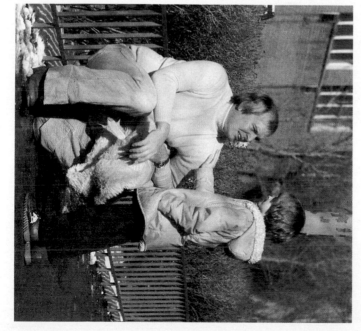

(c)

FIGURE 18–4
After the family turmoil that precedes a divorce, children must deal with dislocations and discontinuities associated with the postdivorce period. One of these discontinuities is the infrequent, and perhaps artificial, contacts with the parent who has not been given custody.

FIGURE 18–5
This mother is teaching her child who is a slow learner how to write her name. Notice how she uses modeling, how the child practices what the mother has modeled, and the mother's reinforcement of the child's progress.

be his strongest reinforcer as he grows. These are his problems as well as what I feel our goals are and what we have to work for.

DR. W.: *The implication when you list all of these behaviors is that the behaviors are there, either too weakly . . .*

MRS. COOPER: *Yes, I feel they are there and could be brought out, but he's not willing to do it, as of now, so this is what I feel are his problems.*
— (Walder and others, 1967, pp. 57–58)

Mrs. Cooper became skillful at recognizing environmental events that might reinforce appropriate responses emitted by Dorian. She planned and wrote up records of her "reinforcement experiments" with him.

We know the following about Dorian already:

A. *He imitates what we say and with some positive reinforcement, successfully learned a great deal of behavior.*

B. *He loves chocolate in any way, shape, or form. He imitates what we say and because of this, and in addition, with positive reinforcers such as the chocolate he has successfully learned a great deal of verbal behavior. This we know.*

C. *He loves chocolate and trains, lights, vacuum cleaners, cleaning objects, dearly.*

D. *He fixates on certain pages of books, and verbalizes quite accurately what he sees there.*

E. *He is beginning to explore the environment and loves to walk, looks into people's homes, and occasionally stops to talk to them.*

— (Walder and others, 1967, p. 59)

Mrs. Cooper's experiments became more and more successful, and her son's autistic behavior, although it was not eliminated, became less a problem.

Other studies have demonstrated that through special tutorial programs parents can become more effective in fostering desirable behavior in children who exhibit the more common types of problem behavior. For example, one child had learned how to command and control the behavior of his parents ("You go over there and I'll stay here"). When his parents learned to identify and differentially respond to his autocratic behavior, its frequency declined. The child became more socially cooperative when his parents ignored his commands; they also gave him special attention when he cooperated. Parents and teachers of highly aggressive boys have been taught to note the occurrence of particular types of undesirable behavior and to reduce their frequency through the use of reinforcement and other appropriate behavioral techniques (Patterson, 1982).

The School

School districts, schools, and classrooms are larger and more complex social systems than families. Often they seem unwieldy and unmanageable. However, in some respects it is more feasible to attack problems of behavior in the school situation than in the home. Dorian's mother invited a behavior modification specialist to visit her home and observe what went on there, but many parents, even while admitting that their families have problems, would be neither eager nor willing to have their privacy invaded by observers.

Teachers, school psychologists, and social workers can cite many instances in which longstanding family problems are not identified until the child reaches school age. But even when a problem is recognized at school, it may not be possible to deal with it effectively. The parent may refuse to cooperate with the school, or the realities of the child's life may make any significant change in his or her condition impossible—for example, if the child's home is unstable because of continual fighting between the parents or because the parents are immature and irresponsible.

Despite such barriers, early-detection projects in schools have attempted to identify children who are likely to have adjustment problems later in life. The results of these projects show that early observation of the child, together with data available to school mental-health workers (for example, nurses' notes, teachers' reports, and test scores), can predict later psychological casualties. In addition, classmates' ratings of each other seem to have predictive value. On the basis of such information, intervention studies have been carried out to help vulnerable children before their problems become serious enough to require clinical help. For example, in one project nonprofessional aides worked under close professional supervision for an entire school year with children who were judged to be at risk for school maladjustment. The children who received this one-to-one contact showed significant changes in a number of areas, including social and academic skills and overall adjust-

ment (Chandler and others, 1984). Special training for teachers, workshops to help parents develop their child-rearing skills, and carefully planned in-school and after-school activity programs can help prevent a significant number of behavior disorders in children.

Dropping Out

Some children are never comfortable in school, and by the time they reach high school they are ready to leave. The dropout problem is a social problem as well as an educational one. In prosperous times, when jobs are not difficult to obtain, the economic cost to the dropout may not seem great. However, when competition in the job market intensifies, poorly educated, unskilled people tend to fall by the wayside.

An example of primary prevention is a study aimed at teaching cognitive and social skills to high school students (Sarason and Sarason, 1981). The school in which the research was carried out had a history of high dropout and delinquency rates and a low percentage of graduates who went on to college. The research was carried out in class sessions as part of a regular course. The basic procedure involved using modeling to demonstrate social and cognitive skills, followed by rehearsal of the modeled behavior. The subjects saw demonstrations of the cognitive antecedents of effective behavior (for example, deciding between alternative courses of action) and effective overt responses (such as how to ask a teacher a question). Repeated emphasis was placed on the links between thought and action. The following is an excerpt from a videotape that was used in the experimental program ("Jim's cognitions" refers to voiceovers).

TOM: *Hey Jim, you want to go down to Green Lake fourth period?*

JIM: *What are you gonna do down at Green Lake?*

TOM: *A bunch of us are gonna take the afternoon off and party it up.*

JIM: *I don't think I can go. Sixth period Mr. Smith is reviewing for the algebra exam.*

TOM: *What about coming over and staying until sixth?*

JIM: *Well, I kind of like Mr. Jones's class. Besides, it's too hard to get to Green Lake and back in an hour and forty minutes. I could come after school.*

TOM: *You know Lydia is going to be there.*

JIM(*with noticeable interest*): *She is?*

TOM: *Yeah. And by the time school is over, who knows if the party will still be there. We might go over to someone's house.*

JIM'S COGNITIONS: *Gee, I really want to go to that*

party. Maybe I can get up the nerve to ask Lydia out. But I should stay for that algebra review, at least. The test will be hard enough without missing the review.

TOM: *You know, it is Friday afternoon and a beautiful day.*

JIM'S COGNITIONS: *I wish Tom would let me make my own decision. This isn't easy. Maybe I could study hard this weekend. Then I won't need to go to the review. But will I really study Saturday?*

TOM: *Well are you going to come?*

JIM: *I don't know, Tom. I'll have to think about it some more. Maybe I'll see you there fourth. If not, I'll probably come later.*

TOM: *Okay, I hope you come.*

One year after the completion of the study, the experimental subjects had better school-attendance records, less tardiness, and fewer referrals to school counselors and psychologists because of behavioral problems than similar students who did not participate in the program.

The Community

After people leave school they are pretty much on their own. Most of their activities are not supervised by authority figures, and a certain degree of independence is expected of them. They are also expected to fit into the community by working and by adhering to its laws, values, norms, and priorities.

Work is the major postschool activity for most people. Finding employment that is satisfying and sufficient to earn a livelihood is obviously a major ingredient in an individual's satisfaction with life. How can maladaptive work behavior be prevented?

A study by Ross and Glaser (1973) compared several variables related to childhood experiences and the home environments of successful and unsuccessful male residents of a ghetto in a large city. Both groups grew up under decidedly disadvantaged circumstances, but while half continued to live in poverty, the other half managed to change their lives for the better in significant ways. There were two successful (A) groups consisting of blacks and Mexican-Americans, and two unsuccessful (B) groups of the same ethnic makeup. The A groups had worked more or less steadily during the 2 years preceding the study; the B groups had been unemployed or underemployed. The investigators hypothesized that parental attitudes and aspirations made the difference between people who did and did not overcome the developmental barriers posed by poverty and discrimination.

Interviews with respondents in the two groups uncovered a number of differences that supported the hypothesis and were consistent for both blacks and Mexican-Americans. Members of the A groups received greater support, encouragement, and discipline at home. They also had developed a sense of self-esteem through involvement in productive activities. The results indicate the need to help relatively unsuccessful people overcome low self-esteem and self-confidence. Another personality characteristic of members of the B groups that might be modified through imaginative programs is their dependence on approval from peers. We might expect that many unproductive people would benefit from a close relationship with nonpeers—teachers, athletic coaches, or employment counselors, for example—who would make demands, motivate achievement, provide information about productive skills, and act as both models and reinforcers of good performance.

Community Agencies

Every person is influenced by the way in which society and its institutions are organized. Although some institutions are concerned with specific segments of the population (for example, day-care centers, schools, social centers for senior citizens), several are capable of reaching all of the society's members. Because of our tendency to take these institutions for granted, we may lose sight of their potential for contributing to personal growth and reducing the likelihood of maladaptation. For example, a public library can be a powerful force in a person's life, and if it provides positive models, it can indirectly contribute to the prevention of maladaptive behavior. Kenneth Clark, an influential educator who grew up in Harlem, found such a model in a librarian at the New York Public Library.

I met Schomburg when I was about twelve years old, a crucial period in my life. It was at this time I clearly recognized that I was not ever going to be able to compete with my classmates in athletic skills.

I went to the library not only to escape the athletic competition, but also to escape the streets.

On one of my trips to the library, I decided that I was going to go upstairs to the third floor to the forbidden and mysterious area reserved for adults. I fully expected to be turned away unceremoniously. As I climbed the last flight of stairs, I felt the excitement of an interloper. I was prepared for the risk of either a polite or a more direct rejection. When I entered the room, a large man, whom I later came to know as Arthur Schomburg, got up from his desk and came over to me and smiled. He didn't ask me what I wanted. He merely put one arm around my shoulder and assumed that I was interested in the books. We went over to a table and sat down and began to talk. . . . We talked about books. We talked about

FIGURE 18–6
Police officers frequently must intervene in family disputes. This officer is trying to calm a domestic disturbance.

wonderful things: about the history of human beings, about the contributions of Negroes which were to be found in books. He showed me portraits of Negroes who had contributed something important.

On that first day of meeting Schomburg, I knew I had met a friend. He accepted me as a human being and through his acceptance helped me to share his love of, and his excitement in, the world of books.

— (Clark, 1965)

Most people deal with everyday crises in the best way they can using available resources. Just as we don't go to the doctor every time we have a sniffle, we don't run to the clinical psychologist every time we are upset. The availability of nonprofessional "therapists" may be one reason for this. For example, people like hairdressers and bartenders do a lot of therapeutic listening to the troubles of their customers (Cowen, 1982). However, some social institutions have been specifically assigned the task of handling crises.

Although they are not usually included in lists of mental-health workers, police officers frequently modify behavior—whether for good or ill and whether they are aware of it or not. Police officers are not in a position to remove the causes of crime, but as their skills in human relations develop, their contributions to the prevention of crime could increase. A crime prevention experiment in New York City has provided some information about the effects of increasing police officers' psychological sophistication and expertise (Bard, 1970). The focus of training and preventive work was on handling family disputes, since a high percentage of violent crimes are committed by close relatives. Another reason for developing more skill in handling family disturbances is that 22 percent of fatalities and 40 percent of injuries to police officers occur while they are intervening in these situations (see Figure 18–6). Psychological training does help police officers handle violence more effectively. In addition, it can help them handle many other problems, such as the usually harmless but often bizarre behavior of former mental-hospital patients, with more tact and discretion.

Suicide Prevention

Aside from the police, in many communities there is a need for specialized programs directed toward people who are going through a personal crisis or share particular types of problems. For example, suicide and crisis prevention centers have been established in many communities (see Figure 18–7). The purpose of these centers is to encourage troubled people to seek help, either through telephone contact or in person. Such efforts may provide a means of reducing social isolation and bringing destructive and self-destructive thoughts out into the open. However, because it usually is not pos-

sible to conduct well-controlled studies of sudden crisis events such as potential suicides, there is continuing debate about the nature and effectiveness of crisis prevention centers. One recent study presented evidence suggesting that suicide-prevention centers do lower suicide rates, particularly among young white females (Miller and others, 1984).

Many suicides can be prevented if friends and relatives recognize the danger signs. Some of these signs are listed in Table 18–2. There is no specific treatment for those who make suicide attempts, because the reasons for those attempts are extremely varied. Therapists must show that they are not surprised or discouraged by the client's suicidal urges. Several strategies are often employed by therapists to deal with the possibility of suicide. One approach is to be very active and tell the client to get rid of pills, guns, ropes, or other potential means of suicide. Therapists must also be available at all times and may ask the client to call if he or she is uncertain about controlling suicidal impulses. Sometimes it is helpful to insist that the client make an explicit promise not to commit suicide. Because people thinking about

FIGURE 18–7

Crisis hotlines and suicide-prevention centers provide help for people who feel unable to cope with events in their lives. Sometimes just talking to an understanding listener is all that is needed. If more help is required, those who staff the hotlines can provide the callers with additional numbers to call for assistance.

TABLE 18-2

Warning Signs of Suicide in Young People

Verbal comments Statements such as "I wish I'd never been born," and "You'll be sorry when I'm gone," should be taken just as seriously as the direct threat, "I'm going to kill myself."

Behavior changes These cover a wide range and include giving away treasured possessions, taking life threatening risks, and having frequent accidents. Other signs may be complaints of intense loneliness or boredom, a marked increase in agitation or irritability, or getting into trouble with school or the police. There may also be the more customary signs of depression: changes in appetite and sleep habits, suddenly dropping grades, complaints of inability to concentrate, and withdrawal from friends and from favorite activities.

Situational factors Inability to communicate with parents, recent problems at school, end of a love relationship, recent involvement with drugs or alcohol all increase the situational risk.

What to do Parents and friends should take action by asking questions such as "Are you very unhappy?" "Do you have a plan about taking your life?" "Do you think you really don't want to live anymore?" Asking direct questions about suicide doesn't put ideas into someone's head. Instead it may be a lifesaving measure if the answers are taken seriously. Both parents and friends often don't believe that such statements might be carried out or they may be too frightened to take action. Although friends are sometimes sworn to secrecy about suicidal thoughts, they should contact a parent or responsible adult immediately if they suspect thoughts of suicide and professional help should be obtained at once. If the suicidal threat seems immediate, the nearest suicide prevention center (usually listed under "suicide" or "crisis" in the phone book) should be contacted.

suicide often are not thinking clearly and see no other options open to them, the therapist can be helpful in suggesting other possibilities to solve the problem. When a therapist or other person is in contact with someone threatening suicide, bargaining may be useful. For instance, someone threatening to jump from a high place can be urged to delay and keep all options open by discussing the problem (see Figure 18–8).

Treatment in the Community

Whether people receive mental-health services in the community or in institutions, society has a definite interest in how those services are provided, their effectiveness, and their cost. The mix of available services can influence not only the recipients' sense of well-being but also their economic productivity. In one study, matched groups of schizophrenic patients in Portland, Oregon, and Vancouver, British Columbia, were compared approximately one year following discharge from a mental hospital (Beiser and others, 1985). Whereas Vancouver had a rich network of accessible community services for the chronically mentally ill, Portland's services at the time of the study were limited. One year after discharge, the Vancouver group experienced fewer readmissions, were more likely to be employed, and reported a higher level of well-being than was the case for the former patients in Portland. These results suggest that the effects of deinstitutionalization depend on the resources available to help former patients.

Many people who would otherwise have to be hospitalized could remain in the community if facilities that provide additional social support and supervision were available. An example of such a facility is the half-way house or community lodge. In one study, a group of institutionalized patients who had volunteered to do so moved from the mental hospital to a lodge in the community (Fairweather and others, 1969). The members decided who their leaders would be and the work that each would perform. Initially, extensive supervision was needed, and the group frequently found it necessary to seek help. However, as time passed, the lodge patients significantly increased their employment level and the length of time they were able to be out of the hospital. The median percentage of time in full employment for the lodge group was as high as 70 percent, while virtually all of the control subjects were totally unemployed.

The Case of Sylvia Frumpkin

The story of Sylvia Frumpkin shows how the community's "help" can sometimes be anything but helpful (Sheehan, 1982). Frumpkin (the name is fictitious, but the story is true) had a long and disheartening journey through what is commonly called "the system." In fact, she encountered the disjointed, fragmented, and ineffective system at every turn. Following her first psychotic break in 1964 at the age of 15, she was repeatedly hospitalized or placed in various types of institutions. At different times she was diagnosed as manic-depressive or as schizophrenic, either undifferentiated or paranoid type. At one time or another she was given individual psychotherapy, antipsychotic medications, lithium, insulin coma therapy, electro-convulsive therapy, "Chris-

tian psychotherapy," and megavitamin therapy. Over the years she saw a constantly changing variety of therapists, often for very short periods. These therapists, often treated her with nearly every available medication, sometimes without reference to her history, and they sometimes changed, suddenly decreased, or altogether stopped her medication in a seemingly arbitrary manner.

Sylvia Frumpkin is not the kind of patient most therapists enjoy; she is slovenly, unappreciative, and uncooperative. She drains the energies of clinical personnel by being loud, abusive, and even violent during the acute phases of her illness. Even when she was not acutely ill, Frumpkin was characterized by a staff member as "arrogant, nasty, and demanding." Nevertheless, as Figure 18–9 shows, Sylvia Frumpkin experienced 45 changes in treatment settings. She was repeatedly bounced back and forth between her family home, various hospital settings, and community residential facilities. She was admitted 27 separate times to 8 different hospitals (state, municipal, general, voluntary, and private), where she spent a total of 9 years. She spent almost 7 years in a state hospital. For slightly less than 6 years she lived with her family, cycling in and out of their home 9 different times. She spent a total of 3 years in several different types of community settings, such as halfway houses, a foster home, a YWCA residence and a religious community. The cost of her care was estimated to be $636,000 in 1982 and would be even greater today if the costs of inflation are taken into account.

Unfortunately, Sylvia Frumpkin's story is not unique. There are an estimated 1.7 to 2.4 million chron-

FIGURE 18–8
Sometimes emergency physical intervention is necessary to prevent suicide. This woman had threatened to jump from a ledge outside her third floor apartment. Police and paramedics had to pull her to safety after their attempts to persuade her to reenter the building failed.

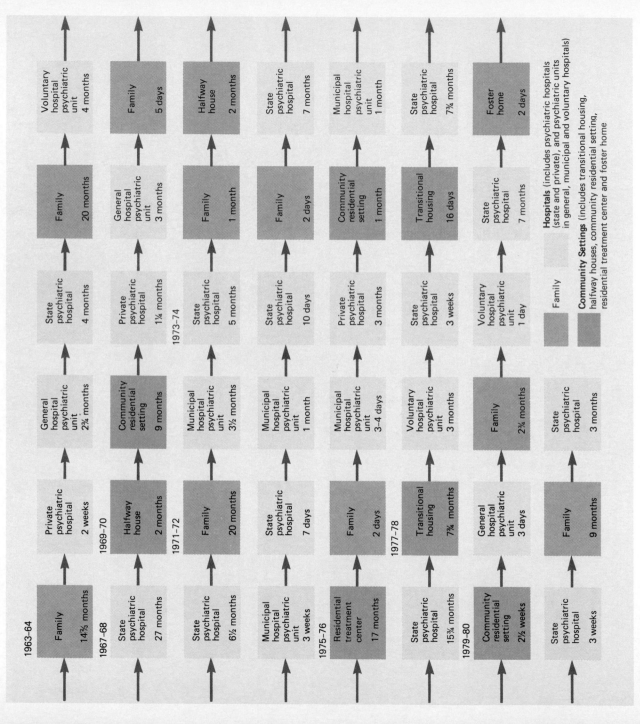

FIGURE 18–9
Sylvia Frumpkin's odyssey as a chronic mental patient, 1963–1980. (Based on Moran, Freedman, & Sharfstein, 1984, p. 889. *Hospital and Community Psychiatry.* Copyright © 1984, the American Psychiatric Association. Reprinted by permission.)

ically mentally ill people in the United States. Policy makers and the public can learn a great deal from the experiences of people like Sylvia Frumpkin. Her story clearly illustrates the profound impact of chronic mental illness on patients, families, and communities, as well as on the staggering costs of providing care. It may well be that Frumpkin would have continued to deteriorate even if the conditions of her treatment had been more favorable, but the behavior of the system certainly seems to have been a contributing factor. In her various hospitalizations, Frumpkin never experienced a prolonged relationship with a caring person. She perceived no one as having her interests continuously at heart during a period of 17 years. Cases like Frumpkin's have led mental-health workers, judges, and other government officials to think about ways to reform both the system and the laws that place disturbed individuals in public institutions.

Experiments designed to improve the mix of available mental-health services are under way in a number of states. For example, the Massachusetts Mental Health Center provides an alternative for patients who traditionally would have been admitted and retained on inpatient services. In the new system all patients who are thought to need inpatient hospitalization are first admitted to a day hospital. Those who do not require residential facilities return to their homes or community living situations at night and on weekends. Those who are admitted for day hospitalization but are found to require 24-hour inpatient care because they are dangerous or unable to care for themselves are transferred to an acute intensive-care unit within the hospital. As soon as is warranted by the clinical situation, these patients are returned to the day hospital or to a day hospital and dormitory-inn. The dormitory-inn is a special facility that provides care for patients for whom the intensive-care unit is no longer appropriate, who need treatment in the day hospital, and who have no other place to sleep. It is a time-limited residence with an anticipated 3-week length of stay (Gudeman and others, 1985). Whether inpatient hospitalization is a question that requires further investigation. However, the development of this type of facility clearly reflects growing awareness of the need for an expanded array of treatment facilities in the community.

Long-term mental-hospital patients do not usually fare well when they return to the community unless effective aftercare programs are available to them. The Vancouver–Portland and community-lodge studies mentioned earlier, as well as other evidence, suggest that long-term patients can help themselves attain an impressive degree of autonomy through carefully planned aftercare programs both in hospitals and in the community. The opportunity for resocialization is an important element of these programs. Of importance, also, is the ability of the program to adapt to the special needs of its residents and workers. Halfway houses can, at a lower cost to society, increase the personal freedom and self-confidence of many former mental-hospital patients and decrease the stigma attached to mental illness.

Although the concept of community care for the chronically mentally ill is a good one, most deinstitutionalized people have simply been dumped into communities that fear them because of their eccentric behaviors and do not look after them in any systematic way. As a consequence, the number of homeless mentally-ill people has greatly increased.

How do the chronically mentally ill become homeless? Obviously, there are many pathways to the streets, but it is useful to look briefly at some of them. The

chronically and severely mentally ill are not proficient at coping with the stresses of this world; therefore, they are vulnerable to eviction from their living arrangements, sometimes because of an inability to deal with difficult or even ordinary landlord–tenant situations and sometimes because of circumstances in which they play a leading role.

In the absence of an adequate case management system, they are out on the streets and on their own. Many, especially the young, have a tendency to drift away from their families or from a board-and-care home; they may be trying to escape the pull of dependency and may not be ready to come to terms with living in a sheltered, low-pressure environment. If they still have goals, they may find an inactive life style extremely depressing. Or they may want more freedom to drink or use street drugs. Some may regard leaving their comparatively static milieu as a necessary part of the process of realizing their goals, but this is a process that exacts its price in terms of homelessness, crises, decompensation, and hospitalizations. Once the mentally ill are out on their own, they will more than likely stop taking their medications. The lack of professional care on the streets and the effects of alcohol and other drug abuse are further serious complications. They may now be too disorganized to extricate themselves from living on the streets—except by exhibiting blatantly bizarre or disruptive behavior that leads to their being taken to a hospital or jail.

Few deinstitutionalized people are given the vocational training, guidance in self-care, recreation, or opportunities for socializing that are required for any sort of meaningful existence. The need for follow-up care, the hard realities of insufficient funding, the impact of patients on communities, and the uncertainties as to what constitutes effective community programs have all been largely ignored. As a result, a growing number of people who would otherwise be enthusiastic about deinstitutionalization have become at least somewhat disillusioned.

For some individuals, hospitalization denies them their freedom and further decreases their ability to cope with their problems. For others, the psychiatric hospital provides a haven where, in a protected atmosphere, they can regroup their defenses for reentry into the community (see Figure 18–10). The following excerpt from a Seattle newspaper illustrates how the deinstitutionalized movement may result in inadequate protection and help.

Rubie Label rapped gently at the door of the small housekeeping unit in the Frye Apartments, which he manages.

There was no answer.

This article stimulated the following letter from a reader.

After reading the article in the paper about the little psychotic lady who is living in abject misery in the hotel on First Avenue (The Times, December 16); I feel compelled to write this letter.

It is not an easy letter to write, as my past history of hospitalization in a mental institution is not one I am proud of or like to recall.

However, I must speak out on the issue of the commitment law in the State of Washington.

The crux of the whole problem of voluntary versus involuntary commitment to a mental hospital seems to lie in the simple fact that a person in the midst of a mental crisis is not capable of making the decision to commit himself to a hospital for treatment.

In a state of mental confusion or breakdown, one's mental processes are in such a muddle that one is unable to make any rational decision about life. Also, most times a mentally confused person has the feeling that if "so-and-so would only keep me, I could make it." Well, so-and-so doesn't have the time, the interest, or the expertise to do or say the things you may need.

Most of the time, one's family and friends are just as confused as you are about what is best to do.

One of the things one is painfully aware of in any mental hospital is that the staff is being paid to care. But at least they care, and if they are up to snuff, they know how to help you.

A large mental hospital is not a happy place to be, but tell me this—what's so great about being in a flea-bitten hotel room where no one knows you exist or cares? Freedom and rights are great rhetoric, but what is freedom to one who is unable to use it for one's own best interests?

Is the right to starve to death in a wretched hotel room, and be so zonked out of your mind that you don't know who you are, really all that precious?

— (Seattle Times, December 25, 1977, p. A13)

The incident described in the newspaper article reflects the lack of community help and supervision for the mentally disturbed; the letter explains why the mental hospital remains a needed haven for some people.

One consequence of the large number of failures of deinstitutionalization has been an increase in readmissions to state hospitals. Patients now stay in the hospital for shorter periods but, because of their inability to function in the community, return more often. About half of the patients who are released from state hospitals are readmitted within a year of discharge.

Label pushed open the door and stepped inside. No one was in the kitchenette. He looked in the sitting room. Empty.

He glanced toward the open bathroom door. A young woman, without clothing, was standing rigid and transfixed in front of the mirror, her back to the doorway, apparently in deep shock.

Label sighed. He wrapped a robe around her, coaxed her gently to a chair and talked constantly to her, "This is Rubie. You're all right now. No one is going to hurt you. Rubie is here now."

She looked at him, wide-eyed, questioning. She began to sob and the tears dampened long dark hair cascading around her face. Label put his arms around her, comforting her.

Afterward, after he had drawn her out of her trance and promised to return, Label stepped outside and leaned a sagging shoulder against the corridor wall. His eyes, too, were wet.

He knew that for this young woman there were no solutions, only problems. She was one of dozens, perhaps hundreds of people with mental problems who are in downtown Seattle now.

Few can be taken in for hospital care. More refused to commit themselves to a hospital. Most are not considered dangerous to themselves or others, the criteria for an involuntary commitment.

—(Seattle Times, December 16, 1977, p. A17)

FIGURE 18–10

Deinstitutionalization may not live up to its potential if the trade-off for not being hospitalized is inadequate housing, isolation, and lack of therapeutic contact.

Legal Aspects of Treatment and Prevention

In this and the previous chapter we have discussed ways to help people to avoid having problems and, if that isn't possible, to overcome them to the extent possible. What can be more humane, more noncontroversial? Because people live in groups, the community has an interest in preventing behavior that is maladaptive. Although historically it has not always been the case, governmental units now have laws that deal with both helping people who behave deviantly and protecting the public from the dangers posed by certain types of deviant individuals (for example, murderers). Actually, trying to help someone can create problems if our judgment of what constitutes help happens to be wrong or the person doesn't want to be helped (at least by us).

Institutionalization

The process of placing a person in an institution is called **commitment**. Prisoners are committed to prisons for punishment, and mental patients are committed to mental hospitals for treatment. **Criminal commitment** of an individual to a mental hospital may occur when a criminal act is legally declared to be a result of insanity and that the interests of society and the individual would be best served by commitment to a mental hospital rather than to a prison. Some mental patients voluntarily commit themselves, but others are involuntarily hospitalized through a legal procedure called **civil commitment**. Civil commitment can only be carried out if a person is judged to be a risk to him or herself or to others. The forced institutionalization of a person poses serious problems. On the one hand, civil commitment aims at providing help, but to do that, it must deprive the person of basic human rights.

Anna May Peoples made the Public Safety Building her home for 2 years, but authorities had to dismiss trespassing charges against her. She was not competent to stand trial and not dangerous enough to institutionalize (see Figure 18-11).

But the 64-year-old transient was arrested again last night, charged again with criminal trespass for being in the Public Safety Building after hours. Officers escorted her out of the building at 10:45 P.M., then arrested her five minutes later when she came back in.

To the consternation of the Police Department, Peoples insists on making her home in the building at Third Avenue and James Street. She bathes in the restroom sinks, dresses in the elevators, and sleeps on the rock-hard floors.

One night, police found her naked in an elevator. Another time, she fell asleep and plunged through a plate-glass door.

Social workers tried to find the woman a home, but Peoples refused help. She preferred the Public Safety Building, despite being dragged out by police on various occasions.

—(Adapted from Guillen, 1982, p. B1).

Peoples is a paranoid schizophrenic who believes people are out to shoot her. Because of that, she said, she took

---

What lessons can be learned from the way deinstitutionalization has been practiced up to now? Perhaps the most important lesson of the bad experiences of the past decade is that deinstitutionalization as it is now being carried out is not helpful to many individuals. As happens so often, society neglects many of the nuts and bolts needed to reach a worthy objective. More money and more trained personnel are needed.

More education is also essential. Public-information programs about mental illness and retardation and more citizen involvement in planning for the reentry of former patients into the community can help make deinstitutionalization a positive experience for both the patients and the community. The entry of formerly institutionalized patients into the neighborhood has frequently been perceived as a threat, even though the overwhelming majority of ex-mental patients and retarded individuals are harmless (Rabkin, 1979). Nothing can arouse negative feelings in a neighborhood more effectively than the proposed establishment of a halfway house or aftercare center in the vicinity. Yet there is no evidence that simply being a discharged mental patient makes a person more likely to commit crimes or endanger the community. However, there is an increasing tendency to place people with criminal records in mental hospitals, and people with previous arrest records are likely to be arrested again after they are discharged from mental hospitals (Steadman, 1981).

The problems of the chronically mentally ill living in the community require a comprehensive system of care that includes:

1. An adequate number of supervised community-housing settings
2. Community clinical services ranging from professional mental-health workers who can provide crisis intervention to hospitalization for acute conditions
3. Recognition of the importance of families in treatment and adequate support for family members as well as for the patient.

FIGURE 18-11
Anna May Peoples, caught between the technicalities of legal incompetence and lack of dangerousness, waits to hear her fate during a court appearance.

refuge in the Public Safety Building. She could not be committed involuntarily because she was not a danger to herself or others.

Criminal Commitment

To convict a person of a crime, the state must establish beyond a reasonable doubt not only that the person committed the prohibited act but also that the act was committed with criminal intent. If it cannot be proven that the person meant to do harm, the insanity defense becomes possible. The aim of the insanity defense is to show that the defendant did not have a "guilty mind" at the time that the crime was performed.

The concept of insanity is often confused with that of competence to stand trial. **Insanity** refers to a person's state of mind at the time that an act was carried out, while **competency** refers to a person's state of mind at the time of a judicial proceeding. In a legal sense, an **incompetent person** is one who lacks the capacity to consult with a lawyer and to understand what legal proceedings are about. Both insanity and competency are legal terms whose applicability in a given case is determined by a judge after considering all evidence, including the opinions of expert witnesses.

During the late nineteenth and early twentieth centuries, it was recognized that a crime did not necessarily have to be seen as a deliberate defiance of social norms; it may be an unconscious response to personal conflicts. The offender might be psychologically disturbed rather than simply wicked. As belief in this interpretation grew, statutes were introduced that permitted the court to defer sentencing decisions until the offender could be studied and recommendations made to the judge. Psychiatrists, psychologists, social workers, and probation officers became advisers to the court.

Sentencing became more flexible, and parole was used increasingly. Along with these developments came the possibility that an accused individual could plead insanity, by which was meant mental incompetence and inability to distinguish right from wrong at the time that a crime was committed.

The number of insanity defenses that are successful is very small. In the entire state of New York, for example, there are on the average fewer than 50 successful insanity defenses each year. Thus, the insanity defense can be contributing only a tiny fraction to the problem of crime in the United States. In part, this is because juries have difficulty applying the fine legal points involved in the insanity defense. The following excerpt from a news article illustrates this point.

Roderick Stoudamire, whose previous trial ended in a hung jury three months ago, was found guilty in Superior Court today of first-degree murder in the stabbing death last summer of a woman jogger at Seward Park.

The jury of six women and six men announced its verdict for the second trial at 10:40 A.M. in a courtroom packed with spectators. They deliberated about five hours.

The jury also found Stoudamire guilty of assaulting two other women joggers.

Stoudamire, 16, had pleaded not guilty by reason of insanity. It was his insanity defense that caused the deadlock in the first trial. After deliberating more than two days, jurors in that case said they were confused by the definition of criminal insanity, and could not decide whether it applied to Stoudamire.

The tall, slender youth sat quietly, usually with a vacant look on his face, as witnesses testified during both of the long and often dramatic trials. He wore the same look this morning when the decision against him was read.

A mistrial was declared in the youth's first trial after jurors announced they were deadlocked. In that trial, 10 said they did not believe Stonamire was legally insane, while the 2 others said they were convinced the youth was schizophrenic and voted to acquit him.
—(Home, 1979, p. C11).

One of the toughest problems with the insanity defense is what to do with those who are acquitted—how to deal humanely with the criminally insane on the one hand and protect the public on the other. At one time the criminally insane were simply committed indefinitely and warehoused along with the rest of the mentally ill. Recently, however, a nationwide trend toward deinstitutionalization, tighter commitment laws, and guaranteed right to treatment have made it almost impossible to imprison the criminally insane in hospitals for long periods.

Insanity is a legal term, not a psychiatric diagnosis. Early English law did not recognize insanity as an excuse for criminal behavior. However, by the thirteenth century proof of criminal intentions was necessary to convict a person of a felony. If accused individuals could prove that they were completely "mad," they could successfully defend themselves against a criminal charge. In 1843 Daniel M'Naghten, a Scottish woodturner, assassinated Edward Drummond, secretary to the prime minister of England (see Figure 18–12). He was found not guilty because the judges stated that he was "labouring under such a defect of reason, from disease of the mind, as not to know the nature and quality of the act he was doing; or, if he did know, that he did not know he was doing what was wrong" (M'Naghten case, 1843).

This rule, the **M'Naghten rule**, became the "right and wrong" test of insanity and was widely adopted. An example of an attempt to invoke this rule occurred in the case of Jack Ruby, who was convicted of the murder of President Kennedy's assassin, Lee Harvey Oswald, in 1964. In appealing his death sentence, Ruby claimed that he suffered from psychomotor epilepsy and that this prevented him from determining right and wrong. However, this claim was rejected by the judge and Ruby was found legally sane. He eventually died in prison.

The M'Naghten rule and subsequent court decisions have been controversial largely because of the difficulty defining precisely what knowing right from wrong really means. In 1962 the American Law Institute (ALI) proposed a set of guidelines that have since been incorporated into the laws of several states. The ALI's guidelines focus on impairment that grows out of a defendant's mental illness and include the following ideas.

FIGURE 18–12
Daniel M'Naghten.

1. *A person is not responsible for criminal conduct if at the time of such conduct as a result of mental disease or defect he lacks substantial capacity either to appreciate the criminality (wrongfulness) of his conduct or to conform his conduct to the requirements of law.*

2. *. . . The terms "mental disease or defect" do not include an abnormality manifested only by repeated criminal or otherwise antisocial conduct.*
—(American Law Institute, 1962, p. 66)

With each passing year, the ALI guidelines have gained increased acceptance throughout the country. In 1983, in the case of *Jones v. United States*, the Supreme Court ruled that people who are found not guilty by reason of insanity can be held indefinitely in a mental hospital under a less rigorous standard of proof of dangerousness than is required for civilly committed individuals. The Court ruled that acquitted insanity defendants "constitute a special class that should be treated differently."

John Hinckley's acquittal by reason of insanity from charges of attempting to assassinate Ronald Reagan caused many people to question the fairness of the insanity defense. The American Psychiatric Association argued that people should be acquitted for insanity only if they have a serious mental disorder such as psychosis. Those who have personality disorders—for example, antisocial personality disorder—or abuse drugs or alcohol should be held responsible for their actions. The Association further stated that expert witnesses should not be allowed to testify about whether the defendant was able to control his or her behavior (*Psychiatric News*, February 4, 1983). The use of expert opinion poses profound interpretive problems (see Box 18–1). So far none of the guidelines that have been proposed for dealing with the problem of insanity have provided a completely satisfactory solution.

Thomas Szasz (1970), a psychiatrist, believes that a verdict of "mentally ill" rather than "guilty" or "not guilty" is dehumanizing because it denies personal responsibility. In one survey, over 80 percent of a sample of people living in midtown Manhattan were judged to be mentally ill to some extent (Srole and others, 1962). Does this mean that over 80 percent of the population is therefore immune from having to accept the consequences of their actions? Perhaps the criminal-justice system should be revised to deal separately with the determination of guilt and with the appropriate type of sentence. In this way a person might be judged guilty yet still be sent to a hospital for treatment instead of prison. The state of California is unusual in that it does provide for two trials—a guilt trial and a penalty trial.

Two factors have restricted this type of judicial innovation. In the first place, the judicial system is already overloaded with cases and so far behind in its work that there is little time to plan and carry out the experiments on which reforms might be based. Second, the decisions of judges and juries are based on varied and often conflicting goals, including rehabilitation of offenders, isolation of offenders who pose a threat to community safety, discouragement of potential offenders, expression of the community's condemnation of the offender's conduct, and reinforcement of the values of law-abiding citizens.

Civil Commitment

All fifty states have civil commitment laws. These laws are based on the doctrine of **parens patriae,** according to which the state can act in what it takes to be the best interest of a minor or of an adult who is incapacitated. The principal features of the process are a petition, a hearing, and a decision about the place to which the individual is to be committed. In some states, the judgments of psychiatrists are decisive in reaching commitment decisions. In others, physicians who are not psychiatrists play dominant roles. Until a short time ago standards for commitment were loosely worded and protections for the patient either did not exist or were ignored. Then, in a 1979 decision (*Addington v. Texas*), the Supreme Court ruled that people may not be committed to mental institutions unless the state has pre-

sented "clear and convincing" evidence that they require hospitalization.

Growing awareness of abuses like the one described in the following newspaper article led to reforms of commitment codes in many states. The patient in this article had been sent to a medical hospital during a severe attack of asthma in 1956. Twenty days later she was committed to a county mental hospital. She was not discharged until 1960, even though the staff of the mental hospital had considered her sane since 1957. *The New York Times* gave the following report of the proceedings at her release trial.

At today's hearing in Judge Pindar's court, Dr. John J. Scott, assistant medical director of the county medical hospital, testified that as far back as 1957, at a hospital staff conference, Miss Dean had been adjudged sane.

Asked why she had not been released in view of her many requests for her freedom since that time, Dr. Scott said that the woman was without relatives and it had been feared that she would become a public charge.

When a patient at the hospital, Miss Dean performed the duties of a registered nurse, without pay.

Miss Dean's release was effected through the effort of a friend, who remembered that Raymond H. Chasan, a lawyer, had won the release of another mental patient in 1947, under somewhat similar circumstances.

—(*New York Times*, July 17, 1960, p. 59)

All civil-commitment laws involve two judgments: whether the individual is suffering from a disabling mental illness and whether he or she is dangerous. The first criterion is relatively easy to establish. The second is more of a problem. Dangerousness refers to the potential to inflict harm on other people as well as on oneself. Because dangerousness involves a prediction of future behavior, its application to individual cases creates enormous problems. Can a clinical expert tell the court whether a person is dangerous and when he or she has stopped being dangerous?

In 1985 a 22-year-old accountant was pushed in front of a speeding subway train at rush hour. A team of some 200 doctors, nurses, and technicians operated on her for 22 hours, trying to save her life and repair her severe head injuries and numerous broken bones. Her assailant, who had been held by another subway rider until police arrived, turned out to be a 19-year-old unemployed woman with a history of mental problems. She had been released from a psychiatric ward less than a month before her crime, despite violent behavior while incarcerated and a psychiatrist's warning that she

BOX 18-1
The Debate Over the Insanity Defense

Will the insanity defense be retained in, or banished from, the federal and state criminal codes throughout the country? Legal and clinical experts—abolitionists and retentionists—continue to disagree. Throughout the controversy, however, one major point seems clear: whatever happens to the insanity defense, the judicial system cannot ignore the mental aberrations that a defendant may have experienced at the time of an unlawful act. The public outcry against "criminals getting away with murder" also cannot be ignored, even though the insanity defense is only frequently successful (see Figure 18-13). Understandably, the public remembers highly publicized cases in which the insanity defense is invoked and someone who has clearly committed a crime is found not guilty by reason of insanity, is released after a short hospitalization, and later commits another crime.

During the trial of John W. Hinckley, Jr., the man who shot Ronald Reagan and an aide, the barrage of contradictory expert testimony damaged the image of psychiatry in the public mind. Those who would abolish the insanity defense believe that one way to end this type of spectacle would be to restrict psychiatric testimony to evidence of mental abnormality that bears on the defendant's conscious awareness and perception—his or her "intent" to commit the crime. Other testimony concerning more subtle impairments of understanding, judgment, or behavior control would no longer be relevant at the guilt stage of the trial, but could be introduced at the time of sentencing. Another proposal calls for a pool of expert witnesses to be selected by the court. These experts would no longer testify for the prosecution or the defense. Instead, the impartial panel would attempt to arrive at a conclusion regarding the defendant's mental state when the crime was committed.

(a)

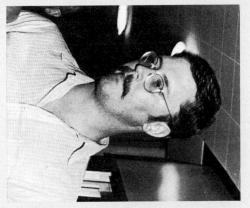

(b)

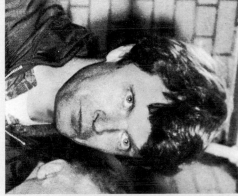

(c)

(d)

FIGURE 18-13

Edmund E. Kemper, III (a) was acquitted by reason of insanity from the charge of murdering his grandparents in 1964, and was released from a mental hospital in 1969 as "cured"; he later murdered six college students, his mother, and one of her friends—for which he was found sane and guilty. Dennis Sweeney (b) was sent to the Mid-Hudson Psychiatric Center when a judge accepted his plea of "not guilty by reason of mental disease" of killing Congressman Allard Lowenstin in 1980. After the slaying of his parents, Gregory Shaddy (c) was acquitted by reason of insanity; he spent 2 years in a hospital and was then pronounced cured and released. The case of John W. Hinckley, Jr. (d) revived debate over the insanity defense after he was acquitted from the charge of attempting to assassinate President Ronald Reagan, and committed to a mental hospital.

was dangerous. On two occasions she had attacked fellow patients and had to be subdued by means of a straitjacket.

Although the psychiatrist in this case was correct in thinking that the 19-year-old woman was dangerous, available evidence suggests that clinicians' predictions of whether a given individual will do something dangerous in the future are often inaccurate. As a group, former mental patients do have a higher arrest record for all types of crime than the general population, but patients who did not have an arrest record *before* hospitalization have a lower arrest rate than the general population. The higher rate of violent crimes committed by released mental patients can be accounted for entirely by patients with a record of criminal activity before hospitalization. Thus, a record of past violence is the best predictor of future violence. By itself, the mental status of released patients does not raise their risk of arrest for committing violent crimes (Monahan, 1981).

Involuntary hospitalization will be controversial as long as the dangerousness criterion is used in civil-commitment proceedings. Recent reforms require that the individual's constitutional rights be protected in a commitment proceeding as they would in any other court action. Steps in that direction include providing the person with a lawyer to protect those rights, limiting the length of confinement, and reviewing the person's progress at specified intervals.

The goal of protecting the rights of people who might be committed to an institution against their will is accepted by all. However, it is by no means clear how to protect those rights while simultaneously assuring the welfare of the individual and of society. Civil-commitment procedures and the concepts underlying them are in a state of flux, and humane procedures in which both lawyers and clinicians play defined roles are needed. At present, civil commitments seem to be increasing in frequency. This trend is being reinforced by recent court decisions that have emphasized the *parens patriae* role of the state in treating a patient for his or her own good. Also contributing to the trend is the failure of many states to develop community treatment networks to supplement hospital systems, as well as health insurance programs that provide only marginal subsidies for outpatient care.

The Rights of Patients

In the not-so-distant past, people were treated as if admission to a mental hospital justified taking away all their rights. However, according to recent court decisions patients' rights must be upheld and adequate treatment must be provided. In a 1971 case that attracted national attention (*Wyatt v. Stickney*), the court ruled

that a state must provide adequate treatment for mental hospital patients who are confined involuntarily. Beyond recognizing the patient's right to treatment, the court specified basic hospital staffing ratios and qualifications and also required individualized treatment plans.

In a 1975 Supreme Court decision (*O'Connor v. Donaldson*), Kenneth Donaldson was awarded compensatory and punitive damages of $38,500 against two staff psychiatrists at the Florida State Hospital because they had not provided adequate treatment for him during the 14 years of his involuntary commitment. The significance of the *O'Connor v. Donaldson* ruling was its recognition that hospitalized people who are not dangerous have a constitutional right to treatment. Whether or not a dangerous patient has a similar right has not yet been decided. The *O'Connor v. Donaldson* decision strengthened the rights of involuntarily hospitalized patients, but it did not make the task of determining whether or not a patient is dangerous any easier.

The courts have opened the door to long-overdue improvement in the treatment of the mentally ill. A federal judge in New Jersey has ruled that an involuntarily committed mental patient who objected to the drug therapy administered to him may not be forced to take the medicine (*Rennie v. Klein*, 1978). Since drugs now constitute the primary mode of behavior control in institutions, and virtually all involuntarily committed patients are routinely given antipsychotic medications, this and similar rulings may have widespread effects on the way in which treatment is defined in state institutions. In addition to strengthening their right to get treatment (and their right to refuse it), the courts have also supported patients' right to receive the least restrictive treatment available. The "least restrictive treatment" is only as restrictive and confining as is necessary to achieve the purposes of the commitments.

Increasingly, both patients and judges are questioning the safety and effectiveness of present-day treatment methods. Physical treatments such as drugs and electro-convulsive therapy do have the potential to cause permanent injury. Some experts also believe that behavior-modification procedures such as token economies may obliterate individuality. In addition, certain patients appear to deteriorate as a result of receiving psychotherapy. Some critics believe that merely being institutionalized is therapeutically counterproductive, regardless of the quality of the institution. Until recently a hospital's power to deny patients the right to examine their own files was taken for granted. Now patients can see their charts, but some hospitals do not voluntarily tell patients that they are entitled to do so.

As the rights of patients have been extended, the requirement of informed consent has been strengthened. **Informed consent** requires that patients receive adequate information about the nature of a planned treatment before they agree to it. The physician must communicate this information in language that is meaningful to the patient, rather than in "doctor talk," and must clearly explain the potential risks and benefits, including any discomfort that might arise from the treatment. Frequently, if the patient is incompetent to evaluate the information provided (for example, because of a psychotic condition), a lawyer assigned to look out for the patient's interests plays a role in the decision-making process. The requirement of informed consent applies to people who serve as subjects in experiments as well as to patients who are undergoing treatment. Patients and experimental subjects both have the right to terminate their participation in treatment or research even if they had previously consented to participate.

Should patients have the right to discontinue treatment that most people would agree was helping them? The difficulty of answering this question can be seen in this daughter's account of her mother's changed behavior after discontinuing the use of antipsychotic medication. Her mother came to New York to join her children after being discharged from a mental institution. She was talking Haldol, an antipsychotic drug.

On Haldol Mother's behavior improved tremendously, and we even harbored false hopes of her return to normal living. We never suspected that she might cease taking medication and regress. . . .

Not only did Mother rediscover art and music in New York, but she soon became familiar with the liberal New York laws regarding "patient's rights." She refused to continue to take Haldol and slowly began the reverse trip to "No Man's Land," where she now dwells. The first sign of her decompensation was a refusal to come to my apartment, and then she rejected me completely. Next the manager of her middle class apartment hotel asked us to remove her. She was annoying the guests with her outbursts. She had become known to all the shopkeepers on the block as "The Crazy Lady of West 72nd Street." Looking like a zombie, she paraded down West 72nd Street, accusing aunts, uncles, and brother of stealing her father's fortune, screaming at people who frightened her. . . .

Whether or not it's preferable for her to be forcefed Haldol and incarcerated in Kansas or allowed to do as she pleases in liberal New York, as destructive as her life is now, is paradoxical. She was not able to enjoy life and pursue her artistic interests in the former situation, but she is even less able to do so in the latter. Without medication, she can only exist. I believe that basically she is less free in her present life,

a prisoner of her delusions and paranoia. My brother, however, disagrees. He thinks that Mother is better off having the choice to live as she wishes, wandering aimlessly in the streets, constructing the world to fit her delusions.

— (Adapted from Lanquetot, 1984, p. 471)

The courts are only beginning to deal with the special problems that arise in the institutionalization of children. Among the questions that must be considered are: How much freedom may parents exercise in seeking to institutionalize a son or daughter? When, and under what conditions, can the state institutionalize children against their will? What procedures are needed to protect the child's rights? What are those rights? The United States Supreme Court has ruled that parents may commit their children to state institutions as long as "neutral fact-finders" approve.

The quality of the treatment provided is an important factor in approving institutionalization for children as well as for adults. For example, questions have been raised concerning the constitutionality of institutions for the mentally retarded that provide little or no special training. It has been argued that all such institutions are unconstitutional because they do not conform to the standard of least restrictive treatment. Retarded people can be helped in much less restrictive environments.

Although it may be a less obvious problem than protection of the rights of institutionalized people, the need to preserve the dignity of those who seek the help of mental-health specialists on an outpatient basis is also important. The need to assure the confidentiality of the interaction between therapist and client is just as great in a community clinic as it is in a state hospital.

Another area in which ethical issues arise is the selection of treatment methods and the goals of treatment. Informed consent is needed before therapeutic programs are begun. The issue of informed consent in therapy has been recognized most clearly in the case of organic or aversive treatments such as electro-convulsive therapy, but it is also relevant to the psychological therapies. Whenever possible, the goals of therapy should be determined jointly by the therapist and the client, without undue influence exerted by the therapist. Should a therapist encourage a young man to go to college because the client's parents, who are paying the therapy bills, want him to? The client should be the main concern of the therapist, but external influences like the parents' desires might become coercive factors in treatment. Clinicians also must not unduly impose their personal values on the therapy they offer to clients. A respectful attitude toward the client, an undogmatic approach, and healthy questioning of therapeutic tactics are important ingredients in all types of treatment.

The Challenge of Prevention

At the beginning of the chapter we said that prevention can take more than one form. It can involve taking the steps needed to keep a disorder from arising in the first place as well as efforts to limit its impact on the life of the individual. In this sense prevention and treatment are closely related. Common to both is the concept of vulnerability. Vulnerability arises when an individual's personal characteristics are insufficient to deal with characteristics of the situation. We have just seen how the mentally disturbed can deteriorate when placed in situations that lack social supports and opportunities to learn needed skills. The challenges of deinstitutionalization and prevention are the identification of opportunities for growth and stability and the provision of such opportunities to people who need them. These opportunities differ depending on the nature of the people to be served. For example, as they grow older, children need situations that give them increasing opportunities to be on their own. On the other hand, the aged usually need increasing care and attention.

Society inevitably must be involved in meeting the challenge of prevention because it controls or influences so many of the situations of modern life. We have seen many examples of the impact of community and social forces on our lives. Certain types of maladaptive behavior (for example, phobias and delusions) can be attacked on an individual basis with the clinical methods we have described (psychotherapy, behavioral therapy, drugs). But lasting solutions to many problems of living require social change. Slum children living in crowded apartments have only limited opportunities to generalize from what they learn in a stimulating school or preschool program. Medication may help deinstitutionalized patients hallucinate less frequently, but they still need a supportive environment and a chance to acquire new social and occupational skills.

Preventing maladaptive behavior and responding therapeutically to it when it does occur require an examination of society, its components, and how they are interrelated. This examination should include elements that a community lacks as well as positive steps that it may take. Examples of such steps are houses for runaway children, drop-in centers for teenagers, and crisis centers. Virtually all such programs have been started by citizens without government support, and, at least initially, on a nonprofessional basis. As a result of such efforts, professionals in many areas have broadened the scope of their clinical services and have increased their involvement in community programs.

Paraprofessionals

Programs have also been created to train and use nonprofessionals and paraprofessionals for significant roles in a variety of community settings. A wide culture-related gap often exists between middle-class professional workers (clinical psychologists, psychiatrists, and social workers) and people from low socioeconomic strata who need help. Much of the success of paraprofessionals seems to be due to similarities between their backgrounds and those of their clients. For this reason, some community psychologists devote a major portion of their activities to training paraprofessionals.

Paraprofessionals vary widely in age, education, and cultural background. They often make up a large part of the staff in neighborhood service centers, residential youth centers, and mental-health programs in both urban and rural areas. There they may serve as bridges between an established agency and a target group in the community that the agency has failed to serve effectively. Although relatively little research has been done on how to select, train, and evaluate the effectiveness of these workers, it has been shown that in some situations paraprofessionals may be as effective as professionals (Hattie and others, 1984). The responsibilities of paraprofessionals and their role in professional and community power structures need to be defined.

Self-Help Groups

Self-help groups can also contribute to prevention. For many human problems there are no easy answers or easy cures, but there is an alternative to coping with them alone. Millions of people whose problems and needs are not met through formal health care, social services, and counseling programs can find the hope and personal support they need in self-help groups. Within these groups, whose members share common concerns, they are offered the understanding and help of others who have gone through similar experiences. People like those in the following examples might find the help they need by contacting the appropriate group.

Margaret and Bill are parents of a young child with cancer. For two years they have shared suffering, dashed hopes, and heartbreak. In spite of caring friends and professional support, they feel alone in their grief.

Jean is a divorced mother who has custody of her three children. She now finds herself overwhelmed by the problems of single parenthood. Her teenage son has become difficult to handle and she is increasingly

TABLE 18-3

Ways in Which Self-Help Groups Help Their Members

1. Emotional support and understanding
2. An accepting reference group that reduces social isolation
3. Information and advice
4. Models on how to cope effectively with stress
5. Enhancement of members' awareness of alternatives available in dealing with problems

Based on Levy, 1976.

FIGURE 18–14

Self-help groups are not intended to replace skilled professionals. Rather, they are based on the belief that some problems of living go beyond the bounds of formal care services. Some self-help groups avoid formal professional guidance or consultation, although many groups have benefited from the informal help of professionals.

Roger has a serious drinking problem. He has been fired from two jobs in the last year and is deeply in debt. He has lost the respect of his family and friends. He entered treatment at an alcoholic clinic but began to drink again two months after the treatment ended. He realizes that his addiction is ruining his life but feels helpless to control it.

Table 18–3 lists some of the ways in which self-help groups help their members.

As social beings, all of us need to be accepted, cared for, and emotionally supported; we also find it satisfying to care for and support those around us. Within the most natural "self-help networks"—families and friends—we establish the one-to-one contact so important to our happiness and well-being. This informal support is such a basic part of our social character that we tend to take it for granted, but it clearly influences our ability to handle distressing events in our lives.

discouraged in trying to provide for her children's needs and the demands of her job.

Many of our daily conversations are actually mutual counseling sessions in which we exchange the reassurance and advice that help us deal with routine stresses. In fact, research scientists have found that there is a strong link between the strength of our social-support systems and our health (see Figure 18–14). Further research is needed to determine when, under what conditions, and for which types of problems self-help groups are effective (Videck-Sherman and Lieberman, 1985). Research is also needed to identify the reasons for success when self-help group are effective.

Community Psychology

Community psychology is concerned with the role of social systems in preventing human distress and maladaptive behavior. Community psychologists attempt to work in settings that have an impact on prevention. For example, they might serve as human-relations consultants to a police department, work to increase the skills of individuals who staff welfare offices, or develop prevention programs in homes or schools. Outreach programs are aimed at either preventing breakdowns or dealing with problems in the community before more drastic treatment programs, such as hospitalization, become necessary. Making communities livable requires good ideas about social planning as well as awareness that various segments of the population, including the aged, minorities, and the unemployed, have special needs. Community psychologists are interested in the environmental facts of life in particular communities as well as the impact of those facts on individual lives.

However, if pitfalls and problems cannot be anticipated, tampering with the mechanisms of society could do more harm than good. As a result, there is an urgent need for indexes of current social and psychological conditions in a community, roughly similar to the economic indicators that public and private officials use in setting economic goals. Some of these indicators are more visible than others. For example, national income statistics provide a measure of the level of material well-being; crime and accident statistics provide clues to the moral condition of society; the infant-mortality figures tell us something about the level of health care. Indicators that are less easily indexed are the effectiveness of an educational system, the influence of mass media on behavior, and the cohesiveness of a neighborhood.

A reliable group of social and psychological indicators would not only tell us where society is at a given time but also provide useful dependent measures of the effects of social, political, and economic programs. The community exerts potent psychological influences on its members, and the task of community planners and behavioral scientists is to make those influences as adaptive as possible for the community's residents.

A FINAL WORD

In Chapter 2 we traced the history of abnormal psychology and noted the enormous conceptual changes that have taken place over the centuries. This concluding chapter, perhaps more than any other in the book, illustrates the optimistic outlook of many researchers and therapists today. It is easy to point out the gaps in our knowledge: Why does schizophrenia occur in the late teens and early twenties? What causes panic attacks? What can be done about senility? But perhaps more significant than the lack of knowledge implied by these questions is the current consensus that (1) the scientific method can fruitfully be applied to them and (2) the resulting knowledge can be used to reduce the occurrence of maladaptive behavior.

There are many leads to effective prevention, but systematic research is needed to develop effective interventions. While the preventive approaches reviewed in this chapter seem promising, only scientific studies can validate them.

The formula for achieving prevention might be written $P = K \times W$. Prevention (P) is achieved when the needed knowledge (K) is available and society has the will (W) to use that knowledge to prevent unwanted outcomes. One of the great achievements of the present era is the widespread awareness that little good and much harm is done by blaming or stigmatizing people for their abnormalities, whether physical or behavioral. One of the great challenges is finding a way to motivate both individuals and society to do things to increase happiness, personal effectiveness, and the common good of the human family. The social need for prevention is, and will continue to be, one of the most powerful motivations of objective research in abnormal psychology.

Study Outline

SITUATION-FOCUSED AND COMPETENCY-FOCUSED PREVENTION

Situation-focused prevention is aimed at reducing or eliminating the environmental causes of disordered behavior, while **competency-focused** prevention is concerned with enhancing people's ability to cope with situations that might lead to maladaptive behaviors.

TYPES OF PREVENTION

1. **Primary prevention** is concerned with the reduction of new cases of mental or physical disorder in a given population. The aim of **secondary prevention** is to reduce the duration, intensity, and disability of an existing abnormal condition. **Tertiary prevention** is aimed at reducing the impairment that may result from a given disorder or event.

2. One of the most serious maladaptive behaviors of childhood is juvenile delinquency. Efforts to prevent delinquency may take the form of programs aimed at improving living conditions and school achievement (primary prevention). Secondary prevention programs teach social and vocational skills to young people who have shown early signs of delinquency, while tertiary prevention involves efforts to change seriously maladaptive behavior.

SITES OF PREVENTION

1. The **family** is important because much of the child's earliest learning and development takes place within the family setting. Many preventive programs that are carried out in a family setting focus on **child abuse**, or physical and psychological harm inflicted on children by

their parents. Behavioral training in impulse control and coping skills can be helpful for parents who want to change their behavior.

2. Another area in which preventive programs have been attempted is **spouse abuse**. Efforts to help abused spouses include not only emergency care, safety, and shelter but also counseling to strengthen their self-related positive cognitions.

3. Divorce often has negative effects on children, who not only have to deal with their own stress but also must cope with parents who are experiencing high levels of stress. The possibility of a good adjustment depends on the quality of the child's relationship with both parents, the quality of life of the divorced family, and the degree to which the divorce resolved the problems that brought it about. Research on custody arrangements has found that children living with the same-sex parent seem to fare better than children living with the opposite sex parent.

4. Prevention programs in school settings have focused on efforts to keep children from dropping out by teaching them cognitive and social skills.

5. Institutions in the community have tremendous potential for contributing to personal growth and reducing the likelihood of maladaptation. Police officers in particular are in a position to modify behavior. In addition, in many communities there are specialized programs directed toward people who are going through a personal crisis or share particular types of problems.

6. The mix of services available in the community can influence not only the recipients' sense of well-being but also their economic productivity. Many people who would otherwise have to be hospitalized could remain in the community if facilities that provide additional social support and supervision were available.

7. Efforts to improve treatment programs include the use of aftercare programs in day hospitals and halfway houses. However, very often deinstitutionalized mental patients are simply released into the community without effective follow-up care. The availability of adequate supervised community-housing settings, a range of mental-health services, and support for family members who care for the chronically mentally ill would help make deinstitutionalization a more positive process and might reduce the problem of homelessness.

LEGAL ASPECTS OF TREATMENT AND PREVENTION

1. The process of placing a person in an institution is called **commitment**. **Criminal commitment** of an individual may occur when a criminal act is legally declared to be a result of insanity. Some patients are involuntarily hospitalized through a legal procedure called **civil commitment**.

2. **Insanity** refers to a person's state of mind at the time that an act was carried out. The number of insanity defenses that are successful is very small. The American Psychiatric Association has suggested that people should be acquitted for insanity only if they have a serious mental disorder such as a psychosis.

3. Civil-commitment laws are based on the doctrine of **parens patriae**, which permits the state to act in what it takes to be the best interest of a minor or of an adult who is incapacitated. In 1979 the Supreme Court ruled that people may not be committed to mental institutions unless the state has presented "clear and convincing" evidence that they require hospitalization. All civil-commitment laws involve two judgments: whether individuals are suffering from disabling mental illness and whether they are dangerous to themselves or others.

4. Recent court decisions have upheld the rights of patients to adequate treatment, specified hospital staffing ratios, and individualized treatment plans. They have also strengthened the requirement of **informed consent**, meaning that patients must receive adequate information about the nature of a planned treatment before they agree to submit to it. The question of whether patients should have the right to discontinue treatment is extremely difficult to answer.

THE CHALLENGE OF PREVENTION

1. Society must be involved in meeting the challenge of prevention because it controls or influences so many of the situations of modern life. Certain types of maladaptive behavior can be attacked on an individual basis, but lasting solutions to many problems of living require social change.

2. Efforts to prevent maladaptive behavior include programs to train and use nonprofessionals and **paraprofessionals**, as well as **self-help groups** whose members benefit from the understanding and help of others who have gone through similar experiences.

3. **Community psychology** is concerned with the role of social systems in preventing human distress and maladaptive behavior. Making communities livable requires good ideas about social planning as well as awareness that certain segments of the population have special needs.

Glossary

Abnormal psychology Study of deviant and maladaptive behaviors.

Abstinence violation effect The reaction of conflict and guilt when an individual fails to resist the temptation to indulge in a behavior that he or she is trying to stop—for example, using alcohol. This response often triggers a binge or total relapse.

Acetylcholine Chemical involved in the transmission of nerve impulses.

Acid Slang term for LSD.

Acquired epilepsy Epilepsy with a known cause, such as injury to the brain through accident or illness.

ACTH See *adrenocorticotrophic hormone.*

Adaptation Dynamic process by which an individual responds to his or her environment and the changes that occur within it; ability to modify one's behavior to meet changing environmental requirements. Adaptation to a given situation is influenced by one's personal characteristics and the type of situation. Term often used in a biological, Darwinian sense.

Adaptive orientation The viewpoint that drug addiction is caused by an interaction between certain personality characteristics and stressful aspects of the environment.

Adjustment An individual's ability to harmonize with the environment.

Adjustment disorder Maladaptive reaction to a particular stressful condition that results in impaired functioning and symptoms in excess of what might be a normal response to the stressor. The reaction must occur soon after the beginning of the stress and the reaction can be expected to decrease when the stressor ceases.

Adjustment disorder with depressed mood Depression that occurs as a result of an identifiable life event and that is expected to disappear when the event's impact ceases. (Not classified as mood disorder.)

Adoption studies An attempt to understand the genetics of a disorder and separate them from the effects of environment by comparing children adopted in infancy whose biological parents are affected by a disorder with adopted children without such heredity.

Adrenal cortex The outer layer of the adrenal gland; a source of hormone secretion in the body.

Adrenal corticosteroids Hormones released by the adrenal cortex which affect the body's response to stress.

Adrenal medulla One of the two principle parts of the adrenal glands, the part of the endocrine system located just above the kidneys. A principle function is the secretion of hormones in emergency-type situations.

Adrenaline A secretion of the adrenal glands; also called *epinephrine.*

Adrenocorticotrophic Hormone (ACTH) Hormone secreted by the pituitary gland that goes to the adrenal cortex to release adrenal corticosteroids, chemicals that stimulate the body's responses to stress.

Affect Emotion, feeling, or mood: pleasant or unpleasant, intense or mild; also, a tone of feeling accompanying a thought.

Affective disorder See *mood disorder.*

Agoraphobia Pathological fear of open spaces.

Alcohol amnestic disorder Another term for Korsakoff's disease or syndrome.

Alcoholism Alcohol dependence or addiction.

Alpha-feroprotein test A blood test used to assess the presence of genetic disorder or neural defects in the fetus.

Alpha wave A particular kind of electrical brain activity often seen when a person is tense and the frequency of which decreases with drowsiness or relaxation.

Alzheimer's disease Chronic brain disorder, occurring as early as the fourth decade of life and involving progressive destruction of nervous tissue, which results in slurring of speech, involuntary muscular movements, and gradual intellectual deterioration with growing lapses of memory.

Amnesia Total or partial loss of memory.

Amnesia, anterograde Loss of the ability to remember new information although memories of past events can be recalled.

Amnesia, retrograde Inability to remember information from the time before the amnesic disorder began.

Amnestic syndrome A memory disturbance without confusion or delirium in which there is both inability to learn new material and to remember information learned in the past.

Amniocentesis Technique of removing a sample of amniotic fluid from a pregnant woman and analyzing it to determine whether there are chromosomal defects in the fetus.

Amphetamines Nervous system (particularly cerebral cortex) stimulants, such as dexedrine, which bring a sense of well-being and exhilaration. The stimulation effect is succeeded by fatigue and depression. Psychologically but probably not physiologically addicting.

Anal stage Stage of psychosexual development in which the child derives intense pleasure from activities associated with elimination.

Anencephaly A condition in which a child is born without a developed brain.

Angina pectoris Periodic chest pains resulting from an insufficient supply of oxygen to the heart. A type of coronary heart disease.

Anomaly A deviation from the norm; an abnormality.

Anorexia nervosa An intense and irrational feeling of being fat that leads to excessive restriction of food intake and weight loss that may be life threatening. Usually occurs in adolescence or early adulthood and is much more common in females than males.

Antianxiety drugs Commonly called *tranquilizers*. Used to calm anxious people.

Antidepressant drugs General term for a number of drugs used to relieve depression and to elevate mood.

Antigens Foreign substances that, when introduced into the body, induce the formation of antibodies and then react with these antibodies in a specifiable manner.

Antimanic drugs A family of drugs based on a compound of lithium carbonate that are used to treat mania, bipolar disorder, and some depressions.

Antipsychotic drugs Group of chemical compounds used to treat individuals who show severely disturbed behavior and thought processes, especially in cases of schizophrenia.

Antisocial personality disorder Characterized by continuous, chronic antisocial behavior, beginning before the age of 15 and continuing into adult life; before the age of 18 such behavior is called a *conduct disorder*. Behavior tends to impair the rights of others and to be characterized by an impaired capacity for close relationships.

Anxiety An affect with both a psychological and physiological side. Generally, an unpleasant emotional state accompanied by physiological arousal and the cognitive elements of apprehension, guilt, and a sense of impending disaster. Distinguished from fear, which is an emotional reaction to a specific or identifiable object.

Anxiety disorder Formerly called *neurosis* or *neurotic disorder*. Characterized by some form of anxiety as the most prominent symptom. Includes panic disorders, phobic disorders, obsessive-compulsive disorder, generalized anxiety disorders, and reactions to stressors.

Aphasia Partial or total loss of the ability to convey thoughts through speech.

Appetitive Referring to a physical craving or desire.

Asexual Characterized by lack of response to sexual stimulation and lack of interest in sexual activity.

Asphyxia Unconsciousness or death caused by a lack of oxygen. May result in retardation or seizures as a result of brain damage.

Assertiveness training Combined cognitive and behavioral approach designed to increase the frequency of aggressive behavior that is socially desirable.

Assessment Information gathering aimed at describing and predicting behavior. Assessment specialists devise tests that measure various aspects of behavior.

Assessment interview Same as diagnostic interview.

Assessment study A study aimed at gathering information to describe a particular group in which variables are not manipulated. Such data can be used for prediction and are usually expressed in the form of correlations between variables.

Assortative mating The tendency for people to marry those who have characteristics similar to their own. For instance, chronic schizophrenics tend to marry individuals who have a schizophrenic spectrum disorder or other psychotic disorder. This genetic loading must be taken into account when estimating genetic risk for a variety of disorders.

Asthma Disorder of a chronic nature, often psychophysiological in nature, characterized by coughing, wheezing, breathing difficulty, and a feeling of suffocating.

Atherosclerosis A disorder caused by a build up of plaque (deposits on the blood vessel walls) that narrow the vessels and result in insufficient blood supply to the heart.

Attention-deficit hyperactivity disorder Inability to focus attention together with an impulsive behavior pattern, which could not be expected from the child's developmental level. Often referred to as *hyperactivity* or by other similar labels.

Attribution A term used by social psychologists to describe the way a person assigns responsibility for cause and effect.

Aura Clouded state of consciousness, accompanied by feelings of unreality, which precedes an epileptic attack. Also, the sensory, motor, or mood disturbance preceding migraine headache.

Authentic behavior Term used by some existential theorists to describe behavior dictated by a person's own goals rather than by the goals of society.

Autistic Term used to describe a certain type of schizophrenic thought pattern characterized by self-centered thinking understandable only to the individual.

Autistic disorder A developmental disorder usually occurring early in childhood characterized by severe impairment in social relationships, communication, and activity. Frequently includes mental retardation.

Autoerotic practices Sexual stimulation practiced by an individual on him or herself.

Autogenic training Gaining psychophysiological equilibrium through passive concentration on a series of self-suggestions of various sensations.

Autonomic reactivity Excessive action of the sympathetic and parasympathetic portions of the autonomic nervous system.

Autonomic system Functional division of the nervous system concerned with visceral activities, smooth muscles, and endocrine glands. Name comes from the fact that it was formerly thought to function independently of the central nervous system.

Autosome Chromosome that does not determine the sex of the individual.

Aversion therapies Group of behavior therapies which attempt to condition avoidance responses in patients by pairing the behavior to be extinguished with punishing stimuli—for example, electric shock, social criticism, drugs that cause vomiting. Also known as *aversive conditioning*.

Avoidance response Attempt to leave a situation in which an aversive stimulus is expected to occur.

Avoidant personality disorder Characterized by social withdrawal based on fear of social rejection.

Axon Part of the cell that transmits impulses away from the cell body and across the synapse to the dendrites of another cell.

Balanced placebo design An experimental design in which some subjects receive an inactive substance and

others a psychoactive substance. Part of each group is led to expect that they have received the other category of substance and part of each group is accurately informed about what substance they are given.

Baquet A water-filled tub used by Mesmer as a focus for treatment of hysterical complaints.

Barbiturates Family of drugs that depress central nervous system action and may be addictive.

Baseline observation Operant conditioning procedure in which an initial rate of some response is established. Can be used for descriptive purposes or as a control condition before introducing behavior modification procedures and subsequent response-rate comparisons.

Bedlam Noisy uproar or confusion. A word derived from conditions at Bethlehem Hospital, an institution for the insane.

Behavioral assessment The objective recording of particular categories of observable behavior prior to beginning behavior therapy. The assessment may take place in specially contrived situations or under real life conditions.

Behavioral coping What a person actually does when confronted by a stressor.

Behavioral medicine An area focused on ways to improve diagnosis, treatment, and rehabilitation by using behavioral techniques to help people adopt generally healthier ways of living and to follow treatment plans for specific problems. Also focuses on helping health care providers improve their service delivery.

Behavior change experiment The test of a therapeutic manipulation to determine whether the individual's maladaptive behavior is lessened.

Behavior genetics Study of the transmission of certain kinds of behavior through selective mating.

Behaviorism School of psychology whose adherents contend that the study of overt and observable behaviors provides the only legitimate data of science. Covert events, such as consciousness, are disregarded or considered only as mediation processes between stimulus and response contingencies.

Behavior modification Type of therapy based on the principles of operant conditioning.

Behavior therapy Includes several techniques of behavior modification based on laboratory-derived principles of learning and conditioning. Behavior therapies focus on modifying overt behaviors with minimal reference to internal or covert events.

Benzodiazepines Group of drugs, such as Librium and Valium, used primarily to treat anxiety.

Bereavement The state of having lost someone through death.

Binet tests Intelligence tests, developed by Alfred Binet, that yield a quantitative estimate of a person's intelligence.

Biofeedback Method for inducing behavioral change in which the client learns to alter autonomic nervous system responses by monitoring them on recording instruments.

Biological perspective Theoretical perspective that suggests that all disorders, physical or behavioral, have biological causes. Causes may lie in heredity, genetic accident, or bodily infection or trauma.

Biopsychosocial model Interactional view that emphasizes the interaction among biological, psychological, and social factors in determining behavior and body functioning.

Bipolar II A type of bipolar disorder in which the person has experienced at least one major depressive episode and one hypomanic episode but has never had a manic episode or cyclothymia.

Bipolar disorder Mood disorder in which the individual experiences both periods of mania and periods of depression. Formerly called *manic-depressive order.*

Bisexuality Attraction to and sexual activity with people of both sexes.

Booster session An additional treatment carried out after a period of time has elapsed since the original treatment series. Intended to counteract any weakening of the treatment effect.

Borderline personality disorder Characterized by impulsive and unpredictable behavior and marked shifts in mood. Instability may affect personal relationships, behavior, mood, and image of self.

Brain deterioration See *dementia.*

Brain electrical activity mapping (BEAM) A technique for study of electrical brain activity in which the electrical impulses are summarized in color maps.

Brainstem Portion of the central nervous system that includes the hindbrain, midbrain, and forebrain up to the thalamus.

Briquet's syndrome Another name for somatization disorder.

Bulimia Episodes of binge eating with the awareness that this behavior is abnormal. Vomiting is often self-induced by the individual at the end of the eating session.

Burnout Condition found most often among people in the helping professions whose work involves intense interpersonal contact. Symptoms includes loss of effectiveness and self-confidence and the general feeling of inability to deal with particular situations.

Caffeine Crystalline compound that is found in coffee, tea, and kola nuts and which acts as a stimulant of the central nervous system and also as a diuretic.

Cannabis Plant whose resin produces a psychoactive substance. In solid form the resin is called *hashish.*

Cardiovascular disorder Disorder affecting the blood vessel system and the heart.

Case study method See *clinical method.*

Catatonic schizophrenia Type of schizophrenic disorder characterized by psychomotor disturbance. Often takes the form of body rigidity or posturing. Other behavior may include waxy flexibility or mutism.

Catecholamines Group of hormones, including epinephrine, norepinephrine, and dopamine, that are important in the response to stress. Some catecholamines are produced in the brain, where they are important in nerve transmission.

Cell body The part of the cell that contains the nucleus.

Central nervous system (CNS) Brain and spinal cord; does not include the nerve trunks and their peripheral connections.

Cerebellum Portion of the brain consisting of two hemispheres located behind and above the medulla; coordinates motor activities and maintains bodily equilibrium.

Cerebral cortex Convoluted layer of gray matter of the brain; outer layer of the cerebrum.

Cerebral hemispheres One of the two lateral halves of the cerebrum or upper part of the brain.

Cerebral ventricles Cavities in the brain that are connected to the central canal of the spinal cord and contain cerebrospinal fluid.

Cerebrovascular accident (CVA) Rupture or blockage of blood vessels in the cerebrum that disrupt or prevent blood flow. Commonly referred to as a *stroke.*

CHD See *coronary heart disease.*

Child abuse Harm, usually physical, deliberately inflicted on children by their parent(s), often by repeated beatings.

Choline acetylcholine transferase Enzyme that forms acetylcholine.

Chorionic villus sampling A method of determining genetic damage in the fetus.

Chromosomal abnormality Abnormality in chromosome structure or number of chromosomes in body cells.

Chromosomes Gene-bearing structures within cells.

Classical conditioning Pavlov's experimental method by which a conditioned stimulus is paired with an unconditioned stimulus. Procedure involves presenting the two stimuli in close temporal proximity. The first, or unconditioned, stimulus elicits a reflex. After a number of trials the second, or conditioned, stimulus acquires the potentiality of evoking a similar reflex.

Classification The establishment of a hierarchical system of categories based on the relationship or presumed relationship among the things to be classified, for instance, disorders of behavior and cognition.

Client-centered therapy Carl Rogers' therapeutic approach, which views the subject matter of psychotherapy as the client's world of immediate experience that

Cognitive rehearsal Procedure in which a client learns to rehearse ways to handle problem situations mentally. Such rehearsal makes it easier for the client to behave effectively in the actual situations.

Cognitive restructuring A technique used by Albert Ellis and other cognitive therapists in which the client is made aware of a connection between unrealistic thoughts and the maladaptive behavior these evoke. Clients are helped to develop more rational ways of looking at their behavior.

Cognitive set A person's habitual way of viewing the world and distorting it in terms of his or her personality characteristics and expectations.

Cognitive triad Description of depression in terms of negative thinking about oneself, the current situation, and the future. Part of Beck's cognitive distortion model.

Coming out Term used by homosexuals to indicate the occasion of openly declaring their sexual orientation.

Commitment, civil Commitment of a person to an institution based on a judgment that the person is a potential danger to him or herself and/or to others.

Commitment, criminal Commitment of a person to an institution based on a judgment that the person is guilty of a criminal act and is also legally insane.

Communication deviance Term referring to the inability of a person to maintain a shared focus of attention with another. Studied in parent–child communications in families with a schizophrenic child.

Community perspective Viewpoint that much maladaptive behavior results from poor living conditions, discrimination, and so on. Emphasis is on preventive activities.

Community psychology Branch of applied psychology concerned with modifying both the individual and the structure of the social system to produce optimal benefits for both society and the individual. Community psychologists are often primarily interested in preventing maladaptive behavior.

Compulsive behavior Characterized by an individual's need to repeat a series of acts again and again even though he or she perceives them as senseless and interfering with desirable activities.

Computerized axial tomography (CT scan) Technique that uses a narrow beam of x-rays to photograph an area of the body from many angles. A computer then analyzes this information to provide a clear picture of soft tissues as well as the tissue seen in conventional x-rays.

Concordance Term describing the degree of relationship among twins and other family members with respect to a given characteristic or trait. They are re-

should be approached from the client's frame of reference. In the Rogerian system, the therapist's main task is to create the opportunity for the individual to achieve a reorganization of his or her subjective world and to reach self-actualization.

Clinical method Case study of the individual through observation. May rely heavily upon intuitive judgments of the clinician rather than upon experimentation and systematic measurement.

Clinical psychologist Psychologist, usually with a Ph.D., who has special training and skills in assessing and treating maladaptive behavior.

Clinical trial The use of a research design including one or more experimental groups and a control group in testing the usefulness of a particular approach in treatment of patients.

Clinician Professional who deals directly with the examination or treatment of patients or clients

Clitoris In females, a small organ at the front of the vulva that is highly sensitive to sexual stimulation. The analogue of the penis in the male.

Clonic phase An aspect of seizure activity in which there is rapid alternation of muscle contractions and muscle relaxation.

Cocaine Stimulant with a number of characteristics in common with the amphetamines.

Codeine Derivative of opium that is less potent than morphine.

Cognitive assessment Specification and enumeration of the typical thoughts that precede, accompany, and follow maladaptive behavior. Used in research and by cognitive behavior therapists especially in working with depressed individuals.

Cognitive-behavior therapy Psychotherapeutic approach that emphasizes the importance of cognitions or thoughts as behavior to be changed. Modifying "self-talk" is the most usual approach.

Cognitive coping skills Particular ways of thinking that aid in behaving effectively in stressful situations.

Cognitive distortion model (*of depression*) Proposed by Aaron Beck and suggests that depression is a disorder of thought.

Cognitive modification Technique whereby individuals learn to modify maladaptive thought patterns or to substitute new internal dialogues for old maladaptive ones.

Cognitive perspective Point of view that considers behavior to be the result of information processing and problem solving. Emphasis is on mental processes of which the individual is aware or can easily become aware.

Cognitive psychology Study of human beings as information processors and problem solvers. Focus has recently been extended from the traditional studies of memory, attention, and problem solving to include

ferred to as *concordant* if they both show a particular trait; if they do not, the pair is described as *discordant* for that trait.

Concussion Head injury that does not cause lasting structural damage. Rate of recovery is proportional to the severity of the injury.

Conditioned response (CR) In classical conditioning, the response that occurs after training has taken place and after the conditioned stimulus has been presented.

Conditioned stimulus (CS) In classical conditioning, the neutral stimulus that does not elicit a response prior to training.

Conditioning See *classical conditioning; operant conditioning.*

Conduct disorder DSM-III-R classification for those under 18 who commit antisocial acts. Adults may also be classified this way if they do not meet the criteria for the antisocial personality disorder.

Confabulation The process of filling in missing memories with fabricated information; to replace forgotten facts with fantasy.

Congenital Characteristics that are either innate or acquired, usually through chemical action, while the child is in the uterus.

Conscious Aspects of one's mental life of which a person is aware at any particular time.

Constitutional Any characteristics acquired by heredity, uterine environment, or illness or injury at or after birth.

Continuous Performance Test Test of sustained visual attention in which the subject is required to indicate whenever a certain stimulus is presented and to ignore all other stimuli.

Contusion Brain condition in which diffuse structural damage has occurred (e.g., rupture of blood vessels). Typically, cerebrospinal fluid pressure is raised, causing such symptoms as coma and stupor.

Conversion disorder Type of somatoform disorder in which there is a loss or change in physical functioning that suggests a physical disorder but seems to be a direct expression of a psychological conflict.

Coping Contending with difficulties and overcoming them.

Coping resources Capabilities that a person has available to call into play in a stressful situation.

Coping skills The characteristic way a person deals with difficulties or stress. Commonly used skills include task-directed activity, working on a problem step by step, appropriate control of emotion.

Coping style Characteristic way a person deals with the stimuli in his or her environment.

Coronary heart disease (CHD) Disorder in which one or more of the coronary arteries is partially or totally obstructed by deposits. This results in a temporary or permanent cut off of blood to portions of the heart muscle.

Correlation Degree of correspondence between two variables; a statistical index of covariation that varies from $+1.00$ to -1.00.

Correlational study Type of research in which the relationship of two or more characteristics is measured. No statement about cause and effect can be made from correlational research.

Cortex Outer layer of an organ such as the cerebrum, cerebellum, or adrenal gland.

Corticotrophin-releasing factor (CRF) Substance secreted by the hypothalamus that releases the chemical ACTH when it reaches the pituitary gland.

Countertransference Psychoanalytic term that refers to the therapist's emotional reactions to the patient. See also *transference.*

Covert Behavior that is internal and not directly observable. Includes unexpressed thoughts and feelings and other conscious and unconscious mental phenomena.

Covert sensitization Behavioral therapy in which anxiety is created toward a particular stimulus situation that is likely to produce undesirable behavior. Usually the stimulus is paired with cognitions relating to the possible negative consequences if the person continues a given behavior. A treatment often used in changing the focus of sexual excitement.

Crisis A decisive turning point in a series of events.

Criteria The standards against which behaviors are measured.

Cross-cultural approach Method of studying the causes of various psychological and physical problems by studying their occurrence in a variety of cultures and then attempting to identify factors that are correlated with high and low frequency of the problems.

Cross-fostering study Method of evaluating hereditary factors in behavioral disorders by comparing frequency of a disorder in groups with genetic vulnerability reared by healthy adoptive parent(s) and groups without known genetic vulnerability reared by adoptive parent(s) who have a particular behavior disorder.

Cross-sectional study Research design in which different groups are sampled at the same time and the results compared. Technique often used to study human development.

CT scan See *computerized axial tomography.*

Culture General values, attitudes, achievements, and behavior patterns shared by members of the same society.

Cyclothymia Disorder that includes both mania and depressive episodes, neither of which meet the criteria for major episodes. Lasts for at least 2 years.

Cytomegalovirus One of a number of viral diseases which, if present in a pregnant woman, may result in retardation and other congenital problems in the child.

Defense mechanism (ego defense) Psychoanalytic term for various psychic operations used by the ego to avoid awareness of unpleasant and anxiety-provoking stimuli. The ego selectively uses defense mechanisms to ward off anxiety originating in the id, the superego, or dangers in external reality.

Deficiency needs According to Maslow, the most basic needs of life, which must be met before higher needs, such as social and intellectual needs, can be considered.

Deinstitutionalization Movement whose purpose is to remove patients from large mental hospitals and to obtain treatment and sheltered living conditions for them in the community.

Delirium Condition characterized by a confused mental state, usually resulting from shock or fever, accompanied by alterations in attention and by hallucinations, delusions, and incoherence.

Delirium tremens Acute delirium caused by overdoses of alcohol and consisting of severe alterations in consciousness and attention. Also referred to as the DTs.

Delusion Incorrect belief maintained despite clear evidence to the contrary.

Delusional disorder The presence of a persistent but not bizarre delusion that is not due to any other mental disorder such as schizophrenia. Apart from the delusion the person's behavior is not obviously unusual.

Dementia Progressive atrophy of brain tissue that results in lapses of memory, poor judgment, and disorientation. Called *presenile dementia* if it occurs before age 65, and *senile dementia* if it begins after age 65.

Dementia paralytica Another term for general paresis.

Dementia praecox Older term for schizophrenia; used by Kraepelin to emphasize the early onset and irreversibility of the disorder as he defined it.

Demographic The description of human populations in terms of growth, density, distribution, and vital statistics.

Dendrite Branched part of a cell that serves as a receptor for nerve impulses from the axons of other cells and transmits them toward the cell body.

Denial Defense mechanism that allows rejection of elements of reality that would be consciously intolerable; negation of experiences or reality through unacceptance.

Deoxyribonucleic acid See *DNA.*

Dependent personality disorder Characterized by an inability to make major decisions and a belittling of a person's own abilities and assets. Intense discomfort is experienced if the person remains alone for more than a brief period.

Dependent variable Aspect of behavior which changes according to manipulation of the independent variable in an experiment.

Depersonalization Feelings of unreality or a loss of personal identity; often experienced as one's being someone else or as watching oneself in a movie.

Depression Pervasive feeling of sadness that may begin after some loss or stressful event, but that continues long afterwards. Inappropriate thought patterns that generalize every event as a calamity are characteristic.

Depressive disorder Depressive symptoms that meet DSM-III-R criteria for either a single episode of major depression, or recurrent episodes. If manic or hypomanic behavior has been observed in the past, depressed symptoms should not be classified as a major depression even if they meet the other criteria.

Depressive neurosis Older term for dysthymic disorder.

Descriptive statistics Procedures used to summarize groups of individual observations. The most common descriptive statistics are measures of central tendency (e.g., mean) and measures of variability (e.g., standard deviation).

Determinism The philosophical idea that all acts are the inevitable result of what has happened before and that human choice or free will plays no role in what happens.

Developmental disorder One of a group of disorders that involve distortions in the development of basic psychological functions that are involved in social skills, language, perception, and motor behavior. The disorder can be pervasive and involve many functions (e.g., autism) or specific and involve only a single aspect of development (e.g., developmental arithmetic disorder).

Developmental model Viewpoint that the process of cognitive development of a retarded person is no different than that of a nonretarded individual. Only the speed of development and the level reached differentiate in the two groups. Contrast with *difference model.*

Dexamethasone Suppression Test Chemical test used in an attempt to differentiate depressed individuals who may be helped by different treatments.

Dexedrine See *dextroamphetamine.*

Dextroamphetamine (e.g., Dexedrine) Stimulant drug sometimes used in the treatment of hyperactivity.

Diagnosis Classification of behavior disorders in terms of relatively homogeneous groups based on similar behaviors or correlates. Shorthand description of the behavioral and personality correlates associated

Diagnostic and Statistical Manual, 3rd Edition Revised, (DSM-III-R) Classification system for abnormal behavior published by the American Psychiatric Association. The system is generally used in the United States for official diagnostic and record-keeping purposes.

Diagnostic interview Interview designed to gather information and assess behavior, usually for the purpose of determining seriousness and outcome or deciding what treatment approach would be appropriate.

Diagnostic Interview Schedule (DIS) Standardized interview format designed to yield information necessary to make a DMS-III diagnosis. At present the schedule covers only a few disorders.

Diastolic Term used to describe the blood pressure reading at the time the heart dilates to allow more blood to enter.

Diazepam One of the benzodiazepines, a group of antianxiety tranquilizers. Known by trade name, Valium.

Difference model Viewpoint that the intellectual functioning of retarded individuals is not only less efficient than that of others but also different. Those who hold this view advocate different teaching approaches for retarded children, not merely simplification of standard methods. Contrast with *developmental model.*

Discordant Term often used in twin studies to describe particular characteristics on which the twins differ. Characteristics that are the same for both are referred to as *concordant.*

Disorganized schizophrenia (hebephrenic) Type of schizophrenia distinguished by incoherent speech and flat, incongruous, or silly affect. Often associated with extreme oddities of behavior such as gesturing or grimacing.

Displacement Defense mechanism in which an emotional attitude is transferred from one object to a substitute object.

Dissociative disorder Sudden, temporary alteration in the functions of consciousness, identity, or motor behavior in which some part of one or more of these functions is lost. If consciousness is affected, the person cannot remember important personal events. If identity is affected, a new identity that dominates behavior is temporarily assumed. If motor behavior is affected, then consciousness and/or identity are also affected. Wandering behavior is the most common resulting motor behavior.

Dizygotic twins Fraternal twins developed from two fertilized eggs. The two individuals have the same genetic relationship as any pair of siblings.

DNA Abbreviation for deoxyribonucleic acid, a complex chemical found in chromosomes within living cell nuclei. The sequence of its units determines genetic inheritance.

Dominant gene Member of the gene pair that determines whether the individual will show the trait controlled by that gene. Other member of the pair may be the same (also dominant) or different (recessive).

Dopamine hypothesis Idea that schizophrenia involves an excess of the neurotransmitter dopamine at certain sites in the brain.

Double-blind method Experimental design used in drug research. Neither the subjects nor the experimenters know whether the medication given to different comparison groups are active or inert (placebos).

Down syndrome Condition related to some inequality in the chromosome pair designated as number 21. Usually associated with a trisomy, or presence of an extra chromosome in addition to the usual pair. Also called trisomy 21.

Drug therapy Use of a variety of psychoactive drugs to treat different types of maladaptive behavior. Drugs are most often used to treat schizophrenia, bipolar disorder, some depressions, and anxiety. Drug treatment is often combined with other types of therapy.

DSM-III-R See *Diagnostic and Statistical Manual.*

DTs See *delirium tremens.*

Dyspareunia (functional) Type of sexual dysfunction in which persistent and recurrent genital pain is associated with coitus without any apparent physical cause.

Dysphoria Feelings of anxiety, depression, and restlessness.

Dysphoric mood Characterized by symptoms of depression, sadness, feeling blue and hopeless.

Dysthymic disorder Chronic depressed mood or loss of pleasure in most usual activities lasting at least 2 years. Does not meet the criteria for a major depressive episode.

Echolalia Meaningless repetition of words.

EEG See *electroencephalogram.*

Efficacy expectation The belief that one can successfully carry out a particular behavior.

Ego In psychoanalytic theory, the part of the psyche which makes up the self or the "I." Part of the psyche that is conscious and most closely in touch with reality and that functions as the "executive officer" of the personality.

Ego boundaries, loss of. A state of being unable to distinguish between oneself and another person as separate individuals each of whom has his/her own unique thoughts and feelings. Often associated with feelings of being controlled by others. May be found in schizophrenic disorder or borderline personality disorder.

Electroconvulsive therapy (ECT) Treatment for depression in which electrical current is passed through a patient's head. Used if a quick treatment is needed because of a high suicide risk or if antidepressant drugs have not been effective.

Electroencephalogram (EEG) Graphic record of minute electrical impulses arising from brain cells. Measured by an electronic device called an *electroencephalograph*.

Encephalitis Inflammation of the white matter of the brain. Symptoms include visual failure, mental deterioration, and spastic paralysis.

Encopresis Repeated voluntary or involuntary bowel movements of normal consistency that occur in inappropriate surroundings and are not a result of any organic disorder.

Endocrine Referring to any of the ductless glands of the body. These pass their secretions directly from the gland cells to the bloodstream.

Endorphin Pain-killing substance that occurs naturally in the brain.

Epidemiology The scientific study of the associations between diseases or behavioral deviations and social class variables, geographical variables, or environmental variables. These associations, derived from the study of large population groups, help to suggest possible causes for the health problems observed.

Epilepsy Transitory disturbance of brain function which is characterized by a sudden onset and loss of consciousness and which may involve tonic and clonic muscle spasms. Epileptic seizures may be minor (petit mal) or major (grand mal) and tend to recur.

Epinephrine One of the hormones secreted by the adrenal medulla, active in emotional excitement and in response to stress.

Erectile disorder Type of sexual disorder in which the male is occasionally or chronically unable to achieve or maintain a penile erection. The condition may have physical or psychological causes. Also known as *impotence*.

Erogenous zone Parts of the body sensitive to sexual stimulation.

Escape response The attempt to get out of an unpleasant or aversive situation.

Etiology Assignment of a cause; scientific study of causes and origins of maladaptive behavior.

Excitement (sexual) The initial response to sexual stimulation marked by vaginal lubrication or penile erection.

Exhibitionism Exposure of the genitals in public for purposes of obtaining sexual pleasure and gratification.

Exhibitionist One who practices exhibitionism.

Existential therapy Type of psychotherapy which uses both humanistic and psychodynamic approaches. Emphasis is placed on each person's ability to affect his or her life course by the particular choices made.

Exit event A psychological loss of social support through death, divorce, or the breakup of a relationship.

Exorcism Expelling of evil spirits.

Experiment A study using the experimental method.

Experimental method Study of the factors influencing a result by the manipulation of one or more experimental variables rather than simply observing what occurs naturally.

Exposure in vivo A technique used in cognitive therapy or desensitization in which the individual practices adaptive cognitions or relaxation behavior in the actual presence of the anxiety-producing object or situation.

Exposure orientation In drug addiction, the idea that addiction is brought about by an environment that provides availability of drugs.

Exposure therapy Behavioral therapy that has as its basic element maintaining contact with or imagining contact with the feared stimulus.

Expressed emotion (EE) A measure of emotional involvement and attitudes of family members when talking about a behaviorally disturbed family member.

External Tendency to see events as caused not by oneself but by outside forces. See also *locus of control*.

Extinction Weakening of a response following removal of reinforcement.

Eye-tracking movements Study of smooth pursuit and saccadic eye movements as an individual attempts to visually follow a rhythmically moving stimulus. One goal of such study is to uncover genetic markers of vulnerability.

Factitious disorder Symptoms, either fabricated or self-induced, that are designed to produce attention and care from medical personnel.

Fading Technique for gradually eliminating cues used in behavior modification after an individual begins to achieve a desired response.

Family study Study of characteristics of a group of related individuals to uncover genetic patterns.

Family systems approach A therapeutic approach in which the disturbance experienced by the client is viewed as the result of the way the family interacts rather than a problem caused by the client alone.

Family therapy Specialized type of group therapy in which the members of the family of the client all participate in group-treatment sessions. The basic idea is that the family, not just the individual client, has to alter behavior to solve the problem.

Fantasized exposure Exposure therapy in which the upsetting stimuli are imagined rather than presented in actuality.

Fetal alcohol syndrome Condition that may occur in the children of alcoholic mothers or mothers who used excessive alcohol during pregnancy. Characterized by retardation and unusual physical characteristics.

Fetishism Sexual deviation in which sexual interest is centered upon some body part or inanimate object which becomes capable of stimulating sexual excitement.

First rank symptoms Group of symptoms described by Kurt Schneider in an attempt to establish clear behavioral criteria for schizophrenia. One of the bases of the DSM-III-R definition of schizophrenic disorders.

Fixation Inappropriately strong attachment for someone or something. Also refers to an abnormal arrest of development during infancy or childhood which persists in adult life as an inappropriate constellation of attitudes, habits, or interests.

Fixed-role therapy Cognitive approach developed by George Kelly in which the client is asked to practice or try out new roles in interpersonal relationships.

Flashback The reexperiencing of hallucinations or other perceptual symptoms which had originally occurred while the person was intoxicated by a psychoactive substance.

Flooding Behavioral therapeutic technique used particularly in the treatment of phobias. Treatment consists of exposing the client to the feared stimulus until the fear response has extinguished.

Follow-up study A method in which individuals listed at one point in time are contacted again at a later time to reassess behavior so that any changes can be noted.

Fragile X syndrome An abnormality of the X chromosome that is the most frequent cause of mental retardation except for Down syndrome.

Free association Basic technique of the psychoanalytic method by which a patient expresses his or her thoughts as freely and in as uninhibited a manner as possible. Free associations provide a natural flow of thought processes unencumbered by interruptions or explanations.

Frigidity Sexual problem in which a female either does not have a swelling-lubrication response when sexually excited or cannot maintain that response until orgasm is reached.

Frontal lobe Portion of each cerebral hemisphere involved in abstract thinking processes.

Fugue state Flight from reality in which the individual may leave his or her present environment and life situation and establish a new lifestyle in another geographical location. Such a person is usually totally amnesic concerning his or her past life, although other abilities remain unimpaired; he or she may appear essentially normal to others.

Fully functioning person Term used by Carl Rogers to describe the optimal level of adjustment at which an individual can function with minimal anxiety.

GABA Term for gamma-amino-butyric-acid, a neurotransmitter. A deficiency of GABA, associated with hereditary causes, is thought to be involved in Huntington's disease.

Galvanic skin response (GSR) Change in the electrical resistance of the skin. This response serves as a dependent variable in conditioning and is used in lie detector tests.

Gastrointestinal disorders Disorders of the digestive system, the stomach, and intestines.

Gay Term used to describe a homosexual lifestyle by those who feel the term homosexual has too many negative connotations.

Gender identity Basic feature of personality encompassing an individual's conviction of being male or female.

Gender identity disorder (transsexualism) Disorder in which the individual has a strong desire to become a member of the opposite sex by changing his or her anatomical structure.

Gender identity disorder of childhood A disorder occurring before puberty in which the child shows intense distress over its assigned sex. Such children may deny their assigned sex or assert that they will develop the genital characteristics of the opposite sex.

Gender nonconformity in childhood Situation in which the child is primarily interested in the activities culturally associated with the opposite sex. Not necessarily associated with later sexual deviance.

Gene Microscopic structure in the chromosome; physical unit of hereditary transmission.

General adaptation syndrome Concept proposed by Selye. Three-stage reaction of an organism to excessive and prolonged stress, including (1) an alarm or mobilization reaction; (2) a resistance stage; and (3) a final stage of exhaustion.

Generalized anxiety disorder Persistent anxiety that lasts at least 1 month and includes several of the following: motor tension, autonomic hyperactivity, apprehensive expectation, vigilance, and scanning. The symptoms do not include phobias, panic attacks, obsessions, or compulsions.

General paresis See *paresis*.

Genetic counseling The giving of information about risk for inheritance of certain disorders based on general information about heredity, knowledge of family history, and genetic characteristics of the person or couple seeking information.

Genetic heterogeneity In genetics, the idea that more than one gene is necessary for the inheritance of a characteristic. However, the genes each have a separate effect, not an additive one.

Genetic specificity A gene pattern that is unique to a particular disorder or group of disorders.

Genital stage According to Freud, if maturation proceeds without problems, after adolescence the individual reaches this stage in which the focus of pleasure is on a mature heterosexual relationship.

Gestalt A unified configuration that has many properties or meanings that could not be derived from the total of its individual parts.

Gestalt therapy Humanistic approach that emphasizes removing distortions in self-perception and in the perception of others. Originated by Perls.

Glove anesthesia Condition in which a person cannot move or feel the part of the arm and hand that a glove would normally cover.

Grand mal Severe form of epilepsy involving major convulsive attacks and loss of consciousness.

Grief Sorrow, usually over a loss.

Group home A sheltered living environment that may be either transitional or permanent. Often used for retarded persons and those with chronic schizophrenia. Emphasis is on self-care and self-regulation to the extent the individual's ability and condition permit.

Group hysteria Hysterical symptoms, often of a conversion disorder-like nature, that seem to spread contagiously through a group of individuals.

Group therapy Psychotherapy of several persons at the same time in small groups.

Guided mastery A therapeutic approach in which the therapist enhances the client's feelings of self-efficacy through modeling, information, or suggestions.

Guided rehearsal Aspect of modeling in which the client practices the previously modeled behavior and is coached by the therapist in order to improve the performance.

Gyri Raised portions of the brain's surface between the sulci (plural of gyrus).

Habituation Decrease of the orienting response after the repeated presentation of a stimuli.

Halfway house Transitional living facility that accommodates, for a short period of time, newly discharged psychiatric patients or those who have functioned maladaptively.

Hallucination Sensory perception in the absence of an external stimulus. Hallucinations are usually visual ("seeing things") but may occur in other sensory modalities as well.

Hallucinogen General name for a group of drugs or chemicals capable of producing hallucinations.

Halo effect Tendency to rate an individual improperly high or low on a particular factor because of

prior information or a general impression of the individual.

Hashish Hallucinogenic substance that is the solidified resin of *cannabis sativa* (marijuana).

Headache, cluster Headaches that occur in groups over a relatively short time period. Each headache is very painful for several minutes and fades away completely within an hour.

Headache, migraine Severe headache caused by a constriction followed by a dilation of the cranial artery. Usually preceded by some sensory or emotional cues called an *aura*. The disorder is thought to have some stress-related components.

Health psychology Area of psychology concerned both with calling attention to ways that disease can be prevented by changing living habits and with helping people modify behavior that increases health risk.

Hebephrenic schizophrenia See *disorganized schizophrenia*.

Helplessness See *learned helplessness*.

Heredity The process by which characteristics of an organism are basically determined by genes received from the parents.

Heroin Extremely addictive opiate derived from morphine.

Herpes virus hominus (herpes simplex) Chronic viral illness which, if present in a pregnant woman, may cause retardation and other congenital malformations in her child.

Heterosexual Characterized by attraction to the opposite sex.

Hierarchy of needs View, especially as described by Abraham Maslow, that certain basic needs of the individual must be met before the person becomes interested in such topics as personal growth and self-actualization.

High-risk study Research strategy entailing the longitudinal study of persons who might be vulnerable to breakdown.

Histrionic personality disorder Characterized by overly reactive behavior of a histrionic, exhibitionistic type. Individuals with this disorder are egocentric and self-absorbed and usually have poor sexual adjustment.

Homeostasis Maintenance of equilibrium and constancy among the bodily processes.

Homosexuality Sexual activity between persons of the same sex.

Hormones Glandular secretions that function as co-ordinators of bodily reactions to external events and body growth and development.

Humanistic-existentialist perspective Idea that all individuals are unique and should be free to make their own choices about life directions. Emphasizes the creative freedom and potential of the individual.

Humanistic therapies Psychotherapies with special

emphasis on human beings' fundamental desires to obtain self-respect and their needs for it. Carl Rogers' approach is an example.

Huntington's disease Uncommon degenerative disease occurring in families. Symptoms include jerking and twisting movement, facial grimaces, and psychotic symptoms. Also called Huntington's chorea.

Hyperactivity See *attention-deficit hyperactivity disorder*.

Hypertension High blood pressure, usually considered a psychophysiologic disorder.

Hypervigilance Tendency to constantly survey the environment for negative stimuli. A coping mechanism often used by avoidant personalities and by anxious individuals.

Hypnosis Altered state of consciousness induced by suggestion. Ranges from mild hypersuggestibility to deep, trancelike states.

Hypochondriasis (Hypochondria) Disorder in which a person is preoccupied by fear of disease and worries a great deal about his or her health without any realistic cause.

Hypomania A disorder characterized by unusual elevation in mood that is not as extreme as that found in mania.

Hypothalamus Part of the brain that lies below the thalamus. Controls various activities of the autonomic nervous system, including regulation of body temperature.

Hypothesis A statement of relationship or cause and effect stated in terms that allow a scientific test.

Hypothesis-testing experiment Evaluation of the correctness of an idea by experimental test.

Hypothetical construct Inferred intermediate mechanism; a concept conceived of as having properties of its own (e.g., a memory trace).

Hysteria Presence of a physical problem without any physical causes. A person with hysteria is called an *hysteric*.

Hysteric Term used by Charcot to describe an individual who complains of organic symptoms such as pain, blindness, or paralysis for which no organic cause can be found.

Id In psychoanalysis, that diversion of the psyche which is a repository of all instinctual impulses and repressed mental contents. Represents the true unconscious or the "deepest" part of the psyche.

Identification Feeling of association with another person or group such that an individual takes on the viewpoint and behavior of the other(s).

Idiot Term formerly used for a retarded individual whose intelligence fell in the lowest measurable range.

Imipramine One of the tricyclic drugs used in the treatment of some depressed individuals.

Immune system Body system that fights disease through inactivation of foreign substances by means of lymphocyte cells.

Implosive therapy Behavior therapy technique based on the principle of extinction. Client is repeatedly presented with strong anxiety-provoking stimuli until he or she no longer reacts in an anxious manner.

Impotence Failure of a male to attain or maintain a penile erection even when sexually excited.

Impulse control disorder A disorder in which the person seems unable to resist impulses (gambling, stealing, fire setting) that do not occur as part of any other disorder.

Impulsive Characterized by a lack of forethought or planning.

Inattention Failure to consistently focus on a stimulus; often results in the tendency to leave tasks unfinished.

Inauthentic behavior According to existential theorists, the determination of behavioral goals by others, not one's self.

Incest Sexual relations between close family members, such as brother and sister or parent and child.

Incidence data A count of the number of new cases that begin during a certain period of time; used in epidemiology. Contrast with *prevalence data*.

Incompetent Legal term used to describe individuals who are not able to understand the meaning of legal proceedings in which they are involved and who are unable to consult with an attorney in a way that might assist their defense.

Increased stress theory Idea that the negative impact of the condition of poverty and crime make mental illness, especially schizophrenia, more likely because of the increased pressures of living. Contrast with *social selection theory*.

Independent variable Experimental factor (e.g., time of food deprivation) that is manipulated or altered in some manner while others are held constant.

Index case See *proband*.

Indoleamine Type of neurotransmitter of the monoamine group—e.g., serotonin—appears especially closely related to mood.

Infantile sexuality View held by Sigmund Freud that children as well as adults have sexual feelings and experience erotic stimulation.

Inferential statistics Methods based on the laws of probability that are used to draw conclusions about relationships among variables studied.

Inflexibility Inability to change; in personality, those coping styles habitually used even if they are unsuitable to a given situation.

Information processing A view of cognitive behavior that compares the human senses and brain function and behavior to a computer.

Informed consent Requirement that patients must be given adequate information about the benefits and

Irrational thought Ideas and beliefs that are derived from emotional response rather than reasoning.

Isolation Defense mechanism by which inconsistent or contradictory attitudes and feelings are walled off from each other in consciousness. Similar to repression, except that in isolation the impulse or wish is consciously recognized, but is separated from present behavior; in repression, neither the wish nor its relation to action is recognized. Intellectualization is a special form of isolation.

Juvenile delinquency Violations of the law committed by adolescents (usually defined as persons 18 years of age or younger).

Kaufman Assessment Battery for Children (K-ABC) Intelligence test designed to reduce cultural bias by use of measures from cognitive psychology and neuropsychology.

Kinsey Report First detailed statistical report that attempted to present the variations in human sexual behavior from a descriptive, scientific view.

Korsakoff's syndrome Chronic brain disorder precipitated by a vitamin deficiency stemming from alcoholism. Characterized by marked disorientation, amnesia, and falsification of memory.

Labeling Cognitive device by which a person classifies his or her own emotional responses as a way of controlling behavior, especially in stress-producing situations. Also, a way people are categorized by others, a way of stereotyping.

La Belle indifference Marked lack of concern about one's disability, occasionally seen in patients with conversion disorder.

Laceration Gross tear or rupture in tissue. Cerebral lacerations may occur through head injuries.

Latency period According to Freud, the period from age 5 until adolescence during which the child's sexual impulses are not a primary focus of his or her pleasure-seeking activities.

Learned helplessness Acquired belief in one's helplessness to deal with a situation or control one's environment. Concept has been applied to explain depression in humans.

Learning perspective Idea that what one experiences is the most important aspect of behavior, which is considered as a product of stimulus–response relationships. One group of learning theorists were called behaviorists.

Lesbianism Female homosexuality.

Librium (chlordiazepoxide) Tranquilizer often prescribed for anxiety problems.

Limbic system Part of the brain that controls visceral and bodily changes associated with emotion; also regulates drive-motivated behavior. Lower parts of the cerebrum.

Lithium (lithium carbonate) Chemical salt used in the treatment of bipolar disorder.

risks of planned treatments before they agree to the procedures.

Innate Characteristics acquired through general inheritance or the mutation of a gene or genes passed on from the parent.

Insanity Legal term connoting mental incompetence, inability to distinguish "right from wrong," and inability to care for oneself.

Insight Self-knowledge; understanding the significance and purpose of one's motives or behavior, including the ability to recognize inappropriateness and irrationality.

Intellectualization A defense mechanism in which a person separates the description or meaning of an event from its emotional impact.

Intelligence test Standardized test used to establish an intelligence-level rating by measuring an individual's ability in a variety of tasks including information, word meaning, concept formation, and various performance skills.

Interactional view of behavior Viewpoint that directs attention to the joint effects or interactions of many of the variables emphasized by different theoretical viewpoints in producing abnormal behavior.

Internal Tendency to see oneself rather than the environment as the cause of events. See also *locus of control*.

Interpersonal factors In therapy refers to the relationship between the therapist and the client as a consequence of the personalities of the two rather than as a result of the techniques the therapist uses.

Interpersonal systems approach A type of therapy that focuses on how the client and family interact rather than focusing on the client alone.

Intervening variable An inferred variable functionally connected with antecedents and consequences; such variables are abstractions and have no properties other than those defined by the empirical data.

Interview See *diagnostic interview*; *therapeutic interview*.

Intravenous injection The injection of a drug or chemical directly into the bloodstream by inserting a hollow needle into a vein.

Intoxication Mental disorder and the presence of maladaptive behavior due to the use and present effect on the body of some substance. The most common behavior changes are inattention and impaired thinking, judgment, emotional control, and motor activity.

Intrapsychic conflict Lack of acceptance of certain areas of thought or emotion that make it necessary for an individual to attempt to keep some material out of awareness.

In vivo exposure A type of exposure therapy that uses actual experience of the feared situation as a way of treating anxiety symptoms.

Locus, gene The characteristic position within a chromosome in which a particular gene pair are located.

Locus of control Personality characteristic described by Julian Rotter in which an individual believes either that he or she has the power to affect the outcome of situations (internal locus of control) or that he or she has little control over what happens (external locus of control).

Longitudinal study Research strategy based on observing and recording the behavior of people over periods of time. Involves obtaining measures on the same people either continuously or at specific or regular intervals.

LSD (Lysergic acid diethylamide) Chemically produced synthetic hallucinogen with psychotomimetic properties.

Lunatic Term used in the past to describe the insane. The word *luna* (moon) refers to the old belief that those who were insane were moonstruck.

Lycanthropy Term for the magical change believed to overcome individuals and cause them to behave like wolves.

Lymphocyte A general term that includes several types of cells in the immune system that fight disease.

Magnetic resonance imaging (MRI) A type of scanning technique that uses the changing form of magnetic fields around the head to map the electrical activity in the brain.

Mainstreaming Practice of assigning retarded and other handicapped children to classes including children of all ability levels and those who are not physically impaired rather than segregating them with others who are similar to themselves.

Major depressive disorder or episode A severe depression characterized by dysphoric mood as well as poor appetite, sleep problems, feelings of restlessness or being slowed down, loss of pleasure, loss of energy, feelings of inability to concentrate or indecisiveness, recurrent thoughts of death or suicide attempts. These occur without mood-incongruent delusions or hallucinations and are not due to schizophrenia, paranoid disorder, organic mental disorder, or recent death of a loved one.

Maladaptive behavior Behavior that deals inadequately with a situation, especially one that is stressful.

Male limited Hereditary pattern that seems to be transmitted only from fathers and only to male offspring.

Malingering Behavior designed to get financial or other rewards by pretending to have some disorder. *Contrast with* factitious disorder.

Mania Euphoric, hyperactive state in which an individual's judgment is impaired.

Manic depressive psychosis *See bipolar disorder.*

Mantra *See meditation.*

MAO inhibitor *See Monoamine oxidase inhibitor.*

Marijuana Substance derived from the leaves or flowering tops of the cannabis plant. Smoking it leads to a dreamy state of altered consciousness in which ideas are disconnected, uncontrollable, and plentiful. Under the influence of marijuana, behavior is impulsive and mood is elevated.

Marital therapy A subtype of group therapy in which a couple meet together with a therapist in an attempt to improve the couple's interaction.

Markers Biological or behavioral characteristics that may make it possible to identify people who are vulnerable to certain disorders.

Masochism Deviation in which sexual pleasure is attained from pain inflicted on oneself, from being dominated, or from being mistreated.

Masochist One who practices masochism.

Masturbation Self-stimulation of the genitals for the purposes of deriving sexual pleasure.

Mediator A link (for example, between a stimulus and the resulting behavior).

Meditation The technique of relaxing through concentrating on a thought, sensation, or special word or mantra.

Medroxyprogesterone acetate (MPA) A chemical used to reduce the level of male sex hormone in the blood which is used experimentally for treating some of the paraphilias. Trade name Depo-provera.

Meninges Any of the membranes enclosing the brain or spinal cord in vertebrates.

Meningitis Inflammation of any or all of the meninges of the brain and spinal cord. Usually caused by a bacterial infection.

Mental age The age equivalent at which a person's intelligence behavior places him or her. Contrasted to chronological age, the person's actual age as determined by birth date. The ratio between the two mental age and chronological age, the mental age score of 70 or below together with a poor level of social functioning. The degree of retardation is further defined. Scores of 50 to 70 or below together with a poor level of social functioning are called mild retardation, 35 to 49 moderate, 20 to 34 severe, and below 20 profound retardation.

Mental retardation Intellectual functioning significantly below average. Generally defined as an intelligence test score of 70 or below together with a poor level of social functioning. The degree of retardation is further defined. Scores of 50 to 70 or below together with a poor level of social functioning are called mild retardation, 35 to 49 moderate, 20 to 34 severe, and below 20 profound retardation.

Mental-status examination An interview, sometimes supplemented with psychological and neurological tests, used to assess an individual's intellectual function and ability to interact appropriately with the environment.

Meta-analysis Technique used to combine the data from many studies in a meaningful way. Has been used to investigate the effects of psychotherapy on clients.

Metacognition A person's knowledge of his or her own cognitive processes and the products of these processes.

Methadone Synthetic chemical whose action is similar to that of morphine. Because its use allegedly does not lead to escalation of dosage, it is prescribed by some authorities as a treatment for heroin addiction.

Methadone maintenance Use of methadone as a substitute for heroin. Methadone prevents withdrawal and suppresses the desire for heroin, although methadone also has undesirable side effects.

Method factors Variations in results that are caused by the way a study was conducted, the type of questionnaire used, or other factors not associated with a real difference in what has been measured.

Methylphenidate Stimulant drug (e.g., Ritalin) sometimes used in the treatment of hyperactivity.

Mileau-limited Term for a hereditary pattern in which a disorder seems to appear only under certain environmental conditions.

Mileau therapy Effort to provide a totally therapeutic environment within an institution by enlisting the efforts of all staff members as providers of some form of therapeutic contact.

Mind Human consciousness as shown in thought, perception, and memory. Reflects the artificial dichotomy often made between mind and body.

Minnesota Multiphasic Personality Inventory (MMPI) Self-report personality questionnaire designed to facilitate psychiatric diagnosis.

M'Naghten rule Legal precedent in English law, originating in 1843, which provides for acquittal if an accused person is found to be not responsible for the crime—that is, if he or she could not distinguish between "right and wrong." The rule did not take into account that a person might be held to be insane even though he or she knew the difference between right and wrong.

Modeling Behavior learned or modified as a result of observing the behavior of others. Learner does not have to make the observed response him- or herself, or be reinforced for making it, to learn the new behavior. Term used interchangeably with observational learning.

Modeling, covert The use of the client's imagination to vividly reproduce his/her carrying out of a sequence of behaviors described by the therapist.

Modeling, live A person acting out a situation in order to teach another person how to behave in those same circumstances.

Modeling, symbolic Using a film or other media to provide information about a new and potentially stressful situation before one experiences the situation oneself.

Monoamine Type of neurotransmitter with a distinctive single amino acid (NH_2) in its molecular structure. There are two types of monoamines: catecholamines and indoleamines.

Monoamine oxidase (MAO) Enzyme in the neuron receptors that inactivates the various amines, including the catecholamines.

Monoamine oxidase (MAO) inhibitor One of a group of drugs used to treat depression. Works by preventing the degrading of monoamines and thus allowing more norepinephrine and serotonin to collect at the receptor sites.

Monogenic (single-gene) theory Refers to theory of inheritance in which a gene at one particular locus (e.g., one site on a chromosome) is sufficient to produce an inherited characteristic.

Monozygotic twins Identical twins developed from one fertilized egg.

Mood disorder One of a group of disorders primarily affecting emotional tone. Can be depression, manic excitement, or both. May be episodic or chronic.

Moral treatment Technique of treating mental-hospital patients which prevailed in the nineteenth century. Emphasized removal of restraints, allowing religious conviction, and ensuring humanitarian treatment.

Morphine Principle derivative of opium, which has been used extensively to relieve pain.

Mosaicism The condition in which all a person's cells do not have the same chromosome count as a result of an error in cell division in the fertilized egg.

Multiaxial classification system System that rates an individual separately on a number of different criteria or axes. The DSM-III-R is an example.

Multifactorial polygenic model Theory that a number of genes from a variety of loci may combine to produce a particular characteristic or disorder.

Multi-infarct dementia Intellectual deficit resulting from a series of minor strokes that occur over a period of time.

Multiple personality Rare form of dissociative disorder characterized by development and existence of two or more relatively independent and coexisting personality systems within the same individual.

Munchausen syndrome A factitious disorder in which the person pretends to have a particular disorder in order to get medical treatment. Involves faking of symptoms, and often self-injury.

Mutant A cell in which the hereditary material has been altered. This mutation may be spontaneous (occurring naturally) or induced by internal factors such as radiation and certain chemicals.

Mutation Sudden change in the composition of a gene, which usually causes abnormal characteristics in the progeny.

Myocardial infarction Tissue damage to the heart muscle from a drastic decrease in the amount of blood that reaches the heart; commonly called a heart attack.

Naloxone A drug that blocks the pain relieving effects of endorphins.

Narcissism Term for self-love or self-absorption derived from the Greek myth about Narcissus who fell in love with what he thought was a water nymph but was in reality his own reflection in a pond.

Narcissistic personality disorder Characterized by a sense of self-importance and a preoccupation with fantasies of unlimited success. Individuals are preoccupied with how well they are doing and how well others think of them. Disorder is often accompanied by depressed mood.

Narcotics Legal term for addicting drugs, the most common of which are the opiates, derived from the Oriental poppy.

Natural disaster Overwhelming event caused by the forces of nature rather than human intervention—for example, a tornado, earthquake, or flood.

Natural fool Old term for a retarded person. It means one who is born deficient in judgment.

Negative symptoms, in schizophrenia Symptoms characterized by behavior deficits such as flattened affect, poverty of speech and apathy. Sometimes called Type II schizophrenia.

Negative transference Feelings of hostility a client carries over from earlier relationships into his or her relationship with a therapist.

Neoanalyst Theorist who agrees with a revised version of Freud's concepts.

Neo-Freudian Pertaining to former followers of Freud who departed in several major doctrinal ways from orthodox psychoanalysis. Whereas ego psychologists view themselves as psychoanalysts, neo-Freudians do not. Prominent among the neo-Freudians are Adler, Jung, and Sullivan. Their writings emphasize the social and cultural determinants of behavior.

Neuroleptic drugs Name for a group of psychoactive drugs that are used to treat schizophrenic disorders. These reduce psychotic symptoms but may have side effects resembling neurological disorders.

Neurologist Specialist in the diagnosis and treatment of disorders of the nervous system.

Neuron Individual nerve cell.

Neuropsychology Branch of psychology dealing with brain-behavior relationships.

Neurosis Older term for what are now called *anxiety disorders.*

Neurotic depression Older term for *dysthymic disorder.*

Neurotransmitter Chemical product of the nervous system that makes possible the movement of the nerve impulse across the synapse.

Nicotine Volatile psychoactive substance that is the chief active chemical in tobacco.

Non compos mentis Latin term meaning not of sound mind and therefore not legally responsible.

Nontranssexual gender identity disorder Persistent discomfort about one's assigned sex; frequently involves cross dressing or fantasies about cross dressing. Differs from transsexualism in that there is no persistent preoccupation to acquire the primary and secondary sexual characteristics of the other sex.

Norepinephrine Hormone also called *noradrenalin,* produced by the adrenal medulla. One of the catecholamine group.

Observational research A method in which no variables are manipulated and relationships are studied as they naturally occur. Contrast with *experimental method.*

Obsessive behavior Characterized by preoccupation with a particular type of thought that keeps occurring repetitively.

Obsessive-compulsive disorder Characterized by recurrent obsessions and/or compulsions, often accompanied by depression or anxiety.

Obsessive-compulsive personality disorder Distinguished by lack of ability to express warmth, a stiff and formal way of relating to others, and extreme perfectionism that leads an individual to focus on details rather than on the whole picture.

Occipital lobe Major division of either cerebral hemisphere located in the dorsal area.

Operant conditioning Form of conditioning in which a desired response occurs and is subsequently reinforced to increase its probability of more frequent occurrence; also called *instrumental conditioning.*

Operant response Response originally occurring rarely that has been increased in frequency through reinforcement.

Opiate Natural or synthetic substance that is similar in action to morphine or other derivatives of the opium poppy.

Opioid Drug with a morphine-like action. Can be either a natural or synthetic substance.

Oral dependent Psychodynamic term to describe individuals who secure a major part of their psychological gratification from such activities as eating, drinking, and smoking, and who may show dependent personality characteristics.

Oral stage First developmental stage of infancy, during which pleasure is derived from lip and mouth contact with need-fulfilling objects (e.g., breast).

Organic affective syndrome Abnormal changes in mood thought to be the result of changes in brain metabolism or toxic conditions.

Organic anxiety syndrome Panic attacks or generalized anxiety thought to be causally related to some specific organic factor.

Organic brain syndrome Group of symptoms characteristic of acute and chronic brain disorders.

Organic defect theory Idea that a particular bodily

organ that is working improperly is the cause of maladaptive behavior.

Organic delusional syndrome Delusional thinking that occurs as the result of some organic condition, often associated with abuse of a variety of substances including amphetamines, cannabis, and hallucinogens.

Organic hallucinosis Hallucinations caused by some organic factor. Often the result of use of hallucinogenic drugs or large quantities of alcohol.

Organic mental disorder Brain dysfunction based on either aging or the ingestion of substances that affect brain activity. May be temporary or permanent.

Organic personality syndrome Diagnosis used when major personality changes occur that are believed to be the result of some change in or injury to brain tissue.

Organismic point of view Pertaining to the organism as a whole rather than to particular parts. Behavior is considered an interrelated and interactive function of the integrated organism.

Organ-susceptibility hypothesis Idea that emotional stress might cause a psychophysiological problem in a particular bodily organ in a particular individual because that organ had some inherent weakness.

Orgasm Third stage of sexual response, which involves rhythmic muscular contractions and high physical arousal. In the male ejaculation of semen takes place during this stage.

Orienting response Measurable psychophysiological changes that come about when a person notices an environmental stimulus and prepares to receive some information from it.

Overanxious disorder A childhood disorder in which excessive or unrealistic worry is observed over at least a 6-month period.

Overgeneralization According to Aaron Beck, characteristic way of thinking found in some depressed individuals. Tendency to exaggerate the meaning of an event into a general principle.

Paradigm A model or example.

Paradoxical intention Therapeutic technique in which the client is instructed to perform behaviors that seem to be counter to the therapeutic goal. For instance, someone who is afraid of crowds may be instructed to go into a crowd and concentrate on feeling as fearful as possible.

Paranoid disorder Disorder characterized by the persistence of delusions that are usually well organized; does not include prominent hallucinations, incoherent speech, thought derailment, or many of the delusions associated with schizophrenia.

Paranoid personality disorder Personality disorder similar in some ways to schizoid personality disorder, but notable for extreme sensitivity in interpersonal relationships; suspicious; jealous, and stubborn behavior; and a tendency to use the defense mechanism of projection.

Paranoid schizophrenia Type of schizophrenia characterized by persistent delusions, often either grandiose or accusatory.

Paraphilia Sexual deviation that involves choice of inappropriate sex partners or inappropriate goals for the sex act. Pedophilia, sadism, and voyeurism are examples.

Paraprofessional Term used to describe workers who have received certain basic training that enables them to perform tasks formerly performed by professional workers. Paraprofessionals often come from the same communities and educational backgrounds as the people whom they treat or aid.

Parasuicide Term used to describe any act that does not end in death in which a person deliberately causes self-injury or takes a drug overdose with the apparent intention of suicide.

Parens patriae Legal doctrine that gives the state power to act in what it believes to be the best interest of an incapacitated adult or a minor.

Parental affective style A measure of negative feelings expressed by family members as the family discusses upsetting problems together. Compare with *expressed emotion*.

Paresis Chronic and progressively deteriorating brain condition caused by syphilitic infection and characterized by loss of cognitive and motor functions, speech disorder, and eventual death.

Parietal (lobe) Middle division of each cerebral hemisphere of the brain, behind the central sulcus, above the fissure of Sylvius, and in front of the parietooccipital fissure.

Parkinson's disease Chronic and progressive neurological disorder characterized by motor tremor, rigidity, loss of vocal power, and psychotic symptoms. Believed to be caused by an acquired defect in brain metabolism.

Partial hospitalization Use of either day, night, or weekend hospital care for patients who do not need 24-hour care. Designed particularly to aid transition back to the community. Also used to prevent complete hospitalization if the family can provide partial care, for instance, outside of their own working hours.

Participant modeling Therapeutic procedure in which the response is first demonstrated for the client, who then produces the same response with suggestions from the therapist.

Passive-aggressive personality disorder Usually characterized by aggressive behavior exhib-

ited in passive ways (e.g., pouting). Three types are often distinguished: (1) passive-aggressive type: hostility and aggression expressed by passive means such as obstructionism, stubbornness, inefficiency, and procrastination; (2) aggressive type: hostility and aggressiveness expressed directly through temper tantrums, destructive behavior, argumentativeness, and negativism; and (3) passive-dependent type: characterized by overdependency, helplessness, indecisiveness, and the childlike tendency to cling to others. Reactions are grouped together on the basis that they seem to represent different reactions to common-core conflicts over dependency and aggression.

Pathology Disease or abnormal physical condition.

PCP (phencyclidine) Hallucinogenic drug popularly known as "angel dust."

Pedophilia Sexual deviation in which an adult desires or engages in sexual relations with a child. May be either homosexual or heterosexual in nature.

Pedophile, fixated A person who begins to display pedophilia during adolescence and usually has no other important sexual relationships.

Pedophile, regressed A person who begins pedophilic behavior only after some negative life events.

Pellagra Chronic disease caused by niacin deficiency. Symptoms include skin eruptions, digestive disturbances, and disturbances of the nervous system which may cause psychoticlike behavior.

Penetrance Percentage of cases in which a particular trait or characteristic, derived from a specific gene, will manifest itself in subsequent organisms of the species.

Pepsinogen Substance found in the gastric system that is converted to a digestive enzyme by hydrochloric acid in the digestive system. Individuals with high natural pepsinogen levels are prone to develop ulcers under stressful conditions.

Peptide A compound containing two or more amino acids linked together in a specific chemical fashion.

Performance anxiety (sexual) High degree of concern in males about the ability to maintain an erection until orgasm. The anxiety has a negative effect on sexual performance.

Performance IQ One of the two subscores of the Wechsler intelligence test series. Reflects ability to solve puzzles, copy designs, and perform other similar tasks.

Peripheral nervous system System that includes all outlying nerve structures not included in the central nervous system.

Personal constructs A term originated by George Kelly for categories used by someone about his or her personal effectiveness in acting in specific or general types of situations.

Personality Particular constellation of attributes that defines one's individuality.

Personality disorder Deeply ingrained, inflexible, maladaptive patterns of thought and behavior which persist throughout a person's life.

Personality inventories Paper-and-pencil tests in which the person describes him- or herself by answering a series of true–false questions or by rating a series of self-descriptive phases. Most personality inventories yield several scores, each of which is intended to describe an aspect of personality.

Personality maladaptation Perception by an individual of personal dissatisfactions and concerns that interfere with happiness but not significantly with social adjustment or work achievement.

Pervasive developmental disorder A life-long disorder in which the quality of the person's social interactions, communication skills, and ability to engage in imaginative activities and other cognitive tasks is impaired. Autistic disorder is the only subtype of this disorder that has been defined so far.

Petit mal Mild form of epilepsy which involves partial alterations of consciousness.

Phallic stage Stage of psychosexual development during which a child begins to perceive his or her body as a source of gratification. Feelings of narcissism are heightened during this period.

Phenobarbitol Barbiturate sometimes used as a sedative and in the control of epileptic seizure activity.

Phenothiazine One of a family of antipsychotic drugs.

Phenylketonuria (PKU) Form of mental retardation caused by a metabolic deficiency.

Phobia Excessive or inappropriate fear of some particular object or situation which is not in fact dangerous.

Phobic disorder Type of anxiety disorder mainly characterized by irrational and highly specific fears (for example, of dirt, water, high places).

Phototherapy The use of exposure to very bright light for several hours a day as a treatment for seasonal depression.

Phrenology Obsolete theory that different psychological behaviors were related to different parts of the brain and that these could be assessed by touching the surface of the skull.

Physical disorder Term used to refer to a medical as opposed to a psychological problem.

Physiognomy The art of judging human character or personality from facial features.

Physiotherapy Treatment of disorders by mechanical means—for example, exercise, heat, light, or massage.

Pica Repeated eating of nonnutritive substances such as paint, clay, animal droppings, or laundry starch at a time when there is no evidence of hunger, malnutrition, or aversion.

Pick's disease Type of progressive dementia caused by atrophy of the cerebral cortex.

Placebo Inactive or inert substance that is presented as effective remedy for some problem in order to determine what role suggestibility plays in symptom change.

Placebo effect Changes in behavior as a result of the expectancy that a placebo, or inactive substance, is an active or "real" drug; type of suggestion effect.

Plaque Abnormal structure found in nerve cells of individuals who have Alzheimer's disease.

Plateau stage Second stage of sexual response, which includes increases in heart rate and muscle tension as well as swelling of genital tissue.

Play therapy Treatment approach used with children; based on the assumption that young children can express thoughts and fantasies more directly in play than through verbal means.

Pleasure principle Psychoanalytic term for the regulatory mechanism for mental life that functions to reduce tension and gain gratification. Principle that governs the functioning of the id to obtain gratification without regard to reality considerations.

Polygenic Theory in genetics that several genes at different loci must interact to produce a particular inherited characteristic.

Polygraph Instrument that measures emotional responses through physiological reactions, such as blood pressure and galvanic skin response. Commonly called a *lie detector*.

Population genetics Study of the ways genes are distributed in a population through the mating of individuals.

Positive reinforcer See *reinforcer*.

Positive symptoms, in schizophrenia Generally, symptoms that show behavioral excesses: hallucinations, delusions, bizarre behavior, and so forth. Sometimes called Type I schizophrenia.

Positive transference Carrying over of positive feelings about other relationships onto the therapist–client relationship.

Positron emission tomography (PT) Technique for studying the dynamic chemical activity of the brain by using a scanning device that produces a series of cross-section images of the brain.

Posttraumatic psychosis Psychotic symptoms that appear suddenly after an injury to the brain or a stressful life event.

Posttraumatic stress disorder Development of symptoms in response to events of such severity that most people would be stressed by them. Symptoms often include a feeling of numbness in response or psychological reexperiencing of the event in thoughts, dreams, or nightmares.

Poverty of content A characteristic of some schizophrenic speech in which little information is transmitted through speaking because of factors such as vagueness of meaning, repetition of phrases, or inappropriate degree of abstraction of the thoughts expressed.

Preconscious Thoughts that are not held in a person's mind at a particuar time but which can easily be brought into awareness.

Premature ejaculation Inability of the male to inhibit ejaculation long enough for his female partner to experience orgasm.

Premorbid adjustment Achievement level and adjustment to interpersonal activities shown by an individual earlier in life before a disorder becomes apparent.

Presenile dementia See *dementia*.

Prevalence data Information concerning the number of cases of a particular disorder that are ongoing at any particular time. Contrast with *incidence data*.

Primary appraisal First stage of assessing the meaning of a situation. In this stage the situation is interpreted as threatening or harmless. In the following stage, secondary appraisal, the individual decides how to deal with the situation.

Primary prevention Efforts at preventing the development of maladaptation by removing factors that might cause it to develop.

Primary process thinking Primary cognitive mode, characteristic of infants and children, that is not based on rules of organization or logic. The presence of primary process thinking, free association in its purest form, is characteristic of the id. Primary process thought is illogical, is entirely pleasure oriented, has no sense of time or order, and does not discriminate between reality and fantasy. Compare with *secondary process thinking*.

Primitive emotion node A hypothetical memory unit that organizes memories related to a particular mood.

Proband Term used in the study of genetics to indicate the individual with a disorder whose heredity is under study.

Problem drinking Term for the pattern of alcohol abuse that does not include alcohol dependence or physiological addiction.

Prognosis Forecast; probable course and outcome of a disorder.

Projection Defense mechanism that involves attributing to others the undesirable characteristics or impulses which belong to but are not acceptable to oneself.

Projective technique Ambiguous stimulus materials that elicit subjective responses of an associative or fantasy nature. So named because an individual is believed to "project" aspects of his or her personality into the task. Tasks may include inkblot interpretation (Rorschach Test), and various associative completion techniques (word association, incomplete sentences).

Prototypal approach The use of a checklist in making a diagnostic decision. If more than a predetermined number of characteristics are found, the diagnosis is made. As a result people with the same diagnosis may have different sets of characteristics.

Psilocybin One of the two psychoactive substances isolated from the psilocybin mushroom.

Psychedelic drugs See *hallucinogen*.

Psychiatric social work Field of social work in which the professional specializes in helping those with maladaptive behaviors in a clinical, usually medical, setting.

Psychiatric social worker A person with a graduate degree in social work and specialized training in treating and practically assisting both patients with behavioral problems and their families.

Psychiatrist Physician with postgraduate training in the diagnosis and treatment of emotional disorders.

Psychic determinism Principle of causality, one of the basic assumptions of psychoanalysis, which states that all events, overt and covert, are determined by prior and often multiple mental events.

Psychoactive drug Term including several types of drugs that may reduce maladaptive behavior. Includes antipsychotic, antianxiety, and antidepressant drugs.

Psychoactive substance A chemical that affects a person's thoughts, emotions, and behavior.

Psychoactive substance-induced organic mental disorder Organic changes that occur as a result of the use of psychoactive substances.

Psychoactive substance use disorder Maladaptive changes in behavior that result from the use of a psychoactive drug.

Psychoanalysis Term has three meanings: (1) theory of psychology and psychopathology developed by Freud from his clinical experiences with patients; (2) procedure for investigating the mental life, conflicts, and coping processes, which employs the techniques of free association, dream analysis, and interpretation of transference and resistance phenomena; and (3) form of therapy that uses the psychoanalytic procedure and the theories of personality and psychopathology just described.

Psychodrama Method of group therapy in which individuals both act out their emotional responses in situations they find difficult and also practice new, constructive roles.

Psychodynamic perspective Point of view that emphasizes thoughts and emotions as the most important determiners of behavior. Basic ideas come from the work of Sigmund Freud.

Psychogenic Adjective referring to symptoms for which an organic cause cannot be specified.

Psychogenic amnesia Disturbance in the ability to recall important personal information in the absence of an organic disorder and without the assumption of a new identity such as that found in a psychogenic fugue.

Psychogenic fugue See *fugue state*.

Psychogenic pain disorder Characterized by severe pain that does not have an identifiable physical cause.

Psychoimmunology Study of the relationship between changes in immune system functioning and psychological events.

Psychological dependence Habit or need that requires continued or repeated administration of a drug to produce pleasure or to avoid conflict.

Psychological hardiness Term used by Kobasa and other researchers to describe people who are more resistant to stress and illness than most people. Research on hardiness is directed toward understanding precisely what characteristics are involved.

Psychological numbing Reduced capacity for emotion, and symptoms of apathy, withdrawal, and depression. These are likely to occur after a disaster.

Psychological perspective View that maladaptive behavior is caused by problems of perception, cognition, or emotion rather than by biological causes.

Psychological tests Procedures to measure in a standardized way some aspect of behavior such as intelligence or personality characteristics.

Psychology of personal constructs The approach of George Kelly, who was interested in helping his clients understand the unique way in which they viewed themselves and other people and also to see that their behavior was designed to fill certain roles. Kelly urged his clients to try out new roles rather than be stuck in nonadaptive ways of interacting.

Psychometric Refers to measures of psychological functioning.

Psychomotor Term used to describe muscular action resulting from prior mental activity, especially conscious mental activity.

Psychomotor epilepsy Trancelike state with recurring episodes of confusion during which repetitive and semiautomatic muscle movements occur. Often accompanied by confusion and visual hallucinations.

Psychopath Term used by Hervey Cleckley to describe antisocial individuals who met a certain set of characteristics including charm, lack of anxiety or guilt, poor judgment, and failure to learn from experience.

Psychopharmacology Study of the effects of drugs on psychological functioning and behavior.

Psychophysiological assessment Measurement of various body functions such as blood pressure, heart rate, breathing, and galvanic skin response in an attempt to understand feelings and emotions. One commercial use is the polygraph or lie detector.

Psychophysiological (psychosomatic) disorder Physical pathology and actual tissue damage that results from continued emotional mobilization of the body during periods of sustained stress.

Psychophysiology of behavior Study of the relationship between observed behavior and the functions of the central and peripheral nervous systems.

Psychosexual disorder Deviant sexual thoughts and/or behavior that are either personally anxiety-provoking, or are injurious to others.

Psychosexual stage One of several developmental stages of life as defined by Sigmund Freud. These differ in terms of the source of primary gratification and include oral, anal, phallic, and genital stages.

Psychosis (plural: psychoses) Disorder that includes any of the following: delusions, hallucinations, incoherence, repeated derailment of thought, marked poverty of thought content, marked illogicality, and grossly disorganized or catatonic behavior.

Psychosis, atypical A disorder in which there are psychotic symptoms (hallucinations, delusions, etc.) but the symptom pattern does not meet the criteria for any of the nonorganic psychotic disorders.

Psychosocial disadvantage Growing up in an intellectually, culturally, and financially impoverished environment.

Psychosocial stressor Feeling of stress arising from relationships with other people in the environment.

Psychosomatic disorder See *psychophysiological disorder.*

Psychosomatic hypothesis Idea popular in the 1930s and 1940s that physical symptoms can be caused by an inability to express strong emotions.

Psychotherapy General term referring to psychological, verbal, and expressive techniques used in treating maladaptive behavior. The client works on resolving inner conflicts and modifying his or her behavior by means of verbal interchanges with the therapist. Insight into feelings and behavior is the goal of most psychotherapy.

Psychotic An adjective indicating the presence of psychosis.

Psychotic disorder A disorder in which there is gross impairment in reality testing and the creation of a new reality. Psychotic disorders include schizophrenia, delusional disorders, some organic mental disorder, and some mood disorders.

PT scan See *positron emission tomography.*

Punishment Aversive stimulus given as a result of an undesired behavior in an attempt to suppress that behavior in the future.

Radical behaviorists Group of learning theorists who think of behavior as entirely a response to environmental stimuli.

Rape Sexual intercourse accomplished by force and without the partner's consent.

Rape, date Rape committed by a person who is a social acquaintance of the person who is raped.

Rape-relief center Organization, often composed in part of volunteers, designed to provide information about medical and legal services for those who have been raped and also to offer psychological support for the victims.

Rape, statutory Crime defined as having sexual intercourse with someone below the age of legal consent. Force is not necessarily involved.

Rating scale Type of test in which a person can indicate on a scale the degree of his or her agreement with each item.

Rational approach Idea that only the use of reason and not experimental evidence or observation is the prime source of truth.

Rational-emotive therapy Therapy developed by Albert Ellis to modify unrealistic and illogical thought.

Rational thinking Based on reasoning and logic, not on observation or experimental evidence.

Reaction formation Defense mechanism that enables the individual to express an unacceptable impulse by transforming it into its opposite.

Reattribution therapy An effort to help clients change their mental explanation about the cause of a particular behavior or situation.

Recall A measure of information retention in which the subject is asked to reproduce as many parts of a previous stimulus as possible.

Recessive gene Member of a gene pair which determines the characteristic trait or appearance of the individual only if the other member of the pair matches it. Compare to *dominant gene.*

Recognition A measure of information retention in which the subject is asked to select which of several stimulus items have been presented previously.

Refractory period (sexual) In males, the period after orgasm when no additional arousal can occur. Females may or may not have a refractory period.

Regress To go backward or return to an earlier level of functioning. Interpreted in psychoanalytic theory as a defense mechanism. See *regression.*

Regression Defense mechanism characterized by a return to earlier and more primitive modes of responding. Through regression, the ego returns to an earlier developmental phase of functioning which had met with some success.

Reinforcement Any event (stimulus) which, if contingent upon response by an organism, changes the probability that the response will be made again. Reinforcements may be positive (reward) or negative (aversive) and may be presented according to a prescribed schedule (continuous, intermittent). May also be primary (drive reducing—e.g., food) or secondary (derived from prior association with a primary reinforcer—e.g., money, praise).

Reinforcer A consequence of behavior that makes it more likely the behavior will occur again. A *positive reinforcer* achieves this result by provoking a reward or pleasure. A *negative reinforcer* is a stimulus that ceases when the desired behavior is performed. See also *punishment*.

Relapse prevention In treatment of alcohol problems from a cognitive viewpoint, the emphasis on identifying problem situations and helping the client to identify coping devices that may give him or her a feeling of control over such situations.

Relaxation training Series of specified exercises that the client learns to perform in order to remove a tension response that may be characteristic in certain situations.

Reliability The tendency of a measure or procedure to produce the same results when administered on two different occasions. Also refers to the internal homogeneity of a multiple-item test.

Remission Cessation of the symptoms of a disorder. Implies that the basic problem may still exist.

REM sleep Stage of sleep characterized by rapid eye movements and a characteristic brain-wave pattern. Reducing the amount of REM sleep can help decrease some types of depressive symptoms.

Repression Psychoanalytic defense mechanism that involves a "stopping-thinking" or not-being-able-to-remember response. Repression actively forces traumatic events, intolerable and dangerous impulses, and other undesirable mental affects out of consciousness into the less-accessible realm of the unconscious.

Resolution phase The period after sexual orgasm in which the arousal decreases and the body's physiological status returns to normal.

Retardation Level of intellectual functioning that is significantly below average and is accompanied by an inability to behave adaptively in society because of this lack of cognitive ability.

Retarded ejaculation Inhibition of the sexual response of males that results in an inability to eject semen even when sexually excited.

Rheumatoid arthritis Chronic joint disease with inflammation caused by immune-system activity.

Rh incompatibility Presence of incompatible substances on the surfaces of red blood cells of a pregnant woman and her fetus. The mother's blood will produce antibodies that may harm the unborn child unless preventative measures are taken.

Ritalin See *methylphenidate*.

Ritualistic behavior Behavior that follows a series of prescribed actions that are repeated even though they may be maladaptive. Thought to be a way of reducing anxiety.

Role playing In psychotherapy, a technique that requires an individual to enact a social role other than his or her own, or to try out new roles. In sociology, an individual's assumption of the role expected of him or her in a particular type of situation.

Rorschach inkblots Projective test developed by Hermann Rorschach in which the individual is shown a series of ambiguous inkblots and asked to describe what is seen in them.

Rubella Virus which, if present in a pregnant woman, particularly during the first 3 months of pregnancy, can cause retardation and other congenital disorders in her child; commonly called *German measles*.

Rumination disorder of infancy Disorder in which partially digested food is brought up into the infant's mouth without nausea or vomiting. The infant loses weight or fails to gain weight after a period of normal functioning.

Saccadic eye movement Quick jerks of the eye interspersed with steady fixations that are under voluntary control.

Sadism Sexual deviation in which sexual gratification is obtained through inflicting physical pain on other people.

Sadist One who practices sadism.

Sadistic personality disorder A longstanding behavioral pattern in which the person seems to enjoy inflicting psychological or physiological suffering on other people or on animals. The disorder differs from sexual sadism because the sadistic behavior is not carried out for sexual arousal.

Schedule A plan of what will happen and the time it is to occur.

Schizoaffective disorder Separate category from either schizophrenia or affective disorders for individuals who show depressive or manic symptoms as well as those of thought disorder.

Schizoid personality disorder Classification used for withdrawn individuals who are not disturbed by their lack of social relationships. These people have flat emotional responses and often seem cold and detached.

Schizophrenia in remission A lessening or disappearance of symptoms that had been apparent when the person was diagnosed as having a schizophrenic disorder. The term reflects the view that schizophrenia is a life-long disease for which there is no cure, only the possibility of at least temporarily reduced symptoms.

Schizophrenia, residual type A stage of schizophrenic disorder in which psychotic features, especially hallucinations or delusions, are no longer prominent although eccentric behavior, illogical thinking, social withdrawal, and so forth continue to be observed.

Schizophrenic disorders Group of disorders that always involves at least one of the following at some time: delusions, hallucinations, or certain characteristics of thought disorder.

Schizophrenic spectrum disorder One of a group of disorders including schizotypal and paranoid personality disorders, and sometimes schizoaffective disorder, atypical psychosis, and paranoid disorder, which are thought by some researchers to be produced by the same genetic factors as schizophrenia. Used as an explanation for the fact that the incidence of narrowly defined schizophrenia alone is less than would be expected by monogenetic theory.

Schizotypal personality disorder Shows some of the symptoms of schizophrenia, but not in as extreme a form. People with this disorder include those formerly diagnosed as having simple schizophrenia. Differs from schizoid personality disorder in that it includes eccentricities of communication and behavior not seen in that group.

Second rank symptoms Those symptoms classified by Schneider as typical of schizophrenia but which are also found in other psychotic disorders.

Secondary appraisal Second stage of appraisal of a situation in which an individual considers the kind of action necessary and whether he or she has the skills to deal with the situation.

Secondary prevention Efforts directed toward detecting early signs or symptoms to prevent a more serious condition.

Secondary process thinking Psychoanalytic concept referring to organized, logical, and reality-oriented adult thinking. Whereas primary process thinking is characteristic of the id and is based on the pleasure principle, secondary process thought is an ego function based on the reality principle.

Self-actualization Synonymous with self-fulfillment. Process by which the development of one's potentials and abilities is achieved.

Self-defeating personality disorder A longstanding behavioral pattern in which a person seeks out situations or relationships that seem bound to end negatively. Such a person avoids situations that are potentially pleasureful or where the outcome may be successful.

Self-determination Viewpoint of existential theorists that individuals have control of their own lives through the choices they make.

Self-help group A group of people with the same problem who meet together to share experiences and ways to handle situations in an attempt to help themselves improve their own ability to cope with these problems.

Self-monitoring Keeping detailed records of one's behavior.

Self-regulation Technique of controlling one's own behavior through internal reinforcement often in the form of cognitions.

Senile dementia See *dementia*.

Sensate focus Approach to sex therapy advocated by Masters and Johnson in which an individual learns to focus on erotic sensation to the exclusion of other stimuli.

Sensorimotor Pertaining to the functions of the sensing and motor activities of the individual—for example, the sensorimotor nerves.

Sentence completion test Projection test in which the client is presented with a series of incomplete sentences and is asked to complete each one.

Separation anxiety disorder Some children's irrational fear of being apart from the parent(s) because of worries of what will happen to themselves or to their parent(s) in their absence.

Serotonin (5HT) One of a group of chemical neurotransmitters that implement neural transmission across the synapse. Thought to be involved in some types of depression.

Sex offender Term used for individuals who come into contact with the legal system because of their practice of sexual deviations that are prohibited by law.

Sex-reassignment surgery Surgery in which male or female genital organs are removed and facsimiles of genital organs of the opposite sex are created. Surgery is usually combined with hormone treatment to modify secondary sexual characteristics.

Sexual disorders Includes two types—paraphilias and sexual dysfunction. The first relates to obtaining sexual satisfaction through inappropriate partners or activities. The second is the inability to carry out normal sexual activities because of physiological difficulties thought to have psychological causes.

Sexual dysfunction Problems in one or more phases of sexual intercourse that decrease the pleasure derived by the participants or make successful culmination impossible.

Shaman Inspired priest or medium who can summon up and communicate with good and evil spirits.

Shaping Basic process of operant conditioning involving the reinforcement of successively closer approximations to a desired behavior.

Simple phobia Relatively rare type of phobia that involves irrational fear not related to either unfamiliar situations or social interactions; for example, fear of shut-in places (claustrophobia) or fear of specific animals.

Simple schizophrenia See *schizotypal personality disorder*.

Skinner box Apparatus designed by B. F. Skinner and used to study operant conditioning. Organism makes a simple response—for example, presses a bar—to obtain a reinforcement.

Sleep disorders Disorders characterized either by problems with the amount, quality, and timing of sleep, or by abnormal events occurring during sleep such as night terrors or sleepwalking.

Smooth pursuit eye movements Type of essentially involuntary movement that occurs when an individual visually follows the movements of a rhythmically moving object such as a pendulum.

Social causation Theory that maladaptive behavior is a result of poor economic circumstances, poor housing, and inadequate social services.

Social facilitation Acquisition of social competence skills through observing the behavior of others.

Social intervention Treatment approach that involves not only interacting with the client but also attempting to modify the client's environment at home or at work.

Social-learning theories Refers to several similar theoretical viewpoints which hold that social behavior and inner thoughts and feelings are learned through social interactions.

Social phobia Type of irrational fear of situations in which a person will be exposed to the scrutiny of others. Most common types are fear of blushing, public speaking, eating in public, writing in public, and using public toilet facilities.

Social role The function a particular person plays in society, which is determined by the particular role he or she fills. Most people have a variety of overlapping social roles, such as an occupational role, several family roles, and perhaps some recreational roles as well.

Social selection theory Idea that the lower socioeconomic class contains many people who drifted there from higher classes because of their poor functioning. Higher incidence of maladaptive behavior in the lower class is explained in this way.

Social skills training Behavioral or cognitive-behavioral therapeutic approach that emphasizes learning more effective ways of interacting with other people in a variety of situations.

Somatic system Part of the peripheral nervous system that sends nerve impulses from the sense organs to the muscles that determine voluntary movement.

Somatic therapy Treatment, such as drugs, surgery, or electroconvulsive therapy, that directly affects a person's physical state.

Somatization disorder (Briquet's syndrome) Disorder characterized by a variety of dramatic but vague complaints that are often chronic but which have no discernible physical cause.

Somatoform disorders Characterized by physical symptoms that suggest a physical disorder but for which there are (1) no organic findings to explain the symptom and (2) strong evidence or suggestion that the symptoms are linked to psychological factors or conflicts; formerly called *hysterical neurosis* or *conversion reaction*.

Specific developmental disorder Problems in specific areas of development not due to another more general disorder such as retardation or autism. Examples are reading disorder, arithmetic disorder, inability to articulate certain sounds clearly.

Spectrum concept The idea that several differently classified disorders may be caused by the same general genetic pattern. These disorders are then considered genetically related.

Speedball Slang term for the injection of a combination of heroin and cocaine.

Spina bifida A condition in which the spinal cord does not close over the nerve column during the prenatal period. The amount of the spinal column that remains open determines how many nerves will be affected. This condition is often associated with an abnormal buildup of pressure of spinal fluid in the brain which can produce retardation unless it is surgically treated.

Splitting Term used to describe the inability of the borderline individual to integrate the positive and negative experiences he or she has with another individual into a coherent relationship.

Spontaneous remission Disappearance of symptoms or maladaptive behaviors in the absence of therapeutic intervention.

Spouse abuse Physical harm done to wives or husbands by their marital partners. Physical assaults by husbands on wives are most common. Abuse may also be psychological.

Squeeze technique Technique used in sex therapy to assist the male in retarding ejaculation by gently squeezing the end of the penis when ejaculation is imminent.

Stanford-Binet Modification of the Binet test developed at Stanford University by Louis Terman and which is the Binet format most often used in North America.

Stereotypy Development of a ritualized or highly repetitive behavior. Sometimes seen as a result of stress or of the use of certain drugs such as amphetamines.

STP (2, 5 dimethoxy-4-methyl amphetamine) Hallucinogenic agent similar to LSD.

Straight jacket Confining garment used to bind the arms tightly against the body. Often used for violent patients.

Stress Feeling or reaction individuals have when faced with a situation that demands action from them, especially action that may be beyond their capabilities.

Stressor Source of stress, pressure, or strain. Something that upsets the equilibrium of an organism.

Stroke See *cerebrovascular accident.*

Sublimation Defense mechanism and developmental concept which involves the refinement or redirection of undesirable impulses into new and more socially acceptable channels. Whereas displacement involves an alteration in choice of object, sublimation alters both the aim (unacceptable drive) and the object to a personally acceptable one.

Substance abuse Use of a psychoactive substance to the degree that a severe and long-lasting impairment in function results.

Substance dependence Category of disorder involving the use of mood- or behavior-modifying substances to the degree that physiological tolerance or withdrawal symptoms can be demonstrated.

Substance-induced organic mental disorder Result of direct effects on the central nervous system of mood- or behavior-modifying substances. Examples are intoxication or drug-withdrawal symptoms.

Substance-use disorder Condition in which regular use of one or more substances that affect the central nervous system produces clear effects in behavior or mood.

Sulci (singular: sulcus) Shallow valleys on the surface of the brain separating the convolutions.

Superego Structure of the psyche in psychoanalytic theory which is developed by internalization of parental standards and by identification with parents. Contains two parts: the ego-ideal and the conscience. The ego-ideal represents the total of positive identifications with accepting and loving parents and desired standards of excellence and good conduct. The conscience includes those attitudes and values which are moralistic (good-bad) in nature.

Support group Group of individuals with the same or similar problems who meet to discuss their problems and how they deal with them.

Supportive therapy Brief form of psychotherapy in which the therapist provides acceptance for the patient and affords him or her some opportunity to be dependent.

Survival guilt Feeling that it is unfair to be alive when others in the same situation have died. Overwhelming feelings of guilt, unworthiness, and helplessness.

Synapse Point at which a nerve impulse passes from an axon of one neuron to the dendrite of another neuron.

Synaptic vesicle Container on the axon terminal button that serves as a storage point for a chemical neurotransmitter.

Syndrome A group of symptoms that often appear together.

Syphilitic infection Chronic infectious venereal disease, transmitted through direct contact, caused by a spirochete, *Treponema pallidum.*

Systemic desensitization Learning-theory-based therapeutic technique in which a client is first trained in muscle relaxation and then imagines a series of increasingly anxiety-provoking situations until he or she no longer experiences anxiety while thinking about the stimuli. Learning principle involved is reciprocal inhibition, according to which two incompatible responses (e.g., anxiety and relaxation) cannot be made simultaneously by one person.

Systolic Term used to describe the blood pressure reading at the time the heart contracts to drive the blood through. Compare to *diastolic.*

Tactile Referring to the sense of touch.

Tangles Abnormal structure found in nerve cells of individuals who have Alzheimer's disease.

Tarantism Uncontrollable urge to dance, believed to be the result of the bite of a tarantula. This was frequent in Southern Italy from the fifteenth to seventeenth centuries.

Tardive dyskinesia Disorder involving uncontrolled body movements, often of the lips and tongue, that may result from treatment with antipsychotic drugs.

Tay-Sachs disease Inherited metabolic disorder, inevitably fatal, that causes progressive deterioration of the nervous system.

Technique factors The particular procedures used by a therapist in treating a client. Distinguished from the effects of the therapist's personality on the treatment.

Temporal lobe Part of the cerebral hemisphere lying behind the temples and below the lateral fissure in front of the occipital lobe.

Tension headache Probably the most common form of headache; characterized by bandlike pains and tender scalp. Gradual in onset and often longlasting. Thought to be a result of stress.

Tertiary prevention Efforts aimed at reducing the impairment that may result from a given disorder.

Test anxiety Unusually apprehensive response to evaluative situations. Often a factor in poor performance because of worry and interfering thoughts.

THC (tetrahydrocannabinol) Major active ingredient in marijuana.

Thematic Apperception Test (TAT) Projective test consisting of somewhat ambiguous pictures. Subject is asked to tell a story about each picture. From these stories personality dynamics are inferred.

Theoretical perspective The particular set of beliefs or ideas that determine what people notice in behavior, how they interpret what they observe, and how they believe problems should be approached.

Therapeutic interview Interaction between a client and therapist although perhaps including other family members as well. Designed to help promote change in behavior and attitudes.

Thorazine Trade name for chlorpromazine, one of a group of phenothiazine drugs used in the treatment of schizophrenia.

Thought stopping A cognitive technique that uses a specific command as a distraction to end a period of obsessive thinking.

Tic Involuntary, repetitive, rapid muscle contractions often occurring in the face. Thought to be related to tension and anxiety.

Tolerance (drug) Condition in which an individual must use increasing doses of a substance to produce the same physiological effect.

Tonic phase Phase of seizure in which the body is extended and stiff and during which reflexes to light and to pressure on the cornea are absent. See also *clonic phase.*

Tranquilizing drugs Drugs (for example, of the chlorpromazine and phenothiazine families) which are used to reduce agitation and anxiety. Drug action inhibits the activities of the hypothalamus.

Transference Psychoanalytic term that refers to the displacement of affect from one person to another. Patterns of feelings and behavior originally experienced with significant figures in childhood are displaced or attached to individuals in one's current relationships (e.g., a psychotherapist). Current person is reacted to as if he or she were some significant other from the respondent's past. Transference reactions may be positive or negative.

Translocation The breaking off of a piece of one chromosome and the attachment of that piece to another chromosome. May result in the transmission of too much genetic material to the child of a person with a translocation.

Transsexualism Intense desire or need to change one's sexual status, including anatomical structure.

Transvestism Sexual deviation in which an individual derives gratification from wearing the clothing of the opposite sex.

Traumatic neurosis Psychological symptoms that occur after a traumatic event but which are not a direct result of physical injury.

Trephination Process of making a circular hole in the skull. In early times this was done to allow evil spirits to escape.

Tricyclics Group of drugs used to treat depression. An example is Imipramine. Common trade names of tricyclic drugs are Tofranil and Elavil.

Trisomy Occurrence in an individual of three chromosomes of one kind rather than the usual pair. Usually associated with an abnormality of some type.

Trisomy 13 Presence of three number 13 chromosomes rather than the usual pair. Occurs in one of every 5000 births and causes severe mental retardation and a number of specific physical defects. Only about 18 percent of affected infants survive the first year.

Trisomy 18 Presence of three number 18 chromosomes rather than the usual pair. The next most common trisomy after trisomy 21. Occurs in one of every 3000 births. Most such infants die before birth; only 10 percent of those born alive survive to age 1. Results in severe retardation and many physical abnormalities.

Trisomy 21 See *Down syndrome.*

Tuberous sclerosis Disorder caused by a dominant gene and characterized by severe retardation, seizures, and the appearance of small, fibrous tumors.

Type-A behavior Term used to describe a personality type hypothesized to be heart-attack prone.

Type-B behavior Term used to describe people who do not show the characteristics of Type-A Personality. Type Bs are less pressured and hard driving than Type As.

Type I schizophrenia See *positive symptoms.*

Type II schizophrenia See *negative symptoms.*

Ulcer Sore on the skin or internal mucous tissue that results in the death of the tissue involved.

Ultrasound scan technique The use of sound waves to produce a visual image of a fetus or of the form and action of body organs. Also called *sonogram.*

Unauthentic behavior According to existentialist theory, that behavior governed not by an individual's desires but by the desires of other people.

Unconditional positive regard Term used by Carl Rogers to emphasize the importance of a therapist's unqualified acceptance of a client as a person of worth.

Unconditioned response (UR) In classical conditioning, the response that occurs automatically, before training, when the unconditioned stimulus is presented.

Unconditioned stimulus (US) In classical conditioning, the stimulus that automatically elicits the desired response before training has taken place.

Unconscious Out of awareness; mental contents that can be brought to awareness only with great difficulty (or not at all).

Undifferentiated type schizophrenia Clearly psychotic symptoms that either do not fit any of the other categories of schizophrenia or that meet the requirements for more than one category.

Undoing Defense mechanism aimed at negating or atoning for some disapproved impulse or act.

Uniplar disorder Term for an affective disorder in which only depression occurs and there is no history of episodes of mania.

Vaginal Pertaining to the vagina, the passage leading

from the external genital opening to the uterus in female mammals.

Vaginismus (functional) Type of sexual dysfunction in women in which an involuntary spasm of the muscles of the outer third of the vagina interferes with sexual activity.

Valium One of the minor tranquilizing drugs often prescribed to reduce anxiety.

Venereal disease Contagious disease for example, syphilis and gonorrhea, contracted through sexual intercourse.

Ventricles System of communicating cavities in the brain that are linked with the central canal of the spinal cord.

Verbal IQ One of the two subscores of the Wechsler intelligence test series. Tests reflect general information or knowledge and the ability to make abstractions.

Vicarious learning Learning that occurs merely by watching the behavior of others.

Voyeur One who practices voyeurism.

Voyeurism (scopophilia) Attaining sexual gratification from observing the sexual behavior of others. Synonymous with *peeping tomism*.

Vulnerability Tendency to react maladaptively, to be insufficiently defended especially in particular situations.

Wechsler tests (WAIS, WISC, WPPSI) Tests of intelligence for adults and children; composed of subtests that tap verbal and nonverbal aspects of intelligence.

Withdrawal Physiological changes, varying from mild to extremely unpleasant, that take place after an individual's discontinuation of a habit-forming substance. The symptoms of heroin withdrawal are perhaps best known.

Word association test Projective technique in which a list of words is presented one by one. Client is asked to respond to each item with the first word that comes to mind.

X-linked dominance Genes carried on the X sex chromosome that determine a characteristic by their presence. Females have two X chromosomes. Males have one X and one Y chromosome. This means that characteristics that are a result of X-linked dominance can occur in males only through inheritance from the mother. In females it can be inherited from either parent.

ABIKOFF, H., & GITTELMAN, R. 1984. Does behavior therapy normalize the classroom behavior of hyperactive children. *Archives of General Psychiatry, 41,* 449–454.

ABRAHAM, K. 1953. Contributions to the theory of the anal character (1921). In K. Abraham, *Selected papers on psychoanalysis.* New York: Basic Books.

ABRAHAM, K. 1968. Notes on the psychoanalytic investigation and treatment of manic-depressive insanity and allied conditions (1911). In K. Abraham, *Selected papers of Karl Abraham.* New York: Basic Books.

ABRAHAM, S. F., & BEAUMONT, P.J.V. 1982. How patients describe bulimia or binge-eating. *Psychological Medicine, 12,* 625–635.

ABRAMS, D. B., & WILSON, G. T. 1979. Effects of alcohol on social anxiety in women: Cognitive versus physiological processes. *Journal of Abnormal Psychology, 88,* 161–173

ABRAMS, S. 1973. The polygraph in a psychiatric setting. *American Journal of Psychiatry, 130,* 94–98.

ABRAMSON, L. Y., METALSKY, G. I., & ALLOY, L. B. (In press.) The hopelessness theory of depression: A metatheoretical analysis with implications for psychopathology research. *Psychological Review.*

ABRAMSON, L. Y., SELIGMAN, M.E.P., & TEASDALE, J. D. 1978. Learned helplessness in humans: Critique and reformulation. *Journal of Abnormal Psychology, 87,* 49–74.

ACHENBACH, T. M., & EDELBROCK, C. S. 1983. *Manual for the child behavior checklist and revised child behavior profile.* Burlington: University of Vermont.

ACHENBACH, T. M., McCONAUGHY, S. H., & HOWELL, C. T. 1987. Child/adolescent behavioral and emotional problems: Implications of cross-informant correlations for situational specificity. *Psychological Bulletin, 101,* 213–232.

ACKERMAN, S. H., MANAKER, S., & COHEN, M. I. 1981. Recent separation and the onset of peptic ulcer disease in older children and adolescents. *Psychosomatic Medicine, 43,* 305–310.

ADLER, G., & BYIE, D. 1979. Aloneness and borderline psychopathology: The possible relevance of child development issues. *International Journal of Psychoanalysis, 60,* 83–96.

ADOLPHI, M., ANGELO, C., MENGHI, P., & NICOLO-CORIGLIANO, A. 1983. *Behind the family mask: Therapeutic changes in rigid family systems.* New York: Brunner/Mazel.

AGETON, S. 1985. *Facts about sexual assault: A research report for teenagers.* Rockville, MD: U.S. Department of Health and Human Services.

AGRAS, W. S., TAYLOR, O. B., KRAEMER, H. C., ALLEN, R. A., & SCHNEIDER, M. S. 1980. Relaxation training: Twenty-four hour blood pressure reductions. *Archives of General Psychiatry, 37,* 859–863.

AIKEN, T. W., STUMPHAUZER, J. S., & VELOZ, E. V. 1977. Behavioral analysis of non-delinquent brothers in a high juvenile crime community. *Behavioral Disorders, 2,* 212–222.

AIMES, P. L., GELDER, M. G., & SHAWN, P. M. 1983. Social phobia: A comparative clinical study. *British Journal of Psychiatry, 141,* 174–179.

AKESSON, H. O. 1986. The biological origin of mild mental retardation. *Acta Psychiatrica Scandinavica, 74,* 3–7.

AKISKAL, H. S. 1985. Interaction of biologic and psychologic factors in the origin of depressive disorders. *Acta Psychiatrica Scandinavica,* Supplementum, No. 319, 131–139.

Alcohol and Health. 1987. Rockville, MD: National Institute of Alcohol Abuse and Alcoholism.

Alcoholism: An inherited disease. 1985. Rockville, MD: National Institute of Alcohol Abuse and Alcoholism.

ALDRICH, C. K. 1966. *An introduction to dynamic psychiatry.* New York: McGraw-Hill.

ALFORD, G. S. 1980. Alcoholics anonymous: An empirical outcome study. In W. R. Miller, ed., *Addictive behaviors,* vol. 5. Oxford: Pergamon Press.

ALLOY, L. B., & ABRAMSON, L. Y. 1979. Judgment of contingency of depressed and nondepressed students: Sadder but wiser. *Journal of Experimental Psychology, 108,* 441–485.

ALLSOP, D., KIDD, M., LANDON, M., & TOMLINSON, A. 1986. Isolated senile plaque cores in Alzheimer's disease and Down's syndrome show differences in morphology. *Journal of Neurology, Neurosurgery, and Psychiatry, 49,* 886–892.

ALTMAN, D. 1982. *The homosexualization of America.* Boston: Beacon Press.

AMBELAS, A. 1987. Life events and mania: A special relationship. *British Journal of Psychiatry, 150,* 235–240.

AMBELAS, A., & GEORGE, M. 1986. Predictability of course of illness in manic patients with positive life events. *Journal of Nervous and Mental Disease, 1974,* 693–695.

American Law Institute. 1962. *Model penal code: Proposed official draft.* Philadelphia: American Law Institute.

American Psychiatric Association. 1968. *Diagnostic and statistical manual of mental disorders,* 2nd ed. Washington, D.C.: American Psychiatric Association.

American Psychiatric Association. 1980. *Diagnostic and statis-*

tical manual of mental disorders, 3rd ed. Washington, D.C.: American Psychiatric Association.

American Psychiatric Association. 1987. *Diagnostic and statistical manual of mental disorders*, 3rd ed. revised. Washington, D.C.: American Psychiatric Association.

ANASTASI, A. 1988. *Psychological Testing.* New York: Macmillan.

ANDERSON, D. J., NOYES, R., Jr., & CROWE, R. R. 1984. A comparison of panic disorder and generalized anxiety disorder. *American Journal of Psychiatry, 141,* 572–575.

ANDERSON, E. A. 1987. Preoperative preparation for cardiac surgery facilitates recovery, reduces psychological distress, and reduces the incidence of acute postoperative hypertension. *Journal of Consulting and Clinical Psychology, 55,* 513–520.

ANDREASEN, N. C. 1988. Brain imaging: Applications in psychiatry. *Science, 239,* 1381–1388.

ANDREASEN, N. C., & GROVE, W. 1979. The relationship between schizophrenic language, manic language, and aphasia. In J. Gruzelier & P. Flor-Henry, eds., *Hemisphere symmetries of function in psychopathology.* Amsterdam: Elsevier/North Holland.

ANDREASEN, N. C., & GROVE, W. M. 1986. Thought, language, and communication in schizophrenia: Diagnosis and prognosis. *Schizophrenia Bulletin, 12,* 348–359.

ANDREASEN, N. C., & POWERS, P. S. 1975. Creativity and psychosis. *Archives of General Psychiatry, 32,* 70–73.

ANDREWS, S., VAUGHN, K., HARVEY, R., & ANDREWS, G. 1986. A survey of practising psychiatrist's view on the treatment of schizophrenia. *British Journal of Psychiatry, 149,* 357–364.

ANONYMOUS. 1965. A practicing psychiatrist: The experience of electroconvulsive therapy. *British Journal of Psychiatry, 111,* 365–367.

ANONYMOUS. 1977. Psychosocial implications of schizophrenic diagnoses (personal account). *Schizophrenia Bulletin, 3,* 4(b).

ANTHONY, E. J. 1975. The influences of a manic-depressive environment on the developing child. In E. J. Anthony & T. Benedek, eds., *Depression and human existence.* Boston: Little, Brown.

ANTHONY, E. J. 1977. Depression and children. In G. D. Burrow, ed., *Handbook of studies of depression.* Amsterdam: Excerpta Medica.

ANTHONY, J. C., FOLSTEIN, M., ROMANOSK, A. J., VON KORFF, M. R., NESTADT, G. R., CHAHAL, R., MERCHANT, A., BROWN, H., SHAPIROS, S., KRAMER, M., GRUENBERG, E. M. 1985. Comparison of the lay Diagnostic Interview Schedule and a standardized psychiatric diagnosis: Experience in Eastern Baltimore. *Archives of General Psychiatry, 42,* 667–675.

APA Task Force on Laboratory Tests in Psychiatry. 1987. The Dexamethasone Suppression Test: An overview of the current status in psychiatry. *American Journal of Psychiatry, 144,* 1253–1262.

ARIETI, S., & BEMPORAD, J. 1978. *Severe and mild depression.* New York: Basic Books.

ARONSON, T. A., & SHUKLA, S. 1987. Life events and relapse in bipolar disorder. The impact of a catastrophic event. *Acta Psychiatrica Scandinavica, 57,* 571–576.

ASAAD, G., & SHAPIRO, B. 1986. Hallucinations: Theoretical and clinical overview. *American Journal of Psychiatry, 143,* 1088–1097.

ASARNOW, J. R., & CALLAN, J. W. 1985. Boys with peer adjustment problems: Social cognitive processes. *Journal of Consulting and Clinical Psychology, 53,* 80–87.

ASARNOW, J. R., CARLSON, G. A., & GUTHRIE, D. 1987. Coping strategies, self-perceptions, hopelessness and perceived family environments in depressed and suicidal children. *Journal of Consulting and Clinical Psychology, 55,* 361–366.

AXLINE, V. M. 1947. *Play therapy: The inner dynamics of childhood.* Boston: Houghton Mifflin.

AYLLON, T., GARBER, S. W., & ALLISON, M. G. 1977. Behavioral treatment of childhood neurosis. *Psychiatry, 40,* 315–322.

ALLYON, T., SMITH, D., & RODGERS, M. 1970. Behavioral management of school phobia. *Journal of Behavior Therapy and Experimental Psychiatry, 1,* 124–138.

BANDURA, A. 1969. *Principles of behavior modification.* New York: Holt, Rinehart & Winston.

BANDURA, A. 1977. Self-efficacy: Toward a unifying theory of behavior change. *Psychological Review, 84,* 191–215.

BANDURA, A. 1978. The self-system in reciprocal determinism. *American Psychologist, 33,* 344–358.

BANDURA, A. 1982. Self-efficacy mechanism in human agency. *American Psychologist, 37,* 122–147.

BANDURA, A. 1986. *Social foundations of thought and action: A social cognitive theory.* Englewood Cliffs, NJ: Prentice Hall.

BANDURA, A., & MENLOVE, F. L. 1968. Factors determining vicarious extinction of avoidance behavior through symbolic modeling. *Journal of Personality and Social Psychology, 8,* 99–108.

BANNON, N. J., & ROTH, R. H. 1983. Pharmacology of mesocortical dopamine neurons. *Pharmacological Reviews, 35(1),* 53–68.

BARD, M. 1970. Alternatives to traditional law enforcement. In F. Korten, S. W. Cook, & J. I. Lacey, eds., *Psychology and the problems of society.* Washington, D.C.: American Psychological Association, 128–132.

BARDEN, H. S., KESSEL, R. & SCHUETT, V. E. 1984. The costs and benefits of screening for PKU in Wisconsin. *Social Biology, 31,* 1–17.

BAREFOOT, J. C., SIEGLER, I. C., NOWLING, J. B., PETERSON, B. L., HANEY, T. L., & WILLIAMS, R. B., Jr. 1987. Suspiciousness, health, and mortality: A follow-up study of 500 older adults. *Psychosomatic Medicine, 49,* 450–457.

BARKER, C., & LEMLE, R. 1984. The helping process in couples. *American Journal of Community Psychology, 12,* 321–326.

BARLOW, D. H., DiNARDO, P. A., VERMILYEA, B. B., VERMILYEA, J., & BLANCHARD, E. B. 1986. Co-morbidity and depression among the anxiety disorders: Issues in diagnosis and classification. *Journal of Nervous and Mental Disease, 174,* 63–72.

BARNES, G. M. 1984. *Alcohol use among secondary school students in New York State.* Buffalo: Research Institute on Alcoholism.

BARON, M., RISCH, N., HAMBORGER, R., MANDEL, B., KOSHNER, S., NEWMAN, M., DRUMER, D., & BELMAKER, R. H. 1987. Genetic linkage between X-chromosome markers and bipolar affective illness. *Nature, 326,* 289–292.

BARON, M., & RISCH, N. 1987. The spectrum concept of schizophrenia: Evidence for a genetic-environmental continuum. *Journal of Psychiatric Research, 21,* 257–267.

BARRETT, D., & FINE, H. 1980. A child was being beaten: The therapy of battered children as adults. *Psychotherapy: Theory, Research and Practice, 17,* 285–293.

BARTAK, L., RUTTER, M., & COX, M. 1975. A comparative study of infantile autism and specific developmental receptive language disorder. I. The children. *British Journal of Psychiatry, 126,* 127–145.

BARTROP, R. W., LUCKHURST, E., LAZARUS, L., KILOH, L. G., & PENNY, R. 1977. Depressed lymphocyte function after bereavement. *Lancet, 1,* 834–836.

BATEMAN, A. W. 1986. Rape: The forgotten victim. *British Medical Journal, 292,* 1306.

BAUER, R. B., STEVENS, C., REVENO, W. S., & ROSENBAUM, H. 1982. L-Dopa treatment of Parkinson's disease: A ten year follow-up study. *Journal of the American Geriatric Society, 30,* 322–325.

BAYER, R., & SPITZER, R. L. 1985. Neurosis, Psychodynamics, and DSM-III. *Archives of General Psychiatry, 42,* 187–195.

BEATRICE, J. 1985. A psychological comparison of heterosexuals, transvestites, preoperative transsexuals, and post operative transsexuals. *Journal of Nervous and Mental Disease, 173,* 358–365.

BECK, A. T. 1967. *Depression: Clinical, experimental and theoretical aspects.* New York: Hoeber.

BECK, A. T. 1970. Role of fantasies in psychotherapy and psychopathology. *Journal of Nervous and Mental Disease, 150,* 3–17.

BECK, A. T. 1976. *Cognitive therapy and the emotional disorders.* New York: International Universities Press.

BECK, A. T., BROWN, G., STEER, R. A., EIDELSON, J. I., & RISKIND, J. H. 1987. Differentiating anxiety and depression: A test of the cognitive content-specificity hypothesis. *Journal of Abnormal Psychology, 96,* 179–183.

BECK, A. T., & EMERY, G. 1985. *Anxiety disorders and phobias: A cognitive perspective.* New York: Basic Books.

BECK, A. T., KOVACS, M., & WEISSMAN, A. 1979. Assessment of suicidal ideation: The scale for suicide ideation. *Journal of Consulting and Clinical Psychology, 47,* 343–352.

BECK, A. T., RUSH, A. J., SHAW, B., & EMERY, G. 1979. *Cognitive therapy of depression.* New York: Guilford.

BECK, A. T., STEER, R. A., KOVACS, M., & GARRISON, B. 1985. Hopelessness and eventual suicide: A ten year prospective study of patients hospitalized with suicidal ideation. *American Journal of Psychiatry, 175,* 559–563.

BECK, J. G., & BARLOW, D. H. 1984. Current conceptualizations of sexual dysfunction: A review and an alternative perspective. *Clinical Psychology Review, 4,* 363–378.

BEERS, C. 1908. *A mind that found itself.* Garden City, NY: Doubleday.

BEISER, M., SHORE, J. H., PETERS, R., & TATUM, E. 1985. Does community care for the mentally ill make a difference? A tale of two cities. *American Journal of Psychiatry, 142,* 1047–1105.

BEITCHMAN, J. H. 1983. Childhood schizophrenia: A review and comparison with adult onset schizophrenia. *Psychiatric Journal of the University of Ottawa, 8,* 25–37.

BELL, A. P., & WEINBERG, M. S. 1978. *Homosexualities: A study of diversity among men and women.* New York: Simon & Schuster.

BELL, A. P., WEINBERG, M. S., & HAMMERSMITH, S. F. 1981. *Sexual preference.* Bloomington: Indiana University Press.

BELLACK, A. S., & MUESER, K. T. 1986. A comprehensive treatment program for schizophrenia and chronic mental illness. Special Issue: Systems aspects of chronic mental illness. *Community Mental Health, 22,* 175–189.

BEMPORAD, J. R. 1983. Cognitive, affective and psychologic changes in the depressed process. *Journal of the American Academy of Psychoanalysis, 11,* 159–172.

BENDER, L. 1938. A visual motor Gestalt test and its clinical use. *American Orthopsychiatric Association, Research Monographs, No. 3.*

BENSON, H. 1977. Systemic hypertension and the relaxation response. *New England Journal of Medicine, 296,* 1152–1156.

BENTLER, P. M., & PRINCE, C. 1969. Personality characteristics of male transvestites. *Journal of Abnormal Psychology, 74,* 140–143.

BERGIN, A. E., & LAMBERT, M. J. 1978. The evaluation of therapeutic outcomes. In S. L. Garfield, & A. E. Bergin, eds., *Handbook of psychotherapy and behavior change,* 2nd ed. New York: John Wiley.

BERKE, J., & HERNTON, C. 1974. *The cannabis experience.* London: Peter Owen.

BERRY, P., GROENEWEG, G., GIBSON, D., & BROWN, R. I. 1984. Mental development of adults with Down syndrome. *American Journal of Mental Deficiency, 89,* 252–256.

BEUTLER, L. E., CRAGO, M., & ARIZMENDI, T. G. 1986. Therapist variables in psychotherapy process and outcome. In S. L. Garfield & A. E. Bergin, eds., *Handbook of psychotherapy and behavior change,* 3rd ed. NY: John Wiley.

BIEBER, I. 1980. *Cognitive psychoanalysis.* New York: Jason Aronson.

BIEBER, I., DAIN, H. J., DINCE, P. R., DRELLICH, M. G., GRAND, H. G., GUNDLACH, R. H., KREMER, M. W., RIFKIN, A. H., WILBER, C. B., & BEIBER, T. B. 1962. *Homosexuality: A psychoanalytic study.* New York: Basic Books.

BLACK, D. W., WARRACK, G., & WINOKUR, G. 1985. The Iowa Record-Linkage Study: II. Excess mortality among patients with organic mental disorders. *Archives of General Psychiatry, 42,* 78–81.

BLACK, D. W., YATES, W. R., & ANDREASEN, N. C. 1988. Schizophrenia, schizophreniform disorder, and delusional paranoid disorders. In J. A. Talbott, R. E. Hales, & S. C. Yudofsky, eds., *Textbook of psychiatry.* Washington, D.C.: American Psychiatric Press.

BLANCHARD, E. B., ANDRASIC, F., NEFF, D. F., ARENA, J. G., AHLES, T. A., JURISH, S. E., PALLMEYER, T. P., SAUNDERS, N. L., & TEDERS, S. J. 1982. Biofeedback and relaxation training with three kinds of headache: Treatment effects and their prediction. *Journal of Consulting and Clinical Psychology, 50,* 562–575.

BLAZER, D., HUGHES, D., & GEORGE, L. D. 1987. Stressful life events and the onset of a generalized anxiety syndrome. *American Journal of Psychiatry, 144,* 1178–1183.

BLEULER, E. 1950. *Dementia praecox or the group of schizophrenias (1911)* (J. Zinkin, trans.). New York: International Universities Press.

BLEULER, M. 1972. *The schizophrenic psychoses in the light of long-term case and family histories.* Stuttgart: Georg Thieme Verlag.

BLEULER, M. 1978. *The schizophrenic disorders: Long term patient and family studies.* New Haven: Yale University Press.

BLOOM, B., HODGES, W., & CALDWELL, R. 1982. A preventive program for the newly separated: Initial evaluation. *American Journal of Community Psychology, 10,* 251–264.

BLUMSTEIN, P. W., & SCHWARTZ, P. 1976. Bisexuality in women. *Archives of Sexual Behavior, 5,* 171–181.

BLUMSTEIN, P. W., & SCHWARTZ, P. 1977. Bisexuality: Some social psychological issues. *Journal of Social Issues, 33(2),* 30–45.

BLUMSTEIN, P. W., & SCHWARTZ, P. 1983. *American Couples.* New York: William Morrow.

BOHMAN, M., CLONINGER, C. R., SIGVARDSSON, S., & VON KNORRING, A. L. 1982. Predisposition to petty criminality of Swedish adoptees I. Genetic and Rh environmental heterogencity. *Archives of General Psychiatry, 39,* 1233–1241.

BOOR, M. 1982. The multiple personality epidemic. *Journal of Nervous and Mental Disease, 170,* 302–304.

BOUSHA, D. M., & TWENTYMAN, C. T. 1984. Mother-child interactional style in abuse, neglect, and control groups: Naturalistic observations in the home. *Journal of Abnormal Psychology, 93,* 106–114.

BOWER, G. H. 1981. Mood and memory. *American Psychologist, 36,* 129–148.

BOWERS, K. S., & MEICHENBAUM, D., eds. 1985. *The unconscious reconsidered.* New York: Wiley Interscience.

BOWLBY, J. 1973. *Separation: Anxiety and anger.* New York: Basic Books.

BOWLEY, J. 1980. *Loss, sadness, and depression.* New York: Basic Books.

BOZETT, F. W. 1981. Gay fathers: Evolution of the gay-father identity. *American Journal of Orthopsychiatry, 51,* 552–559.

BRADLEY, T. B. 1983. Remediation of cognitive deficits: A critical appraisal of the Feuerstein model. *Journal of Mental Deficiency Research, 27,* 79–92.

BRAUN, B. G. (1983). Neurophysic changes in multiple personality due to integration: A preliminary report. *American Journal of Clinical Hypnosis, 26,* 84–92.

BRAUN, B. G. 1984. Toward a theory of multiple personality and other dissociative phenomena. *Psychiatric Clinics of North America, 7,* 171–193.

BRECHER, E. M., & Consumer Reports Books' Editors. 1983. *Love, sex, and aging: A Consumer Union report.* Boston: Little Brown.

BRENNAN, T. 1982. Loneliness at adolescence. In L. A. Peplau & D. Perlman, eds., *Loneliness: A source book of current theory, research and therapy.* New York: John Wiley, 219–290.

BRENNAN, T., & AUSLANDER, N. 1979. *Adolescent loneliness: An exploratory study of social and psychological pre-dispositions and theory,* vol. 1. Boulder, CO: Behavioral Research Laboratory.

BRENNER, M. H. 1973. *Mental illness and the economy.* Cambridge, MA: Harvard University Press.

BRESLOW, N., EVANS, L., & LANGLEY, J. 1985. On the prevalence and roles of females in the sadomasochistic subculture: Report of an empirical study. *Archives of Sexual Behavior, 14,* 303–317.

BRESLOW, N., EVANS, L., & LANGLEY, J. 1986. Comparisons among heterosexual, bisexual, and homosexual male sadomasochists. *Journal of Homosexuality, 13,* 83–107.

BREZNITZ, S. 1988. The seven kinds of denial. In C. D. Spielberger, I. G. Sarason, & P. B. Defares, eds., *Stress and Anxiety,* vol. 11. Washington, D.C.: Hemisphere, 73–90.

BRIER, N. 1986. The mildly retarded adolescent: A psychosocial perspective. *Developmental and Behavioral Pediatrics, 7,* 320–323.

BRODY, G. H., & STONEMAN, Z. 1984. Children with atypical siblings. In B. B. Lahey & A. E. Kazdin, eds. *Advances in child clinical psychology,* vol. 6. New York: Plenum.

BRODY, J. E. 1984. Autoerotic death of youths causes widening concern. *New York Times,* March 27, 17, 20.

BROGA, M. I., & NEUFELD, R. W. 1981. Multivariate cognitive performance variables and response styles among paranoid and nonparanoid schizophrenics. *Journal of Abnormal Psychology, 90,* 495–509.

BROWN, G., & HARRIS, T. 1978. *Social origins of depression: A study of psychiatric disorder in women.* New York: Free Press.

BROWN, G. W., HARRIS, T., & COPELAND, J. R. 1977. Depression and loss. *British Journal of Psychiatry, 130,* 1–18.

BROWN, R. T., BORDEN, K. A., & CLINGERMAN, S. R. 1984. Adherence to methylphenidate therapy in a pediatric popu-lation: A preliminary investigation. Paper presented at the meeting of the NIMH New Clinical Drug Evaluation Unit Program. Key Biscayne, FL.

BROWN, W. T., JENKINS, E. C., COHEN, I. L., FISCH, G. S., WOLF-SCHEIN, E. G., GROSS, A., WATERHOUSE, L., FEIN, D., MASON-BROTHERS, A., RITVO, E., RUTTENBERG, B. A., BENTLEY, W., & CASTELLS, S. 1986. Fragile X and autism: A multicenter survey. *American Journal of Medical Genetic, 23,* 341–352.

BROWNE, A., & FINKELHOR, D. 1986. Impact of child sexual abuse: A review of research. *Psychological Bulletin, 99,* 66–77.

BROWNELL, K. D., HAYES, S. C., & BARLOW, D. H. 1977. Patterns of appropriate and deviant sexual arousal: The behavioral treatment of multiple sexual deviations. *Journal of Consulting and Clinical Psychology, 45,* 1144–1155.

BROWNELL, K. D., MARLATT, G. A., LICHTENSTEIN, E., & WILSON, G. T. 1986. Understanding and preventing relapse. *American Psychologist, 41,* 794–805.

BUCHANAN, A., & OLIVER, J. F. 1977. Abuse and neglect as a cause of mental retardation. *British Journal of Psychology, 131,* 458–467.

BUCHSBAUM, M. S. 1986. Brain imaging in the search for biological markers in affective disorder. *Journal of Clinical Psychiatry, 47,* 7–10.

BUCHSBAUM, M. S., & HAIER, R. J. 1987. Functional and anatomical brain imaging: Impact on schizophrenia research. *Schizophrenia Bulletin, 13,* 115–132.

BURGESS, A. W., & BALDWIN, B. A. 1981. *Crisis intervention: Theory and practice.* Englewood Cliffs, NJ: Prentice-Hall.

BURNSIDE, J. W. 1987. The diary. *Journal of the American Medical Association, 257,* 1802.

CADORET, R. J. 1986. Adoption studies: Historical and methodological critique. *Psychiatric Developments, 1,* 45–64.

CALEV, A. 1984. Recall and recognition in chronic nondemented schizophrenics: Use of matched tasks. *Journal of Abnormal Psychology, 93,* 172–177.

CAMERON, N. 1963. *Personality development and psychopathology.* Boston: Houghton Mifflin.

CAMPBELL, S. S., & GILLIN, J. C. 1987. Sleep measures in depression: How specific? *Psychiatric Annals, 17,* 647–653.

CANCRO, R. 1985. Schizophrenic disorders. In H. I. Kaplan & B. J. Sadock, eds. *Comprehensive textbook of psychiatry,* 4th ed., vol. I. Baltimore: Williams & Wilkins.

CAPUTO, P. A. 1977. *A rumor of war.* New York: Holt, Rinehart & Winston.

CAREY, G., & GOTTESMAN, I. I. 1981. Twin and family studies of anxiety, phobic, and obsessive disorders. In D. F. Klein & J. Rabkin, eds., *Anxiety: New research and changing concepts.* New York: Raven Press, 117–136.

CARPENTER, W. T., JR., HEINRICHS, D. W., & ALPHS, L. D. 1985. Treatment of negative symptoms. *Schizophrenia Bulletin, 11,* 440–452.

CARPENTER, W. T., JR., SACKS, M. H., STRAUSS, J. S., BARTKO, J. J., & RAYNER, J. 1976. Evaluating signs and symptoms: Comparisons of structured interview and clinical approaches. *British Journal of Psychiatry, 128,* 397–403.

CARROLL, B. J. 1985. Dexamethasone Suppression Test: A review of contemporary confusion. *Journal of Clinical Psychiatry, 46,* 13–24.

CARROL, K., & LEON, G. R. 1981. The bulimia-vomiting disorder within a generalized substance abuse pattern. Paper presented at the 15th Annual Convention of the Association for the Advancement of Behavior Therapy, Toronto.

CASPER, R. C., & DAVIS, J. M. 1977. On the course of anorexia nervosa. *American Journal of Psychiatry, 134,* 974–978.

CAUTELA, J. R. 1985. Covert modeling. In A. S. Bellack & M. Hersen, eds., *Dictionary of behavior therapy techniques.* New York: Pergamon.

CHALKLEY, A. J., & POWELL, G. E. 1983. The clinical description of forty-eight cases of sexual fetishisms. *British Journal of Psychiatry, 142,* 292–295.

CHAMBERS, W. J., PUIG-ANTICH, J., HIRSCH, M., PAEZ, P., AMBROSINI, P. J., TABRIZI, M. A., & DAVIES, M. 1985. The assessment of affective disorders in children and adolescents by semistructured interview. *Archives of General Psychiatry, 42,* 696–702.

CHANDLER, C. L. WEISSBERG, R. P., COWEN, E. L., & GUARE, J. 1984. Long-term effects of a school-based secondary prevention program for young maladapting children. *Journal of Consulting and Clinical Psychology, 52,* 165–170.

CHARNEY, D. S., MENKES, D. B., & HENINGER, G. R. 1981. Receptor sensitivity and the mechanism of action of antidepressant treatment. *Archives of General Psychiatry, 38,* 1160–1180.

CHESNEY, M. A., & ROSENMAN, R. H., eds. 1985. *Anger and hostility in cardiovascular and behavioral disorders.* Washington, D.C.: Hemisphere.

CHESS, S. 1978. The plasticity of human development. *American Academy of Child Psychiatry, 17,* 80–91.

CHESS, S., THOMAS, A., & HASSIBI, M. 1983. Depression in childhood and adolescence: A prospective study of six cases. *Journal of Nervous and Mental Disease, 171,* 411–420.

CHRISTENSEN, H., HADZI-PAVLOVIC, D., ANDREWS, G., & MATTICK, R. 1987. Behavior therapy and tricyclic medication in the treatment of obsessive-compulsive disorder: A quantitative review. *Journal of Consulting and Clinical Psychology, 55,* 701–711.

CLARK, D. C., CLAYTON, P. J., ANDREASON, N. C., LEWIS, D., FAWCETT, J., & SCHEFTNER, W. A. 1985. Intellectual functioning and abstraction ability in major affective disorders. *Comprehensive Psychiatry, 26,* 313–325.

CLARK, K. A. 1965. A role for librarians in the relevant war against poverty. Wilson Library Bulletin, Sept. 1965 (Quoted in A. MacLeod, *Growing up in America.*) Rockville, MD: National Institute of Mental Health.

CLARKE, A. M., & CLARKE, A.D.D. 1979. *Early experience: Myths and evidence.* New York: Free Press.

CLAUSEN, J. A. 1987. Health and the life course: Some personal observations. *Journal of Health and Social Behavior, 28,* 337–344.

CLECKLEY, H. 1964. *The mask of sanity,* 4th ed. St. Louis: Mosby.

CLEMENS, S. (Mark Twain) 1923. *Huckleberry Finn.* New York: Harper & Row.

CLONINGER, C. R., BOHMAN, M., & SIGVARDSSON, S. 1981. Inheritance of alcohol abuse. *Archives of General Psychiatry, 38,* 861–868.

COHEN, D. J., CAPARULO, B. K., & SHAYWITZ, B. A. 1978. Neurochemical and developmental models of childhood autism. In G. Serban, ed., *Cognitive defects in the development of mental illness.* New York: Brunner/Mazel.

COHEN, L. H. 1988. *Life events and psychological functioning: Theoretical and methodological issues.* Newbury Park, CA: Sage.

COHEN, R. A. 1975. Manic-depressive illness. In A. M. Freedman, J. I. Kaplan, & B. J. Sadock, *Comprehensive textbook of psychiatry,* 2nd ed. Baltimore, MD: Williams & Wilkins.

COLE, N. 1985. Sex therapy—a critical appraisal. *British Journal of Psychiatry, 147,* 337–351.

COLEMAN, E. 1981–1982. Developmental stages of the coming out process. *Journal of Homosexuality, 7(2/3),* 31–43.

COOPER, J., & SARTORIUS, M. 1977. Cultural and temporal variations in schizophrenia: A speculation on the importance of industrialization. *British Journal of Psychiatry, 130,* 50–55.

COOPER, W. H. 1981. Ubiquitous halo. *Psychological Bulletin, 90,* 218–244.

CORNBLATT, B. A., & ERLENMEYER-KIMLING, L. 1985. Global attentional deviance as a marker of risk for schizophrenia: Specificity and predictive validity. *Journal of Abnormal Psychology, 94,* 470–486.

CORSON, S. A., CORSON, E. O., ARNOLD, L. E., & KNOPP, W. 1976. Animal models of violence and hyperkinesis. In G. Serban & A. Kling, eds. *Animal models in human psychology.* New York: Plenum.

Council on Scientific Affairs, American Medical Association. 1986. Alcohol and the driver. *Journal of the American Medical Association, 255,* 522–527.

Council on Scientific Affairs, American Medical Association. 1986. Polygraph. *Journal of the American Medical Association, 256,* 1172–1175.

Council on Scientific Affairs. 1987. Fundamentals of magnetic resonance imaging. *Journal of the American Medical Association, 258,* 3417–3423.

Council on Scientific Affairs. 1987. Aversion therapy. *Journal of the American Medical Association, 258,* 2562–2566.

COWEN, E. L. 1982. Help is where you find it: Four informal helping groups. *American Psychologist, 37,* 385–395.

COWEN, E. L. 1985. Person-centered approaches to primary prevention in mental health: Situation-focused and competence enhancement. *American Journal of Community Psychology, 13,* 31–48.

COYLE, J. T., PRICE, D.I.C., & DELONG, M. R. 1983. Alzheimer's disease: A disorder of cortical cholinergic innervation. *Science, 219,* 1184–1190.

COYNE, J. C., KAHN, J., & GOTLIB, I. H. 1987. Depression. In T. Jacob, ed., *Family interaction and psychopathology.* New York: Pergamon.

CRAIG, E. M., & MCCARVER, R. B. 1984. Community placement and adjustment of deinstitutionalized clients: Issues and findings. *International Review of Research in Mental Retardation, 12,* 95–122.

CREESE, I., BURT, D. R., & SNYDER, S. H. 1976. Dopamine receptor binding predicts clinical and pharmacological potencies of antischizophrenic drugs. *Science, 192,* 481–483.

CRISP, A. H., & BURNS, T. 1983. The clinical presentation of anorexia nervosa in the male. *International Journal of Eating Disorders, 2,* 5–10.

CROOK, T., & ELIOT, J. 1980. Parental death during childhood and adult depression: A critical review of the literature. *Psychological Bulletin, 87,* 252–259.

CROW, T. J. 1980. Positive and negative schizophrenia symptoms and the role of dopamine. *British Journal of Psychiatry, 137,* 383–386.

CROW, T. J. 1985. The two syndrome concept: Origins and current status. *Schizophrenia Bulletin, 11,* 471–486.

CROWE, M. J., GILLAN, P., & GOLOMBOK, S. 1981. Form and content in the conjoint treatment of sexual dysfunction: A controlled study. *Behaviour Research and Therapy, 19,* 47–54.

CUMMINGS, E. M., IANNOTTI, R. J., & ZAHN-WAXLER, C. 1985. Influence of conflict between adults on the emotions and aggression of young children. *Developmental Psychology,* 21, 495–507.

CUMMINGS, J. L., & ZARIT, J. M. 1987. Probable Alzheimer's disease in an artist. *Journal of the American Medical Association,* 258, 2731–2734.

CURRAN, J. P., & MONTI, P. M., eds. 1982. *Social skills training: A practical handbook for assessment and treatment.* New York: Guilford.

CUSTANCE, J. 1952. *Wisdom, madness and folly.* New York: Pelligrini & Cuddahy.

CUTRONA, C. E., RUSSELL, D. W., & PEPLAU, L. A. 1979. *Loneliness and the process of social adjustment: A longitudinal study.* Paper presented at the American Psychological Association, New York.

CZEISLER, C. A., WEITZMAN, G. D., MOORE-EDE, M. C., ZIMMERMAN, J. C., & KNAUER, R. S. 1980. Human sleep: Its duration and organization depend on its circadian phase. *Science,* 210, 1264–1267.

DARLING, C. A., KALLEN, D. J., & VANDUSEN, J. E. 1984. Sex in transition, 1900–1980. *Journal of Youth and Adolescence,* 13(5), 385–399.

DAVENPORT, Y. B., ADLAND, M. L., GOLD, P. W., & GOODWIN, F. K. 1979. Manic-depressive illness: Psychodynamic features of multigenerational families. *American Journal of Orthopsychiatry,* 49, 24–35.

DAVIS, G. E., & LEITENBERG, H. 1987. Adolescent sex offenders. *Psychological Bulletin,* 101, 417–427.

DAVIS, J. M. 1985. Antipsychotic drugs. In H. I. Kaplan & B. J. Sadock, eds. *Comprehensive textbook of psychiatry,* 4th ed., vol. 2. Baltimore, MD: Williams & Wilkins.

DAWSON, M. E., & NUECHTERLEIN, K. H. 1987. The role of autonomic dysfunctions within a vulnerability: Stress model of schizophrenic disorders. In D. Magnusson and A. Ohman, eds., *Psychopathology: An interactional perspective.* New York: Academic Press.

DAYEE, F. S. 1982. *Private zones.* Edmonds, WA: Charles Franklin Press.

DELUTY, R. H. 1988–89. Physical illness, psychiatric illness and the acceptability of suicide. *Omega: The Journal of Death and Dying,* 1, 79–91.

DEMOS, J. P. 1982. *Entertaining Satan: Witchcraft and the culture of early New England.* New York: Oxford University Press.

DE NIKE, L. D., & TIBER, N. 1968. Neurotic behavior. In P. London & D. Rosenham, eds., *Foundations of abnormal psychology.* New York: Holt, Rinehart & Winston.

DERRY, P. A., & KUIPER, N. A. 1981. Schematic processing and self reference in clinical depression. *Journal of Abnormal Psychology,* 90, 286–297.

DETTERMAN, D. K. 1987. Theoretical notions of intelligence and mental retardation. *American Journal of Mental Deficiency,* 92, 2–11.

DEUTSCH, A. 1948. *The shame of the states.* New York: Arno.

DEUTSCH, S. I., & DAVIS, K. L. 1983. Schizophrenia: A review of diagnostic and biological issues. II. Biological issues. *Hospital and Community Psychiatry,* 34, 423–437.

DEYKIN, E. Y., & MACMAHON, B. 1979. The incidence of seizures among children with autistic symptoms. *American Journal of Psychiatry,* 136, 1310–1312.

DIAMOND, E. L. 1982. The role of anger and hostility in essential hypertension and coronary heart disease. *Psychological Bulletin,* 92, 410–433.

DIDION, J. 1979. *The white album.* New York: Simon & Schuster.

DIGDON, N., & GOTLIB, I. H. 1985. Developmental considerations in the study of childhood depression. *Developmental Review,* 5, 162–199.

DIMSDALE, J. E. 1988. A perspective on Type A behavior and coronary disease. *New England Journal of Medicine,* 318, 110–112.

DODGE, K. A. 1985. Attributional bias in aggressive children. *Advances in Cognitive Behavioral Research and Therapy,* 4, 73–110.

DOHRENWEND, B. P., & DOHRENWEND, B. S. 1982. Perspectives on the past and future of psychiatric epidemiology. *American Journal of Public Health,* 72, 1271–1279.

DOLLARD, J., & MILLER, N. 1950. *Personality and psychotherapy.* New York: McGraw-Hill.

DORIAN, B., & GARFINKEL, P. E. 1987. Stress, immunity and illness—a review. *Psychological Medicine,* 17, 393–407.

DOUGLAS, W. O. 1974. *Go east, young man.* New York: Random House.

DREWNOWSKI, A., YEE, D., & KRAHN, D. 1987. *Bulimia on campus: Incidence and recovery role.* Paper presented at the American Psychiatric Association, Chicago.

DUNNER, D. L. 1987. Stability of Bipolar II affective disorder as a diagnostic entity. *Psychiatric Annals,* 17, 18–20.

DULCAN, M. K. 1986. Comprehensive treatment of children and adolescents with attention deficit disorders: The state of the art. *Clinical Psychology Review,* 6, 539–569.

EASTON, K. 1959. An unusual case of fugue and orality. *Psychoanalytic Quarterly,* 28, 505–513.

EATON, W. W., HOLZER, C. E., III, VON KORFF, M., ANTHONY, J. C., HELZER, J. E., GEORGE, L., BURNAM, M. A., BOYD, J. H., KESSLER, L. G., & LOCKE, B. Z. 1984. The design of the epidemiologic catchment area surveys. *Archives of General Psychiatry,* 41, 942–948.

EBERHARDY, F. 1967. The view from "the couch." *Journal of Child Psychology and Psychiatry,* 8, 257–263.

ECKARDT, M. J., HARFORD, T. C., KAELBER, C. T., PARKER, E. S., ROSENTHAL, L. S., RYBACK, R. S., SALMOIRAGHI, G. C., VANDERVEEN, E., & WARREN, K. R. 1981. Health hazards associated with alcohol consumption. *Journal of the American Medical Association,* 246, 648–666.

EGELAND, J. A., GERHARD, D. S., PAULS, D. L., SUSSEX, J. N., KIDD, K. K., ALLEN, C. R., HOSTETTER, A. M., & HOUSMAN, D. E. 1987. Bipolar affective disorders linked to DNA markers on chromosome II. *Nature,* 325, 783–787.

EICHENWALD, K. 1987. Braving epilepsy's storm. *New York Times Magazine,* January 11, 30–36.

EISENSON, J. 1973. *Adult aphasia: Assessment and treatment.* Englewood Cliffs, NJ: Prentice-Hall.

EISLER, R. M. 1972. Crisis intervention in the family of a firesetter. *Psychotherapy: Theory, research and practice,* 9, 76–79.

ELDRED, S. H., BELL, N. W., LONGABAUGH, R., & SHERMAN, L. J. 1964. Interactional correlates of chronicity in schizophrenia. *Psychiatric Research Report 19,* December 1–12. Washington, D.C.: American Psychiatric Association.

ELIOT, R. S., & BUELL, J. C. 1983. The role of the CNS in cardiovascular disorders. *Hospital Practice,* May, 189–199.

ELKINS, R., RAPOPORT, J., & LIPSKY, A. 1980. Childhood obsessive-compulsive disorder: A neurobiological perspective. *Journal of the American Academy of Child Psychiatry,* 19, 551–554.

ELLENBERGER, H. F. 1970. *The discovery of the unconscious.* New York: Basic Books.

ELLIS, A. 1962. *Reason and emotion in psychotherapy.* New York: Lyle Stuart.

ELLIS, A. 1970. Rational-emotive therapy. In L. Hersher, ed., *Four psychotherapies*. New York: Appleton-Century-Crofts.

ELLIS, E. M., ATKESON, B. M., & CALHOUN, K. S. 1981. An assessment of long-term reaction to rape. *Journal of Abnormal Psychology*, 90, 263–266.

ELMADJIAN, E. 1963. Excretion and metabolism effect in the epinephrine and norepinephrine in various emotional states. *Proceedings of the Fifth Pan-American Conference of Endocrinology*, Lima, Peru.

ENDLER, N. S. 1982. *Holiday of darkness*. New York: Wiley-Interscience.

ENGEL, G. L. 1977. The need for a new medical model: A challenge for biomedicine. *Science*, 196, 129–136.

ERDELYI, M. 1985. *Psychoanalysis: Freud's cognitive psychology*. New York: W. H. Freeman.

ERICKSON, M. F., & EGELAND, B. 1987. A developmental view of the psychological consequences of maltreatment. *School Psychology Review*, 16, 156–168.

ERIKSON, E. H. 1975. *Life history and the historical moment*. New York: W. W. Norton.

ERLENMEYER-KIMLING, L., & CORNBLATT, B. 1987. High risk research in schizophrenia: A summary of what has been learned. *British Journal of Psychiatry*, 21, 401–411.

ERON, L. D. 1987. The development of aggressive behavior from the perspective of a developing behaviorism. *American Psychologist*, 42, 435–442.

ERON, L. D., & Peterson, R. A 1982. Abnormal behavior: Social approaches. In M. R. Rosenzweig & L. W. Porter, eds., *Annual Review of Psychology*. Palo Alto, CA: Annual Reviews.

ESMAN, A. H. 1986. Dependent and passive-aggressive personality disorders. In R. Michels and J. O. Cavenar, Jr., eds., *Psychiatry*, vol. 1. New York: Basic Books.

EYSENCK, H. J. 1952. The effects of psychotherapy: An evaluation. *Journal of Consulting Psychology*, 16, 319–324.

EYSENCK, H. J. 1961. The effects of psychotherapy. In H. J. Eysenck, ed., *Handbook of abnormal psychology*. New York: Basic Books.

EYSENCK, H. J., & Eysenck, S.B.G. 1975. *Manual of the Eysenck Personality Questionnaire*. London: University of London Press.

EYSENCK, H. J. 1987. Anxiety, learned helplessness, and cancer: A causal theory. *Journal of Anxiety Disorders*, 1, 87–104.

FABREGA, H., MEZZICH, J. E., MEZZICH, A. C., & COFFMAN, G. A. 1986. Descriptive validity of DSM-III Depressions. *Journal of Nervous and Mental Disease*, 174, 573–584.

FAIRWEATHER, G. W., SANDERS, D. H., MAYNARD, H., CRESSLER, D. L., & BLECK, D. S. 1969. *Community life for the mentally ill: An alternative to institutional care*. Chicago: Aldine.

FALLOON, I. 1981. Interpersonal variables in behavioral group therapy. *British Journal of Medical Psychology*, 54, 133–141.

FARAONE, S. V., & TSUANG, M. T. 1985. Quantitative models of the genetic transmission of schizophrenia. *Psychological Bulletin*, 98, 41–66.

FARBER, S. L. 1983. *Identical twins reared apart: A reanalysis*. New York: Basic Books.

FARBER, S. S., FELNER, R. D., & PRIMAVERA, J. 1985. Paren-
tal separation/divorce and adolescents: An examination of factors mediating adaptation. *American Journal of Community Psychiatry*, 13, 171–185.

FARINA, A., GHILA, D., BOUDREAU, L. A., ALLEN, J. G., & SHERMAN, M. 1971. Mental illness and the impact of believing others know about it. *Journal of Abnormal Psychology*, 77, 1–5.

FARMER, A., JACKSON, R., McGUFFIN, P., & STOREY, P. 1987. Cerebral ventricular enlargement in chronic schizophrenia: Consistencies and contradictions. *British Journal of Psychiatry*, 150, 324–330.

FAWCETT, J., SCHEFTNER, W., CLARK, D., HEDEKER, D., GIBBONS, R., & CORYELL, W. 1987. Clinical predictors of suicide in patients with major affective disorders: A controlled prospective study. *American Journal of Psychiatry*, 144, 35–46.

FEINGOLD, G. F. 1975. *Why your child is hyperactive*. New York: Random House.

FELDMAN, D. 1987. A social work student's reaction to client suicide. *Social Casework*, 63(3), 184–187.

FERREL, R. B. 1980. Schizophrenia: The diagnoses and misdiagnoses. *Carrier Foundation Letter*, 65(Nov.), 1–5.

FEUERSTEIN, R., RANDY, Y., HOFFMAN, M. B., & MILLER, R. 1980. *Instrumental Enrichment*. Baltimore, MD: University Park Press.

FINKELHOR, D. 1984. *Child sexual abuse: New theory and research*. New York: Free Press.

FINKELHOR, D., & HOTALING, G. 1984. Sexual abuse in the national incidence study of child abuse and neglect: An appraisal. *Child Abuse and Neglect*, 8, 23–33.

FISCHER, G. J. 1986. College student attitudes toward forcible date rape: I. Cognitive predictors. *Archives of Sexual Behavior*, 15, 457–466.

FLAY, B. R., RYAN, K. B., BEST, J. A., BROWN, K. S., KERSELL, M. W., D'AVERNAS, J. R., ZANNA, M. P. 1985. Are social psychological smoking prevention programs effective? The Waterloo study. *Journal of Behavioral Medicine*, 8, 37–59.

FOA, E. B., STEKETKE, G., & YOUNG, M. C. 1984. Agoraphobia: Phenomenological aspects, associated characteristics, and theoretical considerations. *Clinical Psychology Review*, 4, 431–457.

FOLSTEIN, S., & RUTTER, M. 1977. Infantile autism: A genetic study of 21 twin pairs. *Journal of Child Psychology and Psychiatry*, 18, 297–321.

FORD, C. V., & FOLKS, D. G. 1985. Conversion disorders: An overview. *Psychosomatics*, 26, 371–374, 380–383.

FOWLER, R., RICH, C., & YOUNG, D. 1986. San Diego suicide study. *Archives of General Psychiatry*, 43, 962–965.

FRAEBERG, S., ADELSON, E., & SHAPIRO, V. 1975. Ghosts in the nursery: A psychoanalytic approach to the problem of impaired infant-mother relationships. *Journal of the American Academy of Child Psychology*, 14, 387–421.

FRANCES, A. J. (In press.) A critical review of four DSM-III personality disorders: The borderline, avoidant, dependent, and passive-aggressive. In G. Tischler, ed., *DSM-III: An interim appraisal*. Washington, D.C.: American Psychiatric Press.

FRANCES, A. J. 1980. The DSM-III personality disorders section: A commentary. *American Journal of Psychiatry*, 137, 1050–1054.

FRANCES, A. J., & KLEIN, D. F. 1982. Anxious, precise, demanding man seeks help soon after marriage. *Hospital and Community Psychiatry*, 33, 89–90.

FRANCES, A. J., SWEENEY, J., & CLARKIN, J. 1985. Do psychotherapies have specific efforts? *American Journal of Psychotherapy, 39,* 159–174.

FRANCES, A. J. & WIDIGER, T. 1986. The classification of personality disorders: An overview of problems and solutions. *Annual Review of Psychiatry, 5,* 240–257.

FRANK, E., ANDERSON, C., & RUBENSTEIN, D. 1978. Frequency of sexual dysfunction in "normal" couples. *New England Journal of Medicine, 299,* 111–115.

FRANKS, C. 1985. Behavior therapy with children and adolescents. *Annual Review of Behavior Therapy, 10,* 236–290.

FRANKS, L. 1985. The story of "James B." *New York Times Magazine,* Oct. 20, p. 48.

FREEDMAN, B. J. 1974. The subjective experience of perceptual and cognitive disturbances in schizophrenia: A review of autobiographical accounts. *Archives of General Psychiatry, 30,* 333–340.

FREEMAN, B. J., RITVO, E. R., NEEDLEMAN, R., & YOKOTA, A. 1985. The stability of cognitive and linguistic parameters in autism: A five-year study. *Journal of the American Academy of Child Psychiatry, 24,* 459–464.

FREUD, S. 1925. (originally published 1914) On narcissism: An introduction. In J. Strachey, ed., *The standard edition of the complete psychological works of Sigmund Freud,* vol. 4. London: Hogarth.

FREUD, S. 1930. Civilization and its discontents. In J. Strachey, ed., *The standard edition of the complete psychological works of Sigmund Freud,* vol. 21. London: Hogarth.

FREUD, S. 1950. (originally published 1909) Selected papers. In J. Strachey, ed., *The standard edition of the complete psychological works of Sigmund Freud,* vol. 3. London: Hogarth.

FREUD, S. 1951. A letter from Freud (April 9, 1935). *American Journal of Psychiatry, 107,* 786–787.

FREUD, S. 1957. (originally published 1917) Mourning and melancholia. In J. Strachey, ed., *The standard edition of the complete psychological works of Sigmund Freud,* vol. 14. London: Hogarth.

FREUD, S. 1963. *The cocaine papers.* New York: Dunquin.

FREUD, S. 1964. (originally published 1936) A disturbance of memory on the Acropolis. In J. Strachey, ed., *The standard edition of the complete psychological works of Sigmund Freud,* vol. 22. London: Hogarth.

FREUD, S. 1969. *Collected works,* vol. 5. New York: Basic Books.

FRIEDMAN, H. S., & BOOTH-KEWLEY, S. 1987. The "disease-prone personality." *American Psychologist, 42,* 539–555.

FRIEDMAN, M., & ROSENMAN, R. 1974. *Type A behavior and your heart.* New York: Knopf.

FROMUTH, M. E. 1986. The relationship of childhood sexual abuse with later psychological and sexual adjustment in a sample of college women. *Child Abuse and Neglect, 10,* 5–15.

FULLER, R. K., BRANCHEY, L., BRIGHTWELL, D. R., DERMAN, R. M., EMRICK, C. D., IBER, F. L., JAMES, K. E., LACOURSIERE, R. B., LEE, K. K., LOWENSTAM, I., MAANY, I., NEIDERHISER, D., NOCKS, J. J., & SHAW, S. 1986. Disulfiram treatment of alcoholism: A Veterans Administration cooperative study. *Journal of the American Medical Association, 256,* 1449–1455.

GABBARD, G. O. 1985. The role of compulsiveness in the normal physician. *Journal of the American Medical Association, 254,* 2926–2929.

GARDNER, H. 1983. *Frames of mind.* New York: Basic Books.

GARFIELD, S. L., & BERGIN, A. E., eds. 1986. *Handbook of psychotherapy and behavior change,* 3rd ed. New York: John Wiley.

GARMEZY, N., & DEVINE, E. 1984. Project competence: The Minnesota studies of children vulnerable to psychopathology. In N. F. Watt, E. J. Anthony, N. F. Wynne, & J. E. Rolf, eds. *Children at risk for schizophrenia: A longitudinal perspective.* Cambridge: Cambridge University Press, 289–303.

GARNER, D. M., & GARFINKEL, P. E. 1980. Socio-cultural factors in the development of anorexia nervosa. *Psychological Medicine, 10,* 647–656.

GARNER, D. M., GARFINKEL, P. E., SCHWARTZ, D., & THOMPSON, M. 1980. Cultural expectations of thinness in women. *Psychological Reports, 47,* 438–491.

GARVER, D. L. 1987. Methodological issues facing the interpretation of high risk studies: Biological heterogeneity. *Schizophrenia Bulletin, 13,* 525–529.

GEBHARD, P. H. 1972. Incidence of overt homosexuality in the United States and Western Europe. In J. M. Livingood, ed., *National Institute of Mental Health Task Force on Homosexuality: Final Report and Background Papers,* Publication 72-9116. Dept. of Health, Education, & Welfare, 22–29.

GELARDO, M. S., & SANFORD, E. E. 1987. Child abuse and neglect: A review of the literature. *School Psychology Review, 2,* 137–155.

GEORGE, L., & NEUFELD, R.W.J. 1985. Cognition and symptomatology in schizophrenia. *Schizophrenia Bulletin, 11,* 264–285.

GERBNER, G., GROSS, L., MORGAN, M., & SIGNORIELLI, N. 1981. Health and medicine on television. *New England Journal of Medicine, 305,* 901–904.

GERSHON, E. S., HAMOVIT, J., GUROFF, J. J., DIBBLE, E., LECKMAN, J. F., SCEERY, W., TARGUM, S. D., NURNBERGER, J. I., GOLDIN, L. R., & BUNNEY, W. E., JR. 1982. A family study of schizoaffective, bipolar I, bipolar II, unipolar and normal control probands. *Archives of General Psychiatry, 39,* 1157–1167.

GERSHON, L., & SHAW, F. H. 1961. Psychiatric sequelae of chronic exposure to organophosphorous insecticides. *Lancet, 1,* 1371–1374.

GERSTEIN, D. R. 1987. *Toward the prevention of alcohol problems: Government, business, and community action.* Washington, D.C.: National Academy Press.

GIBBONS, F. X. 1985. Stigma perception: Social comparison among mentally retarded persons. *American Journal of Mental Deficiency, 90,* 98–106.

GIBBS, F. A., GIBBS, E. L., & LENNOX, W. G. 1939. Influence of the blood sugar level on the wave and spike formation in petit mal epilepsy. *Archives of Neurology and Psychiatry, 41,* 1111–1116.

GILL, J. J., PRICE, V. A., FRIEDMAN, M., THORESEN, C. E., POWELL, L. H., ULMER, D., BROWN, B., DREWS, F. R. 1985. Reduction in Type-A behavior in healthy middle-aged American military officers. *American Heart Journal, 110,* 503–514.

GITTELMAN, R., & KÄÄÄÄ, D. F. 1984. Relationships between separation anxiety and panic and agoraphobic disorders. *Psychopathology, 17* (supplement), 56–65.

GITTELMAN, R., MANNUZZA, S., SHENKER, R., & BONAGURA, N. 1985. Hyperactive boys almost grown up: I. Psychiatric status. *Archives of General Psychiatry, 42,* 937–947.

GITTELMAN-KLEIN, R., ABIKOFF, H., POLLACK, E., KLEIN, D., KATZ, S., & MATTES, J. 1980. A controlled trial of behavior modification and methylphenidate in hyperactive children. In C. Whalen & B. Henker, eds., *Hyperactive children: The social ecology of identification and treatment.* New York: Academic Press.

GOFFMAN, E. 1959. The presentation of self in everyday life. New York: Doubleday.

GOLD, G. 1974. The White House transcripts. New York: Bantam Books.

GOLDEN, J. C., GRAVER, B., BLOSE, L., BERG, R., COFFMAN, J., & BLOCH, S. 1981. Differences in brain densities between chronic alcoholic and normal control patients. Science, 211, 508–510.

GOLDEN, K. M. 1977. Voodoo in Africa and the United States. American Journal of Psychiatry, 134, 1425–1427.

GOLDMAN, P., & WILLIAMS, D. A. 1978. Black youth, a lost generation? Newsweek, August 7, 22–34.

GOLDSTEIN, M. J. 1985. Family factors that antedate the onset of schizophrenia and related disorders: The results of a fifteen-year prospective longitudinal study. Acta Psychiatria Scandinavica Supplementum, No. 319, 71, 7–18.

GOODWIN, D. W. 1981. Alcoholism and alcoholic psychoses. In H. I. Kaplan & B. J. Sadock, eds. Comprehensive textbook of psychiatry III, 4th ed., vol. 1. Baltimore: Williams and Wilkins.

GOODWIN, D. W. 1986. Genetic factors in the development of alcoholism. Psychiatric Clinics of North America, 9, 427–433.

GOODWIN, F. K., & JAMISON, K. R. 1987. Bipolar disorders. In R. E. Hales and A. J. Frances, eds., American Psychiatric Association Annual Review, vol. 6. Washington, D.C.: American Psychiatric Press.

GOODYER, I., KOLVIN, I., & GATZANIS, S. 1985. Recent undesirable life events and psychiatric disorder in childhood and adolescence. British Journal of Psychiatry, 147, 517–523.

GOSSELIN, C., & WILSON, G. 1980. Sexual variations. New York: Simon & Schuster.

GOTLIB, I. H. & COLBY, C. A. 1987. Treatment of depression. New York: Pergamon Press.

GOTTESMAN, I. I., McGUFFIN, P., & FARMER, A. E. 1987. Clinical genetics as clues to the "real" genetics of schizophrenia. Schizophrenia Bulletin, 13, 23–47.

GOTTLIEB, J., SEMMEL, M. I., & VELDMAN, D. J. 1978. Correlates of social status among mainstreamed mentally retarded children. Journal of Educational Psychology, 70, 396–405.

GOTTSCHALK, L. A. 1978. Psychosomatic medicine today: An overview. Psychosomatics, 19, 89–93.

GOVE, W. R., & HUGHES, M. 1980. Reexamining the ecological fallacy: A study in which aggregate data are critical in investigating the pathological effects of living alone. Social Forces, 58, 1157–1177.

GOULD, M. S., & SHAFFER, D. 1986. The impact of suicide in television movies (Evidence of imitation). New England Journal of Medicine, 316, 690–694.

GOYER, P. I., EDDLEMAN, H. C. 1984. Same-sex rape of non-incarcerated men. American Journal of Psychiatry, 141, 576–579.

GRAHAM, J. R. 1987. The MMPI: A practical guide, 2nd ed. New York: Oxford University Press.

GRANDIN, T. 1984. My experiences as an autistic child and review of selected literature. Journal of Orthomolecular Psychiatry, 13, 144–174.

GRANDIN, T. 1987. Motivating autistic children. Academic Therapy, 22(3), 297–302.

GRAWBOWSKI, J., ed. 1985. Pharmacological adjuncts in smoking cessation. Rockville, MD: National Institute on Drug Abuse.

GREEN, E. 1972. Biofeedback for mind/body self-regulation: Feeling and creativity. Biofeedback and self-control. Chicago Aldine.

GREEN, R. 1974. Sexual identity conflicts in children and adults. New York: Basic Books.

GREEN, R. 1985. Gender identity in childhood and later sexual orientation: Follow-up on 78 males. American Journal of Psychiatry, 142, 339–341.

GREEN, R. 1987. The "sissy boy syndrome" and the development of homosexuality. New Haven: Yale University Press.

GREEN, S., WITKIN, M., ATAY, J., FELL, A., & MANDERSCHEID, R. W. 1986. State and county mental hospitals, United States, 1982–83 and 1983–84, with trend analyses from 1973–74 to 1983–84. Mental Health Statistical Note, No. 176 (U.S. National Institute of Mental Health). Washington, D.C.: U.S. Government Printing Office.

GREEN, W. H., CAMPBELL, M., HARDESTY, A. S., GREGA, D. M., PADRON-GAYOL, M., SHELL, J., ERLENMEYER-KIMLING, L. A comparison of schizophrenic and autistic children. Journal of the American Academy of Child Psychiatry, 23, 399–409.

GREENBERG, B. S., GRAEF, D., FERNANDEZ-COLLADO, C., KORZENNY, F., & ATKIN, C. K. 1980. Sexual intimacy on commercial television during prime-time. Journalism Quarterly, 57(2), 30–37.

GREENBERG, J. 1978. The Americanization of Roseto, Science News, 113, 378–382.

GREENFELD, J. A. 1970. A child called Noah. Life, October 23, 60–72.

GREER, S., & MORRIS, T. 1975. Psychological attributes of women with breast cancer: A controlled study. Journal of Psychosomatic Research, 19, 147–153.

GRENELL, M. M., GLASS, C. R., & KATZ, K. S. 1987. Hyperactive children and peer interaction: Knowledge and performance of social skills. Journal of Abnormal Child Psychology, 15, 1–13.

GROTH, A. N., LONGO, R. E., & McFADIN, J. B. 1982. Undetected recidivism among rapists and child molesters. Crime and Delinquency, 28, 450–458.

GROTH, A. N., & BURGESS, A. W. 1980. Male rape: Offenders and victims. American Journal of Psychiatry, 137, 806–810.

GROTH, A. N. 1979. Men who rape. New York: Plenum Press.

GROVE, W. M., & ANDREASEN, N. C. 1985. Language and thinking in psychosis. Archives of General Psychiatry, 42, 26–32.

GUDEMAN, J. E., DICKEY, B., HELLMAN, S., & BUFFETT, W. 1985. From inpatient to inn status: A new residential model. Psychiatric Clinics of North America, 8, 461–469.

GUILLEN, T. 1982. Competency ruling frees Safety Building squatter. Seattle Times, Jan. 27, B1.

GUMMOW, L., MILLER, P., & DUSTMAN, R. E. 1983. Attention and brain injury: A case for cognitive rehabilitation of attentional deficits. Clinical Psychology Review, 3, 255–274.

GUNDERSON, J. G. 1984. Borderline Personality Disorder. Washington, D.C.: American Psychiatric Press.

GUNDERSON, J. G., & SANARINI, M. C. 1987. Current overview of the borderline diagnosis. Journal of Clinical Psychiatry, 48:8(Supplement), 5–11.

HAAGA, D. A. 1987. Treatment of the Type A behavior pattern. Clinical Psychology Review, 7, 557–574.

HACKETT, T. P., & CASSEM, N. H. 1975. The psychologic reactions of patients in the pre- and post-hospital phases of myocardial infarction. Postgraduate Medicine, 57, 43–46.

HALL, W., GOLDSTEIN, G., ANDREWS, G., LAPSLEY, H., BARTELS, R., & SILOVE, D. 1985. Estimating the economic costs of schizophrenia. *Schizophrenia Bulletin, 11,* 598–610.

HALMI, K. A., OWEN, W., LASKY, E., & STOKES, P. 1983. Dopaminergic regulation in anorexia nervosa. *International Journal of Eating Disorders, 22,* 129–134.

HAMILTON, E., & ABRAMSON, L. 1983. Cognitive patterns and major depressive disorders: A longitudinal study in a hospital setting. *Journal of Abnormal Psychology, 92,* 173–184.

HAMILTON, M. 1982. Symptoms and assessment of depression. In E. S. Paykel, ed., *Handbook of affective disorders.* Edinburgh: Churchill-Livingston.

HAMMEN, C. L. 1985. Predicting depression: A cognitive-behavioral perspective. In P. C. Kendall, ed., *Advances in cognitive-behavioral research and therapy,* vol. 4. Orlando, FL: Academic Press.

HAMMEN, C., & DeMAYO, R. 1982. Cognitive correlates of teacher stress and depressive symptoms: Implications for attributional models of depression. *Journal of Abnormal Psychology, 91,* 96–101.

HANSON, D. M., JACKSON, A. W., & HAGERMAN, R. J. 1986. Speech disturbances (cluttering) in mildly impaired males with the Martin-Bell/Fragile X syndrome. *American Journal of Medical Genetics, 23,* 195–206.

HANSON, J. W., STREISSGUTH, A. P., & SMITH, D. W. 1978. The effects of moderate alcohol consumption during pregnancy on fetal growth and morphogenesis. *Journal of Pediatrics, 92,* 457–460.

HARBIN, H. T. 1980. Episodic dyscontrol and family dynamics. *Advances in Family Psychiatry, 2,* 63–170.

HARDING, C. M., BROOKS, G. W., ASHIKAGA, T., STRAUSS, J. S., & BREIER, A. 1987a. The Vermont longitudinal study of persons with severe mental illness, I: Methodology, study sample and overall status 32 years later. *American Journal of Psychiatry, 144,* 718–726.

HARDING, C. M., ZUBIN, J., & STRAUSS, J. S. 1987b. Chronicity in schizophrenia: Fact, partial fact or artifact. *Hospital and Community Psychiatry, 38,* 477–486.

HARE, E. H. 1985. Old familiar faces: Some aspects of the asylum era in Britain, Part II. *Psychiatric Developments, 4,* 383–392.

HARE, R. 1978. Psychopathy. In H. von Praag, H. Leder, & O. Rafaelson, eds., *Handbook of biological psychiatry.* New York: Marcel Dekker.

HARE, R. D. 1983. Diagnosis of antisocial personality disorder in two prison populations. *American Journal of Psychiatry, 140,* 887–890.

HARE, R. D., & FORTH, A. E. 1985. Psychopathy and lateral preferences. *Journal of Abnormal Psychology, 94,* 541–546.

HARLOW, H. F., & SUOMI, S. J. 1974. Induced depression in monkeys. *Behavioral Biology, 12,* 273–296.

HARRIS, S. L. 1981. A letter from the editor on loss and trust. *The Clinical Psychologist, 34(3),* 3.

HARTLEY, X. Y. 1986. A summary of recent research into the development of children with Down syndrome. *Journal of Mental Deficiency Research, 30,* 1–14.

HARTSOUGH, C. S., & LAMBERT, N. M. 1985. Medical factors in hyperactive and normal children: Prenatal, developmental and health history findings. *American Journal of Orthopsychiatry, 55,* 190–201.

Harvard Mental Health Letter. 1985. Attention deficit disorder, *2(3),* 1–4.

HATHAWAY, S. R., & MCKINLEY, J. C. 1967. *Minnesota Multiphasic Personality Inventory: Manual for administration and scoring.* New York: Psychological Corporation.

HATTIE, J. A., SHARPLEY, C. F., & ROGERS, H. J. 1984. Comparative effectiveness of professional and paraprofes-

sional helpers. *Psychological Bulletin, 95,* 534–541.

HAYNES, S. G., FEINLEIB, M., & KANNEL, W. B. 1980. The relationship of psychological factors to coronary heart disease in the Framingham study: III. Eight-year incidence of coronary heart disease. *American Journal of Epidemiology, 111,* 37–58.

HAZELWOOD, R. R., BURGESS, A. W., & GROTH, A. N. 1981. Death during dangerous autoerotic practice. *Social Science Medicine, 15E,* 129–133.

HAZELWOOD, R. R., DIETZ, P. E., & BURGESS, A. W. 1983. *Autoerotic fatalities.* Lexington, MA: Lexington Books.

Health promotion and disease prevention: United States, 1985. 1988. *Vital and Health Statistics,* Series 10, Number 183. Hyattsville, MD: U.S. Dept. of Health and Human Services.

HELGASON, T. 1979. Prevalence and incidence of mental disorders estimated by a health questionnaire and psychiatric case register. *Acta Psychiatrica Scandinavica, 58,* 256–266.

HELSING, K. J., SZELO, M., & COMSTOCK, G. W. 1981. Factors associated with mortality after widowhood. *American Journal of Public Health, 71,* 802–809.

HELZER, J. E. 1987. Epidemiology of alcoholism. *Journal of Consulting and Clinical Psychology, 55,* 284–292.

HELZER, J. E., ROBINS, L. N., & McEVOY, L. T. 1987. Posttraumatic stress disorder in the general population. *New England Journal of Medicine, 317,* 1630–1634.

HELZER, J. E., ROBINS, L. N., McEVOY, L. T., SPITZNAGEL, E. L., STOLZMAN, R. K., & FARMER, A. 1985. A comparison clinical and diagnostic interview schedule diagnoses. *Archives of General Psychiatry, 42,* 657–666.

HENDEN, H. 1981. Psychotherapy and suicide. *American Journal of Psychotherapy, 35,* 469–480.

HENNEKENS, C. H., WILLETT, W., ROSNER, B., COLE, D. S., & MAYRENT, S. L. 1979. Effects of beer, wine and liquor in coronary deaths. *Journal of the American Medical Association, 242,* 1973–1974.

HENNIGAN, K. M., HEATH, L., WHARTON, J. D., DELROSARIO, M. L., COOK, T. D., & CALDER, R. J. 1982. Impact of the introduction of television on crime in the United States: Empirical findings and theoretical implications. *Journal of Personality and Social Psychology, 42,* 461–477.

HERDT, G. H., ed. 1984. *Ritualized homosexuality in Melanesia.* Berkeley: University of California Press.

HEROLD, E. S., & WAY, L. 1983. Oral-genital sexual behavior in a sample of university females. *Journal of Sex Research, 19,* 327–338.

HESSE, H. 1969. *Peter Camenzind.* New York: Farrar, Straus, and Giroux.

HESTON, L. L., & MASTRI, A. R. 1982. Age of onset of Pick's and Alzheimer's dementia: Implications for diagnosis and research. *Journal of Gerontology, 37,* 422–424.

HESTON, L. L., WHITE, J. A., & MASTRI, A. R. 1987. Pick's disease. *Archives of General Psychiatry, 44,* 409–411.

HETHERINGTON, E. M., COX, M., & COX, R. 1979. Play and social interaction in children following divorce. *Journal of Social Issues, 35,* 26–49.

HINZ, L. D., & WILLIAMSON, D. A. 1987. Bulimia and depression: A review of the affective variant hypothesis. *Psychological Bulletin, 102,* 150–158.

HOENIG, J. 1984. Schneider's first rank symptoms and the tabulators. *Comprehensive Psychiatry, 25,* 77–87.

HOFER, M. A. 1984. Relationships as regulators: A psychobiologic perspective on bereavement. *Psychosomatic Medicine, 46,* 183–197.

HOFFMAN, R. E. 1986. Verbal hallucinations and language

production processes in schizophrenia. *Behavioral and Brain Sciences, 9,* 503–548.

HOFFMAN, R., STOPEK, S., & ANDREASEN, N. C. 1986. A discourse analysis comparing manic versus schizophrenic speech disorganization. *Archives of General Psychiatry, 43,* 831–838.

HOFLING, C. K. 1968. *Textbook of psychiatry for medical practice,* 2nd ed. Philadelphia: Lippincott.

HOGARTY, G. E., ANDERSON, C. M., REISS, D. J., KORNBLITH, S. J., GREENWALD, D. P., JAVNA, C. D., MADONIA, M. J., and the EPICS Schizophrenia Research Group. 1986. Family psychoeducation, social skills training, and maintenance chemotherapy in the aftercare treatment of schizophrenia I. *Archives of General Psychiatry, 43,* 633–642.

HOGARTY, G. E., SCHOOLER, N. R., ULRICH, R., MUSSARE, F., FERRO, P., & HERRON, E. Fluphenazine and social therapy in the aftercare of schizophrenic patients. *Archives of General Psychiatry, 36,* 1283–1294.

HOLDEN, C. 1985. A guarded endorsement for shock therapy. *Science, 228,* 1510–1511.

HOLDEN, C. 1986. Depression research advances: Treatment lags. *Science, 233,* 723–726.

HOLLON, S. D., DeRUBEIS, R. J., & EVANS, M. D. 1987. Causal mediation of change in treatment for depression: Discriminating between nonspecificity and noncausality. *Psychological Bulletin, 102,* 139–149.

HOLROYD, K. A., ANDRASKI, F., & WESTBROOK, T. 1977. Cognitive control of tension headache. *Cognitive Therapy and Research, 2,* 121–133.

HOLZMAN, P. S. 1978. Cognitive impairment and cognitive stability: Toward a theory of thought disorder. In G. Serban, ed., *Cognitive defects in the development of mental illness.* New York: Brunner/Mazel.

HOLZMAN, P. S., SOLOMON, C. M., LEVIN, S., & WATERNAUX, C. S. 1984. Pursuit eye movement dysfunctions in schizophrenia: Family evidence for specificity. *Archives of General Psychiatry, 41,* 136–139.

HOOLEY, J. M. 1985. Expressed emotion: A review of the critical literature. *Clinical Psychology Review, 5,* 119–139.

HORN, W. F., CHATOOR, I., & CONNORS, C. K. 1983. Additive effects of dexedrine and self-control training. *Behavior Modification, 7,* 383–402.

HORNE, J. 1979. Defendant found guilty of murdering jogger. *Seattle Times,* May 31, C11.

HOROWITZ, M. J. 1974. Stress response syndromes. *Archives of General Psychiatry, 31,* 768–781.

HOROWITZ, M. J. 1986. Stress-response syndromes: A review of posttraumatic and adjustment disorders. *Hospital and Community Psychiatry, 37,* 241–249.

HORWITZ, A. V. 1984. The economy and social pathology. *Annual Review of Sociology, 10,* 95–119.

HOUGHTON, J. F. 1980. One personal experience: Before and after mental illness. In J. G. Rabkin, L. Gelb, & J. B. Lazar, eds., *Attitudes toward the mentally ill: Research perspectives.* Rockville, MD: National Institute of Mental Health.

HOUGHTON, J. F. 1982. First person account: Maintaining mental health in a turbulent world. *Schizophrenia Bulletin, 8,* 548–552.

HOYT, M. F., XENAKIS, S. N., MARMAR, C. R., & HOROWITZ, M. J. 1983. Therapists' actions that influence their perceptions of "good" psychotherapy sessions. *The Journal of Nervous and Mental Disease, 171,* 400–404.

HUNT, M. 1974. *Sexual behavior in the 1970s.* Chicago: Playboy Press.

HUNT, W. A., & BESPALIC, D. A. 1974. An evaluation of

current methods of modifying smoking behavior. *Journal of Clinical Psychology, 30,* 430–438.

HURLBURT, R. T., & MELANCON, S. M. 1987. Single case study. Goofed up images: Thought sampling with a schizophrenic woman. *Journal of Nervous and Mental Disease, 175,* 575–578.

IANOCO, W. G., & KOENIG, W. G. R. 1983. Features that distinguish the smooth-pursuit eye-tracking performance of schizophrenic, affective disorder, and normal individuals. *Journal of Abnormal Psychology, 92,* 29–41.

INGRAM, R. E. 1984. Toward an information-processing analysis of depression. *Cognitive Therapy and Research, 8,* 443–478.

INHELDER, B. 1969. *The diagnosis of reasoning in the mentally retarded,* 2nd ed. W. B. Stephens et al., trans. New York: Chandler.

ITL, T. M. 1977. Qualitative and quantitative EEG findings in schizophrenics. *Schizophrenia Bulletin, 3,* 61–79.

ITL, T. M., SALETU, B., & DAVIS, R. 1974. Stability studies of schizophrenics and normals using computer-analyzed EEG. *Biological Psychiatry, 8,* 321–325.

JACK-ROLLER & SNODGRASS, J. 1982. The Jack-Roller at seventy. Lexington, MA: Lexington Books.

JACOB, R. G., WING, R., & SHAPIRO, A. P. 1987. The behavioral treatment of hypertension: Long-term effects. *Behavior Therapy, 18,* 325–352.

JAFFEE, J. H. 1985. Opioid dependence. In H. I. Kaplan & B. J. Sadock, eds., *Comprehensive textbook of psychiatry,* 4th ed., vol. 1. Baltimore: Williams & Wilkins.

JAMISON, K. R., GERNER, R. H., HAMMEN, C., & PADESKY, C. 1980. Clouds and silver linings: Positive experiences associated with primary affective disorders. *American Journal of Psychiatry, 137,* 198–202.

JANICAK, P. G., & BUSHES, R. A. 1987. Advances in the treatment of mania and other acute psychotic disorders. *Psychiatric Annals, 17,* 145–149.

JANIS, I. L. 1958. *Psychological stress: Psychoanalytic and behavioral studies of surgical patients.* New York: Wiley.

JELLINEK, E. M. 1960. *The disease concept of alcoholism.* New Haven: Hillhouse Press.

JEMMOTT, J. B., III, & LOCKE, S. E. 1984. Psychosocial factors, immunologic mediation, and human susceptibility to infectious diseases: How much do we know? *Psychological Bulletin, 95,* 78–108.

JENKINS, J. H., KARNO, M. N., DE LA SELVA, A., SANTANA, F., TELLIS, C., LOPEZ, S., & MINTZ, J. 1986. Expressed emotion, maintenance psychotherapy and schizophrenic relapse among Mexican-Americans. *Psychopharmacology Bulletin, 22,* 621–627.

JENSEN, A. R. 1969. How much can we boost IQ and scholastic achievement? *Harvard Educational Review, 39,* 1–123.

JOEL-NIELSON, N. 1979. Suicide risk in manic-depressive disorder. In M. Schov & E. Strongren, eds., Origin, prevention and treatment of affective disorders. London: Academic Press.

JOHNSON, C. T., & BERNDT, D. J. 1983. Preliminary investigation of bulimia and life adjustment. *American Journal of Psychiatry, 140,* 774–777.

JONES, D. J., FOX, M. M., BABIGAN, H. M., & HUTTON, H. E. 1980. Epidemiology of anorexia nervosa in Monroe County, New York: 1960–1976. *Psychosomatic Medicine, 42,* 551–558.

JONES, K. W., SMITH, D. W., STREISSGUTH, A. P., & MYRIANTHOPOULOS, N. C. 1974. Outcomes in offspring of chronic alcoholic women. *Lancet, 1,* 1076–1078.

JONES, M. C. 1981. Midlife drinking patterns. Correlates and

KENDELL, R. E. 1983. Schizophrenia. In R. E. Kendall & A. K. Zealley, eds., *Companion to psychiatric studies.* Edinburgh: Churchill Livingstone.

KENDLER, K. S. 1983. Overview: A current perspective on twin studies of schizophrenia. *American Journal of Psychiatry, 140,* 1413–1425.

KENDLER, K. S., & GRUENBERG, M. 1984. An independent analysis of the Copenhagen sample of the Danish adoption study of Schizophrenia IV. *Archives of General Psychiatry IV, 41,* 555–564.

KENDLER, K. S., GRUENBERG, M., & TSUANG, M. T. 1985. Psychiatric illness in first-degree relatives of schizophrenic and surgical control patients. *Archives of General Psychiatry, 42,* 770–779.

KENDLER, K. S., HEATH, A., MARTIN, N. G., & EAVES, L. J. 1986. Symptoms of anxiety and depression in a volunteer twin population: The etiologic role of genetic and environmental factors. *Archives of General Psychiatry, 43,* 213–221.

KENYON, K. 1979. A survivor's notes. *Newsweek,* April 30, p. 17.

KERNBERG, O. F. 1970. A psychoanalytic classification of character pathology. *Journal of the American Psychoanalytic Association, 18,* 800–822.

KERNBERG, O. F. 1975. *Borderline conditions and pathological narcissism.* New York: Jason Aronson.

KETY, S. S., ROSENTHAL, D., WENDER, P. H., SCHULSINGER, F., & JACOBSON, B. 1978. The biological and adoptive families of adopted individuals who become schizophrenic: Prevalence of mental illness and other characteristics. In L. C. Wynne, R. L. Cromwell, & S. Matthysse, eds. *The nature of schizophrenia: New approaches to research and treatment.* New York: Wiley.

KEYES, S., & BLOCK, J. 1984. Prevalence and patterns of substance use among early adolescents. *Journal of Youth and Adolescence, 13,* 1–14.

KILMANN, P. R., SABALIS, R. F., GEARING, M. L., BUKSTEL, L. H., & SCOVERN, A. W. 1982. The treatment of sexual paraphilias: A review of outcome research. *Journal of Sex Research, 18,* 193–252.

KINSEY, A. C., POMEROY, W. B., & MARTIN, C. E. 1948. *Sexual behavior in the human male.* Philadelphia: W. B. Saunders.

KINSEY, A. C., POMEROY, W. B. MARTIN, C. E., & GEBHARD, P. H. 1953. *Sexual behavior in the human female.* Philadelphia: W. B. Saunders.

KIPPER, D. A. 1977. Behavior therapy for fears brought on by war experiences. *Journal of Consulting and Clinical Psychology, 45,* 216–221.

KIRBY, E. A., & KHAZINDAR, N. 1985. *Durable and generalized effects of cognitive-behavior modifications with attention deficit disorder children.* (Unpublished manuscript).

KIRIGIN, K. A., BRAUKMAN, C. J., ATWATER, J. D., & WOLF, M. M. 1982. An evolution of teaching—family group homes for juvenile offenders. *Journal of Applied Behavior Analysis, 15,* 1–16.

KLERMAN, G. L. 1984. The advantages of DSM III. *American Journal of Psychiatry, 141,* 539–542.

KLERMAN, G. L. 1987. *The treatment of depressive conditions: Perspectives on depressive disorders.* Rockville, MD: National Institute of Mental Health.

KLERMAN, G. L., LAVORI, P. W., RICE, J., REICH, T., ENDICOTT, J., ANDREASEN, N. C., KELLER, M. D., & HIRSCHFIELD, R.M.A. 1985. Birth-cohort trends in rates of major depressive disorder among relatives of patients with affective disorder. *Archives of General Psychiatry, 42,* 689–693.

antecedents. In D. H. Eichorn, ed., *Present and past in middle life.* New York: Academic Press, 223–242.

JUSTICE, B. 1987. *Who gets sick: Thinking and health.* Houston, TX: Peak Press.

KALIN, N. H. 1979. Genital and abdominal surgery: A case report. *Journal of the American Medical Association, 241,* 2188–2189.

KAMPHAUS, R. W., & REYNOLDS, C. R. 1984. Development and structure of the Kaufman Assessment Battery for Children. *Journal of Special Education, 18,* 213–228.

KAMIMURA, Y., & KUSANO, K. 1981. Habitual physical activity and heart rate level of children with Down's syndrome. *Japanese Journal of Special Education, 19,* 21–27.

KANE, J. M. 1987. Treatment of schizophrenia. *Schizophrenia Bulletin, 13,* 133–156.

KANFER, R., & ZEISS, A. M. 1983. Depression, interpersonal standard setting, and judgments of self-efficacy. *Journal of Abnormal Psychology, 92,* 319–329.

KAPLAN, H. S. 1979. *Disorders of sexual desire.* New York: Simon & Schuster.

KAPLAN, H. S. 1974. *The new sex therapy: Active treatment of sexual dysfunctions.* New York: Quadrangle Books.

KARLINSKY, H. 1986. Alzheimer's disease in Down's syndrome: A review. *Journal of the American Geriatrics Society, 34,* 728–734.

KASHANI, J., & SIMONDS, J. P. 1979. The incidence of depression in children. *American Journal of Psychiatry, 136,* 1203–1205.

KAUFMAN, A. S. 1979. *Intelligence testing with the WISC-R.* New York: John Wiley.

KAUFMAN, A. S., & KAUFMAN, N. L. 1983. *Kaufman Assessment Battery for Children: Interpretive manual.* Circle Pines, NM: American Guidance Service.

KAUFMAN, M. J., AGARD, J. A., & SEMMEL, M. I. 1982. *Mainstreaming: Learners and their environments.* Baltimore: University Park Press.

KAZDIN, A. E, & MASCITELLI, S. 1982. Covert and overt rehearsal and homework practice in developing assertiveness. *Journal of Consulting and Clinical Psychology, 50,* 250–258.

KAZDIN, A. E., & ESVELDT-DAWSON, K. 1986. The interview for antisocial behavior: Psychometric characteristics and concurrent validity with child psychiatric inpatients. *Journal of Psychopathology and Behavioral Assessment, 8,* 289–303.

KEGAN, R. G. 1986. The child behind the mask: Sociopathy as developmental delay. In W. H. Reid, D. Dorr, J. I. Walker, and J. W. Bonner, eds., *Unmasking the Psychopath.* New York: W. W. Norton.

KELLER, M. B. 1987. Differential diagnosis, natural course, and epidemiology of bipolar disorder. In R. E. Hales and A. J. Francis, eds., *American Psychiatric Association Annual Review,* vol. 6. Washington, D.C.: American Psychiatric Press.

KELLNER, R. 1987. Hypochondriasis and somatization. *Journal of the American Medical Association, 258,* 2718–2722.

KELLY, G. A. 1955. *The psychology of personal constructs,* vols. 1 & 2. New York: W. W. Norton

KENDALL, P. C., ed. 1985. *Advances in cognitive-behavioral research and therapy.* Orlando, FL: Academic Press.

KENDALL, P. C., & MARUYAMA, G. 1985. Metanalysis: On the road to synthesis of knowledge? *Clinical Psychology Review, 5,* 79–89.

KENDALL, P. C., & WILCOX, L. E. 1978. Self-control in children: Development of a rating scale. *Journal of Consulting and Clinical Psychology, 47,* 1020–1029.

KLINE, N. S. 1977. Depression. *Swarthmore College Bulletin*, July, 8–11.

KLUFT, R. P. 1984. An introduction to multiple personality disorder. *Psychiatric Annals*, 14, 19–24.

KNOWLES, P.A.L., & PRUTSMAN, T. D. 1968. *The case of Benjie*. Unpublished manuscript, Florida Atlantic University.

KOBASA, S. C., MADDI, S. R., & KAHN, S. 1982. Hardiness and health: A prospective study. *Journal of Personality and Social Psychology*, 42, 168–177.

KOG, E., & VANDEREYCKEN, W. 1985. Family characteristics of anorexia nervosa and bulimia: A review of the research literature. *Clinical Psychology Review*, 5, 159–180.

KOHUT, H. 1971. *The analysis of the self*. New York: International Universities Press.

KOHUT, H. 1977. *The restoration of the self*. New York: International Universities Press.

KOLATA, G. 1987. The poignant thoughts of Down's children are given voice. *New York Times*, December 22, 15.

KOLB, L. D., & BRODIE, H.K.H. 1982. *Modern clinical psychiatry*, 10th ed. Philadelphia: W. B. Saunders.

KONSTANTAREAS, M. M. 1986. Early developmental backgrounds of autistic and mentally retarded children. *Psychiatric Clinics of North America*, 9, 671–687.

KOSTEN, T. R., & ROUNSAVILLE, B. J. 1986. Psychopathology in Opioid Addicts. *Psychiatric Clinics of North America*, 9, 515–532.

KOSTEN, T. R., ROUNSAVILLE, B. J., & KLEBER, H. D. 1987. Multidimensionality and prediction of treatment outcome in opioid addicts: 2.5-year follow-up. *Comprehensive Psychiatry*, 28, 3–13.

KOUMIAN, J. 1981. The use of valium as a form of social control. *Social Science Medicine*, 15E, 245–249.

KOVACS, M. 1985. The natural history and course of depressive disorders in childhood. *Psychiatric Annals*, 15, 387–389.

KOVACS, M., & BECK, A. T. 1977. An empirical-clinical approach toward a definition of childhood depression. In J. G. Schulter-Brandt and A. Raskin, eds., *Depression in childhood: Diagnosing treatment and conceptual models*. New York: Raven Press.

KOVACS, M., BECK, A T., & WEISSMAN, A. 1975. The use of suicidal motives in the psychotherapy of attempted suicides. *American Journal of Psychotherapy*, 29, 363–368.

KRAEPELIN, E. 1909–1913. *Psychiatric*, 8th ed. Leipzig: J. A. Barth.

KRAKOWSKI, A. J. 1982. Stress and the practice of medicine: II. Stressors, stresses, and strains. *Psychotherapy and Psychosomatics*, 38, 11–23.

KRANTZ, D. S., & MANUCK, S. B. 1984. Acute psychophysiologic reactivity and risk of cardiovascular disease: A review and methodologic critique. *Psychological Bulletin*, 96, 435–464.

KRANTZ, S., & HAMMEN, C. L. 1979. Assessment of cognitive bias in depression. *Journal of Abnormal Psychology*, 88, 611–619.

KRINGLEN, E. 1981. Stress and coronary heart disease. *Twin Research 3: Epidemiological and clinical studies*. New York: Alan R. Liss.

KUPFER, D. J., ULRICH, R. F., COBLE, P. A., JARRETT, D. B., GROCHOCINSKI, V. J., DOMAN, J., MATTHEWS, G., & BORBELY, A. A. 1985. Electroencephalographic sleep of younger depressives. *Archives of General Psychiatry*, 42, 806–810.

KURIANSKY, J. B., DEMING, U. E., & GURLAND, B. J. 1974. On trends in the diagnosis of schizophrenia. *American Journal of Psychiatry*, 131, 402–408.

LACKS, P. 1984. *Bender-Gestalt screening for brain dysfunction*. New York: John Wiley.

LADER, M. 1975. The nature of clinical anxiety in modern society. In C. D. Spielberger & I. G. Sarason, eds., *Stress and anxiety*, vol. 1. Washington, D.C.: Hemisphere.

LAFFAL, J. 1965. *Pathological and normal language*. New York: Atherton.

LAGRECA, A. M., STONE, W. L., & BELL, C. R., III. 1983. Facilitating the vocational-interpersonal skills of mentally retarded individuals. *American Journal of Mental Deficiency*, 88, 270–278.

LAING, R. D. 1967. *The Politics of Experience*. New York: Harper Torch books.

LAMBERT, N. M., SANDOVAL, J., & SASSONE, D. 1978. Prevalence of hyperactivity in elementary school children as a function of social system defenses. *American Journal of Orthopsychiatry*, 48, 446–463.

LAMBLEY, P. 1976. The use of assertive training and psychodynamic insight in the treatment of migraine headache: A case study. *Journal of Nervous and Mental Disease*, 163, 61–64.

LANQUETOT, R. 1984. First person account: Confessions of the daughter of a schizophrenic. *Schizophrenia Bulletin*, 10, 467–471.

LARANCE, D. L., & TWENTYMAN, C. T. 1983. Maternal attributions and child abuse. *Journal of Abnormal Psychology*, 92, 449–457.

LATIB, A., CONROY, J., & HESS, C. M. 1984. Family attitudes toward deinstitutionalization. *International Review of Research on Mental Retardation*, 12, 67–93.

LAUDENSLAGER, M. L., & REITE, M. L. 1984. Losses and separations: Immunological consequences and health implications. In P. Shaver, ed., *Review of personality and social psychology*. Beverly Hills, CA: Sage Publications.

LAZARUS, A. A. 1971. *Behavior therapy and beyond*. New York: McGraw-Hill.

LEACH, B. 1973. Does Alcoholics Anonymous really work? In P. G. Bourne & R. Fox, eds., *Alcoholism: Progress in research and treatment*. New York: Academic Press.

LEAF, P. J., WEISSMAN, M. M., MYERS, J. K., HOLZER, C., & TISCHLER, G. 1986. *Psychosocial risks and correlates of major depression in one United States urban community: Progress and challenge*. New York: Guilford Press.

LEAF, P. J., WEISSMAN, M. M., MYERS, J. K., TISCHLER, G. L., & HOLZER, C. E., III. 1984. Social factors related to psychiatric disorder: The Yale Epidemiological Catchment Area Study. *Social Psychiatry*, 19, 53–61.

LEFF, J. 1987. The influence of life events and relatives' expressed emotion on the course of schizophrenia. In D. Magnusson & A. Ohman, eds., *Psychopathology: An interactional perspective*. New York: Academic Press.

LEFF, J., KUIPERS, L., BERKOWITZ, R., & STURGEON, D. 1985. A controlled trial of social intervention in the families of schizophrenic patients: Two-year follow-up. *British Journal of Psychiatry*, 146, 594–600.

LEFF, J., & VAUGHN, C. 1981. The role of maintenance therapy and relatives' expressed emotion in relapse schizophrenia: A two-year follow-up. *British Journal of Psychiatry, 139,* 102–104.

LEFF, J., & VAUGHN, C. 1985. *Expressed emotion in families.* New York: Guilford Press.

LEE, T., SEEMAN, P., TOURTELLOTTE, W. W., FARLEY, I. J., & HORNYKEIWICZ, O. 1978. Binding of ³H-neuroleptics and ³H-apomorphine in schizophrenic brains. *Nature, 274,* 897–900.

LEHMAN, H. E., & CANCRO, R. 1985. Schizophrenia: Clinical features. In H. I. Kaplan & B. J. Sadock, *Comprehensive textbook of psychiatry,* 4th ed., vol. I. Baltimore: Williams & Wilkens.

LEHRER, P. M., & WOOLFOLK, R. L. 1986. Are all stress-reduction techniques interchangeable, or do they have specific effects: A review of the comparative empirical literature. In R. L. Wollfolk & P. M. Lehrer, eds., *Principles and practices of stress management.* New York: Guilford Press.

LEITENBERG, H., GROSS, J., PETERSON, J., & ROSEN, J. 1984. Analyses of an anxiety model and the process of change during exposure plus response prevention treatment of bulimia nervosa. *Behavior Therapy, 15,* 3–20.

LEON, G. R., LUCAS, A. R., COLLIGAN, R. C., FERINANDE, R. J., & KAMP, J. 1985. Sexual, body image, and personality attitudes in anorexia nervosa. *Journal of Abnormal Child Psychology, 13,* 245–257.

LEON, G. R., & PHELAN, P. W. 1984. Anorexia nervosa. In B. Lahey & A. Kazdin, eds., *Advances in Clinical Child Psychology, 8,* 81–111.

LEONARD, W. E. 1927. *The locomotive god.* New York: Appleton-Century-Crofts.

LEVIN, S. M., BARRY, S. M., GAMBARO, S., WOLFINSOHN, L., & SMITH, A. 1977. Variations of covert sensitization in the treatment of pedophilic behavior: A case study. *Journal of Consulting and Clinical Psychology, 45,* 896–907.

LEVINE, S. B. 1980. Psychiatric diagnosis of patients requesting sex reassignment surgery. *Journal of Sex and Marital Therapy, 6,* 164–173.

LEVINE, S. B., & LOTHSTEIN, L. 1981. Transsexualism and the gender dysphoria syndromes. *Journal of Sex and Marital Therapy, 7,* 85–113.

LEVY, L. 1976. Self-help groups: Types and psychological processes. *Journal of Applied Behavioral Science, 12,* 310–323.

LEVY, R. F. 1977. "Male woman" finds self. Washington Post, May 11, C1, C3.

LEVY, R. I., & MOSKOWTTZ, J. 1982. Cardiovascular research: Decades of progress, a decade of promise. *Science, 217,* 121–129.

LEWIN, R. 1988. Cloud over Parkinson's therapy. *Science, 240,* 390–392.

LEWINE, R.R.J. 1984. Stalking the schizophrenia marker: Evidence for a general vulnerability model of psychopathology. In N. F. Watt, E. J. Anthony, L. C. Wynne, and J. E. Rolf, eds., *Children at risk for schizophrenia: A longitudinal perspective.* Cambridge: Cambridge University Press.

LEWINSOHN, P. M., & ARCONAD, M. 1981. Behavioral treatment in depression: A social learning approach. In J. Clarkin & H. Glazer, eds., *Behavioral and directive treatment strategies.* New York: Garland Press.

LEWINSOHN, P. M., & HOBERMAN, H. M. 1982. Depression. In A. S. Bellak, M. Hersen, & A. E. Kazdin, eds., *International handbook of behavior modification and therapy.* New York: Plenum.

LEWINSOHN, P. M., MISCHEL, W., CHAPLAIN, W., & BARTON, R. 1980. Social competence and depression. The role of illusory self-perceptions. *Journal of Abnormal Psychology, 89,* 203–212.

LEWIS, J. F. & MERCER, J. R. 1978. The system of multicultural pluralistic assessment: SOMPA. In W. A. Coulter & H. W. Morrow, eds., *Adaptive behavior: Concepts and measurement.* New York: Grune & Stratton.

LILJEFORS, I., & RAHE, R. H. 1970. An identical twin study of psychosocial factors in coronary heart disease in Sweden. *Psychosomatic Medicine, 32,* 523–542.

LINDEMALM, G., KORLIN, D., & UDDENBERG, N. 1986. Long-term follow-up of "Sex Change" in 13 male to female transsexuals. *Archives of Sexual Behavior, 15,* 187–210.

LINDENMAYER, J. P., KAY, S. R., & FRIEDMAN, C. 1986. Negative and positive schizophrenic syndromes after the acute phase: A prospective follow-up. *Comprehensive Psychiatry, 27,* 276–286.

LINEHAN, M. M. 1981. A social-behavioral analysis of suicide and parasuicide. In J. F. Clarkin & H. I. Glazer, eds., *Depression: Behavioral and directive intervention strategies.* New York: Garland STPM Pres.

LINEHAN, M. M. 1987. Dialectical behavior therapy for borderline personality disorder. *Bulletin of the Menninger Clinic, 51,* 261–276.

LINGJAERDE, O. 1983. The biochemistry of depression. *Acta Psychiatrica Scandinavica Supplementum,* No. 302, 69, 36–51.

LINN, M. V., CAFFEY, E. M., KLETT, C. J., HOGARTY, G. E., & LAMB, H. R. 1979. Day treatment and psychotropic drugs in aftercare of schizophrenic patients. *Archives of General Psychiatry, 36,* 1055–1066.

LINSKY, A. S., STRAUS, M. A., & COLBY, J. P., JR. 1985. Stressful events, stressful condition and alcohol problems in the United States: A partial test of Coles' theory. *Journal of Studies on Alcohol, 46,* 72–80.

LIPOWSKI, Z. J. 1987. Delirium (Acute Confusional States). *Journal of the American Medical Association, 258,* 1789–1792.

LIPSIUS, S. H. 1987. Prescribing sensate focus without proscribing intercourse. *Journal of Sex and Marital Therapy, 13,* 106–116.

LOBATO, D. 1983. Siblings of handicapped children: A review. *Journal of Autism, 13,* 347–364.

LOCKE, S. E., KRAUS, L., HURST, M. W., HEISEL, J. S., WILLIAMS, R. M. 1984. Life change stress, psychiatric symptoms, and natural killer cell-activity. *Psychosomatic Medicine, 46,* 441–453.

LOO, R. 1986. Post-shooting stress reactions among police officers. *Journal of Human Stress, 12,* 27–31.

LORANGER, A. W., OLDHAM, J. M., & TULIS, E. H. 1982. Familial transmission of DSM-III borderline personality disorder. *Archives of General Psychiatry, 39,* 795–799.

LOVAAS, O. I. 1987. Behavioral treatment and normal educational and intellectual functioning in young autistic children. *Journal of Consulting and Clinical Psychology, 55,* 3–9.

LOWE, M. 1985. Rapid smoking. In A. S. Bellack & M. Hersen, eds., *Dictionary of behavior therapy techniques.* New York: Pergamon Press.

LUBORSKY, L., CRITS-CHRISTOPH, P., MCLELLAN, T., WOODY, G., PIPER, W., LIBERMAN, B., IMBER, S., & PILKONIS, P. 1986. Do therapists vary much in their success? Findings from four outcome studies. *American Journal of Orthopsychiatry, 56,* 501–512.

LUMRY, A. E., GOTTESMAN, I. I., & TUASON, V. B. 1982. MMPI State dependency during the course of bipolar psychosis. *Psychiatry Research, 7,* 59–67.

LYNN, R., & HAMPSON, S. 1970. National anxiety levels and prevalence of alcoholism. *British Journal of Addiction, 64,* 305–306.

MACCOBY, E., & MACCOBY, N. 1954. The interview: A tool of social science. In G. Lindzey, ed., *Handbook of social psychology*. Cambridge, MA: Addison-Wesley, 449–487.

MACMILLAN, M. 1986. Souvenir de la Salpetriere: M. le Dr. Freud a Paris, 1885. *Australian Psychologist*, 21, 3–29.

MACTURK, R. H., VIETZE, P. M., MCCARTHY, M. E., MCQUISTAN, S. T., YARROW, L. J. 1985. The organization of exploratory behavior in Down's syndrome and nondelayed infants. *Child Development*, 56, 573–581.

MAGAZINER, J. 1980. *Density, living alone, age and psychopathology in the urban environment*. Unpublished doctoral dissertation, University of Chicago.

MAHONEY, E. R. 1980. Religiosity and sexual behavior among heterosexual college students. *Journal of Sex Research*, 16, 97–113.

MAHONEY, E. R. 1983. *Human Sexuality*. New York: McGraw-Hill.

MALAMUTH, N. M. 1981. Rape proclivity among males. *Journal of Social Issues*, 37, 138–157.

MALATESTA, V. J. 1979. Alcohol effects on the orgasmic-ejaculatory response in human males. *Journal of Sex Research*, 15, 101–107.

MALATESTA, V. J., POLLACK, R. H., CROTTY, T. O., & PEACOCK, L. J. 1982. Acute alcohol intoxication and female orgasmic response. *Journal of Sex Research*, 18, 1–16.

MANSCHRECK, T., & PETRI, M. 1978. The paranoid syndrome. *Lancet*, 2, 251–253.

MANUCK, S. B., MORRISON, R. L., BELLACK, A. S., & POLEFRONE, J. M. 1985. Behavioral factors in hypertension, cardiovascular responsivity, anger, and social competence. In M. A. Chesney & R. H. Rosenman, eds., *Anger and hostility in cardiovascular and behavioral disorders*. Washington, D.C.: Hemisphere.

MARENGO, J. T., HARROW, M., LANIN-KETTERING, I., & WILSON, A. 1986. Evaluating bizarre-idiosyncratic thinking: A comprehensive index of positive thought disorder. *Schizophrenia Bulletin*, 12, 497–510.

MARKMAN, H. J., JAMIESON, K., & FLOYD, F. 1983. The assessment and modification of premarital relationships: Preliminary findings on the etiology and prevention of marital and family distress. In J. Vincent, ed., *Advances in family interventions, assessment and theory*, vol. 3. Greenwich, CT: JAI Press.

MARKOWITZ, J., BROWN, R., SWEENEY, J., & MANN, J. J. 1987. Reduced length and cost of hospital stay for major depression in patients treated with ECT. *American Journal of Psychiatry*, 144, 1025–1029.

MARKS, I. M., & LADER, M. 1973. Anxiety states (anxiety neurosis): A review. *Journal of Nervous and Mental Disease*, 156, 3–18.

MARKS, I. M. 1987. Behavioral aspects of panic disorder. *American Journal of Psychiatry*, 144, 1160–1165.

MARKS, I. M. 1987. *Fears, phobias, and rituals: Panic, anxiety, and their disorders*. New York: Oxford University Press.

MARLATT, G. A., DEMMING, B., & REID, J. B. 1973. Loss of control drinking in alcoholics: An experimental analogue. *Journal of Abnormal Psychology*, 81, 233–241.

MARLATT, G. A., & GORDON, J. R. 1985. *Relapse prevention: Maintenance strategies in the treatment of addictive behaviors*. New York: Guilford.

MARMOR, J. 1980. *Homosexual behavior*. New York: Basic Books.

MARMOR, M. G., & SYME, S. L. 1976. Acculturation and coronary heart disease in Japanese-Americans. *Journal of Epidemiology*, 104, 225–247.

MARTIN, H. P. 1976. *The abused child*. Cambridge, MA: Ballinger.

MARZILLIER, J. S., & BIRCHWOOD, M. J. 1981. Behavioral treatment of cognitive disorders. In L. Michelson, M. Hersen, & S. M. Turner, eds., *Future perspectives on behavior therapy*. New York: Plenum Press.

MASLOW, A. H. 1968. *Toward a psychology of being*, 2nd ed. Princeton, NJ: Van Nostrand.

MASTERS, W. H., & JOHNSON, V. E. 1966. *Human sexual response*. Boston: Little, Brown.

MASTERS, W. H., & JOHNSON, V. E. 1970. *Human sexual inadequacy*. Boston: Little, Brown.

MASTERS, W. H., & JOHNSON, V. E. 1979. *Homosexuality in perspective*. Boston: Little, Brown.

MASTERS, W. H., JOHNSON, V. E., & KOLODNY, R. C. 1985. *Human sexuality*, 2nd ed. Boston: Little, Brown.

MATTHEWS, W. S., BARABAS, G., CUSAK, E., & FERRARI, M. 1986. Social quotients of children with phenylketonuria before and after discontinuation of dietary therapy. *American Journal of Mental Deficiency*, 91, 92–94.

MAY, P.R.A., TUMA, A. H., & DIXON, W. J. 1981. Schizophrenia: A follow-up study of the results of five forms of treatment. *Archives of General Psychiatry*, 38, 776–784.

MCADAMS, J. A. 1985. Messages. *Journal of the American Medical Association*, 254, 1222.

MCCLELLAND, D. C., ROSS, G., & PATEL, V. 1985. Exam stress and immunoglobulin levels. *Journal of Human Stress*, 11, 52–59.

MCGLASHAN, T. H. 1986. Schizotypal personality disorder. *Archives of General Psychiatry*, 43, 329–334.

MCGLASHAN, T. H. 1983. The borderline syndrome. *Archives of General Psychiatry*, 40, 1319–1323.

MCGUE, M., GOTTESMAN, I. I., & RAO, D. C. 1985. Resolving genetic models for the transmission of schizophrenia. *Genetic Epidemiology*, 21, 99–110.

MCGUE, M., GOTTESMAN, I. I., & RAO, D. C. In press. Resolving genetic models for the transmission of schizophrenia. *Genetic Epidemiology*.

MCGUFFIN, P., REVELEY, A., & HOLLAND, A. 1982. Identical triplets: Nonidentical psychosis? *British Journal of Psychiatry*, 140, 1–6.

MCNALLY, R. J. 1987. Preparedness and phobias: A review. *Psychological Bulletin*, 101, 283–303.

MCNEAL, E. T., & CIMBOLIC, P. 1986. Antidepressants and biochemical theories of depression. *Psychological Bulletin*, 99, 361–374.

MCNIEL, D. E., ARKOWITZ, H. S., & PRITCHARD, B. E. 1987. The response of others to face-to-face interaction with depressed patients. *Journal of Abnormal Psychology*, 96, 341–344.

MEDNICK, S. A., CUDECK, R., GRIFFITH, J. J., TALOVIC, S. A., & SCHULSINGER, F. A. 1984. The Danish high-risk project: Recent methods and findings. In N. F. Watt, E. J. Anthony, L. C. Wynne, & J. E. Rolf, *Children at risk for schizophrenia*. Cambridge: Cambridge University Press.

MEDNICK, S. A., MOFFIT, T., POLLACK, V., TALOVIC, S., GABRIELLI, W., & VAN DUSEN, K. T. 1983. "The inheritance of human deviance." In D. Magnusson & V. L. Allen, eds., *Human Development: An interactional perspective*. New York: Academic Press.

MEDNICK, S. A., & SCHULSINGER, F. 1968. Some premorbid characteristics related to breakdown in children with schizophrenic mothers. *Journal of Psychiatric Research*, 6, 267–291.

MELAMED, B. G., & BUSH, J. P. 1986. Parent-child influences during medical procedures. In S. M. Auerbach and A. L. Stolberg, eds., *Crisis intervention within children and families*. Washington, D.C.: Hemisphere.

MELLOR, C. S. 1970. First rank symptoms of schizophrenia. *British Journal of Psychiatry*, 177, 15–23.

MERCER, J. R. 1971. The meaning of mental retardation. In R. Koch & J. C. Dobson, eds., *The mentally retarded child in his family: A multidisciplinary handbook*. New York: Brunner/Mazel, 23–47.

MERIKANGAS, K. R., & WEISSMAN, M. M. 1986. Epidemiology of DSM-III Axis II personality disorders. In A. J. Francis & R. E. Hales, eds., *American Psychiatric Association Annual Review*, vol. 5. Washington, D.C.: American Psychiatric Association.

MILICH, R., & DODGE, K. A. 1984. Social information processing in child psychiatric populations. *Journal of Abnormal Child Psychology*, 12, 471–490.

MILICH, R., WOLRAICH, M., & LINDGREN, S. 1986. Sugar and hyperactivity: A critical review of empirical findings. *Clinical Psychology Review*, 6, 493–513.

MILLER, H. L., COOMBS, D. W., LEEPER, J. D., & BARTON, S. N. 1984. An analysis of the effects of suicide prevention facilities on suicide rates in the United States. *American Journal of Public Health*, 74, 340–343.

MILLER, W. R. 1985. Motivation for treatment: A review with special emphasis on alcoholism. *Psychological Bulletin*, 98, 84–107.

MILLER, W. R., & HESTER, R. K. 1986. Inpatient alcoholism treatment: Who benefits? *American Psychologist*, 41, 794–805.

MILLMAN, R. B. 1986. General principles of diagnosis and treatment. In A. J. Frances and R. E. Hales, eds., *American Psychiatric Association Annual Review*, vol. 5. Washington, D.C.: American Psychiatric Press.

MILLON, T. 1981. *Disorders of personality: DSM-III, Axis II*. New York: Wiley.

MILLON, T. 1986. The avoidant personality. In R. Michels and J. O. Cavenar, Jr., *Psychiatry*, vol. 1. New York: Basic Books.

MILLON, T., & KLERMAN, G. C. 1986. *Contemporary directions in psychopathology: Toward the DSM-IV*. New York: Guilford.

MINTZ, L. I., LIBERMAN, R. P., LEFF, J., & VAUGHN, C. 1985. *Expressed emotion in families*. New York: Guilford Press.

MINTZ, L. I., LIBERMAN, R. P., MIKLOWITZ, D. J., & MINTZ, J. 1987. Expressed emotion: A call for partnership among relatives, patients, and professionals. *Schizophrenia Bulletin*, 13, 227–235.

MINUCHIN, S., ROSMAN, B., & BAKER, L. 1978. *Psychosomatic families: Anorexia nervosa in context*. Cambridge, MA: Harvard University Press.

MIZES, J. S. 1985. Bulimia: A review of its symptomatology and treatment. *Advances in Behavior Research and Therapy*, 1, 91–142.

MIZES, J. S., & FLEECE, E. L. 1984. The effect of progressive relaxation on the urge to binge and actual binges in a bulimorexic female. Paper presented at the 5th Annual Meeting of the Society of Behavioral Medicine. Philadelphia, May.

MOLLER, H. J., VON ZERSSEN, D., WERNER-EILERT, K., & WUSCHNER-STOCKHEIM, M. 1982. Outcome in schizophrenic and similar paranoid psychoses. *Schizophrenia Bulletin*, 8, 99–108.

MONAHAN, J. 1981. *Predicting violent behavior: An assessment of clinical techniques*. Beverly Hills: Sage.

MONEY, J. 1984. Food, fitness and vital fluids: Sexual pleasure from graham crackers to Kellogg's cornflakes. *British Journal of Sexual Medicine*, 11, 127–130.

MONEY, J. 1987. Sin, sickness, or status? Homosexual gender identity and psychoneuroendocrinology. *American Psychologist*, 42, 384–399.

MONEY, J., & BOHMER, C. 1980. Prison sexology: Two personal accounts of masturbation, homosexuality, and rape. *Journal of Sex Research*, 16, 258–266.

MONEY, J., & RUSSO, A. J. 1979. Homosexual outcome of discordant gender identity/role in childhood: Longitudinal follow-up. *Journal of Pediatric Psychology*, 4, 29–41.

MONEY, J., & SCHWARTZ, M. 1977. Dating, romantic and nonromantic friendships and sexuality in 17 early-treated adrenogenital females, age 16–25. In Palee, et al., eds., *Congenital adrenal hyperplasia*. Baltimore: University Park Press.

MORAN, A. E., FREEDMAN, R. I., & SHARFSTEIN, S. S. 1984. The journey of Sylvia Frumpkin: A case study for policymakers. *Hospital and Community Psychiatry*, 35, 887–893.

MORELAND, J., SCHWEBEL, A., BECK, S., & WELLS, R. 1982. Parents as therapists. *Behavior modification*, 10, 250–276.

MORIHISA, J. M., DUFFY, F. H., & WYATT, R. J. 1983. Brain electrical activity mapping (BEAM) in schizophrenic patients. *Archives of General Psychiatry*, 40, 719–728.

MORRIS, A. F., VAUGHN, S. E., & VACCARO, P. 1982. Measurement of neuromuscular tone and strength in Down's syndrome children. *Journal of Mental Deficiency Research*, 26, 41–46.

MORRIS, J. 1974. *Conundrum*. New York: Harcourt, Brace, & Jovanovich.

MORRISSEY, J. P., & GOLDMAN, H. H. 1986. Care and treatment of the mentally ill in the United States: Historical developments and reforms. *American Association of Political and Social Sciences*, 484, 12–28.

MOZAR, H. N., BAL, D. G., & HOWARD, J. T. 1987. Perspectives on the etiology of Alzheimer's disease. *Journal of the American Medical Association*, 257, 1503–1507

MURPHY, E., LINDESAY, J., GRUNDY, E. 1986. Sixty years of suicide in England and Wales. *Archives of General Psychiatry*, 43, 969–976.

MURPHY, L. B. 1974. Coping, vulnerability, and resilience in childhood. In G. V. Coelho, D. A. Hamburg, & J. E. Adams, eds., *Coping and adaptation*. New York: Basic Books.

MURRAY, H. A. 1943. *Thematic Apperception Test: Pictures and manual*. Cambridge, MA: Harvard University Press.

MURRAY, J. B. 1982. The psyche and stomach ulcers. *Genetic Psychology Monographs*, 105, 182–212.

MYERS, J. K., WEISSMAN, M. M., TISCHLER, G. L., HOLZER, C. E., III, LEAF, P. J., ORVASCHEL, H., ANTHONY, J. C., BOYD, J. H., BURKE, J. D., JR., KRAMER, M., & STOLTZMAN, R. 1984. Six-month prevalence of psychiatric disorders in three communities. *Archives of General Psychiatry*, 41, 959–967.

National Academy of Sciences. 1982. *Marijuana and health*. Washington, D.C.: National Academy Press.

National Household Survey on Drugs. 1985. Rockville, MD: National Institute on Drug Abuse.

NEIMEYER, G. J., & NEIMEYER, R. A. 1985. Relational trajectories: A personal construct contribution. *Journal of Social and Personal Relationships*, 2, 325–349.

NAGLER, S., & MIRSKY, A. F. 1985. Introduction: The Israeli high-risk study. *Schizophrenia Bulletin*, 11, 19–29.

MITCHELL, J. E., & ECKERT, E. D. 1987. Scope and significance of eating disorders. *Journal of Consulting and Clinical Psychology*, 55, 628–634.

MIRSKY, A. F., & BAKAY PRAGNAY, E. 1984. Brainstem mechanisms in the processing of sensory information: Clinical symptoms, animal models and unit analysis. In D. E. Sheer, ed., *Attention: Theory, brain functions and clinical applications*. Hillsdale, NJ: Erlbaum.

NEMIAH, J. C. 1978. Psychoneurotic disorders. In A. M. Nicholi, ed., *Harvard guide to modern psychiatry*. Cambridge, MA: Harvard University Press.

NEMIAH, J. C. 1985. Phobic disorders (phobic neuroses). In H. I. Kaplan and B. J. Sadock, eds., *Comprehensive textbook of psychiatry*, 4th ed. Baltimore, MD: Williams and Wilkins.

NEMIAH, J. C. 1985. Obsessive-compulsive disorder (obsessive-compulsive neurosis). In H. I. Kaplan & B. J. Sadock, eds., *Comprehensive textbook of psychiatry*, 4th ed. Baltimore, MD: Williams & Wilkins.

NESS, R. C., & WINTROB, R. M. 1981. Folkhealing: A description and synthesis. *American Journal of Psychiatry, 138*, 1477–1481.

NEUGEBAUER, R. 1979. Medieval and early modern theories of mental illness. *Archives of General Psychiatry, 36*, 477–483.

NICHOLS, P. L. 1984. Familial mental retardation. *Behavior Genetics, 14*, 161–170.

NIETZEL, M. T., & HIMELIEN, M. J. 1986. Prevention of crime and delinquency. In B. A. Edelstein and L. Michelson, eds., *Handbook of Prevention*. New York: Plenum.

NOLEN-HOEKSEMA, S. 1987. Sex differences in unipolar depression: Evidence and theory. *Psychological Bulletin, 101*, 259–282.

NUECHTERLEIN, K. H. 1983. Signal detection in vigilance tasks and behavioral attributes among offspring of schizophrenic mothers and among hyperactive children. *Journal of Abnormal Psychology, 92*, 4–28.

NUECHTERLEIN, K. H., & DAWSON, M. E. 1984. Information processing and attentional functioning in the developmental course of schizophrenic disorders. *Schizophrenia Bulletin, 10*, 160–203.

OATLEY, K., & BOLTON, W. 1985. A social-cognitive theory of depression in reaction to life events. *Psychological Review, 92*, 372–388.

OCHBERG, F. M., ed. 1988. *Post-traumatic therapy and victims of violence*. New York: Brunner/Mazel.

O'CONNELL, R. A. 1986. Psychosocial factors in a model of manic-depressive disease. *Integrative Psychiatry, 4*, 150–154.

O'CONNOR, G. 1976. *Home is a good place: A national perspective of community residential facilities for developmentally disabled persons*. Washington, D.C.: American Association on Mental Deficiency.

O'DONOGHUE, E. G. 1914. *The story of Bethlehem Hospital from its foundation in 1247*. London: T. Fisher.

OGDEN, J. A. H. 1947. *The Kingdom of the Lost*. London: Bodley Head.

OKOLO, C., & GUSKIN, S. 1984. Community attitudes toward community placement of mentally retarded persons. *International Review of Research in Mental Retardation, 12*, 25–66.

OLDHAM, J. M., & FROSCH, W. A. 1986. Compulsive personality disorder. In R. Michels and J. O. Cavenar, Jr. eds., *Psychiatry*, vol. 1. New York: Basic Books.

O'LEARY, K. D., & WILSON, G. T. 1987. *Behavior therapy: Application and outcome*. Englewood Cliffs, NJ: Prentice-Hall.

O'NEAL, J. M. 1984. First person account: Finding myself and loving it. *Schizophrenia Bulletin, 10*, 109–110.

ORNITZ, E. M. 1985. Neurophysiology of infantile autism. *Journal of the American Academy of Child Psychiatry, 24*, 251–262.

PAGEL, M. D., BECKER, J., & COPPEL, D. B. 1985. Loss of control, self-blame, and depression: An investigation of spouse caregivers of Alzheimer's disease patients. *Journal of Abnormal Psychology, 94*, 169–182.

PAINTER, S. L. 1986. Research on the prevalence of child sexual abuse: New directions. *Canadian Journal of Behavioral Science, 18*, 323–339.

PARKES, C. M. 1986. *Bereavement: Studies of grief in adult life*. Madison, CO: International Universities Press.

PARNAS, J., SCHULSINGER, F., SCHULSINGER, H., MEDNICK, S. A., & TEASDALE, T. W. 1982. Behavioral precursors of schizophrenic spectrum: A prospective study. *Archives of General Psychiatry, 39*, 658–664.

PATTERSON, G. R. 1982. *Coercive family process*. Eugene, OR: Castilia Press.

PAUL, G. L. 1969. Chronic mental patient: Current status-future directions. *Psychological Bulletin, 71*, 81–93.

PAUL, G. L., & LENTZ, R. J. 1977. *Psychosocial treatment of chronic mental patients: Milieu versus social-learning programs*. Cambridge, MA: Harvard University Press.

PAUL, S. M. 1985. Toward the integration of neuroscience and psychiatry. In H. A. Pincus & H. Pardes, eds., *The integration of neuroscience and psychiatry*. Washington, D.C.: American Psychiatric Press, 39–52.

PAYKEL, E. S. 1979. Recent life events in the development of the depressive disorders. In R. A. Depue, ed., *The psychobiology of the depressive disorders: Implications for the effects of stress*. New York: Academic Press.

PEELE, S. 1984. The cultural context of psychological approaches to alcoholism: Can we control the effects of alcohol? *American Psychologist, 39*, 1337–1351.

PEELE, S. 1985. *The meaning of addiction: Compulsive experience and its interpretation*. Lexington, MA: Lexington Books.

PELHAM, W. E., & BENDER, M. 1982. Peer relationships in hyperactive children: Description and treatment. In K. Gadow & I. Bialer, eds., *Advances in learning and behavioral disabilities*, vol. 1. Greenwich, CT: JAI Press.

PENNEBAKER, J. W. 1982. *The psychology of physical symptoms*. New York: Springer-Verlag.

PERLS, F. S. 1969. *Gestalt therapy verbatim*. Lafayette, CA; Real People Press.

PERRIS, C. 1987. Toward an integrative theory of depression-focusing on the concept of vulnerability. *Integrative Psychiatry, 5*, 27–39.

PENNEBAKER, J. W., & BEALL, S. K. 1986. Confronting a traumatic event: Toward an understanding of inhibition and disease. *Journal of Abnormal Psychology, 95*, 274–281.

PERRY, J. C., & FLANNERY, R. B. 1982. Passive aggressive personality disorder: Treatment implications of a clinical typology. *Journal of Nervous and Mental Disease, 170*, 164–173.

PERSKY, V. W., KEMPTHORNE-RAWSON, J., & SHEKELLE, R. B. 1987. Personality and risk of cancer: 20-year follow-up of the Western Electric Study. *Psychosomatic Medicine, 49*, 435–449.

PETERSON, C., & SELIGMAN, M.E.P. 1984. Causal explanations as a risk factor for depression: Theory and evidence. *Psychological Review, 91*, 347–374.

PETTI, T. A. 1981. Depression in children: A significant disorder. *Psychosomatics, 22*, 444–447.

PFEFFER, C. R., CONTE, H. R., JERRETT, I., & PLUTCHIK, R. 1980. Suicide behavior in latency age children. *Journal of the American Academy of Child Psychology, 19*, 703–710.

PFOHL, B., & ANDREASEN, N. C. 1986. Schizophrenia: Diagnosis and classification. In R. E. Hales & A. J. Frances, eds., *American Psychiatric Association, Annual Review* vol. 6. Washington, D.C.: American Psychiatric Press.

PHILLIPS, D. P., & CARSTENSEN, L. S. 1986. Clustering of

teenage suicides after television news stories about suicide. *New England Journal of Medicine*, 315, 685–689.

PHILLIPS, D. P., & PAIGHT, D. J. 1987. The impact of televised movies about suicide. *New England Journal of Medicine*, 317, 809–811.

PIERCEY, B. P. 1985. First person account: Making the best of it. *Schizophrenia Bulletin*, 11, 155–157.

PILKONIS, P. A., IMBER, S. D., LEWIS, P., & RUBINSKY, P. 1984. A comparative outcome study of individual, group, and conjoint psychotherapy. *Archives of General Psychiatry*, 41, 431–437.

PILLARD, R. C., & WEINRICH, J. D. 1986. Evidence of familial nature of male homsexuality. *Archives of General Psychiatry*, 43, 808–812.

PINEL, P. 1969. *Traite' medico-philosophique sur l'alienation mentale*, 2nd ed. Paris: Brossen, 1809; as quoted in W. Riese, *The legacy of Philippe Pinel*. New York: Springer.

PLAKUN, E. M., BURKHARDT, P. E., & MULLER, A. P. 1985. Fourteen-year follow-up of borderline and schizotypal personality disorders. *Comprehensive Psychiatry*, 26, 448–455.

PLISZKA, S. R. 1987. Tricyclic antidepressants in the treatment of children with attention deficit disorder. *Journal of the American Academy of Child and Adolescent Psychiatry*, 26, 127–132.

PLUMB, M. M., & HOLLAND, J. 1977. Comparative studies of psychological function in patients with advanced cancer. I. Self-reported depressive symptoms. *Psychosomatic Medicine*, 39, 264–276.

POGUE-GEILE, M. F., & HARROW, M. 1985. Negative symptoms in schizophrenia: Their longitudinal course and prognostic importance. *Schizophrenia Bulletin*, 11, 427–439.

POLICH, J. M., & ARMOR, D. J. 1980. *The course of alcoholism: Four years after treatment*. Santa Monica, CA: Rand.

POMEROY, W. B. 1972. *Kinsey and the Institute for Sex Research*. New York: Harper & Row.

POPE, H. G., JR., JONAS, J. M., HUDSON, J., COHEN, B. M., & GUNDERSON, J. G. 1983. The validity of DSM-III borderline personality disorder. *Archives of General Psychiatry*, 40, 1319–1323.

PRESLY, A. S., GRUBB, A. B., & SEMPLE, D. 1982. Predictors of successful rehabilitation in long-term patients. *Acta Psychiatria Scandinavica*, 66, 83–88.

PRINCE, V. C. 1967. *The transvestite and his wife*. Los Angeles: Argyle Books.

PRIOR, M. R. 1984. Developing concepts of childhood autism: The influence of experimental cognitive research. *Journal of Consulting and Clinical Psychology*, 52, 4–16.

PRIOR, M. R., & McGILLVRAY, J. 1980. The performance of autistic children on three learning set tasks. *Journal of Child Psychology and Psychiatry*, 21, 313–324.

PURCELL, K., BRADY, K., SCHAL, H., MUSER, J., MOLK, L., GORDON, N., & MEANS, J. 1969. The effect on asthma in children of experimental separation from the family. *Psychosomatic Medicine*, 31, 144–164.

RABKIN, J. G. 1979. Criminal behavior of discharged mental patients: A critical appraisal of the research. *Psychological Bulletin*, 86, 1–27.

RACHMAN, S. J., & DESILVA, P. 1978. Abnormal and normal obsessions. *Behavioral Research and Therapy*, 16, 223–248.

RACHMAN, S. J., & HODGSON, R. J. 1980. *Obsessions and compulsions*. Englewood Cliffs, NJ: Prentice-Hall.

RAGLAND, D. R., & BRAND, R. J. 1988. Type A behavior and mortality from coronary heart disease. *New England Journal of Medicine*, 318, 65–69.

RAMEY, C. T., & HASKINS, R. 1981. The modification of intelligence through early experience. *Intelligence*, 5, 43–57.

RAPAPORT, K., & BURKART, B. R. 1984. Personality and attitudinal characteristics of sexually coercive college males. *Journal of Abnormal Psychology*, 13, 216–221.

RAPOPORT, J., ELKINS, R., LANGER, D. H., SCEERY, W., BUCHSBAUM, M. S., GILLIN, J. C., MURPHY, D. L., ZAHN, T. P., LAKE, R., LUDLOW, C., & MENDELSON, W. 1981. Childhood obsessive-compulsive disorder. *American Journal of Psychiatry*, 138, 1545–1554.

A recovering patient. 1986. "Can we talk?": The schizophrenic patient in psychotherapy. *American Journal of Psychiatry*, 143, 68–70.

REDICK, R. W., SITKIN, M. J., & BETHEL, H. 1984. Distribution of psychiatric beds, United States and each state, 1982. *Mental Health Statistical Note*, No. 167, Sept., U.S. Department of Health and Human Services, National Institute of Mental Health. Washington, D.C.: U.S. Government Printing Office.

REICH, W. 1949. (originally published 1933) *Character analysis*. New York: Orgone Institute Press.

REISBERG, B. 1985. Alzheimer's disease updated. *Psychiatric Annals*, 15, 319–322.

REISS, B. F. 1980. Psychological tests in homosexuality. In J. Marmor, ed., *Homosexual behavior*. New York: Basic Books.

REKERS, G. A. 1977. Assessment and treatment of childhood gender problems. In B. B. Lahey & A. E. Kazdin, eds., *Advances in clinical child psychology*, vol. 1. New York: Plenum.

REHM, L. P., KASLOW, N. J., & RABIN, A. S. 1987. Cognitive and behavioral targets in a self-control therapy program for depression. *Journal of Consulting and Clinical Psychology*, 55, 60–67.

REID, W. H. 1986. Antisocial personality. In R. Michels and J. O. Cavenar, Jr., eds., *Psychiatry*, vol. 1. New York: Basic Books.

REID, W. H., & BALIS, G.U. 1987. Evaluation of the violent patient. In R. E. Hales and A. J. Frances, eds., *American Psychiatric Association Annual Review*, vol. 6. Washington, D.C.: American Psychiatric Press.

REID, W. H., DOOR, D., WALKER, J. L., & BONNER, J. W. 1986. *Unmasking the psychopath: Antisocial personality and related symptoms*. New York: Norton.

REMAFEDI, G. 1985. Adolescent homosexuality: Issues for pediatricians. *Clinical Pediatrics*, 9, 481–485.

REMAFEDI, G. 1987a. Male homosexuality: The adolescent perspective. *Pediatrics*, 79, 326–330.

REMAFEDI, G. 1987b. Adolescent homosexuality: Psychosocial and medical implications. *Pediatrics*, 79, 331–337.

Research News. 1987. Brain grafts benefit Parkinson's patients. *Science*, 236, 149.

Research on mental illness and addictive disorders. 1985. *American Journal of Psychiatry*, 142 (supplement), 9–41.

Research on mental illness and addictive disorders: Progress and prospects. 1984. Washington, D.C.: National Academy Press.

REVELEY, A. M. 1985. Genetic counseling for schizophrenia. *British Journal of Psychiatry*, 147, 107–112.

RICE, J., REICH, T., ANDREASEN, N. C., ENDICOTT, J., VANEERDEWEGH, M., FISHMAN, R., HIRSCHFELD, R.M.A., & KLERMAN, G. L. 1987. The familial transmission of bipolar illness. *Archives of General Psychiatry*, 44, 441–447.

RICHMANN, N., STEVENSON, J., & GRAHAM, P. J. 1982. *Pre-school to school: A behavioral study*. London: Academic Press.

RIE, H., & RIE, E. eds. 1980. *Handbook of minimal brain dysfunctions: A critical view*. New York: Wiley.

RIESENBERG, D. 1987. Treating a societal malignancy—rape. *Journal of the American Medical Association*, 257, 726–727.

ROACH, M. 1983. Another name for madness. New York Times Magazine, Jan. 16, 22-31.

ROBERTSON, H. A. 1979. Benzodiazepine receptors in "emotional" and "nonemotional" mice: Comparison of four strains. European Journal of Pharmacology, 56, 163.

ROBINS, C. J. 1988. Attributions and depression: Why is the literature so inconsistent. Journal of Personality and Social Psychology, 54, 847-852.

ROBINS, L. N., HELZER, J. E., CROGHAN, J., & RATCLIFF, K. S. 1981. National Institute of Mental Health Diagnostic Interview Schedule. Archives of General Psychiatry, 38, 381-389.

ROBINS, L. N., & RATCLIFF, K. S. 1980. The long-term outcome of truancy. In L. A. Hersov & I. Berg, eds., Out of School: Modern perspectives on truancy and school refusal. Chichester, England: Wiley.

ROCK, C. L., & YAGER, J. 1987. Nutrition and eating disorders: A primer for clinicians. International Journal of Eating Disorders, 6, 267-280.

ROGENTINE, G. N., VANKAMMEN, D. P., FOX, B. H., DOGHERTY, J. P., ROSENBLATT, J. E., BOYD, S. C., & BUNNEY, W. E., Jr. 1979. Psychological factors in the prognosis of malignant melanoma: A prospective study. Psychosomatic Medicine, 41, 647-655.

ROGERS, C. R. 1951. Client-centered therapy. Boston: Houghton-Mifflin.

ROGERS, C. R. 1959. A theory of therapy, personality, and inter-personal relationships as developed in the client-centered framework. In S. Koch, ed., Psychology: A study of a science, vol. 3. New York: McGraw-Hill.

ROGERS, C. R. 1980. A way of being. Boston: Houghton-Mifflin.

ROGLER, L. H., & HOLLINGSHEAD, A. B. 1965. Trapped: Families and schizophrenia. New York: John Wiley.

ROGERS, R. C., & SIMENSEN, R. J. 1987. Fragile X syndrome: A common etiology of mental retardation. American Journal of Mental Deficiency, 91, 445-449.

ROMER, D., & HELLER, T. 1983. Social adaptation of mentally retarded adults in community settings: A social-ecological approach. Applied Research in Mental Retardation, 4, 303-314.

RORSCHACH, J. 1942. Psychodiagnostic: Methodik und ergebnisse eines wahrnehmungs-diagnostichen experiments, 2nd ed. (P. Lemkau & B. Kronenberg, trans.) Berne & Berlin: Huber. 1932; republished: New York: Grune & Stratton.

ROSEN, J. C. & LEITENBERG, J. 1982. Bulimia nervosa: Treatment with exposure and response prevention. Behavior Therapy, 13, 117-124.

ROSENBAUM, A., & O'LEARY, K. D. 1981. Marital violence: Characteristics of abusive couples. Journal of Consulting and Clinical Psychology, 49, 63-71.

ROSENBLUM, L. A., & PAULLY, G. S. 1987. Primate models of separation-induced depression. Psychiatric Clinics of North America, 10, 437-447.

ROSENHAN, D. L. 1973. On being sane in insane places. Science, 179, 250-257.

ROSENMAN, R. H., BRAND, R. J., JENKINS, C. D., FRIEDMAN, M., STRAUS, R., & WURM, M. 1975. Coronary heart disease in the Western Collaborative Group Study. Journal of the American Medical Association, 233, 872-877.

ROSENSTEIN, M. J., & MILAZZO-SAYRE, L. J. 1981. Characteristics of admissions to selected mental-health facilities. Rockville, MD: U.S. Dept of Health and Human Services.

ROSENSTEIN, M. J., STEADMAN, H. J., MILAZZO-SAYRE, L. J., MacASKILL, R. C., & MANDERSCHEID, R. W. 1986. Characteristics of admissions to the inpatient services of state and county mental hospitals, United States, 1980. Mental Health Statistical Note. No. 177 (U.S. National Institute of Mental Health). Washington, D.C.: U.S. Government Printing Office.

ROSENTHAL, D., ed. 1963. The Genain quadruplets: A case study and theoretical analysis of heredity and environment in schizophrenia. New York: Basic Books.

ROSENTHAL, D., WENDER, P. H., KETY, S. S., SCHULSINGER, F., WELNER, J., & OSTERGAARD, L. 1968. Schizophrenics' offspring reared in adoptive homes. In D. Rosenthal & S. S. Kety, eds., The transmission of schizophrenia. Oxford: Pergamon Press.

ROSENTHAL, N. E., JACOBSEN, F. M., SACK, D. A., ARENDT, J., JAMES, S. P., PARRY, B. L., & WEHR, T. A. 1988. Atenolol in seasonal affective disorder. American Journal of Psychiatry, 145, 52-56.

ROSENTHAL, D., WENDER, P. H., KETY, S. S., SCHULSINGER, F., WELNER, J., & REIDER, R. 1975. Parent-child relationships and psychopathological disorder in the child. Archives of General Psychiatry, 32, 466-476.

ROSIE, J. S. 1987. Partial hospitalization: A review of recent literature. Hospital and Community Psychiatry, 38, 1291-1299.

ROSS, D. M., & ROSS, S. A. 1982. Hyperactivity: Research, theory, and action. New York: John Wiley.

ROSS, H. L., & GLASER, E. M. 1973. Making it out of the ghetto. Professional Psychology, 4, 347-356.

ROSSLER, T., & DEISHER, R. W. 1972. Youthful male homosexuality: Homosexual experience and the process of developing homosexual identity in males aged 16 to 22 years. Journal of the American Medical Association, 219, 1018-1023.

ROSVOLD, H. E., MIRSKY, A. F., SARASON, I. G., BRANSOME, E. D., & BECK, L. H. 1956. A continuous performance test of brain damage. Journal of Consulting Psychology, 20, 343-350.

ROY-BYRNE, P. P., & KATON, W. 1987. An update on treatment of the anxiety disorders. Hospital and Community Psychiatry, 38, 835-886.

ROY-BYRNE, P. P., POST, R. M., UHDE, T. W., PORCU, T., & DAVIS, D. 1985. The longitudinal course of recurrent affective illness: Life chart data from research patients at the NIMH. Acta Psychiatrica Scandinavica Supplementum, 71, 3-34.

RUBENS, R. L., & LAPIDUS, L. B. 1978. Schizophrenic patterns of arousal and stimulus barrier functioning. Journal of Abnormal Psychology, 87, 199-211.

RUBERMAN, J. W., WEINBLATT, E., GOLDBERG, J. D., & CHAUDHARY, B. S. 1984. Psychological influences on mortality after myocardial infarction. New England Journal of Medicine, 311, 552-559.

RUMSEY, J. M., DUARA, R., GRADY, C., RAPOPORT, J. L., MARGOLIN, R. A., RAPOPORT, S. I., & CUTLER, N. R. 1985. Brain metabolism in autism. Archives of General Psychiatry, 42, 448-455.

RUSSELL, D.E.H. 1984. The prevalence and seriousness of incestuous abuse: Step fathers vs. biological fathers. Child Abuse and Neglect, 8, 15-22.

RUTTER, M. 1967. Psychotic disorders in early childhood. In A. J. Coppen & A. Walk, eds., Recent developments in schizophrenia. Oxford, England: Headley Bros.

RUTTER, M. 1980. Changing youth in a changing society. Cambridge: Harvard University Press.

RUTTER, M. 1984. The developmental psychopathology of depression: Issues and perspectives. In M. Rutter, C. E. Izard, & P. Read, eds., Depression in childhood: Developmental perspectives. New York: Guilford Press.

RUTTER, M. 1986. Depressive feelings, cognitions and disorders: A research postscript. In M. Rutter, ed., *Depression in young people*. New York: Guilford Press.

RUTTER, M., COX, A., TUPLING, C., BERGER, M., & YULE, W. 1975. Attainment and adjustment in two geographical areas: I. The prevalence of psychiatric disorder. *British Journal of Psychiatry, 126,* 493–509.

RUTTER, M., & GARMEZY, N. 1983. Developmental psychopathology. In P. Mussen, ed., *Handbook of child psychology,* vol. 4. New York: John Wiley.

RUTTER, M., & GILLER, H. 1984. *Juvenile delinquency: Trends and perspectives.* Harmondsworth, England: Penguin.

RUTTER, M., GRAHAM, P., & YULE, W. 1970. A neuropsychiatric study in childhood. *Clinics in Developmental Medicine,* Nos. 35/36. London: Heinemann.

RUTTER, M., & HERSOV, L. 1985. Child and adolescent psychiatry: Modern approaches. Oxford, England: Blackwell Scientific Publications.

RUTTER, M., & QUINTON, D. 1984. Parental psychiatric disorder: Effect on children. *Psychological Medicine, 14,* 853–880.

RUTTER, M., & SHAFFER, D. 1980. DSM-III: A step forward or back in terms of the classification of child psychiatric disorders. *Journal of the American Academy of Child Psychiatry, 19,* 371–394.

RUTTER, M., TIZARD, I., & WHITMORE, K., eds. 1981. (originally published in 1970) *Education, health and behavior.* Huntington, NY: Krieger.

RUTTER, M. T., & ROBINS, E. 1973. *Male and female homosexuality: A comprehensive investigation.* Baltimore: Williams & Wilkins.

SACKHEIM, H. A., & WEGNER, A. Z. 1986. Attributional patterns in depression and euthymia. *Archives of General Psychiatry, 43,* 553–560.

SAGHIR, M. T., & ROBINS, E. 1973. *Male and female homosexuality: A comprehensive investigation.* Baltimore: Williams & Wilkins.

SALTER, A. C., RICHARDSON, C. M., & KAIRYS, S. W. 1985. Caring for abused preschoolers. *Child Welfare, 64,* 343–356.

SANDLER, J., with A. FREUD. 1985. *The analysis of defense: The ego and the mechanisms of defense revisited.* New York: International Universities Press.

SARASON, B. R., SARASON, I. G., HACKER, T. A., & BASHAM, R. B. 1985. Concomitants of social support: Social skills, physical attractiveness, and gender. *Journal of Personality and Social Psychology, 49,* 469–480.

SARASON, I. G. 1979. Three lacunae of cognitive therapy. *Cognitive Therapy and Research, 3,* 223–235.

SARASON, I. G., JOHNSON, J. M., & SIEGEL, J. M. 1978. Assessing the impact of life stress: Development of the Life Experiences Survey. *Journal of Consulting and Clinical Psychology, 46,* 932–946.

SARASON, I. G., & SARASON, B. R., eds. 1985. *Social support: Theory, research and applications.* Dordrecht, The Netherlands: Martinus Nijhof.

SARASON, I. G., & SARASON, B. R. 1981. Teaching cognitive and social skills to high school students. *Journal of Consulting and Clinical Psychology, 49,* 908–919.

SARASON, I. G., SARASON, B. R., POTTER, E. H. III, & ANTONI, M. H. 1985. Life events, social support, and illness. *Psychosomatic Medicine, 47,* 156–163.

SARASON, I. G., & STOOPS, R. 1978. Test anxiety and the passage of time. *Journal of Consulting and Clinical Psychology, 46,* 102–109.

SASS, L. 1982. The borderline personality. *New York Times Magazine,* August 22.

SAUL, R. A., STEVENSON, R. I., SIMENSEN, R. J., WILKES, G., ALEXANDER, W., & TAYLOR, H. 1982. Fragile X syndrome in South Carolina. *Journal of the South Carolina Medical Association, 78,* 475–477.

SCARR, S. 1981. *Race, social class and individual differences in IQ.* Hillsdale, NJ: Erlbaum.

SCARR, S., & WEINBERG, R. A. 1978. The influence of "family background" on intellectual attainment. *American Sociological Review, 43,* 674–692.

SCHACHT, T. E., & STRUPP, H. H. 1985. Evaluation of psychotherapy. In H. I. Kaplan & B. J. Sadock, eds. *Comprehensive textbook of psychiatry,* 4th ed., vol. 2. Baltimore: Williams & Wilkins.

SCHACHTER, S. 1982. Recidivism and self-care of smoking and obesity. *American Psychologist, 37,* 436–444.

SCHAFER, R. 1948. *Clinical application of psychological tests.* New York: International Universities Press.

SCHAIE, K. W. 1983. The Seattle longitudinal study: A 21-year exploration of psychometric intelligence in adulthood. In K. W. Schaie, ed., *Longitudinal studies of adult psychological development.* New York: Guilford Press.

SCHALLING, D. 1978. Psychopathy-related personality variables and the psychophysiology of socialization. In R. D. Hare & D. Schalling, eds., *Psychopathic behavior: Approaches to research.* Chichester, England: John Wiley.

SCHILDKRAUT, J. J. 1965. The catecholamine hypothesis of affective disorders: A review of supporting evidence. *American Journal of Psychiatry, 122,* 509–522.

SCHILLING, R. F., & SCHINKE, S. P. 1984. Maltreatment and mental retardation. In J. M. Berg, ed., *Perspectives and progress in mental retardation,* vol. 1. Baltimore, MD: University Park Press.

SCHALLOCK, R. L., & LILLEY, M. A. 1986. Placement from community-based mental retardation programs: How well do clients do after 8 to 10 years. *American Journal of Mental Deficiency, 90,* 669–676.

SCHLESINGER, H. J., MUMFORD, E., GLASS, G. V., PATRICK, C., & SHARFSTEIN, S. 1983. Mental Health treatment and medical care utilization in a fee-for-service system: Outpatient mental health treatment following the onset of a chronic disease. *American Journal of Public Health, 73,* 422–429.

SCHLESSER, M. A., & ALTSHULER, K. Z. 1983. The genetics of affective disorder: Data, theory, and clinical applications. *Hospital and Community Psychiatry, 34,* 415–422.

SCHOENMAN, T. J. 1984. The mentally ill witch in text books of abnormal psychology: Current status and implications of a fallacy. *Professional Psychiatry, 15,* 299–314.

SCHOTTE, D. E., & STUNKARD, A. J. 1987. Bulimia vs. bulimic behaviors on a college campus. *Journal of the American Medical Association, 258,* 1213–1215.

SCHUCHTER, S. R., & SISSOK, S. 1984. Psychological reactions to the PSA crash. *International Journal of Psychiatry in Medicine, 14,* 293–301.

SCHUCKIT, M. A. 1987. Biological vulnerability to alcoholism. *Journal of Consulting and Clinical Psychology, 55,* 307–309.

SCHWARTZ, S. 1982. Is there a schizophrenic language? *The Behavioral and Brain Sciences, 4,* 579–588.

SCHWEINHART, L. J., & WEIKART, D. P. 1980. *Young children grow up.* Ypsilanti, MI: High/Scope.

Science Reports: National Institute of Mental Health. 1981. *Treating and assessing the chronically mentally ill.* Rockville, MD: U.S. Dept of Health and Human Services.

SEARL, S., JR. 1978. Stages of parent reaction to the birth of a handicapped child. *Exceptional Parent*, (April), 23–27.

SECHEHAYE, M. 1951. *Autobiography of a schizophrenic girl.* New York: Grune & Stratton.

SEDVALL, G., FARDE, L., PERSSON, A., & WIESEL, F. A. 1986. Imaging of neurotransmitter receptors in the living human brain. *Archives of General Psychiatry, 43*(10), 995–1005.

SELIGMAN, M.E.P. 1974. Depression and learned helplessness. In R. J. Friedman & M. M. Katz, eds., *The psychology of depression: Contemporary theory and research.* Washington, D.C.: V. H. Winston.

SELIGMAN, M.E.P. 1975. *Helplessness: On depression, development, and death.* San Francisco: W. H. Freeman.

SELYE, H. 1976. *The stress of life,* rev. ed. New York: McGraw-Hill.

SHAFFER, J. W., GRAVES, P. L., SWANK, R. T., & PEARSON, T. A. 1987. Clustering of personality traits in youth and the subsequent development of cancer among physicians. *Journal of Behavioral Medicine, 10,* 441–447.

SHAPIRO, D. 1965. *Neurotic styles.* New York: Basic Books.

SHAPIRO, D. 1981. *Autonomy and rigid character.* New York: Basic Books.

SHAW, C. R., ed. 1930. *The Jack Roller.* Chicago: University of Chicago Press.

SHEA, T., GLASS, D., & PILKONIS, J. 1987. Frequency and implications of personality disorders in a sample of depressed out-patients. *Journal of Personality Disorders, 1,* 27–42.

SHEEHAN, S. 1982. *Is there no place on earth for me.* Boston: Houghton Mifflin.

SHEKELLE, R. B., RAYNOR, W. J., OSTFELD, A. M., GARRON, D. C., BIELIAUSKAS, L. A., LIU, S. C., MALIZA, C., & OGLESBY, P. 1981. Psychological depression and 17-year risk of death from cancer. *Psychosomatic Medicine, 43,* 117–125.

SHERMAN, B. 1985. The new realities of "date rape." *New York Times,* Oct. 23, 17.

SHIFFMAN, S. 1982. Relapse following smoking cessation: A situational analysis. *Journal of Consulting and Clinical Psychology, 50,* 71–86.

SHNEIDMAN, E. S. 1980. *Voices of death.* New York: Harper & Row.

SHURE, M. B., & SPIVACK, G. 1982. Interpersonal problem-solving in young children: A cognitive approach to prevention. *American Journal of Community Psychology, 10,* 341–356.

SHURE, M. B., & SPIVACK, G. 1987. Competence-building as an approach to prevention of dysfunction: The ICPS model. In J. A. Steinberg and M. M. Silverman, eds., *Preventing mental disorders: A research perspective.* Rockville, MD: National Institute of Mental Health.

SIEGEL, J. M. 1985. The measurement of anger as a multidimensional construct. In M. A. Chesney and R. H. Rosenman, eds., *Anger and hostility in cardiovascular and behavioral disorders.* Washington, D.C.: Hemisphere.

SIEGEL, S., HINSON, R. E., & KRANK, M. D. 1981. Morphine-induced attenuation of morphine tolerance. *Science, 212,* 1533–1534.

SIGELMAN, C. K., BUDD, E. C., SPANHEL, C. L., & SCHOENROCK, C. J. 1981. When in doubt say yes: Acquiescence in interviews with mentally-retarded persons. *Mental Retardation, 19,* 53–58.

SIEVER, L. J., & COURSEY, R. D. 1985. Biological markers for schizophrenia and the biological high risk approach. *Journal of Nervous and Mental Disease, 173,* 4–16.

SIEVER, L. J., & DAVIS, K. L. 1985. Overview: Toward a dysregulation hypothesis of depression. *American Journal of Psychiatry, 142,* 1017–1031.

SIEVER, L. J., & KENDLER, K. S. 1986. Schizoid/schizotypal/paranoid personality disorders. In R. Michels and J. O. Cavenar, Jr., eds., *Psychiatry,* vol. 1. New York: Basic Books.

SILVERSTEIN, M. L., & HARROW, M. 1981. Schneiderian first-rank symptoms in schizophrenia. *Archives of General Psychiatry, 38,* 288–293.

SIMMONS, K. 1987. Adolescent suicide: Second leading death cause. *Journal of the American Medical Association, 257,* 3329–3330.

SKLAR, L. S., & ANISMAN, H. 1981. Stress and cancer. *Psychological Bulletin, 89,* 369–406.

SKULTANS, V. 1979. *English madness.* London: Routledge & Kegan Paul.

SLOANE, R. B., STAPLES, F. R., YORKSTON, N. J., WHIPPLE, K., & Cristol, A. H. 1975. *Short-term analytically oriented psychotherapy versus behavior therapy.* Cambridge, MA: Harvard University Press.

SMALL, G. W., & NICHOLI, A. M. 1982. Mass hysteria among school children. *Archives of General Psychiatry, 39,* 89–90.

SMITH, D. W., & WILSON, A. A. 1973. *A child with Down's syndrome (mongolism).* Philadelphia: W. B. Saunders.

SMITH, M.L., GLASS, G. V., & MILLER, T. I. 1980. *The benefits of psychotherapy.* Baltimore: Johns Hopkins University Press.

SMITH, R. N. 1982. *Dewey and his times.* New York: Simon & Schuster.

SMITH, T. W. 1982. Irrational beliefs on the cause and treatment of emotional distress: A critical review of the rational-emotive model. *Clinical Psychology Review, 2,* 505–522.

SOLOVAY, M. R., SHENTON, M. E., & HOLZMAN, P. S. 1987. Comparative studies of thought disorders. *Archives of General Psychiatry, 44,* 13–20.

SPANOS, N. P. 1978. Witchcraft in histories of psychiatry: A critical analysis and an alternative conceptualization. *Psychological Bulletin, 85,* 417–439.

SPIEGEL, D., & WISSLER, T. 1986. Family environment as a predictor of psychiatric rehospitalization. *American Journal of Psychiatry, 143,* 56–60.

SPITZER, R. L., FORMAN, J. B., & NEE, J. 1979. DSM-III field trials: I. Initial inter-rater diagnostic reliability. *American Journal of Psychiatry, 136,* 815–817.

SPITZER, R. L., & FORMAN, J. B. 1979. DSM-III field trials: II. Initial experience with the multiaxial system. *American Journal of Psychiatry, 136,* 818–820.

SPITZER, R. L., SKODAL, A. E., GIBBON, M., & WILLIAMS, J.B.W. 1981. *DSM-III casebook.* Washington, D.C.: American Psychiatric Association.

SPITZER, R. L., SKODAL, A. E., GIBBON, M., & WILLIAMS, J.B.W. 1983. *Psychopathology: A casebook.* New York: McGraw-Hill.

SPIVACK, G., PLATT, J. J., & SHURE, M. B. 1976. *The problem-solving approach to adjustment.* San Francisco: Jossey-Bass.

SROLE, L., LANGER, T. S., MICHAEL, S. T., KIRKPATRICK, P., OPLER, M. K., & RENNIE, T.A.C. 1978. *Mental health in the metropolis: The midtown Manhattan study,* rev. ed. New York: New York University Press.

STABENAU, J. R., & POLLIN, W. 1967. Early characteristics of monozygotic twins discordant for schizophrenia. *Archives of General Psychiatry, 17,* 723–734.

STEADMAN, H. 1981. Critically reassuring the accuracy of public perceptions of the dangerousness of the mentally ill. *Journal of Health and Social Behavior, 22,* 310–316.

STEIN, M., SCHLEIFER, S. J., & KELLER, S. E. 1987. Psychoimmunology in clinical psychiatry. In R. E. Hales and A. J. Frances, eds., *American Psychiatric Association Annual Review,* vol. 6. Washington, D.C.: American Psychiatric Press, pp. 210–234.

STERN, S. L., RUSH, A. J., & MENDELS, J. 1980. Toward a rational pharmacotherapy of depression. *American Journal of Psychiatry, 137,* 545–552.

STEUER, J. L., MINTZ, J., HAMMEN, C. L., HILL, M. A., JARVIK, L. F., McCARLEY, T., MOTOIKE, P., & ROSEN, R. 1984. Cognitive-behavioral and psychodynamic group psychotherapy in treatment of geriatric depression. *Journal of Consulting and Clinical Psychology, 52,* 180–189.

STEWART, J. W., WALSH, T., WRIGHT, L., ROOSE, S. P., & GLASSMAN, A. H. 1984. An open trial of MAO inhibitors in bulimia. *Journal of Clinical Psychiatry, 45,* 217–218.

STOFFELMAYR, B. E., DILLAVOU, D., & HUNTER, J. E. 1983. Premorbid functioning and outcome in schizophrenia: A cumulative analysis. *Journal of Consulting and Clinical Psychology, 51,* 338–352.

STONE, M. H. 1980. *The borderline syndromes.* New York: McGraw-Hill.

STONE, M. H. 1986. Borderline personality disorder. In R. Michels and J. O. Cavenar, Jr., eds., *Psychiatry,* vol. 1. New York: Basic Books.

STONE, M. H., & STONE, D. K. (In press.) The natural history of borderline patients. *Journal of Personality Disorders.*

STORR, A. 1980. *The art of psychotherapy.* New York: Methuen.

STROBER, M., & CARLSON, G. A. 1982. Bipolar illness in adolescents with major depression: Clinical, genetic and psychopharmacologic predictors in a three- to four-year prospective follow-up investigation. *Archives of General Psychiatry, 39,* 545–555.

STROEBE, W., & STROEBE, M. S. 1987. *Bereavement and health: The psychological and physical consequences of partner loss.* Cambridge, England: Cambridge University Press.

STROUDEMIRE, A., FRANK, R., HEDEMARK, N., KAMLET, M., & BLAZER, D. 1986. The economic burden of depression. *General Hospital Psychiatry, 8,* 387–394.

STRUNK, R. C., MRAZEK, D. A., FUHRMANN, A.S.W., & LABRECQUE, J. F. 1985. Physiologic and psychological characteristics associated with deaths due to asthma in childhood: A case-controlled study. *Journal of the American Medical Association, 254,* 1193–1198.

STRUBE, M. J., GARDNER, W., & HARTMANN, D. P. 1985. Limitations, liabilities, and obstacles in reviews of the literature: The current status of metaanalysis. *Clinical Psychology Review, 5,* 63–78.

STUBBS, E. G., RITVO, E. R., & MASON-BROTHERS, A. 1985. Autism and shared parental HLA antigens. *Journal of Child Psychiatry, 24,* 182–185.

SUELZE, M., & KEENAN, V. 1981. Changes in family support networks over the life cycle of mentally retarded persons. *American Journal of Mental Deficiency, 86,* 267–274.

STRUPP, H. H., & HADLEY, S. W. 1979. Specific versus nonspecific factors in psychotherapy: A controlled study of outcome. *Archives of General Psychiatry, 36,* 1125–1136.

SUOMI, S. J. 1983. Models of depression in primates. *Psychological Medicine, 13,* 465–468.

SUOMI, S. J., & HARLOW, H. F. 1972. Social rehabilitation of isolation-reared monkeys. *Developmental Psychology, 6,* 487–496.

SUOMI, S. J., & HARLOW, H. F. 1978. Early experience and social development in Rhesus monkeys. In M. E. Lamb, ed., *Social and personality development.* New York: Holt, Rinehart and Winston.

SUTHERLAND, S. 1977. *Breakdown.* London: Granada.

SYMONDS, P. M. 1940. Psychoanalysis, psychology, and education. *Journal of Abnormal and Social Psychology, 35,* 139–149.

SZASZ, T. S. 1970. *Ideology and insanity: Essays on the psychiatric dehumanization of man.* Garden City, NY: Anchor Books.

TALBOTT, J. A. 1985. Medical humanism: A personal odyssey. *Psychiatric News, 2,* 31.

TARGUM, S. D. 1984. Persistent neuroendocrine dysregulation in major depressive disorder: A marker for early relapse. *Biological Psychiatry, 19,* 305–310.

TARVER-BEHRING, S., BARKLEY, R. A., & KARLSSON, J. 1985. The mother-child interactions of hyperactive boys and their normal siblings. *American Journal of Orthopsychiatry, 55,* 202–208.

TAYLOR, J. R., & CARROLL, J. L. 1987. Current issues in electroconvulsive therapy. *Psychological Reports, 60,* 747–758.

TAYLOR, S. E., WOOD, J. V., & LICHTMAN, R. R. 1983. It could be worse: Selective evaluation as a response to victimization. *Journal of Social Issues, 39,* 19–40.

TERMAN, L. M., & MERRILL, M. A. 1937. *Measuring intelligence.* Boston: Houghton Mifflin.

TERMAN, L. M., & MERRILL, M. A. 1960. *Stanford-Binet Intelligence Scale: Manual for the 3rd revision, Form-M.* Boston: Houghton Mifflin.

TERMAN, L. M., & MERRILL, M. A. 1973. *Stanford-Binet Intelligence Scale: 1972 norms edition.* Boston: Houghton Mifflin.

THELMAR, E. 1932. *The maniac: A realistic study of madness from a maniac's point of view,* 2nd ed. London: C. A. Watts.

THOMAS, C. B., & DUSZYNCKI, K. R. 1974. Closeness to parents and the family: Constellation in a prospective study of five disease states—Suicide, mental illness, malignant tumor, hypertension and coronary heart disease. *Johns Hopkins Medical Journal, 134,* 251–270.

THOMPSON, J. W., & BLAINE, J. D. 1987. Use of ECT in the United States in 1975 and 1980. *American Journal of Psychiatry, 144,* 557–562.

THOMPSON, T. L., II. 1982. Headache. In H. I. Kaplan & B. J. Sadock, eds., *Comprehensive Textbook on Psychiatry,* 4th ed., vol. 2. Baltimore, MD: Williams & Wilkins.

THORESEN, C. E., FRIEDMAN, M., GILL, J. K., & ULMER, D. K. 1982. The recurrent coronary prevention project: Some preliminary findings. *Acta Medica Scandinavica, 68,* 172–192.

TIENARI, P., SORRI, A., LAHTI, I., NAARALA, M., WAHLBERG, K. E., MORING, J., POHJOLA, J., & WYNNE, L. C. 1987. Genetic and psychosocial factors in schizophrenia: The Finnish adoptive family study. *Schizophrenia Bulletin, 13,* 477–484.

TISCHLER, G., ed. 1987. *Diagnosis and classification in psychiatry: A critical appraisal of DSM-III.* New York: Cambridge University Press.

TOLSTRUP, K., BRINCH, M., ISAGER, T., NIELSEN, S., NYSTRUP, J., SEVERIN, B., & OLESEN, N. S. 1985. Long-term outcome of 151 cases of anorexia nervosa. *Acta Scandinavica Psychiatrica, 71,* 380–387.

TONER, B. B., GARFINKEL, P. E., & GARDNER, D. M. 1986. Long-term follow-up of anorexia nervosa. *Psychosomatic Medicine*, 48, 520–529.

TOOLAN, J. M. 1981. Depression and suicide in children: An overview. *American Journal of Psychotherapy*, 35, 311–322.

TORGERSEN, S. 1979. The nature and origin of common phobic fears. *British Journal of Psychiatry*, 134, 343–351.

TRAHMS, C. M., & COX, C. 1987. *A babysitter's guide to PKU.* Seattle, WA: Child Development and Mental Retardation Center, University of Washington.

TRAHMS, C. M., COX, C., LUCE, P. 1987. *Games that Teach.* Seattle, WA: Child Development and Mental Retardation Center, University of Washington.

TSAI, L. Y. 1987. Pre-, peri-, and neonatal factors in autism. In E. Shopler and G. B. Mesibov, eds., *Neurobiological issues in autism.* New York: Plenum.

TSUANG, M. T., & VANDERMAY, R. 1980. *Genes and the Mind.* Oxford, England: Oxford University Press.

TURK, D. C., & SALOVEY, P. 1985. Cognitive structures, cognitive processes, and cognitive-behavior modification: II. Judgments and inferences of the clinician. *Cognitive Therapy and Research*, 9, 19–33.

TURNER, S. M., BEIDEL, D. C., & COSTELLO, A. 1987. Psychopathology in the offspring of anxiety disorders patients. *Journal of Consulting and Clinical Psychology*, 55, 229–235.

TWENTYMAN, C. T., ROHRBECK, C. H., & AMISH, P. A. 1984. A cognitive-behavioral model of child abuse. In S. Saunders, ed., *Violent individuals and families: A practitioner's handbook.* Springfield, IL: Charles Thomas.

UHDE, T. W., BOULENGER, J. P., ROY-BYRNE, P., GERACI, M. F., VITONE, B. J., & POST, R. M. 1985. Longitudinal course of panic disorder: Clinical and biological considerations. *Progress in Neuropsychopharmacology and Biological Psychiatry*, 9, 39–51.

U.S. Department of Health and Human Services. 1988. *Health promotion and disease-prevention: United States, 1985.* Vital and Health Statistics, National Health Survey, Series 10, Number 183. Hyattsville, MD: U.S. Government Printing Office.

U.S. Department of Health, Education, and Welfare, Public Health Service. 1979. *Smoking and health: A report of the Surgeon General.* Washington, D.C.: U.S. Government Printing Office (DHEW Pub. No. [PHS]79-50066).

U.S. Department of Health and Human Services. 1981. *Schizophrenia, is there an answer?* Rockville, MD: U.S. Dept. of Health & Human Services.

VAILLANT, G. E. 1973. A 20-year follow-up of New York narcotic addicts. *Archives of General Psychiatry*, 29, 237–241.

VAILLANT, G. E. 1976. History of male psychological health: V. The relation of choice of ego mechanisms of defense to adult adjustment. *Archives of General Psychiatry*, 33, 535–545.

VAILLANT, G. E., & MILOFSKY, E. S. 1982. Natural history of male alcoholism: IV. Paths to recovery. *Archives of General Psychiatry*, 39, 127–133.

VAILLANT, G. E. 1984. The disadvantages of DSM-III outweigh its advantages. *American Journal of Psychiatry*, 14, 542–545.

VALONE, K., GOLDSTEIN, M. J., & NORTON, J. P. 1984. Parental expressed emotion and psychophysiological reactivity in an adolescent sample at risk for schizophrenia spectrum disorders. *Journal of Abnormal Psychology*, 93, 448–457.

VARLEY, C. K. 1984. Diet and the behavior of children with attention deficit disorder. *Journal of the American Academy of Child Psychiatry*, 23, 182–185.

VARNHAGEN, C. K., DAS, J. P., & VARNHAGEN, S. 1987. Auditory and visual memory span: Cognitive processing by TMR individuals with Down's syndrome or other etiologies. *American Journal of Mental Deficiency*, 91, 398–405.

VAUGHN, C. E., & LEFF, J. P. 1976. The influence of family and social factors on the course of psychiatric illness. *British Journal of Psychiatry*, 129, 125–137.

VAUGHN, C. E., SNYDER, K. S., JONES, S., FREEMAN, W. B., & FALLOON, I.R.H. 1984. Family factors in schizophrenic relapse. *Archives of General Psychiatry*, 41, 1169–1177.

VERNON, P. E. 1987. The demise of the Stanford-Binet scale. *Canadian Psychology*, 28, 251–258.

VERONEN, L. J., & KILPATRICK, D. G. 1983. Stress inoculation training as a treatment for rape victims' fears. In D. Meichenbaum and M. Jaremko, eds., *Stress Reduction and Prevention.* New York: Plenum.

VIDEKA-SHERMAN, L., & LIEBERMAN, M. 1985. The effects of self-help and psychotherapy intervention on child loss: The limits of recovery. *American Journal of Orthopsychiatry*, 55, 70–82.

VIRKKUNEN, M. 1983. Insulin secretion during the glucose tolerance test in antisocial personality. *British Journal of Psychiatry*, 142, 598–604.

VISCHI, T. R., JONES, K. R., SHANK, E. L., & LIMA, L. H. 1980. *The alcohol, drug abuse and mental health national databook.* Rockville, MD: Alcohol, Drug Abuse and Mental Health Administration.

VOLKMAR, F. R., & COHEN, D. J. 1985. The experience of infantile autism: A first-person account by Tony W. *Journal of Autism and Developmental Disorders*, 15, 47–54.

VON KORFF, M. R., NESTADT, G., ROMANOSKI, A., ANTHONY, J., EATON, W., MERCHANT, A., CHAHAL, R., KRAMER, M., FOLSTEIN, M., & GROENBERG, E. 1985. Prevalence of treated and untreated DSM-III schizophrenia. *The Journal of Nervous and Mental Disease*, 173, 577–581.

VONNEGUT, M. 1975. *The Eden express.* New York: Bantam Books.

WALDER, L. O., COHEN, S. L., & DASTON, P. G. 1967. *Teaching parents and others principles of behavior control for modifying the behavior of children.* Report to U.S. Office of Education, Washington, D.C.

WALKER, C. E., HEDBERG, A., CLEMENT, P. W., & WRIGHT, L. 1981. *Clinical procedures for behavior therapy.* Englewood Cliffs, NJ: Prentice-Hall.

WALKER, J. I., & BRODIE, H.K.H. 1985. Paranoid disorders. In I. H. Kaplan and B. J. Sadock, eds., *Comprehensive textbook of psychiatry*, 4th ed. Baltimore: Williams & Wilkins.

WALKER, L. E. 1984. *The battered woman syndrome.* New York: Springer.

WALLACE, C. J. 1984. Community and interpersonal functioning in the course of schizophrenic disorders. *Schizophrenia Bulletin*, 10, 233–257.

WALLERSTEIN, J. S. 1986. Women after divorce: Preliminary report from a ten-year follow-up. *American Journal of the Orthopsychiatric Association*, 56, 65–77.

WATSON, J. B. 1925. *Behaviorism.* New York: Norton.

WATT, N. F., ed. 1984. *Children at risk for schizophrenia: A longitudinal perspective.* New York: Cambridge University Press.

WECHSLER, D. 1955. *Manual for the Wechsler Adult Intelligence Scale.* New York: Psychological Corporation.

WECHSLER, D. 1958. *The measurement and appraisal of adult intelligence*, 4th ed. Baltimore: Williams & Wilkins.

WEHR, T. A., GOODWIN, F. K., & WIRZ-JUSTICE, A. 1982. Forty-eight hour sleep–wake cycles in manic-depressive illness. *Archives of General Psychiatry*, 39, 559–565.

WEHR, T. A., & SACK, D. A. 1987. Sleep disruption: A treatment for depression and a cause of mania. *Psychiatric Annals, 17,* 654–663.

WEHR, T. A., SACK, D. A., ROSENTHAL, N. E., & GOODWIN, F. K. 1987. Sleep and biological rhythms in bipolar illness. In R. E. Hales and A.J. Frances, eds., *American Psychiatric Association Annual Review,* vol. 6. Washington, D.C.: American Psychiatric Press.

WEHR, T. A., & WERTZ-JUSTICE, A. 1982. Circadian rhythm mechanisms in affective illness and in antidepressant drug action. *Pharmacopsychiatry, 15,* 31–39.

WEINBERG, T. S. 1978. Sadism and masochism: Sociological perspectives. *Bulletin of the American Academy of Psychiatry and Law, 6,* 284–295.

WEINBERG, T. S., WILLIAMS, C. J., & MOSER, C. 1984. The social constituents of sadomasochism. *Social Problems, 31,* 379–389.

WEINBERGER, D. R. 1984. Computed tomography (CT) findings in schizophrenia: Speculation on the meaning of it all. *Journal of Psychiatric Research, 18,* 477–490.

WEISS, G., HECHTMAN, L., MILROY, T., PERLMAN, T. 1985. Psychiatric status of hyperactives as adults: A controlled prospective 15-year follow-up of 63 hyperactive children. *Journal of American Academy of Child Psychiatry, 24,* 211–220.

WEISSMAN, M. (1987) Epidemiology of depression: Frequency, risk groups, and risk factors. In *Perspectives on depressive disorders.* Rockville, MID: National Institute of Mental Health.

WEISSMAN, M. M., GAMMON, G. D., JOHN, K., MERIKANGAS, R., WARNER, V., PRUSOFF, B., & SHOLOMSKAS, D. 1987. Children of depressed parents: Increased psychopathology and early onset of major depression. *Archives of General Psychiatry, 44,* 847–853.

WEISSMAN, M. M., GERHON, E. S., KIDD, K. K., PRUSSOF, B. A., LECKMAN, J. F., DIBBLE, E., HAMOVIT, J., THOMPSON, W. D., PAULS, D. L., & GUROFF, J. J. 1984. Psychiatric disorder in the relatives of probands with affective disorders. *Archives of General Psychiatry, 41,* 13–21.

WEISSMAN, M. M., WICKRAMARATNE, P., MERIKANGAS, K. R., LECKMAN, J. F., PRUSOFF, B. A., CARUSO, K. A., KIDD, K. K., & GAMMON, G. D. 1984. Onset of major depression in early adulthood. *Archives of General Psychiatry, 41,* 1136–1143.

WEISZ, J., YEATES, K., & ZIGLER, E. 1982. Piagetian evidence and the developmental-difference controversy. In E. Zigler & B. Balla, eds., *Mental retardation: The developmental difference controversy.* Hillsdale, NJ: Erlbaum.

WEISZ, J. R., WEISS, B., WASSERMAN, A. A., & RINTOUL, B. 1987. Control-related beliefs and depression among clinic-referred children and adolescents. *Journal of Abnormal Psychology, 96,* 58–63.

WELLER, E. B., & WELLER, R. A. 1985. Clinical aspects of childhood depression. *Psychiatric Annals, 15,* 368–374.

WENDER, P. H., ROSENTHAL, D., KETY, S. S., SCHULSINGER, F., & WELNER, J. 1974. Cross-fostering: A research strategy for clarifying the role of genetic and experiential factors in the etiology of schizophrenia. *Archives of General Psychiatry, 30,* 121–128.

WERDEGAR, D., SOKOLOW, M., PERLOFF, D. B., RIESS, F., HARRIS, R. E., SINGER, T., & BLACKBURN, H. W., JR. 1967. Portable recording of blood pressure: A new approach to assessments of the severity and prognosis of hypertension. *Transactions of the Association of Life Insurance Medical Directors of America, 51,* 93–173.

WERNER, E. E., & SMITH, R. S. 1982. *Vulnerable but invincible: A study of resilient children.* New York: McGraw-Hill.

WERRY, J. S., REEVES, J. C., & ELKIND, G. S. 1987. Attention deficit, conduct, oppositional and anxiety disorder in children: I. A review of research on differentiating characteristics. *Journal of the American Academy of Child and Adolescent Psychiatry, 26,* 133–143.

WESSON, D. R., & SMITH, D. E. 1977. *Barbiturates: Their use, misuse, and abuse.* New York: Human Services Press.

WEST, J. B. 1984. Human physiology at extreme altitudes on Mt. Everest, *Science, 223,* 784–788.

WESTEFELD, J. S., & FURR, S. R. 1987. Suicide and depression among college students. *Professional Psychology: Research and Practice, 18,* 119–123.

WEXLER, N. S., GUSELLA, J. F., CONNEALLY, P. M., & HOUSMAN, D. 1985. Huntington's disease and the new genetics: A preview of the future for psychiatric disorders. In H. A. Pincus and H. Pardes, eds., *The integration of neuroscience and psychiatry.* Washington, D.C.: American Psychiatric Press.

WHALEN, C. K., HENKER, B., & HINSHAW, S. P. 1985. Cognitive-behavioral therapies for hyperactive children: Premises, problems and prospects. *Journal of Abnormal Child Psychology, 13,* 391–410.

WHITEHEAD, W. E., BLACKWELL, B., & ROBINSON, A. 1978. Effects of diazepam on phobic avoidance behavior and phobic anxiety. *Biological Psychiatry, 13,* 59–64.

WIDIGER, T. A., & FRANCES, A. 1985. Axis II Personality disorders: Diagnostic and treatment issues. *Hospital and Community Psychiatry, 36,* 619–627.

WIDIGER, T. A., FRANCES, A., & TRULL, T. J. 1987. A psychometric analysis of the social-interpersonal and cognitive perceptual items for the schizotypal personality disorder. *Archives of General Psychiatry, 44,* 741–745.

WIDOM, C. S. 1978. A methodology for studying noninstitutionalized psychopaths. In R. D. Hare & D. A. Schalling, eds., *Psychopathic behavior: Approaches to research.* Chichester, England: John Wiley.

WIKLER, L. M. 1986. Periodic stresses of families of older mentally retarded children: An exploratory study. *American Journal of Mental Deficiency, 90,* 703–706.

WIKLER, L. M., WASOW, M., & HATFIELD, E. 1981. Chronic sorrow revisited. *American Journal of Orthopsychiatry, 51,* 63–70.

WIKLER, L. M. 1986. Periodic stresses of families of older mentally retarded children. *American Journal of Mental Deficiency, 90,* 703–706.

WILLE, R. 1981. Ten year follow-up of a representative sample of London heroin addicts: Clinic attendance, abstinence, and mortality. *British Journal of Addiction, 76,* 259–266.

WILLIAMS, J.B.W. 1985. The multiaxial system of DSM-III: Where did it come from and where should it go? II. *Archives of General Psychiatry, 42,* 181–186.

WILLIAMS, J. G., BARLOW, D. H., & AGRAS, W. S. 1972. Behavioral measurement of severe depression. *Archives of General Psychiatry, 27,* 330–333.

WILSON, G. T. 1987. Cognitive studies in alcoholism. *Journal of Consulting and Clinical Psychology, 55,* 325–331.

WINSON, J. 1985. *Brain and psyche: The biology of the unconscious.* New York: Anchor Press.

WISE, T. N. 1985. Fetishism—etiology and treatment: A review from multiple perspectives. *Comprehensive Psychiatry, 26,* 249–257.

WITTCHEN, H., SEMLER, G., & VON ZERSSEN, D. 1985. A comparison of two diagnostic methods. *Archives of General Psychiatry, 42,* 667–684.

WITTROCK, W. C., BEATTY, J., BOGEN, J. E., GAZZANIGA, M. S., JERISON, H. J., KRASHEN, S. D., NEBES, R. D., & TEY-LER, T. J. 1977. The human brain, Englewood Cliffs, N. J.: Prentice Hall.

WOLF, L., & GOLDBERG, B. 1986. Autistic children group: An eight to twenty-four year follow-up study. *Canadian Journal of Psychiatry, 31,* 550–556.

WOLF, S. 1969. Psychosocial factors in myocardial infarction and sudden death. *Circulation, 39(4),* 74–83.

WOLFE, D. A., SANDLER, J., & KAUFMAN, K. 1981. Competency-based parent training program for child abusers. *Journal of Consulting and Clinical Psychology, 49,* 633–640.

WOLKIN, A., JAEGER, J., BRODIE, J. D., WOLF, A. P., FOW-LER, J., ROTROSEN, J., GOMEZ-MONT, F., & CANCRO, R. 1985. Persistence of cerebral metabolic abnormalities in chronic schizophrenia as determined by positron emission tomography. *American Journal of Psychiatry, 142,* 564–571.

WOLPE, J., & RACHMAN, S. J. 1960. Psychoanalytic "evidence": A critique based on Freud's case of Little Hans. *Journal of Nervous and Mental Disease, 131,* 135–147.

WOODRUFF, R. A., JR., GOODWIN, D. W., & GUZE, S. B. 1974. *Psychiatric diagnosis.* New York: Oxford University Press.

WOODY, G. E., MCLELLAN, A. T., LUBORSKY, L., & O'-BRIEN, C. P. 1986. Psychotherapy for substance abuse. *Psychiatric Clinics of North America, 9,* 547–562.

WORTMAN, C. B. 1983. Coping with victimization: Conclusions and implications for future research. *Journal of Social Issues, 39,* 195–221.

WORTMAN, C. B. 1987. Coping with irrevocable loss. In G. R. Vanden Bos and B. K. Bryant, eds., *Cataclysms, crises, and catastrophes: Psychology in action.* Washington, D.C.: American Psychological Association.

WULFF, S. B. 1985. The symbolic and object play of children with autism: A review. *Journal of Autism and Developmental Disorders, 15,* 139–147.

WYNNE, L. C. 1975. Adjustment reaction of adult life. In A. M. Freedman, H. I. Kaplan, & B. J. Sadock, eds., *Contemporary textbook of psychiatry,* vol. 2, 2nd ed. Baltimore: Williams and Wilkins.

WYNNE, L. C., COLE, R. E., & PERKINS, P. 1987. University of Rochester Child and Family Study: Risk research in progress. *Schizophrenia Bulletin, 13,* 463–476.

WYNNE, L. C., SINGER, M. T., BARTKO, J. J., & TOOKEY, M. L. 1977. Schizophrenics and their families: Research on parental communication. In J. M. Tanner, ed., *Developments in psychiatric research.* London: Hodder and Stoughton, 254–286.

YALOM, I. D. 1980. *Existential psychotherapy.* New York: Basic Books.

YOUNG, T. Y., LAWSON, G. W., & GACONO, C. B. 1987. Clinical aspects of phencyclidine (PCP). *The International Journal of the Addictions, 22,* 1–15.

YUWILER, A., GELLER, E., & RITVO, E. 1985. Biochemical studies on autism. In A. Lajtha, ed., *Handbook of Neurochemistry,* vol. 10. New York: Plenum.

YUWILER, A., & FREEDMAN, D. X. 1987. Neurotransmitter research in autism. In E. Schopler and G. B. Mesibov, eds., *Neurobiological issues in autism.* New York: Plenum.

ZETLIN, A. G., & TURNER, J. L. 1985. Transition from adolescence to adulthood: Perspectives of mentally retarded individuals and their families. *American Journal of Mental Deficiency, 89,* 570–579.

ZIGLER, E., BULLA, D., & HODAPP, R. 1984. On the definition and classification of mental retardation. *American Journal of Mental Deficiency, 89,* 215–230.

ZIGLER, E., & LEVINE, J. 1983. Hallucinations vs. delusions: A developmental approach. *Journal of Nervous and Mental Disorder, 171,* 141–146.

ZISOOK, S., ed. 1987. *Biopsychosocial aspects of bereavement.* Washington, D.C.: American Psychiatric Press.

ZUBIN, J., MAGAZINER, J., & STEINHAUER, S. R. 1983. The metamorphosis of schizophrenia: From chronicity to vulnerability. *Psychological Medicine, 13,* 551–571.

ZUBIN, J., & SPRING, B. 1977. Vulnerability—a new view of schizophrenia. *Journal of Abnormal Psychology, 86,* 103–126.

ZUBIN, J., STEINHAUER, S. R., DAY, R., & van KAMMEN, D. P. 1985. Schizophrenia at the crossroads: A blueprint for the 80s. *Comprehensive Psychiatry, 26,* 217–240.

Photo References

Time, Inc. 226 The Seattle Post Intelligencer. 227 Jean-Claude Lejeune/Stock, Boston. 230 Robert V. Ecker, Jr./Stock, Boston. 235 Copyright 1985 Hylands Anatomical Dolls, Inc., Torrance, CA. 237 Laimute Druskis. 239 Billy E. Barnes/Southern Light.

Chapter 9: 247 John Running/Stock, Boston. 249 Bruce M. Wellman/Stock, Boston. 250 Chuck Pulin/Star File. 254 UPI/Bettmann Newsphotos; Culver Pictures. 259 Tim Kelly/Liaison. 260 (a) Frank Siteman/Stock, Boston; (b) Wasyl Szkodzinsky/Photo Researchers. 266 Laimute Druskis.

Chapter 10: 276 Collection of the Whitney Museum of American Art, NY. Photo by Geoffrey Clements. 281 University of California, Los Angeles. 287 The American Mental Health Fund/Ad Council. 297 Stengel & Co., G.m.b.H., Dresden. 301 Drs. Mazziotta, Phelps, et al., UCLA School of Medicine.

Chapter 11: 313 UPI/Bettmann Newsphotos. 315 Irene Springer.

Chapter 12: 347 (a) National Institutes of Health; (b, c, and d) Brookhaven National Laboratories. 348 Karolinska Institutet, Sweden. 354 UPI/Bettman Newsphotos. 357 Courtesy of Dr. Monte S. Buchsbaum. 358 Courtesy of Dr. Monte S. Buchsbaum. 359 Courtesy of Dr. Monte S. Buchsbaum.

Chapter 13: 365 (a) Peter Menzel/Stock, Boston; (b) Laimute Druskis. 367 (a) Peter Arnold, Inc..; (b) Russ Kinne/Comstock. 369 Abigail Heyman/Archive. 374 (left) Mimi Forsyth/ Monkmeyer Press; (right) Lynn Johnson/Black Star. 375 Peter Arnold, Inc. 380 New York Daily News Photo. 382 AP Wide World Photos. 383 Giraudon/Londres, Institut Courtauld.

Chapter 14: 395 (a) Larry Mulvehill/Photo Researchers; (b) Rob Nelson/Picture Graph. 396 (a) Matthew Naythons/Stock, Boston; (b) Frank Siteman/Taurus Photos. 401 John A. Moore, Office of Information Services, University of Washington. 402 (a) Sybil Shackman/Monkmeyer Press; (b) Jeff Jacobson/Archive Pictures. 406 (a) David York/The Stock Shop; Russell Clemens/International Stock Photo. 408 Henry Gris/FPG. 411 AP/Wide World Photos. 414 Mary Ellen Mark/Archive Pictures. 415 Arlene Collins/Monkmeyer Press.

Chapter 15: 431 Bill Binzen/Photo Researchers. 437 Bill Binzen/Photo Researchers. 438 George Goodwin/Monkmeyer Press. 441 Jean Claude Lejeune /Stock, Boston. 446 Beatriz Schiller/International Stock Photo. 447 Steve Shapiro/ Sygma. 451 Michal Heron/Monkmeyer Press.

Chapter 16: 458 Arthur Sirdofsky. 461 Allan Grant. 469 National Institute of Health. 470 (bottom) Courtesy National Syndrome Society. 475 Streissguth, Herman, and Smith, 1978. 479 Alan Carey/The Image Works. 480 David M. Grossman/Photo Researchers. 482 AP/Wide World Photos.

Chapter 17: 487 Ann Chwatsky/Phototake. 490 Mimi Forsyth/ Monkmeyer Press. 494 (a) Charles Gupton/Stock, Boston; (b) Dan McCoy/Rainbow. 497 Irene Springer. 498 Jim Pickerell/ FPG. 500 Linda Ferrer/Woodfin Camp & Associates. 509 (a) Freda Leinwand/Monkmeyer Press; (b) Dr. Rose K. Gantner; (c) Katie Deits/FPG. 515 Gail Creig/Monkmeyer Press.

Chapter 18: 521 Bohdan Hrynewych/Southern Light. 523 (a) Cary Wolinsky/Stock, Boston; (b) Rob Nelson/Stock, Boston; (c) Michal Heron/Monkmeyer Press. 529 (a) Randy Matusow/ Monkmeyer Press; (b) Bruce Roberts/Photo Researchers; (c) Richard Hutchings/Photo Researchers. 530 Paule Epstein. 533 Daemmrich/Stock, Boston. 534 Charles Kennard/Stock, Boston. 535 George Rizer, AP/Wide World Photos. 540 Cole Porter, Seattle Times. 541 The Bethlem Royal Hospital, England. 547 Ethan Hoffman/Archive Pictures.

Chapter 1: 3 Brian Masck/The Muskegon Chronicle. 5 (a) Phototeque; (b) copyright © 1987 Cannon Films Inc. and Cannon International B.V., all rights reserved; (c) Memory Shop. 6 (a) Lenore Weber/Taurus Photos; (b) Laimute Druskis; (c) Will McIntyre/Photo Researchers. 11 New York Public Library Picture Collection. 13 Page Poore. 14 (b) Stacy Pick/Stock, Boston; (c) Joseph Nettis/Photo Researchers; (d) Lawrence Migdale/Photo Researchers; (e) Michal Heron/Monkmeyer Press. 23 University of Wisconsin, Harlow Primate Laboratory. 24 University of Wisconsin, Harlow Primate Laboratory.

Chapter 2: 3 (top) Karl Muller/Woodfin Camp & Associates; (bottom) courtesy of American Museum of Natural History, photo by T. Bierwert. 31 National Museum of Natural History, Smithsonian Institution. 33 The Bettmann Archive. 34 (top) Karales/Peter Arnold; (bottom) the Bettmann Archive. 35 Denver Art Museum, Samuel H. Kress Foundation Collection. 36 Historical Pictures Service. 37 Scala/Art Resource. 38 (left) National Library of Medicine; (right) Victoria and Albert Museum, London. With permission of Bethem Royal Hospital, Kent. 39 (top) The Bettmann Archive; (bottom) Wellcome Institute Library, London. 40 Cornell University Library. 41 Cornell University Library. 42 (top) Katherine Drake, Lunatic's Ball (1848), The Royal College of Psychiatrists, London; (bottom) Colonial Williamsburg Photograph. 43 The Bettmann Archive. 44 National Mental Health Association. 45 Peter Arnold, Inc. 46 Andre Brouillet, Charcot at Salpetiere (1887), National Library of Medicine. 47 Mary Evans/Sigmund Freud Copyrights.

Chapter 3: 57 Alexander Tsiaras, Science Source/Photo Researchers. 59 Alex Webb/Magnum Photos. 64 From Sigmund Freud Copyrights Ltd./The Bettmann Archive. 67 The Bettmann Archive. 73 Courtesy of B.F. Skinner. 74 (a) Elizabeth Crews; (b) Larry Mulvehill/Photo Researchers. 77 Courtesy of Albert Bandura. 80 Courtesy of Carl Rogers Memorial Library.

Chapter 4: 100 Courtesy of the Psychological Corporation. 103 American Guidance Service, Inc. 105 (a) Hans Huber, Medical Publisher, Bern; (b) Ken Karp. 106 (a) Reproduced from Murray, 1943; (b) Ken Karp. 108 (a) Cary Wolinsky/Stock, Boston; (b) Tom Tucker/Photo Researchers. 110 (top) Murray Greenberg/Monkmeyer Press; (bottom) courtesy of Spacelabs.

Chapter 5: 119 Yoav/Phototake. 124 UPI/Bettmann Newsphotos. 125 Frank Johnson, UPI/Bettmann Newsphotos. 132 Bill Bernstein/Phototake.

Chapter 6: 144 Ken Karp. 147 (a) Laimute Druskis; (b) Ken Karp. 148 Ken Karp. 150 Reprinted from Psychology Today magazine, copyright ©1985, American Psychological Association. 151 (a) Mimi Forsyth/Monkmeyer Press; (b) Ken Karp. 152 Ken Karp. 154 Ken Karp. 155 Ken Karp. 157 (a) Phototest; (b) UPI/Bettmann Newsphotos.

Chapter 7: 173 Selye, 1952. 175 (a) Jeff Reed/MediChrome; (b) Lew Merrim/Monkmeyer Press; (c) Hank Morgan/Rainbow. 178 (a) Owen Franken/Stock, Boston; (b) Michael Grecco/Picture Group; (c) Charles Gupton/Stock, Boston; (d) Jon Riley/The Stock Shop. 181 Robert Goldstein/Photo Researchers. 191 (a) Hugh Rogers/Monkmeyer Press; (b) Hugh Rogers/Monkmeyer Press; (c) Chuck Fishman/Woodfin Camp & Associates. 200 Ted Fitzgerald.

Chapter 8: 208 Richard Dellenback. 213 W. Keith McManus/Archive Pictures. 214 Betty Lane/Photo Researchers. 215 Tom McHugh/Photo Researchers. 224 (a) Courtesy of Jerry Bauer; (c) Henry Grossman, People Weekly ©1974,

Rosenblum, L. A., 24
Rosenhan, D. L., 17
Rosenman, R. H., 187, 189
Rosenstein, M. J., 13, 14
Rosenthal, D., 337, 338, 358
Rosenthal, L. S., 398
Rosenthal, N. E., 301
Rosie, J. S., 515
Rosman, B., 447, 448
Rosner, B., 397
Ross, D. M., 431
Ross, G., 182
Ross, H. L., 532
Ross, S. A., 431
Rosvold, H. E., 350
Roth, R. H., 347
Rotrosen, J., 346
Rounsaville, B. J., 412, 413
Rubens, R. L., 348
Rubenstein, D., 219
Ruberman, J. W., 185, 186
Rumsey, J. M., 462
Rush, A. S., 285, 289, 291
Rush, B., 43
Russell, D. E. H., 234
Russell, D. W., 127
Rutenberg, B. A., 468
Rutter, M., 81, 93, 274, 313, 428, 434,
  435, 436, 441, 442, 444, 462,
  463, 481
Ryan, K. B., 522
Ryback, R. S., 398

Sabalis, R. F., 233
Sack, D. A., 298, 300, 301
Sackheim, H. A., 294
Sacks, M. H., 324
Saghir, M. T., 212, 213
Saint Augustine, 34
Saletu, B., 348
Salmoiraghi, G. C., 398
Salovey, P., 75
Salter, A. C., 429
Sanders, D. H., 534
Sandler, J., 67, 527
Sandoval, J., 431
Sanford, E. E., 429
Santana, F., 355
Sarason, B. R., 121, 122, 531
Sarason, I. G., 75, 109, 121, 122, 129,
  350, 531
Sartorius, M., 326
Sass, L., 256
Sassone, D., 431
Saunders, N. L., 181
Scarr, S., 337, 475, 476
Secery, W., 300, 440
Schacht, T. E., 510
Schachter, S., 422
Schafer, R., 106, 107
Schaie, K. W., 371
Schall, H., 195, 196
Schalling, D., 262
Scheftner, W. A., 30, 296, 303
Schildkraut, J. J., 279
Schilling, R. F., 481
Schinke, S. P., 481
Schleifer, S. J., 60
Schlesinger, H. J., 175
Schlesser, M. A., 300
Schneider, M. S., 191
Schoenman, T. J., 35
Schoenrock, C. J., 481
Schooler, N. R., 327
Schotte, D. E., 448, 449
Schuckit, M. A., 399
Schuett, V. E., 467

Schulsinger, F., 337, 338, 343, 351
Schulsinger, H., 351
Schwartz, D., 446
Schwartz, M., 216
Schwartz, P., 209, 215
Schwartz, S., 314, 350
Schwebel, A., 528
Schweinhart, L. J., 435
Scovern, A. W., 233
Seal, S., Jr., 456
Sechehaye, M., 314
Sedvall, G., 347, 348
Seligman, M. E. P., 292, 293
Selye, H., 173
Semler, G., 98
Semmel, M. I., 478
Semple, D., 328
Severin, B., 447
Severin, D., 93, 303
Shaffer, D., 176
Shaffer, J. W., 176
Shakespeare, 32, 37
Shank, E. L., 409
Shapiro, A. P., 191
Shapiro, B., 316
Shapiro, D., 246, 249, 264, 255
Shapiro, S., 15, 98
Sharfstein, S. S., 311, 536
Sharpley, C. F., 546
Shaw, C. R., 262
Shaw, F. H., 279
Shaw, S., 404
Shawn, P. M., 154
Shaywitz, B. A., 460
Shea, T., 254
Sheehan, S., 535
Sheiner, R., 299
Shekelle, R. B., 192
Shenker, R., 432
Shenton, M. E., 351
Sherman, B., 236, 239
Sherman, L. J., 17
Sherman, M., 81
Shibur, L. D., 299, 300
Shiffman, S., 423
Shneidman, E. S., 303
Shore, J. H., 534
Shucter, S. R., 124
Shukla, S., 298
Shure, M. B., 521, 522
Siegel, J. M., 129, 189
Siegel, S., 412
Siegler, I. C., 187
Siever, L. J., 246, 247, 280, 349
Sigelman, C. K., 481
Signorielli, N., 4
Sigvardsson, S., 261, 399
Silove, D., 311
Silverstein, M. L., 320
Simensen, R. J., 468
Simmons, K., 443
Simonds, J. P., 441
Singer, M. T., 253
Singer, T., 110
Sitkin, M. J., 13
Sitkin, B.F., 74, 161
Skinner, E. A., 15
Sklar, L. S., 192
Skodal, A. E., 248, 250, 259, 273, 275
Skultans, V., 48
Skverer, R. G., 301
Sloane, R. B., 506
Small, G. W., 200
Smith, A., 233
Smith, D., 451, 452
Smith, D. E., 409
Smith, D. W., 472, 474
Smith, M. L., 507, 508

Smith, R. N., 2, 77
Smith, R. S., 116
Snodgrass, J., 262
Snyder, K. S., 354
Snyder, S. H., 347
Socrates, 32
Sokolow, M., 110
Solomon, C. M., 349
Soloway, M. R., 351
Sorri, A., 340, 341, 342
Spanos, N. P., 35
Spanhel, C. L., 481
Spiegel, D., 355
Spinoza, B., 37
Spitzer, R. L., 92, 93, 248, 250, 259,
  273, 275
Spitznagel, E. L., 98
Spivack, G., 521, 522
Spring, B., 340
Srole, L., 542
Stabenau, J. R., 336
Staples, F. R., 506
Steadman, H. J., 14
Steadman, H., 539
Steer, R. A., 289, 301
Stein, M., 60
Steinhauer, S. R., 340, 341
Steketee, G., 154
Stern, S. L., 285
Steuer, J. L., 499
Stevens, C., 379
Stevenson, J., 436
Stewart, J. W., 449
Stoffelmayr, B. E., 326
Stokes, P., 446
Stoltzman, R., 11
Stolzman, R. K., 98
Stone, D. K., 256
Stone, M. H., 253, 254, 256
Stone, W. L., 480
Stoneman, Z., 457
Stoops, R., 109
Stopek, S., 352
Storey, P., 346
Storr, A., 249, 503
Stoudemire, A., 273
Straus, M. A., 401
Straus, R., 187
Strauss, J. S., 324, 326, 327
Streissguth, A. P., 474
Strober, M., 442, 449
Stroebe, M. S., 131
Stroebe, W., 131
Strube, M. J., 508
Strunk, R. C., 195
Strupp, H. H., 208, 510
Stubbs, E. G., 463
Stumphauzer, J. S., 524
Stunkard, A. J., 448, 449
Sturgeon, D., 329
Suedzic, M., 456
Suomi, S. J., 24, 285
Sussex, J. N., 298
Sutherland, S., 298
Swank, R. T., 176
Sweeny, J., 283, 509
Syme, S. L., 185
Symonds, P. M., 487
Szasz, T.S., 542
Szelo, M., 132

Tabrizi, M.A., 444
Talbott, J. A., 119
Talovic, S., 262, 343
Targum, S. D., 280, 300
Tarver-Behring, S., 431, 432
Tatum, E., 534

and parental age, 471–472
in Pick's disease, 376
in retardation, 466–468
in schizophrenia, 333–340
Genetic markers, 339, 374–375, 399
Genetic model, 338–340
Genetic specificity, 335–336
Genetic testing, 378
Genetics, 53–55
Genital stage, 65
Gestalt therapy, 491–492
Global Assessment of Functioning Scale (GAF), 91
Glove anesthesia, 199
Gonadal glands, 58
Grandiosity, 251
Grand mal seizure, 383
Grief, 60, 131–132, 285
Group homes, 329
for retarded, 478–479
Group hysteria, 200–201
Group therapy, 376, 498–499, 526–527
cognitive-behavioral type, 499
for psychedelic abuse, 418
Group treatment for alcoholism, 403
Guided rehearsals, 496

Habituation, 348
Halfway houses, 48, 329, 534–535, 537, 539
Hallucinations, 311, 314–316, 320, 324, 358, 392, 463, 503
and amphetamine use, 417
in pellagra, 379
Hallucinogen, 417
Halo effect, 101–102
Hashish, 418
Headache, 181, 193–195, 328, 495
and biofeedback, 181
Health:
alcohol and, 396–398
and marijuana, 420
and psychological factors, 174–176
and psychotherapy, 175
Health care:
and psychotherapy, 175
Health problems:
and alcohol, 395
Health-promotion, 179
Health psychology, 179
Heart attack, 117
and alcohol, 397
and depression, 273
Heartbeat, 111
Heart disease:
in Japan, 184–185
psychological factors in, 182
Type A in, 186–187
Hebephrenic, 320, 325
Heredity, 53–54, 335, 372–375, 377
and alcoholism, 398–400
in anxiety disorder, 167
and autistic disorder, 463
in bipolar disorder, 299, 300
in depression, 277
and epilepsy, 386
and intelligence, 476
in retardation, 466–468, 475–476
in schizophrenia, 357–358
Heroin, 410, 411, 413, 419
Herpes, 474
Hierarchy of needs, 79
High-risk studies, 8, 343–344, 351, 353
Hippocampus, 470
History:
of abnormal psychology, 28–49
of schizophrenic disorder, 318–321

Histrionic personality disorder, 198, 245, 249–250
and hyperactivity, 433
Homelessness, 515, 537
Homeostasis, 174
Homosexual, 223
sexual response in, 210
Homosexuality, 206, 211–215
development of, 216–217
Freud's view of, 216
life styles in, 213–214
and parenthood, 215
and sexual behavior, 216
Homovanillic acid, 347
Hopelessness, 274
and suicide, 443
Hormones, 58–59
and immune system, 60
prenatal influence of, 216
and stress, 122
Hospitalization, 311, 514–516 (see also Institutionalization)
benefits of, 537
for drug addiction, 412
effectiveness of, 515
and family, 353–354
involuntary, 544
stress of, 118
Hospitals:
reform of, 40–44
for treatment, 40–43
Hostility, 354, 431
Humanistic-existential perspective, 52–53, 78–80
on depression, 294–295
Humanistic psychology, 78
Humanistic therapy, 490–492
Humanitarian ideas, 41
Huntington's disease, 377–378
Hyperactive behavior, 259
Hyperactivity, 428, 431 (see also Attention-deficit hyperactivity disorder)
and cocaine, 414
Hyperalertness, 414
Hypertension, 376 (see also Blood pressure)
and retardation, 474
and stroke, 386
Hypervigilance, 146, 263
Hypnosis, 63, 490
Charcot's use of, 46–47
Hypochondriasis, 197–198
Hypomania, 300, 314, 442
Hypomanic episode, 297
Hypothalamus, 58, 62
and anorexia nervosa, 447
and cocaine, 414
Hypothesis, 20
Hypothesis testing, 25–26
Hysteria, 32, 33, 46–47, 63
group, 199–200

Id, 65
Identification, 73
with aggressor, 68
of retardation, 476–477
Illness:
vulnerability to, 122
Immune system, 60–61, 181–182, 195, 463
and alcohol, 398
Immunocompetence, 61
Immunological behavior, 258–259
in Huntington's disease, 377–378
in organic personality syndrome, 377
Implosive therapy, 162, 495
Impotence, 217
Impulse control disorder, 92

Impulsivity, 252, 431
Inattention, 431
Incidence, 11–12
of fetal alcohol syndrome, 474
Incompetence:
legal, 540
Increased-stress theory, 356
Independent variable, 22
Index group, 341
Indolamine theory, 279–280
Infancy:
disorders of, 91
experience in, 23–24
Infections and retardation, 475
Information, 74–75
and depression, 294
processing of, 74–75
and stress, 180
Inhibition, 66
Inkblots, 105
Innate behaviors, 23
Innate factors, 466
Insanity, 540
Insanity defense, 540–545
Insight, 488–489
Insomnia, 409
Institutionalization, 457, 539–545
of children, 545
chronic patient and, 535–536
costs of, 535
criteria for, 9, 17–19
reasons for, 513–514
Intellectual deficits, 344
Intellectual functioning:
in general paresis, 379
in multi-infarct dementia, 376
in Parkinson's disease, 378–379
Intellectualization, 67
Intelligence:
of abused children, 429
in autistic disorder, 459–460
cognitive view, 102–103
developmental view, 102
and fetal alcohol syndrome, 474
neuropsychological approach, 102–103
and oxygen deprivation, 104
and retardation, 463, 464–466
Intelligence assessment:
minority issues in, 104
Intelligence tests, 98–100
minority bias in, 477–478
new approaches to, 478
Interactional perspective, 54–55, 60, 82, 295
on adaptation, 3–4
on addictive behaviors, 58
of brain disorders, 364, 386–387
and heart disease, 187–189
and illness, 172, 174
on opioid abuse, 411–412
Interactive approach, 7
Interpersonal factors, 508
Interpersonal relations:
in borderline personality disorder, 256
in schizophrenia, 317
Interpersonal systems approach, 286
Interpersonal therapy, 295
Interpretation, 489
Intervening variable, 75
Intervention:
clinical, 8
programs for, 476
Interview, 95–98
assessment, 95
diagnostic, 95
role of, 96–97
standardized, 97
therapeutic, 95
Intoxication, 367–368, 392–393, 395
barbiturate, 409

SCHIZOPHRENIA

Code in fifth digit: 1 = subchronic, 2 = chronic, 3 = subchronic with acute exacerbation, 4 = chronic with acute exacerbation, 5 = in remission, 0 = unspecified.

Schizophrenia
295.2x catatonic, ___
295.1x disorganized, ___
295.3x paranoid, ___
Specify if stable type
295.9x undifferentiated, ___
295.6x residual, ___
Specify if late onset

DELUSIONAL (PARANOID) DISORDER

297.10 Delusional (Paranoid) disorder
Specify type: erotomanic
grandiose
jealous
persecutory
somatic
unspecified

PSYCHOTIC DISORDERS NOT ELSEWHERE CLASSIFIED

298.80 Brief reactive psychosis
295.40 Schizophreniform disorder
Specify: without good prognostic features or with good prognostic features
295.70 Schizoaffective disorder
Specify: bipolar type or depressive type
297.30 Induced psychotic disorder
298.90 Psychotic disorder NOS (Atypical psychosis)

MOOD DISORDERS

Code current state of Major Depression and Bipolar Disorder in fifth digit:
1 = mild
2 = moderate
3 = severe, without psychotic features
4 = with psychotic features (specify mood-congruent or mood-incongruent)
5 = in partial remission
6 = in full remission
0 = unspecified

For major depressive episodes, specify if chronic and specify if melancholic type.

For Bipolar Disorder, Bipolar Disorder NOS, Recurrent Major Depression, and Depressive Disorder NOS, specify if seasonal pattern.

Bipolar Disorders

Bipolar disorder
296.6x mixed, ___
296.4x manic, ___
296.5x depressed, ___
301.13 Cyclothymia
296.70 Bipolar disorder NOS

Depressive Disorders

Major Depression
296.2x single episode, ___
296.3x recurrent, ___
300.40 Dysthymia (or Depressive neurosis)
Specify: primary or secondary type
Specify: early or late onset
311.00 Depressive disorder NOS

ANXIETY DISORDERS (or Anxiety and Phobic Neuroses)

Panic disorder
300.21 with agoraphobia
Specify current severity of agoraphobic avoidance
Specify current severity of panic attacks
300.01 without agoraphobia
Specify current severity of panic attacks
300.22 Agoraphobia without history of panic disorder
Specify with or without limited symptom attacks
300.23 Social phobia
Specify if generalized type
300.29 Simple phobia
300.30 Obsessive compulsive disorder (or Obsessive compulsive neurosis)
309.89 Post-traumatic stress disorder
Specify if delayed onset
300.02 Generalized anxiety disorder
300.00 Anxiety disorder NOS

SOMATOFORM DISORDERS

300.70* Body dysmorphic disorder
300.11 Conversion disorder (or Hysterical neurosis, conversion type)
Specify: single episode or recurrent
300.70 Hypochondriasis (or Hypochondriacal neurosis)
300.81 Somatization disorder
307.80 Somatoform pain disorder
300.70 Undifferentiated somatoform disorder
300.70 Somatoform disorder NOS

DISSOCIATIVE DISORDERS (or Hysterical Neuroses, Dissociative Type)

300.14 Multiple personality disorder
300.13 Psychogenic fugue
300.12 Psychogenic amnesia
300.60 Depersonalization disorder (or Depersonalization neurosis)
300.15 Dissociative disorder NOS

SEXUAL DISORDERS

Paraphilias

302.40 Exhibitionism
302.81 Fetishism
302.89 Frotteurism
302.20 Pedophilia
Specify: same sex, opposite sex, same and opposite sex
Specify if limited to incest
Specify: exclusive type or nonexclusive type
302.83 Sexual masochism
302.84 Sexual sadism
302.30 Transvestic fetishism
302.82 Voyeurism
302.90 Paraphilia NOS

Sexual Dysfunctions

Specify: psychogenic only, or psychogenic and biogenic (Note: If biogenic only, code on Axis III)
Specify: lifelong or acquired
Specify: generalized or situational
Sexual desire disorders
302.71 Hypoactive sexual desire disorder
302.79 Sexual aversion disorder